FINANCE ESSENTIALS
THE PRACTITIONERS' GUIDE

FINANCE ESSENTIALS
THE PRACTITIONERS' GUIDE

BLOOMSBURY

Copyright © Bloomsbury Information Ltd, 2012

First published in 2012 by

Bloomsbury Information Ltd
50 Bedford Square
London
WC1B 3DP
United Kingdom

Bloomsbury Publishing, London, Berlin, New York, and Sydney
www.bloomsbury.com

A CIP record for this book is available from the British Library.

Standard edition
ISBN-10: 1-84930-040-2
ISBN-13: 978-1-84930-040-7

Middle East edition
ISBN-10: 1-84930-047-X
ISBN-13: 978-1-84930-047-6

E-book edition
ISBN-10: 1-84930-059-3
ISBN-13: 978-1-84930-059-9

Project Director: Conrad Gardner
Project Manager: Ben Hickling

Cover images copyright © AshDesign, Mdd, Stuart Monk, Roman Sigaev, and Maksim Vivtsaruk.

Typeset by OKS Prepress Services, Chennai
Printed and bound by CPI Group (UK) Ltd, Croydon, CR0 4YY

Contents

Contents

viii Introduction

Finance is an essential skill for any professional in any organization. It doesn't matter whether the organization is large or small, located in North America or Oceania, public or private (or not-for-profit). Individuals at all levels—from new graduate trainees up to the C-suite—need to know core financial skills no matter what their principal job title says they do. But even bankers, controllers, auditors, and others working with numbers every day will find that some financial topics are outside their areas of expertise. This is even truer for those in other departments, such as marketing, sales, operations, production, and human resources; places where there often is a fear of finance.

The field of finance changes rapidly. This has been true since the House of Medici was bankrolling European trade, reportedly the first to use the accounting methodology of double-entry bookkeeping. It's practically a worn-out phrase to say that the world is now changing faster than ever before, but it is true in finance, even if trite. Why? First, the "outside" world is forcing rapid change: the rise of "developing" countries, the uncertainties surrounding sovereign debt even in the eurozone, and large companies going bankrupt (often without much warning), just to give a few examples. Other pressures on management are also changing rapidly, such as shareholder activism, the rising importance of good corporate governance, and even basic business ethics (although there are those who argue that these issues were always important, none will disagree that they are more "front-of-mind" to boards today than even a decade ago). Lastly, there's the concern, especially among financiers and economists, that all the previous knowledge of finance—both academic and applied—couldn't stop the implosion of the markets, and especially some very large banks, in the second half of the first decade of the new millennium. In fact, few financial experts foresaw that repudiation of many traditional financial "truisms" which occurred, and those who did issue warnings were largely ignored.

So what's the solution for an executive or investor who wants to stay current about best practice in finance? You could go back to university to learn new financial techniques. But even that knowledge learned in getting an MBA in a leading business school will have a half-life of, probably, three to five years at most, and will therefore need to be continually refreshed. Alternatively, you could take an apprenticeship with an expert; but his or her expertise is likely to be in a narrow field and soon out-of-date, too. So just what do you do to know more about this changing world of finance, without spending every moment of your waking day in reading the latest book or article on this topic, or attending every financial conference on new developments in the industry?

Read this book.

Well, actually, not. I don't expect that anyone will ever pick up this book and read it from cover to cover. Why? Because that is not how it's been designed. Rather, it is intended to be a comprehensive reference document, organized into several main categories that will provide up-to-date insights from leading financial experts about both basic core knowledge and developing advanced topics in finance. As you access this book, find your areas of interest. Perhaps look at the essays surrounding the specific one you looked for, as the articles in the Best Practice and Checklists sections are organized in topics where related themes are provided together. There are often interesting overlaps as one area of finance relates to another. And then, perhaps, you may just be stimulated to read further.

THE BOOK

The essays in this book are largely taken from a much larger book (of over 2,200 pages), *QFINANCE: The Ultimate Resource*, that was first published in 2009 and is already on its third updated edition. In this book, we have selected from among those essays those which are focused more narrowly on the field of applied finance that provide the reader with suggestions on best practice in today's business world. Do feel free to look at *QFINANCE* as well or its companion website: www.qfinance.com.

This book contains four main sections: Best Practice, Checklists, Calculations and Ratios, and Dictionary. The Best Practice essays and Checklist articles are organized into six major topics—a small enough number to allow for differentiation but large enough to allow you to find similar articles easily without there being too many per section. They are:

- **Balance Sheets and Cash Flow**, which covers issues in budgeting, valuation, costs, liquidity, and hedging.
- **Financial Regulation and Compliance**, which has been growing steadily in the past decade but with renewed attention since 2007–08.
- **Funding and Investment**, ranging from private equity to IPOs, and sovereign wealth funds to microfinance; this section includes developments in *shariah* finance and other developing world markets.
- **Governance and Ethics**, which has changed dramatically in the past decade with increasing demands on boards and those who act as board watchdogs.
- **Mergers and Acquisitions**, traditionally seen as a destroyer of value despite being the growth method of choice for many companies and public sector organizations.
- **Operations and Performance**, which covers the many ways that finance links to broader corporate strategies and systems.

These are extensive subject areas and many a whole book has been written just on some of what is summarized in the two- to six-page essays here. Therefore, each essay provides suggestions for further reading if you do want to dig deeper. But this isn't usually necessary, as I expect that the level of information most often needed will be exactly what is provided. At least, that was the intent of each of the expert authors when asked to write on their assigned topics.

To assist with identifying whether to read further, each essay begins with an executive summary or introduction that outlines the main points of the article. Most also include a real-world case study and a section with specific suggestions on "making it happen."

TOPIC I: BALANCE SHEETS AND CASH FLOW

Every organization exists because of its ability to put its assets to the best use; this incorporates the requirement to be cash-flow-positive (because even a non-profit company will cease to exist if there's no cash available to conduct its activities). This section therefore considers the recommendations for best practice in a wide range of areas. The essays cover issues in the reporting of these balance sheet and cash flow items, as well as assessment of the risks involved with each (and therefore also suggestions on appropriate hedging strategies and risk minimization). Different essays are provided for both the asset and liability sides of the balance sheet. The balance sheet essays cover how to optimize the use of inventories, receivables, payables, intellectual property, intangible assets, and goodwill. Although controversial in some quarters because of their use around the time of the start of the global recession in 2008, the correct way of using structured products to manage liabilities is also explained in one of the essays.

Cash flows often depend on proper planning, and another essay therefore discusses best practice in constructing budgets. One series of articles shows how to calculate investment returns, including an essay that discusses why net present value is so pervasive, along with another comparing it to internal rate of return.

The final group of essays in this section focuses on risk issues, including counterparties, interest rates, and pension schemes. There is a fascinating discussion about whether to hedge currency and other international risks and an explanation about how to navigate a liquidity crisis—both topics that will certainly remain important to every company as increased global market volatility appears to have become the new norm.

Checklists on this topic range from suggestions on how best to calculate and use the weighted average cost of capital (WACC; particularly useful because it shows the rate at which a company must pay to finance its assets) to a description of capital structure theory (as developed by Franco Modigliani and Merton Miller).

TOPIC II: FINANCIAL REGULATION AND COMPLIANCE

We have entered a period of greater financial regulation, and this topic focuses on trends in this field and the necessary responses that companies will need to make in complying with those new and more extensive regulations.

No discussion of corporate financial regulation and compliance would be complete without an analysis of best practice in the audit function, both internal and the activities of external auditors. Audit in any company should be a first-line defense against improper activity, whether those activities are taken consciously by employees or inadvertently because of ignorance or error. But audit need not be only defensive, but rather can serve, if properly implemented, as an enabler of the core business. It is an area which continues to see great change, as discussed in an article about international auditing developments by Professors Christopher Humphrey and Anne Loft.

This second section therefore begins with several essays that look at how the continuous internal audit function (linked to the work of the external auditors and other internal risk functions) can first be implemented but then also designed to be aligned with the company's overall strategy or to prevent fraud. The essays discuss best practice in setting up and maintaining an internal audit group, but also the possible limitations that need to be acknowledged and therefore controlled through other means. Senior management engagement with the audit process is the topic of one essay, and another considers the importance of how internal audit can engage with other stakeholders as well. One of the longer articles in this book discusses why continuous auditing is now considered to be best practice.

Other topics covered in this section include how to classify and treat leases (including following a sale and leaseback, which has become an increasingly common activity in the past few years) and the procedures for reporting financial risk in Islamic finance (although the topic of *shariah* finance is covered in greater length in a series of essays in the next section of the book).

Checklists on regulation and compliance range from suggestions about how to choose an external auditor, a description of the basics of International Financial Reporting Standards (IFRS) and also MiFID (the European Commission's Markets in Financial Instruments Directive), through to the key elements of preparing financial statements and what they contain as well as a description of the growing field of "forensic auditing."

TOPIC III: FUNDING AND INVESTMENT

Without funding, an organization will never expand. This section therefore looks at this critical area with numerous best practice essays that apply to companies from the start-up funding stage (for example, how to assess venture capital funding) to seasoned, publicly listed companies who are ready to consider cross-listing their equity in another country. There are two articles by Professor Aswath Damodaran, first on measuring "country risk" and then on how to apply this at the company level, and another by Professor Javier Estrada, author of *Black Swans and Market Timing*.

There are many different funding and investment options, and therefore there are essays in this section about convertible debt and other equity-linked financing, rights issues, and even microfinancing, plus the tools to optimize the balance between equity and debt instruments.

Effective management of a variety of funding sources is necessary as well. Thus, articles are included on how to manage a diverse portfolio of instruments and the impact and influence that outsider organizations will have on a company today, such as short sellers and activist institutional investors. Risk is inherent in any funding or investment decision (and varies by country and type of instrument, and changes as a company matures), and there are several essays discussing these risk elements and providing recommendations on how a company should respond.

We have included a number of articles about *shariah* financing. These range from a simple introduction to the topic through to more complex discussions of the risks contained in *shariah*-compliant instruments and the rise of Islamic banking. I suspect that such a dedicated discussion of *shariah* financing will soon not be necessary in any book such as this—because it will be more generally known and accepted as just one more asset class—but the six essays contained herein at this time do together comprise a useful primer on the topic for those not yet familiar with it.

Checklists on this topic range from suggestions about how to use different dividend discount models and Monte Carlo simulations correctly, through to some recommendations about how to obtain bank financing and even *shariah* microfinancing.

TOPIC IV: GOVERNANCE AND ETHICS

A decade ago, the topic of "governance and ethics" would not even have appeared in a book on finance. At most, lip service would have been given to the need to check financial decisions with stakeholders other than shareholders and, perhaps, employees. In today's world, especially the post Enron, Parmalat, and Lehman environment, a discussion of governance and ethics is not just politically correct or good business practice, it is essential and regulated. Sarbanes–Oxley in the United States and the Higgs Review in the United Kingdom both demonstrate this.

This section therefore includes suggestions for improving corporate governance from Sir Christopher Hogg, former chairman of the Financial Reporting Council (FRC). Best practice guidelines, including useful case studies, are provided regarding dividend policies and executive compensation (where financial rewards need to match performance) as both of these can and should be tools used to improve good governance.

The fact that there are multiple stakeholders whose concerns must be addressed is the subject of several other very helpful essays in this section. These include the need to balance the demands of different stakeholders, from senior management to stockholders, best practice in corporate social responsibility, and proper board structures to support these efforts.

There is an essay by Sir Adrian Cadbury, the former chairman of Cadbury Schweppes, on this topic of good board practices, including the appropriate roles for all members of the boardroom (nonexecutive directors, executive directors, board committees, and company secretaries).

Checklists on this topic include one for setting up sustainable development policies and others on executive compensation, selecting a board and the dos and don'ts for directors.

TOPIC V: MERGERS AND ACQUISITIONS

The conventional wisdom about mergers and acquisitions is that most of them fail, no matter how you try to define success. Fortunately, this is based on data from deals in the 1980s and 90s; studies about more recent deals show that the success rate has improved to something that approximates 50%. This may be better than previously, but what other business decision would be consistently approved by senior management and boards if the proponents of the venture demonstrated that the success of others in similar endeavors is only 50/50?

Each deal must be decided on its individual merits. There is a growing body of evidence that you can beat the odds: a number of serial acquirers do consistently outperform with their acquisitions. This section of the book therefore provides advice on these best practices, including how to conduct successful integration, the need for effective and deep due diligence, how to identify and minimize the strategic risks from M&A, and the common causes of deal failure.

From the target's perspective, there is an essay on when to sell a business and another on how to value them, and one on the reactions you can expect in the equity markets whether a bidder or target. Deals differ in their structure, and some of the articles focus on specific types of deal, such as management buyouts (MBOs), other leveraged buyouts (LBOs), strategic alliances, and joint ventures.

Checklists include coverage of global M&A regulations, acquisition and disposal planning, and various topics in M&A valuation, among other very useful lists.

TOPIC VI: OPERATIONS AND PERFORMANCE

Finance relates to all areas of company activity, ranging from the overall corporate strategy through to the daily operations of sales, production, human resources, and information technology systems. It is critical that all elements of a company are financially aligned and that each division contributes as expected to the bottom line.

Accordingly, this section addresses these issues. There are articles about aligning corporate structure with strategy, creating company value, incentivizing employees with stock options, and even a discussion of the essentials necessary for export success as a company grows outside its home market. Other essays cover business continuity planning and a variety of specialized risk areas including supply chain, political, and reputation risk, and their importance to an organization at all levels. In addition, there are discussions about the importance of protecting against fraud and a very topical essay on the impact of climate change on businesses.

It has been said that "you can't control what you can't measure," and this section provides articles discussing best practice in a number of different financial and analytical business measurement techniques and tools, such as economic value added, benchmarking, real options, and decision analysis for valuing R&D projects.

Checklists provided include how to conduct stress testing and the value of outsourcing, through to managing bankruptcy and insolvency, should that ever be necessary.

CALCULATIONS AND RATIOS

This section of the book provides over 50 short descriptions of key financial ratios and calculations (basics such as dividend and bond yields, but also some less frequently encountered ones such as the Treynor ratio).

DICTIONARY

Containing over 4,000 terms, the book's dictionary provides key knowledge when uncommon words are used in our essays or in day-to-day work or study.

THE AUTHORS

The people who have contributed the essays to *QFINANCE*, and then to this book, are all experts in their field. They all have careers that have allowed them to research, and in some cases demonstrate, best practice in today's volatile and fast-changing financial markets. Included among the authors are both academics and practitioners (and in some cases, the authors combine teaching and research with business management). They come from leading business schools globally (Harvard Business School, INSEAD (France), London Business School, NYU Stern School of Business, and Yale School of Management) and companies (Clifford Chance, JP Morgan, PKF, the Royal Bank of Scotland, and SAP) from around the world (Germany, Hong Kong, the Middle East, the United Kingdom, and the United States). These authors have decades of professional experience, often with multiple organizations and across continents as well. We are fortunate to have such an esteemed group of contributors willing to share their insights and actionable recommendations.

CLOSING COMMENTS

There are four wishes that I have for users of this book. First, that you find what you're looking for about fresh developments in finance. Many of these essays have been written by well-known practitioners and even those from lesser-known authors have all been selected for their relevance to the world of finance today. These are therefore not pure academic essays, but practical. Each demonstrates what we believe today is "best practice." Second, that you are stimulated by the format of this book, as mentioned above, to look at related topics. In this way, the book can, hopefully, challenge your thoughts in a direction which a website can't—because all too often on the internet we see and read what we searched for, but don't click on the linked topics, assuming these links are even provided. Paging through this book to find what you need will offer you other essays that should prove fascinating and perhaps relevant as well. Third, that you keep this book handy near your desk. As a finance reference, it is unparalleled in its depth and content quality. And fourth, that you come away from using this book with an even better appreciation of the richness of finance as a topic. We have indeed come a long way since the rise of the Medicis in Florence in the 14th century.

Scott Moeller
Professor in the Practice of Finance
Cass Business School, City University London

Contributor Biographies

Seth Armitage is a professor of finance and head of the accounting and finance group at the University of Edinburgh Business School. His research is mainly in the area of corporate finance and includes projects on rights issues and open offers, the cost of capital, the role of banks in funding companies, and mutual financial institutions. He is author of *The Cost of Capital: Intermediate Theory* (Cambridge University Press, 2005). He was on the faculty of the University of Edinburgh from 1989 to 2002, and before rejoining in 2007 he was head of the Department of Accounting and Finance at Heriot-Watt University.

Ilias G. Basioudis is senior lecturer in financial accounting and auditing at Aston Business School. He is also chairman of the Auditing Special Interest Group of the British Accounting Association, a fellow of the UK Academy of Higher Education, and an adjunct senior lecturer at the University of South Australia. Dr Basioudis has published widely in academic and professional journals and his textbook Financial Accounting: a Practical Introduction is recently published by Pearson. His research interests lie primarily in the area of empirical auditing, corporate governance, and accounting education. He is a member of various international accounting associations and is on the editorial board of the *International Journal of Auditing*.

Paul Beretz, CICE (Certified International Credit Executive), is managing director of Pacific Business Solutions, Clayton, CA, a company he created in 1999. In addition, he is a partner of Q2C (Quote to Cash) Solutions. He brings over 30 years of global management experience in telecommunications, semiconductors, forest products, and chemicals. His faculty postings include St Mary's College, California (MA in leadership), University of California, Berkeley, Michigan State University, and Dartmouth College. He has designed and facilitates online courses in international credit and general business. He currently serves on the advisory committee of the Export–Import Bank of the United States.

Harold Bierman, Jr, is Nicholas H. Noyes professor of business administration at the Johnson Graduate School of Management, Cornell University, New York. Professor Bierman's interests are in investment and corporate financial policy decisions. He has consulted for many public organizations and industrial firms and is the author of more than 150 books and articles in the fields of accounting, finance, investment, taxation, and quantitative analysis. In 1985 he was named winner of the prestigious Dow Jones Award of the American Assembly of Collegiate Schools of Business for his outstanding contributions to collegiate management education.

R. Brayton Bowen is author of *Recognizing and Rewarding Employees* (McGraw-Hill) and leads the Howland Group, a strategy consulting and change management firm committed to "building better worlds of work." His documentary series *Anger in the Workplace*, distributed to public radio nationally in the United States, continues to be regarded as a benchmark study on the subject of workplace issues and change. A *Best Practice* editor and contributing author to the hallmark work *Business: The Ultimate Resource* (Bloomsbury Publishing and Perseus Books), he has written for *MWorld*, the online magazine of the American

Management Association. He currently serves as executive adviser for the Center for Business Excellence at McKendree University.

Ian Bremmer's career spans academic, investment, and policymaking communities. His research focuses on states in transition, global political risk, and US foreign policy. Dr Bremmer founded the research and consulting firm Eurasia Group, which today is the preeminent global political risk consultancy. In 2001, he authored Wall Street's first global political risk index, now the Global Political Risk Index (GPRI). Throughout his career, Dr Bremmer has spent much of his time advising world leaders on US foreign policy, including US presidential candidates from both Democratic and Republican parties, Russian Prime Minister Sergei Kiriyenko, and Japanese Prime Minister Shinzo Abe.

Janusz Brzeszczynski is a senior lecturer in the Department of Accountancy, Economics and Finance at Heriot-Watt University, Edinburgh, and specializes in international finance, financial markets, and financial econometrics. Before joining Heriot-Watt, he held a Fulbright scholarship in the United States and worked as a visiting professor in the Department of Economics, Arizona State University. He was also a visiting scholar at the Swiss Institute of Banking and Finance, University of St Gallen, Switzerland, and assistant/associate professor at the Chair of Econometric Models and Forecasts, University of Lodz, Poland. Besides the Fulbright scholarship, he was also awarded an ESKAS post-doctoral scholarship at the Swiss Institute of Banking and Finance and a DAAD doctoral scholarship at Kiel University, Germany. Dr Brzeszczynski has published in a number of finance journals.

Patrick Buchmann is managing director at ThyssenKrupp Management Consulting, Germany, having previously been a principal at the Hamburg office of the Boston Consulting Group. He joined the company in 2001 and is a core group member of the industrial goods, operations, and corporate development practice areas. He is an expert on net working capital optimization. Over the past years he has led and supported a number of international projects, with a focus on the optimization of processes and inventories as well as creditor and debtor management. Buchmann holds a master's degree from the Technical University of Berlin in industrial engineering with emphasis on production technology and logistics, and he studied business administration at the Cass Business School in London.

Terry Carroll headed up corporate finance and advisory services for Broadhead Peel Rhodes, following a highly successful career as finance director and CEO of a range of businesses. He was also for some years a business and financial consultant, working especially with SMEs and growing businesses. A qualified banker, corporate treasurer, and chartered accountant who trained with KPMG, Carroll has experience of many different corporate finance projects, including banking, financing, business restructuring, mergers and acquisitions, MBO/MBI, and venture and private capital. With five books and scores of published articles, he is also an established business author.

Susan Cartwright is professor of organizational psychology and well-being and director of Centre for Organizational Health and Well-Being, having previously been a professor at Manchester

Business School. She worked in industry for 12 years before joining the Manchester School of Management (now MBS) in 1987, where she completed a master's degree in 1988 and a PhD in 1990, which was supported by an ESRC competitive scholarship. Professor Cartwright is a fellow of the British Academy of Management, of which she is currently president. She has been an associate editor of the *British Journal of Management* for more than seven years, is a past editor of the *Leadership & Organization Development Journal*, and is the recipient of the first Meritous Reviewer Award presented by Human Relations.

Peter Casson is a senior lecturer in accounting at the School of Management of the University of Southampton. He graduated with BTech and PhD degrees in psychology from Brunel University and an MSc in occupational psychology from Birkbeck College, University of London. He is a fellow of the Institute of Chartered Accountants in England and Wales. After holding a number of research posts in psychology, he trained as a chartered accountant before starting an academic career in accounting. His research interests are mainly in accounting for financial instruments, stock option compensation, corporate governance, and company taxation.

Andrew Chambers works for Management Audit LLP advising on corporate governance and internal auditing, and is also a professor at London South Bank and Birmingham City universities. Described in an editorial in The Times (September 15, 2006) as "a worldwide authority on corporate governance," until 2010 he chaired the Corporate Governance and Risk Management Committee of the Association of Chartered Certified Accountants. Professor Chambers was dean of what is now the Cass Business School, London where he is professor emeritus. He is a member of The Institute of Internal Auditors' international Internal Audit Standards Board.

Andrew Cox is a corporate governance professional who currently works as an independent consultant, primarily in Australia and the United Arab Emirates. His specialty areas are internal audit, quality assessment of internal audit functions, risk management, business continuity and IT disaster recovery planning. His professional experience also covers other areas including project management, change and capacity building programs, security, strategic planning, IT planning, and industrial relations. His career includes roles as chief audit executive at high profile organizations. He has given presentations on auditing in forums both in Australia and internationally, and has taught auditing in Australia and overseas.

Tom Coyne has been a chief investment strategist at the Index Investor since 2000. He received a BS in economics from Georgetown University and MBA from Harvard University. He began his career at Chase Manhattan Bank in South America, and for many years specialized in turnaround and growth consulting at the MAC Group in London and Bristol Partners in San Francisco. He has also been both the CFO and CEO of a publicly traded environmental technology company in Canada.

Susi Crawford is a senior associate in Clifford Chance's finance practice. She has worked on a number of projects, project financings, and financings in Europe and the Middle East and specializes in Islamic finance. She advised on the first ever *shariah*-compliant swap to use the *wa'ad* structure and continues to advise a number of financial institutions on this structure. In addition to her structured finance practice, she has been the lead associate on a number of significant Islamic finance transactions and continues to work on Islamic finance transactions that use new and innovative structures.

Henrik Cronqvist is the McMahon family chair in corporate finance, George R. Roberts fellow, and associate professor of financial economics at the Robert Day School of Economics and Finance, Claremont McKenna College (CMC), California. He received his PhD in finance from the University of Chicago. Prior to joining CMC, he served on the faculty at the Fisher College of Business, Ohio State University, where he was a recipient of the Pace Setters Research Award. His research and teaching interests are empirical corporate finance, behavioral finance, and individual investor behavior. His work has been published in the top journals in economics and finance, and based on his research he is regularly invited to give seminars at academic conferences and to policy makers, executives, and investment managers, in the United States and overseas. His research has been featured in *The Economist*, the *Financial Times*, and the *Wall Street Journal*.

Aswath Damodaran is a professor of finance at the Stern School of Business at New York University, where he teaches corporate finance and equity valuation. He also teaches on the TRIUM Global Executive MBA program, an alliance of NYU Stern, the London School of Economics, and HEC School of Management. Professor Damodaran is best known as author of several widely used academic and practitioner texts on valuation, corporate finance, and investment management. He is also widely published in leading journals of finance, including the *Journal of Financial and Quantitative Analysis*, *Journal of Finance*, *Journal of Financial Economics*, and the *Review of Financial Studies*.

Graham Dawson studied philosophy, politics and economics at University College, Oxford, and holds a PhD in philosophy from the University of Keele. He is the author of *Inflation and Unemployment: Causes, Consequences and Cures* and of articles in journals including *Philosophy and Economics*, *Risk, Decision and Policy*, *Philosophy*, and *Economic Affairs*. He recently retired from the post of senior lecturer in economics at the Open University and is currently visiting fellow at the Max Beloff Centre for the Study of Liberty at the University of Buckingham.

Bert De Reyck is a professor of management science and innovation at University College London and adjunct professor at the London Business School. Previously, he held positions at the Kellogg School of Management, Northwestern University, and the Rotterdam School of Management. He is an authority on decision-making, risk management, project management, and project portfolio management. Professor De Reyck's awardwinning research has been published in numerous scientific and professional journals, and applications of his work can be found in industries such as pharmaceuticals, energy, and aerospace. He is also a multiple award-winning educator. He is a member of the Institute for Management Science and Operations Research (INFORMS), the Institute of Industrial Engineers (IIE), and the Project Management Institute (PMI).

Todd DeZoort is professor of accounting and accounting advisory board fellow at the University of Alabama. He joined the university's accounting faculty in 2001 and has published 40 articles with many in top academic journals such as *Accounting, Organizations and Society, Contemporary Accounting Research, Auditing: A Journal of Practice & Theory, Journal of Accounting Literature,* and *Behavioral Research in Accounting.* He also has received several research grants from the American Institute of Certified Public Accountants, KPMG's Audit Committee Institute, and the Institute of Internal Auditors. Dr DeZoort is currently a member of the AICPA's reliability task force and an advisory council member at the Academy for Ethics in Financial Reporting.

Shane Edwards is managing director and global head of equity structuring at the Royal Bank of Scotland. His team has won numerous "best in country" and innovation awards and is responsible for structured products across the entire client spectrum from retail investors to large institutions and major hedge funds. Edwards's research on derivatives markets has been published in industry and academic journals, and he is frequently a speaker at derivatives conferences and interviewed by journalists. Prior to the Royal Bank of Scotland, he worked in a similar capacity and as an algorithmic trader at Deutsche Bank, Macquarie Bank, and a private hedge fund. He is one of the youngest ever winners of the Dow Jones' *Financial News* Top 100 Rising Stars in Europe Award.

Marc J. Epstein is distinguished research professor of management at Jones Graduate School of Management at Rice University, Houston, Texas. He was also recently visiting professor and Wyss visiting scholar at Harvard Business School. Prior to joining Rice, Dr Epstein was a professor at Stanford Business School, Harvard Business School, and INSEAD (European Institute of Business Administration). He has completed extensive academic research and has extensive practical experience in the implementation of corporate strategies and the development of performance metrics for use in these implementations. Dr Epstein has extensive industry experience and has been a senior consultant to leading corporations and governments for over 25 years.

Javier Estrada, professor of financial management at Barcelona-based IESE Business School, set the cat among the pigeons with his ground-breaking research, *Black Swans and Market Timing: How Not to Generate Alpha.* Published in 2008, this revealed that investors who seek to time the market are unlikely to reap rewards. His research focuses on risk, portfolio management, investment strategies, emerging markets, and insider trading. The founding editor of the *Emerging Markets Review,* he also has several visiting professorships in Scandinavia and Latin America. His first degree, a BA in economics, was from the National University of La Plata in Buenos Aires, and he has an MSc and PhD from the University of Illinois at Urbana-Champaign.

Frank J. Fabozzi is professor of finance at the EDHEC Business School, France, having previously been at Yale School of Management from 1994 to 2011. He is editor of the *Journal of Portfolio Management* and has authored and edited many acclaimed books, three of which were coauthored with the late Franco Modigliani and one coedited with Harry Markowitz. Professor Fabozzi is a consultant to several financial institutions, is on the board of directors of the BlackRock complex of closed-end funds, and is on the advisory council for the Department of Operations Research and Financial Engineering at Princeton

University. He was inducted into the Fixed Income Analysts Society Hall of Fame in November 2002 and is the 2007 recipient of the C. Stewart Sheppard Award given by the CFA Institute.

Alain Fayolle is professor and director of the entrepreneurship research center at EM Lyon Business School, France. He is also visiting professor at Solvay Brussels School of Economics and Management, Belgium, and HEC Montréal, Canada. His current research work focuses on the dynamics of entrepreneurial processes, the influence of cultural factors on organizations' entrepreneurial orientation, and the evaluation of entrepreneurship education. Professor Fayolle's most recent books are *Entrepreneurship and New Value Creation: The Dynamic of the Entrepreneurial Process* (Cambridge University Press, 2007) and *The Dynamics between Entrepreneurship, Environment and Education* (Edward Elgar, 2008).

Hung-Gay Fung is a professor of Chinese studies at the College of Business Administration of the University of Missouri, St Louis. He holds a BBA (1978) from the Chinese University of Hong Kong and a PhD (1984) from Georgia State University, in both cases majoring in finance with a minor in economics. His teaching areas are investments, risk management, corporate finance, and international investments. His research focuses on international finance, banking, derivative markets, and small business finance. In 1999 he won a best paper award (with G. Lai, R. MacMinn and Bob Witt) given by the Committee on Online Services (COOS) of the Casualty Actuarial Society.

John Gilligan is a corporate finance partner in PKF (UK) LLP and has worked in the private equity and venture capital industry for 24 years. He started his career in 1988 at 3i Group plc as a financial analyst. He joined what is now Deloitte in 1993 and was a partner from 1998 to 2003. He is a special lecturer at Nottingham University Business School and has also taught at Cranfield University Business School. He has a degree in economics from Southampton University and an MBA in financial studies from Nottingham University. He is the coauthor with Mike Wright of *Private Equity Demystified.*

Vidhan Goyal is a professor of finance at the Hong Kong University of Science and Technology. His research interests are in empirical corporate finance, with an emphasis on capital structure and corporate governance. His research papers have been published in the *Journal of Finance, Journal of Financial Economics, Journal of Business, Journal of Financial Intermediation, Finance Research Letters, Journal of Corporate Finance,* and the *Pacific Basin Finance Journal.* Professor Goyal is a member of the American Finance Association, the Western Finance Association, and Beta Gamma Sigma.

Raj Gupta is research director of the Center for International Securities and Derivatives Markets (CISDM) at the University of Massachusetts, Amherst. He is also a visiting faculty at Clark University and has taught finance at the University of Massachusetts, Amherst. Gupta is assistant editor for the *Journal of Alternative Investments* and has published articles in the *Journal of Portfolio Management, Journal of Alternative Investments, Journal of Investment Consulting, Journal of Trading, Alternative Investment Quarterly, IMCA Monitor,* and the *Journal of Performance Measurement.* He is a frequent speaker at industry conferences on topics such as performance measurement, asset allocation, and risk management. He holds a PhD in finance from the University of Massachusetts, Amherst.

Kamal Abdelkarim Hassan is involved in structured products as part of the Treasury, Financial Institutions, and Debt Capital Markets at Kuwait Finance House (Bahrain). He is the former director of technical development at the Accounting and Auditing Organization for Islamic Financial Institutions (AAOIFI), the international self-regulatory organization for the Islamic finance industry. Hassan has over 10 years' experience working in the Islamic finance industry. He holds a MBA in Islamic banking and finance from the International Islamic University Malaysia and a BSc in economics from the London School of Economics. He is a sought-after speaker on Islamic finance, having delivered presentations and lectures at various international conferences.

Andrew Higson is a lecturer in accounting and financial management at the Business School, Loughborough University. After qualifying as a chartered accountant, he studied for a PhD. Dr Higson's research has covered a wide range of topics, including accounting theory, the conceptual framework of financial reporting, the expectations gap in financial statements, external auditing, and fraud. He is on the editorial board of the *Icfai University Journal of Audit Practice*, which is based in Hyderabad, India.

Andrew Hiles is founding director of Kingswell International, consultants and trainers in crisis, reputation, risk, continuity, and service management. He has conducted projects in some 60 countries. He was founder and, for some 15 years, chairman of the first international user group for business continuity professionals and founding director of the Business Continuity Institute and the World Food Safety Organisation. He has contributed to international standards and is the author of numerous books. He edited, and is the main contributor to, *The Definitive Handbook of Business Continuity Management*. Hiles has delivered more than 500 public and in-company workshops and training courses internationally and broadcasts on television, radio, webinars, and podcasts.

Peter Howson is a director of AMR International, a London-based strategic consultancy that specializes in commercial due diligence. His particluar focus is on manufacturing, building, and construction. He has over 20 years of M&A experience, gained both in industry and as an adviser. Previously he worked in corporate finance at Barings, where he focused on domestic and cross-border deals in manufacturing industries. He has also worked for TI Group plc, transforming the company from a UK supplier of mainly commodity engineering products into a global specialist engineering company through a series of acquisitions and disposals. He has also held senior finance and M&A roles with British Steel and T&N.

Christopher Humphrey is a professor of accounting in the Manchester Accounting and Finance Group (MAFG) at Manchester Business School. His main research interests are in the areas of auditing, international financial regulation, public sector financial management, accounting education, and qualitative research methodologies. He is an associate editor of the *European Accounting Review* and sits on a number of editorial boards for international academic journals in accounting, business, and management. He is a co-opted academic member of

the Council of the Institute of Chartered Accountants in England and Wales and is currently writing the official history of the International Federation of Accountants (IFAC) (jointly with Anne Loft, Lund University, Sweden).

Hao Jiang is assistant professor of finance at Rotterdam School of Management, Erasmus University. Dr Jiang's main research areas include asset pricing, investments, the behavior of institutional and individual investors, and international finance. At Erasmus he teaches portfolio management, investments, advanced asset pricing, and behavioral finance. His work will appear in the *Journal of Financial Economics* and he has conducted industry and academic presentations across Europe, the United States, and Asia.

Andreas Jobst is an economist in the Monetary and Capital Markets Department of the IMF in Washington, DC. His work focuses on structured finance, risk management, sovereign debt management, financial regulation, and Islamic finance. As part of IMF missions, he has been responsible for the financial sector coverage of Costa Rica, the Dominican Republic, Germany, Honduras, India, Panama, Switzerland, and the United States. He previously worked at the Federal Deposit Insurance Corporation, Deutsche Bundesbank, the Center for Financial Studies, the European Central Bank, the Bank of England, the Comisión Económica para América Latina y el Caribe of the United Nations, the European Securitization Group of Deutsche Bank, and the Boston Consulting Group. Jobst holds a PhD in finance from the London School of Economics. He has published widely and is associate editor of the *International Journal of Emerging Markets* and the *Journal of Islamic and Middle Eastern Finance*.

Scott S. Johnson is the CEO of SJ Partners, LLC, a middle-market leveraged buyout group. He is on the boards of portfolio companies European Soaps LLC and Audio Messaging Solutions LLC. He previously worked in equity research at Salomon Smith Barney and Merrill Lynch. Johnson earned his BA, MIA (Master of International Affairs), and MBA from Columbia University.

Udo Jung is a senior partner and managing director in the Frankfurt office of the Boston Consulting Group (BCG). He joined BCG in 1990 and leads the operations practice in Europe. His work focuses on performance improvement, value lever management, and cash-flow optimization (including net working capital management) for industrial goods companies, with a focus on the chemical and logistics industries. He supports companies mainly in Europe, the Middle East, and Asia. Dr Jung holds a PhD in business administration and studied at Philipps-University of Marburg in Germany and the University of Illinois, USA.

Dean Karlan is professor of economics at Yale University, president of Innovations for Poverty Action, a research fellow at MIT's Jameel Poverty Action Lab, cofounder and president of StickK.com, and codirector of the Financial Access Initiative, a consortium with funding from the Bill and Melinda Gates Foundation. He holds a PhD in economics from MIT, MBA and MPP from the University of Chicago, and BA in international affairs from the University of Virginia. In 2007 he was a recipient of the Presidential Early Career Award for Scientists and Engineers and in 2008 was awarded an Alfred P. Sloan research fellowship. His research employs experimental methodologies to examine what works and what doesn't in interventions in microfinance and health internationally, and, domestically, in voting, charitable giving, and commitment contracts. Karlan consults for many organizations, including the World Bank, the Asian Development Bank, FINCA International, and the Guatemalan government.

Alison Kemper is completing her PhD in strategic management under the supervision of Roger Martin. She is studying the impact of social ratings on the behavior of firms. For many years she was a leader and activist in the nonprofit sector. She completed her BA in religious studies at Yale College, her MDiv and MTh at Trinity College, Toronto, and her MBA at the Rotman School of Management, University of Toronto.

Peter Killing is professor of strategy at IMD, Lausanne, Switzerland. His major interest is the interface between strategy and leadership. His teaching, research, and consulting activities focus on leaders who are working with their teams to create the right strategy and at the same time set the ground for effective implementation. In the area of mergers, acquisitions, and alliances, Professor Killing has written and edited four books and several articles, including one in the *Harvard Business Review*. He also runs in-company programs for a variety of clients including BMW, Allianz, Sika, and Vestas, the Danish wind turbine company.

Leslie L. Kossoff is an internationally renowned executive adviser specializing in next generation thinking and strategy for executives and their enterprises. For over 20 years she has assisted clients ranging from start-ups to Fortune 50's across industries and sectors in the United States, Japan, and Europe. Her clients include Fidelity Investments, Sony, TRW, Kraft Foods, Baxter Healthcare, the UK National Health Service, Seiko/Epson, 3M, Infonet and GM/Hughes. A former executive in the aerospace/defense and pharmaceutical industries, Kossoff enjoys an outstanding reputation as an invited speaker at conferences worldwide. She is the author of the *Executive Field Guides*, the award winning book, *Executive Thinking*, and more than 100 articles in journals and newspapers, including the *Financial Times* and *CEO Magazine*.

Klaus Kremers is a partner at Roland Berger Strategy Consultants in London. He is also a member of Berger's Restructuring & Corporate Finance Competence Center. Kremers has more than 10 years' experience in strategic, operational, and financial restructuring in turnaround situations. He advises international sponsors/financiers and European corporate clients across a range of industries. Prior to joining Roland Berger in 2000, he worked for KPMG Transaction and Corporate Recovery Services in Frankfurt. He has studied in Germany, the United States, the Netherlands, and the United Kingdom. He holds a degree in international business administration and a master's in business administration with special focus on finance.

Vinod Lall is a professor in the School of Business at Minnesota State University Moorhead, with teaching responsibilities in supply chain management, operations management, management science, project management, and management information systems. Lall has developed and taught online and face-to-face graduate courses in his area of expertise at a number of business schools in Bulgaria, Ecuador, India, Thailand, and the United States. He is active in research and publication, has published numerous papers in peer-reviewed journals, and has presented papers at national and international conferences. He is a certified supply chain professional (CSCP) by APICS, the American Association for Operations Management. Lall is the vice president of education for the Red River Valley chapter of APICS, where he leads APICS certification training classes for a number of regional manufacturing and service organizations.

Meziane Lasfer is professor of finance at Cass Business School, London, which he joined in 1990. He has written extensively on corporate finance, capital markets, and corporate governance issues. His research is widely reported in the financial press and is published in top academic journals such as the *Journal of Finance*, the *Journal of Finance and Quantitative Analysis*, the *Journal of Banking and Finance*, the *Journal of Corporate Finance*, the *Journal of Business Finance and Accounting*, *Financial Management*, the *National Tax Journal*, and *European Financial Management*. He is a visiting professor at University Paris-Dauphine. He teaches extensively masters, PhDs, and executives at Cass and abroad.

Qudeer Latif is head of Islamic finance at Clifford Chance. He has worked with Chance in London, Dubai, and Riyadh, and his practice covers structuring and implementing Islamic instruments across a number of asset classes including those in the capital markets, project finance, acquisition finance, structured finance, and asset finance fields.

Joseph LiPuma is an affiliate professor in strategic management at EM Lyon Business School. He has a BS in mathematics and an MBA from SUNY Buffalo, and received his doctorate in business strategy and policy from Boston University. LiPuma has nearly 20 years of professional experience, including senior management, operating committee and board-level roles. He has established new businesses (information technology consultancies) in both US domestic and international environments. His research focuses on international entrepreneurship, specifically new venture internationalization and its relationship to the manner in which ventures are capitalized. He teaches masters-level courses in strategy, international business, and entrepreneurship.

Roger Lister is a chartered accountant and a professor of finance at Salford University. After reading modern languages as a major open scholar at Oriel College, Oxford, he worked for international accounting firms KPMG and PwC, specializing latterly in corporate taxation with particular interest in the taxation of groups. In his academic posts at Liverpool and Salford universities, Lister has taught accounting, corporate finance, and corporate tax and given specialized courses on capital structure. His research and publications have focused on corporate finance. Recent work has included an interdisciplinary perspective in which he examines alternative cultural models and advocates a role for the arts in business education.

Anne Loft is professor of accounting at Lund University in Sweden. Gaining a PhD from the London Business School in 1986, she moved to Denmark, becoming professor of auditing there in 1997, moving to Lund University in 2005. She was one of the founder editors of the *European Accounting Review* (1992–2000), and is currently an editor of the *International Journal of Auditing*. At present she is writing the official history of the International Federation of accountants (IFAC) jointly with

Christopher Humphrey. Her main research interests are in the accounting profession and in auditing regulation—from both historical and contemporary perspectives.

Steven Lowe is client portfolio manager at JP Morgan and a partner at Pension Corporation Investments. Previously he was a senior credit portfolio manager with Legal and General Investment Management (LGIM), where he focused on structured solutions, derivatives, and investment-grade credit for pension fund clients. Before working at LGIM, he worked at Barclays Global Investors, State Street Global Advisors and Baring Asset Management. Lowe has 15 years of investment experience and was awarded the Chartered Financial Analyst designation in 1997.

Norman Marks is vice president, governance, risk, and compliance at SAP, focusing on thought leadership around internal audit, governance, risk management, compliance, enterprise performance, and business intelligence. Marks has been chief audit executive of major global corporations since 1990 and is a recognized thought leader in the profession of internal auditing. He is the author of two of the most downloaded Institute of Internal Auditors (IIA) products: a guide for management on Sarbanes–Oxley s. 404 and the GAIT methodology for defining the scope for Sarbanes–Oxley of IT general controls. He is the editor of the corporate governance column in the IIA's *Internal Auditing* magazine, a member of the review boards of several audit and risk management publications, a frequent speaker internationally, the author of several award-winning articles, and a prolific blogger. He is a fellow of the Open Compliance and Ethics Group.

Roger Martin has served as dean of the Rotman School of Management since 1998. He also serves as an adviser on strategy to the CEOs of several major global corporations. He has published two books: *The Opposable Mind* (2007) and *The Responsibility Virus* (2002). His third book, *The Design of Business: Why Design Thinking is the Next Competitive Advantage*, will be published in November 2009 (Harvard Business School Press). In 2007, *Business Week* named him one of the 10 most influential business professors in the world. He received his AB from Harvard College, with a concentration in economics, in 1979, and his MBA from the Harvard Business School in 1981.

Thomas McKaig is a widely recognized Canadian author with 30 years of international business experience in 40 + countries. He delivers quality business solutions to clients in five languages. He owns Thomas McKaig International, Inc., found at www.tm-int. com. He speaks internationally on quality management and international trade, and is an adjunct professor, teaching Global Business Today in the Executive MBA program at the University of Guelph. His most recent book is *Global Business Today* (McGraw Hill-Ryerson), with his next international business book due in stores in November 2011. He has served as executive in residence at the University of Tennessee and Universidad de Montevideo, and was worldwide strategic marketing adviser to the United States Treasury Department Bureau of the US Mint's Gold Eagle Bullion coin program.

Scott Moeller is professor in the practice of finance and the founder and director of the M&A Research Centre at Cass Business School, London. He is the author of several best-selling business books and a former senior executive at Deutsche Bank and

Morgan Stanley. While at Deutsche Bank, Professor Moeller held roles as global head of the corporate venture capital unit, managing director of the Global eBusiness division, and managing director responsible for worldwide strategy and new business acquisitions, and while at Morgan Stanley was based first in New York and then Tokyo and Frankfurt. Prior to his career in investment banking, he was a management consultant with Booz, Allen & Hamilton (now Booz & Co). He is a nonexecutive director of several nonprofit and financial services companies in the United States, the United Kingdom, and Continental Europe.

Sendhil Mullainathan is a professor of economics at Harvard University and a director of ideas42, a center devoted to taking insights about people from behavioral economics and using them to create novel policies, interventions, and products. He received his BA in computer science, mathematics, and economics from Cornell University and PhD in economics from Harvard. He conducts research on development economics, behavioral economics, and corporate finance. Professor Mullainathan has published extensively in top economics journals including the *American Economic Review*, the *Quarterly Journal of Economics*, and the *Journal of Political Economy*. He is the recipient of a MacArthur Foundation "genius grant" and of other grants and fellowships from the National Science Foundation, the Olin Foundation, the Alfred P. Sloan Foundation, and the Russell Sage Foundation.

Sue Newell is Cammarata professor of management at Bentley University in Waltham, Massachusetts, and a part-time professor of information management at Warwick University in the United Kingdom. She gained her BSc and PhD from Cardiff University and is currently PhD director at Bentley University. Professor Newell's research focuses on understanding the relationships between innovation, knowledge, and organizational networking (IKON)—primarily from an organizational theory perspective. She was one of the founding members of IKON, a research center based at Warwick University. Newell has published more than 80 journal articles on organizational studies and management and information systems, as well as numerous books and book chapters.

Kevin Ow Yong is an assistant professor of accounting at Singapore Management University. He graduated with a bachelor of accountancy (first class honors) from Nanyang Technological University and a PhD from Duke University. He is a Certified Public Accountant (CPA) and a Chartered Financial Analyst (CFA) holder. His research has been cited in two of Singapore's highest-circulation newspapers, the *Straits Times* and the *Business Times*, as well as in *Pulses* (previously, the *Singapore Stock Exchange Journal*), *Smart Investor*, and *CFO Asia*, a publication of The Economist Group.

Ramesh Pillai is CEO and group managing director of Friday Concepts (Asia). He is also the risk management adviser to AmanahRaya/KWB and a nominee director for Bank Negara Malaysia (Central Bank of Malaysia). Previously he was the risk management adviser to Tabung Haji. He holds a bachelor of economics with accountancy (honours) degree from Loughborough University. A member of the Institute of Chartered Accountants in England and Wales and the Malaysian Institute of Accountants, as well as a Certified Risk Professional, Pillai was also a regional director for the Global Association of Risk

Professionals and is one of the founding members of the Malaysian chapter of the Professional Risk Managers International Association.

Sridhar Ramamoorti has a blended academic–practitioner background spanning over 25 years of academic, auditing, and consulting experience. He earned his BCom from Bombay University, India, and his MAcc and PhD from Ohio State University. Dr Ramamoorti was on the University of Illinois accountancy faculty prior to returning to professional practice with Andersen Worldwide, Ernst & Young, and most recently as a corporate governance partner with Grant Thornton. Widely published, Dr Ramamoorti is a coauthor of the best-selling IIA textbook on internal auditing, *The Audit Committee Handbook*, and served on the COSO (2009) and ISACA (2010) monitoring guidance development teams. A prolific and sought-after speaker, he has presented in over a dozen countries. Dr Ramamoorti was co-chair of the IIA's 2010 Global CBOK Study (2008–11).

Philip Ratcliffe left Oxford University to start his life-long career in internal audit with Unilever, where he qualified as a chartered management accountant. He later became head of internal audit at a number of large multinational companies involved in manufacturing, distribution, and natural resources. He was then chief audit executive at a publicly quoted UK paper and packaging company. A long-term member and fellow of the Institute of Internal Auditors (in the United Kingdom, Brazil, and Belgium), Ratcliffe joined the UK council in 2006, serving as president for 2008–09.

Jenny Rayner is director and principal consultant at Abbey Consulting, which she established in 1999 to provide consultancy and training on the positive management of risk to improve business performance and protect and enhance reputation. Prior to this, her wide-ranging career spanned more than 20 years with ICI and Zeneca in a variety of sales, marketing, purchasing, logistics, supply chain, and general business management roles, and latterly she was a chief internal auditor with ICI. Rayner also writes and lectures on risk management, corporate governance, corporate social responsibility, and reputation.

Luc Renneboog is a professor of corporate finance at Tilburg University, the Netherlands. Before joining Tilburg, he taught at the Catholic University of Leuven and at Oxford University. Dr Renneboog graduated with a BSc/MSc in management engineering from the University of Leuven, followed by an MBA from the University of Chicago, a BA in philosophy from Leuven, and a PhD in financial economics from the London Business School. He has also been a visiting researcher at the London Business School, HEC Paris, and Venice University. He is a widely published author, with research interests are corporate finance, corporate governance, mergers and acquisitions, and the economics of art.

Jeffrey Ridley is visiting professor of auditing at London South Bank University. He teaches and researches internal auditing, corporate governance, corporate social responsibility, and quality management. His experience spans both the public and private sectors over 40 years. Formerly he was manager of internal auditing at Kodak UK, an operational auditor at Vauxhall Motors, and a member of the British colonial audit service in Nigeria. He is a past president of the Chartered Institute of Internal Auditors

(UK and Ireland) and in 2010 was awarded its distinguished service award. He has been a member of the IIA's international board of regents and of its international committee on quality. Currently he is a member of the IIA Research Foundation's board of research advisers and also of the editorial advisory board for the IIA's journal *Internal Auditor*. Ridley's books include *Leading Edge Internal Auditing* and *Cutting Edge Internal Auditing*.

Steve Robinson was director of open executive programs at Henley Business School until the end of 2007. Previously he was with Ashridge Business School for 14 years, latterly as director of executive MBA programs. Robinson has designed and taught on a variety of management development and qualification programs in the United States, Europe, Asia, and Australia. He is the author of the *Financial Times Handbook of Financial Management* and is an external examiner at the Cass Business School, City University, London. He is now an independent educator, writer, and consultant working closely with Duke Corporate Education and with the Henley, Warwick, and Kingston Business Schools.

David Sadtler is an associate of the Ashridge Strategic Management Centre. His research, teaching, consulting, and writing activities are concentrated on questions of corporate-level strategy. A graduate of Brown University (mathematics and economics) and of Harvard Business School, his career has been divided between consulting and industry. Sadtler was the corporate development director and a main board director of London International Group plc, a diversified healthcare company, for eight years and is a two-time alumnus of McKinsey & Company, having served a broad range of clients on questions of strategy in the New York, Amsterdam, and London offices.

Hans-Dieter Scheuermann has extensive experience at SAP, the business software developer, in the areas of financials and insurance solutions. Since 2003 he has headed the SAP Business Solution Architects Group, deploying his 30 years of experience directly in strategic customer relationships. Before assuming his current post, he had global responsibility for the General Business Unit (GBU) Financials. In 1998–2000 he was director of the Industry Business Unit (IBU) Insurance. Prior to that, from 1991 he was head of development for the financials and accounting application. He started his career at SAP in 1978 as a developer for financial accounting solutions. Scheuermann studied mathematics at the University of Heidelberg.

David Shimko holds a PhD in finance from Northwestern University. He has taught finance at the Kellogg Graduate School of Management at Northwestern University, the Marshall School of Business at the University of Southern California, the Harvard Business School, and the Courant Institute at New York University. His professional career included positions at JP Morgan, Bankers Trust, and Risk Capital, an independent risk advisory firm that was sold to Towers Perrin in 2006. Currently, Shimko sits on the board of trustees of the Global Association of Risk Professionals (GARP). He acts as an independent financial consultant and continues to teach part-time at the Kellogg School.

Will Spinney joined the treasury department at Johnson Matthey plc after a brief career in the Royal Navy, and took the first ever Association of Corporate Treasurers (ACT) corporate treasury exams in 1985. He has been a practicing treasurer now for 25 years, working for several companies that have included most recently Eaton Corporation and Invensys plc, where his experience ranged from risk management, cash management, and extensive refinancings to pension investment strategies. He has been a speaker at several ACT conferences and has been involved in education and training programmes with the ACT for several years, both writing resources and as a member of the MCT examination board.

John Surdyk is director of the Initiative for Studies in Transformational Entrepreneurship at the Wisconsin School of Business in Madison, Wisconsin. He has advised companies bringing emerging technologies to market for international consultancies for 10 years. Surdyk spent more than a decade consulting with hightechnology start-ups, Fortune 500 firms, and nonprofit organizations at SRI International in Menlo Park and, later, Navigant Consulting in Chicago. He has also evaluated policy initiatives at the National Center for Environmental Economics at the US Environmental Protection Agency. He now teaches on social entrepreneurship at the University of Wisconsin, Madison.

Amarendra Swarup is a respected commentator and expert on financial markets, alternative investments, asset–liability management, regulation, risk management, and pensions. He was formerly a partner at Pension Corporation, a leading UK-based pension buyout firm, and was at an AAA-rated hedge fund of funds in London before that. Swarup is a CAIA charter-holder and sits on the CAIA examinations council, the AllAboutAlpha.com editorial board, and the Adveq advisory board. He was a visiting fellow at the London School of Economics, setting up the Pensions Tomorrow research initiative, and a member of the CRO and Solvency II committees of the Association of British Insurers. Swarup holds a PhD (cosmology, Imperial College, London) and an MA (natural sciences, University of Cambridge). He has written extensively on diverse topics and is currently writing a book on financial crises throughout history and the common human factors underlying them, to be published by Bloomsbury in 2013.

Aziz Tayyebi works as head of international development for the Association of Chartered Certified Accountants (ACCA), having previously been financial reporting officer for ACCA. Tayyebi is the key technical contributor to ACCA's thought leadership in the field of Islamic finance, contributing articles and discussion papers on the subject and responding to external consultations in this area. He represents the ACCA on the Federation of European Accountants (FEE) task force on XBRL and on the UKTI accounting subgroup on Islamic finance. Previously, he worked as a manager with Ernst & Young, managing a portfolio of audit clients ranging from large privately owned companies to listed companies.

Siri Terjesen holds a PhD from Cranfield School of Management (2006), a master's in international business from the Norwegian School of Economics and Business Administration (Norges Handelshùyskole), where she was a Fulbright scholar (2002), and a BS in business administration from the University of Richmond, Virginia (1997). She is an assistant professor in the Kelley School of Business at Indiana University and a visiting research fellow in the entrepreneurship, growth, and public policy group at the Max Planck Institute of Economics in Jena, Germany. She has been widely published in leading journals and is a coauthor of *Strategic Management: Logic & Action* (Wiley, 2008).

Shaun Tyson is emeritus professor of human resource management at Cranfield University. He holds a PhD from the London School of Economics and is a fellow of the Chartered Institute of Personnel and Development, a fellow of the Royal Society of Arts, and a member of the British Psychological Society. He has written 19 books on human resource management and has published extensively on human resource strategy and policies. He has carried out consultancy assignments and research with a wide range of public and private sector organizations in the United Kingdom and overseas. He chaired the remuneration committee of the Law Society for four years.

Jos van Bommel is associate professor at CEU Cardenal Herrera University, in Valencia, Spain. He was formerly a lecturer in finance at Oxford University's Said Business School and conducts empirical and theoretical research in various areas of corporate finance. He has completed several studies on IPOs, but is also interested in private equity, venture capital, and international finance. He also studies the market's microstructure and investigates the strategic behavior of informed and less informed traders to better understand how information is incorporated into market prices. Dr van Bommel holds a university degree in engineering from the University of Eindhoven, an MBA from the IESE Business School, and a PhD in finance from INSEAD. In between his studies he worked in international sales and marketing.

Daud Vicary Abdullah is the managing director of DVA Consulting. Since 2002 he has focused exclusively on Islamic finance. He is a distinguished fellow of the Islamic Banking and Finance Institute Malaysia (IBFIM), a Chartered Islamic Finance Professional (CIFP), and a former board member of the Accounting and Auditing Organization for Islamic Financial Institutions (AAOIFI). He was the first managing director of Hong Leong Islamic Bank, after which he became chief operating officer and ultimately acting CEO at the Asian Finance Bank. He is now engaged by Deloitte to assist in the setting up of their global Islamic finance practice. Abdullah is a frequent speaker and commentator on matters relating to Islamic finance.

Priscilla Wisner is a distinguished lecturer at the University of Tennessee. She formerly taught at Montana State University and the Thunderbird School of Global Management, and her research has been widely published in journals and books, including *Management International Review* and the *Harvard Business School Balanced Scorecard Report*. She also has more than 15 years' experience of consultancy with corporations. Dr Wisner earned her PhD at the University of Tennessee, an MBA degree from Cornell University, and a BA in international economics from the George Washington University.

S. David Young is a professor at INSEAD (France and Singapore), holds a PhD from the University of Virginia, and is both a certified public accountant (United States) and a chartered financial analyst. His main research interests are value-based management, executive compensation, and corporate financial reporting. Most of his efforts focus on how businesses can align key management systems with the value creation imperative. His research has appeared in a wide range of academic and professional journals, including the *Harvard Business Review*. He is also a consultant, having advised many firms in Europe, North America, and Asia.

xx

Hassan Ahmed Yusuf is operational risk manager at Masraf Al Rayan (Al Rayan Bank), an Islamic financial institution in Qatar. Currently a PhD candidate in Islamic finance at the International Islamic University Malaysia, he holds a MSc in economics from that university. He also holds a MBA in finance from the University of Poona and a BComm degree from Osmania University. He has written a number of published and unpublished articles on Islamic finance, *shariah*, and risk management in economic development. Yusuf is also a member of several risk management associations.

BEST

PRACTICE

Best-Practice Working Capital Management: Techniques for Optimizing Inventories, Receivables, and Payables
by Patrick Buchmann and Udo Jung

EXECUTIVE SUMMARY

- Working capital (also known as net working capital) is a financial metric that measures a company's operating liquidity.
- Working capital is defined as current assets minus current liabilities. A positive position means that a company is able to support its day-to-day operations—i.e., to serve both maturing short-term debt and upcoming operational expenses.
- One of the metric's shortcomings, however, is that current assets often cannot be liquidated in the short term. High working capital positions often indicate that there is too much money tied up in accounts receivable and inventory, rather than short-term liquidity.
- All companies should therefore focus on the tight management of working capital. Inventory, accounts receivable, and accounts payable are of specific importance since they can be influenced most directly by operational management.
- Companies that improve their working capital management are able to free up cash and thus can, for example, reduce their dependence on outside funding, or finance additional growth projects.
- If done right, working capital management generates cash for growth together with streamlined processes along the value chain and lower costs.

INTRODUCTION

Many companies still underestimate the importance of working capital management as a lever for freeing up cash from inventory, accounts receivable, and accounts payable. By effectively managing these components, companies can sharply reduce their dependence on outside funding and can use the released cash for further investments or acquisitions. This will not only lead to more financial flexibility, but also create value and have a strong impact on a company's enterprise value by reducing capital employed and thus increasing asset productivity.

High working capital ratios often mean that too much money is tied up in receivables and inventories. Typically, the knee-jerk reaction to this problem is to apply the "big squeeze" by aggressively collecting receivables, ruthlessly delaying payments to suppliers and cutting inventories across the board. But that only attacks the symptoms of working capital issues, not the root causes. A more effective approach is to fundamentally rethink and streamline key processes across the value chain. This will not only free up cash but lead to significant cost reductions at the same time.

NWC: DEFINITION AND MEASUREMENT

Working capital, also referred to as net working capital (NWC), is an absolute measure of a company's current operative capital employed and is defined as:

(Net) working capital = Current assets − Current liabilities

Current assets are assets which are expected to be sold or otherwise used within one fiscal year. Typically, current assets include cash, cash equivalents, accounts receivable, inventory, prepaid accounts which will be used within a year, and short-term investments.

Current liabilities are considered as liabilities of the business that are to be settled in cash within the fiscal year. Current liabilities include accounts payable for goods, services or supplies, short-term loans, long-term loans with maturity within one year, dividends and interest payable, or accrued liabilities such as accrued taxes.

Working capital, on the one hand, can be seen as a metric for evaluating a company's operating liquidity. A positive working capital position indicates that a company can meet its short-term obligations. On the other hand, a company's working capital position signals its operating efficiency. Comparably high working capital levels may indicate that too much money is tied up in the business.

The most important positions for effective working capital management are inventory, accounts receivable, and accounts payable. Depending on the industry and business, prepayments received from customers and prepayments paid to suppliers may also play an important role in the company's cash flow. Excess cash and nonoperational items may be excluded from the calculation for better comparison.

As a measure for effective working capital management, therefore, another more operational metric definition applies:

(Operative) net working capital = Inventories + Receivables − Payables

− Advances received + Advances made

where:

- inventory is raw materials plus work in progress (WIP) plus finished goods;
- receivables are trade receivables;
- payables are non-interest-bearing trade payables;
- advances received are prepayments received from customers;
- advances made are prepayments paid to suppliers.

When measuring the effectiveness of working capital management, relative metrics (for example, coverage) are generally applied. They have the advantage of higher resistance to growth, seasonality, and deviations in (cost of) sales. In addition to better comparison over time, they also allow better benchmarking of operating efficiency with internal or external peers.

A frequently used measure for the effectiveness of working capital management is the so-called cash conversion cycle, or cash-to-cash cycle (CCC). It reflects the time (in days) it takes a company to get back one monetary unit spent in operations. The operative NWC positions are translated into "days outstanding"—the number of days during which cash is bound in inventory and receivables or financed by the suppliers in accounts payable. It is defined as follows:

$$CCC^1 = DIO + DSO - DPO$$

where:
- days inventories outstanding (DIO) = (average inventories ÷ cumulative cost of sales) × 365 = average number of days that inventory is held;
- days sales outstanding (DSO) = (average receivables ÷ cumulative sales) × 365 = average number of days until a company is paid by its customers;
- days payables outstanding (DPO) = (average payables ÷ cumulative purchasing volume) × 365 = average number of days until a company pays its suppliers.

Optimizing the three components of operative NWC simultaneously not only accelerates the CCC, but also goes hand in hand with further improvements. Figure 1 illustrates how an NWC optimization impacts the value added and free cash flow of a company. However, applying the right measures will not only increase value added by lowering capital employed. Improved processes will also lead to reduced costs and higher earnings before income and taxes (EBIT).

HOLISTIC APPROACH TO WORKING CAPITAL MANAGEMENT

By streamlining end-to-end processes, companies can, for example, reduce stock, decrease replenishment times from internal and external suppliers, and optimize cash-collection and payment cycles. The key is to uncover the underlying causes of excess operative working capital. In order to address the often hidden interdependencies among the different components and achieve maximum savings from a working capital program, companies must analyze the entire value chain, from product design to manufacturing, sales and after-sales support. They must also look for ways to simplify and streamline processes and eliminate waste, always keeping potential trade-offs in mind. For instance, cutting inventories of spare parts or reducing product customization could lead to a major reduction in inventory. But how would these measures affect service quality, market positioning, or other aspects of the business?

Figure 1. Holistic approach to working capital management

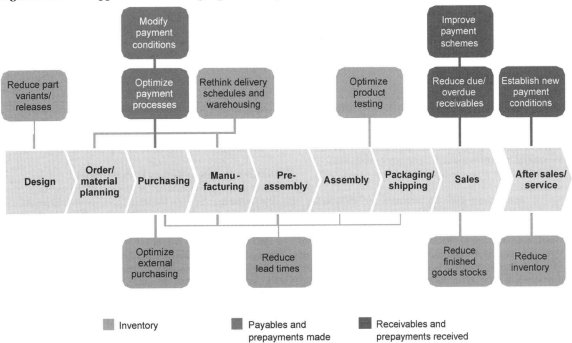

Note: Value chain and relevance of levers may vary with industry and business model
Source: BCG

THE THREE OPERATIONAL
...NTS OF NWC

...the relevant levers of working capital manage-
...now are they applied? In effect, receivables and
...are just different ways of financing inventories.
Co... ...ies need to manage all three components simultaneously across the value chain so as to drive fundamental
reductions in asset levels. Given the wide range of possible
actions, focus is critical. A realistic plan with clear priorities is
the best approach. An overly ambitious agenda can overstrain
internal capabilities and deliver suboptimal results. Instead,
companies should concentrate on the most promising actions
that will not impair flexibility and performance. These actions
will vary depending on industry and competitive situation,
and have to be adapted to country specifics and regulations. In
the following paragraphs some typical (but just exemplary)
levers are described.

Reduce Inventories
Excess inventory is one of the most overlooked sources of
cash, typically accounting for almost half of the savings from
working capital optimization projects. By streamlining
processes within the company—as well as processes involving
suppliers and customers—companies can minimize inventory
throughout the value chain.

- *Enhanced forecast accuracy and demand planning*:
  Improved forecast accuracy and regular updates of
  customer demand lead to a much more reliable planning
  process and help companies not only to reduce their
  inventory but also to improve the ability to deliver.
- *Advanced delivery and logistics concepts*: In order to keep
  inventories at lower levels, top-performing companies
  establish advanced and demand-driven logistics concepts
  with their suppliers, such as vendor-managed inventory,
  just in time (JIT) or just in sequence (JIS), and collaborate
  with their suppliers in terms of a holistic supply chain
  management with mutual benefits.
- *Optimized production processes*: An important lever to
  reduce work-in-progress inventory is the redesign of
  production processes. The main objectives here are to
  reduce non-value-adding time ("white-space reduction")
  and excessive inventory between production steps.
  Promising measures are removing bottlenecks and
  migrating from push concepts to demand-driven pull
  systems.
- *Service level adjustments*: An increased service level for
  products which are critical to the customer (and thus allow
  higher prices) and a decreased service level for products
  which are uncritical to the customer will not only lead to
  optimized stocks. A more sophisticated approach to
  calculating security stocks based on target availability and
  deviations in production and demand will also reduce out-
  of-stock situations for critical parts.
- *Variance management*: Reducing product complexity
  and carefully tracking demand of product variants in
  order to identify low-turning products is one way to
  reorganize and tighten the assortment and concentrate
  on the most important products. Moreover, where
  applicable, components should be standardized.

Customization of products should take place as late in the
process as possible.

SPEED UP RECEIVABLES COLLECTION
Many companies are early payers and late collectors—a
formula for squandering working capital. Other companies—
particularly project-based businesses and manufacturers of
large, costly products with lengthy production cycles—have
cash flow problems caused by a mismatch in timing between
costs incurred and customer payments. Therefore, efficient
management of receivables and prepayments received is
crucial. An optimization can yield significant potential.

- *Invoicing cycle*: The main target in this respect is to get
  invoices to the customers as quickly as possible. Processes
  and systems should be aligned to allow invoicing promptly
  after dispatch or service provision. All disruptions of the
  process by unnecessary interfaces should be eliminated.
  Furthermore, companies should reduce invoicing lead
  times by multiplying their invoicing runs.
- *Early reminders/dunning cycles*: Experience shows that a
  number of customers seem to postpone their payments to
  the receipt of the first payment reminder. Early reminders
  and short dunning cycles thus have a direct impact on late
  payments. Best-in-class companies reduce grace periods to
  a minimum or remind their customers of upcoming
  payments even before the due date. Establishing direct
  debiting with main customers is the most effective means to
  avoid overdue payments.
- *Payment terms*: Renegotiated payment terms will lead to
  reduced DSO. The first step is often a harmonization and
  reduction of available conditions to decrease discretionary
  application. When preparing negotiations, companies
  should analyze their customers' bargaining power and
  specific preferences in order to identify improvement
  potential in the terms and conditions for payments.
- *Payment schedule*: Companies operating in project
  business should introduce more advantageous payment
  schemes that cover costs incurred. Percentage of
  completion (POC) accounting helps to define relevant
  payments along milestones. But also for companies with
  small series productions, the introduction of prepayments
  and advances can significantly improve liquidity.

Rethink Payment Terms with Suppliers
If fast-paying companies are at one end of the spectrum, then
companies that "lean on the trade" and use unpaid payables as
a source of financing are at the other. Between these two
extremes there is a more effective, integrated approach to
payment renegotiation that takes into account all aspects of
the customer–supplier relationship, from price and payment
terms to delivery time frames, product acceptance conditions,
and international trade definitions.

- *Payment cycle*: Payment runs for payables should be
  limited to the required frequency. Here, of course, country-
  and industry-specific business conventions apply. Moderate
  adjustments of payment runs just require some changes in
  the accounting systems, and tend to be a "quick hit."
- *Avoidance of early payments*: Payments before the due
  date should be strictly avoided. Payments should be

Figure 2. Value creation and free cash flow are overarching targets

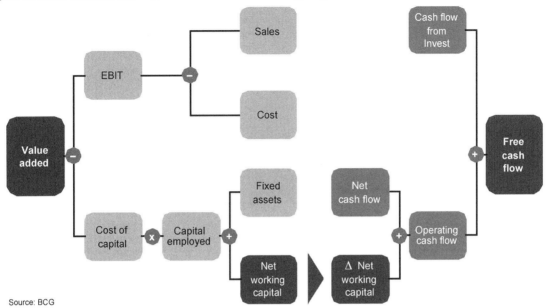

Source: BCG

accomplished with the next payment run after the due date (ex post). Switching from ex ante to ex post payments is common practice and entails an easily implemented lever for increasing payables.

- *Payment conditions*: A DPO increase can often be achieved by renegotiating payment conditions with suppliers. Best-practice approach here is to first get an overview of all payment terms in use and to define a clear set of payment terms for the future. Renegotiations with suppliers are based on these new standard terms. It is critical to take into account supplier specifics. For those with liquidity constraints the focus should lie on prices, whereas for suppliers with high liquidity the payment term can often be extended.
- *Product acceptance conditions*: Connecting the settlement of payables to the fulfillment of all contractual obligations may result in significant postponements of respective payments. Enforcing supplier compliance to stipulated quality, quantity, and delivery dates is also the basis for optimized, demand-oriented supply concepts. Prerequisite is full data transparency on relevant events.
- *Back-to-back agreements*: Balancing the due dates of receivables and payables helps to avoid excessive prefinancing of suppliers and can even lead to a positive cash balance.

Mind the Trade-Offs

Applying best practices of working capital management also means applying value-oriented management of trade-offs between NWC and fixed assets, and between NWC and costs. The isolated treatment of individual levers has its boundaries and, therefore, all elements of tied-up capital across the balance sheet (fixed assets, inventories, receivables, payables, and cash) have to be considered as a whole. For example, it may

be advantageous to acquire a new and more flexible machine (fixed asset) in order to reduce inventories. As another example, negotiations in purchasing cannot only focus on payment targets. The company also has to consider the resulting prices and discount conditions. Therefore, a best-practice NWC optimization is not just a pure reduction of NWC; it is rather a holistic optimization with value creation as the overarching target.

CASE STUDY

A leading industrial conglomerate with worldwide sales presence in all of its divisions recently conducted a comprehensive, group-wide working capital program with a strong commitment to top management levels. Critical success factors were a holistic approach to the entire value chain and the definition of clear and practicable measures, together with employees responsible for implementation on the operational level.

Improvement measures ranged from more easily implemented quick wins, such as optimizing payment processes, to complete restructuring of production processes. Quick wins not only paid off the initiative after a few months, but also served as a beacon for the initiative and proof of concept. The overall NWC reduction added up to more than 40%. Roughly half of the improvement potential was already realized within one year from start of the implementation.

In order to anchor working capital management in the organization, a pragmatic controlling tool was set up and regular reporting cycles were established. Working capital goals were integrated into budgets and incentive programs to further foster sustainability.

Best Practice

Before the program brought the change, a number of initiatives had fallen short of expectations. The main reasons had been an undifferentiated top-down approach, and the lack of a comprehensive perspective on working capital. Thus, the symptoms rather than the root causes of excess accounts receivable and inventory or low positions in payables had been approached and no sustainable results had been achieved.

CONCLUSION

Best-in-class companies understand the company- and industry-specific drivers behind each component of operative working capital, and focus on optimizing the most promising ones. During this process, they consider the entire value chain to reveal the root causes of tied-up cash and take into account all interdependencies between the respective components. They apply a holistic approach in which they do not randomly reduce costs but consider all trade-offs with costs and capital employed to optimize the company value. By applying the appropriate levers for each component, obstacles that slow cash flow can be removed and overall company processes can be improved.

MAKING IT HAPPEN

Since working capital optimization affects many areas of a company, detailed planning and a holistic approach are crucial for the success of a project. The following points provide some success factors of implementation:

* *How should we approach a working capital optimization project?* A benchmarking for the company and for all segments/business units should be conducted in order to identify the most promising areas for improvement and respective units. Following this, the project should start with a few selected pilots. Once these pilots have been executed, knowledge gains can be transferred to other business units, and further projects can be rolled out to the entire company.
* *How do we ensure that a working capital initiative is sustainable?* There are four main aspects to successfully anchoring an NWC project into an organization and making it sustainable: 1. Commitment and resources (sponsorship by top management, clear responsibilities, dedicated teams, internal experts as multipliers). 2. Communication and enabling (conveying motivation and necessity, fostering know-how exchange and best-practice sharing, providing training on NWC principles). 3. Incentives (inclusion in

budget planning, linking variable salary to target achievements, recognizing jobs well done). 4. Controlling (integration into existing reporting formats, tracking target achievement and implementation progress).
* *How long does it take to optimize NWC?* In order to keep a momentum for change and to get a proof of concept, the right mix of quick wins and deep-dive improvements should be aimed for. Quick wins are usually realized within less than a year. They can make up roughly 30% of the overall potential. The overall sustainable optimization takes about three years, depending on company size and industry. According to project experience, the next 40% of the overall potential can be realized in the second year and the rest (about 30%) in the third year.

MORE INFO

Article:
Karaian, Jason. "Dash for cash." *CFO Europe* (July/August 2008). Online at: www.cfo.com/article.cfm/11661328

Websites:
Atradius has further survey data on agreed payment terms and delays: global.atradius.com
CFO and *CFO Europe* magazines have articles on working capital management: www.cfo.com
Dun and Bradstreet has information on payment terms and late payment: www.dnb.com
Intrum Justitia compiles in its European Payment Index Report data on average agreed payment terms and delays in a European country comparison: www.europeanpayment.com

See Also:
★ Best Practices in Cash Flow Management and Reporting (pp. 7–12)
★ Navigating a Liquidity Crisis Effectively (pp. 38–40)
✔ Hedging Liquidity Risk—Case Study and Strategies (pp. 294–295)
✔ Managing Working Capital (pp. 298–299)
✔ Measuring Liquidity (pp. 299–300)
⇄ Working Capital Cycle (pp. 414–415)

NOTE

1 For some businesses (i.e., project business) prepayments should be included as well. Prepayments received should be related to cumulative sales (as receivables). Prepayments paid should be related to the purchasing volume (as payables).

Best Practices in Cash Flow Management and Reporting

by Hans-Dieter Scheuermann

EXECUTIVE SUMMARY

The article compares classical ex post cash flow reporting with modern ex ante cash flow analysis and management. It sets focus on integrated cash management and cash flow forecast and explains how integrated data management works. Insights in optimization of financial supply chains complete the picture.

INTRODUCTION: BENEFITS OF INTEGRATED CASH FLOW INFORMATION

With margins getting squeezed, the optimized use of the resource known as capital has never been more important for companies. At the same time, the globalization of the markets means that new risks must be hedged due to volatile currencies. Risks from interest rates, supply, and quality must become transparent. Customer and vendor credit risk with their link to dependent "risk family trees" after the subprime crisis is obvious. Company performance hinges to a great extent on an efficient and effective internal treasury. Managers need to access accurate company data at the "push of a button," complete transparency and disclosure of risk factors, and integration with all relevant business processes.

CASH FLOW REPORTING

The importance of cash-flow management with the components of cash-flow reporting and cash-flow monitoring has changed dramatically. Cash- flow monitoring has been an important part of managing a company for years, but it always was an ex-post view on the balance sheet. The structure was defined by legislation. So, IAS7 defines indirect cash flow with:

- annual net profit/loss;
- cash flow from operating activities;
- cash flow from investing activities;
- cash flow from financing activities

representing the cash flow. So, cash flow reporting is an established part of a corporate's period end reporting.

CASH FLOW ACCOUNTING AND LIQUIDITY PLANNING

Cash-flow reporting is aided by cash-flow accounting, which records changes in cash flows directly. Incoming and outgoing payments of liquid funds, such as cash in hand and bank savings, are analyzed in real time and recorded according to their cash flow classes in revenues and expenditures.

The primary task of cash accounting is to provide information on a corporate's solvency and internal financing potential. It delivers the actuals and is, therefore, the basis for cash flow analysis and liquidity planning. (Liquidity planning, and its potential integration with sales, personnel, production and investment plans, is beyond the scope of this article.)

INTEGRATED CASH FLOW MANAGEMENT

Modern cash-flow management is based on an ex-ante principle with current information on the cash position and short/medium-term cash forecast. This article focuses on the integration of cash-flow management and optimization of working capital by means of financial supply-chain management.

Integrated Financial Infrastructure

As integrated IT systems map the entire logistical and accounting business process, in terms of its impact on liquidity as well as its risk, they provide crucial benefits for short-term and medium-term liquidity management. Each business transaction is still processed in the company department to which it is functionally assigned. However, different integration levels are updated and aggregated in the background, so that the information can be viewed by the relevant people in the appropriate form. These levels are:

- integration of values and quantities;
- integration of deadlines and time requirements;
- integration of commitments and availabilities;
- cash-flow integration.

This means, for example, that all the stages in the cash-relevant business processes in an integrated accounting system are evaluated in real time, and the expected cash flow can be forecast using information that is always up to date. This is shown in the example of the sales order–invoicing–incoming payment process chain (Figure 1) below. In the sales department, the order is managed using a purely logistical approach.

At the same time, the forecast for the expected cash inflow runs in the background, based on the agreed delivery data and terms of payment. Every commodity transaction change that results in a change to the value (through delivery quantity, price, or term of payment) or to the forecast cash-flow date is immediately and automatically updated in the cash forecast.

When the order is billed, the actual terms of payment and billing amounts as well as the customer's payment history (for example, taking advantage of discounts, tendency to delay payments) are used. This makes the forecast even more accurate. In the cash forecast, the updated values appear in the forecast from invoices process step.

When the actual payments arrive from the customer, for example, as checks, the cash forecast is updated again, this time with the agreed valuation date at the presenting bank. This example shows just how much transparency in terms of cash flow and risk (according to currency, countries, or creditworthiness of customer groups) can be achieved. This forecast accuracy offers great opportunities for intra-enterprise risk netting and managing short term financial transactions.

Figure 1. Integrated views on order to cash process. (*Source*: Finance Best Practice Network Workshop, Milan, January 2009, Hans-Dieter Scheuermann, SAP)

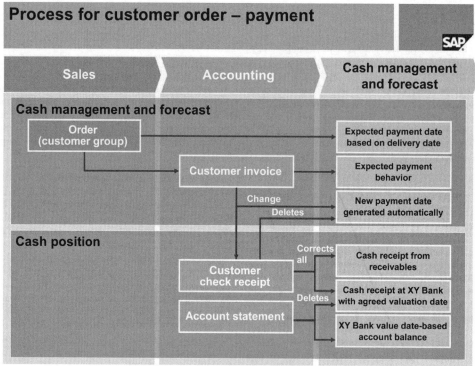

Integrated Business Partners of Supply and Delivery Chain

Like the tight integration of commodity transactions in the logistical supply chain, the exchange of accounting and financial data also becomes more important. By merging traditionally separate financial functions such as accounting and treasury, financial information is obtained. This means that payment advice information, particularly from large customers, is integrated into active cash management at an early stage—and before the actual payment is received—so that planning can be done using reliable data. For the day-to-day processing of accounting functions, data is passed on with the required level of detail, and with the partner assignment characteristics and references, using electronic payment advice notes, and then automatically processed using the recipient's IT system. Standardized encryption and message standards (for example, REMADV in EDIFACT and now XML SEPA Bank Transfer Standards) enable this rationalization at an international level. Electronic connectivity thus becomes an important qualification criterion when companies choose their vendors.

Integrated Bank Partners

Whatever applies to partners in commodity transactions applies to an even greater extent to the bank—the partner in financial transactions—because here, a financial transaction must be up-to-date and secure for it to be successful. The company can thus participate in the information services

offered in the area of financials and, at the same time, meet the need for information required by an active in-house treasury. Electronic communication with the financial partner ensures market transparency and the availability of up-to-date external market data for the company's own computer systems. In addition to providing information on financial market data and the company's own offering, day-to-day processing in money-market and foreign-exchange trading, as well as financial transactions for financial assets and raising cash are predestined for the electronic exchange of information. The flow of information in a money-market transaction is used here as an example:

Money market → Payment order → (Confirmation) → Account statement

Performing a money-market transaction from quotation through to conclusion is still supported for the most part by traditional means of communication such as telephone, telex, and fax. With electronic connectivity, the transaction can be completed more reliably. FOREX marketplaces, such as "360°" in Germany, in which the bank customer triggers the automatic execution of money-market transactions, are becoming more and more relevant. The electronic payment order with non-repudiation status management enables financial transactions to be executed in a timely manner within the planning and value-date deadlines. Reference information is sent with the order and, with confirmation from the bank via the account statement, this information results in reduced administration expenses. Automated controls ensure that the information flow complies with security regulations.

Integrated Cash Management and Treasury, and Accounting Within Your Corporation

Powerful bank accounting functions are required as the basis for intra-enterprise financial controlling. Using a standardized, integrated data basis, processes optimized for accounting are combined with cash-management analyses. Highly developed bank accounting with detailed structuring using subaccounts (settlement accounts) is characterized by:

- administration on an open account basis;
- value-date-based recording of values;
- the storing of parallel currencies;
- automated posting using automatic payment transactions;
- automated processing of money-market and foreign-exchange trading transactions in the treasury back office;
- automatic clearing using electronic bank transactions.

These functions enable the permanent reconciliation, balance-sheet assignment, and evaluation of all items, and are integrated with the automated processing of all payment transactions for the relevant cash and subledger accounts.

In addition, the following options exist for payment transactions:

- manual fast entry of bank statements with the option of clearing current account items;
- the entry, management, and deletion of payment advice notes as value-date-based (pre-) information for all payment orders and/or incoming payments in the form of incoming checks, bank statements, and bill of exchange discounting;
- the creation of check deposit lists with posting proposal, management of outstanding checks, and returns monitoring;
- billing holdings management and commitment management;
- an interest scale calculation with automatic interest settlement and costing-based interest calculation.

The key factor here is that the bank accounting functions are integrated with the general ledger. The networking of cash flows and the customer and vendor processing that is closely linked with this create the integrated database for cash management and forecast, and financial planning.

In the interfaces to modern electronic banking services, manual entry work is further reduced to get closer to the goal of being able to plan ahead as early as possible. Automated controls require human intervention only if defined rules apply or in defined exceptional circumstances.

Specifically, this leads to a key improvement in organizational processes through:

- automated posting of the account statement;
- statement entry with automatic management of the settlement accounts;
- transfer to automatic incoming payments processing in accounts receivable;
- automatic posting of the costs of the payment transaction (bank charges, fees);
- maintaining foreign currency accounts with automatic posting of exchange rate differences.

This enables payment transactions in many areas to be processed more securely, faster, and more effectively. Automatic cash concentration represents a considerable improvement to short-term balance management and planning in the area of bank accounts. Financial transactions can be configured using advice notes and can thus be planned in advance—individually and to the exact day—for the participating accounts.

The following specific features are especially worth mentioning:

- consideration of payment methods and core deposits;
- cross-company summaries;
- multiple levels enabled by grouping accounts;
- possibility to make manual corrections;
- creation of correspondence.

Of course, postings are also made directly to the general ledger accounts, if posting-relevant clearing activities are involved.

In the cash position, you can see all incoming and outgoing payments updated on a daily basis. It comprises all bank-related transactions, differentiated according to the sources of information. To create a planning- and value-date-based cash position over the short term (nought to five days), the actual data must be entered dependent on the value date. This is ensured by integrating bank accounting.

Short-Term and Medium-Term Cash Management and Forecast

In financials, the tasks of adequate and orderly accounting merge with the functions for controlling and safeguarding liquidity and profitability. By including all of a company's payment-related and planning-relevant transactions, and consolidating them across all the corporate functions and units, the cornerstone is set for sound evaluations and analyses.

As an integral part of the application software, Treasury is integrated with the logistical and financial processes. Based on the financial results (banking, accounting and receivables, and collections management), the disclosure of the actual bank balance leads to the cash position.

If you take this observation further and include:

- expected cash flows from completed or planned capital-market-driven foreign-exchange transactions;
- interest-rate adjustment schedules/repayment schedules from granted and received loans;
- receivables and payables;
- planned items available;
- open sales orders;
- current purchase orders

you can extend liquidity forecasting, step by step, into the medium term. As a result of modern transmission technologies and end-to-end partner relationships between the customer, vendor, and bank, the information is available at short notice to any desired degree of detail (for example, automatic transfer and clearing of payment advice notes). The displays in cash management and forecast can be set to any degree of detail and show the development of:

- liquidity as a whole;
- the planned amounts;
- the risk classes

in local and foreign currencies.

Figure 2. The Structure of the Financial Supply Chain (based on a concept by the Aberdeen Group). (*Source*: CFO—The CFO as Business Integrator, Cedric Read, Hans-Dieter Scheuermann)

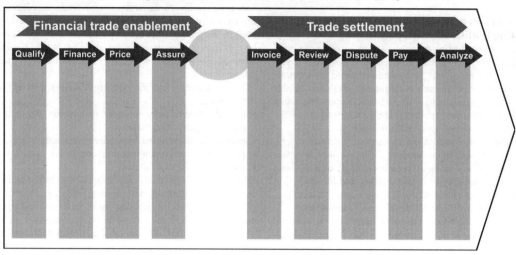

Modern financial supply-chain management presents a good opportunity to test traditional payables and receivables processes in accounting, and to design a meaningful and affordable distribution of tasks as part of an integrated approach to process optimization in O2C (order to cash) and P2P (purchase to pay).

OPTIMIZATION OF WORKING CAPITAL THROUGH FINANCIAL SUPPLY CHAIN MANAGEMENT

The CFO is at the heart of complex internal and external relationships that need to be connected intelligently. As the company's integrating force, they must also take care of all the individual aspects of the financial supply chain (FSC). This chain encompasses all processes and transactions that have a direct impact on cash flow and working capital. As the diagram below illustrates, the financial supply chain starts with the selection of business partners and continues with the payment process, drawing up reports and analyses, and making cash-flow forecasts.

Effective FSC management can be a great blessing for the CFO, because it can positively influence customers, financial forecasting, and working capital. The advantages of successful FSC planning for your company include:
- improved inventory monitoring and cash-flow management;
- reduction in the working capital by 20% and more;
- lower installment payments for the required working capital;
- earlier identification of problems with business transactions;
- more efficient, automated financial systems.

Until recently, the individual financial functions were usually regarded by CFOs not within the context of an integrated supply chain, but rather as separate entities. An integrated approach enables better resource management and makes it easier to adjust the financial supply chain to operational requirements. Such an approach offers CFOs the following benefits:
- integrated cash-flow management;
- more exact profitability forecasts through more up-to-date and precise information about customers;
- better use of the working capital and avoidance of an expensive working capital float;
- greater drilldown depth in financial reports;
- faster and more efficient resolution of payment problems;
- comprehensive overview of business partners;
- improved support for strategic planning.

Moreover, an integrated financial supply chain accelerates the processes between the vendor and the customer, which represents a decisive competitive factor in today's transient business environment.

Financing and invoice processing are usually the most expensive factors in financials, and tie up large amounts of capital. Traditional ERP systems can accompany these processes, but are often not yet integrated with the related systems to customers, vendors, and banks. SAP® Financial Supply Chain Management (FSCM) is a concept that encompasses the entire process—from selecting vendors and customers, through the payment process, reporting, and analysis—in other words, all processes that directly have an impact on cash flow and working capital, and not just within the company, but also throughout the business partner network. A Swiss SAP customer stated: "The SAP solution supports, improves, and optimizes the business processes in the financial supply chain by drastically cutting the days of sales outstanding (DSO), and reducing the cost of finance, ultimately optimizing the working capital."

CASE STUDY
A Swiss pharmaceutical company provides a strong example of modern cash-flow management and reporting beyond

traditional boundaries. A centralized treasury function based on the SAP Technology Infrastructure was not the subject of these experiences, but helped as an enabler. The company saw treasury as a central service provider with the goal of cost reductions and efficiency gains for finance and IT. The core tasks are providing optimal funding and safeguarding business from forex exposures.

In relation to bank relationship management they achieved the goal of reducing bank fees and increasing automation in bank communication. The ease of communication with bank partners, business-wise and IT-wise, was an additional value add.

In protecting the internal supply chain from external challenges (such as financing fees and exchange rates) they secured supply chain finance. The company considers Treasury as a financial supply-chain-oriented one and its in-house bank concept is based on the management mission, which sees the Treasury as a service provider for the business, its vision to partly internalize business of external banks, and its strategic decision for central Treasury to run SAP and "pick up your customer at his front door."

In 2004, the company started the global rollout of this in-house bank concept with key enablers of physical cash pooling with non-resident and bank streamlining to three global cash-management banks with strong IT automation and standardization.

The in-house bank achieved classical benefits in cash pooling by more than 150 affiliates participating in 42 countries and 34 currencies:
- interest savings > CHF5 million;
- ST cash reduced by 80%.

Intercompany payments initialized (volume > CHF22 billion p.a.):
- interest savings and lower bank fees > CHF1 million.

Forex hedging internalized (volume > CHF30 billion p.a.):
- netting gains and margin savings > CHF1 million.

Streamlined banking:
- Fewer bank accounts, smaller Treasury HQ headcount etc.

Additional benefits for the financial supply chain included:
- automation of bank postings, and automated EBS upload and payment file upload host to host;
- intercompany invoicing and reconciliation upgrade by currency streamlining and elimination of local FX P&L, automation of payment allocation (850,000 invoices p.a.), and local finance headcount reduction;
- communication with banks (IT) through elimination of local EBS interfaces, process automation, and standardization—payment interfaces are standardized and file upload is automated.

On their radar screen, they define the outlook towards a payment and collection factory, with further benefits for the financial supply chain. Cross-border payments can be turned

Figure 3. Financial Supply Chain Management Overview. (*Source*: Finance Best Practice Network Workshop, Milan, January 2009, Hans-Dieter Scheuermann)

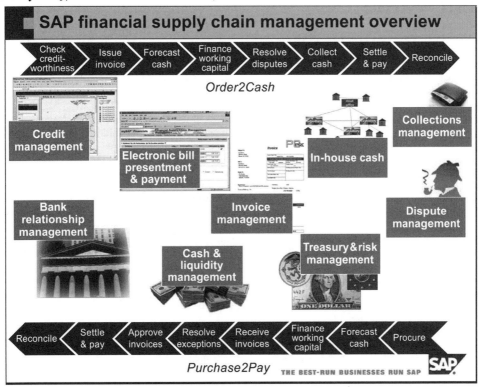

★

Best Practice

into domestic payments, saving bank fees, forex spreads and value-dated, as well enabling the closing of more than 100 bank accounts. IT complexity can be reduced—no more interfaces from local SAP to banks, routing of electronic payments and collections can be done via IHB, and payment workflow can be streamlined and concentrated onto SAP. Centralized cash flow becomes information and transactional-wise. A centrally controlled standardized disbursement channel aids compliance and security when it is SWIFT and SAP-based.

CONCLUSION

SAP FSCM can greatly simplify financial supply-chain management in an organization. With this set of applications, companies can more easily address the multifaceted challenges of managing cash flow and optimizing working capital—two critical elements for successful financial performance today.

The outcome of the experience of this "finance best practice network" shows clearly that traditional cash-flow reporting is "out" and only seen as a complementary communication to stakeholders with no impact on the cash-flow management on an operational level, which is key in today's turbulent financial environment.

MORE INFO

Books:

Kerber, Stephan, and Dirk Warntje. *Cash Accounting and Cash Flow Planning with SAP Liquidity Planner*. Dedham, MA: SAP Press, 2006.
Pfaff, Donovan, Bernd Skiera, and Juergen Weiss. *Financial Supply Chain Management*. Braintree, MA: Galileo Press, 2002.
Read, Cedric, and Dieter Scheuermann. *The CFO as Business Integrator*. Hoboken, NJ: Wiley, 2003.

Website:

SAP Executive Value Network for Finance:
www.sap.com/solutions/business-suite/fbpn/

See Also:

★ Best-Practice Working Capital Management: Techniques for Optimizing Inventories, Receivables, and Payables (pp. 2–6)
✔ Assessing Cash Flow and Bank Lending Requirements (pp. 292–293)
✔ Measuring Liquidity (pp. 299–300)
✔ Preparing a Cash Flow Forecast (pp. 301–302)

Capital Budgeting: The Dominance of Net Present Value
by Harold Bierman, Jr

EXECUTIVE SUMMARY
- The time value of money is highly relevant.
- Net present value (NPV) is a very reliable method of analysis.
- Use incremental cash flows.
- NPV profile is an excellent summary.

INTRODUCTION

A capital budgeting decision is characterized by costs and benefits that are spread out over several time periods. This leads to a requirement that the time value of money be considered in order to evaluate the alternatives correctly. Although to make decisions we must consider risks as well as time value, I restrict the discussion to situations in which the costs and benefits are known with certainty. There are sufficient difficulties in just taking the time value of money into consideration. Moreover, when the cash flows are allowed to be uncertain, I would suggest the use of procedures that are based on the initial recommendations made with the certainty assumption, so nothing is lost by making the assumption of certainty.

A financial executive made the following interesting observation (Bierman, 1986): "The real challenge is creativity and invention, not analysis. Timely execution of projects by entrepreneurial managers is also more critical than sophistication of analytical budgeting techniques."

RATE OF DISCOUNT

We shall use the term time value of money to describe the discount rate. One possibility is to use the rate of interest associated with default-free securities. This rate does not include an adjustment for the risk of default; thus risk, if present, would be handled separately from the time discounting. In some situations, it is convenient to use the firm's borrowing rate (the marginal cost of borrowing funds). The objective of the discounting process is to take the time value of money into consideration. We want to find the present equivalent of future sums, neglecting risk considerations.

Although the average cost of capital is an important concept that should be understood by all managers and is useful in deciding on the financing mix, I do not advocate its general use in evaluating all investments. Different investments have different risks.

DEPENDENT AND INDEPENDENT INVESTMENTS

In evaluating the investment proposals presented to management, it is important to be aware of the possible interrelationships between pairs of investment proposals. An investment proposal will be said to be economically independent of a second investment if the cash flows (or equivalently the costs and benefits) expected from the first investment would be the same regardless of whether the second investment were accepted or rejected. If the cash flows associated with the first investment are affected by the decision to accept or reject the second investment, the first investment is said to be economically dependent on the second.

In order for investment A to be economically independent of investment B, two conditions must be satisfied. First, it must be technically possible to undertake investment A whether or not investment B is accepted. Second, the net benefits to be expected from the first investment must not be affected by the acceptance or rejection of the second. The dependency relationship can be classified further. In the extreme case where the potential benefits to be derived from the first investment will completely disappear if the second investment is accepted, or where it is technically impossible to undertake the first when the second has been accepted, the two investments are said to be mutually exclusive.

STATISTICAL DEPENDENCE

It is possible for two or more investments to be economically independent but statistically dependent. Statistical dependence is said to be present if the cash flows from two or more investments would be affected by some external event or happening whose occurrence is uncertain. For example, a firm could produce high-priced yachts and expensive cars. The investment decisions affecting these two product lines are economically independent. However, the fortunes of both activities are closely associated with high business activity and a large amount of discretionary income for the "rich" people. This statistical dependence may affect the risk of investments in these product lines because the swings of profitability of a firm with these two product lines will be wider than those of a firm with two product lines having less statistical dependence.

INCREMENTAL CASH FLOWS

Investments should be analyzed using after-tax incremental cash flows. Although we shall assume zero taxes so that we can concentrate on the technique of analysis, it should be remembered that the only relevant cash flows of a period are after all tax effects have been taken into account.

The definition of incremental cash flows is relatively straightforward: If the item changes the bank account or cash balance, it is a cash flow. This definition includes opportunity costs (the value of alternative uses). For example, if a warehouse is used for a new product and the alternative is to rent the space, the lost rentals should be counted as an opportunity cost in computing the incremental cash flows of using the space.

The computations in this article make several assumptions that are convenient and that simplify the analysis:
- Capital can be borrowed and lent at the same rate.
- The cash inflows and outflows occur at the beginning or end of each period, rather than continuously during the periods.
- The cash flows are certain, and no risk adjustment is necessary.

In addition, in choosing the methods of analysis and implementation, it is assumed that the objective is to maximize the wellbeing of stockholders, and more wealth is better than less.

TWO DISCOUNTED CASH FLOW METHODS

The two primary discounted cash flow investment evaluation procedures are net present value (NPV) and internal rate of return (IRR). We shall conclude that the net present value method is better than the other possible methods of analyzing investments.

Net Present Value

The two most important measures of investment worth are called the discounted cash flow (DCF), measures. It is desirable to explain the concept of the present value of a future sum because in one way or another this concept is utilized in both these measures.

The present value of $100 payable in two years can be defined as that quantity of money necessary to invest today at compound interest in order to have $100 in two years. The rate of interest at which the money will grow and the frequency at which it will be compounded will determine the present value. I shall assume that funds are compounded annually. Assume that we are given a 0.10 annual rate of interest. Let us examine how the present value of a future sum can be computed by using that rate of interest.

Suppose that an investment promises to return a total of $100 at the end of two years. Because $1.00 invested today at 10% compounded annually would grow to $1.21 in two years, we can find the present value at 10% of $100 in two years by dividing $100 by 1.21 or by multiplying by the present value factor, 0.8264. This gives $82.64. Therefore, a sum of $82.64 that earns 10% interest compounded annually will be worth $100 at the end of two years. By repeated applications of this method, we can convert any series of current or future cash payments (or outlays) into an equivalent present value. Because tables, hand calculators, and computers are available that give the appropriate conversion factors for various rates of interest, the calculations involved are relatively simple.

The net present value method is a direct application of the present value concept. Its computation requires the following steps:
1 Choose an appropriate rate of discount.
2 Compute the present value of the cash proceeds expected from the investment.
3 Compute the present value of the cash outlays required by the investment.
4 Add all the present value equivalents to obtain the net present value.

The sum of the present values of the proceeds minus the present value of the outlays is the net present value of the investment. The recommended accept or reject criterion is to accept all independent investments whose net present value is greater than or equal to zero and to reject all investments whose net present value is less than zero.

With zero taxes, the net present value of an investment may be described as the maximum amount a firm could pay for the opportunity of making the investment without being financially worse off. If no such payment must be made, the expected net present value is an unrealized capital gain from the investment, over and above the cost of the investment used in the calculation. The capital gain will be realized if the expected cash proceeds materialize.

The following example illustrates the basic computations for discounting cash flows—that is, adjusting future cash flows for the time value of money, using the net present value method.

Assume that there is an investment opportunity with the cash flows given in Table 1.

Table 1. An investment's cash flows

Period	0	1	2
Cash flow	−$12,337	$10,000	$5,000

We want first to compute the net present value of this investment using 0.10 as the discount rate. The present value of $1 due zero periods from now discounted at any interest rate is 1.000. The present value of $1 due one period from now discounted at 0.10 is 0.9091 or $(1.10)^{-1}$. The present value of $1 due two periods from now discounted at 0.10 is 0.8264 or $(1.10)^{-2}$.

The net present value of the investment is the algebraic sum of the three present values of the cash flows (Table 2).

Table 2. Present value calculations

(1) Period	(2) Cash flow	(3) Present value factor	Present value (col. 1 × col. 2)
0	− $12,337	1.0000	− $12,337
1	$10,000	0.9091	$9,091
2	$5,000	0.8264	$4,132
	Net present value =	$886	

The net present value is positive, indicating that the investment is acceptable. Any investment with a net present value equal to or greater than zero is acceptable using this single criterion. Since the net present value is $886, the firm could pay an amount of $886 in excess of the cost of $12,337 and still break even economically by undertaking the investment. The net present value calculation is a reliable method for evaluating investments.

Internal Rate of Return

Many different terms are used to describe the internal rate of return concept. Among these terms are: yield, interest rate of return, rate of return, return on investment, present value return on investment, discounted cash flow, investor's method, time-adjusted rate of return, and marginal efficiency of capital. IRR and internal rate of return may be used interchangeably.

The internal rate of return method utilizes present value concepts. The procedure is to find a rate of discount that will make the present value of the cash proceeds expected from an investment equal to the present value of the cash outlays

required by the investment. Such a rate of discount may be found by trial and error. For example, with a conventional investment, if we know the cash proceeds and the cash outlays in each future year, we can start with any rate of discount and find for that rate the present value of the cash proceeds and the present value of the outlays. If the net present value of the cash flows is positive, then using some higher rate of discount would make them equal. By a process of trial and error, an approximately correct rate of discount can be determined. This rate of discount is referred to as the internal rate of return of the investment, or its IRR.

The IRR method is commonly used in security markets in evaluating bonds and other debt instruments. The yield to maturity of a bond is the rate of discount that makes the present value of the payments promised to the bondholder equal to the market price of the bond. The yield to maturity on a $1,000 bond having a coupon rate of 10% will be equal to 10% only if the current market value of the bond is $1,000. If the current market value is greater than $1,000, the IRR to maturity will be something less than the coupon rate; if the current market value is less than $1,000, the IRR will be greater than the coupon rate.

The internal rate of return may also be described as the rate of growth of an investment. This is more easily seen for an investment with one present outlay and one future benefit. For example, assume that an investment with an outlay of $1,000 today will return $1,331 three years from now.

Table 3 shows a 0.10 internal rate of return, and it is also a 0.10 growth rate per year.

Table 3. Cash flow

Beginning-of-time period	Growth of cash investment	Growth	Growth divided by beginning-of-period flow investment
0	$1,000	$100	100 ÷ 1,000 = 0.10
1	$1,100	$110	110 ÷ 1,100 = 0.10
2	$1,210	$121	121 ÷ 1,210 = 0.10
3	$1,331	—	—

The internal rate of return of a conventional investment represents the highest rate of interest an investor could afford to pay, without losing money, if all the funds to finance the investment were borrowed and the loan (principal and accrued interest) was repaid by application of the cash proceeds from the investment as they were earned.

We shall illustrate the internal rate of return calculation using the example of the previous section where the investment had a net present value of $886 using 0.10 as the discount rate.

We want to find the rate of discount that causes the sum of the present values of the cash flows to be equal to zero. Assume that our first choice (an arbitrary guess) is 0.10. In the preceding situation, we found that the net present value using 0.10 is a positive $886. We want to change the discount rate so that the present value is zero. Since the cash flows are conventional (negative followed by positive), to decrease the present value of the future cash flows we should increase the rate of discount (thus causing the present value of the future cash flows that are positive to be smaller).

In Table 4 we try 0.20 as the rate of discount.

Table 4. NPV using 0.20

Period	Cash flow	Present value factor	Present value
0	− $12,337	1.0000	− $12,337
1	$10,000	0.8333	$8,333
2	$5,000	0.6944	$3,472
	Net present value =	**$532**	

The net present value is negative, indicating that the 0.20 rate of discount is too large. We shall try a value between 0.10 and 0.20 for our next estimate. Assume that we try 0.16 (Table 5).

Table 5. NPV using 0.16

Period	Cash flow	Present value factor	Present value
0	− $12,337	1.0000	− $12,337
1	$10,000	0.8621	$8,621
2	$5,000	0.7432	$3,716
	Net present value =	**$0**	

The net present value is zero using 0.16 as the rate of discount, which by definition means that 0.16 is the internal rate of return of the investment.

Although tables give only present value factors for select interest rates, calculators and computers can be used for any interest rate.

NET PRESENT VALUE PROFILE

The net present value profile is one of the more useful devices for summarizing the profitability characteristics of an investment. On the horizontal axis we measure different discount rates; on the vertical axis we measure the net present value of the investment. The net present value of the investment is plotted for all discount rates from zero to some reasonably large rate. The plot of net present values will cross the horizontal axis (have zero net present value) at the rate of discount that is called the internal rate of return of the investment.

Figure 1 shows the net present value profile for the investment discussed in the previous two sections. If we add the cash flows, assuming a zero rate of discount, we obtain

$$-\$12,337 + \$10,000 + \$5,000 = \$2,663$$

The $2,663 is the intersection of the graph with the y-axis. We know that the graph has a height of $886 at a 0.10 rate of discount and crosses the x-axis at 0.16, since 0.16 is the internal rate of return of the investment. For interest rates greater than 0.16, the investment's net present value is negative.

Note that for a conventional investment (negative cash flows followed by positive cash flows), the net present value profile slopes downward to the right.

Figure 1. Net present value profile

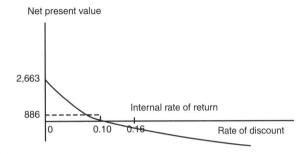

THE ROLLBACK METHOD

On a simple hand calculator that lacks a present value button, it is sometimes convenient to use a rollback method of calculation to compute the net present value of an investment. One advantage of this procedure is that the present values at different moments in time are obtained. Consider the investment in Table 6.

Table 6. The rollback example

Time	Cash flow
1	− $7,000
1	5,000
2	2,300
3	1,100

Assume that the discount rate is 0.10.

The first step is to place the cash flow of period 3 ($1,100) in the calculator and divide by 1.10 to obtain $1,000, the value at time 2. Add $2,300 and divide the sum by 1.10 to obtain $3,000, the value at time 1. Add $5,000 and divide by 1.10 to obtain $7,273, the value of time 0. Subtract $7,000 to obtain the net present value of $273.

CASE STUDY

A chemical company had sales of $14 billion and net earnings of $380 million in 20×1. Sales grew at 8% in the period 2001–20×1 and earnings at 10%.

Management was concerned that the firm's growth rates would fall as its product lines were maturing and the firm was finding it difficult to develop desirable investments. Management wanted the firm to grow at least 10% per year.

The firm used a 15% (after tax) hurdle rate as the required return.

The European plant was designed to manufacture a new proprietary polyethylene terephthalate (PET) that could be used, if successful, to package bottled water. A test tube quantity had been prepared but the new product had never been manufactured.

Demand for water bottles was expected to double in the next six years. The materials currently being used were neither environmentally sound nor safe. The new bottle would also have a better appearance. The average European drinks three times as much bottled water as the average resident in the United States.

The economic analysis presented for this plant was as given in Table 7.

Table 7. Financial analysis for the chemical company

	NPV (0.15)	IRR
Most probable outcome	$80,000,000	0.38
A 20% decrease in expected volume	$50,000,000	0.30
A 10% decrease in gross margin	$70,000,000	0.35
A 20% decrease in volume and 10% decrease in gross margin	$44,000,000	0.20

Question: Should the plant being considered be accepted?

Answer: The plant has risk (the product has never been manufactured), but the likely profits look good. Accept. For all the listed events, the outcomes are acceptable.

CONCLUSION

There are many different ways of evaluating investments. In some situations, several of the methods will lead to identical decisions. We shall consistently recommend the net present value method as the primary means of evaluating investments.

The net present value method ensures that future cash flows are brought back to a common moment in time called time 0. For each future cash flow, a present value equivalent is found. These present value equivalents are summed to obtain a net present value. If the net present value is positive, the investment is acceptable.

The transformation of future flows back to the present is accomplished using the mathematical relationship $(1 + r)^{-n}$, which we shall call the present value factor for r rate of interest and n time periods.

In cases of uncertainty, additional complexities must be considered, but the basic framework of analysis will remain a discounted present value method.

A Stanford Research Institute publication (1966) stated the situation well (p. 3): "The growth in corporate long range planning has intensified interest in corporate objectives, and has created a critical need to evaluate the financial impact of alternative courses of action."

MORE INFO

Books:

Bierman, Harold, Jr. *Implementation of Capital Budgeting Techniques*. Financial Management Survey and Synthesis Series. Tampa, FL: FMA, 1986.

Bierman, Harold, Jr, and Seymour Smidt. *Advanced Capital Budgeting*. New York: Routledge, 2007.

Bierman, Harold, Jr, and Seymour Smidt. *The Capital Budgeting Decision*. 9th ed. New York: Routledge, 2007.

Stanford Research Institute. *Financial Management in Transition*. Menlo Park, CA, 1966.

Articles:

Graham, John R., and Campbell R. Harvey. "The theory and practice of corporate finance: Evidence from the field." *Journal of Financial Economics* 60:2–3 (May 2001): 187–243. Online at: dx.doi.org/10.1016/S0304-405X(01)00044-7

Hastie, K. L. "One businessman's view of capital budgeting." *Financial Management* 3:4 (Winter 1974): 36–44.

See Also:

★ Comparing Net Present Value and Internal Rate of Return (pp. 16–19)

✔ Appraising Investment Opportunities (p. 358)

✔ Understanding the Relationship between the Discount Rate and Risk (pp. 308–309)

⇄ Net Present Value (pp. 400–401)

Comparing Net Present Value and Internal Rate of Return

by Harold Bierman, Jr

EXECUTIVE SUMMARY

- Net present value (NPV) and internal rate of return (IRR) are two very practical discounted cash flow (DCF) calculations used for making capital budgeting decisions.
- NPV and IRR lead to the same decisions with investments that are independent.
- With mutually exclusive investments, the NPV method is easier to use and more reliable.

INTRODUCTION

To this point neither of the two discounted cash flow procedures for evaluating an investment is obviously incorrect. In many situations, the internal rate of return (IRR) procedure will lead to the same decision as the net present value (NPV) procedure, but there are also times when the IRR may lead to different decisions from those obtained by using the net present value procedure. When the two methods lead to different decisions, the net present value method tends to give better decisions.

★

Best Practice

It is sometimes possible to use the IRR method in such a way that it gives the same results as the NPV method. For this to occur, it is necessary that the rate of discount at which it is appropriate to discount future cash proceeds be the same for all future years. If the appropriate rate of interest varies from year to year, then the two procedures may not give identical answers.

It is easy to use the NPV method correctly. It is much more difficult to use the IRR method correctly.

ACCEPT OR REJECT DECISIONS

Frequently, the investment decision to be made is whether to accept or reject a project where the cash flows of the project do not affect the cash flows of other projects. We speak of this type of investment as being an independent investment. With the IRR procedure, the recommendation with conventional cash flows is to accept an independent investment if its IRR is greater than some minimum acceptable rate of discount. If the cash flow corresponding to the investment consists of one or more periods of cash outlays followed only by periods of cash proceeds, this method will give the same accept or reject decisions as the NPV method, using the same discount rate. Because most independent investments have cash flow patterns that meet the specifications described, it is fair to say that in practice, the IRR and NPV methods tend to give the same accept or reject recommendations for independent investments.

MUTUALLY EXCLUSIVE INVESTMENT

If undertaking any one of a set of investments will change the profitability of the other investments, the investments are substitutes. An extreme case of substitution exists if undertaking one of the investments completely eliminates the expected proceeds of the other investments. Such investments are said to be mutually exclusive.

Frequently, a company will have two or more investments, any one of which would be acceptable, but because the investments are mutually exclusive, only one can be accepted. Mutually exclusive investment alternatives are common in industry. The situation frequently occurs in connection with the engineering design of a new installation. In the process of designing such an installation, the engineers are typically faced at a great many points with alternatives that are mutually exclusive. Thus, a measure of investment worth that does not lead to correct mutually exclusive choices will be seriously deficient.

INCREMENTAL BENEFITS: THE SCALE PROBLEM

The IRR method's recommendations for mutually exclusive investments are less reliable than are those that result from the application of the NPV method because the former fail to consider the size of the investment. Let us assume that we must choose one of the following investments for a company whose discount rate is 10%: Investment A requires an outlay of $10,000 this year and has cash proceeds of $12,000 next year; investment B requires an outlay of $15,000 this year and has cash proceeds of $17,700 next year. The IRR of A is 20%, and that of B is 18%.

A quick answer would be that A is more desirable, based on the hypothesis that the higher the IRR, the better the investment. When only the IRR of the investment is considered, something significant is left out—and that is the size of the investment. The important difference between investments B and A is that B requires an additional outlay of $5,000 and provides additional cash proceeds of $5,700. Table 1 shows that the IRR of the incremental investment is 14%, which is clearly worthwhile for a company that can obtain additional funds at 10%. The $5,000 saved by investing in A can earn $5,500 (a 10% return). This is inferior to the $5,700 earned by investing an additional $5,000 in B.

Table 1. Two mutually exclusive investments, A and B

Investment	Cash flows		IRR (%)
0	1		
A	− $10,000	$12,000	20
B	− $15,000	$17,700	18
Incremental (B − A)	− $5,000	$5,000	14

Figure 1 shows both investments. It can be seen that investment B is more desirable (has a higher present value) as long as the discount rate is less than 14%.

We can identify the difficulty just described as the scale or size problem that arises when the IRR method is used to evaluate mutually exclusive investments. Because the IRR is a percentage, the process of computation eliminates size; yet, size of the investment is important.

TIMING

Assume that there are two mutually exclusive investments both requiring the same initial outlay. This case seems to be different from the one we have just discussed because there is no incremental investment. Actually, the difference is superficial. Consider investments Y and Z, described in Table 2. Suppose that Y and Z are mutually exclusive investments for a company whose cost of money is 5%. The IRR of Y is 20%, whereas that of Z is 25%. If we take the present value of each investment at 5%, however, we find that the ranking is in the opposite order. The present value of Z is less than the present value of Y.

Figure 1. Two mutually exclusive investments, A and B

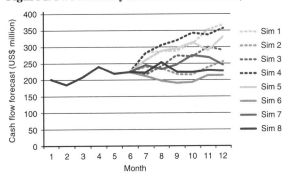

Table 2. Cash flows for two investments, Y and Z

Investment	Cash flows for period			IRR (%)	NPV at 5%
0	1	2			
Y	−$100.00	$20.00	$120.00	20	$27.89
Z	−$100.00	$100.00	$31.25	25	$23.58

Table 3. Incremental comparison of cash flows for investments Y and Z

Period 0	$0.00	Cash flows identical
Period 1	−$80.00	Cash flow of Y is less than that of Z
Period 2	$88.75	Cash flow of Y exceeds that of Z

Suppose that we attempt to make an incremental comparison, as shown in Table 3. We see that the cash flow of Y is $80.00 less in year 1 and $88.75 more than Z in year 2. As before, we can compute the IRR on the incremental cash flow. An outlay of $80.00 that returns $88.75 one year later has an IRR of 10.9%. An investment such as this would be desirable for a company whose cost of money is less than 10.9%. Again, we are really dealing with a problem of the scale of the investment, but in this case, the opportunity for the additional investment occurs one year later.

The same result can be reached by a somewhat different route if we ask how much cash the company would have on hand at the end of the second year if it accepted investment Y or if it accepted investment Z. Both investments give some cash proceeds at the end of the first year. The value of the investment at the end of the second year will depend on what is done with cash proceeds of the first year. Assume that the cash proceeds of the first year could be reinvested to yield 5%. Then investment Y would result in a total cash accumulation by the end of the year of $141 (105% of $20 plus $120). Investment Z would result in a cash accumulation of only $136.25 (105% of $100 plus $31.25).

Figure 2 shows that investment Y is to be preferred as long as the appropriate discount rate is less than 10.9%. If the rate is in excess of 10.9, then Z is to be preferred.

One disadvantage associated with the use of the IRR method is the necessity of computing the IRR on the incremental cash proceeds in order to determine which of a pair of mutually exclusive investments is preferable. If there are more than two mutually exclusive investments, we shall have to conduct an elimination tournament among the mutually exclusive investments. Taking any pair, we compute the IRR on the incremental cash flow and attempt to decide which of the two investments is preferable. The winner of this round would then be compared in the same manner with one of the remaining investments until the grand champion investment is discovered. If there are 151 investments being considered, there will have to be 150 computations, because 150 investments would have to be eliminated.

WHY IRR IS POPULAR

Managers like the IRR method, since they consider it important to know the differential between the proposed

Figure 2. Two mutually exclusive investments, Y and Z

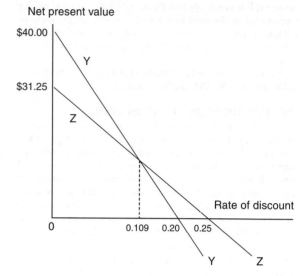

investment's IRR and the required return. This is a measure of safety that allows an evaluation of the investment's return compared to its risk. If an investment has an IRR of 0.30 when the required return is 0.12, this is a large margin that allows for error. An NPV measure does not give the same type of information to management.

CASE STUDY
A DECISION IN MEXICO

A major Mexican steel corporation had a major decision. It could stand relatively pat (a marginal investment of $50,000,000) with its present steel making facilities and earn indefinitely (after maintenance capital expenditures) $8,000,000 per year. This is an IRR of 0.16. The pesos have been translated to dollars.

The alternative is to invest $10,000,000,000 and earn $1,500,000,000 per year indefinitely, an IRR of 0.15.

What should the corporation do if it has a cost of capital of 0.10 for steel making facilities?

The solution is:

$$\text{NPV (stand pat)} = 8,000,000 \div 0.10 - 50,000,000$$
$$= 80,000,000 - 50,000,000$$
$$= \$30,000,000$$

$$\text{NPV (major investment)} = 1,500,000,000 \div 0.10 - 10,000,000,000$$
$$= 15,000,000,000 - 10,000,000,000$$
$$= \$5,000,000,000$$

IRR says stand pat (0.16 is larger than 0.15). NPV says rebuild ($5 billion is larger than $30 million).

★

CONCLUSION

An effective understanding of present value concepts is of great assistance in the understanding of a wide range of areas of business decision making. The concepts are especially important in managerial decision making, since many decisions made today affect the firm's cash flows over future time periods.

It should be stressed that I have only discussed how to take the timing of the cash flows into consideration. Risk and tax considerations must still be explained before the real-world decision maker has a tool that can be effectively applied. In addition, there may be qualitative factors that management wants to consider before accepting or rejecting an investment.

It is sometimes stated that refinements in capital budgeting techniques are a waste of effort because the basic information being used is so unreliable. It is claimed that the estimates of cash proceeds are only guesses and that to use anything except the simplest capital budget procedures is as futile as using complicated formulas or observations of past market levels to determine which way the stock market is going to move next. For example, in 1974 K. Larry Hastie published his classic paper, "One Businessman's View of Capital Budgeting." His position is that firms should avoid excessively complex measurement techniques. He states: "Investment decision making could be improved significantly if the emphasis were placed on asking the appropriate strategic questions and providing better assumptions rather than on increasing the sophistication of measurement techniques" (1974, p. 36).

It is true that in many situations reliable estimates of cash proceeds are difficult to make. Fortunately, there are a large number of investment decisions in which cash proceeds can be predicted with a fair degree of certainty. But even with an accurate, reliable estimate of cash proceeds, the wrong decision is frequently made because incorrect methods are used in evaluating this information.

While it is not possible to make a single estimate of cash proceeds that is certain to occur, it does not follow that incorrect methods of analysis are justified. When all the calculations are completed, judgmental insights may be included in the analysis to decide whether to accept or reject a project.

MORE INFO

Books:

Bierman, Harold, Jr. *Implementation of Capital Budgeting Techniques*. Financial Management Survey and Synthesis Series. Tampa, FL: FMA, 1986.

Bierman, Harold, Jr, and Seymour Smidt. *Advanced Capital Budgeting*. New York: Routledge, 2007.

Bierman, Harold, Jr, and Seymour Smidt. *The Capital Budgeting Decision*. 9th ed. New York: Routledge, 2007.

Stanford Research Institute. *Financial Management in Transition*. Menlo Park, CA, 1966.

Article:

Hastie, K. L. "One businessman's view of capital budgeting." *Financial Management* 3:4 (Winter 1974): 36–44.

See Also:

★ Capital Budgeting: The Dominance of Net Present Value (pp. 12–16)

★ Creating Value with EVA (pp. 255–258)

★ Valuing Start-Ups (pp. 239–243)

✔ Understanding the Relationship between the Discount Rate and Risk (pp. 308–309)

⇄ Internal Rate of Return (p. 396)

⇄ Net Present Value (pp. 400–401)

Fair Value Accounting: SFAS 157 and IAS 39
by Kevin Ow Yong

EXECUTIVE SUMMARY

- Fair value accounting is increasingly being adopted by many countries across the world.
- When financial instruments are not traded in active markets, fair value accounting involves subjective estimations based on valuation models.
- There are many measurement considerations that managers need to be aware of when making subjective valuation estimates of their firms' financial instruments.
- Understanding these measurement issues aids managers in considering how best to manage their firms' assets and liabilities in a fair-value-driven accounting regime.

INTRODUCTION

Recent initiatives by both the International Accounting Standards Board (IASB) and the US Financial Accounting Standards Board (FASB) have increased the use of fair value accounting for financial reporting across many jurisdictions around the world. There are many issues surrounding fair value accounting. This article outlines the main measurement issues contained in the fair value accounting standard used by the FASB (SFAS 157), and that used by the IASB (IAS 39).

THE RATIONALE FOR FAIR VALUE ACCOUNTING

The increasing use of fair value accounting in financial reporting came about because accounting standard setters have debated, and come to the conclusion that fair value appears to meet the conceptual framework criteria better than other measurement bases (for example, historical cost, amortized cost, among others). Notwithstanding this rationale, a major issue with fair value accounting is the difficulty of measurement ("subjective estimates") when financial instruments do not trade in active markets. Both SFAS 157 and IAS 39 provide measurement guidance as to how firms should compute fair value estimates in such a situation.

FAIR VALUE ACCOUNTING BASED ON SFAS 157

SFAS 157 details the framework for measuring fair value for firms reporting their financial statements based on US GAAP. Prior to this standard, there were different definitions of fair value, and limited guidance in the applications of those definitions. SFAS 157 provides a consistent definition of fair value, outlines several types of valuation techniques that can be used to measure fair value, and requires firms to disclose their valuation inputs (the "fair value hierarchy"), in order to increase consistency and comparability in fair value measurements.

The standard defines fair value as "the price that would be received to sell an asset or paid to transfer a liability in an orderly transaction between market participants at the measurement date" (paragraph 5). This definition focuses on the price that would be received to sell the asset or paid to transfer the liability ("exit price"), not the price that would be paid to acquire the asset or received to assume the liability ("entry price"). An orderly transaction assumes that the firm has sufficient time to market the asset. Hence, fair value estimates should not be estimated as in a forced liquidation or distress sale, contrary to some misconceptions about fair value accounting.

SFAS 157 states three valuation techniques which can be used for estimating fair values. They are the market approach, income approach, and/or cost approach (paragraph 18). A market approach typically uses quoted prices in active markets, but other valuation techniques consistent with the market approach include the use of market multiples derived from a set of comparables, and matrix pricing that allows a firm to value securities without relying exclusively on quoted prices.

The second approach is the income approach. The income approach uses valuation techniques to convert future amounts (cash flows or earnings) to a single present value amount. Examples of such valuation techniques include present value discounted cash flows, option pricing models (for example, the Black–Scholes–Merton formula, or a binomial model), and the multi-period excess earnings method. Finally, the cost approach is based on the amount that would be required to replace the service capacity of an asset. From the perspective of a seller, the price that would be received for the asset is determined based on the cost to a buyer to acquire or construct a substitute asset of comparable utility, adjusted for obsolescence such as physical, functional (technological), and economic (external) obsolescence.

SFAS 157 establishes a fair value hierarchy that prioritizes the inputs to valuation techniques that are used to measure

fair value. Broadly speaking, inputs refer to the assumptions that market participants would use in pricing the asset or liability, including assumptions about risk. The standard specifies the use of valuation techniques that maximize the use of observable inputs (i.e., based on market data obtained from sources independent of the firm), and minimize the use of unobservable inputs (i.e., inputs that reflect the firm's own assumptions as to how market participants would price an asset or liability) (paragraph 21).

Specifically, a firm is to use Level 1 inputs (unadjusted quoted prices in active markets) on the assumption that a quoted price in an active market provides the most reliable evidence of fair value. It shall be used whenever available (paragraph 24), except when it is available but not readily accessible (paragraph 25), or when it might not represent fair value at the measurement date (paragraph 26). If observable prices are not available, the firm can value its assets based on Level 2 inputs (observable inputs other than quoted prices included within Level 1). Level 2 inputs are inputs such as (i) quoted prices for similar (but not identical) assets or liabilities in both active and inactive markets, and (ii) inputs other than quoted prices such as interest rates and yield curves, credit risks, default risks, and other inputs that can be derived principally from observable market data by correlation, or other means (market-corroborated inputs). A Level 2 input must be substantially observable for the full term of the asset or liability.

Finally, to the extent that observable Level 2 inputs are not available (for example, situations in which there is little market activity for the asset or liability at measurement date), Level 3 inputs can be applied. These are the firm's own assumptions about how other market participants would price the asset or liability. To ensure that there is information that will enable financial statement users to assess the quality of inputs used to estimate these fair value measurements, the standard requires firms to disclose information (separately for each major category of assets and liabilities), both quantitative information that shows how the fair value measurements are segregated based on the valuation inputs, and qualitative information that details the valuation techniques used to measure fair value. The quantitative disclosures are to be presented in tabular format. An example is given in the Case Study.

FAIR VALUE ACCOUNTING BASED ON IAS 39

IAS 39 details the principles for recognizing and measuring financial instruments for firms that report their financial statements under IFRS. IAS 39 defines fair value slightly differently from SFAS 157. Fair value is defined as "the amount for which an asset could be exchanged, or a liability settled, between knowledgeable, willing parties in an arm's length transaction" (paragraph 9).

There are some subtle language differences between the fair value definition in SFAS 157 versus that in IAS 39. SFAS 157's definition is explicitly based on the concept of an "exit price," whereas IAS 39's definition is based neither on "exit price," nor "entry price." SFAS 157 uses the "market participants" view whereas IAS 39's definition uses the concept of "willing buyer and seller." SFAS 157 states that the fair value of a liability is the price that will be paid to transfer a liability, whereas IAS 39 defines the fair value of a liability as the amount for which it can be settled. The IASB has asked for respondents' views on these differences.

As with SFAS 157, IAS 39 states that fair value estimation is not the amount that a firm would receive or pay in a forced transaction, involuntary liquidation, or distress sale (paragraph A69). Also consistent with SFAS 157, IAS 39 regards the best evidence of fair value as quoted prices in an active market (paragraph 48). Finally, while IAS 39 does not explicitly classify valuation inputs into Level 1, Level 2, and Level 3 categories as specified in SFAS 157, it does specify that the chosen valuation technique should make maximum use of market inputs and rely as little as possible on firm-specific inputs.

Regarding the measurement issues relating to fair value estimation, IAS 39 provides three classifications: Active markets for which quoted prices are available, inactive markets for nonequity instruments, and inactive markets for equity instruments. For financial instruments trading in active markets, the appropriate quoted market of an asset held (or liability to be issued) is the current bid price, whereas for assets to be acquired (or liability held), it is the current ask price. When current bid and ask prices are unavailable, the price of the most recent transaction can be used provided that there has not been a significant change in economic circumstances since the time of the transaction. Furthermore, quoted prices can be adjusted if the firm can demonstrate it is not fair value (for example, distress sales).

In the absence of an active market for a nonequity financial instrument, IAS 39 specifies that the preferred valuation technique to be used is the valuation technique that is shown to be commonly used by market participants to price the instrument (for example, if the valuation technique has been demonstrated to be able to provide reliable estimates of fair value obtained in actual market transactions). The chosen valuation technique needs to be consistent with established economic methodologies for pricing financial instruments, and the firm needs to calibrate the valuation technique periodically by testing it for validity using prices from any observable current market transactions in the same instrument (or based on any available observable market data).

Finally, for equity instruments (and any linked derivatives) that do not have a quoted market price in active markets, IAS 39 specifies that these instruments are to be measured at fair values only if the range of reasonable fair value estimates is not significant, and the probabilities of the various estimates can be reasonably assessed. Otherwise, the firm is precluded from measuring these instruments at fair value.

CASE STUDY

Two examples are given that show how financial assets and liabilities are disclosed, as reported by HSBC Finance Corporation, which is incorporated in the US, and HSBC Bank plc, a UK entity. Evidently, HSBC Finance Corporation categorized and reported the fair values of its assets and liabilities based on the nature of valuation inputs (Note 15 to the accounts). For example, the firm reported US$3,136

million of available-for-sale securities, of which US$354 million were fair value estimates from quoted prices in active markets (Level 1), US$2,743 million were fair value estimates from Level 2 inputs and US$39 million originated from Level 3 valuation inputs.

In contrast, HSBC Bank plc has traditionally reported its fair values by measurement basis (for example, £427,329 million as trading assets) in its Notes on the Financial Statements (Note 15: Analysis of financial assets and liabilities by measurement basis). To provide additional disclosures that are similar to SFAS 157's disclosure requirements, HSBC Bank plc disaggregated its £427,329 million of trading assets into fair value estimates that were derived from quoted prices (£234,399 million), versus those fair value estimates that were based on valuation methods using observable inputs (£185,369 million), and significant nonobservable inputs (£7,561 million).[1]

FURTHER CONSIDERATIONS

Recent illiquidity in some financial markets due to the subprime crisis has highlighted to standard setters the need to provide additional guidance in the measurement of fair value of financial instruments in markets that are not active. The IASB formed an expert advisory panel in mid-2008 to discuss specific issues encountered in the current adverse market environment. Likewise, the FASB issued FSP FAS 157-3, *Determining the fair value of a financial asset in a market that is not active*, to clarify how management's internal assumptions and observable market information should be considered when measuring fair value in markets that are not active, as well as how market quotes such as broker quotes should be considered in measuring fair value.

First, while broker quotes may be an appropriate input when measuring fair value, they are not necessarily determinative if an active market does not exist for the financial market. Thus, the firm should not automatically conclude that a particular transaction price is determinative of fair value. In markets that are not active, managerial judgment is required to evaluate whether individual transactions are forced liquidations or distressed sales.

Having said that, it is also inappropriate to automatically conclude that an inactive market implies the presence of forced transactions. The determination of whether a transaction is forced requires a comprehensive understanding of the circumstances of the transaction. Examples of what may constitute a forced transaction include a legal requirement to transact regardless of market conditions, or a necessity to dispose an asset immediately, even if there is insufficient time to market that asset to be sold. Hence, the presence of an inactive market may simply reflect an imbalance between supply and demand (i.e., more sellers than buyers), and not represent evidence of forced transactions (or distress sales).

Finally, the standard setters also clarify that, regardless of the valuation technique used to estimate fair values, a firm should always include appropriate risk adjustments that take into account credit and liquidity risks. This is because a fair value estimate that does not take into account all factors that market participants would consider in pricing the instrument does not represent a fair estimate of a current transaction price on the measurement date.

GOING FORWARD

The IASB has been working on several long-term projects that will further clarify guidance on fair value measurements. First, to establish a single source of guidance for all fair value measurements required or permitted by existing IFRSs, so as to reduce complexity, and improve consistency in their application. This project is similar in intent to SFAS 157, although it might differ in its requirements and wording. Publication of the exposure draft happened in the second quarter of 2009, and new standard IFRS 13 *Fair Value Measurement* was published in May 2011, to be effective from January 2013.

Second, the IASB is currently working to simplify and improve IAS 39. The board recognizes the need to improve the reporting of financial instruments, and to reduce the complexity of that reporting. In March 2008, the IASB published a discussion paper, *Reducing Complexity in Reporting Financial Instruments*. Going forward, the IASB plans to issue an IFRS to simplify financial instrument reporting, although no specific timeline has been set.

Third, the financial crisis has raised concerns that users need further information on how firms estimate the fair value of their financial instruments when there are only limited market data to support those estimates. In October 2008, the IASB published an exposure draft, *Improving Disclosures about Financial Instruments*, that proposes amendments to IFRS 7 (*Financial Instruments: Disclosures*). The exposure draft proposes disclosure requirements that are similar to the disclosure requirements in SFAS 157, such as having the three-level, fair value hierarchy. Depending on the comments received, the board will deliberate whether to proceed with amending IFRS 7.

Similarly, the FASB has also announced the addition of new FASB agenda projects intended to improve both the application guidance used to determine fair values, and the disclosure of fair value estimates. These projects were added partly in response to recommendations contained in the December 2008 Securities and Exchange Commission's (SEC) report on mark-to-market accounting. The SEC report recommended against suspension of fair value accounting standards, and reaffirmed that investors generally believe fair value accounting increases financial reporting transparency.

CONCLUSION

The trend toward fair value accounting appears to be irreversible. Fair value accounting requires recognition of balance sheet amounts at fair value, and changes in fair values to have an impact on the income statement, or via stockholder equity. Managers should be aware of the various measurement issues involved in valuing the financial instruments in their companies, especially when subjective fair value estimates are involved.

MAKING IT HAPPEN

Managers need to consider some important considerations when implementing fair value accounting. For example:
- The availability of observable market inputs, and how that would affect the estimation of fair values;
- The validity of valuation models used to estimate subjective fair values, given that valuation models might overlook certain key assumptions;
- The possible impact of increased volatility in their firms' earnings, and/or valuations as a result of fair value accounting, and how best to mitigate the increased volatility;
- The potential of systemic risk (or contagion risk) during periods of rapidly falling markets.

MORE INFO

Reports:

FASB. "FASB staff position no. FAS 157-3. Determining the fair value of a financial asset when the market for that asset is not active." October 10, 2008. Online at: www.fasb.org/pdf/fsp_fas157-3.pdf

FASB. "Summary of statement no.157: Fair value measurements." Online at: www.fasb.org/st/summary/stsum157.shtml

IASC Foundation. "Technical summary. IAS 39 Financial instruments: Recognition and measurement." Online at: tinyurl.com/3wynegm [PDF].

IASB Expert Advisory Panel. "Measuring and disclosing the fair value of financial instruments in markets that are no longer active." October 2008. Online at: tinyurl.com/5drmjd [PDF].

US Securities and Exchange Commission. "Report and recommendations pursuant to Section 133 of the Emergency Economic Stabilization Act of 2008: Study on mark-to-market accounting." Online at: www.sec.gov/news/studies/2008/marktomarket123008.pdf

Websites:

Financial Accounting Standards Board (FASB; US): www.fasb.org

IFRS Foundation and the International Accounting Standards Board (IASB): www.ifrs.org

See Also:

★ Effective Financial Reporting and Auditing: Importance and Limitations (pp. 81–83)

✔ International Financial Reporting Standards (IFRS): The Basics (pp. 316–317)

♥ Fair Value Calculations (pp. 392–393)

Introduction to Islamic Financial Risk Management Products

by Qudeer Latif and Susi Crawford

EXECUTIVE SUMMARY

- The main features of Islamic finance and *shariah* scholars are introduced.
- Conventional financial risk management products are viewed as non-*shariah*-compliant, which means that such products are not available to Islamic investors.
- The popularity of Islamic finance has given rise to a demand for *shariah*-compliant financial risk management products for underlying Islamic investments.
- A number of structures of *shariah*-compliant financial risk management products are available in the marketplace, all based around a *murabaha* sale structure.
- The rising popularity of the *wa'ad* structure is discussed.
- The article concludes with a brief summary of the future of *shariah*-compliant financial risk management products.

INTRODUCTION: THE MAIN FEATURES OF ISLAMIC FINANCE

To consider the basics of Islamic financial risk management products it is helpful to summarize the Islamic principles and jurisprudence on which Islamic finance is based.

- **Speculation**: contracts which involve speculation (*maysir*) are not permissible (*haram*) and are considered void. Islamic law does not prohibit general commercial speculation, but it does prohibit speculation which is akin to gambling, i.e. gaining something by chance rather than productive effort.
- **Unjust enrichment**: contracts where one party gains unjustly at the expense of another are considered void.
- **Interest**: the payment and receipt of interest (*riba*) are prohibited, and any obligation to pay interest is considered void. Islamic principles require that any return on funds provided by the lender be earned by way of profit derived from a commercial risk taken by that lender.
- **Uncertainty**: contracts which contain uncertainty (*gharar*)—particularly when there is uncertainty as to the fundamental terms of the contract, such as the subject matter, price, and time for delivery—are considered void.

To ensure adherence to these underlying principles, most banks that sell Islamic products have a board of *shariah* scholars (or will appoint a *shariah* scholar on a product-by-product basis) to ensure the bank's (or product's) compliance with the Islamic precepts.

On the whole, *shariah* scholars in the financial field hold the view that financial risk management products (commonly referred to as hedging arrangements) in the conventional finance space fall into the category of speculation (*maysir*) and uncertainty (*gharar*), both of which are prohibited under the *shariah* and cannot therefore be marketed as *shariah*-compliant products or used in conjunction with Islamic financing.

With the rise in sophistication of Islamic finance in recent years, however, a school of thought has emerged among pre-eminent *shariah* scholars that Islamic investors should be able to enter into hedging arrangements, provided that the financial risk management product is itself structured in a *shariah*-compliant manner and that there is genuine underlying risk arising from an Islamic investment.

The conventional financial risk management products have become an intrinsic part of the mechanics of banking finance and are, to a large part, documented by standard documentation and negotiated without recourse to lawyers. Any *shariah*-compliant financial risk products have to strike the balance of being faithful to the principles of *shariah* while maintaining the user-friendly structure of their conventional counterparts.

THE CONVENTIONAL PRODUCTS

Financial risk management products in the conventional world are, in their basic form, a derivative, and each product is based on the principles that a derivative is a financial instrument whose value derives from that of an underlying asset, and the underlying asset must be capable of being ascribed a market value.

The number of "assets" that can be ascribed a market value and from which, therefore, a derivative can be derived has resulted in a variety of financial risk management products. The commonly known structures are those based on interest and currency rates: i.e. interest rate swaps, cross-currency swaps, and foreign exchange forwards. There are also commodity derivatives based on gold, steel, and other metals. More recently, products known as "exotics" based on the weather and carbon emissions have appeared in the market in response to the requirements of a changing environmental as well as financial climate.

HOW A *SHARIAH*-COMPLIANT PRODUCT IS STRUCTURED

The starting point in structuring an Islamic financial risk management product should be an understanding of the commercial purpose of its conventional counterpart. For example, when structuring a profit rate swap, one must examine the use and structure of the basic interest rate swap. The interest rate swap is a hedging arrangement that is used to limit exposure to possible losses of expected income due to interest rate movements, and there is a similar demand for *shariah*-compliant products to limit exposure in Islamic investments where the profit, rent, or commission is linked in part to interest rate movements.

One must also must consider the non-*shariah* aspects of a conventional financial risk management product and address the same in the Islamic structure. As noted in the introduction, a principle of Islamic finance is that any profit must be earned through trade and taking a risk in a transaction. A common reason why hedging arrangements are seen as non-compliant is that although a financial risk management product is linked to the value of an asset, it does not require ownership risk in the asset itself and any profit earned is earned independently of trade, ownership, or investment in such an asset.

Conventional risk management products are structured along the lines of a synthetic trade that occurs on each payment date. The elements of this synthetic trade are that:

- a party will be obliged to carry out an action (such as the delivery of an asset or the payment of a price) on a certain date; and
- the obligation to carry out such action will vary in accordance with the value of the underlying asset.

This structure has provided the framework for *shariah*-compliant financial risk management products by replacing the synthetic trade with an actual commodity (or any other asset) trade structured along the lines of a *murabaha*. This is a common Islamic structure under which assets can be sold for an express profit and the payment can be deferred.

By using commodity trades, the banks and the counterparty expose themselves to ownership, if only briefly, of an underlying asset. The traded commodity represents the principal amount of the underlying Islamic investment (the "cost price") and is sold at a profit, which is calculated by reference to an interest rate and, if applicable, a margin (the "profit"). As the bank has taken ownership in the underlying asset, it is permitted to on-sell this at the profit, which must be agreed upfront.

A number of structures of *shariah*-compliant products all based on the *murabaha* have appeared in the marketplace with varying degrees of success. A description of the main structures, using the example of a profit (interest) rate swap, are set out below, together with the advantages and disadvantages of each.

Profit Rate Swap Structure No. 1

As in a conventional trade the parties, namely the "bank" and the "counterparty," agree the commercial terms of the future transaction i.e. the trade dates, the fixed rate, the floating rate, the assets to be traded, and the notional cost price. On each trade date, the bank and counterparty will enter into two *murabaha* agreements.

Under the first *murabaha* agreement (the "floating leg"):

- the counterparty will sell to the bank an amount of commodities, the value of which will be the notional cost price;
- the sale price for these commodities will be cost price + profit;
- the profit element will represent the floating rate (calculated against the notional cost price).

Under the second *murabaha* agreement (the "fixed leg"):

- the bank will sell to the counterparty an amount of commodities the value of which will be the notional cost price;
- the sale price for these commodities, will be cost price + profit;
- the profit element will represent the fixed rate (calculated against the notional cost price).

The structure is shown in Figure 1. The net result of these trades is that on each trade date: the amount of commodities sold under each *murabaha* will be the same and the cost price

Figure 1. *Murabaha* structure no. 1

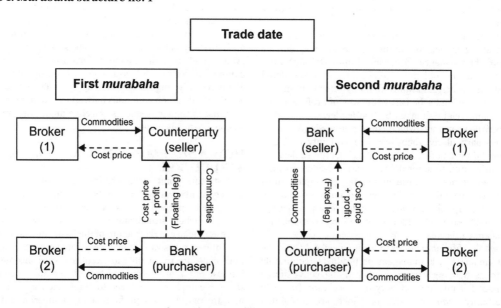

will be the same, and these will effectively be netted off by way of on-sales to a third-party broker; only the profit element will differ; and, as in a conventional interest rate swap, the net beneficiary (of the difference between the fixed and floating rate) is dependent on whether the fixed or floating rate was higher.

The risks associated with this *murabaha* structure are as follows:

Commodity risk. This arises from the bank's and the counterparty's ownership of the commodity. To mitigate this risk, although the ownership lasts for a short period only, many banks require the counterparty to indemnify them against any losses incurred due to ownership of the commodity. Some Islamic institutions see this as undermining the principles of *shariah*, which require that full ownership risk is taken.

Execution risk. This arises due to the fact that, under Islamic principles, parties cannot agree to a future sale (where delivery of the asset and payment of the price are both deferred to a later date). Therefore, the delivery of a commodity must occur on the same day that the *murabaha* contract is concluded. The result of this "parallel *murabaha*" structure depends on both parties' willingness to enter into the *murabaha* agreements on each trade date (whether or not they are the net beneficiary).

Costs. These costs arise from the fact that two new *murabahas* are entered into at the beginning of each "profit" period (with deferred payment provisions) or on the trade date itself (with immediate delivery and payment provisions), throughout the term of the profit rate swap. This exposes each party not only to ownership risk, but also to the brokerage costs associated with a commodity trade (normally the brokerage fees are the liability of the counterparty, who would then be liable for two sets of brokerage fees on each trade date).

Profit Rate Swap Structure No. 2

In recognition of the risks set out above, the "parallel *murabaha*" structure has been developed in such a way as to limit the bank's and the counterparty's exposure to these risks, the key of which is that the fixed-leg *murabaha* is only entered into on day 1 and runs for the life of the profit rate swap, with "fixed" profit under the day-one *murabaha* being paid in installments over a number of deferred payment dates (with no need for further commodity trades to take place or *murabaha* agreements to be entered into).

The deferred payment dates under the fixed-leg *murabaha* will match the trade dates of each floating-leg *murabaha*. Because the floating-leg *murabaha* resets the profit rate a number of times, it has to be re-executed in relation to each trade date in order to give the parties certainty of the cost price + profit, which results in a commodity trade being carried out. The way that structure 2 operates is illustrated in Figure 2.

Figure 2. *Murabaha* structure no. 2

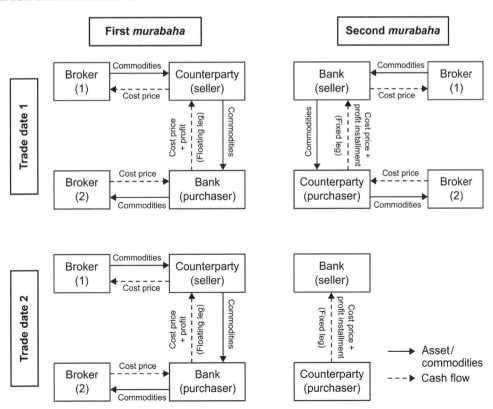

This structure reduces the ownership risk (by reducing the number of commodity trades that are carried out) and the associated costs. It also reduces the execution risk as one half of the trade is entered into on day 1. The parties are, however, still exposed to some execution risk: for example, a party not benefiting from a trade could walk away from the trade and the bank would remain liable to pay out under the fixed-leg *murabaha*.

Profit Rate Swap Structure No. 3

A structure that addresses the execution risk associated with structures 1 and 2 (and mitigates the ownership risk associated with structure 1) has recently appeared on the market and is known as the *wa'ad* structure (Figure 3).

Wa'ad is the Arabic word for promise. A promise, though commonly thought of as a moral obligation, is in most legal systems a legal one. The *wa'ad* structure is based on each party (as promisor) granting the other (as promisee) a unilateral and irrevocable promise to enter into a trade on certain dates for a certain price in the future (effectively a put option). The trade that takes place on a trade date is, like the *murabaha* structure, based on the purchase of commodities (or other assets), and the promise itself is

documented by way of a purchase undertaking (or put option).

These two purchase undertakings cannot be linked in any way, but they can and do contain similar terms such as the trade dates and the commodities to be purchased. The only main difference is the price, which consists of cost price and profit (which will be calculated to reflect the difference between the fixed and floating rates).

The main aspect of the promise is the conditions attached to its exercise by the beneficiary, the promisee. The conditions attached to the exercise mirror those in the conventional hedge that determine which party benefits on a trade date. In an interest rate swap, this would be whether the fixed rate or the floating rate were higher. Depending on which is higher, only one party is able to exercise the purchase undertaking under which they are promisee and require the promisor to carry out a trade, purchase commodities, and pay the promisee the cost price + profit. The net result of the trade mirrors that of the *murabaha* structures in that the cash flows are gained through the purchase and on-sale of commodities, but also that of a conventional trade, where there is only one cash flow representing the difference in the profit.

Figure 3. The *wa'ad* structure

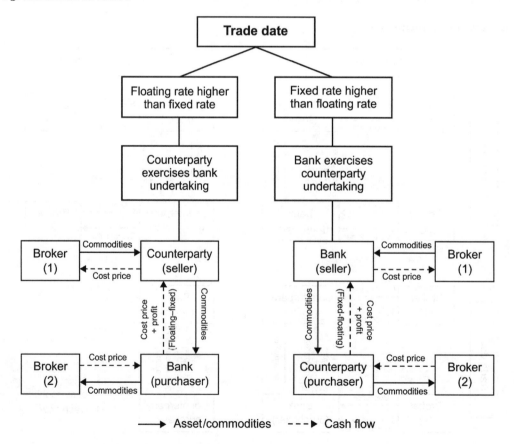

As is the case with structure 2, the benefits are that there is only one trade on any trade date, which lowers the ownership risk and associated costs. The real advantage, however, is that it resolves the issue of execution risk as the party in the money is in "control" of the trade, and once the promise is exercised by the promisee, the contractual obligation to purchase the commodities and pay the cost price + profit arises without need for further execution.

The flexibility of the *wa'ad* structure makes it suitable for a number of products beyond profit rate swaps, as it can be adapted as a foreign exchange forward (with only one purchase undertaking) or cross-currency swap. It can also be drafted as a master agreement together with purchase undertakings, bringing it in line with its conventional counterparts.

CONCLUSION

The Islamic financial risk management products market has gathered such momentum in recent years that the favored structures are constantly under review and revision. Satisfied that the Islamic structure allows payments that mirror those of the conventional trades, bankers are now looking at the other International Swaps and Derivatives Association (ISDA)–style provisions, such as right to terminate, termination events, tax events, and calculation of close-out amounts, and they are demanding the same level of sophistication in the Islamic financial risk management products.

MAKING IT HAPPEN

Before structuring or entering into an Islamic financial risk management product, consider the following points.
- What is the commercial objective of the transaction: i.e. what

position should the parties be in on a trade date and at the end of the transaction? Does the Islamic structure reflect this?
- Which structure is more suitable, considering the costs and the risks involved? This may be determined more by the *shariah* board of the financial institution involved than by commercial preference.
- How should the trade be documented? Who will be carrying out the day-to-day mechanics of the underlying trades, and will they understand the documentation? Conventional financial risk products are often based on ISDA documentation and are carried out by bankers without recourse to lawyers.
- What jurisdiction are you dealing in, and will the documentation be enforceable? What is the situation on insolvency? This will have to be considered when drafting the close-out or unwind mechanics.

MORE INFO

Websites:
International Islamic Financial Market (IIFM): www.iifm.net
International Swaps and Derivatives Association (ISDA): www.isda.org

See Also:
- ★ Investment Risk in Islamic Finance (pp. 27–31)
- ★ Procedures for Reporting Financial Risk in Islamic Finance (pp. 101–103)
- ★ Risk Management of Islamic Finance Instruments (pp. 48–53)
- ✔ Managing Risk in Islamic Finance (pp. 297–298)

Investment Risk in Islamic Finance
by Kamal Abdelkarim Hassan and Hassan Ahmed Yusuf

EXECUTIVE SUMMARY
- The unique risks within the Islamic finance investment space are described, along with the challenges faced in developing procedures and processes to address those risks.
- The categories of *shariah* risk, and the means available to mitigate this risk, are considered.
- Investment opportunities are limited due to the restricted nature of the Islamic investment universe.

INTRODUCTION

At the inception of Islamic finance, Islamic economists advocated change and developed a policy for Islamic banking practice and process, arguing that the main aspect of

conventional banking—*riba* (interest)—required immediate rectification if Islamic banking was to exist. To achieve this goal, profit and loss sharing methods were introduced, along with other products such as *ijarah* (lease) and *murabahah* (cost plus). The rest of the technical banking operational procedure remained almost the same, especially in areas where there was no immediate solution, such as the application of the London Interbank Offered Rate (LIBOR) as a benchmark. This was based on the Islamic maxim *al daruuriyaatu tubihu al mahdurat* (necessity permits the unlawful). Likewise, the application of risk management within Islamic finance is not completely different from its conventional counterpart. Similarly, both Islamic and conventional financing apply the same methodology and technique in regard to risk management. It is essential to note that there are elements of risk, such as *shariah* risk, associated with Islamic finance that do not exist in its conventional counterpart due to the nature of Islamic finance and investment. As such, the challenge for the *shariah*-compliant investment and finance industry is to have procedures and processes in place to deal with risks unique to Islamic finance instruments. Based on the above, we discuss below types of Islamic investment risks unique in Islamic finance, as shown in Table 1.

Table 1. Risks specific to Islamic investment

Shariah risk	Risk associated with not implementing Islamic investment and finance products in accordance with *shariah* principles.
Asset concentration	Investing, financing, or drawing earnings and income in a single market or a single asset class.
Default risk	Risk that a counterparty fails to meet its financial obligations as they fall due.
Rate of return risk	Risk of fluctuations in earnings where expected income targets may not be achieved due to market conditions as Islamic finance and investment concentrates more on equity.
Transparency risk	Risk of not disclosing information necessary for users in regard to financial data, risk management, business conditions, and other necessary information.
Equity investment risk	Risk associated with holding equity investment during unfavorable situations, where decline in investment caused by market conditions in turn gives volatility of earnings of *musharakah* and *mudarabah* investments. (This definition needs more clarity as it appears to include rate of return risk as well.)

UNIQUE RISKS IN ISLAMIC FINANCE

There is no the doubt that the recent financial crisis and the rapid development of financial innovation and engineering of Islamic investment instruments necessitate the need for risk management, control, and vigilant supervision. Islamic finance investment is different from its conventional

counterpart because it is required to comply with *shariah* rules and guidance or it could lose its legitimacy, thereby constituting a *shariah* risk. *Shariah* risk has a deeper, more profound meaning than its current use in the Islamic finance literature, and its scope is changing relative to the pace of Islamic finance development.[1]

SHARIAH RISK AND ITS CATEGORIES

Shariah risk can occur in different stages in Islamic investment. It has subcategories and the impact of each category is different. To understand this better, *shariah* risk can be categorized as follows.

Category 1 relates to the minimum requirements for an investment to be deemed *shariah*-compliant and forms important distinctions between conventional and Islamic investment. Those features that are to be avoided are interest, gambling, and uncertainty. All Islamic investments should be free from dealings with interest, gambling, and excessive uncertainty. Additionally, *shariah* compliance requires abstention from investing in industries where the core business is considered illicit in Islam, such as alcohol, pork, cinemas, gambling industries, and items that are regarded as prohibited in *shariah* (Figure 1).

Failure to comply with the minimum parameters in the first category of *shariah* risk with respect to any potential Islamic investment could have a huge impact, possibly resulting in the dissolution of the invested entity, and could cause huge reputational risk. Hence, the important responsibility of the *shariah* board to check and ensure the details of the investment and declare it legitimate before any investment commitment.

Category 2 of *shariah* risk relates to the process and implementation mechanism of finance investment products. Generally, the process starts with presentation of the financial product to the *shariah* board by the developer of the product. The product description and structure, its underlying asset securities (if any), different types of contracts, charges, fees, and other necessary details are examined by the *shariah* board. Following detailed discussions, the *shariah* board renders its advice.[2] Once the product is completed as the

Figure 1. The investment selection process

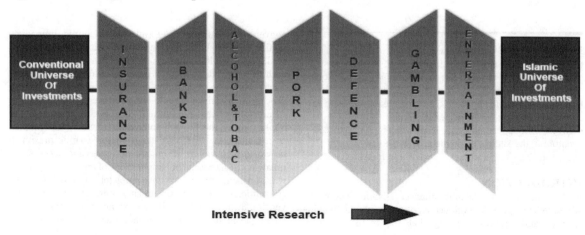

shariah board has advised, legitimacy is given and it hits the market. *Shariah* risk in this category would arise if the product failed to conform to the process approved by the *shariah* board (for instance, the procedure advised by *shariah* is sequential in order, where one step follows its predecessor, while in contrast the implementation team may feel it irrelevant that step 3 should precede step 4).[3] This type of risk is mitigated through a *shariah* auditor or supervisor review of the process and mechanism implemented during the operational process of any product launch.

This type of risk is limited as long as *shariah* audit reviews and corrections are applied immediately. An example of this type of risk is in a *wakalah* contract offer where money is received by a *wakil* (agent) before the offer is accepted by the *muwwakil* (principal). The money cannot be invested before the acceptance of offer is signed, according to the *shariah* guidelines.

Category 3 refers to the situation where the process of a structured product presented to the *shariah* board may not be implemented as advised by the board. Here there could be some additions and/or deletions of the process by the developers which were not included in the information initially presented to the *shariah* board. Such a risk is mitigated by employing a *shariah* auditor review, or additionally making it the practice of *shariah* boards to review products after launch and during normal operations. An example of this type is a structured product approved by *shariah* but where the board has not approved part of the fees or commission received as these were not presented to the board during the initial product presentations. The impact and the risk are that the generated fees or profit not approved by the *shariah* board during that period could be canceled.

Category 4 risk is that some investments may be declared null and void by another group of scholars or a regulatory body, based on the lack of accurate product formulation or their own differing interpretation of *shariah* principles, procedures, and processes. An example of this type is *tawwaruq*,[4] as the legitimacy and the approval of the investment product was based on the *fatwa* given by the *shariah* board. Since the *fatwa* itself is in the form of *ijtihad* (the process of making a legal decision by independent interpretation of the legal sources of the scholar), there are no problems if it is right. If it is wrong, the appropriate corrections will need to be applied thereto without necessarily outlawing the product or the interpretation. This is based on the well-known principle of *fiqh* in Islamic jurisprudence (i.e. if a scholar offers a correct *fatwa*, he or she receives two rewards; if he or she gets it wrong, they get one reward only). In contrast, declaring a product illegitimate requires research and evidence, as financial transactions in Islamic investment are based on what is known. Permissibility of origin[5] and the burden of proof lie with the person asserting that the product is not permissible.

ASSET CONCENTRATION

The Islamic investment universe offers a limited choice of investment products that meet *shariah*-compliant guidelines. As a result, a primary Islamic investment vehicle for many Islamic financial institutions tends to be real estate. This type of concentration leads to risky circumstances, particularly in unfavorable market conditions as we have seen in the subprime mortgage crisis of 2008. Unsurprisingly, within the Gulf Cooperation Council (GCC), banks reached the ceiling investment limit of real estate portfolio. Such a situation clearly highlights asset concentration due to the limited choice of Islamic investment products. Currently, Islamic investment is moving toward more mature levels, and therefore is in dire need of product innovation. The impact of this type of risk could be enormous if there is a sudden change of microeconomic conditions. There are defined guidelines for addressing this risk concentration and controls that can reduce exposure to risk if properly applied and managed.

DEFAULT RISK

Default risk is when a counterparty fails to pay its investment or finance obligation. This is also classified as credit risk in conventional terminology. Similar mitigating frameworks applied in conventional finance may be applied within Islamic investment and finance. Nevertheless, within the conventional investment system, the procedure for granting credit facilities includes background checks and credit history of the past performance of applicants that is facilitated by maintaining good quality data (credit agencies). Within Islamic investment and finance, trust by way of name-lending supersedes conventional credit examination—particularly in the GCC, where a developed credit bureau does not exist. The significant downside of name-lending has long been established (for example, investments without collateral). Risk of default may be higher and, even in the face of existing genuine collateral, issues may arise in determining the real market value when required, and any liquidation of assets could entail a lengthy legal process.

RATE OF RETURN RISK

Islamic investments face rate of return risk due to the fluctuations in microeconomic conditions. Islamic investment could experience greater fluctuations and volatility in rate of return risk due to limited product choices and prefixed income, which are absent in conventional investment. Furthermore, asset classes within Islamic investment are not easily converted to cash and may be subject to commodity price risk, as some of these assets do not have ready or deep secondary markets (*sukuk*—Islamic bonds) and, as such, must be held until maturity.

OTHER RISKS

Investment in Islamic finance faces equity investment risk, largely due to the application of both *mudarabah* and *musharakah* investments. Likewise, there are other risk elements that are interrelated in Islamic investments. For instance, the lack of a wide range of *shariah*-compliant products to absorb the liquidity of Islamic investments could result in an opportunity loss for the investment. Islamic investment products are few considering the amount of available funds available for Islamic investment. This results in a low return on investment as it is invested in short-term products and thus creates mismatch problems, since Islamic investments are in long-term opportunities such as project finance, real estate, and *sukuk*. Furthermore, the lack of tradable instruments in secondary markets could also play a role. The scope of transparency risk in Islamic investment is not confined to lack of reliability, nondisclosure, and inadequate information, but can also include the process of the approval of products in case of dispute, as we have seen in recent court cases. It also includes the stock selection process and details and strategies for stringent risk management process employed to safeguard the interests of all parties—shareholders and depositors alike.

RISK IMPACT OF ISLAMIC FINANCE

The subprime mortgage and subsequent financial crisis in 2008 were blamed on the lack of risk management and the complete ignoring of signs of risk by senior management within financial institutions. Nevertheless, recent cases in the Islamic finance sector highlight that lapses in risk management could have detrimental results on the stability of Islamic finance institutions and damage the reputation of the industry.

The troubled Bahrain-based Gulf Finance House (GFH), once the darling of Islamic finance in the Kingdom, suffered from severe lapses in risk management.[6] Within GFH there was an absence of real diversification. In 2008 and 2009, 78.5% and 83.4% respectively of GFH's assets were concentrated in Gulf countries and were primarily real estate in nature. Furthermore, the fact that the business and earnings of GFH were directly linked to a single asset class (real estate) was a recipe for disaster. One could also argue that the presence of *shariah* risk, evident in methods of implementing *murabahah* transactions within GFH, was not complete given that the basic conditions to disclose price and markup were violated. Likewise, in the case of Dato' Haji Nik Mahmud bin Daud vs Bank Islam Malaysia,[7] *shariah* risk occurred due to the nontransferrence of ownership. This also violated the *shariah* requirement that a seller must own the title of the asset. In the Symphony Gems case,[8] the *murabahah* contract was not a valid *murabahah* contract according to the testimony of Dr Al-Samaan. In a recent case involving the Investment Dar Company (TID) vs Blom Development Bank,[9] TID's legal counsel used *shariah* noncompliance of the contract as a defense—highlighting the significance of *shariah* risk.

MAKING IT HAPPEN

- The risks faced by Islamic investments, such as *shariah* risk and equity investment risk, are unique due to the nature of such investments. Inadequate and insufficient observation of *shariah* investment guidelines could cause a risk that results in the dissolution of the investment and leads to loss of confidence, trust, and reputation of the institution. Consequently, there is a lack of development in the Islamic risk management framework that would enable it to identify, assess, and measure the risks unique to Islamic investment. Even the analysis and structure of presentation of *shariah* risk are borrowed from conventional risk management.
- There is a dire need to have a complete and comprehensive *shariah* risk management framework for Islamic finance that can capture the current process of the Islamic finance structure. Other risks faced by Islamic investment, such as rate of return, credit risk, asset concentration, commodity

risk, and market volatility, can have a huge impact if not managed properly. Contained within the *shariah* principles are adequate measures that provide effective safeguards for Islamic investment.

- However, there remains a need for *shariah* to show adaptability in the face of phenomenal growth, the sophistication of product innovation, and financial engineering. This should hasten changes and the development of a suitable risk management framework that is compatible with the *maqasid al-shariah* (objective of *shariah*).

MORE INFO

Books:

Archer, Simon, and Rifaat Abdelkarim. *Islamic Finance: The Regulatory Challenge*. Singapore: Wiley, 2007.

Iqbal, Zamir, and Abbas Mirakhor. *An Introduction to Islamic Finance Theory and Practice*. Singapore: Wiley, 2007.

Article:

Moghul, Umar F., and Arshad A. Ahmed. "Contractual forms in Islamic finance law and Islamic Investment Company of the Gulf (Bahamas) Ltd. v. Symphony Gems N.V. & others: A first impression of Islamic finance." *Fordham International Law Journal* 27:1 (December 2003): 150–194. Online at: ir.lawnet.fordham.edu/ilj/vol27/iss1/7/

Reports:

Bälz, Kilian. "Sharia risk? How Islamic finance has transformed Islamic contract law." Occasional Publications 9. Islamic Legal Studies Program, Harvard Law School, September 2008. Online at: www.law.harvard.edu/programs/ilsp/publications/balz.pdf

Khnifer, Mohammed, Aatef Baig, and Frank Winkler. "The rise and fall of Gulf Finance House." Design, Implementation and Risk Aspects of Islamic Financial Products and Services module, Reading University, 2010.

Saiful Azhar Rosly. "*Shariah* compliant parameters reconsidered." Paper presented at the Annual Malaysian Finance Association Conference, Kuching, Malaysia, June 4–5, 2008.

See Also:

★ Introduction to Islamic Financial Risk Management Products (pp. 23–27)

★ Procedures for Reporting Financial Risk in Islamic Finance (pp. 101–103)

★ Risk Management of Islamic Finance Instruments (pp. 48–53)

✔ Managing Risk in Islamic Finance (pp. 297–298)

NOTES

1 The scope of *shariah* risk currently applied is often limited to financial transactions, but, given that *shariah* compliance is the distinctive characteristic of Islamic finance, a much broader application of this unique risk is required. As *shariah* should encompass all of an Islamic financial institution's activities, from transactional contracts to staff and vendor contracts, a broader approach to *shariah* risk is required.

2 This is one of the processes for obtaining approval of Islamic finance and investment products from the *shariah* board. Different banks have different processes for obtaining product approval from the *shariah* board. Sometimes a *shariah* compliance officer may make the presentation to the *shariah* board.

3 There was a case in a Gulf bank where written acceptance of an offer was received after the profit of that period was realized, and the *shariah* board canceled the profit from that period.

4 *Tawwaruq* is a controversial product among scholars. Recently a Gulf central bank issued written advice on the use of *tawwaruq* products, the permissible percentages of these relative to other products, and even advising that *tawwaruq* should not be used on credit cards.

5 Under *shariah* law, legality and illegality are based on either prohibition or permissibility. For example, all forms of worship are illegitimate except those allowed by *shariah*. This means that no one can use any form of worship unless that form is permitted by *shariah*. This is unlike the situation with food, where all kinds are permissible except what has been prohibited. That is why, when *shariah* considers items of food, it starts with prohibitions, as permissibility is the basis in matters of food. Similarly, financial transactions are based on permissibility. The outcome is that if the usage of something is based on permissibility, the burden of proof is on the party rejecting such permissibility, and if it is based on prohibition, the burden of proof is on the party permitting such actions.

6 Khnifer *et al.*, 2010.

7 Saiful, 2008.

8 Moghul and Ahmed, 2003.

9 Investment Dar Company vs Blom Development Bank case.

Managing Counterparty Credit Risk
by David Shimko

EXECUTIVE SUMMARY

- Counterparty risk exposure is the financial measure of performance risk in any contract.
- Many contract exposures are managed through operational or legal means; this article focuses on financial risk management.
- Counterparty credit exposure equals *current exposure* (accounts receivable minus collateral) plus an adjustment for *potential future exposure* based on possible increases in future net receivables.
- A comprehensive credit risk management policy addresses counterparty initiation and monitoring, contracting standards, credit authorities and limits, the transaction approval process, credit risk reporting, and reserving and capital policy.
- Credit risk mitigation is best handled through collateral, but there are legal and financial means to mitigate credit risk as well.
- Credit insurance can fit the exposure perfectly, but may be costly.
- Credit default swaps are linked to credit events and payments that may not correspond exactly to counterparty exposures, but may be cheaper than credit insurance.

DEFINING COUNTERPARTY RISK

Counterparty risk is the risk to each party of a contract that the counterparty will not live up to its contractual obligations; it is otherwise known as default risk.

Counterparty risk relates closely to performance risk. It arises whenever one entity depends on another to honor the terms of a contract. If a parts supplier fails to provide steering wheels to General Motors, GM will be damaged because of its inability to deliver complete cars. The resulting profit reduction is defined as the *exposure* that GM runs to its supplier. Similarly, GM runs a credit exposure to its customers who have not yet paid for their cars. This would include dealers and end customers who are financed by GMAC, GM's financing subsidiary.

Normally, performance risk is managed operationally—i.e., GM would use alternative suppliers, reserve supplies of steering wheels, and contractual nonperformance remedies to manage its performance risk. Also, to manage risk to its dealers, it may retain title to vehicles, verify insurance coverage, obtain some advance payment, and use legal means to minimize their collections risk. In addition to these counterparty risk situations, GM will experience counterparty risk from its derivative contracts.

Suppose GM wanted to purchase steering wheels on an ongoing basis from a European supplier, and protect itself from devaluation of the US dollar. It would likely enter a foreign exchange swap transaction with a bank. After entering the contract, rates would continue to change, bringing the contract in-the-money to either GM or the bank. If the dollar were to devalue, the contract would move in-the-money to GM, which would expose GM to the possible failure of the bank to honor its contract. Conversely, if the dollar were to strengthen, the bank would have an in-the-money contract with GM, and subsequently become concerned about GM's possible default risk.

MEASURING COUNTERPARTY RISK

Counterparty risk exposure can be divided into accounts receivable exposure and potential future exposure. If collateral is held as a bond for performance risk, the amount of the collateral is deducted from the gross exposure calculation. If the collateral itself is risky, such as a deposit of traded securities rather than cash, the collateral may not get full credit. Therefore, total credit exposure can be defined as follows:

Current exposure = {max (Accounts receivable
 − Discounted collateral value), 0}

Potential future exposure = Current credit exposure
 + Maximum likely increase in future credit exposure

Figure 1. Exposure distribution for GM

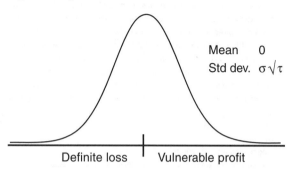

Mean   0
Std dev. $\sigma\sqrt{\tau}$

Definite loss   Vulnerable profit

The maximum likely increase in future credit exposure is defined relative to a timeframe and relative to a statistical confidence interval, typically 95%. To demonstrate this concept simply, assume a potential foreign exchange transaction as an expected value of zero with an annual standard deviation of σ, a duration of τ, and a normally distributed risk. This is illustrated in Figure 1.

The *definite loss* shows in which cases GM will owe money to the bank, while *vulnerable profit* shows cases where the bank may owe money to GM. It is called vulnerable on account of the default risk of the bank. Although the current exposure is zero, the vulnerable profit could be as great as 1.65 standard deviations using a 95% confidence interval. This is also known as the *peak exposure*. The probability-weighted average of all the exposure figures, both zero and positive, is known as the *expected exposure*. For the normal distribution case, the expected exposure is 0.40 times the standard deviation.

To determine the expected loss conditional on default, we need to have two more pieces of information. One is the probability of default, which we will call π. The other is the *loss given default*, i.e., the percentage of the exposure that we never recover, even after settlement or bankruptcy. We call this estimate λ. Given these assumptions, we may summarize:

Peak exposure $= 1.65\sigma\sqrt{\tau}$

Expected exposure $= 0.40\sigma\sqrt{\tau}$

Expected loss $= 0.40\pi\lambda\sigma\sqrt{\tau}$

For example, if GM determines the euro volatility to be 15% per year, the contract to be three months in duration (0.25 years), its bank to have a default likelihood of 10%, and the loss given default to be 50%, its expected loss is $(0.40 \times 0.10 \times 0.50 \times 0.15 \times \sqrt{0.25}) = 0.0015$ times the size of the transaction—i.e., $1500 per million dollars hedged.

In the case of a swap rather than a single forward transaction, the amortization of the swap payments reduces exposure over time, so that it does not necessarily rise with the square root of time. In this case, the peak and expected exposure can be determined as in Figure 2.

The peak exposure can be used to understand how much risk is being taken with respect to the counterparty, whereas the expected exposure is an indicator of expected losses.

Figure 2. Exposure of a swap

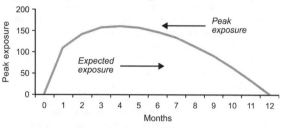

CREDIT RISK MANAGEMENT POLICY

Best practice credit risk management policy includes the following items:

- counterparty initiation and monitoring;
- contracting standards;
- credit authorities and limits;
- transaction approval process;
- credit risk reporting;
- a reserving and capital policy.

Counterparty initiation refers to the first time a company wishes to enter a transaction with a proposed counterparty. The credit department typically reviews available public information, credit agency reports, and counterparty financials before agreeing to trade with the counterparty. The financial status of the counterparty should be continually monitored to detect proactively situations where counterparty credit quality might deteriorate. It is also important to segregate counterparties according to legal entities; trading with a subsidiary of a triple-A company may provide little or no financial protection in the event of a default. Furthermore, one should assume in general that a benefit of trading with one legal entity *cannot* be netted against a loss to another legal entity of the same firm. For example, if a company is owed $1 million by subsidiary X, and owes $1 million to subsidiary Y of the same counterparty, and X defaults, it will still have an obligation to Y.

Contracting standards refer to the types of contracts that may be entered with an appropriately initiated counterparty. For example, in most derivative contracts, a standard contract such as the International Swaps and Derivatives Association (ISDA) contract is used. Even standard contracts require customization, however. The Credit Support Annex (CSA) of the ISDA details the unilateral or bilateral collateral posting requirements of the counterparties. It also typically contains provisions for Material Adverse Changes (MAC) in the credit quality of the counterparties, perhaps calling for more collateral when credit ratings downgrade. Finally, the CSA details rules for termination of contracts—for example, upon failure to supply collateral. ISDA Master Agreements should be established to guarantee netting across different legal entities of the same counterparty.

Credit limits refer to the amount of credit risk that may be taken to approved counterparties with approved contract forms. In most firms, credit limits are set on an aggregate basis by counterparty or credit rating—for instance, the firm is unwilling to take more than $100 million in credit risk to any one bank with a AA rating.

Credit authorities refer to the ability of any individual trader or trading desk to enter into new transactions with a counterparty, considering the possible impact on current or future credit exposure. Best practice firms use some measure of *potential future exposure* in setting their credit limits, although many focus only on *current exposure*. Some firms will also set portfolio concentration limits, for example, restricting the company's credit exposure to a particular industry. In all cases, firms must establish exception policies to deal with situations where credit limits are inadvertently or deliberately breached.

Transaction approval is a verification process to ensure that, before an individual transaction is executed, all of its requirements have been met: Counterparty initiation, contracts, collateral provisions, collateral collection if applicable, and compliance with authorities and with limits. Some firms allow slack in the process, such as transactions under a given materiality threshold with an uninitiated counterparty. These are a practical consequence of business dealings, but credit risk departments should strive to minimize these occurrences.

Credit risk reporting should address credit risk across the firm, whether risk is run in treasury, procurement, or sales. Aggregate receivables, potential future exposure, and aggregate collateral should be brought together in a comprehensive report by a non-netted legal entity. Best practice reporting includes portfolio risk measures, such as aggregate credit exposure, concentrations, and sensitivity of exposure to key economic drivers.

A reserving policy for expected credit losses—to be taken as a charge against earnings and reversed if losses never materialize—should be established by the office of the chief financial officer. This practice ensures that business units are held responsible for credit risk in their contracting processes. Some firms also charge business units for credit risk usage, but practices vary considerably. As a general statement, if a firm puts a price on credit risk, then business units must ensure that the profitability of their projects includes a cost factor for the credit risk being used. In general, the formula to adjust project NPV (net present value) for credit is as follows:

Project NPV = Starting NPV − Expected PV of credit losses
　　　　　　 − Cost of credit risk
　　　　　　 × PV of credit risk consumed for unexpected credit losses

In the marketing department, credit risk calculations are sometimes used as a determinant in product pricing. For example, credit card companies will factor expected collection costs and losses into its fee structure for retail clients.

CREDIT RISK MITIGATION
The most important credit risk mitigation tool is the collection of collateral and ongoing diligence with respect to enforcing collateral requirements. This may include the threat of forced terminations for failure to provide collateral. If collateral is not an option, due to contract limitations, then there are other options.

When a company determines that it has too much exposure to a single counterparty, and it is unable to collect collateral, it may undertake several actions. First, attempts may be made to close out some trading positions with the counterparty, or initiate new trading positions that have the effect of reducing the risk. Second, the company may attempt to novate a contract—i.e., reassign the contract to a different counterparty for some consideration. Third, a firm may try to "book out" a trade if it finds it has identical and offsetting trades to two different counterparties. All of these options require counterparty agreement.

Barring these operational strategies, there are two financial strategies for mitigating credit risk. One is to obtain credit insurance for the actual realized loss to a defaulting counterparty. The other is to enter a credit default swap (CDS), which is essentially a contingent payment triggered by a counterparty credit event and made by a third-party derivatives trading counterparty.

Insurance can be tailored to provide specific coverage of the actual realized loss, but because of its specificity, the insurance company margin can be seen as being excessive by some corporations. Credit default swaps can be cheaper, since they trade in broader over-the-counter (OTC) markets.

Using CDSs to manage credit risk creates three problems. First, in most trading situations, the actual exposure is variable, making it difficult to target 100% protection. Second, in CDS markets, the payment-triggering event may not correspond exactly to a counterparty's default event. For example, when Fannie Mae and Freddie Mac were put into receivership by the US government in 2008, this was classified as a default event in CDSs and synthetic collateralized debt obligations (CDOs), which were built from those CDSs—even though there was no default. Third, as we learned in 2008, CDS spreads can become extremely high and can be subject to their own performance risk, as Lehman Brothers' counterparties discovered.

OTHER CONSIDERATIONS
Contagion. Most models of credit focus on bilateral credit arrangements, without recognizing that credit relationships are multilateral. For example, GM's supplier mentioned above may depend on other suppliers for parts. While the supplier itself may be creditworthy, its own suppliers may not be creditworthy. GM may not know how vulnerable it is to its counterparty's counterparty.

Consequences. While counterparty risk is often measured in terms of the counterparty's failure, it may be the case that default by a counterparty leads to much greater damage for a company. Many financial institutions were compromised in 2008 when the credit crisis caused a domino-like effect of systemic corporate collapse. Counterparty credit risk assessment, therefore, must include all the costs of counterparty failure, including the cost of lost reputation, lower credit rating, and, in the most extreme cases, bankruptcy.

MAKING IT HAPPEN
- Set a corporate policy for credit risk management that recognizes the links to financial strategy.
- Identify corporate contracts and relationships with credit or performance risk.

- Model and quantify the organization's exposure to credit losses.
- Consider operational and financial credit risk mitigation where appropriate.

CONCLUSION
Although a relatively young discipline, credit risk management has matured rapidly. Improved risk measurement and reporting techniques paired with comprehensive credit risk policies can provide extremely effective protection against credit risk losses. The best risk management techniques are operational and legal, with collateral providing the best financial risk mitigation. Credit insurance and credit default swaps offer financial protection against default, but each at its own cost—which must be compared to the benefits of reducing the specific risk it is intended to mitigate.

MORE INFO
Books:
de Servigny, Arnaud, and Olivier Renault. *Measuring and Managing Credit Risk*. New York: McGraw-Hill, 2004.
Saunders, Anthony, and Linda Allen. *Credit Risk Measurement: New Approaches to Value at Risk and Other Paradigms*. 2nd ed. New York: Wiley, 2002.

See Also:
★ Best-Practice Working Capital Management: Techniques for Optimizing Inventories, Receivables, and Payables (pp. 2–6)
★ Minimizing Credit Risk (pp. 142–145)
★ Quantifying Corporate Financial Risk (pp. 45–48)

Managing Interest Rate Risk
by Will Spinney

EXECUTIVE SUMMARY
- Interest rate risk can manifest itself in several different ways.
- It is best managed within the context of the firm and a risk framework.
- Proper evaluation or measurement is key.
- Selection of a good key performance indicator is essential.
- A typical response to interest rate risk is a transfer of risk to another party.
- Many risk transfer tools are available, of which interest rate swaps are the most popular.
- The risk is usually transformed rather than eliminated.

INTRODUCTION
Almost all firms are exposed to interest rate risk, but it can manifest itself in different ways. A proper response to this risk can only come following a full understanding of the context of the firm and its strategy, along with a full evaluation of the risk. Firms should generate a well thought out key performance indicator (KPI) and then apply one or more of the many tools available in the market to transfer interest rate risk.

MAJOR WAYS THAT A FIRM CAN BE AFFECTED
Interest rate risk is the exposure of the firm to changing interest rates. It has four main dimensions:

Changing Cost of Interest Expense or Income
Companies with debt charged at variable rates (for example, based on Libor, and also called floating rates) will be exposed to increases in interest rates, whereas companies whose borrowing costs are totally or partly fixed will be exposed to falls in interest rates. The reverse is obviously true for companies with cash term deposits. This is usually the key risk that firms consider.

Impact on Business Performance by a Changing Business Environment
Changes in interest rates also affect businesses indirectly, through their effect on the overall business environment. In normal times, for example, construction firms enjoy a rise in business activity when interest rates fall, as investors build more when the cost of projects is lower. Conversely, some firms may benefit from high levels of activity that prompt a high interest rate response by central banks. So some firms may have a form of natural hedge against the other forms of interest rate risk, although for any one firm the effect may lead or lag actual changes in rates.

Impact on Pension Schemes Sponsored by the Firm
Pension schemes that carry liability and investment risk for the sponsor have interest rate risk in that liabilities act in a similar way to bonds, rising in value as interest rates fall and vice versa.

Changing Market Values of Any Debt Outstanding
Although a nonfinancial firm will usually report its bonds on issue in financial statements at substantially their face value, early redemptions must be done at the market value. This may be significantly different, as interest rates will change the value of fixed-rate debt. This risk is not commonly considered by most nonfinancial firms.

INTEREST RATE RISK IN THE CONTEXT OF THE FIRM
Investors do expect firms to take risks, especially with regard to their core business competencies. It may be that investors expect the firm to take interest rate risk. On the other hand,

Table 1. The effect of interest rate changes on earnings and interest cover

| | Interest rate | | | | | | |
	4.5%	5.0%	5.5%	**6.0%**	6.5%	7.0%	7.5%
EBIT	100.0	100.0	100.0	**100.0**	100.0	100.0	100.0
Interest	(18.0)	(20.0)	(22.0)	**(24.0)**	(26.0)	(28.0)	(30.0)
Tax	(24.6)	(24.0)	(23.4)	**(22.8)**	(22.2)	(21.6)	(21.0)
Earnings	57.4	56.0	54.6	**53.2**	51.8	50.4	49.0
Interest cover	5.56	5.00	4.55	**4.17**	3.85	3.57	3.33

investors would probably not expect a firm to breach a financial covenant because of rising interest rates.

RISK MANAGEMENT FRAMEWORK

A risk management framework includes the following key stages:
- Identification and assessment of risks;
- Detailed evaluation of the highest risks;
- Creation of a response to each risk;
- Reporting and feedback on risks.

Evaluation is crucial to the management of interest rate risk and will discover exactly how a firm might be affected, thus guiding the response to the risk. Evaluation techniques include: sensitivity analysis, modeling changes in a variable against its effect; and value at risk (VaR) analysis, based on volatilities to calculate the chances of certain outcomes.

Let us look at a simple firm with earnings before interest and tax (EBIT) of 100, borrowings of 400 (all on a floating rate), an interest rate of 6% (as a base case), and a tax rate of 30%, and apply some of these techniques.

Evaluation 1: Sensitivity Analysis

A 1% move in interest rates has an effect of 4 (1% of 400) on the annual interest charge. This is not very helpful because there is no context for the effect.

Evaluation 2: Sensitivity Analysis

A table can be constructed to show the effect on earnings and interest cover (Table 1). In the table items in bold represent the base case, whereas other columns represent the sensitivities to this base case. Earnings are earnings after interest and tax.

This is much more helpful, showing the effect on both earnings and interest cover. If the firm has an interest cover covenant of, say, 3.75, then the table shows a high risk of a breach, depending on how likely a rise in rates might be.

Evaluation 3: Sensitivity Analysis

Suppose now that EBIT displays volatility. We can construct a further table (Table 2) showing interest cover under variations in EBIT and the interest rate. Italic numerals indicate a covenant breach, and the number in bold is the base case described in Table 1.

A drop of 5 in EBIT and a rise of 0.5% in interest rates will cause a breach, a clear risk factor for the firm. If a relationship between EBIT and interest rates can be established, then further conclusions could be drawn.

Sensitivity analysis does not show the probability of these changes, but if they are available—for example from a study of market volatility—a probability distribution for a covenant breach can easily be obtained.

Evaluation 4: VaR

Suppose that investigation of the assets and liabilities in the firm's pension scheme shows that the scheme has a deficit of 50. As an illustration, VaR might tell us that, based on the volatility of the long-term interest rates used to calculate liabilities, and taking into account that the scheme has some bond investments (in which value moves are opposite to liabilities), there is a 1 in 20 chance that the deficit will increase in the next year, because of interest rate changes alone, by 15 or more.

Interest rate risk inside a pension scheme (or other scheme for future employee benefits) often dwarfs interest rate risk inside the firm.

Evaluation should reveal where a firm is sensitive to interest rates. It could be:
- Earnings, perhaps where earnings per share (EPS) is an important issue.
- Cash flow.
- Interest cover ratios, perhaps because of financial covenants.
- Other ratios, such as those used by credit rating agencies.

Table 2. Interest cover under variations in EBIT and interest rate

| | Interest rate | | | | | | |
	4.5%	5.0%	5.5%	**6.0%**	6.5%	7.0%	7.5%
EBIT							
80	4.44	4.00	*3.64*	*3.33*	*3.08*	*2.86*	*2.67*
85	4.72	4.25	3.86	*3.54*	*3.27*	*3.04*	*2.83*
90	5.00	4.50	4.09	3.75	*3.46*	*3.21*	*3.00*
95	5.28	4.75	4.32	3.96	*3.65*	*3.39*	*3.17*
100	5.56	5.00	4.55	**4.17**	3.85	*3.57*	*3.33*
105	5.83	5.25	4.77	4.38	4.04	3.75	*3.50*
110	6.11	5.50	5.00	4.58	4.23	3.93	*3.67*
115	6.39	5.75	5.23	4.79	4.42	4.11	3.83
120	6.67	6.00	5.45	5.00	4.62	4.29	4.00

Table 3. Tools that can be used to transfer interest rate risk

Tool	Description	Comment
Forward rate agreement (FRA)	An FRA is a tool for fixing future interest rates (or unfixing them) over shorter periods, up to say 1–2 years.	A 3v6 FRA allows a firm to fix the three-month Libor (or other reference) rate in three months time. It is dealt over the counter (with banks).
Future	Futures have the same function as FRAs.	Futures are traded on an exchange, and thus have less flexibility.
Cap	A cap is an option instrument. The buyer of a cap pays a maximum interest rate over the life of the cap but enjoys lower rates as they come down. Caps have a premium.	Caps are usually dealt over the counter by firms, and the classic use is for a borrower to buy a cap that is higher than current interest rates, thus providing insurance for the borrower.
Floor	A floor is an option instrument. The buyer of a floor receives a minimum interest rate over the life of the floor but enjoys higher rates as they increase. Floors have a premium.	Floors are usually dealt over the counter by firms, and the classic use is for a depositor to buy a floor that is lower than current interest rates, thus providing insurance for the depositor.
Collar	A collar is a combination of a cap and a floor, thus providing a firm with a corridor of possible interest rates between a maximum and a minimum.	A borrower would buy a cap and sell a floor, usually over the counter, thus creating a "collar," or corridor, of rates.
Interest rate swap	An interest rate swap is probably the most widely used and popular risk transfer instrument in the field of interest rate risk. It changes the nature of a stream of interest payments from floating to fixed or vice versa.	Swaps (as they are usually called) are dealt over the counter and the market is large and (usually) deep. Terms of 5 to 7 years are common with nonfinancial firms, although terms of 30 or more years are often used by pension schemes, reflecting their different maturity horizon.
Swaption	A swaption is an instrument where the buyer of a swaption has the right to enter into an interest rate swap at a particular rate, thus protecting the buyer against adverse movements in long-term rates, while allowing them to benefit from favorable moves.	Swaptions are not very popular with nonfinancial firms but might be used near the time of bond issues, for example.

ESTABLISHING A KPI AND RESPONSE TO THE RISK

Evaluation should lead the firm to establish a KPI for interest rate risk. A good example of a KPI would be: *Interest cover to be greater than 3.75, on a 99% confidence basis, over an 18-month period*. This is better than using a simple interest cover ratio or a fixed/floating ratio as a KPI, because it speaks specifically about the risk to the firm.

The KPI should guide the response to the risk. Possible responses include:

- Avoid: It is hard to avoid interest rate risk.
- Accept: Simply accept the risk and take no further action. This may be suitable if there are no significant issues such as proximate financial covenants.
- Accept and reduce: It may be possible to reduce the risk through internal actions, such as reducing cash balances as far as possible to repay debt.
- Accept and transfer: Many market products are available that enable a firm to change the character of interest payments. This process is called hedging.

ESTABLISHING A POLICY

The factors we have seen should be formalized in a policy, as should approaches to all risks. The policy should set out:

- The overall direction of the policy.
- How the risk is to be measured.
- Who has responsibility for the risk management.
- What procedures should be in place to control the risk.
- A framework for decision-making.
- The key performance indicator.
- A reporting mechanism to view the performance of the policy.

TOOLS AVAILABLE TO TRANSFER INTEREST RATE RISK

There are a large number of tools available for the transfer of interest rate risk (Table 3).

Figure 1. Floating-rate borrower uses swap to convert to a fixed rate

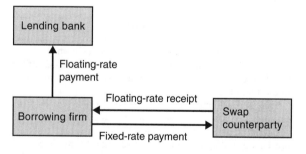

Figure 2. Fixed-rate borrower uses swap to convert to a floating rate

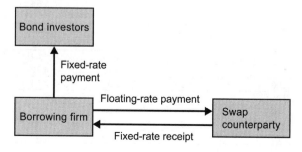

Table 4. Interest cover under variations in EBIT and interest rate for firm that pays fixed swap (see text for details)

	Interest rate						
	4.5%	5.0%	5.5%	6.0%	6.5%	7.0%	7.5%
EBIT							
80	*3.56*	*3.48*	*3.40*	*3.33*	*3.27*	*3.20*	*3.14*
85	*3.78*	*3.70*	*3.62*	*3.54*	*3.47*	*3.40*	*3.33*
90	4.00	3.91	3.83	3.75	*3.67*	*3.60*	*3.53*
95	4.22	4.13	4.04	3.96	3.88	3.80	*3.73*
100	4.44	4.35	4.26	4.17	4.08	4.00	3.92
105	4.67	4.57	4.47	4.38	4.29	4.20	4.12
110	4.89	4.78	4.68	4.58	4.49	4.40	4.31
115	5.11	5.00	4.89	4.79	4.69	4.60	4.51
120	5.33	5.22	5.11	5.00	4.90	4.80	4.71

Interest Rate Swap

This key instrument deserves a little more explanation. It is an instrument that, in its usual form, transforms one kind of interest stream into another, such as floating to fixed or fixed to floating. Each swap has two counterparties, and therefore in each swap one party pays fixed and receives floating, while the other party receives fixed and pays floating.

There are two classic uses of swaps by nonfinancial firms:
- *A floating-rate borrower converts to a fixed rate.* In this case a borrower has floating-rate bank debt and carries out a pay-fixed swap, converting the debt to a fixed rate. This is shown diagrammatically in Figure 1. The two floating-rate streams cancel each other out for the borrower, leaving it to pay only a fixed-rate stream.
- *A fixed-rate borrower converts to a floating rate.* In this case a borrower has fixed-rate bond debt and undertakes a receive-fixed swap, converting the debt to a floating rate (Figure 2). The two fixed-rate streams cancel each other out for the borrower, leaving it to pay only a floating-rate stream.

Let's suppose that our firm from above has responded to the risk of covenant breach by deciding to enter into a pay-fixed swap for 75% of its borrowing. It will pay 6% on the fixed-rate leg of the swap. The interest cover table we considered in Table 2 is now as shown in Table 4.

The italicized cells (covenant breach) now cover the width of the table but are less deep. Our firm has a lower risk of a breach from interest rates alone but has increased the risk from a falling EBIT. As interest rates are believed to be more volatile than EBIT, the overall risk to our firm has been reduced through the transfer of risk.

FIXING PRODUCTS VERSUS OPTIONS

There is a key difference between interest-rate-fixing products (such as swaps) and options. A fixing instrument binds its user to the rate that is set when it is transacted. An option allows the buyer to walk away. So a firm taking out a pay-fixed swap, following which rates decline, is left paying the higher rates. The risk is thus transformed, rather than transferred. Exposure to rising rates has become an exposure to falling rates. Firms must be clear about this when establishing their response to risk.

Accordingly, option products may seem to be an ideal product to deal with interest rate risk, and for those prepared to pay, they can be. However, costs rise with two main factors:
- Time: The longer an option has until expiry, the higher the premium.
- Volatility: The higher the volatility in the underlying risk being hedged, the higher the premium.

Both these factors tend to deter firms from using options and, for the longer term, risk transfer-response interest rate swaps are usually the instrument of choice.

CONCLUSION

The effects of changes in interest rates on a firm can be complex, but techniques are available to evaluate and respond to any risks this presents. A clear reference back to business and financial strategy will put interest rate risk in its context, allow a suitable response, and help the firm to achieve its goals.

MAKING IT HAPPEN
- Assess how the firm is affected by changes in interest rates.
- Evaluate the risk according to the firm's strategy, using tools such as sensitivity analysis or VaR.
- Establish a key performance indicator for the risk.
- Choose whether to avoid or to accept the risk.
- If the choice is to accept, either:
  ○ accept and reduce; or
  ○ accept and transfer, such as with interest rate swaps or options.
- Make frequent reports to give feedback on the risk.

MORE INFO
Books:
Buckley, Adrian. *Multinational Finance.* 5th ed. Harlow, UK: Pearson Education, 2004.
Chapman, Robert J. *Simple Tools and Techniques for Enterprise Risk Management.* Chichester, UK: Wiley, 2006.

Best Practice

Navigating a Liquidity Crisis Effectively
by Klaus Kremers

EXECUTIVE SUMMARY

- Liquidity crises are usually the symptoms of underlying strategic and operational crises that must be tackled to avoid repeated cash crises.
- The levers to address liquidity crises are not just operational and financial but also behavioral.
- CFOs must recognize the liquidity crisis and communicate openly to crucial stakeholders as a first step; they need to build trust with current and new financing stakeholders by producing a predictable rolling liquidity forecast.
- Cash constraints can be addressed by collecting and controlling existing cash, reducing net working capital, and restructuring the balance sheet.
- The control of cash requires very conservative cash authorizations and aggressive control from the financial team on all operations.
- Reducing net working capital is a well-known source of cash, but requires care to avoid deteriorating relationships with clients or suppliers.
- Restructuring the balance sheet is a medium/long-term solution. It mainly involves selling assets and raising/refinancing debt and/or equity.

INTRODUCTION

Until 2007, debt had become very cheap and accessible. Most companies sharply increased their leverage. In Germany, for example, the net-debt-to-EBITDA ratio extremes moved from around 3 in 2002 to around 7 in early 2008. However, a downturn in company performance or an external financial crisis—where lending becomes scarce and borrowing expensive—can make this approach risky.

WHAT IS A LIQUIDITY CRISIS?

A company's liquidity is its ability to quickly pay off its short-term debts as they fall due, and still have enough cash to keep operating. Liquidity crises can be broadly split into company-specific crises, and those driven by external factors—by market or general economic changes. In both cases, the company experiences a loss of investor confidence, making it difficult to raise further cash. If the company has insufficient cash reserves, it can very quickly run into serious difficulty. A familiar vicious circle takes hold, where a company cannot pay its debts because it has no funds, but cannot raise funds as its financial difficulties result in the downgrading of its debt.

HOW TO RESPOND TO A LIQUIDITY CRISIS

Once a company finds itself struggling to meet its short-term obligations, it needs to urgently access sources of cash, both internal and external. The following five-step approach covers the key elements of any response:

1. Tackle the Root of the Crisis

Normally, a liquidity crisis is only the last symptom of pre-existing root issues such as strategic or profitability crises (for example, losing one key customer contract, misalignment of product portfolio and market, a company overstretching itself by entering too many markets). A liquidity crisis needs to be addressed right away, but ignoring the crisis' root causes will merely postpone the next liquidity crisis. In these times of urgency, the support of external advisers can bring highly needed extra resources, experience of crisis management, and an independent perspective.

2. Be Honest

It is essential that a company is honest about its current situation, and creates a climate of transparency. It must comply with any regulatory requirements to inform the market, which can be applicable to listed companies. A CFO only has one chance to put things right with the banks:
- Give an honest assessment of the situation;
- Communicate appropriate information to all stakeholders; banks, shareholders, employees, suppliers, credit insurers, etc. so as not to mislead, or make fraudulent misrepresentations. Be sure to present an accurate picture of the current situation; account for all received bills (from experience, purchase ledgers do not include all received invoices, with many invoices hidden in staff drawers).

3. Gain or regain trust

Regaining the trust of banks, shareholders, and other stakeholders is a prerequisite to maintaining, or raising external funding. This requires communicating robust and

realistic plans, delivering on these plans and building relationships.
- The main tool for trust building is a bullet-proof rolling liquidity forecast on which you will deliver (see Rolling Liquidity Forecast).
- In a liquidity crisis, a company's usual banking relationship can be replaced by a workout banker with different expectations and greater experience of liquidity crises.

4. Harvest Cash
There are three main ways to improve cash position:
1 Collect and control existing cash
2 Reduce working capital
3 Restructure the balance sheet

4.1. Collect and control existing cash
Companies usually have large amounts of cash spread across business entities and regions:
- Know where the cash is and who is responsible for it;
- Establish cash pooling: minimize cash held by operational entities (no cash constraint on operational entities means no tough cash discipline);
- Make managers ask for cash if they want to spend;
- If the company has one main bank lender, try to keep all the company's cash within this bank, to increase transparency.

4.2. Reduce net working capital
Working capital reduction obviously uses three levers: receivables, inventories, and payables. Keep some key points in mind while reducing working capital:
- Fix a deadline for finalizing collection and deciding on write-offs for receivables;
- Promptly claim refunds of taxation, if due;
- Reduce inventories by both reducing replenishment of production inventories, and by selling low-rotation inventories to generate cash;
- Be careful when extending payment conditions for suppliers, and keep in touch with the credit insurer—if they pull the cover, the company would have to prepay its suppliers, with disastrous consequences for its liquidity.

The potential for reduction in working capital is also very much industry-specific, depending on the make-up of the industry's working capital requirements. For example:
- The construction industry has far greater potential for cash realization (up to 20% of working capital employed) than the oil and gas industry (far less than 10% of working capital employed).
- This difference is from the type of long-term contracts normally used in the construction industry, creating significant work in progress and inventory balances.

4.3. Restructure balance sheet
Restructuring the balance sheet is a medium/long-term option, and usually involves third parties. Three main approaches exist:
1 *Reduce investments*: short-term solution of freezing or cancelling investments:
   ○ Before freezing expenditures, critically analyze impacts on future earnings;

○ Investments should be modular as far as possible, so that if a project is curtailed or postponed, the investment already made is itself still viable;
○ The cash return on investment should be a maximum of three years for generic industries (longer for asset intensive industries).
2 *Sell fixed assets*: medium/long-term solution. A liquidity crisis gives the opportunity to redefine the core businesses and sell non-core activities:
   ○ Selling assets always takes much longer than planned—consider it an upside rather than part of the main solution;
   ○ Within the core business, consider the sale and leaseback of assets.
3 *Raise debt and/or equity*: medium to long-term solution. This approach may seem the easiest solution, but at the end of 2008, banks reduced credit lines, and stock markets closed to capital increases.
4 Following the aforementioned steps will better enable the company to raise finance in the future. Remember, too, that keeping the supplier insurers on side and informed indirectly generates a source of credit through creditor balances.

5. Manage Cash Sustainability
Finally, a company needs to ensure a sustainable liquidity position. As mentioned above, strategic and operational root causes for the last crisis must be understood and tackled to avoid reoccurrences of liquidity crises; then companies can implement the following techniques to keep control of liquidity:
- Implementation of KPI-based management that includes liquidity and capital tied-up indicators.
- Active risk management of the business, including operations, legal contracts, financing decisions and structure, investments, and image/reputation. For example, a European pharmaceutical company lacking cash flows decided to finance a €80m factory with short-term loans. Due to poor performance, banks decreased the credit facility, causing a liquidity crisis which forced the company to restructure.
- Change of the company culture:
   ○ Encourage staff to take care of the company's cash as if it were their own;
   ○ Encourage realistic forecasts and planning: use scenario modeling techniques to limit future surprises;
   ○ Change employees' incentivization (long-term focus).
- Ongoing communication with internal and external stakeholders to further build trust and confidence.
- Continuous implementation of a "tool box" of operational measures to optimize cash management, working capital, and information accuracy.
- Further operational, financial and strategic flexibility to enable the company to react early and quickly once issues become apparent.

ROLLING LIQUIDITY FORECAST
- This is not "just another financial report": it shows where your company liquidity is—and will be—when negotiating with external and internal parties.

- All departments communicate their cash impacts (purchasing, sales, operation/investment, etc) and are responsible for impacts and timing.
- Obviously, take into account business seasonality and a reasonable buffer. Avoid surprises, as one cannot ask twice for an extension of credit lines: the CFO's credibility would not survive.
- The frequency with which the forecast is updated depends on the liquidity stretch: daily rolling liquidity plans are usual during periods of high crisis.
- Carrying out these simple steps properly will put the company in favorable light with banks: a Roland Berger study showed that only 30% of companies with a liquidity crisis have implemented a rolling liquidity forecast.

CASE STUDY
ROLAND BERGER

- A mid-sized mechanical engineering company with assets of €500m was in a liquidity crisis following two years of losses. External funding sources had dried up due to poor performance. Our project focused on generating cash from internal sources. A team of four consultants released €51m cash in around six months. The methods used for extracting cash included:
- In the first two months:
  - putting a cash control and liquidity plan put in place;
  - selling raw materials back to suppliers (€6m);
  - postponement of non-essential projects (€4m);
  - review of accounts receivable (€16m) and accounts payable (€2m).
- Over the course of the next four months:
  - cash pooling across sites;
  - giving site managers targets for raising cash—further cut in inventories (€12m);
  - operational and strategic restructuring defined and implementation started, for example loss making activities identified and plans put in place for site and product rationalization.

In the first 12 months, an additional €11m of liquidity was generated through asset disposal, as well as sale and leaseback of fixed assets. Short-term measures allowed the company some breathing space to enable it to find an investor; longer-term measures provided the negotiation basis for the entry of an additional investor. The company is now trading profitably and has a new investor, brought in on reasonable terms.

CONCLUSION

The outlined approach to a liquidity crisis describes the worst-case scenario. In less severe cases, not all levers need to be utilized. Even in good times, however, the best companies are already using most of these tools.

MAKING IT HAPPEN

A few dos and don'ts that management should bear in mind during a liquidity crisis:

Do
- Announce problems early and honestly to all relevant stakeholders.
- Build and monitor a reliable rolling liquidity forecast.
- Develop an action plan early on to demonstrate control of the situation.
- Empower managers to look for potential to extract cash in their areas from the bottom up.
- Maintain regular and open contact with external stakeholders.
- Be honest with employees and involve them in the process.
- Perform financial restructuring in conjunction with operational restructuring.
- Always prepare for the worst: in a crisis situation the worst case is always the real case.

Don't
- Ignore the situation hoping that things will turn themselves around.
- Look for profit instead of liquidity: avoid paying early for cash discounts, and collect value adjusted receivables rather than keep your write-offs down.
- Throw good money after bad: accept sunk cost rather than continuously burn new cash.
- Forget to include an additional buffer for peaks in cash requirements in your liquidity forecast: there will always be unexpected events, and most will hit you.
- Stop spending and investing completely: do not risk a complete breakdown of operations.
- Look for perfect solutions: take a practical approach, and react quickly to avoid rumors spreading and a domino effect.

MORE INFO
Books:

Blatz, Michael, Karl-J. Kraus, and Sascha Haghani. *Corporate Restructuring: Finance in Times of Crisis*. New York: Springer, 2006.

Graham, Alistair. *Cash Flow Forecasting and Liquidity*. Chicago, IL: AMACOM, 2001.

Websites:

Association of Corporate Treasurers (ACT), contingency planning: www.treasurers.org/contingencyplanning

Roland Berger, restructuring: www.rolandberger.com/expertise/functional_issues/restructuring

Turnaround Management Association (TMA): www.turnaround.org

See Also:

Pension Schemes: A Unique and Unintended Basket of Risks on the Balance Sheet

by Amarendra Swarup

EXECUTIVE SUMMARY

- Pension schemes are often the most overlooked part of a company's balance sheet, despite the large hidden and complex risks they can pose. Some of the unique risks within pension schemes are exposure to interest rates, inflation, market risk, and longevity.
- The problem is particularly acute for defined-benefit pension schemes—common in many developed countries—where the benefits are predetermined, are often index-linked, and can be passed on to dependents. The present cost of bearing these risks has risen sharply in recent decades, and many companies have closed their pension schemes to new members.
- In the short term, changing economic, financial, and demographic perceptions can materially alter the valuation of a pension scheme's assets and liabilities from one day to the next, potentially leaving many finance directors with an uncontrolled liability on otherwise well-managed balance sheets.
- The waters can be muddied further by another fundamental problem: for most schemes, liabilities are calculated infrequently using ad hoc or out-of-date assumptions, which can often present a less than prudent valuation of the true costs.
- Options to manage and even reduce these uncertainties are now appearing. The key is to have a proactive and realistic approach to the risks that are being carried on the balance sheet.

INTRODUCTION

The only function of economic forecasting, the late American economist J. K. Galbraith once noted, was to make astrology look respectable. And, knowingly or not, it's a belief that's endemic in the corporate world.

The overriding concern is to find the hidden value in companies—whether in their balance sheet or in their intellectual property—and extract it in the most efficient way possible. Every financial and operational risk is carefully studied and, where possible, mitigated. Lines of credit are negotiated at known terms to suit the company's horizon. Capital structures are continually redrawn to maximize efficiency. Balance sheets are scrutinized line by line and operations are streamlined.

There is no obsession with predicting GDP, or agonizing over the evolution of the labor market over the next decade, for example. No, these are all nebulous questions for economic forecasters to ponder. For the seasoned financial director, the wider economy only matters insofar as it affects that all important cash flow.

Yet, hidden in that otherwise well-managed balance sheet might be a host of unconstrained liabilities that threaten to undo the most meticulous business plan and expose companies to a whole host of unknown risks—all housed within an often overlooked pension plan.

The problem is particularly acute for defined benefit schemes—occupational schemes where the pension benefits are fixed in advance and are often calculated as a proportion of an employee's final salary. Many include provision for dependents such as widows, and can even be indexed to inflation. These proved to be enormously popular in the aftermath of the Second World War, when many companies saw them as an effective way to defer compensation for workers to future years. However, these schemes placed a host of unintended and poorly understood risks with the sponsoring employer, such as exposure to longevity, to future interest rates, and to the capricious whims of financial markets.

In recent decades, as companies found themselves confronted with declining employment and a growing retiree problem, the present cost of bearing these risks has escalated sharply, and many have closed their pension schemes to new members. Furthermore, pension schemes and, in some jurisdictions, their associated healthcare liabilities, are increasingly a growing factor in corporate finance transactions.

A potentially attractive merger or acquisition may become unstuck because of the pension fund, or, worse still, an existing company may hit difficulties as the full cost of the pension obligation becomes known. The abortive takeover of Sainsbury's in the United Kingdom and the well-publicized troubles at General Motors in the United States are but the most visible tip of the proverbial iceberg, and are indicative of a problem that can consign businesses to a slow decline.

But more than just eroding stockholder value in the present, defined benefit schemes are also a danger to a company's long-term survival in an increasingly competitive global economy. Many management teams now face the problem of maintaining a set of financial commitments made in another era, when assumptions and expectations were vastly different. These commitments are difficult to measure—let alone anticipate—and they are tied to the health of the corporate sponsor of the pension fund, which is legally required to underwrite any deficit. If the company does go under, the responsibility of meeting at least part of these liabilities may then be transferred to governments and taxpayers. This may create additional problems, as pension scheme members will likely receive reduced benefits, and the addition of significant numbers of liabilities to the government balance sheet is eventually likely to become politically unpalatable.

A GROWING PROBLEM

Anyone who doubts the potential scale of the problem only has to look at the case of the American Civil War veterans' pension fund—one of the earliest defined benefit schemes. Originally set up during the war to pay pensions to disabled veterans, the scheme was gradually extended to include all veterans and their dependants, making its final payment only in 2004—nearly 140 years after the war ended. By then, the scheme had cost the US government hundreds of billions in today's dollars, and at its peak in the early 1890s, it had even constituted over 40% of the annual federal budget.

It's a stark warning for many pension schemes and their corporate sponsors today.

Any views on interest rates over the next decade? Your debt financing may have excellent terms, and it may seem a moot point, but the pension fund's liabilities and their associated accounting costs will swing violently over the next few decades with movements in the prevailing interest rates. By some estimates, the drop in long-term interest rates from 1999 to 2002 increased the value of pension liabilities by 30–40%.

How about inflation—any thoughts on how it might evolve over the next half century? Many scheme members, particularly in the United Kingdom, have index-linked pensions, and the burden of payments can quickly become onerous. Figures from the UK Office for National Statistics show that from 1970 to 2007, annual employer contributions to pension schemes went up a factor of 53, and they trebled over the last seven years alone of that period (Figure 1). Wage inflation too can rapidly push up costs.

And what about people living longer? For individuals and society, increased longevity is desirable, but living longer can often also create large unanticipated costs. Ever since German Chancellor Otto von Bismarck thought he'd pulled off a politically brilliant move back in 1889, by promising pensions at 70 when the average German lived to less than 50 years of age, the continual improvements in life expectancies have rapidly unraveled the best-laid pension plans. Even more troubling, the current upward trend shows little sign of leveling off, and it is increasingly clear that

Figure 1. Increasing life expectancy in the United Kingdom for 65-year-olds. (*Source*: Office for National Statistics)

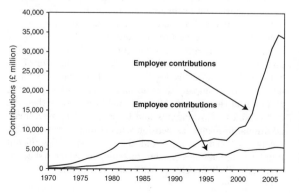

Figure 2. Annual contributions to UK pension schemes by employers and employees 1970–2007. (*Source*: Office for National Statistics)

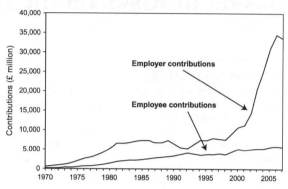

this is the most significant risk to the finances of pension schemes and their sponsors. The rising life expectancies for males and females in the United Kingdom are shown in Figure 2.

In a field typified by extremes, the case of Jeanne Calment is a situation that's humorlessly reminiscent of reality for many pension schemes. When Madame Calment's lawyer agreed in 1965 to pay her an annual income worth one-tenth of the value of her flat on the understanding that he would inherit the property on her death, it seemed like a shrewd bargain. Madame Calment was then 90 years old, and it seemed unlikely that she had much longer to go on this particular journey. Unfortunately, bearing testament to perhaps one of the most misjudged investment decisions ever, Jeanne went on to live to the ripe old age of 122. Along the way, she also became the oldest rap artist ever, releasing an album at 121, but that is unlikely to have provided much consolation to her poor aforementioned lawyer. By then, he was long dead and his widow was still making the payments.

THE DANGERS OF VOLATILE MARKETS

It's a complex basket of risks and, in the short term, changing economic and demographic perceptions can materially alter the valuation of a pension scheme's liabilities from one day to the next. Even the assets are not immune, as many pension schemes have more than half their assets in equities—a consequence of their long-term perspective, adherents argue. In the short term, however, volatility in the markets can materially alter the valuation of a pension scheme from one day to the next. It's a headache for many finance directors, who are left with an uncontrolled liability on otherwise well-managed balance sheets.

It becomes extremely difficult under these circumstances to determine the ability of a defined benefit pension scheme to pay its annuities 40 years down the track. Throw in the increasingly common belief that the economic environment in the coming years is likely to be far less favorable than in recent years, and increased volatility seems inevitable.

In early 2008, for example, Aon Consulting estimated that sharp falls in the FTSE caused UK pension schemes to lose US$60 billion in just a single week, wiping out all the gains made in 2007. More worryingly for companies, equity markets have declined significantly since their highs in mid-2007. Given that these companies are often older, and therefore have a much greater role as pension sponsors than the percentage of market capitalization that they represent, sponsor risk is also an increasingly major concern across the board.

It's a growing headache for many firms, for whom such risks often lie far from familiar territory and who are charged with looking after a broad church of stakeholders, not just pensioners. Though the increased pension fund liabilities are often longer term than most corporate horizons, they must be carried on the company's balance sheet, reducing net asset value and increasing financial leverage. As the corporate sponsor, they generally also have an obligation to fund at least part of these unexpected costs, giving them an uncertain command over their own cash flow and reducing future distributions to investors. The impact can go far beyond the immediate cash flow hit—filtering through to the P&L, lowering profits, hurting competitiveness, and, ultimately, even impacting the share price.

In the case of General Motors, for example, net obligations are estimated to be about US$170 billion across all of GM's US operations, dwarfing its current market cap of US$3 billion. To meet its soaring obligations, the company contributed an astonishing US$30 billion to its US pension plans in 2003 and 2004, but the accounts are still tens of billions of dollars in deficit. Now, pension and healthcare costs make up more of the average GM vehicle's price tag than the steel used to build it. Consequently, the company is inexorably losing ground to a wave of foreign competitors with lower cost bases and less debt on their balance sheets—resulting in a catastrophic decline in stock price for investors, from US$55 in January 2004 to under US$10 today.

MUDDY WATERS

The waters are muddied further by another fundamental problem. For most schemes, liabilities are calculated infrequently, using out-of-date longevity assumptions and ad hoc discount rates, and often presenting a less than prudent valuation of the true costs of delivering pensioners full financial security. As people live longer—15 minutes more for every passing hour by some estimates—and accounting standards move more toward valuing balance sheets on a mark-to-market basis, the immediately calculable costs can rise dramatically as outdated assumptions are revised.

Many pension schemes value their liabilities by using a discount rate that is implicitly linked to the assumed return on their assets. The problem is that they are effectively banking on an uncertain set of future gains to pay off their obligations to millions of current and future pensioners. Even worse, the discount rates vary from scheme to scheme. Some may choose a point in time and a single discount rate for all their liabilities, while others may choose to be more sophisticated and look at evolving discount rates over time. Regardless, most discount rates are ultimately linked to AA-rated corporate bond yields—the result of an implicit belief that returns of this order can be harvested without difficulty.

This is not to say that corporate bonds are not good investments. They are an investment staple with good reason and can provide low-risk returns. However, they are not risk-free, and any prudent investor needs to be cognizant of the default, credit, and liquidity risks that go with the asset class. In recent months, the problem has been highlighted by the credit crunch, which has seen prices of AA corporate bonds collapse and their yields soar. No wonder many schemes were feeling pleasantly flush and in surplus over the last couple of years—their liabilities dramatically lessened over the same time period!

It's a false optimism. The downturn in prices reflects the increasing fear that some of these corporate bonds might default. Even if one claimed that investing everything in AA corporate bonds today could still provide these returns at low risk, there simply aren't enough around. Taking the United Kingdom as an example, the total value of AA corporate bonds floating around the UK financial markets at last count was just over US$142 billion—a fraction of the some US$1,200 billion of liabilities they are supposed to underpin.

It's a troubling mismatch problem. Although there is a tradition of pension schemes and insurers "booking" some potential asset gains in advance, it is important for companies not to bank on future gains to work out their liabilities. An unembellished picture of the liabilities, stripped of any assumed risk premiums, can often be a good guide when setting investment targets and managing the risk on your balance sheet.

The area is also coming under increased regulatory scrutiny, with more stringent accounting standards being imposed. For example, the pensions regulator in the United Kingdom is now pushing schemes to adopt more realistic mortality assumptions that reflect the latest scientific evidence—a change that could equate to an additional cost of US$40 billion for the UK defined benefit industry with every added year of life expectancy. This also presents additional shorter-term risks for sponsors, as they may have to divert extra cash into the scheme to meet these future liabilities via a contribution notice.

SOLUTIONS ON THE HORIZON

Company finance directors must feel victimized. Constrained by ever-growing liabilities on the balance sheet and a volatile pension asset portfolio, they often find themselves on the wrong side of the window when it comes to securing their retirees' benefits. Changing interest rates, rising inflation, and ever-increasing allowances for longevity mean that the liabilities are often a fast-moving target. Throw in a worsening economic environment, and keeping apace is complicated by potentially thorny negotiations with trustees and retirees for additional injections.

So how are trustees and sponsors to manage these new, troubling risks? It's hard enough to judge market returns over the next few years, without crystal ball gazing to estimate the lifespan of all the scheme members under your responsibility—past, present, and future.

The answer today is that it is largely a dark art. The current trend is unlikely to be your friend here; longevity improvements have repeatedly defied the hopeful shackles of successive actuarial models, despite the most Orwellian filtering of data by job, medical history, and even postcode. The latest models—even if true—give scant comfort. For example, by 2050 a 65-year-old UK male might live to be between 86 and 97 years old, up from 83 today.

However, there are options. Like any other risk, these uncertainties can be managed, and even reduced, once understood. The key is to have a proactive and realistic approach to the risks that are being carried on the balance sheet. Sponsors need to engage actively with trustees and walk a fine line between investors' expectations and the funding needs for the pension scheme.

Unique solutions are now appearing in the market. A whole industry has now sprung up in the United Kingdom offering full insurance buyouts, where the pension liabilities are transferred away to dedicated specialists. This can often improve the situation for pension scheme members, as these specialist insurers are tightly regulated, operate within strict investment and asset/liability guidelines, and have to hold capital against any extreme losses.

It also helps troubled sponsors: Securing pension liabilities away from balance sheets improves their ability to raise finance, and removes the situation where, in a falling equity market with a commensurate fall in the valuation of a scheme's assets, a sponsor looking to invest in the business might also find trustees coming cap in hand. Above all, it enables management to get on with running the business, free from the peripheral distractions of administering a pension scheme.

However, insurance buyout valuations use more cautious longevity assumptions and paint a truer picture of the hidden arrears, increasing the liabilities and the premiums required significantly. Like customers outside a Ferrari showroom peering in through the window, it is simply unaffordable for many companies and not available in many countries.

But there are alternatives to help transfer risk. Schemes can execute partial buyouts for some of their liabilities, such as current pensioners. If that overshoots the budget and the deficit is still too large, or the options are not available in your jurisdiction, there are now innovative corporate solutions to help transfer risk, ranging from taking on the entire scheme and its myriad liabilities, to specific solutions for specific risks.

For example, trustees and sponsors can implement bond or swap-based hedging strategies to nullify the impact of interest rates and inflation on their liabilities, and thereby on the balance sheet. There is even a growing market in longevity swaps, allowing people also to hedge this idiosyncratic risk. Although they introduce new risks in lieu, such as the health of the counterparties on the other side of the swap, these steps are cost-effective and can ensure that the larger part of a scheme's risk—its volatile liabilities—is better constrained, while precious assets are freed up to invest in assets with higher returns.

Another alternative is to delegate the holistic management of all the scheme's assets and liabilities to a third-party fiduciary manager, who will manage them on a real-time basis within tight guidelines agreed with the trustees. These specialists will typically hedge all the liabilities where possible and diversify the assets among a range of best of breed providers. This ensures that the funding position is improved, and its ultimate targets, such as a full buyout, are reached in an efficient and structured manner. The asset/liability management approach has proved popular in countries such as The Netherlands, where it has significantly improved funding positions.

It's a rapidly evolving environment, and, with new solutions appearing fast, corporate sponsors can be hopeful of finding innovative ways of managing these new risks on their horizon. Most importantly, they can go back to finding and building businesses—not reading horoscopes.

MORE INFO

Reports:

Eich, Frank, and Amarendra Swarup. "Pensions tomorrow: A white paper." London School of Economics, 2008. Online at: tinyurl.com/4yeym5x [PDF].

Eich, Frank, and Amarendra Swarup. "Longevity: Trends, uncertainty and the implications for pension systems." London School of Economics, 2009. Online at: tinyurl.com/3zaf6rx [PDF].

Website:

London School of Economics—Pensions Tomorrow: tinyurl.com/3qey89z

See Also:

Quantifying Corporate Financial Risk
by David Shimko

EXECUTIVE SUMMARY

- Standard pro forma cash flow analysis considers risk in a crude way, usually with a subjectively determined upside and downside to cash flows.
- Stochastic analysis generates a large number of scenarios to give a better understanding of risk interactions, business linkages, optionality, and contracts designed to mitigate risk.
- Simple models can be built in spreadsheets, but one must take care to model financial assets, commodity prices, interest rates, and exchange rates appropriately.
- Stochastic pro formas can lead to better capital budgeting, valuation, and risk management decisions, particularly when risk is important to decision-making.
- Even the most sophisticated models are still subject to model risk; and they do not likely capture all the risks affecting an enterprise.

EXAMPLE OF A STOCHASTIC PRO FORMA

Consider the case of a company that has experienced six months of cash flows this year and wants to forecast the next six months. The usual way to do this is to predict a cash flow growth rate—expected, high, and low—and to base the analysis on these choices. A sample cash flow projection might be illustrated graphically in Figure 1.

In reality, of course, several different cash flow patterns might emerge for the last six months of the year. Using the same risk model, we could run a large number of simulations and see what the outcomes might be. Eight possible outcomes are plotted in Figure 2.

Clearly the stochastic analysis, albeit more realistic, is not as simple and not as attractive at first blush as deterministic analysis. And there are many situations where stochastic analysis is not needed. Yet there are certain results that one

Figure 1. Deterministic cash flow forecast for last six months

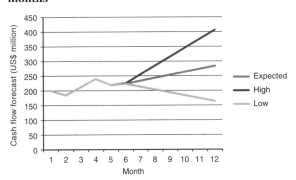

Figure 2. Stochastic cash flow projection for last six months

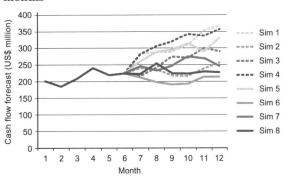

Table 1. Incremental analyses produced by stochastic pro formas

Analysis	Sample question
Probabilities of outcomes	What is the likelihood we will need to borrow?
Risk of outcomes	What is the most likely range for annual cash flows at year-end?
Interactions	If we invest more in capital expenditures only when cash flows are up, how do we reflect that in the analysis, and what impact does it have?
Options	Our loan contracts have floating rates, but the rates are capped. How does this affect the probabilities of different cash flow levels?
Worst case	We probably won't have the worst case revenues and the worst case costs in the same year; how does that reflect on our expectation of the worst case?
Events	There is a 10% chance we get a major contract that will increase our cash flows significantly. How do we incorporate this in the model?
Risk mitigation	The treasurer wants to lock in foreign exchange rates for our foreign buyers. How will this affect cash flow volatility?
Capital structure	What is our capacity to make interest payments on debt with 99% certainty?

can get from stochastic analysis that cannot be gained from deterministic analysis. Table 1 gives some examples.

Stochastic analysis is needed in situations where risk assessment is required, where the future company decisions depend on an unknown variable, where options are present, and when the company wants to study risk mitigation strategies.

Stochastic modeling of the income statement can be done at the aggregate level as it has been demonstrated here, or the components can be broken down into smaller components, such as the prices of products, inputs, interest rates, foreign exchange rates, and the like. The benefit of breaking down the income statement into its market-driven components is that we can find much more information on market-quoted prices and rates. This historical information is usually used as a starting point in determining how best to model these prices and rates.

MODELING MARKET RISK

Risk analysts need to spend significant time and effort to model the risk of the inputs to their stochastic models correctly. Incorrect specifications for market prices will lead to incorrect results. There are several models available to model market price risk. The choice of the best model generally is made by looking at the market's historical performance and making judgments about market price behavior.[1]

For example, if our risk model depends on fluctuations in the stock market index, a popular approach is to represent the index as following a random walk in percentage terms. Thus, any given day's return is normally distributed with a constant mean and standard deviation, and statistically independent from the previous day's return. This approach was popularized in the Black–Scholes (1973) and Merton (1973) papers on option pricing. The random walk works reasonably well, except that with specialized knowledge one could argue that the average return should not be constant, the volatility should not be constant, and there are sometimes events which cause stock prices not to be normally distributed. For this reason, the S&P 500 index may reasonably follow a random walk, but the stock of a small pharmaceutical company will not, since it is prone to occasional major events such as FDA drug approval or discovery of legal liability.

Other market prices, such as interest rates, do not follow random walks. Overly high and overly low interest rates tend to correct over time to equilibrium levels. Although that equilibrium level may change over time, the general character of interest rates is that they are *mean-reverting*—i.e., they revert to a long-run mean over time. The same is true of commodity prices. High commodity prices stimulate production, which causes future prices to fall. Low prices discourage production, causing future prices to rise. Therefore, interest rates and commodities need to be modeled in a similar way. Some currencies exhibit mean-reverting behavior and some do not.

Finally, every market price may have unique characteristics. The volatility of natural gas and heating oil changes by season. Power prices spike rapidly when generation fails and bounce back immediately as generation comes back on line. Careful modeling of critical market price inputs will lead to the best models of stochastic results.

MODELING RISK INTERACTIONS

It is not enough to have good models of security prices, interest rates, foreign exchange rates, and commodity prices. We must also understand how those prices and rates interact. For example, higher security prices are generally correlated with low interest rates. The Australian dollar exchange rate is correlated to gold prices, due to the importance of gold mining in its economy. In many cases, simplistic correlation is fine to establish a linear relationship between changes in the risk variables. However, in other cases, the correlations may not be

linear, requiring a more subtle approach. For some firms, that subtlety will be important enough to build a precise model of the interaction between two risks of importance to the company.

MODELING EVENT RISK

Every corporation is subject to risks from significant events, such as losing a major lawsuit, or obtaining a patent on its proprietary technology. Also, the company can be affected by market-related events, such as the bankruptcy of a key supplier. In many modeling situations, these events play an important role in determining the probability distributions of future cash flows.

It is tempting to think of event risks as being random outcomes, independent of everything else in the model. This is the biggest mistake a modeler can make. The credit crisis of 2008, for example, showed vividly how default risks across investment banks were correlated, owing to the similarity of their risk-taking activities.

AGGREGATING CASH FLOW RISKS TO THE INCOME STATEMENT

Once all the drivers of the income statement have been modeled, they are compiled to the income statement in the same way that a pro-forma income statement would normally be generated. For example, suppose a refinery in Brazil buys crude oil in dollars, sells products in reais, shuts down production when it is not profitable to produce, and runs the risk of operational failures according to some statistical model. In this case, the modeler could build stochastic formulas for the price of crude, the price of products, the dollar foreign exchange rate, the shutdown policy of the firm, and the unplanned outage rates due to operational risk. The result is a determination of net income for each particular simulated environment. These net income numbers can be simulated as many times as required to determine the volatility of cash flows, the value of the shutdown option, and the answer to any of the questions posed above.

MODELING RISKS OTHER THAN CASH FLOW

Some risks may not affect cash flows but could affect earnings, such as a mark-to-market liability. In these cases, similar risk models can be built to model earnings risk, or to model the likelihood of a credit downgrade. Stochastic models can be

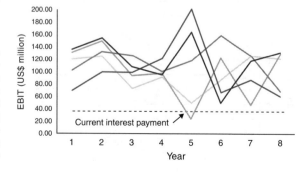

Figure 3. Current EBIT stochastics

Figure 4. EBIT stochastics post-hedging

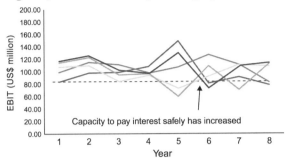

Capacity to pay interest safely has increased

simple or extremely complex, but they all are built fundamentally to make deterministic models more realistic and able to answer questions related to risk, risk management, optionality, capital structure, and much, much more.

CASE STUDY

An ethanol-producing company may be reluctant to issue more debt because of the high volatility of its cash flows and the increased risk of being put into bankruptcy.

A bank has proposed a transaction where the company would reduce its risk by selling its ethanol to customers at a price agreed today—i.e., entering forward contracts. If it did so, the bank would lend additional funds at the same rate. The company is reluctant to accept the bank's proposal because the sales price falls below the level at which the company thinks it can sell ethanol, costing the company $2 million per year. How can the company compare the benefit of higher debt with the cost of selling at a distressed price? And how can the company and the bank determine an appropriate level of additional debt?

A stochastic pro forma analysis could be done for the company before and after the proposed transaction. Before the transaction, the average earnings before interest and tax (EBIT) is estimated at $100 million with a standard deviation of $50 million. Shown in Figure 3 are five outcomes simulated over an eight-year period. The current annual debt service is $49 million.

By selling its ethanol forward, the company expects to lose $2 million per year, but to reduce the standard deviation to $25 million. The resulting stochastics demonstrate that the company can now prudently afford to make higher interest payments without having much risk of failure to pay (Figure 4).

The company can afford to pay $65 million in interest safely, after hedging its results. Should the company accept the hedging program? The answer depends on taxes. If the ethanol company is not in a tax-paying situation, it has lost an expected $2 million per year in value, so it should not hedge unless there are other reasons to do so. A taxpaying firm in the 40% bracket, however, will be able to deduct the interest expense from taxable income, saving $6.4 million per year (40% of 65 minus 49). The taxpaying firm should hedge, barring other considerations that might cause the firm not to want to hedge.

MAKING IT HAPPEN

- Begin with a project or corporate pro forma.
- Consider every assumption and ask if it is vulnerable to risk.
- Produce a risk model to simulate all the assumptions consistently and simultaneously.
- Use this model (stochastic pro forma) to design best and worst cases.
- Simulate outcomes of all key financial variables and communicate the risks.

CONCLUSION

Stochastic pro-forma analysis answers many financial questions that cannot be addressed with usual deterministic pro-forma analysis. The case study demonstrates how hedging and capital structure may be evaluated using stochastic pro formas. Other applications include evaluation of real options,[2] the study of credit ratings, and the development of probability statements around cash flow or earnings.

Like any other type of analysis, poor assumptions lead to poor conclusions. Good simulation models take a great deal of care in specifying the correct models for all the risk drivers and the interactions between them. Finally, more realistic risk-based models lead to better corporate financial decisions.

In the final analysis, however, even a very sophisticated model is still a model, and is therefore subject to model risk. Thus, the model may not fully identify or quantify all risks that affect an enterprise, and can thereby lead to a false sense of security. Accordingly, decision-makers should consider model risk as one of the components of any financial decision based on stochastic pro-forma analysis.

MORE INFO

Articles:

Black, Fischer, and Myron Scholes. "The pricing of options and corporate liabilities." *Journal of Political Economy* 81:3 (May–June 1973): 637–654. Online at: www.jstor.org/stable/1831029

Merton, Robert C. "Theory of rational option pricing." *Bell Journal of Economics and Management Science* 4:1 (Spring 1973): 141–183. Online at: www.jstor.org/stable/3003143

Websites:

Most of the literature in "stochastic processes" is extremely technical and not suitable for the average business reader. Even "stochastic processes in finance" tends to lead to models of security prices and interest rates for building value-at-risk models and option pricing models.

The topic "financial statement simulation" in an internet search engine leads to simulation software providers, such as Palisade, Finance 3.0, and @Risk. These providers offer written materials to supplement their software services. In addition, the reader is invited to request additional materials from the author.

Best Practice

See Also:
★ Best Practices in Cash Flow Management and Reporting (pp. 7–12)
★ Real Options: Opportunity from Risk (pp. 273–276)
✔ Analysis Using Monte Carlo Simulation (p. 327)

NOTES

1 Analysts should never expect that historical price behavior will represent future price behavior—only to realize that there is usually no better source of information for modeling purposes.

2 See the article "Real Options: Opportunity from Risk" in this volume.

Risk Management of Islamic Finance Instruments
by Andreas Jobst

EXECUTIVE SUMMARY

- Derivatives are few and far between in Islamic countries. This is due to the fact that the compatibility of capital market transactions with Islamic law requires the development of *shariah*-compliant structures that guarantee certainty of payment obligations from contingent claims on assets with immutable object characteristics. Notwithstanding these religious constraints, Islamic finance can synthesize close equivalents to conventional derivatives.

- Based on the current use of accepted risk transfer mechanisms, this article explores the validity of risk management in accordance with fundamental legal principles of *shariah*, and summarizes the key objections of *shariah* scholars that challenge the permissibility of derivatives under Islamic law.

- In conclusion, the article offers suggestions for the *shariah* compliance of derivatives.

TYPES OF ISLAMIC FINANCE

Since only interest-free forms of finance are considered permissible in Islamic finance, financial relationships between financiers and borrowers are not governed by capital-based investment gains but by shared business risk (and returns) in lawful activities (*halal*). Any financial transaction under Islamic law implies *direct participation in performance of the asset*, which constitutes entrepreneurial investment that conveys clearly identifiable rights and obligations for which investors are entitled to receive a commensurate return in the form of state-contingent payments relative to asset performance. *Shariah* does not object to payment for the use of an asset as long as both lender and borrower share the investment risk together, and profits are not guaranteed *ex ante* but accrue only if the investment itself yields income—subject to the intent to create an equitable system of distributive justice and promote permitted activities in the public interest (*maslahah*).

The permissibility of risky capital investment without explicit earning of interest has spawned three basic forms of Islamic financing for both investment and trade: (1) synthetic loans (*debt-based*) through a sale–repurchase agreement or back-to-back sale of borrower- or third-party-held assets; (2) lease contracts (*asset-based*) through a sale–leaseback agreement (operating lease) or the lease of third-party-acquired assets with purchase obligation components (financing lease); and (3) profit-sharing contracts (*equity-based*) of future assets. As opposed to equity-based contracts, both debt- and asset-based contracts are initiated by a temporary (permanent) transfer of existing (future) assets from the borrower to the lender, or the acquisition of third-party assets by the lender on behalf of the borrower.

"IMPLICIT DERIVATIVES" IN ISLAMIC FINANCE

From an economic point of view, the "creditor-in-possession"-based lending arrangements of Islamic finance replicate the interest income of conventional lending transactions in a religiously acceptable manner. The concept of *put–call parity*[1] illustrates that the three main types of Islamic finance outlined above represent different ways of recharacterizing conventional interest through the attribution of economic benefits from the ownership of an existing or future (contractible) asset by means of an "implicit derivatives" arrangement.

In *asset-based* Islamic finance, the borrower leases from the lender one or more assets A, valued at S, which have previously been acquired from either the borrower or a third party. The lender allows the borrower to (re-)gain ownership of A at time T by writing a call option $- C(E)$ with time-invariant strike price E subject to the promise of full repayment of E (via a put option $+ P(E)$), plus an agreed premium in the form of rental payments over the investment period. This arrangement amounts to a *secured* loan with *fully collateralized* principal (i.e. full recourse). The present value of the lender's *ex ante* position at maturity is $L = S - C(E) + P(E) = PV(E)$,[2] which equals the present value of the principal amount and interest of a conventional loan. In a more realistic depiction, this put–call combination represents a series of cash-neutral, maturity-matched, risk-free (and periodically extendible), *synthetic* forward contracts

$$\Sigma_{t=1}^{T} [P_t(E) - C_t(E)]$$

over a sequence of rental payment dates t. By holding equal and opposite option positions on the same strike price at inception, there are no objectionable zero-sum gains or uncertainty of object characteristics and/or delivery results.

Overall, the put–call arrangement of *asset-based Islamic lending* implies a sequence of *cash-neutral, risk-free (forward) hedges of credit exposure*. Since poor transparency of S in long-dated contracts could make the time value of $+ P(E)$ appear greater than its intrinsic value, long-term Islamic lending with limited information disclosure would require a high repayment frequency to ensure efficient investor recourse. In *debt-based* Islamic finance, borrower indebtedness from a sale–repurchase agreement ("cost-plus sale") of an asset with current value $PV(E)$ implies a premium payment to the lender for the use of funds over the investment period T and the same investor payoff L.[3] In Islamic profit-sharing (*equity-based*) agreements, the lender receives a payout in accordance with a pre-agreed disbursement ratio only if the investment project generates enough profits to repay the initial investment amount and the premium payment at maturity T. Since the lender bears all losses, this equity-based arrangement precludes any recourse in the amount $+ P(E)$ in the absence of enforceable collateral.

"EXPLICIT DERIVATIVES" AND *SHARIAH*-COMPLIANT RISK MANAGEMENT

Amid weak reliance on capital market financing in many Islamic countries, risk transfer mechanisms are subject to several critical legal hindrances that impact on the way that derivatives redress perceived market imperfections and financing constraints. Although "implicit derivatives" in the form of synthetic forward contracts (see above) are essential to profit generation from temporary asset transfer or profit-sharing in Islamic finance without creating the potential of unilateral gains, and thus are not deemed objectionable on religious grounds, the *explicit* use of derivatives remains highly controversial (Jobst, 2008b).

While "explicit derivatives" remain few and far between in Islamic finance, the implicit forward element of Islamic lending contracts, like forwards in conventional finance, involves problems of double coincidence and counterparty risk due to privately negotiated customization. Parties to forward agreements need to have exactly opposite hedging interests, which *inter alia* coincide in the timing of protection sought against adverse price movements and the quantity of asset delivery. Moreover, forward contracts elevate the risk of one counterparty defaulting when the spot price of the underlying asset falls below the forward price prior to maturity, rendering the contract "out-of-the-money" and making deliberate default more attractive.

Although the premise of eliminating these risks is desirable *per se* under Islamic law, the assurance of definite performance through either cash settlement (in futures), or mutual deferment (in options), as in conventional derivatives contracts, is clearly not as, it supplants the concept of direct asset recourse and implies a zero-sum proposition (Usmani, 1999). Instead, in Islamic finance, the bilateral nature and asset-backing *ensure definite performance* on the delivery of the underlying asset (unlike a conventional forward contract).

By virtue of holding equal and opposite option positions on the same strike price, both creditor and debtor are obliged to honor the terms of the contract irrespective of changes in asset value. Unlike in conventional options, there are no unilateral gains from favorable price movements (for example, "in-the-money" appreciation of option premia) in the range between the current and the contractually agreed repayment amount. Any deviation of the underlying asset value from the final repayment amount constitutes shared business risk (in an existing or future asset).

Shariah scholars take issue with the fact that futures and options are valued mostly by reference to the sale of a nonexistent asset or an asset not in the possession (*qabd*) of the seller, which negates the *hadith* "sell not what is not with you." *Shariah* principles, however, require creditors (or protection sellers) to actually own the reference asset at the inception of a transaction. Futures and options also continue to be rejected by a majority of Islamic scholars on the grounds that "...in most futures transactions, delivery of the commodities or their possession is not intended" (Usmani, 1996). Derivatives almost never involve delivery by *both* parties to the contract. Often parties reverse the transaction and cash-settle the price difference only, which transforms a derivative contract into a paper transaction without the element of a genuine sale. Given the Islamic principle of permissibility (*ibahah*), which renders all commercial transactions *shariah*-compliant in the absence of a clear and specific prohibition, current objections to futures and options constitute the most discouraging form of religious censure (*taqlid*).

Besides the lack of asset ownership at the time of sale, other areas of concern shared by Islamic scholars about *shariah* compliance of derivatives have centered on: the selection of reference assets that are nonexistent at the time of contract; the requirement of *qabd* (i.e. taking possession of the item prior to resale); mutual deferment of both sides of the bargain, which reduces contingency risk but turns a derivative contract into a profitable sale of debt; and excessive uncertainty or speculation that verges on gambling, resulting in zero-sum payoffs of both sides of the bargain (Mohamad and Tabatabaei, 2008; Kamali, 2007; Khan, 1991).

Although Khan (1995) concedes that "some of the underlying basic concepts as well as some of the conditions for [contemporary futures] trading are exactly the same as [those] laid down by the Prophet Mohammed for forward trading," he also acknowledges the risk of exploitation and speculation, which belie fundamental precepts of *shariah*. For the same reasons, several scholars also consider options in violation of Islamic law. Nonetheless, Kamali (2001) finds that "there is nothing inherently objectionable in granting an option, exercising it over a period of time or charging a fee for it, and that options trading like other varieties of trade is permissible *mubah*, and as such, it is simply an extension of the basic liberty that the Qur'an has granted."

However, so far only a few explicit derivative products have been developed by various banks for managing currency and interest rate risk. While recent innovation in this area has focused mostly on highly customized option contracts as well as commodity hedges, cross-currency swaps and so-called "profit-rate swaps" constitute the most widely accepted forms of newly established *shariah*-compliant derivatives (see next section). Given the prohibition of interest income and the exchange of the same assets for profit (which includes the cost-plus sale of debt), for Islamic investors to execute a swap both parties instead agree to sell assets, usually commodities, to each other for deferred payment. In the case of cross-currency swaps, the contractual parties exchange commodities in the form of a cost-plus sale and settle their mutual payment obligations in different currencies according to a predefined installment schedule.

Nonetheless, governance issues—especially *shariah*-compliance of products and activities—constitute a major challenge for the Islamic finance industry in general and risk management in particular. Although *shariah* rulings (*fatwas*) and their underlying reasoning are disclosed, there are currently no unified principles (and no precedents) on the basis of which *shariah* scholars decide on the religious compliance of new products. *Fatwas* are not consolidated, which inhibits the dissemination, adoption, and cross-fertilization of jurisprudence across different countries and schools of thought. Therefore, the fragmented opinions of *shariah* boards, which act as quasi-regulatory bodies, remain a source of continued divergence of legal opinion. In particular, there is considerable heterogeneity of scholastic opinion about the *shariah*-compliance of derivatives, which

testifies to the general controversy about risk management in Islamic finance. In particular, it underscores the difficulties of reconciling financial innovation and greater flexibility in the principled interpretation of different modes of secondary sources supporting religious doctrine: i.e. analogous deduction (*qiyas*), independent analytical reasoning (*ijtihad*), and scholarly consensus (*ijma*).

Recent efforts of regulatory consolidation and standard-setting have addressed the economic constraints and legal uncertainty imposed by both Islamic jurisprudence and the poorly developed uniformity of market practices. Private-sector initiatives, such as an Islamic primary market project led by the Bahrain-based International Islamic Financial Market (IIFM) in cooperation with the International Capital Markets Association (ICMA), have resulted in the adoption of a memorandum of understanding on documentation standards and master agreement protocols for Islamic derivatives. Also, national solutions are gaining traction. In November 2006, Malaysia's only fully fledged Islamic banks, Bank Islam Berhad and Bank Muamalat Malaysia Berhad, agreed to execute a master agreement for the documentation of Islamic derivative transactions (Jobst, 2007 and 2008a). Therefore, market inefficiencies and concerns about contract enforceability caused by heterogeneous prudential norms and diverse interpretations of *shariah*-compliance are expected to dissipate in the near future.

Figure 1. *Murabaha*-based cross-currency swap. (Numbers indicate sequence in which transactions are executed. GCC indicates country in Gulf Cooperation Council)

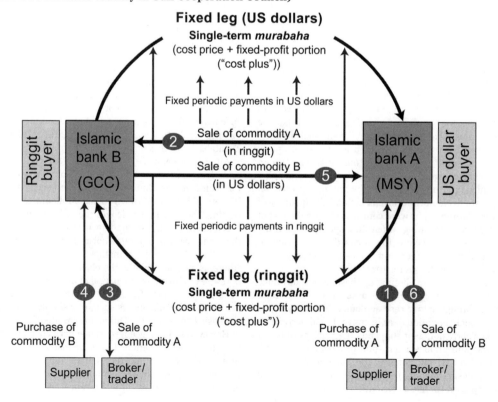

ISLAMIC SWAP TRANSACTIONS: CROSS-CURRENCY AND PROFIT-RATE SWAPS

Shariah-compliant swap transactions are traded bilaterally and combine opposite, maturity-matched *murabaha* contracts with instantaneous (or periodic) transfer of similar assets and delayed payment of the sales price (inclusive of a premium payment for the use of the asset until the maturity date).[4]

Islamic Cross-Currency Swap

Islamic cross-currency swaps (CCS) debuted only recently when Standard Chartered executed the first ever swap transaction of this kind for Bank Muamalat Malaysia in July 2006. The basic structure of a CCS matches two commodity *murabaha* sale contracts that generate offsetting cash flows in opposite currencies with maturities desired by the contracting parties.

The following example illustrates the functioning of a CCS (see Figure 1). Consider the case of a Malaysia-based Islamic bank that raises revenue in Malaysian ringgit but faces payments in US dollars over a certain period of time. To eliminate this foreseeable currency mismatch, the bank could substitute its future outflows in US dollars for outflows in Malaysian ringgit by entering into a CCS with a US dollar-paying counterparty.

Under this contract, the Malaysia-based Islamic bank purchases an amount of commodity A on a *murabaha* basis (i.e. against future installments) denominated in Malaysian ringgit. Simultaneously, an Islamic bank based in a Gulf Cooperation Council (GCC) country buys an amount of commodity B, also under a *murabaha* agreement but denominated in US dollars. By combining the two *murabaha* contracts, each denominated in a different currency, each party will be able to receive cash flows in the desired currency. Finally, both banks sell their respective commodities in order to recoup their initial expense, where the fair value of each commodity (A and B) should wash out at the prevailing exchange rate.

If the parties wanted to hedge term risk (i.e. the risk of the fair market values of the exchanged assets diverging over the life of the transaction), either in addition to the cross-currency swap or as a separate transaction, they would enter into a profit-rate swap. In this Islamic version of an interest-rate swap, the two sides exchange periodic fixed-rate for floating-rate payments. After selling a designated commodity to the protection seller, the protection buyer receives periodic fixed-rate payments in return for floating-rate installments.

Islamic Profit-Rate Swap

This instrument, pioneered by Commerce International Merchant Bank of Malaysia in 2005, allows financial

Figure 2. *Murabaha*-based profit-rate swap[5]

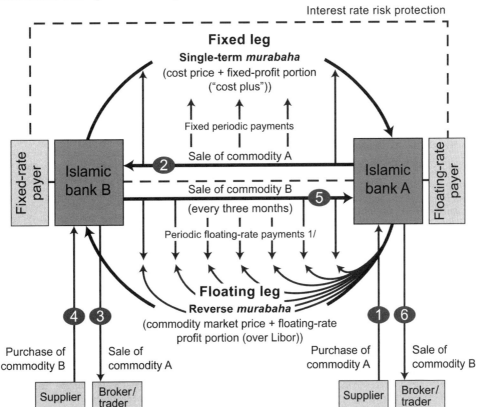

institutions to manage their exposures to fixed and floating rates of return. That is, through the profit–rate swap (PRS), institutions can restructure the nature (fixed vs. floating) of their existing rates of return. As in the CCS, profit-rate swaps are based on the combination of two commodity *murabaha* contracts (see Figure 2). The floating-rate leg involves the periodic *murabaha* sale of a commodity by the protection seller in exchange for future installments at the fair value (market) price plus a *floating-rate profit portion* ("cost-plus") that varies according to changes in some pre-agreed benchmark (for example, some interbank funding rate such as the London or Kuala Lumpur Interbank Offered Rate). The fixed-rate leg stipulates the one-off sale of a commodity by the protection buyer in exchange for a stream of future predetermined payments. As in the cross-currency swap, both parties may sell their commodities in order to recoup their initial disbursement. Note that the floating-rate payer (or interest rate protection buyer) purchases commodity B in periodic increments—unlike the fixed-rate payer (or interest rate protection seller), who receives commodity A in full at inception.

Attempts to design other *shariah*-compliant derivatives, such as total return swaps, have been mired in controversy. One particularly contested structure is based on a dual *wa'ad* (or promise) contract, which swaps the returns of a *shariah*-compliant asset portfolio with those of a designated index or reference investment portfolio, which can contain conventional assets. This Islamic total return swap would allow investors to access returns from assets that are prohibited under *shariah* principles. DeLorenzo (2007) has argued that, in practice, this swap structure does not conform to *shariah* norms, because the returns from the alternative portfolio are not derived from religiously acceptable activities.

MAKING IT HAPPEN
POSSIBILITIES FOR ESTABLISHING *SHARIAH*-COMPLIANCE OF DERIVATIVES AND RISK MANAGEMENT

The heterogeneity of scholastic opinion about the *shariah*-compliance of derivatives is largely a reflection of individual interpretations of *shariah* and different knowledge of the mechanics of derivative structures and risk management strategies. Many policymakers, market participants, and regulators are unfamiliar with the intricate mechanics and highly technical language of many derivative transactions, which hinder a more comprehensive understanding and objective appreciation of the role of derivatives in the financial system and their prevalence in a great variety of business and financial transactions. Risk diversification through derivatives contributes to the continuous discovery of the fair market price of risk, improves stability at all levels of the financial system, and enhances general welfare.

In principle, futures and options may be compatible with Islamic law if they: (1) are employed to address a genuine hedging demand on asset performance associated with a direct ownership interest; (2) disavow mutual deferment without actual asset transfer; and (3) eschew avertable uncertainty (*gharar*) as prohibited sinful activity (*haram*) in a bid to create

an equitable system of distributive justice in consideration of the public interest (*maslahah*). *Shariah*-compliant derivatives would also maintain risk sharing that favors win–win situations from changes in asset value. For instance, the issuance of stock options to employees would be an ideal candidate for a *shariah*-compliant derivative. By setting incentives for higher productivity, firm owners reap larger corporate profits that offset the marginal cost of greater employee participation in stock price performance. However, the *de facto* application of many derivative contracts is still objectionable due to the potential for speculation (or deficient hedging need) to violate the tenets of distributive justice and equal risk sharing subject to religious restrictions on lending and profit-taking without real economic activity and asset transfer.

MORE INFO
Books:
Jobst, Andreas A. "Derivatives in Islamic finance." In Syed Salman Ali (ed). *Islamic Capital Markets: Products, Regulation and Development*. Jeddah, Saudi Arabia: Islamic Research and Training Institute, 2008a; pp. 97–124.
Kamali, Mohammad Hashim. *Islamic Commercial Law: An Analysis of Futures and Options*. Cambridge, UK: Islamic Texts Society, 2001; ch. 10.
Khan, Muhammad Akram. "Commodity exchange and stock exchange in an Islamic economy." In A. H. M. Sadeq *et al.* (eds). *Development and Finance in Islam*. Kuala Lumpur: International Islamic University Press, 1991; pp. 191–212.

Articles:
Jobst, Andreas A. "The economics of Islamic finance and securitization." *Journal of Structured Finance* 13:1 (Spring 2007): 6–27. Online at: dx.doi.org/10.3905/jsf.2007.684860
Jobst, Andreas A. "Double-edged sword: Derivatives and Shariah compliance." *Islamica* (July–August 2008b): 22–25.
Kamali, Mohammad Hashim. "Commodity futures: An Islamic legal analysis." *Thunderbird International Business Review* 49:3 (May/June 2007): 309–339. Online at: dx.doi.org/10.1002/tie.20146
Usmani, Maulana Taqi. "Futures, options, swaps and equity investments." *New Horizon* 59 (June 1996): 10.
Usmani, Maulana Taqi. "What shariah experts say: Futures, options and swaps." *International Journal of Islamic Financial Services* 1:1 (April–June 1999): 36–38.

Reports:
DeLorenzo, Yusuf Talal. "The total returns swap and the 'Shariah conversion technology' stratagem." December 2007. Online at: www.dinarstandard.com/finance/DeLorenzo.pdf
Khan, M. Fahim. "Islamic futures and their markets." Research paper no. 32. Islamic Research and Training Institute, Jeddah, Saudi Arabia, 1995, p. 12.
Mohamad, Saadiah, and Ali Tabatabaei. "Islamic hedging: Gambling or risk management?" Islamic Law and Law of the

Muslim World Paper no. 08-47. New York Law School, August 27, 2008. Online at: ssrn.com/abstract=1260110

NOTES

1 The relation between the put and call values of a European option on a nondividend-paying stock of a traded firm can be expressed as $PV(E) + C = S + P$. $PV(E)$ denotes the present value of a risky debt with a face value equal to exercise price E, which is continuously discounted by $\exp(-rT)$ at a risk-free interest rate r over T years. In our case of a lending transaction, the share price S represents the asset value of the funded investment available for the repayment of terminal value E.

2 The lease payments received from the borrower wash out in this representation.

3 However, some debt-based financing with deferred payment of future claims on existing assets (*salam*), predelivery finance for future assets (*istisna*), or the deferred cost-plus sale of a third party-held asset imply counterparty and market risks from lost recovery value, which could translate to a lower strike price F on the call or put option respectively.

4 The degree of collateralization of each leg of the swap depends on the original ownership of the transferred asset (or, in this case, the exchanged commodities), defining the level of creditor indebtedness. In the standard *murabaha* sales contract, the creditor has either full recourse to the underlying asset and periodic payments (in a sale–repurchase agreement at an initially discounted sales price (cost-plus sale)), or limited recourse to periodic payments only (in a back-to-back cost-plus sale of an asset which the seller acquired previously from a third party). In a *murabaha*-based swap transaction the restrictions on recourse apply, even though both contract parties hold mutually offsetting payment obligations against each other, preventing speculative interest and mitigating the contingency risk of periodic payments.

5 This includes full payment and physical settlement in each period. This structure was pioneered by the Commerce International Merchant Bank of Malaysia in 2005.

To Hedge or Not to Hedge
by Steve Robinson

EXECUTIVE SUMMARY
- How currency risks are created and managed and the types of risk inherent in international trading.
- The techniques for managing currency risks.
- A framework for selecting appropriate techniques in specific business situations.
- An outline and illustration of the use of the main financial derivatives.

INTRODUCTION
Business has become increasingly international, and companies cannot ignore the impact of currency changes on cash flows, profitability, and their asset and liability position. No company is wholly immune—the cash received from exporting is affected by the relationship between the currency used by the customer to pay and the currency in which the cost of providing the product or service is denominated.

Many commodity prices have been volatile, rising and falling dramatically in recent years—driven by exploding or plummeting demand from fast-developing countries. Copper, tin, wheat, platinum, and of course oil, have risen dramatically, and this has had a significant impact on costs for many industries. Declines can be equally sudden, although falling costs often take more time to work through to market prices.

A spectacular result was the sudden collapse of several airline businesses in late 2007 and early 2008. Among them was EOS, a business-class only carrier operating mainly between London and New York, which started only in 2005. Also, Oasis Hong Kong Airlines, an innovative long-haul discount operator between Hong Kong, London, and Vancouver, MAXjet Airways, and some smaller low-cost US carriers, have all ceased trading very suddenly. Although other factors, such as reduced business travel and turbulent financial markets, have had an impact, the price of aviation fuel is the main cost driver, closely followed by the impact of currency changes—airlines pay all their costs in US dollars.

The risks extend beyond the trading sphere. Many banks have had to write down the value of their assets—largely complex "trading" securities. Finance is a global industry, and companies borrow and invest in many currencies. It is not sufficient that only financial people know how currency risks are created and managed.

WHAT ARE THE RISKS?
Currency risk is the net potential effect of exchange rate movements on the cash flow, profit, and balance sheet of a business. There are three types of currency risk:

Economic, Strategic, or Competitive Risk
Economic exposure covers the indirect risk to the profitability and cash flow of a company that arises from changes in

exchange rates. It is likely that ultimately a resultant transaction exposure will arise.

An illustration, relating to the US dollar, the euro, and sterling, could be holidays. For British holidaymakers, holidays in the euro zone and the US dollar zone become more expensive if sterling weakens. The UK holiday industry could benefit from the euro exchange rate if more British stayed in the United Kingdom for their holidays.

Translation Risk

Translation risk arises when amounts denominated in foreign currency are converted to domestic equivalents for financial reporting purposes. There is no immediate cash impact. Translation can affect both the profit and loss account and the balance sheet. Increasingly, converging accounting standards under International Financial Reporting Standards (IFRS), which do not apply to unquoted companies, are removing some previous distortions. The most common accounting policy is to convert trading profit and loss numbers at an average exchange rate during the accounting period, and to convert assets and liabilities at the year-end rate.

Profit and Loss Statement Translation

The profit and loss translation is only a paper figure initially, but it may become a real transaction exposure if cash interest or dividends need to be paid. A company with a large proportion of its income, or of its cash, in other currencies, will have a translation issue, but this can be helped by effective communication to investors, persuading them that short-term currency fluctuations will not necessarily lead to reduced long-term stockholder value creation.

Balance Sheet Translation

The foreign currency assets of the company are not exposed to currency fluctuations unless they are to be sold and the cash converted to another currency. Liabilities denominated in foreign currencies will represent a real exposure when they are due for repayment.

The impact of translation on the gearing level has to be evaluated to ensure that no covenants are breached, even if only technically. A very simple way around this is to match investment in foreign currency assets with loans dominated in equivalent currencies.

The practical difficulty is how far the company can go to protect *reported* earnings, while incurring a cost that will impact on the bottom line. It is also possible that a *real* transaction exposure could be created by a currency borrowing. Also to be considered is the impact of a fair value adjustment, on both the profit and loss bottom line and on reserves in the balance sheet.

Transaction Risk

This risk is that exchange rate movements affect the value of foreign currency cash flows. It is the only risk that has a direct and immediate impact on cash, and arises when a transaction is entered into to convert from one currency to another.

The most common trading situation creating this exposure is the sale or purchase of goods or services on extended payment terms in foreign currencies. Another common

situation arises when dividend or interest payments are paid or received.

This type of risk is usually predictable and quantified, making the protection or hedging process straightforward. Really successful management of currency exposures needs to cope with transactions that have not yet been identified but are likely to occur.

SPECIFIC SITUATIONS
Price List Exposure

Scenario: An exporting company publishes a price list in a local currency. It is commercially impractical to change prices in less than six months.

Risk: A potential exposure is created for up to six months, plus any extended payment term. Actual exposure arises when an invoice is issued.

Possible solutions:

- Small print "right to impose surcharges" clauses. This is legally possible, but commercially highly damaging. Airlines have had to resort to this, but it is easier for them given the high profile of oil price movements and the fact that almost all of the competitors are doing it!

- Hedging a proportion of projected sales, from the date of publication of the price list, is advisable. What proportion is a risk management decision, dependent on the corporate attitude to risk, the corporate memory of past situations, and the degree of volatility between currencies.

Capital expenditure: This investment is usually planned and committed over a long period. There may be no actual transaction exposure until purchase contracts are awarded, so the exposure can be identified, quantified, and handled by a hedging technique.

Tender to Control Exposure

Scenario and risk exposure: Companies that regularly submit tenders for the supply of goods and services are exposed from the date of submitting the tender to the date(s) cash is received. Until an order has been received, this is potential exposure; after that event there is real exposure, and from the invoice date transaction exposure exists.

Possible solutions:

- Using historic data for guidance, assess the success rate from tender to contract. Apply that rate—with a value weighting—to all tenders issued, hedging the proportion that's likely to be successful. Additionally, where good market intelligence exists, add in those contracts likely to be won.

- Treat the exposure after winning the contract as a transaction, and hedge using an appropriate technique.

- Try to offset as many costs as possible by buying in the currency of the payer.

MANAGING CURRENCY RISKS

A range of techniques exists that enable companies to limit their exposure to the effect of fluctuating exchange rates. The decision to protect or hedge is made after an assessment of the significance of the risk to the business of exchange rate movements. The selection of hedging technique is made for each specific situation, following a risk assessment of the impact on the business. Factors considered in the risk assessment are:

- The percentage of the company's turnover that is exposed to currency risk. The greater the proportion of sales paid in international currencies versus the home currency, the greater the risk to the business.
- The individual size of a single exposure. Depending on the volatility of the currency, this could be a very high risk, even threatening the continuity of the business.
- The market position of the company. This is its financial strength and consequent ability to react to competitive pressures.
- The portfolio of currencies in which the company trades, and whether there are potential offsetting transactions.
- The relationship of cost to sales within trading blocs, particularly currencies that move in lockstep with the US dollar—those of Canada, Hong Kong, Malaysia, Singapore, and Saudi Arabia.
- The ability to match the currency of sales with the currency of costs.
- The previous experience of the company in relation to currency losses, and its forecasting experience.
- The level of currency management expertise within the company.

HEDGING TECHNIQUES
Internal
Sometimes known as commercial or natural, these techniques are within the internal management control of the company.
  Pricing:
- In the currency in which the majority of the costs are incurred.
- In the domestic currency of the main competitors, so that comparative prices are less affected by exchange rate variations.
- Inserting an exchange rate variation clause (always difficult commercially) to protect margins.

Matching:
- Setting up an equal and opposite commercial transaction when the original exposure is created—for example, using the currency of a receivable to buy a commodity used by the business.
- Borrow in the same currency as that needed to complete the asset purchase.

Netting:
- A partial alternative to matching—a net amount is still left exposed, but the overall risk is reduced.

Leading and lagging:
- Simply, either delaying payment, or settling early, in anticipation of falling or rising exchange rates. Safe, and simple to manage, but there is a reliance on the accuracy of a forecast.

Intercompany payment discipline:
- Intercompany payables and receivables are real exposure and should be ranked equally for settlement with external liabilities.

- There is no canceling gain or loss situation within a group. When the transaction interacts with the market there will be a gain or a loss—and it will be real.

External
When the use of internal techniques has been exhausted, external ones should be used. There are four main instruments:
- Forward contracts;
- Lending and borrowing;
- Options;
- Swaps.

Forward Contracts
A forward contract is an agreement to exchange a fixed amount of one currency for a fixed amount of another currency at an agreed date in the future. The effective exchange rate is derived from the comparative interest rates of the two currencies being exchanged. Its suitability depends on being able to forecast the currency flows confidently. If the forecast proves not to be accurate, the business has in reality created an exposure rather than protected an existing one, because the forward contract is a binding agreement to deliver a quantity of one currency and receive a quantity of another. The key features of a forward contract are:
- Certainty and simplicity—enabling good cash management;
- Off balance sheet—it does not count as borrowings that affect gearing;
- Normally sourced from a bank.

Lending and Borrowing
As an alternative to a forward contract, the currency could be exchanged immediately in the spot market, i.e. where the transaction is agreed on the "spot" and takes place immediately. The exchange rate is known as fixed, the transaction immediate (two days delivery normally), and the administration and monitoring of forward contracts are avoided. The currency is normally deposited in an interest-bearing currency account until needed.
  Illustration: A forward transaction to buy yen for a capital equipment purchase has been made. Delivery will be late. A way around this problem would be to take delivery of the yen as agreed and put the amount on deposit until needed. As yen interest rates are lower than for sterling, there will be an effective interest cost. If delivery was available earlier and agreed to by the company, yen could be borrowed short term and repaid when the forward contract matured.

Options
An option is the right, but not the obligation, to exchange a fixed amount of one currency for a fixed amount of another within, or at the end of, a predetermined period. In effect, it is a forward contract that can be walked away from, where you lose only the cost of the option, which could be 3–5% of the contract value. It therefore has the advantage of limiting the downside, as the maximum cost is known at the beginning, while leaving unlimited profit potential. These options are ideally suited to translations, where the size or existence of the

exposure is uncertain, for example tender-to-contract or price list exposures.

Illustration: A quantity of a commodity (or currency to pay for it) is needed in three months' time. A dealer is willing to accept US$100 per ton to supply a predetermined quantity at US$2,000 per ton. If the price of this commodity in three months' time is US$1,700 per ton, then the option would be thrown away, the product bought in the spot market, and the cost to the company would be US$1,800 per ton. The tender-to-contract or price list item would have been safeguarded, and the price could even be reduced by US$200 per ton if competitive conditions demanded. If the price of the commodity rose, the cost to the company would be contained. The option could be sold at a profit if the product was not needed, or the loss would in any event be limited to US$100 per ton.

There are two types of option:

- **Calls**—giving the right to buy a currency;
- **Puts**—giving the right to sell a currency.

Currency Options

The exchange rate (known as the strike price) and the expiry date of the option are chosen by the customer at the outset. The cost (known as the premium) of the option is calculated based on these decisions and the volatility of the currency involved. Options can be exchange-traded where they exist in standardized form, or bought over the counter, where they are written to fit a customer's particular circumstances.

There are two styles of option:

- **American option**. The buyer can exercise the option (make the exchange of currencies) at any time up to the expiry date.
- **European option**. This can be exercised on the expiry date only, and is slightly cheaper because of its lack of flexibility.

Options may have a resale value, determined by the same criteria as the original cost. When the exercise price of an option is better than the current spot exchange rate, it is called "in the money"; when it is the other way round, it is "out of the money."

Swaps

Swaps are like long-dated forward contracts. They involve the exchange of a liability now, with the exchange back at a predetermined future time, and the compensation of the other party for costs in the intervening period. Swaps are used primarily to protect an investment or portfolio of borrowings. They involve a back-to-back loan between companies with a matching but opposite need. What is "swapped" is essentially a series of cash flows.

Illustration: A UK company wishes to raise cash to invest in developing its business in the United States. It is quoted in the United Kingdom only, which means it does not have access to US capital markets and it does not have a rating, so it would be extremely difficult to borrow in the United States.

What sources of funds are available?

- Raise equity via a UK rights issue;
- Borrow sterling from a UK bank;
- Borrow in US dollars.

The first two of these options will appear on a balance sheet as sterling liabilities, but the asset will appear as a dollar asset, creating a translation exposure. The returns from the investment will be in dollars, which will create a translation exposure when they are converted to sterling income in the profit statement, and a transaction exposure when they need to be converted to pay interest or dividends in sterling.

A solution is to swap the currency flows for the duration of a loan, paying or receiving a sum of money from the other party, leaving both sides in an equivalent cash flow position but having avoided specific payments in another currency. The loan would revert to the borrowing currency on maturity.

CONCLUSION

Managing currency and related transactions is a core part of corporate risk management within the treasury function. Its importance will continue to demand boardroom time and the highest standard of corporate governance. Massive and unpredictable fluctuations in currency markets have made forecasting more difficult and the need to safeguard the value of assets, liabilities, and transactions is paramount.

MORE INFO

Books:

Arnold, Glen. *Corporate Financial Management*. 4th ed. Harlow, UK: FT Prentice Hall, 2008.

Boakes, Kevin. *Reading and Understanding the Financial Times*. Harlow, UK: FT Prentice Hall, 2008.

Matza, Peter (ed). *The International Treasurer's Handbook 2012*. 22nd ed. London: Association of Corporate Treasurers, 2011.

Shomah, Shani Beverley. *A Foreign Exchange Primer*. 2nd ed. Chichester, UK: Wiley, 2009.

Slatyer, Will. *The Debt Delusion: Evolution and Management of Financial Risk*. Boca Raton, FL: Universal Publishers, 2008.

Websites:

DailyFX: www.dailyfx.com

Reuters Business and Finance: www.reuters.com/finance

Treasury Management International (TMI): www.treasury-management.com

See Also:

★ Political Risk: Countering the Impact on Your Business (pp. 270–273)

✔ Hedging Liquidity Risk—Case Study and Strategies (pp. 294–295)

✔ Identifying and Managing Exposure to Interest and Exchange Rate Risks (pp. 296–297)

Using Structured Products to Manage Liabilities

by Shane Edwards

EXECUTIVE SUMMARY

- Structured products (SPs) are derivative contracts that are tailored for a specific purpose, such as hedging the value of an uncertain future liability.
- The value of a SP is derived from one or many underlying reference asset values, which causes uncertainty in the value of the liability to be hedged.
- SPs are typically transacted between a client and an investment bank, and can take various legal forms.
- The fact that SPs are flexible and can be tailored to client needs distinguishes them from standard derivatives, which have generic fixed terms.
- However, SPs tend to be regarded as more complex financial instruments, and they are more difficult to value than vanilla derivatives.

INTRODUCTION

Only a decade ago, the use of structured products (SPs) was largely confined to sophisticated institutions that used them for risk management purposes. Now SPs are embraced across the client spectrum and are owned by millions—from retail individuals investing in capital-protected equity products, to global corporations that tailor SPs to meet their often complex and highly specific liability management needs.

In the liability management arena, SPs have an important role to play due to their highly customizable nature. They are used by corporate treasurers as a way of actively managing borrowing costs and hedging foreign exchange liabilities. Many companies have also embraced SPs, outside of treasury, to manage expected future liabilities (for example, airlines hedging the price of jet fuel or importers/exporters hedging the foreign exchange rate). SPs are also used by many pension funds as a strategic initiative to manage the asset–liability mismatch and tailor the pension deficit risk profile.

The increased appetite for SPs is a result of improved client education and the rapid pace of innovation at investment banks, where SPs have become a major source of business. The growth in SP volumes is expected to continue its rapid pace in the years ahead.

ANATOMY OF A STRUCTURED PRODUCT

A derivative is a financial instrument that derives its value from one or more underlying reference asset values. Derivatives can range in complexity from very simple with standardized terms (vanilla derivatives), to very complex with highly customized features (exotic derivatives). Broadly, there are three levels of complexity in derivatives, listed here in order of complexity:

Linear derivatives (for example, futures, forwards, zero strike calls), which reflect the performance of an underlying asset on an almost one-to-one basis but without legal ownership of the underlying asset. These derivatives can be simply priced through arbitrage (cost of carry) arguments.

Nonlinear derivatives (for example, call options), where at expiry the price of the derivative will vary linearly with the underlying asset price if the underlying is above a predefined strike level. If this is not the case, the option price will be worth zero. Well-understood models are available that rely heavily on the volatility of the underlying asset to determine the derivative price.

Exotic derivatives, which have path-dependent payouts, restriking features, or hybrid (multiasset class) characteristics. They require sophisticated mathematical models to price and are highly sensitive to calibrations of the underlying probability distribution and correlation assumptions (in the case of multiasset underlyings).

Any of the three derivative types may be regarded as structured products due to the amount of customization that is contained in the contract terms. Common customizations include:

- Underlying assets (underlyings): These may include anything that is transparent and tradable, such as equities, interest rates, foreign exchange rates, commodities, and inflation. Hybrid SPs can be created where multiple asset classes are used.
- Tenor: Clients are able to tailor the maturity of a SP to any extent where the counterparty providing the hedge allows it, which in turn is dictated by the liquidity of the underlying asset. SPs can include features that allow early maturity, such as: puttability (where the client may choose to early-terminate the structure with preagreed payout), callability (where the hedge counterparty can terminate at its discretion), or automatic termination (where maturity will occur once a predefined event has occurred).
- Path dependency: The payouts of many SPs are determined with reference to how the underlyings have performed through the life of the product, and not simply as a function of the final underlying asset level. Examples are Asian options (where the average level of an underlying is calculated) and lookback or barrier options (where the highest or lowest observed levels of an underlying determine the payout).
- Payouts: SPs can have interim payouts (coupons) and/or a final payout at maturity as specified.

- Currency: SP payouts are often requested in currencies other than the currency of the underlying asset; such products are known as quanto or composite options.

LEGAL FORM

A structured product is a legally binding financial contract between a client and an investment bank, stating the specific terms that have been agreed. The legal form of the transaction is referred to as a wrapper, and the most common wrappers are:

Over-the-counter (OTC). This typically means that a client makes an upfront payment equal to the offer price of the SP. In return, the bank (as per the terms of the SP) may pay the client coupons and/or a payment at maturity, all of which are typically dependent on the performance of the underlying reference assets.

Structured note. The client pays the principal amount to the bank at inception. In return, the bank sells the client a note, which is typically a senior unsecured debt obligation of the bank. The note will reflect the terms of the transaction and specify payments, normally including the return of the principal amount at maturity (for principal protected notes), or possibly some principal loss (in the case of nonprincipal protected notes), depending on the performance of the underlying.

Swap. In a swap there is no exchange of principal. Typically, the client will pay floating Libor (minus a spread) and the investment bank will pay periodic amounts contingent on the performance of the underlying.

Other forms. There are myriad wrappers that find preference with certain clients or in certain jurisdictions, depending on the tax consequences, counterparty risk exposure, and local regulation. Other wrappers include structured deposits and UCITS III funds,[1] for example.

CLIENT TYPES AND COMMON USES OF STRUCTURED PRODUCTS IN LIABILITY MANAGEMENT

Due to their flexibility, SPs are chosen in a variety of liability management situations and by an array of users. They are implemented as both a proactive (value enhancing) and a reactive (risk hedging) tool. Some examples are given below for corporate treasurers who manage interest rate exposure, borrowing requirements, and currency exposure, and for pension managers who employ SPs in the asset–liability management framework.

Managing interest rate exposure (reactive example). A corporation has existing floating-rate debt and is concerned that interest rates will increase. It may buy a cap with the same remaining debt maturity, which means it will pay a premium upfront and will receive periodic payments if the floating reference rate is above the agreed cap rate. Thus the company can ensure that its net floating payments will not exceed a capped rate.

Managing interest rate exposure (proactive example). A corporation is aware that its business revenue varies inversely with the level of prevailing interest rates. Working with an investment bank, the treasurer decides to restructure its borrowing and issue an inverse floater, which means that its interest payments will decline as the floating reference rate rises (and its business revenues contract), and its interest payments will rise if floating reference rates fall (and business revenues expand), providing profit stabilization through the economic cycle.

Using SPs for new borrowing requirements (hybrid example). A Japanese company could borrow in US dollars to establish a US-based distribution center for products it manufactures in Japan for a fixed cost in Japanese yen. A major threat to profit is the selling price, which is fixed in US dollars. Again, looking to stabilize profit, the company could buy a SP where it will receive coupons if the dollar depreciates or if the US interest rate rises.

Hedging input prices. Steel is a vital input for automobile manufacturers. In forecasting the budget, auto makers will estimate the number of cars they need to complete over the following period and the associated revenues and costs. Clearly, fluctuating input prices could threaten the bottom line. A variety of SPs can hedge this risk, including a forward purchase agreement that guarantees a fixed price or an option to buy steel at a fixed price in the future, for which the company could pay an upfront premium.

Pension asset–liability management. Pension managers receive plan contributions and must grow the asset base so that it exceeds the expected liabilities that arise from funding the future retirement benefits of fund members. The desire to invest in higher-growth assets (for example, equities) is tempered by the knowledge that they are also higher risk. The fund could invest in low-risk assets (for example, government bonds) and gain exposure to the outperformance of an equity index over a bond index, floored at zero, through a tailored hybrid SP. This would allow it to substantially outperform fixed-income investments during good times, though it would slightly underperform during bad times since the SP premium paid would detract from a bond-only portfolio.

PRACTICAL CONSIDERATIONS

The attributes that make SPs so desirable—namely their flexibility and highly customizable nature—may also be their biggest disadvantage. Some predominant practical considerations are:

- Pricing: This can be complicated and requires mathematical models and computing power. Most structured products are priced in a Monte Carlo framework, which is a statistical technique involving the simulation of many paths for each underlying to assess the expected payout of the SP.
- Mark-to-market valuation: Although many SPs have a clearly defined payout at maturity (intended to match a specific liability, for example), the fluctuations in mark-to-market valuations also depend on other variables. Such variables include changes in the underlying's volatility, correlation, or interest rates. Mark-to-market fluctuations can cause balance sheet volatility, depending on how hedge accounting is implemented.

- Secondary market: A client wishing to terminate an SP before its maturity date may be granted an unwind price from the bank it originally traded with, or enter into a directly opposite trade with another investment bank. This may leave residual credit risk.
- Asset mismatch: Sometimes the precise underlying that constitutes the source of a future liability cannot be used as the underlying for the SP because it is not readily tradable. This is a particular concern with commodity SPs, which are often linked to commodity futures rather than physical commodities.
- Counterparty risk: Many of the typical SP wrappers, such as OTC, note, and swap, contain credit risk—that is, the investment bank may not be able to fulfill its obligations when they fall due. This can be mitigated by requiring the bank to post high-quality collateral against mark-to-market valuations.

CONCLUSION

Structured products represent a powerful instrument for the active management of specific liabilities, a liability portfolio, or asset–liability dilemmas. They can be linked to a wide variety of underlying assets and are fully flexible with regard to maturity date and conditions observed throughout the term. However, there are a number of practical issues that need to be understood, including valuation difficulties, counterparty risk, and mark-to-market fluctuations.

MAKING IT HAPPEN

Most SP experts are found at the major investment banks. As a potential client, a useful starting point is to have clarity on a specific liability or liability portfolio, and an objective that the company would like to achieve—for example, hedging of price uncertainties, smoothed performance over business cycles, or achieving a higher return with less risk on surplus funds. Clients can approach this in a number of ways:

- Advanced clients will often propose the details of an SP to investment banks and ask for pricing and trade terms to see whether they are favorable.
- Less-experienced clients will request a meeting with a bank at which SP experts will propose a range of potentially appropriate products and indicative terms.
- Always conduct a scenario analysis of how the liability portfolio behaves before and after the inclusion of an SP that is being considered, and consider mark-to-market and accounting effects.

- Many courses are available that teach elementary SP pricing. This knowledge will help you to understand how different variables may affect a valuation.

MORE INFO

Books:

Adam, Alexandre. *Handbook of Asset and Liability Management: From Models to Optimal Return Strategies*. Chichester, UK: Wiley, 2007.
Hull, John C. *Options, Futures, and Other Derivatives*. 8th ed. Upper Saddle River, NJ: Pearson, 2011.
Rebonato, Riccardo. *Volatility and Correlation: The Perfect Hedger and the Fox*. 2nd ed. Chichester, UK: Wiley, 2004.
Wilmott, Paul. *Paul Wilmott on Quantitative Finance*. 2nd ed. Chichester, UK: Wiley, 2006.

Articles:

Black, Fischer, and Myron Scholes. "The pricing of options and corporate liabilities." *Journal of Political Economy* 81:3 (May–June 1973): 637–654. Online at: www.jstor.org/stable/1831029
Dupire, Bruno. "Pricing with a smile." *Risk* 7:1 (1994): 18–20.
Heston, Steven L. "A closed-form solution for options with stochastic volatility with applications to bond and currency options." *Review of Financial Studies* 6:2 (Summer 1993): 327–343. Online at: dx.doi.org/10.1093/rfs/6.2.327

Magazines:

Risk, *Structured Products*, *Euromoney*, *Derivatives Week*.

See Also:

★ To Hedge or Not to Hedge (pp. 53–56)
✔ Analysis Using Monte Carlo Simulation (p. 327)
✔ Identifying and Managing Exposure to Interest and Exchange Rate Risks (pp. 296–297)
✔ Swaps, Options, and Futures: What They Are and Their Function (pp. 303–304)
✔ Understanding Asset–Liability Management (Full Balance Sheet Approach) (pp. 305–306)

NOTE

1 Undertakings for Collective Investments in Transferable Securities (UCITS) are a set of European Union directives that allow compliant collective investment schemes to operate freely throughout the European Union. These funds are a versatile legal structure that often includes embedded structured products.

Valuing Pension Fund Liabilities on the Balance Sheet

by Steven Lowe

EXECUTIVE SUMMARY

- Accounting standards affect how pension liabilities are reported in company accounts. FAS 158 requires that the net of pension fund assets and liabilities are reported in the main accounts. Traditional accountancy measures allow a more subjective measurement, and relegate pension information to the accounting notes.
- The real issue is how a company calculates and values the projected liability—which depends on the discount rate selected, the actuarial assumptions relating to future inflation, wage increases, and, most importantly, the expected longevity of employees.
- Different pension stakeholders will favor different liability measures, resulting in differing investment risk tolerances and strategies, which in turn can impact the corporate balance sheet.
- Accounting measures and buyout measures of pension liabilities differ. Finance directors need to be aware of both types of measure, their assumptions, and the interaction between them, as they can impact pension strategies and, consequently, financial reporting.

INTRODUCTION

With a pension plan, companies agree to provide certain benefits to their employees, by specifying either a defined contribution (where a fixed contribution is made to the plan each year by the employer, with no promises as to the future benefits that will be delivered by the plan) or a defined benefit (where the employer undertakes to pay a certain benefit to the employee at some point in the future). Under the latter, the employer has to put sufficient money into the plan each period such that the amounts, with reinvestment, are sufficient to meet the defined benefits due as plan members retire.

With a defined contribution plan, the firm meets its obligation once it has made the prespecified contribution to the plan, and its valuation on the balance sheet is reasonably straightforward. With a defined benefit plan, the firm's obligations are much more difficult to estimate, since they will be determined by a number of variables, including the benefits that employees are entitled to (which will change as their salary and employment status change), the prior contributions made by the employer (and the returns they have earned), the expected retirement date of employees, and the rate of return that the employer expects to make on current contributions.

As these variables change, the value of the pension fund assets can be greater than, less than, or equal to the pension fund liabilities (which include the present value of promised benefits). Recent changes to accounting regulations have increased the transparency of pension funding, and this has sparked an increased debate about the goals of defined benefit pension funds. The stakeholders of a pension fund (sponsor, trustees, and the various classes of pensioner) often have different goals, and therefore require the asset and liability information to be presented using different assumptions. These assumptions can materially affect both profit and loss (P&L) and balance sheet statements.

A pension fund whose assets exceed liabilities is an overfunded plan, whereas one in which assets are less than liabilities is underfunded, and disclosures to that effect have to be included in financial statements. When a pension fund is overfunded the firm has several options: It can withdraw the excess assets from the fund, it can discontinue contributions to the plan, or it can continue to make contributions on the assumption that the overfunding is a transitory phenomenon that could well disappear by the next period. When a fund is underfunded, the firm has a liability that must be recognized on the balance sheet.

ACCOUNTING STANDARDS

In late 2006, the Financial Accounting Standards Board issued its final Statement of Financial Accounting Standards No. 158 (FAS 158), which deals with the rules for reporting the obligations and expenses of pension plans, retiree health plans, nonqualified deferred compensation plans, and other post retirement benefits. Among many changes, FAS 158 moved information about the funded status of pension plans and other postretirement employee benefit plans from the footnotes of the financial statements to the balance sheet itself. The idea behind FAS 158 was to create more transparency and to make information about pension plans and other postretirement employee benefit plans available to investors. It requires companies to include on the balance sheet the full net value of pension assets and obligations. These are to be measured as the difference between the fund assets and the projected benefit obligations. A company does not have to show the full value of assets and the full value of liabilities— just the net of the two. If the fund assets are higher than pension obligation, it will show as an asset; if not, it will be a liability.

Before FAS 158, the effects of certain events, such as plan amendments or actuarial gains and losses, could be given delayed recognition in the balance sheet. Alternatively, market returns could be smoothed over several years rather than recognized at once. As a result, a plan's funded status (plan assets less obligations) rarely reflected the true position and so was not reported on the balance sheet. FAS 158 requires companies to report their plan's funded status, which is likely to cause reported pension liabilities to rise significantly. The traditional actuarial approach is incorporated to a degree in

International Accounting Standard 19 (IAS 19), which means that the balance sheet generated on an IAS 19 basis does not necessarily reflect the full net asset or liability position of the pension plan. Whichever accountancy basis is adopted, the real issue is how to identify the projected benefit obligation.

Typically, the assets held by the sponsor's pension fund are liquid, have publicly accessible pricing data, and are subject to market value fluctuations. The liabilities, however, are rarely traded, are particular to the individual pension scheme, and, depending on the valuation method adopted, can be considerably less volatile. Assets are measured at market value, whereas the discount rate for valuing liabilities is based on the actuaries' assessment of long-run returns on the assets in the pension fund.

CALCULATING ACCOUNTING LIABILITIES

The projected benefit obligation is the actuarial present value of the benefit obligations made by the pension plan. This liability, according to most accounting standards (FRS 17, FAS 87, IAS 19), is calculated by reference to the yield on AA corporate bonds. These in turn are affected by movements in interest rates, and also variations in the cost of credit.

This accounting measure of liabilities makes no allowance for the actual investment policy pursued by the pension scheme. It does, however, include actuarial forecasts of inflation, expected future salary increases, and current longevity assumptions. These assumptions are taken as being best-guess estimations, and often cause keen debate between a corporate sponsor's actuaries and those advising the trustees during the triennial funding discussion. The rate of inflation and forecast salary increases are usually fairly straightforward and based on recent experience, but forecasts of longevity lead to more discussion. Longevity has been increasing exponentially since the Second World War, and actuaries have consistently underestimated life expectancy. Any increase in assumed life expectancy will increase the liability of the pension fund and thus increase the annual contributions required by the sponsor, as well as increasing the total liability on the balance sheet. It is estimated that an increase of one year of life expectancy will add approximately 7% to pension liability. Given that life expectancy for a 65-year-old male is improving at the rate of one year's increase in life expectancy in every five years, this has the potential to have a huge impact on corporate investment plans.

The assumptions made about inflation, salary increases, and longevity are a key subject of discussion when trustees and sponsor debate proposed future funding strategies for the pension plan. The other key topic for discussion should be the expected investment returns from the asset strategy undertaken by the trustees. Both the actuarial assumptions and the investment risk assumed by the pension fund are likely to greatly influence the size and scale of future sponsor contributions.

The funding strategy is normally assessed on a going concern principle, resting on the assumption that the sponsor will be around for many years and is able and willing to provide the support necessary to the pension scheme if the investment strategy produces returns below those expected, or if life expectancy or any of the other actuarial assumptions

exceeds the forecast. There are a number of factors that should be considered by both sponsor and trustees in determining how much risk there is to the ability of the pension fund to meet its future liabilities:

- Covenant or sponsor business risk: The stronger the covenant (the lower the business risk), the more risk can be taken with the pension fund investment and the less conservative the actuarial assumptions need to be.
- Maturity of pension scheme: The longer the funding period (i.e., the younger the potential beneficiaries or pension scheme membership), the more investment risk can be taken without compromising the security of the final benefit payments. Conversely, the higher the longevity risk which a younger scheme incorporates, the greater is the risk that even minor improvements in life expectancy will cause a large movement in the value of future pension promises and, hence, liability on the balance sheet.
- Surplus: The larger the accounting surplus, the more investment risk can be taken. Conversely, with a large deficit there will also be pressure to take increased investment risk.

The minimal risk approach argues that assets should be valued at market prices and that liabilities should be valued consistently using the market returns on appropriate assets and conservative longevity assumptions. The optimal asset allocation would then be determined using horizon matching. This uses bonds, with their reliable cash flows, to meet current and near-maturing pension obligations (using a strategy called cash flow matching), and equity and property, with their growth potential, to match long-maturing liabilities that grow in line with earnings (using a strategy called surplus management). This second strategy is justified because of the long-run constancy of factor shares in national income (which makes capital and land ideal long-term matching assets for a liability that is linked to the return on labor), and because of the positive long-run equity risk premium and mean-reversion in equity returns (which implies that long-run equity returns are more stable than short-run returns). Such an asset allocation should mean that changes in pension liabilities caused by moves in interest rates, inflation, or longevity are matched by a mixture of bond and equity returns, thus immunizing the balance sheet from any unexpected changes in value of either asset or liability metric. With a stable balance sheet, planning future pension contributions can be done with more certainty, thus limiting the impact of volatile contributions on the P&L.

BUYOUT LIABILITY

Another, different, way of calculating the pension position is based on the assets required to buy out the pension liabilities at a specific point in time. This can be thought of as the market price of passing all the liabilities of a pension fund to a specialist insurer. Five years ago, this only happened in the case of insolvency, but increasingly niche insurers are starting to specialize in pooling longevity risk and offering prices to remove all pension assets and liabilities from a sponsor's balance sheet. The buyout deficit shows the additional funds needed if the accrued liabilities were to be settled by purchasing matching annuities from these insurers. Under

UK legislation, this is also the contingent debt that could be served on the sponsor by the trustees of the pension scheme, should the sponsor decide to discontinue the scheme.

The volatility of this measure is dictated by the terms on which insurance companies are prepared to deal. Annuities are usually priced at yields well below the prevailing yields on government bonds and with a cautious view of future longevity trends. Therefore, the liabilities assessed on this measure are significantly higher than those assessed on the accounting and funding measures.

ACCOUNTING IMPACT

The current accounting methodology has three main impacts. First, balance sheets have become more volatile due to the inclusion of net pension assets or liabilities, which are dependent on publicly traded debt prices. This volatility may trigger loan covenants or borrowing limits, or otherwise affect corporate behavior. Second, the P&L retains some volatility due to pension impacts, since changes in the balance sheet funding position affect the level of sponsor contributions and, hence, flow through to the P&L. Finally, financial statements have increased in complexity as noncash pension items are now included. Some items, such as the current service cost and amortization of past service costs within operating cost, the unwinding of the pension liability discount, and the expected return on assets within financing costs, are highly complex in themselves.

CONCLUSION

There is no doubt that the accounting measure has been, and continues to be, hugely influential in corporate decision-making and short-term risk management. It provides the basis for funding discussions with the trustees and is therefore important for cash flow management, particularly in companies where the corporate covenant is not strong. The buyout measure of pension liabilities is becoming more important, since the discharge of all pension obligations by the sponsor is growing in desirability as the full risks of longevity increases are increasingly recognized. Additionally, trustees often find that a buyout, with the security provided by a regulated insurer rather than a corporate sponsor, is a goal for pension funding in itself. Buyout pricing also establishes a target for a closed defined benefit scheme (over a suitable time horizon).

Therefore it is vital that finance directors monitor the development of assets and liabilities using both accounting and buyout measures, as well as understanding the assumptions that each employs and interactions between them.

MAKING IT HAPPEN

- A defined benefit pension scheme is one where the employer promises to pay a certain benefit to the employee on retirement. It is funded by contributions to a pension plan and the investment return on those contributions while the employee is working, which, over time, the employer hopes will match the benefits promised.

- Both the assets and liabilities are accounted for on the corporate balance sheet, introducing a complicated variable into financial reporting that usually has little to do with the main business of the employer.
- Assets are valued using market rates, but future liabilities are valued by selecting a discount rate and making assumptions about future inflation, wage increases, and longevity.
- Each of these factors (inflation, wages, and longevity) can have a large influence not only on the financial information reported, but also on the strategy and risk tolerance of the pension fund and its stakeholders.
- Because of this, it is vital that the employer understands a variety of different measures for the pension liabilities, such as the accounting/funding basis and the buyout liability, as these can impact how the pension fund assets and liabilities are ultimately reported on the balance sheet each year.

MORE INFO

Book:

Fridson, Martin, and Fernando Alvarez. *Financial Statement Analysis: A Practitioner's Guide*. 3rd ed. New York: Wiley, 2002.

Articles:

Financial Education. "Balance sheet recognition of pension liabilities under International Accounting Standards (IAS)." Online at: tinyurl.com/anupfb

Juliens, Dennis. "The impact of pension accounting on financial statements and disclosures." *CFA Institute Conference Proceedings* The Transition to International Financial Reporting Standards (April 2005): 19–24. Online at: dx.doi.org/10.2469/cp.v2005.n3.3484

Zion, David. "Beginning to overhaul the pension accounting rules." *CFA Institute Conference Proceedings Quarterly* 24:2 (June 2007): 38–44. Online at: dx.doi.org/10.2469/cp.v24.n2.4704

Report:

Riley, Leigh C., and Katherine L. Aizawa. "Pension fund issues in the boardroom: Is your pension plan becoming too expensive?" Foley & Lardner, May 2007. Online at: tinyurl.com/7bq2hcn

See Also:

Aligning the Internal Audit Function with Strategic Objectives

by Ilias G. Basioudis

EXECUTIVE SUMMARY

- Due to high-profile scandals at the beginning of the century, regulators and the accounting profession worldwide have put forward a series of initiatives to repair the damage and restore faith in corporate governance.
- Globally, more companies are adopting corporate governance best practice.
- An independent internal audit function is widely recognized as an integral part of a company's strategic objectives, corporate governance, and risk management.
- The internal audit standards issued by the Institute of Internal Auditors serve as authoritative guidance for members of the internal audit profession.
- Internal audit's role is to evaluate the appropriateness and effectiveness of companies' systems and processes, and to identify and manage risks present in the normal course of conducting business activities.

INTRODUCTION

Given today's complex and rapidly changing management climate, companies must implement continuous improvements to achieve efficiency, and assure investors and other concerned parties of solid corporate governance.

The recent scandals at Enron, WorldCom, Parmalat, and others have raised the profile of corporate governance across the globe. Trust in the process of financial accounting, corporate governance, and auditing has been undermined by these high-profile corporate scandals. In response, regulators and the accounting profession worldwide have put forward a series of initiatives to repair the damage and restore faith in corporate governance. Furthermore, companies must continuously implement improvements to achieve effective and efficient management in order to assure the investors, other stakeholders, and concerned parties in general of its good and sound corporate governance. Globally, more companies, governments, states, and regulators are adopting corporate governance best practice, and placing more emphasis on improving corporate governance in companies, which in turn improves the confidence of investors and stakeholders in companies.

Worldwide legislative initiatives, of which the Sarbanes–Oxley Act (US) and Directive No. 8 (EU) are the most famous, make senior management responsible for establishing, evaluating, and assessing over time the effectiveness of risk management processes, systems of internal control, and corporate governance processes. In tandem, companies play a critical role in the national economy, or economies, in which they have activities. A country's competitiveness, wealth, efficiency, and high level of economic growth may depend on the competitive nature of its companies. There is no doubt that a transparent and reasonable corporate governance structure has a positive impact on a company.

The audit committee is a subcommittee of the board of directors, and is widely recognized as an integral part of a company's corporate governance, and, together with the internal audit function, they contribute towards the company implementing continuous improvements. In fact, one line of thought claims that the audit committee, especially in large organizations, could not possibly be effective without an efficient, effective, and independent-minded internal audit function.

As a result, the internal audit function has the potential to be one of the most influential and value-adding services available to a company's senior management and board of directors. Furthermore, with the growing focus on corporate governance issues, organizations are increasingly exploring the potential benefits to be gained from establishing an effective and efficient internal audit function. Company boards must identify the opportunities, risks, and exposures that can determine success or failure. The establishment of an internal audit function can become an integral part of overall strategy, and assist in achieving corporate objectives.

THE PURPOSE AND ROLE OF INTERNAL AUDITING

According to The Institute of Internal Auditors' (IIA) definition of internal auditing, the internal audit function should provide independent, thorough, timely, and objective results of quantitative and qualitative testing to senior management, and, in essence, help evaluate organizational risk management. Internal auditing assists public and private organizations to meet overall corporate objectives by establishing a systematic and disciplined approach to assessing, evaluating, and improving the quality and effectiveness of risk management processes, systems of internal control, and corporate governance processes. This systematic approach and analysis is implemented across all parts of an organization, and the internal auditor reports directly and independently to the most senior level of management. The role of the internal auditor, therefore, is to provide an overall assurance to management that all key risks within an organization are managed effectively, so that the organization can achieve its strategic objectives.

An internal audit function should be independent and unbiased, and hold a neutral position within an organization. The audit function looks beyond the narrow focus of financial statements and financial risks (although these risks are included in the remit of the internal auditor's job), and it may, for example, involve auditing reputational, operational, environmental, or strategic risks. Reputational risks could involve labor practices in host countries; operational risks include poor health and safety procedures; environmental risks might involve pollution generated by a factory; while a strategic risk might involve the board stretching company resources by producing too many products.

An internal audit function should have the ability itself to define the scope of internal audits (after consultation with the internal audit's primary stakeholders), the authority to obtain information and resources, and have an appropriate reporting structure to senior management. The internal audit team members do not test their own work, or the work of persons that they report to. Any actual or potential conflicts of interest that hinder an honest, independent, and unbiased assessment must be disclosed.

INTERNAL AUDIT STANDARDS

In order to operate an internal audit function that is objective, independent, effective, and useful to an organization, it is essential that the internal audit function complies with the International Standards for the Professional Practice of Internal Auditing, developed by the Institute of Internal Auditors. The International Standards are authoritative guidance for the internal audit profession, and are principles-focused. Implementation standards refer to either assurance or consulting activities, and are embedded in the attribute and performance standards. Attribute standards refer to the composition of the audit department in terms of staff expertise and ongoing training, as well as independence and objectivity. Attribute standards also refer to the internal audit department's purpose, authority, and responsibility.

Performance standards refer to how the internal audit function should operate, and how the planning, scope, and reporting activities should be conducted and by whom. The performance standards reflect the purpose of the internal audit function in that they define the activities to be completed, which help make sure that the internal audit function is operating as designed for the benefit of the organization.

Another authoritative guidance issued by the IIA is the Code of Ethics. This is a statement of principles and expectations governing the behavior of individuals and organizations in the conduct of internal auditing, and provides a description of minimum requirements for conduct, and describes behavioral expectations rather than specific activities. The Code of Ethics refers to the integrity, objectivity, confidentiality, and competence of internal auditors.

DESIGNING A STRATEGICALLY FOCUSED INTERNAL AUDIT FUNCTION

How well an organization is able to recognize, understand, and manage its risks plays a critical part in the success, or failure, of the organization, and, consequently, the value it is able to deliver to customers, shareholders, and other stakeholders.

The internal audit function contributes to better overall governance when it operates within a strategic framework established by the audit committee and senior management. Once this strategic framework is in place, the corporation will be well positioned to define the mission, organizational structure, resource model, working practices, and communications protocols for the internal audit function.

Hence, when designing and implementing an effective internal audit function, the corporation's strategic objectives must be followed closely, and not vice versa. In other words, the internal audit's primary stakeholders must determine how the function will deliver the desired value, and what the specified outcomes expected of the new function are to be.

Common internal audit outcomes include:
- assessment of internal control effectiveness and efficiency;
- risk management and control assurance;
- regulatory and corporate compliance assurance;
- legislature readiness assessment and ongoing testing, such as Sarbanes–Oxley Act (US) and Directive No. 8 (EU);
- fostering awareness of risk and control across the organization;
- ability to respond to urgent events.

Once the function is established and the specific outcomes have been identified and defined, the internal audit's stakeholder expectations should be reassessed on a regular basis, and the mission for the internal audit function must be clearly articulated, so that the performance of the function can be evaluated on a regular basis. In addition, a formal mission statement for the internal audit function should be laid out by the head of the audit function, with the cooperation of senior management and the audit committee. The mission statement must also be aligned clearly and directly with stakeholder expectations and the internal audit's specified outcomes, as otherwise it would be of little value and possibly detrimental to achieving corporate strategic performance. Furthermore, the mission statement must be shared and communicated, to achieve full understanding and buy-in among key stakeholders and staff.

Once the mission statement is agreed, a formal strategic plan must be approved. This plan formally defines the value proposition of the new function, the customers it serves, and the value it will create now and into the future. The strategic plan serves as an operational manual of the new function, and as guidance on the key objectives and outcomes of the function, and how they will be achieved. The strategic plan sets a standard against which future decisions and results can be measured. Ideally, the plan should be reviewed at least annually, with changes considered and approved by all primary stakeholders as appropriate. For large companies, a full audit cycle of three years generally may seem appropriate; that is, the whole organization should be audited in an appropriate manner within three years. However, high risk areas should be audited at least annually.

Next, it is critical for the internal audit to develop a systematic process to analyze risk, and ensure that the audit plan is sufficiently broad in scope and executed in a timely manner. Internal auditors should segment the corporation into well-defined, reasonably sized, auditable units (often collectively called the "audit universe"), and then identify, determine, and prioritize/rank the inherent risks in each unit. Even a small business unit is likely to have a range of risks, some of which are higher priority than others. Inherent risks are those present in the normal course of conducting business activities. These include external risks such as changes to global, national, and economic climates, as well as technological, legal, social, and political changes. Inherent risks also include internal factors that warrant special attention, including changes in operating systems, new product launches, entry to new markets, management and organizational changes, and the expansion of foreign operations. Therefore, the risk assessment should evaluate current and prospective risks, particularly where new risks are emerging due to a change in the corporation's strategy or product mix.

The senior management and the audit committee must ensure the risk assessment executed by the audit function is not limited by reference to its own skill sets. In other words, a misalignment must be avoided between the technical competencies necessary to execute the audit plan and the skill sets resident in the internal audit function. An effective way to prioritize processes for audit purposes is to look at a matrix of probability of occurrence versus severity of loss for each of the processes, and develop a risk-based audit plan according to this classification.

Furthermore, other departments and functions within an organization gather intelligence and other important information, and senior management and the audit committee must ensure that the internal auditors are aware of these, and use them accordingly in determining and prioritizing risks. However, it is not necessary that the internal audit's independent view on risks coincide with other functions' perspectives in the organization, and this needs to be recognized and accepted. Senior management and the audit committee should also evaluate whether any "strong" executives or directors outside of the internal audit function, or "strong" business areas within the organization, have played a major role in shaping the internal audit's plan, and, if so, in what way. After the risk assessment is performed and the risk-based audit plan is drawn up, it is then important that timely and comprehensive coverage by the internal audit function is secured in order that the reliability and effectiveness of the internal controls in mitigating the significance and/or likelihood of a risk occurrence are considered. Another step to be taken after the assessment of risks and the audit plan are completed is the creation of current and longer-term budgets for the internal audit function. Budgets must provide sufficient resources for internal auditors to deliver the developed risk-based audit plan, as well as the flexibility to respond to changing business needs.

Budgets should be aligned with corporate strategies, and look to internal audit benchmarks developed by the IIA or other third parties to establish a budgetary baseline as compared to similar internal audit functions within the same industry. The budget should be projected on a three-to-five-year horizon.

The fieldwork should begin as soon as possible, even prior to having all staffing and infrastructure in place. Key stakeholders in an organization want to see demonstrable progress promptly, so it is important to begin conducting the audits without delay, in order for the internal audit function to create immediate value. In a start-up internal audit department, the first three months are important in completing the audits of three to five known high-risk areas, such as general computer systems and controls, inventory management, and other business areas with known internal control problems and challenges.

At times, corporations are impatient for results and, thus, they may choose to outsource all, or nearly all, of the internal audit to a third-party specialist firm. This is in contrast to the IIA's recommendation, which states that internal audit activity should never be fully outsourced, but should be managed from within the organization. Outsourcing can have several advantages, including employing professionals who are more independent as they are not beholden to management for their compensation; access to resources necessary to complete specific high-risk audits; access to an array of technical, up-to-date expertise; and, possibly, knowledge transfer to the organization's employees as the function converts into a full in-house or co-sourced resource model.

On the other hand, full or near-full outsourcing brings with it specific governance challenges for senior management and the audit committee. These problems may include the following: limited communication and level of interaction between the organization and the third-party audit professionals; increased difficulty for the third-party auditors to gain sufficient standing in the corporation; outsourcing is significantly more expensive on a per-hour basis than undertaking the function in-house; and, the corporation has limited ability to influence audit team appointments when the internal audit function is fully outsourced. If some level of dependence on third-party firms for specialist audit skills is necessary for a corporation, then selective use of co-sourcing arrangements should be in place.

By revisiting stakeholder-specified outcomes and the internal audit function's mission statement developed earlier in the start-up process, a balanced staffing model must be adapted to each corporation's needs. Best practice requires corporations to staff their internal audit functions with long-tenured audit career professionals, as well as rotating talented executives from across the organization for two-or three-year rotations in internal audit. Furthermore, the necessary internal audit infrastructure and methodologies should be developed at the same time. These will greatly improve the efficiency, quality, and consistency of the internal audit process, and will provide assurance towards compliance with both the organization's methodologies, policies, and desired outcomes, and the standards developed by the IIA. Corporations should establish routine, robust, and frank lines of communication with their key internal audit professionals. It is imperative that an internal audit function communicates effectively and freely with all its internal stakeholders (and, primarily, with senior management and the audit committee). On a regular, if not daily, basis, the internal audit should seek opportunities for dialogue and communication with the corporation's senior management and the audit committee, creating a strong, clear connection between the internal audit mission and the corporation's strategic issues and risks.

In addition, the external auditors also have a role to play in an organization's corporate governance, and, as such, the audit committee should seek to establish and maintain good links and cooperation between internal and external audits.

Finally, it is important that the internal audit demonstrates results, and its reports are actionable and implemented. The reports should be generated and circulated in a timely fashion after the audit is complete, and senior management and the audit committee should ensure that an effective and timely follow-up to the reports has been implemented.

CONCLUSION

Organizations serve their stakeholders. Senior management's role is to ensure that the organization's resources are managed and applied effectively to meet objectives and responsibilities. A crucial part of this process of governance is the design of appropriate systems and processes in order for them to be able to identify and manage risks effectively and efficiently. Internal audit's role is to evaluate the appropriateness and effectiveness of those systems and processes, whether they are related to finance, IT, brand reputation, health and safety, legal and regulatory compliance, human resources, and/or major projects.

Internal auditors perform their role by working with boards of directors, audit committees, and senior managers to help them understand the consequences of risks and ineffective processes to manage them. They encourage and support managers to have appropriate systems in place. Internal auditors then report to senior management and the audit committee on how effectively these systems of control are operating. In such a way, the corporation succeeds in aligning the internal audit function with its strategic objectives.

MAKING IT HAPPEN

- Define stakeholder expectations.
- Articulate the mission, structure, resource model, working practices, and communication protocols for the internal audit function.
- Develop a formal strategic plan and assess company risks.
- Establish short- and long-term budgets for the internal audit function.
- Launch fieldwork quickly and, concurrently, assess any further needed skill sets.

- Develop internally or acquire (by outsourcing) enabling internal audit infrastructure, methodologies, and technologies.
- Determine clear lines of communication between the internal audit function and all company stakeholders (primarily, however, with senior management and the audit committee).
- Measure the results of the internal audit function.

MORE INFO

Books:

Pickett, K. H. Spencer. *The Essential Handbook of Internal Auditing*. Chichester, UK: Wiley, 2005.

Pickett, K. H. Spencer. *Audit Planning: A Risk-Based Approach*. Hoboken, NJ: Wiley, 2006.

Standard:

Public Company Accounting Oversight Board. "Auditing standard no. 5: An audit of internal control over financial reporting that is integrated with an audit of financial statements." July 25, 2007. Online at: tinyurl.com/ye5sprj

Websites:

Chartered Institute of Internal Auditors (UK and Ireland): www.iia.org.uk

Institute of Internal Auditors (IIA): www.theiia.org

See Also:

★ Contemporary Developments in International Auditing Regulation (pp. 70–74)
★ Role of Internal Auditing at Board Committee Level (pp. 207–210)
★ Starting a Successful Internal Audit Function to Meet Present and Future Demands (pp. 103–108)
✔ Defining Corporate Governance: Its Aims, Goals, and Responsibilities (pp. 341–342)
✔ Understanding Internal Audits (pp. 324–325)

Classification and Treatment of Leases
by Roger Lister

EXECUTIVE SUMMARY

- Accounting bodies, both international and national, require leases to be classified in terms of economic substance rather than legal form.
- Current regulation distinguishes a finance lease from an operating lease. If a lease transfers the risks and rewards of an asset to the lessee, it is a finance lease. Otherwise, the lease is an operating lease. A finance lease appears in the balance sheet; an operating lease may remain off the balance sheet.

- New international and national accounting standards will almost certainly remove the distinction. Except for very short leases, all will go on the balance sheet.
- The change will eliminate a sometimes artificial distinction, but higher reported leverage may have ill effects. Management may avoid otherwise desirable leasing to protect the leverage ratio. Bond covenants may be breached and need to be renegotiated. There may be an incentive to circumvent the standard by taking out a succession of short but renewable leases.
- Tax allowances emphasize legal form, but tax in its detail tends to follow accounting standards. Companies will

therefore need to consider the tax impact of the new standard as it solidifies.

- Anti-avoidance tax legislation proliferates daily and will probably increase as governments seek every opportunity to raise revenue in straitened times. At worst, a measure will be retrospective. Planners should monitor discussion and attempt the difficult task of identifying and anticipating the most likely changes, including anti-avoidance legislation.

INTRODUCTION

Lease accounting is nearer than ever to its goal of reporting substance rather than form. International regulators and their national counterparts agree that right-to-use rather than legal title should determine the classification and treatment of leases. The choice is essentially between disclosing a lease as a financial instrument on the balance sheet or as an operating lease on the income statement.

Financial reporting of leases is addressed in the International Accounting Standards Board's International Accounting Standard IAS 17. The International Accounting Standards Board (IASB) benefits from the participation of many countries, including the US Financial Accounting Standards Board (FASB).

Why lease? Management needs to test conventional answers carefully since some have limited relevance, while others are frankly contestable. Leasing is sometimes promoted for its small initial outlay, even as 100% financing. This ignores the fact that a rational lessor like a lender will seek a cushion of equity to protect the finance provided. A more rational answer is that leasing is advantageous if it provides more finance than the borrowing which it displaces. Management is essentially asking how far, for their company, is leasing a substitute for borrowing and how far a complement. Research suggests that leasing tends to be a substitute for borrowing for larger firms and a valuable complement to borrowing for small and medium enterprises (SMEs). Leasing can help to overcome SMEs' difficulty in conveying their quality to would-be financiers.

In the individual case, management has to investigate the impact of the fact that repossession of a leased asset is easier than foreclosure on the collateral of a secured loan, enhancing the debt capacity of leasing over secured lending. They must also consider how far leasing provides a solution to potential mistrust between asset provider and user with respect to the quality of the asset and the costs of maintenance.

CLASSIFICATION

Currently, the essential distinction is between the finance and the operating lease, but it is virtually certain that under the revised international financial reporting standard due about 2011 this distinction will disappear. The new classification will equate finance and operating leases. All but the shortest contracts will be treated like finance leases. New national standards will probably anticipate, accompany, or follow the new international standard.

A finance lease transfers substantially all the risks and rewards of asset ownership to the lessee and features accordingly in the balance sheet. An operating lease remains off balance sheet. If a lease satisfies any one or more of certain criteria, then it may be a finance lease. These are:

- Ownership of the asset is transferred to the lessee at the end of the lease term;
- The lease contains a bargain purchase option to buy the equipment at less than fair market value;
- The lease term is for the major part of the economic life of the asset even if title is not transferred;
- At the inception of the lease, the present value of the minimum lease payments amounts at least substantially to all of the fair value of the leased asset;
- The leased assets are of a specialized nature such that only the lessee can use them without major modification;
- Any cancellation losses are borne by the lessee;
- The lessee takes gains and losses on the asset's residual value;
- The lessee can rent for a secondary period for less than the market rent.

The international standard, unlike some national standards, does not focus on a numerical percentage of fair asset value (typically 90%).

"Asset" means the lower of the fair value and the present value of the minimum lease payments (MLP). MLP are discounted at the interest rate implicit in the lease if practicable, or else at the enterprise's incremental borrowing rate. Depreciation has to be consistent with that for similar owned assets. If ultimate ownership is unlikely, the asset has to be depreciated over the shorter of the lease term and the life of the asset. The income statement includes depreciation and the finance charge. Rental payments are recognized as part finance charge and part repayment of the liability to the lessor. Repayments of the obligation reduce the liability in the balance sheet.

In the case of operating leases, periodic rentals are charged in total against income on a straight-line basis, unless another systematic basis is more representative of the time pattern of the user's benefit. Any outstanding rentals are reported in the balance sheet, distinguishing maturities and categories of activity.

IAS 17 is further explained in SIC 15, SIC 27 and IFRIC 4 and 12. SIC 15 states that any incentives such as rent-free periods or contributions by the lessor to the lessee's relocation costs should be reported as a reduction of lease income or lease expense. IFRIC (a standard issued post 2001) 4 and 12 consider cases where a right to use, while not a lease in form, may amount to a lease for financial reporting purposes. Examples are outsourcing arrangements, telecommunication contracts that provide rights to capacity, and take-or-pay and similar contracts in which purchasers must make specified payments regardless of whether they take delivery of the contracted products or services.

Current classification and treatment of leasing has already brought financial reporting closer to economic reality, and the new standard will continue this progress. It will break down deceptive barriers between economically similar transactions. However, management needs to recognize potentially perverse effects. Reported leverage will increase if finance and operating leases are both on the balance sheet, possibly causing management to avoid otherwise beneficial leases.

Bond covenants may be nominally breached and have to be renegotiated. Without suitable safeguards, companies may circumvent the standard by taking out short but renewable leases that will in practice span an asset's useful life.

The underlying principle is that treating lease expenses as financing expenses potentially impinges on reported operating income, capital, profitability and cash flow. It is likely that the market will reassess the value of many companies.

In the case of leveraged leasing (not under discussion here), the lessee gains access to the lessor's leveraged capital. The lessor owns the asset but typically provides only some 25% of capital while garnering any tax allowance in full. Institutional lenders provide the balance of the purchase price to the lessor on a non-recourse basis.

An extract from Christian Dior's 2007 accounts illustrates how lease classification appears in practice:"In addition to leasing its stores, the Group also finances some of its equipment through long term operating leases. Some fixed assets and equipment were also purchased or refinanced under finance leases."

SALE AND LEASEBACK

Extra financial reporting issues arise with sale and leaseback. An owner selling and leasing back an asset should in the first instance revise the recorded value of the asset to its economic value. This avoids distortion of the sale and leaseback transactions.

If the asset is sold at fair value and made the subject of an operating lease, any profit belongs in the year's income statement. If the sale is above fair value, the purchaser will charge higher rentals. In this case, the seller's profit on sale must be set against the high rentals by annual installments over the term of the lease or until the time of any rent review if sooner. If the asset is sold at a loss, the loss must be recognized immediately unless the purchaser compensates by below-market rentals, in which case the loss is amortized over the period of use. If the asset is sold at fair value and made the subject of a finance lease, any excess of proceeds over recorded value is amortized over the term of the lease.

TAX

Significant tax changes will come with new accounting standards and increasing anti-avoidance legislation. Legislators and avoiders dodge and weave around pitfalls and opportunities. Management has to monitor and even try to influence discussion and hope that anti-avoidance provisions will not be retrospective.

In the United Kingdom, current detailed regulations[1] as administered by HM Revenue and Customs tend to look to the accounting standards subject to the fundamental difference that the tax definition of finance lease is based on legal title. Thus, a taxable lessor can still pass the benefits of capital allowances to a nontaxable lessee in the form of reduced rentals. Other points include:

- Finance charges are deductible according to any method that gives the lessor a constant return on rentals outstanding.
- If premature termination occurs, individual circumstances will determine whether any payment is an adjustment of

past rentals (revenue expenditure) or a penal charge (capital expenditure).
- Any rebate or further rental arising on the substitution of one finance lease for another in respect of the same asset will also be a revenue item for tax purposes. Where an operating lease becomes a finance lease any transitional payment is treated as a revenue item.
- Rentals on operating leases are tax-deductible.

The above general rules are subject to a continuing stream of anti-avoidance legislation. For example, on November 13, 2008, the UK government announced that it would take action, effective from that date, to prevent a loss of tax on transactions involving the leasing of plant or machinery under long funding leases, on the sale of a company that is an intermediate lessor of plant or machinery, and on rents payable on long funding leases of films.

Anti-avoidance legislation has countered many traditional tax benefits of leasing such as deferral of income, conversion of income into capital, acceleration of capital allowances, and techniques connected with sales and leasebacks. The cat and mouse anti-avoidance game becomes particularly frenetic when it crosses borders. This arises with double-dip leasing, when differing tax treatment of lessor and lessee under different jurisdictions generates allowances in each country. Anti-avoidance has closed off many such opportunities, and the taxpayer's defeat in the Coleman case (see Case Study) illustrates both the complexity of the taxpayer's attempt and the taxpayer's vulnerability.[2]

CASE STUDY
COLEMAN

The British Tax Court imposed the strong proof rule on the taxpayer to show that it was entitled to depreciation deductions on a double-dip leasing transaction, even though the transaction was structured to also obtain a UK tax advantage. Coleman involved a cross-border leasing transaction, in which the parties sought to obtain depreciation deductions on certain leased computer equipment for both UK and US tax purposes. The lease and title to the computer equipment were transferred by a dealer to UK lenders, who were able to write off the computers in one year under UK tax law. The dealer retained an interest in the residual of the lease and (to simplify matters greatly) sold a portion of the residual interest to the US taxpayers. These persons claimed to be the owners of the leased computer equipment for US tax purposes and depreciated their bases in the equipment for US tax purposes. The court held that the record failed, under the strong proof standard, to sustain the petitioners' position that they were the owners of the computer equipment, and that the form of the transaction as a financing should be disregarded.

OPEN ISSUES

Much will be resolved when the new international standards appear, but in the meantime companies should monitor the IASB's discussions of open issues. Sensitive areas under discussion include the following.

Right of Use
The Board favored reporting the lessee's right of use during the term and the accompanying obligation to make specified payments. This seemingly innocuous definition amounts to a preference for a model that does not take account of an obligation to return the physical item. This may be insignificant for a long lease, but is material for a shorter lease.

Measurement of the Lessee's Asset and Liability Under the Lease
The Board decided to recommend that right to use should be initially measured at the present value of the "expected lease payments." They noted that these may differ from minimum lease payments if they include contingent rentals. The discount rate used in calculating the expected lease payments should be the secured incremental borrowing rate.

Options to Extend or Terminate a Lease
The Board decided to propose that options to extend or terminate the lease should be based on an assessment of the lease term, but it did not express a preference among the various frameworks for assessment, for example, a probability-weighted approach, or as to whether the estimated lease term should be trued up on a regular basis. There was a consensus that all contractual, noncontractual, financial, and business factors should be taken into consideration when determining the lease term.

Purchase Option
The Board favored inclusion of the purchase option if exercise of the option was the most likely outcome.

Residual Value Guarantee
The Board decided to propose that the lessee's liabilities should include the obligation to make payments under a residual value guarantee.

In addition to the above, management need to monitor numerous outstanding issues which are to be addressed in the Board's future discussions. These include accounting for sale-leaseback transactions, accounting for subleases, whether a lease should be recognized on execution or asset-delivery, treatment of payments for services within the lease payments and capitalization of initial direct costs.

MAKING IT HAPPEN
Classification and treatment should not dominate the leasing decision. They should be integrated with the decision to achieve an optimal capital structure, including optimal financial mobility. Six important lessons emerge from the present review:
- It remains important to choose between an operating and finance lease contract, but discussions regarding the revised international standard and evolving national standards must be carefully monitored to see how best to contract the lease.
- Opportunities should be taken to contribute to the discussions, especially if there is a chance to head off a result that will harm the company's interests.

- The tax impact of a leasing decision under current provisions is crucially important even though its impact may be less in the short-term insofar as recession makes more businesses zero tax rated.
- Probable changes of tax treatment in response to the new standard must be monitored.
- Anti-avoidance legislation must be anticipated as far as possible—the content of tax cases may provide a first indication.

MORE INFO
Books:
Bragg, Steven M. *Wiley GAAP 2012*. Hoboken, NJ: Wiley, 2011.
International Accounting Standards Board. *International Financial Reporting Standards IFRS 2008: Including International Accounting Standards (IASs) and Interpretations as approved at 1 January 2008*. London: IASB, 2008.

Articles:
Beattie, Vivien, Alan Goodacre, and Sarah Jane Thomson. "International lease-accounting reform and economic consequences: The views of U.K. users and preparers." *International Journal of Accounting* 41:1 (2006): 75–103. Online at: dx.doi.org/10.1016/j.intacc.2005.12.003
Frecka, Thomas J. "Ethical issues in financial reporting: Is intentional structuring of lease contracts to avoid capitalization unethical?" *Journal of Business Ethics* 80:1 (June 2008): 45–59. Online at: dx.doi.org/10.1007/s10551-007-9436-y
Henry, Elaine, Oscar J. Holzmann, and Ya-wen Yang. "Tracking the lease accounting project." *Journal of Corporate Accounting and Finance* 19:1 (November/December 2007): 73–76. Online at: dx.doi.org/10.1002/jcaf.20361

Websites:
Equipment Leasing and Finance Association (ELFA): www.elfaonline.org
Finance and Leasing Association (FLA; UK): www.fla.org.uk
HM Revenue and Customs' information about taxation of leases (UK): www.hmrc.gov.uk/manuals/bimmanual/bim61101.htm
IFRS Foundation and the International Accounting Standards Board (IASB): www.ifrs.org
International Finance and Leasing Association (IFLA): www.ifla.com

See Also:
 Distinguishing between a Capital and an Operating Lease (pp. 387–388)

NOTES
1 HM Revenue and Customs documentation, notably BIM61101–BIM 61185; BLM 00050–38000.
2 *Coleman v. Commissioner*, 87 T.C. 178 (1986).

69

Best Practice

Contemporary Developments in International Auditing Regulation

by Christopher Humphrey and Anne Loft

EXECUTIVE SUMMARY

The contemporary development of international audit regulation is connected to the growing significance of international investors who demand financial reports that are prepared and audited in accordance with globally accepted international standards. International Standards on Auditing (ISAs) are set by the International Auditing and Assurance Standards Board (IAASB), an independent standard setting board working within the International Federation of Accountants (IFAC) and subject to public oversight by international regulators. ISAs have been adopted in many countries, but their practical impact depends centrally on how they are implemented and enforced. Recent years have seen a greater emphasis on such issues.

INTRODUCTION

The development of international audit regulation is closely linked to the development of international accounting regulation. Both have been significantly associated with the globalization of capital markets and growth in importance of international investors. Such investors expect the financial reports of the companies they are investing in to be fair and reliable, with auditors playing a critical role—famously categorized by Paul Volcker in 2002—as the "guardians of truth in markets."

Audit regulation is centrally concerned with the issue of ensuring that auditors are competent and independent. These attributes ensure that auditors are both capable of detecting significant errors and omissions in financial status (competent) and faithfully reporting these to investors/stakeholders in the enterprise (independence).

Broadly defined, audit regulation has the same four basic elements of any regulatory system—namely a concern and involvement with the setting, adoption, and implementation of standards and, through monitoring and enforcement processes, ensuring that such standards are applied in practice.

Following this introductory section, the chapter reviews the setting of international auditing standards (ISAs). This includes the role of international regulatory bodies in supporting this process and the demands they have made of the standard setting body and the international accounting profession more generally. In the third section, issues of compliance and oversight are discussed; including recent developments in international coordination through the International Forum for Independent Audit Regulators (IFIAR). The fourth section examines the role of the big audit firms in international audit regulation, and the final section presents conclusions and some thoughts for the future.

SETTING GLOBAL STANDARDS

International Standards for Auditing (ISAs) are set by the International Auditing and Assurance Standards Board (IAASB), which is situated within the International Federation of Accountants (IFAC)—a private body whose member bodies are the national associations of professional accountants in each country. There are currently (December, 2009) 159 member bodies of IFAC, representing 124 countries and around 2.5 million professional accountants worldwide. IFAC recently celebrated its 32nd anniversary, having been formed in 1977, four years after the International Accounting Standards Committee (IASC), which was the predecessor body of the International Accounting Standards Board (IASB).

The members of the IAASB are a mixture of practicing professional accountants (especially members of the large audit firms) and persons from outside the profession. A number of important global organizations have supported the development and application of ISAs, which are now used in more than 100 countries around the world.[1] These include the Financial Stability Forum (FSF), a body set up by the G7 Finance Ministers and central bank governors in 1999 in the wake of the financial crisis in Asia in 1997/8—and re-established as the Financial Stability Board (FSB) in April 2009.[2] The objective of the FSF/FSB is to strengthen financial systems and ensure the stability of international financial markets, and as part of this remit it has designated 12 key standards and codes as most relevant to strengthening financial systems. Both International Accounting Standards (IASs/IFRS and ISAs are included in this group (the only private standard setters to be included).[3] These 12 standards and codes are seen as "best practices" associated with the legal, regulatory and institutional framework for financial systems.

The International Organization of Securities Commissions (IOSCO) is another important organization in this respect. Despite the FSF/FSB's inclusion of ISAs in its leading globally recognized standards and codes, the endorsement of ISAs by IOSCO has proved to be a more problematic and longstanding issue. A 1992 resolution by IOSCO's Presidents' Committee in support of the use of ISAs was subsequently suspended while "negotiations" continued with IFAC over issues such as the quality of ISAs and the degree of public oversight of the standard setting process.

The EU has also continued to review the feasibility of a formal EU endorsement of ISAs. In 2003, the European Commission issued a Communication entitled "Reinforcing the statutory audit in the EU," announcing that it intended that ISAs would apply to all statutory audits in Europe. It emphasized, though, that this required the public interest to be fully taken into account in the IAASB's standard setting processes, with a subsequent communication reiterating that the EU needs to be content that ISAs are "developed with proper due process, public oversight and transparency" and that IFAC's governance arrangements are adequate to ensure the pursuit of the public interest, specifically that the standards are "conducive to the European public good." In the Statutory Audit Directive issued on May 17, 2006, it repeated this message, whilst at the same time the text of the Directive indicated that it was expected that ISAs should become EU's auditing standards, ultimately to be legally binding in all Member States. The European Commission is currently analyzing the responses to its June 2009 formal public consultation on the adoption of ISAs for statutory audits required by European Community Law, having previously commissioned and published an independent study on the relative costs and benefits of adoption.[4] IFAC has moved towards satisfying such demands over its standard setting processes and governance arrangements by establishing, among other things, an active Public Interest Oversight Board (PIOB) and developing ISAs through the IAASB's "clarity project." The members of the PIOB are selected by leading institutions in the international regulatory community, including IOSCO, the Basel Committee on Banking Supervision (BCBS), the International Association of Insurance Supervisors (IAIS), the European Commission, World Bank and the FSF/FSB. Included in the activities of the PIOB is the monitoring of all meetings of IFAC's public interest standard setting committees, making this a very active process of oversight. With this IFAC appears to have satisfied one of the requirements of the regulators for improving governance arrangements to bring in a clear consideration of the public interest, although it is worth noting that the effectiveness of such governance reforms is currently being evaluated by the above mentioned regulatory and international organizations (commonly referred to as the Monitoring Group).[5]

The IAASB's Clarity Project, started in 2004, and was completed in February 2009.[6] The project's aim was to ensure that ISAs have clear objectives and that each standard distinguishes what the auditor absolutely shall do when carrying out an audit from guidance on how to achieve this.[7] In the process of clarification, some standards were ultimately revised quite considerably (and more than was originally anticipated). In total, the clarity project produced 36 updated and clarified ISAs, together with a clarified International Standard on Quality Control (ISQC). The standards are to be applied to audits of financial statements for reporting periods beginning on or after December 15, 2009.

In June 2009, IOSCO issued a statement that formally encouraged[8] securities regulators to accept audits performed and reported in accordance with the clarified ISAs for cross-border purposes; "recognizing that the decision whether to do so would depend on a number of factors and circumstances in their jurisdiction" (IOSCO, 2009). In much the same way, IOSCO encouraged securities regulators to consider the clarified ISAs when setting auditing standards for national purposes.[9]

According to IFAC, currently 43 countries have adopted ISAs or are required to use them by law, with a further 28 countries having generally adopted them as national standards but with modifications (acceptable to the IAASB) for

specific legislative and regulatory requirements.[10] While ISAs are pushing towards the position of being the global standards for auditing, a significant inclusion in the 55 "other/remaining" countries surveyed by IFAC, is the United States of America—which, as yet, has not abandoned its own auditing standards. Up until 2002 the American Institute of Certified Public Accountants (AICPA) was responsible for setting US auditing standards but, in the wake of the Enron scandal, and others like it, this responsibility was given to a new independent body under the supervision of the Securities and Exchange Commission (SEC). This body, namely, the Public Company Accounting Oversight Board (PCAOB), has it its own processes for setting independent audit standards and also has extraterritorial powers of regulatory reach in relation to audits of US quoted companies. Recent speeches by SEC staff at the 2009 AICPA national conference on current SEC and PCAOB developments have confirmed that the PCAOB does maintain an active interest in ISAs and standard setting developments at the IAASB—and that, in their view, the momentum for international convergence in auditing standards is growing.[11] The chances of ISAs becoming truly "world standards" are also likely to be aided by the SEC's approach towards IFRS. The latest indications are that the SEC will shortly update its "roadmap" proposals for US listed companies to move to IFRS.[12] The international pressure on the SEC would seem to have increased recently, with the G20 in September 2009 notably calling for a "redoubling of efforts" by international accounting bodies to achieve a single-set of "high quality global accounting standards" and for the convergence process to be completed by June 2011.[13]

Finally, in relation to global (auditing) standards, it is important to point out that, while scandals such as Enron regularly illustrate the international significance of both auditor independence and competence, international independence standards remain some way off. While IFAC's Code of Ethics for Professional Accountants[14] provides a potential international regulatory solution in this area, the lack of international consensus on the issue of auditor independence is such that regulation here is more likely to be of national or regional orientation, influenced strongly by related legal structures.

COMPLIANCE AND REGULATORY OVERSIGHT

As was noted at the start of this chapter, a regulatory system is not just about standard setting but also the implementation and enforcement of such standards. Historically, issues of compliance with international auditing standards were not given enormous emphasis at the global level—reflecting a range of factors, including desires to grow the numbers of countries adopting such standards, a limited level of available resources, accepted traditions of self-regulation and professional peer review and the clear positioning of responsibilities for compliance, regulation, and oversight activities at the national rather than the international level.

One of the most active and visible initiatives in this area has been the ROSC (Reports on Standards and Codes) program set up by the IMF and World Bank in 1999, which examines the degree to which emerging and developing countries are using key standards and codes (defined to include ISAs and IASs as benchmark standards for each individual country's reports on accounting and auditing practices). The formal remit is to: "analyze comparability of national accounting and auditing standards with international standards" and "assist the country in developing and implementing a country action plan for improving institutional capacity with a view to strengthening the country's corporate financial reporting regime."[15]

IFAC has increased its focus on global compliance issues with the 2004 launch of its Compliance Program, overseen by the Compliance Advisory Panel (CAP), which seeks to ensure that member bodies are meeting their membership obligations. Formally, this program has three main elements, comprising: an assessment by each member body of their country's regulatory and standard-setting framework; a self-assessment questionnaire of the extent to which each member body is using its best endeavors to adopt international accounting and auditing standards and maintain quality assurance and enforcement regimes to ensure such standards are applied in practice; and the development of action plans to further the global accounting and auditing standards convergence process and address any issues/weaknesses identified in the self-assessment questionnaire. IFAC, "in the interests of transparency," has chosen to post all the responses received from member bodies for full public access on its website.[16]

These initiatives are dealing with the general issue of compliance, but not with the actual compliance of a particular audit firm with ISAs and other standards. In reaction to the problematic audits of Enron, Global Crossing and other large companies, in July 2002, the passing of the Sarbanes–Oxley Act replaced the self-regulation of the US auditing profession with the PCAOB-led system of independent inspection. Similar initiatives have followed in other countries and there is a whole new international emphasis on auditor oversight as an essential feature of audit regulation. This oversight is, for obvious reasons, done at local national level. However, the Sarbanes–Oxley Act did not exclude foreign registrants with US stock exchanges from the requirement from oversight by the PCAOB. This appears to have encouraged a number of (large) countries to establish their own auditor oversight systems in the hope that there will be mutual recognition of each other's systems. This, however, has only occurred to a small extent, resulting in a considerable amount of extra-territorial activity by the PCAOB audit inspectors.

The issue of public oversight has further developed on the international stage through the establishment in September 2006 of the International Forum of Independent Audit Regulators (IFIAR).[17] IFIAR is committed to sharing knowledge and experiences of the audit market and associated regulatory activities between independent national audit regulatory agencies. It seeks to promote collaboration and consistency in regulatory activity and to act as a platform for dialogue with other organizations with an interest in the quality of auditing. There are currently 36 independent national regulators who are members of this new international organization, including the PCAOB. Observers at IFIAR meetings include the FSB, IFAC's PIOB, IOSCO, IAIS, World Bank, European Commission and the Basel Committee, again reflecting the increasingly interlocking nature of international

regulatory relationships (for more discussion, see Humphrey *et al.*, 2009).

The multi-layered nature of such regulatory arrangements is well illustrated by the fact that the European Union itself had previously established a European Group of Audit Oversight Bodies (EGAOB) in December 2005—with the specific remit of ensuring effective coordination of new public oversight systems of statutory auditors and audit firms within the European Union.[18] The press release announcing the EGAOB development cited the view of Commissioner McCreevy that this "group will help to make public supervision systems a reality in all 25 Member States, promoting practical day-to-day co-operation as it goes along. It is a key initiative in our drive to bring EU audit rules into the 21st century and restore faith in the profession." The European Commission reiterated its views on the importance of public oversight, with a Recommendation (May 13, 2008) on external quality assurance for the statutory audit of public interest entities. This expanded the responsibilities of public oversight boards and emphasized that they should play an active role in the inspections of audit firms.

THE GLOBAL REGULATORY INVOLVEMENT OF AUDIT FIRMS

An interesting development with respect to public oversight was the presentation by the CEOs of the six largest global auditing firms at IFIAR meetings in Norway (April 2008) and South Africa (September 2008) to consider global quality monitoring arrangements. This section of the chapter explores what is an evidently growing involvement of the large audit firms in international audit regulation.

During the last two decades, there has been a continued increasing concentration in the international auditing profession, with the large firms getting a greater share of the audit market. The Big Eight firms of the past have reduced to the Big Four today of PwC, KPMG, E&Y, and Deloitte—with the next two largest firms, BDO International and Grant Thornton International, relatively speaking, being quite a lot smaller. Gradually, through a variety of pressures, often driven by major corporate collapses and financial crises, such firms have sought to ensure a greater global consistency in auditing practice, such that an audit, for example, in China by PwC is equivalent to one conducted by the same firm in, say, Sweden. Through internal processes of regulation, they place pressure on parts of their network where audit quality and associated quality control procedures are apparently insufficient, and thus act as an "internal" or "self" regulatory pressure towards harmonizing standards.

The audits undertaken by the, then, Big Five[19] in Asia at the time of the crisis (1997–8) were sharply criticized by the World Bank, and it was this that stimulated the Big Five to set up a Global Steering Committee. One of the aims was to provide a body to deal, on a collective, global basis, with the common professional and regulatory issues they were facing. Another aim was to strengthen IFAC as the global audit standard setter. Under this initiative the large firms supported IFAC financially and were allocated seats on each of IFAC's standard setting boards. In the case of the newly established IAASB (previously the International Auditing Practices Committee) they had five seats out of a total of 18. This greater engagement of the Big Firms with IFAC continued to grow, especially in the wake of the Enron scandal and its aftermath, with the establishment of a new organization, the Global Public Policy Committee (GPPC).

The GPPC comprises the six largest international accounting networks and focuses on "public policy" issues for the profession. The GPPC has a Regulatory Working Group and a Standards Working Group and while much of its work is undertaken in private, it does issue policy papers where it expresses its commitment to working in the public interest and facilitating the functioning of global capital markets (see GPPS, 2006). The global firms' involvement in international regulatory affairs has also seen them expand the scale of financial support that they provide to IFAC, which now receives approximately one-third of its funding from the large firms. The firms can also be seen to be making substantial efforts to further strengthen their own global organization. For instance, it was reported in the *Financial Times* (August 20, 2008) that a number of them had announced restructuring plans to align more tightly member firms within global structures/networks and introduce "enhanced" audit practice standards.[20] The current financial crisis has witnessed a continuing major involvement with global regulatory matters, driven by the direct consequences that auditing work could have for global financial stability through decisions relating to the valuation of "toxic" assets and the auditor's determination as to whether audited enterprises are "going concerns."

MAINTAINING PUBLIC INTEREST IN GLOBAL REGULATION

While the global audit regulatory arena is complex, it is possible to draw out a number of important characteristics. While contemporary audit regulation engages directly with audit practice at the national level, it is being driven primarily by events and strategic action at the global level. The development in this global regulation of audit has been rapid during the current decade and, associated with the identification of reliable financial reporting, is becoming an essential part of a wider international financial architecture. Significant strategic actions have been made by international organizations such as the EU, IOSCO, FSF/FSB, and the World Bank, to aid, support, and increasingly mandate, the usage of international standards on auditing. While these organizations are primarily governmental in character, the main international audit standard setter, the IAASB—under the auspices of IFAC—is classified as private in nature, as are the large audit firms who are also closely involved, albeit in a less public way. This has placed particular emphasis and significance on the development of public oversight regimes as a way of ensuring that international audit standard setting processes are seen to be globally credible and sufficiently responsive to public interest demands (see IFAC, 2008; PIOB, 2008). The policy recommendations emerging from the November 2008 meeting of the G20 likewise have highlighted the importance of regulators serving the public interest and the global importance of making sure that financial markets operate in the most transparent of fashions. The current financial crisis is testing global regulatory structures to their

limit, and it is pretty certain that auditing will remain a fascinating field—both to observe and to debate in an open and constructive fashion. It could be argued that serving the public interest deserves no less.

MAKING IT HAPPEN

For international audit regulation to meet the claims laid out for it in terms of global scope and consistency of application requires a variety of actions and commitments on the part of the international financial regulatory community. Some of the more frequently mentioned priorities include:

- ISAs to be fully endorsed by international financial regulators;
- ISAs to be adopted globally for listed company audits;
- IFAC to continue to operate as an international organization acting in the global public interest;
- Greater global coordination of the work of audit regulatory and oversight bodies;
- Enhanced visibility of the quality and achievements of audit work.

ABBREVIATIONS

ACCA: Association of Chartered Certified Accountants
AICPA: American Institute of Certified Public Accountants
BCBS: Basel Committee on Banking Supervision
CAP: Compliance Advisory Panel
EU: European Union
FSF/(FSB): Financial Stability Forum/ Board
GPPC: Global Public Policy Committee
GPPS: Global Public Policy Symposium
IAASB: International Auditing and Assurance Standards Board
IAIS: International Association of Insurance Supervisors
IFAC: International Federation of Accountants
IFIAR: International Forum of Independent Audit Regulators
IFRS: International Financial Reporting Standard
IMF: International Monetary Fund
IOSCO: International Organization of Securities Commissions
ISA: International Standard on Auditing
ISQC: International Standard on Quality Control
PIOB: Public Interest Oversight Board
PCAOB: Public Company Accounting Oversight Board
ROSC: Report on Standards and Codes (World Bank)
SEC: Securities and Exchange Commission

MORE INFO
Article:

Humphrey, Christopher, Anne Loft, and Margaret Woods. "The global audit profession and the international financial architecture: Understanding regulatory relationships at a time of financial crisis." Accounting, Organizations and Society 34:6–7 (August–October 2009): 810–825. Online at: dx.doi.org/10.1016/j.aos.2009.06.003

Best Practice

Reports:

International Federation of Accountants (IFAC). "Regulation of the accountancy profession." IFAC Policy Position 1. December 2007. Online at: tinyurl.com/2b3wa4e [PDF].

International Federation of Accountants (IFAC). "International standard setting in the public interest." IFAC Policy Position 3. December 2008. Online at: tinyurl.com/27ohv6l [PDF].

International Federation of Accountants (IFAC). "International Federation of Accountants 2008 annual report: Transitioning to a global financial system." February 2009. Online at: web.ifac.org/download/2008_AR_IFAC_Full.pdf

International Forum for Independent Audit Regulators (IFIAR). "Charter." Online at: tinyurl.com/6w9p39e [PDF].

Public Interest Oversight Board (PIOB). "Third public report of the PIOB." May 2008. Online at: tinyurl.com/23byvuu [PDF].

Public Interest Oversight Board (PIOB). "Fourth public report of the PIOB." May 2009. Online at: tinyurl.com/29bm3q3 [PDF].

Technical Committee of the International Organization of Securities Commissions (IOSCO). "Contingency planning for events and conditions affecting availability of audit services: Final report." May 2008. Online at: www.iosco.org/library/pubdocs/pdf/IOSCOPD269.pdf

Website:

International Auditing and Assurance Standards Board: www.ifac.org/auditing-assurance

See Also:

★ Effective Financial Reporting and Auditing: Importance and Limitations (pp. 81–83)

★ Implementing an Effective Internal Controls System (pp. 93–97)

★ Incorporating Operational and Performance Auditing into Compliance and Financial Auditing (pp. 97–100)

✔ International Financial Reporting Standards (IFRS): The Basics (pp. 316–317)

✔ Understanding Internal Audits (pp. 324–325)

NOTES

1 See web.ifac.org/download/2008_IAASB_Annual_Report.pdf
2 See www.fsforum.org/press/pr_090402b.pdf
3 See www.fsforum.org/cos/key_standards.htm
4 tinyurl.com/6qphlq9
5 www.iosco.org/news/pdf/IOSCONEWS162.pdf
6 See www.ifac.org/auditing-assurance/clarity-center
7 www.cnbv.gob.mx/recursos/iosco13.pdf
8 It is an interesting point of debate as to whether such "encouragement" on the part of IOSCO equates with the formal endorsement of ISAs sought, for example, by accounting firms and professional bodies such as PwC, IFAC, ACCA, and the Institut der Wirtschaftsprüfer in Germany—on the grounds that ISAs were already in widespread usage (see IOSCO, 2008).
9 www.iosco.org/library/statements/pdf/statements-7.pdf
10 web.ifac.org/isa-adoption/chart
11 See www.sec.gov/news/speech/2009/spch120709amp.htm
12 The initial proposals suggested an adoption decision in 2011, with mandatory application for US issuers in 2014. The latest indications are that the SEC will announce its current thinking regarding IFRS adoption in early 2010 (see www.sec.gov/news/speech/2009/spch120909ebw.htm).
13 www.pittsburghsummit.gov/mediacenter/129639.htm
14 www.ifac.org/Ethics/Resources.php
15 See www.worldbank.org/ifa/rosc_aa.html
16 See www.ifac.org/ComplianceProgram
17 IFIAR's formal charter can be found at tinyurl.com/6w9p39e [PDF].
18 tinyurl.com/73hsfj9
19 The Big Four plus the now defunct firm of Arthur Andersen.
20 See tinyurl.com/79nk75r

Continuous Auditing: Putting Theory into Practice

by Norman Marks

EXECUTIVE SUMMARY

- Continuous auditing is a topic that is frequently identified as a method for internal auditors to "raise their game" and improve the value they provide to their stakeholders. For example, in their 2010 "State of the internal audit profession study," PricewaterhouseCoopers identifies the ability to leverage technology (including the use of continuous auditing techniques) as one of the eight attributes of a maximized internal audit function.

- In a 2010 study, "What is driving continuous auditing and continuous monitoring today?," KPMG reports, "In a volatile economic environment, a number of key drivers are prompting companies to employ continuous auditing and continuous monitoring techniques to do more than manage risk, including help reduce cost, improve performance, and create value."

- This article defines continuous auditing, discusses the ways in which continuous auditing techniques can be used to provide value, and shares guidance on how to design an effective program. It advises that only after the objectives of a continuous auditing initiative have been determined, and the program designed, should auditors evaluate and acquire software.

INTRODUCTION

The Institute of Internal Auditors (IIA) has issued an excellent global technology audit guide (GTAG) on the topic of continuous auditing. The guide, which we will refer to as GTAG-3, covers a lot of ground, including this definition of continuous auditing:[1]

"Continuous Auditing is any method used by auditors to perform audit-related activities on a more continuous or continual basis. It is the continuum of activities ranging from continuous control assessment to continuous risk assessment—all activities on the control-risk continuum. Technology plays a key role in automating the identification of exceptions and/or anomalies, analysis of patterns within the digits of key numeric fields, analysis of trends, detailed transaction analysis against cut-offs and thresholds, testing of controls, and the comparison of the process or system over time and/or against other similar entities."

Continuous auditing enables an internal audit function to:

- provide the board and management with assurance on a more frequent, if not continuous, basis;
- monitor risks and adjust the audit program to ensure that it addresses what matters to the organization today;
- improve the level of activity, in terms of both volume and period of time, that is audited.

It is important to consider the use and value of continuous auditing within the context of how the IIA defines an internal auditing function:

"A department, division, team of consultants, or other practitioner(s) that provides independent, objective assurance and consulting services designed to add value and improve an organization's operations. The internal audit activity helps an organization accomplish its objectives by bringing a systematic, disciplined approach to evaluate and improve the effectiveness of governance, risk management and control processes."

Taking these two definitions together enables the following points to be made. Each of these will be discussed in this article.

1 Continuous auditing is a method used by internal auditors in support of their assurance and consulting services.
2 Continuous auditing includes activities related to one or more of the following:
   a *Continuous risk assessment* (also known as risk monitoring), including the use of analytical techniques to identify trends, etc., to develop and maintain the periodic audit plan;
   b *Continuous testing of controls* to provide assurance that they operate as intended. GTAG-3 refers to this as "continuous controls assessment";
   c *Continuous testing of transactions*[2] to identify anomalies, exceptions, and potential problems.
3 Although continuous auditing typically leverages technology, continuous auditing activities may include manual testing, reviews of reports, etc.
4 Despite its name, continuous auditing is not necessarily performed continuously. The frequency will depend on a number of factors, including:
   a The frequency with which transactions occur (for example, journal entries are predominantly a month and quarter-end activity);
   b The frequency with which controls are performed;
   c The level of business risk being addressed;
   d The risk that the control may not be performed as intended.

However, few internal audit departments have made major moves into continuous auditing. One of the reasons is that the value is not clear to every chief audit executive (CAE).[3] We will discuss that first.

THE VALUE OF CONTINUOUS AUDITING

Imagine that you are the CAE of a global company and you are called in to see the CEO. He asks for your assessment of the quality of controls over the hedging of currency risk—which you identified as a high-risk area in your last report to the audit committee.

Is it acceptable to reply to the CEO that you will be able to tell him when you have completed the next audit, scheduled in three months? Is it acceptable to report, instead, on the audit your team completed a year ago?

The answer is clearly "no." When it comes to the more significant risk areas (such as the hedging of currency risk mentioned above), the CAE should try to provide assurance when it is needed by the primary stakeholders.

Value Proposition 1: Audit at the Speed of Business

This is the first value proposition for continuous auditing: the ability to provide assurance when it is needed. This can be referred to as "audit at the speed of business." The GTAG-3 refers to it as "continuous controls assessment."

What does internal audit provide assurance on? The Institute of Internal Auditors's "International standards for the professional practice of internal auditing" (IIA, 2010) guides us to provide assurance on the "governance, risk management, and control processes for the organization."[4]

Extending that, *continuous auditing enables an internal auditing function to provide assurance, when it is needed, on the more significant areas of the organization's governance, risk management, and related controls processes.* We can refer to this as "continuous risk and control assurance."

The value to the board and executive management of continuous risk and control assurance is generally very high. Although this dimension of continuous auditing can require the most resources to develop and maintain, the value will frequently far exceed the cost.

The next section will discuss how an internal audit department can use continuous auditing techniques for each of the value propositions. The second value relates to fraud.

Value Proposition 2: Fraud Detection and Control

Internal audit departments have a keen interest in fraud: in the adequacy of controls that prevent or detect fraud, and in investigating potential fraudulent activities. The second value proposition is that *continuous auditing enables the monitoring of risks for indicators of fraud, and of transactions for potential fraudulent activity.*

Continuous testing of transactions to detect potential errors and possible fraudulent activity is generally considered a management activity. However, many internal audit departments have included in their charter the detection of fraudulent activity. Automated techniques can improve the effectiveness and efficiency of a fraud detection program.

Building a business case for continuous fraud detection will depend on the level of risk that fraud represents to the organization, and the quality of existing controls to either prevent or detect significant fraud. The greater the quality of existing controls that can be leveraged, the lower the total cost of a fraud detection program will be.

Value Proposition 3: Continuous Risk Assessment/ Monitoring

The third, but possibly the most important dimension of continuous auditing, is continuous risk assessment or monitoring. The key to an effective internal audit department is to be focused on the risks that are important to the organization *now*. If risk assessment is only performed annually, or even semi-annually, audit engagements may be scoped to address risks that are no longer critical—and the more critical risks may not receive audit attention.

Internal audit departments are moving to more continuous risk assessment, often updating their audit plan on a quarterly basis. Technology can enable many risks to be monitored as frequently as the auditor desires. For example, consider the risk to a global company of sales to customers in Poland. One of the "drivers" of that risk will be the level of sales (or even the pipeline of sales orders) to customers in Poland. As that level rises, so does the risk. Technology can be used to monitor the level of sales or sales orders and send an alert to the audit department if it exceeds a predefined level.

This value proposition can be described as: *continuous auditing can be used to ensure that the internal audit plan remains focused on the more significant risks to the organization as the business changes.* It enables auditing at the speed of business.

Continuous risk monitoring is an essential element in continuous risk and control assurance. Without it, the scope continuous auditing of controls will not be updated as risks change.

Summary

Three value propositions have been identified, each of which will be discussed in more detail below.

- *Continuous risk and control assurance*: Continuous auditing enables an internal auditing function to provide assurance, when it is needed, on the more significant areas of the organization's governance, risk management, and related control processes.
- *Continuous fraud detection*: Continuous auditing enables the monitoring of risks for indicators of fraud, and of transactions for potential fraudulent activity.
- *Continuous risk assessment or monitoring*: Continuous auditing can be used to ensure that the internal audit plan remains focused on the more significant risks to the organization as the business changes.

CONTINUOUS RISK ASSESSMENT OR MONITORING

Although this is the third value proposition, it is a critical element of both continuous risk and control assurance and

continuous fraud detection, so it will be covered first. Why is it so critical? Because without continuously updating internal audit's understanding of risks, auditing (whether continuous or not) is likely to remain focused on what used to be important instead of what is important. The same applies to fraud detection, which should also be driven by the types of fraud and fraud schemes that represent a higher level of risk to the organization.

Ideally, internal audit will be able to leverage an effective risk management program (or ERM, for enterprise risk management) that identifies and assesses risks to the strategies and objectives of the organization. The internal auditor should evaluate whether:

- the ERM program can be relied on to identify the more significant risks to the organization;
- the identification of risks is timely, enabling the internal audit department to adjust the audit plan as needed;
- the assessment of risk levels is reliable.

When these conditions exist, the audit department should work with the risk function to ensure that it receives the information it needs, when it needs it, to maintain the risk-based audit plan.

However, many organizations do not have an ERM program that can be relied upon. Presumably , internal audit has raised this as an issue of critical importance with the board and executive management. But internal audit should not use this as an excuse not to try to maintain an audit plan focused on today's risks.

MAKING IT HAPPEN
A CONTINUOUS RISK MONITORING PROGRAM

One way to build a continuous risk assessment/monitoring program is as follows.

1. Start with the risks you want to monitor. Use the latest risk assessment as a basis.
2. Identify the causes or drivers of the risk. What would cause the risk level (probability or potential impact) to change? For example, if there is a revenue recognition risk related to sales to Thailand, the risk level is likely to rise if the level of sales to Thailand increases.
3. Determine your strategy for monitoring the risk drivers. For example, you can monitor corporate information on orders in the sales pipeline and be alerted when the level (volume or value) is outside a defined range. Why a range? Because if the pipeline is low, the risk level decreases. It is not only increases that should be monitored. The strategy should also include a decision on how often to monitor the risk. If the risk is considered critical and the level is volatile, then monitor more often than if the risk is lower and considered less likely to change.
4. Identify the mechanism(s) that will be used for risk monitoring. Will you rely on existing reports and systems, or will you need to build new capabilities?
5. Define the process for receiving the risk information and responding, generally with updates to the audit plan. How often will you update the plan? Also, a change in a risk level may indicate a need to inquire of management what the

causes of the change are—to confirm the risk level and understand whether related controls and/or activity need prompt audit attention. Some changes in risk levels may indicate an increased level of fraud risk, meriting special attention by internal audit or a fraud department.

6 Step back and decide whether the design to date will be sufficient to monitor the risks. Update the plan, or accept the limitations as appropriate.

7 Build and implement the continuous risk assessment program.

8 Consider how to work with management to identify new or emerging risks, and when to add them to the program.

9 Consider metrics with which to monitor whether the continuous risk assessment program is working effectively.

10 Seek to continuously improve. Perform formal reviews on a formal basis to validate performance, including determining whether the program failed to identify risk changes of significance during the period

CONTINUOUS RISK AND CONTROL ASSURANCE

The idea behind a continuous risk and control assurance (CRCA) program is that internal audit should provide its stakeholders with assurance that the more critical risks to the enterprise are effectively managed—when that assurance is needed.

Building a CRCA program takes time. A typical organization has multiple risks that internal audit will want to address, each of which relies on multiple controls.

Although the decision could be made to provide continuous assurance on only a very few risks and their controls, a larger program that addresses more risks and controls will generally provide a higher return on the investment.

Before considering tools, the CRCA program must be designed. Some internal audit departments are sold tools before they have designed a program, before they have decided how to use the tools—or even whether they are in fact the tools they need. As a result, most of these departments have had limited success.

Design

A CRCA program will include most if not all of the following components, as shown in Figure 1:

- continuous risk monitoring, including the monitoring of key performance indicators (KPI);
- continuous control monitoring;
- continuous transaction or activity monitoring;
- investigation of potential inappropriate activities that have been detected;
- continuous reporting to stakeholders.

The first step, as discussed above, is to decide which business risks will be included in the CRCA program. These will be subject to continuous risk monitoring (see previous section), which has two aspects:

- Monitoring of key performance indicators. A failure to achieve strategies, goals, or performance targets is a strong indicator that risks were not managed effectively, and that

there is a continuing level of risk to achieving goals and objectives.

- Monitoring of risk levels, typically achieved by monitoring the drivers of the risk as discussed earlier. Risk levels are reflected in key risk indicators, or KRI.

Risks are managed through controls. ISO Publication 73 defines a control as a "measure that is modifying risk" and IIA Standard (2010) defines control as "Any action taken by management, the board, and other parties to manage risk and increase the likelihood that established objectives and goals will be achieved."

A higher level of risk is a strong indicator that controls are either not designed or are not working effectively to manage risk within organizational tolerances. The CRCA program should include processes to respond to higher levels of risk, such as reviewing with management the root causes of the higher risk level and whether the system of internal controls remains adequate.

Once the business risks to be addressed are defined, the next step is to identify the controls that are relied on to manage those risks. These are the controls, the *key* controls, that will be tested in the CRCA program. By *key* controls, we mean those controls that have to be in place and operating properly if risks are to be managed. They are not all the controls, just those that if they failed or were not adequately designed would mean that the risks are highly unlikely to be well managed.

Key controls may operate at any level of the organization (corporate, division, location, department, process, etc.) and may be manual or automated. Typically, several controls are required to manage any single risk. If assurance is to be obtained that the risks are well managed, all the key controls have to be addressed in the CRCA program.

If the key controls have not already been identified, consideration should be given to performing an audit. In fact, every time a traditional audit is performed, a deliverable could be the identification of key controls and a strategy for testing them (as described in the rest of this section). This way, the CRCA program is built with confidence that the key controls are properly identified, and a relationship can be developed with operating management that will serve as a foundation for the program going forward.

Testing

After identifying the key controls, the next step is to define how they will be tested. Rather than jump straight to detailed testing techniques, it is better to define the strategy for the testing first. In a CRCA program, many controls will be tested and the overall design of testing will be more efficient— especially when considering how to leverage technology and other techniques (such as management reviews or manual testing)—when all the controls are considered together rather than one at a time. Examples of testing strategies include:

- *Rely on management's continuous monitoring program*— for payroll controls, and for the review of financial trends and significant variances from forecast. Obtain reports monthly to review the results and follow up on any issues.
- *Use software to test controls*—to confirm that all journal entries are approved by a manager, and to verify that all

Figure 1. A continuous risk and control assurance program

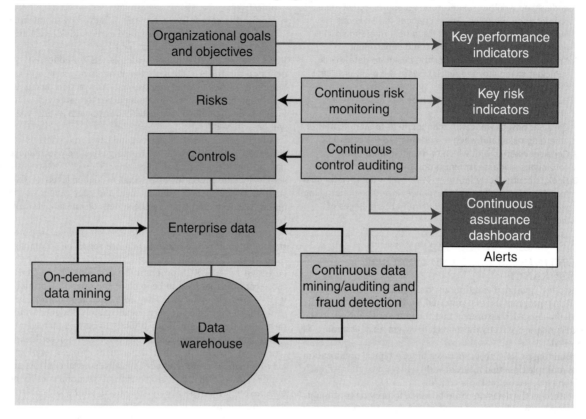

changes to the manufacturing computer system were approved by the IT manager.

- *Use manual testing*—to review actions taken with respect to outstanding items on the bank reconciliation, and to confirm that appropriate cutoff procedures are in place for the annual inventory count.
- *Rely on management self-assessments*—to confirm that the code of conduct has been reviewed with all personnel, and that backup generators are in place and tested periodically.
- *Rely on supervision*—by the IT director of controls over the work of the database administrators, and by the manager of the warehouse of the quality inspection of goods received.
- *Use software to test data*—to validate that all payments to suppliers were consistent with purchase orders and records of goods received, and to identify potential duplicate payments.

One important design consideration is the frequency with which assurance should be provided. Just because it is called *continuous* doesn't mean that the testing and the assurance have to be continuous. They key is that the assurance is provided when it is needed, and that the testing is sufficient to support the assurance.

The best assurance for management that risks are being managed effectively is when assurance can be provided on the condition and quality of the controls in place. Although testing transactions provides assurance that risks have been managed in the past, the level of forward-looking assurance is limited.

The value of assurance is that it provides comfort to the board and stakeholders with respect to current and future activity. While the past provides an indication of what will happen in the future, controls assurance is more powerful and valuable. Testing of controls provides direct evidence that they are performing. Testing of transactions provides, at best, limited indirect evidence.

Testing transactions, even when 100% of transactions are examined, only provides assurance relative to those transactions. It does not provide assurance that the controls are adequate and will ensure the integrity of current and future transactions. Consider a hypothetical analysis of home burglaries which shows that while there were several in neighborhood A, there were none in B. Does that prove that everybody in neighborhood B locked their doors and had effective alarm systems? Clearly not. The fact that transactions were accurate does not prove that there were adequate controls to ensure that they were accurate.

Therefore, a risk and controls assurance program aims to provide as much assurance that the controls are adequate as possible. However, there are limitations, especially to the use of technology to enable the continuous auditing of controls:

- Some controls involve the exercise of judgment, such as the review of journal entries. While technology can test that the journal entries were approved by a manager, they cannot test whether the review was perfunctory or whether appropriate judgment was exercised.
- A number of controls involve physical activities, such as the counting of inventory. Technology can test that a count was taken and adjustments approved by a manager, but it cannot test to ensure that all locations were properly examined.

In many cases these limitations can be addressed by including manual testing as part of the CRCA program. For example:

- a manual review of a sample of journal entries can be performed throughout the year;
- auditors can attend the occasional inventory counting procedure.

Where the limitations involved in testing controls cannot be overcome, the auditor may decide that the indirect assurance from testing transactions is sufficient. This may be the case when the risk if the control fails is considered to be low.

In some companies, management has implemented a continuous monitoring program. This involves direct monitoring by management that assures them that the controls are functioning as intended. When such a program is in place, internal audit should seek to place as much reliance as possible on it. Duplication of effort should be avoided. The auditor should: ·

- Review the scope of management's continuous monitoring program and confirm that it includes the key controls to be covered by the CRCA program.
- Verify that the monitoring by management meets quality and objectivity standards necessary for internal audit reliance. For example, does it simply rely on a manager confirming that he or she has performed the control?
- Determine whether the program produces evidence that can be used by the internal auditor. For example, the program may rely on supervision by a manager that is not documented when it is performed.

For some controls, the auditor may decide to rely on a self-assessment program. This can be valuable, especially where the risk is relatively low, or where direct testing is difficult—such as testing employee awareness of the code of ethics.

The CRCA program design must include consideration of how testing exceptions, or indications that controls may be failing, will be addressed. Most of the time the exceptions will have to be reviewed with management, so that explanations can be obtained and a determination made as to whether the controls have in fact failed—and what actions will be taken in response.

In a few cases, especially where the risk of fraud is considered high, the CRCA program might include "alerts," typically but not necessarily automated, informing internal audit of the control or data exception.

The CRCA program design should include how the results of the testing and monitoring will be summarized for use by internal audit management. What will the summary look like, how often will it be produced (or will it be continuously updated and always available), and how will exceptions be highlighted?

Reporting

Finally, the design has to address how stakeholders will be informed of the quality of risk management and the related controls.

- How often do executive management and the board require reports?
- Do they prefer to receive reports (such as dashboards) or to be notified when there are exceptions?
- What information will be provided to operating management? How often will it be provided, and in what form?

Once the design is complete, the tests can be developed. With respect to the use of technology, the design will determine what the technology needs to achieve and will define the requirements for the selection of the appropriate set of tools. Since the program needs to address all forms of controls, it is unlikely that a single software tool will meet all needs and a combination of tools will be required. For example, one tool may be used as a repository of risk and control information to capture and report the results of testing. Another may be used for risk monitoring and data analytics. Yet another may be used to monitor IT activity when testing IT general controls.

Figure 1 summarizes all the elements of a fully-featured CRCA program.

- The first two rows address the monitoring of key performance indicators (for business objectives) and risk indicators (for risks to those business objectives).
- Controls auditing is the preferred testing approach, but where that is not possible the testing of data (either in the enterprise systems or in a data warehouse or similar) may be included. This is especially true when the risk of fraud is considered (see below).
- The results of the CRCA program have to be collected for reporting within internal audit and to stakeholders. This is shown on the right side of the diagram.

CONTINUOUS FRAUD DETECTION

Many internal audit functions have taken on the responsibility for detecting fraud. Even where strong controls are in place, it is prudent to monitor transactions and look for the signs of potential fraud.

A CRCA program will typically include fraud risks, monitoring their level, testing the controls, and examining activity for potential issues of concern.

A continuous fraud detection program will follow some of the same principles and steps as a CRCA program, even if the continuous auditing activity is limited to fraud detection rather than a full CRCA program:

- Design the program and define your needs before selecting software or developing detailed testing techniques. ·
- Focus on frauds that represent the higher level of risk to the business. According to the Association of Certified Fraud Examiners's latest global fraud study (AC FE, 2010), the average company experiences fraud amounting to 5% of annual revenue. While this is high, care should be taken not to allocate more resources to fraud detection than the risk merits or the detection costs. This can be done by focusing on those fraud risks and schemes that are more likely to be significant to the business.

MAKING IT HAPPEN
AN EFFECTIVE FRAUD DETECTION PROGRAM
The following steps have proven useful in implementing effective fraud detection programs.

1 Identify the fraud risks specific to your organization. Every company is different, and the risks from fraud will vary.
2 Assess each fraud risk for likelihood and potential scale.
3 Select the fraud risks that the program will address.
4 For each risk, identify how the fraud would work: what are the fraud schemes?
5 Determine how an inspection of transactions or other activity (such as trend analysis, comparison of same product margins in different locations, or the detection of transactions approved by the same person who originated the transactions) might detect potential fraud.
6 Design the process for investigating exceptions. Take care to discuss the process with any management personnel who might be involved in reviewing and providing explanations for exceptions.
7 Develop and implement the program.
8 Monitor and adjust the testing procedures as necessary (for example, changing tolerances on any automated tests that are producing false positives).
9 Continue to monitor fraud risks and change the program as needed.
10 Review and continually improve the fraud detection program.

SUMMARY
There are several ways in which continuous auditing techniques can be used to improve the effectiveness of an internal audit program. They include:
- continuous risk and control assurance;
- continuous fraud detection;
- continuous risk assessment.

Before embarking on the continuous auditing journey, the internal audit department should decide what it wants to use continuous auditing for. Will it be for one or more, or for some variant, of the above purposes?

Some departments review the software marketed for continuous auditing or continuous control monitoring and purchase what appears to be the "best." However, they may do this before deciding on the purpose and objectives of their program, which would enable them to define their needs for technology.

Other audit functions understand continuous auditing to be purely an application of technology and do not therefore consider the use of manual testing. Typically, their program becomes one of testing transactions, primarily for potential fraud. It does not provide assurance on the quality of controls, and does not help them to realize their mission of providing assurance and consulting services relating to the effectiveness of governance, risk management, and related control processes.

Finally, some audit departments have left the field entirely. They believe that management should be performing continuous monitoring of controls and that continuous auditing is not necessary. This overlooks the potential for internal audit to review and test management's monitoring program and then rely on it (perhaps supplementing it with its own tests as necessary) to provide their stakeholders with assurance when it is needed by the board and management.

Continuous auditing has great potential. It can move an internal audit from providing assurance based on traditional point-in-time audits to providing assurance when it is needed. But to realize that potential, an internal audit department has to be disciplined.

MORE INFO
Reports:

Association of Certified Fraud Examiners (ACFE). "Report to the nations on occupational fraud and abuse: 2010 global fraud study." 2010. Online at: www.acfe.com/rttn.aspx

Coderre, David. "Global technology audit guide (GTAG) 3: Continuous auditing: Implications for assurance, monitoring, and risk assessment." Institute of Internal Auditors, 2005. Online at: www.theiia.org/guidance/technology/gtag3

Ernst & Young. "Escalating the role of internal audit: Ernst & Young's 2008 global internal audit survey." 2008.

Institute of Internal Auditors (IIA). "International standards for the professional practice of internal auditing (Standards)." Revised October 2010. Online at: tinyurl.com/7we53bq

KPMG. "Continuous auditing/continuous monitoring: Using technology to drive value by managing risk and improving performance." June 2009. Online at: tinyurl.com/5w3huxt [PDF].

See Also:

★ How Can Internal Audit Report Effectively to Its Stakeholders? (pp. 86–90)

✔ Internal Audit Charters (pp. 314–315)

✔ Internal Auditing for Fraud Detection and Prevention (pp. 315–316)

✔ Key Competencies for Internal Auditors (pp. 317–318)

NOTES
1 Unfortunately, there is no universally accepted definition of continuous auditing. Many (including KPMG in its 2009 publication, "Continuous auditing/continuous monitoring") have limited continuous auditing to the use of technology to collect and analyze transactions. The present essay uses the IIA definition.
2 Any activity may be tested, including not only transactions but changes to application code, router or automated control configurations, master data, etc. The term "transaction" is used generically to include any activity subject to testing.
3 In its 2008 global internal audit survey (the latest), "Escalating the role of internal audit," Ernst & Young reported that 42% of respondents to its survey had implemented some level of continuous auditing, mainly to "identify deficiencies, monitor risks and identify potential fraud activities." Reasons for not having already implemented continuous auditing included a "lack of skill sets within internal audit, budget constraints and no perceived value in the program."
4 From the definition of "assurance services" in the Glossary to IIA Standards (2010), p. 18.

Effective Financial Reporting and Auditing: Importance and Limitations

by Andrew Higson

EXECUTIVE SUMMARY
- There is a debate about the specification of the objective of financial statements.
- Clear specification of this objective is important for the financial reporting standard-setters (so they can produce consistent and coherent standards), users (so they understand the nature and scope of financial reporting), external auditors (so they can say whether the financial statements are "fit for purpose"), and educationalists (so they can teach the next generation).
- The lack of clarity about the objective of the financial statements appears to have created a financial reporting expectations gap.
- Perceived defects in financial statements have resulted in a call for real-time financial reporting, but this may have the effect of creating more volatility in share price movements.

INTRODUCTION
The major problem with financial reporting is that people with limited financial knowledge can look at a set of accounts and, by attempting to interpret the numbers, feel that they understand what is happening in an organization. While in simpler times this may have been true, the scale and complexity of modern business, together with the limitations of what can be portrayed in financial statements, means that today's statements may have the capability to mislead as much as they can inform their users.

A large telecom business may have over two hundred million transactions a day in its accounting records, and such a scale of activity is almost beyond human comprehension. The complexity, and uncertainty, surrounding some transactions and financial instruments make their inclusion in the financial statements problematic to say the least. In the past accounting was defined as "an art of recording, classifying and summarizing in a significant manner and in terms of money, transactions and events which are, in part at least, of a financial character, and interpreting the results thereof."[1] The need for financial reporting came about with the development of permanently invested capital (today's share capital), which required a return to be made to the shareholders for their investment over a period of time (usually annually). The separation of ownership and management, especially in larger organizations, gave rise to the need for the accountability of the managers (agents) to the owners (principals), the financial statements being a convenient basis for this. In some jurisdictions financial statements also form a basis for the calculation of taxation. This subdivision of an organization's life into artificial accounting periods may not sound exciting, but it is important. It may not cover all aspects of an organization's activities, but originally this was never intended.

DECISION-USEFULNESS
Since the 1960s, the function of accounting has been increasingly regarded as "to provide quantitative information primarily financial in nature about economic entities that is intended to be useful in making economic decisions, in making resolved choices among alternative courses of action,"[2] and accounting was seen as a service activity.

On a simplistic level, the decision-usefulness approach may be intuitively appealing, but it could also be conceptually flawed and an example of circular reasoning: just because some people may take decisions based on the financial statements, does this mean that decision-usefulness should be specified as the objective of financial statements? When one takes a decision, one should be looking to the future—yet the financial statements say very little about an organization's future. One should also consider the future economic climate, an organization's competitors, and expected technological developments; financial statements say very little about these things. Often short-term investors are more concerned about taking their decision in *anticipation* (buy long, sell short) of the publication of the financial statements rather than waiting for them to come out, reading them, and then taking a decision.

An important component in the debate about the objective of financial statements has been the vagueness of the nature, scope and purpose of accounting "theory." One would have expected developments in financial reporting to have been built on theory and thus be conceptually robust. The focus on unspecified users taking unspecified decisions, at unspecified times, with unspecified results hardly seems an appropriate basis for the production of consistent and coherent financial reporting standards, and consequently there is a danger that the financial reporting standard-setters have been building on shifting sands rather than on firm foundations.

THE CALL FOR REAL-TIME REPORTING
Given the prevailing emphasis on decision-usefulness, and the perceived limitations of financial statements in this respect, some analysts and other external parties have been calling for companies to make real-time accounting data available to them. The argument is that immediate access to, and a greater quantity of, data about a company should improve users' decision-making ability and thus improve market efficiency. However, if companies were to adopt real-time reporting (this presumably would be the reporting of

results on a minute-by-minute basis rather than just putting the annual accounts on the internet), would the results make sense?

There is a danger that there has been a confusion over the "recording" aspect of accounting and the "reporting" aspect of the financial statements. "Raw" accounting data are simply a means of recording in order to keep track of the transactions undertaken by an organization—which is obviously very important for management to do. The periodic financial statements use these accounting data, and related assumptions and conventions, to allocate profit to the appropriate accounting period and to present the financial figures at a point in time (this is after the necessary cut-off adjustments and checks have been made). Given the scale of modern business, one wonders what users would really make of all the data.

To allow outsiders access to real-time "raw" accounting data does raise the question as to how exactly it would lead to greater market efficiency. Indeed, instantaneous access to real-time accounting data may not necessarily result in greater market efficiency—though greater volatility in share price movements would be a distinctly possible consequence.

THE FINANCIAL REPORTING EXPECTATIONS GAP

It is likely there is a financial reporting expectations gap[3] composed of two elements, one being an expectations gap relating to the financial statements, and the other being the audit expectations gap (Figure 1). There has been much discussion of the audit expectations gap (some users of financial statements think that the external auditors are there to detect fraud, that they produce the financial statements, that they check everything recorded by the client's accounting, etc.). The audit expectations gap has been a driving force behind the expansion of the audit report and has focused the debate about the responsibilities of the external auditors.

Compared to the discussion about the audit expectations gap, the possibility of a financial statements expectations gap has almost been ignored.

It is suggested that one element is the already discussed focus of the accountancy profession on the decision-usefulness of financial statements. Just because some people do take decisions based on them, it does not mean that they take the right decision. Another problem is the use of financial statements as an assessment of "performance"; this is because the financial statements *per se* say nothing about the economy, efficiency, and effectiveness of the organizations that produce them. There is also the tension between the long-term development of an organization and the short-term results contained in the financial statements. It is easier for users of financial statements to focus on the short-term figures contained in such statements than to try to look long-term. The broadening of the notion of performance could mean that financial statements would then be recognized for what they are—an attempt to allocate profit to the appropriate accounting period and to indicate the financial position at a point in time—and that they would then enable the debate about what constitutes corporate performance to really begin.

IMPLICATIONS FOR THE EXTERNAL AUDITORS

One might assume that the audit report would be saying that the financial statements are "fit for purpose"; however, traditionally the auditors have said nothing about the decision-usefulness of financial statements. Indeed, the Company Law Review Steering Group report[4] stated: "auditors have no liability to existing shareholders who rely on their report for investment decisions (for example to buy or sell shares), or actual creditors of the company who may make similar decisions about maintaining or withdrawing credit, or potential investors whether of equity or debt, or other

Figure 1. The financial reporting expectations gap. (*Source*: Higson, 2003, p. 13)

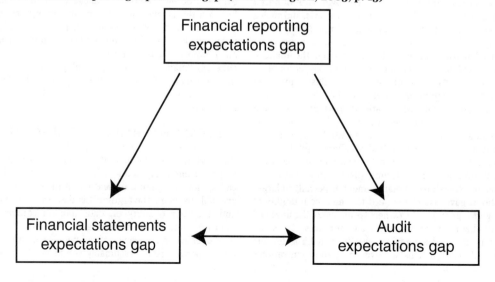

potential creditors (for example trade creditors), who rely on the audit report for a view of the financial position of the company." It is therefore not surprising that in the United Kingdom, following the Bannerman case[5] in 2003, the auditors added a paragraph to their audit report which included the advice that: "Our work has been undertaken so that we might state to the company's members those matters we are required to state to them in an auditor's report and for no other purpose ... we do not accept or assume responsibility to anyone other than the company and the company's members as a body, for our audit work, for this report, or for the opinions we have formed."

The auditors say nothing about corporate economy, efficiency, and effectiveness in their audit report. The users have to try to make their own assessment of these things based on the limited amount of data in the financial statements available to them.

It can be seen that the auditors tend to think of themselves as doing what is required of them (i.e. to follow the auditing standards and ensure that the financial statements have been produced by management in accordance with financial reporting standards), but I wonder how many readers of financial statements will understand this and understand what all these standards mean.

CONCLUSION

The challenges of corporate reporting in the twenty-first century can only be met once there is a real understanding about the nature, scope, and limitations of the financial statements and of the role of the external auditors.

Without a strong theoretical basis, the danger is that the financial reporting standard-setters will merely end up pandering to the perceived needs of the supposed users of financial statements.

The word "performance," in a theatrical sense, could be defined as "an act of make-believe aimed at enchanting an audience." The existence of the financial statements expectations gap may mean that this fate has already befallen the phrase "financial performance" (think about Enron's and WorldCom's financial statements); it is important that it does not befall the phrase "corporate performance."

MAKING IT HAPPEN
AN AGENDA FOR DEVELOPMENTS IN CORPORATE REPORTING

- Give consideration to a tighter and arguably more realistic specification of the objective of the financial statements.

- Increase education about the scope and limitations of financial statements and the external audit.
- Conduct a proper debate about the nature of communicating corporate performance and the assessment of corporate economy, efficiency, and effectiveness.
- Reflect on the usefulness of real-time access to corporate accounting data.

MORE INFO

Books:

Deegan, Craig, and Jeffrey Unerman. *Financial Accounting Theory*. European ed. London: McGraw-Hill, 2006.

Elliott, Barry, and Jamie Elliott. *Financial Accounting and Reporting*. 13th ed. Harlow, UK: FT Prentice Hall, 2009.

Harrison, Walter T., Jr, Charles T. Horngren, and C. William Thomas. *Financial Accounting*. 9th ed. Upper Saddle River, NJ: Pearson, 2012.

Higson, Andrew. *Corporate Financial Reporting: Theory and Practice*. London: Sage Publications, 2003.

Riahi-Belkaoui, Ahmed. *Accounting Theory*. 5th ed. London: Thomson, 2004.

Website:

Corporate Financial Reporting, the author's website: www.accounting-research.org.uk

See Also:

★ Contemporary Developments in International Auditing Regulation (pp. 70–74)

✔ International Financial Reporting Standards (IFRS): The Basics (pp. 316–317)

✔ The Key Components of an Audit Report (pp. 318–319)

NOTES

1 American Institute of Accountants (AIA), Committee on Terminology (1953). *Accounting Terminology Bulletin* No. 1. New York: AIA, 1953; p. 9.

2 Accounting Principles Board (APB). *Statement No. 4: Basic Concepts and Accounting Principles Underlying Financial Statements of Business Enterprises*. New York: AICPA, 1970; para. 40.

3 Higson, 2003.

4 Company Law Review Steering Group. *Modern Company Law for a Competitive Economy: Final Report*. London: DTI, 2001; para. 8.127.

5 Auditing Practices Board Discussion Paper. *The auditor's report: A time for change?* London: Financial Reporting Council, 2007; pp. 11–12.

Engaging Senior Management in Internal Control
by Philip Ratcliffe

EXECUTIVE SUMMARY

- Internal control systems must have the backing of senior management to be effective.
- Internal auditors should make management aware of the importance of sound internal controls, and the serious problems that could arise if they are inadequate.
- The benefits of sound internal controls include efficiency and effectiveness, protection against losses and unpleasant surprises, optimum use of assets, and motivated staff—all in all, they make a major contribution to organizational survival and prosperity.
- Key risks resulting from lack of good internal control are fraud, incorrect accounts, inefficiency and ineffectiveness, damage to the reputation of the organization and its management, and a consequent fall in the value of the company.
- Internal auditors should form their own view of the specific risks facing their organization.
- If the internal control system is inadequate, they should meet with senior management to explain the need for strong, sound controls and their benefits for the organization.

HOW TO GET SENIOR MANAGEMENT TO TAKE INTERNAL CONTROL SERIOUSLY

Top managers in any organization have many calls on their time and attention. Vying for their attention will be customers, suppliers, employees, consultants, and many others. Internal controls can easily be squeezed out of their agenda. The problem this can create is that if senior management does not take control seriously, the "tone from the top" will be wrong—and if the people in charge don't care, then why should anyone else in the organization? Rightly or wrongly, this is the message that will be perceived across the organization, and internal control will suffer.

So, as a corporate auditor, how can you push internal control up the priority list? Showing clearly to management the benefits of strong internal control on the one hand, and the consequences of failure of internal control on the other, is one path to this goal.

Benefits of Control

A key message to communicate to management is that effective, active controls give positive benefits as well as avoiding negative outcomes. Having controls that are effective will ensure that the directions of the board and senior management are implemented as intended; that operations and activities are carried out efficiently and meet their objectives; and that the assets used in an organization are not only properly accounted for, but also that they are used effectively and efficiently for the benefit of the organization.

Procedures which follow sound control principles enable people to carry out their work in an environment that is orderly and satisfying to work in. Good internal control will also protect an organization and its staff against the temptations of dishonesty, fraud, and theft.

Organizations that have sound internal controls will know where they are, and where they are going, because management information controls will tell the organization's management what they need to know when they need to know it. If the first imperative of most organizations is survival, then good internal control can play a major role in achieving that objective. Additionally, and very importantly, there can also be an efficiency dividend for an organization if good, cost-effective internal control systems are in place; for example, when processes are streamlined and well controlled, fewer people may be needed to do the work.

The Impact of Control Failure Inside the Business

All too often, internal control only becomes a concern to top management after it breaks down. Out of the blue comes the sudden discovery of a massive fraud or a major hole in the accounts, or a business segment that was thought to be profitable is dramatically discovered not to be. There is a myriad of such possibilities. Management discovers, painfully, that when there is such a breakdown of control, almost everything else has to be thrown out of the window while the breakdown is investigated. It has to engage with internal auditors, external auditors, consultants, and specialists to uncover the root causes of the problem, as there is no cure without first making a diagnosis. The managers immediately responsible for the failure must be identified, and a conclusion reached on their degree of culpability. And if someone has to be fired, who is going to take on their responsibilities?

Then, senior managers have to make up their minds what to do about the underlying problem. What changes have to be made to ensure that it can never happen again? Should they commission reviews in other similar parts of the organization to gain assurance that the problem isn't endemic elsewhere? Are major investments in systems or capital items needed to fix things? Should procedures be revised? Do staff need retraining or reorganizing? If so, who is going to implement the changes, and where is the money going to come from?

Control Breakdown Can Have External Implications

Another vital aspect is the impact of a breakdown on external relations. Do investors and the stock markets have to be informed? Is a profits warning necessary? How will stakeholders react? What will the (inevitably negative) impact be on the share price, and therefore the value, of the organization? Often such an announcement will create a loss of shareholder value that is many times the original operating loss. At times like these, an executive director may be lucky to keep his job; at the very least, there is a major risk of loss of personal and corporate reputation.

The Opportunity Cost Is Great
On top of this, in a serious case the opportunity cost of the time that management will lose in attending to the consequences of an internal control breakdown can be massive. Strategic issues, tactical issues, business development—all these and many more normal concerns of senior management will have to take a back seat until the problem is resolved. Add to this the loss of reputation and of confidence, inside and outside the organization, because news will inevitably leak out however carefully those involved try to prevent it.

The case here has been made in the context of a commercial organization, but similar considerations apply to all other types of organization, whether governmental, private, or in the not-for-profit sector.

GETTING MANAGEMENT BACKING: WHERE TO START
If the benefits of sound controls are so tangible, and the aftermath of a failure of internal control is so dreadful, how does the corporate auditor make a start on obtaining top management's backing for a regime of sound internal control? Corporate governance regulations in many countries, and best practice, now require organizations formally to analyze and record the risks they face. The purpose of this requirement is, first, to ensure that organizations actually understand their risk profile, as only then can they seriously and properly consider whether they have the right mitigation arrangements in place. Often a management team, in making explicit the risks they face, will discover that initially they do not have a common view as to what the risks are. Only when they have a unified vision can they expect to come up with a coherent and balanced response. Only then can they hope to design and develop a comprehensive internal control system that meets the needs of the organization. The corporate auditor can assist by becoming involved in the risk identification process, by emphasizing to senior management the immediate impact of failure to mitigate the risks (for example, by pointing out that the accounts will be incorrect), and the secondary, but possibly even more drastic, consequences (for example, that a profits warning will have to be issued and the share price will nosedive.)

It is not least by confronting management with the consequences of control failure that it can be helped to take internal control seriously. The internal auditor can help to create an understanding and appreciation of the consequences of control failure by making presentations and having one-to-one meetings with influential people, such as the chairman/president, chief executive, chief financial officer, audit committee chair, other board members, and senior managers. The objective is to create an awareness of internal control in the organization and, through that awareness, to change the attitude to it.

While some risks may be external to the organization and not susceptible to internal control, many can be mitigated by internal controls. In some cultures, management is reluctant to accept the need for internal controls, believing that staff

should be trusted. Internal auditors should point out to such management that trust is not a substitute for internal control. A proper system of internal controls should be considered a force for moral good, in that it effectively removes temptation from employees by ensuring that undesirable behaviors will be promptly detected and corrected; if employees understand this, they will be less likely to attempt to defraud their employer.

CASE STUDY
When a new chief executive officer joined his company, the chief audit executive arranged an early meeting with him. The CAE discussed the internal controls in the organization, demonstrated his knowledge of their strengths and weaknesses, and explained his view of the importance of controls and the vital role to be played by the CEO in setting an example—the tone from the top. As a result, the CEO agreed to have regular meetings to discuss internal controls and to review the assurance provided by internal audit and any resultant need for action, undertakings he subsequently fulfilled. Expectation that these meetings would take place helped to ensure that management throughout the organization gave high priority to internal control and to responding to internal audit findings.

MAKING IT HAPPEN
- Collect evidence about the state of internal controls and any opportunities that exist for improving them.
- Present the benefits of better controls in terms with which management can identify.
- Review the organization's code of conduct or similar document; if none exists, it is worth raising the issue.
- Seek a meeting with the head of the organization and influential members of the board. Have a clear but short agenda. Aim for some specific goals from your meeting. Go prepared with a succinct presentation and some practical recommendations.
- Use the opportunity to argue for the importance of tone from the top where internal control is concerned; if the top people in the company take internal control seriously, so will everybody else. Ask whether they like unwelcome surprises, and what they are prepared to do to avoid them.
- Point up the risks facing the organization, and show how a well-designed control structure can help to avoid or mitigate the worst consequences.
- Don't expect everything to be achieved with just one meeting. Be prepared to keep going back with the same messages until they are not only accepted, but also acted on.

CONCLUSION
Management's role in ensuring effective internal control is vital. Management sets the tone from the top. Unless

management engages and commits, the rest of the organization will not take internal control seriously. The internal auditor can help management to appreciate the importance of internal control by demonstrating its value—not least, the efficiency dividend to an organization if good, cost-effective internal control systems are in place—and by making management aware of the consequences of failures of internal control. The internal auditor can further assist management by highlighting the need to set tone from the top, to allocate sufficient resources for internal control, and to ensure that internal control processes are suitably designed for the needs of the business.

MORE INFO

Book:

Sawyer, Lawrence B., Mortimer A. Dittenhofer, James H. Scheiner, *et al. Sawyer's Internal Auditing: The Practice of*

Modern Internal Auditing. Altamonte Springs, FL: Institute of Internal Auditors, 2003.

Reports:

American Institute of Certified Public Accountants. "Internal control—Integrated framework." May 1994. Order online at: www.theiia.org/bookstore

Financial Reporting Council. "The UK corporate governance code." May 2010. Online at: www.frc.org.uk/corporate/ukcgcode.cfm

See Also:

★ Improving Corporate Profitability Through Accountability (pp. 204–206)
★ Understanding Reputation Risk and Its Importance (pp. 279–282)
✔ Defining Corporate Governance: Its Aims, Goals, and Responsibilities (pp. 341–342)
✔ Understanding Internal Audits (pp. 324–325)

How Can Internal Audit Report Effectively to Its Stakeholders?
by Andrew Cox

EXECUTIVE SUMMARY

- Internal audit has a range of stakeholders who rely on its work, seeking assurance that the organization is running well and that there are effective controls in place.
- Internal audit has a responsibility to its stakeholders to provide reports on the operation of the organization's risk management, control, and governance processes. It also has a responsibility to justify the value of its work and the organization's spending on internal audit resources.
- Internal audit can report on its work to its stakeholders by:
  ○ reporting on the outcomes of its internal audit work;
  ○ reporting on the quality of its internal audit work.
- Together, these elements combine to provide stakeholders with an overall view of the effectiveness of internal audit; one without the other will only provide a partial reporting structure.

INTRODUCTION

Internal audit has a variety of stakeholders who rely on its work. These include: the board of directors; the audit committee; the chief executive officer; senior executives such as the chief financial officer, chief information officer, chief risk officer, etc.; the external auditors; in some cases, regulatory bodies; and stockholders—who, in the case of government organizations, could be the public.

All these stakeholders are seeking assurance that the organization is running well, and that effective controls are in place and operating properly. Internal audit has an important role to play in providing assurance to these stakeholders, but

the trick is how to report the results of its work to them effectively.

ASSURANCE MODELS

Assurance can be equated with the term governance, the four pillars of a good corporate governance framework being—according to the Institute of Internal Auditors—executive management, the audit committee, external audit, and internal audit. Each of these elements relies to an extent on the others, and they all need to be operating effectively to provide overall assurance to stakeholders.

The board of directors will generally want to see a combined assurance model in place for the organization that provides three lines of defense, as shown in Table 1. This demonstrates the interdependencies between the four pillars of good corporate governance and the three lines of defense that go to make up a combined assurance model.

REPORTING ON THE OUTCOMES OF INTERNAL AUDIT WORK

A model for reporting the outcomes of internal audit work could be based on the following four elements: internal audit reports, recommendations for improvement, a communication strategy, and an annual internal audit report. These are discussed below.

Internal Audit Reports

Internal audit reports are the most important part of the work of an internal audit function. The report is the culmination of the effort directed toward an audit of a part

Table 1. Combined assurance model with three lines of defense. (*Source*: National Australia Bank, with amendment)

First line of defense	Second line of defense	Third line of defense
Management controls	**Management of risk**	**Independent assurance**
Real-time focus	Real-time focus + review focus of 1st line	Review focus of 1st and 2nd line
Elements	**Elements**	**Elements**
Policies and procedures	Risk management	External audit
Internal controls	Legal department	Internal audit
Role	**Role**	**Role**
Review compliance	Confirm compliance	Independently confirm
Implement	Recommend	compliance
improvements	improvements	Recommend
		improvements

of the organization. Internal audit can be a costly resource, so reports of its work should demonstrate its value to the organization. Internal audit reports need to be:

- Timely: reports should be issued in a timely manner.
- Accurate: reports should contain accurate information.
- Logical: reports should be logical and valid.
- Clear: reports should be clearly written and easily understood.
- Purposeful: reports should state why the internal audit was performed.
- Written with the audience in mind: reports should be written to suit the intended reader.

The power of a tick cannot be underestimated—it provides balance to an internal audit report. People do not go to work to do a bad job, and they appreciate recognition of good work. What they do not appreciate is an audit report that is negative by exception, says nothing positive, and effectively just gives them stick. So, acknowledge good work, and always say something positive in the report—and not begrudgingly.

Internal audit reports need to tell a story and be insightful. Merely telling people what is wrong cannot be seen as a good use of internal audit resources. That is the easy work, and does not reflect well on internal auditing as a profession. The real value of the work of internal audit comes from an emphasis on cause and effect. It is easy work to find the effect, but much more difficult to ascertain the root cause. Because of this, many internal auditors take the easy way out and just report on what has been found to be operating ineffectively.

Many internal audits could provide additional value to the organization if there was more emphasis on efficiency, effectiveness, economy, and organizational outcomes, with a view to assisting the organization further to improve and streamline business processes.

Recommendations for Improvement

Internal audit reports need to contain recommendations for improvement if they are to have any point, and the recommendations need to be targeted at correcting the root cause.

Locating the cause provides information on accountability relationships, and provides the basis for making improve-

ments. It is important not just to find that something is wrong, but to work out what caused it to be wrong. This can prevent similar problems from happening again. Each recommendation needs to include:

- Whether it is agreed with or not by the audit customer (and if not, why not).
- What the audit customer is going to do about it (action plan).
- By what date the action will be implemented and completed.
- Who will be responsible for implementing the recommendation.

Recommendations contained in internal audit reports also need to be risk rated. In this way, management with the responsibility to implement remedial action will know which recommendations are most important and should be implemented first.

An important task of the internal audit function is to ensure that agreed recommendations arising from internal audit reports are satisfactorily actioned within a reasonable time-frame. If this is not done, its work will be virtually worthless. Many internal audit functions adopt an approach whereby:

- Agreed recommendations from internal audit, external audit, and regulatory bodies are entered into a tracking system and monitored on an ongoing basis by internal audit and the audit committee.
- Management responsible for implementing the recommendations is required to advise internal audit when this is complete, or to provide periodic reports on progress where this may be over a longer period of time.
- Overdue recommendations are reported to the audit committee.
- Internal audit periodically follows up to ensure that implementation has occurred as reported by management. This can be by 100% follow-up, by following up only those recommendations of higher risk, or by following up on a sample basis. A full follow-up audit is not generally necessary.

One point worthy of consideration is the necessity to cover off risks if recommendations are not actioned within a reasonable time-frame. Where a recommendation relates to a higher-risk problem and is not dealt with quickly, the chief audit executive should ask:

- Why has it not been actioned?
- Should the risk rating assigned to the recommendation be increased?
- What fall-back or interim risk management procedures have been put in place to mitigate the risks associated with nonimplementation of the recommendation?
- Should management make a statement accepting the risk associated with nonimplementation of the recommendation?

This information should be reported to each meeting of the audit committee.

Communication Strategy

To develop and maintain a profile within an organization, internal audit should take steps to improve its communication in order to make itself more visible to the wider organization. Some ways in which internal audit might do this include:

Raising awareness
- Have information about internal audit and its achievements posted on the organization's intranet.
- Distribute a small brochure about internal audit, what it does, and its achievements.
- Further develop relationships with stakeholders by making presentations on the work of internal audit to groups within the organization's corporate environment.
- Prepare an annual internal audit report on its activities.

Engaging management
- Consult with internal audit customers prior to the commencement of each internal audit, and request their input to the objectives and scope of the audit.
- Facilitate a risk workshop with internal audit customers in the planning phase of each internal audit.
- When conducting internal audits, internal auditors should spend most of their time in the work areas of their internal audit customers, rather than in the internal audit work area.
- At the completion of internal audit fieldwork, hold a workshop with the audit customer to discuss and agree possible improvement options.
- Provide a balanced reporting format by reporting on what management is doing well, in addition to identifying opportunities for improvement.

Providing value-add
- Plan for each internal audit with a wider view by encompassing objectives relating to efficiency, effectiveness, economy, and organizational outcomes.
- Have involvement in working groups related to strategic developments within the organization in an observer/adviser capacity. It is considered best practice for internal audit to contribute to such forums by providing opinions, and ensuring that controls are considered and built-in to projects and systems under development, rather than after the event via post-implementation reviews, without necessarily compromising the integrity of later audits.

Annual Internal Audit Report

In some organizations, best practice extends to providing the audit committee and management with an annual report of internal audit activities featuring:
- Achievements in the year.
- Analysis of systemic issues identified through the work of internal audit.
- An opinion on the organization's overall risk management, control, and governance environment.

This can provide additional assurance to the audit committee, as well as being beneficial in alerting management to issues and risks identified in internal audits but which may also be occurring in other business areas.

REPORTING ON THE QUALITY OF INTERNAL AUDIT WORK

A model for reporting on the quality of internal audit work could be based on the following four elements: a quality assurance and improvement program, performance measures, review by external audit, and review by regulatory bodies.

Quality Assurance and Improvement Program

The "International Standards for the Professional Practice of Internal Auditing" issued by the Institute of Internal Auditors requires every internal audit function to operate a quality assurance program:

"The chief audit executive must develop and maintain a quality assurance and improvement program that covers all aspects of internal audit activity."

A quality assurance and improvement program is designed to enable an evaluation of internal audit's conformance with the Definition of Internal Auditing and the Standards, and an evaluation of whether internal auditors apply the Code of Ethics. The program also assesses the efficiency and effectiveness of internal audit and identifies opportunities for improvement.

This program should include both internal and external assessments. Internal assessments comprise: ongoing monitoring of the performance of the internal audit activity; and periodic reviews performed through self-assessment or by other persons within the organization with sufficient knowledge of internal audit practices.

External assessments must be conducted at least once every five years by a qualified, independent reviewer or review team from outside the organization. The chief audit executive must discuss with the board the need for more frequent external assessments; and the qualifications and independence of the external reviewer or review team, including any potential conflict of interest. The chief audit executive must communicate the results of the quality assurance and improvement program to senior management and the board.

Performance Measures

Best practice in internal auditing suggests that, like most business units in an organization, internal audit should have performance measures or key performance indicators (KPIs) in place to demonstrate its own level of performance. Best practice also suggests that performance measures need to be specific (clear and concise), measurable (quantifiable), achievable (practical and reasonable), relevant (to users), and timed (having a range or time limit). For more on this, see the case study.

Review by External Audit

As part of its annual external audit of an organization, the external auditors will usually assess the internal audit function on such matters as its organizational status, scope of function, technical competence, and due professional care exercised in its work.

Review by Regulatory Bodies

In many countries, regulatory bodies review the competency and work of internal audit as part of their periodic regulatory review of an organization. These are generally restricted to particular industry groups, for example financial institutions.

Table 2. KPIs prepared by the chief audit executive to assess internal audit. (*Source*: National Australia Bank, with amendment)

	Key performance indicator	Measure	Target	Frequency
	1. Completion of *Internal Audit Plan*			
1.1	Complete planned internal audits as per the approved *Internal Audit Plan* (subject to approved plan amendments)	% of planned internal audits completed within the financial year	95%	Annually
1.2	Complete special and ad hoc management-initiated internal audits and investigations in addition to scheduled internal audits (an allowance for this is contained in the *Internal Audit Plan*)	% of allowance utilized for unplanned ad hoc and management-initiated internal audits and investigations	95%	Annually
1.3	Approved *Internal Audit Plan* to be completed within the approved internal audit budget	% variance from approved budget for the financial year	5%	Annually
	2. Implementation of internal audit recommendations			
2.1	Internal audit recommendations accepted by management	% of recommendations accepted by management (subject to internal audit independence being maintained)	95%	Annually
2.2	Monitor the implementation status of internal audit recommendations by management and report outcomes to the audit committee	Updated status obtained from responsible managers and reported to the audit committee	Quarterly status reports delivered	Quarterly
	3. Formal survey feedback			
3.1	Results of customer feedback surveys following each internal audit	% of survey responses of good or better (averaged)	90%	Annually
3.2	Result of annual feedback survey of members of the audit committee	% of survey responses of good or better (averaged)	90%	Annually
	4. Independent quality review of internal audit			
4.1	Result of external quality assessment of internal audit in accordance with *The International Standards for Professional Practice of Internal Auditing*	Report issued detailing results of review	Consistent with better practice	Five-Yearly

CASE STUDY
MEASUREMENT OF THE INTERNAL AUDIT FUNCTION

The chief audit executive of an organization in Brisbane Australia was seeking ways to measure the work of his internal audit function. He knew that internal audit was doing a good job, but he did not have the evidence to prove it. In thinking how to address this problem, he designed KPIs against which his internal audit function could demonstrate its performance to the audit committee and the organization (Table 2). After all, internal audit assesses the performance of other areas of the organization, so why should it be exempt from having its own performance examined?

The chief audit executive considered these to be the KPIs the audit committee would be interested in to provide an overall assessment of the work of internal audit, and when he asked the audit committee, they agreed. He discounted KPIs such as the number of internal audit recommendations, or the number of internal audit hours delivered, since these can be manipulated and would therefore have little credibility with the committee.

CONCLUSION

Internal audit has a responsibility to its stakeholders to provide reports on the operations of the organization's risk management, control, and governance processes. It also has a responsibility to justify the value of its work and the organization's spending on internal audit resources.

Internal audit can do this in two ways:

- By reporting on the outcomes of its internal audit work.
- By reporting on the quality of its internal audit work.

MAKING IT HAPPEN

The chief audit executive should develop effective reporting mechanisms with the audit committee and other stakeholders. Key reporting tools include:

- Insightful internal audit reports.
- Monitoring of internal audit recommendations, and periodic follow-up to ensure that recommendations have been implemented effectively and in a timely way.
- An internal audit communication strategy.
- An annual internal audit report that covers achievements in the year, an analysis of systemic issues identified through the work of internal audit, and an opinion on the organization's overall risk management, control, and governance environment.
- A quality assurance and improvement program that incorporates both internal and external assessments.
- Key performance indicators measuring the performance of internal audit.

★

- Periodic review of internal audit by external auditors and, where applicable, regulatory bodies.

MORE INFO
Books:

Reding, Kurt F., Paul J. Sobel, Urton L. Anderson, Michael J. Head, *et al. Internal Auditing: Assurance and Consulting Services*. 2nd ed. Orlando, FL: IIA Research Foundation, 2009.

Sawyer, Lawrence B., Mortimer A. Dittenhofer, and James H. Scheiner. *Sawyer's Internal Auditing: The Practice of Modern Internal Auditing*. Altamonte Springs, FL: IIA, 2003.

Report:

Australian National Audit Office. "Public sector internal audit: An investment in assurance and business improvement."

Better Practice Guide. September 2007. Online at: tinyurl.com/7nuerch [PDF].

Standards:

Institute of Internal Auditors. "International standards for the professional practice of internal auditing." October 2010. Online at: tinyurl.com/7qdspr4

Websites:

Institute of Internal Auditors (IIA): www.theiia.org
Institute of Internal Auditors—Australia: www.iia.org.au

See Also:

★ Engaging Senior Management in Internal Control (pp. 84–86)

★ Implementing an Effective Internal Controls System (pp. 93–97)

✔ The Key Components of an Audit Report (pp. 318–319)

✔ Understanding Internal Audits (pp. 324–325)

How to Implement a Standard Chart of Accounts Effectively
by Aziz Tayyebi

EXECUTIVE SUMMARY

A chart of accounts (COA), representing a unique set of codes to record all an entity's transactions consistently, is a well-recognized, fundamental accounting need. Whether it concerns a complex organization with numerous divisions, or an individual applying basic cash accounting, it is essential to be able to collate financial information that is relevant, both for internal management and external parties. This article considers some questions that management should take into account when implementing a standard COA, such as:

- Why update a chart of accounts? An organization may need to adopt a new COA if its industry or country adopts a new set of specific accounting standards. Furthermore, as organizations evolve, it is vital that the COA keeps pace and stays relevant to management.

- What are the options when implementing a chart of accounts? Implementing a new COA can improve an existing system, or involve a completely new development. Management should take care to incorporate all useful accounts from older systems.

- What are the practical considerations when designing a chart of accounts? Management must consider user needs, detailed design specifications, logistics, cost/benefit analysis, and legal requirements.

INTRODUCTION

A chart of accounts (COA) is essentially a set of codes for the consistent classification of financial information. This allows for the systematic production of decision-useful accounting

information for management, such as budgeting, monitoring, and management reporting. Similarly, a standard COA helps to ensure comparability in external financial reporting.

The COA facilitates the recording of all transactions, which are filtered into a unique account code, based on certain criteria. While this criteria is influenced both by internal management needs as well as regulatory requirements, many common types of codes would always be expected, such as revenue, expenses, assets, liabilities, and equity.

WHY UPDATE A CHART OF ACCOUNTS?

A standard COA represents an integral part of an overall financial information system. A COA takes inputs from source accounting documents and journal entries, and allocates that information to a prescribed set of accounts, ultimately producing financial reports, which in turn enable users of that information to track the performance of the business, in a format that best suits their needs.

External Decisions

COAs can change for a number of reasons, including an industry-wide move to standardize accounting terminology. An example of this was the development of a standard COA for not-for-profit organizations (NPOs) in Queensland, Australia. In 2002, Queensland University of Technology (QUT) and Queensland Treasury commenced a project to develop a standard COA for small NPOs that received government funding. The project was commissioned because, at the time, Australia did not provide specific national accounting standards for NPOs. As a result, there was tremendous inconsistency in accounting categories and terms required by government departments in their funding relationships with such organizations. Research from QUT indicated that these inconsistencies created a heavy compliance burden on NPOs when acquitting grants, with many additional costs being incurred in the reporting process . Thus, through an extensive consultation process, a standard COA was launched in Queensland in 2006. The success of the COA, both for NPOs and the funders, through reducing simplification of the reporting process, increasing understanding, and consistency of accounting practices, led to other Australian jurisdictions subsequently commencing similar projects.[1]

A significant number of companies around the world have recently implemented International Financial Reporting Standards (IFRS). For many of those companies, the IFRS implementation was mandated in national legislation. The transition to IFRS involves significant practical and logistical challenges, especially in upgrading and adapting IT systems across the organization. A recent report by KPMG[2] indicated that, "IT costs are generally over 50 per cent of the cost of IFRS conversion," and that changes to the chart of accounts are inevitable.

Other key regulatory requirements, which can have an impact on the COA, revolve around taxation. For larger companies with overseas subsidiaries that will be using the same general ledger system, it is important to consider country-specific requirements when completing the COA, while providing as much consistency as possible.

Organizational Decisions

More commonly, businesses are likely to go through restructuring, make a strategic decision to implement a new IT system, or simply acknowledge that the current COA is not fulfilling the information needs of the business. Whatever the reasons are for change, management needs to assess both the new business requirements, as well as any that were not being met previously.

Similarly when considering the implementation of new reporting systems, it is essential to ensure that the individual components of the financial system, such as invoicing, stock management, and disbursements, are providing the appropriate support to the wider business objectives. This is often why ERM packages are so useful, as they allow information from a common source to be shared across previously disparate departments of the business.

OPTIONS WHEN IMPLEMENTING A CHART OF ACCOUNTS

Essentially, an organization is faced with three choices.
1 Keep the COA from the legacy system in place;
2 Supplement the existing COA with some additional ones;
3 Overhaul the COA and implement the new, changed structures.

From a practical point of view, moving away from the existing chart of accounts also has the significant advantage of offloading redundant codes and accounts which unnecessarily congest it.

In practice, especially when a comprehensive system such as an ERP package is being implemented, the organization faces limited choices. The chances are management will have to consider a whole-scale overhaul of the current system. Thus, it is also essential to ensure that, while this is an opportunity to cleanse the current COA, it is also vital to ensure that the new COA reflects the realities of the business. All-round general ledger systems are, by their nature, more sophisticated, linking various sets of data. Designing an appropriate chart of accounts is a complex process.

PRACTICAL CONSIDERATIONS WHEN DESIGNING A NEW CHART OF ACCOUNTS

As previously described, the COA is only one element in the information system (manual and automated) which aids management decision-making. The COA is, however, a key part, bringing together financial information held within the general ledger, and filtering it into a format that can be used by managers.

The general considerations for implementing a new COA are, unsurprisingly, akin to those that would be assessed when making any significant system changes. Considerations include an assessment of user needs, a detailed design, potential impact assessment and testing, and simulations prior to final running. By thoroughly considering these basic procedures, it should be possible to complete a relatively risk-free, "big bang" approach to the adoption of the new COA. However, in the case of an overall system change, management may decide to run both systems for a period of time in order to ensure that all data is being captured. While costly and time-consuming, the old COA is then still available for cross-reference.

User Needs

Again, reiterating the main reason for having a standard COA, the initial phase of implementation must begin with a thorough analysis of the organization's information requirements. Thus management will need to consider the existing outputs resulting from their present COA, and ensure that all potential stakeholders, within and outside the finance department, are involved in the process.

Understanding the current condition should ensure that relevant COAs are included in the new version, and that shortcomings are remedied. A simulation of the revised COA can then be produced, allowing the stakeholders to preview the resulting information. The main aim of this phase is not to determine what the final reports may look like, but to confirm that the required information is being generated.

Logistical Consideration

Business analysts tend to want as much information as possible, and then decide which information they really need at any given time. This desire, coupled with the wide range of internal and external stakeholders, may make it tempting to include excessive fields in a COA. However, it is generally the case that by widening the net of accounts, the likelihood of error, as well as underutilized codes, will be greater too. Thus, it is also vital to strike the right balance between the user's often-exhaustive demands, and the limitations of an efficient data-capture system.

Typically management may be interested in analyzing performance based on:
• individual product basis and product class;

Best Practice

- separate cost centers;
- geographical segments;
- legal entities.

However, it is the needs of the business that should ultimately dictate the scope of data requirements.

It is also possible that the difficulty and cost of generating some information might ultimately mean that it is not worthwhile. The tendency is that future preparers of information may find it too difficult to provide the inputs regularly, and, therefore, these accounts would again become vacant. Thus, it is imperative to conduct a careful analysis of the process for data capture. While much reporting information can easily be extracted from basic input data from invoices, etc, the consistent splitting of costs and revenues by appropriate cost and activity centers is more challenging.

In order to maintain a consistent application of the COA, it is also important that a thorough guide is in place, outlining how information should be captured and recorded. Again, a regular review of these guidelines should be conducted.

Manual or Electronic Conversion?

In practice, the choice of manual or electronic conversion will be dictated by the type of system being implemented. If a totally new package is introduced, then the standard COA is already inbuilt, and only the process of identifying and/or adding new accounts is required, as discussed above. If the organization is simply implementing a new standard COA only, then the organization is faced with either a manual or an electronic change. Usually, electronic downloading into the accounting software is straightforward—the relevant file is downloaded from the data file into the existing accounting package, which then essentially overlays the existing COA.

A manual conversion requires a thorough comparison between the new standard COA and the existing COA. The process of identifying relevant accounts is, again, critical, although by virtue of the fact that this is not automated, it can be lengthier. A constant review of output reports, such as trial balances, is required.

If the company's financial statements are audited, it is important to consider any requests from auditors, regardless of whether the process is manual or electronic. It is, therefore, important to document any changes to the COA, with an appropriate audit trail in place.

Balancing Cost-Centre Demands and Legal Entity Requirements

Many large organizations have a number of subsidiaries that are legal entities in their own right. While management may make business decisions on quite different aspects, the financial reporting process demands that a COA is able to meet all external reporting requirements, such as statutory and tax reporting. The COA must be set up so that a full trial balance for that individual entity can be obtained.

This can lead to possible conflicts and difficulty, especially where corporate cost centers are managed across a number of reporting entities. It may be that, at a cost-center level, additional detail is required on income-statement accounts, but limited detail is required for balance-sheet classifications—there is no compromise on statutory requirements.

Management should carefully consider how best to set up an accounting company, or a cost center for COA purposes. Typically, when businesses have their own general ledger systems or are legal reporting entities, a separate accounting company approach is the optimal solution. A cost-center approach is more appropriate when an organization is reviewed on the basis of divisional performance, which is supervised by individual mangers themselves.

While a standard COA should be comprehensive enough to allow for all divisional requirements, it should not compromise the compliance requirements of statutory reporting, either for the local entity, or the group as a whole.

CONCLUSION

Changing a COA involves a thorough understanding and analysis of the existing business requirements. However, it is equally important to realize that most businesses constantly evolve, and management information needs may also change. It is, therefore, essential that the implementation process includes a clear vision for future years, and makes the most of available technologies such as eXtensible Business Reporting Language (XBRL), for example. XBRL can benefit the dissemination of financial information from various sources, including various charts of account.

Finally, it is important to be mindful that there is no ideal standard COA. What fits the needs of one organization, and indeed one manager within an organization, may be considerably different for another. What is vital is that a thorough investigation of the needs of the organization as a whole is conducted.

MAKING IT HAPPEN

A correctly structured COA should support the financial and management reporting process, enabling the organization to evaluate its performance in a manner that uses information systems efficiently. Ultimately, a good understanding of the business and its future direction ensures that an optimum COA is developed. It is essential that managers are involved throughout the implementation process. At the centre of the considerations should be:

- Appraising the current system, including the relevance of outputs and accessibility of information, by bringing together managers from relevant departments.
- Understanding the current and potential information needs of the organization and focusing on the overall business strategy and processes, while taking into account external reporting and regulatory requirements.
- Designing and assessing the potential impact of the new COA against those user needs, and adopting an appropriate strategy to move from the old chart.
- Balancing the benefits of numerous financial information demands with the finite resources, both time and costs, required to capture that information, and ensure its accuracy.
- Putting in place a robust framework for operating the COA, including guidance on use (for future employees), regular review of outputs, and methodology for inputs.

MORE INFO

Book:

Potter, Douglas A. *The Automated Accounting Systems and Procedures Handbook*. New York: Wiley, 1991.

Websites:

Queensland University of Technology, experiences of implementing a standard chart of accounts (SCOA): tinyurl.com/72a29fl [via archive.org].

Queensland University of Technology, chart of accounts research project: tinyurl.com/7dr58cq [via archive.org].

See Also:

✔ Assessing Business Performance (pp. 359–360)
✔ International Financial Reporting Standards (IFRS): The Basics (pp. 316–317)
⇄ Management Accounts (pp. 397–398)

NOTES

1 Queensland University of Technology, research program, website
2 KPMG, The Effects of IFRS on Information Systems, 2008

Best Practice

Implementing an Effective Internal Controls System

by Andrew Chambers

EXECUTIVE SUMMARY

- Effective internal control gives reasonable assurance, though not a guarantee, that all business objectives will be achieved. It extends much beyond the aim of ensuring that financial reports are reliable. It includes the efficient achievement of operational objectives and ensures that laws, regulations, policies, and contractual obligations are complied with.

- There is growing appreciation that effective internal control does not evolve naturally. It requires concerted effort on an ongoing basis.

- Often initially stimulated by the requirements of the Sarbanes–Oxley Act (2002), many more businesses are now systematically documenting, testing, evaluating, and improving their internal control processes. We show how to do this.

- In a large organization this more rigorous focus on internal control is likely to encourage greater standardization of similar processes in use in different parts of the organization.

- More effective internal control does not necessarily cost more. Aside from reducing costly risks of avoidable losses and business failures, it is often no more costly to organize business activities in ways that optimize control.

- Better internal controls may enable a business to engage safely in more profitable activities that would be too risky for a competitor without those controls.

INTRODUCTION

In some jurisdictions law or regulation may require effective systems of internal control, with serious penalties for irresponsible failure. The Sarbanes–Oxley Act (2002) requires CEOs and CFOs of companies with listings in the United States to certify their assessment of the effectiveness of internal control over reported disclosures (s302) and financial reporting (s404), with penalties of up to US\$1 million and ten years imprisonment for unjustified certification, or up to US\$5 million and 20 years imprisonment for willful breach of the requirements (s906). The Public Companies Accounting Oversight Board's Auditing Standard No. 5 (2007) requires the company's external auditors themselves to assess the effectiveness of their client's system of internal control over financial reporting, in order to meet the audit requirements of s404 of the Sarbanes–Oxley Act.

Japan and Canada have laws broadly similar to the Sarbanes–Oxley Act. Although not reinforced by the risk of criminal sections, provision C.2.1 of the UK Corporate Governance Code (2010) requires that the board of a company listed on the main market of the London Stock Exchange should satisfy itself that appropriate systems are in place to identify, evaluate, and manage the significant risks faced by the company; and provision C.2.2 requires that the board should, at least annually, conduct a review of the effectiveness of the group's system of internal controls and should report to shareholders that they have done so. The review should cover all material controls, including financial, operational, and compliance controls, and risk management systems. In addition, the UK Financial Services Authority's Disclosure and Transparency Rule DTR 7.2.5 R requires companies to describe the main features of the internal control and risk management systems in relation to the financial reporting process (see Schedule C).

WHAT "EFFECTIVE" MEANS

Although similar requirements exist in many countries, the principal driver for implementing an effective internal controls system should be the enlightened self interest of the company.

Effective internal control is intended to give reasonable assurance of the achievement of corporate objectives at all levels. An internal control framework should be used for the design and evaluation of an internal control system. The COSO

Best Practice

framework is the most widely applied of three published frameworks.[1] COSO (the Committee of Sponsoring Organizations of the Treadway Commission) defines internal control as follows:

"Internal control is broadly defined as a process, effected by the entity's board of directors, management and other personnel, designed to provide reasonable assurance regarding the achievement of objectives in the following categories:

1 Effectiveness and efficiency of operations.
2 Reliability of financial reporting.
3 Compliance with applicable laws and regulations."

Other definitions of internal control categorize the objectives of internal control differently, but fundamentally, effective internal control gives reasonable assurance that all of management's objectives will be achieved. For instance, the King Report (2002)[2] defined internal control as follows:

"The board should make use of generally recognized risk management and internal control models and frameworks in order to maintain a sound system of risk management and internal control to provide a reasonable assurance regarding the achievement of organizational objectives with respect to:

1 Effectiveness and efficiency of operations;
2 Safeguarding of the company's assets (including information);
3 Compliance with applicable laws, regulations and supervisory requirements;
4 Supporting business sustainability under normal as well as adverse operating conditions;
5 Reliability of reporting;
6 Behaving responsibly towards all stakeholders."

Before a conclusion can be reached that internal control is effective, both *results* and *processes* must be considered. For the former, the test is whether there have been any known outcomes attributable to significant breakdowns in internal control. Absence of these does not lead automatically to the conclusion that internal control is effective: it is possible that there may have been breakdowns of internal control yet to be discovered; it is also possible that serious weaknesses exist within the system of internal control that have not yet been exploited. So the second test must also be applied, which is to assess the quality of the control processes or "components."

DESIGN CHARACTERISTICS OF AN EFFECTIVE INTERNAL CONTROLS SYSTEM

The COSO internal control framework recognizes five essential components of any effective internal control system:

- The control environment: Values and culture; tone at the top; policies, organizational structure.
- Information and communication: Reliability, timeliness, clarity, usefulness.
- Risk assessment: Identification, measurement, and responses to threats.
- Control activities: Procedures followed for a control purpose.
- Monitoring: Review of internal control arrangements.

A common failing in designing and evaluating a system of internal control is to focus almost exclusively on control activities, vitally important though they are, overlooking that the other components are also essential. The Securities and Exchange Commission's rule for management's implementation of s404 of the Sarbanes–Oxley Act requires that a recognized internal control framework is applied. Usually it is the COSO framework that is used, and the framework comprises all of these five as being essential components of an effective system of internal control.

General hallmarks of an effective system of internal control include that controls:

- are designed to meet objectives which are clear;
- have regard to competitive issues;
- enable and ensure that performance is measured;
- aid the identification of risks;
- result in unsatisfactory performance being rectified;
- ensure that activities are completed in a timely way;
- mean the right people do the right jobs;
- are cost effective;
- are placed as early in the process as is practical, so that thereafter there is control;[3]
- specify and require appropriate authorization requirements;
- ensure there is an adequate audit trail;
- are "preventative" rather than merely "permissive";
- have no more movements, or steps than are necessary;
- are flexible to allow for adaptation;
- are documented.

Control activities can be categorized as follows:

Preventive controls: *To limit the possibility of an undesirable outcome being realized.* The more important it is that an undesirable outcome should not arise, the more important it becomes to implement appropriate preventive controls. Examples are when no one person has authority to act without the consent of another, or limitation of action to authorized persons (such as only those suitably trained and authorized being permitted to handle media enquiries).

Corrective controls: *To correct undesirable outcomes that have been realized.* Examples are the design of contract terms to allow recovery of overpayment, or contingency planning for business continuity/recovery after events which the business could not avoid.

Directive controls: *To ensure that a particular outcome is achieved or an undesirable event is avoided.* Examples are a requirement that protective clothing be worn, or that staff be trained with required skills before working unsupervised.

Detective controls: *To identify undesirable outcomes "after the event."* Examples are stock or asset checks which detect unauthorized removals, or post-implementation reviews to learn lessons.

Performance controls: *To orientate and motivate the organization's people to focus on the achievement of targets that are appropriate for the achievement of objectives.* Examples are dispatching all orders on the day of receipt of the order, or allowing that less than 2% of production should fail quality control checks.

Investigative controls: To try to understand how the undesirable outcome occurred so as to be able to ensure that it does not happen next time, and to provide a route of recourse to achieve some recovery against loss or damage.[4]

ASSESSING INTERNAL CONTROL EFFECTIVENESS

A widely followed approach to assessing and improving internal control effectiveness has been developed that comprises these steps (see case study 1):

1 Determine the documentation to be used, such as process maps (flowcharts), control registers, and process narratives.
2 Identify the objectives to be achieved.
3 Determine the processes that are key to the achievement of objectives.
4 Learn about each key process, documenting it in narrative, spreadsheet, and/or flowchart form.
5 Within a key process, identify and document the key controls.
6 Judge the potential of each key control to be effective, if followed as intended. Modify the control approach if necessary.
7 Design and document tests to be conducted to assess compliance with each control.
8 Conduct these tests.
9 Interpret the results of these tests. Where necessary, ensure better compliance or modify the control approach if satisfactory compliance is judged impractical.
10 Interpret the control significance of unwanted outcomes that have occurred.
11 Consider the adequacy of the control environment, information and communication, risk assessment, control activities, and monitoring.
12 Conclude on the effectiveness of internal control at the process level.

TESTING INTERNAL CONTROLS

The extent of testing is a compromise between the need for thoroughness and the testing resources available, and will vary according to the criticality of the controls that are being relied upon, the potential for the controls to be circumvented, and the results of initial testing. For controls designed to operate at intervals (such as at week, month, or year ends), initial sample sizes may be as in Table 1. For controls that apply to individual

Table 1. Sample sizes to be used if the control operates at the frequencies shown

Frequency of control	Sample size
Annually	1
Quarterly	2
Monthly	2
Weekly	5
Daily	20
Many times a day	25

Table 2. Sample sizes for transaction controls

Population size	Sample size
1–3	1
4–11	2
12–50	3
51–100	5
101–200	15
201–300	20
Above 300	25 max

transactions Table 2 may be appropriate, which can also be used for interval controls that are used in multiple locations or on multiple occasions.

ONGOING MAINTENANCE OF AN INTERNAL CONTROLS SYSTEM

Changing business requirements will result in modified business processes and the risk that controls within those processes may be abandoned or made less effective. Each modified business process that is key to the achievement of a business objective should be reassessed, applying steps 3 to 6 (above), prior to releasing the new or modified business process for operational use.

For established processes, performance criteria should be established to monitor the quality of performance and the extent to which controls fail.

CASE STUDY 1

A multinational company took the requirement to comply with s404 of the Sarbanes–Oxley Act as an opportunity to assess the effectiveness of its internal control generally, not just internal controls over financial reporting.

First, the accounting processes that could lead to financial misstatements were identified. Second, mission-critical operational processes were identified where there were significant risks of not achieving business objectives and/or risks of misstatement. These accounting and operational processes were documented in process maps (flowcharts), using distinctive symbols to denote what were considered to be key s404 controls, other key financial controls, and key operational controls. These controls were described in a spreadsheet-based control register, supplemented where necessary by further process narrative. From this understanding of each process, deficiencies in control procedures were identified and corrected. Using predetermined, documented test scripts, each key control within a process was then tested for compliance prior to drawing a conclusion about internal control effectiveness of the process.

Initially this work was done by the internal audit function, before being transferred to become an ongoing responsibility of management, working to an annual cycle.

CASE STUDY 2

To be useful, process narrative on internal control must be sufficiently specific to indicate whether control is effective. In the three examples below, only the third is adequate. The reader of the first and second examples will be unclear as to whether it is merely the narrative that is inadequate, or that internal control is inadequate.

Control Documentation Poor

A report on duplicate invoices is produced before payments are made. It is looked at and approved by someone who plays no other part in the order-processing and invoicing procedures.

Control Documentation Average

Each day, before the payments processing run, the senior creditors clerk (SCC) investigates a report on possible

Best Practice

duplicate invoices. The SCC signs and dates this report when the check has been completed, and sends the report to James Smith for second review and final approval. James signs and dates the report to indicate completion of his review and approval of the SCC's investigation.

Neither James nor the SCC has access to the purchase order or invoice-processing SAP modules or the manual parts of those subsystems.

Control Documentation Good

Daily, before the IT-based processing of payments, the SCC personally prints out a possible duplicate payments report from the payables module in SAP (SAP report code 9VDFZ3). This report may indicate five possible types of duplicate (refer to details in the process narrative).

The SCC investigates the possible duplicate invoices as indicated in the report by checking the accuracy of invoice data captured in the SAP accounts payable module against original invoices, making sure that each invoice is valid by reference to source documentation, such as purchase orders , as necessary.

The SCC has no responsibility for other elements of this system, not having any involvement in, or other access to, the processing of purchase orders or invoices—these access rights are blocked to the SCC by the accounts payable module.

When the SCC has completed the investigation, he signs and dates the possible duplicate payments report to indicate that the investigation has been completed. His manager then reviews the possible duplicate payments report, together with the relevant, supporting evidence and comments from SCC's investigation. If the manager is satisfied by the investigation and supporting evidence, he signs and dates the possible duplicate payments report to indicate approval of the SCC's investigation.

MAKING IT HAPPEN

The approach to follow:

1 Adopt and understand a recognized internal control framework.
2 Engage the board, management, and other personnel in the ownership of internal control.
3 Identify the mission-critical business processes.
4 Consider standardizing processes across the business.
5 Document those processes, highlighting the key controls.
6 Consider the effectiveness of the key controls and improve where necessary.
7 Design tests to confirm satisfactory compliance with key controls, and take remedial action as required.
8 In addition to control activities, consider whether the other essential components of an effective system of internal control are sound—for example, the control environment, information and communication, risk assessment, and monitoring.
9 Draw overall conclusions.
10 Use the results from this process as a continuous improvement tool to improve the internal control system.

MORE INFO

Books:

American Institute of Certified Public Accountants (AICPA). *Internal Control over Financial Reporting: Guidance for Smaller Public Companies*. Institute of Internal Auditors Research Foundation, 2006. Order from: www.theiia.org/bookstore

Chambers, Andrew. *Tolley's Internal Auditor's Handbook*. 2nd ed. London: LexisNexis Butterworths, 2009. See especially chapter 6.

Committee of Sponsoring Organizations of the Treadway Commission (COSO). *Internal Control—Integrated Framework*. 2 vols, 1992. Order from: www.coso.org/IC-IntegratedFramework-summary.htm

COSO. *Guidance on Monitoring Internal Control Systems*. 2009. See exposure/review link at: www.coso.org

Articles:

Sneller, Lineke, and Henk Langendijk. "Sarbanes–Oxley Section 404 costs of compliance: A case study." *Corporate Governance: An International Review* 15:2 (March 2007): 101–111. Online at: dx.doi.org/10.1111/j.1467-8683.2007.00547.x

Wagner, Stephen, and Lee Dittmar. "The unexpected benefits of Sarbanes–Oxley." *Harvard Business Review* (April 2006). Online at: tinyurl.com/4jewuc5

Reports:

Canadian Institute of Chartered Accountants. A number of publications in the series *Control Environment—Guidance on Control*. Online at: www.rmgb.ca/publications/index.aspx

COSO. "Enterprise risk management—Integrated framework." 2004. Summary and print requests online at: www.coso.org/ERM-IntegratedFramework.htm

Financial Reporting Council (FRC), UK. "The Turnbull guidance as an evaluation framework for the purposes of Section 404(a) of the Sarbanes–Oxley Act." 2004. Online at: www.frc.org.uk/documents/pagemanager/frc/draft_guide.pdf

FRC. "Internal control: Revised guidance for directors on the Combined Code." October 2005. Online at: www.ecgi.org/codes/code.php?code_id=178

HM Treasury, UK. "The orange book: Management of risk—Principles and concepts." October 2004. Online at: www.hm-treasury.gov.uk/d/3(4).pdf

Institute of Internal Auditors. "Sarbanes–Oxley Section 404: A guide for management by internal controls practitioners." 2nd ed. January 2008. Online at: www.theiia.org/download.cfm?file=31866

Public Company Accounting Oversight Board (PCAOB). "Auditing standard no. 5: An audit of internal control over financial reporting that is integrated with an audit of financial statements." July 2007. Online at: www.pcaobus.org/standards/standards_and_related_rules/auditing_standard_no.5.aspx

Securities and Exchange Commission (SEC). "Commission guidance regarding management's report on internal control over financial reporting under section 13(a) or 15(d)

of the Securities Exchange Act of 1934." June 2007. Online at: www.sec.gov/rules/interp/2007/33-8810.pdf. Subject to amendment issued August 2007: www.sec.gov/rules/final/2007/33-8809.pdf

Website:
Institute of Internal Auditors (IIA): www.theiia.org

See Also:
★ Engaging Senior Management in Internal Control (pp. 84–86)
★ How Can Internal Audit Report Effectively to Its Stakeholders? (pp. 86–90)
✔ Understanding Internal Audits (pp. 324–325)

NOTES
1 Other recognized internal control frameworks are the Canadian "CoCo" framework, and the United Kingdom's Turnbull framework.
2 King Report on Corporate Governance for South Africa (March 2002), "King II," Institute of Directors in Southern Africa. "King III Report and Code" (September 1, 2009) did not include this definition of internal control.
3 For instance, incoming cash should be controlled at the point and time of entry into the business.
4 Institute of Internal Auditors. *Using the Risk Management Process in Internal Audit Planning*. Practice Advisory 2010-2. May 2009; para 4. The meaning PA 2010-2 gives to "investigative controls" is not identical to the meaning we have given in this chapter.

Incorporating Operational and Performance Auditing into Compliance and Financial Auditing
by Andrew Cox

EXECUTIVE SUMMARY
- Almost every audit can also be an operational or performance audit.
- With a bit of creativity, it is not too difficult to include a value-adding element to a compliance or financial audit.
- Operational and performance auditing can provide added value to your organization.
- Including an operational or performance auditing element in your audits can enhance the image of auditing for those being audited and also for management.
- Auditors can increase their job satisfaction through operational and performance auditing.
- The 3Es of economy, efficiency, and effectiveness should be integral components of the internal auditor's work.

INTRODUCTION
"The truth is, 'audit gets no respect.' Quite frankly, if the audit department in question is using yesterday's approach in today's company, has not maneuvered top management and the board into focusing on the company's top five or ten risks, has not caused management to quantify these risks, and has not succeeded in developing authorized bounds of risk tolerance, then it doesn't deserve any respect." Larry Small, President, Fannie Mae, 2000.

This is a great quote, but what a pity it was not applied in recent times when this company got into serious financial difficulty. Perhaps a greater focus on operational and performance auditing might have helped.

What are the big risks for management? Are they likely to be immaterial accounting mistakes, a missing signature on a form, an immaterial asset that cannot be located, people not following a procedure exactly, or perhaps petty cash missing?

Or maybe management is more concerned with making sure the organization is running properly, which means focusing on economy, efficiency, and effectiveness—better known as the 3Es.

OPERATIONAL AND PERFORMANCE AUDITING
What is the difference between operational and performance auditing?
- **Operational audit**. Sometimes called program or performance audits, these examine the use of resources to evaluate whether those resources are being used in the most efficient and effective ways to fulfill an organization's objectives. An operational audit may include elements of a compliance audit, a financial audit, and an information systems audit. This term is mainly used in the private sector.
- **Performance audit**. This is an independent and systematic examination of the management of an organization, program, or function to identify whether the management is being carried out in an efficient and effective manner and whether management practices promote improvement. This term is mainly used in the public sector and may be the same as or similar to an operational audit.

While there may be purists who will argue there is a difference, the reality is that they seek to achieve the same objective. Although operational and performance auditing are generally applied to public sector auditing, and operational auditing is usually applied to private sector auditing, both seek to achieve organizational improvement of the 3Es.

Figure 1. The audit continuum

The Audit Continuum
moving from outputs to outcomes

Outputs → Compliance
Probity
Financial effectiveness
Efficiency
Outcomes Operational and performance

THE AUDIT CONTINUUM

The audit continuum is shown in Figure 1. As we move from basic compliance auditing to more complex forms of auditing such as operational and performance auditing, the complexity of the audit and the difficulty in getting agreement to the audit objectives from the audit customer increases.

THE DIFFERENCES

The differences between operational and performance auditing, and compliance and financial auditing, are shown in Table 1. The real difference is that operational and performance auditing will genuinely add value and seek to improve the bottom line of an organization. Compliance and financial auditing cannot make this assertion, since their focus is generally on whether things are being done in accordance with legislation, regulations, policies, and procedures. Important though this aspect may be, it is unlikely to have the same improvement objective as operational and performance auditing.

Table 1. Differences between operational and performance auditing, and compliance and financial auditing. (*Source*: The State Audit of the United Arab Emirates)

	Operational and performance auditing	Compliance and financial auditing
Purpose	Does performance meet the 3Es?	Is there compliance?
Focus	The organization and its objectives	Accounting transactions
Academic base	Economics, political science, sociology, etc.	Accounting
Methods	Methods vary from audit to audit	Standardized methods
Assessment criteria	Unique for each audit	Standardized criteria
Reports	Varying format	Standardized format

ECONOMY, EFFICIENCY, AND EFFECTIVENESS

What are we seeking to achieve by using performance and operational auditing? The aim is to find out whether business operations are being managed in an economic, efficient, and effective manner; whether procedures for promoting and monitoring the 3Es are adequate; and, importantly, whether improvements can be made.

Economy is concerned with minimizing the cost of resources used (people, materials, equipment, etc.), having regard to the appropriate quality required: i.e., keeping the cost of inputs low without compromising quality. An example could be where healthcare supplies or services of a specific quality are purchased at the best possible price.

Efficiency is concerned with the relationship between goods and services produced (outputs) and the resources used to produce them (inputs): i.e., getting the most from available resources. An example could be where the cost of providing healthcare has been reduced over time. Efficiency is about "doing things right."

Effectiveness is concerned with achieving predetermined objectives (specifically planned achievements) and having the actual impact (output achieved) compared with the intended impact (objective): i.e., achieving the predetermined objective. An example could be where disease rates have fallen as a result of the healthcare provided. Effectiveness is about "doing the right things."

WHAT MANAGEMENT WANTS

Although there are many internal auditors who still believe their job is to tell management what is wrong but not how to fix it, many more enlightened internal auditors have worked out what management is really seeking. This includes such things as:

- help in reducing risk;
- help in improving the business;
- assurance that appropriate governance is in place and working properly;
- internal audits that are relevant and timely;
- internal audits that genuinely add value;
- more value for the money spent on internal audits.

THE STEPS IN PERFORMING AN OPERATIONAL OR PERFORMANCE AUDIT

The sequence of an operational or performance audit is likely to be:

- establish what should be done;
- establish what is being done;
- compare "what should" with "what is";
- investigate significant differences;
- assess the effects of the differences;
- determine the cause of the differences;
- develop audit findings and value-adding options and recommendations.

While the initial steps may not be very different from a compliance or financial audit, the crucial and value-adding steps are: determining the cause of the differences; and developing audit findings and value-adding options and recommendations.

These are the difficult parts. Most compliance or financial auditors can work out an effect, but trying to isolate the cause can be much harder. Hence, many internal auditors find it easier just to report on what is wrong and avoid trying to identify the root cause of a problem.

Often an internal audit recommendation will be something like "Employees should follow the procedures." This is lazy internal audit work and not a particularly enlightened recommendation—it is more of a throwaway line. There may be many reasons why an employee is not following procedures. But not many employees will deliberately disobey a procedure unless it is a bad procedure, or something else is preventing them from complying with it.

PARTNERING WITH MANAGEMENT

There are a number of ways in which internal auditors can promote their services—in particular the benefits of operational and performance auditing. These may include:

- Develop an engagement model and get management buy-in.
- Closely align your internal auditing with the business.
- Plan a risk-based internal audit program developed with management.
- Aim to become an integral part of the organization and to help management improve the business.
- Plan each internal audit with management.
- Facilitate a frank risk assessment with management and stakeholders for each internal audit.
- Formulate insightful objectives for each internal audit, not just "throwaway lines."
- Ask management to agree and sign off the terms of reference for each internal audit.
- Consider using technical experts where internal auditors may not have all the necessary skills for an internal audit.
- Facilitate a workshop with management and stakeholders at the conclusion of an audit to discuss and agree possible improvement options.

REPORTING

As mentioned previously, the real value in an internal audit report is in determining the cause of the differences between "what is" and "what should be," and developing audit findings and value-adding options and recommendations. This is the essence of what operational and performance auditing is all about.

By working closely with management and stakeholders at the conclusion of the audit to discuss improvement options, possibly using a facilitated workshop approach, a much better outcome can be achieved. After all, the people doing the job know a lot more about it than the internal auditor!

CASE STUDY

It is not difficult to turn a compliance audit into a performance audit. In fact, almost every audit can also be an operational or performance audit. And, by being creative, internal auditors can make their internal audit work more interesting and satisfying.

This case study comes from an internal audit conducted in a utilities company that provides electricity, gas, and water to the community. In this company, field staff work overtime. (Overtime is time worked beyond an established limit: i.e., hours worked in excess of the working hours prescribed in the employment agreement.)

The objectives of the audit were to:
- determine who had responsibility for overtime and assess whether this arrangement was working effectively;
- identify the key risks involved with overtime and the mitigation strategies and controls currently in place to manage those risks;
- identify the extent of overtime worked and test whether the key controls were working effectively to manage the identified risks;
- ascertain whether overtime requirements were being effectively communicated to managers and staff;
- review whether management regularly received and acted on feedback on the need for overtime and periodically examined cost-effective alternatives.

The audit covered all the regular auditing matters such as compliance with policy and procedures, sampling and testing overtime calculations, etc., as you would expect in a compliance audit. Since it found that overtime payments were being made correctly in accordance with policies and procedures, the audit was a nonevent. But, with some extra work, analysis of the data showed that:
- most overtime was worked in the electricity division;
- overtime was being worked by around a third of employees, with the number of employees who worked overtime increasing;
- the overall amount of overtime had been steadily increasing in absolute and payroll percentage terms across the organization over the previous four years;
- the electricity and water divisions had overtime budgets for the next year that were below the budgets for the current year (almost certainly optimistically).

Analysis of the causes revealed that:
- there was a countrywide shortage of line workers, resulting in the electricity division being unable to recruit sufficient numbers of people with these skills;
- the electricity division pole replacement program was difficult to run with the number of line workers currently employed by the organization;
- a serious wildfire had destroyed substantial electricity assets.

Once the causes had been identified, the audit recommendations suggested that the organization consider such things as:
- developing a longer-term perspective when formulating future industrial plans for the workforce;
- extending human resources employee self-service to the field employees;
- extending mobile computing to the field for human resources activities and job costing;
- further annualizing salaries to include an overtime component;
- changing the rostering of work crews to true shift work arrangements over 24/7/365.

This added real value to the audit, rather than being a simple compliance audit approach—which would have merely reported that overtime calculations were being made correctly.

Best Practice

CONCLUSION

With a bit of creativity, it is not too difficult to include a value-adding element in a compliance or financial audit:

- Almost every audit can also be an operational or performance audit.
- You can do operational and performance auditing to provide added value to your organization.
- Including an operational or performance auditing element in your audits can enhance the image of auditing with the people being audited and with management.
- You can increase your job satisfaction through operational and performance auditing.

MAKING IT HAPPEN

- Develop an engagement model for your internal auditing, and get management buy-in.
- Closely align your internal auditing with the business, plan a risk-based internal audit program developed with management, and aim to become an integral part of the organization in order to help management improve the business.
- Plan each internal audit with management, and facilitate an up-front risk assessment with management and stakeholders at the commencement of each internal audit—this is a quick and cost-effective way to determine the business processes, risks, and control procedures in place, as well as getting management buy-in.
- Ask management to agree and sign off the terms of reference for each internal audit—be sure that the objectives of an operational or performance audit are insightful and are not just throwaway lines.
- Consider using experts in technical subject areas where internal audit may not have all the skills required for an internal audit.
- Measurement criteria need to be developed; this is much more difficult than a compliance or financial audit and needs to be objective, understandable, comparable, complete, and acceptable.
- Learn the difference between "hard controls" (existence of policies and procedures, documents, payment approvals, segregation of duties, etc.) and "soft controls" (focus on ethics, integrity, competency, relationship building), and learn how to audit soft controls.
- Go outside the organization to get information and consult with external stakeholders.
- Keep the audit focused and timely; if not properly managed, operational and performance audits can take on a life of their own and can end up taking a long time to complete.
- Engage and communicate with management throughout the internal audit.

- Convene a peer review challenge session within internal audit for the draft report; also do this for service providers who perform internal audits for you.
- Get the report "as right as it can be" before taking a draft to management.
- Facilitate a workshop with management and stakeholders at the conclusion of the audit to discuss and agree possible improvement options.

MORE INFO

Books:

Reding, Kurt F., Paul J. Sobel, Urton L. Anderson, Michael J. Head, *et al. Internal Auditing: Assurance and Consulting Services*. 2nd ed. Orlando, FL: IIA Research Foundation, 2009.

Sawyer, Lawrence B., Mortimer A. Dittenhofer, and James H. Scheiner. *Sawyer's Internal Auditing: The Practice of Modern Internal Auditing*. 5th ed. Altamonte Springs, FL: IIA Research Foundation, 2003.

Standards:

Institute of Internal Auditors. "International standards for the professional practice of internal auditing." October 2010. Online at: tinyurl.com/7qdspr4

Websites:

Australian National Audit Office (ANAO): www.anao.gov.au
Institute of Internal Auditors (IIA): www.theiia.org
International Organization of Supreme Audit Institutions (INTOSAI): www.intosai.org
Office of the Auditor-General of Canada: www.oag-bvg.gc.ca

Training Courses and Postgraduate Qualifications:

Institute of Internal Auditors. "Performance based auditing in the public sector." Details online at: tinyurl.com/7dec2nr
Institute of Internal Auditors. "Operational auditing: An introduction through advanced." Details online at: tinyurl.com/86gmema
University of Canberra. "Graduate certificate in performance audit and evaluation." Details online at: tinyurl.com/7ergrx7

See Also:

Procedures for Reporting Financial Risk in Islamic Finance

by Daud Vicary Abdullah and Ramesh Pillai

EXECUTIVE SUMMARY

- Uncertainty is a defining feature of the economic environment. Economic agents' perceptions of risk, together with their willingness and ability to bear it, fundamentally shape decisions, transactions, and market prices. Well-considered decisions should be based on information that helps to highlight existing risks and uncertainties. An important component of the information system of an organization or economy is financial reporting, through which an enterprise conveys information about its financial performance and condition to external users, often identified with its actual and potential claimants. It stands to reason, therefore, that financial reporting should provide a good sense of the impact of those risks and uncertainties on measures of valuation, income, and cash flows.
- It is important to reconcile the perspectives of accounting standard–setters on the one hand, and prudential authorities on the other, on what information should be reported, and on how it should be portrayed. The final goal is a financial reporting system that is consistent, as far as possible, with sound risk management and management practices and that can serve as a basis for well-informed decisions by outside investors as well as prudential authorities.
- Outside investors, be they equity or debt holders, would normally require certain information about the financial performance of a firm so as to guide their decisions. First, they would surely wish to form a view about the firm's past and current profitability, solvency, and liquidity at a given point in time. Second, they would probably also like to develop a picture of the risk profile of those attributes over time and, hence, of their potential future evolution. Third, they might additionally wish to gain a sense of how reliable or accurate those measures are. Combined, these three elements would provide the raw material to inform views about expected returns properly adjusted for risk and for the inevitable uncertainties that surround measurement. These three types of information correspond to the key categories into which the ideal set can be divided—namely, first movement, risk, and measurement error—and they are equally applicable to financial reporting in an Islamic finance environment.

INTRODUCTION

The key elements of Islamic finance can be summarized as follows.

- Materiality and validity of transactions: there is no profit sharing without risk taking, and earning profit is legitimized by engaging in economic venture. Money is not a commodity but a medium of exchange, a store of value, and a unit of measurement.

- Mutuality of risk sharing: clearly defined risk and profit sharing characteristics serve as an additional built-in mechanism. There are clearly laid out terms and conditions.
- Avoidance of *riba* (interest), *maysir* (gambling), and *gharar* (uncertainty).

The key elements of Islamic financial risk can be summarized as follows.

- The reporting of financial risk in an Islamic financial institution (IFI) requires greater transparency and disclosure than its conventional counterpart.
- This is particularly true with respect to additional *shariah* governance and some risk areas that are unique to Islamic finance.
- IFIs have greater fiduciary duties and responsibility to their stakeholders than conventional institutions.
- The additional duties and responsibilities of IFIs are overseen by the IFI's *shariah* board.

First-movement information describes income, the balance sheet, and cash flows at a point in time. It is the type of information with the longest tradition by far in accounting.

Risk information is fundamentally forward-looking. Future profits, future cash flows, and future valuations are intrinsically uncertain. Risk information is designed to capture the prospective range of outcomes for the variables of profit as measured at a particular point in time.

Measurement error information designates the margin of error or uncertainty that surrounds the measurement of the variables of profit, including those that quantify risk. The need for this type of information arises whenever these variables have to be estimated. For instance, measurement error would be zero for first-movement information concerning items that were valued at observable market prices for which a deep and liquid market existed. However, it would be positive if, say, such items were marked to model and/or traded in illiquid markets, since a number of assumptions would need to be made to arrive at such estimates.

There has been a wide array of change and development in Islamic finance in recent years. The Accounting and Auditing Organization for Islamic Financial Institutions (AAOIFI) has tackled several of the pertinent issues in its Financial Accounting Standards (FAS). In particular, FAS 1 relates to general presentation and disclosure in the financial statements of Islamic banks and financial institutions. FAS 5 relates to the disclosure of bases for profit allocation between owners' equity and investment account holders. FAS 17 concerns investment. FAS 22 and FAS 23 deal with segment reporting and consolidation, respectively. AAOIFI Governance Standards 1–6 also provide relevant guidance. In particular, Governance Standard 6, Principles of Governance Section 7, gives guidance in respect of risk management.

Understanding Islamic Banking Risk

IFIs are exposed to all the risks that a conventional one is. However, there are some fundamental differences, particularly in the aspect of *shariah* compliance, where noncompliance can lead to reputational risk and worse.

Typical banking risk exposure includes the following:
- *financial:* balance sheet, capital adequacy, credit, liquidity;
- *operational:* fraud, product, business services, system failure, delivery, and process management;
- *business:* country, reputational, regulatory, legal, macropolicy;
- *event:* political, banking crisis, contagion.

BASIC RISK ANALYSIS

Ratios and analytics are in a constant state of evolution in order to reflect the growing challenges of Islamic finance and the constant stream of new products. In particular, the convergence of international supervisory standards, initiated by the Islamic Financial Services Board (IFSB) since its inauguration in 2002, have contributed to this developing landscape. Typical ratios relate to liquidity, capital adequacy, insider and connected financing, financing portfolio quality, large exposures, and foreign exchange positions.

Peer group benchmarking is a relevant measurement criterion. Here, the behavior of an individual institution can be measured against peer-group trends and industry norms. Significant areas such as profitability, product risk, the structure of the balance sheet, and capital adequacy come to mind. Any significant deviations of the individual institution from what is considered to be the norm must be investigated and understood, as they may well represent an early warning for negative trends in both the IFI and the industry.

What's Different in an IFI?

Islamic contracts and the allocation and sharing of risk. The analysis described above should also include the nature of the Islamic contracts included in the balance sheet and a basic understanding of how the risk is allocated or shared. Therefore a fundamental understanding of the IFI's balance sheet is required.

Liabilities. These include equity capital, reserves, investment accounts (*mudarabah* and *musharakah*) and demand deposits (*amanah*). Money is deposited in investment accounts in the full knowledge that the deposit will be invested in a risk-bearing project, where the profit will be divided between the institution and the depositor on a prearranged profit-sharing ratio. The depositor is also exposed to the risk of loss if the projects invested in do not perform. In many ways these types of deposit have a similarity with an equity investment in the bank, and it is this lack of clarity between shareholders and investors/depositors that can lead to a perception of increased riskiness. IFSB and AAOIFI guidelines have provided significant help in clarifying this issue.

Assets. These include short-term trade finance (*murabahah* and *salam*), medium-term financing (*ijara, istisna*, etc.), long-term partnerships (*musharakah*) and fee-based services (*kifala*, etc.).

These asset and liability contracts carried in the balance sheet of an Islamic financial intermediary give a clear indication of two fundamental differences between Islamic financial intermediaries and their conventional counterparts. First, the relationship between the depositors and the bank is based on profit and loss sharing principles; and second, the asset side of the bank may include "risky" assets such as *mudarabah* and *musharakah* that a conventional bank may not carry.

KEY ELEMENTS OF GOOD CORPORATE GOVERNANCE

Good corporate governance is defined by the set of relationships between the institution's senior management, its board, its shareholders, and other stakeholders.
- Corporate strategy defines how success can be measured.
- Responsibilities include assignment and enforcement.
- Strong financial risk management should be independent of the business, with good internal control and separation of duties.
- Good values and a code of conduct should be well articulated and maintained, especially in the area of related parties.
- Proper incentives must be consistent with objectives, performance, and values.
- The roles of stakeholders must be clearly set out.

The Roles of Stakeholders
- Regulators monitor the statutory environment and help to create an enabling environment.
- *Shariah* boards protect the rights of all stakeholders in accordance with the principles of *shariah*.
- The board of directors sets the direction of the bank and ensures its soundness.
- The executive management executes the direction of the board and has sufficient competence and knowledge to manage the financial risks.
- The board audit committee and internal audit are logical extensions of the board's risk management function. They assist executive management in identifying and managing risk areas.
- External auditors are responsible for validating the results and providing assurance that appropriate governance processes are in place.
- Market participants should accept responsibility for their own investment decisions. They therefore need transparent disclosure of information from financial institutions.
- Shareholders can appoint officers in charge of the governance process, subject to appropriate screening on related party transactions.

THE ROLE OF *SHARIAH*

Shariah boards are unique to IFIs. They have a responsibility to monitor the activities of the financial institution and to ensure compliance with *shariah* principles. As such, the *shariah* board acts as a governance body to protect the rights of the stakeholders in the IFI.

In some jurisdictions, national *shariah* boards have been formed, which work closely with regulators and supervisors in protecting the rights of all investors.

TRANSPARENCY AND DISCLOSURE

Practices in IFIs have improved significantly in recent years, but there is still room for improvement in a number of areas.

- Quantitative methods for the measurement of risk still need improvement. AAOIFI is driving changes in this area.
- The decisions and methodology of the *shariah* boards should be disclosed more publicly. This will enhance the credibility of IFIs and also help to educate the public on the *shariah* decision-making process.
- There needs to be a clear demarcation between equity and depositors' funds.
- The financial information infrastructure requires constant improvement to ensure that a "virtuous cycle" of information continually forces practitioners to adopt sound corporate governance practices.
- Standardized reporting practices throughout IFIs would significantly assist in improving the collectability and analysis of data from them.

CONCLUSION

There are many similarities between conventional and Islamic risk management, as well as some significant differences, which have been highlighted above. The risk management process itself in an IFI does not differ much from conventional banking practices. However, it is the analysis and the identification of the risk environment that differ.

The balance sheet of the IFI needs to be structured in a way that will allow the easy identification of risk, particularly in the area of sources of funding and in the application of those funds for financing purposes.

The role of the *shariah* board is significant in protecting the rights of all stakeholders and ensuring that the business of the IFI is conducted in accordance with the principles of *shariah*.

MAKING IT HAPPEN

Good financial risk management is about changing behaviors and attitudes. Boards and executive management are responsible for setting the implementation process, and regulators are responsible for creating a conducive environment. For example:

- the board must set the direction;

- regulators must ensure a supportive environment that encourages transparency and good market discipline, thereby creating a virtuous cycle;
- the market must value good financial discipline and risk management and must reward compliant companies accordingly;
- all stakeholders must recognize their responsibilities.

MORE INFO

Books:

Greuning, Hennie Van, and Sonja Brajovic Bratanovic. *Analysing and Managing Banking Risk: A Framework for Assessing Corporate Governance and Financial Risk Management.* Washington, DC: World Bank, 2000.

Karim, Rifaat Ahmed Abdel, and Simon Archer (eds). *Islamic Finance: The Regulatory Challenge.* Singapore: Wiley, 2007. See in particular Sundararajan, V. "Risk characteristics of Islamic products: Implications for risk measurement and supervision," pp. 40–68.

Article:

Grais, Wafiq, and Zamir Iqbal. "Corporate governance challenges of Islamic financial Institutions." Paper presented at the Seventh Harvard University Forum on Islamic Finance, 2006.

Websites:

Accounting and Auditing Organization for Islamic Financial Institutions (AAOIFI): www.aaoifi.com

Islamic Financial Services Board (IFSB): www.ifsb.org

Professional Risk Managers' International Association (PRMIA): www.prmia.org

See Also:

★ Introduction to Islamic Financial Risk Management Products (pp. 23–27)
★ Investment Risk in Islamic Finance (pp. 27–31)
★ Risk Management of Islamic Finance Instruments (pp. 48–53)
✔ Managing Risk in Islamic Finance (pp. 297–298)

Starting a Successful Internal Audit Function to Meet Present and Future Demands

by Jeffrey Ridley

EXECUTIVE SUMMARY

- Starting an internal audit function requires a clear and inspiring vision to provide the right direction for its success.
- The services provided by the internal audit role must add value and meet the needs of all its customers, at every level

in the organization. This demands a wealth of knowledge and experience of governance, risk management, and control processes in the function.
- The internal audit charter approved at board level must state the professional standards expected from all staff in the function.

- Internal auditors in the function should be trained to ask the right questions and advise on the impact of present and future change at all levels in the organization, from strategic to operational.
- Quality of performance in the function and its continuous improvement requires a total commitment, measured and reported at board level through key performance indicators, and feedback from its customers.
- The function should contribute to implementation of quality policies in the organization it serves by using its own experience of achieving performance quality.

INTRODUCTION

In 1998 on the occasion of the fifty-year celebration of the establishment of the Institute of Internal Auditors (IIA)'s five chapters in the United Kingdom, I wrote:[1]

"We need to be seen as innovators in the world of regulation, control and auditing. Creativity, innovation and experimentation are now key to our professional success. They must be the vision of all internal auditing functions. This means improving old and developing new products and services for delighted customers, with a focus on their objectives. This means being at the leading edge in all the markets in which we sell our internal auditing services. This means beating our competitors and knowing who these are. This means having the imagination, and foresight into what our organizations will require from us, not just in the year 2000, but also in 2005 and beyond.

In this 50th year celebration of our national institute's past and present teamwork, all IIA—UK [and Ireland] members should continue to set their sights on being inventors of an improved and new internal auditing, to delight all their customers ... and increase its status as an international profession."

Establishing a successful internal audit function requires more than just support and resources approved at board and senior management levels; or an external requirement by government and regulators; or encouragement by external auditors. These are all important drivers and influences for creating the function and setting the boundaries in which it will operate and provide services. But the present and future demands of a successful function require a clear and inspiring vision for the direction of its services, which can only be provided by those who work in the function. It demands their knowledge and experience of risk management, control, and governance processes; their professionalism; their imagination, innovation, and creativity to manage change in what is and will be required from their services. All these attributes are needed if these service providers are to delight all their customers by the quality of their performance. They are needed whether internal auditing is resourced by staff in-house, outsourced, or co-sourced.

CLEAR AND INSPIRING VISION

A vision statement is key to the mission of any organization or function. In 1991 Richard Whitely wrote some inspirational words on vision statements:[2]

- A good vision leads to competitive advantage.

- One way to define vision is ... a vivid picture of an ambitious, desirable state that is connected to the customer and better in some important way than the current state.
- How does this vision represent the interests of our customers and values that are important to us?
- A vision has two vital functions, and they're more important today than ever before. One is to serve as a source of inspiration. The other is to guide decision-making, aligning all the organization's parts so that they work together.
- If your vision is not an impetus to excellence, then it has failed.
- When a company clearly declares what it stands for and its people share this vision, a powerful network is created—people seeking related goals.
- Constantly communicate your vision for your organization to those who work with you and for you. Don't let a day go by without talking about it.

This advice has not dated. It can be seen in many vision statements used by organizations today and will be tomorrow. An inspirational vision for internal auditing in an organization can have a significant impact on those who provide and receive the service. It should be aligned with its organization's vision, creating direction for all its resources, promotion, planning, engagements, and reporting. From the vision should flow the strategic mission of the internal audit role and its business plan, which will set the scene for the resources needed for its achievement. Following the creation of an internal auditing vision statement, all internal auditing staff and senior management should be involved in its development. Seek total organization commitment and board approval for its direction. That direction will set the scene for the services it will provide.

KNOWLEDGE AND EXPERIENCE OF GOVERNANCE, RISK MANAGEMENT, AND CONTROL PROCESSES

No internal audit function can be successful unless it is expert in the principles and practices of management, governance, risk management and control in the sector in which it works and across the supply chains developed by its organization. This expertise demands not only knowledge of what these processes require but also an understanding of the principles on which they are based, experience of how they operate at all levels within an organization, and how they are reported to all stakeholders. This expertise has to be at the management level of internal auditing and with all internal auditors.

Successful organizations assess and manage their economic, environmental, and social risks, mitigating these through appropriate strategies and controls. Successful internal audit functions focus on this corporate social responsibility and its "triple bottom line"[3] in all their engagements—across the entire range of an organization's strategies, policies, processes, and reporting. In many organizations internal auditing is seen as a facilitator in the assessment and management processes addressing these risks. To be successful today, the planning of internal audit engagements and the conducting of assurance and consulting reviews must always be linked to risks and controls in an organization's "triple bottom line."

In 1991, the US Committee of Sponsoring Organizations (COSO) published its integrated control framework exposure draft. This became its risk and control guidance for management and auditors worldwide, published in 1992.[4] Its five integrated elements of "*control environment, risk assessment, control activities, monitoring, and information and communications*" are basic requirements in all risk and control processes. It defines control as a process "designed to provide reasonable assurance regarding the achievement of [effectiveness and efficiency of operations] objectives." Importance of the COSO control elements and key concepts is significant for the mitigation of risks. These have been adopted as best practices by many regulators and organizations. Their importance is even more evident today as organizations embed risk management in their processes, from strategy setting to the achievement of objectives at every level in every operation.

In 2004[5] COSO further developed its framework into an Enterprise Risk Management (ERM) model providing further guidance for the management of risk and control across all levels of an organization. Based on its 1992 control framework, this model demonstrates the importance of embedding each of the 1992 integrated framework elements in the strategic, operations, reporting, and compliance decision-making processes across the whole enterprise. Understanding the description of each of the elements in the ERM model is a good test for management and all auditors in any organization. Such understanding is essential for internal audit success.

The IIA Inc. (2006),[6] in its overview of organizational governance, discusses the internal auditors' role, recommending that "they act as catalysts for change, advising or advocating improvements to enhance the organization's governance structure and practices." Possible steps for the internal auditor to be successful in an organization's governance processes are seen as [*my comments in brackets*]:

1 Review all the relevant internal and external audit policies, codes, and charter provisions, pertaining to organizational governance. [*Look for the key words and phrases about governance.*]

2 Discuss organizational governance with executive management or members of the board. The objective of these discussions is to ensure internal auditors have a clear understanding of the governance structure and processes from the perspective of those responsible for them, as well as the maturity of these processes. [*In these discussions relate direction and control in the organization to the achievement of its vision, mission, and key objectives.*]

3 Discuss options for expanding the role of internal auditors in organizational governance with the board chair, board committee chairs, and executive managers. These discussions could involve explaining the potential actions internal auditors could take and the resources required, as well as the possibility of an assurance gap between the board's assurance requirements and the organization's practices, if internal auditors did not assist in this area. Ensure the internal audit charter is consistent with the expanded role being considered. [*Consider providing education programs on governance for all board, management, and employee training programs.*]

4 Discuss organizational governance topics with other key stakeholders including external auditors and employees of the organization's departments such as legal, public affairs corporate secretary office, compliance, and regulatory affairs. During these discussions, explore their current and future activities as well as how an expanded internal audit role could coordinate with their activities. [*This should also be in every internal audit, not only in the organization but also across all its external relationships.*]

5 Develop a broad framework of the organization's governance structure by identifying potential areas of weakness and concern. [*A real opportunity to be creative in thinking and design.*]

6 Draft a multi-year plan to develop the internal audit role in organization governance areas methodically. [*Another opportunity to be creative.*]

7 Perform a pilot audit in one of the areas noted above. Select a single, well-defined, manageable topic and assess the adequacy of the design and execution of the activities related to the topic. Performing a pilot audit will allow the internal auditor a chance to gauge the organization's response to his or her expanded role and learn how to coordinate more effectively with other stakeholders. [*This should only be the start. It should lead the internal auditor along many paths in many different dimensions.*]

Note how these recommendations link in to the guidance for success in this article.

PROFESSIONALISM

Professional attributes and performance requirements for internal auditing are clearly set out in the IIA's International Standards for Professional Practice of Internal Auditing.[7] These *Standards* and their supporting guidelines have been continuously developed internationally since the 1970s. They represent and are recognized as "best practice" internal auditing and will continue to be revised by international teams to reflect both the needs of internal auditors and the organizations in which they provide their services. All internal auditing charters should require the internal audit role to comply with these standards: not all do! Yet every board would expect its external auditors to comply with developed international standards for external auditing. Why should internal auditing be different?

The *Standards* set out requirements and guidance for internal auditing attributes and performance of work. All are based on defined principles of *Integrity*, *Objectivity*, *Confidentiality*, and *Competency* in its *International Code of Ethics*, first published in 1968 and since revised to meet current and future internal auditing needs for all its members and those who have achieved the status of its qualification *Certified Internal Auditor*.[8]

MANAGING CHANGE

All operations in an organization have a past, a present, and a future. This must be recognized in the planning of all internal auditing services and in each of its engagements. What has happened before and what is happening today will influence what will happen in the future. What happens in the future will also be influenced by more change, not only in the organization but also externally, by many of its stakeholders and events beyond its control. Every test and observation in an internal audit engagement needs to be considered in this scenario of past, present, and future change. Future change is change that can be forecast during the engagement, and change that might be hinted at by events leading to "beyond the horizon." Beyond the horizon is not always an easy prediction to make, but it should be attempted by the internal auditor studying events and issues surrounding the operations being reviewed, and in discussion with board members and management at all levels.

QUALITY OF PERFORMANCE

To be successful an internal audit function must have a total commitment to the quality of its performance and continuous improvement. This is a requirement of the IIA *Standards*. Such commitment will be strongly influenced by its collective knowledge, experience of governance, risk management and control; its professionalism of service; and its ability to question change in the past, present, and future. This can be seen in the cutting-edge internal auditing framework in the figure, developed within the chapters of my book *Cutting Edge Internal Auditing*.[9]

In Figure 1, each of the directional lines demonstrates an importance in the management of internal audit. Each touches and influences the quality of performance in an internal audit function:

- The horizontal line represents the level of knowledge and experience of risk management, control, and governance in the function across the organization's supply chains—supplier through operations to customers, related today to economic, social, and environmental issues and risks. The wider the line the better the service provided by the function and greater the impact on the vertical and diagonal lines and the quality of its performance.
- The vertical line represents the compliance of the function with the IIA International Standards. The deeper the line, the better the compliance and greater the impact on the horizontal and diagonal lines and the quality of its performance.
- The diagonal line represents the function's ability to question change across time past, present, and future, and into beyond the horizon. The wider the line, the greater the involvement of the function in the organization's risk management processes; and the greater the impact on the horizontal and vertical lines and the quality of its performance.

A total commitment to quality by the staff in the function can create opportunities for it to contribute to the organization's quality culture. Gupta and Ray[10] show that "internal auditors can leverage their knowledge of business processes and play

Figure 1. Cutting-edge internal auditing framework

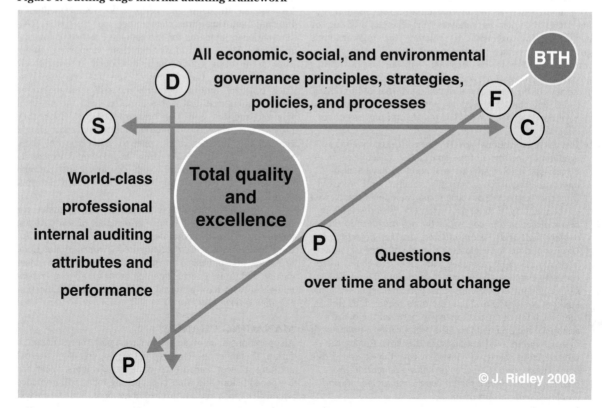

an active role in the development and implementation of [the] Total Quality Improvement process." Their research describes the complete range of quality management tools and techniques used by organizations to implement and measure quality improvement programs showing how a knowledge of these and experience in their use can improve an internal audit activity's services and processes. Their research identifies seven steps (Table 4-22, p. 104) to be undertaken to implement Total Quality Improvement in internal auditing:

1 Development of Mission and Vision Statements and establishing internal audit department objectives.
2 Establishment and implementation of performance measures for various stages of the internal auditing process.
3 Identification of customers of internal auditing departments.
4 Development and implementation of internal auditing customer satisfaction surveys and feedback systems.
5 Benchmarking with other internal auditing departments.
6 Introspective self-analysis.
7 TQM training and education of the internal auditing staff.

Note how these steps have been woven into the guidance in this article for establishing a successful internal audit function to meet present and future needs for all its customers.

MAKING IT HAPPEN

Starting a successful internal auditing function requires a chief audit executive who is experienced in the implementation of professional internal auditing processes and has a full understanding of the principles and practices of management, government, risk management and control. That experience and knowledge must be used to educate the board and senior management in the role that internal auditing should assume to add best value to the organization. That role should be written into a charter, approved at board level, showing its purpose, authority, and responsibility. Once established, the internal auditing function should:

- create an inspiring vision linked to its aimed success;
- develop a plan to achieve its vision, focused on adding value;
- employ and train competent qualified professional staff;
- focus all its engagements on changes in the past, present, future, and beyond the horizon;
- report its findings on a timely basis to appropriate management and the board;
- continuously measure and improve the quality of its services and delight its customers.

CASE STUDY
SCOPE AND TYPES OF WORK IN SUCCESSFUL INTERNAL AUDIT FUNCTIONS[11]

The scope of internal auditing covers all the activities of an organization, without regard for internal boundaries or geographical restrictions. It encompasses the adequacy and effectiveness of governance, risk management, and internal control processes in identifying and responding to all the risks facing the organization. The following are examples of the different types of work that internal audit may undertake:

- giving assurance to the board that the organization's risks have been properly identified and managed in accordance with the approved risk appetite;
- reviewing the activities undertaken by management to implement the ethical policy across the whole organization;
- giving assurance that business continuity and disaster recovery planning, including for mission-critical information systems, are adequate given the risks facing the organization and the risk appetite;
- giving assurance that the purchase process includes adequate controls to ensure agreed levels of competitiveness, cost savings, and quality performance;
- assisting the management team in evaluating the actual return on investments over a given period of time;
- carrying out an internal audit to verify an organization's compliance with labor laws and regulations;
- giving assurance that measures are properly designed and working effectively to address health, safety, and environmental risks on industrial sites;
- verifying that all purchase and sales contracts comply with the organization's policies;
- giving an opinion on the efficiency and effectiveness of the customer complaints process;
- providing advice to management on the design and implementation of risk management processes.

Consider

- How many of these examples of types of work exist in your internal audit function?
- Have you promoted all of these services in your internal audit charter?

MORE INFO
Websites:

Chartered Institute of Internal Auditors (UK and Ireland): www.iia.org.uk
Committee of Sponsoring Organizations of the Treadway Commission (COSO): www.coso.org
European Confederation of Institutes of Internal Auditing (ECIIA): www.eciia.org
Global Reporting Initiative (GRI): www.globalreporting.org
Institute of Internal Auditors (IIA): www.theiia.org

See Also:

★ Aligning the Internal Audit Function with Strategic Objectives (pp. 63–66)
★ Best Practices in Corporate Social Responsibility (pp. 175–179)
★ Incorporating Operational and Performance Auditing into Compliance and Financial Auditing (pp. 97–100)

NOTES

1 Ridley, J. "IIA—UK celebrates 50th." *Internal Auditing* (March 1998): 12.

2 Whiteley, Richard C. *The Customer-Driven Company: Moving from Talk to Action*. London: Basic Books, 1991, pp. 21, 26–28, 32, 37.

3 *Sustainability Reporting Guidelines* 2000–2006.

4 Committee of Sponsoring Organizations. *Internal Control—Integrated Control Framework*. New York: American Institute of Certified Public Accountants, 1992.

5 Committee of Sponsoring Organizations. Enterprise Risk Management—Integrated Framework, New York: American Institute of Certified Public Accountants, 2004.

6 *Organizational Governance: Guidance for Internal Auditors*. Altamonte Springs, FL: Institute of Internal Auditors, 2006.

7 The Institute of Internal Auditors (IIA). *International Standards for the Professional Practice of Internal Auditing*. Altamonte Springs, FL: 2009.

8 See the IIA website (www.theiia.org) for details of this and other internal auditing qualifications.

9 Ridley, Jeffrey. *Cutting Edge Internal Auditing*. Chichester, UK: Wiley, 2008.

10 Gupta, Parveen P., and Manash R. Ray. *Total Quality Improvement Process and the Internal Audit Function*. Altamonte Springs, FL: IIA Research Foundation, 1995.

11 *Internal Auditing in Europe—Position Paper*. Brussels: European Confederation of Institutes of Internal Auditors, 2005.

What Are the Leading Causes of Financial Restatements?

by Todd DeZoort

EXECUTIVE SUMMARY

- Financial restatements are serious corporate reporting failures that have the potential to undermine stakeholder confidence and decisions.

- The quality of corporate governance, risk management, and compliance systems is critical in controlling financial restatement risk within organizations.

- The number of financial restatements increased consistently after the Sarbanes–Oxley Act until 2007, when the number and magnitude of restatements started to decrease.

- The research literature in accounting and finance provides useful evidence about the leading causes of financial restatements, including accounting complexity, transaction complexity, human error, and fraud.

- The effects of restatements are widespread and contingent on the cause of the restatement. Possible restatement effects include negative market reactions, reduced credit access, and turnover within management and the board of directors.

INTRODUCTION

Both the International Accounting Standards Board (IASB) and the Financial Accounting Standards Board (FASB) in the United States highlight the importance of "reliability" as a primary qualitative characteristic necessary to make accounting information useful to users making economic judgments and decisions. Reliability in this context refers to a quality of financial reporting that makes it a verifiable, faithful representation of transactions and events that have occurred within an organization.[1]

Financial restatements represent reporting failures where companies admit that previous financial representations are not reliable. Such reporting failures have various potential causes and effects that can undermine company health and raise questions about the expertise and integrity of individuals that affect reporting, operations, and compliance. In the post-Sarbanes–Oxley era, financial report users (for example, investors, creditors, analysts) have seen an explosion in the number of restatements, giving rise to questions about why so many companies find it difficult to produce accurate information.

UNDERSTANDING FINANCIAL RESTATEMENT TRENDS

Companies face daunting challenges when compiling financial reports that users rely on when making economic decisions. For example, managers preparing financial reports work in highly competitive business environments where they face: complex business transactions; the need to comply with complex accounting rules, regulations, and laws; pressure to control reporting and compliance costs; and powerful incentives to report results in the best possible light. Given the diversity and magnitude of these challenges, huge emphasis has been placed on the importance of quality governance, risk assessment, and compliance (GRC) systems to help companies achieve their objectives and ensure accountability among key players in the financial reporting process.

Financial restatements must be made when financial GRC systems fail and companies file annual or quarterly reports that are not in conformity with generally accepted accounting principles (GAAP). Companies filing misstated financial statements must restate and correct previous reported results. For example, US public companies that file inaccurate reports are required to provide a formal restatement announcement in 8-K filings with the Securities and Exchange Commission (SEC).[2] Further, the SEC highlights that "the restatement process, which may take longer than 12 months, imposes significant costs on investors as well as preparers. During that

Figure 1. Number of restatements in the United States 2001–07. (*Source*: Audit Analytics, 2008)

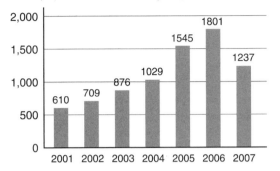

process, companies often go into a 'dark period' and issue very little financial information to the public."[3] Some companies attempt to avoid alarming users by providing "stealth restatements" that are disclosed in quarterly or annual reports without formally filing an 8-K.

Although restatement numbers in the United States increased prior to 2000, the passage of the Sarbanes–Oxley Act of 2002 (SOX) prompted a dramatic increase in the number of financial statements filed each year. The Act (for example, Section 404 on internal controls) created significant focus on the quality of financial governance by management, audit committees, internal auditors, and external auditors.

Interestingly, Figure 1 indicates that the number of financial restatements in the United States dropped in 2007 for the first time since the passage of the SOX, although over 1,200 restatements were still filed. The recent decrease in number of restatements has been accompanied by recent decreases in the average number of issues per restatement and the average income effect. For example, Table 1 reveals that the average income decrease per restatement in 2005 was over US$21.3 million; in 2006 the average income decrease was US$17.8 million. In 2007, the average income decrease dropped to only US$3.6 million.

Table 1. Restatement characteristics. (*Source*: Audit Analytics, 2008)

	Average income effect	Average number of issues	Average restatement period
2005	– US$21.33 million	2.41	746 days
2006	– US$17.81 million	1.97	710 days
2007	– US$3.64 million	1.87	643 days

These trends raise questions about whether financial reporting is actually improving or whether regulators are simply becoming more lenient in their approach.

CAUSES AND EFFECTS OF RESTATEMENTS
The causes of financial restatements vary considerably across cases. However, the accounting research literature (for example, Plumlee and Yohn, 2008; Scholz, 2008) and existing restatements highlight a number of potential causes of restatements, including:

- Complexity of accounting standards and/or transactions. Although there is a growing push to emphasize principles-based standards, companies in the United States still face demands related to rules from an array of authoritative bodies. GAAP involve hundreds of rules provided by IASB for most countries and FASB in the United States.
- Weak financial governance and controls. Contemporary corporate governance frameworks highlight the importance of management, the board of directors/audit committee, internal auditors, and external auditors in ensuring financial reporting reliability. Weak governance and internal controls over financial reporting increase the likelihood of financial reporting failure and restatement.
- Increased auditor and audit committee conservatism. The SOX created a number of new demands on auditors and audit committees. Increased regulation, scrutiny, and legal exposure for auditors and audit committees increase their motivation to be conservative and revisit management's judgments when evaluating financial reporting and specific accounting issues.
- Broad application of materiality. The SEC Advisory Committee on Improvements in Financial Reporting expressed concern that restatements result from overly strict materiality assessments where restatements occur to correct misstatements that investors might not find important.
- Earnings management. Management faces tremendous pressure to meet or beat expectations established by various groups (for example, analysts, directors). GAAP provide a great deal of opportunity for earnings management (for example, in areas related to depreciation, reserves, asset valuation) that is subject to abuse that can lead to restatement.
- Lack of transparency. In complex reporting environments, companies often fail to provide disclosures that are complete and understandable in compliance with GAAP. For example, footnotes that fail to provide clear, sufficient descriptions of company activities and policies undermine financial reporting reliability.
- Fraud. The largest frauds are due to financial reporting schemes where individuals intentionally misstate companies' financial statements.

Plumlee and Yohn (2008) conducted an empirical study of over 3,700 restatements during the period 2003–06, to identify the leading causes of financial restatements. They classified restatement causes as due to either a basic company error, an intentional manipulation, a transaction complexity, or some characteristic of an accounting standard. Their results revealed that over half of the restatements analyzed during the four-year period were due to "basic internal company errors" rather than to the complexity of the transaction or accounting standard.[4]

A closer look at prominent causes of restatements reveals a wide variety of accounting problems, including (but certainly not limited to) expense recognition, revenue recognition, misclassification in financial statements (for example, cash flows), executive compensation (for example, stock options), valuation of estimates (for example, liabilities, reserves), and business combinations (for example, mergers, acquisitions) and reorganizations.

While not necessarily causal, the research literature also provides evidence that highlights a variety of factors that are associated with financial restatements. Research indicates a positive link between short-term incentive compensation (for example, bonuses, stock options) for officers and audit committee members and the likelihood of restatements.[5] Such findings raise critical questions about the use and nature of incentive compensation for management and directors to motivate behavior in the interests of shareholders.

The effects of financial restatements are difficult to pinpoint precisely given the difficulty in controlling for other events (for example, company, industry) that affect companies during the period when restatements occur. However, the research literature provides some overall insights into the types of effects that restatements can have. For example, investors react negatively when their companies announce financial restatements. Studies consistently show a negative market reaction around restatement dates, although evidence suggests that the strength of the reaction depends on a variety of factors (for example, restatement cause, issue).[6] Further, market reactions appear to be less severe in the post-SOX era than they were pre-SOX, suggesting that markets have become more "comfortable" with the restatement environment.

Beyond capital market responses, restatements have the potential to affect companies' efforts to secure credit, with evidence suggesting that restatements are associated with higher interest rates and stricter borrowing terms for restating companies.[8] The research literature also links restatements (and restatement effect on income) to turnover in top management and the board of directors. For example, Srinivasan (2005) finds a positive relation between the magnitude of income-reducing annual restatements and the likelihood of independent director turnover.

CASE STUDY
SAFETY-KLEEN CORPORATION

Safety-Kleen is a North American waste management company that issued a major financial restatement in 2001. In 2000, the company's board of directors initiated an investigation of possible accounting fraud within the company. The next year, Safety-Kleen restated (reduced) previously reported net income by US$534 million for the period 1997–99.[7] The restatement issues included:

- Improper revenue recognition involving contingent contract claims, property sales, and other contingent revenue.
- Inappropriate recognition of gain on derivatives transactions. Safety-Kleen management violated GAAP by inappropriately using cash generated by derivatives transactions to increase interest income and to reduce interest and other operating expenses.
- Inappropriate capitalization and deferral of operating expenses, including capitalizing payroll expenses related to marketing and start-up activities, software development and implementation costs, and repair and maintenance expenses for company trucks.
- Inappropriate reserve and accrual accounting. Company management increased earnings by reducing certain reserve

account balances without sufficient justification. It also reversed certain payroll expense accruals that had been made to account for bonuses that were paid.

In the week surrounding the announcement of Safety-Kleen's investigation, the company's stock price dropped over 70% and its auditor, PricewaterhouseCoopers, withdrew its financial statement audit reports for the previous three years. The company also saw analysts' company recommendations downgraded and its credit ratings reduced and eventually removed by some agencies. Safety-Kleen filed for Chapter 11 (reorganization) bankruptcy in 2000, and underwent a formal SEC investigation and ruling, and several class action lawsuits from external stakeholders.

CONCLUSION

Financial restatements are reporting failures that have a variety of potential causes and effects on markets, organizations, and individuals. Though the number of restatements has been declining in recent years after steady growth post-SOX, a number of events create questions about what the number and nature of restatements will look like in the future. For example, the SEC's Advisory Committee on Improvements to Financial Reporting developed recommendations to consider alternative approaches to assessing materiality to reduce the number of "unnecessary" restatements that investors do not seem to care about. Alternatively, the impending shift to International Financial Reporting Standards in the United States will likely provoke a new wave of restatements because of confusion and abuse related to the transition from the current rules-based approach to accounting and reporting using a more principles-based approach. Ultimately, stakeholders interested in minimizing financial restatement risk need to invest heavily in GRC frameworks that prioritize financial reporting reliability.

MAKING IT HAPPEN

Managing the risk of financial restatements requires strong commitment to a long-term focus on financial reporting governance and internal controls. These processes should prioritize active involvement among a variety of internal and external stakeholder groups that collaborate to address key questions in the area. For example:

- Is financial restatement risk evaluated formally within the company? If so, who is involved in the risk assessment? Explicit periodic restatement risk assessment should include the audit committee, management, internal audit, and external audit.
- What are the key financial restatement risks within the company and industry? Does the organization have a plan for managing the consequences of financial restatements if they occur?
- Are cutting-edge GRC frameworks and practices being implemented around a culture of integrity and expertise to ensure that the design and operation of internal controls over financial reporting are effective?

MORE INFO

Articles:

Archambeault, Deborah S., F. Todd Dezoort, and Dana R. Hermanson. "Audit committee incentive compensation and accounting." *Contemporary Accounting Research* 25:4 (Winter 2008): 965–992. Online at: dx.doi.org/10.1506/car.25.4.1

Graham, John R., Si Li, and Jiaping Qiu. "Corporate misreporting and bank loan contracting." *Journal of Financial Economics* 89:1 (July 2008): 44–61. Online at: dx.doi.org/10.1016/j.jfineco.2007.08.005

Srinivasan, Suraj. "Consequences of financial reporting failure for outside directors: Evidence from accounting restatements and audit committee members." *Journal of Accounting Research* 43:2 (May 2005): 291–334. Online at: dx.doi.org10.1111/j.1475-679x.2005.00172.x

Reports:

Audit Analytics. "Financial restatements: A seven year comparison." February 2008. For purchase online at: www.auditanalytics.com

Audit Analytics. "Financial restatements and market reactions." March 2008. For purchase online at: www.auditanalytics.com

Glass, Lewis & Co. "Restatements: out of sight, out of mind." May 30, 2008. Available from Glass, Lewis & Co. by subscription from: www.glasslewis.com

Government Accountability Office. "Financial restatements: Update of public company trends, market impacts, and regulatory enforcement activities." 2007. Online at: www.gao.gov/new.items/d06678.pdf

Plumlee, M., and T. L. Yohn. "An analysis of the underlying causes of restatements." Working paper, 2008. Online by search at: www.ssrn.com

Scholz, S. "The changing nature and consequences of public company financial restatements 1997–2006. Department of the Treasury, 2008. Online at: www.imanet.org/pdf/USTR.PDF

Securities and Exchange Commission. "Final report of the Advisory Committee on Improvements to Financial Reporting to the United States Securities and Exchange Commission." 2008.

See Also:

★ Effective Financial Reporting and Auditing: Importance and Limitations (pp. 81–83)

✔ International Financial Reporting Standards (IFRS): The Basics (pp. 316–317)

NOTES

1 Financial Accounting Standards Board. FASB Concepts Statement No. 2, "Qualitative characteristics of accounting information," May 1980.

2 The SEC requires companies to file form 8-K to report the occurrence of material events and changes (for example, bankruptcy, change in control of the company, change of audit firm, change in the board of directors).

3 SEC Advisory Committee on Improvements to Financial Reporting. *Final Report of the Advisory Committee on Improvements to Financial Reporting to the United States Securities and Exchange Commission*, August 1, 2008, p. 6.

4 Plumlee, M., and T. L. Yohn. "An analysis of the underlying causes of restatements." Working paper, March 1, 2008.

5 Archambeault *et. al.* (2008).

6 Bhattacharyya, A. "Time for us to consider restatements." *Business Standard (New Delhi)* (February 25, 2008).

7 United States General Accounting Office (GAO). *Financial Statement Restatements: Trends, Market Impacts, Regulatory Responses, and Remaining Challenges*. Washington, DC: GAO, October 2002.

8 Graham *et. al.* (2008).

Acquiring a Secondary Listing, or Cross-Listing
by Meziane Lasfer

EXECUTIVE SUMMARY

- Over the last three decades an increasing number of companies have sourced their equity capital in foreign countries by listing their stock abroad.
- This strategy of parallel listing on both domestic and foreign stock exchanges, referred to as "cross-listing," is used by companies from both developed and emerging markets.
- In 2008, for example, 121 companies from BRIC countries (Brazil (7), Russia (24), India (24), and China (66)) were listed on the London Stock Exchange Alternative Investment Market (LSE-AIM), an equivalent to NASDAQ in the United States.
- Although the major stock markets for cross-listing are in the United States (NYSE and NASDAQ) and London (LSE and LSE-AIM), with a 43% market share in 2007, firms are also likely to cross-list in other markets of the world, such as the Singapore, Euronext, Hong Kong, and Mexico stock exchanges.
- According to the Bank of New York Mellon, during the first half of 2008 more than US$2.4 trillion of depository receipts (DRs) traded on US and non-US markets and exchanges, up 85% from the previous year.

INTRODUCTION

Cross-listing is controversial and raises a number of academic and practitioner questions, particularly: Why and how does a firm cross-list, and does cross-listing create additional value for existing stockholders? The purpose of this article is to discuss the institutional framework of cross-listing, the classification of depository receipts (DRs), the types of DR available in the United States, the reasons why companies list abroad (by contrasting the advantages and disadvantages of raising equity capital in foreign markets), and the cross-listing process.

INSTITUTIONAL BACKGROUND

Companies cross-list by issuing depository receipts. These are certificates that are first issued by the company to a bank in a foreign country, which in turn issues the certificates to investors in that country. Indirectly, DRs represent ownership of home market shares in the overseas corporation. The underlying shares remain in custody in the home country, and DRs effectively convey ownership of those shares. DRs are quoted and normally pay dividends in the foreign country's currency (for example, US dollars or euros). DRs can be established either for existing shares that are already trading, or as part of a global offering of new shares. Each DR normally represents some multiple of the underlying share. This multiple allows the DR to possess a price per share that is appropriate for the foreign market, and the arbitrage normally keeps foreign and local prices of any given share the same after adjustment for transfer costs. DRs can be exchanged for the underlying foreign shares, and vice versa.

CLASSIFICATIONS OF DEPOSITORY RECEIPTS

There are a number of classifications of depository receipts, two of which are:

- Trading location: Global depository receipts (GDRs) are certificates traded outside the United States; American depository receipts (ADRs) are certificates traded in the United States and denominated in US dollars.
- Sponsorship: A sponsored ADR is created at the request of a foreign firm that wants its shares to be traded in the United States. In this case, the firm applies to the Securities and Exchange Commission (SEC) and to a US bank for registration and issuance. In contrast, an unsponsored ADR occurs when a US security firm initiates the creation of an ADR. Such an ADR would be unsponsored, but the SEC still requires all new ADRs to be approved by the firm itself.

TYPES OF LISTING

In the United States there are four types of depository receipt: Levels 1 and 2 apply to cases where the DR is created using existing equity; Levels 3 and 4 apply to cases where new equity is issued, such as an initial public offering (IPO).

Level 1 is the least costly, as the DRs are traded over the counter in the United States, in the pink sheet market. There is little additional disclosure requirement, apart from the translation of the home country's financial statements into English. On average, about 56% of the approximately 1,500 DR programs are classified as Level 1.

Level 2 is relatively more costly. The DRs are traded on the NYSE, NASDAQ, and AMEX exchanges, with greater cost as the initial fee can exceed US$1 million. A cross-listed firm must also reconcile to US GAAP, report quarterly, and meet the listing requirements of the US exchange on which it trades.

Level 3 is similar to Level 2 for existing quoted companies, except that it applies to IPOs; the firm raises new equity capital in a public offering and trades on the NYSE, NASDAQ, or AMEX. A company must meet full SEC disclosure requirements, comply with US GAAP, report quarterly, and meet the listing requirements of the exchange.

Level 4, now referred to as 144A, applies to firms that raise new equity capital through a private placement. The securities are not registered for sale to the public; rather, investors follow a buy and hold strategy. Firms that use this method are exempt from disclosure requirements of a new equity issue in the United States, such as the SEC disclosure and the US GAAP. In April 1990 the SEC approved Rule 144A, which permits qualified institutional buyers to trade privately placed securities without SEC registration. These securities are traded on a screen-based automated trading system known as PORTAL, established to create a liquid secondary market for those private placements.

In other countries, the requirements depend mainly on the type of markets in which the company is going to be cross-listed. For example, requirements to list on the London Stock

Exchange Official List are more extensive than those for the Alternative Investment Market.

The choice between listing in the United States (ADR) and in other markets through GDR depends on a number of factors. In particular, companies are likely to prefer listing in the United States through ADRs only if their objective has a powerful appeal to US retail investors and they are able to cover the significant cost of Sarbanes–Oxley compliance and major exposure to liability for management and board of directors. ADRs are also useful if they can benefit by selling new shares at a premium. Cross-listing through GDR may be cheaper and quicker, and could achieve the same purpose with fewer downsides. For example, cross-listing in the London Stock Exchange involves two main rounds, where the firm receives comments from the UK Listing Authority (UKLA) in about two weeks. Furthermore, since July 2005, the UKLA no longer requires 25% of GDR issues to be distributed to European investors.

As an alternative to depository receipts, companies can have "Euroequity public issue." Under this method, instead of listing a share on the home market and then cross-listing, shares are issued simultaneously in multiple markets. The term Euroequity has nothing to do with Europe per se. Euroequity public issue simply refers to equity issues that are sold globally. Often these are used for very large equity issues, and different tranches are sold in different markets.

WHY DO COMPANIES CROSS-LIST?
In general, companies cross-list when the size of their financial needs exceeds their domestic market capacity. There is a limited liquidity in the domestic market, and the price of stock may be more attractive in a foreign market, especially if there is market segmentation and DRs offer diversification benefits to investors. The existing domestic investors also benefit, since cross-listing is likely to mitigate the agency conflicts with their managers. A company becomes more visible internationally, and the share prices are likely to be more efficient (known as price discovery), because trading happens in two or more markets and more financial analysts follow the cross-listing. However, some costs make cross-listing less attractive. This section provides a summary of the benefits and costs of cross-listing.

Benefits of Cross-Listing
The most widely cited benefit is the reduction in the cost of capital. Cross-listing is likely to reduce the cost of capital, because in close domestic markets the efficient frontier is determined only by the set of domestic assets. Therefore, the equity cost of capital depends on the risk premium of the domestic market portfolio. However, if the firm is cross-listed it can reach foreign investors who will be able to invest in both foreign and domestic firms, and the market risk premium will be lower because the level of diversification that investors can attain in an open capital market is far greater. As a result, a cross-listed firm's cost of capital will be lower. Karolyi (1998) reports that the cost of capital of UK cross-listed firms in the United States decreases by 2.64%, from 15.56% before to 12.91% after cross-listing. The market reaction is also positive when the firm announces the decision to list abroad.

However, it is not clear whether the market reacts positively because of the decrease in the cost of capital or whether it is driven by one or more of the additional benefits of cross-listing. These are:
- Improved liquidity of existing shares and broadening of the stockholder base, with, as a result, a reduced probability of takeovers.
- Establishment of a secondary market for shares used in acquisitions.
- An increase in the firm's visibility and political acceptability to its customers, suppliers, creditors, and host governments.
- Creation of a secondary market for shares that can be used to compensate local management and employees in a foreign subsidiary.
- The recently developed bonding hypothesis, which suggests that managers will adhere to stricter regulatory regimes when their firm is cross-listed, because they will face the regulation and corporate governance codes of their home country as well as the foreign market.

Costs of Cross-Listing
The positive market reaction to cross-listing could also reflect the trade-off between the benefits of cross-listing discussed above and some potential costs, namely disclosure costs. In cross-listing and selling equity abroad, a firm faces two barriers: an increased commitment to full disclosure and a continuing investor relations program. Non-US firms must think twice before cross-listing in the United States. Not only can the disclosure requirements be onerous, but timely quarterly information is also required by US regulators and investors. Costs are likely to be higher for firms that have been accustomed to revealing far less information.

MAKING IT HAPPEN
Over the last few years, an increasing number of firms have listed their shares in foreign markets. The decision to cross-list is strategic and involves the following issues:
- Where to cross-list: Companies can go to the United States and issue American depository receipts (ADRs), or to other non-US stock exchanges by issuing global depository receipts (GDRs).
- The choice of a particular market depends on a number of factors. In particular, the firm needs to know whether its stock is attractive to US investors, and whether it can comply with all the requirements of listing, including stronger information disclosure, before it issues ADRs.
- A firm also needs to understand the reasons for cross-listing before issuing depository receipts. The most fundamental is often financing needs, and the inability of the firm to cover this from the domestic market.
- In general, cross-listing leads to an increase in share prices on the announcement date. Such market reactions are likely to be driven by a number of factors, including a reduction in the cost of capital, a wider geographical range of stockholders, an increase in visibility and financial analysts' coverage, and the adoption of stricter corporate governance codes.

MORE INFO

Articles:

Baker, H. Kent, John R. Nofsinger, and Daniel G. Weaver. "International cross-listing and visibility." *Journal of Financial and Quantitative Analysis* 37:3 (September 2002): 495–521. Online at: dx.doi.org/10.2307/3594990

Coffee, John C., Jr. "Racing towards the top? The impact of cross-listings and stock market competition on international corporate governance." *Columbia Law Review* 102:7 (November 2002): 1757–1831.

Dobbs, Richard, and Marc H. Goedhart. "Why cross-listing shares doesn't create value." *The McKinsey Quarterly* (November 2008). Online at: tinyurl.com/6xonzo

Doidge, Craig, G. Andrew Karolyi, and René M. Stulz. "Why are foreign firms listed in the U.S. worth more?" *Journal of Financial Economics* 71:2 (February 2004): 205–238. Online at: dx.doi.org/10.1016/S0304-405X(03)00183-1

Doidge, Craig, G. Andrew Karolyi, and René M. Stulz. "Has New York become less competitive in global markets? Evaluating foreign listing choices over time." Working paper 13079. National Bureau of Economic Research, May 2007. Online at: www.nber.org/papers/w13079

Karolyi, G. Andrew. "Why do companies list their shares abroad? A survey of the evidence and its managerial implications." *Financial Markets, Institutions and Instruments* 7:1 (February 1998): 1–60. Online at: dx.doi.org/10.1111/1468-0416.00018

Karolyi, G. Andrew. "The world of cross-listing and cross-listings of the world: Challenging conventional wisdom." *Review of Finance* 10:1 (January 2006): 99–152. Online at: dx.doi.org/10.1007/s10679-006-6980-8

Korczak, Adriana, and Meziane A. Lasfer. "Does cross listing mitigate insider trading?" Working paper, Cass Business School, City University, London, 2009.

Leuz, Christian. "Cross listing, bonding and firms' reporting incentives: A discussion of Lang, Raedy and Wilson (2006)." *Journal of Accounting and Economics* 42:1–2 (October 2006): 285–299. Online at: dx.doi.org/10.1016/j.jacceco.2006.04.003

Leuz, Christian. "Was the Sarbanes–Oxley Act of 2002 really this costly? A discussion of evidence from event returns and going-private decisions." *Journal of Accounting and Economics* 44:1–2 (September 2007): 146–165. Online at: dx.doi.org/10.1016/j.jacceco.2007.06.001

Licht, A. N. "Cross-listing and corporate governance: Bonding or avoiding?" *Chicago Journal of International Law* 4 (Spring 2003): 141–164. Online at: cjil.uchicago.edu/past-issues/spr03.html

Pagano, Marco, Ailsa A. Roell, and Josef Zechner. "The geography of equity listing: Why do companies list abroad?" *Journal of Finance* 57:6 (December 2002): 2651–2694. Online at: dx.doi.org/10.1111/1540-6261.00509

Sarkissian, Sergei, and Michael J. Schill. "The overseas listing decision: New evidence of proximity preference." *Review of Financial Studies* 17:3 (Fall 2004): 769–810. Online at: dx.doi.org/10.1093/rfs/hhg048

Websites:

Bank of New York Mellon press releases 2008: www.bnymellon.com/pressreleases/2008/pr071408b.html

Crosslisting.com: crosslisting.com

London Stock Exchange: www.londonstockexchange.com

Open University learning module on cross-listing: tinyurl.com/84tudrj

US Securities and Exchange Commission: www.sec.gov

See Also:

Assessing Venture Capital Funding for Small and Medium-Sized Enterprises

by Alain Fayolle and Joseph LiPuma

EXECUTIVE SUMMARY

• Entrepreneurs and small and medium-sized enterprise (SME) managers capitalize their firms with debt equity investments, or a combination of both.

• Equity investments such as venture capital can erode executive control but can enable access to the investor's knowledge, advice, and networks.

• Venture capital can be provided by business angels, independent venture capital firms (IVCs[1]), corporations, or universities.

• The sources' differing investment objectives, backgrounds, and control mechanisms deliver varying levels of added value to the SME.

• Companies seeking venture capital should select investors whose objectives, potential to add value, and expectations of control mesh most closely with those of the entrepreneur.

INTRODUCTION

Entrepreneurs and SME managers face two key choices when financing their ventures: debt or equity. Debt in the form of personal loans (including credit cards) and bank loans, key sources for most nascent ventures, gives efficient incentives for managers to exert effort and allow entrepreneurs to maintain control. The availability and utility of debt vary significantly with economic conditions, which, in turn, will have an impact on the supply and cost of capital. To a lesser extent, entrepreneurs rely on equity financing,[2] in which parties external to a venture obtain partial ownership (and control) in exchange for financial capital, thus diluting managers' incentives to expend effort. Equity financing is particularly important for high-growth ventures, since the amount of debt financing available may not permit sufficiently rapid growth in volatile industries (for example, technology). Objectives and incentives that are well aligned between investor and manager are the most efficient and facilitate additional value for the venture.

VENTURE CAPITAL

Venture capital (VC) refers to independently managed, dedicated pools of capital which the providers channel into equity or equity-linked investments in privately held, high-growth companies.[3] Worldwide, more than US$30 billion is invested annually as venture capital,[4] with the most intensive use in the United States, Europe, and Israel (with US$28 billion, US$6 billion, and US$0.7 billion invested respectively in 2007).[5] Venture capital represents a bundle of productive, value-adding resources, comprising the human capital (knowledge and experience) and social capital (network) of the venture capitalist—who oversees the investment—in addition to the financial capital. The value and productivity of these nonfinancial aspects of VC can be significant, influencing a venture's offering, geographic diversity, and growth. Venture capitalists can help to professionalize a new venture through representation on the board of directors, executive recruiting, or by exerting rights of control (over, for example, cash flow and liquidation) in exchange for capital. Despite modest levels of investment,[6] venture capital-backed companies[7] accounted for over ten million jobs and US$1.8 trillion in revenue in the United States in 2003[8]—approximately one-sixth of GDP.

Venture capital can come from business angels, independent VC firms (IVCs), corporate venture capital (CVC) programs, and universities. The different ways in which

these are funded, investments are managed, and partners are compensated (see Table 1[9]) result in varying allocations of control rights between the investor and the venture. Angel investors, for example, rarely require representation on corporate boards, whereas IVCs generally do seek directorships. Investment objectives influence the nature of companies in which VCs invest and, correspondingly, the value they are able to add. Independent VC firms invest solely for financial reasons and may best add value to SMEs by helping them to recruit key executives or access additional capital. Corporations that provide CVC often invest for strategic reasons, frequently in ventures with complementary offerings. These corporations are generally multinational, enabling them to add more value in the development of foreign networks of customers, suppliers, and partners. However, CVC investors generally do not invest in early-stage ventures, usually waiting until an IVC invests before committing their resources.

SELECTING THE RIGHT TYPE OF VC

Though only a small percentage of companies receive venture capital,[10] those that do can usually choose its source and should therefore select investors whose objectives, added-value potential, and expectations of control are most in accord with those of the business owner. Since the process of pitching ventures to investors and negotiating terms can be time-consuming, especially for SMEs and young ventures, it is crucial to establish your objectives and target VC sources early on. This may also help to avoid later contract issues, optimize venture capitalist contributions, and increase the venture's value. Questions to consider are:

What stage are we at? At the seed or startup stage, angel financing is best because it comes with fewer strings attached and is easier to "buy out." Angel investors are good stewards and may take active, informal roles in the company. Corporations generally do not invest at early stages, so IVC is most likely at the next stage, with CVC most used in expansion stages.

How big a VC provider do you need? While this answer often depends on capital needs, prestigious or "big name" IVC providers bring broad and helpful networks, in addition to status, that can help when exiting via a public offering or acquisition. However, prominent VCs often require more control over cash flow, voting, board representation, and

Table 1. Characteristics of the different providers of venture capital

	Angel	IVC	CVC	UVC
Typical background	Ex-entrepreneur	Ex-entrepreneur or financial	Large, tech-savvy multinational	Patent holder
Motivation	Financial and "giving back"	Financial	Strategic and financial	Commercialize patents
Fund source	Self	Limited partners	Corporate	University, government
Investment method	Direct	Direct	Direct and indirect	Direct and indirect
General partner compensation	Gain from exit or early buyout	Percentage of valuation increase	Salary plus bonus	Salary plus bonus
Average invested per venture	~US$10,000[a]	~US$8 million[b]	~US$4.5 million[c]	< US$250,000[d]

a Allen, Kathleen A. *Launching New Ventures: An Entrepreneurial Approach*. Boston, MA: Houghton Mifflin Company, 2006.

b PricewaterhouseCoopers/National Venture Capital Association. "MoneyTree™ report." Data: Thomson Reuters.

c *Ibid.*

d Miles, Morgan P., John B. White, and Eve White. "University sponsored venture capital: An exploratory study." *Journal of Business and Entrepreneurship* 13:1 (2001): 129–134.

★

Best Practice

liquidation. Such rights are often contingent on observable performance measures. If the venture does badly, VCs obtain more control, whereas if the venture does well, VCs relinquish most control and liquidation rights.

Do I need a specialized VC provider with specific industry knowledge and contacts? Industry specialization helps VC firms to develop skills for vetting and selecting investments, and for developing relevant industry knowledge and networks. Generalist firms are able to thrive and grow as industries evolve and ebb, and they have cross-industry experience and networks that may benefit nascent ventures.

How much capital do we need, and what do we need the funds for? If funds are needed for initial technology development, CVC, with the associated corporate technology knowledge, may provide access to technical skills. In addition to supplying capital of their own, IVCs are good at helping companies in which they invest to obtain access to other funds because of their legitimacy and the networks they have.

Are we planning to enter foreign markets? The VC industry is globalizing,[11] and since VC providers tend to invest in ventures that are geographically proximate, there is limited foreign investment. In addition, some VC providers tend to eschew investments in internationalized ventures, since they cannot easily monitor their activities. CVC associated with a multinational enterprise may provide foreign market knowledge and assist in market penetration, and permit access to foreign customers, suppliers, and partners who can help to monitor the internationalized venture.

How vulnerable is my intellectual property? Working with a VC provider requires an exchange of detailed information about development projects, product specifications, and marketing plans. Corporations often invest for strategic reasons based on industry or market congruity with new ventures. Such congruity suggests that the investor could easily appropriate the intellectual property of the SME. Research suggests that receiving investments from multiple corporations may limit that risk.

CASE STUDY
TESSERA ENTERPRISE SYSTEMS
Tessera Enterprise Systems, a custom software developer, was founded in Boston in 1995 by an executive team that had previously worked together for three years. Tessera's target market included some of the largest American retail and financial companies, such as Eddie Bauer and Charles Schwab. The founders provided initial funding for the venture, but after one year it was decided that venture capital was required to expand the company. Tessera, however, secured an investment offer from Greylock Management, a prominent Boston-based IVC. Greylock's status added legitimacy to the fledgling venture, permitting it to obtain contracts with target companies such as Charles Schwab, Eddie Bauer, and other prominent clients. Subsequent expansion and third-stage funding from two other prominent IVCs solidified Tessera in the market and led to a corporate expansion to San Francisco. At the same time, Tessera considered establishing an office in Switzerland to serve potential European clients. One of the VC

providers likened internationalization to loading an airplane with stacks of cash and opening the doors while flying over the Atlantic.

Tessera nevertheless pursued its foreign market entry strategy and, while it slowly obtained some European contracts, it did so without the involvement or aid of its IVC investors. Had Tessera sought investment from a technology corporation such as Oracle (on whose products its offerings were often based), it might have been better able to leverage its investor's networks and knowledge to the benefit of its foreign business. A modest capital round was provided by IVCs and a private investor in preparation for an exit. Tessera, originally planning on a public offering and broad foreign expansion, was acquired in 2001 by iXL, an Atlanta-based internet services provider company with offices in San Francisco and London.

MAKING IT HAPPEN
Since VC has the potential to change the nature of resources in an SME so dramatically, entrepreneurs must approach it with a strategic view of how it may best add value, and source it accordingly. At the same time as they assess their financial capital needs, SME managers should do the following:

- Carefully consider the type of advice, information, and network access you want from an investor in the light of current needs and strategic direction.
- Identify VC providers that have great reputations for providing value in a manner consistent with your willingness to cede some control.
- Ask others who have undertaken VC-backed ventures about their experience with investors—both IVC and CVC—and the success and problems they encountered.
- Identify companies that had exits—IPOs and acquisitions—most consistent with your goals and ask about their investors.

CONCLUSION
SMEs and young ventures that receive capital investments can often choose their source. The boundary-spanning role of investors, as both advisers and links to external networks, places VCs in a unique position to add value to a venture. The potential for investors to aid in the growth and development of such ventures demands that entrepreneurs and SME managers make their choice in a considered manner that is consistent with their overall strategy. Careful consideration of investor types can lead to an efficient selection process that provides value throughout the life of the venture.

MORE INFO
Books:
Gompers, Paul A., and Josh Lerner. *The Venture Capital Cycle*. Cambridge, MA: MIT Press, 1999.
Maula, M., and G. C. Murray. "Corporate venture capital and the creation of US public companies: The impact of sources of venture capital on the performance of portfolio companies."

In Michael A. Hitt, Raphael Amit, Charles E. Lucier, and Robert D. Nixon (eds). *Creating Value: Winners in the New Business Environment*. Oxford: Blackwell Publishing, 2002.

McNally, Kevin. *Corporate Venture Capital: Bridging the Equity Gap in the Small Business Sector*. London: Routledge, 1997.

Articles:

Maula, Markku V. J., Erkko Autio, and Gordon C. Murray. "Corporate venture capitalists and independent venture capitalists: What do they know, who do they know and should entrepreneurs care?" *Venture Capital* 7:1 (January 2005): 3–21. Online at: dx.doi.org/10.1080/1369106042000316332

Sapienza, Harry J., Allen C. Amason, and Sophie Manigart. "The level and nature of venture capitalist involvement in their portfolio companies: A study of three European countries." *Managerial Finance* 20:1 (1994): 3–17. Online at: dx.doi.org/10.1108/eb018456

Smith, Gordon. "How early stage entrepreneurs evaluate venture capitalists." *Journal of Private Equity* 4:2 (Spring 2001): 33–45. Online at: dx.doi.org/10.3905/jpe.2001.319981

Van Osnabrugge, Mark, and Robert J. Robinson. "The influence of a venture capitalist's source of funds." *Venture Capital* 3:1 (January 2001): 25–39. Online at: dx.doi.org/10.1080/13691060117288

Websites:

National Venture Capital Association (NVCA): www.nvca.org

European Private Equity and Venture Capital Association (EVCA): www.evca.eu

See Also:

★ Financial Steps in an IPO for a Small or Medium-Size Enterprise (pp. 126–128)

★ Understanding Equity Capital in Small and Medium-Sized Enterprises (pp. 164–169)

✔ Steps for Obtaining Bank Financing (pp. 333–334)

NOTES

1   We wish to emphasize that the acronym "IVC" here refers to formal venture capital investments by independent firms specialized for this purpose. Other literature uses "IVC" to refer to informal venture capital investments.

2   For example, in the United States fewer than 7% of companies obtain outside equity financing, whereas 45% take on outside debt (Robb, Alicia, and David T. Robinson. "The capital structure decisions of new firms: Second in a series of reports using data from the Kauffman firm survey." Kansas City, MO: Kauffman Foundation, 2008). New Zealand businesses are almost six times more likely to seek additional debt financing than equity financing (www.stats.govt.nz), whereas nearly 20 times more Canadian companies sought debt financing than equity financing (www.sme-fdi.gc.ca).

3   Gompers and Lerner (1999).

4   Ernst & Young. "Transition: Global venture capital insights report 2006."

5   PricewaterhouseCoopers/National Venture Capital Association. "MoneyTree™ report." Online at: www.pwcmoneytree.com/MTPublic/ns/index.jsp. Data: Thomas Reuters (accessed March 5, 2009); www.evca.com; and www.investinisrael.gov.il respectively.

6   From 1999 to 2002, less than 0.5% of GDP was invested via venture capital in the United States (OECD report).

7   This includes those that are now public companies, such as Intel, Microsoft, eBay, and Home Depot.

8   Global Insight. "Venture impact 2004: Venture capital benefits to the U.S. economy." June 2004. Online at: tinyurl.com/89x6vcx [PDF].

9   Note that this table is based on examples from the United States. In Europe, for example, research institutes often take the place of universities in conducting research and formulating approaches to the commercialization of intellectual property.

10   For example, in the United States fewer than 0.1% of all companies founded in the 1990s received venture capital (authors' analysis of US data from the NVCA). In Europe, the probability of receiving VC is approximately 0.07% (Achtmann, Eric. "Getting a view of VC in Europe… from the centre." 4th Annual MIT VCPI Conference, Cambridge, MA, December 1, 2001).

11   See, for example: Hall, Graham, and Ciwen Tu. "Venture capitalists and the decision to invest overseas." *Venture Capital* 5:2 (2003): 181–190. Online at: dx.doi.org/10.1080/1369106032000097058; and Manigart, Sophie, Veroniek Collewaert, Mike Wright, Sarika Pruthi, *et al.* "Human capital and the internationalization of venture capital firms." *International Entrepreneurship and Management Journal* 3:1 (March 2007): 109–125. Online at: dx.doi.org/10.1007/s11365-006-0021-0

Asset Allocation Methodologies
by Tom Coyne

EXECUTIVE SUMMARY

• Asset allocation is both a process and a collection of methodologies that are intended to help a decision-maker to achieve a set of investment objectives by dividing scarce resources between different alternatives.

• Theory assumes that asset allocations are made in the face of risk, where the full range of possible future outcomes and their associated probabilities are known. In the real world this is rarely the case, and decisions must be made in the face of uncertainty.

• The appropriate asset allocation methodology to use, in part, depends on an investor's belief in the efficacy of forecasting. Assuming you believe that forecasting accuracy beyond luck is possible, there remains an inescapable trade-off between a forecasting model's fidelity to historical data and its robustness to uncertainty. Confidence in prediction also increases when models based on different methodologies reach similar conclusions. In fact, averaging the results of these models has been shown to raise forecast accuracy.

- The traditional methodology for asset allocation problems is mean–variance optimization (MVO), which is an application of linear programming that seeks to maximize the return for any given level of risk. However, MVO has many limitations, including high sensitivity to input estimation error and difficulty in handling realistic multiyear, multiobjective problems.

- Alternative techniques include equal weighting, risk budgeting, scenario-based approaches, and stochastic optimization. The choice of which to use fundamentally depends on your belief in the predictability of future levels of risk and return.

- Although they are improving, all quantitative approaches to asset allocation still suffer from various limitations. For that reason, relatively passive risk management approaches such as diversification and automatic rebalancing occasionally need to be complemented by active hedging measures, such as going to cash or buying options.

INTRODUCTION

Everyone has financial goals they want to achieve, whether it is accumulating a target amount of money before retirement, ensuring that a pension fund can provide promised incomes to retirees, or, in a different context, achieving an increase in corporate cash flow. Inevitably, we do not have unlimited resources available to achieve these goals. We often face not only financial constraints, but also shortages of information, time, and cognitive capacity. In many cases, we also face additional constraints on how we can employ available resources to achieve our goals (for example, limits to the maximum amount of funds that can be invested in one area, or the maximum acceptable probability of a result below some threshold).

Broadly, these are all asset allocation problems. We solve them every day using a variety of methodologies. Many of these are nonquantitative, such as dividing resources equally between options, using a rule of thumb that has worked in the past, or copying what others are doing. However, in cases where the stakes are high, the allocation problem is complicated, and/or our choice has to be justified to others, we often employ quantitative methodologies to help us identify, understand, and explain the potential consequences of different decision options. This article considers a typical asset allocation problem: how to allocate one's financial assets across a range of investment options in order to achieve a long-term goal, subject to a set of constraints.

THE CORE CHALLENGE: DECISION MAKING UNDER UNCERTAINTY

All investment asset allocation methodologies start with two core assumptions. First, that a range of different scenarios could occur in the future. Second, that investment alternatives are available whose performance will vary depending on the scenario that eventually develops. A critical issue is the extent to which a decision-maker believes it is possible to accurately predict future outcomes. Traditional finance theory, which is widely used in the investment management industry, assumes that both the full range of possible outcomes and their associated probabilities are known to the decision-maker. This is the classic problem of making decisions in the face of risk.

However, when you dig a bit deeper, you find that this approach is based on some questionable assumptions. The obvious question is: how can a decision-maker know the full range of possible future outcomes and their associated probabilities? One explanation is that they understand the workings of the process that produces future outcomes. In physical systems, and even in simple social systems, this may be true. But this is likely not to be the case when it comes to investment outcomes. Financial markets are complex adaptive systems, filled with positive feedback loops and nonlinear effects caused by the interaction of competing strategies (for example, value, momentum, and passive approaches) and underlying decisions made by people with imperfect information and limited cognitive capacities who are often pressed for time, affected by emotions, and subject to the influence of other people. An investor can never fully understand the way this system produces outcomes.

Even without such causal understanding, an investor could still believe that the range of possible future outcomes can be described mathematically, based on an analysis of past outcomes. For example, you could use historical data to construct a statistical distribution to describe the range of possible future outcomes, or devise a formula for projecting a time series into the future. The validity of both these approaches rests on two further assumptions. The first is that the historical data used to construct the distribution or time-series algorithm contain sufficient information to capture the full range of possible future outcomes. The second is that the unknown underlying process that generates the historical data will remain constant, or only change slowly over time. Over the past decade, we have seen repeated evidence that in financial markets these two assumptions are not true, for example in the meltdown of the Long Term Capital Management hedge fund in 1998, the crash of the technology stock bubble in 2001, and the worldwide financial market panic in 2008. In these cases, models based on historical data failed to identify the full range of possible outcomes, or to accurately assess the probability of the possible outcomes they identified. People will live with the consequences of these failures for years.

This is not to say that skilled forecasters do not exist, however. They certainly do. Unfortunately, it is usually easier to identify them with the benefit of hindsight (which also helps to distinguish between skill and luck) than it is to pick them in advance.

This discussion leads to an important conclusion. In the real world, asset allocators must make decisions not in the face of *risk*, but rather under conditions of true *uncertainty*, in which neither the full range of possible future outcomes nor their associated probabilities are fully known in advance. This has two critical implications. First, there is an inescapable trade-off between any forecasting model's fidelity to historical data and its robustness to uncertainty. The more carefully a model is backtested and tightly calibrated to accurately reproduce *past* outcomes, the less likely it is to accurately predict the future behavior of a complex adaptive system. Second, confidence in a forecast increases only when models based on differing methodologies (for example, causal, statistical, time-series, and judgmental forecasts) reach similar conclusions, and/or when their individual forecasts are combined to reduce the impact of their individual errors. In short, decision-making under uncertainty is much harder than decision-making under risk.

Asset Allocation: A Simple Example

Let us now move on to a more concrete, yet still simple, example to illustrate some key issues that underlie the most common asset allocation methodology in use today. Our quantitative data and results are summarized in the following table:

	Asset A	Asset B
Year 1 return	1%	3%
Year 2 return	5%	7%
Year 3 return	9%	20%
Year 4 return	5%	–5%
Year 5 return	1%	8%
Sample arithmetic mean	4.2%	6.6%
Standard error of the mean	1.5%	4.1%
Sample geometric mean	4.1%	6.3%
Sample standard deviation	3.3%	9.1%
Covariance of A and B	0.12%	
Correlation of A and B	0.41	
Asset weight	40%	60%
Expected arithmetic annual portfolio return	5.6%	
Expected portfolio standard deviation	6.1%	
Expected geometric annual portfolio return	4.9%	

Our portfolio comprises two assets, for which we have five years of historical data. In line with industry norms, we will treat each data point as an independent sample (i.e. we will assume that no momentum or mean-reversion processes are at work in our data series) drawn from a distribution which includes the full range of results that could be produced by the unknown return-generating process. As you can see, the sample mean (i.e. arithmetic average) annual return is 4.2% for Asset A and 6.6% for Asset B. So it is clear that Asset B should produce higher returns, right? Wrong. The next line of the table shows the standard error for our estimate of the mean. The standard error is equal to the sample standard deviation (which we'll discuss below) divided by the square root of the number of data points used in the estimate (in our case, there are five). Assuming that the data come from a normal distribution (that is, one in the shape of the bell curve), there is a 67% chance that the true mean will lie within plus or minus one standard error of our sample mean, and a 95% chance that it will lie within two standard errors. In our example, the short data history, along with the relatively high standard deviation of Asset B's returns, means that the standard errors are high relative to the sample means, and we really can't be completely sure that Asset A has a higher expected return than Asset B. In fact, we'd need a lot more data to increase our confidence about this conclusion. Assuming no change in the size of the standard deviations, the size of the standard error of the mean declines very slowly as the length of the historical data sample is increased—the square root of 5 is about 2.2; of 10, about 3.2; and of 20, about 4.5. Cutting the standard error in half—that is, doubling the accuracy of your estimate of the true mean—requires about a fourfold increase in the length of the data series. Considering that 20 years is about the limit of the available data series for many asset classes, you can see how this can create problems when it comes to generating asset allocation results in which you can have a high degree of confidence.

The next line in the table, the sample geometric mean, highlights another issue: As long as there is any variability in returns, the average return in a given year is not the same as the actual compound return that would be earned by an investor who held an asset for the full five years. In fact, the realized return—that is, the geometric mean—will be lower, and can quickly be approximated by subtracting twice the standard deviation squared from the arithmetic mean. In summary, the higher the variability of returns, the larger the gap will be between the arithmetic and the geometric mean.

The following line in the table shows the sample standard deviation of returns for Assets A and B. This measures the extent to which they are dispersed around the sample mean. In many asset allocation analyses, the standard deviation (also known as volatility) is used as a proxy for risk. Common sense tells you that the correspondence between standard deviation and most investors' understanding of risk is rough at best. Most investors find variability on the downside much less attractive than variability on the upside—and they like uncertainty even less than risk, which they can, or think that they can, measure. Also, when it comes to the distribution of returns, it is not just the average and standard deviation that are of interest to investors. Whether the distribution is Gaussian (normal)—that is, it has the typical bell curve shape—is also important. Distributions that are slightly tilted toward positive returns (as is the case with Assets A and B) are preferable to ones that are negatively skewed. Skewness should also affect preference for distributions with a higher percentage of extreme returns than the normal distribution (i.e. ones with high kurtosis). Preference for higher kurtosis should rise as skewness becomes more positive, and fall as it becomes more negative (i.e. as the probability of large negative returns rises). In fact, in our example, Asset B has positive skewness and higher than normal kurtosis (compared to Asset A's lower than normal kurtosis). Hence, some investors might be willing to trade off higher positive skewness and kurtosis against higher standard deviation in their assessment of the overall riskiness of Asset B. This might be particularly true when, as in the case of some hedge fund strategies, the expected returns on an investment have a distribution that is far from normal. However, many asset allocation methodologies still do not take these trade-offs into account, because they either assume that the returns on assets are normally distributed, or they assume that investors only have preferences concerning standard deviation, and not skewness or kurtosis.

Covariance and correlation

Covariance and correlation are two ways of measuring the relationship between the time series of returns on two or more assets. Covariance is found by multiplying each year's return for Asset A by the return for Asset B, calculating the average result, and subtracting from this the product of the average return for Asset A and by the average return for Asset B—or, more pithily, it is the average of the products less the product of the averages. Correlation standardizes the covariance by dividing it by the product of the standard deviation of Asset A's returns, multiplied by the standard deviation of Asset B's returns. Correlation takes a value between minus one (for returns that move in exactly opposite directions) and plus one (for returns that move exactly together). In theory, a correlation close to zero implies no relationship between the returns on the two sets of returns. Unfortunately, most people forget that correlation only measures the strength of the *linear* relationship between variables; if this relationship is *nonlinear*, the correlation coefficient will also be deceptively close to zero. Finally, covariance and correlation measure the average relationship between two return series; however, their relationship under extreme conditions (i.e. in the tails of the two return distributions) may differ from this average. This was another lesson taught by the events of 2008.

Forming a Portfolio

Let us now combine Asset A and Asset B into a portfolio in which the first has a 40% weight and the second has a 60% weight. The second-to-last row of our table shows the expected arithmetic portfolio return of 5.6% per year. This is simply the weighted average of each asset's expected return. The calculation of the expected standard deviation of the portfolio is more complicated, but it highlights the mathematical logic of diversification. The portfolio standard deviation equals the square root of the portfolio variance. The latter is calculated as follows: [(Asset A weight squared multiplied by Asset A standard deviation squared) plus (Asset B weight squared multiplied by Asset B standard deviation squared) plus (two times Asset A weight multiplied by Asset B weight times the covariance of A and B)]. As you can see, the portfolio standard deviation is 6.1%, which is less than 6.8%—the weighted average of Asset A's and Asset B's standard deviations. The cause of this result is the relatively low covariance between A's returns and B's returns (or alternatively, their relatively low correlation of 0.41). The fact that their respective returns apparently move in less than perfect lockstep with each other reduces the overall expected variability of the portfolio return. However, this encouraging conclusion is subject to two critical caveats. First, it assumes the absence of a nonlinear relationship between A's returns and B's returns that has not been picked up by the correlation estimate. Second, it assumes that the underlying factors giving rise to the correlation of 0.41 will remain unchanged in the future. In practice, however, this is not the case, and correlations tend to be unstable over time. For example, in 2008, investors discovered that despite relatively low estimated correlations between their historical returns, many asset classes shared a nonlinear exposure to a market liquidity risk factor. When liquidity fell sharply, correlations rose rapidly and undermined many of the expected benefits from portfolio diversification.

Expected Portfolio Returns

The last line in our table is an estimate of the geometric or compound average rate of return that an investor might be expected to actually realize on this portfolio over a multiyear period, assuming that we have accurately estimated the underlying means, standard deviations, and correlations and that they remain stable over time (all questionable assumptions, as we have noted). As you can see, it is less than the expected arithmetic annual return. Unfortunately, too many asset allocation analyses make the mistake of assuming that the arithmetic average return will be earned over time, rather than the geometric return. In the example we have used, for an initial investment of $1,000,000 and a 20-year holding period, this difference in returns results in terminal wealth that is lower by $370,358, or 12.5%, than the use of the arithmetic average would have led us to expect. This is not a trivial difference.

ASSET ALLOCATION: ADVANCED TECHNIQUES

The basic methodology we have just outlined can be used to calculate asset weights that maximize expected portfolio return for any given constraint on portfolio standard deviation (or other measure of risk, such as value-at-risk). Conversely, this approach can be used to minimize one or more portfolio risk measures for any given level of target portfolio return. These are all variants of the asset allocation methodology known as mean–variance optimization (MVO), which is an application of linear programming (for example, as found in the SOLVER function in an Excel spreadsheet). Although MVO is by far the most commonly used asset allocation methodology, it is, as we have shown, subject to many limitations.

Fortunately, there are techniques that can be used to overcome some, if not all, of the problems highlighted in our example. We will start with alternatives to the MVO methodology, and then look at alternative means of managing errors in the estimation of future asset class returns, standard deviations, covariances, and other model inputs.

Alternative Approaches to Portfolio Construction

The simplest alternative to MVO is to allocate an equal amount of money to each investment option. Known as the $1/n$ approach, this has been shown to be surprisingly effective, particularly when asset classes are broadly defined to minimize correlations (for example, a single domestic equities asset class rather than three highly related ones, including small-, mid-, and large-cap equities). Fundamentally, equal weighting is based on the assumption that no asset allocation model inputs (i.e. returns, standard deviations, and correlations) can be accurately forecast in a complex adaptive system.

Another relatively simple asset allocation methodology starts from the premise that, at least in the past, different investment options perform relatively better under different economic scenarios or regimes. For example, domestic and foreign government bonds and gold have, in the past, performed relatively well during periods of high uncertainty (for example, the 1998 Russian debt crisis and the more recent subprime credit crisis). Similarly, history has shown that inflation-indexed bonds, commodities, and commercial property have performed relatively well when inflation is high, whereas equities deliver their best performance under more normal conditions. Different approaches can be used to translate these observations into actual asset allocations. For example, you could divide your funds between the three scenarios in line with your subjective forecast of the probability of each of them occurring over a specified time horizon, and then equally divide the money allocated to each scenario between the asset classes that perform best under it.

When it comes to more quantitative asset allocation methodologies, research has shown that—at least in the past—some variables have proven easier to predict and are more stable over time than others. Specifically, relative asset class riskiness (as measured by standard deviation) has been much more stable over time than relative asset class returns. A belief that relative riskiness will remain stable in the future leads to a second alternative to MVO: risk budgeting. This involves allocating different amounts of money to each investment option, with the goal of equalizing their contribution to total portfolio risk, which can be defined using either standard deviation or one or more downside risk measures (for example, drawdown, shortfall, semi-standard deviation). However, as was demonstrated by the ineffective performance of many banks' value-at-risk models during 2008, the effectiveness of risk budgeting depends on the accuracy of the underlying assumptions it uses. For example, rapidly changing correlations and volatility, along with illiquid markets, can and did result in actual risk positions that were very different from those originally budgeted.

The most sophisticated approaches to complicated multi-year asset allocation problems use more advanced methodologies. For example, rather than a one-period MVO model, multiperiod regime-switching models can be used to replicate the way real economies and financial markets can shift between periods of inflation, deflation, and normal growth (or, alternatively, high and low volatility). These models typically incorporate different asset return, standard deviation, and correlation assumptions under each regime. However, they are also subject to estimation errors not only in the assumptions used in each regime, but also in the assumptions made about regime continuation and transition probabilities, for which historical data and theoretical models are quite limited.

Rebalancing Strategies

Multiperiod asset allocation models can also incorporate a range of different rebalancing strategies that manage risk by adjusting asset weights over time (for example, based on annual rebalancing, or maximum allowable deviations from target weights). When it comes to identifying the best asset allocation solution for a given problem, these models typically incorporate sophisticated evolutionary search techniques. These start with a candidate solution (for example, an integrated asset allocation and rebalancing strategy), and then run repeated model simulations to assess the probability that they will achieve the investor's specified objectives. An evolutionary technique (for example, genetic algorithms or simulated annealing) is then used to identify another potential solution, and the process is repeated until a stopping point is reached (which is usually based on the failure to find a better solution after a certain number of candidates have been tested or a maximum time limit is reached). Strictly speaking, the best solutions found using evolutionary search techniques are not *optimal* (in the sense that the word is used in the MVO approach)—meaning a unique solution that is, subject to the limits of the methodology, believed to be better than all other possible solutions. In the case of computationally hard problems, such as multiperiod, multiobjective asset allocation, it is not possible to evaluate all possible solutions exhaustively. Instead, much as for real life decision-makers, stochastic search models aim to find solutions that are robust—ones that have a high probability of achieving an investor's objectives under a wide range of possible future conditions.

ESTIMATING ASSET ALLOCATION INPUTS

A number of different techniques are also used to improve the estimates of future asset class returns, standard deviations, correlations, and other inputs that are used by various asset allocation methodologies. Of these variables, future returns are the hardest to predict. One approach to improving return forecasts is to use a model containing a small number of common factors to estimate future returns on a larger number of asset classes. In some models, these factors are economic and financial variables, such as the market/book ratio, industrial production, or the difference between long- and short-term interest rates. Perhaps the best known factor model is the CAPM (capital asset pricing model). This is based on the assumption that, in equilibrium, the return on an asset will be equal to the risk-free rate of interest, plus a risk premium that is proportional to the asset's riskiness relative to the overall market portfolio. Although they simplify the estimation of asset returns, factor models also have some limitations, including the need to forecast the variables they use accurately and their assumption that markets are usually in a state of equilibrium.

The latter assumption lies at the heart of another approach to return estimation, known as the Black–Litterman (BL) model. Assuming that markets are in equilibrium enables one to use current asset class market capitalizations to infer expectations of future returns. BL then combines these with an investor's own subjective views (in a consistent manner) to arrive at a final return estimate. More broadly, BL is an example of a so-called shrinkage estimation technique, whereby more extreme estimates (for example, the highest and lowest expected returns) are shrunk toward a more central value (for example, the average return forecast across all asset classes, or BL's equilibrium market implied returns). At a still higher level, shrinkage is but one version of model averaging, which has been shown to increase forecast accuracy in multiple domains. An example of this could be return estimates that are based on the combination of historical data and the outputs from a forecasting model.

When it comes to improving estimates of standard deviation (volatility) and correlations, one finds similar techniques employed, including factor and shrinkage models. In addition, a number of traditional (for example, moving averages and exponential smoothing) and advanced (for example, GARCH and neural network models) time-series forecasting techniques have been used as investors search for better ways to forecast volatility, correlations, and more complicated relationships between the returns on different assets. Finally, copula functions have been employed with varying degrees of success to model nonlinear dependencies between different return series.

CONCLUSION

In summary, although they are improving and becoming more robust to uncertainty than in the past, almost all quantitative approaches to asset allocation still suffer from various limitations. In a complex adaptive system this seems unavoidable, since their evolutionary processes make accurate forecasting extremely difficult using existing techniques. This argues strongly for averaging the outputs of different methodologies as the best way to make asset allocation decisions in the face of uncertainty. Moreover, these same evolutionary processes can sometimes give rise to substantial asset class over- or undervaluation that is outside the input assumptions used in the asset allocation process. Given this, relatively passive risk management approaches such as diversification and rebalancing occasionally need to be complemented with active hedging measures such as going to cash or buying options. The effective implementation of this process will require not only paying ongoing attention to asset class valuations, but also a shift in focus from external performance metrics to achieving the long-term portfolio return required to reach one's goals. When your objective is to outperform your peers or an external benchmark, it is tempting to stay too long in overvalued asset classes, as many investors painfully learned in 2001 and again in 2008.

MAKING IT HAPPEN

- Using broadly defined asset classes minimizes correlations and creates more robust solutions by reducing the sensitivity of results to deviations from assumptions about future asset class returns, which are the most difficult to forecast.
- Equal dollar weighting should be the default asset allocation, as it assumes that all prediction is impossible.
- However, there is considerable evidence that the relative riskiness of different asset classes is reasonably stable over time and therefore predictable. This makes it possible to move beyond equal weighting and to use risk budgeting. There is also evidence that different asset classes perform better under different economic conditions, such as high inflation or high uncertainty. This makes it possible to use scenario-based weighting.
- Techniques such as mean–variance optimization and stochastic search are more problematic, because they depend on the accurate prediction of future returns. Although

new approaches can help to minimize estimation errors, they cannot eliminate them or change the human behavior that gives rise to bubbles and crashes. For that reason, all asset allocation approaches require not only good quantitative analysis, but also good judgment and continued risk monitoring, even after the initial asset allocation plan is implemented.

MORE INFO

Books:

Asset Allocation:

Bernstein, William. *The Intelligent Asset Allocator: How to Build Your Portfolio to Maximize Returns and Minimize Risk.* New York: McGraw-Hill, 2001.

Darst, David M. *The Art of Asset Allocation: Principles and Investment Strategies for Any Market.* 2nd ed. New York: McGraw-Hill, 2008.

Fabozzi, Frank J., Petter N. Kolm, Dessislava A. Pachamanova, and Sergio M. Focardi. *Robust Portfolio Optimization and Management.* Hoboken, NJ: Wiley, 2007.

Ferri, Richard A. *All About Asset Allocation: The Easy Way to Get Started.* New York: McGraw-Hill, 2006.

Gibson, Roger C. *Asset Allocation: Balancing Financial Risk.* New York: McGraw-Hill, 2000.

Michaud, Richard O., and Robert O. Michaud. *Efficient Asset Management: A Practical Guide to Stock Portfolio Optimization and Asset Allocation.* 2nd ed. New York: Oxford University Press, 2008.

Swensen, David F. *Pioneering Portfolio Management: An Unconventional Approach to Institutional Investment.* New York: Free Press, 2009.

Forecasting:

Mlodinow, Leonard. *The Drunkard's Walk: How Randomness Rules Our Lives.* New York: Pantheon Books, 2008.

Osband, Kent. *Iceberg Risk: An Adventure in Portfolio Theory.* New York: Texere, 2002.

Rebonato, Riccardo. *Plight of the Fortune Tellers: Why We Need to Manage Financial Risk Differently.* Princeton, NJ: Princeton University Press, 2007.

Taleb, Nassim Nicholas. *The Black Swan: The Impact of the Highly Improbable.* New York: Random House, 2007.

Articles:

There are many academic papers on asset allocation and portfolio construction methodologies. The best single source is www.ssrn.com. SSRN is also a good source for papers on markets as complex adaptive systems by authors including Andrew Lo, Blake LeBaron, Cars H. Hommes, and J. Doyne Farmer.

Websites:

In addition to web-based tools based on mean–variance optimization, there are many vendors of more sophisticated asset allocation software. All of the following employ advanced techniques beyond simple MVO:

AlternativeSoft: www.alternativesoft.com

EnCorr: tinyurl.com/6lemmun

New Frontier Asset Allocation Suite:
    www.newfrontieradvisors.com
SmartFolio: www.smartfolio.com
Windham Financial Planner: www.windhamcapital.com

See Also:
★ Viewpoint:Investing in a Volatile Environment: A Black Swan
   Perspective (pp. 129–130)

Equity Issues by Listed Companies: Rights Issues and Other Methods
by Seth Armitage

EXECUTIVE SUMMARY
- A rights issue is a method by which a listed company can issue new shares. The principle of a rights issue is that stockholders are offered new shares in proportion to their existing holdings. If stockholders do not want to buy the new shares, they can sell their rights on the stock market.
- The main alternative issue methods are the firm-commitment offer, the private placement or placing, and the open offer. These methods have been replacing rights issues in several countries.
- The average reaction of a company's share price to firm commitments is negative, but it is positive for placements and open offers. The reaction to rights issues varies by country.
- The aim for a company is to have a smooth issue that raises the intended amount of capital for a competitive fee and at a minimum discount.

INTRODUCTION
This article is about issues of shares to investors by companies that are already listed on a stock exchange. Such issues are often called rights issues, although in fact the rights issue is only one of several issue methods used. Other methods will also be discussed here. A generic term for issues by listed companies is seasoned equity offers (SEOs).

TYPES OF OFFER
Rights Issue
The principle of a rights issue is that the company offers the new shares to its existing stockholders in proportion (pro rata) to the number of shares owned by each stockholder. In most countries this is a requirement of company law. The stockholder's right of first refusal over the new shares is known as the preemption right. If a stockholder does not want to buy some or all of the new shares to which he or she is entitled, he or she can sell the rights to them on the stock market during a prescribed offer period. In the United Kingdom this period is three weeks.

The offer price of the new shares is usually set at a large discount to the market price of the existing shares just before the issue is announced. This discount means that the rights are likely to be worth something during the offer period. A numerical example is helpful in understanding the rights issue mechanism:

Company X:

Number of existing shares	10 million
Number of new shares	5 million
Price of existing shares before offer is announced	$12
Offer price	$9

In this example, Company X is issuing one new share for every two existing shares in what is known as a "one-for-two" issue. The new equity to be raised is $45 million. The offer period starts on the ex-rights date, when the existing shares cease to carry the one-for-two entitlement to the new shares. If the underlying value of the company does not change, the share price will fall to the theoretical ex-rights price (TERP) on the ex-rights date. The TERP is the weighted average value of the old and the new shares. In the example, the TERP is $11:

$$\frac{(10 \text{ million} \times \$12 + 5 \text{ million} \times \$9)}{15 \text{ million}} = \$11$$

At this market price, each right to one new share will be worth $2; that is, $11 − $9.

An important point about rights issues is that a stockholder is as well off whether or not he sells the rights. If he does not sell, and he buys the new shares, he loses $10 per old share when they go ex-rights, but gains $2 per new share because the offer price is $2 below the market price ex-rights. If he sells the rights, he still loses $10 per old share but gains $2 in cash per new share. However, this ignores the cost of selling rights, which can be substantial if the company's shares are illiquid.

The majority of rights issues are underwritten. This means that the investment bank arranging the issue will find sub-underwriters, usually investing institutions, to buy the shares at the offer price, or will buy them itself if necessary. The deeper the discount, the less likely it is that the underwriters will be called upon.

Firm-Commitment or Public Offer
In the United States, rights issues by commercial companies (as opposed to investment companies) have been rare since the 1970s. The standard method for larger issues is the firm-commitment offer. After the issue is announced, there is a

book-building period of about one month, during which a syndicate of investment banks invites applications for the new shares and the share registration document is finalized. With a shelf offering, the new shares will already have been registered with the Securities and Exchange Commission. There is no pro rata offer to existing stockholders.

The offer price is set the day before the shares are issued. The offer price used to be the same as, or very close to, the prevailing market price. But, during the 1990s, it became common to set the offer price at a discount to the market price of about 2.5%. Firm-commitment offers are underwritten by the syndicate of investment banks that market the issue. Non-underwritten public offers are known as "best efforts" offers. Both rights issues and firm commitments are accompanied by a prospectus—a marketing document and memorandum that contains information required by the relevant regulatory authority.

In recent years, a variant known as the accelerated bookbuilt offer has become more common. The offer is announced and bids from investors are invited very quickly, often by the end of the same day. Accelerated bookbuilding tends to be used by large companies to raise small amounts in relation to their size.

Private Placement or Placing

A third type of offer is the private placement. In the United States, private placement refers to the sale of a block of shares by private negotiation, usually to one or two investors only and for a fairly small amount (a few million dollars). Placements are less onerous to arrange than firm commitments, because the shares are not offered to investors in general and no prospectus is required. Most placements are made at a discount, the average being around 15% in the United States. Many placements are now private investment in public equity (PIPE) issues, in which the shares placed can be resold more quickly than in a conventional placement. In the United Kingdom the term "placing" is used for any sale of shares that does not involve a pro rata offer to existing stockholders. Larger placings will have 20 or 30 placees.

Open Offer

An open offer combines a pro rata offer to existing stockholders with a private placing. Although stockholders retain their preemption rights, the rights cannot be traded and are therefore worthless unless the stockholder chooses to buy new shares. This type of offer is now standard in the United Kingdom but appears to be unique to that country.

ASPECTS OF PRACTICE
Market Reaction to SEOs

The share price of US industrial companies falls by around 3% on average when a firm-commitment offer is announced. The stock market reaction to rights issues is mixed; it is negative in some countries and positive in others. A negative reaction is surprising on the face of it, since a company would not be expected to go to the expense of a share issue unless it had a good use for the money, i.e. a positive net present value investment.

The leading explanation (Myers and Majluf, 1984) is that news of an SEO indicates that the issuer is more likely to be overvalued than undervalued. An undervalued company is one in which the market value of the equity is less than the managers' assessment of its value. If the managers are correct, issuing shares when the company is undervalued means that existing stockholders who do not buy will lose out to new investors, who will obtain shares at below the full-information price. Some undervalued companies will choose not to issue as a result, even if they need the money for a worthwhile investment. Therefore, companies that choose to issue are more likely to be overvalued, and the market price will fall as a result.

However, the market reaction to private placements, placings, and open offers is positive on average. These issue methods potentially involve detailed investigation of the issuer by placees or underwriters, who have access to private information about the company. So one explanation for the positive reaction is that the willingness of these well-informed agents to buy or underwrite certifies a minimum value for the issuer. Another explanation is that in some placements an active placee is introduced, i.e. an agent who brings know-how or an intention to intervene in the company, and the market reacts positively to news of a placement to such an investor.

Decline of the Rights Issue

The decline of rights issues in the United States, the United Kingdom, Japan, and elsewhere is somewhat puzzling. The firm-commitment method that replaced them in the United States is more expensive and does not offer an obvious advantage. Most placings are made at a sizeable discount, which means that stockholders who are not invited into the placing lose out. Possible disadvantages of rights issues include the cost of selling large blocks of rights, delays in the issue process compared with placings, and less effective certification of value than in an open offer or placing.

Rights issues work best when most of the new shares will be bought by existing stockholders willing to take up their rights. There is then little need to find other buyers. They are therefore frequently used by family-controlled firms. Rights issues also work well for the largest companies, with very liquid shares, because it is cheap and easy to sell rights on the market.

Long-Run Underperformance Following SEOs

Companies that raise new equity tend to underperform in relation to other companies matched by industry, size, and risk over a three- to five-year horizon. This underperformance occurs for both returns on the shares and operating profit. The same finding applies to companies that make or have made an initial public offer. One explanation is that, on average, companies successfully time their issue for when they are overvalued.

Issue Costs

The total cost of a firm-commitment offer in the United States is, on average, 7% of the amount raised, ignoring any discount.

The cost of a rights issue or open offer in the United Kingdom is 6% on average. Much the largest components of the cost are the fees to the lead bank and to the underwriters. The cost is relatively more for smaller companies, partly because there are clear economies of scale and partly because they are riskier.

Discounts

Discounts to the market price are a cost to nonsubscribing stockholders, except in a rights issue. Why are discounts needed? First, investors tend to buy large blocks, which could be costly to sell in future. There is a strong empirical relationship between depth of discount and the bid–ask spread of the issuer's shares. Second, the value of many issuers is rather uncertain; in the academic jargon, there is high information asymmetry. There was a major shift in the 1990s in the type of company listed on stock exchanges, away from well-established companies with a successful track record, toward smaller firms that are still in the product development stage. The discount could also provide compensation for costs of investigating the issuer, or for future costs of active monitoring.

MAKING IT HAPPEN

- An equity issue is an expensive process and time-consuming for senior management.
- Key practical aspects include the choice of lead investment bank and other professional-service firms (for example, lawyers), the type of issue, the size and timing of the issue, whether to have it underwritten, the content of the prospectus, the level of fee, the offer price discount, and who the main buyers (future stockholders) will be.
- Companies are largely in the hands of the lead investment bank once the issue process is under way, but they can (and do) shop around when selecting the lead bank. When making the choice and negotiating the terms of the issue, company managers should be aware of the terms on which recent SEOs have been made by companies of a similar size. The fees and discount should be competitive.
- The company should aim for a smooth issue that raises the intended amount and is sold to a group of investors who are, or plan to be, long-term holders of the shares.

CASE STUDY
BRADFORD AND BINGLEY'S "RIGHTS REISSUE," MAY–JUNE 2008

The rights issue of Bradford and Bingley plc, a British mortgage bank, was among the most extraordinary in living memory. On May 14, 2008, Bradford and Bingley announced that it was to raise £300 million via a 19-for-25 issue at an offer price of 82p—a discount of 48% on the preannouncement share price. However, on June 4, 2008, while the offer period was still running, the bank unexpectedly announced a profit warning, the resignation of its chief executive, and a restructuring of the issue. In particular, the offer price was cut to 55p to avoid the share price dropping below the offer price after the profit warning. A price cut mid-offer is extremely rare, but without it the underwriters would have been left holding much of the issue at a loss, and they might have sought to escape their obligations by invoking the "material adverse change" clause in the underwriting agreement.

In a further twist, Bradford and Bingley arranged for Texas Pacific Group (TPG), a private equity investor, to buy shares at 55p via a placing, acquiring a 23% stake and two seats on the board. TPG's shares were not offered to existing stockholders and were therefore not part of the rights issue proper. TPG's involvement as a potentially active investor was generally welcomed. At the same time, some institutional stockholders were annoyed at not being given the chance to invest more at 55p. As one said, "If there was no TPG, the whole thing would have collapsed. But it comes at a huge price for investors."[1]

MORE INFO
Book:

Eckbo, B. Espen, Ronald W. Masulis, and Øyvind Norli. "Security offerings." In B. Espen Eckbo (ed). *Handbook of Corporate Finance: Empirical Corporate Finance*. Vol. 1. Amsterdam: Elsevier, 2007; 233–373. A thorough review of research on SEOs.

Article:

Myers, Stewart C., and Nicholas S. Majluf. "Corporate financing and investment decisions when firms have information that investors do not have." *Journal of Financial Economics* 13:2 (June 1984): 187–221. Online at: dx.doi.org/10.1016/0304-405X(84)90023-0

Report:

Myners, Paul. "Pre-emption rights: Final report." UK Department of Trade and Industry, February 2005. Online at: www.berr.gov.uk/files/file28436.pdf. The pros and cons of rights issues from a practitioner's perspective.

See Also:

★ Acquiring a Secondary Listing, or Cross-Listing (pp. 112–114)
★ Understanding the True Cost of Issuing Convertible Debt and Other Equity-Linked Financing (pp. 169–172)
✔ Obtaining an Equity Value Using the Weighted Average Cost of Capital (WACC) (pp. 331–332)

NOTE
1 *Financial Times* (June 6, 2008).

Financial Steps in an IPO for a Small or Medium-Size Enterprise
by Hung-Gay Fung

EXECUTIVE SUMMARY

- The firm forms an underwriting syndicate by selecting a lead underwriter and co-managers. Typically, for small and medium-sized firms underwriters charge a fee of 7% of the issue value. In the United States, a firm registers with the Securities and Exchange Commission (SEC) for the IPO issue, and when it has received approval it distributes a preliminary prospectus, known as a "red herring," to the public.
- The firm has to select an exchange on which to list its stock.
- The firm and the underwriter arrange road shows to promote the issue and to find out more about market demand; later this will provide useful information for setting the offer price and determining how many shares should be issued.
- After the IPO trading, the lead underwriter provides market research on the issue and other relevant information.

WHY AN IPO?

An initial public offering (IPO) of stocks is a share offering to the public by a small or medium-sized enterprise (SME) undertaken to raise additional cash for future growth or to enable existing stockholders to cash out by selling part of their holdings. Among other things, a successful IPO will provide a company with an objective valuation of its stock, create a good public image of the company—thus lowering its cost of borrowing—and provide it with a pool of publicly owned shares for future acquisitions of other companies. However, there are also drawbacks to being a public company, such as loss of freedom (including costly disclosure requirements and close monitoring by the public and government) and, if a takeover is threatened, potential loss of control.

TYPES OF IPO

There are many types of IPO, illustrating the different management and owner compensation contracts in firms.

- The plain vanilla IPO is undertaken by a privately held company, mostly owned by management, who want to secure additional funding and determine the company's fair market value.
- A venture capital-backed IPO refers to a company in which management has sold its shares to one or more groups of private investors in return for funding and advice. This provides an effective incentive scheme for venture capitalists to implement their exit strategy after they have successfully transformed a firm in which they invested so that it is financially viable in the market.
- In a reverse-leveraged buyout, the proceeds of the IPO are used to pay off the debt accumulated when a company was privatized after a previous listing on an exchange. This process enables owners who own majority shares to privatize their publicly trading firms, which are undervalued in the market, thus realizing financial gains after the public was informed of the high intrinsic value of the private firm.
- A spin-off IPO denotes the process whereby a large company carves out a stand-alone subsidiary and sells it to the public. A spin-off may also offer owners of the parent firm and hedge funds the opportunity to capitalize mispricing in both the subsidiary and parent if the market is not efficient enough. An interesting example in the United States was the spin-off of uBid by Creative Computers in 1998, which enabled arbitragers to capitalize the mispricing between the two listed companies.

THE IPO PROCESS
Overview

The first task of management is to select the underwriters who will be responsible for the new issue. This is done roughly three months before the IPO date. The underwriters provide the issuing firm with procedural and financial advice. Later they will buy the stock and then sell it to the public. The company, with the aid of lawyers, accountants, and underwriters, submits a registration statement to a regulatory body (such as the Securities and Exchange Commission (SEC) in the United States) for approval of the public offering. The registration statement is a detailed document about the company's history, business, and future plans. Specifically, the SEC requires information on the details of the company (form S-1), its financial history (form S-2), and expected cash flows (form S-3). The company must be able to back up the information provided to the SEC.

In the United States, about six weeks prior to the IPO issue the SEC reviews and approves the content of the disclosure to the public; this becomes the preliminary prospectus and is also called the "red herring." In December 2006, the SEC set new rules on what information must be included about a public company's executive compensation, including the level of executive pay, the benchmark used, and what quantitative or qualitative methods are employed in determining that pay.[1] The prospectus is a legal document describing the securities to be offered to participants and buyers. It is advised on and distributed by the underwriters, and provides information such as the types of stock to be issued, biographies of officers and directors with detailed information about their compensation, any litigation in place, and any other material information.

After publication of the prospectus the company, with the help of the underwriting syndicate, prepares for roadshows to meet potential investors—primarily institutional investors in major cities like New York, San Francisco, Boston, Chicago, and Los Angeles. Roadshows may sometimes be arranged for overseas investors. After the SEC approves registration of the IPO, the underwriters and the company will agree on the amount and price of the issue. On the day prior to the IPO issue the exact price of the shares to be issued is announced by the underwriter. After the IPO, the lead underwriter provides stock liquidity and research coverage.

The IPO date is followed by a "lockup" period, the duration of which varies across different issues and markets, but is in the region of 180 days for a typical issue. After this "insiders," who include the underwriters, are allowed to sell their shares. Insiders may or may not hold on to stock they own, depending on their motives and objectives. However, the lockup period appears to exert no control on those who bought shares at the market-offered IPO price, although there are regulatory restrictions on the types of clients to whom the firm can sell stock.

Selection of Underwriters
The board of a firm planning to launch an IPO will first meet with potential candidates for underwriters among investment banks and then select the lead underwriter. The choice of underwriter is based on criteria that include: a preliminary valuation of the firm based on its financial information; and the characteristics of the underwriter, such as previous IPO experience, strengths and weaknesses, client network, research capabilities, and support for post-IPO issues. Discounted cash flow analysis and earnings multiples (such as the price/earnings ratio) are typically used to come up with the preliminary value of the company.

Citigroup was ranked first among underwriters in 2007, arranging US$617.6 billion of offerings, and JPMorgan Chase was second with US$554.1 billion. Deutsche Bank was ranked third and Merrill fourth in underwriting volume.[2] Citigroup has been top of the list for the past eight years. As a result of the global recession that began in 2008 the underwriting volume has declined, while fees have increased.

Types of Underwriting
The management of the IPO firm selects the underwriters and decides on the type of underwriting it wants. There are two types of underwriting: *firm commitment*, and *best efforts*. If the underwriter enters a firm commitment with the company, the underwriter is confident about the issue and is willing to buy all the shares if there is insufficient demand. In a firm commitment offering, the underwriters will buy the IPO shares at a discount in the range 3.5–7.0% and then sell them on to the public at the full offer price.

In a best efforts case, the investment bank will only do as much as it reasonably can to sell the shares and will return unsold equity to the firm. This practice is common for less liquid securities. However, if there is excess demand, the bank will ask for a "greenshoe" option, allowing it to buy additional stock from the IPO firm. Typically, a lead underwriter asks other investment banks to form an underwriting syndicate to take care of the IPO issue before final approval by the SEC. The syndicate serves to expand the marketing of the company's stock issue and to reduce the overall risk of the lead bank. The syndicate members are involved in the underwriting either

through a commitment to sell the shares or just in marketing of the shares.

Underwriters may face legal consequences if a new issue goes wrong. Therefore, they have to present accurate and fair facts about the firm to investors, because otherwise they may be sued for misrepresentation, or for failing to carry out due diligence. Some underwriters may allocate stocks of popular new issues to their important corporate clients; this is known as "spinning," and is deemed to be unethical and illegal.

Underwriters charge different spreads, and domestic and overseas spreads may differ. The average underwriting fee (spread) runs between about 3.3% and 7% in the United Kingdom and the United States (Brealey, Myers, and Allen, 2008).

Selection of an Exchange
Different exchanges have different listing requirements. In general, they require minimum levels of pretax income, net tangible assets, and number of stockholders. For example, a New York Stock Exchange listing requires an income of either US$2.5 million before federal income taxes for the most recent year or US$2 million pretax for the each of the preceding two years. The firm must have been profitable in the two years before a listing.

The NASDAQ (National Association of Securities Dealers Automated Quotations), the largest electronic screen-based equity securities trading market in the United States, has lower listing requirements than the NYSE. Other markets, such as the NASDAQ Small Cap Market and the American Stock Exchange, offer even lower listing requirements (www.inc.com/guides/finance/20713.html). Thus, an IPO firm needs to assess its own strengths and weaknesses in order to pick the right exchange on which to list its shares.

A firm also needs to select a trading symbol for use on the exchange. For example, Microsoft trades as MSFT. A fee, which varies for each exchange, has to be paid for the services provided.

Subscription Procedure
IPO shares are distributed in different ways to investors. One approach is an open auction, where investors are invited to submit bids stating the number of shares they wish to purchase and the price they will pay for them. The highest bidders get the securities. The Google IPO of US$1.7 billion in 2004 and the Morningstar IPO of US$140 million in 2005 used this open auction method.

The bookbuilding method is the most commonly used in the United States today and is gaining popularity and dominance across the globe (Degeorge, Derrien, and Womack, 2007). During the roadshows, the investment banker asks institutional investors and individual clients about their intention to buy the shares. Each bid indicates the number to be purchased, and may include a limiting price. Such information is recorded in a "book," from which the name bookbuilding is derived. These indications of interest provide valuable information, because all bids are compiled to ascertain the market demand for the security. Although these bid indications are not binding, the investment banker can utilize the information to set the final offer price, which is made known on the day before the actual issue (Cornelli and Goldreich, 2003).

The appeal of the bookbuilding method, despite its higher underwriting costs, is that investment banks provide better promotion and research coverage of the IPO than other IPO issuing procedures. Thus, the networking of the bank with clients helps to enhance the image of the issuing firm. Chief financial officers appear to prefer this approach to IPOs despite the higher cost.

IPO COST AND PRICING
Underpricing
Besides the substantial underwriting cost and direct costs of lawyers, printers, accountants, etc., the IPO firm has to bear notional losses due to the underpricing of the issue—i.e., the IPO price is less than the true price of the stock. If the offering price is less than the true value of the issue, original stockholders effectively provide a bargain to the new investors. The finance literature shows that investors that buy at the issue price on average realize high returns (for example, 18%) over the following days. This high return from underpricing is common across the world—especially in China, which provides the highest return of 257% (Loughran, Ritter, and Rydqvist, 1994).

Underpricing, which is most likely to be seen with the bookbuilding method, can be justified as follows. First, a low offer price makes it probable that shares will later be traded at a higher price in the market, thus enhancing the firm's ability to raise capital in future. That is, underpricing ensures that the IPO is successful and that those who want to buy the issue will follow the same underwriter among those in the market. Second, it is a way to avoid the winner's curse—the feeling of investors that they have paid too much. Simply, underpricing makes it more likely that an IPO will be successful. It appears that stockholders of the IPO firm focus more on likely gains in wealth from later stock price increases than on any short-term loss from underpricing (Loughran and Ritter, 2002).

New Price and Stock Issue
Suppose that an IPO firm has 10 million shares with a current valuation of $100 million, that it wants to raise $70 million for the issue, and that it has to pay $4.9 million for the direct cost of issuance, which is in general about 7% of the issue value (Hansen, 2001). The post-issue price, P_{new}, which includes underpricing, and the number of new shares to be issued, N, will be determined simultaneously. That is, the dollar amount of the new issue will cover the fund required and the direct cost to be paid, while the augmented value of the firm will include the old and new assets of the firm. P_{new} and N can be determined as follows:

$$P_{new} \times N = \$70,000,000 \text{ (new fund)} + \$4,900,000 \text{ (issue cost)} \quad (1)$$

$$(10,000,000 + N) \times P_{new} = \$100,000,000 \text{ (old assets)} \\ + \$70,000,000 \text{ (new assets)} \quad (2)$$

Solving these two equations (1) − (2) yields the new price of the IPO, $P_{new} = \$9.51$. The number of new shares to be issued, $N = 7,875,920$.

MAKING IT HAPPEN
- An IPO is a time-consuming process.
- The success of an IPO depends on the successful selling of the firm to the investment banks, to the regulator, to the analysts, and to the public.
- During the six-month IPO process the firm's operations need to be on autopilot cruise control as management will be totally tied up during this time.

MORE INFO
Books:
Brealey, Richard A., Stewart C. Myers, and Franklin Allen. *Principles of Corporate Finance.* 10th ed. Boston, MA: McGraw-Hill, 2010.
Killian, Linda, Kathleen Smith, and William Smith. *IPOs for Everyone: The 12 Secrets of Investing in IPOs.* Hoboken, NJ: Wiley, 2001.

Articles:
Cornelli, Francesca, and David Goldreich. "Bookbuilding: How informative is the order book?" *Journal of Finance* 58:4 (August 2003): 1415–1443. Online at: dx.doi.org/10.1111/1540-6261.00572
Degeorge, François, François Derrien, and Kent L. Womack. "Analyst hype in IPOs: Explaining the popularity of book-building." *Review of Financial Studies* 20:4 (July 2007): 1021–1058. Online at: dx.doi.org/10.1093/rfs/hhm010
Hansen, Robert S. "Do investment banks compete in IPOs? The advent of the '7% plus contract.'" *Journal of Financial Economics* 59:3 (March 2001): 313–346. Online at: dx.doi.org/10.1016/S0304-405X(00)00089-1
Loughran, Tim, Jay R. Ritter, and Kristian Rydqvist. "Initial public offerings: International insights." *Pacific-Basin Finance Journal* 2:2–3 (1994): 165–199. Online at: dx.doi.org/10.1016/0927-538X(94)90016-7
Loughran, Tim, and Jay R. Ritter. "Why don't issuers get upset about leaving money on the table in IPOs?" *Review of Financial Studies* 15:2 (Spring 2002): 413–444. Online at: dx.doi.org/10.1093/rfs/15.2.413

Websites:
Hoover's IPO Central: www.hoovers.com/global/ipoc
Inc. magazine articles on IPOs: www.inc.com/guides/finance/20713.html

See Also:
★ Assessing Venture Capital Funding for Small and Medium-Sized Enterprises (pp. 114–117)
★ IPOs in Emerging Markets (pp. 131–133)
★ Price Discovery in IPOs (pp. 148–151)

NOTES
1 See *Wall Street Journal* (December 8, 2008).
2 See *International Herald Tribune* (January 1, 2008).

Viewpoint: Investing in a Volatile Environment: A Black Swan Perspective

by Javier Estrada

★

INTRODUCTION

Javier Estrada, who is professor of financial management at Barcelona-based IESE Business School, was a tennis coach in his native Argentina before moving to live and work in Spain in 1993. He set the cat among the pigeons in global investment circles with his ground-breaking research, "Black swans and market timing: How not to generate alpha," which conclusively revealed that investors who seek to time the market are unlikely to reap rewards. His research focuses on risk, portfolio management, investment strategies, emerging markets, and insider trading. The founding editor of *Emerging Markets Review*, he holds visiting professorships in Scandinavia and Latin America. As wealth management adviser at Sports Global Consulting, Estrada advises professional sports-players on their investments. His favorite football team is Club Atlético River Plate. A fan of hard-rock bands, including Queen, Kansas, and Led Zeppelin, he plays electric guitar in his spare time. His first degree, a BA in economics, was from the National University of La Plata in Buenos Aires, and he also holds MSc and PhD degrees from the University of Illinois at Urbana-Champaign.

HEALTHY EATING AND INVESTING

We all know that eating properly is essential for our health. Most of us are aware that certain types of food are good for us while others are best avoided. We are also aware of the trade-off between the desirable long-term goal of being fit and healthy and the pain associated with denying ourselves foods that we really like. We also know that patience and discipline are required.

What does healthy eating have to do with investing, you may well ask? Arguably, there are plenty of similarities. Anyone who has gone into a bookstore in search of a book on healthy eating will have been confronted by rows and rows of books, each outlining a different miracle diet.

Anyone looking for a book on investing has a similar experience. Shelf after shelf bulges with books outlining "high-return, low-risk" strategies. Each gives the impression that all we need do is to follow the indicated path to instant riches. If only life were as easy! If it was, I would not be writing these lines and you would not be reading them—we would probably both be enjoying the Caribbean sun.

A BALANCED DIET

Most of us recognize that eating healthily is going to require a long-term commitment and the making of certain sacrifices (we must kiss goodbye to all those tasty 600-calorie blueberry muffins), and that there is no such thing as a painless shortcut. The same applies to investing.

In reality, the only way to generate high long-term investment returns is to endure some risks in the short term, with the associated pain that comes from sleepless nights as our portfolio value bounces about. There is no such thing as a "high-return, low-risk" strategy. Sadly, the same "no pain, no gain" rule applies both to eating and to investing.

And yet, when it comes to investing, many investors are seduced by "get rich quick" schemes. They often get blinded by the lights of easy money and delude themselves into thinking that gain can be achieved without pain.

For the purpose of this article, I would like to group the investment strategies people are offered into two types: in one group are the "exciting" active investment strategies, which usually promise high returns but claim to achieve them with little or no risk; in the second group are the more boring and conservative passive strategies, which usually promise no gain without pain.

The two approaches can be evaluated from several standpoints, not all of which lead us to the same conclusions. I will evaluate them here through the prism of my own recent research into the so-called "black swans" in financial markets.

BLACK SWANS

A black swan is an event that has three main attributes: First, it is an outlier, lying outside the realm of regular expectations because nothing in the past can convincingly point to its occurrence; second, it carries an extreme impact; and third, despite being an outlier, plausible explanations for its occurrence can be found after the fact, thus giving it the appearance of being both explainable and predictable. In summary, a black swan has three characteristics: rarity, extreme impact, and retrospective predictability.

The black swan perspective of investing is based on three main ideas. The first is that an extremely small number of trading days have a disproportionate impact on long-term investment performance—this is an empirical fact. The second is that, although being invested on the good days and not invested on the bad days would yield extraordinary returns, investors are extremely unlikely to get the timing right. And third, because attempts to time the market are doomed to fail in the long term (in fact, their main consequence is likely to be higher transaction costs), investors are better off holding a properly diversified investment portfolio for the long term.

A PATH TO POVERTY?

Curiously, this is exactly the same recommendation that is put forward by advocates of the efficient market theory of investment. However, the black swan perspective assumes neither market efficiency nor normally distributed returns. Instead, it argues that return distributions have very fat tails and are therefore far from being normal. It also argues that mistakenly assuming that returns are normally distributed can lead to a massive destruction of wealth, as it leads investors to underestimate risk substantially.

Let's first examine the facts. My own research (Estrada, 2008) reveals that a tiny number of days can have an exceptional impact on long-term portfolio performance.

Across 15 developed markets, being out of the market on the ten days when the biggest stock market rallies occurred would have resulted in portfolios being 51% less valuable than if the money had been passively invested. Not being invested in these markets during their ten worst days would have resulted in portfolios being 150% more valuable than a passive investment would have been.

Given that these ten days represent less than 0.1% of the days in the average developed market I considered, the conclusion is obvious: A negligible proportion of days determines a massive creation or destruction of wealth, and the odds of successfully and consistently predicting the right days to be in and out of the market are nil.

In emerging markets, a tiny number of days have an even bigger impact on portfolio performance. My own research (Estrada, 2009) reveals that across 16 emerging markets, missing the ten best days would have resulted in portfolios being 69% less valuable than if the money had been passively invested. Not being invested on the ten worst ten days would have resulted in portfolios being 337% more valuable than a passive investment would have been. Given that ten days represent 0.15% of the days in the average emerging market I considered, the conclusion is again stark: The probability of successfully and consistently getting the timing right is negligible.

At times of high stock market volatility, like those we experienced during 2008, investors are often tempted to try and take advantage of large daily swings. In such turbulent times many investors attempt to capture outsized returns by frequently jumping in and out of the market, or from one market to another. But investors who engage in this sort of active trading, particularly in a volatile environment, are largely relying on luck rather than on a sound financial strategy.

Investors should bear in mind that the odds are heavily stacked against them; they should also remember that, while the additional transaction costs of their active trading strategy are certain, outsized returns are, at best, a hope.

I run a program on portfolio management for individuals (as opposed to institutions) that aims to give unsophisticated investors some basic tools with which to manage their savings. In this program I tell participants about the two "sad truths" of financial markets. I call them sad truths because these are two statements that most investors would prefer were false. Unfortunately, however, both are true.

PATIENCE IS A VIRTUE

The first statement is that the higher the required return, the greater must be the exposure to risk. The second is that the higher the exposure to risk, the longer must be the investment horizon. Deep inside, participants know that these statements are true, but a part of each of them would prefer to go on believing in painless shortcuts.

In the program, I also tell participants that they should stop focusing on forecasting. I give them many reasons why they should forget about trying to second-guess the market, which stock to buy or sell, or which currency is going to appreciate. I give them plenty of reasons why they should start focusing on asset allocation instead. As with the "sad truths," they instinctively know this advice to be right, but more often than not their next question is whether I think the dollar is going to appreciate or the market is going to fall. Oh, well…

Some investors may well question the wisdom of being passively invested in an environment such as that in 2008, when markets displayed exceptional levels of volatility and were apparently going nowhere but down. But hindsight is 20:20. It is very easy to say now that we should have cashed out at the beginning of 2008, but it did not look that obvious at the time. Trends, in fact, are not obvious until they are well in place. Black swans are unpredictable, and we only know when one has hit us after the event.

As mentioned at the beginning, eating healthily and investing have much in common; in both, the long-term goal is desirable, but the "getting there" is the problem. Most investors know what they have to do along the way; most know that pain is a part of the process; most know that patience and discipline are essential; and yet most are tempted into shortcuts ("miracle diets" or "high-return, low-risk" strategies), even though they probably recognize that these may ultimately be dead ends. When it comes down to healthy eating or investing, there is simply no gain without pain.

Black swans do exist, both in the natural world and in the financial markets. Those in nature are just a curiosity, but those in financial markets have critical implications for investor behavior. Volatile markets invite investors to engage in a losing game. And yet, at the end of the day, black swans render market timing a goose chase.

MORE INFO
Books:

Estrada, Javier. *Finance in a Nutshell: A No-nonsense Companion to the Tools and Techniques of Finance*. Harlow, UK: FT Prentice Hall, 2005.

Mandelbrot, Benoit B., and Richard L. Hudson. *The (Mis)Behavior of Markets. A Fractal View of Risk, Ruin and Reward*. London: Profile Books, 2005.

Taleb, Nassim Nicholas. *The Black Swan. The Impact of the Highly Improbable*. New York: Random House, 2007.

Articles:

Estrada, Javier. "Black swans and market timing: How not to generate alpha." *Journal of Investing* 17:3 (Fall 2008): 20–34. Online at: dx.doi.org/10.3905/joi.2008.710917

Estrada, Javier. "Black swans in emerging markets." *Journal of Investing* 18:2 (Summer 2009): 50–56. Online at: dx.doi.org/10.3905/joi.2009.18.2.050

See Also:
★ Asset Allocation Methodologies (pp. 117–123)

IPOs in Emerging Markets

by Janusz Brzeszczynski

EXECUTIVE SUMMARY

- IPO activity in emerging markets depends strongly on the macroeconomic environment, business cycles, and stock market phases.
- The number of IPOs increases during bull markets and decreases during bear markets.
- Companies launching IPOs during bull markets can count on raising more capital than if they go public in a bear market.
- There is usually a time lag of about a year between changes in stock market index returns and the subsequently observed IPO activity.

INTRODUCTION

An initial public offering (IPO) is the sale of a company's shares to the public for the first time, leading to a stock exchange listing. This process is known also as a public offering, or "going public."

The main reason for IPOs is the need for fresh capital to finance various business activities, such as the development of new products or expansion into new markets. Most IPOs are launched by relatively small but dynamic companies, which grow too fast to be financed only in traditional ways such as by bank loans. Nevertheless, many big privately owned companies also decide to become publicly traded.

Decisions about an IPO are predominantly based on the actual capital requirements and the expansion plans of the management, but the timing of the IPO is very strongly determined by the current macroeconomic environment, business cycles, and stock market phases.

IPOs are considered to be risky for both the issuers and the investors. The issuers may miscalculate the value of the company and choose the wrong time to go public. In this event, the amount of capital raised from the IPO will be less than expected, and control of the company may be lost by diluting the shares of previous stockholders in the new ownership structure after the IPO. However, when an IPO is successful, a company can raise more capital than anticipated, and the original stockholders may still be able to control the company.

As for the risks faced by the investors, first, they may make errors in assessing the company value, and second, it is very difficult to predict how the share price will behave once the company is listed on the stock exchange. Investors normally have access only to limited historical data, which makes the valuation and the appraisal of the firm's financial situation rather difficult. Moreover, the majority of IPOs are companies that are experiencing a transitory growth stage. This creates even more uncertainty about their value in the future. Last but not least, the stock market before and after an IPO may behave in an erratic way and exhibit high volatility, which in a short period of time may lead to either unexpected profits or unexpected losses.

INITIAL PUBLIC OFFERINGS

The main advantage of an IPO is that the company is not obliged to return the capital raised from the investors. The downside is that new stockholders are entitled to a share of future profits (usually in the form of a dividend). The stockholdings of the existing owners will be diluted in the new ownership structure, and in many cases they may even lose control over the company. However, they expect their shares to become more valuable after the IPO, when the company should be able to generate higher profits from the capital raised in the IPO process.

In an IPO the issuers are usually assisted by underwriting firms, such as investment banks, which help to decide on the best offer price and the timing of the offer. They also deal with the legal aspects of the entire process. Furthermore, the underwriter approaches investors with offers to sell the shares of the IPO company.

The sale of shares in an IPO may take place using different methods. These are: Dutch auction, firm commitment, best efforts, bought deal, or self distribution of stock. When the IPO is successful and the underwriters sell the shares, they are rewarded by a commission calculated as a certain percentage of the value of the shares issued and sold.

The number of new IPOs in any market always depends on business cycles. One of the best examples is the dot-com bubble in the United States during the 1990s, when share prices were rising sharply and many young companies from the high-tech sector were seeking capital through IPOs. After the companies were listed on the stock market, their share prices sky-rocketed—and continued to do so until the bubble burst.

The value of the IPO of a company is usually relatively high in comparison to alternative methods of financing such as bank loans. The largest IPOs in history so far have been: Industrial & Commercial Bank of China (US$21.6 billion) in 2006; NTT Mobile Communications (US$18.4 billion) in 1998; Visa Inc. (US$17.9 billion) in 2008; and AT&T Wireless (US$10.6 billion) in 2000.

Pricing of Public Offers

In order to sell a large number of new shares and raise significant amounts of capital, an IPO has to offer investors a strong incentive to buy. That is why most IPOs tend to be underpriced. On one hand, a consequence of this is that investors who buy the shares at the offering price can earn substantial returns, and this tends to happen over a relatively short period of time. On the other hand, when an IPO is severely underpriced the result may be what is known as "money left on the table." This term is used to describe the situation when the company experiences a relative loss of capital, i.e. the loss of money that could have been raised from the market in an IPO if the shares had been offered and sold at a higher price.

If the shares are overpriced, the underwriters may not be able to sell all of them. They then face the problem of acquiring the shares themselves—which is even more troublesome when the current market price is lower than the issuing price.

The public offering price (POP) is the price at which IPOs are offered to the public by an underwriter. Several factors affect this price, including data about a company's financial situation (past, current, and forecasted), macroeconomic conditions and stock market trends (current and predicted), as well as information about investor confidence.

A preliminary registration statement filed with the securities commission, which describes a new IPO, is called a "red herring." It does not include the price or issue size and it may be updated many times before it becomes the final prospectus. The process of soliciting orders to buy an IPO before its registration is approved by the securities commission is known as "gun jumping." An advertisement published by the underwriters giving information about the details of an IPO is called a "tombstone." The first recommendation issued by an underwriter for an IPO is known as the "booster shot." Its aim is to promote the new shares of the IPO company and to increase the chance of its successful sale to the public. The underwriters cannot, however, promote the IPO during the "quiet period," which is the period of time following the filing with the securities commission and before the registration statement. The term "quiet period" refers also to a certain number of days after an IPO is listed on the stock market, during which the company and those underwriters directly engaged in the IPO are not allowed to issue any financial forecasts or recommendations for the company concerned.

IPOs in Emerging Markets

In many emerging markets the term "going public" may seem confusing. In countries that did not have free-market economies in the past, and where government ownership was dominant over private ownership, most companies that launched IPOs were in fact privatized, because they were sold by the government to *private* investors through the stock market. Hence, they were in fact going private rather than going public.

A problem in emerging market financial systems is that many small, young private firms that have good investment opportunities can show little evidence of past business and financial performance. They therefore face serious problems

when they want to attract external finance for new ventures. This is because in these countries either firm financing is intermediated or the capital markets are underdeveloped. Furthermore, in many emerging markets the legal and regulatory environment is rather weak, and financial intermediaries tend to give priority to large companies that have a relevant track record and own a certain value of physical assets which can be used as collateral for loans. There is also a danger that intermediaries may favor firms controlled by politicians. In emerging markets, the development of public equity markets has been found to be beneficial for the financial systems. It is believed that public capital markets are more immune to the influence of politicians and other lobbying groups.

The development of capital markets in emerging market countries, combined with their dynamic macroeconomic growth in recent years, has triggered IPO activity on their stock exchanges. However, it is worth distinguishing between the various sources of capital that are being invested in IPOs. In many emerging markets the limited availability of capital has been a major problem. Even though the economic growth of emerging countries in recent years has helped in the accumulation of capital from domestic sources, much of the capital invested in IPOs has its origin in developed countries. An important role here is played by venture capital companies, which often use an IPO as their exit strategy. However, the activity of venture capital funds may differ from country to country—it is, for example, traditionally higher in Asian markets and lower in the emerging market countries in Europe.

A typical IPO process in an emerging market starts when a company enters a high growth phase and the management decides that there is a momentum in the firm's life during which a relatively large amount of new capital can be raised for further expansion. It is then that the shares can be sold via an IPO at prices that result in high multiples of the most commonly used financial ratios, such as price/earnings ratio (P/E), or price/book value ratio (P/BV). Other typical reasons why companies decide to become public in emerging markets and launch an IPO are easier access to capital in the future, increased liquidity of their shares, and, last but not least, visibility and prestige when they are listed on the stock market.

Figure 1. New IPOs versus stock market returns in Poland in the period 1997–08. (*Source*: Warsaw Stock Exchange and author's calculations. The data exclude the NewConnect market segment)

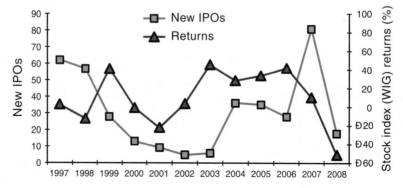

The number of IPOs in emerging markets is variable over time and depends on many key factors, among which the macroeconomic environment and the rate of growth of the economy are the dominant ones. There is evidence to show that IPO activity in emerging markets is related to phases of the stock market, which in turn are connected to business cycles. Bull and bear market periods always depend on the macroeconomic indicators and the prospects of economic growth.

Macroeconomic activity also affects the degree of underpricing of IPOs. Although this effect tends to be more significant in emerging market countries than in developed economies, it is in fact always time-varying in its nature, and depends periodically on macroeconomic conditions. Nevertheless, there are cases in which the underpricing was so severe that the share price on the first day of listing reached a level more than 100% higher than the offer price in the IPO—in well-established markets the underpricing is typically below 20%.

CASE STUDY
IPOS IN THE EMERGING MARKET IN POLAND

Figure 1 shows the number of new IPOs and the main stock market index (WIG) returns for the Polish stock market over a period of 12 years from 1997 to 2008. An important feature of this graph is the one-year shift of new IPOs relative to the situation in the stock market, where the pattern of volatility of index returns clearly leads the IPO activity. The correlation coefficient between those two variables is only 0.0244 (2.44%) when IPOs and stock market index returns are analyzed simultaneously, but increases to as high as 0.5683 (56.83%) when the WIG returns are lagged by one year.

Following the period 2003–06, during which the WIG index increased at an annual rate of nearly 40%, in 2007 the number of new IPOs jumped to 81 from an annual average of less than seven in 2001–2003 and 33 in 2004–2006. When global stock markets collapsed in 2007 and continued to seek new bottoms in 2008 (events that were reflected in the returns of the Polish market index WIG), the number of new IPOs in 2008 fell more than fourfold to less than 20 from the peak of just over 80 the year before.

This finding shows that decisions about IPOs are strictly dependent on stock market phases and that IPOs tend to increase when share prices are rising and to decrease when they fall. The relationship is not simultaneous, with some lagged effect being observed that may be linked to the length of time decision-makers need to assess the profitability of a new IPO, given the financial environment and predictions of how much capital can be raised from the stock market at current prices.

CONCLUSION

The number of IPOs in emerging markets and the profitability of the public offers are related to macroeconomic conditions (both global and local), business cycles, and stock market activity. In most emerging market countries there is a time lag between movements of the stock market index and decisions to launch new IPOs.

The correct timing of an IPO is very important for a company that plans a public offering. An IPO may raise different amounts of capital from investors depending on whether stock markets are in a bull or a bear phase.

MAKING IT HAPPEN

- Emerging markets are not immune to trends in global financial markets. Hence, it is important for company executives who plan IPOs in these countries to have a good understanding of the global macroeconomic environment and of the financial linkages with developed countries.
- There are research institutes that sell forecasts of future macroeconomic trends and predictions of stock market performance. Forecasts of the world economy are also offered by such institutions as the World Bank, the International Monetary Fund, and the United Nations, as well as by central banks and the finance ministries of individual countries.
- Any decision to launch an IPO should be very carefully analyzed using not only past financial data for the company, but also macroeconomic forecasts. These may provide valuable information about future economic growth, which is likely to impact stock market activity and share prices directly.
- Timing an IPO correctly may lead to substantial gains if the IPO shares sell at a high price. Poor timing may result in the loss of capital if stock market prices are too low.

MORE INFO
Articles:

Beck, Thorsten, Asli Demirgüç-Kunt, and Vojislav Maksimovic. "Financial and legal constraints to firm growth: Does firm size matter?" *Journal of Finance* 60:1 (February 2005): 137–177. Online at: 10.1111/j.1540-6261.2005.00727.x

La Porta, Rafael, Florencio Lopez-de-Silanes, and Guillermo Zamarippa. "Related lending." *Quarterly Journal of Economics* 118:1 (February 2003): 231–268. Online at: dx.doi.org/10.1162/00335530360535199

Rajan, Raghuram G., and Luigi Zingales. "The great reversals: The politics of financial development in the 20th century." *Journal of Financial Economics* 69:1 (July 2003): 5–50. Online at: dx.doi.org/10.1016/S0304-405X(03)00125-9

Shleifer, Andrei, Rafael La Porta, Florencio Lopez-de-Silanes, and Robert W. Vishny. "Legal determinants of external finance." *Journal of Finance* 52:3 (July 1997): 1131–1150. Online at: www.afajof.org/journal/jstabstract.asp?ref=11724

Websites:

International Monetary Fund (IMF): www.imf.org
United Nations (UN): www.un.org
World Bank: www.worldbank.org

See Also:

★ Financial Steps in an IPO for a Small or Medium-Size Enterprise (pp. 126–128)
★ Price Discovery in IPOs (pp. 148–151)

134

Managing Activist Investors and Fund Managers
by Leslie L. Kossoff

EXECUTIVE SUMMARY

- Organizations not previously of interest to activist investors or hedge funds should prepare to be targeted.
- Be proactive in understanding why investors become agitators, and address their concerns before they escalate.
- Organizational governance—particularly the combined chairman/CEO position—and financial management will be the easiest targets for activists.
- Activists often succeed because they communicate better than management—particularly to tagalong investors who become part of the proxy fight.
- Unlocking stockholder value and simultaneously developing and executing on a long-term strategy will give activists less reason to agitate and less success with tagalongs; executive management will then have a less volatile financial landscape within which to work.

INTRODUCTION

Whether or not your organization has been a target in the past for activist investors and fund managers, you have to plan on it becoming a fact of life from now on—things have changed.

It used to be that only a few organizations were hit by activist investor activity. From the almost prophetic, and beautifully constructed, Benjamin Graham move on Northern Pipeline in 1951, to Carl Icahn's dramatic moves on Yahoo! during the "Microhoo" (Microsoft–Yahoo!) debacle of 2008, activist investors were a rarity—something other organizations had to deal with. A problem for the really Big Boys. Not everyone else. Not you.

Not any longer.

Whether or not you have any known activist investors currently rearing their heads, you'll have to plan for when they show up—because they will. If you work it right, proactively, as well as when the activism hits, you'll manage your way through those very choppy waters and find a safe haven at the end.

WHY INVESTORS BECOME ACTIVIST

Historically, the reason that most activist investors became active was because they saw something wrong with the way things were being managed. The value of the company was not fully represented in the share value. Management was taking the organization in a direction—usually with a direct correlation to falling share value or dividends—that was making the investors unhappy.

But those reasons are historical, and they were retrospective. One of the big changes is that now investors become activists *proactively*. They see things on the horizon that they don't like, and they act accordingly. Not only may they not be happy with what has happened in the past, they're also not happy about what they see coming next.

For management, that is a wake-up call in the best possible way. It puts the onus on you to look at those components of your business that might lead investors to become activist—and take action accordingly. Because if they're seeing something they don't like, either they need to understand why it is the right thing for the business to do, or you need to take a different, objective, look at what they're not liking so that you can determine the relative merit of what they see.

Also, by looking at the organization the way the activists do, you will see other weaknesses—in everything from your strategy, to your operations, to your financial management—that might be the next focus of their attention. You don't want that; you want to make the fix before they ever have the chance to raise their voices.

TOO GOOD AN OPPORTUNITY TO MISS

And then there are those activist investors who get in because they see something that your company has to offer that is just too good an opportunity to miss. It may be because they have a history of being activist and simply see a new opportunity on which to bring their activist skills and financial acumen to bear. Or it may be because your company is such a good target for some other opportunity which you're not considering (like M&A) that they want to get in and make fast money. Whatever the reason, they'll find a way.

Activist investors have a profile. They are identifiable, as is their methodology. Part of that methodology is to get others who own shares in your company to tag along. In most cases, they can't pull off what they want on their own. They need proxy votes. That being the case, they're making a case to their counterparts that you have to counter in its entirety.

Activist investors identify where your organization is exposed. That's where their opportunities lie. Then, once they've got a handle on where, from their perspective, you're going wrong, their next move is to start communicating that shortfall to others they can bring on board. They create the tagalongs. Tagalongs start out knowing nothing more than what they are told. Many of them, on seeing where the activists are going, will become involved in finding out information for themselves—but those tend to be the larger investors who already have analysts working your organization or your sector anyway. If the activists can get enough small investors involved and on side, they'll win.

On your side is that if you can identify those activist investors and fund managers with large stockholdings in your firm, you will be able, with a high sense of assurance, to begin figuring out what their strategy will be. Track their track record.

Then, if you've done your homework and figured out where your exposure lies, you'll be able to address those problems before the activists can take the initiative. You will also be in a stronger position to tell all your investors—especially those proxy candidates—exactly what you're doing, and why the management is on top of the problems and opportunities that everything from economic conditions to global competition are throwing your way.

Activists can't win if management is doing its job—and well.

THE EASY TARGETS

There are some problems which organizations create for themselves that are easy pickings for the activists—and provide some of the highest exposure for management. Now and going forward, corporate governance is the easiest target that activist investors will be able to find.

Since the Sarbanes–Oxley Act of 2002, the question of whether the same person can be both chairman and chief executive officer, and still ensure that the organization is safe for its stockholders, is—and will continue to be—the easiest target of all. It doesn't matter in which country the organization is headquartered. All that matters is that it is publicly traded and that stockholders should not fear that having the same person in the two roles, with their different responsibilities, is creating an increase in risk.

Activist investors and fund managers are looking for situations where the board is perceived as being entrenched. Unfortunately, even if having the same person as your chairman and CEO is the best thing that's happened to your organization in years, from an outside perspective it looks like cronyism on the board. This is a situation that many will associate with lack of transparency and with untrustworthy and inadequately considered decisions.

That puts the onus on the chief executive and the board, *in toto*, to ensure that stockholders see a level of transparency in governance that goes beyond what existed before. Transparency of voting structures—and even a periodic, situational decision to rescue him or herself by the chairman/chief executive—will go far to calm what could otherwise give rise to very contentious criticisms of the board and how the company is managed at the top.

Issues surrounding everything from operational decisions to, most particularly, executive compensation and bonuses will also be fodder for the activists, both now and in the future. The tolerance for perceived cronyism and mismanagement is lower than ever—and is likely to stay that way.

In effect, just as politicians have to deal with a 24-hour news cycle, so too do corporate executives. There is no rest and no hiding from activists once they decide they want to engage.

CASE STUDY
MICROSOFT/YAHOO!

It was bad enough for Yahoo! when Microsoft decided to make an unsolicited offer for its takeover. Initially offering US$31 per share—a 62% premium over the then share price—Microsoft had decided to expand its internet presence through a big acquisition. This was even though Microsoft, at number three in the search engine business, with Yahoo! in second place, had little or no chance of coming close to the big beast, Google, for the advertising revenues that were there to be had.

When Carl Icahn decided to get into the fray, however, all the rules changed. Buying 5% of Yahoo!, Icahn started actively lobbying for the so-called Microhoo (or Micro-Hoo) deal to go through. He wanted those premiums—especially when Microsoft upped its offer price to US$33 per share.

But Jerry Yang, Yahoo!'s chief executive, and Roy Bostock, its nonexecutive chairman, didn't want to sell—at least not at that price. They had other plans, with and without Google. As a result a three-way fight started, but after a while it wasn't altogether clear who was on whose side—especially because so much of the fight was conducted using the business media.

The proxy fight was about to begin. Icahn was fighting to remove all the current members of Yahoo!'s board, including Yang, and to replace them with a new set chosen by him. But at that point Microsoft decided that neither was it willing to pay the price Yahoo! was asking, nor was it comfortable doing a deal with Icahn tacitly setting the terms. The fight to create Microhoo was over before it began.

That was in 2008.

For Icahn, holding 5% and looking for a way to ensure his shares would gain value in the future, he had to create an alternate win and he did so. His initial demands and wins were changes to the board of directors and a new CEO. The Yahoo! board expanded from 10 seats to 11, with one current board member stepping down, and three new board members—one of which was to be Icahn, the other two selected from his list of alternates to be added. Carol Bartz became CEO in 2009 and one of her first deals was an alliance collaborating on Microsoft's search engine, Bing.

On the face of it, Icahn was right. The Microsoft deal was the best deal going. Now, the question is how long Icahn continues to support Bartz in her new strategic direction for the company.

AVOIDING THE ACTIVISTS' GLARE

A clear-cut corporate strategy for addressing stockholder concerns will do more to avoid the possibility of successful activism than anything else.

First, the stockholders need to see, on an ongoing basis, that the company is dedicated to unlocking stockholder value; that it is committed to finding new ways to make their investment pay off for them—now and in the future.

That is achieved by ensuring that the long-term strategic objectives that are set are not only well communicated, but are also fully executed to the stockholders' satisfaction. By setting and delivering on those long-term objectives, executive management can build long-term investor trust and commitment, leading to a much less volatile financial landscape for the companies' operations.

And, finally, it's all about communication. Activists become activists—particularly the successful ones—by doing a better job of getting their message across to stockholders than corporate management does. By working diligently to ensure that stockholders not only have the information they need, but never feel that anything is being withheld from them, the chances of activists getting involved and their capability to bring in others can be severely reduced.

Ultimately it's all about good management, and about thinking like an activist before they can make their arguments stick. By being proactive and objective about the company—and then doing the right things—you'll stop the activists getting a toehold. More importantly, they'll have no reason to try to do so.

MAKING IT HAPPEN

- Before the activists get the chance, take an objective look at where the business is exposed, and then take action to correct those deficiencies.
- Identify activist investors who already own shares in the company, then research how, and on what particular issues, they have agitated in the past.
- Be proactive in taking steps to address the activists' issues—from leveraging, to corporate governance, management structure, strategy execution, and more—to reduce the activists' opportunities to act.
- Recognize that activism is now future-oriented—not just retrospective and based on the board's previous decisions. Make sure that forward planning and the ability to execute and deliver are sound.
- Message well and continuously to your stockholders, so that it is the company's message that gets the most traction—not that of the activists.

MORE INFO

Books:

Burke, Edmund M. *Managing a Company in an Activist World: The Leadership Challenge of Corporate Citizenship*. Westport, CT: Praeger, 2005.

Schroeder, Alice. *The Snowball: Warren Buffett and the Business of Life*. London: Bloomsbury, 2008.

Articles:

Greenwood, Robin, and Michael Schor, "When (not) to listen to activist investors." *Harvard Business Review* 86:1 (2008). Online at: tinyurl.com/29yah3f

Levin, Timothy W., and Phillip T. Masterson. "Implications of hedge funds as activist investors: No longer flying under the radar." *Investment Lawyer* 13:10 (October 2006): 19–26.

Website:

The Icahn Report: www.icahnreport.com

See Also:

★ Creating Value with EVA (pp. 255–258)
★ The Role of Institutional Investors in Corporate Financing (pp. 154–158)
✔ Defining Corporate Governance: Its Aims, Goals, and Responsibilities (pp. 341–342)

Measuring Company Exposure to Country Risk

by Aswath Damodaran

EXECUTIVE SUMMARY

- Following the piece on "Measuring Country Risk," we focus on a related question: Once we have estimated a country risk premium, how do we evaluate a company's exposure to country risk?
- In the process, we will argue that a company's exposure to country risk should not be determined by where it is incorporated and traded.
- By that measure, neither Coca-Cola nor Nestlé are exposed to country risk. Exposure to country risk should come from a company's operations, making country risk a critical component of the valuation of almost every large multinational corporation.

INTRODUCTION

If we accept the proposition of country risk, the next question that we have to address relates to the exposure of individual companies to country risk. Should all companies in a country with substantial country risk be equally exposed to country risk? While intuition suggests that they should not, we will

begin by looking at standard approaches that assume that they are. We will follow up by scaling country risk exposure to established risk parameters such as betas (β), and complete the discussion with an argument that individual companies should be evaluated for exposure to country risk.

THE BLUDGEON APPROACH

The simplest assumption to make when dealing with country risk, and the one that is most often made, is that all companies in a market are equally exposed to country risk. The cost of equity for a firm in a market with country risk can then be written as:

$$\text{Cost of equity} = \text{Risk-free rate} + \beta\,(\text{Mature market premium}) + \text{Country risk premium}$$

Thus, for Brazil, where we have estimated a country risk premium of 4.43% from the melded approach, each company in the market will have an additional country risk premium of 4.43% added to its expected returns. For instance, the costs of equity for Embraer, an aerospace company listed in Brazil, with a beta[1] of 1.07 and Embratel, a Brazilian telecommunications company, with a beta of 0.80, in US dollar terms would be:

Cost of equity for Embraer = 3.80% + 1.07(4.79%) + 4.43% = 13.35%

Cost of equity for Embratel = 3.80% + 0.80(4.79%) + 4.43% = 12.06%

Note that the risk-free rate that we use is the US treasury bond rate (3.80%), and that the 4.79% figure is the equity risk premium for a mature equity market (estimated from historical data in the US market). It is also worth noting that analysts estimating the cost of equity for Brazilian companies, in US dollar terms, often use the Brazilian ten-year dollar-denominated rate as the risk-free rate. This is dangerous, since it is often also accompanied with a higher risk premium, and ends up double counting risk.

THE BETA APPROACH

For those investors who are uncomfortable with the notion that all companies in a market are equally exposed to country risk, a fairly simple alternative is to assume that a company's exposure to country risk is proportional to its exposure to all other market risk, which is measured by the beta. Thus, the cost of equity for a firm in an emerging market can be written as follows:

Cost of equity = Risk-free rate + β (Mature market premium + Country risk premium)

In practical terms, scaling the country risk premium to the beta of a stock implies that stocks with betas above 1.00 will be more exposed to country risk than stocks with a beta below 1.00. For Embraer, with a beta of 1.07, this would lead to a dollar cost of equity estimate of:

Cost of equity for Embraer = 3.80% + 1.07(4.79% + 4.43%) = 13.67%

For Embratel, with its lower beta of 0.80, the cost of equity is:

Cost of equity for Embratel = 3.80% + 0.80(4.79% + 4.43%) = 11.18%

The advantage of using betas is that they are easily available for most firms. The disadvantage is that while betas measure overall exposure to macroeconomic risk, they may not be good measures of country risk.

THE LAMBDA APPROACH

The most general, and our preferred, approach is to allow for each company to have an exposure to country risk that is different from its exposure to all other market risk. For lack of a better term, let us term the measure of a company's exposure to country risk to be lambda (λ). Like a beta, a lambda will be scaled around 1.00, with a lambda of 1.00 indicating a company with average exposure to country risk and a lambda above or below 1.00 indicating above or below average exposure to country risk. The cost of equity for a firm in an emerging market can then be written as:

Expected return = R_f + β (Mature market equity risk premium) + λ (Country risk premium)

Note that this approach essentially converts our expected return model to a two-factor model, with the second factor being country risk, with λ measuring exposure to country risk.

Determinants of Lambda

Most investors would accept the general proposition that different companies in a market should have different exposures to country risk. But what are the determinants of this exposure? We would expect at least three factors (and perhaps more) to play a role.

1 *Revenue source*: The first and most obvious determinant is how much of the revenues a firm derives from the country in question. A company that derives 30% of its revenues from Brazil should be less exposed to Brazilian country risk than a company that derives 70% of its revenues from Brazil. Note, though, that this then opens up the possibility that a company can be exposed to the risk in many countries. Thus, the company that derives only 30% of its revenues from Brazil may derive its remaining revenues from Argentina and Venezuela, exposing it to country risk in those countries. Extending this argument to multi-nationals, we would argue that companies like Coca-Cola and Nestlé can have substantial exposure to country risk because so much of their revenues comes from emerging markets.

2 *Production facilities*: A company can be exposed to country risk, even if it derives no revenues from that country, if its production facilities are in that country. After all, political and economic turmoil in the country can throw off production schedules and affect the company's profits. Companies that can move their production facilities elsewhere can spread their risk across several countries, but the problem is exaggerated for those companies that cannot move their production facilities. Consider the case of mining companies. An African gold mining company may export all of its production but it will face substantial country risk exposure because its mines are not movable.

3 *Risk management products*: Companies that would otherwise be exposed to substantial country risk may be able to reduce this exposure by buying insurance against specific (unpleasant) contingencies and by using deriva-tives. A company that uses risk management products should have a lower exposure to country risk—a lower lambda—than an otherwise similar company that does not use these products.

Ideally, we would like companies to be forthcoming about all three of these factors in their financial statements.

Measuring Lambda

The simplest measure of lambda is based entirely on revenues. In the last section, we argued that a company that derives a smaller proportion of its revenues from a market should be less exposed to country risk. Given the constraint that the average lambda across all stocks has to be 1.0 (someone has to bear the country risk!), we cannot use the percentage of revenues that a company gets from a market as lambda. We can, however, scale this measure by dividing it by the percentage of revenues that the average company in the market gets from the country to derive a lambda.

$$\frac{\left(\lambda_i - \% \text{ of revenue in country}_{Company} \right)}{\% \text{ of revenue in country}_{Average\ company\ in\ market}}$$

Consider the two large and widely followed Brazilian companies—Embraer, an aerospace company that manufactures and sells aircraft to many of the world's leading airlines, and Embratel, the Brazilian telecommunications giant. In 2002, Embraer generated only 3% of its revenues in Brazil, whereas the average company in the market obtained 85% of its revenues in Brazil.[2] Using the measure suggested above, the lambda for Embraer would be:

$$\lambda_{Embraer} = \frac{3\%}{85\%} = 0.04$$

In contrast, Embratel generated 95% of its revenues from Brazil, giving it a lambda of

$$\lambda_{Embratel} = \frac{95\%}{85\%} = 1.12$$

Following up, Embratel is far more exposed to country risk than Embraer and will have a much higher cost of equity.

The second measure draws on the stock prices of a company and how they move in relation to movements in country risk. Bonds issued by countries offer a simple and updated measure of country risk; as investor assessments of country risk become more optimistic, bonds issued by that country go up in price, just as they go down when investors become more pessimistic. A regression of the returns on a stock against the returns on a country bond should therefore yield a measure of lambda in the slope coefficient. Applying this approach to Embraer and Embratel, we regressed monthly stock returns on the two stocks against monthly returns on the ten-year dollar-denominated Brazilian government bond and arrived at the following results:

$$Return_{Embraer} = 0.0195 + 0.2681\ Return_{Brazil\ dollar\text{-}bond}$$

$$Return_{Embratel} = -0.0308 + 2.0030\ Return_{Brazil\ dollar\text{-}bond}$$

Based upon these regressions, Embraer has a lambda of 0.27 and Embratel has a lambda of 2.00. The resulting dollar costs of equity for the two firms, using a mature market equity risk premium of 4.79% and a country equity risk premium of 4.43% for Brazil are:

Cost of equity for Embraer = 3.80% + 1.07(4.79%) + 0.27(4.43%) = 10.12%

Cost of equity for Embratel = 3.80% + 0.80(4.79%) + 2.00(4.43%) = 16.49%

What are the limitations of this approach? The lambdas estimated from these regressions are likely to have large standard errors; the standard error in the lambda estimate of Embratel is 0.35. It also requires that the country have bonds that are liquid and widely traded, preferably in a more stable currency (dollar or euro).

Risk Exposure in Many Countries
The discussion of lambdas in the last section should highlight a fact that is often lost in valuation. The exposure to country risk, whether it is measured in revenues, earnings, or stock prices, does not come from where a company is incorporated but from its operations. There are US companies that are more exposed to Brazilian country risk than is Embraer. In fact, companies like Nestlé, Coca-Cola, and Gillette have built much of their success on expansion into emerging markets. While this expansion has provided them with growth opportunities, it has also left them exposed to country risk in multiple countries.

In practical terms, what does this imply? When estimating the costs of equity and capital for these companies and others like them, we will need to incorporate an extra premium for country risk. Thus, the net effect on value from their growth strategies will depend upon whether the growth effect (from expanding into emerging markets) exceeds the risk effect. We can adapt the measures suggested above to estimate the risk exposure to different countries for an individual company.

We can break down a company's revenue by country and use the percentage of revenues that the company gets from each emerging market as a basis for estimating lambda in that market. While the percentage of revenues itself can be used as a lambda, a more precise estimate would scale this to the percentage of revenues that the average company in that market gets in the country.

If companies break earnings down by country, these numbers can be used to estimate lambdas. The peril with this approach is that the reported earnings often reflect accounting allocation decisions and differences in tax rates across countries.

If a company is exposed to only a few emerging markets on a large scale, we can regress the company's stock price against the country bond returns from those markets to get country-specific lambdas.

CONCLUSION
A key issue, when estimating costs of equity and capital for emerging market companies relates to how this country risk premium should be reflected in the costs of equities of individual companies in that country. While the standard approaches add the country risk premium as a constant to the cost of equity of every company in that market, we argue for a more nuanced approach where a company's exposure to country risk is measured with a lambda. This lambda can be estimated either by looking at how much of a company's revenues or earnings come from the country—the greater the percentage, the greater the lambda—or by regressing a company's stock returns against country bond returns—the greater the sensitivity, the higher the lambda. If we accept this view of the world, the costs of equity for multinationals that have significant operations in emerging markets will have to be adjusted to reflect their exposure to risk in these markets.

MORE INFO
Book:
Falaschetti, Dominic, and Michael Annin Ibbotson (eds). *Stocks, Bonds, Bills and Inflation*. Chicago, IL: Ibbotson Associates, 1999.

Articles:

Booth, Laurence. "Estimating the equity risk premium and equity costs: New ways of looking at old data." *Journal of Applied Corporate Finance* 12:1 (Spring 1999): 100–112. Online at: dx.doi.org/10.1111/j.1745-6622.1999. tb00665.x

Chan, K. C., G. Andrew Karolyi, and René M. Stulz. "Global financial markets and the risk premium on US equity." *Journal of Financial Economics* 32:2 (October 1992): 137–167. Online at: dx.doi.org/10.1016/0304-405X(92)90016-Q

Damodaran, Aswath. "Country risk and company exposure: Theory and practice." *Journal of Applied Finance* 13:2 (Fall/Winter 2003): 64–78.

Godfrey, Stephen, and Ramon Espinosa. "A practical approach to calculating the cost of equity for investments in emerging markets." *Journal of Applied Corporate Finance* 9:3 (Fall 1996): 80–90. Online at: dx.doi.org/10.1111/j.1745-6622. 1996.tb00300.x

Indro, Daniel C., and Wayne Y. Lee. "Biases in arithmetic and geometric averages as estimates of long-run expected returns and risk premium." *Financial Management* 26:4 (Winter 1997): 81–90. Online at: www.jstor.org/stable/3666130

Stulz, René M. "Globalization, corporate finance, and the cost of capital." *Journal of Applied Corporate Finance* 12:3 (Fall 1999): 8–25. Online at: dx.doi.org/10.1111/j.1745-6622. 1999.tb00027.x

Report:

Damodaran, Aswath. "Measuring company risk exposure to country risk: Theory and practice." September 2003. Online at: tinyurl.com/77ozxll [PDF].

NOTES

1 We used a bottom-up beta for Embraer, based upon an unlevered beta of 0.95 (estimated using aerospace companies listed globally) and Embraer's debt-to-equity ratio of 19.01%. For more on the rationale for bottom-up betas, read the companion paper on estimating risk parameters, "Measuring Country Risk."

2 To use this approach, we need to estimate the percentage of revenues both for the firm in question and for the average firm in the market. While the former may be simple to obtain, estimating the latter can be a time-consuming exercise. One simple solution is to use data that are publicly available on how much of a country's gross domestic product comes from exports. According to the World Bank data in this table, Brazil got 23.2% of its GDP from exports in 2008. If we assume that this is an approximation of export revenues for the average firm, the average firm can be assumed to generate 76.8% of its revenues domestically. Using this value would yield slightly higher betas for both Embraer and Embratel.

Measuring Country Risk
by Aswath Damodaran

EXECUTIVE SUMMARY

• As companies and investors globalize and financial markets expand around the world, we are increasingly faced with estimation questions about the risk associated with this globalization.
• When investors invest in Petrobras, Gazprom, and China Power, they may be rewarded with higher returns, but they are also exposed to additional risk.
• When US and European multinationals push for growth in Asia and Latin America, they are clearly exposed to the political and economic turmoil that often characterize these markets.
• In practical terms, how, if at all, should we adjust for this additional risk? We review the discussion on country risk premiums and how to estimate them.

INTRODUCTION

Two key questions must be addressed when investing in emerging markets in Asia, Latin America, and Eastern Europe. The first relates to whether we should impose an additional risk premium when valuing equities in these markets. As we will see, the answer will depend upon whether we view markets to be open or segmented and whether we believe the risk can be diversified away. The second question relates to estimating an equity risk premium for emerging markets.

SHOULD THERE BE A COUNTRY RISK PREMIUM?

Is there more risk in investing in Malaysian or Brazilian equities than there is in investing in equities in the United States? Of course! But that does not automatically imply that there should be an additional risk premium charged when investing in those markets. Two arguments are generally used against adding an additional premium.

Country risk can be diversified away: If the additional risk of investing in Malaysia or Brazil can be diversified away, then there should be no additional risk premium charged. But for country risk to be diversifiable, two conditions must be met:

1 The marginal investors—i.e., active investors who hold large positions in the stock—have to be globally diversified. If the marginal investors are either unable or unwilling to invest globally, companies will have to diversify their operations across countries, which is a much more difficult and expensive exercise.

2 All or much of country risk should be country-specific. In other words, there should be low correlation across markets. If the returns across countries are positively correlated, country risk has a market risk component, is not diversifiable, and can command a premium. Whereas studies in the 1970s indicated low or no correlation across markets, increasing diversification on the part of both investors and companies has increased the correlation numbers. This is borne out by the speed with which troubles in one market can spread to a market with which it has little or no obvious relationship—say Brazil—and this contagion effect seems to become stronger during crises.

Given that both conditions are difficult to meet, we believe that on this basis, country risk should command a risk premium.

The expected cash flows for country risk can be adjusted: This second argument used against adjusting for country risk is that it is easier and more accurate to adjust the expected cash flows for the risk. However, adjusting the cash flows to reflect expectations about dire scenarios, such as nationalization or an economic meltdown, is not risk adjustment. Making the risk adjustment to cash flows requires the same analysis that we will employ to estimate the risk adjustment to discount rates.

ESTIMATING A COUNTRY RISK PREMIUM

If country risk is not diversifiable, either because the marginal investor is not globally diversified or because the risk is correlated across markets, we are left with the task of measuring country risk and estimating country risk premiums. In this section, we will consider two approaches that can be used to estimate country risk premiums. One approach builds on historical risk premiums and can be viewed as the *historical risk premium plus approach*. In the other approach, we estimate the equity risk premium by looking at how the market prices stocks and expected cash flows—this is the *implied premium approach*.

Historical Premium Plus

Most practitioners, when estimating risk premiums in the United States, look at the past. Consequently, we look at what we would have earned as investors by investing in equities as opposed to investing in riskless investments. With emerging markets, we will almost never have access to as much historical data as we do in the United States. If we combine this with the high volatility in stock returns in such markets, the conclusion is that historical risk premiums can be computed for these markets, but they will be useless because

of the large standard errors in the estimates. Consequently, many analysts build their equity risk premium estimates for emerging markets from mature market historical risk premiums.

$$\text{Equity risk premium}_{\text{Emerging market}} = \text{Equity risk premium}_{\text{Mature market}} + \text{Country risk premium}$$

To estimate the base premium for a mature equity market, we will make the argument that the US equity market is a mature market and that there is sufficient historical data in the United States to make a reasonable estimate of the risk premium. Using the historical data for the United States, we estimate the geometric average premium earned by stocks over treasury bonds of 4.79% between 1928 and 2007. To estimate the country risk premium, we can use one of three approaches:

Country Bond Default Spreads

One of the simplest and most easily accessible country risk measures is the rating assigned to a country's debt by a ratings agency (S&P, Moody's, and IBCA all rate countries). These ratings measure default risk (rather than equity risk), but they are affected by many of the factors that drive equity risk—the stability of a country's currency, its budget and trade balances and its political stability for instance.[1] The other advantage of ratings is that they can be used to estimate default spreads over a riskless rate. For instance, Brazil was rated Ba1 in September 2008 by Moody's and the ten-year Brazilian ten-year dollar-denominated bond was priced to yield 5.95%, 2.15% more than the interest rate (3.80%) on a ten-year US treasury bond at the same time.[2] Analysts who use default spreads as measures of country risk typically add them on to the cost of both equity and debt of every company traded in that country. If we assume that the total equity risk premium for the United States and other mature equity markets is 4.79%, the risk premium for Brazil would be 6.94%.[3]

Relative Standard Deviation

There are some analysts who believe that the equity risk premiums of markets should reflect the differences in equity risk, as measured by the volatilities of equities in these markets. A conventional measure of equity risk is the standard deviation in stock prices; higher standard deviations are generally associated with more risk. If we scale the standard deviation of one market against another, we obtain a measure of relative risk.

$$\text{Relative standard deviation}_{\text{Country X}} = \frac{\text{Standard deviation}_{\text{Country X}}}{\text{Standard deviation}_{\text{US}}}$$

This relative standard deviation when multiplied by the premium used for US stocks should yield a measure of the total risk premium for any market.

$$\text{Equity risk premium}_{\text{Country X}} = \text{Risk premium}_{\text{US}} \times \text{Relative standard deviation}_{\text{Country X}}$$

Assume, for the moment, that we are using a mature market premium for the United States of 4.79%. The annualized standard deviation in the S&P 500 between 2006 and 2008, using weekly returns, was 15.27%, whereas the standard deviation in the Bovespa (the Brazilian equity index) over the same period was 25.83%.[4] Using these values, the estimate of a total risk premium for Brazil would be as follows:

$$\text{Equity risk premium}_{Brazil} = \frac{4.79\% \times 25.83\%}{15.27\%} = 8.10\%$$

The country risk premium can be isolated as follows:

$$\text{Country risk premium}_{Brazil} = 8.10\% - 4.79\% = 3.31\%$$

While this approach has intuitive appeal, there are problems with comparing standard deviations computed in markets with widely different market structures and liquidity. There are very risky emerging markets that have low standard deviations for their equity markets because the markets are illiquid. This approach will understate the equity risk premiums in those markets.

Default Spreads and Relative Standard Deviations

The country default spreads that come with country ratings provide an important first step, but still only measure the premium for default risk. Intuitively, we would expect the country equity risk premium to be larger than the country default risk spread. To address the issue of how much higher, we look at the volatility of the equity market in a country relative to the volatility of the bond market used to estimate the spread. This yields the following estimate for the country equity risk premium.

$$\text{Country risk premium} = \frac{\text{Country default spread} \times \sigma \text{ Equity}}{\sigma \text{ Country bond}}$$

To illustrate, consider again the case of Brazil. As noted earlier, the default spread on the Brazilian dollar-denominated bond in September 2008 was 2.15%, and the annualized standard deviation in the Brazilian equity index over the previous year was 25.83%. Using two years of weekly returns, the annualized standard deviation in the Brazilian dollar-denominated ten-year bond was 12.55%.[5] The resulting country equity risk premium for Brazil is as follows:

$$\text{Additional equity risk premium}_{Brazil} = \frac{2.15\% \times 25.83\%}{12.55\%} = 4.43\%$$

Unlike the equity standard deviation approach, this premium is in addition to a mature market equity risk premium. Note that this country risk premium will increase if the country rating drops or if the relative volatility of the equity market increases. It is also in addition to the equity risk premium for a mature market. Thus, the total equity risk premium for Brazil using this approach and a 4.79% premium for the United States would be 9.22%.

Both this approach and the previous one use the standard deviation in equity of a market to make a judgment about country risk premium, but they measure it relative to different bases. This approach uses the country bond as a base, whereas the previous one uses the standard deviation in the US market. It also assumes that investors are more likely to choose

between Brazilian government bonds and Brazilian equity, whereas the previous approach assumes that the choice is across equity markets.

Implied Equity Premiums

There is an alternative approach to estimating risk premiums that does not require historical data or corrections for country risk but does assume that the market, overall, is correctly priced. Consider, for instance, a very simple valuation model for stocks:

$$\text{Value} = \frac{\text{Expected dividends next period}}{(\text{Required return on equity} - \text{Expected growth rate})}$$

This is essentially the present value of dividends growing at a constant rate. Three of the four inputs in this model can be obtained externally—the current level of the market (value), the expected dividends next period, and the expected growth rate in earnings and dividends in the long term. The only "unknown" is then the required return on equity; when we solve for it, we get an implied expected return on stocks. Subtracting out the risk-free rate will yield an implied equity risk premium. We can extend the model to allow for dividends to grow at high rates, at least for short periods.

The advantage of the implied premium approach is that it is market-driven and current, and it does not require any historical data. Thus, it can be used to estimate implied equity premiums in any market. For instance, the equity risk premium for the Brazilian equity market on September 9, 2008, was estimated from the following inputs. The index (Bovespa) was at 48,345 and the current cash flow yield on the index was 5.41%. Earnings in companies in the index are expected to grow 9% (in US dollar terms) over the next five years, and 3.8% thereafter. These inputs yield a required return on equity of 10.78%, which when compared to the treasury bond rate of 3.80% on that day results in an implied equity premium of 6.98%. For simplicity, we have used nominal dollar expected growth rates[6] and treasury bond rates, but this analysis could have been done entirely in the local currency. We can decompose this number into a mature market equity risk premium and a country-specific equity risk premium by comparing it to the implied equity risk premium for a mature equity market (the United States, for instance).

- Implied equity premium for Brazil (see above) = 6.98%.
- Implied equity premium for the United States in September 2008 = 4.54%.
- Country specific equity risk premium for Brazil = 2.44%.

This approach can yield numbers very different from the other approaches, because they reflect market prices (and views) today.

CONCLUSION

As companies expand operations into emerging markets and investors search for investment opportunities in Asia and Latin America, they are also increasingly exposed to additional risk in these countries. While it is true that globally diversified investors can eliminate some country risk by diversifying across equities in many countries, the increasing correlation across markets suggests that country risk cannot be entirely diversified away. To estimate the country risk premium, we considered three measures: the default spread on a government

★

Best Practice

bond issued by that country, a premium obtained by scaling up the equity risk premium in the United States by the volatility of the country equity market relative to the US equity market, and a melded premium where the default spread on the country bond is adjusted for the higher volatility of the equity market. We also estimated an implied equity premium from stock prices and expected cash flows.

MORE INFO

Book:

Falaschetti, Dominic, and Michael Annin Ibbotson (eds). *Stocks, Bonds, Bills and Inflation*. Chicago, IL: Ibbotson Associates, 1999.

Articles:

Booth, Laurence. "Estimating the equity risk premium and equity costs: New ways of looking at old data." *Journal of Applied Corporate Finance* 12:1 (Spring 1999): 100–112. Online at: dx.doi.org/10.1111/j.1745-6622.1999.tb00665.x

Chan, K. C., G. Andrew Karolyi, and René M. Stulz. "Global financial markets and the risk premium on US equity." *Journal of Financial Economics* 32:2 (October 1992): 137–167. Online at: dx.doi.org/10.1016/0304-405X(92)90016-Q

Indro, D. C., and W. Y. Lee. "Biases in arithmetic and geometric averages as estimates of long-run expected returns and risk premium." *Financial Management* 26:4 (Winter 1997): 81–90. Online at: www.jstor.org/stable/3666130

Report:

Damodaran, Aswath. "Equity risk premiums (ERP): Determinants, estimation and implications." October 2008. Online at: tinyurl.com/7qaq2z9 [PDF].

See Also:

★ Measuring Company Exposure to Country Risk (pp. 136–139)
★ Political Risk: Countering the Impact on Your Business (pp. 270–273)
✔ Identifying and Managing Exposure to Interest and Exchange Rate Risks (pp. 296–297)
✔ Understanding the Relationship between the Discount Rate and Risk (pp. 308–309)

NOTES

1 The process by which country ratings are obtained is explained on the S&P website at www2.standardandpoors.com/aboutcreditratings

2 These yields were as of January 1, 2008. While this is a market rate and reflects current expectations, country bond spreads are extremely volatile and can shift significantly from day to day. To counter this volatility, the default spread can be normalized by averaging the spread over time or by using the average default spread for all countries with the same rating as Brazil in early 2008.

3 If a country has a sovereign rating and no dollar-denominated bonds, we can use a typical spread based upon the rating as the default spread for the country. These numbers are available on my website at www.damodaran.com

4 If the dependence on historical volatility is troubling, the options market can be used to get implied volatilities for both the US market (about 20%) and for the Bovespa (about 38%).

5 Both standard deviations are computed on returns: returns on the equity index and returns on the ten-year bond.

6 The input that is most difficult to estimate for emerging markets is a long-term expected growth rate. For Brazilian stocks, I used the average consensus estimate of growth in earnings for the largest Brazilian companies which have ADRs listed on them. This estimate may be biased as a consequence.

Minimizing Credit Risk
by Frank J. Fabozzi

EXECUTIVE SUMMARY

- Credit risk encompasses credit default risk, credit spread risk, and downgrade risk.
- Market participants typically gauge credit default risk in terms of the credit rating assigned by rating agencies.
- Factors that are considered in the evaluation of a corporate borrower's creditworthiness are: the quality of management; the ability of the borrower to satisfy the debt obligation; the level of seniority and the collateral available in a bankruptcy proceeding; and covenants.
- Credit risk transfer vehicles allow the redistribution of credit risk.
- Securitization is a credit risk transfer vehicle for corporations that is accomplished by selling a pool of loans or receivables to a third-party entity.
- Credit derivatives are a form of credit risk transfer vehicle.

INTRODUCTION

Financial corporations and investors face several types of risk. One major risk is credit risk. Despite the fact that market participants typically refer to "credit risk" as if it is one-dimensional, there are actually three forms of this risk: credit default risk, credit spread risk, and downgrade risk.

Credit default risk is the risk that the issuer will fail to satisfy the terms of the obligation with respect to the timely payment of interest and repayment of the amount borrowed. This form of credit risk covers counterparty risk in a trade or derivative transaction where the counterparty fails to satisfy its obligation. To gauge credit default risk, investors typically rely on credit ratings. A *credit rating* is a formal opinion given by a company referred to as a *rating agency* of the credit default risk faced by investing in a particular issue of debt securities. For long-term debt obligations, a credit rating is a forward-looking assessment of the probability of default and the relative magnitude of the loss should a default occur. For short-term debt obligations, a credit rating is a forward-looking assessment of the probability of default. The nationally recognized rating agencies include Moody's Investors Service, Standard & Poor's, and Fitch Ratings.

Credit spread risk is the loss or underperformance of an issue or issues due to an increase in the credit spread. The credit spread is the compensation sought by investors for accepting the credit default risk of an issue or issuer. The credit spread varies with market conditions and the credit rating of the issue or issuer. On the issuer side, credit spread risk is the risk that an issuer's credit spread will increase when it must come to market to offer bonds, resulting in a higher funding cost.

Downgrade risk is the risk that an issue or issuer will be downgraded, resulting in an increase in the credit spread demanded by the market. Hence, downgrade risk is related to credit spread risk. Occasionally, the ability of an issuer to make interest and principal payments diminishes seriously and unexpectedly because of an unforeseen event. This can include any number of idiosyncratic events that are specific to the corporation or to an industry, including a natural or industrial accident, a regulatory change, a takeover or corporate restructuring, or corporate fraud. This risk is referred to generically as *event risk* and will result in a downgrading of the issuer by the rating agencies.

FACTORS CONSIDERED IN ASSESSING CREDIT DEFAULT RISK

The most obvious way to protect against credit risk is to analyze the creditworthiness of the borrower. In performing such an analysis, credit analysts evaluate the factors that affect the business risk of a borrower. These factors can be classified into four general categories—the quality of the borrower; the ability of the borrower to satisfy the debt obligation; the level of seniority and the collateral available in a bankruptcy proceeding; and restrictions imposed on the borrower.

In the case of a corporation, the quality of the borrower involves assessing the firm's business strategies and management policies. More specifically, a credit analyst will study the corporation's strategic plan, accounting control systems, and financial philosophy regarding the use of debt. In assigning a credit rating, Moody's states:

"Although difficult to quantify, management quality is one of the most important factors supporting an issuer's credit strength. When the unexpected occurs, it is a management's ability to react appropriately that will sustain the company's performance."[1]

The ability of the borrower to meet its obligations begins with the analysis of the borrower's financial statements. Commonly used measures of liquidity and debt coverage combined with estimates of future cash flows are calculated and investigated if there are concerns. In addition, the analysis considers industry trends, the borrower's basic operating and competitive position, sources of liquidity (backup lines of credit), and, if applicable, the regulatory environment. An investigation of industry trends aids a credit analyst in assessing the vulnerability of the firm to economic cycles, the barriers to entry, and the exposure of the company to technological changes. An investigation of the borrower's

various lines of business aids the credit analyst in assessing the firm's basic operating position.

A credit analyst will look at the position as a creditor in the case of a bankruptcy. The US Bankruptcy Act comprises 15 chapters, each covering a particular type of bankruptcy. Of particular interest here are Chapter 7, which deals with the liquidation of a company, and Chapter 11, which deals with the reorganization of a company. When a company is liquidated, creditors receive distributions based on the *absolute priority rule* to the extent that assets are available. The absolute priority rule is the principle that senior creditors are paid in full before junior creditors are paid anything. For secured creditors and unsecured creditors, the absolute priority rule guarantees their seniority to equity holders. However, in the case of a reorganization, the absolute priority rule rarely holds because in practice unsecured creditors do in fact typically receive distributions for the entire amount of their claim and common stockholders may receive something, while secured creditors may receive only a portion of their claim. The reason is that a reorganization requires the approval of all the parties. Consequently, secured creditors are willing to negotiate with both unsecured creditors and stockholders in order to obtain approval of the plan of reorganization.

The restrictions imposed on the borrower (management) that are part of the terms and conditions of the lending or bond agreement are called *covenants*. Covenants deal with limitations and restrictions on the borrower's activities. Affirmative covenants call on the debtor to make promises to do certain things. Negative covenants are those that require the borrower not to take certain actions. A violation of any covenant may provide a meaningful early warning alarm, enabling lenders to take positive and corrective action before the situation deteriorates further. Covenants play an important part in minimizing risk to creditors.

CREDIT RISK TRANSFER VEHICLES

There are various ways that investors, particularly institutional investors, can reduce their exposure to credit risk. These arrangements are referred to as *credit transfer vehicles*. It should be borne in mind that an institutional investor may not necessarily want to eliminate credit risk but may want to control it or have an efficient means by which to reduce it. The increasing number of credit risk transfer vehicles has made it easier for financial institutions to reallocate large amounts of credit risk to the nonfinancial sector of the capital markets.

For a bank, the most obvious way to transfer the credit risk of a loan it has originated is to sell it to another party. The bank management's concern when it sells corporate loans is the potential impairment of its relationship with the corporate borrower. This concern is overcome with the use of *syndicated loans*, because banks in the syndicate may sell their loan shares in the secondary market by means of either an *assignment* or a *participation*. With an assignment, a syndicated loan requires the approval of the obligor; that is not the case with a participation since the payments by the borrower are merely passed through to the purchaser, and therefore the obligor need not know about the sale.

Two credit risk vehicles that have increased in importance since the 1990s are securitization and credit derivatives. It is important to note that the pricing of these credit risk transfer instruments is not an easy task. Pricing becomes even more complicated for lower-quality borrowers and for credits that are backed by a pool of lower-quality assets, as recent events in the capital markets have demonstrated.

SECURITIZATION

Securitization involves the pooling of loans and/or receivables and selling that pool of assets to a third-party, a special purpose vehicle (SPV). By doing so, the risks associated with that pool of assets, such as credit risk, are transferred to the SPV. In turn, the SPV obtains the funds to acquire the pool of assets by selling securities. When the pool of assets consists of consumer receivables or mortgage loans, the securities issued are referred to as *asset-backed securities*. When the asset pool consists of corporate loans, the securities issued are called *collateralized loan obligations*.

A major reason why a financial or nonfinancial corporation uses securitization as a fund-raising vehicle is that it may allow a lower funding cost than issuing secured debt. However, another important reason is that securitization is a risk management tool. Although the entity employing securitization retains some of the credit risk associated with the pool of loans (referred to as retained interest), the majority of the credit risk is transferred to the holders of the securities issued by the SPV.

CREDIT DERIVATIVES

A financial derivative is a contract designed to transfer some form of risk between two or more parties efficiently. When a financial derivative allows the transfer of credit exposure of an underlying asset or assets between two parties, it is referred to as a *credit derivative*. More specifically, credit derivatives allow investors either to acquire or to reduce credit risk exposure. Many institutional investors have portfolios that are highly sensitive to changes in the credit spread between a default-free asset and a credit-risky asset, and credit derivatives are an efficient way to manage this exposure. Conversely, other institutional investors may use credit derivatives to target specific credit exposures as a way to enhance portfolio returns. Consequently, the ability to transfer credit risk and return provides a tool for institutional investors—the potential to improve performance. Moreover, corporate treasurers can use credit derivatives to transfer the risk associated with an increase in credit spreads (i.e., credit spread risk).

Credit derivatives include credit default swaps, asset swaps, total return swaps, credit linked notes, credit spread options, and credit spread forwards. In addition, there are index-type or basket credit products that are sponsored by banks that link the payoff to the investor to a portfolio of credits. Credit derivatives are over-the-counter instruments and are therefore not traded on an organized exchange. Hence, credit derivatives expose an investor to counterparty risk, and this has been the major concern in recent years in view of the credit problems of large banks and dealer firms who are the counterparties.

Credit derivatives also permit banks to transfer credit risk without the need to transfer assets physically. For example, in a collateral loan obligation, a bank can sell a pool of corporate loans to a special purpose vehicle (SPV) in order to reduce its exposure to the corporate borrowers. Alternatively, it can transfer the credit risk exposure by buying credit protection for the same pool of corporate loans. In this case, the transaction is referred to as a *synthetic collateralized loan obligation*.

An understanding of credit derivatives is critical even for those who do not want to use them. As Alan Greenspan, then the Chairman of the Federal Reserve Board, in a speech on September 25, 2002, stated:

"The growing prominence of the market for credit derivatives is attributable not only to its ability to disperse risk but also to the information it contributes to enhanced risk management by banks and other financial intermediaries. Credit default swaps, for example, are priced to reflect the probability of net loss from the default of an ever broadening array of borrowers, both financial and non-financial."[2]

CASE STUDY

A *credit-linked note* (CLN) is a security, usually issued by an investment-grade-rated corporation, that has an interest payment and fixed maturity structure similar to a standard bond. In contrast to a standard bond, the performance of the CLN is linked to the performance of a specified underlying asset or assets as well as that of the issuing entity. There are different ways that a CLN can be credit linked, and we will describe one case here.

British Telecom issued on December 15, 2000, a CLN with a coupon rate of 8.125% maturing on December 15, 2010. The terms of this CLN stated that the coupon rate would increase by 25 basis points for each one-notch rating downgrade of British Telecom below A–/A3 suffered during the life of the CLN. The coupon rate would decrease by 25 basis points for each rating upgrade, with a minimum coupon set at 8.125%. In other words, this CLN allows investors to make a credit play based on this issuer's credit rating. In fact, in May 2003, British Telecom was downgraded by one rating notch and the coupon rate was increased to 8.375%.

CONCLUSION

While market participants typically think of credit risk in terms of the failure of a borrower to make timely interest and principal payments on a debt obligation, this is only one form of credit risk: credit default risk. The other types of credit risk are credit spread risk and downgrade risk. When evaluating the credit default risk of a borrower, credit analysts look at the quality of the borrower, the ability of the borrower to satisfy the debt obligation, the level of seniority and the collateral available in a bankruptcy proceeding, and covenants. Credit risk transfer vehicles include securitization and credit derivatives. Credit derivatives include credit default swaps, asset swaps, total return swaps, credit linked notes, credit spread options, credit spread forwards, and baskets or indexes of credits.

MAKING IT HAPPEN

Controlling credit risk requires not just an understanding of what credit risk is and the factors that affect a borrower's credit rating but other important implementation issues. These include:

- establishing the credit risk exposure that a corporation or institutional investor is willing to accept;
- quantifying the credit risk by using the latest quantitative tools in the field of credit risk modeling;
- understanding the various credit risk transfer vehicles that can be employed to control credit risk;
- evaluating the merits of different credit risk transfer vehicles to determine which are the most appropriate for altering credit risk exposure.

MORE INFO

Books:

Anson, Mark J. P., Frank J. Fabozzi, Moorad Choudhry, and Ren-Raw Chen. *Credit Derivatives: Instruments, Pricing, and Applications.* Hoboken, NJ: Wiley, 2004.

Fabozzi, Frank J., Moorad Choudhry, and Steven V. Mann. *Measuring and Controlling Interest Rate and Credit Risk*. 2nd ed. Hoboken, NJ: Wiley, 2003.

Articles:

Fabozzi, Frank J., and Moorad Choudhry. "Originating collateralized debt obligations for balance sheet management." *Journal of Structured Finance* 9:3 (Fall 2003): 32–52. Online at: dx.doi.org/10.3905/jsf.2003.320318

Fabozzi, Frank J., Henry A. Davis, and Moorad Choudhry, "Credit-linked notes: A product primer." *Journal of Structured Finance* 12:4 (Winter 2007): 67–77. Online at: dx.doi.org/10.3905/jsf.12.4.67

Lucas, Douglas J., Laurie S. Goodman, and Frank J. Fabozzi. "Collateralized debt obligations and credit risk transfer." *Journal of Financial Transformation* 20 (2007): 47–59. Online at: tinyurl.com/86xlppd

Websites:

DefaultRisk.Com—for credit risk modeling and measurement: www.defaultrisk.com

Vinod Kothari's credit derivatives website: www.credit-deriv.com

See Also:

★ Countering Supply Chain Risk (pp. 253–255)
★ Managing Counterparty Credit Risk (pp. 31–34)

NOTES

1 Moody's Investor Service. "Industrial company rating methodology." *Global Credit Research* (July 2008): 6.

2 Speech titled "World Finance and Risk Management," at Lancaster House, London, United Kingdom.

Optimizing the Capital Structure: Finding the Right Balance between Debt and Equity

by Meziane Lasfer

EXECUTIVE SUMMARY

- Just over 50 years ago Miller and Modigliani (1958) showed that under a certain set of conditions—namely perfect capital markets with no taxes and agency conflicts—a firm's capital structure is irrelevant to its valuation.
- Their results are controversial and have raised a large number of questions from academics and practitioners.
- This article summarizes the main issues underlying the choice by firms of an appropriate capital structure, taking into account their specific fundamentals as well as macroeconomic factors.
- It presents the benefits and costs of borrowing, describes how to assess these to arrive at the basic trade-off between debt and equity, and examines conditions under which debt becomes irrelevant.

TYPES OF FINANCING

There are three financing methods that companies can use: debt, equity, and hybrid securities. This categorization is based on the main characteristics of the securities.

Debt Financing

Debt financing ranges from simple bank debt to commercial paper and corporate bonds. It is a contractual arrangement between a company and an investor, whereby the company pays a predetermined claim (or interest) that is not a function of its operating performance, but which is treated in accounting standards as an expense for tax purposes and is therefore tax-deductible. The debt has a fixed life and has a priority claim on cash flows in both operating periods and bankruptcy. This is because interest is paid before the claims to equity holders, and, if the company defaults on interest payments, it will be declared bankrupt, its assets will be sold, and the amount owed to debt holders will be paid before any payments are made to equity holders.

Equity Financing

Equity financing includes owners' equity, venture capital (equity capital provided to a private firm in exchange for a share ownership of the firm), common equity, and warrants (the right to buy a share of stock in a company at a fixed price during the life of the warrant). Unlike debt, it is permanent in the company, its claim is residual and does not create a tax advantage from its payments as dividends are paid after interest and tax, it does not have priority in bankruptcy, and it provides management control for the owner.

Hybrid Securities

Hybrid securities are securities that share some characteristics with both debt and equity and include, for example, convertible securities (defined as debt that can be converted into equity at a prespecified date and conversion rate), preferred stock, and option-linked bonds.

THE IRRELEVANCE PROPOSITION

In 1958 Modigliani and Miller demonstrated that, under a certain set of assumptions, the choice between any of these securities (referred to as capital structure or leverage) is not relevant to a company's valuation. The assumptions include: no taxes, no costs of financial distress, perfect capital markets, no interest rate differentials, no agency costs (rationality), and no transaction costs. These assumptions are, in fact, the main drivers of capital structure and gave rise to the trade-off theory of leverage.

THE TRADE-OFF OF DEBT

In this so-called Miller–Modigliani framework, firms choose their optimal level of leverage by weighing the following benefits and costs of debt financing.

Benefits of Debt

There are two main advantages of debt financing: taxation, and added discipline.

Taxation: Since the interest on debt is paid before taxation, whereas dividends paid to equity holders are usually paid from profit after tax, the cost of debt is substantially less than the cost of equity. This tax-deductibility of interest makes debt financing attractive. Suppose that the debt of a company is $100 million and the interest rate is 10%. Every year the company pays interest of $10 million. Suppose that the corporation tax rate is 30%. If the company does not pay tax, its interest will be $10 million and the cost of debt will be 10%. However, if the company is able to deduct the tax on this $10 million from its corporation tax payment, then the company saves $10 million × 30% = $3 million in tax payments per year, making the effective interest payment only $7 million. If the debt is permanent, every year the company will have a $3 million tax saving, referred to as a tax shield. We can compute the present value (PV) by discounting annual value by the cost of debt, as follows:

$$\text{PV of tax shield} = \frac{k_d \times D \times t_c}{k_d} = D \times t_c$$

where k_d is the cost of debt, D is the amount of debt, and the product of k_d and D gives the amount of the interest charge. t_c is the corporation tax rate. We simplify the ratio by k_d to obtain the present value of the tax shield as the product of the amount of debt and the corporation tax rate. Thus, the value of a company that is financed with debt and equity (such a company is referred to "levered") should be equal to its value if it is financed only with equity plus the present value of the tax shield. We can write this value as:

Value of levered firm with debt D = Value of nonlevered firm + $D \times t_c$

These arguments suggest that the after-tax cost of debt can be computed as 10% × (1 − 30%) = 7%.

Added discipline: In practice, the managers are not the owners of the company. This so-called separation of managers and stockholders raises the possibility that managers may prefer to maximize their own wealth rather that of the stockholders. This is referred to as the agency conflict. In general, debt may make managers more disciplined because debt requires a fixed payment of interest, and defaulting on such payments will lead a company to bankruptcy.

Costs of Debt

Debt has a number of disadvantages, including a higher probability of bankruptcy, an increase in the agency conflicts between managers and bondholders, loss of future financial flexibility, and the cost of information asymmetry.

Expected bankruptcy cost. Given that debt holders can declare a company bankrupt if it defaults on its interest payment, companies that have a high level of debt are likely to have a high probability of facing such a default. This probability is also increased when a company is operating in a high business risk environment. Debt financing creates financial risk. Thus, companies that have high business risk should not increase their risk of default by taking on a high financial risk through their use of debt. Evidence indicates that much of the loss of value occurs not in the liquidation process but in the stage of financial distress, when the firm is struggling to pay its bills (including interest), even though it may not go on to be liquidated.

Agency costs: These costs arise when a company borrows funds and the managers use the funds to finance alternative, usually more risky, activities than those specified in the borrowing contract to generate higher returns to stockholders. The greater the separation between managers and lenders, the higher the agency costs.

Loss of future financing flexibility: When a firm increases its debt substantially, it faces difficulties raising additional debt. Companies that can forecast their future financing needs accurately can plan their financing better and may not raise additional funds randomly. In general, the greater the uncertainty about future financing needs, the higher the costs.

Information asymmetry: When companies do not disclose information to the market, their information asymmetry will be high, resulting in a higher cost of debt financing.

Redeployable assets of debt: Lenders require some sort of security when they fund a company. This security is referred to as collateral. Lenders accept assets that can be resold or redeployed into other activities, such as property (real estate), as collateral. In general, the lower the value of the redeployable assets of debt, the higher are the costs.

FINANCING CHOICES AND A FIRM'S LIFE CYCLE
Although companies may prefer to use internal financing to minimize the issuance (transaction) costs, the trend in financing depends critically on the firm's life cycle.

Start-ups are small, privately owned companies. They are likely to be financed by owners' funds and bank borrowings. Their funding needs are high, but their ability to raise external funding is limited because they do not have sufficient assets to offer as security to finance providers. They will try to seek private equity funding. Their long-term leverage is likely to be low as they are mainly financed with short-term debt.

Expanding companies are those that have succeeded in attracting customers and establishing a presence in the market. They are likely to be financed by private equity and/or venture capital in addition to owners' equity and bank debt. Their level of debt is low and they have more short-term than long-term debt in their capital structure.

High-growth companies are likely to be publicly traded, with rapidly growing revenues. They will issue equity in the form of common stock, warrants, and other equity options, and probably convertible debt. They are likely to have a moderate leverage.

Mature companies are likely to finance their activities by internal financing, debt, and equity. Their leverage is likely to be relatively high but will depend on the costs and benefits of debt and their fundamental factors, such as business risk and taxation.

CONCLUSION
This article discussed the different financing methods companies can use and then argued that their choice depends on the costs and benefits of debt financing and the firm's life cycle. For example, whereas start-up companies are likely to be financed with private personal funds, making their leverage low, mature companies tend to have high leverage because they are able to mitigate the costs of debt and gain from the tax benefits. In addition to these factors, in practice firms may choose their financing mix by mimicking comparable firms, or they may adopt the average level of debt of all the companies in their industry. These methods are not highly recommendable as they may result in a suboptimal choice. In other cases they follow a financing hierarchy, where retained earnings are the preferred option, followed by external financing in the form of debt, and then equity. This preference is driven by the transaction and monitoring costs.

MAKING IT HAPPEN
The choice of financing is strategic and involves the following issues:
- Both low- and high-debt financing are suboptimal. Companies should aim for the most advantageous level of debt financing, whereby the costs are minimized and the benefits are maximized.

- The costs of debt include a greater probability of bankruptcy, an increase in the agency conflicts between managers and bondholders, a loss of future financial flexibility (including the availability of collateral assets), and information asymmetry costs.
- The benefits relate mainly to tax shields and the added discipline to mitigate the agency conflicts between stockholders and managers.
- This equilibrium applies primarily to mature companies. Start-ups and growth companies are likely to have lower leverage as their borrowing capacity is low. It also applies to companies that normally pay dividends and do not accumulate cash for reinvestment in order to avoid the need to raise external financing.
- The recent financial crisis has highlighted another issue in debt financing, namely liquidity. Leverage concepts were developed mainly in times when debt financing was fully available. In the current credit crisis this is no longer the case. Companies therefore now have to pay an extra liquidity cost to raise additional capital. The question is whether this is a temporary situation or a permanent one, in which case debt will become more costly and leverage will be lower than in the past.
- Another challenge of debt financing relates to the ethics of the use of excessive debt financing, particularly by financial institutions. Pettifor (2006) was able to foresee the current crisis, tracing debt financing back to early times and arguing that religions are against debt because it results in usury. She provides interesting arguments, challenging the whole structure of debt financing, payment of interest, and interest tax deductibility. Possibly a new structure of debt that is linked to the profitability of assets and incurs no interest will emerge from the current crisis.

MORE INFO
Books:
Damodaran, Aswath. *Applied Corporate Finance*. 3rd ed. Hoboken, NJ: Wiley, 2010.
Pettifor, Ann. *The Coming First World Debt Crisis*. Basingstoke, UK: Palgrave Macmillan, 2006.

Articles:
Graham, John R., and Campbell R. Harvey. "How do CFOs make capital budgeting and capital structure decisions?" *Journal of Applied Corporate Finance* 15:1 (Spring 2002): 8–23. Online at: dx.doi.org/10.1111/j.1745-6622.2002.tb00337.x
Lasfer, Meziane A. "Agency costs, taxes and debt: The UK evidence." *European Financial Management* 1:3 (November 1995): 265–285. Online at: dx.doi.org/10.1111/j.1468-036X.1995.tb00020.x
Modigliani, Franco, and Merton H. Miller. "The cost of capital, corporation finance and the theory of investment." *American Economic Review* 48:3 (June 1958): 261–297. Online at: www.jstor.org/stable/info/1809766

Websites:
About.com article "Debt financing—Pros and cons": tinyurl.com/856j35k

★

Answers.com article "Debt financing":
  www.answers.com/topic/debt-financing

See Also:

★ Understanding the True Cost of Issuing Convertible Debt and Other Equity-Linked Financing (p. 169)

✔ Conflicting Interests: The Agency Issue (pp. 338–339)
✔ Understanding and Using Leverage Ratios (p. 335)
✔ Understanding Capital Structure Theory: Modigliani and Miller (pp. 306–307)
⇄ Debt/Equity Ratio (pp. 384–385)

Price Discovery in IPOs
by Jos van Bommel

EXECUTIVE SUMMARY

- When a company goes public, the issuer's intermediating investment bank (aka the underwriter, bookrunner, or lead manager) expends efforts and resources to discover the price at which the firm's shares can be sold.
- Buy-side clients also expend effort and resources to value the firm. The market price will be a weighted average of the many resulting value *estimates*.
- To discover the price at which the issue can be sold, the issuer helps buy-side clients with their analysis by providing a prospectus and meeting with their analysts during road show meetings.
- To extract newly produced information from the market, the issuing team asks selected buy-side clients for their indications of their interest.
- Investment banks compensate buy-side clients for their costly analysis by setting the price at a discount from the expected market price.
- In addition, investment banks allocate more shares to those buy-side clients who are more helpful in the price discovery exercise. Because of the repeated interaction between banks and their clients, free riding is curtailed, and price discovery is optimized.

PRICE DISCOVERY

The most important, yet most difficult, part of the initial public offering (IPO) process is setting the offer price. In an IPO, the issuer, aided by an intermediating investment bank, plans to sell a relatively large number of shares of common stock in which there is at that point no market. However, they know that soon after the IPO process the secondary market will impute all the information in the market in an efficient manner. Investors who believe the price to be too high will sell; investors who believe the price to be too low will buy. The key outcome of this competitive trading is the *market price* of the stock.

Naturally, the issuing team (the issuer and its investment bank would like to know the market price in advance. If they had a crystal ball, they would set the price at a small discount (say 3%) to the future market price, so as to generate sufficient interest from buy-side clients, and place the issue. In fact this is exactly what issuers do when they sell securities which already have a market price. Unfortunately, there is no

secondary market for IPO shares, and neither are there crystal balls.

To estimate the market price as best as they can, issuers and their advisers conduct a costly analysis to estimate the value of the firm. We call this process *price discovery*.

Note that not only do the issuer and its investment bank analyze the firm. Prospective investors also conduct costly analysis to predict the future market price. Naturally, a good estimate of the future market price gives them a substantial advantage in their dealings with the issuer: If they have strong indications that the offer price is set too high, they stay away from the offering. If they believe the price to be below the future market price, they sign up for IPO shares enthusiastically.

ENTERPRISE VALUATION

There are two main methods to estimate the market value of the firm: multiple analysis, and discounted cash flow (DCF) analysis.

Multiple Analysis

When employing the multiple method, analysts gather performance measures of the firm. A popular measure is *earnings* or *net income*. They multiply these performance measures with *multiples*. The appropriate multiple for a firm's earnings is the *price–earnings ratio*, or P/E. The multiples are obtained from similar firms, (so-called *proxies*, or *pure-plays*). For example, if listed paper manufacturers trade at an average P/E of 9, and we want to estimate the value of an unlisted paper company that recently reported a net income of $1 million, we would estimate the market price to be $9 million. Because this single estimate is bound to be imprecise, analysts collect *many* performance measures so as to get *many* estimates. Popular accounting performance measures are earnings, sales, operating income (EBIT), and cash flow (EBITDA). Apart from these, analysts use industry-specific performance measures such as passenger miles (for airlines), overnight stays (for hotels), or page visits (for internet companies). By employing more and more multiples, analysts aim to arrive at an ever more precise estimate of the market price.

Discounted Cash Flow Analysis

A more fundamental valuation method is discounted cash flow analysis. In an efficient market, securities should be worth the present value of the future cash payments that accrue to the shareholders. Since cash today is always more valuable than cash tomorrow, investors discount projected future cash flows at the opportunity cost of capital. For example, if investors want to value a one-year promissory note of $100, and the one-year interest rate is 10%, they conclude that the note is worth $100/1.10 = $90.91. If future cash flows are uncertain (risky), investors use a higher discount rate (see p. 896 to see how the discount rate depends on risk).

Apart from deciding on an appropriate discount rate, investment analysts forecast the company's *free cash flows*, which are defined as the cash generated by operations less the cash dedicated to new investments. Often, young companies do not distribute cash flows to their financiers, but instead solicit cash from the financial markets. In fact, this is an important reason for doing an IPO in the first place. Naturally, the investments are expected to add to the future cash flows. Hence, analysts often predict negative free cash flows early in life, but expect them to become positive as the firm matures.

Forecasting a firm's free cash flows is difficult. To obtain reasonable conjectures, analysts make a *model* to project the revenues, expenses, and investments. Analysts' models can be very sophisticated. They analyze the products or services that the company provides, conduct industry analysis to gauge where the company stands vis-à-vis its competitors, consult market forecasts (of the firm's products and production costs), interview the firm's executives and other employees (as far as this is allowed by the laws that govern financial markets), and conduct sensitivity analysis.

Whatever method investment analysts use to estimate the market value of as yet untraded securities, valuing financial securities is a task that requires skill and effort.

ESTIMATES ARE OFTEN WRONG

Being an investment analyst does not just require hard work, it is also a risky job. After all, despite our best efforts, estimates often turn out to be wrong. That is the nature of *estimates*.

Each valuation is different. Analysts use different multiples, different proxies, and give different weights to individual multiple estimates. DCF valuations are highly sensitive to the many assumptions incorporated into a model, and to the discount rate used to arrive at a present value. Clearly, if we have many independent estimates, the highest estimate is likely to be too high and the lowest estimate is probably too low. If we assume that the estimates are unbiased, the true market value will lie somewhere in the middle.

Hence, there are two ways to engage in price discovery. The first is to help analysts to make more precise estimates. To do this, the issuer and its intermediaries (investment bank, auditor, legal advisers) provide buy-side analysts with a detailed prospectus, which explains the structure of the issue (for example, how many shares are sold), describes the company's business, and presents recent financial performance. In addition, they invite analysts to information sessions on the firm's products and managers. During such road-show presentations, the company presents its business plan, its managers, and its products to prospective investors. An important part of the road-show meetings is the question and answer session, during which analysts can pepper the issuing team with questions so as to fine-tune their models and estimates.

The second way to improve the price discovery is to involve more buy-side clients and more analysts. A statistical property called the *law of large numbers* says that if we have more estimates, the average of these will be closer to the true value. The problem, however, is that if we invite too many prospective investors, it will adversely affect the incentives to produce information.

SOUNDING OUT THE MARKET

When buy-side clients have done their analysis and have become "informed," issuers will find it easier to sell them their securities. However, there are still important differences in opinion among clients. Extracting these opinions is not an easy task. Clearly, buy-side clients will be reluctant to part with their hard-earned information. Nevertheless, issuers can *sound out the market* by individually targeting large and well-informed buy-side clients. They do this by ringing them up, and asking them for their opinions and indications of interest. The investment bank writes down indicative orders in a book of orders. This exercise is called *book-building*. Indicative orders can take three main forms. First there are *strike orders*, which indicate a demand that is independent of the price. Second, there are *limit orders*, such as "I sign up for 150,000 shares as long as the price is not higher than $10." Finally, there are *step* orders, which are combinations of several limit orders. For example, "If the price is set at $9 or below, we want 130,000 shares; if it is set at $10 or less, we

Figure 1. Example of an order book. During book-building, the lead manager calls up prospective buy-side clients and asks them for indicative orders. This results in an aggregate demand curve. However, the bookrunner knows that not all indications of interest are equally sincere, and he or she has to gauge what the *real demand* is—i.e. the demand that is not due to strategic overbidding (due to anticipated rationing). Notice that the real demand is invisible. Investment bankers use their experience and judgment to estimate it

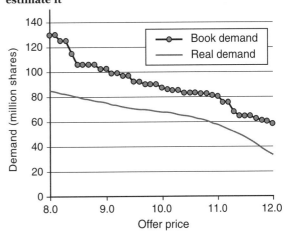

want 80,000 shares; and if you set it higher, we don't want any shares."

After one or two weeks of making phone calls, the bookrunner will have compiled a book of orders, which forms a downward sloping demand curve (see Figure 1). Naturally, this demand curve represents very valuable information for the price discovery process.

SETTING THE PRICE

One would think that the issuing team can now simply set the price so that demand equals supply. If all orders were genuine, this would be the optimal strategy. However, the new shareholders would feel fooled if, after expending significant efforts to analyze the firm, they received no surplus in return. To reward large and sophisticated buy-side clients for their analysis of the firm, investment banks set the offer price at a discount from the expected market price. Historically, the average discount, which translates into an average *initial return* (the return from the offer price to the market price) has been around 15%. Initial returns have been extensively studied. Average discounts differ between countries and time periods. All studies, however, find that smaller and more difficult to value IPO firms tend to be discounted more, which is consistent with the "compensation for analysis efforts" story.

The promise of a discount can be made credible because of the investment bank's reputation and its repeated interaction with the market's buy-side. For example, because Fidelity knows that Goldman Sachs will price IPO shares at a reasonable discount, they are willing to expend effort to analyze the IPO firm.

The problem with setting the offer price at a discount is that it attracts "free riders." It seems that investors who simply signed up for all IPOs would, on average, make a profit because of the discount. For this reason, investment banks only invite large and sophisticated investors to submit orders in the book. From experience and repeated interaction, investment bankers know whose indicative orders are most informative. Still, even among the invited bidders there is a temptation to overbid. Because they know that the shares will be set at a discount, buy-side clients want to bid for as many shares as possible. In other words, even the orders of the repeat clients may not be entirely genuine. An important task for the investment bank is to distinguish the *real* demand from the *book* demand (Figure 1). They can never do this perfectly, but, through skill and judgment, experienced bookrunners can assess the seriousness of book orders. So, after closing the book, the issuer compiles the book demand curve, gauges where the real demand is, and then sets the price at a small discount.

The price is set during the *pricing meeting*, which typically takes place on the evening before the actual floatation. During the pricing meeting the issue is officially underwritten, so that the bookrunner becomes legally liable for placing the shares. By scheduling this important meeting shortly before the actual selling day, the bookrunner reduces the risk of being stuck with IPO shares on its books. In the example of Figure 1, the issuers may set the price at $9.50, so as to place all the shares, and leave some money on the table for the buy side analysts.

ALLOCATING THE SHARES

As mentioned, the IPO process is a repeated game for buy-side clients and investment banks. Both parties to the price discovery process develop long-term relationships. Investment bankers know which buy-side analysts provide the most accurate indications of interest, and reward them with higher allocations. One way to gauge the quality of the buy-side analysts is to monitor their order submission strategy and their trading behavior after the IPO. Strike orders may indicate poor analysis, while limit or step orders are better signals for price discovery. If a client often asks for large allocations, but then quickly sells ("flips") its shares in the secondary market, this is an indication of poor analysis. Orders that are submitted in the early stage of the book-building indicate confidence and informed decision-making. Hence, it is not surprising that we see that clients who put in limit or step orders early, and do not flip their shares in the secondary market, receive higher allocations on average.

THE OVER-ALLOTMENT OPTION

Almost all IPOs have an *over-allotment option*, also known as a *greenshoe*, named after the company that first used this mechanism. The over-allotment option gives the bookrunner the right to buy a specified number of additional shares from the issuer and sell them on to the buy-side. Or, they have the right to *over-allocate*. Typically, the option is for 15% of the offering size. In practice, the underwriter always over-allocates, so that after the offering the bank is technically "short": they have sold shares they do not yet own. The bookrunner will exercise the over-allotment option if the price in secondary market trading increases beyond the offering price, which is usually the case. If, however, the price in the secondary market comes under pressure (i.e. there is a lot of flipping), the underwriter buys back the shares in the open market.

This is sometimes referred to as *price support* or *price stabilization*. The over-allotment option is therefore a clever way to adjust the supply of shares to the uncertain demand for shares. By keeping track of flippers, bookrunners can monitor buy-side clients and gauge their quality for the price discovery process.

BOOK-BUILDING VERSUS AUCTIONS

The book-building mechanism has become the standard way of selling shares in initial public offerings. The characteristic difference from other IPO mechanisms is the close and personal interaction between relatively few players on both sides of the transaction. These cozy relationships, and the subsequent preferential allocations, sometimes make small investors, issuers, and regulators uneasy about the book-building mechanism. Naturally there is the chance that investment banks and buy-side clients collude to set the offer price low and share the profits of large initial returns. Although there certainly have been instances of doubtful allocations of conspicuously underpriced shares, the book-building mechanism has survived and is widely accepted. The key advantage is that it results in more *information production*.

An obvious alternative to book-building is the auction. Due to its fair and transparent nature, the auction mechanism has been used in several countries, including the United Kingdom,

Denmark, and France. However, evidence shows that they are less effective in achieving a high price and a liquid aftermarket. Empirical studies have found that book-built IPOs have, on average, lower initial returns, especially if they were floated by prestigious investment banks.

The Google IPO and a stylized example (see Case Studies) further illustrate how targeted information exchange between relatively few informed players may be more effective for price discovery than an impersonal auction.

CASE STUDIES
The Google IPO
When Google went public in August 2004, it announced upfront that the price would be determined by a competitive Dutch auction in which everybody could participate on equal terms. Large and small investors were invited to submit their limit and step orders through the internet. The price would be set at the point where the 19.6 million shares could be sold. Large institutional investors openly grumbled and complained about the "cheap" way in which Google was selling its shares, saying that they would not bother to get out of bed for an auction.

The result was that, due to the lack of a targeted information exchange, the market price was not fully discovered. The auctioneers set the offer price at US$85. When secondary market trading began, the price shot to above US$100 within days, and above US$200 within months, which suggested that Google did not get the full value for its shares. Many industry watchers (and the author of this article) believe that if Google had opted for a standard book building method, its shares may have fetched a higher price in the primary market.

Illustration of Targeted Information Exchange
Imagine that you receive a surprise inheritance from a distant uncle. The inheritance is a trunk full of foreign coins. Most are post-war coins from various countries, but your seven-year-old son has spotted some gold, silver, and very ancient coins. You are not much of a coin collector and are strapped for cash,

so you decide to sell the coins. To do this you go to a coin collectors' fair. At the fair there is an auction session where you can put your coins up for sale. Alternatively, you can approach the three largest collectors, let each have a close look at your collection, explain your situation, and ask them for their offer. If your collection is difficult to value (as a company is), the second route may well get you a higher price.

MORE INFO
Books:
Draho, Jason. *The IPO Decision: Why and How Companies Go Public*. Cheltenham, UK: Edward Elgar Publishing, 2006.
Gregoriou, Greg N. *Initial Public Offerings: An International Perspective*. Oxford: Butterworth-Heinemann, 2006.

Article:
Benveniste, Lawrence M., and Walid Y. Busaba. "Bookbuilding versus fixed price: An analysis of competing strategies for marketing IPOs." *Journal of Financial and Quantitative Analysis* 32:4 (1997): 383–403. Online at: dx.doi.org/10.2307/2331230

Websites:
IPO Financial Network (IPOfn) news, analysis, and resources: www.ipofinancial.com
IPO Monitor—Coverage of IPOs and secondary equity offerings: www.ipomonitor.com
IPO Renaissance Capital—research and investment management services on newly public companies: www.ipohome.com

See Also:
★ Acquiring a Secondary Listing, or Cross-Listing (pp. 112–114)
★ Financial Steps in an IPO for a Small or Medium-Size Enterprise (pp. 126–128)
★ IPOs in Emerging Markets (pp. 131–133)
✔ Understanding the Relationship between the Discount Rate and Risk (pp. 308–309)

Rigidity in Microfinancing: Can One Size Fit All?
by Dean Karlan and Sendhil Mullainathan

EXECUTIVE SUMMARY
• Despite rapid growth in outreach, microfinance providers often have yet to reach a large proportion of the market of poor households.
• One explanation may be that microfinance practitioners have been slow to implement innovations to the standard lending methodologies.
• By tailoring products to clients' needs and repayment capacity, flexible microfinance has the potential to reach many more clients at lower cost. This can be proven with randomized evaluations of flexible lending contracts.
• Further work is needed to understand how this will impact on clients.

INTRODUCTION
In the span of a single decade microfinance has gone from being virtually unknown—to bankers, to development workers, and, most of all, to the poor—to being a household

word. Ask anyone today to describe microfinance and most likely you will get a common answer: "That's when banks lend to groups of poor women to start little businesses." Much of this increase in awareness is thanks to the tireless work of industry advocates who have traveled the world convincing development organizations and funders that microfinance offers the best hope for large numbers of poor families to move out of poverty.

Practitioners, broadly speaking, have been offered three choices:

1 Grameen Bank-style solidarity lending, with 12-month loans offered to groups of five poor women;
2 FINCA-style village banking, with a four-month loan divided among a larger group of about 30 poor women; or
3 ACCION-style individual lending to the moderately poor.

On most other features, these options are strikingly similar. All three target entrepreneurs with capital for sewing machines, chickens, tortilla presses, and the like. And all emphasize operational efficiency through product standardization, and good repayment through frequent regular payments that start shortly after the loans are disbursed. Here we discuss ideas that can be seen as "tweaks" to the above standard models. These tweaks increase the flexibility with an aim to improving the quality of the service received by the client.

LENDING FLEXIBILITY
Problems with the Standard Model

Looking back on the evolution of microfinance one begins to wonder if perhaps its advocates might have been too successful in their messaging. By sticking to this script, the industry may have stifled creativity and individualism in the development of financial services for the poor. Consider the repayment schedule adopted with near universality for group-lending clients: weekly payments that start only one or two weeks after disbursement of the loan. This despite the fact that microfinance institution (MFI) managers are well aware that most of their clients' enterprises will not start generating returns so rapidly.

Why is this important? Being poor is not just about having too little income—it is about having an insecure income. The income of the poor can vary dramatically from day to day, month to month, season to season. The poor have good weeks and bad weeks. But microloans, like all loans with fixed repayments, are made on the basis of the borrower's ability to repay in their *worst week*. Otherwise they would end up in arrears at some point during the loan cycle. This rigidity has several ramifications. First, by basing borrowers' repayment capacity on bad weeks, instead of average weeks, it greatly limits the size of the loans the poor can borrow. If I earn 50 rupees some weeks and 550 rupees other weeks, my debt capacity is not based on my average income of 300 rupees but on the 50 rupees that I can afford to pay in the bad weeks. As a result, borrowers with variable income and little recourse outside of money lenders to smooth that variability will be given a debt capacity that is much lower than ideal.

Second, it may screen out many potential borrowers entirely: for example, any entrepreneur who pictures a week in which she might have slow sales or a household emergency. Or existing clients may leave because they experience too

many "close calls" and then drop out to avoid going into default. Incidentally, these should be the bank's best customers—they are clients of such strong integrity that they refuse to borrow for fear of defaulting! Third, it precludes potential innovations like bullet loans for agriculture (a bullet loans is a loan where payment of the entire principal of the loan, and sometimes the principal and interest, is or are due at the end of the loan term).

These limitations help to explain why, despite years of growth, MFIs still fulfill only a small fraction of the financial needs of the poor. This year the Microcredit Summit Campaign has reported that its members reach a total of 150 million borrowers (Daley-Harris, 2009). This is a stunning achievement, and yet only a dent in the estimated two billion households that lack access to financial services. The need to identify ways to reach this market with appropriate financial services cannot be ignored.

How to Be Flexible: Some Suggestions

How can we practically implement flexibility in the current structure of microfinance? A full portfolio of flexible financial products has yet to be developed, but there are some promising ideas. We give three examples, each highlighting a different element of flexibility. First, we observe that flexibility can be *prebuilt* into the contract. For example, in India the monsoon is a difficult time for everyone. Contracts could reflect this by reducing payments during this period in a prespecified manner. Similarly, dairy farmers face two months a year without milk. Again, the contract could prespecify a smaller loan payment during this period. Prespecification of flexibility has many benefits. Notably, clients are not led to believe that they can negotiate down other payments. The flexibility is not after-the-fact. It is actually a "rigid" flexibility, with tightly delineated rules. As a result, it also eases technological and logistical concerns of management information systems, cash management, and loan officer fraud.

Second, one could provide a less rigid flexibility by prespecifying a number of low payment periods, but not their timing. For example, one could give clients several tokens and tell them that each token can count for one weekly payment. In this way, the client agrees to a slightly higher payment each week in return for getting a few difficult weeks—of their own choosing—off. Again, the creation of a token ought to ease the logistical problems of MIS, cash management, and fraud. Yet it still provides the borrower with a great deal of flexibility.

Finally, consider an MFI that feels that its borrowers could handle 2,000-rupee larger loans than they currently receive. Should it just increase the initial loan size? What if instead it told all borrowers that they would be eligible for a second 2,000-rupee loan at any point during the cycle? This second loan might actually help the client more than simply increasing the initial loan by 2,000 rupees since it gives the client a safety valve in case of emergencies.

Why Have People Been Afraid of Flexibility?

Fixed-debt contracts may be problematic, but there are sensible reasons for using them. First, a flexible payment stream may generate many operational headaches. For instance, portfolio monitoring requires clear information on default status. It may be difficult (or impossible) to distinguish between someone exercising their flexibility and someone who is intending to default further. The faster lenders deal with default, it is often believed, the better they are able to recover the loans. Furthermore, depending on how the flexibility is structured, it could cause confusion in the field. It is easier to train staff to collect equal and constant weekly payments. The flexibility should be such that staff can easily understand and implement it.

Second, cash management problems may arise. If clients experience correlated shocks (for example floods or droughts), they may (should!) use the flexibility to help smooth out those shocks. This has implications for the lender if it is seeing a shortfall in repayment at the exact moments it wants to have more cash on hand to lend to individuals. Third, flexibility may put the lender at risk of loan officer fraud. The loan officer, for instance, could claim that the client exercised her "flexibility" when in fact she repaid. (As noted above, this can be mitigated by prespecifying the payment schedule: if the client is expected to pay 50 rupees in a given week, the MIS will raise a flag if any other payment is recorded.)

Last, varying contracts might weaken the repayment discipline of borrowers. Some argue that the key difference between debt programs and savings programs is that debt provides a commitment to make weekly payments, whereas with savings there is no such commitment. Thus, this is one reason why rotating savings and credit associations (ROSCAs) and chit funds exist, to provide individuals with a commitment to save. If the debt requirement allows some flexibility, some fear that this will erode the repayment discipline. Borrowers may forget which weeks to pay and which not, or find it hard to turn on and off the habit of putting money aside to pay the loan. Either way, the fear is that having a few weeks off will lead to lower repayment when the payments are required.

These costs of flexible contracts are often better articulated than the benefits. Yet qualitatively the benefits could be huge. Will these products work? Will operational hurdles prevent them from working? Will they erode repayment discipline and increase default? Or will they allow for much larger loan sizes and greater client income growth? We simply do not know. A common retort is that borrowers can use other sources of income or debt to fill in the gaps. This misses the basic point about the financial policy for the poor: these alternatives either do not exist or are very expensive. Why cede this important and potentially lucrative financial service without ever testing the water? There is only one way to know if microfinance can be more flexible: by testing. As with any new idea, there is no way to know how well it works without careful experimentation. As we note above, the point is not that flexibility will impose no costs on the organization. Flexible products may be trickier to implement, or they might have ambiguous effects, like increasing portfolio-at-risk while increasing profitability. The challenge for MFIs is to find those aspects of flexibility which can expand their reach and impact without hampering continued growth.

To examine these theories in a practical way, at Innovations for Poverty Action (IPA) we use randomized control trials to test new products and services for the poor. To determine whether the benefits of a new idea outweigh its costs we measure its impact, benchmarked against the traditional methodology.

FLEXIBILITY WORKS: SOME EXAMPLES
Group versus Individual Liability

For years a central part of the conventional wisdom of microfinance was that microfinance worked because of group liability: banks could safely lend to poor borrowers with no collateral because they would guarantee each others' loans. True, repayment rates among microfinance clients have been impressive. But, like the inflexible repayment schedules, there may be costs as well as benefits: How many potential clients might be deterred by the group-liability contract? How many don't borrow because they don't want to be responsible for other people's loans? We used a randomized control trial to measure the effects. Working with a rural bank in the Philippines, Giné and Karlan (2008) randomly selected groups of their microfinance clients to switch from group liability to individual liability, with all other aspects of the loan contract remaining constant. Following up three years later, the authors found no increase in default among individual-liability clients. On the other hand more clients had joined the individual-liability groups, suggesting that on average clients much prefer individual liability. In an expansion of that study, the authors tested with new clients by randomly marketing in some villages individual-liability loans, and in other villages group-liability loans. Again, there was no difference in default. The bank officers were much less willing to make individual liability loans, suggesting that the flexibility was perceived as too much for their staff, and they restricted the supply of credit. Whether it was right or not we cannot tell, since we do not know whether those not approved for loans would have defaulted or not.

Repayment Frequency

In another study that tested one of the key assumptions of microfinance contracts, Field and Pande (2007) experimented with altering the frequency of payments, from weekly to monthly. After one year, they found no change in default. This simple test has vast implications: if clients can meet far less often with no effect on repayment, MFIs can drastically reduce their staff costs. Those savings can be passed along to clients, potentially making credit more affordable to the poor. And more clients may join if there's less of a burden on their own time. Naturally, more time may yield different results, and proper testing and patience can help us to learn the answer to these important questions.

EVALUATING FLEXIBLE CONTRACTS

This same type of analysis can be applied to carefully examine the flexible lending contracts we describe above. In each case a (randomly selected) group receiving the innovation would be compared to clients offered only the traditional contract. The analysis can go much beyond simply "does it work?" The treatment and control groups can be evaluated on any number of dimensions: repayment, client retention, MFI profitability, etc. For example, flexibility might actually *save* on loan officer time. If every monsoon we know that clients have a tough time paying, might it not be more cost-effective to have lower or less frequent payments during that period rather than use valuable loan officer time to chase down "delinquent" clients?

Further, flexible contracts may greatly increase the impact of the loan. Clients with rigid contracts may take actions which reduce the return on their investments. Owners of milk animals may underfeed during difficult times. Asset owners may sell off (productive) assets to repay debts. Freedom from Hunger, through its MAHP program, is helping the MFIs CARD, CRECER, and Bandhan to offer emergency health loans to their clients. It would be useful to evaluate this type of product to determine whether it is able to prevent the destruction of this value. Potentially, such a product could be as useful as the initial loan itself. Or if clients can't handle the additional debt burden, it could have negative spillovers, destabilizing their borrowing groups. If the impact is positive, however, the increased income from retaining productive assets could allow the MFI to further increase loan size.

CONCLUSION

Rigorous evaluations will become only more important as new technologies are developed to improve the efficiency and scale of microbanking. These same technologies, such as handheld computers for loan officers, have the potential to greatly increase the flexibility offered to clients—by making on-the-spot credit decisions, or handling variable repayment amounts, for example. We have focused here on one issue in particular: the flexibility or rigidity of debt products; but with the deployment of any new technology we are faced with the same unknown: how well does it work? The goal of our research around the world, as with the Innovations for Poverty Action, the Financial Access Initiative, and the Massachusetts Institute of Technology Abdul Latif Jameel Poverty Action

Lab, is to bring about consensus about the circumstances under which different products and features and services are optimal for clients and institutions. Related work will shed more light on other important aspects of flexibility, including loan tenure, loan size, group size, and guarantee requirements.

MORE INFO

Article:

Field, Erica, and Rohini Pande. "Repayment frequency and default in micro-finance: Evidence from India." *Journal of the European Economic Association* 6:2–3 (April–May 2008): 501–509. Online at: tinyurl.com/772j6be [PDF].

Reports:

Daley-Harris, Sam. "State of the Microcredit Summit Campaign report 2009." Washington, DC: Microcredit Summit Campaign, 2009. Online at: tinyurl.com/73dm2zy [PDF].

Giné, Xavier, and Dean S. Karlan. "Group versus individual liability: Long term evidence from Philippine microcredit lending groups." Working paper. May 2009. Online at: tinyurl.com/7a6hklh [PDF].

Websites:

Innovations for Poverty Action (IPA): www.poverty-action.org
Financial Access Initiative (FAI): financialaccess.org
Abdul Latif Jameel Poverty Action Lab (J-PAL): www.povertyactionlab.com

See Also:

✔ Islamic Microfinance (pp. 330–331)
✔ Steps for Obtaining Bank Financing (pp. 333–334)

The Role of Institutional Investors in Corporate Financing
by Hao Jiang

EXECUTIVE SUMMARY

- Institutional investors have become increasingly important in global capital markets.
- In equity markets, institutional investors tend to prefer liquid stocks with larger market capitalization, higher turnover, and higher price levels.
- Institutional investors particularly favor stocks in popular equity indexes, giving them higher valuations because their performance is typically benchmarked against those indexes.
- In bond markets that are mainly populated by institutional investors, there is a clear clientele effect.
- Private equity funds are an important source of capital for entrepreneurial firms.

INTRODUCTION

Institutional investors have become increasingly important in global capital markets. As of the end of December 2007, total assets under management by major global institutional investors reached US$81.90 trillion. In particular, mutual funds, pension funds, and insurance companies managed US$26.2, 28.2, and 19.9 trillion of assets, respectively, while assets managed by nontraditional managers such as hedge funds, sovereign funds, and private equity funds experienced dramatic growth, reaching US$2.3, 3.3, and 2.0 trillion in 2007 (Figure 1). In comparison, the world equity markets amounted to US$60.8 trillion, and the aggregate value of corporate bonds outstanding in the United States, the largest corporate bond market, was US$5.8 trillion in 2007. Clearly, for any successful corporate managers who raise capital to

Figure 1. Assets under management by different types of institutional investors in 2007. (*Source*: International Financial Services London)

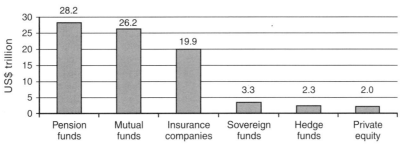

MAJOR INSTITUTIONAL PLAYERS

Institutional investors are a heterogeneous group of investors that populate the global capital markets. Based on their legal type, institutional investors can be broadly classified into mutual funds, pension funds, insurance companies, sovereign funds, hedge funds, and private equity funds.

A mutual fund is an investment vehicle that buys a portfolio of securities selected by a professional investment adviser to meet a specified financial goal (investment objective). Between 2000 and 2007, the total net assets of mutual funds grew from US$6.96 to 12.02 trillion in the United States, from US$3.29 to 8.98 trillion in Europe, from US$1.13 to 3.67 trillion in Asia-Pacific, and from US$16.92 to 95.22 billion in Africa (Figure 2).

A pension fund is a pool of assets forming an independent legal entity that are bought with the contributions to a pension plan for the exclusive purpose of financing pension plan benefits. Table 1 lists the world's 20 largest pension funds as ranked by *Pensions & Investments*. Insurance companies and banks are also important types of institutional investor that constitute the traditional asset managers.

Paralleling the growth of traditional institutions is the universe of nontraditional institutional investors. Among them, a sovereign wealth fund (SWF) is a state-owned investment fund composed of financial assets such as stocks, bonds, real estate, or other financial instruments funded by foreign exchange assets. Table 2 shows the top sovereign wealth funds across the world.

A hedge fund is an unregulated pool of money managed by an investment advisor, the hedge fund manager, who typically has the right to have short positions, to borrow, and to make extensive use of derivatives. Hedge fund managers receive both fixed and performance fees. Table 3 shows the top ten hedge funds based on assets under management ranked by Institutional Investor in 2007.

A private equity fund is a pooled investment vehicle which invests its money in equity securities of companies that have not "gone public" (i.e. are not listed on a public exchange). Private equity funds are typically limited partnerships with a fixed term of ten years (often with annual extensions). At inception, institutional investors such as pension funds and endowments (limited partners) commit a certain amount of capital to private equity funds, which are run by the general partners. Table 4 is a list of the ten largest private equity firms in the world as ranked by Private Equity International in 2008.

THE ROLE OF INSTITUTIONAL INVESTORS IN CORPORATE FINANCING

Institutional investors supply capital for firms seeking to raise finance from both publicly traded securities markets and from the private domain.

Figure 2. Total net assets of mutual funds around the world. (Source: *2008 Investment Company Fact Book*, Washington, DC: Investment Company Institute, 2008)

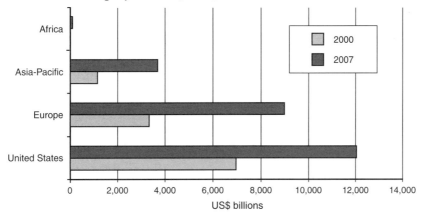

Table 1. The world's top 20 pension funds based on total assets. (*Source: Pensions & Investments*; Watson Wyatt, 2006)

Rank	Fund	Country	Assets (US$ million)
1	Government Pension Investment	Japan	870,587
2	Government Pension	Norway	235,849
3	ABP	Netherlands	226,974
4	National Pension	Korea	214,184
5	California Public Employees	US	195,978
6	Pension Fund Association	Japan	183,352
7	Federal Retirement Thrift	US	167,165
8	Local Government Officials	Japan	137,153
9	California State Teachers	US	133,988
10	New York State Common	US	131,861
11	GEPF	South Africa	124,167
12	Postal Savings Fund	Taiwan	117,265
13	Florida State Board	US	114,935
14	General Motors	US	114,271
15	New York City Retirement	US	105,860
16	Ontario Teachers	Canada	99,490
17	Texas Teachers	US	94,384
18	New York State Teachers	US	87,353
19	Public Schools Employees	Japan	85,224
20	PGGM	Netherlands	84,986

Institutional Investors as Holders of Publicly Traded Securities

Given their large portfolio size, institutional investors naturally become dominant holders of publicly traded securities. According to the 13F filings that institutional investors are required to lodge with the Securities and Exchange Commission (SEC), institutional investors hold over 68% of the total market value of US common stocks.

According to the "Flow of Funds" data provided by the Federal Reserve, institutional investors hold approximately 86% of corporate bonds in the US corporate bond markets. Therefore, their investment behavior will have a significant influence on the pricing of these securities. For corporate managers who raise money from capital markets, it is important to understand the demand structure of institutional investors for publicly traded securities.

Despite their apparent heterogeneity, institutional investors share common characteristics because of the legal environment that they face as fiduciaries, and because of the demand for liquidity resulting from the large sizes of their portfolios and the need to reduce transaction costs. As a group, institutional investors exhibit preferences for certain stock characteristics in their equity portfolio. In particular, they tend to prefer stocks with larger market capitalization, higher turnover ratios, and higher levels of price. In other words, institutional investors are willing to pay a higher premium for stocks with these characteristics.[1]

Because most institutional investors benchmark their performance against certain indices, they naturally exhibit preferences for stocks in popular equity indexes. In the US market, when stocks are included into the S&P500 Index, the most prevalent equity index, the prices of those stocks tend to experience a 2–3% increase over a short period of time.

Firms with access to the corporate bond market tend to issue bonds as a means of debt financing. Based on the credit quality of the issue, corporate bonds can be classified into investment-grade and noninvestment-grade (high-yield or junk bonds, which are rated Ba and below by Moody's, or BB and below by Standard & Poor's). For corporate bond issuers, it is important to recognize the tendency of different classes of corporate bonds to attract different types of institutional investor—namely the clientele effect—in corporate bond markets.

Table 2. The world's largest sovereign wealth funds. (Ranking by Sovereign Wealth Fund Institute, 2008)

Country	Fund	Assets (US$ billion)	Inception	Origin
UAE: Abu Dhabi	Abu Dhabi Investment Authority	875	1976	Oil
Saudi Arabia	SAMA Foreign Holdings	433.0	n/a	Oil
Singapore	Government of Singapore Investment Corporation	330	1981	Noncommodity
China	SAFE Investment Company	311.6		Noncommodity
Norway	Government Pension Fund—Global	301	1990	Oil
Kuwait	Kuwait Investment Authority	264.4	1953	Oil
China	China Investment Corporation	200	2007	Noncommodity
Russia	National Welfare Fund	189.7	2008	Oil
China: Hong Kong	Hong Kong Monetary Authority Investment Portfolio	173	1998	Noncommodity
Singapore	Temasek Holdings	134	1974	Noncommodity
UAE: Dubai	Investment Corporation of Dubai	82	2006	Oil
China	National Social Security Fund	74	2000	Noncommodity
Qatar	Qatar Investment Authority	60	2003	Oil
Libya	Libyan Investment Authority	50	2006	Oil
Algeria	Revenue Regulation Fund	47	2000	Oil
Australia	Australian Future Fund	43.8	2004	Noncommodity
US: Alaska	Alaska Permanent Fund	39.8	1976	Oil
Kazakhstan	Kazakhstan National Fund	38	2000	Oil
Ireland	National Pensions Reserve Fund	30.8	2001	Noncommodity
South Korea	Korea Investment Corporation	30	2005	Noncommodity
Brunei	Brunei Investment Agency	30	1983	Oil

Table 3. The world's top ten hedge funds. (Ranking by Institutional Investor, 2007)

Rank	Fund	Location	Firm capital (US$ million)
1	JP Morgan Asset Management	New York, NY	44,700
2	Bridgewater Associates	Westport, CT	36,000
3	Farallon Capital Management	San Francisco, CA	36,000
4	Renaissance Technologies Corp.	East Setauket, NY	33,300
5	Och-Ziff Capital Management Group	New York, NY	33,200
6	DE Shaw Group	New York, NY	32,240
7	Goldman Sachs Asset Management	New York, NY	29,206
8	Paulson & Co	New York, NY	28,979
9	Barclays Global Investors	London, UK	26,227
10	GLG Partners	London, UK	23,900

Table 4. The world's ten largest private equity firms. (Ranking by Private Equity International, 2008)

Rank	Firm	Headquarters	Capital raised 2003–2008
1	The Carlyle Group	Washington, DC	52
2	Goldman Sachs Principal Investment Area	New York, NY	49.05
3	Texas Pacific Group	Fort Worth, TX	48.75
4	Kohlberg Kravis Roberts	New York, NY	39.67
5	CVC Capital Partners	London, UK	36.84
6	Apollo Management	New York, NY	32.82
7	Bain Capital	Boston, MA	31.71
8	Permira	London, UK	25.43
9	Apax Partners	London, UK	25.23
10	The Blackstone Group	New York, NY	23.3

Institutional investors generally place restrictions on investing in noninvestment-grade bonds. For example, the National Association of Insurance Commissioners (NAIC) imposes on insurance companies an upper limit of 20% of their assets for investment in high-yield bonds. Pension funds often impose limits on the value of a portfolio that can be invested in high-yield bonds. US investment-grade bond mutual funds place a limit of 5% of assets for investments in junk bonds and must sell any security if it falls below a B rating. However, there are institutional investors that specialize in junk bonds such as hedge funds with strategies in distressed assets and high-yield bond mutual funds. A recent study shows that when a bond receives a downgrade from investment to speculative grade there is a persistent price decline of 2%, whereas similar downgrades that do not cross the junk bond threshold do not experience such persistent price drops. This result suggests the importance of investor clientele for the pricing of corporate bonds.[2]

Institutional Investors as Fund Intermediaries for Private Firms

For entrepreneurial firms at the early stage of their life cycle, private equity funds comprise an important source of financing. Two primary categories of private equity funds are venture capital funds and leveraged buyout funds. In particular, venture capital funds provide equity capital for firms that are not yet profitable and lack tangible assets. Typically, such venture capital funds are active investors and play a primary role in shaping the top management team of the companies in which they invest.

Unlike venture capital funds that invest in young, fast-growing private companies, leveraged buyout funds invest in established companies and facilitate the process of purchasing an entire company or a controlling part of the stock of a company involving large amounts of debt—a "leveraged buyout." During the past two decades, both types of private equity funds have played an increasingly important role in corporate financing.

CASE STUDY
HEDGE FUNDS AND THE TURMOIL OF THE CONVERTIBLE BONDS MARKET

Convertible bonds, which give holders an option to exchange the bonds for a specified number of shares of common stocks, are an importance source of capital for many firms. Among various reasons, managers favor convertible bonds because they are less costly than a direct share issuance, and because firms to which straight debt and equity are not available can still raise money in the convertible bond market. SEC Rule 144A, effective in 1990, allows firms to issue securities to qualified institutional buyers (QIBs) without having to register these securities. This regulation significantly accelerates the capital-raising process from more than one month in the public market to one or two days in the 144A market from announcement to closing. As a result, nearly all convertible bonds in recent years have been issued via the 144A market.

According to the SDC Global New Issues database, convertible bond issuance amounted to US$50.2 billion in 2006, increasing more than six-fold from US$7.8 billion in 1992. It is generally believed that hedge funds that conduct convertible arbitrage are the major players in the convertible bond markets, purchasing more than 70% of convertible bonds in the primary market.

In late 2004 and early 2005, large institutional investors in convertible hedge funds, unimpressed with the performance of hedge funds in 2004, started to withdraw capital from those funds. To meet investor redemptions, hedge funds sold convertible bonds, causing their prices to fall relative to their fundamental values, which in turn lowered the returns on convertible hedge funds. From January to May of 2005, the Credit Suisse/Tremont Convertible Arbitrage Hedge Fund Index decreased by 7.2%.[3] The lower returns on convertible hedge funds triggered further investor redemptions and more selling of convertible bonds, forming a vicious cycle. The price of convertible bonds dropped significantly below fundamental values. The maximum discount of convertible bonds was 2.7% in May 2005.[4] A gradual price recovery took place in 2006.

CONCLUSION

The dramatic expansion of institutional investors in global capital markets demonstrates the changing savings pattern of households in the global economy. As such, corporate managers who wish to raise funds to finance the growth of their firms must understand such institutionalization in the global fund markets. In equity markets, institutional investors tend to prefer liquid stocks with larger market capitalization, higher turnover, and higher price levels. Because the performance of institutional investors is typically benchmarked against certain indexes, stocks in popular equity indexes are particularly favored by institutional investors and are thus priced at a higher valuation ratio. In bond markets that are mainly populated by institutional investors, there is a clear clientele effect. Banks, insurance companies, pension funds, and investment-grade bond mutual funds place severe restrictions on the holdings of high-yield bonds, whereas hedge funds and high-yield bond mutual funds provide capital for high-yield issuers. Lastly, private equity funds are an important source of capital for entrepreneurial firms.

MAKING IT HAPPEN

Institutional investors have dominated global capital markets. As a result, the assets under their management constitute an important source of capital for corporate managers.

- To attract institutional investors in equity markets, liquidity of shares is a major consideration. In particular, larger market capitalization, higher turnover, and higher price levels are important in attracting institutional holdings. Index membership is a strong sweetener.
- In bond markets, investment-grade bonds have a broader institutional investor base, whereas the issuance of high-yield bonds relies on capital providers such as specialized bond mutual funds and hedge funds.
- For entrepreneurial firms that seek both capital and strategic support, private equity funds appear to be increasingly important.

MORE INFO

Books:

Davis, E. Philip, and Benn Steil. *Institutional Investors*. Cambridge, MA: MIT Press, 2004.

Jaeger, Robert A. *All About Hedge Funds: The Easy Way to Get Started*. New York: McGraw-Hill, 2003.

Pozen, Robert C. *The Mutual Fund Business*. 2nd ed. Boston, MA: Houghton Mifflin, 2002.

Pratt's Guide to Private Equity & Venture Capital Sources. New York: Thomson Reuters, 2008.

Websites:

Dow Jones LP Source Galantes: www.dowjones.com/privatemarkets/gal.asp

Institutional Investor: www.institutionalinvestor.com

Investment Company Institute (ICI): www.ici.org

Pensions & Investments: www.pionline.com

Preqin: www.preqin.com

Private Equity International (PEI): www.peimedia.com

Sovereign Wealth Fund Institute (SWFI): www.swfinstitute.org

Towers Watson: www.towerswatson.com

See Also:

★ Managing Activist Investors and Fund Managers (pp. 134–136)

★ Valuing Pension Fund Liabilities on the Balance Sheet (pp. 60–62)

NOTES

1 Gompers, Paul A., and Andrew Metrick. "Institutional investors and equity prices." *Quarterly Journal of Economics* 116:1 (February 2001): 229–259. Online at: dx.doi.org/10.1162/003355301556392

2 Da, Zhi, and Pengjie Gao. "Clientele change, persistent liquidity shock, and bond return reversal after rating downgrades." Working paper. University of Notre Dame, February 14, 2009. Online at: ssrn.com/abstract=1280834

3 Based on the author's calculations.

4 Mitchell, Mark, Lasse Heje Pedersen, and Todd Pulvino. "Slow moving capital." *American Economic Review* 97:2 (May 2007): 215–220. Online at: dx.doi.org/10.1257/aer.97.2.215

The Role of Short Sellers in the Marketplace
by Raj Gupta

EXECUTIVE SUMMARY

- This article examines the role of short-sellers in the marketplace. The process of short-selling involves three major participant groups: the lenders, the agent intermediaries, and the borrowers.
- First, the history of short-selling is discussed briefly. This includes the enactment of the Securities Exchange Act of 1934, the adoption of the uptick rule following concentrated short-selling in 1937, and the relaxation of that rule in 2007.
- Next, the short-sale process is discussed. Five categories of short positions are identified. These categories include general collateral, reduced rebate, reduced rebate and fail, fail only, and buy-in.
- Third, the borrowers are identified and their activities are discussed. These borrowers include hedge funds, mutual funds, ETF counterparties, and option market-makers.

- Fourth, the lenders are identified and their motivations for lending are discussed. The primary lenders include mutual funds and pension funds.
- Fifth, historical statistics on the universe of lendable securities and the percentage of loaned equities are presented. A dramatic increase in the level of loaned securities is observed for the period 2006 to the second quarter of 2008 followed by significant declines in the third and fourth quarters of 2008. Since then, the level of loaned securities has gradually increased by 12%.
- Finally a brief review of the academic literature on short-selling is conducted.

INTRODUCTION

The term "short-selling" or "shorting" is used to describe the process of selling financial instruments (such as equities or futures) that the seller or holder does not actually own but borrows from various sources. If the value of the instrument declines, the short-seller can repurchase the instrument at a lower price and cover the loan. Short-sellers have long played the crucial role of price discovery in financial markets. If short-selling were not allowed, traders with negative views of certain stocks would at best avoid those stocks. However, short-selling allows them to generate returns based on their views if they are correct, hence making short-selling an important aspect in price discovery. Companies in certain countries where short-selling is not allowed may also list on the exchanges of countries where it is allowed. After the crash of 1929, the US Congress created the Securities and Exchange Commission (SEC) by enacting the Securities Exchange Act of 1934. Following an inquiry into the effects of concentrated short-selling during the market break of 1937, the SEC adopted Rule 10a-1. Rule 10a-1(a)(1) stated that, subject to certain exceptions, a listed security may be sold short:

- at a price above the price at which the immediately preceding sale was effected ("plus tick"); or
- at the last sale price if it is higher than the last different price ("zero-plus tick").

This implied that short sales were not permitted on minus ticks or zero-minus ticks, subject to narrow exceptions. The operation of these provisions was commonly described as the "tick test." Both the New York Stock Exchange (NYSE) and the American Stock Exchange (Amex) had elected to use the prices of trades on their own floors for the tick test. In 2007, the Commission voted to adopt amendments to Rule 10a-1 and Regulation SHO that removed Rule 10a-1 as well as any short sale price test of any self-regulatory organization (SRO). In addition, the amendments prohibited any SRO from having a price test. The amendments included a technical amendment to Rule 200(g) of Regulation SHO that removed the "short-exempt" marking requirement of that rule.

On July 15, 2008, the SEC issued an emergency order related to short-selling securities of 19 substantial financial firms,[1] which took effect July 21, 2008. This order stated that any person executing a short sale in the publicly traded securities of 19 financial firms, using the means or instrumentalities of interstate commerce, must borrow or arrange to borrow the security or otherwise have the security

available to borrow in its inventory prior to executing the short sale. On September 19, 2008, the SEC, acting in concert with the UK Financial Services Authority, took temporary emergency action[2] to prohibit short-selling in 799 financial companies to protect the integrity and quality of the securities market and strengthen investor confidence. This ban was lifted on October 8, 2008.

In this article we will examine the role of short-sellers. The profile of short-sellers includes hedge funds and other speculators, proprietary desks of bank holding companies, options market-makers, and, in recent years, mutual funds that execute 1X0/X0 strategies. We will discuss the academic literature on short sales, illustrate the short-sale process, examine the role of various participants in the process including lenders such as mutual funds and pension funds, agent intermediaries such as prime brokers, and borrowers such as hedge funds, mutual funds, and options market-makers, and we will present statistics on the universe of lendable and loaned securities. We find that the level of securities loaned versus the total universe of lendable securities increased dramatically during the period 2006 to the second quarter of 2008, followed by significant declines in the third and fourth quarters of 2008.

THE SHORT-SALE PROCESS

There are generally three groups of players in the short-sale process. The groups are securities lenders, securities borrowers (short-sellers), and agent intermediaries.

Securities lenders: Securities lenders are institutions with securities portfolios of sufficient size to make securities lending worthwhile. Generally these institutions include mutual funds, insurance companies, pension funds, and endowments. The lending activities of these groups are discussed in greater detail later.

Securities borrowers: Securities borrowers are institutions that engage in short-selling either as part of their trading strategies or to hedge their risk exposures. These institutions include hedge funds, mutual funds, ETF counterparties, and option market-makers. We will examine these groups in detail in the next section.

Agent intermediaries: Agent Intermediaries are institutions that facilitate the lending and borrowing of securities. These institutions may include custodian banks, broker-dealers, and/or prime brokers. We will examine the functions of these groups later.

The process illustrated in Figure 1 works well if there are plenty of shares available to borrow. However, one must consider another possibility: What if shares desired for borrowing purposes are unavailable? Several academic articles have examined impediments to the short-selling process. Evans, Geczy, Musto, and Reed (2009) group short positions from an unnamed options market-maker into five categories: general collateral, reduced rebate, reduced rebate and fail, fail only, and buy-in. These categories as defined in their database as follows:

- *General collateral* indicates that a stock has been loaned at the normal rebate rate, i.e. the stock is easy to borrow.
- *Reduced rebate* indicates that the rebate rate is below the general collateral rate, i.e. the stock is special.

160

Figure 1. The short-sale process

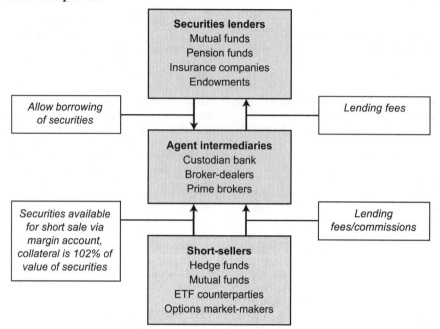

- *Reduced rebate and fail* indicates that some shares have been borrowed at a reduced rebate and that the market-maker failed to deliver some shares that were sold short.
- *Fail only* indicates that the market-maker failed to deliver any of the shares in this short position.
- *Buy-in* indicates that the counterparty of the short-sale transaction is forcing delivery on some or all of the shares in the short position.

One would expect a significant majority of short positions to fall into the general collateral category. More than 90% of the short positions in the database used by Evans *et al.* (2009) fell into that category.

THE KEY SHORT-SELLERS

In this section we will examine the key short-sellers. While certain participants may engage in short-selling by virtue of their trading strategy, others may engage in short sales to hedge their risk exposures (see Figure 1 for an illustration of the short-sale process). We will examine in detail each of these groups below.

Hedge Funds and Other Speculators

Several hedge fund strategies employ shorting stocks as part of their strategy. In the case of convertible arbitrage, the arbitrageur generally takes long positions in convertible bonds and sells short the underlying stock. In the case of equity strategies, managers may use fundamental or quantitative analysis to sell stocks short. Long/short equity strategies generally comprise the bulk of the hedge fund universe both in terms of assets under management as well as number of funds. In the case of merger arbitrage, managers sell short the

acquiring company, while short-biased strategies engage in short-selling of seemingly overvalued stocks.

Bank Holding Companies

Prior to the recent requests by Goldman Sachs and Morgan Stanley to change their status to bank holding companies, investment banks borrowed stock for their proprietary trading desks.[3] However, these and other banks will continue to borrow stock for their proprietary trading desks and other functions.

Short and Ultra-Short Exchange-Traded Funds

In recent years, several exchange-traded funds have been established that offer either the inverse or twice the inverse of the returns on a certain index. These exchange-traded funds are generally referred to as short-ETF or ultra-short ETF. The funds generally achieve their short exposure using derivatives such as swaps. Although these funds generally do not short underlying stocks, they retain the ability to do so if necessary.

ETF Counterparties

One of the primary instruments that the short- and ultra-short exchange-traded funds described in the previous section use to achieve their exposures is swaps. The counterparty in the swap transaction may choose to hedge its exposures by shorting stocks.

Mutual Funds

In recent years several firms have launched 1X0/X0-type funds. Generally, the equities owned by the fund equal 1X0% of its net asset value, while the equities shorted equal X0% of the fund's net asset value. Although the vast majority of

1X0/X0-type funds are offered through separate accounts, there are several mutual funds that are available to the public.

Option Market-Makers
Options market-makers short-sell securities on a regular basis for hedging purposes. They are, however, exempt from locating shares before short-selling.

THE KEY EQUITY LENDERS
In this section we will examine the key lenders. These institutional lenders include mutual funds, pension funds, insurance companies, and endowments (see Figure 1 for an illustration of the short-sale process). Generally, the lending activities take place through an intermediary agent such as a custodian bank or broker-dealer. These intermediary agents pool securities from various lenders who are unable to lend securities directly. Most broker-dealers combine their security-lending activities with their prime-brokerage operations. We will examine each of these groups next.

Mutual Funds
The US mutual fund industry managed around US$12 trillion in assets as of year-end 2007. Stock mutual funds accounted for 54% of the total mutual fund industry. In light of the actions of the SEC relating to the banning of short sales on the securities of 799 financial firms, two major mutual funds, Vanguard Group Inc. and State Street Corp., imposed additional restrictions that halted the lending of their shares.[4] However, lending fees received by mutual funds can be substantial and permanent restrictions may impact revenues.

Pension Funds
Equities form a major component in the asset allocation of defined contribution (DC) plans. According to Pensions & Investment online,[5] more than 50% of assets in corporate DC plans are allocated to equities, while significant percentages are allocated by public and union DC plans as well. Defined benefit plans have a significant percentage of assets allocated to equities as well. Pension funds participate significantly in the equity-lending market.

The reasons for lending securities include not only the offsetting of custody and administrative costs but also the generation of revenue. The infrastructure to support securities lending varies from lender to lender. Lenders sometimes impose credit restrictions. As noted earlier, certain lenders imposed restrictions on borrowing activities in light of the SEC rules prohibiting short-selling.

SUMMARY DATA ON SHORT SALES
In previous sections we examined the various aspects of the short-sale process and the key players. In this section we will look at the data on short sales. Figure 2 presents statistics on total lendable equities worldwide. The data were obtained from the Risk Management Association.[6]

The universe of lendable equities (or lendable assets, represented on the left axis in Figure 2) denotes the total dollar value of equities available for lending worldwide. These include North American, European, and Pacific-rim equities (including Australia) along with other equities not included in the aforementioned categories. The figures are reported as aggregate assets without consideration of client- or bank-imposed guidelines. The universe of loaned assets (right axis

Figure 2. Universe of lendable (left axis) versus loaned (right axis) equities worldwide

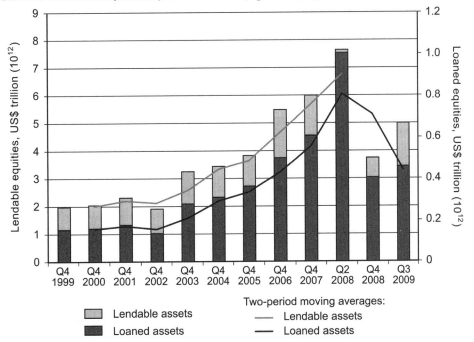

in Figure 2) represents the total dollar value of equities loaned worldwide.

One of the interesting aspects is the growth in the universe of lendable assets from around US$2 trillion in 1999 to more than US$7 trillion at the end of the second quarter of 2008. Expectedly, the universe shrank between 2001 and 2002 and then experienced a steady increase.

The level of loaned assets worldwide has followed a similar pattern. However, the level of loaned assets experienced a dramatic increase, from less than US$600 billion at the end of 2006 to over US$1 trillion at the end of the second quarter of 2008. The numbers definitively capture the sentiments of short-sellers leading up to the third and fourth quarters of 2008.

The significant increases in the levels of loaned equities in the years 2006–08 suggest a negative outlook on the stock market on the part of certain traders. In fact, the first signs of the subprime debacle can be traced back to early 2007. Stock prices of bond insurers such as Ambac and MBIA recorded their all-time highs in early 2007 before declining precipitously to 15-year lows in 2008, losing more than 90% of their value. The stock prices of erstwhile investment banks such as Bear Stearns and Lehman Brothers also followed similar patterns before the former merged with JP Morgan and the latter filed for bankruptcy. Further, Fannie Mae, Freddie Mac, American International Group (AIG), Merrill Lynch, Citigroup, Wachovia, and American Express among many others also witnessed precipitous declines in the value of their equities. These numbers, as well as media reports, suggest that short-biased traders such as certain hedge funds correctly predicted the decline of these companies, thus generating enormous capital appreciation for their investors (such as

pension funds, endowments, and foundations). The two-period moving average lines show this more explicitly.

In Figure 3 we explore levels of lendable assets for North America, Europe, and the Pacific Rim. Not surprisingly, North American and European equities represent a significant portion of the total dollar value of lendable equities worldwide. In Figure 4 we explore levels of loaned assets for the same regions. Again, the total dollar value of loaned North American and European equities represents a significant portion of the universe.

By the end of 2008 the level of loaned equities dropped to around 408 billion dollars, a fall of almost 60%. Numerous factors contributed to this decline, including the meltdown of equity markets, the ban on short-selling of financial stocks, and the self-imposed restrictions on stock lending by various financial institutions. It is also interesting to note that the levels of loaned assets have gradually increased to around 458 billion dollars as of the third quarter 2009, an increase of around 12%.

LITERATURE REVIEW

A plethora of academic articles have examined various aspects of short-selling. In this section we will examine some of these articles and their contribution to the literature.

Seneca (1967) examined the net effects of large short positions using data between 1946 and 1965 and found that short sales acted as a predictor of stock prices. Baron and McDonald (1973) explored the risk–return patterns of reported short positions. Using data from the NYSE over the period 1961–66, they found that stocks with more idiosyncratic risk had higher short interest. Brent, Morse, and Stice (1990) examined the increase in short interest over the period

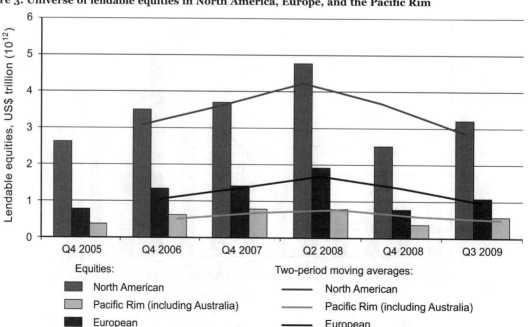

Figure 3. Universe of lendable equities in North America, Europe, and the Pacific Rim

Equities:
- North American
- Pacific Rim (including Australia)
- European

Two-period moving averages:
- North American
- Pacific Rim (including Australia)
- European

Figure 4. Universe of loaned equities in North America, Europe, and the Pacific Rim

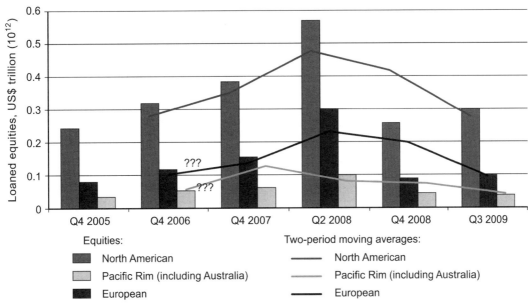

1974–86. They found that stocks with convertible securities, options, and high betas tended to have more shares held short. Further, Figlewski and Webb (1993) examined the effects of options on short sales. Using data from the Center for Research in Security Prices (CRSP) and Interactive Data Corp. (IDC) over the period 1969–85, they found that options facilitated short-selling.

More recently Geczy, Musto, and Reed (2002) have examined short-selling costs and constraints. Using data from an unnamed custodian bank over the period 1998–99, they found that short-selling frictions appear strongest in merger arbitrage. Bris, Goetzmann, and Zhu (2007) investigated the relation between short sales and market efficiency in world markets. Using data from various investment banks[7] over the period 1990–2001, they found that markets where short-selling is prohibited display significantly less negative skewness. Boehmer, Jones, and Zhang (2008) considered whether short-sellers are informed. Using data from CRSP and the NYSE over the period 2000–04, they found that short-sellers are well informed and contribute to efficient stock prices. Diether, Lee, and Werner (2008) studied the trading strategies used by short-sellers. Using data from various exchanges for 2005, they found that short-sellers in both NYSE and NASDAQ stocks increased their short-selling activity after periods of positive returns. Finally Evans, Geczy, Musto, and Reed (2009) explored whether options market competition tends to oligopoly as stocks become difficult to short. Using data from a large options market-maker over the period 1998–99, they found that market-makers profit when they fail to deliver stock.

CONCLUSION
In this article we examined the role of short-sellers in the marketplace. We showed that the process of short-selling involves three major participant groups: the lenders, the agent intermediaries, and the borrowers. We discussed the history of short-selling, including the enactment of the Securities Exchange Act of 1934, the adoption of the uptick rule in 1937, and the relaxation of that rule in 2007. We then discussed the short-sale process and identified five categories of short positions. Further, we discussed the profile of borrowers and lenders and provided historical statistics on the percentage of lendable securities and loaned equities. We observed a dramatic increase in the level of loaned securities between 2006 and the second quarter of 2008, followed by a dramatic decline by the fourth quarter of 2008. Finally, we presented a brief review of the academic literature on short-selling.

MORE INFO
Articles:
Boehmer, Ekkehart, Charles M. Jones, and Xiaoyan Zhang. "Which shorts are informed?" *Journal of Finance* 63:2 (April 2008): 491–527. Online at: dx.doi.org/10.1111/j.1540-6261.2008.01324.x

Brent, Averil, Dale Morse and E. Kay Stice. "Short interest: Explanations and tests." *Journal of Financial and Quantitative Analysis* 25:2 (June 1990): 273–289. Online at: dx.doi.org/10.2307/2330829

Bris, Arturo, William N. Goetzmann, and Ning Zhu. "Efficiency and the bear: Short sales and markets around the world." *Journal of Finance* 62:3 (June 2007): 1029–1079. Online at: dx.doi.org/10.1111/j.1540-6261.2007.01230.x

Diether, Karl B., Kuan-Hui Lee, and Ingrid M. Werner. "Short-sale strategies and return predictability." *Review of Financial Studies* 22:2 (February 2009): 575–607. Online at: dx.doi.org/10.1093/rfs/hhn047

Evans, Richard B., Christopher C. Geczy, David K. Musto, and Adam V. Reed. "Failure is an option: Impediments to short selling and options prices." *Review of Financial Studies* 22:5 (May 2009): 1955–1980. Online at: dx.doi.org/10.1093/rfs/hhm083

Figlewski, Stephen, and Gwendolyn P. Webb. "Options, short sales, and market completeness." *Journal of Finance* 48:2 (June 1993): 761–777. Online at: www.jstor.org/stable/2328923

Geczy, Christopher C., David K. Musto, and Adam V. Reed. "Stocks are special too: An analysis of the equity lending market." *Journal of Financial Economics* 66:2–3 (November–December 2002): 241–269. Online at: dx.doi.org/10.1016/S0304-405X(02)00225-8

McDonald, John G., and Donald C. Baron. "Risk and return on short positions in common stocks." *Journal of Finance* 28:1 (March 1973): 97–107. Online at: www.jstor.org/stable/2978171

Seneca, Joseph J. "Short interest: Bearish or bullish." *Journal of Finance* 22:1 (March 1967): 67–70. Online at: www.jstor.org/stable/2977301

Websites:

Australian Securities Lending Association (ASLA): www.asla.com.au

High short interest stocks: www.highshortinterest.com

International Securities Lending Association (ISLA): www.isla.co.uk

NASDAQ short interest: www.nasdaqtrader.com/asp/short_interest.asp

Pan Asia Securities Lending Association (PASLA): www.paslaonline.com

Risk Management Association (RMA): www.rmahq.org/RMA

Securities Industry and Financial Markets Association (SIFMA): www.sifma.org

ShortSqueeze.com: www.shortsqueeze.com

See Also:

✔ Swaps, Options, and Futures: What They Are and Their Function (pp. 303–304)

NOTES

1 These companies include BNP Paribas Securities Corp. (BNPQF or BNPQY), Bank of America Corporation (BAC), Barclays PLC (BCS), Citigroup Inc. (C), Credit Suisse Group (CS), Daiwa Securities Group Inc. (DSECY), Deutsche Bank Group AG (DB), Allianz SE (AZ), Goldman Sachs Group Inc. (GS), Royal Bank ADS (RBS), HSBC Holdings PLC ADS (HBC and HSI), JPMorgan Chase & Co., (JPM), Lehman Brothers Holdings Inc. (LEH), Merrill Lynch & Co., Inc. (MER), Mizuho Financial Group, Inc. (MFG), Morgan Stanley (MS), UBS AG (UBS), Freddie Mac (FRE), and Fannie Mae (FNM).

2 For more information see www.sec.gov/news/press/2008/2008-211.htm

3 The US House of Representatives on December 11, 2009, passed a 1,279-page Bank Reform bill (Financial Stability Improvement Act of 2009) that seeks to prohibit proprietary trading if it puts the firm's safety and soundness at risk. See "Winners and losers in the Bank Reform bill." *Wall Street Journal* "Dear Journal" blog (December 11, 2009). Online at: tinyurl.com/6f89h7c. To become law, the bill would have to pass the Senate, which would be a tall order.

4 See "2 mutual fund firms act to halt short sales." *Boston Globe* (September 23, 2008). Online at: tinyurl.com/4yze4w

5 For more information see www.pionline.com

6 For more information see www.rmahq.org/RMA

7 The term "investment bank" ceased to exist in 2008 when the last two remaining investment banks, Goldman Sachs and Morgan Stanley, asked the Federal Reserve to be converted to bank holding companies following the failures of Bear Stearns and Lehman Brothers and the announcement of the merger of Merrill Lynch with Bank of America.

Understanding Equity Capital in Small and Medium-Sized Enterprises

by Siri Terjesen

EXECUTIVE SUMMARY

- Equity capital or financing is funding raised by a business in exchange for a share of the ownership.
- Equity financing enables firms to obtain money without incurring debt, or without needing to repay a specific amount of money at a particular time.
- There are four stages of equity investment: seed, early-stage, expansion, and late-stage financing.
- Equity capital sources differ in terms of timing, amount provided, type of firm funded, extent of due diligence, contract type, expectations of timing and payback, and monitoring of business decisions.

INTRODUCTION

Entrepreneurs may require both debt and equity financing, and often start their firms by financing growth through equity. Equity capital is money invested in the venture with no legal obligation on the entrepreneur to repay the principal amount or to pay interest on it; however, it requires sharing the ownership and profits with the funding source, and possibly also paying dividends to equity investors.

After value has been built, entrepreneurs may consider debt financing, which involves a payback of the funds (with interest) for use of the money. In short, debt places a burden of repayment and interest on the entrepreneur, whereas equity capital forces the entrepreneur to relinquish some degree of ownership and control.

The stages of equity financing are depicted in Figure 1. In the first stage, known as the seed stage, entrepreneurs tend to raise capital from their own savings, though they may also seek informal investment from family, friends, business angels, and public sources. Entrepreneurs may then choose to pursue formal equity capital through rounds of early-stage, expansion, and late-stage financing. This may be followed by an initial public offering (IPO) and, finally, raising of finance from public markets and banks. Summary details of the financing stages are as follows:

- Seed financing is the initial funding to develop a business concept, for example by expenditure on research, product development, and initial marketing to reach early-adopter customers. Companies that receive seed funding may be in the process of incorporation, or may have been in operation for a while.
- Early-stage financing is sought by companies that have completed the product/service development stage and test marketing but require additional financing to expand.
- Expansion financing is provided when the company is poised to grow rapidly. The funds may be used to increase production capacity, marketing, or product development, and/or provide additional working capital.
- Late-stage funding refers to pre-IPO investments to strengthen a company's positioning and to gain endorsements from top venture capital (VC) firms as the company prepares to list.

At any stage, equity investment can come from informal or formal sources. However, it is more usual to access informal sources in the seed and early stages, and formal sources in the expansion and late stages.

INFORMAL EQUITY SOURCES
Informal and Angel Investment

Informal investment refers to equity provided by individuals. In addition to accessing their own savings and those of family, friends, and even neighbors, entrepreneurs seek informal "angel" investors who provide financial capital as well as business expertise for running a company.

As shown in Figure 2, the rates of informal investment vary dramatically around the world, from a high of 13% in Uganda to a low of 0.5% in Japan. Business owners are approximately four times more likely to make informal investments than are non business-owners (Bygrave and Hunt, 2005). As can be seen in the figure, many informal investors have experience as owners/managers of their own businesses.

Although the profile of angel investors varies, in developed economies, angels tend to have entrepreneurship experience, be retired from their own firm or a corporation, and have net incomes in excess of US$100,000 a year. Most angels invest in companies within a two-hour traveling distance of their home, and therefore the informal investment market is geographically diverse. On average, the angel capital market is approximately ten times the size of the formal venture capital market. Indeed, small firms are eight times more likely to raise finance from business angels than from formal institutions.

Business angels tend not to have any previous relationship with the entrepreneur, and are often more objective. Angel investors can be passive (backing the judgment of others) or active (hands-on, with advice or direct management input to help the business to establish itself). Angels tend to invest as individuals or as part of a larger group, and generally as a part-time interest rather than as a full-time job (as is the case of venture capitalists). In addition to financial goals, informal investors often seek other, nonfinancial returns, among them the creation of jobs in areas of high unemployment,

Figure 1. The stages of equity financing

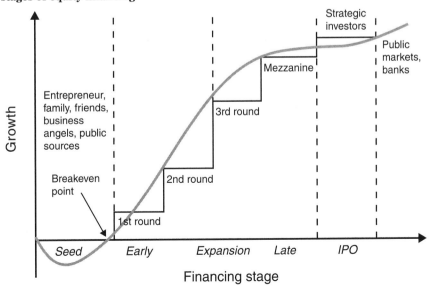

Figure 2. Rates of informal investment around the world. (*Source*: Global Entrepreneurship Monitor data)

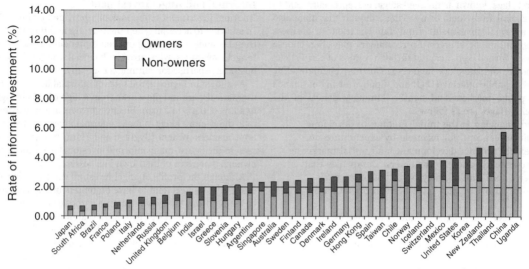

development of technology for social needs (for example, medical or energy), local revitalization, provision of assistance to indigenous peoples, and just personal satisfaction from the assistance they give to entrepreneurs.

Business angels prefer to fund high-risk entrepreneurial firms in their earliest stages. They fill the so-called equity gap by making their investments in precisely those areas where institutional venture capital providers are reluctant to invest. Angels may also prefer to fund the smaller amounts (within the equity gap) that are needed to launch new ventures, and they invest in almost all industry sectors. Angels tend to be more flexible in their financial decisions, and also tend to have different criteria, longer investment horizons ("patient" money), shorter investment processes, and lower targeted rates of return than venture capitalists. Business angel funding can make a firm more attractive for other sources of finance. However, business angels are less likely to make follow-on investments in the same firm.

FORMAL EQUITY SOURCES
Venture Capital

Venture capitalists can be a valuable and powerful source of equity funding for new ventures, providing, in addition to capital, help with a full range of financial services for new or growing ventures. These include market research, strategy, management consulting, contacts with prospective customers/-suppliers/others, assistance in negotiation and with management and accounting controls, employee recruitment, risk management, and counseling on regulations. Venture capitalists tend to have ambitious expectations for both the return on and the increase in their investment, as shown in Table 1.

The process of seeking venture capital financing includes the following four stages:

- Initial screening to assess the firm's ability to meet the VC's particular requirements.
- Detailed reading of the business plan.

- Verbal presentation to the venture capitalist.
- Final evaluation, including visiting suppliers, customers, consultants, and others; the venture capitalist then makes a final decision.

This four-step process screens out approximately 98% of all venture plans, with the remaining 2% receiving some degree of financial backing. Venture capitalists reach a go/no-go decision in an average of 6 minutes on the basis of the initial screening, and in less than 21 minutes on the basis of an overall proposal evaluation. The main factors in their decision are the firm's expected long-term growth and profitability, although an entrepreneur's background and characteristics are also taken into account.

Venture capitalists tend to agree on an exit strategy at the time of investment, with the following five main mechanisms:
- Trade sale to another company.
- Repurchase of the venture capital shares by the investee company.
- Refinancing or purchase of the venture capital equity by a longer-term investment institution.
- Stock market listing.
- Involuntary exit.

Table 2 summarizes the differences between business angels and venture capitalists.

Table 1. Typical returns on investment (ROI) and increase on initial investment sought by venture capitalists. (*Source*: Terjesen and Frederick, 2007)

Stage of business	Expected annual ROI (%)	Expected increase on initial investment
Seed	60 +	10–15 times
Early	40–60	6–12 times
Expansion	30–50	4–8 times
Late	25–40	3–6 times
Turnaround situation	50 +	8–15 times

Table 2. Differences between business angels and venture capitalists. (*Source*: Terjesen and Frederick, 2007)

Differential factor	Investor type	
Business angel	Venture capitalist	
Personal	Entrepreneurs	Investors
Firms funded	Small, early-stage	Large, mature
Due diligence done	Minimal	Extensive
Location of investment	Of concern	Not important
Contract used	Simple	Comprehensive
Monitoring after investment	Active, hands-on	Strategic
Exiting the firm	Of lesser concern	Highly important
Rate of return	Of lesser concern	Highly important

Table 3. Advantages and disadvantages of IPO funding. (*Source*: Terjesen and Frederick, 2007)

Advantages	Disadvantages
Stronger capital base	Pressure for short-term growth
Improves other financing prospects	Disclosure and confidentiality
Better placed to make acquisitions	Costs—initial and ongoing
Diversification of ownership	Restrictions on management
Increased executive compensation	Loss of personal benefits
Increased company and personal prestige	Trading restrictions

Initial Public Offering

As the firm grows, managers may consider an initial public offering (IPO), which is when a company's shares are first sold to the public. An IPO is often the first time people outside the company have the opportunity to buy its shares; hence, IPOs are referred to as "going public" or "floating" the company. An IPO has advantages and disadvantages. The advantages are:

- *Amount and efficiency of capital raised*: Selling shares is one of the fastest ways to raise large sums of capital in a short period of time.
- *Liquidity*: A public market provides liquidity for owners, who can readily sell their shares.
- *Value*: The market puts a value on the company's shares, which in turn allows a value to be placed on the company.
- *Image*: Publicly traded companies are often perceived to be stronger by suppliers, financiers, and customers.

However, an IPO also has several disadvantages:

- *Cost*: IPO expenses are significantly higher than for other sources of capital due to fees for accounting, legal services, prospectus printing and distribution, and the cost of underwriting the shares. The cost can easily exceed US$1 million.
- *Disclosure*: An IPO requires detailed public disclosure of company affairs, but new firms may prefer to keep this information private. Furthermore, the paperwork involved in meeting regulation requirements and providing regular information about performance may drain large amounts of management time, energy, and money that could be better invested in opportunities for company growth.
- *Stockholder pressure*: Stockholders are interested in a strong performance record on earnings and dividends, and so may put pressure on managers to focus on short-term performance. If managers do this, it can be at the expense of long-term growth and improvement.

The advantages and disadvantages of IPO funding are summarized in Table 3.

Should a firm decide to pursue an IPO, it is important that it be aware of laws with respect to securities and investments, which vary across countries but include the following common elements.

Investor information: Firms must provide investors with key information.

Investment banker or underwriter: Most firms select a lead investment banker to sell the new shares, usually at fees of about 7% of the issue value.

Ownership structure: The shares sold in the IPO are designated as primary shares, which are new shares, and secondary shares, which were previously owned by existing stockholders, usually the founders and managers of the firm. The size of the new issue relative to the existing shares and their distribution change the ownership structure. The IPO often results in moving from management by firm founders toward professional management of the firm. The IPO generally occurs when the founder's entrepreneurial activities are coming to an end, but often he or she will play a role in the future of the company.

Lockup provisions: When going public, IPOs almost always commit to a lockup period, whereby insiders (major stockholders, directors, and senior officers) are prohibited from selling shares without the written permission of the lead underwriter until a certain amount of time has passed. On average, the waiting time is 180 days. These lockup provisions control the supply of shares sold during the period after the IPO by insiders or existing stockholders who might have inside knowledge and, thus, unfair advantage.

Presence of venture capitalists: Many firms may be financed by VCs, who take an ownership position and have partial control over the entrepreneurs. The IPO may change this control as the VC distributes the shares to their limited partners. The use of an IPO may be a cheaper form of financing than that provided by VCs, and will certainly provide liquidity to the existing pre-IPO stockholders.

Issue size: With the fixed costs of an IPO to create a liquid market, the number of new shares in the IPO should be large enough to provide sufficient liquidity, but small enough so that the issuing firm does not raise more cash than it can profitably use.

Mechanisms for pricing IPOs: IPOs may be priced through auctions, fixed-price offers, or book-building. In auctions, the market-clearing price is determined after bids are submitted. In a fixed-price offer, the price is set prior to the allocation. If there is excess demand, shares are rationed on a pro rata or lottery basis. In book-building, the investment bankers canvas potential buyers and then set an offer price. Book-building is now the predominant mechanism by which IPO shares are sold around the world.

Prospectus: If a company is raising capital by offering its shares to the public for the first time, it will issue a disclosure document called a prospectus. The prospectus is a formal written offer to sell shares and provides an investor with the information necessary to make an informed decision. All negative information must be clearly highlighted and explained. Some of the specific detailed information that must be presented includes: the history and nature of the company, its capital structure, a description of any material contracts, a description of the securities that are being registered, the salaries of major officers and directors and the price paid for any security holdings they may have, underwriting arrangements, an estimate of and planned use for the net proceeds to be raised, audited financial statements, and information about the competition with an estimate of the probability that the firm will survive.

CASE STUDY
AN ANGEL IN ENGLAND

Anita Roddick started her own business, The Body Shop, creating and selling beauty products. Roddick was keen to open a second shop in Chichester, but the bank turned down her request for a loan. In desperation, Roddick asked her friend Aidre, who was helping to manage the first store, for help. Aidre had a boyfriend named Ian Bentham McGlinn, who had some spare cash from operating a local garage. Scottish born McGlinn offered Roddick £4,000 in 1976 in return for 50% equity in the business. Anita accepted the offer but wrote to her husband Gordon (who was on a two-year hike in South America) to inform him of the offer. Gordon wrote back suggesting that she "not do it, not give away half the company," but it was too late.

With his equity investment, McGlinn became a business angel and sat on the board of The Body Shop, resigning just before it was floated on the stock market in 1984. At the time of the flotation McGlinn was worth £4 million, but he avoided the press by taking a holiday in Portugal. By 1991, McGlinn's 52 million shares were worth £150 million, though his dividends were worth only £638,000 annually. The Roddicks and McGlinn together owned 56% of The Body Shop, preventing a takeover. In 1996, McGlinn sold 3.5% of the business for £12 million. When L'Oréal took over The Body Shop in 2006, McGlinn's 22% stake was worth £137 million. As of 2007, Ian McGlinn was ranked no. 28 on the *Sunday Times* Rich List, with an estimated worth of £146 million.

MAKING IT HAPPEN

When approaching venture capitalists, entrepreneurs must remember that VCs are inundated with potential business opportunities. It is therefore advisable to keep the following in mind.

Do
- Prepare all your materials before soliciting firms.
- Send a business plan and a covering letter first.
- Contact several firms with this material.
- Keep phone conversations brief—prepare a one-minute and a three-minute pitch.

- Remain positive and enthusiastic about your company and its product or service.
- Know your minimum deal and walk away if necessary.
- Negotiate a deal you can live with.
- Investigate the venture capitalist's previous deals and current portfolio structure.

Don't
- Don't expect a response.
- Don't dodge questions.
- Don't give vague answers. Know what you can and cannot disclose before you start talking, so that you do not stumble over awkward questions.
- Don't switch off—be an active listener as you will always learn something.
- Don't hide significant problems.
- Don't expect immediate decisions.
- Don't become fixated on pricing.
- Don't embellish facts or projections.

When considering an IPO, managers should ask the following questions:
- Can the company run without you while you are managing the IPO process? The work leading up to a public offering is time-intensive and can deflect your focus away from everyday operations, ultimately hurting the business. If the company lacks a strong management team, it can be helpful to appoint an interim CFO with experience of taking companies, preferably small, through the rigors of going public.
- Can you get to a market capitalization of US$100 million within three years of going public? The value of a public company is a multiple of what it earns. If the result isn't near US$100 million, staying private may be best. This number is a good indicator because it is the level of earnings at which the company can attract brokers and investors.
- Are you building a company with high gross and operating margins? High margins are important because they keep companies out of the volume game. For a company to reach critical mass in earnings with low margins, it must generate enormous sales growth.
- Can your business deliver double-digit sales and earnings growth? The competition among public companies, mutual funds, and other investment networks is fierce. Investors won't look twice at a company that doesn't grow fast enough to warrant the use of their time and money.
- Are you building a family business? If the succession plan for the business is set in stone to be passed on to the kids, public may not be the right route. Families measure the success of a business generation by generation. Money movers are interested in the quarter-to-quarter progress.
- Can the business be built inexpensively? The main reason companies go public is to raise initial funds for major growth. As a result, sales and growth need to reflect the use of the first round of financing. If another round of financing is needed to achieve the original plan, investors may look elsewhere.

MORE INFO

Books:

Cendrowski, Harry, James P. Martin, Louis W. Petro, and Adam A. Wadecki. *Private Equity: History, Governance, and Operations*. Hoboken, NJ: Wiley, 2008.

Gadiesh, Orit, and Hugh MacArthur. *Lessons from Private Equity Any Company Can Use*. Cambridge, MA: Harvard Business School Press, 2008.

Terjesen, Siri, and Howard Frederick. *Sources of Funding for Australia's Entrepreneurs*. Raleigh, NC: Lulu, 2007.

Report:

Bygrave, William D., with Stephen A. Hunt. "Global entrepreneurship monitor 2004 financing report." Babson College and London Business School, 2005.

Websites:

Global Entrepreneurship Monitor (GEM) data: www.gemconsortium.org

US Small Business Administration on equity financing: tinyurl.com/7boyfzm

See Also:

★ Assessing Venture Capital Funding for Small and Medium-Sized Enterprises (pp. 114–117)
★ Financial Steps in an IPO for a Small or Medium-Size Enterprise (pp. 126–128)
★ Optimizing the Capital Structure: Finding the Right Balance between Debt and Equity (pp. 145–148)

★

Best Practice

Understanding the True Cost of Issuing Convertible Debt and Other Equity-Linked Financing
by Roger Lister

EXECUTIVE SUMMARY

- Convertible securities (CSs) combine debt and equity. In option terms, CSs are a call option on a specified number of shares whose exercise price is the debt claim forgone in exchange for the shares. CSs are also like a stock with a put option whose exercise price is the market value of the convertible.

- Some critics insist that CSs are uneconomic because they address several habitats of investors at the same time. Others say that they comprise flexible, non-dilutive, easily executed, and cheap finance, which appeals to many professional investors including hedge funds.

- The basic formula defines the cost of CSs but ignores tax and dividends. The formula produces a weighted average of the cost of the debt and the cost of a call option on the issuer's shares.

- Management's task is to measure the cost of CSs with the formula while allowing for the real world influences that the basic model ignores.

- Cost-influencing factors include dividends, tax, and resolution of agency costs.

INTRODUCTION

Convertible securities (CSs) and other equity-linked instruments combine debt and equity. Depending on the terms and the issuer's future performance, CSs can range from almost pure equity to an option-free bond. In option terms, a CS can be viewed in two ways. It amounts to a straight bond with a call option on a specified number of shares. It is also effectively a share with a put option whose exercise price is the market value of the convertible.

Some iconoclasts persistently argue that CSs and other equity-linked instruments are essentially uneconomic. Classically championed by Tony Merrett and Allen Sykes, critics maintain that by jointly approaching the equity and fixed interest markets a company must offer costly conversion rights to attract the equity investor while giving virtually the same rights to the fixed interest investor who values them less. Likewise, issuers must give fixed interest investors an acceptable income. In short, CSs contradict the advantage of specialization whereby capital-raising is tailored to habitats of investors. The iconoclasts invoke studies like Ammann, Fehr, and Seiz (2006) to the effect that negative equity returns follow the announcement and issue of CS.

Loss of interest on the part of one habitat can lead to greater interest from the other. The mini-boom in convertibles in the spring of 2009 occurred as the reduced value of the equity element led to higher yields becoming available to investors interested in debt. At the same time some straight equity investors crossed over into convertibles attracted by the combination of yield and equity option.

A counterargument is that CSs are flexible, non-dilutive, easily executed, and cheap finance. CSs appeal to professional investors, including hedge funds which exploit arbitrage opportunities.

Rating agencies such as Fitch see sense in both viewpoints and hold that the desirability of CSs depends more strongly than other sources of finance on individual corporate circumstances and market context. Fitch (2006) concludes:

"Issuers must find continuing compelling reasons for such issuance ... The lower costs of such issuance compared with the cost of issuing equity are certainly supportive, as are the gradual standardization, transparency and consistency of documentation, market practice and the activities of the agencies. On the other hand, issuers and their advisers must always strive to satisfy several constituencies, including regulators, legal and tax authorities, the agencies and finally, investors. Investor appetite underpinned the buoyant corporate activity of recent years. However, that appetite arose in an environment of low interest rates that will not persist indefinitely."

What is the true cost of CSs? Definition is less difficult than measurement. Having defined the parameters and influences on cost, management must frankly ask whether their measurements are so unreliable as to make them a dubious basis for decision-taking. Of course this applies across financial management, but it is particularly acute for the cost of capital.

THE COST FORMULA

The cost of a CS is a weighted average of the cost of its debt element and the cost of a call option on the issuer's shares, since the investor in a CS is a lender and the holder of a call option on the value of the firm. The difference between a conversion right and a regular call option is that a CS holder gets new shares upon exercise. It follows that if the price at which the CS holder is entitled to shares is below market price, then the value of all corporate equity, including the convertor's, is diluted. This explains why a convertible warrant is worth less than a straight call option on the company's shares whose exercise leaves existing equity intact.

The market will discount each element to the present using appropriate required rates of return. The cost of CS is an average of the rates weighted by each element's share of total market value.

The starting point is the textbook formula (see, for example, Copeland, Weston and Shastri, 2004, Chapter 15) which can be summarized as follows.

These are the essential terms: k_{cv} is the cost of convertible debt; B is the value of debt element; W is the value of equity element, being the value of a call option on the company's shares; $B + W$ is the value of the convertible security; k_b is the required rate of return on debt; and k_c is the required rate of return on a call option on the company's shares. See below.

Using the capital asset pricing model,

$$k_c = R_f + [E(R_m) - R_f]\beta_c$$

where k_c is the required rate of return on a call option on the company's shares with the same maturity as the CS; R_f is the risk-free rate of return for a bond with the same maturity as the CS; $E(R_m)$ is the expected rate of return on a portfolio comprising all the shares in the market; β_c is the systematic risk of the call option expressing its correlation with the market. β_c is computed by reference to the β of an underlying share of the company adjusted to option using the Black–Scholes option pricing program:

$$k_{cv} = k_b \left(\frac{B}{B + W} \right) + k_c \left(\frac{W}{B + W} \right)$$

The basic Black–Scholes option pricing scheme assumes that the issuer pays neither dividends nor tax (see, for example, Berk and DeMarzo, 2007, Chapters 21, 22, 23; Brealey and

Myers, 2007, Part 6; and packages like the London Business School's).

FACTORS INFLUENCING COST

In the real world, dividends, tax, and mitigation of agency costs influence the cost of a CS.

Dividends: If a company pays dividends then the value of the call option C changes. A call option on a dividend-paying share suffers, since a cash dividend liquidates some corporate value and the proceeds go to shareholders but not option holders. The larger the dividends, the more the option suffers. Option holders who try to anticipate this by early exercise gain dividends but lose interest on the exercise price.

Options on dividend-paying stocks with assumed-continuous or, more realistically, discrete dividends can now be valued (Chandrasekhar and Gukhal, 2004), but only with protracted and complex mathematics beyond the present scope.

Tax: The impact of tax on cost is unique for every issuer, holder, and regime. Tax impinges on C, the value of the call, on β, its systematic risk and on k_b, the cost of debt. The impact in any particular case depends on:

- the issuer and holder's tax regime;
- interacting intra-group regimes;
- corporate, inter-corporate, and personal taxes at critical decision points;
- the taxable status of issuer, holder, and associates;
- how issuer and holder prioritize tax allowances.

Some aspects of recent relevant tax regulations for the United Kingdom are illustrative. The issue price is split between debt and equity. The debt element is valued by discounting comparable straight debt at the interest rate that would have been payable had the security contained no equity conversion feature. The difference between this value and the issue price of the security is treated as being either an equity instrument or an embedded derivative, according to whether the company can only issue shares or whether it has the discretion to pay cash. In the former case the conversion right is treated as an equity issue and is disregarded for tax. In the latter case it is in principle taxable as an embedded derivative. If so, a chargeable gain or allowable loss will arise when the company pays cash to the holders. The gain or loss is determined by a formula based on the difference between the book value of the equity element and the amount paid.

Any difference between the deemed issue price of the debt element and the amount payable on its redemption is amortized and is tax-deductible over the life of the security.

A company can get a high and timely tax deduction by paying high interest on a CS with a short life. This reduces k_b, the cost of debt. However if CS holders are taxable, their personal tax may negate the deduction: if debt is tax-inefficient relative to equity, such investors will require compensation by way of a higher return.

Furthermore tax benefits may be truncated by bankruptcy, voluntary conversion by bondholders, or a company decision to force conversion. If cross-border jurisdiction is involved it becomes necessary to examine how CSs would be categorized under relevant tax treaties, EC directives, and double taxation resulting from any inconsistent classification.

Figure 1. Annual global convertible issuance, data through March 10, 2004. (*Source*: Standard & Poor's Global Fixed Income Research, Thomson Financial)

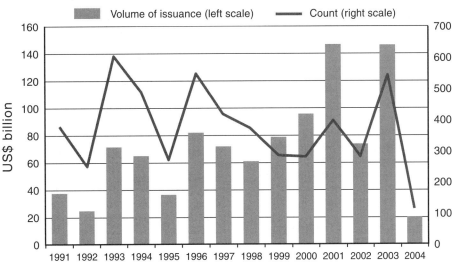

Mitigation of agency costs: Agency costs are costs of conflict among different classes of investor and between managers and investors. They reflect opportunities for equity to exploit debt and for managers to invest sloppily, forgo good investments, shirk, and enjoy perks. Endangered parties impose monitoring costs on the shareholders. If the endangered party is a lender, then the cost of debt rises. With CSs an equity sweetener reduces the monitoring costs by aligning the interests of debt and equity.

CSs can reduce the managerial incentive to overinvest in poor, low-return projects. For example, consider the second of two interdependent risky investments, which is only beneficial if the first succeeds. Either finance can be borrowed at the outset for both projects or CSs can be issued that will be sufficient for the first project while providing enough for the second on conversion. If all goes well, the second project will be duly financed by conversion. If the first project fails, the value of the CS will fall, nobody will convert, and management will be able to repurchase the debt at its low value in the open market. Indeed Mayers (2003) has observed a correlation between conversion and spates of corporate investment. If all had been borrowed upfront and if the first project failed, management might be tempted to invest the unused borrowings in easy, unprofitable projects.

A TREND AND ITS REVERSAL

A suitably selected trend illustrates in combination a number of the factors discussed. Such was the boom of 2003 (*Economist*, 2003) and the subsequent fall.

The factors that prompted the surge in the early 2000s to issuance to a near-historic high are concerned with cost, capital structure, value, financial mobility, and market context:

- The market had no appetite for equity, and at the same time companies were suffering from unpalatable gearing levels. CSs with a low coupon provided financial mobility and

some reassurance to anxious investors and garnered tax advantage.
- Hedge funds were attracted to CSs because they perceived a bargain insofar as the issue price underestimated the volatility of the equity, which meant that the call option, C in the basic formula, was undervalued.
- Hedge funds bought the convertible, sold the debt, and kept the undervalued call option. They then sold shares short to exploit underestimated volatility.

A reversal of the trend came when

- the volatility of equities declined;
- companies grew wise to the excessive cost of CSs that they were suffering;
- for tax reasons dividends increased, and this hurt short sellers who had to pay the dividends to their purchaser.

The above trend and its reversal illustrate an underlying decision process. An issue of convertibles may be based on perceived market opportunity as above. Alternatively it may be a reaction against the relative costs of issuing straight equity or straight debt. Onerous regulation may further militate against either or both straight instruments.

MAKING IT HAPPEN

The decision to issue CSs follows the answers to a series of questions.

- Is there presently a "hot convertible debt window" in the market or are there contraindications?
- Do the causes of the window or the contraindications apply to us?
- What is our debt capacity? If we are near its limits will CSs bust us or will they enable us to stretch our borrowing?
- Can we tailor CSs to our real investment needs? Can we at the same time mitigate agency costs?

Best Practice

- What tax-planning opportunities do CSs offer? Should we prioritize other tax benefits?
- Measurement of the parameters of the cost of capital is notoriously difficult. How reliable are our estimates? For example, how stable is our beta and how reliable is our estimate of volatility?

MORE INFO

Books:

Berk, Jonathan, and Peter DeMarzo. *Corporate Finance*. Boston, MA: Pearson Addison Wesley, 2007.

Bhattacharya, Mihir. "Convertible securities and their valuation." In Frank J. Fabozzi (ed). *The Handbook of Fixed Income Securities*. New York: McGraw-Hill, 2005; 1393–1442.

Brealey, Richard A., Stewart C. Myers, and Franklin Allen. *Principles of Corporate Finance*. 10th ed. Boston, MA: McGraw-Hill, 2010.

Copeland, Thomas, Fred Weston, and Kuldeep Shastri. *Financial Theory and Corporate Policy*. 4th ed. Boston, MA: Addison-Wesley, 2004.

Tuckman, Bruce, and Angel Serrat. *Fixed Income Securities: Tools for Today's Market*. 3rd ed. Hoboken, NJ: Wiley, 2011.

Articles:

Ammann, Manuel, Martin Fehr, and Ralf Seiz. "New evidence on the announcement effect of convertible and exchangeable bonds." *Journal of Multinational Financial Management* 16:1 (February 2006): 43–63. Online at: dx.doi.org/10.1016/j.mulfin.2005.03.001

Asquith, Paul. "Convertible bonds are not called late." *Journal of Finance* 50:4 (September 1995): 1275–1289. Online at: www.afajof.org/journal/jstabstract.asp?ref=11557

Campbell, Cynthia J., Louis H. Ederington, and Prashant Vankudre. "Tax shields, sample selection bias, and the information content of conversion-forcing bond calls." *Journal of Finance* 46:4 (September 1991): 1291–1324. Online at: www.afajof.org/journal/jstabstract.asp?ref=11156

Economist. "Convertible bombs." November 14, 2002. Online at: www.economist.com/node/1446299?story_id=E1_TQQGNJJ

Economist. "Options and opportunities." July 17, 2003. Online at: www.economist.com/node/1927089?story_id=E1_TJNSDRJ

Fitch Ratings. "Guide to hybrid securities." July 18, 2006. Online at: www.gtnews.com/feature/138_2.cfm

Laurent, Sandra. "Convertible debt and preference share financing: An empirical study." Working paper. 2005. Online at: ssrn.com/abstract=668364

Gukhal, Chandrasekhar Reddy . "The compound option approach to American options on jump-diffusions." *Journal of Economic Dynamics and Control* 28:10 (September 2004): 2055–2074. Online at: dx.doi.org/10.1016/j.jedc.2003.06.002

See Also:

★ Equity Issues by Listed Companies: Rights Issues and Other Methods (pp. 123–125)

★ Optimizing the Capital Structure: Finding the Right Balance between Debt and Equity (pp. 145–148)

★ The Role of Short Sellers in the Marketplace (pp. 158–164)

★ Understanding Equity Capital in Small and Medium-Sized Enterprises (pp. 164–169)

✔ Swaps, Options, and Futures: What They Are and Their Function (pp. 303–304)

Balancing Senior Management Compensation Arrangements with Shareholders' Interests

by Henrik Cronqvist

EXECUTIVE SUMMARY

- Appropriately designed executive compensation schemes can add substantial value for the firm's shareholders.
- Base salaries should be competitive with those awarded by similar-sized firms in the industry in order to attract and retain superior top-executive talent.
- Most perquisite-type compensation is now outdated, fails to align manager–shareholder interests in any obvious way, and should be avoided.
- Annual cash bonuses should be based on measures that can't be easily manipulated through accounting practices adopted by management.
- Long-term, equity-based compensation in the form of stock options or grants is the most effective way to harmonize the interests of senior management and shareholders.
- It is important to anticipate increased disclosure and scrutiny of executive compensation structures by the media when a particular compensation structure is being designed.

INTRODUCTION

The board of directors, and specifically the compensation committee (or remuneration committee), has the challenging task of designing a compensation structure for the chief executive officer (CEO) and other senior managers that balances their interests with those of the shareholders. The general idea is to make an executive's pay sensitive to the value created for the firm's shareholders. In this way, everyone shares the common goal of maximizing shareholder value.

Corporate executives can in principle be compensated in three different ways:
- base salary and perquisites, or "perks";
- annual cash bonus;
- shares.

No one form will perfectly align the interests of senior management and shareholders. The task of designing a value-adding compensation structure is therefore about identifying the mix between these different forms of compensation that best incentivizes senior management to create value for the shareholders.

DESIGNING A VALUE-ADDING COMPENSATION STRUCTURE

The base salary is the starting point for the compensation package and is commonly set through benchmarking based on a survey of similar-sized firms in the company's industry. Because of risk aversion, most executives will not accept a purely performance-based pay package. Though not sensitive to company performance, the base salary can still play a key role in attracting and retaining superior managerial talent.

Perks such as country club membership and private use of a corporate aircraft used to be common. There is, however, a trend towards the use of fewer perks, mainly because of increased disclosure and scrutiny by media and "watch-dog" groups.[1] For example, in an article with the headline "Only the little people pay for lawn care," columnist Gretchen Morgenson of the *New York Times* wrote that Donald J. Tyson, the former CEO of Tyson Foods, received US$84,000 in compensation for "lawn maintenance costs" during 1997–2001.[2] Though the perk was an insignificant portion of his pay during this period, the public's perception of its size can be much more significant than its monetary value. Perks perceived as excessive can cause customer resentment and, as a result, adversely affect both brand and shareholder value.

In contrast to base salary and perks, annual cash bonuses are conditional on short-term financial or nonfinancial goals being met by the firm or individual senior managers. Executives' bonuses, other than for the CEO, should be based on their particular business unit's performance, though a part may be based on overall firm performance or cooperation among executives managing different business units.[3] Nonfinancial targets can include successfully launching a new product line, meeting a certain customer satisfaction level, or appointing a new chief financial officer (CFO). These objectives should be specific, attainable, and measurable in the short run. Examples of financial performance targets are earnings per share (EPS), earnings before interest, taxes, depreciation, and amortization (EBITDA), and economic value added (EVA). Regardless of which measure is chosen, a particular threshold has to be attained before a minimum bonus is paid. If the performance is above that threshold, the bonus should increase in increments up to a prespecified maximum. One advantage of annual cash bonuses is that they are one-time compensation for past, realized performance— unlike base salary raises, which are permanent.

Using accounting-based performance targets, such as EBITDA, carries two potential risks. First, short-term performance measures can result in myopic behavior by management: For example, managers trading off short-term earnings growth at the expense of creating shareholder value through valuable R&D projects. Second, accounting-based measures can lead to earnings management, and in the extreme case even manipulation, in order to boost current earnings.

Equity-based compensation, in the form of options or stock, can be used to circumvent some of the problems with short-term, accounting-based cash bonuses. Stock options are the most common form of long-term incentive pay. These allow the executive to purchase a certain number of shares at a prespecified exercise price, commonly the stock price on the day of the option grant, and with a specific period length, often 10 years.

To see how stock options can consolidate manager and shareholder interests, suppose that the stock price at the time of a grant of 250,000 options to a CEO is $50. If the stock price doubles over a couple of years, the CEO will make a profit of $12.5 million (250,000 shares × ($100 − $50)). In contrast, suppose that the stock price declines to $25. Then the options are said to be "underwater" and worth nothing, but the CEO does not lose any money. If the CEO creates value for the shareholder by taking actions that result in the stock price going up, he or she will be rewarded with a slice of that value added. Granted stock options commonly vest (reach a point where they cannot be taken away) over time according to a schedule, or after the firm meets certain performance targets. Executives cannot exercise options before they have vested.

One problem with stock options is that they reward executives even if the reason for the firm's stock price increase is completely beyond their control. Suppose that the world market price of oil increases significantly; the stock prices of oil companies increase too, but for reasons that have no relation to anything an oil executive may have done. One potential solution is to benchmark the exercise price of executive stock options to the overall stock market or to a portfolio of firms in the firm's industry—i.e. oil companies in this example. In practice, however, such indexed executive stock options are extremely rare.

Another form of equity-based compensation is stock grants. One argument in favor of stock grants is that options provide executives with an asymmetric incentive because their value goes to zero if the stock price falls below the exercise price; the value of a stock grant does not go to zero. Restricted stock is a form of stock grant that involves common stock of the firm, but with the condition that a certain period of time, for example 10 years, has to pass or a target has to be met before the executive can sell the shares. Performance shares are another form of stock grant. These consist of common stock granted to an executive provided that specific firm perform-ance targets, for example EPS, are met. The performance shares become more valuable if the stock price goes up after the grant is made.

In addition to the three forms of compensation discussed above, severance pay packages, also referred to as "golden parachutes," are also common. There are several reasons why appropriately designed severance pay for a firm's CEO can be in the interests of value-maximizing shareholders. First, shareholders want to avoid a situation in which a CEO is resisting a value-enhancing takeover of the firm because the executive's job will then be eliminated. A golden parachute can provide an incentive for a CEO to step down rather than trying to fight a takeover threat. Second, the severance pay can compensate the CEO for signing a restrictive and lengthy noncompete contract with the firm. Such a contract can be in the interest of value-maximizing shareholders, especially in R&D-intensive industries, because it prevents the individual who knows the most about the corporation's business practices from sharing them with the competition.

CASE STUDY
EQUITY-BASED COMPENSATION AT DISNEY

Based on his 1989 employment agreement with the Walt Disney Company, CEO Michael Eisner was granted millions of stock options as part of his compensation package. If shareholder value could be created through Eisner's actions, then he would be rewarded with a slice of that value added. Billions of dollars of shareholder value was indeed created: The stock price doubled between 1992 and 1998. Eisner's base salary was US$750,000 in 1998, and his cash bonus was US$5 million, based on an EPS growth target. He also exercised previously granted and vested stock options and realized a total profit of about US$570 million. Since Eisner was central to the creation of over US$10 billion of shareholder value, it makes sense that he should have been rewarded appropriately.

But this compensation structure can be questioned. Was more than half a billion dollars in rewards really necessary to create a strong incentive for Eisner? Was such compensation "reasonable" from the perspective of the public, in particular the ordinary working person who is also a Disney customer?

The problem is that Disney's stock performed much less impressively from the late 1990s until Eisner resigned in 2005, to the extent that, from 1998 to 2001, more than half of the shareholder value created before 1998 was lost. In 2001 Eisner received US$1 million in base salary but no cash bonus because he did not meet the short-term accounting performance targets. Nor did he exercise any stock options.

Stock option grants may incentivize a CEO to create shareholder value, but this case also emphasizes potential problems associated with them of which boards have to be aware. In particular, option grants can result in mega-payoffs that can be next to impossible to explain to the public. Also, there is nothing shareholders can do once stock options are granted, even if most or all of the previously created value is subsequently destroyed during the tenure of the very same CEO.

MAKING IT HAPPEN

A review of the compensation structure for senior management should focus on the following:

- How can the interests of senior management and shareholders be harmonized? Annual cash bonuses make executives focus on year-to-year performance targets. Grants of options and restricted stock provide long-term incentives to create shareholder value.
- What are the advantages of stock grants over options? Because options, unlike restricted stock grants, reward superior performance but do not penalize poor performance, they can result in excessive risk-taking.
- What can be done to avoid a debate about excessive CEO pay? Perks that do not align manager and shareholder interests should not be provided. The board also has to consider the likelihood of mega-payoffs from the proposed compensation scheme.

CONCLUSION

The design of an executive compensation structure is crucial when providing managerial incentives to create shareholder value, but in practice it is a very challenging task. Management compensation should be sensitive to a firm's performance, should reward superior current performance, and should provide incentives for similar strong results in the future. At the same time, it should prevent the firm from paying a premium for poor performance. Because compensation of senior management in public firms is subject to increased disclosure requirements and scrutiny by media and various interest groups, public perception of what constitutes "reasonable" pay is another important factor to consider.

MORE INFO

Books:

Ellig, Bruce R. *The Complete Guide to Executive Compensation*. New York: McGraw-Hill, 2007.

Lipman, Frederick D., and Steven E. Hall. *Executive Compensation Best Practices*. Hoboken, NJ: Wiley, 2008.

Website:

Benchmarking executive and director compensation: www.equilar.com

See Also:

★ Creating Value with EVA (pp. 255–258)

★ Employee Stock Options (pp. 258–260)

★ Executive Rewards: Ensuring That Financial Rewards Match Performance (pp. 194–198)

✔ Assessing Business Performance (pp. 359–360)

✔ Creating Executive Compensation (pp. 340–341)

NOTES

1 An example is CIO-AFL's Executive PayWatch, www.aflcio.org/corporatewatch/paywatch

2 Morgenson, Gretchen. "Only the little people pay for lawn care." *New York Times* (May 1, 2005). Online at: tinyurl.com/7klhule

3 For example, Citigroup recently announced that a part of senior managers' bonuses will be determined by how well they interact with other executives during meetings of a division's management committee. See the *Financial Times* (October 14, 2008).

Best Practices in Corporate Social Responsibility

by Alison Kemper and Roger Martin

EXECUTIVE SUMMARY

- Business leaders throughout the world are under increasing pressure to make socially responsible decisions even as they comply with legal requirements and generate sufficient profits.
- Corporate social responsibility (CSR) decisions demand new skills: managers must understand not only the responsibilities demanded of all firms, but also the opportunities they introduce.
- While the marketplace does not reward all good deeds, thoughtful strategies can increase the likelihood that firms increase their value while creating positive outcomes for society.
- In this essay, we review the complexity of the issue, the opportunities CSR presents, and one approach to identifying CSR opportunities.

MANAGING IN COMPLEXITY—CIVIL VS STRATEGIC

As business has become increasingly global, the values and principles that guide managers are no longer local. Raw materials from Canada and Indonesia are transformed by manufacturers in India and Brazil under contract to firms in the United States and Germany. Social activists, investors, accountants, workers, politicians, environmentalists, regula-

tors, and customers in each and every location work to influence management's decisions. Normal business practices in one location can be objectionable to customers and investors in other areas, while labor and environmental principles in one region appear to be protectionist to businesses in other regions.[1] Companies would like to do the right thing but seldom have reliable means to choose a direction or level of investment.

For most companies, CSR presents complex problems and great opportunities. CSR allows companies to engage in sophisticated nonmarket strategies that can influence customers, regulators, and employees. It also can reveal firm weaknesses. There are no global laws. There is no single right way. Firms must distinguish the legitimate demands of multiple governments, assess the claims of diverse groups, and identify the significant problems they can best resolve.

WHAT WORKS?

Many researchers have looked for the elusive factor that will turn a firm's good deeds into profits, searching in vain for missing magic. The right answer to the question "Does doing result in doing well?" is "It depends." Firms that select a specific type of social or environmental opportunity consistent with their identity and strategy will reap rewards. Firms which make choices based on the most recent request for help or on a particular manager's enthusiasm will likely not.

Figure 1. CSR value curve. (*Source*: IBM Institute for Business Value)

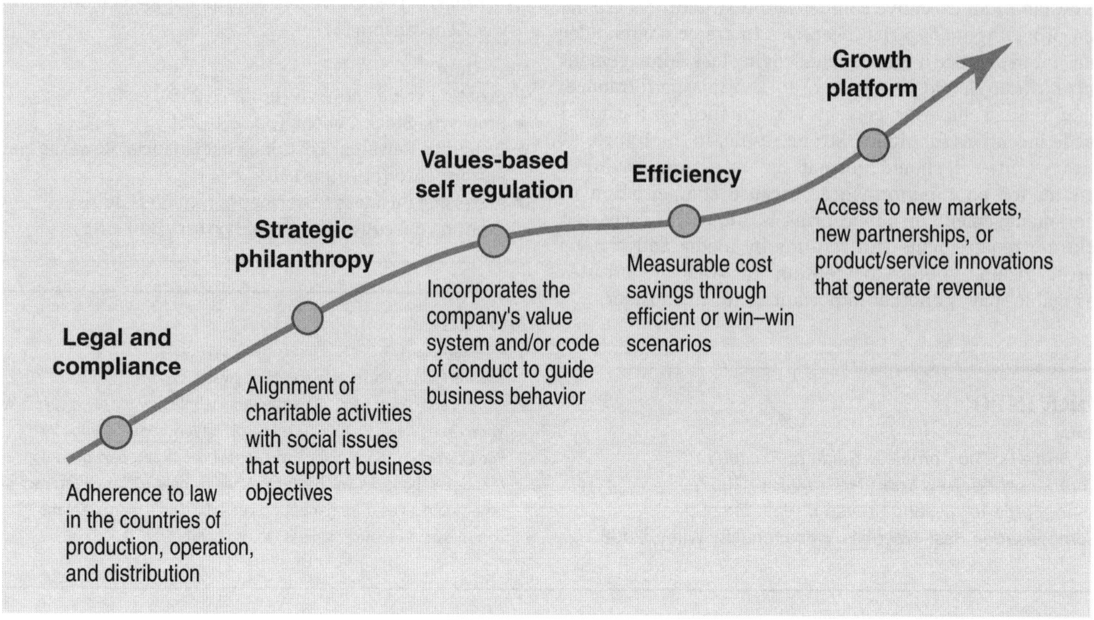

The most critical factors in the success of any firm's CSR strategy are not about CSR. A successful CSR strategy builds on basics. First, a firm must be viable in order to create an effective, valuable approach to society and the environment. It is unlikely that a good CSR strategy will reverse bad business decisions. Second, firms must meet their legal and regulatory commitments. Compliance is essential. Enron's ethics policies were widely admired, but the company was nevertheless in violation of the law. Third, firms must meet basic expectations of their industry and the communities in which they operate. A company known for spilling toxic effluent is unlikely to make gains from sponsoring a children's sports team. This sequence of responsibility is illustrated in the CSR value curve IBM has described (Figure 1).

IBM recommends that firms ask their employees, suppliers, and customers what kind of CSR strategy would be optimal. Engagement with these groups helps managers identify their best strategies in many settings. The IBM report suggests that consulting these groups will also help identify good CSR strategies. This is consistent with recent economic theory that makes the case for strategic approaches not only to financial gains, but also to social output.[2]

Meeting the demands of disparate social agents disperses the energy and creativity of the firm. Deliberate, strategic choices maximize social effectiveness and firm opportunities.

THE ROLE OF FINANCIAL FIRMS

Financial institutions can choose to play another, powerful role: increasingly often, they determine whether new initiatives carry more social and environmental risks than potential economic benefits.[3] Good analysts will be able to see the ways in which future growth prospects are enhanced or reduced by the social and environmental characteristics of the firms and projects they finance.

Financial analysts and investors now recognize that a firm's ability to work with indigenous people and their property rights is critical to the success of new mineral extraction projects. Corporate finance professionals in companies like Procter & Gamble know that their sustainability principles must be factored into their investment decisions and growth forecasts.[4]

The special role of the financial industry is apparent in the appearance of two CSR codes focused solely on finance. *The Equator Principles* and *Principles for Responsible Investment* both offer guidance to finance professionals who are faced with projects of great potential value and risk. Financial professionals who identify a broader set of risks and rewards will be more effective.

How Would *You* Have Responded?

Imagine that on September 1, 2007 you were one of the following:

- A financial analyst in New York focusing on the global toy industry;
- A banker reviewing loan applications for coating process machinery in Shanghai;
- Plant manager of a coating factory in Guanyao;
- Chief of manufacturing export regulations in Beijing;
- Regional manager of Toys "R" Us retail operations in California;
- Global brand manager of Thomas & Friends Wooden Railway Toys;
- Research director at Al Tawfeek, a leading provider of *shariah*-compliant investment funds.

Figure 2. The virtue matrix

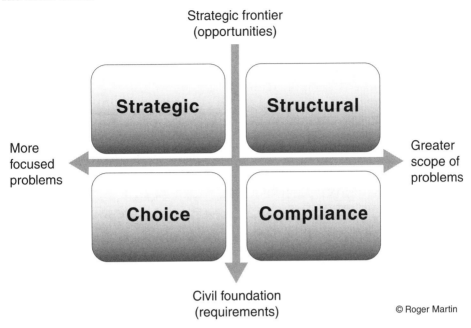

Strategic frontier
(opportunities)

Strategic

Structural

More
focused
problems

Greater
scope of
problems

Choice

Compliance

Civil foundation
(requirements)

© Roger Martin

From the perspective of the person whose position is most similar to yours, first list the strategic opportunities and risks you see in the situation you face. Then consider these issues:

1 What do governments require? Do you need to ensure that these requirements are being met?
2 What do consumers and other groups expect of businesses in this situation? Does your work meet their expectations?
3 Where are the opportunities for a single firm or brand to gain advantage over its competitors? Can you identify and harness them?
4 Where is there no likelihood of profit but a great likelihood of harm? Is this impossible to resolve by firms that must make profits? Can your organization contribute to a resolution?
5 From your professional standpoint, do you support a market solution based on competitive dynamics? Do you think that voluntary industry codes will work? Would you support increased regulation?

What are the issues here? Why did the Chinese toy debacle happen? Why did the incentives allow this to happen repeatedly? What can prevent its recurrence?

CASE STUDY
THOMAS THE TANK ENGINE RUNS OFF THE RAILS

The spring of 2007 was promising for the global toy industry. In early June 2007, RC2 (RCRC), the manufacturer of Thomas & Friends Wooden Railway Toys, was trading at over US$45 per share, the highest level it had ever reached. Mattel's stock also reached historic highs in spring 2007. In May, a trade journal announced that "China's coatings industry is benefiting from the country's thriving consumer goods market, to which it supplies almost 4.5 M tonnes/y of paint... In the electronic and computerized toys segment, coatings suppliers will be hoping to tap the country's 290 M children."[5] Painted toys were a key segment of China's manufacturing sector, and the global demand for colorful, inexpensive toys seemed insatiable.

In 2007, China's manufacturers accounted for approximately 80% of the world market for toys and employed more than 4 million workers.[6] Their business depended on the tight ties in the value chain: the links between consumers, the brands, and their personalities, the toy company giants, the Hong Kong brokers, and the Chinese manufacturers were close and profitable.

Everything changed in mid-June, when RC2 recalled 1.5 million Thomas toys that had been sprayed with lead paint.[7] RC2's share price dipped below US$40 on the news. The markets began to discount other toy companies: Mattel dropped from US$28 to US$26 in June, and eventually to US$22. Hasbro went from historic highs of US$32 in June 2007 to US$28 for the remainder of 2007.

The toys were pulled from shelves throughout Asia, the European Union, Canada, and Australia as well. It was not the first such recall: Of the 24 US recalls earlier in 2007, all were of Chinese manufacture. Once lead had been found in the paint on RC2's Thomas trains, parents, politicians, and retailers began to search through the toy aisles for more. By early August, they had found it. Mattel recalled two batches of toys costing in excess of US$30 million.

Chinese and US officials battled over the issue: were there enough safeguards on Chinese exports? Which government was at fault?

Best Practice

The Hong Kong industrialists were devastated. Companies were banned from exporting goods. One toy manufacturer, Cheung Shue Hung, committed suicide.[8] The industry was in disarray from shop floors in Guanyao to retail shelves in Toronto.

Good intentions had failed. In spite of all the safeguards, millions of lead-contaminated toys were sold to families around the world. Toy companies lost millions of dollars of capitalization. Cheung was dead. It was time to move up from good intentions to effective action.

MAKING IT HAPPEN
THE VIRTUE MATRIX[9] AS AN ACTION FRAMEWORK

By distinguishing four types of "virtue," companies can approach CSR effectively. When a firm recognizes the specific type of social activity demanded, it can respond optimally. Roger Martin's "virtue matrix" maps out these four kinds of virtue, each of which demands a different decision-making logic.

To identify and enact CSR strategies, a broad-based working group of managers can ask:

- *Compliance:* What are the firm's legal and regulatory requirements?
- *Choice:* Which codes of conduct and other expectations govern the choices of business in this context?
- *Strategic:* What problems can be tackled that will enhance the value, brand, or profits of a specific firm?
- *Structural:* What are the problems that no business can solve alone?

The best business opportunities lie in the area where a firm's unique resources and skills match social and environmental gaps or needs. Competitive advantage does not emerge from compliance with the law, from tackling systemic issues single-handedly, or from meeting the demands of civil society. Each of those must be addressed as distinct ways of doing good.

This need not be a mysterious process. Mapping the demands and opportunities requires environment scanning and research, capacities that businesses use daily. IBM suggests asking employees and suppliers to make recommendations. For most firms, there are likely to be many more opportunities to do good than there is capacity.

Having gathered a planning team and a list of options, a firm might then match each idea to a quadrant in the virtue matrix and assign a priority

- Compliance issues are the most straightforward: Noncompliance is too risky for most businesses.
- Choice issues are more complex. What are the social norms? Are there any rankings or indices that give firms information about their competitive position with regard to the issues? What kind of identity does the firm wish to project? What can it afford?
- Structural issues demand the alignment of firms, governments, industries, and/or civil groupings. Each structural problem identified demands the formation of a working group or coalition. A firm can then ask if the potential benefit to a resolution warrants participation in such a group.

- Finally, strategic opportunities can be evaluated for their potential benefit to the reputation, position, or profits of a firm. Their implementation can be assessed through the same processes as are used for other business strategies.

By categorizing each type of CSR, a firm can make better decisions.

MORE INFO

Books:

Crane, Andrew, Abagail McWilliams, Dirk Matten, Jeremy Moon, *et al.* (eds). *The Oxford Handbook of Corporate Social Responsibility.* Oxford: Oxford University Press, 2008.

Kline, John M. *Ethics for International Business: Decision Making in a Global Political Economy.* London: Routledge, 2005.

Prahalad, C. K., Michael E. Porter, and Charles Handy (eds). *Harvard Business Review on Corporate Responsibility.* Boston, MA: Harvard Business School Press, 2003.

Vogel, David. *The Market for Virtue: The Potential and Limits of Corporate Social Responsibility.* Washington, DC: Brookings Institution, 2005.

Websites:

Global organizations

International Finance Corporation on sustainability: www.ifc.org/sustainability

Organisation for Economic Co-operation and Development (OECD): www.oecd.org

United Nations. See especially the United Nations Global Compact, starting here: www.un.org/partners

United Nations Conference on Trade and Development (UNCTAD); search on "ISAR" to find the webpages of the Intergovernmental Working Group of Experts on International Standards of Accounting and Reporting: www.unctad.org

World Bank. The bank's website has many useful resources, including CSR links and information on the Inclusive and Sustainable Business Program and Business Fighting Corruption. Search from the home page: www.worldbank.org

Accounting and reporting standards

AA1000: www.accountability.org/standards/

Global Reporting Initiative (GRI): www.globalreporting.org

ISO 14000: tinyurl.com/23tamv

Social Accountability 8000 (SA8000): tinyurl.com/4xhlv95

Other sources

Business for Social Responsibility (BSR): www.bsr.org

Equator Principles, a benchmark for the financial industry to manage social and environmental issues in project financing: www.equator-principles.com

Ethical Corporation: www.ethicalcorp.com

Industry Canada: www.ic.gc.ca

Principles for Responsible Investment (PRI), a UN-based initiative which provides a framework to integrate responsible investment into mainstream decision-making: www.unpri.org

Forum for Sustainable and Responsible Investment (US SIF): ussif.org

Wikipedia on CSR:
    en.wikipedia.org/wiki/Corporate_social_responsibility
World Business Council on Sustainable Development
    (WBCSD): www.wbcsd.org

NOTES

1 Kline (2005).
2 Husted, B. W., and Jose De Jesus Salazar. "Taking Friedman seriously:
   Maximizing profits and social performance." *Journal of Management*
   Studies 43:1 (January 2006): 75–91. Online at:
   dx.doi.org/10.1111/j.1467-6486.2006.00583.x
3 See the Equator Principles: www.equator-principles.com
4 Procter & Gamble. "P&G 2007 global sustainability report." Online at:
   tinyurl.com/n7csrg [PDF].
5 "China has enormous potential in paint and coatings for cars, electronics
   and computerized toys." *ICIS Chemical Business* (May 21, 2007). Online
   at: tinyurl.com/3qn4qhk
6 Chen, Shu-Ching Jean. "Trapped in the Chinese toy closet." Forbes.com
   (August 21, 2007). Online at: tinyurl.com/3jg3va5
7 Chen, Shu-Ching Jean. "Subcontractor at heart of Fisher-Price toy
   recall is apparent suicide." Forbes.com (August 13, 2007). Online at:
   tinyurl.com/44lumrb
8 *Ibid.* 2007.
9 Martin, Roger L. "The virtue matrix: Calculating the return on corporate
   responsibility." *Harvard Business Review* 80:3 (March 2002): 68–75.
   Online at: tinyurl.com/43lgcvx

★

Business Ethics
by Sue Newell

EXECUTIVE SUMMARY

• Business ethics focuses on identifying the moral standards
  of right and wrong as they apply to behavior within
  and across business institutions and other related
  organizations.
• Corporations sometimes behave unethically, having a
  harmful effect on people or the environment.
• Unethical behavior is typically not caused by a single "bad
  apple," but is a result of complex interactions between
  individuals, groups, and organizational cultures.
• Ethical behavior can be defined either as behavior that
  maximizes happiness and minimizes harm or as behavior
  that is motivated by principles of duty.
• While behaving unethically may have some short-term
  benefit for a company, in the long term it will harm
  stakeholder support.
• Long-term sustainability comes from concentrating on the
  triple bottom line: that is, social, environmental, and
  financial performance (Elkington, 1998).

INTRODUCTION

Look in the newspaper on virtually any day of the week and
you will find at least one business scandal in which a
corporation appears to have violated the rules or standards of
behavior generally accepted by society. Company finances
have been manipulated in order to show a better balance sheet
than actually exists, toxic waste has been allowed to flow into a
river, bribes have been paid to secure a business deal, child
labor has been used to assemble a product, discriminatory
practices have prevented the employment or promotion of
members of a particular group. When businesses behave
unethically, they act in ways that have a harmful effect on
others and in ways that are morally unacceptable to the larger
community. This is very serious because corporate power and
impact are increasing as corporations become larger (indeed,
global) and as profit-making concerns take over functions that
were once publicly controlled, such as the railroads, water
utilities, and healthcare. Increasingly, it is the private sector
that determines the quality of the air we breathe, the water we
drink, our standard of living, and even where we live and how
easily we can move around.

COMMON ETHICAL PROBLEMS WITHIN CORPORATIONS

Given the increasing social impact of business, business ethics
has emerged as a discrete subject over the last 20 years.
Business ethics is concerned with exploring the moral
principles by which we can evaluate business organizations
in relation to their impact on people and the environment.
Trevino and Nelson (2004) categorize four types of ethical
problems that are commonly found in business organizations.

First are the *human resource problems*: These relate to the
equitable and just treatment of current and potential employees. Unethical behavior here involves treating people unfairly
because of their gender, sexuality, skin color, religion, ethnic
background, and so on.

Second are ethical problems arising from *conflicts of
interest*, when particular individuals or organizations are
given special treatment because of some personal relationship
with the individual or group making a decision. A company

might get a lucrative contract, for example, because a bribe was paid to the management team of the contracting organization, not because of the quality of its proposal.

Third are ethical problems that involve *customer confidence*. Corporations sometimes behave in ways that show a lack of respect for customers or a lack of concern with public safety. Examples here include advertisements that lie (or at least conceal the truth) about particular goods or services, and the sale of products, such as drugs, where a company conceals or obfuscates negative data about safety and/or efficacy.

Finally, there are ethical problems surrounding the *use of corporate resources* by employees who make private phone calls at work, submit false expense claims, take company stationery home, etc.

The financial scandals that have rocked the corporate world in recent years (Enron, WorldCom, Parmalat, Lehman Brothers, for example) have involved a number of these different ethical issues. In these cases, senior managers have engaged in improper bookkeeping, making companies look more financially profitable than they actually are. As a consequence the stockholder value of the company increases, and anyone with stock profits directly. Among those profiting will be those making the decisions to manipulate the accounts—and so there is a conflict of interest. However, the fallout from the downfall of these companies affects stockholders, employees, and society at large negatively, with innocent people losing their retirement reserves and/or savings, and employees losing their jobs.

Another category can be added to this list—ethical problems surrounding the *use of the world's environmental resources*. Many organizations have externalized the costs associated with their negative impact on the environment, whether in relation to their own operations to produce goods and services, or in terms of the use and later the disposal of the goods that they have sold. Externalizing means that organizations do not themselves pay for the environmental costs that they create. For example, carbon dioxide emissions, a by-product of energy use for all kinds of organizations, are now recognized as contributing to global warming; computer equipment contains toxic waste that pollutes the land where it is dumped; and packaging of all kinds, including plastic bags that are handed out by supermarkets, are creating mounting problems as local authorities run out of landfill sites. Increasingly, ethical business is seen to require that a business takes into account and offsets its "environmental footprint" so that it engages in sustainable activity. Sustainability broadly means that a business meets the needs of the present without compromising the ability of future generations to meet their needs.

ACCOUNTING FOR ETHICAL AND UNETHICAL BEHAVIOR

While it may be very easy to identify and blame an individual or small group of individuals, to see these individuals as the perpetrators of an unethical act—the "bad apple"—and hold them responsible for the harm caused, is an oversimplification. Most accounts of unethical behavior that are restricted to the level of the individual are inadequate. Despite popular belief, decisions harmful to others or the environment that are

made within organizations are not typically the result of an isolated, immoral individual seeking to gain personally. Although an individual's level of moral maturity or the locus of control (for example, the degree to which they perceive they control their behaviors and actions) are factors, we also need to explore the decision-making context—the group dynamics and the organizational practices and procedures—to understand why an unethical decision was made.

Group dynamics influence the decision-making process. A particularly important group-level influence is *groupthink*, a phenomenon identified by Irving Janis (1982) in his research on US foreign policy groups. The research demonstrates the presence of strong pressures towards conformity in these groups: individual members suspend their own critical judgment and right to question, with the result that they make bad and/or immoral decisions. Janis defines groupthink as "the psychological drive for consensus at any cost that suppresses dissent and appraisal of alternatives in cohesive decision-making groups."

The degree to which decisions are ethical is also influenced by organizational culture or climate. Organizational ethical climates can differ; some are more egoistic, others are more benevolent, still others are highly principled, and these contexts can shape a manager's ethical decision-making. Smith and Johnson (1996) identify three general approaches that organizations take to corporate responsibility:

- **Social obligation**: The corporation does only what is legally required.
- **Social responsiveness**: The corporation responds to pressure from different stakeholder groups.
- **Social responsibility**: The corporation has an agenda of proactively trying to improve society.

In a company in which the dominant approach to business ethics is social obligation, it is likely to be difficult to justify a decision based on ethical criteria; morally irresponsible behavior may be condoned as long as it does not break the law. Legal loopholes, for example, may be exploited in such a company if these can benefit the company in the short term, even if they might have a negative influence on others in society.

ETHICAL DILEMMAS

Sometimes it is clear that a business has behaved unethically—for example, where a drug is sold illegally, the company accounts have been falsely presented, or where client funds have been embezzled. Of more interest, and much more common, are situations that pose an ethical dilemma—situations that present a conflict between right and wrong or between values and obligations—so that a choice is necessary. For example, a corporation may want to build a new factory on a previously undeveloped and popular tourist site in a location where there is large-scale unemployment among the local population. Here we have a conflict between the benefits of wealth and job creation in a location in which these are crucial and the cost of spoiling some naturally beautiful countryside. Philosophers have attempted to develop prescriptive theories providing universal laws that enable us to differentiate between right and wrong, and good and bad, in these situations.

PRESCRIPTIVE ETHICAL THEORIES

Essentially there are two schools of thought. The consequentialists argue that behavior is ethical if it maximizes the common good (happiness) and minimizes harm. The opposing nonconsequentialists argue that behavior is ethical if it is motivated by a sense of duty or a set of moral principles about human conduct—regardless of the consequences of the action.

Consequentialist Accounts of Ethical Behavior

Philosophers who adopt the consequentialist approach (sometimes also referred to as utilitarianism) consider that behavior can be judged ethical if it has been enacted in order to maximize human happiness and minimize harm. Jeremy Bentham (1748–1832) and John Stuart Mill (1806–73) are two of the best-known early proponents of this view. Importantly it is the common good, not personal happiness, that is the arbiter of right and wrong. Indeed, we are required to sacrifice our personal happiness if doing so enhances the total sum of happiness. For someone faced with a decision choice, the ethical action is the one that achieves the greatest good for the greatest number of people after weighing the impact on those involved. Common criticisms of this approach are that it is impossible to measure happiness adequately and that it essentially condones injustice if this is to the benefit of the majority.

Nonconsequentialist Accounts of Ethical Behavior

Philosophers who adopt a nonconsequentialist approach (also referred to as deontological theory) argue that behavior can be judged as ethical if it is based on a sense of duty and carried out in accordance with defined principles. Immanuel Kant (1724–1804), for example, articulated the principle of *respect for persons*, which states that people should never be treated as a means to an end, but always as an end in themselves; leading to the easy to remember maxim—do as you would be done by. The idea here is that we can establish moral judgments that are true because they can be based on the unique human ability to reason. One common criticism of this approach is that it is impossible to agree on the basic ethical principles of duty or their relative weighting in order to direct choices when multiple ethical principles are called into question at the same time, or when decisions cut across cultures with different ethical principles.

WHY BEHAVING ETHICALLY IS IMPORTANT FOR BUSINESS

Choosing to be ethical can involve short-term disadvantages for a corporation. Yet in the long term it is clear that behaving ethically is the key to sustainable development. When you're faced with an ethical dilemma in which the immoral choice looks appealing, ask yourself three questions:

1 **What will happen when (not if) the action is discovered?** Increasingly, the behavior of corporations is under scrutiny from their various stakeholders—customers, suppliers, stockholders, employees, competitors, regulators, environmental groups, and the general public. People are less willing to keep quiet when they feel an injustice has been done, and the internet and other media give them the means to make their concerns very public, reaching a global audience. Corporations that behave unethically are unlikely to get away with it, and the impact when they are discovered can be catastrophic. This leads to the second question.

2 **Is the decision really in the long-term interests of the corporation?** Many financial services companies in the United Kingdom generated short-term profits in the 1990s by mis-selling personal pensions to people who would have been better off staying in their company's pension plan. However, in the long term these companies have suffered by having to repay this money and pay penalties. Most significantly, the practice has eroded public confidence. The same is true of many banks and mortgage brokers in the first part of the 21st century when they sold mortgages to individuals who could not afford to repay their debts. The eventual result was that large numbers defaulted, causing a meltdown in the global financial system beginning in 2008.

3 **Will organizations that behave unethically attract the employees they need?** Corporations that harm society or the environment are actually harming their own employees, including those who are making the decisions. For example, corporations that pour toxins into the air are polluting the air their employees' families breathe. Ultimately, a business relies on its human resources. If a company cannot attract high-quality people because it has a poor public image based on previous unethical behavior, it will certainly flounder.

Behaving ethically is clearly key to the long-term sustainability of any business. Focusing on the triple bottom line—the social and environmental as well as the economic impact of a company—provides the basis for sound stakeholder relationships that can sustain a business into the future.

MAKING IT HAPPEN

While the two approaches to evaluating behavior described above are clearly different, they can be integrated to create a checklist that will help an individual or group make sound ethical decisions.

- Gather the facts: What is the problem, and what are the potential solutions?
- Define the ethical issues. This is a step that is often neglected, so that the ethical dilemmas raised by a particular decision are never even considered.
- Identify the various stakeholders involved.
- Think through the consequences of each solution: What happiness or harm will be caused?
- Identify the obligations and rights of those potentially affected: What is my duty here? Can I uphold my duty to avoid doing harm and make reasonable efforts toward that end?
- Check your gut feeling.

The last step is crucial. Those involved need to ask themselves what they would feel like if friends or family found out they had been involved in making a particular corporate decision, whether personally or collectively.

MORE INFO

Books:

Elkington, John. *Cannibals with Forks: The Triple Bottom Line of 21st Century Business*. Gabriola Island, BC: New Society Publishers, 1998.

Janis, Irving L. *Groupthink: Psychological Studies of Policy Decisions and Fiascoes*. 2nd ed. Boston, MA: Houghton Mifflin College, 1982.

Smith, Ken G., and Phil Johnson. *Business Ethics and Business Behaviour*. Boston, MA: International Thomson Business Press, 1996.

Trevino, Linda K., and Katherine A. Nelson. *Managing Business Ethics: Straight Talk About How to Do It Right*. 5th ed. Hoboken, NJ: Wiley, 2010.

Velasquez, Manuel G. *Business Ethics: Concepts and Cases*. 7th ed. Upper Saddle River, NJ: Pearson Education, 2011.

Websites:

Aspen Institute: www.aspeninstitute.org
Bentley University Center for Business Ethics: cbe.bentley.edu
Business in Society Gateway: www.businessinsociety.eu
Institute of Business Ethics (IBE): www.ibe.org.uk
International Business Ethics Institute: business-ethics.org

See Also:

★ Best Practices in Corporate Social Responsibility (pp. 175–179)

★ CSR: More than PR, Pursuing Competitive Advantage in the Long Run (pp. 187–189)

★ The Impact of Climate Change on Business (pp. 267–270)

★ Improving Corporate Profitability Through Accountability (pp. 204–206)

Corporate Board Structures
by Vidhan Goyal

EXECUTIVE SUMMARY

- Firms choose their board structures based on a value-maximizing process.
- Large and outsider-dominated boards are optimal for complex firms (such as large firms, firms with multiple business segments, and complex operational and financial structures). Conversely, small and insider-dominated boards are optimal for small, young, and high-growth firms.
- CEOs who also hold the title of chairman appear to have greater influence on the board. In firms with combined titles, boards do not dismiss poorly performing CEOs at the same rate as they do in firms with CEO and chairman titles vested in different individuals.
- Politically connected directors add substantial value to the firms. They matter more in firms in which politics plays an important role, such as firms where sales to government, exports, and lobbying are greater.
- Women in the boardroom have a positive impact on how firms are governed. Women have fewer attendance problems, and they improve the attendance behavior of male directors.

INTRODUCTION

The job of the board is to control the managerial succession process (involving hiring, assessing, promoting, and if required, dismissing the CEO), and to provide high-level counsel to top management.

There is a widespread skepticism of the effectiveness of boards. Recent accounting scandals at firms such as Enron, WorldCom, and Parmalat have resulted in intense scrutiny of the function of boards. Critics point out that corporate boards have failed primarily because of poor board structures. Top management and board members are tied together though a web of personal and business connections, compromising a board's ability to monitor firms. Michael Jensen puts it more bluntly by stating that, in large US corporations, "even the outside directors basically see themselves as employees of the CEO... And this means that, in American companies, the CEO effectively has no boss."[1]

Many scholars, regulators, legislators, and investors are, therefore, calling for a reform of corporate boards. The codes of conduct for good corporate governance frequently recommend that boards should be small, and comprised largely of independent directors.[2] TIAA-CREF, one of the largest pension funds, will only invest in firms that have boards consisting of a majority of outside directors. CalPERS, another large pension fund, recommends that the CEO should be the only inside director on the board. The Sarbanes-Oxley Act of 2002 mandates that audit committees of boards should consist entirely of outside directors. The stock exchanges, such as the NYSE and the NASDAQ, require listed firms to use a majority of outside directors. These intense institutional, regulatory, and legislative pressures are indeed working. YiLin Wu, for example, shows that after firms are publicly named for poor governance by CalPERS, the number of inside board members declines, and board sizes shrink.[3] Governance activists have also been calling for boards to elect their directors annually, to separate the CEO and chairman positions, and for greater diversity on boards.

This article reviews the literature that inquires into whether differences in board structures affects the way in which boards conduct themselves, and whether boards affect firm performance. Board sizes and board compositions differ across firms. Many firms continue to operate with large boards and boards with high insider representation. Boards are often elected on staggered terms, and it is common in large corporations to have the CEO and chairman positions vested in the same individual. If these board structures are suboptimal, as the critics of existing board structures claim, then why do they persist? Should we compel all firms to conform to a single model of board structure?

The emerging academic evidence suggests that the conventional wisdom on board structures is misguided. Recent work suggests that boards are organized according to a value-maximizing calculus. This work carefully highlights the trade-offs associated with different board structures, and shows that the observable variation in board structures reflects careful attention to these tradeoffs. Firms choose the board structures that suit their circumstances.

CAUSES AND CONSEQUENCES OF BOARD STRUCTURES
Board Size
It is often asserted that small boards are more effective than large boards. For example, Martin Lipton and Jay Lorsch argue that, "[W]hen a board has more than 10 members it becomes more difficult for them all to express their ideas and opinions."[4] Michael Jensen takes up this theme, and conjectures that "keeping boards small can help improve their performance. When boards get beyond seven or eight people they are less likely to function effectively and are easier for the CEO to control."[5] These conjectures are supported by David Yermack, who finds that smaller boards are associated with higher firm value.[6]

A careful examination of the forces affecting board structures reveals that firms face a trade-off in determining board sizes. As boards become larger, the directors collectively possess more information that is important for both monitoring and advisory functions. Each prospective director brings additional information to the board. Consequently, larger boards have more aggregate information about product markets, technology, regulation, financing choices, and mergers and acquisition opportunities.

However, the costs of decision-making increase as boards become large, because of higher coordination costs and the free-rider problems associated with larger boards. With an increase in board size, each member considers its influence on board decisions to be of lesser significance. This reduces the director's incentives to incur the private costs of acquiring information and actively monitoring top management. In other words, the decision to add a new member to the board is determined by a trade-off between the additional information that a prospective director brings to the board against the increased coordination costs and free-rider problems.

Large firms with more diverse operations find the additional information that a prospective director brings more valuable. Large firms and those with more complex operations have a higher volume of activity and larger information requirements. These firms frequently engage in mergers and acquisitions, and more often use sophisticated financing

techniques. Thus, large firms benefit from the specialized information that new board members bring to the firm.

On the other hand, young, fast-growing firms with lots of intangible assets should optimally keep their boards small. A primary reason is that large information differences exist among managers and outside directors in young and high-growth firms. These information differences increase monitoring costs. By keeping their boards small, firms ensure that board members will have sufficient private interest to bear the high costs of monitoring. In addition, young and high-growth firms will find the slow and deliberate decision-making associated with large boards more costly. Young and high-growth firms, particularly those operating in more volatile environments, face rapid technological changes and unstable market shares. Smaller boards are likely to be more nimble, providing these firms with the flexibility to react quickly.

The empirical evidence is consistent with these predictions. Kenneth Lehn, Sukesh Patro, and Mengxin Zhao examined a sample of 81 firms that survived over the period 1935–2000, and show that "two variables, firm size and growth opportunities, explain a large amount of cross-sectional and inter-temporal variation in the size and composition of boards."[7] Audra Boone, Laura Field, Jonathan Karpoff, and Charu Raheja studied the development of corporate boards during the first 10 years after a firm's initial public offering.[8] They found that as firms become larger, older, and start to add more segments, boards become larger. Conversely, boards become smaller as a firm's environment becomes noisier, as R&D expenditures increase, and as growth opportunities become more abundant.

Recent work by Jeffrey Coles, Naveen Daniel and Lalitha Naveen showed that firm value is increasing in board size in firms with greater advising needs (such as large firms, diversified firms, and high debt firms).[9] Their evidence suggests that certain classes of firms actually benefit from larger boards, contrary to the calls from governance activists requiring all boards to reduce their sizes.

Board Composition
Typically, boards of directors can be divided into two groups—inside directors (management), or outside directors (non-management). Inside directors are full-time employees of the firm, while outside directors are not employed by the firm. Often, outside directors are taken to be independent, but sometimes they are not because of business or personal relationships with the firm or the CEO. On average, outside directors make up about 55–60% of the total directors of large US firms. This proportion has increased in the last decade, particularly for listed firms, since the enactment of the Sarbanes–Oxley Act of 2002, which led to an increase in the number of outside directors on US firms.

Conventional wisdom suggests that outsider-dominated boards are more effective boards. Following up on this conventional wisdom, there is a general push from institutional investors, regulators, and legislators towards more independent boards. Martin Lipton and Jay Lorsch suggested that there be at least two independent directors for every affiliated director. Michael Jensen goes even further and writes that, "it is almost impossible for those who report directly to the CEO to participate openly and critically in effective evaluation and monitoring of the CEO..., the only inside board member should be the CEO." A large number of codes of conduct for good governance put forth by various countries recommend firms to have a majority of independent directors on their boards.

Similar to our discussion of board sizes, a serious consideration of trade-offs reveals that firms choose the board composition that is optimal for their circumstances. Independent-outsider-dominated boards serve important advisory and monitoring functions. CEOs of large firms, firms with diverse operations, and firms with complex operating and financing structures have greater need for advice. These firms benefit more from the specialized expertise outside directors bring to the firm. At the same time, small, young, high-growth firms will find it optimal to have fewer outside directors. The reason is that information problems are relatively more severe in small and high-growth firms. Outside board members find it relatively costly to obtain information that is relevant for monitoring and advisory functions. These information differences also slow down decision-making associated with outsider-dominated boards in small, young, high-growth firms.

The available evidence suggests that, indeed, outside directors are effective monitors. Michael Weisbach finds that in firms with outsider-dominated boards, poorly performing CEOs are removed at a relatively higher frequency compared to that in firms with insider-dominated boards.[10] However, the size of these effects remains controversial.

The research cited earlier also finds systematic cross-sectional variation in board independence. Large firms, firms with diversified operations, and high-debt firms have more independent boards. Small, young, and high-growth firms have boards that consist largely of insiders.[11]

Classified Boards

Boards also differ in the terms they offer to their directors. A majority of US firms have classified boards, which stagger the annual election of director slates. With classified boards, directors are grouped into distinct classes (typically three), with a single class of directors standing for re-election each year. Thus, in classified boards, directors serve for three-year terms. In firms with a single class of directors, directors are elected for one-year terms. Almost 60% of major US firms have classified boards.

Many scholars criticize classified board structures for their anti-takeover properties. Paul Gompers, Joy Ishii, and Andrew Metrick suggest that board classification is "one of the few provisions that clearly retains some deterrent value in modern takeover battles."[12] Similarly, Lucian Bebchuk and Alma Cohen criticize board classification by arguing that it raises the expected costs of bidders contemplating a hostile change-in-control bid.[13] They argue that by insulating management from takeovers, classified boards entrench management, and, consequently, reduce shareholder wealth.

On the other side of the debate, several commentators point out the advantages of classified boards. By providing multi-year terms, classified boards increase board stability and board independence. If directors are elected to multi-year terms, they will have greater incentives to invest in the information required to monitor managers actively, and to provide advice and guidance to top managers. John Wilcox argued that classified boards increase board stability, and enhance director independence by insulating directors from outside pressures.[14] Thomas Bates, David Becher, and Michael Lemmon argued that in takeover situations, board classification can facilitate bargaining for a greater share of transaction surplus.[15]

The costs and benefits of classified boards are likely to vary across firms. Seoungpil Ahn, Vidhan Goyal, and Keshab Shrestha argued that staggered terms are likely to be most useful when firms have greater advising needs, and outside directors can more effectively monitor managers.[16] Advising needs are often greater in firms with a greater scope and complexity of operations. These firms are more likely to benefit from classified boards. Classified boards tend to be less useful, even value-destroying, in firms where monitoring managers by outside directors is particularly difficult. Outsider-controlled boards are generally less effective in monitoring firms that are relatively opaque (firms with high R&D intensity or with lots of intangible assets). Staggering the terms of these insider-controlled boards would further entrench management, and it is optimal for these firms to have a single class of directors.

These views continue to remain controversial. It is unclear whether classified boards actually reduce the likelihood of a firm becoming a takeover target, as recent research by Thomas Bates, David Becher, and Michael Lemmon showed that takeover targets with a classified board are acquired at an equivalent rate to targets with a single class of directors. Moreover, target firms with classified boards do obtain a larger proportional share of the total value gains in merger and acquisition transactions.

Research by Seoungpil Ahn, Vidhan Goyal, and Keshab Shrestha showed that certain classes of firms actually benefit from board classification, as their market value is higher when they adopt classified boards. In particular, firms with greater advising needs (large and more complex operations) and low monitoring costs (low R&D intensity) have higher market value when they adopt classified boards.

OTHER BOARD ATTRIBUTES
CEO–Chairman Duality

In a large fraction of major US firms, CEOs also hold the title of chairman of the board. Many commentators have called for a prohibition of the CEO serving as chairman, based on the argument that this structure gives CEOs greater control at the expense of other board members. Michael Jensen argued that "the function of the chairman is to run board meetings and oversee the process of hiring, firing, evaluating, and compensating the CEO. Clearly, the CEO cannot perform this function apart from his or her personal interest... for the board to be effective, it is important to separate the CEO and chairman positions."

Indeed, CEOs who also hold the chairman title have greater power. For example, Vidhan Goyal and Chul Park found that in firms with combined titles, boards do not dismiss poorly performing CEOs at the same rate compared to firms where the CEO and chairman titles are vested in different individuals.[17] Overall, the evidence in the literature confirms that combined titles provide CEOs with greater influence in the firm. There is little evidence, however, that combining or separating CEO and chairman titles leads to any appreciable differences in corporate performance.[18]

Politically Connected Boards

Boards can also add value through the connections they provide with politicians. Anup Agarwal and Charles Knoeber showed that firms in which politics matter more tend to have a larger number of political directors.[19] These politically experienced directors are more common in firms where sales to government, exports, and lobbying are greater. Similarly, firms that are exposed to costly environmental regulation appoint more directors with backgrounds in law. Firms also respond to changes in regulation by adjusting board composition. In the 1990s, as retail competition in electricity became an increasingly political issue, outside directors with political backgrounds increased in number and importance on the boards of US electric utilities.

Politically connected boards add substantial value to the firms. The stock prices of firms nominating politically connected directors to their boards increase on the announcement dates of such nominations. Research by Eitan Goldman, Jörg Rocholl, and Jongil So showed that in the 2000 presidential election in the US, companies with political connections to the Republican Party increased in value upon the Republican win, while companies with connections to the Democratic Party suffered a drop in value.[20] If politically connected boards add value in countries with strong legal systems, as has been shown in the existing research, the added value of politically connected directors would be even larger in other countries with relatively weak legal systems.

Women in the Boardroom

Boards worldwide are under increasing pressure to choose female directors. Renée Adams and Daniel Ferreira confronted the issue of whether women directors affect the functioning of boards.[21] The evidence suggests that women have fewer attendance problems than men. In fact, having women directors on boards improves the attendance behavior of male directors. Boards with greater gender diversity meet more often, and offer more performance-based pay to board members. Overall, women have a positive impact on how boards are governed.

CONCLUSION

In the last 10 years, boards have become more independent and diligent. Contributing to this change is the increased pressure from institutional investors, greater regulation, litigation threats from shareholders, and new exchange requirements regarding the composition of boards. Data show that the proportion of outside directors on boards is now larger than in previous decades. Importantly, outside directors nominated to boards since 2000 are relatively more independent, more of them have financial acumen, and

more of them are women. The increasing independence of boards has changed the way boards operate. A direct impact of this can be seen in the shortening of CEO tenure in the last decade, compared to earlier periods.

Overall, the academic evidence suggests that a "one size fits all" approach to board structures is misguided. A large part of variation in board structures can be explained by underlying firm characteristics suggesting that there is an underlying economic logic at work in determining these structures. Greater regulation on board structures may force firms towards an inefficient board structure, imposing heavy deadweight costs on firms and their shareholders.

MAKING IT HAPPEN

- Large, multidivisional firms should optimally choose bigger and more independent boards. Small, young, fast-growing firms should optimally choose smaller boards.
- Large and multidivisional firms, where boards have a greater number of outside directors, should consider staggering the election of directors. By contrast, small, young, fast-growing firms should consider electing their directors every year.
- The titles of CEO and chairman should be vested in different individuals.
- Politically experienced directors add substantial value in firms that sell to the government, or those which are exposed to costly regulation. Women on boards positively affect the governance of firms. Boards with more women meet more often and offer more performance-based pay to board members.

MORE INFO

Books:

Harvard Business Review on Corporate Governance. Boston, MA: Harvard Business School Press, 2000.

Macey, Jonathan R. *Corporate Governance: Promises Kept, Promises Broken*. Princeton, NJ: Princeton University Press, 2008.

Monks, Robert A. G., and Nell Minow. *Corporate Governance*. Chichester, UK: Wiley, 2008.

Articles:

Ahn, Seoungpil, Vidhan K. Goyal, and Keshab Shrestha. "The differential effects of classified boards on firm value." Working paper, National University of Singapore, HKUST, and Nanyang Technological University, April 22, 2009. Online at: tinyurl.com/78keth3 [PDF].

Boone, Audra L., Laura Casares Field, Jonathan M. Karpoff, and Charu G. Raheja. "The determinants of corporate board size and composition: An empirical analysis." *Journal of Financial Economics* 85:1 (July 2007): 66–101. Online at: dx.doi.org/10.1016/j.jfineco.2006.05.004

Coles, Jeffrey L., Naveen D. Daniel, and Lalitha Naveen. "Boards: Does one size fit all?" *Journal of Financial*

Economics 87:2 (February 2008): 329–356. Online at: dx.doi.org/10.1016/j.jfineco.2006.08.008

Goyal, Vidhan K., and Chul W. Park. "Board leadership structure and CEO turnover." *Journal of Corporate Finance* 8:1 (January 2002): 49–66. Online at: dx.doi.org/10.1016/S0929-1199(01)00028-1

Jensen, Michael C. "The modern industrial revolution, exit and the failure of internal control systems." *Journal of Finance* 48:3 (July 1993): 831–880. Online at: www.jstor.org/stable/2329018

Lehn, Kenneth M., Sukesh Patro, and Mengxin Zhao. "Determinants of the size and structure of corporate boards: 1935–2000." *Financial Management* 38:4 (Winter 2009): 747–780. Online at: dx.doi.org/10.1111/j.1755-053X.2009.01055.x

Website:

European Corporate Governance Initiative (ECGI): www.ecgi.org

See Also:

★ Identifying the Right Nonexecutive Director (pp. 201–204)
✔ Creating Executive Compensation (pp. 340–341)
✔ Defining Corporate Governance: Its Aims, Goals, and Responsibilities (pp. 341–342)
✔ Directors' Duties: A Primer (pp. 342–343)

NOTES

1 "US corporate governance: Accomplishments and failings: A discussion with Michael Jensen and Robert Monks." *Journal of Applied Corporate Finance* 20:1 (Winter 2008): 28–46. Online at: dx.doi.org/10.1111/j.1745-6622.2008.00167.x
2 The codes of conduct for good governance can be accessed from the homepage of the European Corporate Governance Institute (www.ecgi.org).
3 Wu, YiLin. "The impact of public opinion on board structure changes, director career progression, and CEO turnover: Evidence from CalPERS' corporate governance program." *Journal of Corporate Finance* 10:1 (January 2004): 199–227. Online at: dx.doi.org/10.1016/S0929-1199(03)00024-5
4 Lipton, Martin, and Jay W. Lorsch. "A modest proposal for improved corporate governance." *Business Lawyer* 48 (1992): 59–77.
5 Jensen, Michael C. "The modern industrial revolution, exit and the failure of internal control systems." *Journal of Finance* 48:3 (July 1993): 831–880. Online at www.jstor.org/stable/2329018
6 Yermack, David. "Higher market valuation of companies with a small board of directors." *Journal of Financial Economics* 40:2 (February 1996): 185–211. Online at: dx.doi.org/10.1016/0304-405X(95)00844-5
7 Lehn, Kenneth M., Sukesh Patro, and Mengxin Zhao. "Determinants of the size and structure of corporate boards: 1935–2000." *Financial Management* 38:4 (Winter 2009): 747–780. Online at: dx.doi.org/10.1111/j.1755-053X.2009.01055.x
8 Boone, Audra L., Laura Casares Field, Jonathan M. Karpoff, and Charu G. Raheja. "The determinants of corporate board size and composition: An empirical analysis." *Journal of Financial Economics*. 85:1 (July 2007): 66–101. Online at: dx.doi.org/10.1016/j.jfineco.2006.05.004
9 Coles, Jeffrey L., Naveen D. Daniel, and Lalitha Naveen. "Boards: Does one size fit all?" *Journal of Financial Economics* 87:2 (February 2008): 329–356. Online at: dx.doi.org/10.1016/j.jfineco.2006.08.008
10 Weisbach, Michael S. "Outside directors and CEO turnover." *Journal of Financial Economics* 20 (January–March 1988): 431–460. Online at: dx.doi.org/10.1016/0304-405X(88)90053-0
11 See Boone *et al.* (2007), Coles *et al.* (2008), and Lehn *et al.* (2009).
12 Gompers, Paul, Joy Ishii, and Andrew Metrick. "Corporate governance and equity prices." *Quarterly Journal of Economics* 118:1 (February 2003): 107–155. Online at: dx.doi.org/10.1162/00335530360535162
13 Bebchuk, Lucian A., and Alma Cohen. "The costs of entrenched boards." *Journal of Financial Economics* 78:2 (November 2005): 409–433. Online at: dx.doi.org/10.1016/j.jfineco.2004.12.006
14 Wilcox, J. C. "Two cheers for staggered boards." *Corporate Governance Advisor* 10 (2002): 1–5.
15 Bates, Thomas W., David A. Becher, and Michael L. Lemmon. "Board classification and managerial entrenchment: Evidence from the market for corporate control." *Journal of Financial Economics* 87:3 (March 2008): 656–677. Online at: dx.doi.org/10.1016/j.jfineco.2007.03.007
16 Ahn, Seoungpil, Vidhan K. Goyal, and Keshab Shrestha. "The differential effects of classified boards on firm value." Working paper, National University of Singapore, HKUST, and Nanyang Technological University, 2009. Online at: papers.ssrn.com/sol3/papers.cfm?abstract_id=1265078
17 Goyal, Vidhan K., and Chul W. Park. "Board leadership structure and CEO turnover." *Journal of Corporate Finance* 8:1 (January 2002): 49–66. Online at: dx.doi.org/10.1016/S0929-1199(01)00028-1
18 See Brickley, James A., Jeffrey L. Coles, and Gregg Jarrell. "Leadership structure: Separating the CEO and chairman of the board." *Journal of Corporate Finance* 3:3 (June 1997): 189–220. Online at: dx.doi.org/10.1016/S0929-1199(96)00013-2
19 Agarwal, Anup, and Charles R. Knoeber. "Do some outside directors play a political role?" *Journal of Law and Economics* 44:1 (April 2001): 179–198. Online at: www.jstor.org/stable/10.1086/320271
20 Goldman, Eitan, Jörg Rocholl, and Jongil So. "Do politically connected boards affect firm value?" *Review of Financial Studies* 22:6 (June 2009): 2331–2360. Online at: dx.doi.org/10.1093/rfs/hhn088
21 Adams, Renee B., and Daniel Ferreira. "Women in the boardroom and their impact on governance and performance." Working paper, University of Queensland, London School of Economics, CEPR, and ECGI. 2008. Online at: papers.ssrn.com/sol3/papers.cfm?abstract_id=1107721

CSR: More than PR, Pursuing Competitive Advantage in the Long Run
by John Surdyk

EXECUTIVE SUMMARY

- Consumers increasingly expect companies to act in "responsible" ways.
- Because of their scale and reach, companies have unusual opportunities to address social concerns in innovative and productive ways.
- Evidence suggests that corporate social responsibility (CSR) practices produce long-term benefits with financial performance gains.
- Advancing CSR is made easier with modern risk management tools, reporting guidelines, and committed leadership and employees.

THE EMERGENCE OF CORPORATE SOCIAL RESPONSIBILITY

Global greenhouse gas emissions continue to rise. Diseases wreak havoc across entire continents. An entire host of seemingly intractable issues confront governments throughout the world, which are sometimes unable to effect positive changes. With the emergence of companies as some of the most powerful institutions for innovation and social change, more shareholders, regulators, customers, and corporate partners are increasingly interested in understanding the impact of these organizations' regular activities upon the community and its natural resources. With the world's largest 800 nonfinancial companies accounting for as much economic output as the world's poorest 144 countries, the importance of these organizations in addressing trade imbalances, income inequality, resource degradation, and other issues is clear. While companies are not tasked with the responsibilities of governments, their scale and their ability to influence these issues necessitate their involvement and create opportunities for forward-looking organizations to exercise great leadership.

In public opinion surveys, consumers admit that they prefer to buy products and services from companies they feel are socially responsible (72%) and that they sell shares of those companies they feel don't pass muster (27%). Challenging Nobel laureate Milton Friedman's notion that companies' only responsibility is to make profit, executives are increasingly seeking ways to combine economic gain with social well-being in ways that will produce more customer loyalty, better relationships with regulators, and a host of other advantages. CSR practices may, in fact, prove pivotal to the success of a company.

Sometimes described simply as "doing well by doing good," corporate social responsibility initiatives gained traction in the 1990s as consumer interest in management practices erupted in the wake of several substantial incidences of executive malfeasance and of escalating environmental challenges. While originally focused on environmental factors, CSR reports increasingly include social measures. Likewise, company leaders today express interest in business models that weave together explicit goals for profit, environmental performance, and social factors, at the same time recognizing that these efforts will likely yield no short-term financial benefits but rather long-term performance improvements.

A CLOUDY CONCEPT BEGINS TO CRYSTALLIZE

The phrase "corporate social responsibility" (CSR) describes both:

- a social movement;
- a collection of specific management practices and initiatives.

Business leaders, government professionals, and others use these principles and tools to assess and report on organizations' impact on society.

Globally, CSR is an evolving concept without a clear definition, yet it describes a set of corporate obligations and practices somewhere on the spectrum between traditional charitable giving on the one hand and merely strict compliance with laws on the other.

While operating definitions remain elusive, the term "CSR" generally refers to a company's efforts to include social and environmental concerns explicitly in its decision-making, along with a commitment to increasing the organization's positive impact on society. Beneath these efforts is a realization that improved CSR reporting and better risk-management systems generally promote the transparency and accountability essential to good company governance and improved financial performance. These systems, in effect, enable a company to anticipate and respond to opportunities when it senses that society's expectations aren't being met by its performance.

BENEFITS FROM CSR

The benefits of corporate social performance reporting spread over an entire organization.

Areas of greatest gain for a company's market value, operational efficiency, access to capital, and brand value typically come from:

- Establishing ethics, values, and principles for the organization;
- Improving environmental processes or reducing environmental impact;
- Improving workplace conditions.

Other efforts, such as better governance measures, also tend to yield positive benefits for companies.

Best Practice

Table 1. Benefits of CSR

Business Area	Reduce Costs	Create Value
License to Operate	More favorable government relations; reduced shareholder activism; reduced risk of lawsuits	Increased community support for the company's operations ("a bank account of goodwill")
Reputational Capital	Reduced negative consumer activism/ boycotts; positive media coverage/"free advertising"; positive "word-of-mouth" advertising	Increased customer attraction; increased customer retention
Human Resources	Increased employee retention and morale	Enhanced recruitment; increased productivity
Finance		Social screens and investment funds are attracted to companies perceived as good social performers

MAKING CSR REAL

Traditional rhetoric about "private versus public" responsibilities is diminishing while companies operate more and more with an understanding of an acknowledged (if tacit) role to play in society. In the United States, many people feel companies should be doing more to improve society through changing their business practices.

Although implementing CSR initiatives in modern companies is a daunting prospect because of their increasingly complex and global operations, many CSR management frameworks have moved onto the international stage. Approximately 400 companies—including many of the world's largest—use all or some of the Global Reporting Initiative (GRI), and combined environmental and social reports are increasingly common alongside companies' regular sustainability reports. Launched in 1997 by the Coalition of Environmentally Responsible Economies, the GRI report contains 50 core environmental, social, and economic indicators for a broad range of companies. It also offers additional modules with distinct metrics for companies, depending on their industry sector and operations. The price range for producing a report spans from US$100,000 for a basic GRI to more than US$3 million for complex organizations like Shell.

Other major initiatives and reporting standards provide helpful guidance and principles; among them are:
• The United Nations Global Compact;
• Global Environmental Management Initiative;
• International Standards Organization guidelines (for example, ISO14000).

The continued growth of the socially responsible investment movement, especially in the United States and Europe, is stimulating companies' adoption of GRI and other instruments. In the United States alone, capital available to socially responsible companies reached US$2.29 trillion in 2005.

CASE STUDY

Beginning with US$1,000 in a garage in 1990, Greg Erickson founded a new energy bar company, Clif Bars, Inc., in Berkeley, California. Committed to exercising environmental stewardship, Greg made expensive investments in organic ingredients and renewable energy while pursuing progressive employment practices such as six-month sabbaticals for employees. Refusing acquisition overtures from other companies, Clif Bars' commitments to corporate responsibility laid a strong, long-term foundation for the growing US$100 + million company and its meteoric rise against titans like Kellogg and Quaker Oats.

CHALLENGES TO CSR

The majority of corporations in the world do not produce any reports on their CSR practices. Executives often cite several concerns, including:
• Fear that they may undertake a CSR program while competitors do not, meaning they incur expenses and refocus management talent that may put them at a competitive disadvantage.
• No feeling of urgency to act on many societal issues.
• No accepted standard of what type of information should be reported or at what depth.
• Concern that if they only achieve goals they largely establish for themselves, they may appear only half-heartedly committed—or they may even open themselves to lawsuits.
• Trouble identifying stakeholders, meaning the audience for their reports may be ambiguous, which may, in turn, undermine the quality of the reporting generally.
• Belief that traditional philanthropy fulfils an organization's commitment to society.
• Reporting on the entire scope of a company's impact on society and the environment is increasingly complex.

Recognizing "that one size does not fit all," more companies are exercising greater discretion in reporting initiatives to highlight key information for their sector or the parts of the world in which they operate.

HOW TO GET STARTED

These principles must be grounded in an organization for CSR management frameworks to yield their maximum benefit.
• Ensure long-term organizational commitment by involving the top leadership *and* the employees.
• Don't adopt every reporting system: select one that makes the most sense for your industry and scale.
• Carefully identify stakeholders to help develop feedback loops so you can adjust your course.
• Consider benchmarking against peer companies.
• Communicate your results widely.
• Don't be afraid to revise standards or develop new metrics of your own.

CONCLUSION

Evidence is mounting that CSR provides tangible benefits and lasting competitive advantage to organizations. While difficult to implement, corporate social responsibility practices and frameworks provide companies with a chance to influence the rules of competition positively while playing a crucial—and increasingly expected—role in the world.

MAKING IT HAPPEN

There is no consensus among government bodies, companies, or consumers about what precisely constitutes a definition—or even a consistent set of management topics—under the umbrella of corporate social responsibility. Several intergovernmental bodies, company federations, and nonprofits have advanced competing definitions. Among the most influential are:

- *World Bank*. "Corporate Social Responsibility, or CSR, is the commitment of business to contribute to sustainable economic development, working with employees, their families, the local community, and society at large to improve their quality of life, in ways that are both good for business and good for development."
- *World Economic Forum*. "Corporate Citizenship can be defined as the contribution a company makes to society through its core business activities, its social investment and philanthropy programs, and its engagement in public policy. The manner in which a company manages its economic, social, and environmental relationships, as well as those with different stakeholders, in particular shareholders, employees, customers, business partners, governments, and communities, determine its impact."
- *Business for Social Responsibility*. "CSR is operating a business in a manner that meets or exceeds the ethical, legal, commercial, and public expectations that society has of business. CSR is seen by leadership companies as more than a collection of discrete practices and occasional gestures, or initiatives motivated by marketing, public relations, or other business benefits. Rather, it is viewed as a comprehensive set of policies, practices, and programs that are integrated throughout business operations, and decision-making processes that are supported and rewarded by top management."
- *Center for Corporate Citizenship at Boston College*. "Corporate Citizenship refers to the way a company integrates basic social values with everyday business practices, operations, and policies. A corporate citizenship company understands that its own success is intertwined with societal health and well-being. Therefore, it takes into account its impact on all stakeholders, including employees, customers, communities, suppliers, and the natural environment."

- *International Business Leaders Forum*. "Corporate Social Responsibility means open and transparent business practices that are based on ethical values and respect for employees, communities, and the environment. It is designed to deliver sustainable value to society at large as well as to shareholders."
- *United Nations*. While not advocating a particular definition of corporate social responsibility, the United Nations uses the term "global corporate citizenship" to describe international companies' obligations to respect human rights, improve labor conditions, and protect the environment. The UN Research Institute for Sustainable Development, which follows academic work in this area, typically concentrates on ethical issues and principles guiding how a company's management engages stakeholders.

FUN FACTS

The Institute of Business Ethics published a study of FTSE 250 companies, providing evidence that those with an ethical code in place for over five years generated greater economic value and market value than their peers over the period 1997–2000.

For 79% of fund managers and analysts surveyed in 2003, the management of social and environmental risks has a positive impact on a company's market value in the long term.

MORE INFO

Book:
United Nations Conference on Trade and Development. *Disclosure of the Impact of Corporations on Society: Current Trends and Issues*. New York: United Nations, 2004. Online at:
www.unctad.org/en/docs/iteteb20037_en.pdf

Websites:
Business for Social Responsibility (BSR): www.bsr.org
CSR Network: www.csrnetwork.com
Ethical Corporation: www.ethicalcorp.com
SustainAbility: www.sustainability.com
World Business Council for Sustainable Development (WBCSD): www.wbcsd.org

See Also:
★ Best Practices in Corporate Social Responsibility (pp. 175–179)
★ Business Ethics (pp. 179–182)
★ Understanding Reputation Risk and Its Importance (pp. 279–282)
✔ Creating a Sustainable Development Policy (pp. 339–340)
✔ Social Return on Investment (pp. 345–346)

Best Practice

Dividend Policy: Maximizing Shareholder Value
by Harold Bierman, Jr

EXECUTIVE SUMMARY
- Dividend policy (or distribution policy) distributes some amount of cash (possibly zero) to its investors.
- Retained earnings is a very tax efficient (zero dividend) policy.
- If cash is to be distributed, with most tax systems and taxed investors, share repurchase is the preferred method.
- The choice of method is important on several different dimensions.

INTRODUCTION

The amount of dividends can affect stock prices. Barsky and De Long (1993) stated: "… changes in current and expected future dividends can account for the bulk of long-run stock price fluctuations, although much less so for short-term price movements."[1]

The title of this paper could be "Distribution Policy," since dividends are not the only way of implementing a policy aimed at financially rewarding a firm's stockholders. The various methods of distributing cash (or not distributing cash), listed in order of preference from an economic–finance perspective of maximizing shareholder wealth, are:
- retained earnings;
- share repurchase;
- sale of firm (or part of a firm);
- LBOs (buyouts);
- cash dividends with a dividend reinvestment plan (DRIP);
- cash dividends.

RETENTION: TAX DEFERRAL

It has been proven that, with enough assumptions, dividend policy is not relevant to the valuation of the common stock equity of a firm. However, the proof assumes zero investor taxes; thus it does not apply to a real-world situation in which such taxes exist. With income taxes, an investor benefits from being able to defer the payment of taxes as well as from the fact that some types of income (capital gains) for individuals may be taxed at lower rates than other types of income (dividends).

If a company retains $100, earns 0.10 in one period, and then pays a dividend of $110, the investor taxed at a rate of 0.40 will net: $110 \times (1 - 0.4) = \$66$.

If the same company had paid a dividend of $100 and if the investor also could earn 0.10 before tax and 0.06 after tax on the $60 after tax proceeds, the investor receiving the $100 dividend ($60 after tax) would have after one period: $60 \times 1.06 = \$63.60$.

The investor is better off by $2.40 with the one-period delay in cash distribution. The investor "defers" $40 of taxes that

earn 0.10, or $4. The $4 is taxed ($1.60) and the investor is better off by $2.40.

If desired, one could compute the return necessary for the firm to justify retention. It would be equal to the after-tax return (0.06) available in the market to the investor. Thus, if the corporation could earn 0.06 and then pay a dividend, the investor would net: $100 \times 1.06 \times (1 - 0.4) = \$63.60$. This is the same as the investor would net with an immediate cash dividend.

If the planning horizon is n periods instead of one period, then 0.06 still measures the return that the firm must earn to justify retention. If the earning opportunities available to the corporation are greater than 0.06, retention is more desirable than an immediate dividend.

If the planning horizon is n periods, the dollar advantage of tax deferral increases. For example, if the firm can earn 0.10 and the time horizon is 20 years with retention and then a tax rate of 0.40, the investor has:

$$\$100 \times 1.10^{20} \times (1 - 0.4) = \$100 \times 6.73 \times 0.6 = \$404$$

With an immediate $100 cash dividend and the investment of $60 by the stockholder to earn 0.06 after tax for 20 years, the investor would have:

$$\$60 \times 1.06^{20} = \$60 \times 3.207 = \$192$$

With a planning horizon of 20 years, the advantage of tax deferral is $212 for the retention of the $100 earnings. There will be 19 other years between now and the end of the 20 years that will generate comparable tax deferral savings (although of decreasing amounts).

CAPITAL GAINS

To this point, we have assumed that all income is taxed at one rate. Now we assume that a capital gains tax rate of 0.20 applies to capital gains income. This assumes that retention of earnings leads to stock price increases and that these increases can be realized by investors as capital gains.

Returning to the 20-year horizon, with retention and then capital gains taxation of 0.20, the investor would have:

$$\$100 \times 1.10^{20} \times (1 - 0.20) = \$100 \times 6.73 \times 0.80 = \$538$$

The cash dividend and an after-tax earning rate of 0.06 again leads to a value of $192 after 20 years.

The net advantage of retention is $538 - \$192 = \$346$. Capital gains taxation increases the value of retention from the $212 obtained above to $346.

Again, if we considered the tax consequences of the dividend decision for all subsequent years, the value of the difference would be even larger. Tax deferral and capital gains are two powerful factors that must be considered in deciding a distribution policy.

SHARE REPURCHASE

A number of explanations of the motivation behind share repurchase (where a company buys its own stock) have been suggested. It has been argued, for example, that firms buy back their own shares to have them available to acquire other companies or to fulfill the obligations of stock option plans. Unquestionably, some repurchasing has been done for these reasons. Income tax considerations may make it possible for firms to acquire other companies more cheaply for stock than for cash, and the use of stock options and restricted stock as forms of executive compensation have been widespread. However, the growth of share repurchasing cannot be explained by merger and stock option plans. There is no essential reason why firms should use repurchased shares for these purposes, rather than newly issued shares.

Corporations also repurchase shares with the intention of retiring them, or at least holding them indefinitely in the treasury. It has been suggested that firms with excessive liquid assets have one or more of the following motives to repurchase shares:

- repurchasing shares is the best investment that can be made with these assets;
- repurchasing shares has beneficial leverage effects;
- repurchasing shares, rather than paying dividends, has a significant tax advantage for stockholders.

Is a firm's purchase of its own common stock an investment? There are authors who think so: "The repurchase of its own stock by a company is an investment decision—plain and simple."[2]

Share Repurchasing as an Investment

Share repurchasing does not possess the same general characteristics as other acts of investment by a firm—for instance, purchasing plant and equipment. Normal investments increase the size of the firm and do not decrease the stockholders' equity balance. A firm's repurchase of its own common stock, on the other hand, reduces the size of the enterprise. Specifically, the cash balance is decreased and the stockholders' equity balance is reduced. In short, repurchasing shares has few characteristics which identify it as a normal investment.

While share repurchasing is clearly not an investment by the firm, there is a change in the relative proportions of ownership if some stockholders sell their shares and some do not sell. The investors who do not sell are implicitly making an investment compared with the investors who do sell. Also, investors not selling make an investment in the firm compared with what would have happened if they had received a cash dividend.

Even though share repurchasing is not an investment, it may be the best use of corporate cash from the point of view of the present investors. This may be the case if the present stock price is below the intrinsic value of the shares.

Taxes and Share Repurchasing

The tax laws can provide powerful incentives for firms with excess liquid assets to repurchase shares rather than pay dividends. The tax code may lead individuals to prefer capital gains to ordinary income, assuming that the top marginal rate of taxation on ordinary income is higher than the rate on capital gains.

Consider now a corporation with excess cash that it desires to pay out to stockholders in the form that will be most attractive from its shareholders' point of view. If it distributes the assets as dividends, they will represent ordinary income to shareholders, and will be taxed accordingly. If, on the other hand, the corporation buys back shares, the tax basis of the stock will be regarded as a return to the shareholders' capital and will not be taxed at all, while that portion of the return which is taxed—i.e., the capital gain—will be subject to a lower rate than ordinary income. In addition, the investor who merely wants to reinvest and does not sell is not taxed at all.

Abby Cohen (1994) captures the essence of this thought:[3] "First, shareholders are not thrilled by the prospect of double taxation on cash dividends. Many prefer that corporations 'pay out' the cash indirectly to shareholders in the form of share repurchases, rather than in the form of cash dividends."

Given these incentives for returning cash to stockholders by repurchasing shares, a relevant question would seem to be: Why, if the tax law is as described, do firms pay dividends? One important answer is that many stockholders do not pay tax on the dividends they receive (for example, Cornell University and low-income retirees). A second reason (related to the first) is that the receipt of cash dividends to low-tax investors reduces the transaction costs for those investors who need cash. But even if one were to accept the above explanations, the basic question still remains. Why do firms pay dividends to investors who are taxed at high ordinary income tax rates?

Example

A firm has 100,000 shares outstanding and $100,000 available for distribution. Should it pay a dividend or repurchase shares? Assume that the personal tax rate is 0.36 and the capital gains tax rate is 0.20. The initial stock price is $20. Assume that the tax basis is also $20. There is an investor who owns 1,000 shares. With a $1,000 cash dividend for this investor we have:

Dividend

Cash received	$1,000
Tax (0.36)	$360
Net	$640

If the company acquires $100,000/20 = 5,000$ shares and the investor tenders 0.05 of the 1,000 shares held, we have:

Stock repurchase

Cash received (50 × $20)	$1,000
Tax	$0
Net	$1,000

There is a $360 cash flow advantage for share repurchase compared to a cash dividend.

With a zero tax basis and a 0.20 tax rate, we have for the share repurchase:

Stock repurchase

Cash received	$1,000
Tax (0.20)	$200
Net	$800

Not selling, the investor's percentage ownership goes up from 0.01 to 0.0105 (that is, 1,000/95,000). The investor has a choice of receiving cash (selling some stock) or increasing the relative investment in the firm.

When capital gains and ordinary income have different tax treatment, the value of the firm's stock is influenced by the form of its cash distribution. In addition, with share repurchase and a positive-tax basis, part of the cash distribution is not taxed. There are three factors at work that cause the buying back of shares to be more profitable than dividend payments (from the stockholders' point of view) under any reasonable set of assumptions that includes taxation of income. For one thing, part of the distribution under the share-repurchasing arrangement is considered a return of capital and is not taxed. Secondly, that part of the distribution subject to tax (i.e., the capital gain) is generally taxed at a lower rate than ordinary income. Finally, the investor can avoid all taxes by not selling.

Stock Option Plans

Share repurchase programs by corporations enhance the value of stock options compared to cash dividends by forcing the stock price up relative to a cash dividend of equal dollar amount (the number of shares outstanding is reduced). The stock price effect is not a real advantage to the investor, but it is an advantage to the holders of stock options.

For example, suppose a firm has one million shares outstanding selling at $40 per share. The value of the stock equity is $40 million. If it pays a $4 million cash dividend, the value of the stock equity will be $36 million. Then, as a result of the cash dividend:

Stock price per share	$36
Cash received	$4
Total value to investor per share	$40

The investor is indifferent to the share repurchase and dividends (with zero taxes), but the holder of the stock options prefers the share repurchase.

The firm could buy 100,000 shares with the $4 million. The value of the firm after purchase will be $36 million, and the stock price per share will be $40 (that is, $36,000,000/900,000 = $40). The investor is indifferent to share repurchase and cash dividend (with no taxes), but the holder of a stock option prefers the $40 market price with share repurchase to the $36 price with cash dividends.

The stock price after one year is interesting. Assume that the stock equity is again $40 million (the firm made earnings of $4 million during the year).

Having paid a $4 million dividend last year, the stock value per share would be $40. If the firm had repurchased 100,000 shares instead of a dividend, the stock value per share would be $40,000,000/900,000 = $44.44.

A share repurchase program, all things equal, will result in an increasing stock price through time compared to the price with dividends being paid. With a stock option contract (not adjusted for share repurchases) the increase in stock price resulting from a share repurchase strategy rather than a cash dividend is valuable for the holder of the stock option.

Of course, the owner of an exercisable option can convert it to stock and receive any dividend that is paid. This will require a cash outlay equal to the option's exercise price. Also, the cash dividend is taxed. With the stock repurchase by the firm and the owner not exercising the option, the tax on the cash dividend is avoided and the cash outlay of the option's exercise price is delayed.

A Flexible Dividend

One tax advantage of stock repurchase in lieu of cash dividends is that investors who do not want to convert their investments into cash do not sell their stock back to the corporation. By not selling, they avoid realization of the capital gain and do not have any taxation on the increment to the value of their wealth (they also avoid transaction costs).

The investors who want to receive cash sell a portion of their holdings, and even though they pay tax on the gain, it is apt to be less than if the cash distribution were taxed as ordinary income. By using stock repurchase as the means of the cash distribution, the company tends to direct the cash to those investors who want the cash and bypass the investors who do not need cash at the present time. Also, the tax consequences are favorable for investors.

THE SIGNALING EFFECT OF REPURCHASE

Would management be more likely to launch a share repurchase program if the firm's stock is overvalued or undervalued? While many companies implement share repurchase programs irrespective of whether the stock price is too low or too high, there is evidence that firms are more likely to buy stock that is undervalued by the market. Thus, some investors will consider the start of a stock buyback program as a signal that management thinks the stock is undervalued. Two studies that find evidence supporting this signaling effect are Dann (1981) and Vermaelen (1981).

Investors Like Dividends

The attitude of investors is an important factor to be considered. Consistently increasing dividends are generally welcomed by investors as indicators of profitability and safety. Uncertainty is increased by lack of dividends or dividends that fluctuate widely. Grigoli (1986) agrees with this conclusion: "Because investors value stable dividends, it may not be in a corporation's best interests to raise dividends to unsustainable levels."[4]

Dividends are thought to have an information content; that is, an increase in dividends means that the board of directors expects the firm to do well in the future. This "signaling effect" might favorably affect the firm's common stock price. On the other hand, if income expectations do not justify the optimism, the indication of a more positive future than is justified by the facts is not likely to lead to a favorable outcome.

Since trust officers can only invest in securities with a consistent dividend history, firms like to establish a history of dividends so that they can make the "trust legal list." This consideration sometimes leads to the payment of cash dividends before the firm would otherwise start paying a dividend.

Another important reason for the payment of dividends is that a wide range of investors need the dividends for consumption purposes. Although such investors could sell a portion of their holdings, this latter transaction has relatively high processing costs compared with cashing a dividend check. The presence of investors desiring cash for consumption makes it difficult to change the current dividend policy. One group of investors may benefit from a change in dividend policy, but another group may be harmed. Although we see that income taxes paid by investors tend to make a retention policy more desirable than cash dividends, the presence in the real world of zero tax and low tax investors needing cash dictates that we consider each situation individually and be flexible in arriving at a dividend policy.

There are stockholders who desire cash. A dividend supplies cash without the investor incurring brokerage expense. If cash is retained by the corporation, the stockholders wanting liquidity will have to sell a fraction of their holdings to obtain cash, and this process will result in brokerage fees. Retired individuals living off their dividends and tax-free universities are apt to prefer dividend-paying corporations to corporations retaining income. While a 100% earnings payout cash dividend has the advantage of giving cash to those investors who desire cash, the policy also results in cash being given to those investors who do not desire cash, and who must incur brokerage fees to reinvest the dividends, and who pay taxes.

Dividend Changes and Signaling

A study by Liu, Szewczyk, and Zantout (2008) shows that "there is no compelling evidence of a post-dividend-reduction or post-dividend-omission price drift" (p. 987).

Assume that a firm's stock is fairly priced. Let us assume that this firm's management thinks that if dividends are increased, the market will conclude that this is a favorable signal and the stock price will increase significantly. If the stock was fairly priced to begin with, the stock price after the dividend increase will be too high. This means that with no other changes, the new stockholders will earn less than the firm's required return on stock. Thus, if a stock is fairly priced initially, an increase in dividends that leads to an unjustifiable stock price is not desirable since it leads to investor returns that are less than those required by the new stockholders.

CASE STUDY
MICROSOFT (2003–04)

In 2003, the US tax rates on dividends and capital gains were reduced to a maximum rate of 0.15. Microsoft had over US$40 billion in cash.

In January 2003, Microsoft issued its first cash dividend of US$0.02 per quarter. Some investors thought the dividend too low. Others thought the company should have repurchased more shares rather than pay a cash dividend. In July 2004, the company announced a special US$3 cash dividend. With almost 11 billion shares outstanding, this dividend would require a cash outlay of US$33 billion.

CONCLUSION

If investors in a high tax bracket expect the price of a stock to increase because of improved earnings (and a higher level of future dividends), they will be willing to pay more for a stock knowing that if their expectations are realized the stock can be sold and be taxed at the relatively lower capital gains tax rate. Whereas the lower capital gains tax rate tends to increase the value of a share of stock, we have shown that another powerful factor arises from the ability of the stockholder to defer paying taxes if the corporation retains income rather than paying dividends. Tax deferral is an extremely important advantage associated with the retention of earnings by a corporation.

The present tax law allows deferral of tax payment (or complete avoidance) on capital gains, and recognized gains may be taxed at a lower rate than ordinary income. Dividend policies of firms have relevance for public policy in the areas of taxation of both corporations and individuals. As corporate managers adjust their decision-making to include the tax law considerations, the makers of public policy must decide whether the results are beneficial to society.

It is not being argued that all firms should discontinue dividend payments. There is a place for a variety of payout policies, but there is a high cost to investors for all firms attempting to cater to the dividend and reinvestment preferences of an average investor. However, it is entirely appropriate that not all corporations appeal to all investors and that corporations design their common stock (and other securities) in the same way they design their consumer products. A corporation should have a financial personality resulting from its various financial policies (especially capital structure and dividend policies) that is attractive to a given group of investors, and is inappropriate for other groups. Corporate securities should have clienteles.

Define the price (and value) of a share of common stock as being equal to the present value of the next dividend (assumed to be declared and paid one period from now) and the price of the share at the time the dividend is paid. If we keep repeating the substitution process, we find that the value of the firm is equal to the present value of all future dividends, where the word "dividend" is used to include all cash distributions made from the firm to its investors. We replace the price at each future moment in time by the dividends that causes the stock to have value.

A board of directors acting in the interests of the stockholders of a corporation sets the dividend policy of a firm. The ability of an investor to defer income taxes as a result of the company retaining earnings is an important consideration. In addition, the distinction between ordinary income and capital gains for purposes of income taxation by the federal government accentuates the importance of investors knowing the dividend policy of the firm whose stock they are considering purchasing or have already purchased. In turn, this means that the corporation (and its board) has a responsibility to announce its dividend policy and to attempt to be consistent in its policy, changing only when its economic situation changes significantly. In the particular situation in which a firm is expanding its investments rapidly and is financing this expansion by issuing securities to its stockholders, the payment of cash dividends is especially vulnerable to criticism.

MORE INFO

Book:

Bierman, Harold, Jr. *Increasing Shareholder Value: Distribution Policy, A Corporate Finance Challenge.* Norwell, MA: Kluwer Academic Publishers, 2001.

Articles:

Barsky, Robert B., and J. Bradford De Long. "Why does the stock market fluctuate?" *Quarterly Journal of Economics* 108:2 (May 1993): 291–311. Online at: dx.doi.org/10.2307/2118333

Black, Fisher. "The dividend puzzle." *Journal of Portfolio Management* 2:2 (Winter 1976): 5–8. Online at: dx.doi.org/10.3905/jpm.1976.408558

Dann, Larry Y. "Common stock repurchases: An analysis of returns to bondholders and stockholders." *Journal of Financial Economics* 9:2 (June 1981): 113–138. Online at: dx.doi.org/10.1016/0304-405X(81)90010-6

Liu, Yi, Samuel H. Szewczyk, and Zaher Zantout. "Under-reaction to dividend reductions and omissions." *Journal of*

Finance 63:2 (April 2008): 987–1020. Online at: dx.doi.org/10.1111/j.1540-6261.2008.01337.x

Miller, Merton H., and Franco Modigliani. "Dividend policy, growth, and the valuation of shares." *Journal of Business* 34:4 (October 1961): 411–433. Online at: www.jstor.org/stable/2351143

Rundell, C. A. "From the thoughtful businessman." *Harvard Business Review* 43:6 (November–December 1965): 39.

Vermaelen, Theo. "Common stock repurchase and market signaling." *Journal of Financial Economics* 9:2 (June 1981): 139–183. Online at: dx.doi.org/10.1016/0304-405X(81)90011-8

Reports:

Cohen, Abby Joseph. "No problem with dividend growths." Goldman Sachs Portfolio Strategy. August 12, 1994; p. 1.

Grigoli, Carmine J. "The great corporate de-financing." Merrill Lynch. March 1986; p. 5.

See Also:

✔ Calculating Total Shareholder Return (pp. 329–330)
✔ Setting Up a Dividend Policy (p. 302)
✔ Using Dividend Discount Models (p. 337)
⇄ Dividend Yield (pp. 388–389)

NOTES

1 Barsky and De Long (1993).
2 Rundell (1965), p. 39.
3 Cohen (1994), p. 1.
4 Grigoli (1986), p. 5.

Executive Rewards: Ensuring That Financial Rewards Match Performance
by Shaun Tyson

EXECUTIVE SUMMARY

• Executive pay is used to attract and retain executives, and to drive performance.

• Business strategy objectives are cascaded down the organization and used as performance targets for the variable element in the reward package, in order to provide a clear line of sight.

• Reward packages for executive pay include base pay, short-term incentives, benefits, long-term incentives, and perks. Base pay is determined by the market rate in similar organizations.

• Variable pay incentives usually take the form of an annual bonus scheme, or, in the case of long-term incentives, deferred bonus and/or stock option plans.

• Reward packages are decided by remuneration committees as an important aspect of good corporate governance; the decisions are made by nonexecutive directors, with transparent reporting in annual reports. In the United Kingdom stockholders vote on the report.

INTRODUCTION

Effective management of executive rewards resides at the heart of a network of pressures and issues of central relevance to the management of organizational performance. These pressures can be represented diagrammatically to show how stockholder interests and corporate governance issues impact on business performance, objective setting, the motivation of executives, and the position of the organization as an employer

Figure 1. Reward at the centre of internal and external pressures

in specific labor markets; and how all of these are affected by corporate values/culture and vision (Figure 1).

However, the economic events of 2008 have reminded us all that these issues are conditioned by the broader economic climate in which corporations operate, where survival is more risky and uncertain. The recession which began with a massive banking crisis and near financial collapse, has affected the UK especially, because of the reliance on the financial sector revenues, and the significance of the City of London to the UK economy. Recovery and emergence from recession began in the US, Germany, Japan and other major economies however, in 2009. One of the consequences of the recession has been a search for more international regulation of the financial sector, in particular control over rewards associated with risk taking. The topic of executive rewards must be seen as a dynamic field, and this caveat informs all that follows. Nevertheless, there are systematic and enduring influences in the linkages between reward and performance.

We will examine rewards to show the major impact of reward policies and practices on organizational performance. This article takes rewards from the organizational perspective, and the starting point is an examination of the significance of corporate values, vision, and the culture of rewards.

CORPORATE VALUES/CULTURE/VISION

Corporate values and vision statements are an explicit expression of the formal values and vision of the organization, including the sometimes implicitly preferred behaviors and attitudes of managers in their leadership roles. These values may be published but, if not explicitly stated, will still emerge in the actions of senior managers and the founders. The objectives of a reward policy can be summarized as:

- Building stockholder value (or sustaining value for the citizen in the public sector).
- Being competitive in the recruitment of executives.

- Motivating and retaining executives.
- Being cost-effective.
- Being seen as fair by employees.
- Providing a degree of security for employees.

How these objectives are interpreted in any organization is contingent on that organization's values and the nature of its objectives—for example, profit maximization, market share, and service provision.

A number of authors have suggested that there are specific best practices to drive a philosophy of rewards that will support the corporate vision. For example *The New Pay*, by Schuster and Zingheim (1996), was a reward ideology that emphasized the strategic role of rewards and the supremacy of the marketplace. Key features of *The New Pay* were:

- Emphasis on external market-sensitive pay rather than annual increases.
- Risk-sharing partnership with employees rather than entitlements.
- Variable, performance-based pay.
- Flexibility in pay systems.
- Lateral promotions rather than career paths.
- Employability, not job security.

Later, the same authors argued that there are general reward principles that include aligning rewards with business goals; extending the "line of sight" of all employees to see the relationship between individual performance, corporate performance, and their rewards; and recognizing the market value of the individual with base pay, while rewarding results with variable pay (Zingheim and Schuster, 2000).

These ideas have gained currency over the last 20 years. Even though the economic storm now raging across the globe challenges some of this received wisdom, the ideas remain consistent with the prevailing concepts of market capitalism.

RELATING BUSINESS PERFORMANCE TO REWARDS

According to economic logic, there is a clear and consequential relationship, or line of sight, between the economic climate, the organization's performance, and the rewards provided (Figure 2).

Certain linkages, such as that between strategies and accountabilities, are critical. The diagram demonstrates the importance of line of sight. There is also the question of how quickly strategies, accountabilities, and rewards can adapt in response to changes in the economic climate.

Objective Setting and Targets

Objectives are normally "cascaded" down from the business strategy—each business unit or department having agreed short-term (next year) and longer-term (three to five year) plans. Objectives are usually both financial and qualitative. Financial objectives are typically total stockholder returns (TSR) and return on capital employed (ROCE). Budget targets are also often used, as well as share price. In remuneration planning, the performance objectives should be measured, and they should be designed to drive the business forward: "Paying for value creation is the most reliable way of generating it" (Credit Suisse First Boston). Targets are usually discussed and agreed at the annual performance review.

The Reward Package

Reward packages are pay policies aimed at achieving behaviors and actions by senior managers that accomplish business objectives. A package consists of base pay, short-term incentives, benefits, long-term incentives, and perks (perquisites). Base pay is decided by reference to pay rates in comparable organizations (see below), and usually according to internal relativities decided by the job evaluation scheme in use.

The decision of where to be in the market is a matter for corporate policy (for example, at the market median, or the upper quartile rate), reflecting labor market pressures and attraction and retention strategies. Short-term incentives are usually annual bonus schemes. Long-term incentive plans (LTIPs) use stock options and/or bonuses, merit pay, company-wide share plans, and the like.

Benefits include pensions to which the employer makes a contribution, private health plans, life insurance, and similar personal benefits. Perks are fringe benefits such as status cars, concierge services, use of company accommodation, etc. In most countries such perks are taxable as benefits in kind, although the package as a whole should be constructed to be as tax-effective as possible. Benefits may be flexible, so that individuals can choose a mix of benefits and perks within the agreed total value package. In some organizations there will also be the opportunity to sacrifice a proportion of salary for benefits.

Reward specialists structure executive reward packages taking into account the proportion of the base pay to variable pay available in the bonus opportunities, and typically they seek to balance the various elements in the package to drive the performance (both short and long term) required to achieve corporate objectives. The trend is toward variable pay based on performance being a high proportion of the total reward package, especially as managers become more senior. In this way senior managers take a larger risk with their rewards, since variable rewards are related more directly to the performance of the business in market conditions, which may vary for any number of reasons. Irrespective of these market conditions, directors and senior managers are accountable for profit, cost, and market share objectives.

LTIPs are normally constructed using bonus and stock option plans. Stock options give the right to purchase a defined quantity of stock at a stipulated price over a given period, according to predetermined eligibility requirements. There may be stock appreciation rights—the share award is triggered by increases in the share price, at a time chosen by the executive in the time period allowed.

Stock options have been popular as a way to retain key executives, to provide them with a stake in the company, and, at a time when share prices were rising, the opportunity to acquire real wealth. The change from a bull to a bear market has diminished enthusiasm for stock option schemes because the schemes depend on rising share prices so that executives can gain in wealth either by owning an appreciating asset, or by selling the shares and realizing the difference between the stipulated price (the strike price) and the enhanced market price.

Various performance conditions may be attached to the granting of a stock option or bonus. These include improvements in TSR, ROCE, EPS, and EBITDA (earnings before interest, taxation, depreciation, and amortization), usually in

Figure 2. Linkages between objectives and rewards

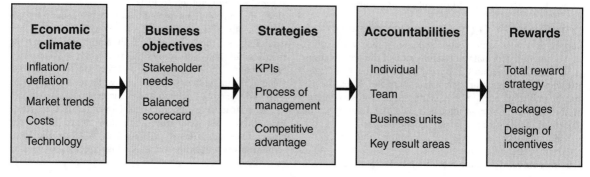

Economic climate	Business objectives	Strategies	Accountabilities	Rewards
Inflation/ deflation	Stakeholder needs	KPIs	Individual	Total reward strategy
Market trends	Balanced scorecard	Process of management	Team	Packages
Costs			Business units	Design of incentives
Technology		Competitive advantage	Key result areas	

Table 1. Example of a reward package: BP executive directors as at December 2007. (*Source*: IDS *Executive Compensation Review* 326 (April 2008): 12)

	Salary p.a.	Annual bonus	Benefits	Performance shares	Total
Chief executive	£877,000	£1,262,000	£14,000	Zero vested	£2,153,000
Chief finance officer	£591,755	£781,117	£5,036	Zero vested	£1,377,908

the corporate figures produced for the annual accounts. Table 1 is an example from BP in 2007 to show how the package works.

There is an annual bonus scheme. Performance measures and targets were set at the beginning of the year. Bonus opportunities were: on target (120%), and maximum (150%), of salary. The remuneration committee can, in exceptional circumstances, increase these payments, or reduce them to zero if appropriate. Targets for 2007 and 2008 were: half of the bonus is based on financial measures (EBITDA, ROCE, and cash flow), the other half on nonfinancial measures and individual performance. Nonfinancial targets were safety and people (including values and culture); individual performance targets were results and leadership.

The LTIP had three elements: shares, stock options, and cash; up to 5.5 times salary could be awarded in performance shares. Performance measured in TSR was compared to other oil companies. Although in this particular case shares were not vested (i.e. not passed into the ownership of the executives for 2007, due to operational problems that affected performance compared to other oil companies), high performance in previous years had resulted in substantial numbers of shares being vested. This demonstrates how the package reflects performance.

CORPORATE GOVERNANCE ISSUES
Reward for Failure
Much attention has been paid to excessive pay increases and bonuses for senior executives, especially where these appear to be awarded regardless of the corporate performance achieved.

Criticism of directors for receiving massive bonus and termination payments typically happens when there seems to be an element of reward for failure. UK directors of FTSE 100 companies are paid more than directors of those companies in the rest of the FTSE, but they do not receive the massive sums seen in Fortune 500 companies in the United States. There is a tradition of higher rewards in financial services. A big bonus culture existed in financial services among those dealing in the markets, as well as in the boardroom. Whether this was a cause of the recession is not yet clear, but it may have increased the propensity of managers and traders to take higher risks.

Although executive pay increases have tended to be modest, as with other workers during the recession, in 2009, UK and US CEOs were receiving base pay increases and bonus payments in some industry sectors. In the United Kingdom, CEOs of larger companies saw bonus payments cut by around a third, down to around £500,000, according to IDS. In February 2009, President Obama stated he would cap bank executives' pay at $500,000, and forbid bonuses to banks which had received Government aid.

In the United Kingdom and the United States, public outrage at the idea that those banks which had received

bailouts from the State should pay bonuses prompted a response from politicians. A widely held view was that there was a link between reward structure and the acceptance of excessive risk which had produced the financial crisis. The UK Financial Services Authority launched a new Code for Pay and Reward to be effective from January 2010, providing advice on how to mitigate risk, when awarding bonuses. This favors deferred bonus payments, with performance and claw back provisions attached.

Stockholder activism among both institutional stockholders, such as the Association of British Insurers, and small stockholder groups means that stockholders are likely to be consulted before new schemes are introduced. The court of public opinion is assisted by a vigilant press and the transparency rules. Accounting rules are now generally applied that require the cost of stock options and LTIPs to be fully expensed in the accounts. Increased volatility in share prices and the massive fall from the last quarter of 2008 onward have made stock options much less attractive, so there is less likelihood of big payouts at a later time when the executive cashes in the shares.

Base pay and total rewards are typically decided according to the market capitalization, the total number of employees, and the financial turnover of a business with respect to its industry comparators, but they are also, of course, contractually negotiated. Pressure from institutional investors and the press/media has created interest among the general public in this area, fueled by a number of high-profile cases where corporate failure has not been reflected in reductions in bonus or reward. As a consequence, director-level rewards are now very highly regulated and scrutinized compared to other employee groups.

Remuneration Committees
There is a convergence in corporate governance arrangements, based on the principles of transparency, the need to justify pay awards, the independent judgments of a remuneration committee, an accent on the process rather than on the content of rewards, and compliance with the rules as a condition of being listed on the appropriate stock exchange. Some of these principles were found in the original voluntary rules of the stock exchanges (for example in the Combined Code of the London Stock Exchange). Statutory provision has reinforced these rules—Directors' Remuneration Report Regulations 2002 (UK), Sarbanes–Oxley 2002 (US), SEC rules (US), NRE Act 2001 (France), and in Germany, the Cromme Code (2002). The UK regulations of 2002 require listed companies to have a remuneration committee of independent (nonexecutive) directors, which must produce and publish a report as part of the annual company report. This must include a statement of reward policy, the role of the remuneration committee, proposals for directors' pay going forward, and must include a graph showing comparisons in

terms of TSR with a named broad equity index over the previous five years, stating the reasons for selecting the index. Stockholders must be given the opportunity to vote on the remuneration committee report at the AGM. The stockholders' vote is not binding, but it would be unusual for a company and CEO to implement a pay award to the directors if this was voted down.

MAKING IT HAPPEN

- Effective reward policies for senior managers and directors can only be created if there is a clear line of sight between their performance goals and the business objectives. This requires:
  ○ strategic planning and accurate budgeting;
  ○ clear accountabilities, cascaded down the business;
  ○ realistic, measurable, demanding performance targets for the short and long term.
- Job evaluation techniques such as the Hay system can help to review accountabilities systematically.
- Base pay should be decided from market data on rates, with comparator organizations in the same industry sector that have similar market capitalization and employee numbers.
- Variable pay is used to recognize and drive performance. Short-term performance will need bonus schemes to be designed with annual performance targets, and there are design decisions to be made about whether there should be a threshold performance level, any weighting on particular targets, etc. Bonus is normally a percentage of base pay (typically 20%–40%). Long-term incentives might include a deferred bonus paid out after two or three years, with further performance conditions attached, and/or stock option schemes.

- Decisions on rewards are made by remuneration committees for director-level pay in quoted companies, with annual public reporting and stockholder involvement.

MORE INFO

Articles:
Balkin, David B., and Lius R. Gomez-Mejia. "Matching compensation and organizational strategies." *Strategic Management Journal* 11:2 (February 1990): 153–169. Online at: dx.doi.org/10.1002/smj.4250110207
Cascio, Wayne F., and Peter Cappelli. "Lessons from the financial services crisis." *HR Magazine* 54:1 (January 2009): 46–50. Online at: tinyurl.com/7uqkjcg

Websites:
Hay Group global management consulting: www.haygroup.com
Mercer HR and finance consultancy: www.mercer.com
Thomson/Sweet & Maxwell Incomes Data Services (IDS): www.incomesdata.co.uk
Towers Watson global professional services: www.towerswatson.com

See Also:
★ Balancing Senior Management Compensation Arrangements with Shareholders' Interests (pp. 173–175)
★ Corporate Board Structures (pp. 182–186)
★ Creating Value with EVA (pp. 255–258)
★ Employee Stock Options (pp. 258–260)
✔ Assessing Business Performance (pp. 359–360)
✔ Creating Executive Compensation (pp. 340–341)

Human Risk: How Effective Strategic Risk Management Can Identify Rogues
by Thomas McKaig

EXECUTIVE SUMMARY

- Corporations and high-level risk management are built around the people in organizations—and people are fallible.
- The need to evaluate human risk is clear: Stories abound of rogue employees in large and small organizations who have destroyed their entire firm.
- At the extreme, rogue firms, such as Enron, can destroy shareholder value and employees' lives.
- Building a quality-based organization helps to drive out rogues, but that's not the only way.
- Control measures need to be in place.
- Legal measures, the spotlight of publicity, and backing up corporate policies with firm action are all effective tools.

INTRODUCTION

Best practices in strategic risk management are intended to prevent weaknesses within corporations causing damage or even pulling down the firm. However, effective strategic risk management tools and techniques became harder to implement as business operations grow, become more complex, and operate in multiple locations. The controls that might have once been deemed acceptable in keeping employees within corporations on the same page begin to be less effective in cases of corporate restructurings that split businesses into smaller business units, and where employees are prodded into making deeper contributions to the bottom line.

Technology has not necessarily been a savior in this type of situation. Although technology has provided a platform for enhancing competitive advantage for business, it has also been a tool used by smart, capable, yet ill-intentioned employees to steal and distort overall results.

In the age of managerial cutbacks and increased workloads, a lot of things can happen that go unnoticed by overburdened managers. Interview techniques intended to keep rogues out of the workplace are—in spite of all the high-end questionnaires and intensive interview techniques that may be used—oftentimes ineffective, as potential employees are extremely savvy about modern interview techniques. Players in the job market are often familiar with the drill. Job hunters pass through many revolving interview doors, allowing them to hone their skills on how to dupe the interview process. Some interviewers may be incompetent or show poor judgment. HR departments are not foolproof, and it is only realistic to accept the fact that rogues in the workplace are here to stay. HR people will sometimes catch potential wrongdoers at the gatepost through psychological tests and other forms of due diligence involving intuition and criminal checks. But don't count on it.

Newspapers are full of stories about accountants who pad the books and give kickbacks to friends and family. Unhappy workers can damage product on the assembly line. A fired employee can show up at the workplace intent on payback for the injustice he or she feels they have suffered (in the United States this is called "going postal"). A multinational manager away from the watchful eyes of the home office can withhold information and deliver selective reports. Expense accounts can be padded. Goods can be pilfered from warehouses.

Given the current economic and political shocks, the last thing a company needs is to find itself in the news on account of the excessive creativity of one or more of its employees. Managers must face the fact that rogues will enter their organizations. So the question becomes: What can be done about it before the damage is done?

Keep in mind that human risk is about more than employees stealing from a firm; it can include individuals making unsound business decisions because nobody told them otherwise. Mistakes can be just as bad as deliberate fraud, as the following case shows.

CASE STUDY
AN INVITATION TO ROGUE EMPLOYEES

The example of a small Costa Rican bank serves to illustrate this point. At the height of the opening of Costa Rica's financial markets to foreign financial institutions in 1995 there was a rush to change operations practice. In the pre-free market era, Costa Rican banks could do as they pleased and were immune to punishment even when there were banking scandals and losses that were large for Costa Rica's fragile economy during the 1980s and 1990s. Old-style banks, accustomed to getting away with providing poor customer service and having lax internal controls, found that their business environment was changing with the pending legislative changes, set to open Costa Rica's financial markets to the world.

With poor leadership at the helm, and a lack of almost any strategic management initiative, employees were forced to take on new and undefined roles in their bank. Most of these

were ill-suited to employees who were given inadequate training and guidance for their new tasks.

As part of rising to the challenge of this expected competition from foreign banks, and in light of the assumed effectiveness of recently ordered ATM machines, the bank we are considering decided that a lean and mean (and ill-informed) policy of rampant firing would be an acceptable cost-saving measure. Half of the bank's staff lost their jobs, and those who remained quickly became demoralized. The newly installed bank machines did not function properly. Friday afternoon payday waits grew to two hours from the already unacceptable 15–30 minutes.

Internal communications broke down. In place of the usual courteous conversations, vitriolic emails flew from one cubicle to the next—seeding the environment for "surprise actions" from a growing league of unhappy, overworked, and demoralized employees. With no controls in place, an inexperienced bank teller authorized a loan of US$1 million to a long-standing customer—based solely on the fact that the teller liked the man and felt that he could be trusted with the money. For a small bank with a net worth of US$37 million, this inappropriate loan decision was the start of a string of poor management decisions that led to its implosion. Throughout this process the business culture undermined any attempts to implement benchmarking studies or best-practice management solutions. The "generous" employee was not fired and kept his duties with a severe reprimand. The future of the bank was sealed, and eventually it went down.

AT THE EXTREME

At the extreme end of the spectrum, there is a widespread pattern of "pushing the boundaries" of everything from accounting rules to disclosure rules for public companies, lax internal controls, managements that focus on doing deals rather than managing, outright fraud and theft, and incentive systems that reward the wrong actions.

Enron followed this pattern. The case of Enron shows how a combination of intellectual laziness and groupthink by a large number of employees, consultants, and analysts allowed a group of greedy and ambitious individuals to get away with massive fraud. Enron was not a case of one or two people at the top undertaking a complex scheme unbeknown to others, but rather a case of many individuals who knew what they were supposed to do, but didn't do it. This was a case of analysts who never really questioned how Enron made its money, of accountants who didn't ask simple questions, and of employees and board members who saw dubious things but were afraid to stand up and ask the questions they should have.

STRATEGIC RISK MANAGEMENT: A VIEW

What is risk management, and how does it apply to the actions of employees? According to Kent D. Miller, "'risk' refers to variation in corporate outcomes or performance that cannot be forecast ex ante."[1] The key element here is to recognize that there is true uncertainty about human risk, or indeed any risk. The fact that an organization has survived to today without major scandal does not guarantee that it is safe in the future.

So what to do? According to Miller, effective risk management responses frequently include avoidance (which we have noted is almost impossible with the case of human risk), control (to be addressed in a moment), and cooperation and imitation (which can be achieved through quality initiatives).

QUALITY INITIATIVES CAN HELP

An organization is only as good as its parts—in this case the human parts. One fractured link in the chain means one vulnerable corporation. The quality aspect of management can be evoked to work hand in hand with problem prevention, but it is all too often overlooked.

Typically quality applies to (but is not limited to) reducing or eliminating defects in manufactured products. Beyond this, management also needs to invoke quality principles that smooth the internal environment. When intra-corporate communication channels are damaged, the ensuing misinformation may foster rogue behavior within the organization. Many quality experts cite training, transparency, empowerment, and clear communication as vital steps in building a quality organization.

Whether dealing with production issues or those relating to customer service, quality initiatives espoused by management thinkers like Armand V. Feigenbaum, J. M. Juran, Philip B. Crosby, and Frank Gryna can help a business. Firms that include quality as a core value, and reinforce this value through everyday practice, have experienced reductions down to zero of defects on production lines, lower worker turnover, higher levels of worker empowerment through training, more worker satisfaction, greater productivity, and a positive outlook on the company. Valuing people as the key drivers of both quality and performance is important to a firm and can go a long way toward identifying rogues and frustrating their efforts.

Quality starts with managers. Being an ethical role model is a key function of any leader. And the good news is that nothing special has to be done to become such a positive model. However, when leadership falters it can open the door to a rogue hit, doing as much damage to the corporation as a rogue wave can do to a ship at sea. You have to work at good leadership.

But the emphasis on quality alone is not enough. Control mechanisms, including both financial and performance audits, are important for preventing and uncovering potential problems. The really effective tools are punishment and brandishing the legal arsenal available to the company. Such measures reassure the public. A corporation just can't hunker down to avoid embarrassment. Swift and fair measures will fill the void of those strategic management initiatives that fail to catch rogue employees and will serve as a heavy reminder to others who may be about to embark on a negative course of action.

To many, the idea of punishment seems to be a return to management's dark past in the days of command and control. This is not the case. Taking corrective action, including negative reinforcements and punishments, is a legitimate function of managers, just as much as positive reinforcements are. Corrective actions can include firings, admonishments, wage deductions, and suspension without pay. People in authority are chary about digging in their heels to fight for what is ethically and obviously right for fear of being politically incorrect, or worse, manifestly insensitive. Many in decision-making positions prefer a course of inaction because they lack the gumption required to stay the course. If a manager has documented proof (paper or electronic) of wrongdoing by an employee, and particularly in a unionized environment, there is little that a union can do to "rescue" the employee from receiving the appropriate reprimand, short of the union condoning such rogue behavior.

CONCLUSION

A manager faces many risks—from industry-wide risks such as currency and interest rate risks, to department-specific risks such as accounting and treasury risks. Most of these risks can be quantified, though we are finding out that many of the numbers assigned to these risks are little more than educated guesses. Unfortunately the identification, measurement, and quantification of human risk are difficult and challenging. In spite of our best efforts, and in spite of pundits who spout an arsenal of "proof" to the contrary, reliable numbers cannot be assigned to human risk. Nor can risk be completely eliminated from an organization. But quality initiatives and control mechanisms can go a very long way to minimize exposure.

MAKING IT HAPPEN

- Learn to live with the uncertainty of any risk, especially human risk.
- Place renewed emphasis on what is already being done, including audits (financial and performance), internal financial controls, and clear financial reporting.
- Vigilantly tweak and enforce the control mechanisms already in place. Think about expanding and/or adding controls.
- Revisit your own role as a highly visible manager. Are corporate controls short-sighted, or are they clearly structured so as to prevent deceit, fraud, and rogues from doing future damage?
- Identify high-risk areas in your firm—from inventory to treasury areas. Think about safety and security measures in addition to internal controls.

MORE INFO

Books:

Crosby, Philip B. *Completeness: Quality for the 21st Century*. New York: Dutton, 1992.

Feigenbaum, Armand V. *Total Quality Control*. 4th ed. New York: McGraw-Hill, 2004.

Gryna, Frank, M. *Quality Planning & Analysis: From Product Development Through Use*. 4th ed. New York: McGraw-Hill, 2000.

Hill, Charles W. L., and Thomas McKaig. *Global Business Today*. 2nd Canadian ed. Whitby, ON: McGraw-Hill Ryerson, 2009.

Juran, J. M., and Frank M. Gryna (eds). *Juran's Quality Control Handbook*. 4th ed. New York: McGraw-Hill, 1988.

Mintzberg, Henry. *Managers Not MBAs: A Hard Look at the Soft Practice of Managing and Management Development*. San Francisco, CA: Berrett-Koehler Publishers, 2004.

Articles:

Becker, David M. "Testimony concerning new regulatory tools to control the activities of rogue individuals in the financial services industries." Given before the Subcommittee on Oversight and Investigations and the Subcommittee on Financial Institutions and Consumer Credit, US House of Representatives, March 6, 2001. Online at: www.sec.gov/news/testimony/ts042001.htm

Boak, Joshua. "Rogue trader rocks firm: Huge wheat futures loss stuns MFGlobal." *Chicago Tribune* (February 29, 2008).

Clark, Andrew. "From ethical champion to rogue interloper—BP's American nightmare: Accidents and allegations of market fixing destroy environmentalist image." *Guardian (London)* (November 16, 2006). Online at: tinyurl.com/273svw2

Gunther, Will. "In the crosshairs: Limiting the impact of workplace shootings." *Risk Management* 55 (November 2008). Online at: tinyurl.com/7drc3me

Johnston, David Cay. "Staff says IRS concealed improper audits and rogue agent." *New York Times* (May 1, 1998). Online at: tinyurl.com/aqf9tr

Malakian, Anthony. "Internal controls need to be tightened." *Bank Technology News* (April 2008). Online at: www.americanbanker.com/btn/21_4/-349038-1.html

Prince, C. J. "To catch a thief: Employee fraud hits growing businesses hardest. Here's what you can do to make sure there's not a thief among you." *Entrepreneur Magazine* (September 2007). Online at: tinyurl.com/77wpu2r

Report:

KPMG. "An approach to mitigating rogue trading risks." 2008.

Website:

CBC News coverage of the Conrad Black affair: www.cbc.ca/news/background/black_conrad

See Also:

✔ Establishing a Framework for Assessing Risk (p. 313)
✔ Internal Auditing for Fraud Detection and Prevention (pp. 315–316)
✔ Understanding Internal Audits (pp. 324–325)

NOTE

1 Miller, Kent D. "A framework for integrated risk management in international business." *Journal of International Business Studies* 23:2 (June 1992): 311–331. Online at: dx.doi.org/10.1057/palgrave.jibs.8490270

Identifying the Right Nonexecutive Director
by Terry Carroll

EXECUTIVE SUMMARY

• In the past, some have seen NED posts as a sinecure.
• Risk, diligence, and compliance factors may have changed this.
• Companies and prospective NEDs need the role to be seen as more professional.
• Remuneration for the right NED should reflect the increased "risk premium."
• NEDs should protect all stakeholders and apply sound corporate governance.
• Independence is paramount.
• Governance regulations and best practice continue to evolve.
• Successive Companies Acts have growing impact and change demands.
• The "right" NED needs wider skills and relevant business and sector experience.
• A range of sources exists, but thorough evaluation and selection are required.
• The quantity of candidates may reduce but the quality should increase.

INTRODUCTION

The "Credit Crunch" has thrown up many challenges and controversies. The extraordinary losses at Société Générale were reminiscent of the Barings debacle. The unaccountable losses suffered by many banks, especially in America, also beg serious questions about nonexecutive directors (NEDs). Never have times been tougher, or the challenges greater—and not just for banks but for all companies. Never has there been a clearer need for the right NEDs.

This article examines the challenges for all companies from a British perspective and suggests some key characteristics that are needed in the "right" NED. It also looks at wider aspects of the role, and where and how suitable candidates may be found.

GOVERNANCE AND MORE GOVERNANCE

On March 22, 2007, Naguib Kheraj resigned as finance director of Barclays, quoted by *Accountancy Age* as being "sick of compliance." As an executive director he was required to understand the same governance and regulatory matters as a NED.

In the past, some saw the role of NED as a sinecure. Now they may be rethinking that jaundiced view, as the toll of legislation, regulation, compliance, and the globalized economy increase the risk for those who occupy the role. There may still be some who approach the task altruistically, but, in general, to attract the best this increased risk should be reflected in higher remuneration.

Whether or not reward and recognition have been motivators in the past, the growing risk, diligence, and compliance factors may now be more important considerations in the mind of a prospective NED.

THE ROLE OF THE NED

In its simplest terms, the NED is there to protect the interests of the owners of the business. But now, major considerations such as health and safety, derivatives, new legislation concerning companies and employment, and risk management have added immeasurably to the potential legal and practical consequences for a NED—and, correspondingly, to the risks. These are in addition to the economic and commercial challenges that may have been the greatest for years.

To the layperson, the remuneration a NED receives may seem generous. Often it is the FTSE100 companies that hit the headlines in this respect. Not far below this level, NED packages are much more modest, and, although the scale and complexity may not be as vast as for big companies, the weight of regulation and compliance is similar.

The 2003 Higgs Review[1] drew on many of the strands of corporate governance that had been developing since the Cadbury Report in 1992.[2] It created a wholesome debate about the composition and responsibilities of the board. NEDs are now expected to play a more active role in the corporation, while being required to maintain their independence.

Two days a month is a reasonable expectation for a NED, whose day rate may be equal to that of a management consultant. But how can any diligent person be expected to perform their board and committee duties, spend time in the company, *and* keep up to date with information that, if ignored or overlooked, may land them in court, in two days per month?

COMBINED CODE OF CORPORATE GOVERNANCE

Every company needs NEDs, but not all can afford them. The law is pretty much the same for most companies; governance and guidance vary little except for small companies and quoted companies. It would do no harm for more companies to embrace the standards of the Combined Code,[3] whether or not they are required to. It would improve any company and is a useful starting point to guide any prospective NED.

RISK AND REWARD

"For some, the burden of being a NED in a public company is too onerous in terms of time and the potential financial or reputational risk. A point of inflexion is reached when good candidates say 'no thanks.' In this increasingly litigious world, NEDs should be adequately rewarded for their effort in proportion to the risks they run." Virginia Bottomley, Head of Practice at Odgers Ray & Berndtson.

As the demands and the potential exposure grow, so there is a commensurate increase in the risk factor. Ignorance or incompetence is no excuse; insurance and indemnity only go so far. Remuneration should increase to recognize the risk factor and reward the professional.

While NEDs are not responsible for, or engaged in, the day-to-day management, they are nevertheless subject to legal duties and responsibilities similar to those of the executives and are similarly liable for dismissal. Furthermore, it is also recommended that their remuneration should *not* be a significant proportion of their overall income.

So, will we see the emergence of the "professional" NED? A growing number are striking a balance between number of appointments and diligence. Enlightened companies encourage executive directors to accept NED appointments elsewhere to widen their perspective and personal development.

EVOLUTION OF THE ROLE

According to the Higgs Review, NEDs should:

- contribute to and constructively challenge the development of company strategy;
- scrutinize management performance;
- satisfy themselves that financial information is accurate and ensure that robust risk management is in place;
- meet at least once a year without the chairman or executive directors;
- be prepared to attend AGMs and discuss issues relating to their roles;
- have a greater exposure to major shareholders.

If only it was that simple. And according to Higgs, 60% of NEDs are still recruited with no formal process.

NEDs are, however, increasingly being sourced through search and selection. Since Higgs, diversity has been a more significant factor. Many would-be NEDs may prefer to go into private companies, where there are fewer governance requirements and financial rewards can still be attractive. Also, government and public bodies have opened themselves to advertised selection, but the fees they offer are much lower or even zero.

Executive secondment and private companies are a good proving ground. There is still, however, an apparent shortage of suitably qualified NED candidates. Organizations such as Directorbank (www.directorbank.com) have attempted to address this challenge.

The best boards should provide the newly recruited NED with a formal induction and an ongoing training program, whatever the degree of experience. Key aspects would include strategy, governance and regulation, and, of course, an introduction to the company itself, and its key people, products, and services.

This still leaves the onus on the individual to keep up to date and prepare diligently. Some take the view that this would require up to 30 days a year.

KEY ISSUES

According to Ernst & Young's annual survey in 2006, ("Concerns that keep Non-Executives awake at night"; *E&Y*

Newsletter, June 2006) NEDs now spend up to 40% of their time on governance. The matters that most preoccupy them are:

- understanding a new sector;
- audit and finance;
- overseas knowledge;
- technology and security;
- remuneration policy in the company as a whole;
- the company's reputational risk.

Furthermore, a MORI poll cited in the same survey suggested that people were less likely to accept a NED appointment, and much less likely to accept an appointment as chair of the audit committee, than a year before.

INDEPENDENCE

Best practice and regulation dictate the need for independence. It's not just about individual thinking, because teamwork between the NEDs and with the executive is highly desirable. Share options as incentives for NEDs are, however, actively discouraged for quoted companies, and performance-related rewards should be geared to the share price rather than profits or sales.

The NED is required to judge and act in the best interests of the shareholders, yet, ironically, this begins with having the company's best interests at heart. Those who seek personal reward or recognition as a result of their directorship may not instinctively make impartial judgments where the company's interests should prevail.

Above all, integrity, teamwork, and trust across the board are paramount. Consensus is ideal, with a vote hardly ever needed. Consequently, these qualities matter most of all in the selection of the chairman of the board or audit committee.

THE EFFECTS OF THE 2006 COMPANIES ACT

The Companies Act 2006 came into effect in the United Kingdom in October 2008. While it codified the guidance and requirements from many sources, ultimately it made the duties even more significant and onerous. Alongside this, you have the extension of the crime of "corporate manslaughter" to the company itself, thereby effectively doubling the directors' liability.

The Act clearly sets out the seven general duties of directors:

1 A duty to act in accordance with the company's constitution, and to use powers only for the purposes for which they were conferred.
2 A duty to promote the success of the company for the benefit of its members. In doing this the directors are required to take account of:
   ◦ the likely long-term consequences of their decisions;
   ◦ the interests of the company's employees;
   ◦ the need to foster the company's business relationships with suppliers, customers, and others;
   ◦ the impact of the company's operations on the community and the environment;
   ◦ the desirability of maintaining a reputation for high standards of business conduct;
   ◦ the need to act fairly as between members of the company.
3 A duty to exercise independent judgment.
4 A duty to exercise reasonable care, skill, and diligence.
5 A duty to avoid conflicts of interest.
6 A duty not to accept benefits from third parties.
7 A duty to declare to the company's other directors any interest a director has in a proposed transaction or arrangement with the company.

It is likely that the new provisions will cause the greatest difficulty for directors who sit on more than one board. The Act introduces a new statutory right of shareholders to sue directors, in the company's name, to recover on the company's behalf loss it has suffered as a result of the directors' negligence, default, breach of duty, or breach of trust.

The new statutory right, or "derivative action," will undoubtedly make it easier for shareholders to take directors to court. Considerable concern has been expressed that this, taken together with the statutory statement of duties—particularly the detailed list of factors to which directors are to have regard—will lead to significant risks for directors.

Even if directors are able to obtain indemnity or insurance, the above requirements not only codify the requirements of best practice or regulation from a number of different sources, they also increase individual risks and exposure significantly.

One might wonder why anyone would want to be a nonexecutive director. The risks, responsibilities, and liabilities have increased considerably, as has the amount of knowledge and understanding now required of them.

Nevertheless, there will always be a supply of would-be NEDs, and not just for the money. We shall inevitably see the growth of the profession of director, which the United Kingdom's Institute of Directors has done much to foster, through collectivization and training. There will always be some people who either wish to carry their executive experience into semi-retirement or have the personal and professional qualities to perform the role. In addition, there is a ready supply from the executive ranks of other companies.

SO HOW DO YOU FIND AND IDENTIFY THE RIGHT NEDS?

First, all companies of a certain size should encourage their executive directors to seek a NED appointment elsewhere as part of their personal development. This opportunity not only helps them grow as individuals and executives, it also gives them an acute insight into what is required of those fulfilling such roles.

While it is not beyond the whit of a chairman to seek out people with directly relevant sectoral experience and/or skills, there is no reason why this process should be any different from that of selecting executives. Search consultants have been playing an increasing role in identifying and selecting suitable candidates, but ultimately it is for the board to apply an appropriate and objective recruitment and selection process for the right candidate.

It has been too often said in the past that there aren't enough good and suitable candidates. Certainly, not only the diligent governance requirements, but also the personal qualities needed, justify significant expense and a rigorous process of selection.

Ultimately, the fundamental role of NEDs is to protect the interests of the owners of the business. They need to be dispassionate, courageous, and of the highest integrity. The remuneration may not always have compensated for the potential corporate and personal risks, but maybe this is because they weren't always recognized either. Now the British Government and others are ensuring that these considerations are paramount.

ESSENTIAL CHARACTERISTICS

Ideally, a prospective NED should have experience relevant to the business or to the sector in which it operates. However, alongside this goes a set of professional skills. If you can identify the core executive roles, it would be ideal to have an equivalent "shadow" on the board. This is most evident in the case of the finance director. A senior professional from another company, or maybe a retired executive director, can be a coach, mentor, and sounding board.

Above all, the board needs to be capable of acting as a team—NEDs and executives together, comprehensive and all-embracing; neither shy of their collective responsibility to the shareholders, nor of their commitment to the long-term success of the enterprise.

Executive directors may be rigorously reviewed and vetted for their relevant skills; but those required of the NED go one step beyond. If the post ever was a sinecure, it should be no longer. Not only the future of the company, but that of a country's economy and wider reputation lie in the hands of this new generation. The chairman and his colleagues may realize that they are protecting interests beyond their own and those of the owners in having a thorough, objective, and professional identification and selection process for their new NED colleagues.

STILL INTERESTED?

The growth of regulation and the duties of governance may drive some prospective NEDs away. If Naguib Kheraj found life too onerous as an executive director, what might many who contemplate putting themselves forward as candidates for a nonexecutive directorship think? Others, increasingly professional, may be drawn by the challenge, complexity, and variety, together with the intellectual and increasingly appropriate financial reward for a job diligently and well done.

MORE INFO

Website:

Directorbank, for executive and non-executive recruitment: www.directorbank.com

See Also:

★ Corporate Board Structures (pp. 182–186)
✔ Defining Corporate Governance: Its Aims, Goals, and Responsibilities (pp. 341–342)
✔ Directors' Duties: A Primer (pp. 342–343)

NOTES

1 Higgs, Derek. *Review of the Role and Effectiveness of Non-Executive Directors*. London: The Stationery Office, 2003.
2 *Report of the Committee on the Financial Aspects of Corporate Governance.* "The Cadbury Report." London: Gee, 1992.
3 Financial Reporting Council (FRC). *The Combined Code on Corporate Governance.* London: FRC, 2008.

Improving Corporate Profitability Through Accountability

by Marc J. Epstein and Priscilla Wisner

EXECUTIVE SUMMARY

- Traditional measures of performance are of limited use to modern businesses, being rooted in evaluating past performance. They are a poor guide to true value, often missing the key factors that promote long-term worth.
- It is essential to include the leading financial and nonfinancial indicators of performance that drive long-term value. This provides broader and more sophisticated information that highlights future trends.
- Effectively managing and communicating a broader set of performance measures reduces uncertainty, ensures better relationships with stockholders and analysts, and enables improved financial performance.
- Full accountability and disclosure, combined with improved measures and new systems to drive the process throughout the organization, create greater value for stakeholders, promoting future success.

INTRODUCTION

Improved governance requires the right employees, the right culture and values, and the right systems, information, and decision-making. Unfortunately, most organizations are attempting to steer their information-age businesses using industrial-age measurements. Managers have struggled for decades with accounting systems that fail to measure many of the variables that drive long-term value. The historical lagging indicators of performance that are commonly used by accountants are of limited value in determining the value of businesses for external stakeholders, and are of little use in guiding the business internally. Financial data on profitability and return on investment are valuable measures of corporate performance, but they are lagging indicators that measure past performance. A broader set of financial measures is necessary (for example, measurement of intangible assets such as intellectual capital and research-and-development value), in addition to an expanded set relating to customers, internal processes, and organizational measures.

The metrics must include the *leading* financial and nonfinancial indicators of performance that are the drivers and predictors of future financial performance. For example, fines and penalties may be a leading indicator of corporate reputation, employee turnover is a leading measure of future recruitment and training costs, and product quality is a leading measure of customer satisfaction, which in turn is a leading measure of market share. Each of these factors (reputation, employee-related costs, customer satisfaction, and market share) impacts financial performance.

IMPROVED INTERNAL AND EXTERNAL REPORTING

Just as companies expand their performance measurement parameters, they must also expand their performance reporting models. Employees, stockholders, financial analysts, activists, customers, suppliers, government regulators, and others increasingly demand detailed information about corporate activities, and the internet has made the dissemination of that information easier and faster. No longer can managers claim they don't have the information. The data are easy to collect, and it's essential to have broader and more forward-looking information to effectively manage the diverse issues that managers now confront daily. Managers should collect this broader array of information on activities and impacts both inside and outside the company, and select a set of data to provide adequate disclosure to their various stakeholders. External stakeholders need a broader set of information to effectively evaluate corporate performance, and voluntary disclosure of this information is critical for corporate accountability. This accountability, both inside and outside the company, through an effective corporate communications strategy, is an essential element of effective and responsible corporate governance.

Proactively managing external disclosures should be a fundamental part of corporate communications strategy. By externally disclosing a more comprehensive set of measures, company executives are seizing the initiative to describe the company's strategy, set expectations, increase transparency, and ensure goal alignment between the company and a broad set of stakeholders. Disclosing performance measures allows investors and other stakeholders to view the company through the eyes of management. A clear, comprehensive communications strategy is highly valued by stockholders and analysts alike.

CASE STUDY

The Campbell Soup Company has continually improved corporate governance.

Changes undertaken in the early 1990s required a majority of directors to come from outside the organization. All directors must stand for election every year and must own at least 6,000 shares of stock within three years of election. Among other provisions, interlocking directorships are not allowed and insiders are banned from certain key committees. In 1995, the board began a rotating yearly performance evaluation of directors, board committees, and the board as a whole. In 2000, the board approved a new director compensation program to closely link director compensation to the creation of stockholder value; only 20% is paid in cash (tied to attendance at meetings). The full set of Campbell Soup's governance standards and current performance review are disclosed in the annual proxy statement to stockholders.

The Cooperative Bank, based in the United Kingdom and with 4,000 employees, has won numerous awards for the high degree of transparency and accountability the company has exhibited. The bank has identified six partners in its quest for corporate value: stockholders, customers, staff and their families, suppliers, national and international societies, and past and future generations of cooperators. The company surveys all stakeholder groups to determine the critical elements in creating value for each, and performance targets are set on the basis of this information. In 2003, 70 targets were established in three principal areas: delivering value, social responsibility, and ecological sustainability. The Cooperative Bank 2004 Sustainability Report states that 33 targets were fully achieved, acceptable progress was made on 22, and 15 were not achieved. The bank reports progress on each target, providing data and management commentary, and establishes targets for the coming year.

CONCLUSION

Once a company has decided to improve corporate governance, measure a broader set of indicators of past and future success, and report internally and externally, managers must develop systems to drive these decisions through the organization. Leading companies are developing integrated, closed-loop planning, budgeting, and feedback systems to help align strategy implementation with corporate performance. While leadership at the top is critical, buy-in at the shop floor level is essential for the success of any system implementation. Metrics must be linked to strategy and must be consistent throughout the organization. Companies are increasingly stating desires to become more customer focused or more socially responsible, yet many are still basing employee rewards on meeting revenue and profit goals. If companies expect employees to be more customer focused or more socially or environmentally responsible, part of overall performance evaluations and rewards should be on the basis of customer focus or social responsibility.

Accountable managers encourage not only continuous judgment, but continuous improvement. They insist that everyone in the organization participate in decision-making. They implement a culture of constant learning and insist on building learning organizations. Accountable managers communicate constantly, setting a tone of forthright feedback and transparency.

Full accountability comes only when a company combines a strong governance structure, improved and broad measurement of relevant performance impacts, timely and full internal and external reporting, and comprehensive management systems to drive the accountability model throughout the organization. By combining these elements companies are creating value for the stakeholders whose support they need in order to prosper—customers, investors, employees, suppliers, communities, the public, regulators, and other government officials.

MAKING IT HAPPEN

The rewards from building the accountable organization are much like those from building the quality organization—the more committed the managers and workers and the better integrated the concept with company line operations, the greater the benefit. As a first step, managers must build accountable systems and practices within the company. Then they can build bridges to the outside. As they move toward full accountability—well-governed, measured, managed, and publicly responsive—they will position themselves to reap many benefits:

- Executing strategy: the accountable organization articulates each strategy and tactic with specific measures that align direction in ways that broader objectives cannot. The hard measures then give managers objective feedback on what the strategy execution is achieving.
- Improving decision-making: the accountable organization generates a wealth of information on performance, which in turn informs decision-making through facts, not intuition. People inside and outside the company can make more effective decisions to further company strategy and goals.
- Empowering people: the accountable organization thins the ranks of middle managers that distil and convey information and empowers decision-making authority to the front lines. As management articulates what it wants with concrete quantitative measures, workers have clear guidance of goals and objectives and how they relate to strategy.
- Accelerating learning: the accountable organization installs feedback systems that yield rapid-fire learning from people both across and outside the company. The company with the most feedback loops—internal and external—is the most successful.
- Communicating the story: the accountable organization delivers its story of value with credible financial and nonfinancial numbers. As senior managers report more numbers externally, exposing performance transparently, stockholders and analysts have less reason to undervalue their stock.

- Inspiring loyalty: the accountable organization markets its value on a basis of reliable performance measures. The no-smoke-and-mirrors approach spurs cooperation and inspires the loyalty of investors, customers, suppliers, employees, business partners, and communities.

MORE INFO

Books:

Epstein, Marc J., and Bill Birchard. *Counting What Counts: Turning Corporate Accountability to Competitive Advantage*. Cambridge, MA: Perseus, 2000.

Epstein, Marc J., and K. O. Hanson (eds). *The Accountable Corporation*. Westport, CT: Praeger Publications, 2006.

Monks, Robert A. G. *The Emperor's Nightingale: Restoring the Integrity of the Corporation in the Age of Shareholder Activism*. Cambridge, MA: Perseus, 1999.

Ward, Ralph D. *Improving Corporate Boards: The Boardroom Insider Guidebook*. New York: Wiley, 2000.

Articles:

Botosan, Christine A. "Disclosure level and the cost of equity capital." *Accounting Review* 72:3 (July 1997): 323–349. Online at: www.jstor.org/stable/248475

Epstein, Marc J., and Krishna Palepu. "What financial analysts want." *Strategic Finance* (April 1999): 48–52.

Healy, Paul M., Amy P. Hutton, and Krishna G. Palepu. "Stock performance and intermediation changes surrounding sustained increases in disclosure." *Contemporary Accounting Research* 16:3 (Fall 1999): 485–520. Online at: dx.doi.org/10.1111/j.1911-3846.1999.tb00592.x

Hutton, Amy. "Beyond financial reporting—An integrated approach to corporate disclosure." *Journal of Applied Corporate Finance* 16:4 (Fall 2004): 8–16. Online at: dx.doi.org/10.1111/j.1745-6622.2004.00003.x

Sengupta, Partha. "Corporate disclosure quality and the cost of debt." *Accounting Review* 73:4 (October 1998): 459–474. Online at: www.jstor.org/stable/248186

Report:

Engen, Travis, and Samuel DiPiazza. "Beyond reporting: Creating business value and accountability." World Business Council on Sustainable Development, June 2005. Online at: tinyurl.com/7e8t72v

Role of Internal Auditing at Board Committee Level

by Sridhar Ramamoorti

EXECUTIVE SUMMARY

- Boards of directors and their committees, despite receiving extremely summarized and condensed information, now have a well-established responsibility for managing the overall organizational risk.
- The effective management of risk is a prerequisite for ensuring good corporate governance.
- Because governance seems to be so intertwined with risk, one strategy might be to leverage the internal audit function to work with different board committees and provide risk-relevant information.
- The independent audit committee fulfills a vital role in corporate governance. The audit committee can be a critical component in ensuring quality reporting and controls, as well as the proper identification and management of risk.
- A summary of internal audit–audit committee interactions is provided through the perspective of *20 Questions Directors Should Ask of Internal Audit*.
- The internal audit function has long been serving as the "eyes and ears" as well as the "arms and legs" of the audit committee of the board.
- Internal audit role plays a critical role in keeping the audit committee abreast of the latest developments and goings-on of the company, and without such assistance, the audit committee cannot realistically fulfill its risk oversight responsibilities.

INTRODUCTION

In the aftermath of the Wall Street financial crisis, one of the major areas that has been identified as needing improvement is corporate governance. Boards of directors and their committees, despite receiving extremely summarized and condensed information, now have a well-established responsibility for managing the overall organizational risk (Kolb and Schwartz, 2010). A critically important element that was lacking before and during the financial crisis was relevant risk intelligence—most boards were caught off-guard and were truly surprised by the turn of events. Recent guidance from the Information Systems Audit and Control Association (ISACA, 2010) highlights the importance of risk monitoring by noting that "better monitoring means fewer surprises."

The effective management of risk is a prerequisite for ensuring good corporate governance. Organizations exist to achieve their goals and objectives; however, because these goals and objectives have to be achieved in the context or environment of risk, they are not always assured (McNamee and Selim, 1998). Although the practice of risk management, on an enterprise-wide basis, is fundamentally the responsibility of executive management, the internal auditing function is typically charged with examining and reporting on risk exposures, as well as on the quality of the organization's risk management efforts. The board has oversight responsibility with respect to management and, by extension, has responsibility for both effective risk management and governance.

It is evident that organizations worldwide need to strengthen their governance mechanisms. Nevertheless, placing the governance burden in its entirety on the board of directors is an unrealistic position to advocate, given the infrequency of meetings and their limited knowledge of business operations on a day-to-day basis. Because governance seems to be so intertwined with risk, one strategy might be to leverage the internal audit function to work with different board committees and provide risk-relevant information. In this article we will focus on the internal audit function supporting the audit committee with respect to enterprise risk management.

INTERNAL AUDIT–AUDIT COMMITTEE INTERACTIONS

Treating the internal audit function as one of the cornerstones of corporate governance, Swanson (2010) says that "internal auditing can provide strategic, operational and tactical value to an organization's operations." He proceeds to emphasize that audit committee members should not only empower the internal audit function by providing it with resources and encouraging it to take on a leadership role, but that they should also actively oversee its performance. To help formulate the right perspective and ensure that these interactions are ideal, he usefully refers to a publication by the Canadian Institute of Chartered Accountants, *20 Questions Directors Should Ask of Internal Audit* (Fraser and Lindsay, 2008). It is worthwhile to excerpt these 20 questions across six categories, *viz.*

1 *Internal audit's role and mandate*
   a Should we have an internal audit function?
   b What should our internal audit function do?
   c What should be the mandate of the internal audit function?
2 *Internal audit relationships*
   a What is the relationship between internal auditing and the audit committee?
   b To whom does internal auditing report administratively?
3 *Internal audit resources*
   a How is the internal audit function staffed?
   b How does internal auditing get and maintain the expertise it needs to conduct its assignments?
   c Are the activities of internal auditing appropriately coordinated with those of the external auditors?
4 *Internal audit process*
   a How is the internal audit plan developed?

b What does the internal audit plan not cover?

c How are internal audit findings reported?

d How are corporate mangers required to respond to internal audit findings and recommendations?

e What services does internal audit provide in connection with fraud?

f How do you assess the effectiveness of your internal audit function?

5 *Closing questions*

a Does internal auditing have sufficient resources?

b Does the internal audit function get appropriate support from the CEO and senior management team?

c **Are you satisfied that this organization has adequate internal controls over its major risks?**

d Are there any other matters that you wish to bring to the audit committee's attention?

e Are there other ways in which internal auditing and the audit committees could support each other?

6 *Audit committee overall assessment*

a Are we (the audit committee) satisfied with our internal audit function?

(Item 5(c) above has been bolded to indicate that in a very significant way enterprise risk management does pertain to the audit committee, and this is the focus of the next section of this article).

ENTERPRISE RISK MANAGEMENT

Risk is best considered at the portfolio, aggregate, or organization- or enterprise-wide level. Enterprise risk management (ERM) is a process-driven methodology combined with tools that enable senior management to visualize, assess, and manage significant risks that may adversely impact the attainment of key organizational objectives (see COSO, 2004). ERM risks can be categorized as follows.

• *Strategic*: affects the achievement of strategic goals and objectives.

• *Compliance*: affects compliance with federal, state, and local laws, rules and regulations.

• *Reputational*: affects public perception and reputation, including employee morale.

• *Financial*: affects assets, technology, financial reporting, and auditing.

• *Operational*: affects ongoing management processes and procedures.

As noted above, it makes sense for the internal audit function to be viewed as the ideal group within an organization to work on ERM issues that are pertinent to each of the committees of the board. The International Professional Practices Framework (IPPF) issued by the Institute of Internal Auditors (IIA, 2011a) supports such an arrangement.

The IPPF Standard 2120 (see below) can be interpreted as follows.

• Implementation of this standard helps assess whether risk management processes are effective and encapsulates the internal auditor's assessment of:

  ○ whether organizational objectives support and align with the organization's mission; whether significant risks are identified and assessed;

  ○ whether appropriate risk responses are selected that align risks with the organization's risk appetite; and

  ○ whether relevant risk information is captured and communicated in a timely manner across the organization, enabling staff, management, and the board to carry out their responsibilities.

• The internal audit activity may gather the information to support this assessment during multiple assurance and/or consulting engagements. The results of these engagements, when viewed together, provide an understanding of the organization's risk management processes and their effectiveness.

• Risk management processes are monitored through ongoing management activities, separate evaluations, or both (see also COSO, 2009).

All that is needed is a requirement that the internal audit function considers direct reporting to different board committees—the governance, nominating, compensation, and audit committees—in their review of risk management efforts undertaken, their effectiveness, and any significant residual exposures.

APPLICABLE PROFESSIONAL STANDARDS

2120 Risk Management

The internal audit activity must evaluate the effectiveness and contribute to the improvement of risk management processes.

2120.A1 The internal audit activity must evaluate risk exposures relating to the organization's governance, operations, and information systems regarding the:

• Reliability and integrity of financial and operational information;

• Effectiveness and efficiency of operations and programs;

• Safeguarding of assets;

• Compliance with laws, regulations, policies, procedures, and contracts.

2120.A2 The internal audit activity must evaluate the potential for the occurrence of fraud and how the organization manages fraud risk.

2120.C1 During consulting engagements, internal auditors must address risk consistent with the engagement's objectives and be alert to the existence of other significant risks.

2120.C2 Internal auditors must incorporate knowledge of risks gained from consulting engagements into their evaluation of the organization's risk management processes.

2120.C3 When assisting management in establishing or improving risk management processes, internal auditors must refrain from assuming any management responsibility by actually managing risks.

Source: IIA, 2011b.

BOARD COMMUNICATIONS

Although internal audit work plans and programs may be conducted at a detailed level, most board members are unlikely to appreciate the results and findings of assurance engagements at that level of granularity. They would like for internal audit to aggregate their findings and recommendations and present them in a "big picture" fashion. In other words, the chief audit executive (CAE) must consciously work at making board briefings relevant to their corporate governance mandate. Key audit risks may be highlighted in this connection, keeping in mind the level of communications that are appropriate when dealing with board committees (Orsini, 2004).

Some of these risks, as highlighted by Orsini (2004), are outlined below.

- *Risk of missing the big picture*: Organization-wide governance and enterprise-wide risk management necessarily involve looking at risk at an aggregate, macro-level, so that the organizational (risk) profile assessed and opined upon is comprehensive and strategic.
- *Risk of missing the dynamics of change*: The auditors use a maturity-capability model and factor in the current stage of development in the executive management agenda. For instance, it would be helpful for them to use a control baselining methodology in order to track effectively any changes in people, processes, and technology, as well as the overall risk profile (see COSO, 2009).
- *Risk of subjective second-guessing of management*: Audit assessments are based on formal analyses and typically eschew opinions, hearsay, rumor, etc., that are "notoriously unreliable." However, where there exists an "execution capability" concern based on track record, it may be appropriate to drive outcomes and accountability by making critical assessments of management integrity and leadership.
- *Risk of providing insightful but not actionable intelligence*: Audit assessments of (governance) risk exposures should not merely be insightful, but meaningful, practical, and actionable. Thus, if the organization lacks the means to respond effectively or in a timely fashion because it lacks the tools, or because the solutions are simply too costly or would take too long to implement, it is imprudent for the internal auditor to raise the issue (as an extension of the idea of second-guessing management).

ASSISTING THE AUDIT COMMITTEE: A BROAD MANDATE AND MYRIAD OPPORTUNITIES FOR INTERNAL AUDIT

The report of the National Association of Corporate Directors' Blue Ribbon Commission on Audit Committees (NACD, 2000) provided the following rationale for why corporations need audit committees:

"The independent audit committee fulfills a vital role in corporate governance. The audit committee can be a critical component in ensuring quality reporting and controls, as well as the proper identification and management of risk."

Internal auditing can not only play a critical role in helping establish and define appropriate risk oversight expectations, but also identify the source(s) of information and associated monitoring processes to meet these expectations. Clearly, the audit committee of the board must be the conduit for such information.

Bromark and Hoffman (1992) note that the role of the audit committee is expanding because of the need to meet the challenges of constantly changing business conditions. They highlight the following primary responsibilities of the audit committee:

- assisting the board to fulfill its oversight responsibilities as they relate to the financial reporting process and the internal structure;
- maintaining, by way of regularly scheduled meetings, direct lines of communication between the board, financial management, the independent accountant, and internal audit.

Additional responsibilities quoted in Braiotta *et al.* (2010) include the following:

- reviewing corporate policies related to compliance with laws and regulations, ethics, conflict of interests, and the investigation of misconduct and fraud;
- conducting periodic reviews of current pending litigation of regulatory proceedings bearing on corporate governance in which the corporation is a party;
- coordinating annual reviews of compliance with corporate governance policies through internal audit or the company's independent accountants;
- performing or supervising special investigations;
- reviewing executive expenses;
- reviewing policies on sensitive payments;
- reviewing past or proposed transactions between the corporation and members of management; · reviewing the corporation's benefits programs;
- assessing the performance of financial management.

The internal audit function has long been serving as the "eyes and ears" as well as the "arms and legs" of the audit committee of the board. In the context of the above detailed list of responsibilities of the audit committee, it is evident that the internal audit role plays a critical role in keeping the audit committee abreast of the latest developments and goings on of the company.

CONCLUSION

Audit committees have typically been viewed as the group within the board structure with responsibility for risk oversight. As such, they end up relying to a large extent on the internal audit function to assure them about management's effectiveness in assessing, measuring, and responding to the array of risks that affect the organization. Although internal audit must undertake certain types of assurance engagements in this connection, establish safeguards to preserve independence and objectivity in other circumstances, and eschew taking on those activities that would compromise its independence and objectivity, it is clear that it does have a substantive role to play with respect to ERM. Without such involvement, it would simply not be possible for the audit committee to discharge its own ERM oversight function effectively.

MORE INFO

Books:

Braiotta, Louis, Jr, R. Trent Gazzaway, Robert Colson, and Sridhar Ramamoorti. *The Audit Committee Handbook*. 5th ed. Hoboken, NJ: Wiley, 2010.

Information Systems Audit and Control Association (ISACA). *Monitoring Internal Control Systems and IT: A Primer for*

Best Practice

Business Executives, Managers and Auditors on How to Embrace and Advance Best Practices. Rolling Meadows, IL: ISACA, 2010.

Institute of Internal Auditors (IIA). *International Professional Practices Framework*. Altamonte Springs, FL: IIA Research Foundation, 2011a.

Kolb, Robert W., and Donald Schwartz (eds). *Corporate Boards: Managers of Risk, Sources of Risk*. Chichester, UK: Wiley, 2010.

McNamee, David, and Georges M. Selim. *Risk Management: Changing the Internal Auditor's Paradigm*. Altamonte Springs, FL: Institute of Internal Auditors Research Foundation, 1998.

National Association of Corporate Directors (NACD). *Report of the NACD Blue Ribbon Commission on Audit Committees*. Washington, DC: NACD, 2000.

Swanson, Dan. *Swanson on Internal Auditing: Raising the Bar*. Ely, UK: IT Governance Publishing, 2010.

Articles:

Bromark, Ray, and Ralph Hoffman. "An audit committee for dynamic times." *Directors and Boards* 16:3 (Spring 1992). Online at: tinyurl.com/65txg4o

Orsini, Basil. "Auditing governance: The Canadian government offers an audit tool for addressing the risks in implementing management reform." *Internal Auditor* (June 2004). Online at: tinyurl.com/6xaagbv

Reports:

Committee of Sponsoring Organizations of the Treadway Commission (COSO). "Enterprise risk management—Integrated framework." September 2004.

Committee of Sponsoring Organizations of the Treadway Commission (COSO). "Guidance on monitoring internal control systems." February 2009.

Fraser, John, and Hugh Lindsay. "20 questions directors should ask about internal audit." 2nd ed. Canadian Institute of Chartered Accountants, 2008. Online at: www.theiia.org/download.cfm?file=2927 [PDF].

Standards:

IIA. "International standards for the professional practice of internal auditing (Standards)." Rev. ed. Altamonte Springs, FL: IIA, 2011b. Online at: tinyurl.com/42kad8u

See Also:

★ Engaging Senior Management in Internal Control (pp. 84–86)

✔ The Role of the Audit Committee (pp. 322–324)

✔ Understanding Internal Audits (pp. 324–325)

Acquisition Integration: How to Do It Successfully

by David Sadtler

EXECUTIVE SUMMARY

- Successful integration of an acquisition by the acquiring company is often the most important determinant of the overall success of the acquisition process.
- Gaining financial control of the acquired company and tight cash management are essential from the start.
- Integrating management processes and systems can be difficult and time-consuming, but it is essential if the newly acquired management team is to be involved and empowered.
- Use all available sources of information to make key management appointments as quickly as possible.
- Ensure that the key drivers of value creation are known to all involved in the project, and that the process of searching, negotiating, and integrating reflects the most important of them.
- Move as quickly as possible when integrating.

INTRODUCTION

Acquisitions of any size are a major undertaking for both the acquirer and the target. Substantial returns—in particular returns in excess of the cost of capital employed in the entire initiative—are required not only to create stockholder value, but also to justify the enormous investment of managerial time and effort that goes into a takeover. Many acquisitions succeed. Indeed, many corporate acquirers do a large number of deals and become really good at it. Making money through acquisition, for them, is a key skill to be nourished and developed. But, as repeated studies have demonstrated all too well, many acquisitions—according to some, the vast majority—fail to justify the investment involved.

The success or otherwise of acquisitions is a much studied field, and we can therefore readily identify the principle causes of failure and disappointment.[1] Among them are the payment of excessive prices, missing problems during the due diligence phase, and even the use of faulty financial logic. But perhaps the biggest contributor to the failure of acquisitions is inadequate attention to the process of integrating the newly acquired business.

MAJOR CAUSES OF FAILURE

- Paying too much—especially likely in an auction.
- Targeting the wrong company because the value creation logic is inadequate.
- Power struggles among top management and disagreement about who is to be the boss.
- Cultural obstacles, especially in cross-border deals.
- Incompatibility of IT systems.

- Applying obsolete strategic rationales such as sector diversification, vertical integration, financial synergy, and gap-filling.
- Resistance by regulatory authorities and pressure groups.
- Use of faulty financial logic—i.e. getting the numbers wrong.
- Sloppy due diligence.
- Poorly planned and executed acquisition integration.

Successful integration requires that four tasks be done well. The more attention and skill that is marshaled for this purpose, the better the result is likely to be. The four tasks are: assuming financial control, integrating processes and systems, making key managerial appointments, and ensuring that the value creation logic for the acquisition drives the whole process. Inattention to any of them can cause big trouble.

THE FOUR KEY TASKS OF SUCCESSFUL INTEGRATION

1. Assume Financial Control

Serious acquirers know that it is essential to assume immediate control over financial performance and cash management. In some cases, the target may have been left vulnerable to acquisition by poor financial management. Such businesses will need special attention in this area.

This phase involves steps such as installing corporate financial reporting procedures and clarifying expenditure-level authority. In some cases it may also involve more frequent reporting of critical cash flow components, until the required systems are bedded in and the management team of the acquired business becomes familiar with what is expected of it. For example, weekly sales figures may temporarily require early scrutiny to ensure that commercial performance has not deteriorated owing to the demands of the acquisition experience. This phase lends itself to detailed checklists and procedures, constructed with expert help and developed and honed through corporate experience.

2. Integrate Processes and Systems

If the newly acquired business is to play its part in the larger organization, its principal managerial processes—business planning, budgeting, capital expenditure approval, and human resource management—must be integrated with those of the acquirer, so that the target can begin to function as part of the larger whole as quickly as possible. The sooner operational managers can become familiar and comfortable with the new process requirements, the better able they will be to concentrate their efforts on securing competitive advantage and on realizing the benefits expected from the combination of the two organizations.

A major and sometimes seemingly overwhelming aspect of this phase of integration is that of bringing together IT systems. In recent years the IT structures of large organizations have become more all-embracing and, in the case of so-called enterprise systems, may even constitute the digital backbone of the entire business. In such circumstances the criticality of ensuring that the target's systems are quickly and effectively integrated with those of the acquirer is obvious. But sometimes the process is simply too difficult. A number of mergers and acquisitions in the so-called bancassurance sector have floundered because of IT integration problems. The prime rationale for such mergers is usually that of cross-selling—selling the products of the acquirer to the customers of the acquired company and vice versa. This is a difficult goal to achieve at the best of times, and one that is critically dependent on the effective interfacing of the merging organizations' IT systems. When this does not happen, the merger is bound to be a financial disappointment.

3. Make Key Appointments

The aim here is to do the best possible job in the shortest possible time by putting the right people in charge of the newly acquired business and moving aside those who have not made the cut. Some will say it is not possible for corporate overseers to know which managers are best for the key jobs until they have been observed in action for some time. The existing management team—the same people who perhaps failed to perform well enough to keep their business independent—may thus be left in place.

Typically, the most demanding step in this phase is the decision about who is to run the new business. Who is to be the boss? All possible sources of information about prospective candidates must be pressed into service. Managers who have experienced prior dealings with the candidate should be interviewed, the directors of the acquired business surveyed, and even individual performance reviews scrutinized. Getting this right is perhaps the most important task of all. If the right candidate is appointed, delays and failures in other areas are more likely to be remedied to everyone's satisfaction. But the wrong appointment can result in long-lasting problems and disappointment.

The object must be to find the right trade-off between speed and the effectiveness of the managerial appointment process. This may mean acting with less certainty, as opposed to delaying the decision until everyone is completely satisfied with the selection.

4. Ensure the Primacy of Value Creation

Most of all, acquirers must be crystal clear about the value creation rationale for the acquisition, and they must ensure that this thinking drives the entire acquisition process, including that of integration. All involved in the acquisition—analysts, negotiators, professional advisers, the top management of the acquiring company, and those who will be responsible for integration—must be clear about how the acquisition is to make money for the stockholders of the acquirer, and must be constantly reminded of this throughout the process.

The value creation rationale is first proposed, clarified, agreed, and approved when acquisition criteria are developed and target candidates are identified. The thinking behind how the combination with the prospective target is to enhance competitive advantage and thus generate superior returns must be clear. That rationale should drive the contract-negotiating process and the due diligence work which backs it up, so that the important drivers of value creation continue to be reflected along the way.

Finally, the small number (perhaps only two or three) of initiatives that will create the value must be given the highest priority when it comes to integrating the new business. The sooner these initiatives are successfully completed, the greater the payoff, owing to the greater present value of the cash flows achieved.

MAKING IT HAPPEN

- Design the entire acquisition process to focus on the key drivers of value creation, and ensure that the integration process deals with each as a high priority.
- Prepare a complete plan to action the four key areas—financial control, the introduction of new processes and systems, key appointments, and the pursuit of value creation—as soon as ownership changes hands.
- Develop a cadre of specialists to speed the acquisition process so that operational managers can focus on the business itself.
- Don't delay. Move fast.

OTHER FACTORS THAT CONTRIBUTE TO SUCCESS

Finally, a comment about speed. There is widespread agreement among serial acquirers that moving as quickly as possible is best. It may be tempting to keep the pressure off the acquired organization, at least temporarily, because they have been through a demanding and possibly anxious time. But momentum can be lost, benefits delayed, and the acquired management team even led to believe that the acquirers are less than serious about achieving the projected financial benefit. Speed is best.

One major UK retailer got this one wrong. To its credit, it was quite clear about its value creation rationale for the acquisition, which was that of implementing its proven EPOS (electronic point of sale) systems in the acquired company. It saw from its observation of the company—and confirmed this during the diligence process—that introducing its technology would impart major operational benefit to the target company. Inventories would be reduced, stockouts would decline, and overall customer satisfaction would increase. But it delayed implementation, reasoning that steps to integrate the target into its organization and enabling the new employees to become comfortable in their new surroundings were necessary for good morale. Sensing a lack of commitment to change, the acquired company's supply chain and IT specialists took the initiative to bolster their systems and make it hard for any subsequent changeover—along with the potential for staff reductions in the process. Operational integration was delayed for over a year and the financial benefits suffered accordingly.

The corporate development director, who had been the project manager for the acquisition, commented that this was the biggest mistake in the entire process and that it would never happen again.

In larger organizations, and especially those that regard acquisitions as a key source of future growth and competitive advantage, specialists are often developed to perform the tasks of integration. Dedicated teams can reduce the possibility of delays of the kind described above. Smaller companies, and those with less experience, may not have the luxury of maintaining a dedicated staff, but if deals become a way of life, it is probably advisable that a specialized group be formed to capture the company's experience and institutionalize emerging best practice.

CONCLUSION

Integration is a tough and demanding job, but one that frequently spells the difference between success and failure in an acquisition. The task must be treated as one of the highest priority and responsibility apportioned to the people best suited to doing it. If this is done, and if the four tasks enumerated above are handled quickly and effectively, the chances of financial, strategic, and operational success will be that much higher.

MORE INFO
Books:

Galpin, Timothy J., and Mark Herndon. *The Complete Guide to Mergers and Acquisitions: Process Tools to Support M&A Integration at Every Level*. San Francisco, CA: Jossey-Bass, 2007.

Sadtler, David, David Smith, and Andrew Campbell. *Smarter Acquisitions: Ten Steps to Successful Deals*. Harlow, UK: Pearson Education, 2008.

See Also:

★ Due Diligence Requirements in Financial Transactions (pp. 216–220)

★ Maximizing a New Strategic Alliance (pp. 233–235)

★ Why Mergers Fail and How to Prevent It (pp. 243–245)

✔ M&A Regulations: A Global Overview (pp. 348–349)

✔ Planning the Acquisition Process (pp. 350–351)

NOTE

1 The major causes of acquisition failure are dealt with at some length in Sadtler *et al.* (2008).

Coping with Equity Market Reactions to M&A Transactions
by Scott Moeller

EXECUTIVE SUMMARY

- Overall, stock returns to acquirers tend to be negative or insignificant—in contrast to target companies, where stockholders can benefit greatly.
- Companies that believe they may be targets can influence the value of an ultimate acquisition through the design of defensive techniques and by how they react to bids when they occur. Similarly, acquirers can influence the target share prices through their actions prior to the bid.
- Most acquirers are overconfident in their ability to conduct acquisitions successfully.
- Careful planning, including a robust internal and external communications plan, is required to mitigate the impact on equity markets of acquirers.
- Many factors influence equity market reactions to an M&A bid, including how friendly or hostile the bid is, the financing structure of the bid, the relative size of the two companies, and whether the transaction is a merger or an acquisition.
- Deals conducted in the most recent merger wave appear to have taken some of these issues into account and show better relative performance (relative to the market) than deals conducted in the 1980s and 1990s.

INTRODUCTION

It would be nice if the markets were to react consistently in response to the announcement of M&A deals. But they don't. At least not always. But you can depend on one thing: In the short run, shareholders of target companies benefit more than those of the acquiring company.

It is important to know how to cope with the likely equity market reaction to the announcement of a deal. First of all, you need to understand what those likely reactions will be ... and then to work out whether there is anything that can be done to influence the market. Bidders can mitigate the likely negative market reaction to their share price, and targets may be able to provoke even higher bids.

This article discusses public companies only—as these are naturally the only ones with an "equity market reaction." However, one can properly extrapolate their experience to private companies as well. While most advisers and principals in privately held companies take into account the experience of publicly held companies, the reaction of the equity markets regarding the bidder's share price is not dependent on whether the target is public or private. Either way, the shareholder value of bidders declines, on average, following the announcement of a large acquisition.

"Most mergers fail. If that's not a bona fide fact, plenty of smart people think it is. McKinsey & Company says it's true. Harvard, too. Booz Allen & Hamilton, KPMG, A.T. Kearney—the list goes on. If a deal enriches an acquirer's shareholders, the statistics say, it is probably an accident." *New York Times*, February 28, 2008

EQUITY MARKET REACTIONS FOR TARGETS

Relatively few deals make money for the bidding company's shareholders. The market rather consistently shows that bidding companies lose money for their shareholders, or at best break even around the time of the announcement of a takeover, whereas target companies attract offer premiums that typically range from 20% to 40%. Stock prices often rise above the offer price if a competing bidder is anticipated.

These returns are relatively consistent in the United States and the United Kingdom, with the data for other countries less clear but indicating similar results. When the bidder and target returns are combined, the overall shareholder wealth effects are typically found to be insignificant over the short term and positive over the longer term.

In the absence of a competing bid, when a takeover is announced the target company's stock price typically rises to a level *below* the offer price, but slowly rises to approach the bid price as time approaches the closing date when the final deal is consummated, which for most deals is 3–6 months after the announcement date (Figure 1). This is because there is some risk that the deal will not go through or will be repriced (usually lower) because of negative information that the bidder finds while conducting due diligence on the target (see "Due Diligence Requirements in Financial Transactions" for a discussion of the best ways to conduct due diligence in M&A deals).

INFLUENCING TARGET COMPANY STOCK PRICES

The target company itself can have an influence on the potential price offered in a number of ways:
- By having a strong defense in place to protect the company from an unsolicited takeover bid. Such defenses can include so-called poison pills (including under-funded pension plans), shares owned by insiders or in friendly hands, golden and silver parachutes not just for senior management but for a wider group of employees (often called "tin parachutes"), and a history of successfully fending off hostile bidders. Research has shown that these defenses, especially poison pills, do result in higher premiums for target companies.
- Most of these defenses are put in place to make it more difficult (that is, expensive), but not impossible, to be purchased. For example, Mellon Bank put in place tin parachutes for all its employees following an unsuccessful hostile bid by the Bank of New York in 1998; when later, in 2006, a friendly deal was proposed and accepted by Mellon Bank, the senior managers and employees were requested to waive their golden, silver, and tin parachute rights in order to put them on an equal footing with the Bank of New York employees, who had no such employment provisions.
- By letting the market know that a high threshold premium value will be required for any unsolicited bid before the board of directors will recommend it to the shareholders. Yahoo! used this technique when it successfully fended off an unwelcome bid from Microsoft in early 2008 that had a 62% premium associated with it (a so-called "bear hug" offer, which designates an offer above the typical premium range of 20–40%).
- By encouraging competing bids. By opening up the purchase of the company to an auction, the directors admit that the company is for sale and will likely lose its independence, but that they are actively seeking the highest possible price. After Morrisons, the supermarket chain in the United Kingdom, made a formal offer to purchase Safeway for £2.4 billion in January 2003, an auction for Safeway ensued with competing bids from Asda (controlled by Wal-Mart) and J. Sainsbury. There was a feeding frenzy that included Tesco, retail magnate Sir Philip Green, and venture capitalists Kohlberg Kravis Roberts. The price that Morrisons ultimately paid for Safeway was £3.0 billion.

Bidders can also influence the target company's share price, naturally wanting to keep the price of the target down. The

Figure 1. Movement of target company share price

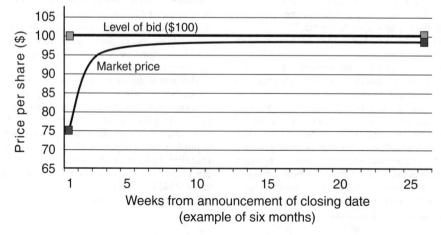

most common technique is to conduct a "street sweep," whereby the target company's shares (or a controlling interest in the target) are purchased in a blitzkrieg that gives the market and the target's management no time to react before the takeover is effectively complete. This is very difficult to conduct in practice, and is most successful when a small number of shareholders control a large percentage of the target's shares or where the bidder already has a large ownership in the target. Thus, for example, Malcolm Glazer, who for a long time had been holding 28% of the publicly listed football club Manchester United, purchased a similarly sized holding from Cubic Expression in May 2004, and thus in one purchase came to control the club.

Many bidders, when purchasing their toeholds in potential targets, will publicly announce that they have no interest "at this time" in making a bid for the entire company, maintaining that their holding is a financial interest only "because the shares represent an attractive investment." This was the position declared by Malcolm Glazer in the Manchester United case from the time he first disclosed a 3% ownership in the club in March 2003 up until the time he bought the shares that gave him control in 2005. In his case, the market expected a bid for the entire company, but his public position nevertheless may have lowered the price he ultimately had to pay for that controlling interest.

In all of these situations, it must be noted that proper legal advice must be taken in order not to fall foul of the many regulations and laws that prohibit market manipulation.

EQUITY MARKET REACTIONS FOR BIDDERS

The shareholders of acquiring companies are not as fortunate as those of the targets. On average, their shares decline in value around the time the company announces its intention to take over another company. Thus, in the example above, when Morrisons launched its surprise bid for Safeway (at a 30.3% premium to the prior day's close), its shares declined 14.3%, and when J. Sainsbury entered with its competing bid, its own share price declined on the day by 3.5%. The shareholders of neither bidder benefited, in distinct contrast to Safeway's shareholders.

Because of the relative consistency over time of stock market movements in response to deal announcements, the market will assume that future deals will do the same, including that only 30–40% of all deals are successful, that mid- and long-term shareholder wealth declines by 10–35%, and that the share prices for acquirers and targets move within certain ranges (on average) around the announcement day. Merger arbitrageurs—whether in hedge funds or investment banks—take large positions knowing that bidders' share prices tend to drop immediately after a deal announcement and that targets will see share price appreciation. This then becomes a virtuous (or vicious, for the bidder) cycle, where the movement in the share prices is magnified by this arbitrage activity.

In many cases these movements in share price can lead to extreme changes in share ownership. For example, when the Deutsche Börse (the largest stock exchange at the time in mainland Europe) made a bid for the London Stock Exchange in 2004, the Anglo-American arbitrageurs rapidly became the largest group of shareholders, displacing the long-term German shareholders, whose ownership was reduced to only a third. It was these arbitrageurs who forced the Deutsche Börse CEO to drop the bid in March 2005, leading to a 30% price rise in the Deutsche Börse shares as it became less and less likely that the deal would succeed.

As with the Deutsche Börse CEO who didn't anticipate this change, most managers seem to be oblivious to facts which appear to be obvious to those outside the company. A DLA Piper survey in 2006 showed that 81% of corporate respondents rated their M&A experience as fairly or highly successful, and over 90% of venture capitalists felt the same, yet we know that 60–70% of all deals fail.

INFLUENCING THE STOCK PRICE OF THE BIDDER

In most M&A situations, the bidder controls the timing of when the bid is publicized. The notable exception to this is when there is a market leak, but even in these situations the leak either happens early in the negotiations when it is easier to deny to the press that any deal is pending (as the negotiations have not progressed sufficiently far for a deal to be in place) or late enough in the proceedings that an emergency communication plan should already be in place for just such a situation.

The announcement event is therefore not a surprise to the bidder. Through proper planning and the use of external advisers (including investment banks, but also specialist public relations firms), positive spin on the deal can be delivered to the market: Benefits to all stakeholders are emphasized; new markets are announced; product innovations are forecast. Support from clients, suppliers, and even outside parties (such as local government) can be rallied. Potential problems will have been anticipated, and strategies to neutralize these will have been developed and disclosed.

Nevertheless, to paraphrase Robert Burns, "The best laid plans of mice and men / Go oft awry." In M&A deals, there are ultimately just too many individuals involved and there is just so much that can go wrong that much often does. Therefore, the press turns negative, equity analysts forecast too much dilution of earnings, cash flow declines, and clients, suppliers, employees, and even managers become very worried about their positions—and naturally assume the worst.

Thus the acquirer must have a very robust communications plan at the ready. Not every contingency will be anticipated, but many can be. Most important is to have teams in place to be able to respond quickly to any false rumors and to replace immediately any such gossip with fact. The company needs to stay in control—as best it can—during the entire deal process. The most effective way to do this is to have a continuous stream of positive stories prepared for periodic, if not even daily, release. Constant communication with the staff of both bidder and target can go a long way towards allaying anxiety and even panic.

One must remember that those who can benefit from the flip side will be acting accordingly as well: these include competitors who see opportunities to grab market share and even valued staff, and trading arbitrageurs who have made bets in the market that the share price will fall. These arbitrageurs certainly have been very successful in pushing down the price of acquirers in many deals, as in the above example where the Deutsche Börse was forced to drop its bid for the London Stock Exchange.

OTHER FACTORS AFFECTING EQUITY VALUES

The above discussion "averages" the results for many companies. Individual deals and individual companies will show different results and provide different returns over time from these averages, and takeover and defensive tactics will also need to be customized for each situation.

There are also other factors that will impact on the equity markets for both the target and bidder's share price. When cash is used to finance the deal instead of issuing more shares, the returns to the bidder are usually higher. In countries such as the United States, where tender offers (often hostile) are common, these do better than friendly mergers. The smaller the target is in relation to the acquirer, the more likely it is that the bidder's share price will not decline relative to the market.

There are also differences in short- and long-term shareholder value effects. This article has looked principally at the short-term effects around the time of deal announcement, but if a longer-term perspective is taken (more than six months), then the negative returns to the bidder are reduced, although still typically remaining negative. Also, one can look at the combined returns when the bidder and target are taken together over the longer term: in this case as noted earlier, history shows that the overall shareholder wealth effects are typically positive.

CONCLUSION

Despite the doom and gloom of the analyses that have looked at the success of companies that merge or acquire, there is some hope: Several recent studies (from Towers Perrin/Cass Business School, McKinsey, and KPMG) have shown that acquiring companies since 2003 are doing better with their deals. Not much, but at least measurably so. Some of the suggestions we've made in this article have been recently more widely adopted by the market. There *is* more focus on careful deal selection and corporate governance. Post-merger

integration *is* receiving attention even before the deal closes, and sometimes even before announcement. There is hope—and evidence—with some of these recent studies that perhaps equity markets may start to award an equity premium to companies that acquire well.

MAKING IT HAPPEN
THE KEY FACTORS

- Understand that the premium offered to the target is only one aspect of the deal's success, and that it is often overshadowed by other factors, especially people issues.
- Formulate a plan for addressing surprises. Try to identify all the ways that the deal could fail … and then look for still more ways it could go wrong.
- Do not be overconfident in your ability to integrate an acquisition successfully. Prior experience is helpful, but not sufficient. Each deal is different.
- Proper legal advice should always be taken.
- Plan for a dynamic deal process where changes will need to be made to the acquisition strategy.
- Incorporate a robust communications plan into any deal.

MORE INFO
Books:

Gaughan, Patrick A. *Mergers, Acquisitions, and Corporate Restructurings.* 5th ed. Hoboken, NJ: Wiley, 2010.
Moeller, Scott, and Chris Brady. *Intelligent M&A: Navigating the Mergers and Acquisitions Minefield.* Chichester, UK: Wiley, 2007.
Sudarsanam, Sudi. *Creating Value from Mergers and Acquisition: The Challenges.* Harlow, UK: FT Prentice Hall, 2003.

See Also:
★ Acquisition Integration: How to Do It Successfully (pp. 211–213)
✔ Planning the Acquisition Process (pp. 350–351)
✔ Using the Market-Value Method for Acquisitions (pp. 355–356)

Due Diligence Requirements in Financial Transactions
by Scott Moeller

EXECUTIVE SUMMARY

- There is an urgency for companies to conduct intensive due diligence in financial deals, both before announcement (when it should be easy to call off the deal) and after.
- Traditional due diligence merely verifies the history of the target and projects the future based on that history; correctly

applied due diligence digs much deeper and provides insight into the future value of the target across a wide variety of factors.
- Although due diligence does enable prospective acquirers to find potential black holes, the aim of due diligence should be this and more, including looking for opportunities to realize future prospects for the enlarged corporation through

leveraging of the acquiring and the acquired firms' resources and capabilities, identification of synergistic benefits, and post-merger integration planning.
- Due diligence should start from the inception of a deal.
- Areas to probe include finance, management, employees, IT, legal, risk management systems, culture, innovation, and even ethics.
- Critical to the success of the due diligence process is the identification of the necessary information required, where it can best be sourced, and who is best qualified to review and interpret the data.
- Requesting too much information is just as dangerous as requesting too little. Having the wrong people looking at the data is also hazardous.

INTRODUCTION
This is not your father's due diligence.

Due diligence is one of the two most critical elements in the success of a mergers and acquisitions (M&A) transaction (the other being the proper execution of the integration process), according to a survey conducted in 2006 by the Economist Intelligence Unit (EIU) and Accenture. Due diligence was considered to be of greater importance than target selection, negotiation, pricing the deal, and the development of the company's overall M&A strategy.

But not even a decade ago, when due diligence was conducted in financial transactions, the focus was almost always limited to financial factors, pending law suits, and information technology (IT) systems. Today, those areas remain important, but they must be supplemented during the due diligence process by attention to the assessment of other factors: management and employees (and not just their contracts, but how good they actually are in their jobs), commercial operations (products, marketing, strategy, and competition—both existing and potential), and corporate culture (can the companies actually work together when they're merged?). But even these areas are now mainstream when due diligence is conducted. Newer areas of due diligence are developing rapidly: risk management, innovation, and ethical (including corporate social responsibility) due diligence.

The 2006 EIU/Accenture survey also found that although due diligence is considered as a top challenge by 23% of CEOs in making domestic acquisitions, this rises to 41% in the much more complex cross-border transactions, which make up the majority of financial transactions, even in today's depressed markets.

ORGANIZING FOR DUE DILIGENCE
It's a two-way street: Buyers must understand what they are buying; and targets must understand who's pursuing them and whether they should accept an offer.

To be successfully conducted, due diligence must have senior management involvement and control, often assisted by outside experts such as management consulting firms, accountants, investment banks, and maybe even specialist investigation firms.

To quote from a PricewaterhouseCoopers report issued in late 2002: "We always have to make decisions based on imperfect information. But the more information you have and the more you transform that into what we call knowledge, the more likely you are to be successful."

That said, there is only a certain amount that can be handled by the number of people involved, the time restrictions under which they are working, and the quality and variety of resources available to them. Moreover, there is the danger of being overloaded by too much information if those involved do not have good management and analytical methods they can deploy.

By and large, it is not the quantity of information that matters so much as its quality and how it is used. Although diligence may not be cheap (as a result of fees charged for often highly complex work by professional services firms), the alternative of litigation or the destruction of stockholder value (as a consequence of having been "penny wise and pound foolish" in the execution of the due diligence process) may prove far more costly in the long run.

THE DUE DILIGENCE PROCESS
Although due diligence may be only one part of an acquisition or investment exercise, in many ways it is by far the most significant aspect of the M&A process. Done properly, acquirers should be better able to control the risks inherent in any deal, while simultaneously contributing to the ultimate effective management of the target and the realization of the goals of the acquisition.

As an instrument through which to reveal and remedy potential sources of risk, due diligence—by confirming the expectations of the buyer and the understanding of the seller—enables firms to formulate remedies and solutions to enable a deal to proceed. In many ways, due diligence lends comfort to an acquirer's senior management, the board, and ultimately the stockholders, who should all insist on a rigorous due diligence process, which provides them with relative (though not absolute) assurance that the deal is sensible, and that they have uncovered any problems pertaining to it that may derail matters in the future.

Ideally, due diligence should start during the conception phase of the deal, and initially it can use publicly available information. It should then continue throughout the merger process as further proprietary information becomes available. Full use of the due diligence information collected would mean that it is not just used to make a go/no-go decision about whether the acquisition should proceed and to determine the terms of the deal, but that the findings from due diligence should also be incorporated in the planning for the postmerger integration.

Clearly it is easier to obtain high-quality data if the deal is friendly; in unfriendly deals due diligence may never progress further than publicly available data. This lack of access to internal information has scuppered many a deal—for example, the takeover attempt by Sir Philip Green of Marks & Spencer in 2004.

THE SCOPE OF DUE DILIGENCE[1]
Before undertaking due diligence—given the typical time, cost, and data constraints—it is important to focus on areas that are

likely to have the most impact on value. Thus, due diligence should be tailored to:

- the type of transaction;
- the motivation for doing the deal;
- plans for the target once acquired;
- the impact on the existing operations of the acquirer.

Some basic questions to ask include:

- Is the acquirer a strategic or a financial buyer?
- How fully integrated will the target be once acquired, and in what time frame?
- Is the whole company being acquired?
- Does the target represent new product lines, marketing channels, or geographic territories, or is there overlap with the acquirer's existing operations?
- Will certain functional operations of the target be eliminated?
- Will the IT systems of the target be retained?
- How will the rating agencies respond to the transaction?

TYPES OF DUE DILIGENCE INFORMATION

Each industry has its own special due diligence requirements. For example, an insurance company will need a review of major policies, actuarial assumptions, and sales practices, whereas the purchase of a bank would require a review of its marking policies and risk management systems.

As noted above, one starts with external sources. Although these rarely provide a sufficient overview of an organization at the level required to obtain a proper understanding, secondary sources do equip management with valuable information, allowing them to strategize and develop honed, and more focused, questions for their further internal due diligence on the prospective acquisition.

In spite of the centrality of financial, legal, cultural, and other areas of due diligence, examples abound of transactions that were completed without effective due diligence being done through lack of time, or because management was overconfident in its ability to understand the target, resulting in devastating losses of stockholder value.

Financial Due Diligence

Financial due diligence enables companies to obtain a view of an organization's historical profits, which can then be used as a canvas on which to paint a picture of the company's financial future. Developed around an array of building blocks—including auditing and verifying financial results on which an offer is based, identifying deal breakers, reviewing forecasts and budgets, pinpointing areas where warranties or indemnities may be needed, and providing confidence in the underlying performance, and therefore future profits, of a company—financial due diligence allows the bidder to make the proper offer for the target, or perhaps uncover reasons for not proceeding with the deal.

Legal Due Diligence

As companies expand into hitherto commercially less experienced parts of the world in search of new markets and products (such as China, Vietnam, or certain countries in the Middle East and Africa), the requirement to conduct effective and sufficient legal due diligence work can prove more trying,

and in certain cases near impossible. Nevertheless, the need to check title over assets that are being sold, and to ensure that the entity being acquired is legitimate and free of any contractual or legal obstacles which might derail the M&A process, will undoubtedly remain pivotal to the due diligence process no matter where the target resides. Governmental regulatory concerns, such as monopolies, employment law, taxes, etc., will also be investigated as part of the legal due diligence.

Commercial Due Diligence

Given that companies are bought not for their past performance but for their ability to generate profits in the future, acquirers must use commercial due diligence to obtain an objective view of a company's markets, prospects, and competitive position. As noted by Towers Perrin in a discussion of operational due diligence, there is a "need to look at all the relevant sources of value to avoid unpleasant surprises."[2] This means a deeper query into certain operations that heavily determine a target's ultimate value to the acquirer—i.e. growth opportunities and resulting future income.

Whether obtained to reduce risk associated with the transaction, to help with the company valuation, or to plan for post-merger integration, commercial due diligence enables acquirers to examine a target's markets and performance—identifying strengths, weaknesses, opportunities, and threats. Focused on the likely strategic position of the combined entity, commercial due diligence, by reviewing the drivers that underpin forecasts and business plans, concentrates on the ability of the target's businesses to achieve the projected sales and profitability growth post acquisition.

Despite the seemingly obvious pivotal benefits that commercial due diligence can bring to acquiring organizations, *Competitive Intelligence Magazine* reported in 2003 that "only 10% of respondents to an Accenture survey of M&A practitioners said that their due diligence process included four or more sources from outside the company."

Innovation Due Diligence

Linked closely to commercial risk but meriting special attention is the due diligence of the research and development (R&D) process. This is more than just an analysis of intellectual property rights. Many non-industrial companies may not have explicit R&D groups, but still remain dependent on the development of intellectual property to maintain their business growth. It must be understood how this is encouraged.

Management Due Diligence

Naturally, acquirers need to perform discrete investigations in order to evaluate both the competence of the target's management and the quality of their past performances, and to ensure that the management of the target and acquirer are compatible. One would think that this would be recognized by any acquirer today, but one acquisition team recently told us that their senior management felt confident enough in their own ability to conduct their management due diligence that they could do this "over a cup of tea," basically, by eyeing the management team from across the table. Nevertheless, in the rush to do deals in the peak merger year of 2007, many of the largest deals properly included extensive management surveys, including 360 degree appraisals, psychometrics, and even investigative reporting.

Cultural Due Diligence

Since one of the more difficult areas for integrating two companies concerns combining their corporate cultures, due care needs to be applied to ensure cultural fit. Indeed, cultural fit is so important that 85% of underperforming acquisitions blame different management attitudes and culture for the poor performance of the combined entities, as reported at a conference in 2006 by Towers Perrin and Cass Business School. Thus, by assessing soft factors such as a company's leadership style, corporate behavior, and even dress code, an acquirer may be able to build an accurate picture of a target's values, attitudes, and beliefs, and so determine if there will be a good cultural fit within their own organizational structure.

Ethical Due Diligence

There is an emerging area, best described as ethical due diligence, that overlaps in many ways with management and cultural due diligence but is not to be confused with legal due diligence. The most obvious requirement of ethical due diligence is to determine whether management have engaged in unethical professional acts (as defined, usually, by the ethical standards of the acquiring company), but it also necessarily includes assessment of the corporate social responsibility activities of the company.

Risk Management Due Diligence

It is critical to understand how the target reports and monitors its inherent business risks. The events in financial and real estate markets in the past several years highlight the need to check carefully not just all risk management systems, but also the *culture* of risk in a company.

CASE STUDY
FAILURE IN DUE DILIGENCE: VERISIGN'S PURCHASE OF JAMBA

In June 2004, VeriSign acquired privately held Berlin-based Jamba for US$273 million. VeriSign was an internet infrastructure services company which provided the services that enabled over 3,000 enterprises and 500,000 websites to operate. Through its domain name registry it managed over 50 million digital identities in more than 350 languages. Revenues exceeded US$1 billion dollars in the previous year. VeriSign had extensive experience with acquisitions, having made 17 acquisitions prior to Jamba, including four that were valued at more than this particular purchase.

Jamba had millions of subscribers and was the leading provider of mobile content delivery services in Europe. It was best known for the Crazy Frog character used in the most successful ring tone of all time.

But, beneath the surface, trouble was brewing that could easily have been uncovered by even the most rudimentary

due diligence: complaints to regulators had noted that Jamster, the UK and US rebranding of Jamba, was targeting children, despite the fact that Jamster's mobile content services were intended for adult customers only. Perhaps more disturbingly, only days before the acquisition VeriSign discovered that a significant portion of Jamba's profits came from the distribution of adult content in Germany—despite a VeriSign policy of not supporting adult or pornographic companies. There were backlashes in Germany over other issues and Jamba was forced to make a declaration of discontinuance regarding many of its contracts. Other legal actions were pending in Germany and the United States.

Unsurprisingly, Jamba's revenues peaked early the following year.

CASE STUDY
NO CULTURAL FIT FOR SONY IN THE MOVIE INDUSTRY

In 1988, Sony (a Japanese electronics manufacturer) acquired Columbia Pictures (an American moviemaker) for US$3.4 billion. With cultures that could scarcely have been more different, the acquisition—which involved little consideration of cultural fit between the two entities—failed to live up to commercial expectations, with Sony famously writing down US$2.7 billion on the deal by 1994.

CONCLUSION

According to the EIU/Accenture survey, only 18% of executives were highly confident that their company had carried out satisfactory due diligence. This is probably due to the lack of attention given to this critical aspect of a deal, or to the view that it is merely a box-ticking exercise conducted by outside advisers.

In short, the probing of a wide variety of due diligence areas should provide a counterbalance to the short-termism of traditionally limited financial and legal due diligence, helping acquirers to understand how markets and competitive environments will affect their purchase, and confirming that the opportunity is a sensible one to undertake from a commercial and strategic perspective, especially in cross-border deals.

MAKING IT HAPPEN

Key factors in conducting informative and timely due diligence are:

- Identifying the critical areas to probe: financial, legal, business, cultural, management, ethical, risk management, etc.
- Identifying the most important information to collect in those areas, as there is never enough time to look at everything in as much detail as one might want.
- Identifying the right sources for the desired information.

★

Best Practice

- Identifying the right people to review the data: this should include those who know most about that area and also those who will be managing the business post acquisition.

Due diligence should not be a mere confirmation of the facts. Bridging the strategic review and completion phases of any merger or acquisition exercise, the due diligence process allows prospective acquirers to understand as much as possible about the target company, and to make sure that what it believes is being purchased is actually what is being purchased. The due diligence process digs deeper *before* the point of no return in consummating a deal.

MORE INFO

Books:

Howson, Peter. *Due Diligence: The Critical Stage in Mergers and Acquisitions*. Aldershot, UK: Gower Publishing, 2003.

Moeller, Scott, and Chris Brady. *Intelligent M&A: Navigating the Mergers and Acquisitions Minefield*. Chichester, UK: Wiley, 2007.

Sudarsanam, Sudi. *Creating Value from Mergers and Acquisition: The Challenges*. Harlow, UK: Pearson Education, 2003.

Article:

May, Michael, Patricia Anslinger, and Justin Jenk. "Avoiding the perils of traditional due diligence." *Outlook Journal* (July 2002). Online at: tinyurl.com/67mh4cj [PDF].

Website:

Intelligent Mergers—Scott Moeller's blog: intelligentmergers.com

See Also:

★ Acquisition Integration: How to Do It Successfully (pp. 211–213)

★ Coping with Equity Market Reactions to M&A Transactions (pp. 213–216)

★ CSR: More than PR, Pursuing Competitive Advantage in the Long Run (pp. 187–189)

✔ M&A Regulations: A Global Overview (pp. 348–349)

✔ Planning the Acquisition Process (pp. 350–351)

NOTES

1 Adapted from: Fell, Bruce D. "Operational due diligence for value." *Emphasis* (2006/3): 6–9. Online at: tinyurl.com/d7w36t

2 *Ibid.*

Going Private: Public-to-Private Leveraged Buyouts
by Luc Renneboog

EXECUTIVE SUMMARY

- Listed firms go private through a leveraged buyout (LBO)—for example, a management buyout or an institutional buyout).
- Reasons for going private are the value of the tax shield, increased incentives for management through equity ownership, to reduce cash flows, to avoid the direct and indirect costs of maintaining a listing, or as an anti-takeover device.
- At announcement of the LBO of a listed firm, the premium (the offer price relative to the pre-buyout share price) amounts to about 40% and abnormal returns to about 25%.
- Good candidates for LBOs have stable cash flows, low and predictable capital investment needs, a liquid balance sheet with collateralizable assets, an established market position, and are in a recession-proof industry.

INTRODUCTION

When a listed company is acquired and subsequently delisted, the transaction is referred to as a public-to-private or going-private transaction. As most such transactions are financed by substantial borrowing, which is used to repurchase most of the outstanding equity, they are called leveraged buyouts (LBOs). An overview of the different types of LBO is given in Table 1.

Four categories are generally recognized: management buyouts (MBOs), management buyins (MBIs), buyin management buyouts (BIMBOs), and institutional buyouts (IBOs).

WHY DO LISTED FIRMS GO PRIVATE?
Reduction of Stockholder-Related Agency Costs

The central dilemma of principal-agent models is how to get the manager (the agent) to act in the best interests of the stockholders (the principals) when the agent has interests that diverge from those of the principals and an informational advantage.

- The *incentive realignment* hypothesis states that the gains in stockholder wealth that arise from going private are a result of providing more rewards for managers (through an increased ownership stake) that induce them to act in line with the interests of investors. Furthermore, in the case of an institutional buyout, the concentration of ownership leads to improved monitoring of management.
- The *free cash flow* hypothesis suggests that the expected stock returns follow from debt-induced mechanisms that force managers to pay out free cash flows. Free cash flow is the cash flow in excess of that required to fund all projects that have positive net present value (NPV) when discounted at the appropriate cost of capital. The high leverage does

Table 1. Summary definitions of types of public-to-private transaction

Term	Definition
LBO	*Leveraged buyout.* Acquisition in which a nonstrategic bidder acquires a listed or non-listed company utilizing funds containing a proportion of debt that is substantially above the industry average. If the acquired company is listed, it is subsequently delisted (in a going-private or public-to-private transaction)
MBO	*Management buyout.* An LBO in which the target firm's management bids for control of the firm, often supported by a third-party private equity investor
MBI	*Management buyin.* An LBO in which an outside management team (often backed by a third-party private equity investor) acquires a company and replaces the incumbent management team
BIMBO	*Buyin management buyout.* An LBO in which the bidding team comprises members of the incumbent management team and externally hired managers, often alongside a third-party private equity investor
IBO	*Institutional buyin.* An LBO in which an institutional investor or private equity house acquires a company. Incumbent management can be retained and may be rewarded with equity participation
Reverse LBO	A transaction in which a firm that was previously taken private reobtains public status through a secondary initial public offering (SIPO)

not allow managers to grow the firm beyond its optimal size (so-called "empire building") and at the expense of value creation.

Tax Benefits
The substantial increase in cash flow creates a major tax shield, which increases the pre-transaction (or pre-recapitalization) value. After the buyout, firms pay almost no tax for a period of at least five years. Consequently, the (new) stockholders gain, but the government loses out.

Reduction of Transaction Costs
The cost of maintaining a stock exchange listing is very high. Although the direct costs (fees paid to the stock exchange) are relatively small, the indirect costs of being listed are substantial (for example the cost of complying with corporate governance/transparency regulations, which requires larger accounting/legal departments, the cost of investor relations managers, and the cost of management time in general, etc.). For a medium-sized listed company these indirect costs are estimated at US$750,000–1,500,000 annually. The going-private transaction eliminates many of the transaction costs.

Wealth Transfers from Bondholders to Stockholders
Gains in stockholder wealth that arise from going private result from the expropriation of value belonging to pre-transaction bondholders. There are three mechanisms through which a firm can transfer wealth from bondholders to stockholders: an unexpected increase in the asset risk (the asset substitution risk); large increases in dividends; or an unexpected issue of debt of higher or equal seniority, or of shorter maturity. In a going-private transaction, the last mechanism in particular can lead to substantial expropriation of bondholder wealth if protective covenants are not in place.

Defense Against Takeover
Afraid of losing their jobs if a hostile suitor takes control, the management may decide to take the company private. Thus, an MBO is the ultimate defensive measure against a hostile stockholder or tender offer.

Undervaluation
As a firm is a portfolio of projects, there may be asymmetric information between the management and outsiders concerning the maximum value that can be realized with the assets in place. If management believes that the share price is undervalued in relation to the firm's true potential, they may privatize the firm through an MBO. Alternatively, if an external party believes that it is able to generate more value with the assets of the firm, the firm may be taken over by means of an IBO or MBI.

HOW HIGH ARE THE PREMIUMS PAID IN LBOS
The premiums (relative to the pre-transaction share price) are in line with those on ordinary takeover transactions: over the last 25 years they have been in the range of 35% to 45%. The cumulative average abnormal returns (CAARs) calculated over two months around the event date (the announcement of the going-public transaction) average around 25%, which is similar to those of ordinary takeover transactions. The abnormal returns are equal to the realized returns corrected for the market movement (the return of the market index) and the riskiness of the firm (the beta).

THE PHASES OF THE BUYOUT PROCESS
Figure 1 shows the structure of the buyout process, the main research questions for each phase of the process, and their explanations. The first phase (Intent) consists of the identification of good LBO candidates; the second phase (Impact) comprises the actual LBO and an analysis of the expected returns; the third phase (Process) consists of the value creation while the firm is privately listed; and the fourth phase (Duration) concerns the duration of the private phase until the main shareholder exits through an IPO or trade sale. At every phase, eight main hypotheses or triggers can be examined: realignment of incentives, acquisition of control, reduction of free cash flow, wealth transfers from various stakeholders, tax benefits, a reduction of transaction costs, the importance of takeover defense mechanisms, and undervaluation of the target firm.

What makes firms good buyout candidates? The "Intent" phase encompasses the characteristics of firms prior to their decision to go private and compares these characteristics to those of firms which remain publicly listed. Out of the eight value drivers (mentioned above) to go public in the United States, the reduction in taxation resulting from the tax shield is the main one. Thus, firms with a high tax bill may consider

Finance Essentials

222

Best Practice

Figure 1. Phases and hypotheses of going private

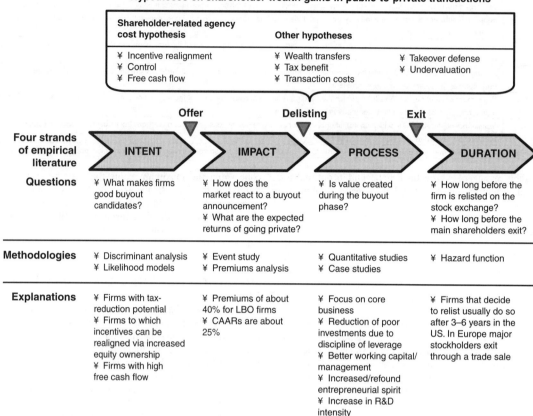

going private with a lot of leverage *provided that* a stable cash flow stream enables the firm to service the debt. In addition, firms with substantial free cash flow (excess cash) that could lead to value-destroying investments have also been shown to be prime candidates for a public-to-private transaction. In the United States, decisions to go private in the 1980s were frequently motivated by anti-takeover defense strategies.

How does the market react to a buyout? The *impact* of an LBO offer can be estimated by analyzing the immediate stock price reaction or the premiums paid to pre-transaction stockholders. The CAARs and premiums reflect the expected value creation when the firm becomes privately held. They are larger at the announcement for firms in which pre-transaction managers hold small equity stakes, which implies that the buyout may induce a realignment of incentives. Furthermore, the fact that the buyout will reduce large free cash flows triggers positive share price returns. Also, for firms paying a large amount of tax, the buyout announcement leads to positive abnormal returns. Finally, bondholder wealth transfers appear to exist but are playing only a very limited role in the wealth gains of pre-buyout stockholders.

Is value created during the private phase? Once a company is privatized, what post-buyout processes lead to more wealth creation? The post-transaction performance improvements

are in line with those expected at the announcement of a going-private transaction. The causes of the performance and efficiency improvements are primarily the organizational structure of the LBO (high leverage and strong (managerial) ownership concentration). In the private phase, a firm's productivity increases due to a focused strategy and the avoidance of excess growth. Post-buyout performance improvements arise from an improved quality of the R&D function and intensified venturing activities. This revamped entrepreneurial spirit follows from reduced stockholder-related agency costs. Also typical of firms that go private is a significant improvement in the management of working capital.

How long is it before a firm is relisted on the stock exchange? An investor may decide to end a company's private status through an exit via a SIPO (secondary initial public offering, or reverse LBO). Especially in the United States, some firms seem to use the organizational form of a privatization transaction as a temporary shock therapy to enable them to restructure efficiently, while others view the LBO as a sustainable and superior organizational form. Firms that do a reverse LBO have usually been private for three to six years. In Europe, major stockholders usually do not exit via a SIPO but perform a trade sale. The longevity of private ownership and its determinants are studied in the literature on *duration*.

CASE STUDY
SAFEWAY AND KROGER

One of the key characteristics of going private through an LBO is the high-leverage structure that results. Nevertheless, the discipline of high leverage can also be induced by a leveraged recapitalization without privatization. Denis (1994) investigated the difference between the two approaches by contrasting two grocery store firms—Kroger, which undertook a recapitalization, and Safeway, which took the LBO route. The higher leverage and the pressure to generate cash led to a performance increase at Kroger, but the performance improvement at Safeway was significantly higher. Why should this have been so?

• Top managers at Safeway put part of their wealth at stake and hold substantial equity stakes (amounting to a total of about 20%) such that every managerial decision has a significant direct impact on their wealth. In addition, management is even more directed towards a focus on value as its bonuses are linked to the market value of assets and managers receive stock options.

• There is a major external stockholder (the private equity firm Kohlberg Kravis Roberts, or KKR) that monitors the firm closely and ensures that management does not maximize its private benefits at the expense of other stockholders and the firm itself.

• Safeway restructured the board to consist of management and representatives of KKR, who provided expertise on corporate restructuring.

• Safeway restructured its operations more drastically than Kroger, closing stores that did not generate sufficient operational cash flows. It also cut back on discretionary expenses, such as advertising and maintenance, to meet its short-term debt obligations, and it cut non-core business.

• Safeway removed leverage-induced cash flow streams as fast as possible through asset sales in order to increase capital expenditures.

CONCLUSION

Firms that undergo leveraged (management) buyouts have significant advantages over publicly listed firms. First, the high leverage creates value through the tax shield. Second, the management is incentivized to focus on value creation because it (co-) owns the firm (in the case of a MBO/MBI) or because strict monitoring of the incumbent management is induced by the major stockholders (in the case of an IBO). The organizational structure reduces the firm's free cash flow such that money is not squandered by investing in negative-NPV projects. The private status of the firm requires little information disclosure compared to a listed firm, which allows the firm to avoid expenses related to compliance with the regulations on corporate governance/transparency.

It should be emphasized that not every firm is a good candidate for LBO. The requirements are: stable cash flows,

low and predictable capital investment needs, a liquid balance sheet with collateralizable assets, an established market position, and being in a recession-proof industry.

MAKING IT HAPPEN

• Establish whether the firm is a suitable candidate for privatization via an LBO:
  ○ Does it have a stable stream of operational cash flows that is sufficient to service the post-transaction debt even in a recession?
  ○ Does it have a large debt cushion, and liquid and collateralizable assets?
  ○ Does it have, and will it be able to maintain, a stable market share?
  ○ Is the economic value of the plant, property, and equipment high, and is future capital expenditure modest?

• Contact an investment bank or LBO specialist (private equity group) to write a prospectus that contains the valuation of the company and maps the risks.

• Take on bank debt (issue bonds) to finance the deal and buy out the pre-transaction stockholders (and bondholders). This results in a small equity stake and a capital structure that has 70–80% of debt on total assets.

• Once it has been privatized, restructure the firm (for example through asset sales), focus on the core business, improve the efficiency of its operations, and increase the efficiency of working capital management.

MORE INFO

Books:

Amihud, Yakov (ed). *Leveraged Management Buyouts: Causes and Consequences*. Washington, DC: Beard Books, 2002.

Wright, Mike, and Hans Bruining (eds). *Private Equity and Management Buy-Outs*. Cheltenham, UK: Edward Elgar, 2008.

Articles:

Denis, David J. "Organizational form and the consequences of highly leveraged transactions: Kroger's recapitalization and Safeway's LBO." *Journal of Financial Economics* 36:2 (October 1994): 193–224. Online at: dx.doi.org/10.1016/0304-405X(94)90024-8

Renneboog, Luc, Tomas Simons, and Mike Wright. "Why do public firms go private in the UK? The impact of private equity investors, incentive realignment and undervaluation." *Journal of Corporate Finance* 13:4 (September 2007): 591–628. Online at: dx.doi.org/10.1016/j.jcorpfin.2007.04.005

Simons, Tomas, and Luc Renneboog. "Public-to-private transactions: LBOs, MBOs, MBIs and IBOs." Working paper no. 94/2005. European Corporate Governance Institute, August 2005. Online at: ssrn.com/abstract=796047

Wright, Mike, Luc Renneboog, Tomas Simons, and Louise Scholes. "Leveraged buyouts in the UK and continental

Europe: Retrospect and prospect." *Journal of Applied Corporate Finance* 18:3 (Summer 2006): 38–55. Online at: dx.doi.org/10.1111/j.1745-6622.2006.00097.x

Websites:
Centre for Management Buy-Out Research (CMBOR; now at Imperial College London): tinyurl.com/89svv2l
The MBO Guide: www.mboguide.co.uk

See Also:
★ Comparing Net Present Value and Internal Rate of Return (pp. 16–19)
★ Leveraged Buyouts: What, Why, When, and How (pp. 230–233)
✔ Management Buyouts (pp. 349–350)
✔ Understanding Anti-Takeover Strategies (p. 354)

Identifying and Minimizing the Strategic Risks from M&A
by Peter Howson

EXECUTIVE SUMMARY
- The high failure rate of acquisitions can be mitigated considerably by dealing with the strategic risks that are present at every stage of the acquisition process.
- It is best to start with a well-developed business strategy, a clear idea of the place of mergers and acquisitions (M&A) in this strategy, and an acquisition target that furthers strategic aims.
- Before embarking on negotiations, acquirers should avoid the risk of overpaying by setting a price above which they will not go.
- Before negotiating the final details, due diligence should be used as a final confirmation of the strategy and the target's fit.
- The most important thing is to make sure that the post acquisition plan is put together early and in as much detail as possible. Acquirers need to add value, and they can only do this if they are clearly focused on the sources of extra value and how to realize them right from the very start.

INTRODUCTION
M&A is extremely risky. Studies carried out over the last 30 years suggest that the failure rate is above 50% and probably close to 75%. However, by identifying and acting to minimize the strategic risks early on in the process, the rewards can be spectacular.

There are four stages in the M&A process:
- acquisition strategy;
- due diligence;
- negotiation;
- post-acquisition integration.
Strategic risks are present in each.

Acquisition Strategy
M&A is glamorous. Market analysts see M&A as a sign of a dynamic management and mark up share prices accordingly. For management, M&A can be a means of bolstering short-term performance and/or masking underlying problems. It is hardly surprising that the failure rate is so high when the mystique of M&A encourages acquirers to rush into acquisitions.

M&A Is a Strategic Tool
This brings us to the first strategic risk—a failure to recognize that M&A is a strategic weapon. Strategy is all about giving customers what they want, and to do it better or more cheaply than anyone else. It is about competitive advantage gained through superior capabilities and resources. M&A should fit into this framework.

Given the high risk of failure, acquirers should ask themselves if acquisition is the best means of achieving aims. There will generally be a trade-off between risk and time. Acquisition is the highest-risk route to corporate development, but it is often the quickest. Acquisition should be examined alongside all the other options—organic development, joint venture, merger, etc.

Is the Timing Right?
Implementation is the key to successful strategy and this is the clue to the next strategic risk—is this the right time to be acquiring? Getting the transaction done and integrating it afterwards will take up a disproportionate amount of time, resource, and expertise. This means making sure that there is:
- a strong base business (if existing operations are struggling, acquisitions will only add to the problems);
- the resources to add value (where there are insufficient resources to manage an acquisition, the chances of adding value are slim).

Select the Right Target
The next risk may sound obvious, but one of the biggest ever M&A disasters stemmed in part from selecting the wrong target. In 1991 AT&T, the US telecommunications company, bought NCR for US$7.48 billion. AT&T was implementing a so called "3Cs strategy" where communications, computers, and consumer electronics were expected to coalesce into a new market. It bought NCR to provide a capability in computers. But NCR was not a computer company. Its core business was in retail transaction processing and banking systems, and it happened also to manufacture a range of "me too" personal

computers. While this may be an extreme example, it is not uncommon for buyers to misunderstand the target company's capabilities.

Due Diligence

The strategic risks in due diligence all stem from making the focus of due diligence too narrow.

The success of any acquisition depends on buyers creating value. Due diligence presents a potential buyer with the access and information it needs to confirm that a transaction can be a long-term success. This means using due diligence not just as an input to the sale and purchase agreement but, more importantly, also to confirm both the robustness of synergy assumptions and their deliverability. As people will deliver the extra value, buyers should also make sure that due diligence covers cultural and people issues.

Negotiation

In negotiation, the strategic risk is overpaying. Buyers are almost certainly going to have to pay a premium for the control of a company. The challenge is to make sure that the synergies are big enough to cover both the premium and the deal costs. Work out a price in advance and, as it is all too easy to get carried away, always set a maximum walk-away price before negotiations begin.

Post-Acquisition Integration

The major cause of acquisition failure is poor integration. Integration is poorly carried out because it gets forgotten. Doing the deal may be sexy, but integration is where the real money is made or lost. The strategic risks stem from not starting work on the integration plan early enough in the process. As integration is central to valuation, the integration plan must be put together well before negotiations begin, and the other golden rules of acquisition integration also demand an early plan:

- Integrate quickly to minimize uncertainty. In particular, integration changes related to personnel need to be made as soon as possible; early communication is paramount; and there should be early victories to demonstrate progress.

- Do not neglect the soft issues. The culture of a company is the set of assumptions, beliefs, and accepted rules of conduct that define the way things are done. These are never written down, and most people in an organization would be hard pressed to articulate them. However, they can substantially increase post-acquisition costs or hold back performance
- Manage properly. Buyers should appoint an integration manager. Like any other big project, acquisitions need one person to be accountable for the project's success.

CASE STUDY

In 1996, Federal-Mogul, a US auto parts company, appointed a new Chairman and Chief Executive, Dick Snell, whose view was that in the automotive industry, a firm must be big.

Automobile makers were focusing on assembly, branding, and marketing, and were encouraging parts manufacturers to play a bigger role in the design and development of components. They were also encouraging the larger suppliers to supply modules and systems rather than components.

Federal-Mogul's "growth by acquisition" strategy had the simple aim of increasing sales from US$2 billion to US$10 billion in six years. The company already made gaskets and seals, but not enough to market a full engine or transmission-sealing package. Federal-Mogul also made engine bearings, but did not have the ability to market the bearings as a system complete with pistons, piston rings, connecting rods, and cylinder liners.

Federal-Mogul first bought T&N Plc (in 1997), a supplier of engine and transmission products and Europe's leading supplier of gaskets. With sales of US$3 billion, T&N was bigger than Federal-Mogul itself. Soon after (in 1998), Federal-Mogul paid US$720 million for privately held Fel-Pro Inc., of Skokie, IL. Fel-Pro was a leading brand of replacement sealing products. Following these two acquisitions, Federal-Mogul had a US$1 billion global sealing business and the basis for providing an integrated engine package. Later that year, Federal-Mogul went on to buy Cooper Automotive for US$1.9 billion. Cooper added three completely new product areas (see Table 1).

Table 1. Federal-Mogul's acquisitions

	Existing operations (as of 1996)	1997: T&N acquisition	1998: Fel-Pro acquisition	1998: Cooper Automotive acquisition
Engine and transmission				
Engine bearings	X	X		
Pistons and piston rings		X		
Seals	X	X	X	
Camshafts	X	X		
Other				
Lighting	X			
Fuel pumps	X			
Friction (brake and clutch pads)		X		
Powdered metals		X		
Ignition				X
Chassis				X
Wiper blades				X

In July 1998, Federal-Mogul's share price was US$72. By September 2001 it was US$1. On October 1, 2001, the company filed under Chapter 11 of the US Bankruptcy Code. What went wrong?

OVERAMBITIOUS STRATEGY

Following the Fel-Pro acquisition, the logical thing would have been to continue building the engine and transmissions business. Instead, Federal-Mogul kept its electrical businesses and the friction businesses acquired with T&N, and went on to add three entirely new product ranges. Focusing only on revenue and growth rarely, if ever, produces a strong organization and financial results over the long term.

PROBLEMS PICKED UP IN DUE DILIGENCE NOT ACTED ON

T&N had at one time manufactured building products containing asbestos, and for years it paid out an increasing number of compensation claims for asbestos-related diseases. Following the takeover, the number of asbestos claims against T&N and its former subsidiaries exploded. In October 2001 there were 365,000 asbestos claims pending. By the end of 2001, Federal Mogul had paid out US$1 billion in claims.

While Federal-Mogul was aware of the asbestos issue, Federal-Mogul leaders did minimal due diligence, failed to appreciate just how serious it was, and believed that, because it operated in the United States, it would be able to manage the litigation better.

POOR INTEGRATION

Federal-Mogul paid a high price for T&N and the other big acquisitions, promised too much, and failed to deliver. Federal-Mogul leadership repeatedly promised the market that integration would bring tens of millions of dollars worth of synergies. In fact, according to a stockholder class action, the company's integration activities destroyed the acquired businesses. The class action claimed that, "After an acquisition, the Company would slash sales staff at the acquired company, close manufacturing and warehouse facilities, reduce investment in research and development, reduce customer service and implement aggressive sales practices."

Federal-Mogul's management lacked an understanding of how international businesses operate. It was obsessed with the Detroit Big Three and dismissive of the other vehicle assemblers, yet the strategic logic of acquiring parts manufacturers should be to broaden geographic reach and bring closer relationships with vehicle assemblers.

Federal-Mogul management also failed to appreciate that the rest of the world was not like the United States and, in particular, that Europe was not like a group of US states. Federal-Mogul centralized all its operations, including customer service. When Federal-Mogul moved aftermarket operations to the United States, it was surprised that its telecom ordering system did not recognize overseas telephone numbers. In contrast, T&N had given a great deal of autonomy to its regions.

Finally, Federal-Mogul lost key staff by insisting that anyone who stayed had to move to Detroit. Most former T&N leaders opted to take the money. While it is not impossible to buy a

company larger than yourself, it is difficult to manage something the size of T&N without retaining most of the management team—and T&N was actually quite good at managing asbestos claims.

Federal-Mogul emerged from Chapter 11 bankruptcy on December 27, 2007 after a financial reorganization designed to protect it from asbestos claims.

MAKING IT HAPPEN

- Think of M&A as a means to gain competitive advantage rather than short-term improvements in financials.
- M&A is the most risky form of corporate development, so be sure to consider alternatives such as organic growth or joint ventures.
- M&A will divert resources from the existing business, so make sure it is strong before embarking on acquisitions.
- Be sure to understand the target company—what it does, how it operates, how it makes money—and be able to articulate why it fits the strategy.
- Do not neglect soft issues like management and culture. Do not assume that "they are just like us," because they won't be.
- Prepare a detailed integration plan in advance.
- Keep the due diligence scope wide. Always use it to confirm the sources of added value identified and quantified in the integration plan.
- Never be lured into overpaying. Set a clear walk-away price and do not exceed it.
- Once the deal is done, communicate immediately, clearly, consistently, and abundantly to everyone concerned. Do not forget external parties, above all customers.
- Implement changes quickly and smoothly and do not underestimate the size of the task.

MORE INFO

Books:

Camp, Jim. *Start with NO: The Negotiating Tools that the Pros Don't Want You to Know*. New York: Crown Business, 2002.

Carey, Dennis, *et al. Harvard Business Review on Mergers and Acquisitions*. Boston, MA: Harvard Business School, 2001.

Cleary, Patrick J. *The Negotiation Handbook*. Armonk, NY: ME Sharpe, 2001.

Freund, James C. *Smart Negotiating: How to Make Good Deals in the Real World*. New York: Fireside, 1993.

Howson, Peter. *Due Diligence: The Critical Stage in Acquisitions and Mergers*. Aldershot, UK: Gower Publishing, 2003.

Howson, Peter. *Commercial Due Diligence: The Key to Understanding Value in an Acquisition*. Aldershot, UK: Gower Publishing, 2006.

Howson, Peter. *Checklists for Due Diligence*. Aldershot, UK: Gower Publishing, 2008.

Howson, Peter, with Denzil Rankine. *Acquisition Essentials*. London: Pearson Education, 2005.

Hubbard, Nancy. *Acquisition: Strategy and Implementation*. Basingstoke, UK: Palgrave Macmillan, 1999.

Hunt, J. W., S. Lees, J. J. Grumbar, and P. D. Vivian. *Acquisitions: The Human Factor*. London: London Business School and Egon Zehnder International, 1987.

Lajoux, Alexandra Reed, and Charles Elson. *The Art of M&A Due Diligence: Navigating Critical Steps and Uncovering Crucial Data*. New York: McGraw-Hill, 2000.

Rankine, Denzil. *Why Acquisitions Fail: Practical Advice for Making Acquisitions Succeed*. London: Pearson Education, 2001.

Article:

Davy, Jeanette A., Angelo Kinicki, John Kilroy, and Christine Scheck. "After the merger: Dealing with people's uncertainty." *Training and Development Journal* 42 (November 1988): 57–61.

Report:

KPMG. "Unlocking shareholder value: Keys to success." London: KPMG, 1999. Online at: tinyurl.com/3yn35rz [PDF].

Websites:

Commercial due diligence—AMR International: www.amrinternational.com

Financial due diligence—BDO Stoy Hayward: www.bdo.co.uk

See Also:

★ Acquisition Integration: How to Do It Successfully (pp. 211–213)

★ Due Diligence Requirements in Financial Transactions (pp. 216–220)

★ Why Mergers Fail and How to Prevent It (pp. 243–245)

✔ Assessing Business Performance (pp. 359–360)

✔ Planning the Acquisition Process (pp. 350–351)

Joint Ventures: Synergies and Benefits
by Siri Terjesen

EXECUTIVE SUMMARY

- A joint venture (JV) is a formal arrangement between two or more firms to create a new business for the purpose of carrying out some kind of mutually beneficial activity, often related to business expansion, especially new product and/or market development.

- An important first step is for each firm's managers to review the firm's business and corporate strategies to determine synergy with the objectives of a joint venture.

- A second key step is to assess the suitability of the potential joint venture partner(s) for fit with the firm's strategy, and compatibility during the life of the JV.

- There are four basic JV types: consolidation (deep combination of existing businesses); skills-transfer (transfer of some key skill from one partner); coordination (leveraging complementary capabilities of all partners); and new business (combining existing capabilities, not businesses, to create new growth).

- JVs can offer an array of benefits to partner firms through access to new and/or greater resources including markets, distribution networks, capacity, staff, purchasing, technology/intellectual property, and finance.

- JV risks can arise from disparate communication, culture, strategy, and resources, and result in loss of control, lower profits, conflict, and transferability of key assets.

- NUMMI is an example of a successful JV offering mutual benefits to its partners, General Motors (GM) and Toyota.

- To succeed, JV partners must mitigate potential risk factors, including poor communication, different objectives, imbalanced resources, and cultural clashes.

INTRODUCTION

A joint venture (JV) is a formal arrangement between two or more firms to create a new business for the purpose of carrying out some kind of mutually beneficial activity, often related to business expansion, especially new product and/or market development. A JV is the most popular type of contractual alliance among firms; other types include formal long-term contracts, informal alliances, and acquisitions. JVs may take the form of a corporation, limited liability company (LLC), partnership, or other structure. The 100 largest JVs worldwide account for more than US$350 billion in revenues (Bamford, Ernst & Fubini, 2008). An increasing number of JVs involve foreign partners, in part due to laws in some countries that require foreign firms to partner with local firms in order to conduct business in that country.

SYNERGY TO STRATEGY

An important first step is for management to review the firm's business and corporate strategies to determine synergy with the objectives of a joint venture. In this process, managers can apply a range of strategy methodologies such as SWOT (strengths, weaknesses, opportunities, and threats), Porter's Five Forces, stakeholder analysis, and the value chain to assess the firm's strategy and future vision. Managers may then determine that the joint venture is not the most optimal organizational form for achieving the firm's objectives, and that another form, such as a long-term contract, may offer a better strategic fit.

A second key step is to assess the suitability of the potential joint venture partner(s) for fit with the firm's strategy, and compatibility during the life of the JV. Key questions here include:

- Does the potential JV partner share the same business objectives and vision for the joint venture?

- Is the potential partner firm trustworthy and financially secure?
- Does the potential partner firm already have JV partnerships with other firms? If so, how are these performing?
- How would you rate the potential partner firm's performance in terms of production, marketing, customers, personnel, innovation, and reputation?
- What are the general strengths and weaknesses of the potential partner? How do they complement our firm?
- What benefits might the potential partner firm realize from the JV?
- What risks might we be exposing our firm to in the JV?

A joint venture should only be formed when the parties mutually agree that this form offers the best possibility of optimizing opportunities.

Thirdly, the parties set out JV terms in a written agreement which addresses structure (for example, if it should be a separate business or not), objectives, financial and other resource contributions (of each partner), including the transferability of any assets or employees to the JV, ownership of intellectual property created in the JV, management and control responsibilities and processes, sharing/re-allocation of liabilities/profits/losses, resolution of disputes, and exit strategy. Joint ventures can be flexible, covering only a limited life span or a limited scope of firm activities.

Four basic types of JVs and their respective benefits are (Bamford, Ernst & Fubini, 2004):

- Consolidation JV: value derived from deep combination of existing businesses.
- Skills-transfer JV: value derived from the transfer of some key skill from one partner to the JV (or to the other JV partner).
- Coordination JV: value derived from leveraging the complementary capabilities of all partners.
- New business JV: value derived from combining existing capabilities, not businesses, to create new growth.

JOINT VENTURE BENEFITS

Joint ventures can offer an array of benefits to partner firms through access to new and/or greater resources including markets, distribution networks, capacity, staff, purchasing, technology/intellectual property, and finance. Often, one firm supplies a key resource such as technology, while the other firm(s) might provide distribution or other assets. The following are key resources that can be shared:

Access to markets: JVs can facilitate increased access to customers. One JV partner might, for example, enable the partner to sell other goods/services to their existing customers. International JVs involve partners from different countries, and are frequently pursued to provide access to foreign markets.

Distribution networks: Similarly, JV partners may be willing to share access to distribution networks. If one partner was previously a supplier to the other, then there may be opportunities to strengthen supplier relationships.

Capacity: JV partners may take advantage of increased capacity in terms of production, as well as other economies of scale and scope.

Staff: JVs may share staff, enabling both firms to benefit from complementary, specialized staff. Staff may also transfer innovative management practices across firms.

Purchasing: As a result of their increased resource requirements, JV partners may be able to collectively benefit from better conditions (for example, price, quality, or timing) when purchasing.

Technology/intellectual property: As with other resources, JV partners may share technology. A JV may also enable increased research, and the development of new innovative technologies.

Finance: In a joint venture, firms also pool their financial resources, potentially eliminating the need to borrow funds or seek outside investors.

Taken together, the benefits suggest an improved competitive position for the JV, and each of the partners.

JOINT VENTURE RISKS

There are, however, a number of risks related to joint ventures that can result in loss of control, lower profits, conflict with partners, and transferability of key assets. In fact, studies in the 1980s and 1990s revealed failure rates of 49% and 47% (Bamford, Ernst, Fubini, 2004). More recent work reports failure rates varying from 2% to 90%, depending on the partners involved (see, for example, Perkins, Morck & Yeung, 2008). JV risks stem from many sources, including the following:

Communication: The firms may not communicate their objectives clearly, resulting in misunderstanding. These communication issues can be exacerbated by geographic and cultural distance among partner firms, and by the use of language such as "us versus them."

Strategy: The firms may have divergent strategies for the joint venture, and fail to reach a set of mutually agreeable objectives regarding business and exit strategies. Risks can also emerge from a lack of agreed processes regarding governance, accountability, decision-making, HR, and conflict resolution.

Imbalanced resources: The firms may bring imbalanced resources to the table, a source of great conflict. Another source of conflict may be that the JV disproportionately allocates resources among the firms. For example, one firm may find that its technology is being appropriated by another firm.

Culture: The JV partner firms may have distinct corporate (and in the case of cross-border JVs, national) cultures and management styles, resulting in poor integration and cooperation.

CASE STUDY
NUMMI JOINT VENTURE

Established in Fremont, California, in 1984, the New United Motor Manufacturing Inc. (NUMMI) was a joint venture between General Motors (GM) and Toyota. The NUMMI JV began as an experiment. The allure for GM was a chance to learn how to build cars, especially of a small size and high quality, using Toyota's "lean" production system. Toyota was interested in testing its production methods in an American setting. According to Eiji Toyoda, then the Chairman of Toyota Motor Company: "Competition and cooperation is the underlying principle of the growth of the world economy. Our joint venture is founded on this approach. We hope to make this project a success as a model of economic cooperation between Japan and the United States—one that contributes to the American economy." (*Source*: NUMMI, archived at tinyurl.com/7a47z7d).

To start the joint venture, US$450 million in funding was required. GM contributed its plant in Fremont, which it had closed in 1982. Toyota provided US$100 million of start-up capital. The remaining capital was raised by NUMMI as an independent Californian corporation. The US Federal Trade Commission (FTC) approved the formation of the company for an initial 12-year period, stating that the venture would offer a wider range of automobile choices to customers. The 12-year limit was eventually lifted, and NUMMI continues to operate. Ford and Chrysler opposed the joint venture and filed an unsuccessful lawsuit to block NUMMI.

NUMMI invited former GM workers to apply for jobs, and expressed a special "need for employees willing to contribute to an atmosphere of trust and cooperation." Following a rigorous hiring assessment, the new employees attended orientation sessions about NUMMI's concept, system, principles, policy, and philosophy. Team members were introduced to NUMMI's core values, which are based on teamwork, equity, involvement, mutual trust and respect, and safety. Approximately 450 group and team leaders traveled to Toyota's Takaeoka plant in Japan to spend three weeks learning in the classroom and on the job about Toyota's production system, team building, union–management relations, and safety. NUMMI's first effort was the Chevrolet Nova, built by 700 team members in 1984. NUMMI has established a collaborative partnership with United Auto Workers (UAW) in which UAW agrees to be a cooperative and active participant in labor-management relationships, to accept Toyota's production methods, and to work to improve productivity and quality. NUMMI has been presented as a case-study model of labor-management cooperation to the International Labor Organization Conference.

NUMMI's unique corporate learning and cultural environment optimized the best of GM, Toyota, and nearby Silicon Valley. The JV is considered to have been instrumental in introducing the Toyota production system and a team-based working environment to the US automobile industry. NUMMI remains a key source of innovative knowledge about quality, continuous improvement, and human resource management. NUMMI closed in 2010 and the manufacturing plant is now owned by Tesla Motors.

CONCLUSION

As the NUMMI case study illustrates, JVs offer benefits to both partners as well as other stakeholders—providing customers with more and a higher quality variety of car choices and manufacturers, with a model of labor-management relations. There are, however, many risks to be considered.

Interrelationships among small and large firms are increasingly common, and offer unique benefits to each partner. For a small firm, a joint venture may offer a unique opportunity to grow quickly with other small firms, or to partner with a larger firm. Often the large partner benefits from the smaller firm's flexibility and intellectual property, while the small partner benefits from increased access to markets, reputation, and other key resources. Increasingly, JV partners of all sizes join together as a defensive response to blurring industry boundaries.

MAKING IT HAPPEN

To succeed, JV partners must mitigate several potential sources of risk: poor communication, different objectives, imbalanced resources, and cultural clashes. Firstly, JV partners must establish clear communication channels at the top of the firms involved, and also with employees whose daily work is related to the joint venture. This communication is often facilitated through regular, face-to-face meetings to establish not only the benefits from the JV, but also the risks if the JV does not work. Secondly, it is essential that partners agree on objectives and milestones. Key performance indicators (KPIs) can be established to measure performance and provide early warning guidance. Imbalanced resources, such as different levels of financing or expertise, can also lead to conflict. Finally, each firm has a unique culture, and cultural clashes in management style may become apparent. These issues may be exacerbated across foreign JV partners as a result of language and cultural differences. Flexibility and an open approach to trying to make things work are essential.

MORE INFO

Books:
Child, John, David Faulkner, and Stephen Tallman. *Coopera-tive Strategies: Managing Alliances, Networks, and Joint Ventures*. 2nd ed. Oxford: Oxford University Press, 2005.
Wallace, Robert L. *Strategic Partnerships: An Entrepreneur's Guide to Joint Ventures and Alliances*. New York: Kaplan Publishing, 2004.

Articles:
Bamford, James, David Ernst, and David G. Fubini. "Launching a world-class joint venture." *Harvard Business Review* (February 2004): 90–100. Online at: tinyurl.com/6w7lrlg
Perkins, Susan, Randall Morck, and Bernard Yeung. "Inno-cents abroad: The hazards of international joint ventures with pyramidal group firms." NBER Working Paper 13914 (April 2008). Online at: www.nber.org/papers/w13914
Steensma, H. Kevin, Jeffrey Q. Barden, Charles Dhanaraj, Marjorie Lyles, and Laszlo Tihanyi. "The evolution and internalization of international joint ventures in a transitioning economy." *Journal of International Business*

230

Studies 39:3 (April 2008): 491–507. Online at:
dx.doi.org/10.1057/palgrave.jibs.8400341

Website:
Google's latest joint venture news: tinyurl.com/7v2653c

Best Practice

See Also:
★ Maximizing a New Strategic Alliance (pp. 233–235)
✔ Structuring and Negotiating Joint Ventures (pp. 352–353)

Leveraged Buyouts: What, Why, When, and How

by Scott S. Johnson

EXECUTIVE SUMMARY

- A leveraged buyout (LBO) is the acquisition of a company financed by debt.
- The use of debt multiplies both the potential return and risk.
- LBOs require active and liquid credit markets.
- Stable, mature businesses with predictable—and ideally recurring—revenues are generally the best LBO targets.
- LBO returns are maximized by buying low and selling high, properly capitalizing the buyout, and maximizing profitable and high-quality growth during the hold period.

WHAT

A leveraged buyout (LBO) is the acquisition of a company financed by debt. It is not unlike the typical purchase of a residence where the majority of financing is derived from a mortgage, and the balance from cash (equity) contributed by the buyer.

The use of debt in an LBO leverages the equity return, providing the equity holder with the possibility of higher returns at the cost of higher risk. Debt levels have averaged 72% of total capital from 1996 to 2008, according to Standard & Poor's. Debt levels vary due to numerous factors, including the vibrancy of credit markets, the ability of the company to support debt, and the strategy of the given LBO.

Although select transactions that could be considered LBOs occurred prior to the 1980s, this acquisition strategy grew in popularity in the 1980s when ample debt financing became available, in particular with the rise of the sub-investment grade, or "junk" debt market. Over the past decade, the strategy has seen even more activity with more than US$100 billion raised by private equity funds. Buyouts have, in fact, become a material element in mergers and acquisitions. From 2004 to 2008, US buyout volume was US$1 trillion, according to Standard & Poor's, though activity has of course significantly decreased with the recession of the world's economies and credit markets.

LBOs can involve the acquisition of an entire company or a division of a company. In some cases, management, usually with the financial backing and transactional expertise of a private equity group, buys out its own entity, which is then more specifically referred to as a management buyout (MBO). Yet another permutation is leveraged recapitalization,

whereby some equity plus debt are used to provide liquidity to shareholders, either to buy their shares outright, or provide cash to them (not unlike a residential mortgage refinancing).

Figure 1. Case study: Sample LBO vs all equity acquisition

	LBO	All equity
Initial acquisition		
Profit	$10	
Multiple	6.0×	
Value	$60	
Capitalization		
Debt	4.0×	0.00×
	$40.0	$0.0
Equity	2.0×	6.00×
	$20.0	$60.0
Return after year-5 sale		
Value	$96.63	
Less: debt	($40.00)	$0.0
Equity value	$56.63	$96.63
Annual return	23.1%	10.0%
Return on capital	1.8×	0.6×
Profit after five years:		
Annual growth	10.0%	
Cumulative growth	161.1%	
Year-5 profit	$16.11	
Year-5 sale price:		
Year-5 profit	$16.11	
times multiple of	6.0×	
gives sale price	$96.63	

Note: Excludes transaction and closing fees and assumes no principal amortization or cash generated.

Figure 2. Case study: Effect of profit decline

	LBO	All equity
Base profit	$10.00	
Decline in profit	25%	
New profit	$7.50	
Interest	$5.00	$0.00
Profit after interest	$2.50	$7.50
Decline in profit after interest	-75.0%	-25.0%
Debt	$40.00	
Interest rate	12.5%	
Interest expense	$5.00	

WHY

Although the leveraged buyout entails risk, given the challenges of servicing debt, significant returns are possible without the need for material growth.

Furthermore, the need to generate sufficient cash flow for debt service imposes discipline. Companies that, pre-LBO, were inefficient, or overloaded with expenses are forced to streamline their operations and cost structure to succeed. At the same time, the need to service debt can generate short-term decision-making that may not always be in the best long-term interest of the business. However, the World Economic Forum's "Global impact of private equity report 2009"[1] estimated that the extra productivity from 1,400 private equity transactions of US manufacturing concerns raised output by US$4 billion, to US$15 billion per year from 1980 to 2005 (expressed in inflation-adjusted 2007 dollars).

CASE STUDY
HOW DEBT CAN MAGNIFY BOTH RETURNS AND RISK

Let's take a company with $10 in profit and assume it is acquired for six times profit, or $60. In the LBO of this company, $40 of the purchase price is financed with debt and $20 is an equity investment, so equity is one-third of the total capital. In the unleveraged scenario, $60 of equity—100% of the consideration—is used to acquire the company.

If the company is sold at the end of five years, and profits have grown at a compound annual growth rate of 10% to $16 (a cumulative growth of 60%), and the purchase price multiple remains six times, the business is sold for $97. In the unleveraged scenario, the annual return is equal to the profit growth, i.e., 10% per annum and 60% on a cumulative basis.

On the other hand, the LBO equity return is much higher. In the LBO, the company sale price value (its enterprise value, or EV) is still $97. Of the $97, the first $40 is returned to the debt holders to pay off their principal, leaving $57 for the equity. Unlike the unleveraged case, where the sale price is 60%

greater than the investment, here the $57 is 183% greater than the $20 investment.

The annual return in the LBO is more than double the unleveraged deal: 23% vs 10% (see Figure 1). Please note that this scenario is an oversimplification, with numerous factors such as transaction costs, working capital, and annual cash flow generation excluded (even when those factors are included, the LBO continues to outperform the unleveraged deal approximately 2:1).

Our case study also illustrates the risks of the leveraged buyout strategy. Without any interest expense or debt principal due, the unleveraged company in our simplified example can weather substantial declines in operating profit, and still maintain positive cash flow. Conversely, if the leveraged company sees a decline of profits of just 25%, its profits after interest expense fall three times that level, or 75%. If the leveraged company had material levels of capital expenditures, or debt principal repayments (which are both post-tax items), it may not be able to service its cash needs. The likely result would be a cash squeeze, which would have negative or potentially disastrous implications (see Figure 2).

WHEN

LBOs are most commonly considered when a candidate company can support the required leverage, and credit markets can provide such leverage.

Good LBO candidates operate in relatively stable businesses with consistent business models. These are generally mature companies with positive cash flow, and an established operating and profitability history. Earlier-stage companies, or those that require continued cash investments to achieve their objectives are generally not good candidates.

Furthermore, companies with a cyclical business, or those materially exposed to major exogenous risks such as technological obsolescence or fashion risk, are also less-optimal buyout candidates. Explicitly recurring revenue businesses (i.e., contractual) or implicit (for example, regularly repurchased consumables) are good targets. Sectors that often exhibit these characteristics and have yielded successful buyouts include consumer, business services, defense, and media.

HOW

LBO returns can be generated from five factors as follows:

1 **Buying low**. The lower the entry valuation level, the greater margin of safety provided for investors. Furthermore, a company acquired at a lower valuation will require less debt to achieve the optimal debt-to-capital mix. On the other hand, higher quality and larger companies often have greater growth prospects, are generally more stable, and thus usually sell for higher valuations. When valuations are high, buyers take the risk that even if the business is properly capitalized and shows good growth, exit valuation levels could be lower and will not be sufficient to generate an acceptable return. While careful analysis can help determine if the steps below are to be a success, entry valuation is critical, as it is a factor that is controllable at the beginning of the LBO.

2 **Maximizing equity returns by minimizing equity investment to prudent levels**. An LBO investor must

first decide the maximum leverage the business can support, and then try to finance the deal to that level, but not more. In strong credit markets, LBO investors should resist the temptation to overleverage their portfolio companies. In weak credit markets, investors need to ensure that, at lower debt levels, they can still achieve their minimum return hurdles (often accomplished by "buying lower"). What is the appropriate debt level? This clearly varies. Two helpful benchmarks to consider are the overall leverage, and the ability of the company to support its debt, and other obligations. Debt levels are often measured as a multiple of earnings before interest, taxes, depreciation, and amortization (EBITDA), a simplified proxy for cash flow. Debt-to-EBITDA levels for buyouts have historically varied by year, largely as a function of the state of the debt markets. In 2007, average debt to EBITDA was 6.0x, but fell to 4.8x in 2008, and averaged as low as 3.5x in 2001, according to Standard & Poor's. LBO investors will also be concerned with their buyout's ability to service its debt. The fixed-charge covenant ratio (FCCR) is a common measure used to measure debt service levels. The FCCR is the ratio of a company's cash flow to its fixed charges, which typically include taxes, interest, capital expenditures, and debt principal payments. Lenders often seek minimum FCCR levels of 1.10–1.35x. Debt levels also vary due to the structure of the debt offered. In larger transactions, publicly traded bonds, which can form the bulk of the financing, do not typically carry principal amortization, allowing for greater debt capacity. In smaller transactions, debt is typically provided in two tranches: senior debt, typically from banks, and "mezzanine debt," which is subordinate to the senior debt and carries higher rates of interest and sometimes includes equity participation in the form of warrants. Senior debt in such structures often includes principal amortization, which can impose material burdens on a company. Thus, the financing structure makes a material difference in the level of debt a company can support. In particular, debt capital structures that have less (or no) principal amortization are more conducive to higher debt levels, as the total debt servicing costs are much lower (especially when it is considered that debt principal repayments are post-tax obligations). Debt levels are also a function of the strategy of the buyout group. Some groups tend to use comparatively less debt, so they have "dry powder" to more easily execute add-on acquisitions and weather shortfalls.

3 **Maximizing quality organic growth before exit**. Generally, the more growth that occurs during the holding period, the more valuable the company will be at exit. However, a company must be careful to focus on generating "good" revenue. While "good" revenue may vary from company to company, it generally entails business that preserves or bolsters a company's competitive advantages and margins, does not create unnecessarily high customer concentration, is ideally of a recurring nature, still yields a good return on investment net of

capital expenditures and working capital requirements, and is the type of business that would appeal to a potential buyer. To achieve these goals, the buyout group relies on its partnership with management. Furthermore, the buyout investor must carefully use the correct management incentives to generate the desired results. These programs usually revolve around the use of longer-term equity incentives that help shape management's overall motivation, and minimize short-term decision-making. For a typical buyout CEO, the annual compensation will be lower than a corporate position, but if the buyout is successful, the payout can be much higher than what would have been possible as a corporate employee.

4 **Making profitable add-on acquisitions or divestitures as appropriate**. Buyout investors may seek to grow a business through acquisition, or sell off divisions as appropriate. The buyout investor must carefully weigh the return on capital that will be generated by incremental investment, as well as the cash that could be generated from a divestiture, which would likely be used to deleverage the business.

5 **Selling high**. After an investment holding period of typically three to seven years, a buyout firm will seek to exit its investment, so that the proceeds may be returned to its own investors. If growth has been positive and consistent, and industry trends and valuation levels are favorable, the buyout firm should achieve a good return on its investment. However, the reality is that valuation levels years after a deal is consummated are well outside of the control of the buyout firm, so having a flexible timetable, entering the deal at a reasonable valuation level, improving the performance of the company during the holding period, and appropriately capitalizing the company are essential to executing a profitable LBO.

MAKING IT HAPPEN

- Do your diligence. While confirmatory diligence to verify financial and operating assumptions is critical, exploratory diligence is often not given enough focus. The buyout investor should, in particular, understand the sustainability of a company's competitive advantages, and make sure they understand not just the recent history of a company's sector, but the sector's outlook, and what underlying threats may exist to that sector.

- Debt structure. While the price of debt is critical, equally if not more important are the terms of that debt. Key areas worth considering include the maturity date of the debt, the level of principal amortization, if any, and how a given lender may act as a partner (especially if results are poor, and covenants are violated).

- "Skin in the game." While a buyout investor can provide management equity upside, through the use of stock options, having a management team invest their own cash in the deal—putting "skin in the game"—confirms management's confidence in the opportunity, and binds them to both the upside and downside.

MORE INFO

Report:
Standard and Poor's. "A guide to the loan market."
September 2011. Online at:
www.lcdcomps.com/d/pdf/LoanMarketguide.pdf

Websites:
Association for Corporate Growth (ACG), the predominant
industry association for the middle market buyout industry:
www.acg.org
The Deal, magazine and online resource: www.thedeal.com
The Private Equity Analyst, a periodical published by Dow
Jones: www.dowjones.com/privatemarkets/pea.asp

Private Equity Growth Capital Council (PEGCC):
www.pegcc.org

See Also:
★ Going Private: Public-to-Private Leveraged Buyouts
(pp. 220–224)
✔ Management Buyouts (pp. 349–350)
✔ Understanding and Using Leverage Ratios (p. 335)

NOTE
1 www.weforum.org/pdf/cgi/pe/Full_Report2.pdf, p. 44.

Maximizing a New Strategic Alliance
by Peter Killing

EXECUTIVE SUMMARY
- Over 60,000 strategic alliances have been formed in the past decade. About half were joint ventures. Only 40% meet or exceed their partners' expectations.
- To be successful with strategic alliances you must be clear about your objectives, get the alliance design right, and manage the alliance effectively after it is formed.
- There is an important difference between shallow and deep alliances, and you should know which type you need and why.
- Alliance success depends in large part on skilled managers who are good with people, have a high tolerance for ambiguity and conflict, and are patient yet persistent.
- The clearest sign of alliance success is growing trust between the partners.

INTRODUCTION
More than 60,000 strategic alliances were formed in the 1990s. About half of these were joint ventures. The other 50% were nonequity arrangements such as technology licensing agreements, joint marketing arrangements, and joint research or development projects. Most of these alliances were international, so it's no surprise to learn that the world's largest multinationals are heavy alliance users: IBM (254 alliances), General Motors (138), Mitsubishi (233), Toshiba (147), Philips (207), and Siemens (200) are just some examples.

Clearly the ability to create and manage strategic alliances is an important skill for most management teams. If you cannot make effective use of alliances in today's world, you will be at a serious competitive disadvantage.

GETTING IT RIGHT
A 1999 study by Andersen Consulting indicates that only 40% of alliances achieve or exceed the initial expectations of their partners, which suggests there's a lot of room for

improvement. One of the reasons for the relatively low success rate is that there are many different aspects of the design and management of alliances that you need to get right, from clearly understanding your objectives, to managing the alliance after it is formed. They can be grouped into three sequential steps:
- **Clarify objectives**. What do we need and for how long? Is an alliance the best way to get what we need?
- **Design the alliance**. What type of alliance should we create? What should our role be?
- **Manage after the deal is done**. How do we effectively manage the alliance? Can we build trust?

Clarify Objectives and the Need for the Alliance
The first challenge is to be clear about what your company needs to fulfill its strategy, which may be different from what others in your industry need. The second challenge is to decide whether an alliance is the best way to get what you need. Three common reasons for forming alliances are:
- **To enter new markets**. One of the classic purposes of joint ventures is to enter foreign markets. Typically the foreign company finds the local market attractive but does not feel confident enough to enter without local knowledge, and so takes a local partner. In some countries the government insists on such a relationship. In China, for example, joint ventures between foreigners and local companies are prevalent. Often, as foreign companies gain confidence in their ability to operate locally, they end the joint venture by buying out their local partner and creating a wholly-owned subsidiary. In this case the alliance is a step on the road to something else.
- **To create new technology and set industry standards**. In technology-intensive industries like computing and telecommunications, companies often use alliances to attempt to create a new technology that will become the industry standard. An example is Symbian, a joint venture formed in 1998 by Psion, Ericsson, Nokia, and

Motorola. Symbian's objective is to create an operating system for wireless devices to exchange information efficiently. Microsoft has also shown an interest in this area and has considered building its own alliance around its CE operating system with partners including NTT DoCoMo and British Telecom. The competition has shifted from company versus company to alliance versus alliance.

- **To shape consolidation**. In consolidating industries such as airlines, telecoms, and the automotive industry, alliances are often formed between companies that fear they are too small to continue independently (and that do not want to be taken over) and those that intend to play a dominant role in the consolidation. The alliance between Fiat and GM was formed for precisely this reason. This deal involves cross-ownership holdings between the two companies, two 50–50 joint ventures, and a variety of smaller cooperative arrangements. Fiat also had an option to sell itself to GM (before agreeing a "divorce" worth US$2 billion in 2005). The immediate motives behind such alliances are to gain economies of scale and global reach, to eliminate excess capacity, and to keep the smaller company out of the hands of predators.

Why Use an Alliance?

Alliances are often the least-preferred choice of the companies that enter them. Many companies would rather enter a new market themselves, or perhaps make an acquisition. GM, for example, would probably have preferred to buy Fiat, but the company was not for sale. Alliances are often seen as difficult to manage, ambiguous in terms of control and decision-making (and as a result slow moving), and requiring an extraordinary amount of management time and attention. The usual motives, positive and negative, for proceeding with an alliance are:

Positive

- to harness the partner's energy and knowledge;
- to set an industry standard by involving partners;
- to learn something;
- to gain economies of scale or global reach;
- to reduce risk;
- to gain speed.

Negative

- government insists on alliance;
- acquisitions are too expensive or not available;
- it's the only financially affordable alternative;
- the company fears being acquired;
- an alliance will prevent a competitor's acquisition of, or alliance with, the partner;
- closing the business is too expensive; an alliance provides a more graceful exit.

You should be clear on your own motives as well as your partner's. There are no data on this issue, but alliances formed for positive motives may have a higher success rate.

Design the Alliance

There are many types of alliance. The simplest are straightforward license agreements and shared marketing deals; the most complex are multipart arrangements such as cross-ownership positions, joint ventures, and cooperative projects between partners. Faced with an abundance of choice, managers entering an alliance need to make a key decision: whether they want a shallow alliance or a deep alliance.

Shallow Alliances—Traveling Light

A shallow alliance might be thought of as a flirtation—a low-commitment alliance that doesn't have a lot of resources devoted to it and that can be broken on short notice. As an example, think of current airline alliances such as the Star and One World alliances, which seem to feature new partners every month. Or consider Cisco and its internet-related businesses. Cisco often cannot judge if a young company's fledgling technology will prove to be important a year later. The shallow alliance solution is to buy 10% of the company's stock in a friendly transaction and get a seat on the board and an option to buy the remainder of the equity. The assigned board member can then assess the company's management, its market prospects, and its technology. If it looks good, they buy the rest of the company. If not, they leave. Shallow alliances thus create options for companies in fast-changing industries in which the way ahead is not clear. The alliances are not usually intended to be permanent.

Deep Alliances—Commitment

At the other end of the spectrum are deep alliances involving high levels of financial and managerial commitment by the partners. Deep alliances feature many links between the partners, usually including one or more seats on the board of directors, cross-ownership positions, at least two or three joint ventures, and many less formal but important cooperative projects. Deep alliances are generally slower-moving than shallow alliances, more difficult to manage, and more difficult to end. The benefits of success can be high, but so can the costs of failure. Deep alliances are not for the timid.

Manage After the Deal Is Done

Once you've formed an alliance, you'll sooner or later discover that you have brought together partners with different ways of doing things and somewhat different objectives, priorities, and performance standards. These differences make the management of alliances a difficult task. The single most important thing you can do to maximize the probability of success is to assign some of your very best people to work on it. "Best" means managers with excellent people skills, cross-cultural sensitivity, and a tolerance for ambiguity and frustration. Alliance managers need to be patient, yet persistent.

Six months into the life of your alliance you should look closely at the relationship between the partners. Is trust starting to develop? If not, why not? Where are the trouble spots? Many texts advise that when choosing a partner you should choose someone you trust. This is difficult to do unless you have worked together before. The real question is whether or not you can develop trust over time. The best predictor of the future performance of any alliance is the current level of trust between the partners.

Finally, don't assume that the alliance is done when the deal is signed. This is just the beginning. Be flexible and open to change and learning. There will be plenty of opportunity for both.

★

MAKING IT HAPPEN

Strategic alliances are increasingly popular, even necessary; however they are often a high-risk strategy. It is worth viewing the alliance in three distinct phases:

- **Before the deal is struck:** The vital period when goals are considered, resources prepared, and partners considered. Internal agreement on the goals, strategy, and resources to be used is important, as is choosing the right partner and evaluating them thoroughly through due diligence.
- **Negotiating the deal:** The terms of the agreement and, significantly, the expectations of each partner and the *spirit* of the agreement, will be decisive in determining the effectiveness of the alliance.
- **Post-agreement management:** Successful agreements are those that are consistently and attentively resourced, managed, and valued. If they are not, they are unlikely to survive normal commercial pressures.

Some key questions to consider include:

- Have you formally assessed the aims and benefits of the strategic alliance?
- How does the alliance fit with your overall commercial strategy?
- Who needs to be informed of the alliance—and when?
- Have you sought the advice of professional advisers?
- Have you taken time to understand the target and the commercial implications?
- To what extent should the alliance be integrated into your existing business? Who will lead this?
- Do you have a fully costed and resourced plan for managing the alliance? What are the targets and success criteria for the alliance?

MORE INFO

Books:

Cauley de la Sierra, M. *Managing Global Alliances: Key Steps for Successful Collaboration*. Reading, MA: Addison-Wesley, 1995.

Doz, Yves L., and Gary Hamel. *Alliance Advantage: The Art of Creating Value through Partnering*. Cambridge, MA: Harvard Business School Press, 1998.

Lewis, Jordan D. *Trusted Partners: How Companies Build Mutual Trust and Win Together*. New York: Free Press, 2000.

Website:

Alliance Strategy offers resources and readings on alliance strategy and management. It is maintained by Ben Gomes-Casseres, author of *The Alliance Revolution*: www.alliancestrategy.com

See Also:

★ Due Diligence Requirements in Financial Transactions (pp. 216–220)

★ Why Mergers Fail and How to Prevent It (pp. 243–245)

✔ M&A Regulations: A Global Overview (pp. 348–349)

✔ Structuring and Negotiating Joint Ventures (pp. 352–353)

Maximizing Value when Selling a Business
by John Gilligan

EXECUTIVE SUMMARY

- *Advisers advise, principals decide*. Advisers may not understand industry-specific risks and are therefore badly placed to make judgments on some risk issues. Be prepared to debate with your own advisers and to overrule them if your knowledge is superior, no matter how much they are being paid.
- *Don't buy a dog and bark yourself*. Corporate sales are complex and risky. Appoint experienced advisers and get them to manage the process under your control.
- *Information*. The importance of information cannot be overemphasized. Buyers are motivated by fear and greed: The quality, tone, and flow of information critically impact both motives.
- *Valuation*. Agree what the walkaway price is with your advisers before starting a process, review it constantly, and be prepared to walk away if necessary.
- *Competitive tension*. The best deals are achieved where more than one buyer with cash (but not an uncontrollable host) wants to purchase a business. Use this rivalry to

maximize the bids received and to eliminate risks that might prevent the buyer from delivering the deal.

- *Blunderbuss versus rifle shot*. Most businesses have a limited target population of buyers who may pay a strategic premium. The approach when marketing needs to favor those most likely to pay the best price.
- *Financial bidders are active*. In the past 20 years more businesses worldwide have probably been sold to private equity firms than any other type of acquirer. Use them to create competitive tension.
- *Auctions have to be managed*. Theory and practice suggest that many tactics in auctions are counterintuitive. Think through what you are going to do and clearly communicate it to potential purchasers.
- *Say nothing*. There are always matters that are uncertain in any deal. Staff are always unsettled by uncertainty. It is best to say nothing at all to them, but if you do decide to explain what is happening, you must be completely honest. But remember, any ambiguity is interpreted negatively.
- *Only the fittest survive*. Transactions are long and often tedious. Do not let boredom, fatigue, or lack of patience

deflect you from your final goal, especially when the winning line is near.

- *The one that got away*. The world is full of people who nearly did the best deal ever. To achieve success, you need to give and take; it is not a war, it is a negotiation.

INTRODUCTION

All corporations seem complex to those looking in from the outside. The cocktail of relationships, contracts, and assets coming together to generate value is different in every company, and the process of realizing the value embedded in that cocktail requires planning, foresight, and pragmatic judgment. Failure to sell a business that has been publicly put up for sale can destroy huge amounts of value. Each situation is unique and no text can provide a comprehensive guide, any more than you could write the complete guide to sailing in all weathers. This article will deal with general principles and strategies, not technical details. Furthermore, it will address the question of *how* to sell a business, not *why* you should sell a business.

ADVISERS—WHAT THEY DO, WHAT THEY DON'T DO

It would be perverse not to believe that corporate finance advice is valuable. Here is one casual, empirical data point that supports this view: Private equity firms, many themselves ex-corporate financiers, and whose core business is buying and selling companies, almost always use advisers. The question is not *whether* to appoint advisers; it is what should they be tasked with doing, and what is the limit of their role. Their role is not to make decisions. They are there to limit the number of decisions the vendor has to make regarding the key commercial factors that make deals happen. Good advisers should be prepared to debate decisions and use their experience to guide their clients toward the paths of least resistance. However, only the owners can make the final decisions.

Having described what advisers don't do, the natural question is: So what *do* they do? The answer to this is—pretty much everything except making the final commercial decisions. Expect advisers to prepare, collate, and analyze data that will be presented to potential purchasers. They should project manage every aspect of the sale process, providing a clear and coherent strategy to achieve a successful outcome with an acceptable level of risk. This is the necessary skill set of any adviser and it enables the company to concentrate on delivering to its customers, not preparing itself for sale. As the saying goes, "Don't buy a dog and bark yourself."

The added value in corporate finance comes in three ways. First is the ephemeral thing called judgment. As one partner of a major British practice used to describe it, having a good "bullshit detector" helps. Second is the ability to take the burden away from the client. Advisers should do all the heavy lifting, leaving their clients to concentrate on the business itself and the key decisions. Finally, and of crucial importance in many deals, advisers need to be able to access the right people in the right places who may wish to acquire the business.

INFORMATION—WHAT YOU SAY, AND HOW YOU SAY IT

In 2001 three US economists, Akerlof, Steiglitz, and Spencer shared the Nobel Prize in economics. Their body of work deals with an area formally known as "information asymmetry," or more colloquially: What do you do when I know things you don't know? This section tries to answer a simple question: If a purchaser can't tell a good car from a bad car, how can a seller get a premium for a good car? The same problem arises when you are selling a company, only more so. Companies are the most complex things that are traded, and selling one may transfer all the future and historical risks and rewards to the new owner. If you cannot persuade the new owner that the net value of those risks and rewards is quantifiable and positive, you won't sell the business. This is one of the commonest areas in which transactions fail. A failure to think through the strategy of managing and transmitting information results in transactions falling apart further down the line, as purchasers narrow the information asymmetry in due diligence and find that what they were told originally is not what they found to be true subsequently.

There are a number of ways to deal with information asymmetry. The simplest and crudest solution is to ignore the issue entirely. Provide limited data and tell purchasers to rely on their own judgment. In essence, this is what happens in an unsolicited hostile takeover, and may well be the reason that so many hostile approaches subsequently turn out to be failures.

To bridge the asymmetry you can either transmit information (under a suitable confidentiality agreement) or agree to take residual risks away from the purchaser by, for example, giving warranties. At the extremes, the negotiating positions are either: "We will give you access to do whatever due diligence you like, but we are not warranting anything," or "We will warrant that the information we give to you is materially correct, but you are not getting any more access than that." The approach to this question needs to be decided early on since it flows through the entire transaction approach and materially influences the form of legal agreement that will emerge at the end of the process. It is also important to communicate your approach to purchasers clearly and consistently. If you do not, they will impose their view on you and purchasers will seek both a belt and suspenders: full access, and full warranties.

VALUATION … IS IN THE EYE OF THE BEHOLDER

In theory, the value of any asset is the present value of its future cash flows. To maximize value, you need to show the maximum future cash flow and the minimum cost of capital. This leads to the infamous "hockey stick" projections—projections that reverse a declining trend and rise thereafter. These are fed into a spreadsheet and out pops a valuation. The danger of believing your own propaganda is that you set unrealistic targets. You must aim high, but not every attempt can be a world record.

In addition to DCF (discounted cash flow) valuations, advisers should prepare a variety of analyses. Comparable transactions that have occurred recently and analysis of comparable quoted companies valuations are the most frequently seen.

Figure 1. Typical business sale process

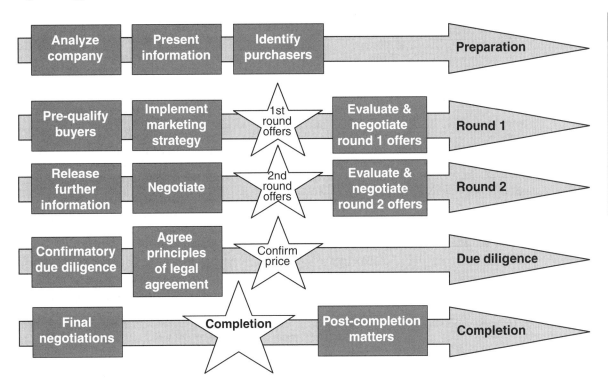

Another way to discover what advisers think your business is really worth is to look at where their fee proposal starts to generate significant uplift. Where fees are correlated to value, you can often work out the implicit valuation of any adviser from their fee proposal.

It is frequently contended that the most important output of the theoretical valuation process is not the maximum number calculated, but that it validates a "walkaway" price—the price at which the vendor will simply stop the process and refuse to sell. This number needs to be at the forefront of your mind in any negotiation. It also needs to be refreshed periodically if the prospects for the business or its markets change materially.

It is also important to remember that all these analyses are simply checking out the potential valuation. To actually achieve a transaction at a particular valuation, you normally need competitive tension or a compelling strategic premium.

COMPETITIVE TENSION—CREATING FEAR, ENCOURAGING GREED

Once you have surveyed the landscape, the task is to identify and communicate with those purchasers most likely to place a valuation on the business that they can afford to pay and which exceeds the walkaway price. When considering the number of parties to approach to create a market, again there are two extremes: blunderbuss or rifle shot.

The blunderbuss approach says that since you never know who might be looking for a business like yours, you should maximize the probability of hitting the target by firing as widely as possible. The downside is that circulating information widely makes a confidential process most unlikely.

The rifle shot approach targets a limited number of buyers, maximizing the probability of reaching those specific purchasers wishing to acquire the business. You risk missing a purchaser that you don't know of, but the process can be managed much more efficiently in a small and tightly controlled market.

Whichever approach is used, maximum tension requires only a few, well-funded potential purchasers to emerge from the initial marketing. There is not much to gain from an auction with seven purchasers compared to an auction with six, but it is much harder to efficiently manage a large number of parties. The number of parties taken into the final process needs to be consistent with the information strategy adopted. It's no use offering open access with no warranties to a large number of bidders; it is unmanageable in practice.

The special case of a market with one buyer presents different challenges. Here there are different ways to motivate a deal. In a market of one, you have to adopt either the "takeaway sale," or enter a courtship.

The takeaway sale is a tactic used by realtors and used car salesmen across the globe. You quickly show your wares and then you rapidly remove them. The message is clear: It is a once in a lifetime opportunity to buy this house/car/company, and it won't come again; act quickly. This is a risky approach. If the purchaser doesn't believe you, your negotiating position can be seriously undermined if they react with a studied show of indifference to the opportunity presented. However when it does work, it can produce spectacular results because a strategic premium is paid by the purchaser.

Courtship is subtler and has its own risks and rewards. It involves exploring possibilities and exchanging information and plans to build a consensus on the way forward and what that means in terms of valuation. When the logic of bringing two companies together is compelling, two questions often arise: First, which is the diner and which is the dinner? Second, even if the cake is bigger, you still have to negotiate how it is going to be shared. A courtship strategy requires a significant investment of senior management time and emotion.

The biggest risk in a failed courtship is, as we all know, the effect of a broken heart. The impact on corporations of a failed courtship should not be underestimated: It can paralyze a corporation just as surely as it can turn a teenager into a gibbering wreck.

FINANCIAL PURCHASERS—ELEPHANTS OR DUNG BEETLES

Financial buyers come in many forms and provide liquidity to many different markets. The private equity (PE) industry contains both large strategic purchasers (elephants) and opportunists, who seek to snap up companies when no strategic purchaser emerges (dung beetles). Whichever strategy they are pursuing, and despite being much misunderstood and maligned, over the past 20 years financial purchasers have acquired more companies than trade acquirers. Any vendor who does not consider the PE market as a potential purchaser may be missing, at a minimum, a valuable source of competitive tension, and possibly the optimal purchaser.

AUCTIONS—THEORY AND PRACTICE

In a traditional, so-called English auction, bidding stops when the last but one bidder drops out. The vendor receives fractionally more than the second highest bidder was willing to pay. There are various ways to attempt to capture the value that the highest bidder might have paid. For example, a reverse auction (also known as a Dutch or clock auction) operates by the price declining until it is accepted by a bidder. This results in the so-called winner's curse—the only thing that the purchaser knows for certain is that they paid more than anyone else would have.

A counterintuitive solution to the problem was proposed by US economist William Vickrey. In a Vickrey auction, sealed bids are received and the asset is sold to the highest bidder, but at the price bid by the second highest bidder. This system ensures that each bidder bids their own true valuation, rather than speculating on the possible bids of other parties. The theoretical underpinnings are outside the scope of this chapter, but Vickrey was (jointly) awarded the 1996 Nobel Prize in economics for his work in this area.

Information from the first round of bids can be used to intensify informed competitive tension in subsequent rounds.

For example, in a group of four second-round bidders, all the bidders might be informed of the value of the third highest bid received in round one. This tells the two highest bidders that they were one of two, but not who was highest. It tells the third highest bidder that they were third, and similarly tells the fourth highest that they are playing catch-up. The information provided by the first-round bids gives each party a clear steer on their position in the process and a strong guide regarding the landscape of the bids.

In practice much of auction theory is of only partial relevance to any corporate sale because the theory is predicated on the assumption that completion of the transaction occurs simultaneously with acceptance of the bid. In practice, of course, there is usually confirmatory due diligence and negotiation of legal agreements to follow.

DEFENDING THE PRICE

Whereas the auction process is designed to drive up the price, the period between accepting an offer and completion is usually defensive. The purchaser may try to find a justification to "chip" the price, and will rarely give any credit for positive variances against any plans they have relied on in the bid. The standard negotiating position of any purchaser when faced with positive information is, "We anticipated improvements in our original bid."

Negative variances are rarely anticipated in a bid and often result in variations to the terms of the indicative offer. Be aware that the legal status of an indicative offer varies from country to country. Whereas most UK and US acquirers view indicative offers relatively lightly, many non-Anglo-Saxon countries view the making of any offer, however qualified it may be, as significant and, in some jurisdictions, potentially legally binding. It helps to understand this when judging both the offers received and the ability to meet any timetable that you might have set for purchasers.

A contract race may alleviate exposure to price chipping, but it requires purchasers to risk paying significant fees in pursuit of a transaction that they have (on average) around a 50% possibility of completing. They may not wish to play that game. Furthermore, the process may increase acquisition risk for the purchaser due to the uncertainty caused to the business, resulting in a reduced final price.

The ability to defend the price depends on the relationship between the purchasers' and vendors' teams, and the effective implementation of the information strategy agreed at the start of the process. If the "hockey stick" projections are not being met, expect a conversation about price to occur.

DEALING WITH STAFF

Companies are possibly the only assets you can sell where the value of the asset is dependent on the goodwill of the people employed in the business. It is extremely difficult to maintain complete secrecy in any transaction. The requirement to collate information not routinely produced often causes questions to be asked. Similarly, e-mails and telephone calls from unfamiliar advisers may trigger suspicion. Uncertainty invariably causes discontent, and transactions involve great uncertainties. Against this background, it is generally advisable to say nothing to staff unless required to do so.

Any ambiguous information is often interpreted negatively, causing even more speculation and disruption. The alternative is to communicate honestly, including all the unknowns and uncertainties, giving legitimacy to the speculation but fanning the uncertainty.

Once a deal is certain, communication with staff must form a key part of the post-transaction integration plan.

MAKING IT HAPPEN

Any transaction involves extensive amounts of work and lengthy negotiations peppered with key decisions. There are periods of little apparent activity followed by periods characterized by long meetings that often drag into the night. Transactions are done by people, not by processes, and it is of utmost importance that the key decision-makers do not let boredom, frustration, or fatigue cloud their judgment. Many deals have failed because the principals or their advisers could not keep their head when the finish line was in sight.

Risks often seem more significant when you stare at them for too long. At the end of any transaction there are often negotiations regarding matters that no senior manager would normally consider material. Principals need to use commercial judgment to cut through any of these issues that are holding up a deal.

Finally, the world of mergers and acquisitions (M&A) is full of people who nearly did the best deal ever. M&A is often spoken about using the language of conflict, with winners and losers. In fact, it is about negotiation, a process that requires give and take. There is no point in beating your "opponent" at the negotiating table if all you end up with is a large bill for an aborted transaction.

MORE INFO

Books:

Brealey, Richard A., Stewart C. Myers, and Franklin Allen. *Principles of Corporate Finance*. 10th ed. Boston, MA: McGraw-Hill, 2010.

Gilligan, John, and Mark Wright. *Private Equity Demystified— An Explanatory Guide*. London: Institute of Chartered Accountants in England and Wales, 2008.

Glover, Christopher G. *Valuation of Unquoted Companies*. London: Gee Publishing, 2004.

Horner, Arnold, and Rita Burrows. *Tolley's Tax Guide*. London: LexisNexis (published annually).

Klemperer, Paul. *Auctions: Theory and Practice*. Princeton, NJ: Princeton University Press, 2004.

Wasserstein, Bruce. *Big Deal: Mergers and Acquisitions in the Digital Age*. New York: Warner Books, 2000.

Article:

Akerlof, George A. "The market for 'lemons': Quality uncertainty and the market mechanism." *Quarterly Journal of Economics* 84:3 (August 1970): 488–500. Online at: dx.doi.org/10.2307/1879431

See Also:

★ Comparing Net Present Value and Internal Rate of Return (pp. 16–19)

★ Due Diligence Requirements in Financial Transactions (pp. 216–220)

✔ Planning the Disposal Process (pp. 351–352)

✔ Understanding the Weighted Average Cost of Capital (WACC) (pp. 309–310)

Valuing Start-Ups
by Aswath Damodaran

EXECUTIVE SUMMARY

• Young and start-up companies pose the most problems in valuation, for a variety of reasons.

• Start-ups have a limited history, are generally not publicly traded, and often don't survive to become successful commercial enterprises.

• Faced with daunting estimation challenges, analysts often fall back on simplistic forecasts of revenues and earnings, coupled with high discount rates, to capture the high failure rate.

• In this article I suggest that traditional valuation models can be used to yield better estimates of the value of these firms.

INTRODUCTION

Although the fundamentals of valuation are straightforward, the challenges in valuing companies shift as they move through their life cycle: from the initial idea and start-up business, often privately owned, to young growth companies, either public or on the verge of going public, to mature companies with diverse products and serving different markets, and finally to companies in decline, marking time until they disappear. At each stage we may be called on to estimate the same inputs—cash flows, growth rates, and discount rates—but with varying amounts of information and different degrees of precision.

DETERMINANTS OF VALUE

If we accept the premise that the value of a business is the present value of the expected cash flows from its assets, there are four broad questions that we need to answer in order to value any business:

1. What are the cash flows generated by existing assets?

If a firm has significant investments that it has already made, the first inputs into valuation are the cash flows from these existing assets. In practical terms, this requires estimates of: how much the firm generated in earnings and cash flows from these assets in the most recent period; how much growth (if any) is expected in these earnings/cash flows over time; and how long the assets will continue to generate cash flows.

2. How much value will be added by future investments?

For some companies, the bulk of the value will be derived from investments they are expected to make in the future. To estimate the value added by these investments, you have to make judgments on both the magnitude of these new investments relative to the earnings from existing assets; and the quality of the new investments, measured in terms of excess returns, i.e. the returns the firm makes on the investments over and above the cost of funding them.

3. How risky are the cash flows, and what are the consequences for discount rates?

Neither the cash flows from existing assets nor the cash flows from growth investments are guaranteed. When valuing these cash flows, we have to consider risk somewhere, and the discount rate is usually the vehicle we use. Higher discount rates are used to discount riskier cash flows, and thus give them a lower value than more predictable cash flows.

4. When will the firm become mature?

The question of when a firm is mature (i.e. when the growth in earnings/cash flows is sustainable forever) is relevant because it determines the length of the high-growth period and the value we attach to the firm at the end of the period (the terminal value). It is a question that may be easy to answer for a few firms, including larger and more stable firms that are either already mature businesses or close to it, and firms that derive their growth from a single competitive advantage with an expiration date (for instance, a patent).

A framework for valuing any business that takes into account these four considerations is shown in Figure 1.

Although these questions may not change as we value individual firms, the ease with which we can answer them may change, not only as we look across firms at a point in time, but also across time—even for the same firm.

VALUING YOUNG COMPANIES

Every business starts with an idea stimulated by a market need that an entrepreneur sees (or thinks that he or she sees) and a way of filling that need. Although many ideas go nowhere, some individuals take the next step of investing in the idea.

The capital to finance the project usually comes from personal funds (from savings, friends, and family), and if things work out as planned the result is a commercial product or service. If the product or service finds a ready market, the business will usually need more capital, and the providers of this are often venture capitalists, who provide funds in return for a share of the equity in the business. Building on the most optimistic assumptions, success for the investors in the business may ultimately be manifested as a public offering to the market or sale to a larger entity.

ESTIMATION ISSUES

At each stage in the process we need estimates of value. At the idea stage, the value may never be put down on paper, but it is the potential of realizing this value that induces the entrepreneur to invest time and money in developing the idea. At subsequent stages of the capital-raising process, valuations become more important because they determine what share of ownership the entrepreneur will have to give up in return for external funding. At the time of the public offering, the valuation is key to determining the offering price.

From the template for valuation that we developed in the last section, it is easy to see why young companies also pose the most daunting challenges. There are few or no existing assets, and almost all of the value is based on the expectations of future growth. The current financial statements of the firm provide no clues about the potential margins and returns that may be generated in the future, and there are few historical data that can be used to develop risk measures.

To complete our consideration of estimation problems, we should remember that many young firms do not make it to the stable growth stage. Estimating when this will happen for firms that do survive is difficult. In addition, these firms are often dependent on one or a few key people for their success, and losing them can have a significant effect on value.

Figure 2 summarizes these valuation challenges.

Given these problems, it is not surprising that analysts often fall back on simplistic measures of value, guesstimates, or on

Figure 1. The fundamental questions in valuation

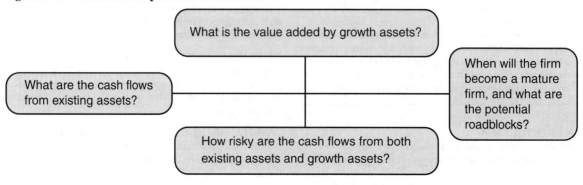

Figure 2. Estimation issues for young and start-up companies

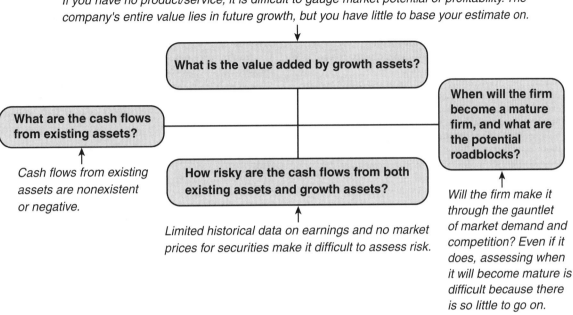

Making judgments on revenues/profits is difficult because you cannot draw on history. If you have no product/service, it is difficult to gauge market potential or profitability. The company's entire value lies in future growth, but you have little to base your estimate on.

What is the value added by growth assets?

What are the cash flows from existing assets?

Cash flows from existing assets are nonexistent or negative.

How risky are the cash flows from both existing assets and growth assets?

When will the firm become a mature firm, and what are the potential roadblocks?

Will the firm make it through the gauntlet of market demand and competition? Even if it does, assessing when it will become mature is difficult because there is so little to go on.

Limited historical data on earnings and no market prices for securities make it difficult to assess risk.

rules of thumb to value young companies. In the process, though, they risk making serious valuation errors.

MEETING THE ESTIMATION CHALLENGE

Given the challenges we face in estimating cash flows and discount rates for the purpose of valuing young companies, it should come as no surprise that many analysts use shortcuts, such as applying multiples to expected future earnings or revenues, to obtain dubious estimates of value. We believe that staying within the valuation framework and making the best estimates of cash flows is still the best approach.

CASH FLOWS AND GROWTH RATES

For many young companies, the biggest challenge in estimating future cash flows is that there is no historical base of any substance to build on. However, we can still estimate expected cash flows using one of two approaches:

Top-Down Approach

In this approach, we begin with the potential market for the firm's products and services and work backwards:
- Estimate the share of this market which the firm hopes to gain in the future and how quickly it can reach this share; this gives expected revenues in future years.
- Make a judgment on the profit margins the firm should see once it attains the targeted market share; this provides the earnings that it hopes to generate each period.
- Finally, evaluate what the firm needs to invest to accomplish this objective; this represents the capital that it

has to reinvest in the business, which is a cash drain each year.

Generally, as the firm's revenues grow and it moves toward the target margins, we should expect to see losses in the earlier years become profits in the later ones. With high growth, it is entirely possible that cash flows will stay negative even after profits turn the corner, since the growth will require substantial reinvestment. As growth subsides in the later years, the reinvestment will also decline and cash flows will become positive.

The key to succeeding with this approach is getting the potential market share and target margin right, and making realistic assumptions about reinvestment needs.

Bottom-Up Approach

For those who believe that the top-down approach is too ambitious, the alternative is to start with what the young company can generate as output, given its resource constraints, and make estimates of the revenues and profits that will be generated as a consequence. This is more akin to a capital budgeting exercise than to a valuation, and the valuation will depend on the quality of the forecasts of earnings and cash flows.

The projected earnings and cash flows from both approaches are dependent on the promoters of the company not only being able to come up with a product or service that meets a need, but also that they can adapt to unexpected circumstances at the same time as delivering their forecast results.

DISCOUNT RATES

The absence of historical data on stock prices and earnings makes it difficult, but not impossible, to analyze the risk of young companies. To make realistic estimates of discount rates, we need to be able to do the following:

Assess Risk from the Right Viewpoint

The risk in an investment can vary, depending on the point of view that we bring to the assessment.

- For the founder/owner who has his or her entire wealth invested in the private business, all risk that the firm is exposed to is relevant risk.
- For a venture capitalist who takes a stake in this private business as part of a portfolio of many such investments, there is a diversification effect, where some of the risk will be averaged out in the portfolio.
- For an investor in a public market, the focus will narrow even more, to only the risk that cannot be diversified away in a portfolio.

As a general rule, the discount rates we obtain using conventional risk and return models, which are built for the last setting, will understate the risk (and discount rates) for young companies, which are usually privately held.

Focus on the Business/Sector, Not on the Company

Since young firms have little operating history and are generally not publicly traded, it is pointless trying to estimate risk parameters by looking at the firm's history. We can get a much better handle on risk by looking at the sector or business of which the firm is a part and evaluating the riskiness of publicly traded firms in the same sector at different stages in the life cycle.

Adjust Risk Measures and Discount Rates as the Firm Matures (At Least in the Projections)

Our task in valuation is not to assess the risk of a young firm today, but to evaluate how that risk will change as the firm matures. In other words, as revenues grow and margins move toward target levels, the risk that we assess in a company and the discount rates we use should change consistently: lower growth generally should be coupled with lower risk and discount rates.

TERMINAL VALUE

In most discounted cash flow valuations, it is the terminal value that delivers the biggest portion of the value. With young firms this will be doubly so, partly because the cash flows in the early years are often negative and partly because the anticipated growth will increase the size of the firm over time.

Consider Scaling Effects and Competition

When firms are young, revenue growth rates can be very high, reflecting the fact that the revenues being grown are small. As revenues grow, the growth rate will slow, and assessing how quickly this will happen becomes a key part of valuing young companies. In general, the speed with which revenue growth will decelerate as firms get larger will depend on the size of the overall market and the intensity of competition. In smaller markets, and with more intense competition, revenue growth will decline much more quickly and stable growth will approach sooner.

Change the Firm's Characteristics to Reflect Growth

As a firm moves from start-up to stable growth, it is not just the growth rate that changes, but the other characteristics of the firm as well. In addition to the discount rate adjustments we mentioned in the last section, mature firms will also tend to reinvest less and have lower excess returns than younger firms.

Consider the Possibility That the Firm Will Not Make It

Most young firms do not make it to become mature firms. To get realistic estimates of value for young firms, we should consider the likelihood that they will not make it through the life cycle, either because key employees leave or because of capital constraints.

CONCLUSION

It is far more difficult to estimate the value of a young company than a mature company. There is little history to draw on and the firm's survival is often open to question. However, that should not lead us to abandon valuation fundamentals or to adopt fresh paradigms. With a little persistence, we can still estimate the value of young companies. These values may not be precise, but the lack of precision reflects real uncertainty about the future of these companies.

MAKING IT HAPPEN

To value young growth companies:

- Assess the potential market and the company's likely market share (if successful).
- Estimate what the company has to do (in terms of operations and investments) to get to this market share.
- Estimate the cash flows based on these assessments.
- Evaluate the risk in the investments and also how it will change as the company goes through the growth cycle, and convert the risk into discount rates.
- Value the business and the various equity stakes in that business.

MORE INFO

Books:

Damodaran, Aswath. *The Dark Side of Valuation; Valuing Old Tech, New Tech, and New Economy Companies*. Upper Saddle River, NJ: Prentice Hall, 2001.

Gompers, Paul, and Josh Lerner. *The Venture Capital Cycle*. 2nd ed. Cambridge, MA: MIT Press, 2006.

Metrick, Andrew. *Venture Capital and the Finance of Innovation*. Hoboken, NJ: Wiley, 2007.

Guideline:
Multiple authors. "International private equity and venture capital valuation guidelines." August 2010. Online at: www.privateequityvaluation.com

Website:
Damodaran Online: www.damodaran.com

See Also:
★ Comparing Net Present Value and Internal Rate of Return (pp. 16–19)
✔ Assessing Cash Flow and Bank Lending Requirements (pp. 292–293)
✔ Basic Steps for Starting a Business (pp. 361–362)
✔ Preparing a Cash Flow Forecast (pp. 301–302)
✔ Understanding the Relationship between the Discount Rate and Risk (pp. 308–309)

★

Best Practice

Why Mergers Fail and How to Prevent It
by Susan Cartwright

EXECUTIVE SUMMARY

- Mergers and acquisitions (M&A) are increasing in frequency, yet at least half fail to meet financial expectations.
- The United States and the United Kingdom continue to dominate M&A activity. As the number of cross-border deals increases, however, many other national players are entering the field, further highlighting the issue of cultural compatibility.
- Financial and strategic factors alone are insufficient to explain the high rate of failure; greater account needs to be taken of human factors.
- The successful management of integrating people and their organizational cultures is the key to achieving desired M&A outcomes.

INTRODUCTION

The incidence of M&A has continued to increase significantly during the last decade, both domestically and internationally. The sectors most affected by M&A activity have been service- and knowledge-based industries such as banking, insurance, pharmaceuticals, and leisure. Although M&A is a popular means of increasing or protecting market share, the strategy does not always deliver what is expected in terms of increased profitability or economies of scale. While the motives for merger can variously be described as practical, psychological, or opportunist, the objective of all related M&A is to achieve synergy, or what is commonly referred to as the 2 + 2 = 5 effect. However, as many organizations learn to their cost, the mere recognition of potential synergy is no guarantee that the combination will actually realize that potential.

MERGER FAILURE RATES

The burning question remains—why do so many mergers fail to live up to stockholder expectations? In the short term, many seemingly successful acquisitions look good, but disappointing productivity levels are often masked by one-time cost savings, asset disposals, or astute tax maneuvers that inflate balance-sheet figures during the first few years.

Merger gains are notoriously difficult to assess. There are problems in selecting appropriate indices to make any assessment, as well as difficulties in deciding on a suitable measurement period. Typically, the criteria selected by analysts are:

- profit-to-earning ratios;
- stock-price fluctuations;
- managerial assessments.

Irrespective of the evaluation method selected, the evidence on M&A performance is consistent in suggesting that a high proportion of M&As are financially unsuccessful. US sources place merger failure rates as high as 80%, with evidence indicating that around half of mergers fail to meet financial expectations. A much-cited McKinsey study presents evidence that most organizations would have received a better return on their investment if they had merely banked their money instead of buying another company. Consequently, many commentators have concluded that the true beneficiaries from M&A activity are those who sell their shares when deals are announced, and the marriage brokers—the bankers, lawyers, and accountants—who arrange, advise, and execute the deals.

TRADITIONAL REASONS FOR MERGER FAILURE

M&A is still regarded by many decision makers as an exclusively rational, financial, and strategic activity, and not as a human collaboration. Financial and strategic considerations, along with price and availability, therefore dominate target selection, overriding the soft issues such as people and cultural fit. Explanations of merger failure or underperformance tend to focus on reexamining the factors that prompted the initial selection decision, for example:

- payment of an overinflated price for the acquired company;
- poor strategic fit;
- failure to achieve potential economies of scale because of financial mismanagement or incompetence;
- sudden and unpredicted changes in market conditions.

This ground has been well trodden, yet the rate of merger, acquisition, and joint-venture success has improved little. Clearly these factors may contribute to disappointing M&A outcomes, but this conventional wisdom only partly explains what goes wrong in M&A management.

THE FORGOTTEN FACTOR IN M&A

The false distinction that has developed between hard and soft merger issues has been extremely unhelpful in extending our understanding of merger failure, as it separates the impact of the merger on the individual from its financial impact on the organization. Successful M&A outcomes are linked closely to the extent to which management is able to integrate members of organizations and their cultures, and sensitively address and minimize individuals' concerns.

Because they represent sudden and major change, mergers generate considerable uncertainty and feelings of power-lessness. This can lead to reduced morale, job and career dissatisfaction, and employee stress. Rather than increased profitability, mergers have become associated with a range of negative behavioral outcomes such as:

- acts of sabotage and petty theft;
- increased staff turnover, with rates as high as 60% reported;
- increased sickness and absenteeism.

Ironically, this occurs at the very time when organizations need and expect greater employee loyalty, flexibility, cooperation, and productivity.

PEOPLE FACTORS ASSOCIATED WITH M&A FAILURE

Studies like the one conducted by the Chartered Management Institute in the UK have identified a variety of people factors associated with unsuccessful M&A. These include:

- underestimating the difficulties of merging two cultures;
- underestimating the problem of skills transfer;
- demotivation of employees;
- departure of key people;
- expenditure of too much energy on doing the deal at the expense of postmerger planning;
- lack of clear responsibilities, leading to postmerger conflicts;
- too narrow a focus on internal issues to the neglect of the customers and the external environment;
- insufficient research about the merger partner or acquired organization.

DIFFERENCES BETWEEN MERGERS AND ACQUISITIONS

In terms of employee response, whether the transaction is described as a merger or an acquisition, the event will trigger uncertainty and fears of job losses. However, there are important differences. In an acquisition, power is substantially assumed by the new parent. Change is usually swift and often brutal as the acquirer imposes its own control systems and financial restraints. Parties to a merger are likely to be more evenly matched in terms of size, and the power and cultural dynamics of the combination are more ambiguous. Integration is a more drawn-out process.

This has implications for the individual. During an acquisition there is often more overt conflict and resistance, and a sense of powerlessness. In mergers, however, because of the prolonged period between the initial announcement and actual integration, uncertainty and anxiety continue for a much longer time as the organization remains in a state of limbo.

CULTURAL COMPATIBILITY

The process of merger is often likened to marriage. In the same way that clashes of personality and misunderstanding lead to difficulties in personal relationships, differences in organizational cultures, communication problems, and mistaken assumptions lead to conflicts in organizational partnerships.

Mergers are rarely a marriage of equals, and it's still the case that most acquirers or dominant merger partners pursue a strategy of cultural absorption; the acquired company or smaller merger partner is expected to assimilate and adopt the culture of the other. Whether the outcome is successful depends on the willingness of organizational members to surrender their own culture, and at the same time perceive that the other culture is attractive and therefore worth adopting.

Cultural similarity may make absorption easier than when the two cultures are very different, yet the process of due diligence rarely extends to evaluating the degree of cultural fit. Furthermore, few organizations bother to try to understand the cultural values and strengths of the acquiring workforce or their merger partners in order to inform and guide the way in which they should go about introducing change.

MAKING IT HAPPEN

Making a good organizational marriage currently seems to be a matter of chance and luck. This needs to change so that there is a greater awareness of the people issues involved, and consequently a more informed integration strategy. Some basic guidelines for more effective management include:

- extension of the due diligence process to incorporate issues of cultural fit;
- greater involvement of human resource professionals;
- the conducting of culture audits before the introduction of change management initiatives;
- increased communication and involvement of employees at all levels in the integration process;
- the introduction of mechanisms to monitor employee stress levels;
- fair and objective reselection processes and role allocation;
- providing management with the skills and training to sensitively handle M&A issues such as insecurity and job loss;
- creating a superordinate goal which will unify work efforts.

CASE STUDY

Paul Hodder was involved as director of human resource management in the formation of Aon Risk Services, a merger of four rather different retail-insurance-broking and risk-management companies. A major theme of their integration process was the formation of a series of task groups to review and identify best practice. Another part involved an organization-wide training program to provide individuals with life skills to help them initiate and cope with change, to improve teamwork, and to develop support networks. Enthusiasm for the program provided several hundred change champions to lead change projects and assume support and mentoring roles. Good communication of early wins and successes has reassured organizational members that the changes are working and are beneficial.

CONCLUSION

Despite thorough pre-merger procedures, mergers continue to fall far short of financial expectations. The single biggest cause of this failure rate is poor integration following the acquisition. The identification of the target company, the subsequent and often drawn-out negotiations, and attending to the myriad of financial, technical, and legal details are all exhausting activities. Once the target company has been acquired, little energy or motivation is left to plan and implement the integration of the people and cultures following the merger. It seems nonsensical to waste all the resources and energy that have gone into the merger through inadequate planning of the integration stage of the process, yet all too often organizations do just that. Without a properly planned integration process or its effective implementation, mergers will not be able to achieve the full potential of the acquisition.

MORE INFO

Books:

Cartwright, Susan, and Cary L. Cooper. *Managing Mergers, Acquisitions and Strategic Alliances*. 2nd ed. Woburn, MA: Butterworth-Heinemann, 1996.
Cooper, Cary L., and Alan Gregory (eds). *Advances in Mergers and Acquisitions*. Vol. 1. New York: JAI Press, 2000.
Stahl, Gunter, and Mark E. Mendenhall (eds). *Mergers and Acquisitions*. Stanford, CA: Stanford University Press, 2005.

See Also:

★ Acquisition Integration: How to Do It Successfully (pp. 211–213)
★ Identifying and Minimizing the Strategic Risks from M&A (pp. 224–227)
★ Maximizing a New Strategic Alliance (pp. 233–235)

Aligning Structure with Strategy: Recalibrating for Improved Performance and Increased Profitability

by R. Brayton Bowen

EXECUTIVE SUMMARY

- Aligning organizational structure with corporate strategy requires financial "rethinking."
- In difficult economic times, it is not unusual for organizational leaders to demand across-the-board cuts of some arbitrary percentage to achieve bottom-line results.
- Unfortunately, that approach often cuts into the "muscle" of critical functions that are vital to the successful performance of the enterprise and its future viability.
- As an alternative, activity-based cost accounting quantifies the cost of specific work activities throughout organizational systems.
- This approach to redesign helps the organization recalibrate how and where work can be better aligned with corporate direction.
- The enterprise can achieve not only better organizational performance with this method, but also bottom-line efficiencies that improve financial results.

INTRODUCTION

Phlebotomy—the ancient practice of bloodletting—seemed logical when medical science centered on the belief that four humors made up the human body: yellow bile, black bile, phlegm, and blood. It was thought at the time that an ailing person could be brought to good health by vomiting, purging, starving, and bloodletting. Unfortunately, in the latter instance, any number of the sick bled to death! By today's medical standards, the practice is considered quackery. Now when a patient is ill, the condition is diagnosed extensively until the source of the problem is identified. If an operation is required, the repair is made with surgical precision.

Oddly enough, phlebotomy continues to be practiced on the body "corporate" in any number of organizations, where the four key elements are considered to be: capital, equipment, product (services), and people. A poor-performing organization, like an ailing patient in ancient times, is "bled" of its people resource. If the economy turns down, more blood is let, until the enterprise either recovers, or dies. In rough economic times, it is not unusual for organizational leaders to demand across-the-board cuts of some arbitrary percentage to achieve bottom-line results—not unlike phlebotomy, where cuts were made on almost all parts of the body. Unfortunately, that approach often cuts into the "muscle" of critical functions that are vital to the successful performance of the enterprise, and its future viability. And, the reality is that once an organization goes through a major bloodletting, a.k.a., "downsizing," "rightsizing," or "rationalizing," management will resort to

doing it again and again. Invariably, the organization fails to achieve its performance objectives, and the scars of phlebotomy serve only to remind the employees who remain that they too may be the subjects of such savagery in the future. Trimming excess resource is certainly necessary from time to time, but keeping trim and fit on a regular basis should be the norm.

DESIGNING FROM THE OUTSIDE IN
Why Are We in Business?

Ask anyone why he or she is in business, and the answer ultimately is "to make money." Certainly, that should be the final result, but the mission is "to serve customers," and the outcome should be "customer satisfaction." Without customers, there is no business. Consequently, the design of an organization must be built from the outside in. In other words, it must begin with the end-customer in mind. Adrian Slywotzky makes the point in

Ask anyone why he or she is in business, and the answer ultimately is "to make money." Certainly, that should be the final result, but the mission is "to serve customers," and the outcome should be "customer satisfaction." Without customers, there is no business. Consequently, the design of an organization must be built from the outside in. In other words, it must begin with the end-customer in mind. Slywotzky and Morrison (1997; p. 23) make the point: "The value of any product or service is the result of its ability to meet a customer's priorities."

Structuring a business strategically requires a careful analysis of what the customer priorities are. To design from the outside in, it is important to know what the customer values: does the customer have a need, either actual or perceived? How much is the customer willing to pay? How quickly does he or she want delivery? Does the customer expect ongoing support? Does the product (service) fulfill a lifestyle or ego need? Does the customer wish to participate in an interactive process of design and fabrication? Will the customer return for replacement and/or enhanced products (services)?

When businesses make across-the-board cuts without regard to customer priorities, it is as though they have compromised the outcome for the customer and jeopardized the integrity of the relationship for the future. Entire industries have reneged on their promises of product quality and customer commitment, for example General Motors promised a unique customer relationship with its Saturn division; now it is eliminating the line to save money. Delta Airlines has continuously cut services and increased fees, reportedly to survive, while management has continued to receive generous compensation and pension benefits; today is it merging with Northwest. Circuit City, a big box retailer, lost its way with customers a long time ago. Today, it is out of business. Cost-cutting measures for all these businesses were applied without regard to the ultimate value proposition for the customer.

WHAT IS THE "ESSENCE" OF THE BUSINESS?

Continuous realignment requires the ongoing process of taking time out of the design, fabrication, and delivery cycles. Time savings equal cost savings. Increasing the value proposition for customers and shareholders requires the ongoing process of assessing the cost of doing business, as well as the return on investment. But, downsizing structure for the sole purpose of reducing cost, in and of itself, is not a sustainable strategy. Form must follow function. Structure must follow strategy. Consequently, any restructuring must begin with outcomes in mind, and the quintessential outcome in business is the value proposition for the customer. So, recognizing that businesses change constantly, how does one go about the process of continuous realignment? Rather than across-the-board cutting—like phlebotomy—consider the alternative: activity-based costing, more commonly referred to as "ABC" accounting. This approach more accurately assigns value to discrete activities, business functions, cross-organizational processes, and, ultimately, specific products and services. It even identifies the cost of what is not being done, like "waiting for instructions" or "idling in traffic." Indeed, it is a process that encourages long-range thinking and strategic decision-making rather than short-term, knee jerk reacting.

STRUCTURAL REDESIGN
Begin with Outcomes in Mind

Establish expectations from the outset by beginning with the outcomes to be realized, for example: · The proposed redesign will be aligned with the organization's vision, mission, values, and major strategies;

- The overall design will enhance the value proposition for the customer;
- Opportunities for income generation will be identified, and a more effective allocation of resources will be proposed according to the income opportunities identified;
- The new structure will be at least 80% aligned with the primary, value-adding initiatives of the organization;
- Organizational members will be empowered to work in self-directed work teams to enhance the exchange of diverse opinions and the sharing of ideas and solutions;
- The number of organizational levels will be reduced to facilitate the rapid transference of information;
- Quality assurance and continuous improvement will be built into the collective cognition and processes of the new organizational design.

Of course, one of the expected outcomes might be a targeted reduction in the cost of people resources; but even if it is not a stated outcome, typically an organization will realize a 10% reduction in the cost of human resources as a result of more efficient and effective organizational design.

Once outcomes have been established, the next step is to identify all work activities.

TAKING STOCK OF WORK ACTIVITIES AND THEIR IMPORTANCE

Taking stock requires identification of every work activity performed throughout the organizational system. For example, in the area of finance (partial list):

- Accounts payable;
- Accounts receivable;
- General accounting.

In the area of manufacturing (partial list):

- Requisitioning materials;
- Assembling parts;
- Testing finished products.

The next step is to identify those activities that are "primary," i.e., value-adding and essential to the organization's primary mission; and those that are "secondary," albeit important, but, nevertheless, ancillary to the core mission of the organization. Hence, for a marketing firm, an example of a primary activity would be "advertising layout," while an example of a secondary activity would be "accounting." (If an enterprise is in the business of advertising, it is not in the business of accounting; therefore, accounting is a secondary activity.) In the final stage of design, it is important to retain 80–90% of the primary activities for the integrity of the organization. Only the most important support activities should be retained, roughly 10–20%. The remaining support activities would be targeted for outsourcing and/or elimination. In this way, the essence of the organization is preserved and, indeed, strengthened.

THE PROCESS OF REDESIGNING

To ensure acceptance of proposed changes in the new structure and enhance the effectiveness of the design itself, utilization of a cross-organizational/cross-functional design team is recommended. Using the inventory of activities suggested above, the design team proceeds with surveying the organization to determine what activities are being performed by people throughout the organizational system, as well as the amount of time expended in performing each activity. This survey feedback is integrated with a reporting system that contains a comprehensive listing of all positions, and the payroll associated with each person. The process is also effective in capturing non-productive time. Once data collection is complete, and the data are integrated with the payroll reporting system, reports can be generated that allow the design team to assess what work is being done currently, where it is being done, who is doing it, and what the associated costs are. Armed with this knowledge, the design team can go on to look at design alternatives that better align with the outcomes expressed at the outset of the process.

SAMPLE REPORTS

Data can be arrayed in several formats to provide the right information to facilitate the redesign process for the team.

The Activity Cost by Function report (Table 1) allows team members to see the actual cost of each function within the organization. The High to Low Activity Cost report (Table 2) gives an instant snapshot of where the organization is spending its money. In the example shown, 80% of the payroll cost is being expended on 27% of the total activities performed within the system. And, finally, Table 3, identifying

Table 1. Activity costs by function

Code	Activity description	Cost US$ (000)	Cost %	FTE	Avg. time
0400	**Finance**	**238.3**	**16.1**	**12.36**	**26.3**
0401	Accounting	88.9	6.0	5.02	15.2
0249	Accounting – general	7.7	0.5	0.35	5.8
0250	Accounting – revenue	4.3	0.3	0.10	5.0

Table 2. Activity costs—High to low

Code	Activity description	Cost US$ (000)	Cost %	Cumulative %	FTE people	Avg. time
0001	Managing	179.8	12.1	12.1	2.55	14.2
0356	Marketing	75.1	5.1	37.3	2.20	44.0
0534	Customer service	68.0	4.6	41.9	4.38	24.3
	...	...	...	...	...	...
	# OF ACTIVITIES: 29	**1,186.2**			**46.44**	

27% of 109 activities cost 80% of payroll

Table 3. Activity costs by primary and support designation

Code	Activity description	Cost US$ (000)	Cost %	FTE	Avg. time
0100	**Primary Work**	**606.6**	**40.9**	**24.63**	**58.6**
0315	Product development	161.2	10.9	6.20	36.5
0356	Marketing	75.1	5.1	2.20	44.0
	...	...	...	...	...
0200	**Support Work**	**876.6**	**59.1**	**32.97**	**55.9**
0249	Accounting – general	7.7	0.5	0.35	5.8
0250	Accounting – revenue	4.3	0.3	0.10	5.0
	...	...	...	...	...

Primary and Support work, provides a ready assessment of how aligned organizational activities are with the primary mission, vision, and strategies of the organization. Ideally, primary activities account for 80–90% of all the activities in the organization. Typically, at the start of a redesign process, it is not unusual to see only 55–65% alignment. The difference between the actual and ideal allocation constitutes the "gap" in alignment that then has to be addressed in the redesign process.

CONTINUOUS REDESIGN

Building quality into the system means incorporating the ability of organizational members to redesign continuously—taking time and cost out of organizational processes, while imbedding flexibility and resiliency into the fabric of the corporate being. Embracing this competency and cultivating its continuous application can potentially stave off the need for major restructuring in the event of severe economic downturns, or increased competitive forces in the marketplace. Indeed, as many times as GE's Appliance Division faced potential closing, continuous reengineering and structural redesign prevented the threat from ever being realized.

CONCLUSION

In a global economy flexibility, adaptability, and quick response times are critical attributes for any organization that wishes to compete in today's competitive environment. Traditional accounting methods and other management metrics fail to capture the true cost of organizational processes, "hidden work," and even "non-work." Activity-based cost accounting provides a level of accountability and transparency that is not achievable with more traditional systems. Moreover, the team-based approach suggested here not only builds relationships among organizational members and understanding throughout the organizational system, it also facilitates the management of change, as design team participants prepare themselves for the implementation of changes in organizational structure they have designed. And, finally, this approach allows for continuous and systematic analysis of the organization and its processes to ensure the ongoing alignment of organizational structure with the strategic goals and desired outcomes of the enterprise.

MAKING IT HAPPEN

Aligning organizational structure with strategic goals and objectives requires intelligent planning and detailed analysis. The benefits of an ABC approach to organizational design far exceed those realized as a result of executive fiats or corporate bloodletting. The following steps are needed to ensure optimum results:

- Determine the desired outcomes of any restructuring—begin with the end in mind.
- Plan to design from the outside-in, by identifying customer needs and expectations.
- Assemble a cross-organizational and cross-functional team to conduct the analysis and propose structural change.
- Identify and catalog the unique work activities that exist throughout the organizational system.
- Conduct a comprehensive analysis of the work that is being done, capturing cost, people units, and time quantities.
- Compare the feedback with personnel data, specifically pay and hours worked.
- Generate meaningful management reports that will allow intelligent analysis by the team.
- Train the team in organizational design concepts that will result in a more horizontal organization and self-direction.
- Secure management approval of the changes and encourage continued analysis of organizational processes and related structures.

MORE INFO

Books:

Bruns, William J., and Robert S. Kaplan (eds). *Accounting and Management: A Field Study Perspective*. Boston, MA: Harvard Business School Press, 1987.

Ostroff, Frank. *The Horizontal Organization: What the Organization of the Future Actually Looks Like and How It Delivers Value to Customers*. Oxford: Oxford University Press, 1999.

Pfeffer, Jeffrey. *The Human Equation: Building Profits by Putting People First*. Boston, MA: Harvard Business School Press, 1998.

Slywotzky, Adrian J., and David J. Morrison. *The Profit Zone: How Strategic Business Design Will Lead You to Tomorrow's Profits*. New York: Times Books, 1997.

Website:
The Howland Group, Inc.: www.howlandgroup.com

See Also:
★ Reducing Costs through Production and Supply Chain Management (pp. 276–279)
★ Using Financial Analysis to Evaluate Strategy (pp. 287–290)
✔ Assessing Business Performance (pp. 359–360)
✔ Assessing the Value of Outsourcing and Offshoring (pp. 360–361)

Best Practice

Business Continuity Management: How to Prepare for the Worst
by Andrew Hiles

EXECUTIVE SUMMARY
- No organization is immune from disaster.
- Business continuity management (BCM) is an integral part of corporate governance.
- A business continuity plan (BCP) can protect your brand, reputation and market share.
- The prerequisite discipline of risk and impact assessment reveals critical dependencies and threats to them, enabling preventative measures to be taken.
- Risk and impact assessment identifies and prioritizes mission-critical activities and the timeframe in which they must be resumed; it can also provide new risk insights to improve your business performance.

GLOSSARY
BC: Business continuity
BCM: Business continuity management
BCP: Business continuity plan
BIA: Business impact assessment
DRP: A plan for the continuity or recovery of information and communications technology (ICT)
MCA: Mission-critical activities
Risk appetite: The level of loss that an organization is prepared to tolerate
RTO: Recovery time objective
RPO: Recovery point objective (of data or transactions)

INTRODUCTION
Over five years even a well-managed organization has an 80% chance of suffering an event that damages its profits by 20%.[1]

The cause could be equipment downtime, failure of utilities or supply chain, terrorism, fire, flood, explosion, or adverse weather. Whatever the cause, without a business continuity plan (BCP), the result is the same: damage to reputation, brand, competitive position, and market share. Sometimes this damage, and subsequent losses, are severe enough to lead to permanent closure.

Yet such loss can be minimized, or even avoided, by implementing a business continuity management (BCM) system which includes developing a BCP.

Quite simply, those organizations that have a BCP tend to survive a major adverse incident, while those without a BCP tend to fail.

WHAT IS BCM?
According to one definition, BCM is: a "holistic management process that identifies potential impacts that threaten an organization and provides a framework for building resilience and the capability for an effective response which safeguards the interests of its key stakeholders, reputation, brand and value creating activities."[2]

Information and communications technology (ICT) disaster recovery is an important and integral part of BCM—but only one part. BCM covers all mission-critical activities (MCAs)—operations, manufacturing, sales, logistics, HR, finance, etc.—not just the technology.

THE BC PROJECT
BCM starts as a project, but, once the BCP has been developed, audited and exercised, it becomes an ongoing program needing regular maintenance and exercise.

The project activities are illustrated in Figure 1.

MAKING BC HAPPEN
Phase One
The BC project should start with a clear understanding of the needs of the stakeholders and the support of the board. BC policy needs to be set.

A high-level steering group needs to be set up to decide priorities and define the scope of the project. For instance, is the objective to be "business as usual"—or will it just cover the 20% of goods or services that generates 80% of the profits? Will it cover all customers, or just the most important ones? Does it embrace all locations, or just head office? How far does it go down into the supply chain? Will it cover only local

Figure 1. BCP project structure

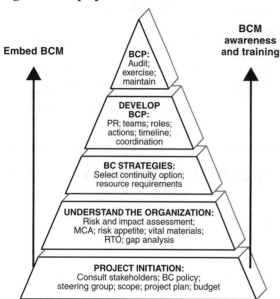

Embed BCM

BCM awareness and training

BCP: Audit; exercise; maintain

DEVELOP BCP: PR; teams; roles; actions; timeline; coordination

BC STRATEGIES: Select continuity option; resource requirements

UNDERSTAND THE ORGANIZATION: Risk and impact assessment; MCA; risk appetite; vital materials; RTO; gap analysis

PROJECT INITIATION: Consult stakeholders; BC policy; steering group; scope; project plan; budget

disasters, or is it to cope with wide-area disasters—hurricanes, major floods, etc.?

Next, a project plan should be developed, identifying the milestones and deliverables of the project. These include:

- risk and impact assessment;
- agreeing BC strategies;
- developing the BCP and implementing contingency arrangements;
- audit and exercising the BCP.

A budget can be established for Phase One from a knowledge of how many sites are to be covered, how many people are to be interviewed, how many processes are to be included at each site, and an assessment of time for research and report-writing.

Risk and impact assessment can be broken down into subactivities:

- identification of assets and threats to them;
- weighting threats for probability and impact (in cash and non-cash terms);
- identification of MCAs and their dependencies;
- establishing the recovery time objective (RTO) for each (the maximum acceptable period of service outage);
- establishing the recovery point objective (RPO) for each (the timestamp to which data and transactions have to be recovered);
- identifying the resources needed for recovery and the timeframe in which they are required;
- identifying any gaps between the RTO, RPO, and actual capability (for example, the IT backup method may not permit recovery within the RTO);
- establishing the organization's appetite for risk;
- making recommendations for risk management and mitigation;
- making recommendations to close any gaps revealed.

The risk and impact assessment is usually conducted by analysis of building plans and operational layouts; review of reports on audit, health, safety, and environmental and operational incidents; interview of key personnel; and physical inspection.

Once these activities have been completed, possible contingency arrangements can be considered. The instinctive reaction is to replicate existing capability—but there may be more cost-effective options.

Holding buffer stock could cover equipment downtime. Increased resilience and "hardening" of facilities may reduce risk to an acceptable level. Items or services could be bought in, rather than undertaken in-house. Contracts could be placed with commercial BC service vendors for standby IT, telecommunications, and work area recovery requirements.

The risk and impact assessment then forms the basis for a cost–benefit analysis of the contingency options and allows a BC strategy to be recommended and agreed.

This report, incorporating the findings and recommendations from the risk and impact assessment, forms a natural closure to Phase One. Usually there is a natural break while recommendations are considered and the budget for Phase Two is agreed.

Phase Two

Once the BC strategy has been agreed, the BC plan can be started, bearing in mind what constraints may be placed on your organization by emergency services, public authorities, regulators, and landlords and other occupants (if you occupy a building with more than one tenant).

Incident and emergency management plans (for instance, evacuation, fire, bomb threat, etc.) need to be consistent with the BCP, and there needs to be escalation processes from them into the BCP. Triggers should also be identified for escalation from customer complaints, failure of service-level agreements, problem and incident management processes, etc., into the BC process.

The BC organization may not necessarily mirror the normal organization—for instance, multidiscipline teams may be appropriate—and the BC manager or coordinator may not usually hold the level of authority they are accorded under disaster invocation.

Typically the board will be separated in two: one to manage the ongoing business, the other to deal with the disaster situation. The emergency, crisis or business continuity management team (BCMT) will include board-level decision-makers. These include members from business and support units, and the BC manager (effectively the project manager for recovery) will report to them.

Business and support unit teams, including ICT, will report on recovery progress and seek clarification, information, and support from the BC manager. The BC manager will resolve any priority clashes within his or her authority and refer others to the BCMT.

Table 1 is a partial example of a BC organization. Additional BC teams will be created as necessary to cover each MCA, business or support unit. The overview at Table 1 needs to be amplified by detailed action plans covering each BC team.

Table 1. Partial example of a BC organization

BC Management team	IT team	Base site recovery team
Leader: BC management team leader Alternate	*Leader:* TBD Alternate: TBD	*Leader:* TBD Alternate: TBD
Members: CFO Alternate COO Alternate PRO Alternate Marketing director Alternate Estates manager Alternate: TBD Admin support: TBD	*Members:* Applications manager Alternate PC servers/LAN manager Alternate Data/voice communications manager Alternate: TBD Admin support: TBD	*Members:* Office services manager Alternate PC servers/LAN Alternate: TBD Data/voice communications Alternate: TBD Damage assessment/salvage Alternate Loss adjuster: TBD Admin support: TBD
Reports: BC manager Alternate	*Roles:* Recovery of all platforms, systems applications and data at standby site: TBD Data/voice communications recovery at standby site: TBD	*Roles:* Damage assessment, limitation and salvage Recovery at base site Recovery of operational capability at base site IT, data/voice communications recovery at base site
Roles: Consider group (corporate) impacts. Manage recovery. Coordinate all team action. Consider safety and security and environmental issues. Decide on priorities. Reassure media and authorities.		

TBD – to be determined

The BCP coordinator is not necessarily the same person who will be BC manager once the BCP is completed. The BCP coordinator's role is to ensure that all BCPs are completed consistently and comprehensively.

The BCPs should not be scenario-based, since the disaster is unlikely to fit neatly into any scenario envisaged. Instead, they should be based on a worst-case scenario: total loss of MCAs. However, if they are developed in a modular fashion, only that part which is relevant need be invoked if a lesser disaster happens.

The BCP coordinator will draft a BCP for the BCMT and for his or her BC activities, including BCP invocation procedure, and will provide advice and guidance to the business and support unit BC coordinators.

Next, a template BCP should be developed that can be used for each team. Once they have had training, BCP development coordinators for each business and support unit complete these. A support program can be created for their guidance as they develop their BCPs.

Each BCP should spell out assumptions so they may be challenged (for example, an assumption that more than one site will not suffer a disaster at the same time; or that skilled people will be available post-disaster).

The minimum content should include:
- prioritized MCAs and a credible action plan for their recovery within RTO and RPO;
- lists of team members, alternates, roles, and contacts;
- resource requirements and when and how they are to be obtained;
- contact details of internal and external contacts;
- information on relevant contracts and insurance;
- reporting requirements;
- instructions on handling the media;
- any useful supporting information (such as damage assessment forms; maps and information about alternate sites; detailed technical recovery procedures).

Once the BCPs have been developed they can be audited, reviewing each BCP for comprehensiveness, clarity, and accuracy. This also ensures that interrelationships between BCPs are reflected in the counterparty BCP.

Rigorous exercises probe BCP effectiveness under different disaster scenarios and provide realistic training for BC team members.

Lessons from BC audit and tests should be incorporated into the BCPs. Where this has not yet been done, a list should be provided at the beginning of the BCP stating what weaknesses were found to exist; who is responsible for rectifying them; and the timeframe for doing so.

The BCP may take many forms: hard copy; handheld devices; memory sticks; etc. Whatever the format, it should be kept secure, and steps should be taken to ensure that only the current version can be held.

CASE STUDY
BUNCEFIELD

Buncefield Oil Storage Terminal supplied fuel to London Heathrow from pipelines transporting fuel from the north of England. It was owned by Hertfordshire Oil Storage Ltd, a joint venture between Total and Texaco. Other businesses were attracted to the site—Marylands Industrial Park—because of its low cost.

Around 06:00 hours on Sunday, December 11, 2005, an explosion occurred, measuring 2.4 on the Richter scale; it was heard as far away as France and the Netherlands.

The Buncefield incident was the biggest explosion, and the accompanying fire was the biggest fire, in peacetime Europe. Twenty-five different fire services tackled the blaze with 600 fire fighters.

The explosion and subsequent fire:
- destroyed some 5% of UK petrol stocks and destroyed 20 fuel tanks;
- injured 200 people; 2,000 were evacuated;
- damaged more than 300 houses and required 10 buildings to be demolished;
- caused all the schools in the county to be closed;
- cost local businesses and local authorities £1 billion: it impacted 600 businesses and prevented 25,000 staff from getting to work;

★

Best Practice

- disrupted global air traffic schedules and local transport;
- caused businesses to suffer disruption of supply;
- caused many organizations to invoke their BC plans;
- made big retailers re-assess their supply chain issues;
- forced companies to make public statements to protect their share value;
- created major environmental impact from millions of gallons of burning oil, which required more than three million gallons of contaminated firewater with up to 40 different contaminants to be disposed of; it took 500 tankers five weeks to move it.

Other impacts were equally devastating:

- By January 10, 2006, data recovery and communications restoration was still ongoing.
- By January 11, 2006, 75 businesses employing 5,000 people were still unable to use their premises.
- Insurance cover was inadequate to cover losses.
- In August 2006, 2,700 claimants sued for a billion pounds in a case that will cost £61 million.
- Supermarket chain Sainsbury's closed three stores damaged by fire.
- Brewers Scottish & Newcastle lost £10 million of stock.
- Retailer Marks & Spencer closed a food depot, disrupting deliveries to retail outlets.
- Fujifilm, 3Com Corporation, and Alcom buildings were damaged.
- Andromeda Logistics' distribution centre was evacuated: operations resumed on December 12 from their alternative distribution center.
- Shares in British Petroleum, a bystander, briefly dived.
- ASOS (As Seen On Screen), an online fashion retailer, lost its new warehouse with £5.5 million stock (19,000 orders were refunded).
- British Airport Authority rationed aviation fuel at Heathrow: airlines diverted to other European airports to refuel.
- Broadcasts on BBC radio and television news urged motorists to avoid panic buying of fuel.
- The HQ of XL Video, a video producer for trade shows, events, television, and concerts suffered structural damage. They had 12 projects to load on the Monday morning. Their BCP diverted projects: all shows were shipped on December 12.
- IT outsourcing company Northgate Information Solutions Ltd had backups ready for collection at 07:00 hours daily, but the fire happened at 06:00. Local tax payments went uncollected, and billing information for utility companies was lost.

Hertfordshire County Council's crisis management plan worked: it had been used at the two rail incidents at Potters Bar and Hatfield and been thoroughly tested in October 2005.

CONCLUSION

Wise executives have long known the importance of risk and impact assessment and the need for contingency planning. With today's threats, this has never been more important. Buncefield proved the need to:

- develop a BCP to protect reputation, brand, and share value and market share;
- communicate to key stakeholders;
- communicate to emergency services and staff;
- keep investors and customers informed;
- have alternative sites for operations and for a control center;
- read and understand the emergency plans of the local authorities;
- ensure that key standby resources are in place, such as information (status, contacts); accommodation (operations and work area); and reserves (stock, spare equipment, etc.).

Buncefield cost local businesses £70 million, much of it uninsured. It is imperative to check insurance cover. The impact of a major disaster could last for months, or even years.

MORE INFO

Books:

Hiles, Andrew. *Business Continuity: Best Practices—World-class Continuity Management.* Brookfield, CT: Rothstein Associates, 2007.

Hiles, Andrew. *The Definitive Handbook of Business Continuity Management.* 2nd ed. Chichester, UK: Wiley, 2007.

Hiles, Andrew N. *Enterprise Risk Assessment and Business Impact Analysis: Best Practices.* Brookfield, CT: Rothstein Associates, 2002.

Von Roessing, Rolf. *Auditing Business Continuity—Global Best Practices.* Brookfield, CT: Rothstein Associates, 2002.

Websites:

Association of Contingency Planners (ACP): www.acp-international.com

Business Continuity Institute (BCI): www.thebci.org

Continuity Central: www.continuitycentral.com

Disaster Recovery Institute (DRI) International: www.drii.org

Standards:

BS 25999 Business Continuity Management (UK)

HB 221 Business Continuity Management (Australia)

NFPA 1600 Emergency Management and Business Continuity (USA)

See Also:

★ Understanding Reputation Risk and Its Importance (pp. 279–282)

✔ Applying Stress-Testing to Business Continuity Management (p. 357)

✔ Establishing a Framework for Assessing Risk (p. 313)

✔ Identifying Your Continuity Needs (pp. 363–364)

NOTES

1 Oxford Metrica, www.oxfordmetrica.com

2 British Standards Institute/Business Continuity Institute Publicly Available Specification 56.

Countering Supply Chain Risk
by Vinod Lall

EXECUTIVE SUMMARY

- Business strategies such as outsourcing, lean manufacturing, and just-in-time lead to efficiency gains but at the same time expose the supply chain to higher risks.
- There are different sources of risk in a modern supply chain. Recognizing and appropriately managing these risks is necessary for a glitch-free functioning of the supply chain.
- Supply chain risk management strategies must be holistic and integrated with the whole supply chain environment.
- Firms must have dedicated budget line items for supply chain risk management activities.
- Failure mode effects analysis (FMEA) can be used to assess supply chain risks.

INTRODUCTION

In March 2000, a fire at a Philips semiconductor factory damaged some components used to make chips for mobile phones. Ericsson and Nokia—two of Philips' major customers—responded to the event in very different ways. Ericsson decided to let the delay take its own course, while supply chain managers at Nokia monitored the situation closely and developed contingency plans. By the time Philips discovered that the fire had contaminated a large area that would disrupt production for months, Nokia had already lined up alternative suppliers for the chips. Ericsson used Philips as a sole supplier and faced a severe shortage of chips, leading to delay in product launch and huge losses to its mobile phone division.

Today's global supply chains are complex and lean while efficiently delivering products and services to the marketplace. These supply chains involve a rigid set of transactions and decisions that span over longer distances and more time zones with very little slack built into them. As a result they are susceptible to several types of risk. These risks include operational risk due to demand variability, supply fluctuations and disruption risk due to natural disasters, terrorist attacks, pandemics, and breaches in data security. Such risks disrupt or slow the flow of material, information, and cash, and put billions of dollars at stake due to stock market capitalization, failed product launches, and the possibility of bankruptcies. In the above example, Ericsson lost 400 million euros after the Philips semiconductor plant caught fire; another example occurred when Apple lost many customer orders during a supply shortage of memory chips after an earthquake in Taiwan in 1999. Supply chain executives and managers must visualize and have a clear understanding of these risks along the entire supply chain, starting from the sourcing of raw materials to the delivery of the final product or service to the consumer. Once these risks are identified, they need to be scored on the likelihood of occurrence, and their impact must be quantified. Resources must then be used to mitigate or eliminate elements of high risk.

TYPES OF SUPPLY CHAIN RISK

Supply chain risks can be classified into different types depending on their origin. These include supply risk, demand risk, internal risk, and external environment risk.

Supply risk: These are the risks on the supply/inbound side of the supply chain. Supply risk may be defined as the possibility of disruptions of product availability from the supplier, or disruptions in the process of transportation from the supplier, to the customer. A supplier may be unavailable to complete an order for a number of reasons, including problems sourcing necessary raw materials, low process yield due to increased scrap, equipment failure, damaged facilities, or the need to ration its limited product among several customers. Transportation disruptions occur while products are in transit and add to the delivery lead time. They may be caused by delays in customs clearance at borders, or problems with the mode of transportation, such as the grounding of air traffic.

Demand risk: Demand risk is the downstream equivalent of supply risk and is present on the demand/outbound side of the supply chain. It may be due to an unexpected increase or decrease in customer demand that leads to a mismatch between the firm's forecast and actual demand. Increase in customer demand leads to depletion of safety stocks, resulting in stock-outs, back orders, and the need to expedite. A fall in customer demand leads to increased costs of holding inventory and, inevitably, price reductions. Other sources of demand risk are dependence on a single customer, customer solvency, and failure of the distribution logistics service provider.

Internal risk: This is the risk associated with events that are related to internal operations of the firm. Examples include fire or chemical spillage leading to plant closure, labor strikes, quality problems, and shortage of employees.

External environment risk: These risk elements are external to and uncontrollable from the firm's perspective. Examples include blockades of ports or depots, natural disasters such as earthquakes, hurricanes or cyclones, war, terrorist activity, and financial factors such as exchange rates and market pressures. These events disrupt the flow of material and may lead to plant shutdown, shortage of high-demand items, and price increases.

STRATEGIES FOR SUPPLY CHAIN RISK MANAGEMENT

Strategies for managing risk must be a part of supply chain management and must include processes to reduce supply chain risks that at the same time increase resilience and efficiency. Firms typically use basic strategies of risk-bearing, risk avoidance or risk mitigation, and risk transference to another party. The goal of risk-bearing is to reduce the potential damage caused by the materialization of a risk, and to be successful requires that early warning systems be installed along the supply chain. The main goal of risk avoidance is to reduce the probability of occurrence of a risk by being proactive, while under risk transfer the potential impact of risk is transferred to another organization such as an insurance company.

MITIGATING SUPPLY CHAIN RISKS

A firm could use strategic and tactical plans under four basic approaches to mitigate the impact of supply chain risks. These approaches include supply management, demand management, product management, and information management. The task of managing supply chain risk is difficult as approaches that mitigate one risk element can end up exacerbating another. Also, actions taken by one partner in the supply chain can increase the risk for another partner.

Supply Management

Supply risks can be reduced by building a web of internal and external sources. Strategically, firms should focus their core competencies on new products and ideas and the engineering necessary to reduce time-to-market. They should continue to manufacture strategic, high-value, long-life products that have relatively low demand volatility while outsourcing non-strategic, low-value manufacturing and logistics services. It is important to be very selective in building a strong web of vendors and closely managing the vendor network. For each new product, the firm must capitalize on the varying expertise of its vendor network and use expected time-to-market, quality level and price to select a vendor from the network.

Tactical plans under supply management focus mostly on supplier selection and supplier order allocation. For this, firms should develop a profile of their supply bases to get a more complete picture of the supply side of the chain. This profile should include a wide range of supplier information including the total number of suppliers, the location and diversity of suppliers, and flexibility in the volume and variety of supplier capacities. Analysis of these data will help firms identify vulnerabilities in their supply chains so they can strategize, create contingency plans, conduct trade-off analysis of issues such as single sourcing, and, if needed, identify and line up backup sources.

Demand Management

Strategic plans under demand management focus on product pricing, while tactical plans are used to shift demand across time, across markets, and across products. One product pricing strategy is called the "price-postponement strategy," whereby the firm decides on the quantity of the order in the first period and then determines the price in the second period after observing updated information about demand. Shifting demand across time is known as "revenue management" or "yield management," whereby firms usually set higher prices during peak seasons to shift demand to off-peak seasons. One technique for shifting demand across markets is called "solo-rollover by market;" this involves selling new products in different markets with time delays, leading to non-overlapping selling seasons. To shift demand across products, firms use pricing and promotion techniques to entice customers to switch products or brands.

As with the supply side, firms must also develop a profile of the demand side to analyze the outbound side of the supply chain. Analysis of the demand side will identify dangers such as those associated with overreliance on a single distribution center to serve a large market, or the risks of having a highly concentrated customer base.

Supply Chain Reserves Management

Firms can deal with supply chain risks by holding reserves of inventory and capacity in the supply chain. Managers must decide carefully on the optimal location and size of these reserves as an undisciplined approach may lead to increased costs and hurt the bottom line.

Product Management

Firms can look at their internal networks and develop a profile of their products, processes, and services. Analysis of data in this profile can help to determine if there is a good mix of products and services and if there are risks in processes such as those used for fulfilling orders.

Information Management

Information technology tools can be used to understand and manage risk better by providing visibility into planned events and warnings for unplanned events in the entire supply chain. Firms must manufacture low-risk products first and use improved forecasts to produce the riskiest products very close to the selling season. This requires the use of reliable data and better forecasting methods. Key members in the supply chain must have easy and timely access to accurate information on such measures as inventory, demand, forecasts, production and shipment plans, work in process, process yields, capacities, backlogs, etc. This offers more opportunities to all parties to respond quickly to sudden changes in the supply chain and requires the implementation of information technology solutions that interface business data and processes end to end.

The collaborative planning, forecasting, and replenishment (CPFR) model is often used to induce collaboration and coordination through information sharing between supply chain partners such as retailers and manufacturers. Under CPFR, the manufacturer generates an initial demand forecast based on market intelligence on products, and the retailer creates its initial demand forecast based on customer response to pricing and promotion decisions. Both parties share their initial demand forecasts and reconcile the differences to obtain a common forecast. Once both parties agree on the common forecast, the manufacturer develops a production plan and the retailer develops a replenishment plan.

MAKING IT HAPPEN

It is critical to have an easy-to-use tool to identify and manage supply chain risk. FMEA is a well-documented and proven risk management tool that is used to evaluate the risk of failures in product and process designs. It can be used to evaluate supply chain risk using the following process steps:

- **Step 1**. Identify the categories of supply chain risk.
- **Step 2**. Identify potential risks in each category.
- **Step 3**. Use a rating scale of 1–5 to rate the opportunity, probability, and severity for each risk. The opportunity score

for a risk is the frequency with which it occurs. One-time risk events receive an opportunity score of 1, while commonly occurring risk events are assigned an opportunity score of 5. The probability score is the score for the expected likelihood that a risk event will actually happen, so high probability scores are used when the probability of a risk event occurring is large. The severity score indicates the level of impact if the risk materializes. Low-risk events cause a minimum impact on the supply chain and receive a low severity score. Risk events that have a significant impact on the supply chain in terms of cost, time, and quality are assigned a high severity score.

- **Step 4**. For each potential risk, calculate the risk priority number (RPN) as RPN = Opportunity × Probability × Severity.
- **Step 5**. Use Pareto analysis to analyze risks by RPN. Pareto analysis is a formal technique used where many possible courses of action are competing for the attention of the problem-solver. The problem-solver estimates the benefit delivered by each action and then selects the most effective action.
- **Step 6**. Develop action plans to mitigate risks with high RPN.
- **Step 7**. Use another cycle of FMEA to reassess the risks.

CONCLUSION

The pursuit of new markets for products and of new sources for components is making supply chains longer and more complex. With this expansion comes increased risk, which may result in disruptions to the supply chain. These disruptions may be unexpected and statistically rare, but they must be understood, identified, and managed.

MORE INFO

Books:

Chopra, Sunil, and Peter Meindl. *Supply Chain Management: Strategy, Planning, and Operations*. 4th ed. Upper Saddle River, NJ: Prentice Hall, 2009.

Sheffi, Yossi. *The Resilient Enterprise: Overcoming Vulnerability for Competitive Advantage*. Cambridge, MA: MIT Press, 2007.

Websites:

Council of Supply Chain Management Professionals: cscmp.org

Supply-Chain Council: www.supply-chain.org

See Also:

★ Reducing Costs through Production and Supply Chain Management (pp. 276–279)

✔ Creating a Risk Register (pp. 362–363)

✔ Establishing a Framework for Assessing Risk (p. 313)

Creating Value with EVA
by S. David Young

EXECUTIVE SUMMARY

- Economic value added (EVA) can serve as the cornerstone of a value-based management system.[1]
- EVA is more than a performance metric. It also represents a mindset that focuses management attention on the value-creation imperative.
- EVA is profit as economists think about profit. It differs from the conventional accounting-based approach in that it imposes charges for the use of all capital, including equity.
- The value of the firm equals capital employed, plus the present value of future EVAs. By motivating managers to increase future EVA, companies can promote value-creating behavior.
- When managers are evaluated and paid on the basis of EVA, they have stronger incentives to improve operational and capital efficiency, dispose of unprofitable business, achieve more optimal capital structures, and invest in value-creating projects.

INTRODUCTION

The value-based management movement is based on two assumptions. The first is that the main aim of any business in a market economy is to maximize shareholder value. The second is that markets are too competitive for companies to create such value by accident. They must plan for it. And that means having the right culture, systems, and processes in place so managers make decisions in ways that deliver better returns to shareholders.

At the very least, corporate functions must be informed by value-based thinking—planning, capital allocation, operating budgets, performance measurement, incentive compensation, and corporate communication. EVA is a tool for achieving this. EVA is a measure of performance, but its uses extend further. When implemented properly, and especially if tied to management compensation, it is a powerful way to promote shareholder value.

EVA: A DEFINITION

EVA is a measure of profit. Not the accounting profit we are accustomed to seeing in a corporate income statement, but profit as economists define it. Both are measured net of operating expenses; they differ only in the treatment of capital costs. While income statements recognize only the interest paid to bankers and bondholders, EVA recognizes all capital costs, including the opportunity cost of shareholder funds.

The difference between accounting profit and economic profit can be seen in Figure 1. On the left side is profit as it appears on the typical income statement, where EBIT is earnings before interest and tax (a popular term for pre-tax

---

★

Best Practice

operating income), I is interest expense, T is income taxes, and IC is invested capital. Net income is simply operating income, with interest and taxes removed. Note that the only capital cost included in the profit measure is interest expense (the amount of debt multiplied by the interest rate).

EVA, or economic profit, also starts with EBIT. Income taxes are subtracted to produce net operating profit after tax, or NOPAT. But instead of subtracting interest, EVA charges for the use of *all* capital, including equity finance. While accounting profit charges only for the cost of debt, capital charges for the calculation of EVA equal the product of invested capital and the cost of capital (COC). The cost of capital, popularly known as the weighted-average cost of capital (WACC), is a function of the cost of debt and equity weighted for their relative proportions in the company's capital structure.

Economic profit is based on an idea generated by the English economist Alfred Marshall in the late 19th century: for investors to earn true economic profits, sales must be sufficient to cover all costs, including operating expenses (such as labor and materials) and capital charges. Such economic profits are the basis of value creation. Indeed, as management guru Peter Drucker has written, "EVA is based on something we have known for a long time: what we generally call profits, the money left to service equity, is usually not profit at all. Until a business returns a profit that is greater than its cost of capital, it operates at a loss."[2]

It can be mathematically proven that the worth of a business must equal invested capital—the sum of fixed assets, cash, and working capital—plus the present (or discounted) value of future EVA. Value determined in this way is mathematically equivalent to the value estimates produced by discounted cash flow models. The upshot: as capital market expectations of corporate EVA increase, so do share prices. Companies can thus use EVA targets to motivate managers to deliver the financial results that capital markets want. This approach is especially useful for executives one or two levels below top management, managers who have little direct influence over share price and for whom stock options are less effective.

EVA-DRIVEN COMPANIES AND FINANCIAL PERFORMANCE

So, what exactly have EVA companies done to improve financial performance and deliver superior returns to shareholders? The clues can be seen in the definition of EVA. EVA equals after-tax operating profit minus capital costs, with capital costs equal to invested capital multiplied by the WACC.[3] However, EVA can be expressed in a different, yet equivalent, way.

When operating profit is divided by invested capital, it yields a measure called return on invested capital (ROIC). The difference between ROIC and WACC, multiplied by capital employed, equals EVA:

EVA = (ROIC − WACC) × Capital employed

Holding other variables constant, EVA increases when ROIC increases; when WACC decreases; when capital employed increases (assuming profitable growth); or when capital employed decreases (in the case of money-losing assets). Evidence from EVA adopters shows several ways to achieve improvements:

- Increasing asset turnover. For example, EVA companies are more likely to drive reductions in inventory and speed up the collection of receivables.
- Repairing assets. Many companies discover that managers on EVA incentive plans are inclined to overhaul existing assets rather than request capital to buy new ones. Also, when additional capacity is required, managers are more likely to acquire used assets.
- Structuring deals that require less capital. For example, Armstrong, an American plastics and floor products company, had always insisted on a controlling stake in any acquisition. After adopting EVA, the company began to define the minimum amount of capital it could put into a deal and still get what it wanted.
- Disposing of unprofitable businesses. Well-managed companies have always done this, but EVA-driven bonus plans create a sense of urgency to use assets more efficiently by, for example, shedding chronic money-losing operations.

Figure 1. Accounting profit (EBIT) versus economic profit (EVA)

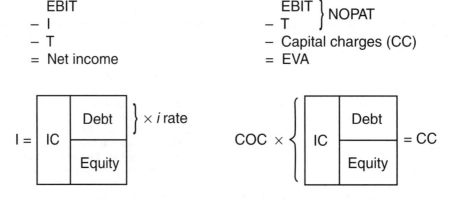

IC = Invested capital

- Increasing debt financing. Senior managers tend to "underlever" their businesses, which means they rely too much on equity finance and not enough on debt. As a result, companies fail to take advantage of valuation tax shields that can increase after-tax cash flows to capital providers. EVA changes such behavior because, when managers are charged for capital, they have powerful incentives to design capital structures that minimize the cost of capital. For the underlevered company, this means taking on debt, which is precisely what many companies have done after adopting EVA.

- Investing in profitable growth. The net present value (NPV) of future cash flows for a proposed capital investment is mathematically equivalent to the present value of incremental EVAs. Therefore, future EVA will increase to the extent that investments are made in projects with positive NPV. However, because the short-term effect of investment may be to cause EVA to decline, companies must take special care to ensure that senior managers have long-term incentives to create value. This need explains, in part, why companies continue to rely on stock options. Equity participation, if structured properly, provides incentives for managers to seek out investments that will boost EVA in the future even if short-term results are compromised.

The first three of the above actions increase EVA through improvements in ROIC. Disposing of unprofitable businesses increases EVA, provided that improvements in the spread between ROIC and WACC more than compensate for the reduction in invested capital. Increasing financial leverage increases EVA by reducing the WACC, assuming that the company is underlevered when it begins taking on more debt. Investing is profitable, and increases EVA, as long as the ROIC for new investments exceeds the WACC.

EVA AND MANAGERIAL COMPENSATION

Although EVA is a potentially powerful tool for creating value-creating incentives, there are some limitations and drawbacks to its use. For example, capital charges might compel managers to forgo potentially value-creating projects out of fear that short-term EVA will suffer. Simply put, because EVA is a single-period measure of performance, managers with EVA-linked bonuses may willingly sacrifice long-term competitiveness in the interests of pursuing short-term targets. Another potential drawback is found in attempts to bring EVA into levels of the firm below the level of strategic business units. Inevitably, contentious and arbitrary cost allocations and transfer prices are required to calculate EVA. In such cases, even the most ardent proponents of EVA have found that performance indicators that represent components or predictors of EVA are more appropriate than EVA itself for incentivizing behavior.

CASE STUDY
SPX—CORPORATE TRANSFORMATION THROUGH EVA

SPX is a large US auto parts and industrial products company. It was a chronic underperformer in the early 1990s, with low profits and a languishing share price. After a change of CEO in

1995, the company adopted EVA as the centerpiece of its change program. By the end of the following year a dramatic improvement in performance was evident.

After adopting EVA, SPX engaged in a broad range of actions, all with one overriding purpose: the creation of shareholder value. For example:
- In the first year after adopting EVA, inventories were cut by 15%, despite higher sales.
- SPX's portfolio of businesses underwent important changes. Several business units were sold, not because they were unprofitable but because strategic reviews revealed that the businesses were worth more to other companies. Meanwhile, several key value-enhancing acquisitions were made.
- Divisions were consolidated for greater operating efficiency. Substantial cost savings were realized.
- Several finance-based initiatives were undertaken. For example, the quarterly dividend was eliminated in favor of stock repurchases, a more tax-efficient way of returning cash to shareholders.

The above actions were neither unusual nor dramatic. Any good executive knows what they are. What makes this company's experience so instructive is that it was able to create a business culture that put value creation at the center of all key management processes and systems. Most critically, senior management bonuses were linked to EVA improvement. It's this link that provided managers with the incentive to aggressively pursue value-creating initiatives. Perhaps the key issue in any business is not whether its managers are capable of creating value, but whether they are motivated to do so.

CONCLUSION

Great business leaders, past and present, have always known about EVA without calling it that. EVA reveals to the rest of us the insights the best business managers have always had at a deep intuitive level. To make the most of this powerful tool for value creation, managers should know that EVA is much more than a measurement system. It's also an instrument for changing managerial behavior. Implementing value-based principles requires acceptance and understanding among all managers, who not only must appreciate why value creation is so important but also must grasp the fundamental concepts underlying value creation. One of the great virtues of EVA is that it makes sound finance theory accessible, so that operating managers, including those with no background or experience in accounting or finance, can incorporate insights from these disciplines into the way they run their businesses.

MAKING IT HAPPEN

Because EVA is really about changing behavior and attitudes, the implementation process must begin with the board and the CEO. However, the CFO's advice and counsel will carry a lot of weight on several key implementation issues. For example,
- How will EVA be calculated? Some companies choose to make adjustments to the standard EVA measure. Finance professionals must decide which adjustments, if any, are appropriate for their own business.

- Are changes needed to the company's accounting and IT systems? Often, significant upgrades are needed to deliver divisional EVA figures in a timely fashion.
- How far down the organizational hierarchy will EVA be calculated? The rule of thumb in most companies is to limit EVA to large business units. Of course, EVA can be calculated at lower levels, but the measurement process will likely be compromised by the arbitrary nature of transfer pricing and overhead allocation practices. Instead, companies tend to rely on other key performance indicators.
- Which managers will have bonuses linked to EVA? Most users limit EVA-linked bonuses to senior managers for the same reasons noted above (i.e., the difficulty of calculating EVA below the level of strategic business units).
- Who will need training in EVA and how will the training needs be executed? Anyone whose performance evaluation or pay is affected in any way by EVA needs to understand the measure—how it's constructed and the steps they can take to improve it.

MORE INFO

Books:

Koller, Tim, Marc Goedhart, and David Wessels. *Valuation: Measuring and Managing the Value of Companies*. 5th ed. Hoboken, NJ: Wiley, 2010.

Martin, John D., and William J. Petty. *Value Based Management*. Boston, MA: Harvard Business School Press, 2000.

Young, S. David, and Stephen F. O'Byrne. *EVA and Value Based Management: A Practical Guide to Implementation*. New York: McGraw-Hill, 2001.

Website:

Value-Based Management: www.valuebasedmanagement. net/methods_eva.html

See Also:

★ Capital Budgeting: The Dominance of Net Present Value (pp. 12–16)
★ Comparing Net Present Value and Internal Rate of Return (pp. 16–19)
★ Dividend Policy: Maximizing Shareholder Value (pp. 190–194)
✔ Understanding the Weighted Average Cost of Capital (WACC) (pp. 309–310)
⇄ Economic Value Added (p. 391)

NOTES

1 EVA is a registered trademark of Stern Stewart & Company.
2 Drucker, Peter. *Classic Drucker*. Boston, MA: Harvard Business School Press, 2008; p. 107.
3 Some companies prefer to calculate EVA on a pre-tax basis, especially for division performance measurement.

Employee Stock Options
by Peter Casson

EXECUTIVE SUMMARY

- Employee stock options are call options on the employer company's common stock, and are usually not transferable.
- Most employee stock options have a vesting period, during which the holder is not unconditionally entitled to the option, with options vesting at the end of the period if performance conditions are met.
- Employee stock options may be used by companies to recruit, retain, and provide incentives to employees and executives. Companies with weak cash flows that cannot afford to pay employees the market rate entirely in cash may use stock options in lieu of cash.
- Companies may use employee stock options to capture tax or accounting benefits associated with them.

INTRODUCTION

Employee stock options are a component of the compensation package of many employees and executives. As well as providing a mechanism for linking pay with the performance of the company's stock price, stock options can facilitate the recruitment and retention of employees. The effectiveness of stock option compensation derives from the basic characteristics of options and from particular features found in many employee stock options. This article describes the essential features of employee stock options and explores the ways in which they are used by companies.

CHARACTERISTICS OF EMPLOYEE STOCK OPTIONS

Employee stock options are call options granted by an employer on the company's common stock. Call options are contracts that give holders the right, but not the obligation, to acquire stock at a specified price (the exercise price), either on a specified date or over a specified period. The fair value of a call option has two components. The first, known as intrinsic value, is the amount that the holder would receive were the option to be exercised today. This amount, which cannot be negative, is the greater of zero and the difference between the fair value of the underlying stock and the exercise price of the option. The second, known as time value, is the difference between the fair value and the intrinsic value of the option.

The fair value of a call option on a company's common stock is sensitive to changes in:

- The fair value of the underlying stock—the value of the option rises with increases in the fair value of the stock.

- The expected volatility of the returns on the underlying stock—the value of the option increases with increases in expected volatility.
- The risk-free rate of interest—the value of the option increases with increases in the risk-free rate.
- The time until the option expires—the value of the option decreases as time to expiry decreases.
- The dividends expected to be paid on the underlying stock over the life of the option—the value of the option decreases with increases in the expected dividend payments.

Stock options granted to employees usually have an exercise price equal to the fair value of the underlying stock on the date the option is granted, and have a life of seven to ten years. Stock options generally have additional features that affect their fair value. First, there is usually an initial period, often three years, after the grant of the option (the vesting period), during which the employee is not unconditionally entitled to the option. Rather, the employee's entitlement to the option at the end of the vesting period only comes about if performance conditions are met. The performance condition for employees is usually to remain in the employment of the grantor company during the vesting period. Options, especially those granted to senior executives, may have additional performance conditions relating to company and/or personal performance. Second, once vested, options are usually forfeited if the employee leaves the grantor company. However, it is usual for employees to be able to exercise options within a period, often 90 days, after leaving the company. The forfeiture provision normally means that employees are forced into an early exercise of in-the-money options. Third, employee stock options are usually nontransferable, which means the employees can only realize value by exercising the option and selling the stock. In so doing, they forego the time value of the option.

WHY COMPANIES USE EMPLOYEE SHARE OPTIONS

Companies grant stock options to attract, retain, and motivate employees and executives. In addition, start-up companies and companies with weak cash flows may grant stock options to compensate for the below-market cash wages that they can afford. Finally, options may be granted to capture taxation and/or accounting benefits.

Stock options attract employees and executives for the following reasons. First, individuals whose abilities match the needs of the company may be attracted by stock options because they believe that their abilities will improve company performance and that this will be reflected in an enhanced stock price. Second, the offer of stock options may attract those employees who are most optimistic about the company's future prospects. Their optimism may lead them to overvalue the options, so reducing the company's overall employment costs. Finally, stock options may attract relatively less risk-averse employees who meet the needs of the company.

Employee stock options can be used as a way to increase employee retention. The vesting conditions usually found in the options encourage employees to remain with the company until the options become exercisable. In addition, employees will forego the time value of vested options if they are forced

into early exercise by leaving the company. Finally, as employees build up a portfolio of options over time, it becomes more costly for a competitor to attract the company's employees, as the competitor may have to compensate them for the value foregone from forfeiting unvested options or from suboptimally exercising options.

Holders of employee stock options have an incentive to act in a way that increases the value of the options. The fair value of employee stock options is, as described above, sensitive to the company's stock price, the expected volatility of the stock, and the dividends expected to be paid on the stock during the life of the options. Employees may act, through enhanced performance, to increase company performance, and that in turn may be reflected in the stock price. Although grants of stock options to CEOs and senior executives may be effective in increasing company performance, the incentive effects of grants to other employees are questionable, as there are significant free-rider problems. The other incentive effects are confined to options held by senior executives, especially CEOs. Senior executives holding stock options may make riskier investment decisions and/or increase the company's leverage with a view to increasing the expected stock volatility. Stock options may also reduce the dividend on the company's stock.

Stock options may be used by start-up companies and companies experiencing cash constraints. Here employees may sacrifice part of their cash compensation in exchange for stock options. Although financial institutions are usually seen to be in a better position than employees to bear the risks associated with lending, employees may be willing to do so because: (1) options attract risk-seeking individuals, who, if the company fails, will move to another company; (2) they possess superior knowledge and so perceive the risk differently to financial institutions; or (3) they do not understand the risks.

Companies may use stock option compensation because of preferential tax policies, although this depends on the tax regime of the country in which the employee and the company are resident. Stock option compensation may, depending on the jurisdiction, be taxed at the time of grant, or at the time the option is exercised, or when the stock acquired on the exercise of the option is subsequently sold. Employees may be charged either to income tax or to capital gains tax on their stock option compensation. Finally, stock option compensation by the company may or may not be tax-deductible. A country's tax regime may offer favorable tax treatment to stock option schemes that have particular features. In such cases, the provisions of the tax regime may shape the option schemes that companies use.

Stock option compensation may also be used because of the way it is accounted for in company financial statements. The accounting treatment of stock options was seen in the past to be advantageous when stock options were recorded at their intrinsic value at the time of grant. As options are usually granted with an exercise price equal to the fair value of the stock on the date of grant, the intrinsic value of the option is zero. This meant that there was no charge against income. However, both international and US accounting standards now require companies to charge the fair value of stock options, as measured at the time of grant, against income.

Best Practice

CASE STUDY
BG GROUP PLC[1]

BG Group plc is a UK-listed company engaged in the discovery, extraction, transmission, distribution, and supply of natural gas. BG has about 5,000 employees, more than 60% of whom are located outside the United Kingdom. The company operates two stock option schemes, a company share option scheme (CSOS) and a sharesave scheme. The CSOS is open to UK and overseas employees above a certain grade. The number of CSOS options granted to individuals depends on their past performance and their expected contribution to the company. The CSOS scheme aims to "drive real earnings growth over the long term." Options granted under this scheme, which have an exercise price equal to the fair value of the company's shares at the time of grant, have a vesting period of three years, and vested options may be exercised at any time until the tenth anniversary of the grant. Options vest to the extent that there has been real growth in earnings per share (EPS) over the vesting period. All the options will vest if EPS growth over the vesting period is at least 30% more than growth in the retail prices index (excluding mortgage payments) (RPIX), and half the options will vest if EPS growth is at least 15% more than RPIX growth.

The sharesave scheme, which is approved by the UK tax authority, allows eligible employees to acquire shares in the company using the proceeds of a tax-exempt monthly savings plan. BG Group uses the scheme as a way of encouraging share ownership in the company.

CONCLUSION

The structure of employee stock options facilitates their use by companies to attract, retain, and motivate employees and executives. In particular, the vesting provisions provide incentives for employees to remain with the company. Employee stock options have a role in aligning employees' and executives' interests with those of stockholders. Performance conditions attached to the vesting of some stock options may also align the objectives of employees with those of the company. The structure of stock options may be shaped to take advantage of tax and/or accounting rules.

MAKING IT HAPPEN

The decision to establish stock options schemes usually rests with the board of directors, and it may require stockholder approval. In designing a scheme it is necessary to consider:
- Why the company wants an employee stock option scheme.
- Which employees should be included within the scheme.
- The characteristics of the stock options. This includes consideration of the exercise price, the vesting period (if any), vesting conditions, the forfeiting of vested options if the employee leaves the company, and the life of the option.
- The tax and accounting implications of the scheme.

MORE INFO

Book:
Wheeler, Peter R. *Stock Options + Grants: The Executive's Guide to Equity Compensation*. Sunnyvale, CA: AdviserPress, 2004.

Article:
Hall, Brian J. "Six challenges in designing equity-based pay." *Journal of Applied Corporate Finance* 15:3 (Spring 2003): 21–33. Online at: dx.doi.org/10.1111/j.1745-6622.2003. tb00458.x

Website:
National Center for Employee Ownership (NCEO; US): www.nceo.org

See Also:
★ Balancing Senior Management Compensation Arrangements with Shareholders' Interests (pp. 173–175)
★ Executive Rewards: Ensuring That Financial Rewards Match Performance (pp. 194–198)
✔ Assessing Business Performance (pp. 359–360)
✔ Creating Executive Compensation (pp. 340–341)

NOTE
1 Information from BG Group plc Annual Report 2007.

Essentials for Export Success: Understanding How Risks and Relationships Lead to Rewards
by Paul Beretz

EXECUTIVE SUMMARY
- The global business environment can present opportunities for rewards for the exporter if international risk attributes can be determined and mitigated.
- Exporters who want to succeed should be able to identify and evaluate their "IQ" (international qualities).
- The risk elements of country, currency, and culture can significantly impact global business transactions.
- Relationship-building and the ability to sustain those relationships are necessary qualities for reaping rewards.

INTRODUCTION

More and more, companies located throughout the world are recognizing that the way to sustain long-term growth is not by continuing to emphasize local, in-country markets. Whether it be for better or worse, global business is a factor that can provide businesses with the opportunity to consider new and challenging markets. In 2008, we saw that severe credit and financial issues could spread quickly, and that no part of the world was immune. Therefore, an understanding of the key risk factors that can lead to rewards is essential.

How should a business assess world markets? One initial approach for exporters is to determine their "IQ," or international qualities, before either entering or expanding their overseas markets.

RATING YOUR COMPANY'S "IQ"

The "IQ" test shown in Figure 1 will address your company's readiness to compete in the global marketplace. For each question, give your company a letter grade (A–F, or U for "Unknown") and state the reason(s) for your grade. Grade A = 90–100%, B = 80–89%, and so on.

RISKS FACING THE EXPORTER

An exporter will face many risks once the decision to sell in overseas markets is made. Key risk areas, in particular, are known as the "three Cs"—country, currency, and culture.

Country Risk

Figure 2 outlines the dimensions of country risk when goods or services are sold globally. Exporters may wish to use the chart to classify the major risk issues and attributes of each risk by country.

Theses are the questions to ask when determining the dimensions of country risk:

- What currency will you be selling in? Is the decision a competitive one? Are you equipped internally to deal in multicurrencies?
- Do you know the laws in specific countries? (For example, a joint venture in China must balance imports with exports, or else it could be barred by the government from obtaining hard currency.)
- What is the recent political history (that could influence the availability of funds or internal stability)? This will include government takeover of properties, whether with or without compensation, operational restrictions, or damage to property or personnel.
- What is the current economic environment in the country? Have there been local currency devaluations recently?
- Have there been border disputes that could escalate military readiness and therefore impact the availability of hard currency, both within the country's borders and as funds leaving the country? If the exporter's customer base is expanding through direct investment abroad, will there be access to the invested capital and will earnings be able to

Figure 1. The "IQ" test

"IQ" question	Grade	Reason
What percentage of your revenues do you expect from the country(ies) you will be exporting to?		
What do you expect as your market share and industry ranking in that/those country(ies)?		
Will you establish direct sales relationships with your major customers?		
Will you ever expect to be considered a company that is "part" of the country you are exporting to?		
Have you analyzed all the cultural, currency, and country issues you will encounter in exporting to a particular country?		
What is your knowledge of the market for your product in a given country?		
What is your knowledge of the economic structure and the current state of the economy in a new country?		
Have you analyzed the legal system in a new country for the legality of your contracts or relationships? Can you cancel a relationship with a distributor or an agent if necessary? Is your documentation of sale legally binding?		
Once the sale is made, and payment is not forthcoming, what are your options in achieving payment? Practically, culturally, and legally, what are the norms?		

Figure 2. Dimensions of country riskBeretzExport_Fig2

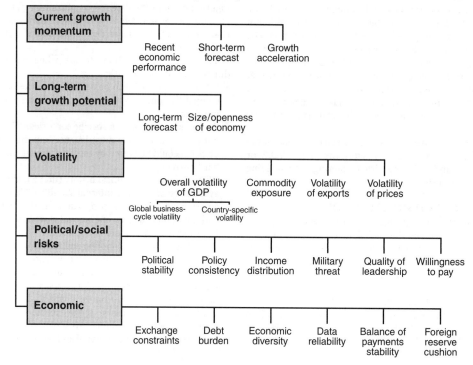

be repatriated? This could impact cash flow and the ability to meet its trade obligations.

Currency Risk

Exporters have to consider selling in foreign currencies to offshore customers. In this competitive environment, an exporter needs flexibility in determining the currency that is billed to the customer. In a volatile global economy, however, billing a buyer in a currency that differs from the seller's own currency can be fraught with risk: When payment is due, has the value of the currency fallen in value against the seller's currency?

One approach for the exporter is to deal in the foreign exchange (FX) market, which is an enormous, sophisticated, and efficient global communications system operating around the clock to enable international transactions. Large commercial banks are the dominant players in the FX market, serving as intermediaries between supply and demand; corporations are the principal end-users. FX transactions are speculative by nature and thus can be volatile, thereby increasing risk.

Three basic transactions for managing FX risk are *spot transactions*, *forward transactions* and *options*. *Spot transactions* are purchases or sales of foreign currency for "immediate" delivery. *Forward transactions* carry a specified price and stipulated future value date for the exchange of currencies. They are used most often to cover future foreign currency payables and anticipated receipts. *Options* are a more suitable tool for "hedging" risk when a foreign customer's commitment is not firm. Buyers pay a premium for the option to exchange foreign currency at a predetermined

rate ("strike price"). Options are bought and sold on the "exchange-traded" (less flexible, less expensive) and "over the counter" (more flexible, more expensive) markets, and they allow buyers to take advantage of favorable changes in currency rates while guarding against adverse changes.

The prudent financial manager recognizes that currency risk is a major factor in the export decision.

Culture Risk

The proactive, truly globally oriented exporter living in today's competitive marketplace understands that business decision making is a form of art as much as a science. All the evaluation tools available cannot take the place of experience. It is essential to possess a fundamental, analytical approach to the export selling process. The "art" form of today's global business process includes an understanding of how the cultures and negotiation processes of different countries become part of the arsenal of tools in making an intelligent decision. How the culture of each country or region impacts the risk is material to the ultimate business decision.

A lack of awareness—whether it be intentional or not—can impact the business relationship, impede the negotiations, and end the opportunity to complete the business transaction. Does the exporter understand customs and practices regarding whether or not to shake hands and what clothes to wear? Does the exporter know about presenting business cards (in different languages)—and not writing on the card? Mistakes that involve eating and drinking have been known to end a business opportunity; many Westerners do not know that in certain Chinese provinces the act of putting chopsticks in a rice bowl means "death" to the person on the other side of the table. In many world cultures, the customer expects the eldest representative of the exporter to be involved in negotiations (such elders are known as the "gray-haired gods"), even if this person is not the most astute.

CASE STUDIES
Country Risk
A large forest products company based in the United States had solid business relations with five distributors located in a Latin American country. These distributors, in total, owed US$10 million to the exporter, all within payment terms. When the central bank of the country froze all payments leaving the country, the government bank instructed all vendors selling into the country that they would have to wait five years for any repayment of debt. The country manager of the forest products company, who had developed excellent relations with several key executives at the central bank over the years, was able to discount the US$10 million debt with a global bank located outside the country. The result? The exporter was paid 95 cents on the dollar within 60 days. In addition, future sales were paid through an escrow account with the same bank. What is the moral of the story? Even though the five customers were well financed and deemed extremely creditworthy, a country calamity impacted their ability to process business normally. Without the relationship the forest products country manager had developed, the exporter would have had to wait five years for payment.

Currency Risk
Tyco International Ltd, based in Bermuda, with headquarter operations in Princeton, NJ, US, is a maker of safety, industrial, and construction products. According to a *Wall Street Journal* article of November 12, 2008 ("Tyco warns currencies, costs will hit earnings"), the company said that in September and October 2008 it saw about a 20% devaluation in currencies of foreign countries where the company did business. The chief executive estimated that these exchange rate fluctuations could reduce fiscal revenue in 2009 by about US$2 billion and reduce annual earnings by about 38 cents per share. Tyco generates about 50% of its revenue abroad.

Culture Risk
A large chemical company had been negotiating a licensing agreement with a Middle-Eastern country for close to a year. As the final meeting was drawing to a close, a junior member of the exporter's team asked the customer's executives present at the meeting if everything was "OK" and, at the same time, made the standard Western gesture meaning the same thing.

In the customer's culture this hand signal was an insulting and vulgar sign, so the customer took offense and walked out of the meeting. It took numerous apologies from the exporter and another six months to restore the relationship before the transaction was eventually consummated.

HOW RELATIONSHIPS CAN LEAD TO REWARDS FOR THE EXPORTER
Awareness, attitude, and anticipation are crucial. In the global business environment, the observant exporter should know how to watch and listen, rather than expect the transaction to happen "now." Relationship building is not only critical with offshore customers, but also imperative with a company's own "internal" customer—the branch office or agent in that country of business. Many exporters demonstrate hubris in their belief that how they do business in their own country is how it is best to do business in the country of the potential importer.

The proactive, successful exporter desiring to succeed in other lands will study behavior, learn about verbal and nonverbal differences that exist, and often will use a "go-between" in order to create the desired relationship. The person who is the intermediary may be one's own country manager; or it could be a banker, business owner, or government employee in a key position in the country who understands how to help achieve the connection between the two parties. Any person-to-person relationship, especially in the business world, has a better chance of succeeding when trust is both understood and established. This need for relationship means that a feeling of complete trust and confidence must exist, not only that the other party will not take advantage of them, but also that they can presume upon the indulgence of the other.

Trust, as part of relationship-building, is paramount in much of the negotiating process. In China, *guanxi* literally means "relationships" and is understood as the network of relationships among various parties that cooperate together and support one another. In Japan, *shokaijo* can mean a letter of introduction, indicating that the status of the exporter is confirmed with the Japanese customer or contact, as opposed to a "cold" call. It provides more of a "guarantee" that the exporter is connected to the business process in Japan. *Jeito* (in Brazil) is the way a businessperson, though local contacts and experiences, is given the chance to succeed.

MAKING IT HAPPEN
To understand how to navigate both the risks and the relationships to reap the rewards, the exporter should:
- Be proactive in determining the ("IQ") international qualities of their own organization.
- Evaluate the risk dimensions of the particular country (or countries) where they want to do business.
- Know enough about how to assess currency risks to know when to call the experts.
- Study, study, and study some more the cultural mores of the countries in which they do business.
- Observe, listen, and learn from their mistakes.

CONCLUSION
The exporter needs to evaluate their "IQ." Once that process is completed, the exporter should identify the critical risk factors of country, currency, and culture with the business trans-action. Woven into these risk factors are the attributes of relationships. By carefully evaluating the risks and ensuing relationships, an exporter can reap rewards.

MORE INFO

Books:

Coface. *2012 Coface Handbook of Country Risk*. London: GMB Publishing, 2012.

Morrison, Terri, Wayne A. Conaway, and Joseph J. Douress. *Dun & Bradstreet's Guide to Doing Business Around the World*. Paramus, NJ: Prentice Hall, 2000.

Websites:

Country risk—Investopedia: www.investopedia.com/terms/c/countryrisk.asp

Culture risk—WiseGeek: www.wisegeek.com/what-is-a-faux-pas.htm

Currency risk—Investopedia: www.investopedia.com/terms/c/currencyrisk.asp

Finance, Credit and International Business Association (FCIB): www.fcibglobal.com

International Education Systems: www.marybosrock.com/faux_pas.html

See Also:

★ Measuring Company Exposure to Country Risk (pp. 136–139)

★ Measuring Country Risk (pp. 139–142)

★ Political Risk: Countering the Impact on Your Business (pp. 270–273)

★ To Hedge or Not to Hedge (pp. 53–56)

Five Routes to Greater Profitability for Small and Medium Enterprises

by Thomas McKaig

EXECUTIVE SUMMARY

- Use your business plan as a road map for your company's success.
- Remember that increasing revenue does not automatically mean increased profits.
- Keep your costs in check.
- Use quality initiatives throughout your organization.
- Profitability depends on human issues, not just balance sheet measures.

INTRODUCTION

Although the routes to profitability discussed in this article are particularly important to the small or medium-sized enterprise (SME), they are broadly applicable to firms of any size. When reviewing these five key steps, ask yourself how many you can implement in your firm—or in your division or team if you work in a larger enterprise.

Review the following five points, and see how *your* business stacks up.

FIVE ROUTES TO GREATER PROFITABILITY

1. Use your business plan as a road map, day in and day out

Some entrepreneurs view their business plan merely as a document to raise initial capital. After this has taken place, the plan gets pushed aside as day-to-day events become more pressing. In other cases, the entrepreneur may never have prepared a formal business plan, as the initial capital was raised from their own resources or from other friendly sources. Both these situations represent lost opportunities to benefit from what a business plan can provide. *A good plan helps you to define your objectives and lets you know where you stand in relation to those objectives*. It helps managers

at all levels to allocate scarce resources. It also helps you to take corrective action when circumstances change—as they will.

Don't keep your business plan to yourself—share it with your employees. A good business plan can improve priority setting for your employees, can promote action orientation, and can improve coordination between groups, divisions, and teams (see route 5).

Even though entrepreneurs are bombarded by people promising the one best business plan (just as job seekers are constantly exposed to sources promising the one best business resume), there is no real magic in creating a business plan. Any plan should include:

- A summary of why the company is in business (its mission), and how it is different from its competitors (its competitive advantage).
- An industry analysis, including the nature of the industry, and the economic and regulatory trends that can or may affect it.
- A market description, noting the current and future size of the market, and the strengths and weaknesses of competitors.
- A description of the product or service being offered, and how it will be produced and sold.
- A marketing strategy.
- Management and human resources, and any particular staffing issues.
- Financial forecasting for the short term (less than one year), medium term (1–3 years), and long term (3–5 years).
- Key benchmarks or milestones, both quantitative and qualitative, for the next six months, one year, and three years.

The future almost never unfolds in the way we predict, which means that a business plan is not a static document. A good plan will actually lead to increased flexibility to meet changing circumstances while keeping focus on the main objectives of the firm. Management should review the plan at least annually, look to it for guidance whenever necessary, and make changes when circumstances warrant.

2. Don't chase revenue

One of the realities for a business of any size is that even though revenue might be the top line on the income statement, it is not always the most important line. Increasing revenues do not automatically mean rising profits. The best illustration of this is the numerous small and medium-sized dot-com companies of the late 1990s that never survived long enough to become larger companies. They constantly searched for growing revenues, or growth of market share, assuming that profits would somehow naturally and eventually follow from this top-line growth. It didn't, and they went out of business, even if they enjoyed near total domination of a particular market segment.

Profits are what ultimately matter, not revenue. Although increasing revenue may bring profits, you can actually increase profits by *reducing* revenue and focusing on the key products or customers that are most profitable. Ask yourself what would happen if you decided not to chase those marginal customers that you may currently have. It is possible to get lean and see your profits rise. In these tough economic times, remember that growing revenues demands increased capital, which may not be available to your firm today at terms that you can live with.

3. Minimizing costs is at least as important as maximizing revenue

The start-up small business entrepreneur is often an expert at controlling costs—by making do or by doing without, or by postponing major expenditures. This skill can often be lost as a firm grows, but it is remains important whether the firm employs 2, 20, or 200 people.

In these tough economic times, look to carry less inventory, examine the potential for savings through cash management, and look at savings that may be available in your existing supplier contracts. Ask your suppliers what they are willing to give you to keep your business. Entrepreneurs are used to pushing and asking for discounts and better terms, but this is a skill set that often falls by the wayside as a firm grows.

For some firms, labor is a major cost component. Examine the feasibility of offshoring some functions, or outsourcing others. Defer bonuses if necessary, both for labor and for management. Make cuts strategically. Cutting an arbitrary 10% from each department is almost certainly suboptimal. One department may have plenty of slack, so you may be able to cut by 20%, whereas another—perhaps your accounting or other support service—might be very tight and should not be cut at all.

An issue related to costs and revenues is the profit margin of your firm. Look at yield management issues, if applicable, and look at the prices you charge. Can these be increased (for added revenue); can they be cut (to gain market share); or can your pricing terms be adjusted?

4. Use quality initiatives when dealing with stakeholders, especially employees and customers

Quality has become such a buzz word that for many people it has little meaning any more, or they misinterpret the word as a synonym for expensive. We tend to think that only expensive products have quality, or that only expensive company processes can produce quality goods and services. Neither of these is true.

According to Armand Feigenbaum, *quality initiatives are a powerful tool to increase overall business profitability and the positive cash flow of a business.* Quality can help in three ways. First, it can help the salability of your product or service by producing a product that meets your customers' wants, and at a price that allows you a substantial profit. Second, it can aid in the producibility of your product, as quality control helps in both the designing and the manufacturing of a product. Finally, quality contributes to the productivity of your firm, since it emphasizes positive control of quality rather than reactive detection and reworking of any failures. Quality initiatives also help in the incoming materials area of your firm, increasing production rates by reducing wasted effort.[1]

5. Work to align the interests of employees with your organization

Non-balance-sheet issues can be very important to your bottom line. However, many entrepreneurs are not managers, and some may have difficulty understanding that not all their employees are as willing to work 24/7 like the company's founders and first employees.

Employee benefits are one way of attracting and retaining employees. However, traditional benefits are particularly difficult for small and medium-sized firms, which cannot offer the same types of employee benefits that their larger competitors can. For example, almost no new SME can offer a traditional defined-benefit pension plan to its employees, as it is simply not cost-effective to do so. Complex health and dental plans, which need a large employee base, may also not be feasible for the firm. A small firm may, then, offer an employee share ownership program (ESOP) if its shares are publicly traded. This can take the place of other benefits the small firm cannot offer, and it can also help to align the interests of the employee with the organization as a whole.

Not every potential employee is willing to trade the safety of a pension plan for stock in the firm, so a key component of any human resource strategy is to pick the right people through the hiring process. Choosing people who understand the entrepreneur's mindset will help to ensure a proper fit in your organization. Having the right people on board will make motivation and employee retention much easier.

The small or medium-sized firm is often characterized by an environment where job titles are constantly changing, and where written job descriptions do not always exist. In such a situation, it is particularly difficult to keep employees focused on your goals and not theirs. One method that can help is management by objectives (MBO). This is often merely thought of as a way of assessing employee performance, but in fact it is much more. The MBO process is a four-step procedure whereby the manager and employee jointly set out clear objectives for each employee (having regard to the firm's overall objectives, as defined in the business plan), jointly establish a plan by which these objectives will be met, identify clear standards for measurement, and define a method for reviewing performance results.

Such a process helps all employees to get to know the organization's objectives and how each person fits within the organization, it aids coordination between divisions of the growing firm, and it frees senior management time for matters other than day-to-day tasks of employee supervision.

CASE STUDY 1
What Not to Do

The firm was a small company in the medical publishing field offering print publications to doctors and other healthcare professionals throughout the country. Profits were substantial, but growth was slow, as the company's market was mature and mostly saturated—almost every doctor, dentist, and pharmacist already received its publications. Thus, growth for the foreseeable future was likely to be very modest, matching the growth of healthcare professionals, estimated to be 1–3% annually for the next decade.

A new company president decided that this growth was not enough. In a field where the company's competitors were being bought up by large multinational firms, the president decided to "get big to get bought out." New sales staff were brought on board and motivated with a new commission schedule that was entirely based on the revenue brought in (the previous schedule looked at both project revenue and project profits). Bonuses were given for new sources of revenue that the company had not pursued before.

Staff found that the company became fixated on sales to such new sources of revenue whether or not a product could actually be delivered, and whether or not it could be done profitably. The company quickly branched out into conferences, online publishing, and related media. None of these efforts made money. Staff complained that sales staff would drop new projects on to their desks that had been presold but which had not been planned for and were never produced. Key staff left quickly, and customers became upset that the products promised to them were not delivered on time. Instead of growing, the company quickly shrank and was eventually bought by a large competitor but at a price far below what the company would have sold for before it began its ill-judged chase after revenues.

CASE STUDY 2
Motivating Creative Employees

European Business Television (EBTV) creates corporate profiles, TV broadcasts, viral advertisements, and webcasts. It specializes in corporate profiles and has recently added the Middle East to its market focus. Rashid Ahmad started the company in 2006 and owns 74% of the company. EBTV employees own 20%. Rashid gives equity to his employees if they stay with the company for 12 months.

Ahmad feels that for his (creative) business to prosper and grow, there has to be a direct connection between his employees having fun and their achieving success—the soft issues noted above. For example, at EBTV, 20% of an employee's day (which is long, as is typical in the industry) is

spent having fun. From playing table tennis to trying new media technology, there is a balance in the workplace between the business and creative environments.

Ahmad hires dynamic individuals and encourages them to bring up and test new ideas. The management structure is flat, employees are empowered to make decisions. He also does not keep the firm's profits to himself, and pays above-average wages to his employees.

CONCLUSION

These five paths to profitability are broadly applicable to firms of any size and are useful at almost any stage in a company's life cycle. So how do you and your firm measure up?

MAKING IT HAPPEN

- No business plan should be carved in stone. Situations can and do change, affecting your business plan. Take out your plan and review it. Are there new competitors today? Is your firm now going in a different direction? How have the economy and the pricing environment changed? What are you going to do to adapt?
- In the rush to book new sources of revenue, don't neglect to ask a key question—can the client pay? And if they pay today, will they be around to pay tomorrow?
- Similarly, remember not to rush the search for completely new sources of revenue. There is never only one good deal left out there. There is always time for due diligence.
- In today's difficult economic environment it will be difficult to motivate employees when cuts have to be made. If you have to make employee cuts, cut once, and cut deep if you have to. It is better to get layoffs out of the way as quickly as possible, rather than leave employees hanging and wondering as one 10% cut in staff is followed by another, and then another.

MORE INFO

Books:
Balderson, D. Wesley. *Canadian Entrepreneurship and Small Business Management*. 8th ed. Whitby, ON: McGraw-Hill Ryerson Higher Education, 2011.
Carnall, Colin. *Managing Change in Organizations*. 5th ed. Harlow, UK: Pearson Education, 2007.
Carpenter, Mason A., and W. Gerard Sanders. *Strategic Management: A Dynamic Perspective. Concepts and Cases*. 2nd ed. Upper Saddle River, NJ: Prentice Hall, 2009.
Feigenbaum, Armand V. *Total Quality Control*. 3rd ed. New York: McGraw-Hill, 1991. (See also 4th ed, published 2004.)
Timmons, Jeffrey A., and Stephen Spinelli. *New Venture Creation: Entrepreneurship for the 21st Century*. 8th ed. McGraw-Hill Irwin, 2008.

Reports:
KPMG. "Managing for growth and profitability." 2009. Online at: tinyurl.com/7mdw64e [via archive.org]
Schiller, Bradley R., and Philip Crewson. "Entrepreneurial origins: A longitudinal inquiry." Washington, DC: US Small

Business Administration. Summary online at:
www.sba.gov/advo/research/rs152.html

Towers Perrin. "Taking the pulse of business and workforce
challenges." April 2008. Online at: tinyurl.com/djqtfx

Websites:
European Commission on "craft and micro-enterprises":
tinyurl.com/7b6kx8e

M Institute blog posts on "growth in medium enterprises":
tinyurl.com/8xnpe9j

See Also:
✔ Assessing Business Performance (pp. 359–360)
✔ Basic Steps for Starting a Business (pp. 361–362)
✔ Preparing a Cash Flow Forecast (pp. 301–302)

NOTE
[1] Feigenbaum (1991), pp. 19–20.

The Impact of Climate Change on Business
by Graham Dawson

EXECUTIVE SUMMARY

- The impact of climate change on business—or the monetary value of the costs that may be incurred by affected parties and the benefits that they may accrue—is difficult to assess with any degree of precision.
- The Stern Review and the United Nations Intergovernmental Panel on Climate Change (IPCC) have reported the results of running complex computer models that integrate climate science and economics with the aim of predicting the economic impact of climate change far into the future.
- There is no agreement concerning the appropriate discount rate or the monetary value of effects where market prices are not available.
- Uncertainty also surrounds the rate, and carbon-intensiveness, of the growth of the world economy for decades and even centuries ahead, while the hypothesis of anthropogenic climate change itself continues to be controversial.

THE GLOBAL IMPACT OF CLIMATE CHANGE ON PEOPLE

The standard approach to assessing the economic impact of climate change on business requires giving a monetary value to the costs that may be incurred by those affected and the benefits that may accrue to them.

The most comprehensive attempt to do this is the Stern Review (2007), commissioned by the UK government, which predicts severe impacts from an average global temperature rise of 2–3°C within the next 50 years or so. These impacts include an increased risk of flooding from melting glaciers, followed by disruption to water supplies, affecting up to one-sixth of the world's population, mainly in the Indian subcontinent and parts of China and South America. In higher-latitude areas, such as Northern Europe, agricultural yields may increase with a temperature increase of 2–3°C, but declining yields, especially in Africa, could leave hundreds of millions of people without sufficient food. Increased mortality from heat-related deaths and the spread of tropical diseases is predicted, although there will be fewer deaths from exposure to cold. With warming of 3–4°C, thermal expansion of the oceans is predicted to cause rising sea levels, which could lead to inundation of low-lying coastal land, displacing "tens to hundreds of millions" of people. The risks are greatest for Southeast Asia (Bangladesh and Vietnam), small islands in the Caribbean and the Pacific, and large coastal cities, such as Tokyo, New York, Cairo, and London. Extreme weather events may become more frequent.

CASE STUDY
WHAT WOULD THIS MEAN FOR BUSINESS ACTIVITY IN, FOR EXAMPLE, THE UNITED STATES?

If predictions such as those reported by Stern prove to be accurate, business will be forced to adapt to changes in climate. Adaptation would involve a range of measures of varying cost. In the United States, temperature increases of up to 2–3°C might cause the wheat belt to shift northward into Canada; US farmers in the Midwest would have to plant new crop varieties, a fairly routine adjustment. In northern areas, winter deaths from exposure to the cold would fall and tourism might increase. Further south, the melting of snow could make the water supply to California and the Mississippi basin more erratic, causing more acute problems for agriculture. Deaths from exposure to heat and the cost of air conditioning and refrigeration would increase. At higher temperatures, southern parts of the United States would see an increased risk of extreme weather events, requiring substantial investment to defend low-lying cities, such as New Orleans and New York, from flooding.

MODELING THE COSTS OF CLIMATE CHANGE

It is easy enough to put a monetary value on some of these impacts. For example, there is a lot of expensive real estate with known market prices in major coastal cities such as London, New York, and Tokyo. Moreover, without offices or factories for people to work in, or homes for them to live in, output would fall, at least for a while. Declining crop yields (adjusted for higher prices) and also fish stocks would reduce the value of world output. Standard practice is to estimate the loss of output consequent upon people's incapacity for paid and unpaid work.

Quantifying these predicted impacts of climate change in monetary terms requires degrees of certainty and precision that may not be attainable. Both the science and the economics of climate change are subject to considerable uncertainty and are therefore deeply controversial.

The impacts of climate change on business depend on the magnitude of temperature changes associated with different concentrations of CO_2 and other greenhouse gas (GHG) emissions, according to the scientific hypothesis of anthropogenic climate change. The earliest studies of the economic impact of climate change assumed a doubling of atmospheric concentrations of CO_2 by 2050, and estimated the costs of the resulting increase in global mean surface temperature at approximately 2% of world gross domestic product (GDP).

Subsequent modeling of the economic impact of climate change has sought to integrate scientific models of the global climate and economic models of future world economic growth. The anthropogenic hypothesis holds that most of the observed rise in temperature has been caused by GHG emissions from fossil fuel use in economic activity. The future path of GHG emissions depends on the rate of growth of world economic activity and how that growth is divided between more and less carbon-intensive processes. So predicting the future path of GHG emissions, and hence the impact of climate change on business, involves modeling the rate of growth of the world economy well into the future.

The United Nations Intergovernmental Panel on Climate Change (IPCC) occupies a near-monopoly position in disseminating climate science to policy makers throughout the world. It does not predict future temperature increases and their impacts but prepares a number of illustrative outcomes, using integrated assessment models (IAM). Models of world economic growth and consequent GHG emissions are combined with climate science models, showing the links between those GHG emissions and temperature change.

The Stern Review used PAGE2002, an IAM designed by the UK government in 2000 and modified two years later. Stern claims that the overall costs and risks of business-as-usual (BAU) climate change would be equivalent to losing 5–20% of global GDP each year, "now and forever," but this may not be as apocalyptic as it sounds.

Stern explains the different stages by which this estimate of the economic impact of climate change was reached. The model is run to simulate a period of 200 years or more and "produces a mean warming of 3.9°C relative to pre-industrial in 2100." The first stage indicates that the costs and risks of climate change that can be quantified in terms of market values (basically, lost output) would be equivalent to losing at least 5% of global GDP each year, "now and forever."

At this point, Stern departs from most other models by adding in "non-market" impacts on the environment and human health. Nonmarket impacts are those that cannot be given a monetary value by referring to a market price (for instance, the price of land lost to coastal flooding). The costs of disease or of lost agricultural land in subsistence economies, for example, do not have a market price. Including this second stage increases the total cost from 5% to 11% of global GDP.

These estimates are highly controversial. Since standard practice is to estimate health impacts in terms of lost output from incapacity to work, applying this and other techniques to estimate the cost of nonmarket impacts is subject to considerable uncertainty. It has also been argued that the degree to which both disease and casualties from natural disasters are related to income rather than environmental factors is not taken into account.

The third stage adds amplifying feedback effects, including the risk of catastrophic climate change, which increase the potential total cost from 11% to 14% of global GDP. Finally, Stern considers the view that a disproportionate burden of climate change would fall on poor regions. If this were given a stronger relative weight, the total cost of global warming could increase to "around 20%" of global GDP. Stern arrives at such a large adjustment for poor regions because he assumes that vulnerability to climate change is independent of development, but it seems more likely that such vulnerability depends on the capacity to adapt and hence on the level of development.

UNCERTAINTIES IN THE ECONOMIC VALUATION OF IMPACTS
"Now and Forever"

The phrase "now and forever" invites examination. The effects of climate change are expected to occur year by year over a very long period of time. The Stern Review calculates the present value of the costs of climate change by averaging the total costs over the number of years the model runs at a rate of discount. Nordhaus ran the Stern model to calculate the costs of climate change, including nonmarket and catastrophic impacts that take Stern's estimate up to 14% of world output, for each year the model covers. According to Nordhaus, the model projects a mean loss of only 0.4% of world output in 2060, rising to 2.9% in 2100 and 13.8% in 2200. Losses averaging about 1% over the period 2000–2100 become about 14% "now and forever" because the losses in the distant future are extremely high (and a low discount rate is used). Nordhaus argues that, "using the [Stern] *Review*'s methodology, more than half of the estimated damages now and forever' occur after the year 2800."

Discounting

For most people, $100 is worth more today than $100 next year because there is a degree of uncertainty about what might happen between now and next year; they would prefer to have $100 to spend right now to having it at some point in an uncertain future. In other words, the *present value* of that $100 payable to you in 10 years is less than $100 paid to you now. Similarly, the expected future costs, no less than the benefits, of an event or occurrence should be discounted, i.e. reduced in value, in order to estimate their present value.

Since many economic impacts of climate change are not expected to occur until decades or even centuries into the future, their occurrence is inevitably subject to a degree of uncertainty. The impacts of catastrophic climate change may never happen, so economists discount, or reduce the value of, their costs. As you add up the costs of climate change year by year, you might want to adjust downward those expected in later years—that is, you might want to *discount* them to reflect the uncertainty of their occurrence. The higher the rate at which you discount such costs, the lower will be their present value.

The discount rate used may influence the results of a model more than any other parameter or value used in the model. There is no agreement about the appropriate rate of discount to use, and Stern argues that any discount rate greater than zero unfairly devalues the interests of future generations. He sets the "pure time preference rate" at zero, on the grounds that a future generation has the same claim on our ethical attention as the current one. Based on a zero pure time preference rate, the discount rates used in Stern's running of PAGE2002 are lower than those used in most other models and do much to explain why Stern's "baseline" cost of 5% of world GDP is higher than the results of other models (typically 1–2% of world GDP). Other ethical approaches are at least as convincing. For example, agent-relative ethics holds that agents naturally value people who are linked to them by kinship or proximity above strangers who are remote in space or time. This approach implies a higher discount rate, which would reduce the loss from "business as usual" in Stern's model substantially below 5% of world GDP.

The estimate is an annual average for an indefinite future; losses are low for the first 50 years or so, and using unusually low discount rates produces a high present value for the catastrophic losses predicted for 2200 and beyond. By that time, given rates of world economic growth sufficient to cause the projected carbon emissions and climate change, it is reasonable to assume that most people will be very much better off than the current generation, although not quite as much better off as they would have been in the absence of climate change.

Scenarios of Future World Economic Growth

How much better off would these future generations be, and which groups of people would gain most? What will the world economy look like 100 years from now? Wisely, the IPCC has demurred from making any such prediction, offering instead six illustrative scenarios of possible future courses that the world economy might take. In 2007 the IPCC reported the "best estimates and likely ranges for global average surface air warming for six… emissions marker scenarios." The best estimate for the low scenario is 1.8°C, and the best estimate for the high scenario is 4.0°C. The important point here is that scenarios are descriptions of possible outcomes to which no probability can be attached. Of the six scenarios, the IPCC asserts that that: "All should be considered equally sound." If it is impossible to assess the risk of any of the associated impacts, there is radical uncertainty.

It is widely believed that the impact of an increase in global temperature of less than 2°C will be mild, and that cereal yields will actually increase in temperate regions. With a global temperature increase of 4°C, the impacts are projected to be catastrophic, with up to 80 million people exposed to malaria, and up to 300 million more affected by coastal flooding each year, with rising risks of extreme weather events. But, on the

IPCC's own admission, it is impossible to say whether the impact of climate change will be mild or catastrophic.

Uncertainty in Climate Science

Uncertainty also surrounds the science of climate change. In its most recent report, the IPCC claims that there is 90% certainty that most of the increase in global mean temperature since the middle of the twentieth century has been caused by the observed increase in greenhouse gas concentrations in the atmosphere. This is actually a rather cautious and vague claim, because it is consistent with a significant role for natural causes being the reason for the rise in global temperature. In the decade since 1998 global temperature has not risen, and critics of the IPCC argue that the scientific evidence for dangerous change is far from overwhelming.

Conclusion

The impact of climate change on business, or the monetary value on the costs that may be incurred by affected parties and the benefits that they may accrue, is difficult to assess with any degree of precision.

The Stern Review and IPCC have reported the results of running complex computer models that integrate climate science and economics with the aim of predicting the economic impact of climate change into the remote future. However, there is no agreement concerning (i) the appropriate discount rate and (ii) the monetary value of effects where market values are unavailable. Uncertainty also surrounds the rate, and carbon-intensiveness, of the growth of the world economy for decades and even centuries ahead, while the hypothesis of anthropogenic climate change itself continues to be controversial.

MAKING IT HAPPEN

Business may be affected by policies to mitigate climate change as much as by climate change itself. In the negotiations for the Kyoto Protocol, which seeks to establish a global framework for reductions in GHG emissions, the fossil fuel producers and users resisted aggressive reductions, while insurance companies and renewable energy producers were more favorably disposed toward them. It is not clear whether aggressive mitigation policies will survive the financial crisis of 2008, with many policy makers more concerned to reduce the effects of the expected global recession than the more distant threats posed by climate change.

MORE INFO
Books:
Lawson, Nigel. *An Appeal to Reason: A Cool Look at Global Warming*. London: Duckworth, 2008.
Nordhaus, William. *The Challenge of Global Warming: Economic Models and Environmental Policy*. New Haven, CT: Yale University Press, 2007. Online at: nordhaus.econ.yale.edu/dice_mss_072407_all.pdf

Singer, S. Fred, and Dennis T. Avery. *Unstoppable Global Warming: Every 1500 Years*. Lanham, MD: Rowman & Littlefield, 2006.

Stern, Nicholas. *The Economics of Climate Change: The Stern Review*. Cambridge, UK: Cambridge University Press, 2007.

Articles:

Beckerman, Wilfred, and Cameron Hepburn. "Ethics of the discount rate in the Stern Review." *World Economics* 8:1 (2007): 187–210. Online at: tinyurl.com/7adyfc8

Brittan, Samuel. "On climate change and good sense." *Financial Times* (February 9, 2007). Online at: www.samuelbrittan.co.uk/text268_p.html

Byatt, Ian, Ian Castles, Indur M. Goklany, David Henderson, *et al*. "The Stern Review: A dual critique. Part II: Economic aspects." *World Economics* 7:4 (2006): 199–232. Online at: tinyurl.com/7dsdfrr

Carter, Robert M., C. R. de Freitas, Indur M. Goklany, David Holland, *et al*. "The Stern Review: A dual critique. Part I: The science." *World Economics* 7:4 (2006): 167–198. Online at: tinyurl.com/7dsdfrr

Tol, Richard S. J., and Gary W. Yohe. "A review of the Stern Review." *World Economics* 7:4 (2006): 233–250. Online at: tinyurl.com/826yrz4

Reports:

Goklany, I. M. "Death and death rates due to extreme weather events: Global and US trends 1900–2006." In *Civil Society Report on Climate Change*. London: International Policy Press, 2007; pp. 47–60. Online at: www.csccc.info/reports/report_20.pdf

House of Lords. "The economics of climate change." HL Paper 12-1, Select Committee on Economic Affairs 2nd Report of Session 2005–06. London, 2005.

Intergovernmental Panel on Climate Change, Working Group 1. "Climate change 2007: The physical science basis. Summary for policymakers." 4th Assessment Report (IPCC WG1 AR4 Report). 2007. Online at: tinyurl.com/88uagec [via archive.org].

Reiter, Paul. "Human ecology and human behaviour: Climate change and health in perspective." In *Civil Society Report on Climate Change*. London: International Policy Press, 2007; pp. 21–46. Online at: www.csccc.info/reports/report_20.pdf

US Climate Change Science Program (CCSP). *Our Changing Planet: The US Climate Change Science Program for Fiscal Year 2009*. Online at: www.climatescience.gov/infosheets/ccsp-8

Websites:

Global and Development Environment Institute at Tufts University: www.ase.tufts.edu/gdae

Intergovernmental Panel on Climate Change (IPCC): www.ipcc.ch

Science and Environmental Policy Project (SEPP): www.sepp.org

United Nations Environment Programme (UNEP) climate change pages: www.unep.org/climatechange/

US Climate Change Science Program (CCSP), integrating federal research on global change and climate change: www.climatescience.gov

See Also:

★ Best Practices in Corporate Social Responsibility (pp. 175–179)

★ Business Ethics (pp. 179–182)

★ CSR: More than PR, Pursuing Competitive Advantage in the Long Run (pp. 187–189)

✔ Creating a Sustainable Development Policy (pp. 339–340)

✔ Identifying Your Continuity Needs (pp. 363–364)

Political Risk: Countering the Impact on Your Business

by Ian Bremmer

EXECUTIVE SUMMARY

- Business decision-makers must understand the political dynamics within the emerging market countries in which they operate.
- We can measure a state's stability—the ability of its government to implement policy and enforce laws despite a shock to the system.
- Essential to managing any type of risk is the development of a detailed and effective hedging strategy.
- Companies should not accept too much risk exposure within any one country or region.
- Rules of the game can change quickly in developing countries, and the cultivation of "friends in high places" isn't always a strong enough hedge.
- Operating in some developing countries comes with reputational risks at home.
- Too many companies have historically relied for insight into local politics and culture on employees who have lived in a particular country for only a short time—or have even merely traveled there.
- Those doing business in developing states need to have credible emergency response plans in place when events outside their control shut down supply chains, prevent local workers from coming to work, or otherwise disrupt operations.
- Developing strategies to recruit and train local managers serves several useful purposes.
- Devoting a share of profits to investment in local schools and universities, infrastructure, and charities can generate stores

of goodwill, which is sometimes essential for cooperation with local workers and government officials.

- In some countries, foreign companies should be wary of transferring proprietary information to local partners or developing it inside the country.
- A foreign firm must look beyond what its local competitors are capable of producing today. It must anticipate how those capabilities are likely to develop over time.
- Conditions sometimes force companies to cut their losses and head for the exit. Ensuring that process is as painless and inexpensive as possible forms a crucial part of any sound risk mitigation strategy.
- Political risk can be managed. It should not be avoided altogether.

INTRODUCTION

Over the past several years, and across a broad range of companies, corporate decision-makers seeking opportunities overseas have learned that it is not enough to have a knowledge of a foreign country's economic fundamentals. They also have to understand the forces and dynamics that shape these countries' politics. This is especially true for emerging markets, where politics matters at least as much as economic factors for market outcomes. Of course, understanding that political risk matters is one thing. Knowing how to use it is another.

STABILITY

Starting with the basics, when committing a company to risk exposure in an emerging market country, it's essential to understand how political risk impacts the underlying strength of its government. There are two key elements to consider: stability and shock. Shocks are especially tough to forecast, because there are so many different kinds and because shocks are, by definition, unpredictable. We can't know when an earthquake will strike Pakistan, an elected leader will fall gravely ill in Nigeria, or a previously unknown group will carry out a successful terrorist attack in Indonesia.

But we can take the measure of a state's stability, which is defined as a government's ability to implement policy and enforce laws despite a shock to the system. The global financial crisis, a potent shock, has inflicted heavy losses on Russia's stock market. But Prime Minister Vladimir Putin has amassed plenty of political capital over the past several years, and President Dmitry Medvedev, his handpicked successor, basks in Putin's reflected glow. Neither need fear that large numbers of Russian citizens will turn on them anytime soon. In addition, a half-decade of windfall energy profits has generated more than US$500 billion in reserves, ready cash that can be used to bail out stock markets, banks, and, if necessary, an unpopular government. That's why, for the near-term, Russia will remain stable.

Pakistan is a different story. The country's newly elected government has a range of rivals and enemies. Inflation, power shortages, and a wave of suicide attacks have undermined the ruling Pakistan Peoples Party's domestic popularity. The financial crisis leaves the country at risk of debt default, forcing the government to negotiate a loan

package with the International Monetary Fund that could impose austerity measures—the kind that helped topple civilian governments in Pakistan in the 1990s. The country is less stable than Russia, because it is much more vulnerable to the worst effects of shock.

President Luiz Inácio Lula da Silva has bolstered Brazil's stability over the past several years by quelling fears of left-wing populism with responsible (and predictable) macro-economic policies. The Chinese Communist Party's ability to generate prosperity at home via three decades of successful economic liberalization has helped its leadership to build durable near-term stability.

But Nigeria's future stability remains at the mercy of President Umaru Yar'Adua's failing health, as historical tensions between northern Muslims and southern Christians combine with ongoing security challenges in the oil-rich Niger Delta region to prevent his government from building a national reputation for competence, vision, and strength. Iran's theocrats and firebrand president Mahmoud Ahmadi-nejad have effectively used the international conflict over the country's nuclear program to shore up support for the government in the face of high inflation and gasoline rationing. Underlying political factors in all these countries have a substantial impact on stability—and, therefore, on the country's business climate.

DIVERSIFY

Yet it is not sufficient to possess broad insights into state stability. If corporate decision-makers are to design a credible business strategy that mitigates political risk and maximizes profit opportunities, they have to look deeper at the vulnerabilities that are peculiar to each country, each province, each community. Essential to managing any type of risk is the development of a detailed and effective diversification strategy. Given the political volatility within many developing world states—countries that will generate a large share of global growth over the next several decades—this kind of strategy is especially important. Even within a country as relatively stable as China, a closer look at internal political dynamics can identify various kinds of risk.

Two years ago, US officials worried publicly over a spike in sales of Russian arms to China. Dire predictions of a developing Russian–Chinese military axis became common-place. But in 2007, sales of Russian arms to China fell by some 62%. Was it because the two governments had some sort of behind-the-scenes falling out? Did the Chinese leadership suddenly doubt the quality of Russian-made products? In reality, the arms sales slowed because China had mastered the design of many of the weapons, and Chinese companies began to produce them in sufficient quantities that demand for foreign-made weaponry fell sharply.

This is a cautionary tale, one that reminds us that any company betting heavily on long-term access to Chinese consumers (or to customers in many other developing countries) may be making a big mistake. There is plenty of money to be made in China for the next several years, but putting too many eggs in a single basket remains as risky as ever. For businesses with supply chains in China and other developing states, it's also important to build redundancies that are not overly exposed within any one region within these countries.

There are other, less obvious, components of a solid diversification strategy. Multinational companies should use all the leverage that their home governments and international institutions can provide to ensure that the governments of the countries in which they accept risk exposure protect their intellectual property rights, enforce all local laws intended to safeguard their commercial interests, and maintain open markets. Rules of the game can change quickly in developing countries, and the cultivation of "friends in high places" isn't always by itself an effective plan.

KNOW THE COUNTRY
Gaining insight into a country's political, economic, social, and cultural traditions is essential for a successful risk-mitigation strategy. Where should this insight come from? Too many companies have historically relied on employees who have lived in a particular country for only a short time—or may even have done no more than travel there. Turning to the guy who backpacked through country X during college for useful information about its politics and culture—not as rare a phenomenon as you might think—is no substitute for the knowledge that can be gained from local workers themselves and from trained political risk analysts.

DESIGN AN EMERGENCY RESPONSE
Generally speaking, emerging market countries are more vulnerable than rich world states to large-scale civil unrest, public health crises, and environmental disasters. Those doing business in developing states need credible emergency response plans in place when events outside their control shut down supply chains, prevent local workers from coming to work, or otherwise disrupt operations. Some businesses have designed technology plans that allow workers to work from home. In cases when circumstances force foreign workers to leave the country, locals should have the necessary training and skills to assume their responsibilities for an extended period. The added expense and time for training are well worth the cost. In some countries, they're essential.

INVEST IN LOCAL WORKERS
Developing strategies to recruit and train local managers serves several useful purposes. First, it gives the host country government an investment in the success of a foreign-owned business. Every job created by a foreign firm is one that local government doesn't have to create. All governments want to keep unemployment at a minimum. Second, it gives local citizens a stake in the foreign company's success and helps to build solid relationships within the community. Some multinational firms have formed mutually profitable partnerships with local colleges and universities that give companies a fertile recruiting ground and ambitious students opportunities for work.

INVEST IN THEIR COMMUNITIES
Devoting a share of profits to investment in local schools and universities, infrastructure, and charities can generate stores of goodwill, which is sometimes essential for cooperation with local workers and government officials. Yet, sensitivity to the local culture matters too. In many developing states, suspicions that Western (especially American) companies have a political or ideological agenda can undermine efforts to promote trust. Contributions to local quality of life should be seen to come without strings attached.

PROTECT INTELLECTUAL PROPERTY
In some countries, foreign companies should be wary of transferring proprietary information to local partners or developing it inside the country. Forging alliances with local partners in joint ventures often serves as an effective risk mitigation strategy, but today's partner can become tomorrow's competitor, and a foreign firm can't always count on local courts or officials to safeguard its assets. Ironically, some foreign multinationals with long-term plans to remain inside a particular emerging market country have invested in local innovation. In the process, they have given locals an incentive to press their own government for stronger legal protections for intellectual property rights. Others have pooled their lobbying efforts with both local businesses and other foreign firms. When lobbying a government, strength in numbers can make a difference.

KNOW THE LOCAL COMPETITION
Successful firms understand their comparative advantages. But a foreign company must look beyond what its local competitors are capable of producing today. It must anticipate how those capabilities are likely to develop over time. Identifying the markets in which a firm's core competencies are likely to deliver profits for the foreseeable future is essential for long-term risk-mitigation strategies.

In many emerging market countries, local companies are often better at large-scale efficient manufacturing than at designing products, marketing them, and delivering them to the customer. Knowing how quickly the local competition can climb the value chain helps with the design of an intelligent, long-term business strategy.

KNOW WHERE TO FIND THE EXITS
Many companies have made lots of money in emerging markets. But as Wall Street veterans like to say, "Don't confuse brilliance with a bull market." Some companies have gotten away with ignoring the need for solid risk-management strategies and have simply ridden the wave produced by the inevitable rise of emerging market economies.

Yet, as skepticism of globalization grows in some developing countries, as their governments respond to domestic political pressure by rewriting rules to favor local companies at the expense of their foreign competitors, and as the challenges facing multinational companies operating inside these countries become more complex, it's important to have an exit strategy. There are plenty of developing states that are now open for business and investment. They have different strengths and vulnerabilities. Too much risk exposure in any one of them can create unnecessary risks. Conditions sometimes force companies to cut their losses and head for the door. Ensuring that this process is as painless and inexpensive as possible forms a crucial part of any sound risk-mitigation strategy.

DON'T FORGET THE POWER OF PERCEPTION

Operating in some developing countries comes with reputational risks at home. Several US companies have faced tough domestic criticism for doing business with governments that are accused of violating international labor, environmental, and human-rights standards. For a company's leadership, clearly communicating what the company will and won't do to gain market access in certain countries—and strict adherence to these standards of conduct —can help to minimize this risk.

POLITICAL RISK INSURANCE

As a last resort, a firm can purchase political risk insurance from providers like the Multilateral Investment Guarantee Agency, an arm of the World Bank, or the US government's Overseas Private Investment Corporation. But this should be a last resort strategy, because high premiums, substantial transaction and opportunity costs, and the complexities of establishing a valid claim have taught many companies that it is far more cost-effective to prevent or pre-empt bad outcomes than to rely heavily on plans to cope with their aftermath.

A LITTLE TOLERANCE IS A GOOD THING

It's useful to remember that having a good exit strategy does not require you to use it. Doing business in developing states comes with risk. But refusing to enter these markets or pulling out at the first sign of trouble comes with a high cost to opportunity. Foreign companies will be earning solid profits within emerging market states for many years to come. Political risk can be managed. It should not be avoided altogether.

MORE INFO

Books:

Bracken, Paul, Ian Bremmer, and David Gordon (eds). *Managing Strategic Surprise: Lessons from Risk Management and Risk Assessment*. New York: Cambridge University Press, 2008.

Howell, Llewellyn D. (ed). *Handbook of Country and Political Risk Analysis*. 3rd ed. East Syracuse, NY: Political Risk Services Group, 2002.

Moran, Theodore H. (ed). *Managing International Political Risk*. London: Blackwell Publishing, 1999.

Moran, Theodore H., Gerald T. West, and Keith Martin (eds). *International Political Risk Management: Meeting the Needs of the Present, Anticipating the Challenges of the Future*. Washington, DC: World Bank Publications, 2007.

Wilkin, Sam (ed). *Country and Political Risk: Practical Insights for Global Finance*. London: Risk Books, 2004.

Articles:

Bremmer, Ian, and Fareed Zakaria. "Hedging political risk in China." *Harvard Business Review* 84:11 (2006): 22–25. Online at: hbr.org/2006/11/hedging-political-risk-in-china/ar/1

The Economist. "Insuring against political risk." April 4, 2007. Online at: www.economist.com/node/8967224?story_id=8967224

Henisz, Witold J., and Bennet A. Zelner. "Political risk management: A strategic perspective." Online at: tinyurl.com/89rekyj

Stanislav, Markus. "Corporate governance as political insurance: Firm-level institutional creation in emerging markets and beyond." *Socio-Economic Review* 6:1 (January 2008): 69–98. Online at: dx.doi.org/10.1093/ser/mwl036

Report:

PricewaterhouseCoopers. "Integrating political risk into enterprise risk management." 2006. Online at: tinyurl.com/ksjp7g

Websites:

Eurasia Group, global political risk advisory and consulting firm: www.eurasiagroup.net

Multilateral Investment Guarantee Agency (MIGA)'s Political Risk Insurance Center: www.pri-center.com

PricewaterhouseCoopers: www.pwc.com. Enter "political risk" in search box to find articles and resources.

See Also:

★ Measuring Company Exposure to Country Risk (pp. 136–139)
★ Measuring Country Risk (pp. 139–142)
★ To Hedge or Not to Hedge (pp. 53–56)
✔ Creating a Risk Register (pp. 362–363)
✔ Establishing a Framework for Assessing Risk (p. 313)

Real Options: Opportunity from Risk
by David Shimko

EXECUTIVE SUMMARY

Real options arise from the ability of economic agents to adjust their behavior to maximize the values of their assets or contracts.

- Common examples are the right to make, expand, contract, defer, or cancel an investment or contract.
- Value real options by considering the value of the asset or contract with and without the ability to adjust.
- In some cases, the Black–Scholes model can be used to approximate the value of real options directly.
- Real options generally increase in value as uncertainty about the future increases.
- Real options can be proprietary or shared, simple or compound, restructurable or not.
- Real options have real value; many corporate valuations cannot be explained except for the presence of real options.

WHAT IS A REAL OPTION?

The origin of the term "real option" derives from financial options. For example, the right to buy a house for a fixed period of time at a fixed price is a call option,[1] except that the underlying asset is a real asset, not a financial asset. Business people and economists discovered that many business processes involve options, and that financial mathematics can be brought to bear to value those options. Some popular examples include:

- the right to make an investment, such as the option to build a plastics plant in China;
- the right to expand or contract an investment based on changes in market conditions, such as a plant design that accommodates changes in production rates at very low cost;
- the right to defer an investment, such as the right to wait for better market conditions to develop a property;
- the right to accelerate an investment;
- the right to cancel a contract;
- the right to produce or not to produce a product, such as the right of a petroleum refinery or electricity power plant to produce or not produce fuel or power;
- the right to choose how to undertake an investment, such as a gold producer's right to choose the mining strategy that maximizes its value.

"Option" and "optimize" share the same root, the word "opt"—meaning, of course, "to choose." Therefore, the value of a real option can be thought of as the value of any right to choose, when compared with following a strategy where no such right is conferred. This suggests the mathematical relation:

Value of real option = Value of strategy with decision rights
                       − Value of strategy without decision rights

In some cases, the option value may be computed directly, as shown in Example 1.

Example 1

A company has a one-year option to acquire an oil-producing property for $100 million. The present value of the drilling profits is currently estimated to be $100 million, and the oil reserves are currently being depleted at the rate of 2% per year. The present value assessment varies according to the price of oil, with a percentage volatility (standard deviation) of 15% per year. If the interest rate is 4%, what is the value of the option?

To value the option, it is helpful to see how the real option resembles a standard financial call option. The owner of an equity call option has the right to buy a stock at a predetermined price (the strike price) for a predetermined period of time. The stock pays dividends which the option holder will not receive if the option is unexercised. Stock volatility makes the option valuable—the more volatile the stock, the greater the value of deciding to buy later at a fixed price. In the case of the oil option, the "stock value" is the present value of the profits, the "volatility" is the percentage variation in the present value, the "strike price" is the acquisition price of the property, and the "dividend" is the depletion of the oil reserve.

As a first approximation, an analyst might use the Black–Scholes formula of stock option pricing to value the real option. Using any online calculator, and the inputs below, the resulting call option value is $6.82 million.

Stock price	$100
Dividend	2%
Exercise price	$100
Volatility	15%
Interest rate	4%
Time	1 year
Call option value	$6.82

Some real options fit the Black–Scholes framework nicely, but most real options have degrees of complexity that are not captured by the option pricing model.

Example 2

A developer owns a piece of land that is currently used as a parking lot. The present value of the parking lot revenues is $5 million. He can convert the land into an apartment building and net an additional $5.5 million in present value. Or he can convert the parking lot into an office building and net an additional $6 million in present value. What is the value of the property in this case?

1 $5 million, since it currently being used as a parking lot.
2 $11 million, since the office project is more profitable than the apartment project.
3 The value of the highest current net present value (NPV) usage of the land.
4 None of the above.

The answer is clearly not 1; a parking lot is worth more than the present value of its current income since it has demonstrated valuable alternative uses. Answer 2 is tempting, but it is wrong if there are any other projects more valuable. Answer 3 may be correct, but also could be incorrect because of the use of the word "current." It may have a more valuable use in the future and, under some conditions, it would be worthwhile to wait to develop the land until that possibility materializes.

The correct answer is generally 4, since the value of the land is equal to or higher than its current value in the highest use. The reason for this is that conditions change over time. If the property owner waits a year, they may find that residential real estate grows faster than commercial, or vice versa. At some point, however, it is optimal to make the irreversible decision as to how to convert the property. In those cases, the value of waiting is zero.

Because the property owner has the right to wait to invest, this confers additional value to investment until the moment when it is no longer optimal to wait, and the option is exercised.

PROPERTIES OF REAL OPTIONS

In many situations, increased project risk reduces project value. This is particularly true when a company has constrained capital and increased risks put the company's survival in jeopardy.

Real options have the opposite effect. Like financial options, they generally increase in value the more uncertain the values of the underlying variables. They generally increase in value the longer the time an option can be deferred. And they increase in value as the cost to exercising falls.

Real options also tend to mitigate project risk, since the project owner has the right to modify strategy midcourse. This can help avoid the worst outcomes for the project, providing a kind of operational hedge against downside risk.

VALUING REAL OPTIONS

When an option pricing formula cannot be applied, there are two other ways to value real options: One using backward induction (best for decision trees) and one using simulation (best for problems with continuous input price changes). As an example of option valuation using backward induction, consider the following game, similar to the American television show *The Price is Right*.

Backward Induction

The contestant is given $50 and has to make a decision whether to keep the $50 or pay $50 to choose one of three boxes. One box has a valuable prize worth $100, but the other two boxes have nothing. After choosing a box, the host reveals an empty box and offers the contestant a chance to switch. What is the value of the player's option to switch?

The tree in Figure 1 summarizes the decision problem.

If the contestant always keeps their box of choice, the expected value is 33.33 since there is a ã chance of getting $100. If they switch after seeing an empty box, there is a ã chance they changed an empty box for a valuable one, and a ã chance they changed a valuable box for an empty one.

Using backward induction, we confirm that switching is the best strategy, and since the value of that is greater than $50, the value of the game is $66.67. The value of the game without the right to switch is $50, since it is optimal not to play the game. Therefore, the value of the option to switch in this case is $16.67 (= 66.67 − 50).

Simulation

More generally, real options are valued using stochastic modeling and some form of optimization theory. For example, plastics can be produced from natural gas or from naphtha. To value a plant that has the option to choose its feedstock, it is necessary to simulate price fluctuations in natural gas and naphtha and determine how the company would optimize its feedstock strategy depending on the prices realized. This problem is complex because switching is costly and cannot be accomplished instantaneously.

Clearly, there is always value in having the ability to switch feedstocks; however, that value may be very small if the costs of switching are high or the volatility of feedstock prices is low.

Figure 1. Decision problem summary

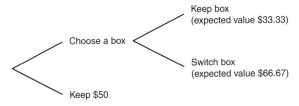

Choose a box

Keep box (expected value $33.33)

Switch box (expected value $66.67)

Keep $50

Generally we can say that the value of the switching option is the difference in value between the plant that can switch its feedstock and the value of the plant that cannot.

NPV AND REAL OPTIONS

Many companies make avoidable NPV mistakes. According to the textbook approach, for example, a manufacturing firm should update its production methods if the present value of the benefits exceeds the present value of the costs. This is not necessarily correct. If new and better innovations are being made available over time, management may find an even better renovation alternative. If they repeatedly renovate every time they make a small gain, they will have lost the opportunity to have made a big gain on the best possible renovation.

For this reason, the NPV rule must consider the value of the option to wait to renovate. The NPV rule can be adjusted by including the lost option as a cost or by requiring the present value of benefits to exceed a predetermined multiple of the present value of the costs. This problem was first analyzed rigorously by McDonald and Siegel (1986).[2]

ADVANCED REAL OPTIONS

The options discussed so far were proprietary to a particular economic agent. In some cases, real options are shared, introducing an element of game theory into their valuation. For example, the option to enter a new market may be shared by one's competitors, and the value of the option depends on competitor strategy. Also, some options are compound rather than simple; in these cases, one exercises an option to obtain another option, which adds a layer of analytical complexity, but the financial intuition remains the same.

CASE STUDY

In 1998, the NYSEG's Homer City power plant, an 1,884 megawatt coal-fired plant located on the border of New York and Pennsylvania, sold for a price of US$955 per kilowatt of capacity. Similar plants, Dunkirk and Huntley, sold for about a third of that price. What was the difference? Was it a problem of irrational exuberance on the part of the bidders, or was there something else going on?

It turns out that because of its location, the Homer City plant had the option of delivering power into New York, and into Pennsylvania and Ohio, giving it the opportunity to benefit from price discrepancies in the three regions. At one hour's notice, the plant could decide to sell in whichever market had the higher price. This real option owned by the NYSEG accounted for roughly two thirds of the market value of the plant. This case was analyzed by Robert Ethier.[3]

MAKING IT HAPPEN

- Identify an aspect of a business where managers respond differently to different market conditions. It may be evidence of the existence of a real option.

- Value the option by considering how the company behaves with and without the flexibility.
- Evaluate the cost/benefit of increases or reductions in flexibility using the same framework.
- Apply this methodology to other corporate situations, and the valuation of acquisitions and divestitures.

MORE INFO

Books:

Copeland, Tom, and Vladimir Antikarov. *Real Options, Revised Edition: A Practitioner's Guide*. New York: WW Norton, 2001.

Kodukula, Prasad, and Chandra Papudesu. *Project Valuation Using Real Options: A Practitioner's Guide*. Fort Lauderdale, FL: J. Ross Publishing, 2006.

Mun, Jonathan. *Real Options Analysis: Tools and Techniques for Valuing Strategic Investments and Decisions*. 2nd ed. New York: Wiley, 2005.

Schwartz, Eduardo S., and Lenos Trigeorgis. *Real Options and Investment Under Uncertainty: Classical Readings and Recent Contributions*. Cambridge, MA: MIT Press, 2001.

Trigeorgis, Lenos. *Real Options: Managerial Flexibility and Strategy in Resource Allocation*. Cambridge, MA: MIT Press, 1996.

Website:
Links to articles, papers, and other resources on real options: www.puc-rio.br/marco.ind/ro-links.html

See Also:
★ Comparing Net Present Value and Internal Rate of Return (pp. 16–19)
✔ Understanding Real Options (pp. 367–368)
⇄ Time Value of Money (p. 411)

NOTES

1 A financial call option is the right to buy a security at a predetermined price for a predetermined time period. A put is the right to sell a security at preset terms.
2 McDonald, Robert, and Daniel Siegel. "The value of waiting to invest." *Quarterly Journal of Economics* 101:4 (November 1986): 707–728. Online at: dx.doi.org/10.2307/1884175
3 Ethier, Robert G. "Valuing electricity assets in deregulated markets: A real options model with mean reversion and jumps." February 1999. Viewable on the New York State Library website at: www.nysl.nysed.gov

Reducing Costs through Production and Supply Chain Management
by Vinod Lall

EXECUTIVE SUMMARY

- There are numerous drivers of production and the supply chain, and there are several processes under each driver. These processes are associated with high overheads and offer opportunities for cost reduction.
- Cost reduction requires a complete knowledge and mapping of all costs, cycle times, purchases, inventories, suppliers, customers, logistics, and other service providers throughout the supply chain.
- Cost reduction in the supply chain often requires trade-off analysis amongst conflicting alternatives using the total cost approach.
- Successfully achieving supply chain cost savings requires the use of cross-functional teams with representation from marketing, design, procurement, production, distribution, and transportation employing an organized approach.

INTRODUCTION

IKEA, the Swedish home products retailer, is known for its good-quality, inexpensive products, which are typically sold at prices 30–50% below those of its competitors. While the price of products from other companies continues to rise over time,

IKEA claims that its retail prices have been reduced by a total of 20% over the last four years. At IKEA, the process of cost reduction starts at product conception and continues throughout the process of design, sourcing of materials and components, production, and distribution. For example, the "Bang" mug has been redesigned many times to realize shipping cost savings. Originally, 864 mugs would fit into a pallet. After redesign a pallet held 1,280 mugs, and with a further redesign 2,024 mugs could be squeezed into a pallet, reducing shipping costs by 60%.

Organizations today are looking for opportunities to improve operational efficiencies and reduce cost without having a negative effect on customer service levels. Production and supply chain management can help to reduce costs by connecting every unit in the supply chain, fostering collaboration among supply chain partners, and offering visibility into the demand and supply side of the chain.

Production and supply chain management involves a number of drivers through which acquired raw materials are converted into finished goods for sale to customers. In turn, these drivers involve several processes that offer opportunities for cost reduction. Common drivers include procurement, design of the supply chain, inventory, transportation, warehousing, and collaboration. Cost reduction requires timely and improved decision-making for common processes under each driver.

PROCUREMENT

Procurement, also known as purchasing, is the process of acquiring raw materials, components, products, services, and other resources necessary either for the production processes themselves or for the support of production processes. Procurement processes ensure that supplies are available in the right place, in the right quantity, and at the right time. Buyers can play a major role in reducing supply chain costs by taking actions to reduce costs incurred in the flow of products from the suppliers to the ultimate customers. Some of the actions are discussed below.

Buyers must increase the flow of information throughout the supply chain, from the customer to the manufacturer and on to the supplier. This will make each entity in the chain aware of the inventory carried by the others and work towards the reduction of inventory without sacrificing customer service levels. Buyers must also take action to reduce cycle times, which will make the supply chain more responsive. To achieve a reduction in lead times, buyers must track and measure supplier lead-times, analyze trade-offs that result from lead time reduction, and then negotiate shorter lead times. Another action buyers can undertake to reduce supply chain cost is to select suppliers on the basis of their total supply chain capability and not just price, lead time, and quality levels.

DESIGN OF SUPPLY CHAIN

There are several principles under design of the supply chain that can help to reduce costs. These include component commonality, component modularity, and postponement.

Component commonality: The principle of component commonality focuses on the design and use of common components for families of products. When there are a large number of products in a supply chain, the inventory of components will naturally be large. Component commonality calls for the use of common components in a variety of products. This reduces costs not only by reducing inventory cost but also through reduced material cost, reduced production cost, and reduced product obsolescence. For example, a computer manufacturer can design common components such as memory and disk drives and use different combinations of these components to produce different finished products.

Component modularity: The principle of component modularity recommends that common subsystems be designed as modules to meet a broad range of feature requirements. This reduces the number of components that must be produced, kept in materials and repair parts inventory, and integrated into the product during the production process. This reduces procurement, manufacturing, and inventory costs, leading to a lower supply chain cost. Manufacturers of electronic products, for example, use the principle of modularity to design and assemble printers, computers, and so on.

Postponement: Postponement means delaying the bringing of products into their final form until close to the point of sale, when customer demand is known with greater accuracy. This results in a better match between supply and demand, leading to reduced costs mainly through inventory reductions. For example, a traditional garment manufacturer might dye the thread before knitting it into sweaters, whereas a garment manufacturer using postponement would postpone dying until the last point in the supply chain, when customer color preferences are known with a greater degree of certainty.

INVENTORY

Inventory resides at several locations in a supply chain, and the goal of inventory management is to reduce or eliminate inventory wherever it exists in the supply chain. This increases the velocity of movement of material through the chain, reducing the time from the point where material enters to the point of final consumption or sale. Slow movement of material leads to higher average inventories throughout the supply chain and results in higher inventory carrying costs. Techniques that can help reduce these costs include the following.

The first technique is to use models such as vendor-managed inventory (VMI) and drop-shipments to reduce the number of locations where inventory is stored. With VMI the buyer of a product provides certain information to a vendor of that product, and the vendor takes full responsibility for maintaining an agreed level of inventory of the material, usually at the location where the buyer uses it.

Second, the same strategy should not be used to manage and control all inventory items regardless of their value. Instead, use ABC analysis (not the same as activity-based costing) to classify inventory into different classes and to maintain appropriately safe stock levels based on the class. ABC analysis makes use of Pareto's Law and classifies inventory into classes A, B and C. A-class items are high in value and low in number, requiring tight control, while C-class items are low-value, high-number items that can be loosely controlled. Items classed as B include medium-value, medium-number items and typically require a blanket policy for control.

Other inventory management techniques include reducing the amount of transportation/pipeline inventory, and application of lean and just-in-time techniques to reduce or eliminate waste.

TRANSPORTATION

Transportation is used to move products from one location in the supply chain to another and is a significant component of the supply chain cost. A responsive transportation system can help to lower supply chain costs by achieving a high level of product availability at a reasonable price. A common technique for making a transportation system responsive is "cross-docking." Under cross-docking, products from a supplier are aggregated into trucks that arrive at distribution centers. At these centers the process of cross-docking means that products are exchanged between different trucks so that each truck leaving for a given retail location is loaded with products from several suppliers.

Transportation planners can reduce supply chain costs by reducing transportation costs by selecting low-cost modes of transport and using software to plan optimal routes and delivery schedules. The various modes of transport include water, rail, truck, intermodal, and air, and package carriers such as DHL, FedEx, and UPS. Having a low-cost supply chain depends closely on the selection and use of an appropriate mode of transport. Water is typically the least expensive, although slowest, whereas air is the most expensive and fastest. Transportation planners often use the approach of total cost analysis to select the best mode. This requires finding the total cost for each mode of transportation and using the mode that has the lowest total cost. The total cost is made up of, and considers, the trade-off between the cost of transport, cost of inventory at the origin, cost of inventory in the pipeline, and cost of inventory at the destination. Several companies develop and provide software that helps planners to construct transportation routes and schedules. Planners also use satellite-based global positioning systems to lower costs while still maintaining a responsive transport system.

WAREHOUSING

Warehouses are locations in the supply chain to and from which inventory is transported. Supply chain planners can help to reduce costs by making good decisions about warehousing strategies, such as the location and capacity of warehouses, and operational decisions such as the functions to be performed at the warehouse, the order-fulfillment methodology to be used, etc.

When deciding on the location of warehouses, planners use a trade-off analysis to choose between a large centralized location, which is more efficient, and multiple decentralized locations that offer a higher level of responsiveness. A number of factors including the quality, cost and availability of the workforce, tax effects, and proximity to customers are used in the analysis. Capacity decisions typically involve decisions on the need for and amount of extra capacity. Warehouses with excess capacity offer flexibility at a cost, while those with little excess capacity are more efficient. Trade-off analysis is also used to make decisions on warehouse capacity. Operational decisions deal with day-to-day processes such as stock placement, stock picking, and cycle counting. Warehouse planners use warehouse management system (WMS) software to plan and execute these processes.

COLLABORATION

Collaboration in a supply chain focuses on joint planning, coordination, and process integration between the firm and its suppliers, customers, and other partners such as the logistics providers. In addition to cost reduction, collaboration offers the advantages of business expansion to other areas, increased return on assets, improved customer service, reduced lead times, increased reliability and responsiveness to market trends, and a shorter time to market. Several options are available for achieving collaboration in a supply chain. These include:

- systems that transmit information between partners using technologies such as fax, e-mail, electronic data interchange (EDI), or extensible markup language (XML);
- systems such as electronic hubs and portals that facilitate the procurement of goods or services from electronic marketplaces, catalogs, and auctions;

- systems such as collaborative planning, forecasting and replenishment (CPFR) that permit shared collaboration rather than just a simple exchange of information amongst the supply chain partners.

The three systems identified above offer different levels of benefits and are associated with varying levels of expected costs. Organizations need to examine and quantify the benefits and costs of the alternative systems before selecting an appropriate system.

CASE STUDY
TRANSPORTATION ANALYSIS PAYS OFF FOR COMPUTER PRODUCTS FIRM

A leading US manufacturer of computer accessories makes many products in China and then funnels them into a single distribution center on the West Coast that serves hundreds of retail clients. The company contracted with various freight services to send the products to retail customers using different modes of transportation, including small-package air, small-package ground, less-than-truckload, truckload, and heavy-weight air freight. The company wanted to have a better understanding of transportation processes and to control transportation costs. To do so, it hired the services of UPS Consulting (UPSC).

UPSC undertook a careful analysis and helped the manufacturer to reduce its domestic transportation costs by approximately 30% by the following means:

- negotiation of better rates with new freight service providers;
- setting up a returns program with a single carrier that picks up and returns the product using the most cost-effective transportation mode;
- development of a user-friendly one-page guide to carrier and mode selection that matches the weight and size of a parcel shipment with the preferred shipping method;
- helping employees to understand shipping parameters;
- establishing a compliance system that requires weekly meetings to review shipping activities and handle any special issues that arise.

CONCLUSION

This article has explored major sources of cost savings in a production and supply chain and identified some techniques used by supply chain personnel such as buyers, inventory managers, and transportation planners. The techniques identified were discussed by grouping supply chain processes under the common supply chain drivers of procurement, design of the supply chain, inventory, transportation, warehousing, and collaboration.

MORE INFO
Books:

Chopra, Sunil, and Peter Meindl. *Supply Chain Management: Strategy, Planning & Operations*. 4th ed. Upper Saddle River, NJ: Prentice Hall, 2009.

Jacobs, F. Robert, and Richard B. Chase. *Operations and Supply Management: The Core*. Boston, MA: McGraw-Hill/Irwin, 2008.

Websites:
Council of Supply Chain Management Professionals (CSCMP): cscmp.org
Supply Chain Council (SCC): www.supply-chain.org

UPS Supply Chain Solutions: www.ups-scs.com

See Also:
★ Countering Supply Chain Risk (pp. 253–255)
✔ Assessing the Value of Outsourcing and Offshoring (pp. 360–361)
✔ Understanding Economic Efficiency Theory (pp. 346–347)

Understanding Reputation Risk and Its Importance
by Jenny Rayner

EXECUTIVE SUMMARY
- Reputation is a critical intangible asset; it is an indicator of past performance and future prospects.
- Reputation is based on stakeholders' perceptions of whether their experience of a business matches their expectations.
- Knowing your major stakeholders, how they perceive you, and what they expect of you is vital in managing reputation risk.
- Everyone working for an organization bears some responsibility for upholding its reputation.
- Reputation risk is anything that could *impact* reputation—either negatively (threats) or positively (opportunities).
- Risks to reputation should be integrated into the business's enterprise risk management (ERM) framework so that they receive attention at the right level and appropriate actions are taken to manage them.

INTRODUCTION
Reputation is the single most valuable asset of most businesses today—albeit an intangible one. A 2007 global survey[1] rated damage to reputation as the top risk, although half the respondents admitted that they were not prepared for it. Hard-earned reputations can be surprisingly fragile in the globalized, technologically interconnected 21st century. The trust and confidence that underpin them can be irrevocably damaged by a momentary lapse of judgment or an inadvertent remark.

That is why understanding reputation risk has become a key focus for businesses in all sectors. It is now recognized that reputation risks need to be managed as actively and rigorously as other more quantifiable and tangible risks.

REPUTATION AND ITS VALUE
Reputation is an accumulation of perceptions and opinions about an organization that reside in the consciousness of its stakeholders.

An organization will enjoy a good reputation when its behavior and performance consistently meet or exceed the expectations of its stakeholders. Reputation will diminish if an organization's words and deeds are perceived as failing to meet stakeholder expectations, as illustrated by the reputation equation below.[2]

$$\text{Reputation} - \text{Experience} = \text{Expectations}$$

Reputation has intrinsic current value as an intangible asset. Although reputation will not appear as a discrete balance sheet item, it represents a significant proportion of the difference between a business's market and book values (less any quantifiable intangibles such as licenses and trademarks). Since intangibles usually represent over 70% of market value, reputation is often a business's single greatest asset.

Reputation also plays a pivotal role in a business's future value by influencing stakeholder behavior and, hence, future earnings potential and prospects. A good or bad reputation can affect stakeholder decisions to maintain or relinquish their stake—be they investors, customers, suppliers, or employees. The "corporate halo" effect of a reputable business can help to differentiate products in a highly competitive sector, may allow premium pricing, and can be the ultimate deciding factor for a prospective purchaser of services. A strong reputation can help to attract and retain high-quality employees and can deter new competitors by acting as a barrier to market entry. Reputation can also shape the attitude of regulators, pressure groups, and the media towards a business and can affect its cost of capital.

Perhaps the greatest benefit of a good reputation is the buffer of goodwill it provides, which can enable a business to withstand future shocks. This "reputational capital," or "reputation equity," underpins stakeholder trust and confidence and can persuade stakeholders to give a business the benefit of the doubt and a second chance when the inevitable unforeseen crisis strikes.

DEFINING REPUTATION RISK
Reputation risk should be regarded as a generic term embracing the risks, from any source, that can *impact* reputation, and not as a category of risk in its own right. Regulatory noncompliance, loss of customer data, unethical employee behavior, or an unexpected profit warning can all damage reputation and stakeholder confidence.

Reputation risk is not only about downside threats, but also about upside opportunities. Climate change, for example, is a potential business threat, but many firms have spotted and exploited the flip-side opportunity for competitive advantage by developing green technologies and promoting themselves as environmentally friendly, thereby enhancing their reputation.

Reputation risk can therefore be defined as: "Any action, event, or situation that could adversely or beneficially impact an organization's reputation."

IDENTIFYING REPUTATION RISKS

The most crucial stage of the reputation risk management process is *identifying* the factors that could impact reputation. Risks have to be recognized and understood before they can be managed. Considering the seven drivers of reputation is a useful starting point, as these are also fertile sources of threats and opportunity to reputation (see Figure 1).

Businesses should consider not only the risks under their direct control, but also risks in the "extended enterprise" relating to suppliers, subcontractors, business partners, advisers, and other stakeholders. Could the values, business practices, or activities of its partners expose the business to reputation risk by association?

One way of approaching this is to consider the expectations of each major stakeholder group against the drivers of business reputation to develop a "heat map" of potential trouble spots and zones of opportunity. Major mismatches between expectations and experience can be analyzed to highlight areas where action is needed to bridge the gaps.

Asking the following questions may also help to uncover reputation risks:
• What newspaper headline about your business would you least (or most) like to see? What could trigger this?
• What could threaten your core business values or your license to operate? Such risks can seriously damage reputation and lead to an irreversible loss of stakeholder confidence.
• Could there be collateral risk arising from the activities of another player in your sector? If so, the reputation of your own business may be vulnerable and come under intense stakeholder scrutiny.
• Could reputation risk exposure arise from an acquisition, merger, or other portfolio change? A mismatch of values, ethos, culture, and standards resulting in inappropriate behavior could seriously damage reputation. Conversely, if the acquisition target enjoys a superior reputation, it could provide a competitive edge.

EVALUATING, RESPONDING TO, MONITORING, AND REPORTING RISKS

Once risks to reputation have been identified, they can be evaluated, appropriate risk responses developed, and the risks monitored and reported.

Risks to reputation can be *evaluated* in the usual way by considering the likelihood of the risk occurring and the impact if it does. The reputational impact of such risks should be considered explicitly, alongside financial or other impacts. This can be done by the use of a word model which explains reputational impact in a way that is relevant and meaningful for a given business. Table 1 provides an example

Figure 1. The seven drivers of reputation. (*Source*: Rayner, 2003)

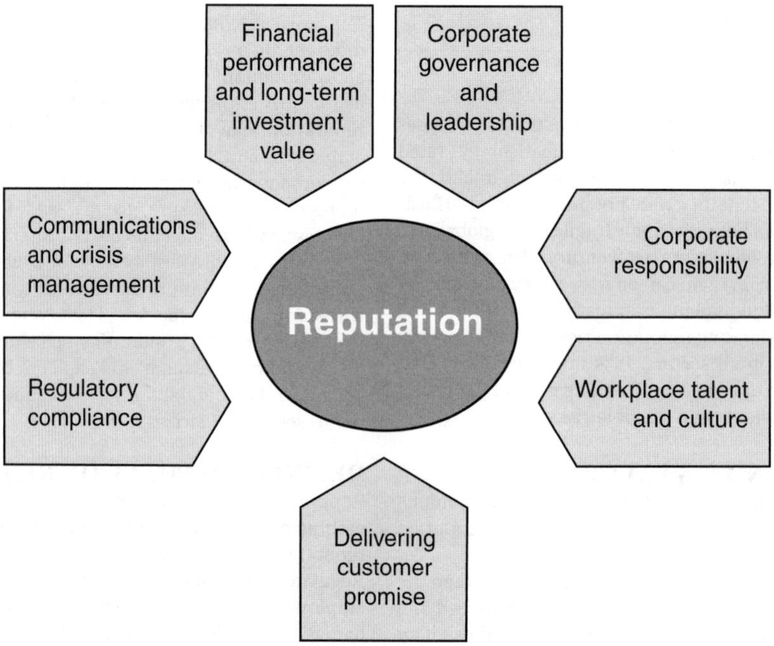

Table 1. Sample reputation impact assessment criteria

Low	Moderate	High	Very high
Local complaint or recognition Minimal change in stakeholder confidence Impact lasting less than one month	Local media coverage Moderate change in stakeholder confidence Impact lasting between one and three months	National media coverage Significant change in stakeholder confidence Impact lasting more than three months Attracts regulator attention or comment	National headline/ international media coverage Dramatic change in stakeholder confidence Impact lasting more than 12 months or irreversible Public censure or accolade by regulators

of a four-point reputation impact scale that caters for both threats and opportunities.

In assessing reputational impact, the view of relevant stakeholders should be considered to ensure that the impact is not underestimated. That is why understanding stakeholders and what they regard as current and emerging major issues lies at the heart of reputation risk management.

Reputational impact can sometimes be quantified in monetary terms—for example, expected reduced income resulting from loss of customers or license to operate; or impact on share price or on brand value. The true ultimate impact can be difficult to estimate as the immediate consequence may be only a relatively small financial penalty (for example, a fine for pollution). However, the event may, over time, have an insidious effect which erodes the business's reputation (for example, because of a perception that the business is not concerned about the environment).

Response plans should be developed to manage the more significant risks that present unacceptable exposure to the business. The gap between experience and expectation can be bridged by improving the business's performance or behavior and/or by influencing stakeholder expectations so they are more closely aligned with what the business can realistically deliver. As reputation is based on stakeholder perception, focused and clear communication to stakeholders is vital so that their perception will accurately reflect business reality.

A business may have done everything possible to anticipate and guard against reputational threats, but if a crisis strikes and the business response is inappropriate, its reputation may still end up in tatters. Having an effective and well-rehearsed generic crisis management plan that can be quickly adapted and implemented to suit specific circumstances is therefore a key component of an effective reputation risk management strategy.

Once risks to reputation have been identified and responses agreed and implemented, the risks can be regularly *monitored* by management to ensure that responses are having the desired effect. Finally, the up-to-date status of the risks should be *reported* at the right level to inform decision-making and enable external disclosure to stakeholders.

ROLES AND RESPONSIBILITIES

The board of a business is the ultimate custodian of a business's reputation. However, managing reputation risk successfully requires a team effort across the business from executive and nonexecutive directors, senior and middle managers, public relations staff, risk and audit professionals, and key business partners.

Everyone employed by and indirectly working for a business should be expected to uphold the business's values and bear some responsibility for spotting emerging risks that could impact reputation. The telltale signs of an imminent crisis are often missed because personnel are not risk-aware: a spate of customer complaints, safety near-misses or supplier non-conformance, a sudden rise in employee turnover, or pressure group activity. These can act as crucial early warning indicators which allow a business to take corrective action and avert disaster.

CASE STUDY
CITIGROUP

In September 2004 the Financial Services Agency (FSA), Japan's bank regulator, ordered Citigroup to close its private banking business in the country following "serious violations" of Japanese banking laws. An FSA investigation found that inadequate local internal controls and lack of oversight from the United States had allowed large profits to be "amassed illegally." The bank had failed to prevent suspected money laundering and had misled customers about investment risk. The punishment meted out by the FSA was particularly severe as a previous inspection in 2001 had exposed similar compliance weaknesses, which Citigroup had not corrected.

Citigroup's then chief executive, Charles Prince, visited Japan in October 2004 in an attempt to repair the company's tarnished image. Bowing, he apologized for the activities of his senior staff, saying that they had put "short-term profits ahead of the bank's long-term reputation." He pledged to improve oversight, change the management structure, increase employee training on local regulations, and set up an independent committee to monitor progress. He said: "Under my leadership, lack of compliance and inappropriate behavior simply will not be tolerated and we will take direct action to ensure that proper standards are upheld and that these problems do not reoccur."

That same month French retailer Carrefour fired Citigroup as a financial adviser on the sale of its Japanese operations to prevent its own reputation from being tarnished by association.

CONCLUSION

A good reputation hinges on a business living the values it claims to espouse and delivering consistently on the promise to its stakeholders. Being "authentic," being "the real thing," has never been so important. Pursuing short-term gain at the expense of long-term business reputation and stakeholder interests is no longer acceptable practice.

Successfully managing reputation risk is both an inside-out and an outside-in challenge. The inside-out component requires business leaders to establish an appropriate vision, values, and strategic goals that will guide actions and behaviors throughout the organization. The outside-in component requires the business to scan the external environment continuously and canvass stakeholder opinion to ensure it is on a track that will secure the continuing support, trust, and confidence of its stakeholders.

Active and systematic management of the risks to reputation can help to ensure that perception is aligned with reality and that stakeholder experience matches expectations. Only in this way can a business build, safeguard, and enhance a reputation that will be sustainable in the long term.

MAKING IT HAPPEN
The key components of reputation risk management are:

- Clear and well-communicated business vision, values, and strategy that set the right ethical and stakeholder-aware tone for the business.
- Supporting policies and codes of conduct that guide employee behavior and decision-making so that goals are achieved in accordance with business values.
- Extension of the business's values and relevant policies to key partners in the supply chain.
- Dialogue and engagement to track the changing perceptions, requirements, and expectations of major stakeholders continuously.
- An effective enterprise-wide risk management system that identifies, assesses, responds to, monitors, and reports on threats and opportunities to reputation.
- A culture in which employees are risk-aware, are encouraged to be vigilant, raise concerns, highlight opportunities, and act as reputational ambassadors for the business.
- Transparent communications that meet stakeholder needs and build trust and confidence.
- Robust and well-rehearsed crisis management arrangements.

MORE INFO
Books:

Atkins, Derek, Ian Bates, and Lyn Drennan. *Reputational Risk: Responsibility Without Control? A Question of Trust*. London: Financial World Publishing, 2006.

Fombrun, Charles J., and Cees B. M. van Riel. *Fame and Fortune: How Successful Companies Build Winning Reputations*. Upper Saddle River, NJ: FT Prentice Hall, 2003.

Larkin, Judy. *Strategic Reputation Risk Management*. Basingstoke, UK: Palgrave MacMillan, 2003.

Rayner, Jenny. *Managing Reputational Risk: Curbing Threats, Leveraging Opportunities*. Chichester, UK: Wiley, 2003.

Article:

See articles in *The Geneva Papers on Risk and Insurance Issues and Practice* 31:3 (July 2006). Online at: tinyurl.com/8y9lksb

Reports:

Coutts and Company. "Face value: Your reputation as a business asset." London: Coutts and Company, 2008.

Economist Intelligence Unit. "Reputation: Risk of risks." White paper. 2005.

Resnick, Jeffrey T. "Reputational risk management: A framework for safeguarding your organization's primary intangible asset." Opinion Research Corporation, 2006.

Websites:

John Madejski Centre for Reputation, Henley Business School, University of Reading: tinyurl.com/7l5zqba

Reputation Institute: www.reputationinstitute.com

See Also:

★ CSR: More than PR, Pursuing Competitive Advantage in the Long Run (pp. 187–189)

★ Human Risk: How Effective Strategic Risk Management Can Identify Rogues (pp. 198–201)

✔ Defining Corporate Governance: Its Aims, Goals, and Responsibilities (pp. 341–342)

NOTES
1 Aon's Global Risk Management Survey, based on responses from 320 organizations in 29 countries.

2 Oonagh Mary Harpur in Chapter B4 of *Corporate Social Responsibility Monitor*. London: Gee Publishing, 2002.

Using Decision Analysis to Value R&D Projects
by Bert De Reyck

EXECUTIVE SUMMARY
- Valuing R&D projects is a critical component of project portfolio management.
- Traditional methods for valuing financial assets cannot be easily used for valuing R&D projects, as they are very different in nature.
- Decision analysis is widely used for valuing projects in R&D-intensive industries such as pharmaceuticals and energy.
- Using decision trees, one can determine a project's expected net present value (eNPV) and downside risk, two essential ingredients for determining whether or not to proceed with the project.

INTRODUCTION

Project portfolio management, the equivalent of financial portfolio management but focused on R&D projects rather than financial assets, often relies on decision analysis methods to value projects rather than traditional financial valuation methods such as net present value (NPV). In finance, the idea of managing portfolios of assets goes back a long time, with the first formal methods being developed in the 1950s. Simply put, assembling a portfolio of stocks, bonds, and other financial instruments balances the risk a manager is taking with any one of the investments. Over time, this same idea has also taken hold for managing a portfolio of R&D projects, where it is referred to as *project portfolio management*.

Project portfolio management considers the company's set of projects in a holistic way, providing an overview of the potential value, as well as the inherent risks of both the projects a company is currently engaged in and those it plans to initiate in the future. By means of project portfolio management, risks can be reduced through diversification of the product portfolio and value enhanced by identifying synergies between projects. Companies in the pharmaceutical and energy industries, for instance, have long recognized the value of project portfolio management, and they are using sophisticated methods and software tools to support this process.

Project portfolio management comprises the following functions:[1]

- determine a viable project mix;
- balance the portfolio;
- monitor the projects in the portfolio;
- analyze and enhance project performance;
- evaluate new opportunities against the current portfolio, taking into account capacity and funding capabilities;
- provide information and recommendations to decision-makers.

THE DIFFERENCE BETWEEN FINANCIAL AND R&D PORTFOLIO MANAGEMENT

Financial portfolios and project portfolios are very different in nature. The main characteristics of investing in financial instruments include:

Divisible investments: Financial instruments allow investment in small portions of an asset, rather than being all or nothing.

Simple interdependencies: The interrelationships between different investment opportunities can typically be captured by: The correlation between the assets' returns; and their financial value, as established by the financial markets.

Passive participation: Investing in financial instruments is typically a passive form of participation: The decision is mainly whether or not to invest, and how much.

Availability of information: Much information is available about financial assets in the form of historical performance and fundamental analyses concerning the future outlook.

Tradability: Most financial instruments are tradable assets, resulting in agreed-on valuations and opportunities to sell assets that do not fit your portfolio.

Clear objectives: The main objective is to maximize the risk–return performance of your portfolio.

Contractual clarity: Clearly defined terms exist for investing in a financial instrument, outlining the rights of the parties involved relying on established market rules.

These characteristics are not shared by a portfolio of R&D projects, which can be characterized as follows:

Discrete investments: Investments in projects are non-divisible, increasing the impact of an investment decision on your portfolio.

Complex interdependencies: Complex interdependencies and interactions exist between projects. Project outcomes are subject to synergies—for example, through the sharing of proprietary knowledge—and investment decisions may affect the options available in related projects.

Active participation: Investing in projects requires active management. Besides making a go/no-go decision and setting a budget, numerous decisions will have to be made during the project lifetime that will impact the outcome.

Lack of information: Since projects are largely unique, not much information is available on related past projects or for the prediction of future performance.

Nontradability: Projects cannot be easily sold, resulting in a lack of valuation information and lock-in situations.

Fuzzy objectives: Projects are typically governed by a multitude of objectives, both financial and nonfinancial, and typically include qualitative objectives.

Contract ambiguity: Project investments may result in disagreement concerning who is entitled to which benefit, with multiple stakeholders holding different views.

As a result, conclusions derived from finance cannot simply be transferred to other areas, nor can their methods be used without adaptation. That is why a variety of approaches have been proposed for valuing R&D projects, which is *the* central issue in managing a portfolio of R&D projects. The most commonly used is *decision analysis*, in which decision trees are used to represent the project's potential outcomes and their likelihood.

DECISION ANALYSIS: A DEFINITION

A central component in decision analysis is the concept of a decision tree. An example of a decision tree is given in Figure 1. In the figure:

- The squares, circles, and triangles represent points in time, which proceeds from left to right.
- The squares, or decision nodes, indicate decisions to be made, and the circles, or chance nodes, indicate the time when the result of an uncertain event becomes known. The triangles, or end nodes, indicate the end of the time horizon.
- The branches indicate the stage that follows, depending on which decision is made or which scenario unfolds.
- A probability is given on top of each branch that emanates from a chance node. This indicates the likelihood of that particular outcome materializing, given that all the preceding steps have already happened. These uncertainties are outside your control. The probabilities of all the branches emanating from a chance node sum to one.
- Below each branch that emanates from a decision or chance node a monetary value can be added to indicate the cash

in- or outflows associated with that particular decision or outcome.

- To the right of the end node two numbers are shown, the upper one representing the likelihood of ending up in that particular scenario, and the lower one the cumulative monetary value.

A key insight resulting from a decision-tree analysis is the so-called *expected value*. Starting at the right of the tree and working back to the left, we perform two types of calculations:

- At each chance node (circle), we compute an expected value as the sum of the probability-weighted expected values associated with the successor nodes.
- At each decision node (square), we determine the highest expected value of the successor nodes. The branch(es) resulting in the highest expected value are indicated by "TRUE," the others by "FALSE," indicating a preferred set of actions based on maximizing the expected value of the project.

Continuing this process, we arrive at the root node of the tree with the *expected value* of the decision tree. The term "expected value" is rather confusing, however, as this value should never be *expected*. In fact, it may even be impossible to obtain, and is merely a probability-weighted average of all the potential outcomes.

USING DECISION ANALYSIS TO VALUE R&D PROJECTS

Decision trees are a natural tool to value R&D projects, as these projects typically consist of several phases. Each project phase can be associated with a stage-gate, a point at which one decides whether or not to continue with the project, depending on the results of the earlier phases and new information obtained about the future. The results of each stage can be represented by a chance node in a decision tree, with the option to abandon the project as a decision node. Other chance nodes can be added to represent possible competitor actions, legislation uncertainties, and global economic

conditions. Decision nodes can be added to represent different possible actions, including the injection of more funds and resources in case of favorable developments, accelerating the project to bring forward its market launch date, etc.

As R&D projects typically take several years to complete, it is essential that the cash flows in the decision tree are discounted at an appropriate rate to take into account the firm's cost of capital. As each chance and decision node corresponds to a point in time, this can be accomplished by discounting each cash flow associated with a chance or decision node appropriately. When all cash flows are discounted, the expected value will then become an *expected net present value*, or eNPV.

Again, the eNPV should not be expected, but is merely a probability-weighted average of all the potential results, discounted at an appropriate cost of capital. Nevertheless, the eNPV is a crucial number, indicating the value of the project, because it considers all possible scenarios and how likely they are. In principle, if the eNPV of a project is positive, the project will add value and should be undertaken. Although for a one-time project the eNPV should not be expected, the strategy of pursuing projects with positive eNPV will, in the long run, result in the highest possible profit for your organization. If, however, the eNPV is negative, other and better uses for the required funds and resources can be found.

A second deliverable of a decision-tree analysis for R&D projects, apart from the eNPV, is the risk profile, which shows the potential outcomes and their likelihood. Of particular interest is the potential downside, the worst possible result with a nonzero likelihood. If this downside is large enough to cause potential financial distress to the company, then perhaps the project should not be pursued after all, despite a potential positive eNPV. If the worst-case scenario is very unlikely, another useful metric can be used, namely the value-at-risk (VaR). The VaR indicates the loss that could result from a project with a certain probability, for example 5%. So if the VaR

Figure 1. Example of decision-tree analysis for a R&D project

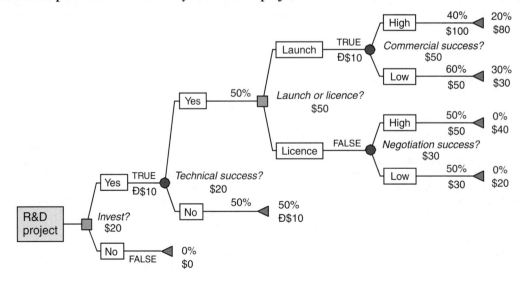

Figure 2. Decision tree for the Phytopharm project

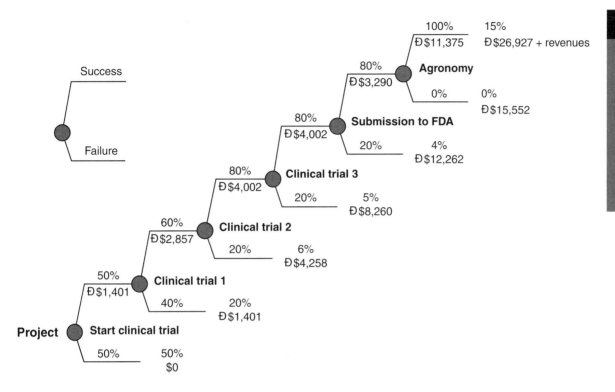

Figure 3. Example of a tornado diagram

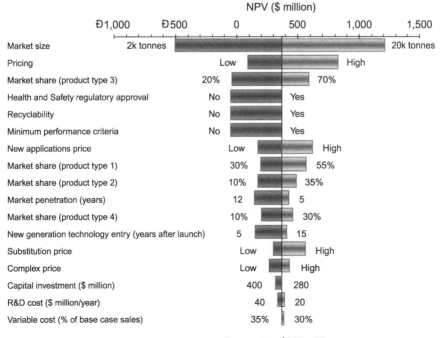

Base value: $360 million

of an R&D project is $10 million, this means that we estimate a 5% chance of losing $10 million or more if we pursue the project. Again, this could be a reason for rejecting a project that would otherwise be interesting (because of a positive eNPV), depending on the risk appetite and liquidity of the company.

CASE STUDY
PHYTOPHARM PLC
All of the world's leading life sciences companies use decision-analytic approaches to value their portfolio of R&D projects. In fact, many have a decision-analysis group, responsible for reviewing the R&D portfolio. They typically use a wide variety of criteria to assess R&D projects, including financial value measured by the projects' net present value, sales, and growth potential, with a special focus on potential blockbusters, pipeline balance over time and over different therapeutic areas, risk, unmet medical need, and strategic fit, expressed as a desire to build strength in certain therapy areas. An array of tools is used to support this analysis, including net present value, decision analysis, and Monte Carlo simulation.

Before a pharmaceutical drug can be approved for production and marketing, stringent scientific procedures must be followed in several stages to ensure patient safety. The drug development process is typically composed of basic research (approximately two years), pre-clinical testing (approximately three years), clinical trials (approximately six years, consisting of phases I, II, and III), followed by a review by regulatory authorities. A new pharmaceutical drug that is being investigated can fail to make it through any one of these stages due to potential harmful side effects or insufficient proof of effectiveness. On average, only one in five medicines that enters clinical trials is launched; and only 1 in 10,000 compounds in the research phase makes it to the market.

Due to the massive resources required to perform the late-stage clinical trials, smaller firms such as biotech companies or university spin-offs typically only perform the first steps of pharmaceutical research and development. If the product passes these first few stages, the product is outlicensed to partners with the financial, R&D, and marketing capabilities to further develop and launch it in the market. This was the case for Phytopharm plc, a pharmaceutical and functional food company based in Cambridgeshire, England.

Several years ago, Phytopharm acquired the exclusive license to develop and market a natural appetite suppressant derived from the *Hoodia gordonii* succulent, a cactus that grows in the Kalahari Desert. In 2004, Phytopharm's senior management was preparing to start negotiations for outlicensing this product, which had shown promise in early pre-clinical and clinical trials and successfully passed proof-of-principle. Although Phytopharm's senior management was confident that the product could be very successful, it needed a comprehensive and flexible methodology to rigorously predict and value the product's potential. A choice was made to use decision analysis as it provided transparency and flexibility, useful characteristics in a negotiation environment.

Figure 2 shows how the project was represented as a decision tree, with the different chance nodes corresponding to the different stages that had to be successfully navigated before the product could be marketed (all numbers are disguised and for illustrative purposes only). Decision nodes (not shown) could be added to represent decisions such as abandoning the development in case of unfavorable clinical trial results or commercial outlook, or choosing between different alternative technologies or markets.

In December 2004, Phytopharm licensed the product to Unilever for US$40 million and an undisclosed royalty on the sales of all products containing the extract. Unfortunately, in November 2008, Unilever decided to abandon the product due to a recent clinical study that provided unsatisfactory results. This possibility was foreseen in the decision-tree analysis, and had been incorporated when calculating the project's value at the time of licensing[2].

CONCLUSION
Decision analysis and decision trees are widely used for valuing R&D projects, because they are ideally suited to deal with the phased nature of R&D investments. Traditional financial valuation methods are based on assumptions that are not realistic in a R&D environment. The key deliverables of a decision-tree analysis of a R&D project is the project's expected net present value (eNPV) and its value-at-risk (VaR), two crucial criteria when deciding whether or not to pursue a project and include it in the organization's portfolio. The general rule is that the eNPV should be positive, and the VaR not so high that it may cause financial distress in case of an unfavorable outcome.

MAKING IT HAPPEN
There are several challenges when using decision trees for valuing R&D projects. For example:
- Which discount rate should be used? Traditional finance theory suggests that a discount rate should be used that reflects the cost of capital of a typical project. The question, however, is what to do when a project is not very typical. And what if the risk changes profoundly over the life cycle of the project? These issues are currently the topic of heated debate, both in R&D organizations and business schools. Note, however, that since the possibility of failure is already explicitly included in a decision-tree analysis, this risk should not be used to further increase the discount rate used to evaluate the project. The only risk that should be considered is the nondiversifiable market risk of the project, i.e., the correlation of the project and market returns.
- When a project contains many stages, with numerous uncertainties and possible decisions, a decision tree can easily "explode" and become unwieldy. Therefore, it is recommended that before carrying out a decision-tree analysis, a sensitivity analysis is performed to determine the main causes of uncertainty, which can then be incorporated in the decision tree. A so-called tornado diagram, which visualizes the key risks in a horizontal bar chart that resembles a tornado, can be used to determine these key risks. An example is shown in Figure 3.

- The validity of any conclusions drawn from a decision analysis depends heavily on the quality of the information used in the analysis. The principle "garbage-in-garbage-out" applies in this context. A common issue that has been observed is the tendency for people to be overconfident, in the sense that we all typically underestimate the magnitude of risks that we are facing. This has led to many criticizing the value-at-risk concept for performing a financial risk assessment, as none of these models could predict the magnitude of the current financial crisis. Therefore, it is essential that sufficient attention is paid to the quality of the data used in the analysis.
- A chance node in a decision tree can distinguish several possible outcomes, but it cannot specify a continuous range of outcomes. This, of course, can be approximated by defining numerous separate outcomes, but doing this will result in the tree "exploding." A better approach is to combine decision-tree analysis with a Monte Carlo simulation, which is ideally suited for analyzing risks with a continuous range of potential outcomes.

Winston, Wayne L., and S. Christian Albright. *Practical Management Science*. 3rd ed. Cincinnati, OH: South-Western College Publishing, 2006.

Websites:

Decision Analysis Society, a subdivision of the Institute for Operations Research and Management Science (INFORMS): www.informs.org/Community/DAS

Palisade Corporation, a provider of decision-analysis software, used to create the examples in this article: www.palisade.com

Strategic Decisions Group, a strategy consulting firm specializing in decision analysis and founded by, among others, the father of decision analysis, Professor Ronald A. Howard of Stanford University: www.sdg.com

See Also:

★ Real Options: Opportunity from Risk (pp. 273–276)
✔ Analysis Using Monte Carlo Simulation (p. 327)
✔ Understanding Real Options (pp. 367–368)
✔ Understanding the Weighted Average Cost of Capital (WACC) (pp. 309–310)

MORE INFO
Books:

Savage, Sam L. *Decision Making with Insight*. 2nd ed. Cincinnati, OH: South-Western College Publishing, 2003.

NOTE

1 Kendall, Gerald I., and Steven C. Rollins. *Advanced Project Portfolio Management and the PMO: Multiplying ROI at Warp Speed*. Boca Raton, FL: J. Ross Publishing, 2003.

Using Financial Analysis to Evaluate Strategy
by David Sadtler

EXECUTIVE SUMMARY

- Financial analysis is widely used to assess investment proposals, but less commonly to evaluate strategy.
- Strategy, both at business unit level (are we competing successfully?) and at the corporate level (does this portfolio of businesses make sense for the shareholders?), needs continuing evaluation.
- Business-level strategy can be judged by economic value added (EVA) analysis.
- Corporate-level strategy can be assessed by breakup analysis.
- Line managers are not necessarily motivated to do these analyses; it is thus up to others, especially the nonexecutive members of the board, to advocate them

INTRODUCTION

Many well-known tools and techniques of financial analysis are used by investors, stockbrokers, and corporate managers to assess corporate performance. Their use is particularly prevalent in mergers and acquisitions and in the analysis of capital expenditure. But how often do we say: "Let's do some financial analysis to see if this strategy is any good. Let's take a view on the corporate portfolio and the extent to which value is added by the corporate center and use financial tools to do it." In my experience, this doesn't happen much.

When companies undertake an acquisition, extensive financial analysis accompanies the investigation by managers, the proposals put to the board, and, if necessary, the story that is told to investors and the financial community. Comparisons are made with valuations of similar businesses and with transactions of a similar nature. Discounted cash flow techniques are used to assess the impact of different outcomes and the extent to which the investment is likely to recover the cost of capital employed in it. So the use of financial analysis for decision-making in the corporate environment is well known and widespread. Indeed, the essence of the core technique—present value and discounted cash flow analysis—has been around for at least 50 years. The tools are well known, credible, and widely accepted.

What about using financial analysis to assess strategy? In nearly all companies there are two levels of strategy that must be kept under constant surveillance by the custodians of stockholder investment. First, the viability of the individual businesses must be constantly examined. Are they earning satisfactory returns—or, indeed, returns in excess of the cost of capital employed in them? Second, does the corporate portfolio make sense? Would some parts of the business be better off elsewhere? There are straightforward tools to help in answering these questions and they should be regularly applied by the board of directors.

Why then does such an analysis not seem to be a widespread and regular practice? I think that the answer is pretty obvious. Top managers often do not want to admit that some parts of their business portfolio are unviable or that they are not the right owners. It's an agency problem, where management's motives diverge from the interests of the stockholders. But there are others whose job it is to question performance and to be sure that these agency problems do not stand in the way of the interests of stockholders. Nonexecutive directors on the board of directors are in this position, as are representatives of the investment community who decide on whether to advocate support for the organization. But to assess strategy—both at the corporate level and at the level of the individual business—they need suitable tools.

CORPORATE-LEVEL STRATEGY

Corporate-level strategy, as comprehensively described in the writings and teachings of the Ashridge Strategic Management Centre (see the More Info section) involves ensuring that value is added by the corporate center to each and every business unit within the portfolio. A number of useful frameworks and techniques have been available for some time to test the quality and intensity of corporate value added. Managers at both the business unit level and at the corporate center can be challenged to explain the exact nature of corporate value added (what do you do to make this business more successful and thus more valuable?). Long-term competitive performance (market share in key segments) can be used to assess the center's role in ensuring lasting commercial and financial viability. Comparison of the management structure and style with key comparator companies (especially those with more successful financial performance) can be used to assess both strengths and weaknesses in value added.

It is thus possible to take a reading on whether or not the corporate owners are doing an adequate job. The owners must address two questions: first, do we really add substantive value to each of our businesses; and, second, what businesses should we be in?

But these tests are *qualitative*. They make use of individual judgments, recollections, and viewpoints. While often pertinent and relevant, they can also be dreadfully biased. An alternative is to make the evaluation a *quantitative* one.

A straightforward financial tool is available to assess the overall success of the parenting capability of any big company, namely, breakup analysis. Breakup analysis takes an arm's length view of the market value of each of the company's businesses and compares the total of these values with corporate market capitalization, which is the value the marketplace places on the corporation as a whole. If the latter is less than the former, corporate strategy isn't working. The market is saying that the corporate center is *destroying* value. Synergies are not believed.

HOW TO DO A BREAKUP ANALYSIS

1 Subdivide the company into discrete businesses, focusing on particular customer groups and operating in identifiable industries. You will know that you are defining the business at the right level when it is easy to identify comparable companies.

2 Determine a baseline profit-after-tax figure for each business. Outside analysts will be constrained by the availability of reported information, but insiders should have all the necessary information. If profit performance has been uneven, use the budgeted figure for the coming year tempered by a judgment about how likely it is to be realized.

3 Corporate overhead costs, if allocated, should be removed from the cost basis of the individual businesses, subject to the limitation that any activities which would have to be added in were the business to be operating on its own must be accounted for. One famous Dutch electrical equipment company assesses a fixed charge for corporate-level R&D on all businesses. If the business in question demonstrably receives little benefit from such services, the charge should be reduced (or eliminated if the business is not really research-dependent) accordingly.

4 Identify comparable companies whose stock is publicly traded. Make a judgment about whether the business being analyzed deserves a rating below, equal to, or above that of the average of comparable companies. Decide on an earnings multiple and calculate *pro forma* market value accordingly.

5 Take note of the current market capitalization of the company as a whole. Make a judgment about whether any exceptional circumstances have caused a temporary departure from the norm. Determine a baseline market capitalization figure. For example, the sudden appearance of very bad news (like a financial scandal) concerning a key competitor can sometimes cause a selloff of major sector participants until the market's nervousness is allayed. Such an apparent "blip" must be considered.

6 Compare this latter figure with the total of the *pro forma* market values of the individual businesses and compare the two figures, after adjusting for borrowings at the corporate level.

Stockbroker analysts often perform similar analyses when judging whether a company is a plausible takeover candidate.

Perhaps the most famous example of a failed corporate-level strategy was that characterizing Imperial Chemical Industries (ICI) in the 1980s, at the time Britain's largest industrial company. ICI was a dominant player in basic chemicals, a notoriously cyclical and increasingly competitive business, where returns have often been unsatisfactory. It also owned a highly successful pharmaceuticals business which produced most of ICI's profit. Outside observers noted that an arm's length valuation of the pharmaceutical business alone was worth more than all of ICI together.[1] This is just another way of saying that the corporate-level strategy was a failure (or that the chemicals business was worth less than nothing). Had ICI's board made this calculation and honestly confronted it, it would have broken the company up itself rather than waiting for a threat from outside to necessitate it.

BUSINESS UNIT STRATEGY

Similarly, many tools and techniques are available to assess the viability of strategy at the level of each business in the corporate portfolio. Each company has its own favorite measures, against which managerial bonuses are often paid. Much attention is paid to these measures, and therefore what they are, and the objectivity with which they have been selected, is important for stockholders. Alas, there are many ways to rig the numbers to make the outcome appear satisfactory even if the reality is somewhat different.

But there is one measure that is hard to rig. Economic value added (EVA) analysis simply calculates business profitability after the imposition of a charge for the capital employed in the business. The tools for doing this are highly developed and, indeed, are championed by a number of consulting firms. The measures can be applied to any business in any company. A division earning $10 million pretax on turnover of $100 million and capital employed in the business of $60 million might, at first glance, be viewed as displaying creditable performance. But at a 35% tax rate and with a cost of capital of 12%, EVA is negative ($10 million × 65% − 0.12 × $60 million = $6.5 million − $7.2 million = − $0.7 million).

The implications of such an analysis are clear. If a business consistently demonstrates negative EVA, it is "parasitical"—eroding stockholder wealth. New investment is folly unless a fundamental game change can credibly be expected to result in positive EVA.

There is the possibility that it is not the fault of the operating management team. Some industries, in the aggregate, produce negative EVA. Airlines are the classic example. Warren Buffett recently observed that the total profitability for the entire industry since its inception has been zero. No one in their right mind would start an airline now. Since deregulation in 1978, there have been at least 100 bankruptcies in the airline businesses.[2] Management teams operating in one of these unhappy industries may actually be doing a good job on a relative basis but, alas, not for their stockholders or for the economy as a whole. How is it possible that an entire industry, perhaps with one or two exceptions, can fail to earn an "economic rent"? How can investors continue to commit capital to industries in which acceptable returns are unlikely? A number of explanations have been offered.

In developed economies major employers, with the major political pressure they can bring to bear, often prop up failing performers and keep marginal plants open, as in the car industry. Barriers to exit can be formidable, especially in industries where capital equipment is only of use in that industry and lasts a long time. Measures of profitability may be misleading. Managerial bias and incentives can prevent problems from being addressed in an objective way. Managers in unsatisfactory industries may not want to admit to the situation because it could make them look foolish—or worse, unemployable. And investors may simply be incompetent. It is not enough to suggest that they might simply buy stocks with high dividend yields on the basis of a very low valuation of assets. Any investor looking to the longer term, as most institutional investors seem to do, will eventually focus on total stockholder return. Term lenders presumably do the same. They'll want capital investment to pay out.

HOW TO CALCULATE EVA

1 The formula to calculate EVA is fairly simple. The formula is: EVA = net operating profit after taxes less the after-tax cost of capital employed.

2 The operating profit includes deductions from revenues for the cost of goods sold and for the operating expenses. Interest expense is then subtracted to cover the cost of the debt capital used, income taxes are then subtracted, and, finally, a cost for the equity capital is subtracted from the net income after tax to obtain the EVA.

3 The cost of equity capital can be derived by using any one of several approaches. Perhaps the simplest approach is to use the interest rate that a company can borrow at and then add a risk premium. The risk premium is added because investors require a higher return to invest in stock than they require for bonds. This is often called the bond yield plus risk premium approach. A typical equity risk premium is about 4%, so if a company can borrow at 10% its cost of equity capital would be 14%. Alternatively, use the weighted average cost of capital (WACC), a figure that is often well known to big companies and available from public data sources.

Alternatively, the cause of negative EVA may simply be poor management and a consistently weak competitive position. The managers of such a business are simply not offering a product or service which pleases enough customers for the business to be viable. We call this a failed competitive strategy.

Whether the problem at business unit level is participation in a low-profit industry or a failed competitive strategy, the business does not deserve further investment. It should be liquidated in the best way possible. Such businesses are likely to display longer-term negative EVA.

OBJECTIONS

Understandably, there are those who resist the notion of assessing strategy at either level by means of quantitative measures and analysis. Many such arguments claim unfairness, or a lack of true comparability. We see this for example in the daily news, when head teachers complain about league tables (often, of course, because the tables give their school a low rank) because, they say, the circumstances of their school are exceptional. They may even be right. But the school's performance is still lousy.

Similarly, business people will often argue in this way against the imposition of regular objective checks.

CONCLUSION

Financial calculations of the kind described above which give a clear indication of failed strategy at either the corporate or business unit level require action.

- Failed corporate strategies call for remedies ranging from reinvigorated management to structural breakup. It is up to the board to decide on the seriousness of the problem and the nature of the appropriate remedies. Failure to take appropriate action will often result in stockholder dissatisfaction and attempts by outsiders to restructure the company.
- Failed business unit strategies likewise demand action, since continuing on this basis constitutes a *de facto* drain on capital. Obviously, this cannot continue indefinitely.

Best Practice

Whatever the remedy, the key is a managerial realization that "business as usual" is not an option.

- This thinking and approach to analysis is simple. Good stewardship demands that these questions are raised regularly and acted on.

MORE INFO

Books:

Collis, David J., and Cynthia A. Montgomery. *Corporate Strategy: A Resource-Based Approach*. 2nd ed. Boston, MA: McGraw-Hill/Irwin, 2005.

Goold, Michael, Andrew Campbell, and Marcus Alexander. *Corporate-Level Strategy: Creating Value in the Multibusiness Company*. New York: Wiley, 1994.

Johnson, Gerry, Kevan Scholes, and Richard Whittington. *Exploring Corporate Strategy: Text and Cases*. 8th ed. Harlow, UK: Pearson Education, 2008.

Sadtler, David, Andrew Campbell, and Richard Koch. *Break Up! When Large Companies Are Worth More Dead Than Alive*. London: Capstone, 1997.

Stern, Joel M., John S. Shiely, and Irwin Ross. *The EVA Challenge: Implementing Value Added Change in an Organization*. New York: Wiley, 2004.

Article

Campbell, Andrew, Michael Goold, and Marcus Alexander. "Corporate strategy: The quest for parenting advantage." *Harvard Business Review* (March–April 1995): 120–132. Online at: tinyurl.com/6oeww7f

Websites:

Ashridge Strategic Management Centre, linked from Ashridge Business School home page: www.ashridge.org.uk

Investopedia article on EVA: www.investopedia.com/university/EVA

See Also:

★ Improving Corporate Profitability Through Accountability (pp. 204–206)

⇄ Economic Value Added (p. 391)

NOTES

1 Geoffrey Owen and Trevor Harrison. "Why ICI chose to demerge." *Harvard Business Review* (March–April 1995): 133–142.

2 Jon Bonné. "Airlines still struggle with paths to profit: After 100 years, it's no easier to get rich flying planes." msnbc.com (December 12, 2003).

CHECKLISTS

Assessing Cash Flow and Bank Lending Requirements

DEFINITION

Lack of cash flow is a major cause of a business failing as, even though it may be turning a profit, if the money does not flow in on time the business will not be able to settle its debts. Cash flow is basically the measure of a company's financial health, showing the amount of cash generated and used by a company in any given period. Cash flow is essential to ensure solvency, as having enough cash ensures that creditors and employees can be paid on time. Banks require companies to show the difference between sales and costs within a specified period, which acts as an indicator of the performance of a business better than the profit margins. Sales and costs, and therefore profits, do not necessarily coincide with their associated cash inflows and outflows. Even though a sale has been secured and goods delivered, payment may be deferred as a result of credit to the customer, yet suppliers and staff still have to be paid and cash invested in rebuilding depleted stocks. The net result is that although profits may be reported, the business may experience a short-term cash shortfall.

The main sources of cash flow into a business are receipts from sales, increases in bank loans, proceeds of share issues and asset disposals, and other income, such as interest earned. Cash outflows include payments to suppliers and staff, capital and interest repayments for loans, dividends, taxation, and capital expenditure. Cash flow planning entails forecasting and tabulating all significant cash inflows and analyzing in detail the timing of expected payments, which include suppliers, wages, other expenses, capital expenditure, loan repayments, dividends, tax, and interest payments.

A computerized cash flow model can be used to compile forecasts, assess possible funding requirements, and explore the financial consequences of other strategies. Computerized models can help prevent major planning errors, anticipate problems, and identify opportunities to improve cash flow and negotiate loans.

Banks must ensure that a business is viable, which entails asking pertinent questions. Lenders will insist on up-to-date information on the type of industry, management capabilities and experience, business plans and daily operations, key competition, and PR and marketing plans. They have to know that the business makes sense and can repay a loan, and what security is available in case of insolvency. Companies have to keep within their cash limits regardless of anticipated business. Business factoring is an alternative to bank loans—a factoring company buys your credit invoices and provides you with immediate cash in exchange for a small fee ranging between 1.5% and 5.0%. Factoring is more flexible than a bank loan.

ADVANTAGES

Ensuring good cash flow through a company helps to:
- increase sales;
- reduce direct and indirect costs and overhead expenses;
- raise additional equity;
- gain the confidence of banks and potentially secure more loans.

DISADVANTAGES
- If your profit margins are already low, you might not be able to afford bank fees.
- Banks have a tendency to increase fees and charge for late payments.

ACTION CHECKLIST

It is essential to keep track of your cash and not allow any surplus to sit idle. Accounts must be carefully monitored and cash invested to maximize returns. There are many ways to increase cash flow:

✔ reducing credit terms for historically slow payers;

✔ reviewing customer payment performance;

✔ becoming more selective when granting credit;

✔ seeking other ways to pay rather than all in one installment, such as deposits or staggered payments;

✔ reducing the amount of time of the credit terms;

✔ invoicing immediately the work has been done;

✔ improving collection systems for billing;

✔ adding late payment charges.

DOS AND DON'TS
DO

Do understand the way your company works, using a detailed analysis of banking procedure and taking into consideration:
- overdraft facilities and investment accounts;
- the number of monthly transactions;
- the number of written monthly checks;
- how customers pay you;
- the suitability of electronic banking for your business;
- cash access facilities;
- interest income;
- overall expenses and fees.

DON'T
- Don't overestimate sales forecasts.
- Don't underestimate costs.
- Don't underestimate delays in payments.
- Don't forget to check your debtors' credit histories carefully.

MORE INFO
Books:

Fight, Andrew. *Cash Flow Forecasting*. Oxford: Butterworth-Heinemann, 2006.

Mulford, Charles W., and Eugene E. Comiskey. *Creative Cash Flow Reporting and Analysis: Uncovering Sustainable Financial Performance*. Hoboken, NJ: Wiley, 2005.

Reider, Rob, and Peter B. Heyler. *Managing Cash Flow: An Operational Focus*. Hoboken, NJ: Wiley, 2003.

See Also:
★ Best Practices in Cash Flow Management and Reporting (pp. 7–12)
✔ Preparing a Cash Flow Forecast (pp. 301–302)
✔ Steps for Obtaining Bank Financing (pp. 333–334)
⇔ Discounted Cash Flow (pp. 386–387)

Estimating Enterprise Value with the Weighted Average Cost of Capital

DEFINITION

Enterprise value (EV) is a fundamental metric for measuring a company's market worth and is often used in place of market capitalization. The standard formula for EV is the market capitalization *plus* debt, minority interest, and preferred shares, *minus* total cash and cash equivalents. Because enterprise value is more comprehensive than market capitalization and takes debt into account, it is considered to be a more accurate representation of a company's value and often viewed as the theoretical takeover price.

Estimating enterprise value with the weighted average cost of capital (WACC) also takes the share price into account. WACC is the rate at which a company must pay to finance its assets. It is the minimum return that a company needs to earn from its existing asset base in order to satisfy its creditors, owners, and any other of its capital providers, and to keep its stock price constant.

WACC is used to discount expected cash flows during the excess return period to arrive at the aggregate of the organization's cash flow from operations. The company's residual value is calculated by dividing the net operating profit after tax by its WACC (based on an assumed terminal growth rate of 0%). Enterprise value is the sum of cash flow from operations, the residual value, and the short-term assets.

ADVANTAGES

- Using WACC to calculate a company's enterprise value gives the most accurate figure possible for the value of a company. Some investors follow a value philosophy and look for companies that generate a lot of cash flow compared with their enterprise value. In general terms, businesses that do this are likely to require less additional reinvestment. With plenty of cash, the owners can take the profit out of the business and invest it elsewhere or pay dividends to investors.

DISADVANTAGES

- The main disadvantage is that enterprise value is not as easy to calculate as market capitalization. The latter is a simple multiplication of the number of shares by the shares' unit value, whereas enterprise value takes other, less-tangible factors into account, making the calculation more elusive.

ACTION CHECKLIST

✔ Understand the reasons why you want to value a company. Is it to buy the company or to buy the stock?

✔ Assess whether you really need very accurate figures. The enterprise value calculation will provide these, but adding in the WACC will give an even more accurate result.

DOS AND DON'TS
DO

- Use enterprise value with WACC if you are considering buying a company.

DON'T

- Don't overcomplicate your calculations if you just want a ballpark figure. In that case, use market capitalization.
- Don't add cash in to the value of a company—take it away.

MORE INFO
Books:

Koller, Tim, Marc Goedhart, and David Wessels. *Valuation: Measuring and Managing the Value of Companies*. 5th ed. Hoboken, NJ: Wiley, 2010.

Koller, Tim, Marc Goedhart, David Wessels, and Erik Benrud. *Valuation Workbook: Step-by-Step Exercises and Tests to Help You Master Valuation*. 5th ed. Hoboken, NJ: Wiley, 2011.

Checklists

See Also:
✔ Obtaining an Equity Value Using the Weighted Average Cost of Capital (WACC) (pp. 331–332)
✔ Understanding the Weighted Average Cost of Capital (WACC) (pp. 309–310)

✔ Using the Market-Value Method for Acquisitions (pp. 355–356)
⇄ Enterprise Value (pp. 391–392)

Hedging Liquidity Risk—Case Study and Strategies

DEFINITION

The concept of "liquidity risk" tends to be very loosely defined. It is used most commonly with reference to the banking and finance industry, but it is an important issue for all companies. Broadly, liquidity risk is the danger that it will be difficult or impossible for an organization to sell an asset in order to provide capital to meet short-term financial demands.

A company needs to remain solvent; the liquidity risk is in the secondary market for its assets, which may not be sellable in time to meet short-term financial commitments, or will be sold at a price considerably below the perceived current market value. The problem may arise as the result of a liquidity gap or mismatch. This means that the dates for inflow and outflow of funds do not match up, creating a shortage.

Systemic liquidity risks arise from external factors. National or international recessions and credit crunches have the largest general impact on liquidity. Capital market disruptions, however, are more common. The collapse of the Russian ruble in 1998, for instance, created a global liquidity crisis, with a capital flight to quality away from the highly speculative Russian stock market.

Generally, liquidity is abundant during times when the economy is booming. During a downturn the impact on companies may increase if they continue with strategies based on the assumption that the high liquidity will continue indefinitely.

CASE STUDY

A company has outgoings of $8,000,000 per month against income from sales of $10,000,000. It faces a number of threats to its liquidity: for example, the price of the commodity it sells has fallen by 25%, leaving its income at $7,500,000 against $8,000,000 outgoings, and it has to find a way to raise the additional $500,000.

Some major customers have axed or cut their orders, leaving the company with a surplus of products to sell on the market. It has lost $4,000,000 in "normal" monthly sales and now has to offload products it is forced to sell, below cost, at 50% of the expected price simply to pay its bills ($6,000,000 in expected sales plus $2,000,000 to meet monthly obligations of $8,000,000).

The company chose to secure its position and iron out liquidity problems in the following ways:
• It held cash to cover some of the shortfall, but it lost the potential income from this capital.

• It set up a line of credit with its bank to help cover the shortfall.
• It sold off some assets in order to meet its financial obligations. This is risky as assets that have to be sold in a hurry may not realize their book price.

All this assumes that the company assessed its liquidity risks accurately and market conditions did not change.

STRATEGIES

Threats to a company's liquidity seldom happen in isolation but are intertwined with other financial risks. If, for example, a company fails to receive a payment, it may be forced to raise cash elsewhere or default on its payments. In this scenario, credit risk and liquidity risk are linked.

The aim of a liquidity management strategy is to minimize the cost of capital, allowing efficient access to capital and money markets at competitive prices during times of "normal" activity. Concurrently, the strategy should provide high levels of liquidity during periods when the financial markets are impaired.

The latter part of the strategy is often described as "life insurance." At a simple level this can mean organizing lines of credit well in advance of market turmoil, which is the cheapest option. However, the activities of a company and the market it operates in are dynamic. There will be periods when it is cash-rich and others when it is cash-poor. As cash is the ultimate liquid asset, there will be periods when it can "self-insure" and times when it will need to approach an external source for insurance.

ACTION CHECKLIST

✔ Examine predicted cash flows for the company. Look for any major negatives. Their impact can be stress-tested by analyzing the effect of a default by the major parties.

✔ Ensure that inflows and outflows match as far as possible.

✔ Assess the risk profile of the company before deciding what measures to put in place. In general liquid assets have a lower rate of return.

✔ Start a process of scenario testing. What happens if there is a default within an income stream?

✔ Ensure that the impacts of rare events are tested too. They may be unusual in isolation, but the more there are, statistically the higher the probability that one will occur.

MORE INFO
Books:
Fiedler, Robert. *Liquidity Modelling*. London: Risk Books, 2011.

Matz, Leonard, and Peter Neu (eds). *Liquidity Risk Management*. Singapore: Wiley, 2007.

See Also:
★ Navigating a Liquidity Crisis Effectively (pp. 38–40)
✔ Managing Working Capital (pp. 298–299)
✔ Measuring Liquidity (pp. 299–300)
⇄ Liquidity Ratio Analysis (pp. 396–397)

How to Manage Your Credit Rating

DEFINITION
A credit rating is an assessment of the creditworthiness of an entity such as an individual, a corporation, or even a country. Credit ratings are worked out from past financial history as well as current assets and liabilities, and are used to inform a potential lender or investor about the probability of the entity being able to pay back a loan. However, in recent years credit ratings have been used more widely. They have, for example, been used to make adjustments to insurance premiums or to establish the amount of a leasing deposit.

Credit reference agencies compile credit histories on individuals using information from sources such as electoral registers, court judgments, and lenders. Anyone applying for credit can expect to have their request recorded for the credit agencies to access and use. Financial institutions compile their own credit ratings for companies. The best known credit raters are Fitch, Moody's, and Standard & Poor's, which produce credit ratings for listed companies, banks, and even countries.

Credit reference agencies do not make the decision on whether to offer credit to would-be borrowers. It is for the lenders to reach a decision using information amassed by the credit agencies, combined with their own lending criteria and knowledge.

Having a bad credit rating limits your borrowing options. Court judgments, defaults on payments, and bankruptcy orders will all reduce your credit rating score. This applies equally to individuals and businesses. Where a credit applicant has a poor credit rating, credit may still be obtained through the subprime market, where the borrower is charged much higher rates of interest.

ADVANTAGES
Managing your credit rating can help to:
• ensure that you have access to credit in the future;
• enable you to take out a mortgage or loan;
• give you peace of mind.

DISADVANTAGES
• Repeated applications for credit (particularly unsuccessful ones) are recorded on your file.
• Repeated checks of your credit rating are recorded on your file.

ACTION CHECKLIST
✔ Buy access to your credit history and use it to check your credit rating.
✔ Make sure that any spent court judgments are recorded as such on your file.
✔ Ensure that any annulled or discharged bankruptcy order is recorded as such on your file.
✔ Keep up with all payments.

DOS AND DON'TS
DO
• Understand what your credit rating is.
• Check for errors in your credit rating, and have them amended.
• Work to make your credit history better if it has been poor in the past.
• Ask a potential lender if you fit their profile of a typical successful credit applicant as this may help you to avoid an actual credit check.
• Pay your creditors on time. If you miss a payment, inform your creditor straight away.
• Make sure you are on the electoral register.
• Make sure you complete credit card application forms correctly.
• Make your credit card, store card, loan, and mortgage repayments on time.
• Consider asking a family member or friend with a good credit rating to co-sign for a small loan or credit card. This can help your own rating.

DON'T
• Don't miss any payments.
• Don't check your credit record too often.
• Don't apply for loans too often, especially if you have a doubtful credit record.
• Don't avoid having any credit—no credit record is as bad as a poor credit record.

Checklists

MORE INFO

Books:

de Servigny, Arnaud, and Olivier Renault. *The Standard & Poor's Guide to Measuring and Managing Credit Risk*. New York: McGraw-Hill, 2004.

Ong, Michael K. (ed). *Credit Ratings—Methodologies, Rationale and Default Risk*. London: Risk Books, 2002.

See Also:

✔ Basic Steps for Starting a Business (pp. 361–362)
✔ Managing Bankruptcy and Insolvency (p. 365)
✔ Steps for Obtaining Bank Financing (pp. 333–334)

Identifying and Managing Exposure to Interest and Exchange Rate Risks

DEFINITION

The successful management of a portfolio includes maximizing returns from shifts in exchange and interest rates, which in turn requires an appreciation of the associated exposures. Not knowing the exposure can leave the portfolio open to significant risk.

Exchange rate risk is the risk arising from a change in the price of one currency against another. Companies or institutions that trade internationally are exposed to exchange rate risk if they do not hedge their positions. There are two main risks associated with exposure to exchange rates.

- Transaction risk arises because exchange rates may change unfavorably over time. The best protection is to use forward currency contracts to hedge against such changes.
- Translation risk concerns the accounts, and the level of risk is proportional to the amount of assets held in foreign currencies. Over a period of time, changes in exchange rates will cause the accounts to become inaccurate. To avoid this, assets need to be offset by borrowings in the affected currency.

The significance of the exposure will depend on the portfolio's weightings and operations. Identifying the level of risk in the above exposures should help with selecting a suitable defense strategy.

Interest rate risk relates to changes in the floating rate. Failure to understand exposure to interest rates can lead to substantial risk. The two main areas of concern here should be borrowings and cash investments. The best way of appreciating exposure to changing interest rates is to stress-test various scenarios. How, for example, would a change in rate from 4% to 6% affect your ability to borrow?

MITIGATING THE RISK

Exchange Rate Exposure

Other than the two strategies mentioned above, good strategies for minimizing exchange rate exposure involve employing one or more of the following products.

- **Spot foreign exchange**: An obligation to buy/sell a specified quantity of currency at the current market rate to be settled in two business days.
- **Structured forwards**: Exchange forwards embedded with, generally, more than one currency option. This adaptation allows a more effective hedge and should

improve the exchange rate within the client's perception of the market.
- **Currency options**: An option to the right to buy/sell a certain amount of currency at a specific exchange rate on or before a specific future date.

Interest Rate Exposure

Once identified, the risks can be minimized using the following methods:

- **Interest rate swap**: A method for changing the interest rate you earn/pay on an agreed amount for a specified time period.
- **Cross-currency swap**: An exchange of principal and interest payments in separate currencies.
- **Forward rate agreement**: Two parties fix the interest rate that will apply to a loan or deposit.
- **Interest rate caps**: The seller and borrower agree to limit the borrower's floating interest rate to a specified level for a period of time.
- **Structured swap**: An interest rate/cross-currency swap embedded with one or more derivatives. This allows the client to minimize exposure on their perception of the market.

ADVANTAGES

- The one key advantage to identifying exposure to interest and exchange rate fluctuations is the ability to minimize possible losses in the event that your view of the market is wrong. This approach will also minimize the chance of unexpected events disrupting the investment strategy.

DISADVANTAGES

- As with any hedge strategy, minimizing possible losses also reduces potential gains. Only those who are supremely confident in their forecasts and with a cushion to absorb losses should consider taking any extra risk to maximize returns.

ACTION CHECKLIST

✔ Plan your approach. Establish what your aims are when dealing with exchange rates/foreign currencies. Decide on your strategies for dealing with interest rate exposure.

Checklists

Create risk registers that set out clear procedures for dealing with risks as they arise.

✔ Calculate what losses you can afford, or what profits you need to make, and stick to them.

DOS AND DON'TS

DO
- Set realistic targets.
- Stick to your strategy.
- Research best strategy and implementation.

DON'T
- Don't be overoptimistic.
- Don't alter your strategy midway.
- Don't expose yourself to excessive risk.

MORE INFO

Books:

Fornés, Gastón. *Foreign Exchange Exposure in Emerging Markets: How Companies Can Minimize It*. Basingstoke, UK: Palgrave Macmillan, 2009.

Friberg, Richard. *Exchange Rates and the Firm: Strategies to Manage Exposure and the Impact of EMU*. Basingstoke, UK: Macmillan, 1999.

See Also:

★ Managing Interest Rate Risk (pp. 34–38)
★ To Hedge or Not to Hedge (pp. 53–56)
✔ Swaps, Options, and Futures: What They Are and Their Function (pp. 303–304)

Managing Risk in Islamic Finance

DEFINITION

There are differences between Islamic finance and conventional finance, but some fundamental principles involved in managing risk apply equally to both. In particular, rigorous risk management and sound corporate governance help to ensure the safety of financial institutions in both the Islamic and non-Islamic worlds.

The key difference between Islamic finance and conventional finance is that Islamic finance involves risk sharing rather than risk transfers. Thus, all parties involved in a transaction must share the rewards and the risks equitably. Furthermore, institutions in the former category must ensure that their activities are always compliant with the restrictions imposed by *shariah* law. This is complicated by the fact that scholars can and do change their minds over what is permitted under *shariah*.

Islamic institutions are confronted with unique risks as a result of the asset and liability structures that compliance with *shariah* law imposes upon them.

Operational risk is significant for *shariah* financial institutions due to their specific contractual features.

Liquidity risk is also more complicated than in conventional finance. This is because Islamic bank funding comes from personal customer accounts, the vast majority of which are on call or very short notice. In addition, until very recently, hedging risk by using conventional methods was not in compliance with *shariah*. Furthermore, there is no central receiver and provider of liquidity to and from the Islamic financial market. Finally, and again unlike the conventional market, most debt is not tradable.

In addition, some of the tools used to manage risk in Western financial institutions either cannot be used or have limited use in the Islamic world because they contravene *shariah* law. Thus, derivatives have been few and far between in Islamic countries, despite their widespread use in the West

to protect against market volatility. Islamic institutions have had limited access to derivative products, mainly because *shariah* law requires the underlying assets in any transaction to be tangible. This excludes most of the mainstream derivative instruments.

However, Islamic finance is developing apace, and products are being launched that can have useful risk management attributes and even mimic risk tools used in the West without contravening *shariah* law.

In March 2010, for example, the Bahrain-based International Islamic Financial Market, in cooperation with the International Swaps and Derivatives Association, launched the *Tahawwut* (Hedging) Master Agreement, which gives the global Islamic financial industry the ability to trade *shariah*-compliant hedging transactions such as profit-rate and currency swaps, which are estimated to represent most of the current Islamic hedging transactions.

Under *shariah* principles, the *tahawwut* or hedge must be strictly linked to underlying transactions and cannot be a transaction that has the sole purpose of making money from money. The lack of hedging products for managing risk has put many investors and institutions involved in Islamic finance at a disadvantage.

The *Tahawwut* Master Agreement should pave the way for quicker and cheaper Islamic risk management and more frequent cross-currency transactions. The contract creates a standard legal framework for over-the-counter (OTC) derivatives in the Islamic market, whereas currently contracts are arranged on an ad-hoc basis.

ADVANTAGES

- The lack of risk tools that are widely used in the West, such as derivatives, and the avoidance of certain sectors, such as banks, means that Islamic financial markets have a low correlation to other financial markets. This has provided protection from market turbulence, such as that seen during the subprime crisis.

- Many argue that the use of risk tools such as derivatives does not protect against volatility but simply increases it, while financial institutions earn vast profits through their deployment to the detriment of clients. Thus the lack of such tools in Islamic finance may benefit investors.

DISADVANTAGES

- The Islamic finance industry is governed by a patchwork of national banking regulations, its own standard-setting bodies, and scholars interpreting Islamic laws, making contracts much more complicated.
- Islamic scholars are split on the legitimacy of risk tools such as derivatives: some see them as permissible instruments to hedge risk, but others regard them as speculative transactions, which Islam forbids.
- While Islamic banks have avoided the complex instruments that were central to the credit crisis, they have still been susceptible to the downturn. Nonperforming loans and investment impairments in the region have mounted, partly due to inadequate risk-monitoring systems.

ACTION CHECKLIST

✔ Ensure that risk-management tools and systems are in place to ensure high standards of corporate governance and transparency.

✔ Establish whether compliance with *shariah* law creates unique risks, and create systems and tools that can monitor and protect against such threats.

DOS AND DON'TS
DO

- Ensure that any risk-management methods are compliant with local *shariah* rules governing finance. Rules can vary widely from one jurisdiction to another.

- Establish whether *shariah*-compliant tools for managing risk are available. The market is developing at a very rapid pace.

DON'T

- Don't ignore the fundamentals of risk management, including credit and counterparty checks.
- Don't assume that *shariah* law governing financial management is rigid. It is partly a question of interpretation, and there are usually solutions to even the most complex problems.

MORE INFO
Books:

Akkizidis, Ioannis, and Sunil Kumar Khandelwal. *Financial Risk Management for Islamic Banking and Finance*. New York: Palgrave Macmillan, 2008.

Iqbal, Zamir, and Abbas Mirakhor. *An Introduction to Islamic Finance*. Singapore: Wiley, 2007.

Report:

Grais, Wafik, and Matteo Pellegrini. "Corporate governance and shariah compliance in institutions offering Islamic financial services." Policy research working paper WPS4054. World Bank, November 2006. Online at: go.worldbank.org/D0UR4GDR30

See Also:

★ Introduction to Islamic Financial Risk Management Products (pp. 23–27)
★ Investment Risk in Islamic Finance (pp. 27–31)
★ Procedures for Reporting Financial Risk in Islamic Finance (pp. 101–103)
★ Risk Management of Islamic Finance Instruments (pp. 48–53)
✔ Understanding and Calculating the Total Cost of Risk (pp. 304–305)

Managing Working Capital

DEFINITION

Working capital, also known as net working capital, is a measurement of a business's current assets, after subtracting its short-term liabilities, typically short term. Sometimes referred to as operating capital, it is a valuation of the assets that a business or organization has available to manage and build the business. Generally speaking, companies with higher amounts of working capital are better positioned for success because they have the liquid assets that are essential to expand their business operations when required.

Working capital refers to the cash that a business requires for its day-to-day operations—for example, to finance the conversion of raw materials into finished goods that the company can then sell for payment.

Among the most important items of working capital are levels of inventory, accounts receivable, and accounts payable. Working capital can be expressed as a positive or a negative number. When a company has more debts than current assets, it has negative working capital. When current assets outweigh debts, a company has positive working capital.

The requirement for working capital depends on the type of company. Some companies are intrinsically better off than others. Examples include retailers (which have a fast turnover of cash) and insurance companies (which receive premiums before having to settle claims).

Manufacturing companies, on the other hand, can incur considerable upfront costs for materials and labor before they receive payment. For much of the time, these companies spend more cash than they generate.

A company will try to manage cash by:

- identifying the cash balance that allows it to meet day-to-day expenses but minimizes the cost of holding cash;
- finding the level of inventory that allows for continuous production but lessens the investment in raw materials and reduces reordering costs;
- identifying the appropriate source of financing, given the cash-conversion cycle.

It may be necessary to use a bank loan or overdraft. However, inventory is preferably financed by credit arranged with the supplier.

If a company is not operating efficiently, this will show up as an increase in the working capital. This can be judged by comparing the amounts of working capital from one period to another. Slow collection and inventory turnover may signal an underlying problem in the company's operations.

ADVANTAGES

- Proper management of working capital gives a firm the assurance that it is able to continue its operations and that it has sufficient cash flow to satisfy both maturing short-term debt and upcoming operational expenses.

DISADVANTAGES

- If a company's current assets do not exceed its current liabilities, then it may run into trouble paying back creditors in the short term.
- A declining working-capital ratio over a longer time period could also be a red flag that merits further analysis. For example, it could be that the company's sales volumes are decreasing and, as a result, its accounts receivable are diminishing.

ACTION CHECKLIST

✔ Check the amount of working capital. If a company is not operating in the most efficient manner (for example slow collection), it will show up as an increase in working capital. This can be understood by comparing the working capital from one period to another. Slow collection may signal a fundamental problem in the company's management.

✔ Is your 'performance indicator' for credit control better than those of other businesses in the same sector?

✔ Invoices should always be accurate in every detail and to the penny when quoting amounts. Inaccuracy is an excuse to query and delay payment. Also aim to send out your invoice the day after delivery of the goods.

✔ Chase debtors—Money that customers still owe cannot be used meet other obligations.

DOS AND DON'TS
DO

- Check that a company has sufficient working capital, as this is an indicator of the success of the business. Lack of working capital may not only mean that a company is unable to grow, but also that it has too little cash to meet its short-term obligations.

DON'T

- Don't allow working capital to fall below the level at which the company has more debts than current assets.

MORE INFO
Books:

Berman, Karen, and Joe Knight, with John Case. *Financial Intelligence: A Manager's Guide to Knowing What the Numbers Really Mean*. Boston, MA: Harvard Business School Press, 2006.

Downes, John, and Jordan Goodman. *Finance and Investment Handbook*. 8th ed. Hauppauge, NY: Barron's Educational Series, 2010.

Articles:

García-Teruel, Pedro Juan, and Pedro Martínez-Solano. "Effects of working capital management on SME profitability." *International Journal of Managerial Finance* 3:2 (March 2007): 164–177. Online at: dx.doi.org/10.1108/17439130710738718

Tooling and Production. "Conserve working capital." June 2008. Online at: tinyurl.com/36eugve

Website:

Working capital reduction case study from Hackett Group: www.thehackettgroup.com/casestudies/cytec/

See Also:

★ Best-Practice Working Capital Management: Techniques for Optimizing Inventories, Receivables, and Payables (pp. 2–6)
✔ Measuring Liquidity (pp. 299–300)
⇄ Working Capital Cycle (pp. 414–415)

Checklists

Measuring Liquidity

DEFINITION

Liquidity refers to the ability of an asset to be easily converted to cash without bringing about a major movement in price and with the lowest loss in value. Liquidity also refers to a company's ability to meet its obligations in terms of possessing sufficient liquid assets.

Checklists

Various ratios are used to measure liquidity. These include: the current ratio, which is the simplest measure and is calculated by dividing total current assets by total current liabilities; and the quick ratio, calculated by deducting inventories from current assets and then dividing by current liabilities. Although the two ratios are similar, the quick ratio provides a more accurate assessment of a business's ability to pay its current liabilities. The quick ratio cuts out all but the most liquid of current assets. Inventory is the most notable omission, because it is not as speedily convertible to cash.

For example, Table 1 using the quick ratio on the balance sheet.

Table 1. Example balance sheet

Cash	$55,000	Accounts payable	$25,000
Equities/ securities	$15,000	Expenses (accrued)	$20,000
Accounts receivable	$45,000	Notes payable	$10,000
		Debt	$15,000
Total current assets	**$115,000**	**Total current liabilities**	**$70,000**

Total current assets ($115,000) divided by total current liabilities ($70,000) = 1.65. Therefore, for every dollar of liabilities, the company has $1.65 in liquid assets to meet those obligations. As a general guide, companies with a quick ratio of greater than 1.0 are considered satisfactorily able to meet their short term liabilities. Liquidity is a measure of the ability of a debtor to pay their debts. It is crucial that a business has enough cash on hand to meet accounts payable, interest expenses, and other bills as and when they become due.

ADVANTAGES

- The quick ratio is a reasonable marker of a business's short term liquidity. The quick ratio gauges a company's ability to meet its short term obligations with its most liquid assets. The higher the quick ratio, the better the position of the business.
- A high or increasing quick ratio usually signifies that a business is experiencing above average growth, is rapidly changing receivables into cash, and is able to cover its financial obligations.

DISADVANTAGES

- The current ratio is the simplest measure and is calculated by dividing total current assets by total current liabilities. However, the current ratio does include inventory, which is often not as swiftly redeemable for cash and is often sold on credit.
- Simple liquidity ratios do not give information about the level and timing of cash flows, which really establish a company's ability to pay liabilities when due.

ACTION CHECKLIST

✔ Check whether a business has a low or decreasing quick ratio. This normally suggests that the business

✔ is over leveraged, unable to maintain or increase its sales, settling its bills too quickly, or collecting its receivables too slowly.

✔ Capital requirements, which differ from industry to industry, can have an effect on quick ratios. Therefore, make liquidity comparisons among companies within the same industry.

✔ Take into account factors such as type of industry (long/short cycle), allowances for bad debt, and payment and collection procedures.

DOS AND DON'TS
DO

- When using liquidity ratios to compare a business with others in an industry, allow for any material differences in accounting policies between the compared company and industry norms.
- Determine whether liquidity ratios were calculated before or after adjustments were made to the balance sheet or income statement. In some cases, these adjustments can significantly affect the ratios.

DON'T

- Don't forget that, although the current ratio is the simplest measure, it does include inventory, which is often not as swiftly redeemable for cash and is often sold on credit.
- Don't forget to take into account factors such as type of industry (long/short cycle), allowances for bad debt, and payment and collection procedures.

MORE INFO
Books:

Fiedler, Robert. *Liquidity Modelling*. London: Risk Books, 2011.

Matz, Leonard, and Peter Neu (eds). *Liquidity Risk Management*. Singapore: Wiley, 2007.

International Monetary Fund (IMF). *Financial Soundness Indicators: Compilation Guide*. Washington, DC: IMF, 2006. Online at: www.imf.org/external/pubs/ft/fsi/guide/2006/

Article:

Scordis, Nicos. "The value of smoothing cash flows." *Risk Management* 55:6 (June 2008). Online at: tinyurl.com/3cgho6d

See Also:

★ Navigating a Liquidity Crisis Effectively (pp. 38–40)

✔ Hedging Liquidity Risk—Case Study and Strategies (pp. 294–295)

✔ Managing Working Capital (pp. 298–299)

⇄ Liquidity Ratio Analysis (pp. 396–397)

Preparing a Cash Flow Forecast

DEFINITION

A cash flow forecast aims to predict a company's future financial liquidity over a specific period of time, using tried and tested financial models. While cash normally refers to the liquid assets in a company's bank account, the forecast usually estimates its treasury position, which is cash plus short-term investments minus short-term debt. The cash flow itself refers to the change in the cash or treasury position from one period to the next. The cash flow forecast is an important way to value assets, work out budgets, and determine appropriate capital structures. It will provide a good indicator of a company's financial health for potential investors.

Several methods are generally used to forecast cash flow—one direct, and three indirect. The direct method is most suitable for short-term forecasts of anywhere from 30 days up to a year, since it is based on actual data from which the projections are extrapolated. The data used are the company's cash receipts and disbursements (R&D). Receipts primarily include accounts from recent sales, sales of other assets, proceeds of financing, etc. Disbursements include salaries, payments for recent purchases, dividends, and debt servicing. Many of the R&D entries are based on projected future sales.

The other methods all use a company's projected income statements and balance sheets as their basis. The first method is adjusted net income (ANI), which first examines the operating income (EBIT or EBITDA), then looks at changes on the balance sheet such as receivables, payables, and inventory to forecast cash flow. The pro forma balance sheet (PBS) method looks at the projected book cash account—if the projections for all other balance sheet accounts are correct, then the cash flow will also be correct. Both these methods can be used to make short-term (up to 12 months) and long-term (multiple year) forecasts. Since they use the monthly or quarterly intervals of a company's financial plan, they must be adjusted to account for the differences between the book cash and the actual bank balance, and these may be significantly different.

The third method uses the accrual reversal method (ARM), which reverses large accruals (revenues and expenses that are recognized when they are earned or incurred, disregarding the actual receipt or dispersal of cash) and calculates the cash effects based on statistical distributions and algorithms. This allows the forecasting period to be weekly or even daily. It can also be used to extend the R&D method beyond the 30-day horizon because it eliminates the inherent cumulative errors. This is the most complicated of all methods and is best suited for medium-term forecasts.

ADVANTAGES

- Cash flow projections offer a useful indicator of a company's financial health.
- Cash flow forecasts enable you to predict the peaks and troughs in your cash balance, helping you to plan borrowings, and they tell you how much surplus cash you

may have at a given time. Most banks insists on forecasts before considering a loan.

DISADVANTAGES

- A cash flow forecast never tells the whole story about a company's financial situation and should not be relied on as the sole indicator.

ACTION CHECKLIST

✔ Be realistic when inputting your estimates. An acceptable method is to combine sales revenues for the same period 12 months earlier with predicted growth.

✔ Choose suitable accounting software to help you prepare a cash flow forecast. Check that it will enable you to update your projections if there is any change in market trends or your company's fortunes. Good software simplifies planning for seasonal peaks and troughs and can also calculate for "what if" scenarios.

DOS AND DON'TS

DO

- Use the most appropriate method, depending on how long you want your forecasting horizon to be.
- Remember that a cash flow forecast can only determine the short-term sustainability of a company. The longer the forecast horizon, the higher the chance of an inaccurate projection.
- Bear in mind that the forecast is dynamic—you will need to adjust it frequently depending on business activity, payment patterns, and supplier demands.

DON'T

- Don't rely solely on a cash flow forecast to determine a company's financial stability—look at the other financial statements and forecasts, such as an income statement and a balance sheet, to see what's actually going on.
- Don't forget to incorporate warning signals into your cash flow forecast. For example, if predicted cash levels come close to your overdraft limits, this should sound an alarm and trigger action to bring cash back to an acceptable level.

MORE INFO

Books:

Coyle, Brian. *Cash Flow Forecasting and Liquidity*. London: Global Professional Publishing, 2001.

Fight, Andrew. *Cash Flow Forecasting*. Burlington, MA: Butterworth-Heinemann, 2005.

Checklists

Loscalzo, William. *Cash Flow Forecasting: Guide for Accountants and Financial Managers*. Maidenhead, UK: McGraw-Hill, 1982.

See Also:

Setting Up a Dividend Policy

DEFINITION

A dividend is a payment made to a stockholder by a company from any earned profits (i.e. not from any other surplus). Companies generally use profit for two things—to reward stockholders for investing in the company or to reinvest in the business (known as retained earnings). Most companies generally reinvest a portion of the profit and pay out the rest in dividends. From the company's perspective, the payment of dividends is the division of an asset among stockholders.

Dividends are paid out on after-tax income, although the dividends received by stockholders are usually treated as taxable income for tax purposes, depending on their country of residence. Dividends are usually settled on a cash basis, although payment often is in the form of a check. However, many companies pay dividends in the form of additional shares or offer a dividend reinvestment program that enables stockholders to use the cash dividend to buy more shares in the company.

The dividend is normally paid out as a fixed amount per share. Thus, each stockholder receives a dividend in proportion to his or her holding. Most companies pay dividends on a fixed schedule, such as quarterly, half-yearly, or annually. However, a company can declare a dividend whenever it chooses—this is usually known as a special dividend to distinguish it from the regular payouts.

When setting up your dividend policy, key decisions will be how frequently to pay out, what percentage of profit to distribute among stockholders, and whether you will offer them other options, such as stocks in lieu of cash. Once the policy is in place, it needs to be communicated clearly to all stockholders so that they know how often and in what form dividends will be distributed. Policies can always be amended. For example, if the company's profits are badly hit one year, the board may decide not to pay dividends but to reinvest all the profit in the hope of better subsequent profits.

It is usual to publish the policy as a distinct corporate document for distribution in printed form. Many companies also publish the dividend policy on their websites. Amendments to the policy should be distributed in the same way.

ADVANTAGES

- Having a clear and transparent policy is essential for attracting stockholders. They are putting trust into a company by investing in it, and the company returns that trust by being open about what investors can expect to receive in return.

- It is also important that any changes to the dividend policy, whether temporary or permanent, are communicated clearly and in a timely fashion to stockholders.

DISADVANTAGES

- The only real disadvantage of a dividend policy is that some stockholders may be exposed to double taxation. In such a situation, stock repurchases may be more efficient if the tax rate for capital gains is lower.

ACTION CHECKLIST

✔ Determine how frequently you will pay out dividends. Be realistic about this—don't announce quarterly dividends if you know the cash flow patterns mean that a payout can only be made half-yearly.

✔ Have your policy written up professionally by someone experienced in the field.

✔ Ensure that the policy document is checked for compliance with all relevant financial regulations and laws in your territory of jurisdiction.

DOS AND DON'TS

DO

- Keep the dividend policy up to date and ensure that stockholders receive regular mailings about any changes.
- Inform stockholders well in advance of each payment date what percentage of profit the payout will be.

DON'T

- Don't amend dividend policy without good reason or telling your stockholders why.

MORE INFO

Books:
Baker, H. Kent. *Dividend Policy: Its Impact on Firm Value*. Hoboken, NJ: Wiley, 2009.
Frankfurter, George M., and Bob G. Wood, with James Wansley. *Dividend Policy: Theory and Practice*. San Diego, CA: Academic Press, 2003.

Manos, Ronny. *Capital Structure and Dividend Policy: Evidence from Emerging Markets*. Saarbrücken, Germany: VDM Verlag, 2008.

See Also:

Swaps, Options, and Futures: What They Are and Their Function

DEFINITION

A swap is a derivative in which two parties agree to exchange a set of cash flows (or leg) for another set. A notional principal amount is used to calculate each cash flow; these are rarely exchanged by the parties. A swap is usually used to hedge a risk, such as an interest-rate risk, or to speculate on a price change. It may also be used to access an underlying asset in order to earn a profit or loss from any change in price while avoiding posting the notional amount in cash or collateral.

An option is a financial instrument that gives the holder the right to engage in a future transaction on an underlying security or futures contract. The holder is under no obligation to exercise this right. There are two main types of option. A call option gives the holder the right to purchase a specified quantity of a security at a fixed price (the strike price) on or before the specified expiration date. A put option gives the holder the right to sell. If the holder chooses to exercise the option, the party who sold, or wrote, the option is obliged to fulfill the terms of the contract.

Futures are traded on a futures exchange and represent an obligation to buy or sell a specified underlying instrument on a specified date (the delivery date or final settlement date) in the future at a specified price (the futures price). The settlement price is the price of the underlying asset on the delivery date. Both parties to a futures contract are legally bound to fulfill the contract on the delivery date. If the holder of a futures position wishes to exit their obligation before the delivery date, they must offset it either by selling a long position or buying back a short position. Such an action effectively closes the futures position and its contractual obligations.

ADVANTAGES

- The use of derivatives means that some financial risks can be transferred to other parties who are more willing or better suited to take or manage those risks and can thus be a useful tool for risk management.
- Purchasing derivatives can be a safer choice if there is a possibility of a looming bear market as they are hedged, unlike equities.
- Buying now at a future price can be cheaper than buying at market price in the future, bearing in mind that the spot price could be less expensive.
- A long call option requires no obligation when it is due.

DISADVANTAGES

- If the market changes dramatically, it is possible to lose financially if the derivatives are being used as a speculative instrument.
- If you hold the put option on a derivative, you are obliged to adhere to it if the holder of the call chooses to exercise their right to sell or buy.

DOS AND DON'TS
DO

- Take time to consider which derivative is most suitable for the transaction you have in mind.
- Consult a financial intermediary or seek other expert guidance if you are unsure.

DON'T

- Don't enter into a contract that will lock you in if there's the slightest possibility that you may need to exit before its expiration date.

MORE INFO
Books:

Arditti, Fred D. *Derivatives: A Comprehensive Resource for Options, Futures, Interest Rate Swaps, and Mortgage Securities*. Boston, MA: Harvard Business School Press, 1996.
Cox, John C., and Mark Rubinstein. *Options Markets*. Englewood Cliffs, NJ: Prentice Hall, 1985.
Hull, John C. *Options, Futures, and Other Derivatives*. 8th ed. Upper Saddle River, NJ: Pearson, 2011.
Redhead, Keith. *Financial Derivatives: An Introduction to Futures, Forwards, Options and Swaps*. London: Prentice-Hall, 1996.

Articles:

Black, Fischer, and Myron S. Scholes. "The pricing of options and corporate liabilities." *Journal of Political Economy* 81:3 (May–June 1973): 637–654. Online at: www.jstor.org/stable/1831029
Cox, John C., Stephen A. Ross, and Mark Rubinstein. "Options pricing: A simplified approach." *Journal of Financial*

Checklists

304

Economics 7:3 (September 1979): 229–263. Online at: dx.doi.org/10.1016/0304-405X(79)90015-1

Moran, Matthew. "Stabilizing returns with derivatives." *Journal of Indexes* (4th Quarter 2002): 34–40. Online at: tinyurl.com/3rwqgqp

Schneeweis, Thomas, and Richard Spurgin. "The benefits of index option-based strategies for institutional portfolios." *Journal of Alternative Investments* 3:4 (Spring 2001): 44–52. Online at: dx.doi.org/10.3905/jai.2001.318987

See Also:
★ The Role of Short Sellers in the Marketplace (pp. 158–164)
✔ Identifying and Managing Exposure to Interest and Exchange Rate Risks (pp. 296–297)
✔ Understanding Asset–Liability Management (Full Balance Sheet Approach) (pp. 305–306)

Understanding and Calculating the Total Cost of Risk

DEFINITION

Risk exists virtually everywhere in business—from the obvious, easily insurable risks such as cover for property assets to more obscure, yet not insignificant, risks such as the loss of key employees to illness. However, in an effort to cover as many bases as possible, some companies channel resources into their risk management operations, potentially raising questions over whether these units are delivering good value for stakeholders in the company. The total cost of risk (TCOR) is a tool for measuring the overall costs associated with the running of the corporate risk management operation, including all insurance premiums, risk control and financing costs, administrative costs, and any self-retained losses incurred, relative to other key measures such as overall company revenues, total headcount, and its asset base. Over time, TCOR therefore provides a yardstick to assess how a company's risk-related costs are changing relative to the overall growth rate of the business. In turn, management can then explore potential ways to assess how the company's TCOR is changing relative to industry benchmarks, typically with the use of data derived from research—e.g., "physical" risk research conducted by trade groups and industry organizations. Given that the cost considerations are uppermost in the oil distribution business, yet food producers may focus more on liability insurance risks, working with these industry bodies can be the best way to obtain relevant and comparable risk-related cost data.

ADVANTAGES

- Calculating the total cost of risk can help companies to highlight inconsistencies in their approach to risk management.
- The process can also identify areas where the cost of managing a particular risk may be excessive relative to risks elsewhere, potentially leading to reallocation of some elements of the risk management budget.
- By highlighting inefficiencies in the risk management process, TCOR can also generate direct cost savings.

DISADVANTAGES

- Truly comparable TCOR data can be difficult to access, though trade bodies can help. However, prized data on direct competitors—such as a key rival also pushing into a new, high-growth market segment—are plainly sensitive and therefore not generally available.
- TCOR analysis can be mistakenly seen purely as a cost-cutting exercise.

ACTION CHECKLIST

✔ Use a basic framework to break down costs into component categories such as risk financing, risk administration, risk compliance costs, and self-insured losses.

✔ Identify existing costs for each category, expressed as a percentage of overall company revenues.

✔ Use any available data from industry bodies for comparison with your existing TCOR figures in each category.

✔ Consider possible reasons for differences between your company's numbers and industry-wide figures.

✔ Establish targets for each category for future years.

DOS AND DON'TS

DO

- Remember that industry benchmarks may not always be truly comparable with your company in every aspect.
- Consider whether some minor risks could be covered in-house.
- Make use of specialist software to help you arrive at decisions on issues such as risk retention, as risk management budgeting is by nature complex.

DON'T

- Don't ignore the value added by the risk management function when making budgeting decisions. This is a mistake. Risk management should not be seen purely as a cost.
- Don't expect that TCOR analysis will lead to immediate cost savings. This could lead to disappointment. Be prepared to invest in risk management tools which will deliver financial benefits over time.

- Don't see the management of risk-related costs as an issue for which all possible solutions lie within the company. Explaining your objectives and priorities to external risk management specialists and insurance brokers could be very productive.

MORE INFO
Books:
Frenkel, Michael, Ulrich Hommel, Gunter Dufey, and Markus Rudolf. *Risk Management: Challenge and Opportunity*. 2nd ed. Berlin: Springer, 2005.

Merna, Tony, and Thaisal F. Al-Fani. *Corporate Risk Management: An Organisational Perspective*. Chichester, UK: Wiley, 2008.

Report:
Green, Andrew, Randy Garber, and Jim Hanna. "The real cost of risk: Reducing cost and schedule overruns at the US Department of Defense." AT Kearney, 2010. Online at: tinyurl.com/3lj529w [PDF].

Website:
Risk and Insurance Management Society (RIMS): www.rims.org

See Also:
★ Quantifying Corporate Financial Risk (pp. 45–48)
✔ Establishing a Framework for Assessing Risk (p. 313)
✔ Managing Risk in Islamic Finance (pp. 297–298)

Understanding Asset–Liability Management (Full Balance Sheet Approach)

Checklists

DEFINITION
Asset–liability management, or ALM, is a means of managing the risk that can arise from changes in the relationship between assets and liabilities. ALM was originally pioneered by financial institutions in the 1970s as interest rates became increasingly volatile. This volatility had dangerous implications for financial institutions. Some, for example, had sold long-term guaranteed interest contracts—some guaranteed rates of around 16% for periods up to 10 years. However, when short-term interest rates subsequently fell, these institutions, such as the Equitable in the US, were crippled. Prior to the 1970s, interest rates in developed countries varied little and thus losses accruing from asset–liability mismatches tended to be minimal.

Following the experience of equitable and other institutions, financial firms increasingly focused on ALM, whereby they sought to manage balance sheets in order to maintain a mix of loans and deposits consistent with the firm's goals for long-term growth and risk management. They set up ALM committees to oversee the ALM process. Today, ALM has been adopted by many corporations, as well as financial institutions. ALM now seeks to ascertain and control three types of financial risk: Interest rate risk, credit risk (the probability of default), and liquidity risk, which refers to the danger that a given security or asset cannot be traded quickly enough in the market to prevent a loss (or make a predetermined profit).

But ALM also now seeks to address other risks, such as foreign exchange risks and operational risks (covering areas such as fraud and legal risks, as well as physical or environmental risks). The techniques that are now applied by ALM practitioners have also developed, reflecting the growth of derivatives and other complex financial instruments. ALM now includes hedging, for example, whereby airlines will seek to hedge against movements in fuel prices and manufacturers will seek to mitigate the risk of fluctuations in commodity prices. Meanwhile, securitization has allowed firms to directly address asset–liability risk by removing assets or liabilities from their balance sheets.

ADVANTAGES
- ALM can help protect a financial institution or corporation against a variety of financial and nonfinancial risks.
- The mere process of identifying risks enables businesses to be better prepared to deal with these risks in the most cost-effective way.
- ALM ensures that a company's capital and assets are used in the most efficient way.
- It can be used as a strategic and business tool to improve earnings.

DISADVANTAGES
- ALM is only as good as the people on the ALM committee and the operational procedures that they follow.
- ALM can prove costly in terms of both the time required of employees and the investment required in management tools such as IT and techniques such as hedging.

ACTION CHECKLIST
✔ Establish an ALM committee to oversee the process.

✔ Ensure the committee has the necessary tools and techniques for measuring and managing rate, credit, and funding risk. This should include a computer system that enables the monitoring of funding sources and credit exposures.

✔ Acquire a managerial accounting system that can control the information fed into the computer system.

✔ Establish a reward and penalty system to manage those employees who are taking rate, credit, funding and other risks.

Checklists

DOS AND DON'TS

DO

- Talk to one of the many consultancy firms that specialize in ALM, and that can advise on establishing an ALM committee and improving its performance.
- Ensure those appointed to the ALM committee have the necessary knowledge and experience to perform their tasks.
- Constantly monitor the performance of your committee.

DON'T

- Don't seek to cut costs in terms of investing in management tools and personnel.
- Don't forget that risks are constantly changing and developing. Make sure your ALM committee has the skills to deal with the latest developments.

MORE INFO

Books:

Buckley, Adrian. *Multinational Finance*. 5th ed. Harlow, UK: FT Prentice Hall, 2003.

Dermine, Jean, and Youssef F. Bissada. *Asset and Liability Management: The Banker's Guide to Value Creation and Risk Control*. 2nd ed. Harlow, UK: FT Prentice Hall, 2007.

Tilman, Leo M. (ed). *Asset Liability Management of Financial Institutions: Maximising Shareholder Value through Risk-Conscious Investing*. London: Euromoney, 2003.

Article:

Buehler, Kevin S., and Anthony M. Santomero. "How is asset and liability management changing? Insights from the McKinsey survey." *RMA Journal* 90:6 (March 2008): 44–49. Online at: tinyurl.com/3pyjwml [PDF].

Website:

Institute of Risk Management (IRM): www.theirm.org

See Also:

★ Managing Counterparty Credit Risk (pp. 31–34)
★ Managing Interest Rate Risk (pp. 34–38)
★ Minimizing Credit Risk (pp. 142–145)
★ Using Structured Products to Manage Liabilities (pp. 57–59)
✔ Identifying and Managing Exposure to Interest and Exchange Rate Risks (pp. 296–297)

Understanding Capital Structure Theory: Modigliani and Miller

DEFINITION

The Modigliani–Miller theorem states that, in the absence of taxes, bankruptcy costs, and asymmetric information, and in an efficient market, a company's value is unaffected by how it is financed, regardless of whether the company's capital consists of equities or debt, or a combination of these, or what the dividend policy is. The theorem is also known as the capital structure irrelevance principle.

A number of principles underlie the theorem, which holds under the assumption of both taxation and no taxation. The two most important principles are that, first, if there are no taxes, increasing leverage brings no benefits in terms of value creation, and second, that where there are taxes, such benefits, by way of an interest tax shield, accrue when leverage is introduced and/or increased.

The theorem compares two companies—one unlevered (i.e. financed purely by equity) and the other levered (i.e. financed partly by equity and partly by debt)—and states that if they are identical in every other way the value of the two companies is the same.

As an illustration of why this must be true, suppose that an investor is considering buying one of either an unlevered company or a levered company. The investor could purchase the shares of the levered company, or purchase the shares of the unlevered company and borrow an equivalent sum of money to that borrowed by the levered company. In either case, the return on investment would be identical. Thus, the price of the levered company must be the same as the price of the unlevered company minus the borrowed sum of money, which is the value of the levered company's debt. There is an implicit assumption that the investor's cost of borrowing money is the same as that of the levered company, which is not necessarily true in the presence of asymmetric information or in the absence of efficient markets. For a company that has risky debt, as the ratio of debt to equity increases the weighted average cost of capital remains constant, but there is a higher required return on equity because of the higher risk involved for equity-holders in a company with debt.

ADVANTAGES

- In practice, it's fair to say that none of the assumptions are met in the real world, but what the theorem teaches is that capital structure is important because one or more of the assumptions will be violated. By applying the theorem's equations, economists can find the determinants of optimal capital structure and see how those factors might affect optimal capital structure.

DISADVANTAGES

- Modigliani and Miller's theorem, which justifies almost unlimited financial leverage, has been used to boost economic and financial activities. However, its use also resulted in increased complexity, lack of transparency, and higher risk and uncertainty in those activities. The global financial crisis of 2008, which saw a number of highly leveraged investment banks fail, has been in part attributed to excessive leverage ratios.

MORE INFO

Books:

Brealey, Richard A., Stewart C. Myers, and Franklin Allen. *Principles of Corporate Finance*. 10th ed. Boston, MA: McGraw-Hill, 2010.

Stewart, G. Bennett. *The Quest for Value: A Guide for Senior Managers*. New York: HarperBusiness, 1991.

Articles:

Miles, James A., and John R. Ezzell. "The weighted average cost of capital, perfect capital markets, and project life: A clarification." *Journal of Financial and Quantitative Analysis* 15:3 (September 1980): 719–730. Online at: dx.doi.org/10.2307/2330405

Modigliani, Franco, and Merton H. Miller. "The cost of capital, corporation finance, and the theory of investment." *American Economic Review* 48:3 (June 1958): 261–297. Online at: www.jstor.org/stable/1809766

Modigliani, Franco, and Merton H. Miller. "Corporate income taxes and the cost of capital: A correction." *American Economic Review* 53:3 (June 1963): 433–443. Online at: www.jstor.org/stable/1809167

See Also:

★ Optimizing the Capital Structure: Finding the Right Balance between Debt and Equity (pp. 145–148)
✔ Steps for Obtaining Bank Financing (pp. 333–334)

Understanding the Cost of Capital and the Hurdle Rate

DEFINITION

The cost of capital is the rate of return that an investor expects to earn on his or her investment. If an investment is to be worthwhile, the expected return on capital must be greater than its cost. In other words, the *risk-adjusted* return on capital (that is, incorporating not just the projected returns, but the probabilities of those projections) must be higher than the cost of capital.

Cost of capital is made up of two elements: debt and equity. The cost of debt is, in the simplest terms, the amount of interest paid on the debt. The interest cost is historical, but investor expectations may also influence the actual cost (i.e. investors may accept a higher cost in the short term where the long-term gains are better). Other factors may also affect the cost of debt. The interest rate usually includes the risk-free rate plus a risk component, which takes into account the probability of default on the debt.

The cost of equity is more complex. The traditional calculation used is that of dividend capitalization, whereby the dividends per share are divided by the current market value of the stock plus the dividend growth rate. Thus, the cost of equity is equal to the compensation demanded by the market in exchange for ownership of the asset and bearing the risk of ownership.

The cost of capital is often used as the discount rate, i.e. the rate at which the projected cash flow is discounted to determine the net present value.

The weighted average cost of capital (WACC) is a method of measuring a company's cost of capital. The total capital is taken to be the value of a company's equity (if there are no outstanding warrants and options, this is equal to the company's market capitalization) plus the cost of its debt (this must be continually updated as the cost of debt changes every time there is a change in the interest rate). When calculating the WACC, the equity in the debt-to-equity ratio is the market value of all equity, rather than the shareholders' equity on the balance sheet.

The hurdle rate is the minimum rate of return, when applying a discounted cash flow analysis, that an investor requires before they commit to an investment. A company may apply it when deciding whether to undertake a project, or a bank when extending loans. It must be equal to the incremental cost of capital. It is known as the hurdle rate because the amount of return determines if the investor is "over the hurdle" and ready to invest.

ADVANTAGES

- Using a hurdle rate can help take the emotion out of making a decision on investment by focusing purely on the financial aspects. When an investment looks exciting, it can be easy to overlook the risks or a potentially poor rate of return. A risk premium can be appended to the hurdle rate if evaluation of the investment shows that specific opportunities inherently contain high levels of risk.

DISADVANTAGES

- A major downside to using a hurdle rate is that, inevitably, some profitable projects will be rejected. Additionally, if the hurdle rate is too high, a company may only favor projects that are profitable in the short term rather than taking a long-term view. Thus it can make companies seem conservative and deter them from investing in innovation where the returns are uncertain.

MORE INFO

Book:

Ross, Stephen A., Randolph W. Westerfield, and Jeffrey Jaffe. *Corporate Finance*. 9th ed. Boston, MA: McGraw-Hill, 2010.

Articles:

Modigliani, Franco, and Merton H. Miller. "The cost of capital, corporation finance, and the theory of investment." *American Economic Review* 48:3 (June 1958): 261–297. Online at: www.jstor.org/stable/1809766

Yee, Kenton K. "Aggregation, dividend irrelevancy, and earnings-value relations." *Contemporary Accounting Research* 22:2 (Summer 2005): 453–480. Online at: dx.doi.org/10.1506/GEH4-WNJR-G58F-UM0U

See Also:

✔ Appraising Investment Opportunities (p. 358)
✔ Assessing Cash Flow and Bank Lending Requirements (pp. 292–293)
✔ Understanding the Relationship between the Discount Rate and Risk (pp. 308–309)
✔ Understanding the Weighted Average Cost of Capital (WACC) (pp. 309–310)

Understanding the Relationship between the Discount Rate and Risk

DEFINITION

The discount rate is the percentage by which a discounted cash flow (DCF) valuation is reduced in each time period beyond the present. Estimating a suitable discount rate is difficult and is an uncertain part of DCF. The problems are magnified by the fact that small changes in the interest rate can cause large changes in value for the final result down the line.

The discount rate used in financial calculations is commonly taken to be equal to the cost of capital. Adjustments can be made to the discount rate to take into account associated risks for uncertain cash flows. Examples of discount rates applied to various types of companies show a wide range:

Start-up companies seeking new money	50–100%
Early start-ups	40–60%
Late start-ups	30–50%
Mature companies	0–25%

High discount rates apply to more risky companies, for a number of reasons:
• Stocks are not traded publicly, so there is a reduced market for ownership.
• The number of willing investors is limited.
• The risk that start-ups will fail is higher.
• Forecasts by the business owners may be overoptimistic.
When a business has made a profit and is deciding whether to reinvest it in the business or pass it to stockholders, it must consider the discount rate. In an ideal world, reinvestment now guarantees larger profits later, and the amount of extra profit required by stockholders in the future, so that they will agree to reinvestment now, based on the stockholder's

discount rate. The capital asset pricing model (CAPM) is a way of estimating stockholders' discount rates. These rates are usually applied by businesses to their decisions on reinvestment by calculating the net present value of the decision. If a company uses the CAPM to work out the discount rate, it must first determine the equity cash flows that are subject to this rate.

The capital asset pricing model takes three variables into account when calculating a discount rate:

Risk-free rate: This is the return (as a percentage) from investing in risk-free securities, for example government bonds.

Beta: Beta is a measurement of how the stock price of a company reacts to a change in the market. A beta figure greater than 1 means that the stock price of the company changes more than the rest of the market. A beta below 1 means that the stock price is stable and does not respond wildly to changes in the market. A beta of less than zero means that the stock price moves in the opposite direction to the market, taking leveraging effects into account.

Equity market risk premium: This is the return on investment above the risk-free rate that investors require.

The discount rate is calculated as follows:

Discount rate = Risk − free rate + Beta × Equity market risk premium

The relationship between the discount rate and risk needs to be considered when performing a DCF analysis because any adjustment of the discount rate needs to allow for risk in future cash flows, and investors need to understand the trade-off between the amount of risk and expected future returns. A higher expected return is usually accompanied by a higher risk. Risk-averse investors usually prefer to hold a risk-free asset that has an expected return that is lower than that of a risky asset. Thus the discount rate would have to rise in order to attract risk-averse investors.

ADVANTAGES
- Applying risk to discount rates gives a better understanding of risks and returns.
- Considering the risk associated with a company gives an investor a better chance of understanding the risk associated with the investment.

DISADVANTAGES
- Many low-level investors may not wish to consider the complexity of the relationship of discount rates to risk.
- Becoming too concerned about risk could mean missing out on a spectacular future return.

ACTION CHECKLIST
When considering an investment, consider the position of the company:

✔ What are the expected rates of return?

✔ What are the risks involved?

✔ Do the rates of return compensate for those risks?

DOS AND DON'TS
DO
- Ensure that the risks associated with the expected returns are taken into account and understood.

- Understand the calculations involved in determining discount rates.
- Understand the nature of the company that is seeking inward investment—i.e. its level of maturity.

DON'T
- Don't ignore the risks.

MORE INFO
Books:
Bailey, Martin J., and Michael C. Jensen. "Risk and the discount rate for public investment." In Michael C. Jensen (ed). *Studies in the Theory of Capital Markets*. New York: Praeger, 1972.
Pannell, David J., and Steven G. M. Schilizzi (eds). *Economics and the Future: Time and Discounting in Private and Public Decision Making*. Cheltenham, UK: Edward Elgar Publishing, 2006.

See Also:
★ Valuing Pension Fund Liabilities on the Balance Sheet (pp. 60–62)
✔ Preparing a Cash Flow Forecast (pp. 301–302)
✔ Understanding the Cost of Capital and the Hurdle Rate (pp. 307–308)

Understanding the Weighted Average Cost of Capital (WACC)

DEFINITION
The weighted average cost of capital (WACC) measures the capital discount of a company's income and expenditure. It is a component of the formula used for calculating the expected cost of new capital and it represents the rate that a company is expected to pay to finance its assets. It is thus the minimum return that a company must earn on its existing asset base to satisfy its creditors, owners, and other providers of capital.

WACC is calculated by taking into account the relative weight of each component of a company's capital structure. The calculation usually uses the market values of the components, rather than their book values, which may differ significantly. Components may include equity (both common and preferred), debt (straight, convertible, or exchangeable), warrants, options, pension liabilities, executive stock options, and government subsidies. More exotic sources of financing, such as convertible/callable bonds or convertible preferred stock, may also be included in a WACC calculation if they are present in significant amounts as the cost of these is usually different from plain vanilla financing methods. For a company

with a complex capital structure, calculating WACC can be a time-consuming exercise.

The equation used to calculate WACC uses the cost of each capital component multiplied by its proportional weight as follows:

$$WACC = E/V \times R_e + D/V \times R_d \times (1 - T_c)$$

where R_e is the cost of equity, R_d is the cost of debt, E is the market value of the firm's equity, D is the market value of the firm's debt, $V = E + D$, E/V is the percentage of financing that is equity, D/V is the percentage of financing that is debt, and T_c is the corporate tax rate.

To determine the value of each component it is assumed that the weight of a source of financing is simply its market value (rather than the book value, which may be significantly different) divided by the sum of the values of all the components. The easiest component to calculate is the market value of the equity of a publicly traded company, as this is simply the price per share multiplied by the number of outstanding shares. Likewise, the market value of preferred shares is easy to determine and is calculated by multiplying the cost per share by number of outstanding shares. The market value of a company's debt is also easy to discover if a company has publicly traded bonds. However, many companies have debt in the form of bank loans, whose market value is not easily found. However, the market value of debt is often fairly close to the book value, at least for companies that have not experienced significant changes in credit rating. Thus, calculation of WACC typically uses the book value of any debt.

On the cost side, the cost of preferred shares is calculated by dividing the periodic payment by the price of the preferred shares. The cost of ordinary shares is typically determined using the capital asset pricing model. The cost of debt is usually the yield to maturity on the company's publicly traded bonds, or the rates of interest charged by the banks on recent loans. The cost of debt can be cut further as a company can usually write off taxes on the interest it pays on the debt. Thus, the cost of debt is calculated as yield to maturity multiplied by (1 minus the tax rate).

Because governments usually allow tax to be deducted from interest, there is an inherent bias towards debt financing. However, the cost of financial distress, such as bankruptcy, tilts any bias towards equity financing. In theory, therefore, the ideal debt-to-equity ratio in a company is usually the point at which any tax benefits accrued by debt financing are outweighed by the costs of financial distress.

MORE INFO

Books:

Armitage, Seth. *The Cost of Capital: Intermediate Theory.* Cambridge, UK: Cambridge University Press, 2005.
Johnson, Hazel. *Determining Cost of Capital: The Key to Firm Value.* London: FT Prentice Hall, 1999.
Pratt, Shannon P., and Roger J. Grabowski. *Cost of Capital: Applications and Examples.* 4th ed. Hoboken, NJ: Wiley, 2010.

Website:

Formularium on WACC calculation: formularium.org/en/10.html?go=96.169

See Also:

✔ Estimating Enterprise Value with the Weighted Average Cost of Capital (pp. 293–294)
✔ Obtaining an Equity Value Using the Weighted Average Cost of Capital (WACC) (pp. 331–332)
✔ Understanding the Cost of Capital and the Hurdle Rate (pp. 307–308)
⇄ Weighted Average Cost of Capital (p. 414)

Avoiding Conflict of Interest in Internal Audits

DEFINITION

Every year a company undergoes an external audit and will also undertake a program of internal auditing. Using external auditors to carry out internal audit work can lead to a conflict of interest. A conflict of interest may also occur when an internal auditor has a personal or professional involvement or association with the area that is subject to the audit.

There are two essential elements that apply to ensure that such conflicts of interest are avoided: independence and objectivity. *Independence* can be achieved by having an appropriate written internal audit charter that ensures the independence of auditors. The chief audit executive should report directly to the audit committee. Also, it is advisable that internal auditors do not have any operational responsibilities. The independence of an internal auditor appointed by the management of a company may be called into question if he or she is involved in reviewing the conduct of the management.

The *objectivity* element is ensured by the professionalism of the internal auditors. This is achieved by having a well-written and implemented internal audit charter. Recruiting and appointing the right internal auditor is of the essential. Maintaining good professional relations between the internal audit function and management is also extremely important. A good management team will be interested in a good audit process that will objectively highlight any positive or negative aspects of the way a company is managed. An internal auditor has a professional and ethical obligation to disclose any involvement on his or her part in an activity that could give rise to a conflict of interest.

The same firm should never be appointed to do both the internal audit and the external audit. Using different audit firms will not only avoid a conflict of interest but will provide independent opinions and reports that the management and shareholders can use to assess the business of the company.

ADVANTAGES

- Having an independent external audit helps an organization to assess the state of its business and to put in place measures to improve and develop it.
- Making sure that internal auditors are not involved in operational responsibilities avoids potential conflicts of interest.

DISADVANTAGES

- External auditors are expensive, but trying to cut costs by using the same auditors for both internal and external audits can lead to conflicts of interest and may in the end increase costs.
- In certain circumstances, a company will be required to change its external auditor after a fixed period and avoid using the same audit company for both internal and external audit work.

ACTION CHECKLIST

✔ Carefully assess your options for internal and external auditors. Obtain as much information from as many sources as you can before appointing auditors.

✔ Consider a selection bidding process and examine each bid carefully before making a decision.

DOS AND DON'TS

DO

- Establish good communication between management and auditors.
- Avoid conflicts of interest by choosing separate internal and external auditors.
- Encourage internal auditors to disclose any involvement in activities that might give rise to conflicts of interest.
- Consider reputation: a more expensive external auditor may offer better value for money in the medium to long term.

DON'T

- Don't make decisions that endanger the impartiality of an audit solely on the basis of financial considerations.
- Don't appoint internal auditors that have had management functions in the company.

MORE INFO

Books:

Gray, Iain, and Stuart Manson. *The Audit Process: Principles, Practice and Cases*. 5th ed. Andover, UK: South-Western Cengage Learning, 2011.

Pastor, Joan. *Conflict Management and Negotiation Skills for Internal Auditors*. Altamonte Springs, FL: Institute of Internal Auditors Research Foundation, 2007.

Websites:

Chartered Institute of Internal Auditors (UK and Ireland): www.iia.org.uk

Institute of Internal Auditors (IIA): www.theiia.org

See Also:

★ How Can Internal Audit Report Effectively to Its Stakeholders? (pp. 86–90)

✔ Conflicting Interests: The Agency Issue (pp. 338–339)

✔ Internal Audit Charters (pp. 314–315)

✔ Understanding Internal Audits (pp. 324–325)

Checklists

Choosing an External Auditor

DEFINITION

An external audit is an unbiased, independent review of a company's business and financial situation conducted by an external auditor. Public organizations and publicly traded firms are usually required to have an external audit conducted yearly. The firm's management is responsible for the selection and appointment of an external auditor.

There are many external audit firms to choose from. Public organizations and publicly traded firms must undergo a stringent process of appointing an external auditor that usually involves tenders and bids. The external auditors who are invited to tender are persons or companies with an in-depth knowledge of audit, finance, and management. The invitation to tender and bid must contain a clear description of the company and its audit requirements. It will explain the type of business the company undertakes, will specify what type of audit it is seeking, and should also give a clear description of the company's internal audit controls, administrative procedures, and management.

Once the bids are submitted the organization or company will start to analyze them. Certain bigger organization might put in place an evaluation committee to examine the bids and to ensure a transparent and fair selection process.

There are many factors to consider in the decision, including the auditor's reputation, past experience, and staff.

If the bids and tenders submitted are not sufficient to arrive at a decision, interviews and consultations can be organized to allow the evaluation committee to make better-informed decisions during the selection process.

Once the external auditor has been selected and appointed, the appointment is confirmed through a written agreement between the company and the external auditor. The agreement deals with the scope of the audit and its timing, cost, and standards, and it will also contain information relating to the obligations of the auditor and the support that the company will provide.

External audit regulations around the world differ. In the United States companies can use only certified public accountants to undertake their audit, while in Commonwealth countries, such as the United Kingdom, Canada, Australia, and New Zealand, the regulations demand the use of a chartered accountant.

ADVANTAGES

- An external audit helps an organization to assess the state of its business and to put in place measures to improve and develop it.
- External audits assess its risk management policies and help to deter fraud.
- Appointing the right external auditors will ensure a smooth and thorough examination of the company and a transparent and thorough audit.

DISADVANTAGES

- External auditors can be expensive. Plan your budget accordingly and make sure you negotiate a reasonable fee.
- In certain circumstances a company will be required to change its external auditor yearly or after a fixed period.

ACTION CHECKLIST

✔ Take time to recruit the best external auditors. Obtain as much information from as many sources as you can before appointing an external auditor.

✔ Consider a selection bidding process and examine each bid carefully before making a decision.

✔ Communicate clearly to your external auditors what you would like to achieve from the auditing process. Explain your business plans and aims and allow the external auditors transparency in examining documents and speaking with key staff.

DOS AND DON'TS
DO
- Establish good communication between management and external auditors.

DON'T
- Do not appoint external auditors based only on cost—consider other factors such as reputation and experience; a more expensive auditor may offer better value for money in the medium to long term.
- Do not underestimate the need for proper training of directors and employees to help them to fulfill their duties.

MORE INFO
Book:
Porter, Brenda, David J. Hatherly, and Jonathan Simon. *Principles of External Auditing*. 3rd ed. Hoboken, NJ: Wiley, 2008.

Articles:
Fan, Joseph P. H., and T. J. Wong. "Do external auditors perform a corporate governance role in emerging markets? Evidence from East Asia." *Journal of Accounting Research* 43:1 (March 2005): 35–72. Online at: dx.doi.org/10.1111/j.1475-679x.2004.00162.x
Wang, Kun, and Zahid Iqbal. "Auditor choice, retained ownership, and earnings disclosure for IPO firms: Further evidence." *International Journal of Managerial Finance* 2:3 (2006): 220–240. Online at: dx.doi.org/10.1108/17439130610676484

See Also:
★ Contemporary Developments in International Auditing Regulation (pp. 70–74)
★ Effective Financial Reporting and Auditing: Importance and Limitations (pp. 81–83)
✔ The Key Components of an Audit Report (pp. 318–319)

Establishing a Framework for Assessing Risk

DEFINITION

Instituting a framework for identifying risks (or opportunities), assessing their probability and impact, and determining which controls should be in place can be critical to achieving the company's business objectives. Identifying and proactively addressing risks and opportunities helps businesses to defend themselves. Debt rating agencies and regulators are also increasingly stipulating that companies institute risk-identifying frameworks.

Enterprise Risk Management (ERM) is a name given to the structures, methods, and procedures used by organizations to identify and combat risk. The setting up and monitoring of ERM is typically performed by management as part of its internal control activities, such as appraisals of analytical reports or management committee meetings with relevant experts to make sure that the risk-response strategy is working and that the objectives are being achieved.

Once the risks have been identified and assessed, management chooses a risk-response approach. This may include:

- Avoidance: Leave risky activities.
- Reduction: Lessen their probability or impact.
- Share or insure: Diminish risk by transferring or sharing.
- Accept: In response to a cost–benefit analysis, take no action.

The most widely used ERM frameworks are COSO (from an organization that prepares audit-related reports) and RIMS (The Risk and Insurance Management Society). Both use methods for identifying, analyzing, responding to, and scrutinizing risks or opportunities within the internal and external settings of the business.

ADVANTAGES

- ERM allows an enterprise to identify and prioritize the risks that might be facing the organization.
- An improved understanding of the risks—both systemic and non-systemic—facing businesses can help in contingency planning for when the unexpected happens.
- Robust identification of risks can protect businesses from events that might otherwise threaten the viability of the entity.

DISADVANTAGES

- Protracted risk-framework evaluation could be counterproductive if the fruitless pursuit of perfection leaves the company exposed to the very risks it hoped to avoid.
- Evaluating risks depends on judgments, estimates, and interpretation. Risks are often intangible issues that might be highly relevant but cannot be easily measured.

ACTION CHECKLIST

✔ Overcome resistance to the introduction or upgrading of risk frameworks by ensuring that the board and managers are conscious of the fact that it is in everyone's interest to be aware of business risks.

✔ Encourage an open environment when establishing a risk framework. Some risks are obvious, but stakeholders or managers of individual business sectors may sometimes know more about hidden risks.

✔ Engage key business stakeholders and managers in the evaluation of risks and when seeking the best resolutions for those risks.

DOS AND DON'TS

DO

- Regularly update risk-assessment frameworks, as these can help to keep management informed of the constantly changing business environment and its risks.
- Spell out in clear terms the risks that the organization may be facing, their probability, and their potential impact.

DON'T

- Don't take risks for granted; just because a risk has been the same in the past, there is no guarantee that it will be the same in the future. Only by fully understanding the risks and updating risk frameworks can you counteract the dangers.
- Don't get bogged down by risk frameworks. Risk is sometimes a natural and acceptable part of doing business.

MORE INFO

Books:

Baxter, Keith. *Risk Management: Fast Track to Success*. Harlow, UK: FT Prentice Hall, 2010.

Leitch, Matthew. *Intelligent Internal Control and Risk Management: Designing High-Performance Risk Control Systems*. Aldershot, UK: Gower, 2008.

Websites:

American Accounting Association (AAA): aaahq.org
Society of Actuaries (SOA): www.soa.org

See Also:

★ Quantifying Corporate Financial Risk (pp. 45–48)
✔ Creating a Risk Register (pp. 362–363)
✔ Understanding Internal Audits (pp. 324–325)

Checklists

Internal Audit Charters

DEFINITION

An internal audit charter is a formal document approved by the audit committee. It should be developed by the chief audit executive and agreed at the highest level of the organization. Standards published by the Institute of Internal Auditors (IIA) require that there be an internal audit charter, but there is no fixed requirement for what it should contain. At a minimum, the IIA standards require a charter to define the purpose, authority, and responsibility of the internal audit function. A charter establishes internal audit's position within an organization and authorizes it to access records, personnel, and physical property that are relevant to internal audit work. It can be used, for example, by an auditor when a manager in a remote part of the business questions the auditor's need to access particular documents, computer records, or personnel. A charter is particularly useful in large organizations but it is important to remember that such situations can also occur in smaller organizations.

The IIA refers to the need for a charter but does not provide specific guidance on what it should contain. IIA Standard 1000 says:[1]

"The internal audit charter is a formal document that defines the internal audit activity's purpose, authority, and responsibility. The internal audit charter establishes the internal audit activity's position within the organization, including the nature of the chief audit executive's functional reporting relationship with the board; authorizes access to records, personnel, and physical properties relevant to the performance of engagements; and defines the scope of internal audit activities. Final approval of the internal audit charter resides with the board."

ADVANTAGES

- A charter can be used in a positive fashion to describe the aims of internal audit.
- It can also be used to defend the audit against hostile managers or staff.
- A charter compels departments that need to be audited to cooperate with the auditor. Without this charter or similar authority, managers might not see the need for an audit and might refuse the auditor's requests.

DISADVANTAGES

- Such a formal document might not be necessary in a small organization.

ACTION CHECKLIST

✔ Develop a precise definition of internal auditing. This should be formally worded and include the objectives of the internal audit function. It may be possible to use the definition outlined by a body such as the IIA.

✔ Ensure that the charter makes it clear that internal audit engagements will cover the following four areas: reliability and integrity of financial and operational information;

effectiveness and efficiency of operations; safeguarding of assets; and compliance with laws, regulations, and contracts.

Here is a suggested checklist for use in formulating an internal audit charter. The charter should:

✔ detail the purpose, authority, and responsibility of the internal audit function, together with the scope of its activities;

✔ establish internal audit's position within the organization;

✔ define the nature of the assurance services that will be provided by internal audit;

✔ include a definition of internal auditing;

✔ define the nature of the assurance services that will be provided by internal audit;

✔ authorize access to records, personnel, and physical property relevant to the performance of engagements;

✔ specify a periodic review of internal audit performance and of the charter itself;

✔ be approved by the audit committee.

DOS AND DON'TS

DO

- Ensure that the role of the internal audit function is clearly set out and that it is distinguished from management's responsibilities. Management should, for example, be responsible for establishing procedures to prevent fraud, while the auditors should be responsible for establishing the effectiveness of those procedures.
- Ensure that the charter is simple and unambiguous.
- Make sure that senior management supports the charter or serious problems could ensue.
- Keep the charter short and to the point.

DON'T

- Don't forget to revisit the charter periodically to ensure that it remains relevant to the organization's needs.

MORE INFO

Books:

Moeller, Robert R. *Brink's Modern Internal Auditing: A Common Body of Knowledge*. 7th ed. Hoboken, NJ: Wiley, 2009.

Pickett, K. H. Spencer. *The Internal Auditing Handbook*. 3rd ed. Chichester, UK: Wiley, 2010.

Website:
Institute of Internal Auditors (IIA): www.theiia.org

See Also:
★ Aligning the Internal Audit Function with Strategic Objectives (pp. 63–66)
★ Starting a Successful Internal Audit Function to Meet Present and Future Demands (pp. 103–108)

✔ Avoiding Conflict of Interest in Internal Audits (p. 311)
✔ Understanding Internal Audits (pp. 324–325)

NOTE
1 IIA. "1000—Purpose, authority, and responsibility." Online at: tinyurl.com/65dspxb

Internal Auditing for Fraud Detection and Prevention

DEFINITION

Fraud protection is a key concern for businesses, and internal audits can play a major role in both detecting and preventing fraud. According to the Institute of Internal Auditors (IIA), for example, "internal auditors support management's efforts to establish a culture that embraces ethics, honesty, and integrity" and "they assist management with the evaluation of internal controls used to detect or mitigate fraud, evaluate the organization's assessment of fraud risk, and are involved in any fraud investigations." This is because, although it is management's responsibility to design internal controls to prevent, detect, and mitigate fraud, the internal auditors are "the appropriate resource" for assessing the effectiveness of the measures that management has implemented. Consequently, the IIA says that depending on directives from management, the board, audit committee, or other governing body, internal auditors can play a variety of consulting, assurance, collaborative, advisory, oversight, and investigative roles in an organization's fraud management process. Internal auditors are well placed to deter and detect fraud because they are highly proficient in techniques used to evaluate internal controls. These skills, "coupled with their understanding of the indicators of fraud, enables them to assess an organization's fraud risks and advise management of the necessary steps to take when indicators are present," concludes the IIA.

ADVANTAGES

- As a part of their assurance activities, internal auditors watch for potential fraud risks, assess the adequacy of related controls, and make recommendations for improvement. They can help also to benchmark statistics related to the probability of occurrence and consequences of fraud.
- Internal auditors are exposed to key processes throughout the organization and have open lines of communication with the executive board and staff. They are thus able to play an important role in fraud detection.
- Since internal auditors report directly to the board or governing body, they have the independence and objectivity necessary for them to undertake investigations of a sensitive nature.

DISADVANTAGES

- Although internal auditors may have a direct role in investigating fraud, they generally lack the expertise of professionals whose primary responsibility is detecting and investigating fraud.

ACTION CHECKLIST

✔ Consult the internal auditors on methods to ensure integrity within the organization and involve them in communicating or interpreting those methods. Internal auditors can also help to develop training related to integrity policies and fraud prevention and detection.

✔ Ensure that the internal auditors have key competencies for this work through specialized training and related experiences. They can also gain certification as fraud or forensic investigators.

✔ Ensure that the chief audit executive is responsible for responding to issues raised on ethics that may lead to detection of fraud.

DOS AND DON'TS

DO
- Establish a culture of integrity, as it is a critical component of fraud control. Executive management must set the highest levels of integrity as a benchmark.
- Ensure that you comply with IIA standards on this issue. In January 2009, for example, the IIA implemented a new standard making auditing for fraud mandatory for internal auditors.
- Make sure that your internal auditors consider using technology-based audit and other data analysis techniques in line with IIA standards.

DON'T
- Don't rely solely on internal auditors to root out and deter fraud. Simple procedures such as vetting employment candidates thoroughly can be highly effective and relatively cheap ways of preventing fraud.

Checklists

MORE INFO

Books:

Pickett, K. H. Spencer. *The Internal Auditing Handbook*. 3rd ed. Chichester, UK: Wiley, 2010.

Rezaee, Zabihollah, and Richard Riley. *Financial Statement Fraud: Prevention and Detection*. 2nd ed. Hoboken, NJ: Wiley, 2010.

Vona, Leonard W. *Fraud Risk Assessment: Building a Fraud Audit Program*. Hoboken, NJ: Wiley, 2008.

Reports:

Coram, Paul, Colin Ferguson, and Robyn Moroney. "The importance of internal audit in fraud detection." Paper presented at AFAANZ Conference, July 2–4, 2006, Wellington, New Zealand. Online at: tinyurl.com/6fvsvxl [PDF].

IIA. "Internal auditing and fraud." December 2009. Online at: tinyurl.com/4vsycok

Websites:

Chartered Institute of Internal Auditors (UK and Ireland): www.iia.org.uk

Institute of Internal Auditors (IIA): www.theiia.org

See Also:

★ Human Risk: How Effective Strategic Risk Management Can Identify Rogues (pp. 198–201)

✔ What Is Forensic Auditing? (pp. 325–326)

Checklists

International Financial Reporting Standards (IFRS): The Basics

DEFINITION

The increasing pace of globalization over recent years has forced the pace for the adoption of truly comparable and consistent international accounting standards. A decade ago, national versions of Generally Accepted Accounting Principles (GAAP) were commonplace. Nowadays, IFRS has gained broad acceptance and is used in over 100 countries. The United States is moving towards the convergence of US GAAP and IFRS, with the present timetable indicating that the set of standards will be applied to large public companies in 2014, though some should have the option to make the move even earlier. Since early 2008, IFRS has been allowed in the United States without reconciliation for foreign private issuers. The Securities and Exchange Commission's (SEC's) roadmap suggests that the decision over the future adoption of IFRS should be made in 2011, though the SEC has suggested that this timescale may be subject to delays.

Presently, the widespread use of US GAAP rather than IFRS can create difficulties for financial analysts, given the challenges in making financial comparisons. However, the timelines for change are far from clear. A joint initiative by the Financial Accounting Standards Board (FASB) and the International Accounting Standards Board (IASB) is aiming to converge existing standards into a single set of standards. In contrast, IFRS has been a requirement in Europe for listed companies since 2005.

In light of the increasingly international trend of IFRS, some emerging economies have been quick to adopt IFRS as their national version of GAAP.

First adopted in 2001, IFRS includes many of the International Accounting Standards (IAS) previously set by the IASB with the objective of improving the level of transparency of companies' finances. IFRS also generally includes the International Financial Reporting Interpretations Committee (IFRIC) interpretation and that of its predecessor, Standing Interpretations Committee (SIC), prior to March 2002. While the impact of the adoption of the IFRS on company accounts varies between countries, the set of standards imposes very strict disclosure requirements on companies. Intended to improve the visibility of companies' liabilities, IFRS requires the full disclosure of pension-related obligations, while executive remuneration visibility is also tackled, with IFRS dictating that stock options granted to executives must be included in the accounts. IFRS also has implications for the way companies account for their fixed assets, setting requirements over the fair value of assets. The impact of the adoption of IFRS can also have significance in areas such as merger and acquisition strategy, the provision of bank covenants, and distributions.

ADVANTAGES

- IFRS improves the level of comparability between the accounts of companies across different countries.
- The stringent disclosure requirements improve the visibility of liabilities such as future pension costs and employee stock schemes.
- The adoption of IFRS can provide greater reassurance for investors, credit rating agencies and lenders, potentially giving companies access to lower-cost capital in line with the lower risk.

DISADVANTAGES

- The adoption of IFRS can bring significant additional short-term costs to businesses, such as fees to pay specialist external accountants.
- As adjustments to comply with IFRS can make year-on-year performance comparisons difficult for investment analysts, potentially creating uncertainty and stock price volatility, companies must also devote resources to the preparation of accounts using the legacy conventions.

ACTION CHECKLIST

✔ Consider the benefits of introducing IFRS to management reporting, bringing improved quality and consistency to internal company information on which key decisions are based.

✔ Multinationals should examine the benefits of adopting IFRS throughout their organization to improve international comparability.

✔ Companies should be prepared to utilize external expertise to help with the transition to IFRS conventions.

DOS AND DON'TS

DO

- Companies adopting IFRS should budget for higher short-term costs.
- Aim to embed the principles of IFRS throughout all levels of an organization to extract maximum benefit.
- Explore the potential benefits in using XBRL (Extensible Business Reporting Language) in financial reporting.

DON'T

- Don't see IFRS as a "threat;" it can bring long-term material benefits, such as higher investor confidence and lower-cost capital.
- Don't ignore IFRS until you are obliged to adopt it by regulators. An understanding of IFRS can help companies

to prepare for its adoption, and can offer firms the flexibility to adopt IFRS at a time that works to their advantage.

MORE INFO

Articles:

Daske, Holger. "Economic benefits of adopting IFRS or US-GAAP—Have the expected cost of equity capital really decreased?" *Journal of Business Finance and Accounting* 33:3–4 (April/May 2006): 329–373. Online at: dx.doi.org/10.1111/j.1468-5957.2006.00611.x

Hail, Luzi, Holger Daske, Christian Leuz, and Rodrigo Verdi. "Mandatory IFRS reporting around the world: Early evidence on the economic consequences." *Journal of Accounting Research* 46:5 (December 2008): 1085–1142. Online at: dx.doi.org/10.1111/j.1475-679X.2008.00306.x

Websites:

American Institute of Certified Public Accountants (AICPA) on IFRS: www.ifrs.com

International Accounting Standards Board (IASB): www.iasb.org

See Also:

★ Best Practices in Cash Flow Management and Reporting (pp. 7–12)
★ Effective Financial Reporting and Auditing: Importance and Limitations (pp. 81–83)

Key Competencies for Internal Auditors

DEFINITION

Internal auditors work in many organizations in the public and private sectors. They can either be trained while working or will possess an internal audit or accountancy qualification before applying for an internal audit position. However, other qualifications can also be useful as the work is varied, challenging, and draws on a broad range of skills.

However, there is a range of key competencies that are required if internal auditors are to carry out their function effectively. These will vary depending on the seniority of the auditor. The requirement in terms of qualifications varies from country to country. In the United Kingdom, for example, an internal auditor is likely to hold the Chartered Institute of Internal Auditors Diploma in Internal Audit Practice (PIIA) or equivalent. Senior internal auditors should hold the Institute's Advanced Diploma in Internal Auditing and Management (MIIA) or equivalent.

According to the UK government,[1] an internal auditor should have the following competencies.

- Understands the principles of the identification, assessment, and management of risk, including that arising from the extended enterprise nature of organizations.

- Is able to identify and critically evaluate the elements of governance and risk management in an organization.
- Is aware of and understands the organization's risk management strategy.
- Understands the relationship of risk management to corporate governance.
- Is able to review and provide advice and recommendations on the implementation of the risk management strategy.
- Understands the organization's high-level objectives, how these are funded, and key related risks.
- Identifies and understands how operational objectives link into the higher-level objectives.
- Understands the relationship between internal audit and risk management, including the choice of roles available to internal audit depending on the risk maturity of the organization and its possible impact on corporate governance.
- Understands the specific risks related to operational activities and is able to contribute to the review of risks in operational areas.
- Is able to relate the organization's risk appetite to the appropriateness of controls and is able to undertake

reviews to assess their effectiveness and report to management accordingly.

- Understands the principles of performance measurement and output targets designed to deliver objectives.

ADVANTAGES

- Possessing key competencies enables internal auditors to do their job effectively.
- Possession of these competencies helps internal audit staff to gain the confidence and respect of senior management and of other staff they come into contact with. This is important if they are to carry out their professional duties effectively.

DISADVANTAGES

- Inevitably there will be costs involved in ensuring staff have the correct training and skills.

ACTION CHECKLIST

✔ Ensure that your internal auditors have a continuing commitment to learning. Business and technology are ever-changing, as are the political and regulatory environments in which a business operates.

✔ Before developing a training and development plan, ensure that training and development are linked to the organization's goals as well as those of personnel.

DOS AND DON'TS
DO

- Assess the competency level of each internal auditor, identify the gaps that need remediation, and develop an individual development plan for each internal auditor.
- Ensure that internal audit staff have an ability to manage projects and to work on their own initiative.

- Link the key competencies required by an internal auditor with your organization's personal development and appraisal systems.
- Ensure that internal audit staff have good written and verbal communication skills and are capable of interacting with senior management.

DON'T

- Don't forget to conduct a post-audit assessment, which should look at a variety of issues, including scoring auditors against key competencies.

MORE INFO
Books:

IIA Research Foundation. *Core Competencies for Today's Internal Auditor*. Altamonte Springs, FL: IIA Research Foundation, 2010.

Moeller, Robert R. *Brink's Modern Internal Auditing: A Common Body of Knowledge*. 7th ed. Hoboken, NJ: Wiley, 2009.

Pickett, K. H. Spencer. *The Internal Auditing Handbook*. 3rd ed. Chichester, UK: Wiley, 2010.

Website:

Chartered Institute of Internal Auditors (UK and Ireland): www.iia.org.uk

See Also:

✔ Avoiding Conflict of Interest in Internal Audits (p. 311)
✔ Establishing a Framework for Assessing Risk (p. 313)
✔ The Role of the Audit Committee (pp. 322–324)
✔ Understanding Internal Audits (pp. 324–325)

NOTE

1 Assurance, Control and Risk Team/PSG Competency Framework Working Group. "Government internal audit competency framework." HM Treasury, March 2007. Online at: tinyurl.com/7bfsmra [PDF].

The Key Components of an Audit Report

DEFINITION

An audit is the examination and verification of an organization's financial statements and records. Audits provide independent and impartial opinion as to whether the information is presented objectively. Most organizations—privately held businesses, publicly owned corporations, and nonprofit organizations—have to prepare financial reports, which are audited. These reports assist owners and managers to make decisions, and help to show the company's financial status to stockholders, employees, regulators, and the public.

When reviewing an audit report on a company, key questions include: What is the source of its revenue? Where, and on what, does it spend its income? How much profit is it earning?

The answer lies in the company's financial statements, and, by law, all public companies have to make these statements freely available to everyone.

These financial statements can be broken down into two key components: the profit-and-loss statement (or income statement) and the balance sheet.

The profit-and-loss statement tells us whether the company is making a profit. It indicates how revenue is transformed into net income. Profit-and-loss statements cover a period of time—usually a year or part of a year.

The balance sheet is a snapshot of a business's financial health at a specific moment in time—usually the close of an accounting period. A balance sheet shows assets, liabilities, and stockholders' equity/capital. Assets and liabilities are divided into short-term and long-term obligations. The balance sheet does not show the flows into and out of the accounts during the period. A balance sheet's assets should equal liabilities plus owners' equity.

There are two kinds of audit: internal and external.

Internal audits ensure that the management of the business is meeting internal goals such as productivity, quality, compliance controls, consistency, and cost, as well as external goals such as customer satisfaction and market share.

External audits are carried out by outside auditors, who do not have any ties to the organization or its financial statements. The outside auditor checks the financial statements prepared by management for balance, and also to see whether the company is adhering to professional standards and Generally Accepted Accounting Principles (GAAP).

ADVANTAGES
- External audits improve understanding of underlying business trends and provide an objective opinion as to whether the information is presented fairly.
- Internal audits let managers know whether a business can expand or needs to adopt a more conservative approach. Can it deal with the normal ebbs and flows in revenue, or should it take immediate steps to bolster cash reserves?
- Internal audits focus on processes within the business, and can identify and help to analyze trends, particularly in the area of receivables and payables, i.e. is the receivables cycle lengthening? Can receivables be collected more aggressively? Is some debt uncollectible?

DISADVANTAGES
- Results sometimes depend on the accounting methods used. Measuring and reporting give management considerable discretion and the opportunity to influence an audit's results.
- Internal audits are not always carried out rigorously and the figures may not reflect the true financial position of the company. Salaries for internal audit staff are paid for by the organization. This can lead to questions about objectivity.

ACTION CHECKLIST
✔ Carefully analyze any profit-and-loss statements for differences during the reporting period. Anomalies might be due to seasonal or other variations, or may indicate deeper problems.

✔ When reviewing internal audits, be prepared to be involved in a long and detailed process of analysis. Some areas will need clarification by experts.

✔ Check which GAAP are used in the internal audit of the business in which you are interested.

✔ Internal audits are not infallible. If you are unsure about specific areas or numbers, don't hesitate to ask for clarification.

DOS AND DON'TS
DO
- Make sure that you take the time and effort to analyze the audit. If in doubt, consult an independent auditor.
- Use your judgment when reviewing internal audits; results do not always tell the whole story.

DON'T
- Don't assume that all audits truly reflect a company's financial position; they only reflect the auditor's opinion.

MORE INFO
Books:
Cardwell, Harvey. *Principles of Audit Surveillance*. Philadelphia, PA: R. T. Edwards, 2005.
President's Council on Integrity and Efficiency, US General Accounting Office. *Financial Audit Manual*. Darby, PA: DIANE Publishing, 2000.
Wealleans, David. *The Quality Audit for ISO 9001:2000: A Practical Guide*. Burlington, VT: Gower Publishing, 2005.

Websites:
American Accounting Association (AAA): aaahq.org
Institute of Internal Auditors (IIA): www.theiia.org

See Also:
✔ Choosing an External Auditor (p. 312)
✔ Establishing a Framework for Assessing Risk (p. 313)
✔ Internal Audit Charters (pp. 314–315)
✔ Understanding Internal Audits (pp. 324–325)

Checklists

MiFID—Its Development and Aims

DEFINITION
The European Commission's Markets in Financial Instruments Directive (MiFID, EU Directive 2004/39/EC), was implemented on November 1, 2007, replacing the Investment Services Directive, and applies to all 27 EU member states plus Iceland, Norway, and Liechtenstein. Each country must incorporate MiFID either into local law or into the rules of the local regulatory handbook, depending on how financial regulation is applied in that state.

The objective of MiFID, apart from increased harmonization, is to boost innovation and competition across the financial markets within the European Union and adjoining states, improve liquidity in the markets, and reduce costs for issuers and investors.

REGULATORY APPROACH

As the key plank of the European Commission's Financial Services Action Plan, MiFID's 42 measures bring significant changes to how EU financial service markets operate. Whereas previous EU financial service legislation focused on "minimum harmonization and mutual recognition," MiFID's "maximum harmonization" principle places emphasis on home state supervision within a level playing field. The EU "passport" approach has been retained, but the old "concentration rule," which let member states require investment firms to route client orders through regulated markets, has been abolished.

MiFID's various articles cover almost all tradable financial products, with the exception of certain foreign exchange trades. This includes commodity and other derivatives such as freight, climate, and carbon derivatives, which were not covered by the Investment Services Directive. Any investment firm operating in Europe's financial markets is affected.

MiFID distinguishes between "investment services and activities" (core services) and "ancillary services" (non-core services). Details of these can be found in Annex 1 Sections A and B of the MiFID Level 1 Directive. A company providing core services is subject to MiFID in respect of both these and also ancillary services and can use the MiFID passport to provide them to other member states. However, a company engaged only in ancillary services is not subject to MiFID and cannot benefit from the MiFID passport.

GOOD PRACTICE

MiFID sets out various elements of good practice, such as how an investment firm should protect its customers or retain records. These apply to whatever is being traded. The following areas form the key aspects of the directive.

Authorization, Regulation, and Passporting

Companies are authorized and regulated in their "home state," typically the country in which they are registered. They can use the passport to provide services to customers in other member states.

Client Categorization and Order Handling

Companies must categorize clients as "eligible counterparties," professional clients, or retail clients (these have increasing levels of protection). Clear procedures must be in place to categorize clients and assess their suitability for each type of investment product. There are stringent requirements on the information to be collected when accepting client orders, to ensure that the company is acting in its clients' best interests, and on how orders from different clients may be aggregated. Appropriate investment advice or suggested financial transactions must be verified before being given.

Pre- and Post-Trade Transparency

Before trading, operators of continuous order-matching systems must aggregate their order information on liquid shares available at the five best price levels on the buy and sell side. The best bids and offers of market-makers must be made available for quote-driven markets. Post-trade, companies must publish the price, volume, and time of all trades in listed shares, even where conducted outside of a regulated market, unless certain requirements are met to allow for deferred publication.

Best Execution

Companies must take all reasonable steps to obtain the best possible result in the execution of a client order. This includes not just the execution price but also cost, speed, likelihood of execution, likelihood of settlement, and any other relevant factors.

Systematic Internalizers

A systematic internalizer is a company that executes orders from its clients against its own book or against orders from other clients. Under MiFID, systematic internalizers are treated as mini-exchanges and are thus subject to pre-trade and post-trade transparency requirements.

MORE INFO

Books:

Casey, Jean-Pierre, and Karel Lannoo. *The MiFID Revolution*. Cambridge, UK: Cambridge University Press, 2009.

Nelson, Paul. *Capital Markets Law and Compliance: The Implications of MiFID*. Law Practitioner Series. Cambridge, UK: Cambridge University Press, 2008.

Skinner, Chris (ed). *The Future of Investing in Europe's Markets after MiFID*. Chichester, UK: Wiley, 2007.

Websites:

European Commission on MiFID: tinyurl.com/yyulyz
MiFID resources: www.mifidirective.com

See Also:

★ Contemporary Developments in International Auditing Regulation (pp. 70–74)

✔ International Financial Reporting Standards (IFRS): The Basics (pp. 316–317)

Preparing Financial Statements: Balance Sheets

DEFINITION

A balance sheet is a snapshot of a business's financial health at a specific moment in time, usually at the close of an accounting period. A balance sheet comprises assets, liabilities, and stockholders' equity/capital. Assets and liabilities are divided into short-term and long-term obligations. On a balance sheet, assets should equal liabilities plus owners' equity.

- Assets: Current assets are those that can be converted to cash in one year or less. Common current assets include cash, account receivables, inventory (products manufactured or even work in progress held for sale in the normal course of business), prepaid expenses, and investment securities. Long-term assets are assets that companies retain for an extended time, such as land, plant, and machinery. Long-term assets earn income and/or are held to manage the companies in which the investment is made. Intangible assets also come under the broad category of long-term assets. Intangible assets are those that have no physical or tangible characteristics, for example patents, trademarks, copyrights, and goodwill.

- Liabilities: Current liabilities are debts to outsiders that should be paid within one year. Some common items that fall into this category are accounts payable and accrued liabilities, such as salaries and wages that have been incurred but not yet paid. Long-term liabilities are obligations that do not have to be met within one year. These might include long-term notes, bonds, and mortgages.
- Stockholders' equity/capital: The difference between the assets and the liabilities is referred to as stockholders' equity. Equity is the amount of capital that would remain once the liabilities were satisfied.

ADVANTAGES
- A balance sheet helps managers to decide if the business is in a position to expand, if it can easily handle the normal financial ebbs and flows of revenues and expenses, or if it should take immediate steps to boost cash reserves.
- Balance sheets can identify and analyze trends, particularly in the area of receivables and payables. Is the receivables cycle lengthening? Can receivables be collected more aggressively? Is some debt un-collectable? Has the business been slowing down payables to forestall a cash shortage?

DISADVANTAGES
- A balance sheet shows a snapshot of a company's assets, liabilities and stockholders' equity at the end of the reporting period. It does not show the flows into and out of the accounts during the period.
- Some numbers depend on judgments, estimates, and interpretation. Intangible assets are factors that might be highly relevant but cannot be reliably measured.
- Financial standards are not always applied to the letter, and balance sheets may not be a true reflection of the financial position of the company.

ACTION CHECKLIST
✔ Quantify in financial terms how decisions based on the balance sheet could impact on the business.

✔ Obtain as much information as possible and compare financial ratios before committing to expensive decisions.

✔ Be prepared to be involved in a long and complicated process of analysis. Some gray areas will not be resolved by financial ratios.

DOS AND DON'TS
DO
- Involve managers and key stakeholders in the company when evaluating balance-sheet findings.
- Determine whether ratios were calculated before or after adjustments were made to the balance sheet. In many cases, these adjustments can significantly affect the ratios.

DON'T
- Don't fall into the trap of thinking that financial ratios are infallible when analyzing balance sheets using ratios; use research to confirm results.
- Don't rely on factors that cannot be reliably measured. Some numbers, such as those for intangible assets, depend on judgments, estimates, and interpretation.

MORE INFO
Websites:
HM Treasury (UK): www.hm-treasury.gov.uk
Institute of Management Accountants: www.imanet.org
US Treasury: www.treasury.gov

See Also:
✔ Assessing Business Performance (pp. 359–360)
✔ Assessing Cash Flow and Bank Lending Requirements (pp. 292–293)
✔ Preparing a Cash Flow Forecast (pp. 301–302)
✔ Preparing Financial Statements: Profit and Loss Accounts (P&Ls) (pp. 321–322)

Checklists

Preparing Financial Statements: Profit and Loss Accounts (P&Ls)

DEFINITION
A profit and loss account, also known as an income statement or a statement of revenue and expense, is a financial statement that indicates how revenue (money received from the sale of products and services before expenses are taken out) is

transformed into net income (the result after all revenues and expenses have been accounted for). The important thing to remember about P&Ls is that they represent a period of time (usually a year or part of a year), rather than being snapshots. They should indicate to managers and investors whether a company made a profit or a loss during the period of time being reported. This contrasts with the balance sheet, which represents a single moment in time.

P&Ls can be broken into two groups: revenues and expenses. Both the revenues and expenses are recorded in the year (or other time period) that they are earned or accrued, not when the revenue is actually received or the expenses paid.

Revenues are the income the business receives in exchange for the products or services it provides. In most cases, revenues are associated with the sale of goods or services. Some of the more common sources of revenue are sales revenue, service revenue, and interest revenue.

The recorded expenses reflect the amount of resources used in earning the reported revenue. Some common examples of expenses are: salaries, research and development, bad debt, depreciation for the current year, and taxes.

For the investor, P&Ls also report earnings per share (EPS). This calculation shows how much money stockholders would receive if the company decided to distribute all of its net earnings for the period reported.

ADVANTAGES

- P&Ls should help investors and creditors to determine the past performance of the enterprise, predict future performance, and assess the enterprise's capability to generate future cash flow.
- P&Ls, along with balance sheets, are the most basic elements required by potential lenders, such as banks, investors, and vendors. Lenders will use the financial information contained in P&Ls to determine credit limits.
- P&Ls can also track dramatic increases in product returns or the cost of goods sold as a percentage of sales. They can also be used to determine income tax liability.

DISADVANTAGES

- Factors that might be highly relevant but cannot be reliably measured (for example brand recognition and customer loyalty) are not reported in P&Ls.
- Some numbers depend on the accounting methods used. The use of current costs or exit prices leaves room for manipulation. Measuring and reporting give management considerable discretion and the opportunity to influence results.
- Some numbers depend on judgments, estimates and interpretation.

ACTION CHECKLIST

✔ Use financial ratios on the P&Ls to evaluate the overall financial condition. Financial-ratio analysis will gauge viability, liabilities, and projected future performance.

✔ Carefully analyze any P&Ls for differences during the reporting period. Anomalies might be due to seasonal or other variations, or may indicate deeper problems.

✔ Consult and question managers and key business stakeholders in the evaluation process for P&Ls.

DOS AND DON'TS
DO
- Make sure that you have used the financial ratios when analyzing profit and loss accounts. If in doubt, consult an expert analyst.
- Consider seeking the help of specialist consultants.
- Check for any changes in accounting policies or anomalies that occurred during the period. Carefully examine any departures from industry norms.

DON'T
- Don't take shortcuts. Accounting can be a complicated process and remember that any undiscovered problems might cost more in the long run.
- Don't rely on accounting standards to protect you from fraud.
- Don't assume that P&Ls are a true reflection of a company's financial position. Measuring and reporting permit considerable discretion and the opportunity to influence results.

MORE INFO
Websites:
American Accounting Association (AAA): aaahq.org
Business Link (UK): www.businesslink.gov.uk

See Also:
✔ Assessing Business Performance (pp. 359–360)
✔ Assessing Cash Flow and Bank Lending Requirements (pp. 292–293)
✔ Preparing a Cash Flow Forecast (pp. 301–302)
✔ Preparing Financial Statements: Balance Sheets (pp. 320–321)

The Role of the Audit Committee

DEFINITION
The audit committee is an operating committee that deals with financial reporting and disclosure of the financial situation of a company. Since the Sarbanes–Oxley Act of 2002, the committee's role has become essential to a company's financial wellbeing. Depending on the size of a company and

whether it is private or public, the audit committee is composed of three to six members with financial, accounting, and auditing experience.

The role of an audit committee is varied. The committee reviews the internal auditors' report and makes recommendations to the board of directors based on its findings. It also reviews the chairman's statement of internal control of a company.

The audit committee performs a reporting and accounting role by overseeing external auditors, reviewing their report and management letter.

Another important role of the audit committee is to assess the risk management of a company by reporting directly to the executive board of a company on the effectiveness of the risk management arrangements and making recommendations. For this the audit committee will familiarize itself with the risk management procedures of a company, review any corporate governance statements, and assess the internal and external audit reports of the company.

Each member of the audit committee should declare any potential conflict of interest that may arise out of the business of the company. In order to be able to fulfill their role, members of the committee must have a good understanding of the company's objectives and priorities. Ideally, the members as a group should bring expertise to the audit committee in various disciplines such as finance and law and in the industry in which the company operates. They must have a clear picture of their appointment, including duration and time commitments. The members must also understand how their individual performance will be reviewed.

ADVANTAGES
- An audit committee is an oversight body that is independent of management.
- An audit committee sets standards in respect of governance, risk management, and controls.
- It performs a reporting and accounting role as well as assessing the risk management of a company.

DISADVANTAGES
- Getting the right expertise to serve on an audit committee can be difficult.
- Setting appropriate terms of reference and giving the committee sufficient authority to be effective can be problematic.
- An audit committee is another corporate overhead.

ACTION CHECKLIST
✔ An audit committee should have an independent chairman and comprise an appropriate mix of people, skills, and experience relevant to company operations. Appointees should include nonexecutive directors and independent members.

✔ The committee should have a charter (terms of reference), a code of conduct, and a register of members' interests. Institute a procedure for dealing with conflicts of interest.

✔ There should be a thorough process for appointing committee members.

✔ The full audit committee should meet regularly, with a written agenda that is distributed in advance.

✔ Agenda items should address key governance matters of the company.

✔ Written records (minutes) should be kept of audit committee meetings.

✔ Consider an evaluation process to assess the effectiveness of the audit committee.

✔ The audit committee should meet with representatives of external and internal auditors at least once a year without management being present.

✔ The audit committee should prepare an annual report for the board of directors on governance, risk management, controls, and fraud.

DOS AND DON'TS
DO
- Review the chairman's statement regarding the internal control of a company.
- Submit the internal auditors' annual report to the audit committee for their consideration.
- Review the external auditors' report and management letter.
- Implement the recommendations made by the audit committee.
- Periodically monitor reports on risks.
- Make sure that the corporate objectives of the company are mapped against risks.

DON'T
- Don't ignore the findings of the audit committee or any recommendations it may make.
- Don't make decisions solely on financial grounds that may endanger the impartiality of audit committee have regard to the reputation of the members of the audit committee and their professionalism.

MORE INFO
Books:
Ruppel, Warren. *Not-for-Profit Audit Committee Best Practices*. Hoboken, NJ: Wiley, 2006.
Verschoor, Curtis C. *Audit Committee Essentials*. Hoboken, NJ: Wiley, 2008.

Articles:
Bugalla, John, Janice Hackett, Mary Lynn McPherson, and Kristina Narvaez. "Audit committees monitor control

Checklists

functions, risk committees provide oversight of a strategic function." *BoardMember.com* (November 2010). Online at: tinyurl.com/6gkojc3

George, Nashwa. "The role of audit committees in the public sector." *CPA Journal* (August 2005). Online at: www.nysscpa.org/cpajournal/2005/805/essentials/p42.htm

See Also:
★ Implementing an Effective Internal Controls System (pp. 93–97)
✔ Establishing a Framework for Assessing Risk (p. 313)
✔ The Key Components of an Audit Report (pp. 318–319)

Understanding Internal Audits

DEFINITION

The Institute for Internal Auditors (IIA) defines internal auditing as "an independent, objective assurance and consulting activity designed to add value and improve an organization's operations." An internal audit "helps an organization accomplish its objectives by bringing a systematic, disciplined approach to evaluate and improve the effectiveness of risk management, control and governance processes."

The following comprise a set of guidelines for initiating an internal audit:

- Clarify guidelines and expectations with management (for example, purpose, timing, scope).
- Set up an audit committee and, with its help, develop an audit charter.
- Consider an appropriate budget and staffing model.
- Formulate reporting responsibilities for the internal audit function.
- Initiate a risk assessment, with management and audit committee involvement.
- Develop an internal audit plan in response to the risk assessment.
- Determine staffing requirements.
- Carry out the audit plan, including a monitoring and follow-up system.
- Update the risk assessment plan as circumstances change.
- Enhance and modify the audit function to meet the organization's changing needs.

If an evaluation of internal controls is to be effective, the audit function should be properly financed. When making staffing decisions, companies should look at their risk profiles. A business facing a significant number of risks or particularly complex risks will require various types of specialist expertise. A chief audit executive heads most internal audit departments, with specialist support staff.

ADVANTAGES

- Internal audits improve understanding of underlying business trends by giving independent objective financial information.
- Internal audits let managers know if a business can expand or needs to pull back, if it can deal with the normal revenue ebbs and flows, or if it should take immediate steps to boost cash reserves.
- Internal audits can identify and help to analyze trends, particularly in the areas of receivables and payables. For example, is the receivables cycle lengthening? Can

receivables be collected more aggressively? Is some debt uncollectable?

DISADVANTAGES

- Results sometimes depend on the accounting methods used. Measuring and reporting give management considerable discretion and opportunity to influence results.
- Internal audits are not always rigorously carried out, and figures may not be a true reflection of the financial position of the company.
- Salaries for internal audit staff are paid for by the organization; this can lead to bias.

ACTION CHECKLIST

✔ When reviewing internal audits be prepared to be involved in a long and detailed process of analysis where some areas will need clarification by experts.

✔ Check which Generally Accepted Accounting Principles (GAAP) are used in the internal audit of the business area or country in which you have an interest.

✔ Internal audits are not infallible. If you are unsure about specific areas or numbers, don't hesitate to ask for clarification.

DOS AND DON'TS
DO

- Make sure that you take the time and effort to analyze the internal audit and, if in doubt, consult an external expert.
- Use your judgment when reviewing internal audits; numbers do not always tell the whole story.

DON'T

- Don't leave out the boring bits; number crunching is not always effortless or interesting, and often it is tempting to skip parts. Sometimes, however, the truth lies in the detail.

MORE INFO
Websites:
HM Treasury (UK): www.hm-treasury.gov.uk
Institute of Internal Auditors (IIA): www.theiia.org
US Treasury: www.treasury.gov

See Also:
★ Aligning the Internal Audit Function with Strategic Objectives (pp. 63–66)
★ Contemporary Developments in International Auditing Regulation (pp. 70–74)
★ Starting a Successful Internal Audit Function to Meet Present and Future Demands (pp. 103–108)
✔ Internal Audit Charters (pp. 314–315)
✔ The Key Components of an Audit Report (pp. 318–319)

What Is Forensic Auditing?

DEFINITION

Forensic auditing is a blend of traditional accounting, auditing, and financial detective work. Technology has an increasingly important role to play, with complex data analysis techniques employed to help flag areas that warrant further investigation.

Forensic auditing offers a toolset that company managers can use to help detect and investigate various forms of white-collar financial impropriety and inappropriate or inefficient use of resources. As company structures and controls become ever more complex, so too does the scope for employees with specialized knowledge of the way control systems work to bypass them. In the past, various forms of auditing have been employed after a major control breach has come to light, but executives are now increasingly looking at forensic auditing to help identify vulnerabilities in financial control.

ADVANTAGES

- Forensic auditing strengthens control mechanisms, with the objective of protecting the business against financial crimes, be they potentially catastrophic one-off events that could threaten the viability of the business, or smaller-scale but repetitive misappropriations of company assets over a number of years.
- Forensic auditing can play an important role for companies under review by regulatory authorities and can also be invaluable to ensure regulatory compliance. For example, forensic auditing can be useful in helping companies to ensure that their anti-money laundering procedures are both effective and robust.
- Forensic auditing can help protect organizations from the long-term damage to reputation caused by the publicity associated with insider crimes. A forensic audit also provides a sound base of factual information that can be used to help resolve disputes, and can be used in court should the victim seek legal redress.
- Forensic auditing can improve efficiency by identifying areas of waste.
- Forensic auditing can help with the detection and recording of potential conflicts of interest for executives by improving transparency and probity in the way resources are used, in both private and public entities.

DISADVANTAGES

- A poorly managed forensic audit could consume excessive management time and could become an unwelcome distraction for the business.

- Forensic audits can have wide-ranging scope across the business. Under certain circumstances, the scope of the audit may need to be extended, with an increase in its budget.
- Some employees can interpret a proactive forensic audit as a slight on their integrity, rather than as a means to improve control procedures for the benefit of the business.

ACTION CHECKLIST

✔ Understand your risks, routes to their potential exploitation, and the tools available to detect abuses, fraud, or wastage.

✔ Analyze numerical data, comparing actual costs against expected costs.

✔ Investigate possible reasons for inconsistencies.

✔ Consider whether covert detection techniques might be more appropriate when investigating cases of possible fraud. Higher-profile full forensic audits can deter future fraud but could also reduce the likelihood of witnessing the culprit carrying out a fraudulent act.

✔ External auditing specialists with extensive experience of complex forensic audits can offer industry-specific experience, auditing management expertise, and advanced interviewing techniques. A combination of these external specialists and companies' internal accountants/auditors can achieve shorter audit timescales and lower levels of disruption to the business.

DOS AND DON'TS
DO

- Remember that well-resourced forensic auditing processes can help to identify misreporting at many levels of an organization.
- Bear in mind that regular proactive forensic audits can help businesses to ensure that their processes stay robust.
- Be prepared to widen the scope of a forensic audit to ensure maximum effectiveness.

Checklists

- See forensic auditing as a continuous process, rather than a one-off event. On completing one audit, restarting the process could uncover something that was previously overlooked.
- Be prepared to share the findings of the forensic audit with other areas of your company, and take into account industry best practice to improve efficiency and combat fraud.

DON'T

- Don't lose sight of the objective of a forensic audit. The cost can be high, but the potential cost of not undertaking an audit and implementing its findings can be even higher.
- Don't fall into the trap of overlooking the importance of the "forensic" element of the audit. With the results of such a process deemed suitable for inclusion in legal proceedings, the high potential costs of the forensic audit process could easily be recovered from dispute resolution or higher levels of loss recovery.

MORE INFO

Book:

Cardwell, Harvey. *Principles of Audit Surveillance*. Reprise ed. Philadelphia, PA: RT Edwards, 2005.

Article:

Brannen, Laurie. "Top of mind: Is a forensic audit in your future?" *Business Finance* (June 2007). Online at: tinyurl.com/6aunj87

Website:

Institute of Forensic Accounting and Investigative Audit (IFAIA): www.ifaia.org

See Also:

★ Implementing an Effective Internal Controls System (pp. 93–97)
✔ Internal Auditing for Fraud Detection and Prevention (pp. 315–316)
✔ Nonperformance and Breach of Contract (pp. 366–367)
✔ Understanding Internal Audits (pp. 324–325)

Checklists

Analysis Using Monte Carlo Simulation

DEFINITION

The Monte Carlo method of simulation uses repeated random sampling to obtain results and is generally used for simulating physical and mathematical systems. It is best suited to calculations using a computer, due to the reliance on repetitive computations and its use of random (or pseudo-random) numbers. It is most often used when it is not possible to reach an exact result using a deterministic algorithm. Monte Carlo simulation is useful for modeling situations that have a good deal of uncertainty in the inputs, and this includes calculations of risks in business.

There is no single Monte Carlo method—the term covers a wide range of approaches to simulation. However, these approaches use a certain pattern in which:

1 A domain of possible inputs is defined;
2 Inputs are randomly generated from the domain;
3 Using the inputs, a deterministic computation is performed;
4 The results are aggregated from the individual computations to give a final result.

Monte Carlo simulation randomly samples inputs to produce many thousands of possible outcomes, rather than a few discrete scenarios as produced, for example, by deterministic modeling using single-point estimates. Monte Carlo results also give probabilities for different outcomes. Lay decision-makers can use Monte Carlo to determine confidence levels for a graphical representation.

In finance, Monte Carlo methods are used in the following areas:

- By financial analysts in corporate finance, project finance, and real option analysis to construct probabilistic financial models.
- To generate many possible price paths to value options on equity.
- To value bonds and bond options.
- To evaluate a portfolio.
- In personal finance planning.

Monte Carlo methods are flexible and can take many sources of uncertainty, but they may not always be appropriate. In general, the method is preferable only if there are several sources of uncertainty.

ADVANTAGES

- Using Monte Carlo simulation is quite straightforward.
- It can provide statistical sampling for numerical experiments using a computer.
- In optimization problems, Monte Carlo simulation can often reach the optimum and overcome local extremes.
- It provides approximate solutions to many mathematical problems.
- Monte Carlo analysis produces a narrower range of results than a "what if" analysis.

DISADVANTAGES

- Monte Carlo simulation is not universally accepted in simulating a system that is not in equilibrium (i.e. in a transient state).

- A large number of samples is required to reach the desired results. This can be time-consuming compared to using a spreadsheet program, such as Excel, which can generate a simple calculation fairly quickly.
- A single sample cannot be used in simulation; to obtain results there must be many samples.
- The results are only an approximation of the true value.
- Simulation results can show large variance.

ACTION CHECKLIST

✔ Consider the problem. Does it have many sources of uncertainty?

✔ Is there an analytical solution? If so, use that.

✔ Choose the software you will use for Monte Carlo simulation.

✔ Decide on the inputs and generate the results.

DOS AND DON'TS

DO

- Use Monte Carlo simulation where an analytical solution either does not exist or is too complicated.
- Use it where there are lots of uncertainties.

DON'T

- Don't use Monte Carlo simulations that might require months or years of computer time—it is not worth it.
- Don't use Monte Carlo simulations where an analytical solution exists and is simple. In this case it is easier to use the analytical solution to solve the problem.

MORE INFO

Books:

Fishman, George S. *Monte Carlo: Concepts, Algorithms, and Applications*. New York: Springer, 2003.

McLeish, Don L. *Monte Carlo Simulation and Finance*. Hoboken, NJ: Wiley, 2005.

Mooney, Christopher Z. *Monte Carlo Simulation*. Thousand Oaks, CA: Sage Publications, 1997.

Website:

Monte Carlo simulation basics from Vertex42: tinyurl.com/2l9qzf

See Also:

Checklists

Applying the Gordon Growth Model

Checklists

DEFINITION

The Gordon growth model is a tool that is commonly used to value stocks. Originally developed by Professor Myron Gordon and also known as Gordon's growth model, the aim of the method is to value a stock or company in today's terms, using discounted cash flows to take into account the present value of future dividends.

The model requires three inputs:

- D: The expected level of the stock's dividend one year ahead
- R: The rate of return the investor is seeking
- G: The assumed constant rate of future dividend growth in perpetuity.

The formula is as follows:

$$\text{Gordon growth stock valuation per share} = \frac{D}{R} - G$$

ADVANTAGES

- The main strength of the Gordon growth model is that the valuation calculation is easily performed using readily available or easily estimated inputs.
- The model is particularly useful among companies or industries where cash flows are typically strong and relatively stable, and where leverage patterns are also generally consistent.
- The model is widely used to provide guideline fair values in mature industries such as financial services and in large-scale real-estate ventures. The model can be particularly appropriate in the valuation of real-estate investment trusts, given the high proportion of income paid out in dividends and the trusts' strictly defined investment policies.

DISADVANTAGES

- Although the model's simplicity can be regarded as one of its major strengths, in another sense this is its major drawback, as the purely quantitative model takes no account of qualitative factors such as industry trends or management strategy. For example, even in a highly cash-generative company, near-future dividend payouts could be capped by management's strategy of retaining cash to fund a likely future investment. The simplicity of the model affords no flexibility to take into account projected changes in the rate of future dividend growth.
- The calculation relies on the assumption that future dividends will grow at a constant rate in perpetuity, taking no account of the possibility that rapid near-term growth could be offset by slower growth further into the future. This limitation makes the Gordon growth model less suitable for use in rapidly growing industries with less predictable dividend patterns, such as software or mobile telecommunications. Its use is typically more appropriate in relatively mature industries or stock-market indices where companies demonstrate more stable and predictable dividend growth patterns.

ACTION CHECKLIST

✔ The Gordon growth model is generally more effective among companies and industries where dividend payments tend to be high—ideally, close to free cash flow to equity (FCFE). FCFE is a measure of how much cash a company can afford to pay out to shareholders after allowing for factors such as debt repayments and various expenses. Consider whether the entity to be valued exhibits such high dividend payments before making use of the model.

✔ Take into account other company-specific factors before applying the model to particular stocks. For example, consider how changes to the regulatory environment could affect a company's prospects.

✔ In the case of individual company valuations, consider whether a shift in the management's geographical horizon or major investment programs could affect cash flow and future dividend patterns. Remember that the Gordon growth model does not take into account possible fluctuations in future dividend growth rates.

DOS AND DON'TS
DO

- Understand the underlying characteristics of the company, industry, or market index before deciding whether to use this model.
- If appropriate, use the model for easily calculated outline valuations.
- Consider the benefits of using other valuation tools in conjunction with or as alternatives to the Gordon growth model.

DON'T

- Don't use the model for companies, industries, or market indices where growth rates are rapid or leverage is subject to sudden swings.
- Don't make the mistake of blindly applying the model to companies in isolation.
- Don't totally ignore nonquantitative factors that could have a major bearing on future valuations.

MORE INFO
Books:

Gordon, Myron J. *The Investment, Financing, and Valuation of the Corporation*. Westport, CT: Greenwood Press, 1982.

Hitchner, James R. *Financial Valuation: Applications and Models*. 3rd ed. Hoboken, NJ: Wiley, 2011.

Articles:

Jackson, Marcus. "The Gordon growth model and the income approach to value." *Appraisal Journal* 62:1 (Spring 1994): 124–128.

Kiley, Michael T. "Stock prices and fundamentals: A macroeconomic perspective." *Journal of Business* 77:4 (October 2004): 909–936. Online at: dx.doi.org/10.1086/422629

Website:

Myron J. Gordon's homepage: www.rotman.utoronto.ca/~gordon

See Also:

★ Valuing Start-Ups (pp. 239–243)

✔ Using Dividend Discount Models (p. 337)

⚏ Discounted Cash Flow (pp. 386–387)

Calculating Total Shareholder Return

DEFINITION

When assessing the performance of stocks, inexperienced investors risk falling into the trap of looking purely at stock price movements, in the process ignoring the value of dividends which may be paid. Total shareholder return (TSR) over a period is defined as the net stock price change plus the dividends paid during that period. While it is possible that a stock could deliver a negative price performance over a certain period yet still generate a positive total shareholder return should the dividend paid outweigh the stock price fall, in practice this happens only rarely. In most markets, the dividend yield indicators are low, with the result that stock prices are generally the key driver of TSR. However, the importance of the dividend component of the total return calculation is typically more significant in traditionally higher-yielding areas of the stock market such as utilities, tobacco companies, and beverage producers.

Total shareholder return over a period can be calculated as follows:

Total Shareholder Return % = Stock price$_{end of period}$

- Stock price$_{start of period}$

+ Dividends paid ÷ Stock price$_{start of period}$

Importantly, when calculating TSR, we must take account of only the dividends that our period of ownership of the stock entitles us to receive, so we need to take account of the stock ex-dividend date rather than the dividend payment date. It could be that we own the stock on the day when the dividend is actually payable, yet we would only be entitled to receive the dividend had we owned the stock on the ex-dividend day.

An alternative ways of thinking of total shareholder return is the internal rate of return of all cash flows paid to investors during a particular period. However, whichever method we choose to calculate total shareholder return, the result essentially represents an indication of the overall return generated for stockholders, expressed in percentage terms. In all cases, the "dividends paid" element of the calculation should also include any special cash payments returned to stockholders, as well as any stock buyback programs. The figure should also take account of any special one-off dividend payments, as well as regular dividend payouts.

ADVANTAGES

- TSR represents a readily understood figure of the overall financial benefits generated for stockholders.
- The figure can be interpreted as a measure of how the market evaluates the overall performance of a company over a specified period.
- Given that TSRs are expressed in percentage terms, the figures are readily comparable between companies in the same sector.

DISADVANTAGES

- TSRs can be calculated for publicly traded companies at the overall level, but not at a divisional level.
- The calculation is not "forward looking" in that it reflects the past overall return to shareholders, with no consideration of future returns.
- TSR is externally focused in that it reflects the market's perception of performance; it could, therefore, be adversely impacted should a share price of a fundamentally strong company suffer excessively in the short term.

ACTION CHECKLIST

✔ Calculate the share price change over the specified period plus any dividends paid to generate a simple TSR calculation.

✔ If necessary, be prepared to make adjustments for special events such as share buybacks and/or splits in stocks' prices.

✔ Investors can use TSR percentages to make comparisons against industry benchmarks.

✔ From a company perspective, remuneration packages can be linked to TSR.

DOS AND DON'TS

DO

- Consider how TSR calculations might be applied to mutual funds as well as company stocks, thus taking account of income paid out by yield-orientated funds when looking at their annual performance.
- However, remember that TSR reflects past performance rather than a perception or indication of future returns.

Finance Essentials

DON'T

- Don't forget that past performance shouldn't be taken as the best guide to future returns.
- Don't look to calculate TSR for privately held companies as the calculation requires stock price inputs.

MORE INFO

Books:

Ward, Keith. *Marketing Strategies: Turning Marketing Strategies into Shareholders Value*. Burlington, MA: Butterworth-Heinemann, 2004.

Young, David S., and Stephen F. O'Byrne. *EVA and Value Based Management*. New York: McGraw-Hill, 2000.

Articles:

Elali, Wajeeh. "Contemporaneous relationship between EVA and shareholder value." *International Journal of Business Governance and Ethics* 2:3–4 (October 2006): 237–253. Online at: dx.doi.org/10.1504/IJBGE.2006.011157

Gardner, Tim, and Eric Spielgel. "Total shareholder return: Planning a perfect future." *Public Utilities Fortnightly* 144:1 (January 2006): 45–50. Online at: tinyurl.com/5wdc5no [PDF].

See Also:

★ Dividend Policy: Maximizing Shareholder Value (pp. 190–194)
⇄ Earnings per Share (pp. 389–390)
⇄ Return on Investment (pp. 408–409)
⇄ Return on Stockholders' Equity (pp. 409–410)

Islamic Microfinance

DEFINITION

Islamic microfinance refers to a system of localized finance arrangements set up as an alternative source of funds for small, low-income Islamic clients. Typically, users of Islamic microfinance have little or no collateral, as they do not possess significant assets, and would therefore be excluded from other forms of financing, including Islamic bank financing. Thus, Islamic microfinance provides a means of accessing funds for those who are unlikely to qualify for other forms of finance, yet are still seeking full compliance with Islamic law and the Islamic way of life.

In essence, key Islamic microfinance contracts are based on *musharakah* and *mudarabah*, while microfinance users can also take advantage of *takaful* Islamic insurance.

Musharakah can be used either for assets or working capital. In principle it involves an equity participation in a business. The parties involved will share any profits or losses resulting from the business according to a pre-established ratio.

A *mudarabah* contract is basically a trustee financing scheme. The financier invests the funds while the other party supplies the expertise for the project. The contract requires rigorous following and transparency to ensure a fair distribution of profits.

Takaful insurance is based on the principle of shared responsibility and has been practiced in one form or another for well over 1,000 years. As a mutual-style concept, *takaful* does not function on conventional profit-making lines. It derives from the Arabic word *kafalah*, which means a joint guarantee. According to the *takaful* principle of insurance, each member of a scheme contributes to a fund that is used to help in case of need such as accidents, loss of crops, or death.

ADVANTAGES

- Islamic microfinance can play an important role in helping to address poverty in parts of the Muslim world.

- Islamic microfinance contracts can be operated individually or combined, giving greater flexibility to their application.
- Islamic microfinance contracts provide an alternative to low-income Muslim clients.
- *Musharakah* and *mudarabah* are the most approved contracts under shariah law and their application is encouraged by *shariah* scholars.
- *Takaful* is flexible in its range of applications, covering areas such as residences, places of business, cars, and inventory, as well as accident and life cover.

DISADVANTAGES

- *Mudarabah* arrangements require a high level of regulation and transparency to ensure a fair distribution of profits, so can be expensive to operate.
- Some Muslims may be uncomfortable with the scope for *takaful* to be used for investment purposes on the basis that investors are effectively speculating that low accident payouts will generate a surplus or profit.
- In general, Islamic microfinance is seen as more a social support system based on philanthropic principles rather than a business.
- Like other forms of microfinance, Islamic microfinance needs support to ensure its sustainability. Typically this support entails some form of ongoing subsidy such as a *waqf* endowment.

ACTION CHECKLIST

✔ Assess carefully the contracts and products offered and whether they are too expensive to operate. Often smaller-scale transactions cost more to operate, process, and regulate than larger ones.

Checklists

✔ Investigate and understand local customs and financial practices, as these can vary widely between countries and even regions.

✔ Gain an understanding of local cultural attitudes to maximize the potential of microfinance; for example, some schemes have more success than others in introducing microfinance to women.

✔ Certain Muslim countries actively encourage Islamic microfinance. Potential users should investigate whether state support is offered to promote local microfinance schemes.

DOS AND DON'TS
DO
- Encourage communication and dialogue between shariah experts and the financiers in order to ensure that the products offered are compliant with *shariah* law.
- Understand that there will be differences between schemes in different countries according to local attitudes and conventions.
- Be realistic in assessing that Islamic microfinance has potential for growth but currently is still exercised on a very small scale.

DON'T
- Don't underestimate the help that local religious leaders can give in explaining to the local population that the financial contracts offered are *shariah*-compliant, which will increase confidence in the use of the products.

• Don't assume that limited-income clients will accept any products offered on unattractive terms; they often drive a hard bargain.

MORE INFO
Books:
Al-Harran, Saad. *An Islamic Microfinance Enterprise: The Financial Vehicle That Will Change the Face of the Islamic World*. London: Xlibris, 2008.
Nenova, Tatiana, and Cecile Thioro Niang. *Bringing Finance to Pakistan's Poor: Access to Finance for Small Enterprises and the Underserved*. New York: World Bank Publications, 2009.

Articles:
Abdul Rahman, Abdul Rahim. "Islamic microfinance: A missing component in Islamic banking." *Kyoto Bulletin of Islamic Area Studies* 1:2 (December 2007): 38–53. Online at: hdl.handle.net/2433/70892
Ahmed, Habib. "Financing microenterprises: An analytical study of Islamic microfinance institutions." *Islamic Economic Studies* 9:2 (March 2002): 27–64.

Websites:
Consultative Group to Assist the Poor (CGAP): www.cgap.org
Microfinance Management Institute (MMI): www.themfmi.org

See Also:
★ Rigidity in Microfinancing: Can One Size Fit All? (pp. 151–154)
✔ Managing Risk in Islamic Finance (pp. 297–298)

Checklists

Obtaining an Equity Value Using the Weighted Average Cost of Capital (WACC)

DEFINITION
Equity value is a market-based measure of the value of a company. In mergers and acquisitions, equity value is a more accurate measure of the value of a company than is market capitalization because equity value incorporates all equity interests in a firm. In contrast, market capitalization is calculated by multiplying the number of common shares currently outstanding by the share price.

WACC influences the calculation of equity value because the cost of financing any debt will reduce the company's nominal value. Valuation of a business using WACC means using the market value of equity, not its book value.

The example below shows how using WACC to calculate the debt value actually reduces the value of the debt and therefore reduces the company's overall equity value.

Example
Let us assume that a company has five million shares outstanding and that each share has a current market value of $8. The market capitalization of this company is thus $5,000,000 \times \$8 = \$40,000,000$.

Now let us assume the company has a debt value of $10 million and a WACC of 15%. The WACC equity value is calculated as follows:

Equity value =
Market capitalization + [Debt value × (1 − WACC)]
$= \$40,000,000 + [\$10,000,000 \times (1 - 0.15)]$
$= \$40,000,000 + \$8,500,000$
$= \$48,500,000$

If WACC were not used in this calculation, the equity value of the company would simply be the sum of market capitalization and the debt value—that is, $50 million.

WACC is particularly used in acquisitions or financing business operations, and is also the method used to determine the discount rate for valuing a company using the discounted cash flow method.

ADVANTAGES
- Calculating equity value using WACC takes into account the market capitalization *plus* the debt *plus* the cost of financing that debt.

DISADVANTAGES
- WACC is not easy to obtain because of the different types of data that have to be found. It is a complicated measure that requires a lot of detailed company information.

ACTION CHECKLIST
✔ A company with an investment return that is greater than its WACC is creating value. Conversely, a company with a return less than WACC is losing value and investors should look elsewhere.

✔ WACC should be recalculated annually in order to maintain correct figures.

DOS AND DON'TS
DO
- Use the market value of equity to value a business.
- Use the WACC if you are considering buying a business or if you are a value investor.

DON'T
- Don't use the book value of the equity to value a business.
- Don't invest in a company with a rate of return less than the WACC.

MORE INFO
Books:

Loos, Nicolaus. *Value Creation in Leveraged Buyouts: Analysis of Factors Driving Private Equity Investment Performance.* Wiesbaden, Germany: Deutscher Universitäts-Verlag (DUV), 2006.

Stewart, G. Bennett, III. *The Quest for Value: A Guide for Senior Managers.* 27th ed. New York: HarperCollins, 1991.

Articles:

Miles, James A., and John R. Ezzell. "The weighted average cost of capital, perfect capital markets and project life: A clarification." *Journal of Financial and Quantitative Analysis* 15:3 (September 1980): 719–730. Online at: dx.doi.org/10.2307/2330405

Yee, Kenton K. "Earnings quality and the equity risk premium: A benchmark model." *Contemporary Accounting Research* 23:3 (Fall 2006): 833–877. Online at: dx.doi.org/10.1506/8M44-W1DG-PLG4-8E0M

See Also:

✔ Estimating Enterprise Value with the Weighted Average Cost of Capital (pp. 293–294)

✔ Understanding the Weighted Average Cost of Capital (WACC) (pp. 309–310)

Weighted Average Cost of Capital (p. 414)

Sovereign Wealth Funds—Investment Strategies and Objectives

DEFINITION
Sovereign Wealth Funds' (SWFs) investment decisions are typically made with one of two goals in mind: Either the funds are seeking an attractive rate of return in purely economic terms, or they are hoping to generate strategic benefits for their country. In the former case, SWFs regularly describe themselves as passive investors in that they do not seek to influence or control the companies they invest in, sometimes preferring to avoid holding voting shares at all. In contrast to typical private equity investors, SWFs are also frequently happy to put their faith in existing company management, rather than aiming to parachute their own executives onto the board. When a SWF invests in a company for strategic benefits, commonly in sectors such as financial services or leisure, the objective is usually to gain insights into the management's operational expertise with a long-term view of helping to develop or grow a related industry in the fund's own country.

While many SWFs may emphasize that their investment strategies tend to be longer term and more "hands off" than the average private equity investor, there are signs that some SWFs are prepared to work more closely with these more active investors to help achieve their investment goals. For example, Abu Dhabi-based Mubadala's 2007 purchase of a 7.5% stake in Carlyle, and news that China Investment Corporation (CIC) had raised its stake in Blackstone to around 12.5% in late 2008, raised the prospect of further cooperation between SWFs and private equity groups.

Though many SWFs have demonstrated their willingness to hold a geographically diverse spread of assets, few have historically provided much insight into the precise investment strategies they employ to achieve their stated objectives. However, Norway's GPF-G Fund (Government Pension Fund—Global), the world's second-largest SWF (after the Abu Dhabi Investment Authority), is the notable exception, providing regular updates on its holdings and demonstrating a high level of commitment to ethical investing. Nevertheless, the SWFs' general perceived lack of investment transparency and doubts over their commitment to high standards of corporate governance standards have done little to help the image of SWFs. Though political pressure is growing in some jurisdictions for greater standards of transparency and improved disclosure from SWFs with the potential to acquire assets of significant national importance or prestige, there is evidence that many SWFs would prefer to work within more loosely worded "best practice" investment frameworks. In October 2008, the International Working Group of Sovereign Wealth Funds presented a proposed set of principles guiding the operations of SWFs to the International Monetary Fund's (IMF) policy-focused International Monetary and Financial Committee. Both the IMF and the Organisation for Economic Co-operation and Development (OECD) are set to present their own proposals in reports due in 2009.

ADVANTAGES

- The long-term and "hands-off" nature of investments by SWFs can make them attractive shareholders for some companies.
- SWFs have been a particularly valuable source of immediate capital injections into financial institutions whose balance sheets have been in urgent need of strengthening.
- High levels of investable cash give SWFs the ability to capitalize on opportunities generated by market swings, with the meaning SWFs can be a stabilizing influence during times of market volatility.

DISADVANTAGES

- Doubts persist in some quarters over the motives behind some SWFs investments, particularly those made for long-term strategic reasons.
- Political concerns are frequently raised over the prospect of key national resources falling under the control of secretive overseas investors, particularly in view of most SWFs' poor disclosure standards.

ACTION CHECKLIST

✔ By moving towards the adoption of best practice guidelines to be proposed by the IMF and the OECD, it should be possible to alleviate some concerns over the lack of transparency and disclosure of most SWFs.

✔ By taking non-voting shares only, SWFs can help to overcome objections over the motivation for some of their more politically sensitive investments.

DOS AND DON'TS

DO

- Recognize the increasing scope for private equity and SWF investors to cooperate on investment projects.
- Appreciate that the generally poor level of transparency of SWFs does little to alleviate concerns over their motives when making overseas investments.

DON'T

- Don't be afraid of improved disclosure; follow the example of Norway's pension SWF.
- Don't overlook the role of SWFs, as cash-rich, long-term investors, in helping to stabilize volatile markets and recapitalize struggling companies.

MORE INFO

Book:
Hassan, Adnan. *A Practical Guide to Sovereign Wealth Funds*. London: Euromoney Institutional Investor, 2008.

Articles:
Jen, Stephen. "Sovereign wealth funds: What they are and what's happening." *World Economics* 8:4 (2007): 1–7. Online at: tinyurl.com/77avvaw
Raphaeli, Nimrod, and Bianca Gersten. "Sovereign wealth funds: Investment vehicles for the Persian Gulf countries." *Middle East Quarterly* 15:2 (Spring 2008): 45–53. Online at: tinyurl.com/ybyjbt2

Websites:
International Working Group of Sovereign Wealth Funds: www.iwg-swf.org
Opalesque Sovereign Wealth Funds Briefing: www.opalesque.com/SWF_Briefing/
Sovereign Wealth Fund Institute: www.swfinstitute.org

Steps for Obtaining Bank Financing

DEFINITION

A major problem for both emerging and established companies is the cost of raising capital. Can the owners obtain bank financing instead of incurring dilution by giving up additional ownership in the company? An owner of a promising business may perceive itself as being creditworthy, however a bank will require "proof," for example in the form of a full quarter or year of sustained profitability, depending on the industry and levels of profitability. Decision makers at the bank will judge the company on a number of factors, including the following ratios:

- *Leverage/gearing*: to guarantee the company is sufficiently capitalized, i.e. total liabilities divided by tangible net worth.
- *Liquidity*: to guarantee sufficient working capital; measured by current ratio, i.e. current assets divided by current liabilities.
- *Debt service coverage*: to guarantee the company has sufficient operating cash flow to cover principal and interest and any capital leases.

Companies will need to present a written business plan explaining business objectives in detail, operating plans, projected earnings for the next one to five years, marketing strategy, and other relevant information. Marketing strategies must be outlined in detail to lend credence to sales projections. The first two years of projections should be detailed by month or by quarter to measure the projected performance against financial ratios. These projections should be composed of balance sheets, income statements, and cash-flow statements. The bank will also want to know:

- How much money do you need?
- How do you plan to use the money? (For example, to buy new assets, to pay off debts, or to pay operating expenses?)
- How long will it take you to repay the loan? (Use your cash flow projections to help plan the repayments.)
- What loan repayments can you afford to make without damaging the business?
- What can you offer as security for the loan? (Bankers generally require personal guarantees from the owners.)

The bank will also want to determine whether the management has the skills to run the business. Typical questions include: is the manager/owner talented enough to direct the company? Are the sales team knowledgeable about the industry and have they demonstrated successful sales growth in other companies? Does the financial officer have an in depth understanding of the financial background of the company? Do the management team get on well together and complement each other?

ADVANTAGES

- Bank financing allows the owners to keep a major interest in the company, instead of diluting interest by selling shares. Looking for bank financing will force the owners to focus on detailed projections. In order to present a written business plan, the owners must concentrate on the strategic planning that is vital to a business's survival. Building a successful relationship with the bank will help with future business expansion.

DISADVANTAGES

- Research, preparation, and presentation of the details required by the bank will take time away from the day to day functions of running the business.

- The company will be leveraged and therefore subject to detailed bank scrutiny during the period of the loan.
- An unfavorable payback period.

ACTION CHECKLIST

✔ Prepare a detailed business plan explaining objectives, operations, marketing strategy, and projected earnings for the next five years.

✔ Make sure you are not taking on too much debt. There is no sense in taking out a loan that will squeeze out your profits and bleed your business dry. Check your leverage/gearing and liquidity ratios and then capacity for debt service coverage.

✔ Prepare answers to the bank's key questions. For example, how much money do you need? How do you plan to use the money? How long will it take you to repay the loan? What will you use as security for the loan?

DOS AND DON'TS
DO

- Get expert advice when preparing your proposal. Getting a bank loan for an emerging company or even an established business is not always simple.

DON'T

- Don't go to the bank thinking that you'll get the loan just because you have a good idea. You will need to take a rigorously detailed proposal.

MORE INFO
Books:

Burk, James E., and Richard P. Lehman. *Financing Your Small Business: From SBA Loans and Credit Cards to Common Stock and Partnership Interests*. Naperville, IL: Sourcebooks, 2006.

Sisson, Robert. *Financing the Small Business: A Complete Guide to Obtaining Bank Loans and All Other Types of Financing*. Cincinnati, OH: Adams Media Corporation, 2002.

Timmons, Jeffry A., Stephen Spinelli, and Andrew Zacharakis. *How to Raise Capital: Techniques and Strategies for Financing and Valuing Your Small Business*. Maidenhead, UK: McGraw-Hill Professional, 2005.

See Also:

★ Assessing Venture Capital Funding for Small and Medium-Sized Enterprises (pp. 114–117)
✔ Assessing Cash Flow and Bank Lending Requirements (pp. 292–293)
✔ Basic Steps for Starting a Business (pp. 361–362)

Checklists

Understanding and Using Leverage Ratios

DEFINITION

Leveraging is a way to use funds whereby most of the money is raised by borrowing rather than by stock issue (for a company) or use of capital (by an individual). At its most basic, leveraging means taking out a loan so that you can invest the money and hoping your investment makes more money than you will have to pay in interest on the loan.

The leverage ratio is used to calculate the financial leverage of a company. This information gives an insight into the company's financing methods, or it can be used to measure the company's ability to meet its financial obligations. There are a number of different ratios, but the main factors involved are debt, equity, assets, operating income, and interest expenses.

The most commonly used ratio is debt to equity (D/E, or financial leverage), which indicates how much the business relies on debt financing. In normal circumstances the typical D/E ratio is 2:1, with only one-third of the debt in the long term. A high D/E ratio might show up possible difficulty in paying interest and capital while obtaining extra funding. As an example, if a company has $10 million of debt and $20 million of equity, it has a D/E ratio of 0.5 ($10 million ÷ $20 million).

Another leveraging ratio can be used to measure the operating cost mix. This helps to indicate how any change in output may affect operating income. There are two types of operating costs: fixed and variable. The mix of these will differ depending on the company and the industry. A high operating leverage can lead to forecasting risk. For example, a tiny error made in a sales forecast could trigger far bigger errors when it comes to projecting cash flows based on those sales.

There is also interest coverage, which measures a company's margin of safety and indicates how many times the company can make its interest payments. This figure is calculated by dividing earnings prior to interest and taxes by the interest expense.

ADVANTAGES

- Leveraging means borrowing money to invest. Anyone who takes out a mortgage is effectively leveraging. By paying a deposit to obtain a loan, you can buy a home that otherwise you would not be able to afford. Although property prices can and do fall periodically, over the long term property usually increases in value. If it does, you can sell the property and make a profit on your original mortgage loan.
- Leveraging enables an individual or a company to gain access to larger capital sums to make investments, with the aim of making a profit by doing so.
- Strategies in leveraging run from basic to highly sophisticated, and the degree of risk varies in the same way. The benefits of leveraging will depend on your financial situation, your objectives, and your attitude to risk.

DISADVANTAGES

- Anything that has the potential to make money involves some risk. Gains can be better than normal; losses can be worse. A change in interest rates can have an effect on your

profit too. There is a risk that your investment will not make enough profit to pay off the interest on your loan.
- You can mitigate the risks by diversifying your portfolio, thereby guarding against high losses, although this will probably limit opportunities to make spectacular gains. A fixed-rate loan can protect against a rise in interest rates.

ACTION CHECKLIST

✔ Are you comfortable borrowing money that you might struggle to pay back?

✔ Are you comfortable with high risk in your finances?

✔ Are you confident that interest rates will not rise to add further risk to your borrowings?

✔ Are you confident your investment will make more than the interest you have to pay back on your loan?

DOS AND DON'TS

DO

- Look at leveraging as a way of using other people's money (by way of a loan) to make your own investments.
- Understand how your loan works and what and when you will have to pay back.
- As much research as you can. And then more research.

DON'T

- Don't get involved with leveraging if you are uncomfortable with financial risk.
- Don't choose an investment without a full understanding of what you are investing in.

MORE INFO

Books:

Marr, Bernard. *Strategic Performance Management: Leveraging and Measuring Your Intangible Value Drivers*. Oxford: Butterworth-Heinemann, 2006.

Matthäus-Maier, Ingrid, and J. D. von Pischke (eds). *Microfinance Investment Funds: Leveraging Private Capital for Economic Growth and Poverty Reduction*. Berlin: Springer-Verlag, 2006.

Militello, Frederick C., and Michael D. Schwalberg. *Leverage Competencies: What Financial Executives Need to Lead*. Upper Saddle River, NJ: FT Prentice Hall, 2002.

See Also:
★ Going Private: Public-to-Private Leveraged Buyouts (pp. 220–224)
★ Leveraged Buyouts: What, Why, When, and How (pp. 230–233)
⇄ Capitalization Ratios (pp. 380–381)

Checklists

336 Understanding Fixed-Charge Coverage

DEFINITION

Fixed-charge coverage is a financial ratio that is used to gauge the quality of a bond issue or the ability of a project to meet its debt repayments. It is calculated by dividing total fixed charges into the net income (or earnings before interest and tax) available for these charges. The fixed charges are gross interest, contractual payments under operating leases, and preference dividends.

Thus, a fixed-charge coverage ratio would look like this:

$$\text{Fixed} - \text{charge coverage} = \text{EBIT} + \frac{\text{Fixed charge}}{\text{Fixed charge} + \text{Interest}}$$

where EBIT is earnings before interest and tax, and the fixed charge is before tax.

Generally, the greatest fixed charge a company is likely to face is the interest on its debt. However, the fixed-charge coverage ratio assumes particular importance if the company you are evaluating spends heavily on leases, such as leases on buildings and equipment. A lease payment is effectively the same thing as a debt payment, and it should be taken just as seriously. The lower a company's net income, the greater the negative impact of the lease payments on the ratio.

Overall, the lower the ratio, the worse is the financial position of the company. Bond issues can contain covenants that set limits on how low the fixed-charge coverage ratio can fall. Such a covenant is designed to provide the lender with protection, so that the borrower's financial position will remain more or less the same as it was when the loan was made. Thus, a bond may contain a covenant that prevents the fixed-charge coverage ratio from falling below 2.

ADVANTAGES

- The fixed-charge coverage ratio is readily identifiable.
- It provides a straightforward measure of the financial health of a company.

DISADVANTAGES

- There is no standardized procedure for determining either fixed charges or the net income available for these charges.
- Other ratios may provide a better indicator of a company's financial health.

ACTION CHECKLIST

✔ Identify the fixed-charge coverage ratio from the company's accounts.

✔ If it is less than 1, speak to the company's managers immediately to ascertain how they plan to meet their fixed-cost obligations.

DOS AND DON'TS

DO

- Remember that if a company has a fixed-charge coverage of less than 1, it cannot meet its fixed obligations through earnings and thus must rely on other funds, such as extra borrowings or drawing down working capital.
- Remember that this ratio often comes into play if you have a working-capital loan; the lender will insist that a specific fixed-charge coverage ratio is maintained or your loan will be recalled.
- Remember to try to gauge the attitudes of managers toward taking on more debt as the existing debt matures.

DON'T

- Don't just rely on the fixed-charge coverage ratio. Other ratios that can be used to measure a company's ability to meet its debt obligations include the interest coverage ratio and the debt service coverage ratio.
- Don't ignore the pro forma coverage ratio. It has essentially the same components as the fixed-charge coverage ratio but is forward looking. It can tell you whether this year's earnings (if repeated) would be able to cover what must be paid in the coming year.

MORE INFO

Books:

Geddes, Ross. *Valuation and Investment Appraisal*. London: Financial World Publishing, 2002.

Holmes, Geoffrey, Alan Sugden, and Paul Gee. *Interpreting Company Reports and Accounts*. 10th ed. Harlow, UK: FT Prentice Hall, 2008.

The Ultimate Small Business Guide: A Resource for Startups and Growing Businesses. New York: Basic Books, 2003.

Article:

Goodacre, Alan. "Operating lease finance in the UK retail sector." *International Review of Retail, Distribution and Consumer Research* 13:1 (2003): 99–125. Online at: dx.doi.org/10.1080/0959396032000065373

Website:

American Bankruptcy Institute (ABI): www.abiworld.org

See Also:

✔ Assessing Cash Flow and Bank Lending Requirements (pp. 292–293)

⇄ Interest Coverage (pp. 395–396)

Using Dividend Discount Models

DEFINITION

Dividend discount models are essentially tools that have been developed to value a stock on the basis of estimated future dividends, discounted to reflect their value in today's terms.

Many variations of dividend discount models exist, but their central basis is the following formula:

$$\text{Estimated valuation} = \frac{D}{R-G}$$

where D is present dividend per share, R is discount rate, and G is dividend growth rate.

Variations on the standard model can be used, depending on the company's stage in the growth cycle, but the common theme of dividend discount models is that the resulting estimated valuation is compared with the share's prevailing market price to determine whether the share is presently trading above or below its fair value.

ADVANTAGES

- Dividend discount models attempt to put a valuation on shares, based on forecasts of the sums to be paid out to investors. This should, in theory, provide a very solid basis to determine the share's true value in present terms.
- Dividend discount models can be of great use over the short to medium term, making use of widely available company research over timescales of up to five years.
- In stable industries, dividend discount models can still be of value over the longer term if investors are prepared to make the assumption that current dividend payout policies will remain in place.

DISADVANTAGES

- Standard dividend discount models are of no value in determining the estimated value of companies that don't pay dividends. This is typically not a problem in mature industries such as utilities and food, but the models are generally of less value in industries such as technology and mobile telecoms, where investors commonly look for share price appreciation rather than high dividend payments.
- The ability of a company to maintain a certain rate of dividend growth over the longer term can be extremely difficult to forecast accurately. Dividend discount models rely heavily on the validity of the data inputs, making them of questionable value given the challenges associated with accurately forecasting growth rates beyond five or so years.
- When used for longer-term analysis, the valuations provided by dividend discount models take no account of the possibility of a deliberate change to a company's dividend policy. This can further compromise the usefulness of dividend discount models over the longer term.

ACTION CHECKLIST

✔ Make every effort to establish the integrity and validity of the data to be input into a dividend discount model. The calculation relies on the accuracy of the source data, making the result very susceptible to inaccurate inputs.

✔ Consider using a dividend discount model as a screening tool, such that stocks that are apparently undervalued according to the model could scrutinized more closely using alternative valuation techniques.

DOS AND DON'TS
DOS

- Recognize the limitations imposed by the assumption made by standard dividend discount models that dividend growth rates will be fixed in perpetuity.
- Consider whether a multistage dividend discount model would be more appropriate. These models take account of the various stages in a company's development, from growth to maturity.

DON'TS

- Don't attempt to use standard dividend discount models for growth-orientated companies that have yet to establish dividend payouts.
- Don't invest purely on the basis of the result of a single dividend discount model calculation in isolation. Given the total reliance on the data inputs, using a wider range of valuation tools could result in better investment decisions.

MORE INFO
Books:
Correia, Carlos, David Flynn, Enrico Uliana, and Michael Wormald. *Financial Management*. 6th ed (spiral-bound). Lansdowne, South Africa: Juta, 2007.
Pinto, Jerald E., Elaine Henry, Thomas R. Robinson, and John D. Stowe. *Equity Asset Valuation*. 2nd ed. Hoboken, NJ: Wiley, 2010.

Articles:
Beneda, Nancy L. "Estimating free cash flows and valuing a growth company." *Journal of Asset Management* 4:4 (December 2003): 247–257. Online at: dx.doi.org/10.1057/palgrave.jam.2240106
Foerster, Stephen R., and Stephen G. Sapp. "The dividend discount model in the long-run: A clinical study." *Journal of Applied Finance* 15:2 (Fall/Winter 2005): 55–75. Online at: ssrn.com/abstract=869545

Report:
Harris, Robert S., Kenneth M. Eades, and Susan J. Chaplinsky. "The dividend discount model." Darden case no. UVA-F-1234. Darden Business School, University of Virginia, 1998. Online at: ssrn.com/abstract=909419

See Also:
✔ Applying the Gordon Growth Model (pp. 328–329)
✔ Estimating Enterprise Value with the Weighted Average Cost of Capital (pp. 293–294)
⇄ Dividend Yield (pp. 388–389)

Checklists

Conflicting Interests: The Agency Issue

DEFINITION

Those running a company should be committed to delivering maximum returns to its stockholders. However, vested interests can sometimes play a role in decision making, frequently managers' personal interests. The way in which a company's stock is dispersed across various stockholder groups can also have a significant bearing on the nature of the specific corporate governance issues it faces. In many developing countries, as well as in some parts of Europe, company stock ownership can be concentrated within a relatively narrow group of investors—certainly when compared with the wider stock-ownership base that is typical in the United States. This concentration of ownership can heighten the risk that the company board is pressurized to make a particular decision—for example, by a powerful industrialist or oligarch with widespread interests and considerable influence, who attempts to steer a company's board down a particular route, potentially to the detriment of other stockholders.

Even in countries where stockholder bases are generally more diversified, conflicts of interest can still arise between company principals and boards of directors in cases where those making decisions are influenced by self-interest. Managers should in all cases inform the board of any potential conflict of interest between themselves and stockholders in advance. Stakeholders can then be made aware of the potential conflict of interest through a disclosure statement, while the board should take appropriate action to ensure that the interests of stockholders are not compromised. This could involve independent monitoring of management decision making or the insistence that the relationship behind the potential conflict of interest is severed.

ADVANTAGES

- Correctly anticipating potential conflicts of interest gives corporate governance professionals the scope to instigate procedures that will ensure probity and help to protect stockholders.
- A well-diversified stockholder base and thorough research by investment analysts into a company's decision making can help to remind managers that any actions they take to put their own interests ahead of the wider stockholder base could be exposed, making them vulnerable to removal from their positions.
- Companies seen to be operating in an inappropriate manner can rapidly lose stockholder support, exposing them to the risk of a hostile takeover. This risk can create an element of "self-policing" by managers who would otherwise be tempted to put their own interests ahead of those of the wider stockholder base.

DISADVANTAGES

- Aiming for complete protection against the impact of the agency issue is unrealistic. Steps can be taken to try to address the main risks, but in practice major stockholders may still hold considerable influence.

- Striking the balance between rewarding top-performing managers and allowing them excessive influence over their own remuneration levels can be difficult.
- Operating an effective and robust corporate governance program can be expensive, with the costs ultimately carried by the stockholders.

ACTION CHECKLIST

✔ The establishment of an independent remuneration committee is often an important step toward adequately rewarding top-performing executives and satisfying large institutional stockholders that the company's resources are being used appropriately.

✔ Aim to align executive compensation with stockholders' interests by granting managers stock options.

✔ Other elements of executive compensation can be linked to factors such as sales or earnings growth.

✔ The establishment of a management monitoring program can help to counter the risk of pressure from dominant external stockholders and protect the interests of other stockholders by scrutinizing executives' decisions.

DOS AND DON'TS

DO

- Ensure that executive remuneration is set by an independent committee with an understanding of competitors' compensation levels.
- Be prepared to permit the remuneration committee to grant stock options to managers to incentivize them to deliver maximum returns for stockholders.

DON'T

- Don't see scrutiny by external investment analysts as a threat: the greater threat to a company's stock price could come from suspicions that managers are feathering their own nests, rather than working to deliver maximum stockholder value.
- Don't skimp unnecessarily on the costs of establishing appropriate structures to oversee executive remuneration and decision making. Disquiet over the probity of decision making can trigger a loss of confidence among key institutional stockholders. In terms of executive remuneration, excessive levels could trigger a stockholder revolt, while companies that under-remunerate executives risk the upheaval of losing key talent to rivals.

MORE INFO

Books:

Sullivan, John D., Jean Rogers, Catherine Kuchta-Helbling, and Aleksandr Shkolnikov (eds). *In Search of Good Directors: A Guide to Building Corporate Governance in the 21st Century*. 3rd ed. Washington, DC: Center for International Private Enterprise, 2003.

Luo, Yadong. *Global Dimensions of Corporate Governance*. Malden, MA: Blackwell Publishing, 2007.

Organisation for Economic Co-operation and Development (OECD). *OECD Principles of Corporate Governance*. Paris: OECD, 2004. Online at: www.oecd.org/daf/corporateaffairs/principles/text

Website:

International Corporate Governance Network (ICGN): www.icgn.org

See Also:

✔ Defining Corporate Governance: Its Aims, Goals, and Responsibilities (pp. 341–342)

✔ Directors' Duties: A Primer (pp. 342–343)

✔ Governance Practices in Family-Owned Firms (pp. 343–345)

Creating a Sustainable Development Policy

DEFINITION

The Brundtland Commission coined what has become the most often quoted definition of sustainable development as being development that "meets the needs of the present without compromising the ability of future generations to meet their own needs."

A sustainable development policy is a model of resource use that aims to meet human requirements while preserving the environment, so that these needs can be met not only in the present but also for the indefinite future. It is a means of trying to resolve the conflict between various competing goals, and it involves the simultaneous pursuit of economic prosperity, environmental quality, and social equity.

Businesses are becoming increasingly interested in sustainable development, and many companies are taking steps to ensure that they conduct themselves in a socially responsible manner. Some are even introducing codes of conduct for their suppliers, to ensure that other companies' policies or practices do not tarnish their own reputation.

The positive outcomes that can arise when businesses adopt a policy of social responsibility include:

- enhanced brand image and increased sales and customer loyalty;
- greater productivity and quality;
- improved ability to attract and retain employees;
- possible improved financial performance, with lower operating costs;
- reduced regulatory oversight;
- access to capital;
- product safety and reduced liability.

The payback to the community and the general public includes:

- improved charitable contributions;
- more employee volunteer programs;
- business involvement in community welfare, education, and employment programs;
- product safety and quality;
- greater material recycling;
- better product durability and functionality;
- greater use of renewable resources.

Whereas traditional business models were all about profit, sustainable development recognizes that without happy, healthy people to staff a business and the natural environment able to sustain those people, the supply of resources for the business is simply unsustainable over the long term. Therefore, environmental management tools—including life-cycle assessment and costing, environmental management standards, and eco-labeling—are now commonly integrated with business plans in enterprises worldwide.

ADVANTAGES

- "At the most fundamental level, the sustainability of human societies is a function of the relationship between ecosystem energy production, human energy expropriation and the ecosystem transformations that result from human withdrawals of energy and matter and additions of waste and pollution." (Freese, 1997).

DISADVANTAGES

- Although it is possible to replace some natural resources, it is unlikely that it will ever be possible to replace ecosystem benefits, such as the protection provided by the ozone layer.
- The evolutionary loss of some biodiversity is irreversible.
- The use of fossil fuels, for example, is not sustainable. But how does society plan to eliminate the use of petroleum products?
- Under sustainable development, all resources must be regulated and controlled in order to meet the needs of the present generation as well as those of all future generations. How do you plan to regulate and control the use of resources by all individuals, families, and businesses?
- Sustainable development is for rich nations. When you don't have enough to eat, you don't worry about sustainability.

Checklists

ACTION CHECKLIST

✔ If you are considering integrating environmental projects with business plans, carefully study the potential business risks and obtain as much information from as many sources as you can before committing to an expensive process.

✔ Encourage an environment of openness about the kinds of risk facing the business from sustainable development policies. Some risks are obvious, but managers of individual business units may sometimes know more about hidden risks.

✔ Involve key business stakeholders in the evaluation of sustainable development and the alternative solutions.

DOS AND DON'TS

DO
• Carefully plan and implement the integration of sustainable development policies.

DON'T
• Don't make the mistake of being attracted to sustainable development policies without being sure that the conversion process has been thoroughly understood.

MORE INFO

Books:
Mawhinney, Mark. *Sustainable Development: Understanding the Green Debates*. Oxford: Blackwell Publishing, 2002.

Organisation for Economic Co-operation and Development (OECD). *Sustainable Development: Critical Issues*. Paris: OECD, 2001.

Schmandt, Jurgen, and C. H. Ward. *Sustainable Development: The Challenge of Transition*. Cambridge, UK: Cambridge University Press, 2000.

Websites:
DEFRA (UK) on sustainable development: sd.defra.gov.uk

International Institute for Sustainable Development (IISD): www.iisd.org

Sustainability links: www.dmoz.org/Science/Environment/Sustainability

See Also:
★ Best Practices in Corporate Social Responsibility (pp. 175–179)

★ Business Ethics (pp. 179–182)

★ CSR: More than PR, Pursuing Competitive Advantage in the Long Run (pp. 187–189)

✔ Social Return on Investment (pp. 345–346)

Creating Executive Compensation

DEFINITION

The level of executive remuneration has risen sharply in many of the World's developed economies over recent decades, with the pay gap between those at the top of the corporate tree and those at the bottom growing ever wider. While this growing divide may trouble some on ideological grounds, the need to set compensation levels at the right level to attract and to retain talented executives has never been greater. Moves to link executive remuneration to performance have found increasing favor over recent years. The objective is to reward executives on the basis of their achieving predetermined measures of the success of the business. While middle-ranking managers may benefit from bonuses linked to relatively simplistic targets such as annual sales increases, the performance-related element of top executives' remuneration can often be more complex, depending on a variety of factors that include company earnings, outright share price performance, and share price performance relative to the company's peer group.

In the United States, executives can expect to benefit from a combination of salary, bonus, stock options, stock grants, and a range of long-term incentive contracts. Over recent years executives have increasingly benefited from a shift to offer stock options.

Specialist independent remuneration committees have increasingly been established by leading listed companies wishing to strike the balance between rewarding top talent and making sure that shareholders' interests are well served. This approach typically stands up well to shareholder scrutiny by distancing executives from the role of effectively setting their own levels of remuneration.

Cultural factors can also have a considerable influence over the acceptable boundaries for top-level managerial pay. Remuneration packages which aggressively leverage private-sector executive remuneration to performance have been widely accepted in countries such as the United States for several decades, though in more conservative countries such as Japan the link between pay and performance has historically been more tentative. However, recent moves by activist investors to extract better shareholder returns in Japan have seen the performance culture penetrate through to boardroom salaries. In other countries such as the United Kingdom, elements of performance-related pay have also percolated into the remuneration packages of senior public service workers as a result of the need to compete with the increasingly incentive-driven private sector for top managerial talent.

ADVANTAGES
• A balanced, well-structured executive remuneration package can help to attract and retain key decision makers.

- Transparency in executive remuneration can find favor with institutional shareholders and is an important element in sound corporate governance.
- A mix of short and long-term performance-related elements can provide further incentives for executives to deliver success. Granting longer-term share options can help to further align executives' and shareholders' interests.

DISADVANTAGES

- The perception that executives may be excessively rewarded for moderate or poor performance can be very damaging to morale among lower-ranking employees.
- Poorly conceived incentive schemes can skew performance toward particular targets that may not necessarily align with the success of the business.
- During boom years, the pay scales in remuneration structures can be equivalent to an arms race as companies compete to attract recognized industry talent. This potentially leaves companies committed to paying excessive rewards for apparent failure during leaner times.

ACTION CHECKLIST

✔ Gain a full understanding of how existing remuneration policies operate before rushing to implement changes.

✔ Study the remuneration arrangements employed by the wider market and compare those used by your own company.

✔ Consider the cultural factors within your company which could effectively limit acceptable multiples between the potential remuneration of executives and that of lower-ranking employees.

✔ Introduce some element of performance-related pay to avoid alienating key workers at lower levels of the corporate structure.

✔ Consider how the performance strength of individual executives can be judged in relation to the overall performance of the company or division.

DOS AND DON'TS
DO

- Make sure that any new proposed executive reward scheme is in keeping with the culture of the company.
- Target consistency and fairness in creative executive compensation. Inflated remuneration to tempt talent from rivals could generate ill-feeling.
- Consider the tax implications before introducing changes to remuneration policies.

DON'T

- Don't underestimate the resources needed to effectively develop and manage executive remuneration policies.
- Don't aim for a remuneration structure which incentivizes managers to shift focus to hitting short-term targets. Opportunities to deliver long-term benefits could be missed.

MORE INFO
Book:
Berger, Lance A., and Dorothy R. Berger. *The Compensation Handbook*. 5th ed. New York: McGraw-Hill, 2008.

Article:
Cahill, Miles B., and Alaina C. George. "Executive compensation incentives in a volatile market." *American Economist* 49:2 (Fall 2005): 33–43. Online at: www.jstor.org/stable/25604323

Website:
Mercer Consulting Executive Remuneration Perspective: www.mercer.com/perspective

See Also:
★ Balancing Senior Management Compensation Arrangements with Shareholders' Interests (pp. 173–175)
★ Executive Rewards: Ensuring That Financial Rewards Match Performance (pp. 194–198)

Defining Corporate Governance: Its Aims, Goals, and Responsibilities

DEFINITION

In order for a company to exist, it has to be set up and registered with the appropriate company authority. Once registered, the company is regarded as a legal person, with legal rights and obligations. A company's existence and organization are continuously scrutinized through a well-established set of rules, laws, and policies that govern the way in which the company is run and controlled. This is known as corporate governance.

Companies can be private or public. Public companies, under certain circumstances, can choose to list their shares on a stock exchange or alternative investment markets. The corporate governance rules apply to every company, whether private or public. However, the larger and more complex a company is, the more closely its decisions are scrutinized. For multinational companies corporate governance has extended internationally, with rules and regulations that cooperate at cross-border levels.

Corporate governance exists to protect the shareholders of a company. It also aims to preserve the reputation of a company and its business against any fraudulent acts committed by its directors and officers. The directors of a company must always make decisions objectively, in the best interests of the company's business and its shareholders. They have the responsibility to run the company successfully and bring in profits for the shareholders. They have to do this ethically, within the framework of laws and regulations that govern the running of a company.

Companies must file yearly accounts that are subject to public notice. Accounts and the auditing of accounts by independent auditors are important aspects of corporate governance. They ensure the smooth running of the business and its good reputation.

ADVANTAGES

- A system of corporate governance gives the shareholders confidence that a company is well monitored and that its directors are acting in the best interests of the company and its shareholders.
- Corporate governance guards against defrauding of shareholders and the company's business.

DISADVANTAGES

- The bigger the company, the more it will be scrutinized. The need to comply with numerous corporate governance requirements is expensive and can deter the directors from their main priority, which should be running the business in the best interests of the shareholders.
- Too much supervision could restrict the independence of a company in the way it runs its business.

ACTION CHECKLIST

✔ Be well informed about any corporate governance rules.

✔ Be prepared to put in place a thorough system of auditing and risk management.

DOS AND DON'TS

DO

- Obtain advice from your legal advisers and accountants regarding the best system of auditing and risk management to put in place and the consequences of a breach of the rules.

DON'T

- Don't ignore compliance with the rules of corporate governance. The consequences could be not only financial penalties for the company but also criminal responsibility for the directors.
- Don't overlook the importance of setting up proper procedures to deal with the consequences of a breach.

MORE INFO

Books:

Keasey, Kevin, Steve Thompson, and Michael Wright. *Corporate Governance: Accountability, Enterprise and International Comparisons*. Chichester, UK: Wiley, 2005.

Solomon, Jill. *Corporate Governance and Accountability*. 3rd ed. Chichester, UK: Wiley, 2010.

Article:

Lee, Soo Hee, Jonathan Michie, and Christine Oughton. "Comparative corporate governance: Beyond 'shareholder value'." *Journal of Interdisciplinary Economics* 14:2 (June 2003): 81–111.

Websites:

Corporate Board corporate governance magazine: www.corporateboard.com

Financial Reporting Council (FRC; UK): www.frc.org.uk

Institute of Chartered Accountants in England and Wales (ICAEW): www.icaew.com

Institute of Chartered Accountants in Scotland (ICAS): www.icas.org.uk

See Also:

★ Improving Corporate Profitability Through Accountability (pp. 204–206)
✔ Conflicting Interests: The Agency Issue (pp. 338–339)
✔ Directors' Duties: A Primer (pp. 342–343)
✔ Governance Practices in Family-Owned Firms (pp. 343–345)

Directors' Duties: A Primer

DEFINITION

Directors have important and powerful positions in a company. The stockholders entrust them with the running of the company, and this is why the law requires directors to comply with certain duties.

Directors have a duty to act within their powers for a proper purpose, which is underlined in the bylaws of the company.

They also have a duty to promote the success of the company and, in doing this, must balance the interests of the stockholders, employees, suppliers, and customers of the company. The law does not define success, but in general this is agreed to mean increasing the value of the company and its business.

The directors are required to exercise independent judgment when making their decisions. They also have a duty to exercise reasonable care, skill, and diligence in the performance of their duties. An experienced director will be expected to exercise a higher degree of care, skill, and diligence in the performance of his or her activities.

Directors have a duty to avoid conflicts of interest. What constitutes a conflict of interest is a complex issue, but in general it refers to transactions between a director and third parties, rather than between a director and the company. Directors have a duty not to accept benefits from third parties if they give rise to a conflict of interest. Benefits in this sense include money and benefits in kind, such as corporate hospitality. It is advisable to obtain specific legal advice in respect of conflicts of interest, as this subject can be quite controversial and difficult to assess.

Directors have a duty to declare any interest in proposed transactions or arrangements with the company. They must disclose any such interest to the board of directors and, in certain circumstances, obtain the approval of the stockholders. This includes transactions involving the director or any person connected with the director, such as a spouse or children, and the company.

ADVANTAGES
- Directors' duties enhance the role of a company's directors and guide their direction of the company's business.
- These duties also reduce the risk of fraud and nonperformance, in the interests of the stockholders.
- The duties give stockholders and investors the confidence to invest in companies and enable them to follow the directors in the performance of their responsibilities.

DISADVANTAGES
- Compliance with directors' duties can be expensive in terms of both time and money. It requires an active training program and professional advice.

ACTION CHECKLIST
✔ When accepting an appointment as a director of a company, make sure you understand the consequences of the appointment.

✔ Obtain specific information about the company itself and the duties imposed upon directors by the bylaws of the company, as well as the company laws in the country where the company is incorporated.

✔ If necessary, obtain legal advice regarding the consequences of your appointment, and the duties, obligations, and responsibilities you will have as a director under the law.

✔ Most jurisdictions require a transparency in any personal interest a director may have in the company, and it will oblige the director to declare any conflict of interest it may have with the business of the company.

343

DOS AND DON'TS
DO
- Put in place a good training program that will keep the directors up to date with their duties.
- Obtain legal and professional advice regarding any changes in the legislation governing directors' duties.

DON'T
- Don't ignore the importance of complying with directors' duties and responsibilities. Doing so could be damaging both to the directors in question and to the company.
- Don't underestimate the need for proper training of directors and professional advice to help them fulfill their duties.

MORE INFO
Books:
Loose, Peter, Michael Griffiths, and David Impey. *The Company Director: Powers, Duties and Liabilities*. 11th ed. Bristol, UK: Jordan Publishing, 2011.
Mitchell, Philip. *Tolley's Director's Duties*. Croydon, UK: Tolley Publishing, 2007.
Webster, Martin (ed). *The Director's Handbook: Your Duties, Responsibilities and Liabilities*. 3rd ed. London: Kogan Page, 2010.

Article:
Cooke, Peter. "Duties of directors in new Companies Act 2006: Legal Q&A." *Personnel Today* (May 8, 2007). Online at: tinyurl.com/3wpukru

Websites:
Institute of Directors (IoD; UK): www.iod.com
National Association of Corporate Directors (NACD; US): www.nacdonline.org

See Also:
★ Corporate Board Structures (pp. 182–186)
★ Identifying the Right Nonexecutive Director (pp. 201–204)
✔ Conflicting Interests: The Agency Issue (pp. 338–339)
✔ Creating Executive Compensation (pp. 340–341)
✔ Defining Corporate Governance: Its Aims, Goals, and Responsibilities (pp. 341–342)

Checklists

Governance Practices in Family-Owned Firms

DEFINITION
Corporate governance practices have come under greater scrutiny in recent years, particularly in the wake of the 2001 corporate debacle that was the collapse of the energy trader Enron. Even at the opposite end of the capitalization spectrum, family-owned businesses have not entirely escaped

344

some suspicious investors' attention, leading to increased pressure for reform. Many businesses owned largely by families have responded by making the governance practices more formal, while generally increasing the transparency of their operations.

Family ownership of listed companies is commonplace, with wealthy families continuing to own large stakes in listed companies. In some European countries, powerful families effectively control their family-owned companies using voting rights that exceed their actual economic stake in the business.

Family-owned businesses benefit from a stronger personal bond between the owners and the actual business, and between the owners and employees, with the result that the family owners can be less focused on short-term earnings growth and more on long-term strategic development. However, governance structures within family businesses typically evolve with the development of the business—a process formalized in the model of family-business growth and governance developed in the late 1990s by Kelin Gersick, John Davis, Marion Hampton and Ivan Lansberg. This widely accepted model identifies three stages of transition of family businesses:

1. Founder or controlling owner stage
Management and ownership are in the hands of one individual or a couple benefiting from the input of close advisers such as accountants and legal professionals. Governance is typically informal, although the personal attitudes of the owner(s) are often reflected in the way the business operates.

2. Sibling partnership stage
With the approaching retirement of the founder(s), control passes to the next family generation. Governance is frequently complicated by the involvement of a wider base of stakeholders than at the founder stage. Some governance needs are best overseen by a board of directors or a separate advisory body.

3. Cousin consortium
Control of the business becomes further diversified as the siblings pass control of the business to their own children. Some may exit the business completely, potentially selling their stake to outsiders and conceivably diluting the family interest to the extent that the business may no longer be regarded as a family operation. In other cases, some siblings may seek to concentrate control by buying out other stakeholders. The need for an independent governance structure increases considerably.

ADVANTAGES
- Greater transparency can improve the public perception of how family-controlled businesses hope to serve the needs of all stakeholders.
- Understanding the development pattern of a business can help to identify how its governance needs are changing.
- The centralized nature of family ownership can help to keep the costs of corporate governance lower than is the case for firms with wider public share ownership.

DISADVANTAGES
- Some investors may be skeptical as to how committed family-run businesses are to equally serving the interests of all shareholders.
- Some growing family businesses can be slow to recognize the need to put in place measures to satisfy outsiders.
- Liquidity in family-owned companies is often tighter than in other companies, with some families creating legal barriers to the disposal of stock. This can lead to greater resistance to the transparency demanded by modern corporate governance standards.

ACTION CHECKLIST
✔ Family businesses should play to their greatest strength—the ability to pursue a strategy for longer-term gain.

✔ Family-owned businesses should also resist short-term industry fads and instead focus on building a long-term market presence.

✔ It is necessary to be aware of the risk that some stakeholders in family businesses might languish in the comfort zone away from mainstream shareholder pressure and instead pursue their personal goals on the business's time and at the expense of other stakeholders.

DOS AND DON'TS
DO
- Recognize how governance needs evolve over time.
- Appreciate that an external perspective can help family members better understand the need for more formal governance procedures to reassure non-family investors.
- Understand that accepting the accountability to an independent governance board can bring real advantages to the business.

DON'T
- Don't fall into the trap of thinking that corporate governance only amounts to protecting the reputation of the family.
- Don't ignore the benefits that external accountability can bring, such as an increased incentive to drive the company's strategy.

MORE INFO
Articles:
Steier, Lloyd P., James J. Chrisman, and Jess H. Chua (eds). Special issue on "Entrepreneurial management and governance in family firms." *Entrepreneurship Theory and Practice* 28:4 (June 2004): 295–411. Online at: tinyurl.com/3tujmkc

Checklists

Ward, John L. "Governing family businesses." *eJournal USA* (February 2005): 38–41.

Website:
International Finance Corporation (IFC) on corporate governance: www.ifc.org/corporategovernance

See Also:
✔ Defining Corporate Governance: Its Aims, Goals, and Responsibilities (pp. 341–342)

Social Return on Investment

DEFINITION

Analyzing the return on an investment in financial terms is intuitively relatively easy, yet many investments can deliver other forms of return that are more difficult to express purely in terms of money.

The social return on investment (SROI) refers to the total social, environmental, and economic value of an activity undertaken by a nonprofit organization or business. SROI has developed from both cost/benefit analysis and social accounting, though the formal concept was originated by the Roberts Enterprise Development Fund, a San Francisco-based philanthropic fund that invests in institutions and organizations working for social returns rather than purely profit.

Social return on investment aims to support a better understanding and management of the outcomes of an existing or potential project. Different individuals or bodies involved in the project, often referred to as stakeholders (for example, those managing, funding, working for, or benefiting from the activity), may place a different emphasis on the relevance of each benefit of SROI.

What sets SROI apart from conventional social accounting is that it aims to put a monetary value on the combined benefits of the activity with a view to maximizing the use of resources. For example, an SROI study could demonstrate that for every $1 invested in a particular social project, a return of $5 was achieved from sources such as healthcare benefits, reduced welfare payments, or lower delinquency rates in the local community. SROI performed retrospectively, known as evaluative SROI, assesses outcomes that have already occurred with a view to judging their overall effectiveness, whereas forecast SROI can be useful in planning terms given its aim of helping to assess the likely total future social, environmental, and economic value of a project or activity.

ADVANTAGES

- Helps to assess the total value of projects for society.
- The analysis supports a long-term view of the overall social, environmental, and economic benefits an activity can generate.
- Can be a valuable tool in promoting existing or potential projects by helping to attract new funding.
- The technique can also help those bodies funding existing projects to understand the full value of benefits delivered.
- Thorough SROI analysis can also identify possible undesirable consequences of projects, providing an early opportunity to change strategy or put in place measures to address negative outcomes.

DISADVANTAGES

- SROI is dependent on subjective considerations, so attitudes to monetary values may differ between stakeholders. Putting a monetary value on some benefits can be extremely difficult.
- Adopting an SROI approach to a project can involve significant resources, both in terms of time and level of commitment.
- Estimating the amount of time needed to implement SROI can be difficult as this depends on the availability of the required data and the skill set of those involved in the study.
- The findings of SROI can lack credibility to any parties who are opposed to the project in the first place; given its reliance on subjective inputs, opponents may see SROI as a means to justify spending on a "pet" project.

ACTION CHECKLIST

✔ When considering investing in a project or activity, give an overall thought to the value and implications it might have for society as a whole.

✔ Ensure that you are communicating effectively with all stakeholders so that they understand what you are measuring, how you are doing it, and what you are hoping to achieve.

✔ Make use of impact maps to foster a better understanding among stakeholders of the relationship between the availability of resources, the possible uses of those resources, and the likely results.

✔ Don't overstate the value of the project—attributing unrelated benefits to the project in an SROI study could undermine the whole credibility of the analysis.

✔ Be transparent about the assumptions you are making—SROI is not an exact science and shouldn't be portrayed as such.

DOS AND DON'TS

DO

- Plan thoroughly and understand what you aim to achieve from your study.
- Identify who all the stakeholders are and understand their goals and objectives.
- Make reasonable and balanced projections and stick to your aims and plans.
- Ensure that any judgments involved in SROI are fully documented to ensure transparency.
- Where resources permit, look to underpin the credibility of your analysis by inviting an independent third party to validate your findings.

DON'T

- Don't think of SROI as an exact science—values are subjective as different stakeholders may have different priorities in terms of outcome.
- Don't become obsessive about the ratio of "money spent versus the total value of benefits received"—rather, use SROI analysis as a basis for a better understanding of the likely outcomes of a project.
- Don't undermine the integrity of your findings by trying to put a value on unrelated outcomes that have little or nothing to do with the project.
- Don't underestimate the value of effective results reporting—present your analysis to stakeholders and encourage ongoing communication with them.

MORE INFO

Books:

Nicholls, Jeremy, Susan Mackenzie, and Alibeth Somers. *Measuring Real Value: A DIY Guide to Social Return on Investment*. London: New Economics Foundation, 2007.

Scholten, Peter, Jeremy Nicholls, Sara Olsen, and Brett Galimidi. *Social Return on Investment: A Guide to SROI Analysis*. Amstelveen, The Netherlands: Lenthe Publishers, 2006.

Article:

Rotheroe, Neil, and Adam Richards. "Social return on investment and social enterprise: Transparent accountability for sustainable development." *Social Enterprise Journal* 3:1 (2007): 31–48. Online at: dx.doi.org/10.1108/17508610780000720

Websites:

ClearlySo, an online marketplace for social business and enterprise, commerce, and investment: www.clearlyso.com

Social ROI, a social entrepreneurship blog: socialroi.com

SROI Network, the social return on investment website: www.thesroinetwork.org

Understanding Economic Efficiency Theory

DEFINITION

Conventional economic efficiency theory states that companies should structure their output to achieve the lowest possible cost per unit produced. Given the combination of fixed and variable costs typical in business, low levels of output are inefficient because fixed costs are shared out across a relatively small number of units. At the other extreme, although above-optimal production can, in theory, generate economies of scale, in practice this apparent benefit is often more than offset by additional costs related to the overstressing of existing systems. In the short term, the point of maximum operational efficiency is achieved at the level of output at which all available economies of scale are taken advantage of, yet short of the level at which the diseconomies of overstraining existing systems come into play. Over the longer term, however, the optimal level of productive efficiency can be raised by increasing the capacity of existing systems.

The second element of conventional economic efficiency theory relates to the way existing resources are allocated. The logic is that high levels of competition among producers should prevent them from making excessive profits by raising their selling prices to an unreasonable level above their marginal costs. At the company level, maximum allocative efficiency is achieved when the firm produces the optimal output level of a combination of goods or services to maximize the benefit to the company as a whole. The theory takes account of the fact that company resources are finite and can be used only once, with the result that using a quantity of a material for one purpose involves an opportunity cost—that is, it denies the company the chance to use the same material for another purpose. Allocative efficiency is achieved only when no other pattern of utilization of resources can deliver a better overall result in terms of the welfare of all interested parties. This point of maximum allocative efficiency, at which improvements in one aspect of usage can only be achieved at the expense of losses elsewhere, is sometimes referred to as the Pareto optimal allocation of resources.

ADVANTAGES

- The theory provides a basic framework to help understand the various factors that are associated with existing operating costs.

- An understanding of the main principles of the theory could provide scope for managers to find ways of making some elements of their business work more efficiently.

DISADVANTAGES

- The theory encourages managers to take a "static" view of their business, with no regard to the possibilities offered by innovation. The rapid pace of technological development over recent years has highlighted this shortcoming in classic economic efficiency theory.
- The focus on the lowest possible cost can give an overly simplistic representation of the way businesses operate, although the theory retains value in some low-technology, noninnovative manufacturing applications.

ACTION CHECKLIST

✔ Analyze your company's cost structure, determining which costs are fixed and which are largely variable; in practice most costs tend to be semivariable in nature.

✔ Consider the levels of production that are likely to begin to put serious strain on existing infrastructure to the point that diseconomies of scale begin to appear. It may be that lessons can be learned from the way systems performed during past periods of temporary high demand.

✔ Study how finite resources are being put to work at present. Excessive downtime of resources, including human resources, should be investigated in an effort to bolster allocative efficiency.

DOS AND DON'TS

DO

- Make use of the theory to gain a greater understanding of various cost and resource utilization patterns within companies. However, remember that an excessive focus on miniscule cost improvements could distract management from changing industry trends, potentially allowing competitors to capitalize on exciting new opportunities.
- Consider whether present resource allocation has more to do with past needs and in-house politics than present or future

requirements. Remember that, as the business environment evolves, company resource allocation decisions should reflect changing demands on the business.

DON'T

- Don't use economic efficiency theory in isolation. Remember that taking a static view of your business is unlikely to be the best preparation for change.
- Don't ignore human factors when seeking greater efficiency. Demoralizing staff in the pursuit of insignificant cost savings could generate unforeseen human resource costs.
- Don't lose sight of wider opportunities to make a quantum leap in efficiency, rather than the small incremental improvements that are typically achieved using economic efficiency theory. Innovation, particularly related to technology, can deliver substantial efficiency benefits.

MORE INFO

Books:

Quinzii, Martine, and Sujaya Parthasarathy (trans). *Increasing Returns and Efficiency*. New York: Oxford University Press, 1993.

Ravenscraft, David J., and Frederic M. Scherer. *Mergers, Sell-Offs, and Economic Efficiency*. Washington, DC: Brookings Institution, 1987.

Zerbe, Richard O., Jr. *Economic Efficiency in Law and Economics*. Cheltenham, UK: Edward Elgar Publishing, 2001.

Article:

Ng, Yew-Kwang. "Increasing returns and economic organization: Introduction." *Journal of Economic Behavior & Organization* 55:2 (October 2004): 129–136. Online at: dx.doi.org/10.1016/j.jebo.2004.05.001

See Also:

★ Aligning Structure with Strategy: Recalibrating for Improved Performance and Increased Profitability (pp. 246–249)
★ Five Routes to Greater Profitability for Small and Medium Enterprises (pp. 264–267)
★ Reducing Costs through Production and Supply Chain Management (pp. 276–279)

Checklists

M&A Regulations: A Global Overview

DEFINITION

Mergers and acquisitions (M&A) has become a mundane expression, used daily in the media. In order to operate successfully in a global economy, corporations have become transnational and have to perform at a multinational level. To achieve such expansion, corporations acquire other companies or merge with them. These large corporations are publicly owned, listed on stock exchanges or alternative markets around the world, and engage in M&A activities that are thoroughly regulated by governments to protect the shareholders of target companies.

The laws and regulations governing M&A are very complex and strict. High levels of expertise and specialist advice are required, and corporations use several teams of lawyers who specialize in the jurisdictions involved in M&A.

In 2003, the European Parliament published a directive that regulated the way in which securities were to be offered to the public or admitted to trading. This became known as the EU Prospective Directive. Its scope was to harmonize and homogenize capital markets within the European Union. In essence, the directive allows a company that issues shares in more than one EU member state to be governed by a single member state, rather than by each member state in which the shares are offered.

In the United States, federal securities laws and regulations are generally applicable if US investors own securities in a foreign target company. In the United States, the Securities and Exchange Commission is the body that supervises and oversees the most important participants in the securities world, such as securities exchanges, dealers, brokers, and mutual funds. Its most important role is to promote disclosure and transparency of market information by maintaining fair dealing and ensuring protection against fraud.

In Australia, the responsibility belongs to the Australian Stock Exchange and the Australian Securities and Investments Commission, while the relevant body in the United Kingdom is the London Stock Exchange.

In September 2006 the Regulations on Foreign Investors' Mergers and Acquisitions of Domestic Enterprises came into force in China, as a direct result of an increase in M&A transactions and the general opening up of the country.

Japan has recently eased regulation on foreign investment by introducing legislation that allows foreign-owned companies to invest in Japanese companies through stock-for-stock (share-for-share) exchanges with the Japanese subsidiaries of those companies.

ADVANTAGES

- M&A regulations protect shareholders and investors in the acquirer and target company.
- In general M&A regulations allow for the harmonization and homogenization of international markets and thus maintain transparency, fair dealing, and protection against fraud.

DISADVANTAGES

- M&A regulations are very complex.
- Specialist financial and legal advice is always required when participating in M&A activity.
- The cost of an acquisition is usually high, and specialist advice only adds to this cost.

ACTION CHECKLIST

✔ Recognize the complexity of M&A regulations.

✔ Seek specialist professional advice at an early stage when considering a possible M&A deal.

✔ Appreciate that while the costs of enlisting professional help to explore global M&A opportunities can be high, the long-term rewards from successful international deals can be considerably higher.

DOS AND DON'TS

DO

- Carefully balance the implications of a developing business against the advantages and disadvantages of acquiring an existing one before committing to any expense.
- Obtain relevant advice regarding the acquisition or merger.
- Research the market carefully before making a decision.

DON'T

- Don't underestimate the need for proper research and professional advice.
- Don't ignore the importance of integrating the new operations within the existing business; otherwise the consequences could be costly.
- Don't be afraid to decide against the acquisition if the signs are that it will not be a good investment.

MORE INFO

Books:

McGrath, Michael. *Practical M&A Execution and Integration: A Step by Step Guide To Successful Strategy, Risk and Integration Management*. Chichester, UK: Wiley, 2011.

Sherman, Andrew J. *Mergers and Acquisitions from A to Z*. 3rd ed. New York: AMACOM, 2011.

Report:

Khalili, Anita, Uvarshanie Nandram, Mariana Trindade, Pratik M. Patel, Roger Conner, and Jill Lewandosky. "2012 M&A outlook." Bloomberg, 2011. Online at: media.bloomberg.com/bb/avfile/ru20IiusvjMM

Websites:
Beyond the Deal: www.beyondthedeal.com
Reuters M&A news: www.reuters.com/finance/deals/mergers

See Also:
★ Due Diligence Requirements in Financial Transactions
   (pp. 216–220)

✔ Planning the Acquisition Process (pp. 350–351)
✔ Understanding Anti-Takeover Strategies (p. 354)

349

Management Buyouts

DEFINITION

A management buyout (MBO) is the acquisition of a business by its management. The management will usually buy the target business from its parent company. The management will incorporate a new company to buy the business or shares of the target company. The transaction usually involves another party, a venture capitalist, which, together with the management, will invest in the new company. A venture capitalist is a company or fund that invests in unquoted companies. The investment usually takes the form of an equity stake.

In an MBO it is very important to establish whether the parent company, the vendor, is willing to sell. The management are usually in a very good position to buy, since they already understand the business they intend to acquire. Funding the acquisition usually requires not only the personal financial commitment of the managers but also additional funding in the shape of a loan or an equity investment.

It is essential that the management establish a coherent business plan, which will help not only in obtaining the funding required for the MBO but also in convincing the parent company that the managers are the best buyers for the business. As for investors, what they need is assurance that the business will be able to continue successfully and that it will provide them with a profitable return on their investment.

In an MBO, confidentiality while negotiations are taking place between the parent company and the management team is essential. The consequences of a leak could be damaging to the business and its staff.

ADVANTAGES

- An MBO will give the management the chance to run their business.
- The new company will have a highly motivated management team, who are not only eager to make a profit but also have a deep knowledge of the business they will be running.
- Since the management understand and have been involved in the running of the business to be acquired, the commercial due diligence that is usually undertaken when a company is acquired should be easier and less time-consuming.

DISADVANTAGES

- An MBO involves a very serious financial commitment and acceptance of risk by the management. The management

will move from being employees to being owners of the business. If the business is not successful, they will feel it directly.
- Even though the commercial due diligence required could be less extensive, the legal and financial affairs of the business still need to be examined. This will involve advice and expense.
- Since acquisition by an MBO is highly leveraged (i.e. has a high proportion of debt relative to equity), this does not put the new company in the best position to compete on price.

ACTION CHECKLIST

✔ Think carefully about the business before you acquire it. Obtain as much information from as many sources as you can before committing to an expensive due diligence process.

✔ Know your market and make sure that you have analyzed the consequences of owning your own business.

✔ Be prepared for a long and complicated due diligence process, which could prove time-consuming as well as costly.

✔ Economize by negotiating a reasonable rate with your legal and financial advisers, but remember that it is better to incur costs by conducting a thorough investigation than to accept a level of service that may fail to reveal potentially costly liabilities.

✔ Always be aware of confidentiality while the MBO is being planned, as any leak can affect the confidence of the staff and affect the performance of the business.

DOS AND DON'TS
DO
- Involve your lawyers and accountants in the evaluation of both the risks and potential benefits of an MBO, as well as in the due diligence process.

- Negotiate your rates and make a contingency plan for any cost overrun.
- Draw up an accurate and achievable business plan.

DON'T

- Don't make the mistake of being attracted by the idea of owning a business without fully weighing up the risks you might be taking.
- Don't underestimate the importance of finance and the financial commitment that owning a business will entail. The risks to the owners of a business are high if the business does not perform.
- Don't forget that many of the banks that offer finance will be looking for collateral for the loan, and the managers could be required to provide personal guarantees that will affect their personal wealth if things do not work out.

MORE INFO

Books:

Sharp, Garry. *Buy Outs: A Guide for the Management Team*. London: Euromoney Institutional Investor, 2002.

Wright, Mike, and Hans Bruining. *Private Equity and Management Buy-Outs*. Cheltenham, UK: Edward Elgar Publishing, 2008.

Website:

MBO Guide: www.mboguide.co.uk

See Also:

★ Going Private: Public-to-Private Leveraged Buyouts (pp. 220–224)

★ Leveraged Buyouts: What, Why, When, and How (pp. 230–233)

Checklists

Planning the Acquisition Process

DEFINITION

After a buyer decides to acquire a business, the process starts with the search for a suitable business. The targeted business could be known to the buyer or could be a competitor of the buyer. It could also be advertised for sale in a trade journal or newspaper, or the buyer could be approached directly by the seller or its intermediary.

After finding a business, the buyer must assess its value in order to establish the best offer price. If the business to be acquired is part of a company, it will have to file yearly accounts, which are of public record.

Every business is affected by cash flow, profit and loss, and how its finances are run. The balance sheet and accounts will give a good indication of all these elements. A buyer should also look at: the overall market within which the targeted business operates; the business's performance and reputation; its competitors; and any other interested buyers. Another element to look at is the legislation in the country where the business operates. The logistics of acquiring a national business and an international business can be very different. A buyer should obtain information on the management of the targeted business. If a business is well managed, it is usually successful and well reputed. The buyer should also consider the workforce.

The buyer should consider the advantages the acquisition will have upon its own business and should start planning how it will be integrated within its own company.

In order to consider the purchase more thoroughly, more detailed investigations should be made. During this process, the buyer may well like to involve advisers who will provide a more thorough and objective valuation. However, this assistance may be expensive.

This investigation should give a buyer an idea of the value of the business and of the offer to make to the seller. The initial information will be verified by the later due diligence process, which takes place with the permission and cooperation of the seller. The buyer will approach the seller either directly or via its advisers and make an offer for the business. Negotiations on the price will usually commence, with the buyer and seller subsequently signing a document called heads of term. This will deal with the main points of the acquisition, such as price, warranties to be given by the seller and other essential conditions. The buyer and its advisers will have to sign a confidentiality agreement, which will protect the data disclosed by the seller and will give the buyer access to more detailed information from the seller's private records. The due diligence process can last a few weeks, depending on the amount and complexity of the information to be investigated. The buyer will look in detail at all the business's contracts with clients and suppliers, insurance, employees' records, any intellectual property and IT issues, and any existent litigation. A buyer should also look at the business premises, any licenses, and environmental issues. Separately, the buyer's accountants will investigate the financial details of the business. At the end of the due diligence process, the buyer will usually receive a legal due diligence report from its lawyers and a financial due diligence report from its accountants. These, together with the buyer's own commercial and business assessment, will provide a very clear picture of the business and will allow the buyer to decide whether the acquisition is worth making or not.

ADVANTAGES

A well-informed and prepared buyer:

- Will be in a better position to decide whether the target business is worth buying in the first place.
- Will be able to decide on an accurate valuation of the business and make a competitive offer price.

- Will have a thorough understanding of the business to be sold and will, therefore, be able to conduct more advantageous negotiations.
- Will be better able to help in running and integration of the business once the acquisition is made.

DISADVANTAGES

- Initial investigations and later due diligence could be costly, and may show that the business is not worth acquiring.
- An acquisition involves huge effort and a concentration of resources, which sometimes could be used to improve its own business.

ACTION CHECKLIST

✔ Consider carefully any business you might acquire. Obtain as much information from as many sources as you can before committing to an expensive due diligence process.

✔ Know your market and make sure that you have analyzed the consequences for your own business of the acquisition of another.

✔ Be prepared for a long and complicated due diligence process, taking time and being costly.

✔ Economize by negotiating a reasonable rate with your legal and financial advisers, but remember that it is better to incur costs by conducting a thorough investigation than to accept service that may fail to reveal potentially costly liabilities.

DOS AND DON'TS

DO

- Involve your solicitors and accountants in the evaluation of both the risks and potential benefits of an acquisition, as well as in the due diligence process.
- Negotiate your rates and make a contingency plan for any cost overrun.
- Plan carefully the integration of the new business within your own.

DON'T

- Don't make the mistake of being attracted by a business that has not been thoroughly investigated.
- Don't overlook the importance of negotiating complex warranties and indemnities that would protect you in the event that underlying liabilities are discovered.

MORE INFO

Book:

Dewhurst, John. *Buying a Company: The Keys to Successful Acquisition*. London: Bloomsbury Publishing, 1997.

Article:

Rowan-Robinson, Jeremy, and Norman Hutchinson. "Compensation for the compulsory acquisition of business interests: Satisfaction or sacrifice." *Journal of Property Valuation and Investment* 13:1 (1995): 44–65. Online at: dx.doi.org/10.1108/14635789510077287

See Also:

★ Acquisition Integration: How to Do It Successfully (pp. 211–213)

✔ M&A Regulations: A Global Overview (pp. 348–349)

✔ Using the Market-Value Method for Acquisitions (pp. 355–356)

Checklists

Planning the Disposal Process

DEFINITION

The preparation for the disposal process starts after the seller has decided to sell the business. There can be several reasons why someone might want to sell his business. The business could need substantial investment, and selling a percentage of shares – and, therefore, a share in the business – would bring in the necessary finance to help develop the business overall. Lifestyle factors could also be involved: a seller may want to sell the whole of his business because of a wish to retire or to do something completely different.

Whatever the reason for the sale, preparing a business for disposal requires time and effort, and it can be expensive. In certain circumstances, a buyer may only be interested in the goodwill of the business sold and certain of its assets. A seller should be aware that such a sale would leave him with the rest of the business, including its liabilities. Usually, the best time

to sell a business is when it is doing well, has a good set-up and is running smoothly, bringing in high profits, and has a successful financial and management record. Then a seller can fully capitalize on its success. In some cases, the buyer of a business is its own management team. This is known as a management buy-out (MBO).

A seller should start preparing for the sale long in advance. He or she needs to make sure that all papers, legal documents and contracts, permits for the business, and its books are in good order. He or she should involve professional advisers, legal and financial, as early as possible. Their help and advice will be required during the disposal process, but they can also provide useful tips when preparing the business for sale.

Staff knowledge of the planned sale is not necessary at this stage. Usually, managers are told because his or her cooperation is required when preparing the sale, but spreading the knowledge of the potential sale through the entire workforce could have a negative influence on the running of the business, as staff could begin to worry about work security.

With the advice of accountants, a seller should consider any tax issues that will affect a disposal, so that the tax burden is minimized. Any buyer will be interested in a well-run business with a good grip on its credit and creditors. A seller should consider renegotiating inefficient contracts with clients and utility providers and should sort out any existent and potential litigation.

ADVANTAGES

- A well-prepared seller will be in a better position to negotiate a good price for the business.
- A well-prepared seller will be in a better position to assess what warranties they will be able to give to the buyer without submitting himself or herself to unexpected risk.
- An MBO could be more advantageous for a seller, as the managers know the business inside out.

DISADVANTAGES

- The initial investigations and later due diligence process could be expensive, both financially and in terms of time, if the acquisition does not go ahead.
- Preparing for a sale will involve huge effort and a concentration of resources, which sometimes could be used to improve the business itself.
- Selling is frequently emotionally difficult on a seller.
- In an MBO, less money is usually offered for a business, because managers may not have access to good finance.

ACTION CHECKLIST

✔ Consider carefully the need to sell and why you want to sell. It may well be that the timing is not ideal and that waiting could be advantageous.

✔ Be prepared for a long and complicated due diligence process, which could prove time consuming as well as costly.

DOS AND DON'TS

DO

- Involve your solicitors and accountants in the evaluation of both the risks and potential benefits of a disposal, as well as the due diligence process.
- Negotiate your rates and make a contingency plan for any cost overrun.
- Plan carefully the tax implications of the disposal.

DON'T

- Don't make the mistake of selling at the wrong time if waiting a while could bring a higher price.
- Don't overlook the importance of mitigating your liabilities under any warranties and indemnities given to the buyer, obtaining advice, and understanding your business.

MORE INFO

Books:

Smith, Ian. *Financial Techniques for Business Acquisitions and Disposals*. 2nd ed. Hawksmere Report Series. London: Thorogood Publishing, 1998.

Steingold, Fred S. *The Complete Guide to Selling a Business*. 3rd ed. Berkeley, CA: Nolo, 2007.

Articles:

Card, Jon. "Selling your business." *Growing Business*. Online at: tinyurl.com/7ymdwhw

Gole, William J., and Paul J. Hilger. "Managing corporate divestiture transactions." *Journal of Accountancy* (August 2008): 48–51. Online at: tinyurl.com/3keqrwy

See Also:

★ Maximizing Value when Selling a Business (pp. 235–239)

Structuring and Negotiating Joint Ventures

DEFINITION

Joint ventures are set up for many reasons: to carry out a specific project or simply to assist with the growth and continuation of a business.

The parties to a joint venture can be individuals, partnerships, companies, or other organizations or associations. In certain cases, the joint venture can be created through the incorporation of a company that becomes a party to the joint-venture agreement. In other cases, the parties can sign a collaboration agreement.

The parties must think carefully about what they are trying to achieve through the joint venture. Do the parties want to

have a period of exclusive negotiation, will they require a confidentiality undertaking, and will they sign a letter of intent to solidify their intention as a preamble for negotiations?

Things to consider include whether the joint venture will have any limitations in terms of territory in which it will operate. Also, what consents, approvals, licenses, and permits are necessary for the joint venture to operate? If the joint venture will operate at a cross-border level, in which jurisdictions will it be established? Consider also whether there are any laws governing foreign ownership or investment. Are they any exchange controls in force? What relevant taxes and duties are imposed?

The parties to a joint venture can provide their own funding for the joint venture or use external sources for funding. The parties' investment can be cash or payment in kind, such as expertise and resources. The parties must agree the percentage in which they will benefit from the joint venture. They must also agree working-capital requirements, any losses, and think about any expansion costs.

If the joint venture is through a company, the parties must agree the extent to which participation in the joint venture is transferable. Should the joint-venture company be wound-up if one of the parties wants to come out of it?

The joint venture will have to be thoroughly organized. The parties will agree the composition of the board and how the board will operate and vote.

Another very important consideration is whether the parties will be prohibited from competing with the joint venture at all or just in that particular territory.

Deadlock provisions are essential in a joint-venture agreement. This is when the parties cannot agree on certain voting issues and a decision cannot be taken. The joint-venture agreement must deal with this and set up a procedure to be followed in the event of a deadlock. For example, a voting deadlock at board level can be solved by giving a casting vote to the chairman or by involving an independent expert or arbitrator. The agreement must also establish the duration of the joint venture and how it can be terminated. In the event of termination, the agreement must deal with the distribution of assets, the discharge of any outstanding contracts, and the liabilities of the joint venture.

ADVANTAGES

- A joint venture allows two competitors to join forces, increase their market exposure, and compete at a higher level against other, more powerful companies in the same industry.
- It also allows two connected businesses to cooperate on a joint project in a certain market.

DISADVANTAGES

- Negotiating a joint venture can be complex and time consuming. It involves thorough research of the market and territory in which the products will be sold or the project will be organized.
- Joint ventures can be expensive to set up initially.

ACTION CHECKLIST

✔ Study any joint venture you might set up carefully. Obtain as much information from as many sources as you can before committing to an expensive joint-venture agreement. Plan it carefully and set up a realistic business plan with your business partner.

✔ Know your market and make sure that you have analyzed the consequences for your own business of entering into a joint-venture agreement.

✔ Economize by negotiating a reasonable rate with your legal advisers, but remember that it is better to incur costs by obtaining legal advice than to enter into a joint venture under terms that you do not understand.

DOS AND DON'TS
DO

- Choose your partner in the joint venture carefully, as you will be legally bound for a set period of time, under obligations that will prove costly if they are not successfully performed.
- Involve your solicitors in the evaluation of both the risks and potential benefits of entering into a joint venture.
- Negotiate your rates and make a contingency plan for any cost overrun.
- Plan carefully how the joint-venture will operate, how the profits will be distributed and who will take responsibility for what.

DON'T

- Don't make the mistake of being attracted by the idea of a joint venture that has not been thoroughly planned and thought through.
- Don't overlook the importance of setting up a contingency plan in case the joint venture will not work and the relationship breaks down.

MORE INFO
Books:

Glover, Stephen I., and Craig M. Wasserman (eds). *Partnerships, Joint Ventures and Strategic Alliances*. Business Law Corporate Series. New York: Law Journal Press, 2004.

Walmsley, John. *Handbook of International Joint Ventures*. London: Graham & Trotman, 1982.

Article:

Geringer, J. Michael, and Louis Hebert. "Measuring performance of international joint ventures." *Journal of International Business Studies* 22:2 (June 1991): 249–263. Online at: dx.doi.org/10.1057/palgrave.jibs.8490302

See Also:

★ Joint Ventures: Synergies and Benefits (pp. 227–230)
★ Maximizing a New Strategic Alliance (pp. 233–235)

Checklists

Understanding Anti-Takeover Strategies

DEFINITION

Anti-takeover strategies come in a number of different guises. Terms such as "shark repellent" and "poison pill" are used to describe the defensive methods or tactics that companies use to attempt to prevent mergers, i.e. the joining of two or more businesses into one, or hostile takeovers, when a business is acquired against the management's or shareholders' wishes.

Anti-takeover strategies are designed to make a company unattractive to predators. They do this in the following ways:

- A shareholder rights plan or poison pill has two different strategies. The "flip-in" allows existing shareholders to purchase more shares at a discount in order to dilute the value of the shares, while the "flip-over" allows shareholders to purchase the bidder's shares at a discount.
- A provision in the company's charter or articles allows shareholders to sell their shares to the bidder for more than the market price.
- A company takes on sufficient debts to make it unattractive, as a bidder would be responsible for those debts.
- The business issues bonds that have to be redeemed at a higher price if the company is taken over.
- The company offers its employees stock options, high bonuses, and exceptional severance pay that would cost a bidder dearly.
- Staggered elections to the board of directors over a period of years can mean that a potential bidder is faced with a hostile board of directors until new elections can be held.

In some jurisdictions, such as the United Kingdom, anti-takeover strategies are illegal or some control on their use is mandated. However, in the United States, where they are legal, the recent economic decline and fear of becoming an acquisition target have renewed interest in anti-takeover strategies in all their forms.

ADVANTAGES

- Anti-takeover strategies are useful when a company feels that its stock has become undervalued and that it may become the target for a takeover.
- Anti-takeover strategies are useful when the predator company's intentions are to acquire the company and then load the company with so much debt that it is unviable.
- Short-term poison pills may help businesses through difficult financial periods when they could be vulnerable as targets.

DISADVANTAGES

- Anti-takeover strategies are sometimes used to entrench management and prevent shareholders from selling their stock and maximizing its price.

- Board members sometimes hide behind poison pills to retain their positions.

ACTION CHECKLIST

✔ Check that the use of anti-takeover strategies is legal in the country or jurisdiction in which the company is operating.

✔ Determine which method would provide the greatest protection without hurting the company's value.

✔ Avoid tying the company to stock options, high bonuses, and exceptional severance pay for employees you might later want to fire.

✔ If you are taking on debts or issuing bonds to make the company unattractive, make sure that you can service those debts even if the economy turns down.

DOS AND DON'TS
DO
- Consult with partners, directors, lawyers and accountants before initiating anti-takeover strategies.

DON'T
- Don't use anti-takeover strategies unless you are sure that they won't backfire and leave the company vulnerable.

MORE INFO
Books:
Frank, Werner L. *Corporate War: Poison Pills and Golden Parachutes*. Charleston, SC: CreateSpace, 2011.
MacIntosh, Julie. *Dethroning the King: The Hostile Takeover of Anheuser-Busch, an American Icon*. Hoboken, NJ: Wiley, 2010.
Ricardo-Campbell, Rita. *Resisting Hostile Takeovers: The Case of Gillette*. Westport, CT: Praeger, 1997.

See Also:
★ Coping with Equity Market Reactions to M&A Transactions (pp. 213–216)
✔ M&A Regulations: A Global Overview (pp. 348–349)
✔ Using the Market-Value Method for Acquisitions (pp. 355–356)

Checklists

Using the Market-Value Method for Acquisitions 355

DEFINITION

The capitalization of a publicly traded company is calculated simply by multiplying the market price per share by the number of shares in issue.

For the purposes of valuing a potential acquisition, however, the basic market-value method involves the study of a range of related companies, ideally at a similar stage in the growth cycle and in the same industry or sector, to determine a range of price-to-earnings (P/E) ratios for comparable companies. The resulting lowest and highest of these P/E ratios can subsequently be used to establish a base valuation band for the target company. Alternatively, an average P/E for the group could be used to calculate a central valuation.

This base valuation method assumes that the prevailing market prices across the group of comparable companies fully reflect all available information relating to their businesses and prospects, as the "efficient" market has already priced in all relevant valuation information.

In almost all acquisitions, the valuation will then need to be upwardly adjusted to reflect an appropriate acquisition premium. The level of this premium typically depends on transaction ratings, which are researched based on factors such as the P/Es that are eventually paid for comparable deals, frequently adjusted to reflect present market conditions.

ADVANTAGES

- The market-value method is widely recognized, and was adopted as the industry-standard method of valuing companies ahead of acquisitions. Although other approaches have found favor more recently, the market-value method remains a standard valuation tool for the due-diligence processes undertaken ahead of acquisitions.
- The method provides a fundamentally sound basis for company valuation as long as a number of truly comparable companies can be identified.

DISADVANTAGES

- Because of its reliance on prevailing market prices, the method is applicable only to publicly traded companies. Alternative valuation tools must be employed to establish the values of private companies.
- While P/E ratios are relatively easy to establish for actively traded large-cap stocks, smaller, less liquid stocks may attract infrequent share transactions. For example, microcap stocks traded on junior or fledgling markets may experience sparse trading activity at times, making P/E ratios more difficult to assess.
- Disputes can arise over which companies should be included in the comparables category for calculating P/Es. Because of the lack of hard and fast rules, a prospective buyer could lean towards comparables with lower P/Es, while a more optimistic seller might prefer to include related companies with more demanding P/E multiples.

- The appropriate level for an acquisition premium can be difficult to determine. Proposed acquisition valuations often need to be revised upwards to improve the chances of success of a deal.

ACTION CHECKLIST

✔ Before relying on the market-value method, you need to be satisfied that the underlying market is truly efficient. Be aware that some scope exists, particularly among less liquid, sparsely traded smaller companies, for unscrupulous manipulation of market prices ahead of an acquisition.

✔ Consider the potential benefits of using a range of P/Es across comparable companies to give a wider valuation band.

✔ Research the acquisition premiums paid in comparable acquisitions, making adjustments for changes to the operating environment.

DOS AND DON'TS
DO

- Make every effort to achieve a non-contentious valuation using reasonable comparisons with other companies in the industry.
- Pay close attention to the risk of potential accounting differences between comparable companies, as these could have significant impacts on the resulting average P/E ratios.
- Be prepared to revise the proposed acquisition price depending on stakeholder reaction. In many cases, an improved valuation can have a significantly higher prospect of securing the acquisition.

DON'T

- Don't blindly attempt to use P/E ratios from large-cap companies when seeking to apply the market-value method to smaller companies. Large differences in ratios frequently occur across the capitalization spectrum and can lead to major valuation errors.
- Don't overlook other means of valuing target companies. Although the market-value method was traditionally the industry standard, discounted cash flow techniques have increasingly found favor in recent years, to the extent that they have now largely displaced the market-value approach in all but due-diligence processes.

MORE INFO
Books:

Hitchner, James R. *Financial Valuations: Applications and Models*. 3rd ed. Hoboken, NJ: Wiley, 2011.

Checklists

356

Reed, Stanley Foster, Alexandra Lajoux, and H. Peter Nesvold. *The Art of M&A: A Merger Acquisition Buyout Guide*. 4th ed. New York: McGraw-Hill, 2007.

Article:

Weaver, Samuel C., Robert S. Harris, Daniel W. Bielinski, and Kenneth F. MacKenzie. "Merger and acquisition valuation: Panel discussion." *Financial Management* 20:2 (Summer 1991): 85–96. Online at: www.jstor.org/stable/3665732

See Also:

★ Coping with Equity Market Reactions to M&A Transactions (pp. 213–216)

★ Valuing Start-Ups (pp. 239–243)

✔ Estimating Enterprise Value with the Weighted Average Cost of Capital (pp. 293–294)

✔ Planning the Acquisition Process (pp. 350–351)

Checklists

Applying Stress-Testing to Business Continuity Management

DEFINITION

Business continuity management (BCM) is an important component of the risk management framework for regulated institutions. It increases the resilience to business disruption that may arise from internal or external events and should reduce any adverse impact on business operations, as well as profitability and reputation.

Business operations have become increasingly complex over the years, increasing their vulnerability to disruption by outside events. BCM has thus become an essential part of a company's risk management framework. A whole industry has sprung up devoted to supporting companies on BCM issues.

Although major disruptions to business are rare, few have forgotten the events of 9/11, which resulted in massive disruption to business. External threats from terrorism, computer crime, and viruses are unlikely to go away. Businesses need to put in place continuity plans that are consistent with the scale of their operations.

Stress-testing is crucial to an organization's BCM and its planning for risk management. Stress-testing and scenario analysis both provide management with the information it needs to assess and adjust risks to the organization and to mitigate them effectively. They enable firms to understand how they should deal with certain threats, pick up on any shortfalls, and implement actions to improve their processes for BCM.

Wider use of BCM, stress-testing, and scenario analysis would have a beneficial effect on the robustness of the world's financial systems. There is, however, no simple formula for a company to follow for its own stress-testing and scenario analysis. Depending on its size and global reach, each organization must formulate its own strategies and plans for testing its BCM processes.

ADVANTAGES

Stress-testing of business continuity management should:
- reduce the impact of disruptions to business operations in the event of a problem;
- increase protection to stakeholders and beneficiaries;
- promote confidence in the organization and the whole financial system.

DISADVANTAGES
- The cost of planning and actions.
- The time spent on the whole process.

ACTION CHECKLIST
✔ Put a BCM strategy in place.

✔ Set up methods and routines for stress-testing and scenario analysis.

✔ Carry out regular tests.

✔ Determine follow-up points.

✔ Carry out any necessary actions to improve the BCM plan.

DOS AND DON'TS
DO
- Review your BCM plans and processes regularly.
- Identify actions to update your BCM as appropriate.
- Follow up these actions.

Don't
- Don't leave your BCM proposals unmonitored once you have put them in place.
- Don't restrict stress-testing to specific threats.

MORE INFO
Books:

Hiles, Andrew (ed). *The Definitive Handbook of Business Continuity Management*. 3rd ed. Chichester, UK: Wiley, 2010.

Osborne, Andy. *Practical Business Continuity Management: Top Tips for Effective, Real-World Business Continuity Management*. Evesham, UK: Word4Word, 2007.

Journal:

Journal of Business Continuity & Emergency Planning. Online at: www.henrystewart.com/jbcep.aspx

Websites:

Continuity Central: www.continuitycentral.com
UK Cabinet Office on business continuity: tinyurl.com/77z8rst

See Also:
★ Business Continuity Management: How to Prepare for the Worst (pp. 249–252)
★ Countering Supply Chain Risk (pp. 253–255)
✔ Creating a Risk Register (pp. 362–363)
✔ Identifying Your Continuity Needs (pp. 363–364)

Checklists

Appraising Investment Opportunities

DEFINITION

As a rule, one of the most critical decisions for any business is long-term investment. This investment can be the purchase of land, buildings, machinery, or other assets in the expectation of earning an income over and above the funds committed. Appraisals are performed to find out whether such investments will yield returns to an organization over a period of time. The appraisals look at the outflows and inflows of funds, the duration of the investment, the scale of risk attached, and the cost of acquiring the funds.

The critical questions in an investment appraisal are:

- What is the extent of the investment, and can the business meet the expense?
- How long will it take to pay back the investment?
- When will the investment start to yield returns?
- What is the return on the investment?
- Would the money be better employed elsewhere?

The methods used when conducting an investment appraisal are:

- Payback: The amount of time needed to repay the initial investment.
- Average rate of return: The profits from an investment as a percentage of the initial capital cost.
- Net present value: Uses opportunity cost (i.e. the cost of an alternative choice when making a decision that must be given up in order to follow a certain action) to put a value on cash inflows from the capital invested.
- Internal rate of return: The annual percentage return on an investment when the sum of the discounted cash inflows over the life of the investment is equal to the sum of the capital invested.

ADVANTAGES

- Investment appraisals allow managers to make long-term plans on the projects that will yield the best returns for the business.
- Payback is easily understood and calculated.
- Average rate of return is easily understood and employs commonly used accounting rules.
- Net present value recognizes that a business incurs costs, such as interest on borrowing.
- Internal rate of return shows how well an investment will perform under different interest rates.

DISADVANTAGES

- The feasibility of the investment appraisal depends on many unknowns, for example the viability of information, financial analysis, and the management skills on which the project is based.
- Payback does not take into account optimal payback time or the effect on profitability.
- Average rate of return does not take into account the duration of the investment or the timing of cash flows.
- Net present value is sensitive to the discount rate applied.
- Management may focus on maximizing the internal rate of return and not net present value.

ACTION CHECKLIST

✔ Identify the key investment objectives for the organization and plan around those objectives.

✔ Have realistic in-depth budgets been calculated?

✔ Will rapid technological change make plant and machinery obsolete sooner and, therefore, will the payback period need to be shortened?

✔ Are resources invested in the most profitable objectives, and what alternatives are available?

✔ Has a risk analysis been carried out on the project to take into account risks and their impact?

DOS AND DON'TS
DO

- Take into account the duration and timing of cash flows.
- Consider how emerging risks necessitate regular reviews, and how risks such as new technology might affect the long-term viability of the project.
- Involve key stakeholders in an investment appraisal.
- Consider seeking the help of specialist consultants.

Don't

- Don't make the mistake of being attracted to a project that has not been thoroughly investigated and appraised.
- Don't take risks for granted; although a risk may have been the same in the past, there is no guarantee that it will be the same in the future.

MORE INFO
Books:

Langdon, Ken. *Investment Appraisal*. Oxford: Capstone, 2002.
McLaney, Eddie. *Business Finance: Theory and Practice*. 9th ed. Harlow, UK: Pearson Education, 2011.
Pettinger, Richard. *Investment Appraisal: A Managerial Approach*. Basingstoke, UK: Palgrave Macmillan, 2000.

Websites:

International Federation of Accountants (IFAC): www.ifac.org
Institute of Internal Auditors (IIA): www.theiia.org

See Also:

★ Best-Practice Working Capital Management: Techniques for Optimizing Inventories, Receivables, and Payables (pp. 2–6)
★ Capital Budgeting: The Dominance of Net Present Value (pp. 12–16)
★ Using Decision Analysis to Value R&D Projects (pp. 282–287)
✔ Understanding the Relationship between the Discount Rate and Risk (pp. 308–309)

Assessing Business Performance

DEFINITION
Regular assessments of business performance are vital. It is easy to lose direction and focus only on the day-to-day development of your business. Longer-term and more strategic planning is necessary to get the most out of your business and market opportunities.

Companies need to:
- Review their activities and reevaluate the products that they make or the services they provide. Why are these products or services successful? Are they priced correctly? What could be improved? Is there a market for new or complementary products or services?
- Assess business efficiency. How do you compare with the competition? Are your IT systems adequate? How flexible are your structures? How well do you address customers' needs? Do you have in place an appraisal system for investment opportunities?
- Assess staff. Do you have a high turnover of staff? Are they motivated? Are their skills adequate, or do they need retraining?
- Redefine goals. Where is the business now, where is it going, and how is it going to get there?
- Companies should review their financial statements to help assess their performance:
- The profit and loss statement tells the company whether it is making a profit, as it indicates how revenue is transformed into net income.
- The balance sheet shows assets, liabilities, and shareholders' equity/capital.
- The cash flow forecast or statement identifies the sources and amounts of cash coming into and going out of a business over a given period.

Another way to assess a company's performance is to employ ratio analysis, which uses a combination of financial and/or operating data as a basis for making comparisons with other companies:
- Liquidity ratios give a measure of how readily a company can meet its obligations.
- Profitability ratios give an indication of the earnings and profitability potential of a company.
- Asset management ratios gauge how efficiently a company can change assets into sales.
- Debt management ratios indicate how debt-leveraged a company is, and how it can manage the debt in terms of assets and operating income.
- Dividend/market value ratios measure how well a company uses its assets to generate earnings.
- Profitability ratios indicate earnings and potential profitability.

ADVANTAGES
- Regularly assessing business performance allows for longer-term and more strategic planning, which is necessary to optimize business and market opportunities.
- Ratio analysis permits analysts to read between the lines of financial statements and identify a company's strengths and weaknesses.
- Financial ratios provide lead indications of potential problem areas and allow corrective measures to be taken.

DISADVANTAGES
- Profit and loss statements do not report factors that might be highly relevant but cannot be reliably measured (for example, brand recognition and customer loyalty).
- A balance sheet shows a snapshot of a company's assets, liabilities, and shareholders' equity. It does not show the flows into and out of the accounts during the period.
- Financial ratios are based on past performance; they cannot take into account future events.

ACTION CHECKLIST
✔ What direction should the company take over the next three to five years?

✔ What are the company's markets, and how should it compete?

✔ How can the company gain market advantage and compete better in the future?

✔ What resources will be needed in assets, finance, staff, etc.?

✔ Obtain as much information and compare as many ratios as you can when assessing a business's performance.

DOS AND DON'TS
DO
- Determine whether ratios were calculated before or after adjustments were made to the balance sheet or income statement, such as nonrecurring items and inventory or pro-forma adjustments. In many cases, these adjustments can significantly affect the ratios.

Don't
- Don't rely solely on ratios when taking decisions. Use market research to confirm the results.
- Don't fall into the trap of thinking that financial ratios are infallible.

MORE INFO
Books:
Porter, Les, and Steven Tanner. *Assessing Business Excellence*. 2nd ed. Oxford: Butterworth-Heinemann, 2004.

Checklists

Young, Peter C., and Steven C. Tippins. *Managing Business Risk: An Organization-Wide Approach to Risk Management*. New York: AMACOM, 2000.

Websites:
JIT Software: www.jit-software.com
Value Based Management.net:
www.valuebasedmanagement.net

See Also:
★ Using Financial Analysis to Evaluate Strategy (pp. 287–290)
✔ Preparing Financial Statements: Balance Sheets (pp. 320–321)
✔ Preparing Financial Statements: Profit and Loss Accounts (P&Ls) (pp. 321–322)
✔ What Is Benchmarking? (pp. 369–370)

Checklists

Assessing the Value of Outsourcing and Offshoring

DEFINITION

The increasingly competitive global business environment and the pace of technological innovation over the last decade have had huge ramifications for the way companies operate. As national borders have shed some of their significance in commercial terms, companies have sought out new ways to focus on their core strengths while seeking to delegate other activities to external parties with specialist expertise in particular fields. Thus, companies with a competitive edge in design could, for example, outsource their manufacturing to a contractor, while other businesses focusing on sectors such as mobile telecoms may choose to outsource their billing and call-centre operations to a specialist third party. However, companies must recognize that, as customers will judge *them*—rather than the outsourcing specialist—by the overall experience they have in buying and using their products, they must ensure that the outsourced services meet the standards expected by customers, or the reputation of the company will suffer.

The increased use of offshoring—the transfer of business processes abroad—over recent years has been further driven by rapid advances in data networking and storage technology. Rather than simply outsource services to specialists in the same country, many companies have seized on opportunities to offshore support services to countries such as India and China, taking advantage of the availability of labor capable of doing the work to the required standard. In most instances, the primary incentive for offshoring is cost, given that the average wage in many developing countries is considerably lower than that demanded by Western employees. However, specialists in the provision of offshoring services claim that using overseas suppliers brings companies other benefits, such as a sharper focus on core activities, better operational efficiency, and improved cultural awareness.

Nevertheless, while offshoring can bring many benefits, the use of overseas external service providers entails some risks. Fraudsters have been quick to investigate opportunities of their own, recognizing that they too can take advantage of cost savings by attempting to bribe employees who have access to secure data, including customer account details. Companies that fall victim to such fraud can run the risk of considerable damage to their reputation and loss of customer confidence.

ADVANTAGES

- Outsourcing and offshoring can bring significant cost benefits.
- Using high-quality specialist external providers can allow companies to capitalize on their strengths and, indirectly, help to improve customers' experiences.
- The use of outsourcing and offshoring can free local employees to focus on strategic planning and other activities.
- External providers can help a company's competitiveness by delivering greater flexibility and responsiveness than would be available in-house.

DISADVANTAGES

- Some in-house employees—even those involved in core activities—could see the use of external specialists as the "thin end of the wedge," taking the view that ultimately their own roles could be outsourced. This could impact on their morale, leading to poor performance.
- Should an external supplier fail to deliver, it is the client company's reputation that stands to suffer most.
- Outsourcing and offshoring can raise control and data security issues.

ACTION CHECKLIST

✔ Choose your service suppliers with care, performing adequate checks on their capabilities and conducting due diligence as required.

✔ Do not select partners purely on the basis of price; consider a range of factors including their experience, track record, financial stability, and the robustness of the company's technology and equipment.

✔ Consider the strength of the local infrastructure—including communications, security, and the availability of resources—when assessing whether to offshore production facilities to a particular overseas location.

✔ Be open with your own employees about the logic behind using external specialists for non-core services.

✔ Whenever possible, test external providers' capabilities with limited trials before increasing your reliance on them.

✔ Ensure that procedures are in place to monitor customer satisfaction levels as external suppliers are introduced, particularly where customers have direct exposure to third-party service providers.

DOS AND DON'TS
DO
- Consider how offshoring production to rapidly developing countries such as China and India could improve your ability to service rising demand in local markets as the spending power of domestic consumers in emerging markets grows.
- Discuss your needs with specialist intermediary consulting companies with direct experience in managing offshore outsourcing. Though this adds to costs, paying for sound advice can prove considerably less expensive than the impact of a poor choice of external provider. Remember that specialist consultants can advise on which activities are most suitable for outsourcing as well as the best choice of external supplier.

Don't
- Don't see outsourcing and offshoring as exclusively cost-cutting exercises.
- Don't expect the decision to offshore to deliver a constant level of benefits. For example, recognize that higher wage

inflation for skilled specialists in developing countries is likely to narrow the gap between salaries in developed and developing economies.

MORE INFO
Books:
Kehal, Harbhajan S., and Varinder P. Singh. *Outsourcing and Offshoring in the 21st Century: A Socio-Economic Perspective*. Hershey, PA: Idea Group, 2006.
Plunkett, Jack W. *Plunkett's Outsourcing & Offshoring Industry Almanac*. Houston, TX: Plunkett Research, 2010.

Articles:
Farrell, Diana. "Offshoring: Value creation through economic change." *Journal of Management Studies* 42:3 (May 2005): 675–683. Online at: dx.doi.org/10.1111/j.1467-6486.2005.00513.x
Harland, Christine, Louise Knight, Richard Lamming, and Helen Walker. "Outsourcing: Assessing the risks and benefits for organisations, sectors and nations." *International Journal of Operations and Production Management* 25:9 (2005): 831–850. Online at: dx.doi.org/10.1108/01443570510613929

Website:
McKinsey Quarterly on outsourcing: www.mckinseyquarterly.com/Operations/Outsourcing

See Also:
★ Aligning Structure with Strategy: Recalibrating for Improved Performance and Increased Profitability (pp. 246–249)
★ Reducing Costs through Production and Supply Chain Management (pp. 276–279)
✔ Assessing Business Performance (pp. 359–360)

Basic Steps for Starting a Business

DEFINITION
You think you have a winning idea that's going to make you a fortune. But before you jump in head first, you should carry out some research to see whether your idea really is feasible. That means finding out who your competitors will be and whether there is an opening in the market for your product or service. Do you have the necessary skills to run the business? Gathering and analyzing this information will help you formulate your business plan and goals.

Your initial research should focus on these key questions:
- Is your idea feasible?
- Do you have the financial capacity to carry out the project?
- Is there a market for your product or service?
- How will you protect your idea?
- Who are your competitors, and what differentiates your product from theirs?

Once you have answered these questions satisfactorily, you should draw up a business plan. Most financial institutions provide business plan templates. Alternatively, you could use an off-the-shelf computer program. Your plan should contain:
- a summary describing the elements of your business;
- a description of your business concept;
- an analysis of your business within the market in order to decide how and where your company or products or services fit;
- strategies and goals for the market, and for overcoming the competition you face;
- an outline of how your products or services match your strategies and goals;
- information on how you will market your products;
- an estimate of your sales forecasts;
- what type of financing you will need, who will provide it, and at what cost.

Researching and writing your business plan may seem like a colossal task, but with thorough preparation you will have all the relevant information available and evaluated before you open your doors. As you go through the planning process, you will develop your knowledge and understanding of the proposed business, improve your chances of success, and reduce your risk of failure as a start-up owner. In short, you will be ready to run your business and equipped to compete.

First impressions count, and an accurate, easy-to-read, and well-organized text will convey professionalism and credibility. Have your figures checked by an accountant and the text proofread.

Naming your business accurately is important. Word play might be clever or funny, but it could add to the difficulty customers have in remembering and finding you. It's also tempting to abbreviate your business name to make communications and correspondence easier, but an acronym doesn't say what you do. The general rule is: Keep it simple and try to describe what you do.

ADVANTAGES

- Starting a business allows you to be your own boss and lets you make the decisions that shape your success.
- You get to choose how long and how hard you work.
- The owner receives all the profits, meaning that all earnings go to the sole proprietor.
- If the business is successful, you may be able to reap a tidy sum on retirement by selling the business at a profit.

DISADVANTAGES

- All the responsibility falls on your shoulders. Good or bad, you have to take decisions that may affect the livelihood of your family and employees.
- If you incur debts of any sort, you may have to repay them out of your personal income and assets.
- You may find it difficult to go on vacation or be absent from work for long.

ACTION CHECKLIST

✔ First, do some basic research to see whether your idea really is feasible. Ask yourself whether you have the financial capacity to carry out the project. Is there a market for your product or service, and how will you protect your idea? Who are your competitors, and what distinguishes your product

from theirs? If the answers are positive, start to build a detailed business plan.

✔ Second, ask yourself whether you are made of the right stuff to run your own business. Do you have the character, temperament, drive, and staying power?

DOS AND DON'TS
DO

- Take the time to draw up an effective business plan. It might take a month or two, but it will not only help you assess your business idea, it will also tell you whether you are ready and able to carry it out.

Don't

- Don't use your savings to set up in business without researching and evaluating your ideas. Many chambers of commerce have successful retired business people who will be happy to give you advice on a volunteer basis.

MORE INFO
Books:

Adams, Bob. *Adams Streetwise Small Business Start-Up: Your Comprehensive Guide to Starting and Managing a Business*. Holbrook, MA: Adams Media, 2002.

Kennedy, Joe. *The Small Business Owner's Manual: Everything You Need to Know to Start Up and Run Your Business*. Franklin Lakes, NJ: Career Press, 2005.

The Ultimate Small Business Guide: A Resource for Startups and Growing Businesses. London: Bloomsbury Publishing, 2004.

Websites:

Canada Business: www.canadabusiness.ca/eng/
US Small Business Administration: www.sba.gov

See Also:

★ Assessing Venture Capital Funding for Small and Medium-Sized Enterprises (pp. 114–117)
✔ Assessing Cash Flow and Bank Lending Requirements (pp. 292–293)
✔ Steps for Obtaining Bank Financing (pp. 333–334)

Creating a Risk Register

DEFINITION

A risk register, also sometimes called a "risk log," is usually used when planning for the future. Future plans may include project plans, organizational plans, or financial plans. Risk registers are used in the area of risk management.

Risk management is a method of managing risks or uncertainty relating to a perceived threat. Risk management

will usually involve having strategies in place to deal with risks, whether by avoiding the risk, transferring it elsewhere, reducing its effect, or dealing with the consequences. Financial risk management deals with risks that can be managed using traded financial instruments.

Risk management uses risk registers to identify, analyze, and manage risks in a clear, concise way. A risk register usually takes the form of a table—however long or wide that may end up being.

A risk is an event that, if it occurred, would have an adverse (or positive) impact on a project, investment, or similar. The risk register contains information on each risk that is identified. One of the main skills in risk management is to successfully identify all possible risks. The risk register should contain, in summarized form, the planned response in the event that a risk materializes, as well as a summary of what actions should be taken beforehand to reduce a particular risk. Much financial legislation, such as Basel II, also impels organizations to take steps to reduce risk. Risks are often ranked in order of likelihood, or of their impact. The risk register lists the analysis and evaluation of the risks that have been identified.

ADVANTAGES
- A risk register can identify and make provision for dealing with risks, enabling an organization to save millions if things go wrong.
- Should a risk materialize, there is already a set list of actions to run through immediately to start minimizing the consequences.
- An organization can have the confidence to press on with a project or investment knowing that procedures to deal with any risks arising have been put in place.

DISADVANTAGES
- Much time, effort, and money can be spent on creating risk registers to deal with events that will never occur.

ACTION CHECKLIST
✔ Establish a risk management team. The team should meet regularly to discuss the risks associated with each project, investment, etc., to review procedures, and to ensure that the risk register is kept up to date. Appoint a team member to keep abreast of any legislative requirements that may affect the risk register.

✔ Identify and list all potential risks, and decide on the likelihood of their occurrence. Determine the expected impact if they do occur. Identify any interdependencies with other risks and what knock-on effects there may be.

✔ Decide who will bear the risk.

✔ Identify countermeasures to mitigate the risk before it occurs.

✔ Keep track on the risk register of the current status of any risk that has occurred and what action is being taken.

DOS AND DON'TS
DO
- Create a risk register for each new project or investment.
- List each risk as a separate entry in the register's table.
- Identify an "owner" for each risk, i.e. a person who will be in charge of resolving the risk.
- Follow up on actions and status for each risk identified.
- Revisit the risk register regularly to evaluate any changes to the likelihood of a risk and its potential impact. Changes to projects and investments should also be evaluated for their effect on previously assessed risks or new risks that may arise.

Don't
- Don't ignore the possibility of risks becoming a reality.
- Don't lose track of the risk register.

MORE INFO
Books:
Ackermann, Fran. *Systemic Risk Assessment: A Case Study*. Management Science Theory Method and Practice Series. Glasgow, UK: Department of Management Science, University of Strathclyde, 2003.
Bateman, Mike. *Tolley's Practical Risk Assessment Handbook*. 5th ed. Boston, MA: Elsevier, 2006.
Brinded, Malcolm. *Perception vs Analysis: How to Handle Risk*. Eighth Annual Royal Academy of Engineering Lloyd's Register Lecture. London: Royal Academy of Engineering, 2000.

Journal:
Risk Management. Published quarterly by Palgrave Macmillan. Online at: www.palgrave-journals.com/rm

Website:
Institute of Risk Management (UK): www.theirm.org

See Also:
★ Countering Supply Chain Risk (pp. 253–255)
★ Quantifying Corporate Financial Risk (pp. 45–48)
★ Understanding Reputation Risk and Its Importance (pp. 279–282)
✔ Establishing a Framework for Assessing Risk (p. 313)
✔ Understanding and Calculating the Total Cost of Risk (pp. 304–305)

Identifying Your Continuity Needs

DEFINITION
In order for a company to be prepared to recover from the impact of a disaster such as a fire, flood, or explosion, it has to identify its key functions and the risks that are faced. Critical activities and resources can be identified through a business impact analysis (BIA), while a concurrent risk assessment will aid recognition of threats.

The aim of analysis is to create two types of plan, which may overlap. An incident management plan covers the initial impact, including procedures such as evacuation. The longer-term business continuity plan prepares an organization to keep delivering key products and services afterwards.

Plans have to be tested to ensure that they work. Staff also have to be trained in the procedures. The frequency of planning exercises depends on the speed of change within an organization and the outcome of previous drills where weaknesses have been identified.

The British Standards Institution (BSI) has developed a standard BS 25999 "Business continuity." In North America the equivalent is the National Fire Protection Association's NFPA 1600 "Standard on disaster/emergency management and business continuity programs." Globally, the International Organization for Standardization (ISO) has published the ISO/PAS 22399:2007 "Guideline for incident preparedness and operational continuity management."

ADVANTAGES
- Having a continuity plan in place gives peace of mind. You may never need it, but it's there if the worst happens.

DISADVANTAGES
- Failing to prepare for disaster could result in serious financial loss or even bankruptcy if there is a major incident.

ACTION CHECKLIST
1. Undertake a business impact analysis
- Identify the products and services that will suffer the greatest impact as a result of disruption.
- Break the results down to analyze the impact on output from disruptions lasting 24 hours, up to two days, up to a week, and up to two weeks.
- Identify the so-called "maximum period of tolerable disruption" of service and product delivery that the organization can cope with before its viability is threatened.
- Set a recovery time for each of the key products and services, allowing for unforeseen difficulties.
- Create a document listing the activities required to deliver the key products and services.
- Ensure that the necessary resources are allocated to meet the requirements.

2. Carry out a risk assessment
- Identify the risks to the organization, including loss of staff, key suppliers, utilities, access to premises, IT, and telecommunications systems.
- Establish the likelihood of each risk.
- List existing arrangements for dealing with the risks.
- List arrangements that should be put in place to deal with the risks.
- Assign a likelihood score to each risk.

3. Decide what action the organization should take for each of the identified risks; for example:
- Deal with the risk by planning to continue service and product delivery at an acceptable minimum level.
- Tolerate the risk if the cost of its reduction outweighs the potential benefits.
- Transfer the risk to a third party or take out insurance.

- Terminate the activity. In some circumstances, particularly where an item is time-sensitive, it may be appropriate to suspend delivery.

4. Develop, publish, and circulate plans
- Establish an overall plan then decide how many plans are required within that. This will depend on the size and scope of the organization.
- State the purpose and scope of each plan.
- Identify who owns each plan and is responsible for its maintenance.
- List the individuals and their roles within the plan.
- Describe the circumstances, methods, and who is responsible for invoking the overall plan and its individual components.
- List appropriate contact details.
- For the initial response to an incident, list the tasks, responsibilities, and methods by which they are to be communicated.
- For business continuity, outline critical activities, the process by which they are to be recovered, and the timescale.

5. Test, maintain, and review plans
- Parts of the plan can and should be tested, such as back-up power, contact lists, and the process of activation.
- Staff should be brought together for training to discuss plans and identify weaknesses.
- Scenario-based desktop exercises can be used to validate plans and train key staff.
- Live exercises can cover one aspect of a plan, such as evacuation, or to test a full plan.

MORE INFO
Reports:

British Standards Institution (BSI). "Business continuity." BS 25999. November 2006/November 2007. Online at: tinyurl.com/qnvdas

International Organization for Standardization (ISO). "Societal security—Guideline for incident preparedness and operational continuity management." ISO/PAS 22399:2007. November 2007. Online at: www.iso.org/iso/catalogue_detail?csnumber=50295

National Fire Protection Association (NFPA). "Standard on disaster/emergency management and business continuity programs." NFPA 1600. 2010. Online at: tinyurl.com/3gpxeze

Websites:

UK Government business continuity guidance: tinyurl.com/c6cgkt

US Federal Emergency Management Agency on business recovery planning: www.fema.gov/business/

See Also:

★ Business Continuity Management: How to Prepare for the Worst (pp. 249–252)

✔ Applying Stress-Testing to Business Continuity Management (p. 357)

Managing Bankruptcy and Insolvency

DEFINITION

An insolvent company is one that cannot pay its debts. Cash flow insolvency is the inability to pay debts as they fall due, while balance sheet insolvency occurs when a company has negative net assets and its liabilities exceed the assets. A company can be cash flow insolvent but balance sheet solvent if its assets are illiquid, particularly against short-term debt. Conversely, a company could have negative net assets on the balance sheet but still be cash flow solvent if income can meet debt obligations. Bankruptcy (liquidation in the United Kingdom) occurs when a court rules that a company is unable to pay its creditors. Creditors can force bankruptcy by filing a suit in court against the company in debt, but more usually a company will initiate bankruptcy proceedings itself.

Insolvency law around the world varies, but is generally aimed at protecting creditors' interests and keeping a business afloat. As companies generally want to avoid bankruptcy, the usual practice today is for an insolvent company to file for "bankruptcy protection" (in the United Kingdom, the equivalent is for the company to go into what is called "administration"). An administrator can be appointed by the company directors, or creditors can ask a court to appoint one (without petitioning for bankruptcy). The administrator's job is rescue the business and maintain it as a going concern. To this end, administrators work to restructure the business and its debts in order to pay off creditors and ensure the company emerges in good financial health for the future.

Bankruptcy may follow insolvency, but can also be initiated without going into administration. Bankruptcy laws vary enormously around the world, but all legislation has the aim of winding up the company and paying off creditors. Receivers are appointed by the court to manage this process. The largest creditors will have priority as the debts, or portions of them, are cleared. Some—particularly customers who bought goods but never received them—may never see their money again.

ADVANTAGES

- Appointing administrators is often the smartest option for an insolvent company, as it keeps the company trading and encourages managers to face up to the challenges of learning from their previous errors.
- Bankruptcy may be the best option for a smaller company if its debts are too big to be managed by administration, although there are downsides (see below).

DISADVANTAGES

- Public knowledge of financial problems can cause reputational damage to an insolvent company, possibly hampering the restructuring process and causing customers to decline to do business.
- In many jurisdictions, company directors are banned from running a business for a set period of time if they are involved in a bankruptcy. In some jurisdictions, company directors may be forced to surrender personal assets to clear company debts.
- In some jurisdictions, being made bankrupt can make it very difficult for a company owner to start a new business in the future.

ACTION CHECKLIST

✔ If you need to appoint administrators, choose a firm that has a strong track record in turning ailing businesses around.

✔ It may be worth asking a different firm of accountants to give a second opinion on the company's books to see if there is any other way forward.

DOS AND DON'TS
DO
- Weigh up all the options before embarking on any course of action.
- Take appropriate advice, including consulting your bank and other financial advisers.

Don't
- Don't rush into making a decision to go bankrupt as other options may be better.
- Don't forget that bankruptcy fraud (concealment of assets, concealment or destruction of documents, making false statements, etc) is a crime.

MORE INFO
Books:
Gilson, Stuart C. *Creating Value through Corporate Restructuring: Case Studies in Bankruptcies, Buyouts and Breakups*. New York: Wiley, 2001.
Hunter, Muir. *Going Bust?: How to Resist and Survive Bankruptcy and Winding Up*. St Albans, UK: XPL Publishing 2007.
Marsh, David, and Roger Sproston. *Bankruptcy Insolvency and the Law: A Straightforward Guide*. 6th ed. Brighton, UK: Straightforward Publishing, 2010.

See Also:
★ Optimizing the Capital Structure: Finding the Right Balance between Debt and Equity (pp. 145–148)
✔ Identifying Your Continuity Needs (pp. 363–364)

Nonperformance and Breach of Contract

DEFINITION

A contract is a legally binding agreement between two or more parties. In certain circumstances, a party may not perform its obligations under the contract or may fail to fulfill other terms of the contract. This constitutes a breach of contract, which, if not remedied, can give the other party the right to claim damages.

Contracts can be written or oral and have expressed terms or implied terms. Written contracts are easier to prove than oral contracts.

If a contract has been breached, the party that has been affected by the breach may be entitled, in certain circumstances, to compensation. In general, a party will only be entitled to compensation by way of damages if it can prove that it has suffered a clear financial loss. There is no compensation for distress or hurt feelings.

The person claiming that the contract has been breached (the claimant) has the onus to prove his/her claim. Claims must be well documented and justified.

The courts take the view that a claim is not a means of turning a loss into a profit. The aim is to put the claimant back in the position in which he or she would have been if a certain event had not occurred. The claimant must show that he/she suffered an actual loss caused by the breach, that the loss is not too remote and is recognized as giving rise to entitlement to compensation, and that there is enough evidence that justifies the damages demanded. In certain circumstances and jurisdictions, such as the United States, the courts can force the breaching party to make a payment as a punishment for the breach of contract. These payments are known as punitive damages.

Damages might not be the only remedy sought by the claimant or awarded by the courts. It may be that the court will oblige the party that has breached to specifically perform and execute the contract.

A party that has either breached a contract or suffered a breach should communicate immediately with the other party to explain or discover why the breach has occurred. In many cases, keeping the lines of communication open can prevent the expense and stress of a court action. There are other ways of dealing with a dispute, such as mediation or conciliation, before a court action is considered.

If all such attempts fail, then, as a last resort, a party can sue for breach of contract and damages.

ADVANTAGES

- Contracts are entered into for all sorts of reasons. Respecting the terms of contracts will ensure the smooth running of a business and will help to create a good reputation for a business or individual.

DISADVANTAGES

- Nonperformance and breach of contract can have severe consequences for the reputation of a business or individual. In certain circumstances, a court decision against an individual or business can negatively influence their credit rating.
- The damages awarded for breach of contract, as well as the litigation itself, can be costly.
- Oral contracts are difficult to prove.

ACTION CHECKLIST

✔ Study carefully any contract you might enter into. Read the contract's terms and conditions, and ensure that you understand them before you commit.

✔ If the terms and conditions offered are not suitable or are too onerous, you may be able to change them through negotiation.

✔ Economize by negotiating a reasonable rate with your legal advisers, but remember that it is better to incur costs by obtaining legal advice than to enter into a contract with terms that you do not understand.

✔ If you are a consumer, obtain information and advice from relevant consumer protection bodies before entering into a contract.

DOS AND DON'TS
DO
- Read carefully the terms and conditions of any contract.
- If necessary, involve your solicitors in the evaluation of both the risks and potential benefits of entering into a particular contract.
- Negotiate your terms and make a contingency plan for any cost overrun.
- Remember that a claim is not a way of turning a loss into a profit.

Don't
- Don't make the mistake of being attracted by a contract with terms you do not understand.
- Don't enter into a contract if you do not intend to respect its terms.
- Don't think that you can automatically obtain damages if a contract is breached by the other party.
- Don't overlook the importance of negotiating warranties and indemnities that would protect you in the event that underlying liabilities in the contract are discovered.

MORE INFO
Books:

Blum, Brian A. *Contracts: Examples and Explanations.* 5th ed. New York: Aspen Publishers, 2010.
Farnsworth, E. Allan. *Contracts.* 4th ed. Aspen Student Treatise Series. New York: Aspen Publishers, 2004.

Articles:
Pearce, David, and Roger Halson. "Damages for breach of contract: Compensation, restitution and vindication." *Oxford Journal of Legal Studies* 28:1 (Spring 2008): 73–98. Online at: dx.doi.org/10.1093/ojls/gqm023

Shavell, Steven. "Damage measures for breach of contract." *Bell Journal of Economics* 11:2 (Autumn 1980): 466–490. Online at: tinyurl.com/y9dlqnl

Website:
Attorney/client matching service: www.legalmatch.com

See Also:
★ Human Risk: How Effective Strategic Risk Management Can Identify Rogues (pp. 198–201)
✔ Assessing Business Performance (pp. 359–360)

Understanding Real Options

DEFINITION

Real options, sometimes also referred to as strategic options, are a tool that can be employed in capital budgeting analysis to help companies make better critical strategic decisions. As with financial market traded options, real options can be valued using pricing models. Real options give the holder the right but, importantly, not the obligation, to take a particular course of action. Real options are a mechanism by which a business can attempt to place an actual value on the choice of taking a particular option, and can play a valuable role in helping a company assess the financial implications of various strategic options. Real options are commonly used when dealing with the decision to initiate a new project or to abandon an existing project, depending on how, over time, actual events have differed from the original forecast. Used in conjunction with discounted cash flow techniques, real options provide businesses with a model as to how a certain course of action is likely to impact the business. Without the inclusion of real options, conventional discounted cash flow techniques can provide an incomplete assessment of the viability of a project, as they ignore the option to change course during the life of the project, perhaps taking a charge to abandon, delay, downscale, or even upscale the project.

Potential applications for real options as a decision-support model are many and varied. For example, an energy company may decide to proceed with a production operation if—and only if—the price of crude oil exceeds a level that makes the project commercially worthwhile. While standard discounted cash flow calculations may make the project appear risky and unattractive, the use of real options adds the ability to study the effects of changing course in return for a charge. This course could substantially increase the attractiveness of the venture, by factoring in the cost of the option of an effective escape from a completely negative outcome. Real options effectively make the project less risky by eliminating the "black or white" choice of one or the other. In this energy company example, real options might remove the risk of being stuck with the production costs for the life of the project, even if oil prices slipped to an unfavorable level. By attaching probability and costings on particular strategic options, the inclusion of real options can have significant impacts on expected net present value (NPV) calculations.

In addition to project viability analysis, real options can play an important role in applications such as process input options (for example, to help decide between various options in raw material sourcing), output mix options (for example, switching production from one product to another), production shutdown analysis, and output expansion options, as well project timing decision-making. The study of real options is an exciting, growing field of academic and business research, and the use of real options looks set to become a feature of mainstream business decision-making during the years ahead.

ADVANTAGES

- Real options are a powerful, flexible methodology, bringing together strategic planning with capital budgeting.
- The use of real options can give a business a significant strategic advantage, given their role in helping to identify the optimal timing for a project.
- The use of real options brings a dynamic element to the decision-making process, and can simulate this decision-making process throughout the project life cycle.
- Real options can help companies to avoid the potential pitfalls of pushing ahead with a new venture too early.

DISADVANTAGES

- Given that real options can be more conceptual than discounted cash flow techniques, real options can be more difficult to value with certainty.
- There is a view in some quarters that reliance on the use of real options exposes decision-making to managers' existing personal strategic biases.
- As with any methodology, calculations using real options rely on the quality and reliability of the input data.

ACTION CHECKLIST

✔ Maximize the full potential of the real options methodology by putting all possible strategic options into the mix, not just the obvious ones.

✔ Qualify the list to ensure that all strategic options are actually viable.

✔ Make use of conventional discounted cash flow techniques.

✔ Assign initial inputs for real options.

✔ Make use of options modeling software to derive pricing information.

Checklists

Checklists

DOS AND DON'TS

DO

- Utilize real options analysis alongside conventional techniques to demonstrate the full value of the model.
- As a project progresses, be prepared to refine/amend earlier numerical assumptions.
- Utilize NPV calculations to help verify your strategic analysis.

Don't

- Don't ignore the value of educating managers and staff about the basic concepts behind real options analysis.
- Don't interpret the results of calculations as "gospel" on which the entire future of a business should be staked.

MORE INFO

Book:

Mun, Johnathan. *Real Options Analysis: Tools and Techniques for Valuing Strategic Investments and Decisions.* 2nd ed. Hoboken, NJ: Wiley, 2006.

Articles:

Boyarchenko, Svetlana, and Sergei Levendorski. "Practical guide to real options in discrete time." *International Economic Review* 48:1 (February 2007): 311–342. Online at: dx.doi.org/10.1111/j.1468-2354.2007.00427.x

Tong, Tony W., and Jeffrey J. Reuer. "Real options in multinational corporations: Organizational challenges and risk implications." *Journal of International Business Studies* 38:2 (March 2007): 215–230. Online at: dx.doi.org/10.1057/palgrave.jibs.8400260

Website:

Real options software provider: www.realoptionsvaluation.com

See Also:

★ Capital Budgeting: The Dominance of Net Present Value (pp. 12–16)
★ Real Options: Opportunity from Risk (pp. 273–276)
★ Using Decision Analysis to Value R&D Projects (pp. 282–287)

Understanding Strategy Maps

DEFINITION

A strategy map, devised by Professors Robert S. Kaplan and David P. Norton, is a business management tool aimed at forging a strong link between a company's long-term strategies and its shorter-term operational activities. The concept of strategy mapping was originally developed by Kaplan and Norton in the "balanced scorecard," a means of assessing how successful a company is in terms of delivering on stated goals. While the basic notion of the balanced scorecard is "what you can't measure, you can't manage," further work aimed to help companies reassess their strategic goals. Kaplan and Norton subsequently shifted their focus to the principle of "what you can't measure, you can't describe" as a means to better utilize companies' intangible assets to help them achieve their objectives. The principle of strategic mapping of long-term strategy with shorter-term operational activities, previously merely one element of the balanced scorecard, was elevated to become a central strategy management tool.

Strategy maps aim to illustrate how a company links its macro strategy objectives with its key day-to-day operational elements from the four different perspectives: financial, customer, internal processes, and learning and growth. The financial element focuses primarily on enhancing the cost structure and utilizing assets towards greater productivity, while the customer element encourages companies to understand what sets them apart from their competitors. Though all elements of the strategy framework aim to improve areas such as attitudes to quality, service, partnerships, and company branding, the internal processes element aims to develop better product and service characteristics. Finally, the learning and growth element aims for companies to consider the skills and technologies that are needed to support the company's strategy. In all cases, the strategic mapping process seeks to engrain the appreciation of cause and effect. What can be improved on a "day-to-day level" is significant as, cumulatively, improvements can help improve a company's daily operational activities, helping it to achieve its longer-term strategic objectives. To better demonstrate the connections, the strategy map features a series of arrows linking objectives with individual operational activities.

ADVANTAGES

- Strategy mapping demonstrates to employees how seemingly minute improvements to operational activities can, cumulatively, contribute towards major efficiency and strategic objectives.
- Strategy mapping provides a clear, visual demonstration as to how short-term operational and medium- to long-term strategic objectives are closely aligned, helping to ensure greater "buy-in" from employees at all levels.
- Strategy mapping helps to demonstrate how a company's intangible assets can improve stockholder value.
- Strategy mapping provides a potential solution for managers unable to identify why certain strategies are not delivering tangible performance improvements.

DISADVANTAGES

- Strategy mapping requires "buy in" from individuals across all levels of the organization. If management fails to convince the workforce of the potential benefits of a successful medium- to long-term outcome, employees may feel disenfranchised from the potential benefits of improved corporate performance.

- Though strategic in its macro focus, strategy mapping is unlikely to deliver a single, massive leap forward in any single aspect. Rather, the considerable ultimate benefits of strategic mapping are often comprised of many, seemingly minor, single aspects.

ACTION CHECKLIST

✔ Ensure that everyone within the organization appreciates that strategy mapping is a technique which aims to align individuals' actions with the strategic objective.

✔ As improvements are likely to be incremental, ensure that the benefits are recognized and built on through an emphasis on the feedback/learning input.

DOS AND DON'TS

DO

- Aim to align personal performance improvement goals with those of the company.
- Base remuneration on goals related to improvements in the performance of the overall business. Setting individual performance objectives with related incentive payouts could be counterproductive if individuals shift their focus from delivering collective benefits to the pursuit of personal objectives.

Don't

- Don't expect giant and immediate leaps forward in terms of operational efficiency, finances or customer experiences. Strategic mapping is more likely to generate numerous, gradual, incremental improvements across the organization.

- Don't set remuneration based on individual targets. Agree only on personal performance goals when you are confident that achieving them will contribute to overall performance improvement across the business.

MORE INFO

Books:

Kaplan, Robert S., and David P. Norton. *Balanced Scorecard: Translating Strategy into Action*. Boston, MA: Harvard Business School Press, 1996.

Kaplan, Robert S., and David P. Norton. *Strategy Maps: Converting Intangible Assets into Tangible Outcomes*. Boston, MA: Harvard Business School Press, 2004.

Articles:

Irwin, D. "Strategy mapping in the public sector." *Long Range Planning* 35:6 (December 2002): 637–647. Online at: dx.doi.org/10.1016/S0024-6301(02)00158-9

Kaplan, Robert S., and David P. Norton "Having trouble with your strategy? Then map it." *Harvard Business Review* (September–October 2000). Online at: tinyurl.com/33zoowa

Scholey, Cam. "Strategy maps: A step-by-step guide to measuring, managing and communicating the plan." *Journal of Business Strategy* 26:3 (2005): 12–19. Online at: dx.doi.org/10.1108/02756660510597065

Website:

Balanced Scorecard Institute: www.balancedscorecard.org

See Also:

★ Using Financial Analysis to Evaluate Strategy (pp. 287–290)
✔ Assessing Business Performance (pp. 359–360)
✔ What Is Benchmarking? (pp. 369–370)

What Is Benchmarking?

DEFINITION

Benchmarking is a tool for analyzing an organization or company's processes and activities to see if they represent best practice. The aim of benchmarking is always to raise an organization's performance to the highest standard.

As the idea is to evaluate the outcome of specific activities, the comparisons do not have to be drawn from competitors. It may be possible to use generic benchmarks based on data from processes that are common across an industry, or functional benchmarks for processes that exist in many unrelated industries. Alternatively, internal benchmarking can compare common activities across the different divisions of an organization.

If it is felt that the most effective data will come from similar businesses, there are two possible approaches: collaborative benchmarking, which is when two or more companies share information on processes; and competitive benchmarking, where the performance of competitors is analyzed. The latter is frequently carried out by a third party.

It is not unusual for competing companies to share benchmarking data. It is not necessary to publish commercially sensitive information in order for a number of companies within an industry to benefit from improvements in efficiency.

The benchmarking information will come from a variety of sources, including interviews, surveys, and published data. Care has to be taken that not only is the information directly comparable, but also that it includes all the relevant areas. It is not uncommon for companies to become fixated on cost-cutting, for example, while ignoring customer care, perhaps because it is less easy to measure.

Once the results of a benchmarking exercise have been presented and agreed, the information can be used as a basis for changes that should improve the organization's processes. These can then provide a baseline for the next round.

ADVANTAGES

- Benchmarking can provide tangible and measurable improvements for an organization.
- It opens up organizations to different ways of operating.
- It provides an objective measure of the success of an organization's processes.
- It encourages focus on key areas for improvement.

DISADVANTAGES

- Benchmarking can be expensive and time-consuming.
- Comparisons may be inappropriate for some processes.
- It can give an organization the answers it wants to hear.
- Comparisons just show that one organization is different from another.
- It can just encourage a process of playing catch-up rather than innovation.

Checklists

ACTION CHECKLIST

1. Planning the benchmarking project

- First understand your own business before making comparisons with others.
- Look at the business units within your organization and identify their outputs.
- Decide which are the key processes to benchmark, ensuring that any improvements will be apparent to customers.

2. Select targets

- Look for processes in your own and other industries that match those of your own organization.
- Identify the organizations that are best in class for those processes by talking to customers, analysts, trade publications, and suppliers.

3. Decide methodology

- As there are so many types of process to be measured, information will come from a variety of sources, including structured interviews, surveys, and publicly available data.
- Make sure your analysis compares "apple with apples" and is as accurate as possible.

4. Collect data and analyze discrepancies

- Establish what is best practice for each benchmarked process.
- Compare the gaps between your organization's performance and those benchmarked processes.

5. Make improvements

- Modify processes to equal or raise your company's performance above that of the highest standard measured.

DOS AND DON'TS

DO

- Pick variables that are relatively easy to measure.
- Ensure that the processes being measured are directly comparable.
- Put sufficient human and financial resources into the project.
- Focus on variables that will respond to actions.
- Produce a succinct summary of benefits for senior management.

Don't

- Don't spread your net too wide by selecting unmanageable areas to research.
- Don't assume your competition's success is solely due to the differences you've measured.
- Don't forget about less easily measured areas such as customer satisfaction.

MORE INFO

Books:

McNair, Carol J., and Kathleen H. J. Leibfried. *Benchmarking: A Tool for Continuous Improvement*. New York: HarperBusiness, 1992.

Watson, Gregory H. *Strategic Benchmarking Reloaded with Six Sigma: Improving Your Company's Performance Using Global Best Practice*. Hoboken, NJ: Wiley, 2007.

Zairi, Mohamed. *Effective Management of Benchmarking Projects: Practical Guidelines & Examples of Best Practice*. Oxford: Butterworth-Heinemann, 1998.

Website:

Global Benchmarking Network:
www.globalbenchmarking.org

See Also:

✔ Assessing Business Performance (pp. 359–360)
✔ Assessing the Value of Outsourcing and Offshoring (pp. 360–361)

CALCULATIONS

AND

RATIOS

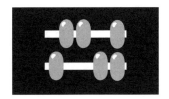

372 Accounts Receivable Turnover

One of several measures used to assess operating performance, accounts receivable turnover also helps in appraising a company's credit policy and its cash flow.

WHAT IT MEASURES

The number of times in each accounting period, typically a year, that a company converts credit sales into cash.

WHY IT IS IMPORTANT

A high turnover figure is desirable because it indicates that a company collects revenues effectively, and that its customers pay bills promptly. A high figure also suggests that a company's credit and collection policies are sound.

In addition, the measurement is a reasonably good indicator of cash flow, and of overall operating efficiency.

HOW IT WORKS IN PRACTICE

The formula for accounts receivable turnover is straightforward. Simply divide the average amount of receivables into annual credit sales:

$$\text{Receivables turnover} = \text{Sales} \div \text{Receivables}$$

If, for example, a company's sales are $4.5 million and its average receivables are $375,000, its receivables turnover is:

$$4,500,000 \div 375,000 = 12$$

TRICKS OF THE TRADE

- It is important to use the average amount of receivables over the period considered. Otherwise, receivables could be misleading for a company whose products are seasonal or are sold at irregular intervals.
- The measurement is also helpful to a company that is designing or revising credit terms.
- Accounts receivable turnover is among the measures that comprise asset utilization ratios, also called activity ratios.

MORE INFO

Book:
Salek, John G. *Accounts Receivable Management: Best Practices*. Hoboken, NJ: Wiley, 2005.

See Also:
Asset Utilization (pp. 375–376)

Alpha and Beta Values of a Security

Both alpha and beta are investment measures used to quantify risk and reward.

WHAT THEY MEASURE

A security's performance, adjusted for risk, compared to overall market behavior.

WHY THEY ARE IMPORTANT

Just as coaches would expect their most accomplished athletes to perform at a higher level than others, investors expect more from higher-risk investments. Alpha and beta give investors a quick indication of just how risky a stock or fund is.

Alpha is defined as "the return a security or a portfolio would be expected to earn if the market's rate of return were zero."

Beta is a means of measuring the volatility (or risk) of a stock or fund in comparison with the market as a whole. The beta of a stock or fund can be any value, positive or negative, but usually is between +0.25 and +1.75.

Alpha expresses the difference between the return expected from a stock or mutual fund, given its beta rating, and the return actually produced. A stock or fund that returns more than its beta would predict has a positive alpha, while one that returns less than the amount predicted by beta has a negative alpha. A large positive alpha indicates a strong performance, while a large negative alpha indicates a dismal performance.

HOW THEY WORK IN PRACTICE

To begin with, the market itself is assigned a beta of 1.0. If a stock or fund has a beta of 1.2, this means its price is likely to rise or fall by 12% when the overall market rises or falls by 10%; a beta of 0.7 means the stock or fund price is likely to move up or down at 70% of the level of the market change.

In practice, an alpha of 0.4% means the stock or fund in question outperformed the market-based return estimate by 0.4%. An alpha of − 0.6% means the return was 0.6% less than would have been predicted from the change in the market alone.

Both alpha and beta should be readily available on request from investment firms, because the figures appear in standard performance reports. It is always best to ask for them, because calculating a stock's alpha rating requires first knowing a stock's beta rating, and calculating beta is a challenge! It is based on linear regression analysis, the week-to-week percentage changes in the given stock's price, and the corresponding week-to-week percentage price change in a market index, over a given period of time, often 24 to 36 months. In short, beta calculations can involve mathematical complexities.

If it's any consolation, calculating alpha is far less taxing, provided the requisite data are available. The formula is:

$$\text{Alpha} = \text{Actual return} - \text{Risk-free return} - \text{Beta} \\ \times (\text{Index return} - \text{Risk-free return})$$

If a mutual fund with a beta rating of 1.1 returned 35%, while its benchmark index returned 30%, and a US Treasury bill returned 4% (T-bill returns are usually used as the "risk-free investment"), then the fund's alpha would equal 2.4%, based on the formula:

$$35\% - 4\% - 1.1 \times (30\% - 4\%) = 31\% - 1.1 \times 26\%$$
$$= 31\% - 28.6\%$$
$$= 2.4\%$$

TRICKS OF THE TRADE

- The underlying rationale for both alpha and beta is that the return of a stock or mutual fund should at least exceed that of a "risk-free" investment such as a US Treasury bill.
- Stocks of many utilities have a beta of less than 1. Conversely, most high-tech, NASDAQ-based stocks have a beta greater than 1; they offer a higher rate of return but are also risky.

- Alpha is often used to assess the performance of a portfolio manager. However, a low alpha score doesn't necessarily reflect poor performance by a fund manager, any more than a high alpha score means that a manager's performance is outstanding. At times, factors beyond a manager's control affect alpha values.

MORE INFO

Reports:

Schwab Performance Technologies. "Troubleshooting an incorrect alpha." September 24, 2007. Online at: schwabpt.com/downloads/docs/pdflibrary/spt010543.pdf

Schwab Performance Technologies. "Troubleshooting an incorrect beta." September 24, 2007. Online at: schwabpt.com/downloads/docs/pdflibrary/spt010480.pdf

Amortization

Amortization is often regarded as being the same as depreciation, but although the two accounting practices can be difficult to distinguish, there are differences between them. Amortization is also used in connection with loans, although that is not the primary focus here.

WHAT IT MEASURES

Amortization is a method of recovering (deducting or writing off) the capital costs of intangible assets over a fixed period of time. Its calculation is virtually identical to the straight-line method of depreciation.

Amortization also refers to the establishment of a schedule for repaying the principal and interest on a loan in equal amounts over a period of time. Because computers have made this a simple calculation, business references to amortization tend to focus more on the term's first definition.

WHY IT IS IMPORTANT

Amortization enables a company to identify its true costs, and thus its net income, more precisely. In the course of their business, most enterprises acquire intangible assets such as a patent for an invention, or a well-known brand or trademark. Since these assets can contribute to the revenue growth of the business, they can be—and are allowed to be—deducted against those future revenues over a period of years, provided the procedure conforms to accepted accounting practices.

For tax purposes, the distinction is not always made between amortization and depreciation, yet amortization remains a viable financial accounting concept in its own right.

HOW IT WORKS IN PRACTICE

Amortization is computed using the straight-line method of depreciation: divide the initial cost of the intangible asset by the estimated useful life of that asset. For example, if it costs

$10,000 to acquire a patent and it has an estimated useful life of 10 years, the amortized amount per year is $1,000.

$$10,000 \div 10 = \$1,000 \text{ per year}$$

The amount of amortization accumulated since the asset was acquired appears on the organization's balance sheet as a deduction under the amortized asset.

While that formula is straightforward, amortization can also incorporate a variety of noncash charges to net earnings and/or asset values, such as depletion, write-offs, prepaid expenses, and deferred charges. Accordingly, there are many rules to regulate how these charges appear on financial statements. The rules are different in each country, and are occasionally changed, so it is necessary to stay abreast of them and rely on expert advice.

For financial reporting purposes, an intangible asset is amortized over a period of years. The amortizable life—"useful life"—of an intangible asset is the period over which it gives economic benefit. Several factors are considered when determining this useful life; for example, demand and competition, effects of obsolescence, legal or contractual limitations, renewal provisions, and service life expectations.

Intangibles that can be amortized include:

- **Copyrights**, based on the amount paid either to purchase them or to develop them internally, plus the costs incurred in producing the work (wages or materials, for example). At present, a copyright is granted for the life of the author plus 70 years. However, the estimated useful life of a copyright is usually far shorter than its legal life, and it is generally amortized over a fairly short period.
- **Cost of a franchise**, including any fees paid to the franchiser, as well as legal costs or expenses incurred in the acquisition. A franchise granted for a limited period should

Calculations

be amortized over its life. If the franchise has an indefinite life, it should be amortized over a reasonable period, not to exceed 40 years.

- **Covenants not to compete**: an agreement by the seller of a business not to engage in a competing business in a certain area for a specific period of time. The cost of the not-to-compete covenant should be amortized over the period covered by the covenant unless its estimated economic life is expected to be shorter.
- **Easement costs** that grant a right of way may be amortized if there is a limited and specified life.
- **Organization costs** incurred when forming a corporation or a partnership, including legal fees, accounting services, incorporation fees, and other related services. Organization costs are usually amortized over 60 months.
- **Patents**, both those developed internally and those purchased. If developed internally, a patent's "amortizable basis" includes legal fees incurred during the application process. Normally, a patent is amortized over its legal life, or over its remaining life if purchased. However, it should be amortized over its legal life or its economic life, whichever is the shorter.
- **Trademarks, brands, and trade names**, which should be written off over a period not to exceed 40 years. However, since the value of these assets depends on the changing tastes of consumers, they are frequently amortized over a shorter period.
- Other types of property that may be amortized include certain intangible drilling costs, circulation costs, mine development costs, pollution control facilities, and reforestation expenditures. They can even include intangibles such as the value of a market share or a market's composition: an example is the portion of an acquired business that is attributable to the existence of a given customer base.

TRICKS OF THE TRADE

- Certain intangibles cannot be amortized, but may be depreciated using a straight-line approach if they have a "determinable" useful life. Because the rules are different in each country and are subject to change, it is essential to rely on specialist advice.
- Computer software may be amortized under certain conditions, depending on its purpose. Software that is amortized is generally given a 60-month life, but it may be amortized over a shorter period if it can clearly be established that it will be obsolete or no longer used within a shorter time.
- Under certain conditions, customer lists that were purchased may be amortized if it can be demonstrated that the list has a finite useful life, in that customers on the list are likely to be lost over a period of time.
- While leasehold improvements are depreciated for income tax purposes, they are amortized when it comes to financial reporting—either over the remaining term of the lease or their expected useful life, whichever is the shorter.
- Annual payments incurred under a franchise agreement should be expensed when incurred.
- The internet has many amortization loan calculators that can automatically determine monthly payment figures and the total cost of a loan.

MORE INFO
Websites:
Financial Accounting Standards Board (FASB): www.fasb.org
US Copyright Office: www.copyright.gov
US Patent and Trademark Office: www.uspto.gov

Annual Percentage Rate

Different investments typically offer different compounding periods, usually quarterly or monthly. The annual percentage rate, or APR, allows them to be compared over a common period of time, namely one year.

WHAT IT MEASURES
The APR measures either the rate of interest that invested money earns in one year, or the cost of credit expressed as a yearly rate.

WHY IT IS IMPORTANT
It enables an investor or borrower to compare like with like. When evaluating investment alternatives, naturally it's important to know which one will pay the greatest return. By the same token, borrowers want to know which loan alternative offers the best terms. Determining the annual percentage rate provides a direct comparison.

HOW IT WORKS IN PRACTICE
To calculate the APR, apply this formula:

$$APR = (1 + i \div m)^m - 1$$

where i is the interest rate quoted, expressed as a decimal, and m is the number of compounding periods per year. For example, if a bank offers a 6% interest rate, paid quarterly, the APR would be calculated this way:

$$
\begin{aligned}
(1 + 0.06 \div 4)^4 - 1 &= (1 + 0.015)^4 - 1 \\
&= 1.015^4 - 1 \\
&= 1.0614 - 1 \\
&= 0.0614 \\
&= 6.14\%
\end{aligned}
$$

TRICKS OF THE TRADE

- As a rule of thumb, the annual percentage rate is slightly higher than the quoted rate.
- When using the formula, be sure to express the rate as a decimal (that is, 6% becomes 0.06).
- When expressed as the cost of credit, remember to include other costs of obtaining the credit in addition to interest, such as loan closing costs and financial fees.
- APR provides an excellent basis for comparing mortgage or other loan rates; lenders are required to disclose it.
- When used in the context of investment, APR can also be called the "annual percentage yield," or APY.

MORE INFO

See Also:

⇄ Nominal and Real Interest Rates (pp. 401–402)

Asset Turnover

Another of the asset utilization ratios, asset turnover measures the productivity of assets. In some circles it is also referred to as the earning power of assets.

WHAT IT MEASURES

The amount of sales generated for every dollar's worth of assets over a given period.

WHY IT IS IMPORTANT

Asset turnover measures how well a company is leveraging its assets to produce revenue. A well-managed manufacturer, for example, will make its plant and equipment work hard for the business by minimizing idle time for machines.

The higher the number the better—within reason. As a rule of thumb, companies with low profit margins tend to have high asset turnover; those with high profit margins have low asset turnover.

This ratio can also show how capital intensive a business is. Some businesses, such as software developers, can generate tremendous sales per dollar of assets because their assets are modest. At the other end of the scale, electric utilities, heavy industry manufacturers, and even cable TV companies need a huge asset base to generate sales.

Finally, asset turnover serves as a tool to keep managers mindful of the company's balance sheet along with its profit and loss account.

HOW IT WORKS IN PRACTICE

Asset turnover's basic formula is simply sales divided by assets:

Sales revenue ÷ Total assets

Most experts recommend using average total assets in the formula. To determine this figure, add total assets at the beginning of the year to total assets at the end of the year and divide by two.

If, for instance, annual sales totaled $4.5 million, and total assets were $1.84 million at the beginning of the year and $1.78 million at the year end, the average total assets would be $1.81 million, and the asset turnover ratio would be:

4,500,000 ÷ 1,810,000 = 2.49

A variation of the formula is:

Sales revenue ÷ Fixed assets

If average fixed assets were $900,000, then asset turnover would be:

4,500,000 ÷ 900,000 = 5

TRICKS OF THE TRADE

- This ratio is especially useful for growth companies to gauge whether or not they are growing revenue (for example) turnover, in healthy proportion to assets.
- Asset turnover numbers are useful for comparing competitors within industries. Like most ratios, they vary from industry to industry. As with most numbers, the most meaningful comparisons are made over extended periods of time.
- Too high a ratio may suggest overtrading: too much sales revenue with too little investment. Conversely, too low a ratio may suggest undertrading and an inefficient management of resources.
- A declining ratio may be indicative of a company that overinvested in plant, equipment, or other fixed assets, or is not using existing assets effectively.

MORE INFO

See Also:

⇄ Asset Utilization (pp. 375–376)
⇄ Return on Assets (p. 408)

Asset Utilization

Appraising asset utilization is a multi-task exercise conceived and performed in the spirit of "one manages what one measures." There is plenty to measure.

WHAT IT MEASURES

How efficiently an organization uses its resources and, in turn, the effectiveness of the organization's managers.

WHY IT IS IMPORTANT

The success of any enterprise is tied to its ability to manage and leverage its assets. Hefty sales and profits can hide any number of inefficiencies. By examining several relationships between sales and assets, asset utilization delivers a reasonably detailed picture of how well a company is being managed and led—certainly enough to call attention both to sources of trouble and to role-model operations.

Moreover, since all the figures used in this analysis are taken from a company's balance sheet or profit and loss statement, the ratios that result can be used to compare a company's performance with individual competitors and with industries as a whole.

Many companies use this measure not only to evaluate their aggregate success but also to determine compensation for managers.

HOW IT WORKS IN PRACTICE

Asset utilization relies on a family of asset utilization ratios, also called activity ratios. The individual ratios in the family can vary, depending on the practitioner. They include measures that also stand alone, such as accounts receivable turnover and asset turnover. The most commonly used sets of asset utilization ratios include these and the following measures.

Average collection period is also known as days sales outstanding. It links accounts receivable with daily sales and is expressed in number of days; the lower the number, the better the performance. Its formula is:

Average collection period = Accounts receivable ÷ Average daily sales

For example, if accounts receivable are $280,000 and average daily sales are $7,000, then:

280,000 ÷ 7,000 = 40 days

Inventory turnover compares the cost of goods sold (COGS) with inventory; for this measure, expressed in "turns," the higher the number the better. Its formula is:

Inventory turnover = Cost of goods sold ÷ Inventory

For example, if COGS is $2 million and inventory at the end of the period is $500,000, then:

2,000,000 ÷ 500,000 = 4

Some asset utilization repertoires include ratios like debtor days, while others study the relationships listed below.

Depreciation/Assets measures the percentage of assets being depreciated to gauge how quickly product plants are aging and assets are being consumed.

Depreciation/Sales measures the percentage of sales that is tied up covering the wear and tear of the physical plant.

In either instance, a high percentage could be cause for concern.

Income/Assets measures how well management uses its assets to generate net income. It is the same formula as return on assets.

Income/Plant measures how effectively a company uses its investment in fixed assets to generate net income.

In these two instances, high numbers are desirable.

Plant/Assets expresses the percentage of total assets that is tied up in land, buildings, and equipment.

By themselves, of course, the individual numbers are meaningless. Their value lies in how they compare with the corresponding numbers of competitors and with industry averages. A company with an inventory turnover of 4 in an industry whose average is 7, for example, surely has room for improvement, because the comparison indicates that it is generating fewer sales per unit of inventory and is therefore less efficient than its competitors.

TRICKS OF THE TRADE

- Asset utilization is particularly useful to companies considering expansion or capital investment: if production can be increased by improving the efficiency of existing resources, there is no need to spend the sums expansion would cost.
- Like all families of ratios, no single number or comparison is necessarily cause for alarm or rejoicing. Asset utilization proves most beneficial over an extended period of time.
- Studying all measures at once can devour a lot of time, although computers have trimmed hours into seconds. Managements in smaller organizations may conduct asset utilization on a continuing basis, tracking particular measures monthly to stay abreast of operating trends.

MORE INFO
See Also:
⇄ Accounts Receivable Turnover (p. 372)
⇄ Asset Turnover (p. 375)

Basis Point Value

WHAT IT MEASURES

The basis point value (BPV) expresses the change in value of an asset or financial instrument that results from a 0.01 percentage change in yield. BPV is commonly used to measure interest rate risk, and may be referred to as a delta or DV01.

WHY IT IS IMPORTANT

Basis point value is extremely important in assessing the impact of changes to the value or rate of a financial instrument such as an asset or portfolio. Simply stating an absolute percentage can be unclear—a 1% increase to a 10% rate might refer to an increase to 10.1% or 11%, for example.

Basis points can be used to measure changes and differentials in interest rates and margins. For example, a floating interest rate might be set at 25 BPV above Libor. If Libor is 3.5%, this means the floating rate will be 3.75%. Basis points are also useful in describing margins, because percentage changes may be very small or unclear—even while they might have a considerable impact on the bottom line.

BPV is commonly used in financial markets to measure interest rates, and specifically the risk associated with a particular rate. It is popular because it is relatively simple to calculate and can be applied in any scenario where you have a known cash flow.

HOW IT WORKS IN PRACTICE

At its most basic, BPV is 1/100th of 1%. Therefore, there are 30 basis points between a bond with a yield of 10.3% and 10.6%. To calculate simple BPV, therefore, use this formula:

$$BPV = Yield \times 0.0001, \text{ or } 1\% \text{ of } 1\%$$

It is often useful to take the calculation a step further to define the price value of a basis point (PVBP), which is the change in value of a bond or other financial instrument given a change of one basis point value. Sometimes this is also known as "dollar valuation of 01" or DV01.

To calculate PVBP, apply the following calculation:

$$PVBP = \text{Initial price} - \text{Price if yield changes by 1 BPV}$$

In the financial market, a basis point is used to refer to the yield that a bond or investment pays to the investor. For example, if a bond yield moves from 7.45% to 7.65%, it is said to have risen 20 basis points.

For example, if a bank raises interest rates from 2.5% to 2.75%, you would calculate PVBP as follows:

$$0.25 \times 0.0001 \times 100 = 0.025\% \text{ change}$$

(This is the difference in yield from the account created by a movement of 1 basis point).

TRICKS OF THE TRADE

- Large financial institutions use highly specialized and sophisticated computer systems to calculate the impact of basis point changes (the DV01 figure) in real-time. These figures can be calculated in spreadsheets, but they are difficult to produce accurately, particularly for complex bonds.
- In the bond market, a basis point is used to refer to the yield that a bond pays to the investor. For example, if a bond yield moves from 1.45% to 1.65%, it has risen 20 basis points. Investors will commonly compare bond yields by weighting them according to the BPV.

MORE INFO
Website:
Barbican Consulting guide to BPV:
www.barbicanconsulting.co.uk/quickguides/bpv

Bond Yield

A bond is a certificate that promises to repay a sum of money borrowed, plus interest, on a specified date, usually years into the future. National, state, and local governments issue bonds, as do corporations and many institutions.

Short-term bonds generally mature in up to 3 years, intermediate-term bonds in 3 to 10 years, and long-term bonds in more than 10 years, with 30 years generally being the upper limit. Longer-term bonds are considered a higher risk because interest rates are certain to change during their lifetime, but they tend to pay higher interest rates to attract investors and reward them for the additional risk.

Bonds are traded on the open market, just like stocks. They are reliable economic indicators, but perform in the reverse direction to interest rates: if bond prices are rising, interest rates and stock markets are likely to be falling, while if interest rates have gone up since a bond was first issued, prices of new bonds will fall.

WHAT IT MEASURES

The annual return on this certificate (the rate of interest) expressed as a percentage of the current market price of the bond.

WHY IT IS IMPORTANT

Bonds can tie up investors' money for periods of up to 30 years, so knowing their yield is a critical investment consideration. Similarly, bond issuers need to know the price they will pay to incur their debt, so that they can compare it with the cost of other means of raising capital.

HOW IT WORKS IN PRACTICE

Bonds are issued in increments of $1,000. To calculate the yield amount, multiply the face value of the bond by the stated rate, expressed as a decimal. For example, buying a new 10-year $1,000 bond that pays 6% interest will produce an annual yield of $60:

$$1,000 \times 0.06 = \$60$$

The $60 will be paid as $30 every six months. At the end of 10 years, the purchaser will have earned $600, and will also be repaid the original $1,000. Because the bond was purchased when it was first issued, the 6% is also called the "yield to maturity."

This basic formula is complicated by other factors. First is the "time-value of money" theory: money paid in the future is worth less than money paid today. A more detailed computation of total bond yield requires the calculation of the present value of the interest earned each year. Second, changing interest rates have a marked impact on bond trading and, ultimately, on yield. Changes in interest rates cannot affect the interest paid by bonds already issued, but they do affect the prices of new bonds.

TRICKS OF THE TRADE

- **Yield to call**. Bond issuers reserve the right to "call," or redeem, the bond before the maturity date, at certain times and at a certain price. Issuers often do this if interest rates fall and they can issue new bonds at a lower rate. Bond buyers should obtain the yield-to-call rate, which may, in fact, be a more realistic indicator of the return expected.
- **Different types of bond**. Some bonds are backed by assets, while others are issued on the strength of the issue's good standing. Investors should know the difference.

- **Zero-coupon bonds**. These pay no interest at all, but are sold at a deep discount and increase in value until maturity. A buyer might pay $3,000 for a 25-year zero bond with a face value of $10,000. This bond will simply accrue value each year, and at maturity will be worth $10,000, thus earning $7,000. These are high-risk investments, however, especially if they must be sold on the open market amid rising interest rates.
- **Interest rates**. Bond values fall when interest rates rise, and rise when interest rates fall, because when interest rates rise existing bonds become less valuable and less attractive.

MORE INFO

See Also:

⇄ Yield (p. 416)

Book Value

No-nonsense number-crunchers adore this measure because it presents the value of common stock equity based on historical values and thus helps separate fact from fiction and fancy.

WHAT IT MEASURES

A company's common stock equity as it appears on a balance sheet.

WHY IT IS IMPORTANT

Book value represents a company's net worth to its stockholders, based on the difference between assets and liabilities plus debt. Typically, book value is substantially different from market value, especially in high-tech and knowledge-based industries whose primary assets are intangible and therefore do not appear on the balance sheet.

When compared with its market value, a company's book value helps to reveal how it is regarded by the investment community. A market value that is notably higher than book value indicates that investors have a high regard for the company. A market value that is, for example, a multiple of book value suggests that investors' regard may be unreasonably high—as was shown in the painful plunge of dot-com companies in 2000 and 2001.

The reverse is also true, of course; indeed, it may suggest that a company's stock is a bargain.

A companion measure is book value per stock. It shows the value of the company's assets that each stockholder theoretically would receive if a company were liquidated.

HOW IT WORKS IN PRACTICE

To calculate book value, subtract a company's liabilities and the value of its debt and preferred stock from its total assets. All of these figures appear on a company's balance sheet. For example:

Total assets	$1,300
Current liabilities	– $400
Long-term liabilities, preferred stock	– $250
Book value	**$650**

Book value per stock is calculated by dividing the book value by the number of stocks issued:

Book value per stock = Book value ÷ Number of stocks issued

If our example is expressed in millions of dollars and the company has 35 million stocks outstanding, the book value per stock would be $650 million divided by 35 million:

650 ÷ 35 = $18.57

TRICKS OF THE TRADE

- Related terms include:
  - adjusted book value or modified book value, which is book value after assets and liabilities are adjusted to market value
  - tangible book value, which also subtracts intangible assets, patents, trademarks, and the value of research and development
  - The rationale is that these items cannot be sold outright
- Book value can also mean the value of an individual asset as it appears on a balance sheet, in which case it is equal to the cost of the asset minus any accumulated depreciation.
- Though often considered a realistic appraisal, book value can still contain unrealistic figures. For example, a building

might be fully depreciated and have no official asset value but could still be sold for millions, or four-year-old computer equipment that is not fully depreciated might have asset value but no market value, given its age and advances in technology.

MORE INFO
See Also:
⇄ Market/Book Ratio (pp. 399–400)

Capital Asset Pricing Model

Although at first glance it looks likes a simple formula, the capital asset pricing model (CAPM) represents an historic effort to understand and quantify something that's not at all simple: risk. Conceived by Nobel economist William Sharpe in 1964, CAPM has been praised, appraised, and assailed by economists ever since.

WHAT IT MEASURES
The relationship between the risk and expected return of a security or stock portfolio.

WHY IT IS IMPORTANT
The capital asset pricing model's importance is twofold.

First, it serves as a model for pricing the risk in all securities, and thus helps investors evaluate and measure portfolio risk and the returns they can anticipate for taking such risks.

Second, the theory behind the formula also has fueled—some might say provoked—spirited debate among economists about the nature of investment risk itself. The CAPM attempts to describe how the market values investments with expected returns.

The CAPM theory classifies risk as being either diversifiable, which can be avoided by sound investing, or systematic, that is, not diversified and unavoidable due to the nature of the market itself. The theory contends that investors are rewarded only for assuming systematic risk, because they can mitigate diversifiable risk by building a portfolio of both risky stocks and sound ones.

One analysis has characterized the CAPM as "a theory of equilibrium" that links higher expected returns in strong markets with the greater risk of suffering heavy losses in weak markets; otherwise, no one would invest in high-risk stocks.

HOW IT WORKS IN PRACTICE
CAPM holds that the expected return of a security or a portfolio equals the rate on a risk-free security plus a risk premium. If this expected return does not meet or beat a theoretical required return, the investment should not be undertaken. The formula used to create CAPM is:

$$\text{Expected return} = \text{Risk-free rate} + (\text{Market return} - \text{Risk-free rate}) \times \text{Beta value}$$

The risk-free rate is the quoted rate on an asset that has virtually no risk. In practice, it is the rate quoted for 90-day US

Treasury bills. The market return is the percentage return expected of the overall market, typically a published index such as Standard & Poor's. The beta value is a figure that measures the volatility of a security or portfolio of securities compared with the market as a whole. A beta of 1, for example, indicates that a security's price will move with the market. A beta greater than 1 indicates higher volatility, while a beta less than 1 indicates less volatility.

Say, for instance, that the current risk-free rate is 4%, and the S&P 500 index is expected to return 11% next year. An investment club is interested in determining next year's return for XYZ Software Inc., a prospective investment. The club has determined that the company's beta value is 1.8. The overall stock market always has a beta of 1, so XYZ Software's beta of 1.8 signals that it is a riskier investment than the overall market represents. This added risk means that the club should expect a higher rate of return than the 11% for the S&P 500. The CAPM calculation, then, would be:

$$4\% + (11\% - 4\%) \times 1.8 = 16.6\%$$

What the results tell the club is that given the risk, XYZ Software Inc. has a required rate of return of 16.6%, or the minimum return that an investment in XYZ should generate. If the investment club doesn't think that XYZ will produce that kind of return, it should probably consider investing in a different company.

TRICKS OF THE TRADE
- As experts warn, CAPM is only a simple calculation built on historical data of market and stock prices. It does not express anything about the company whose stock is being analyzed. For example, renowned investor Warren Buffett has pointed out that if a company making Barbie™ dolls has the same beta as one making pet rocks, CAPM holds that one investment is as good as the other. Clearly, this is a risky tenet.
- While high returns might be received from stocks with high beta shares, there is no guarantee that their respective CAPM return will be realized (a reason why beta is defined as a "measure of risk" rather than an "indication of high return").
- The beta parameter itself is historical data and may not reflect future results. The data for beta values are typically gathered over several years, and experts recommend that only long-term investors should rely on the CAPM formula.

- Over longer periods of time, high-beta shares tend to be the worst performers during market declines.

MORE INFO
Article:
Burton, Jonathan. "Revisiting the capital asset pricing model." *Dow Jones Asset Manager* (May/June 1998): 20–28. Online at: www.stanford.edu/~wfsharpe/art/djam/djam.htm

Website:
Contingency Analysis resource for trading, financial engineering, and financial risk management: www.contingencyanalysis.com

See Also:
✔ Understanding the Relationship between the Discount Rate and Risk (pp. 308–309)

Capital Expenditure

WHAT IT MEASURES

Capital expenditure (capex) refers to the money a business spends purchasing or upgrading fixed assets for future business benefit. Capital expenditure can include money spent for new property that will be resold, or which might be kept for one or more years. Capital expenditure also includes money spent to improve property (or inventory) that you already own. Under international reporting standards, property is considered to be improved only if the money you spend increases or restores an item's value, prolongs its useful life, or enables the item to be used for a new purpose.

WHY IT IS IMPORTANT

Understanding capital expenditure is a vital part of assessing a company's free cash flow. Basically, if a company spends a lot on capital expenditure but doesn't show a corresponding rate of growth, it is considered a less attractive investment. Ideally, healthy companies should generate enough positive cash flow to fund dividends/growth as well as capital expenditure.

HOW IT WORKS IN PRACTICE

To enable cash flow to be properly assessed it is important to calculate accurately the amount of funds necessary to support capital expenditure—and for the business to continue to operate. This is known as capex per share.

First, you should discount any capital expenditure that is discretionary—such as real estate, which might otherwise be leased.

Then use the following formulas to calculate capex per share based on net cash outflow attributable to property, divided by the weighted average number of ordinary shares in issue during the year:

$$\text{Capital expenditure} = \text{Total asset purchases} - \text{Property asset purchases} - \text{Nonproperty asset sales}$$

and

$$\text{Capex per share} = \text{Capex} \div \text{Weighted average of shares in issue}$$

TRICKS OF THE TRADE

- Remember that few companies have smooth capex investment over time. Most companies will have a lean capex year, followed by a year or two of heavy investment. Wherever possible, use an average capex calculation—a single figure can be extremely misleading.
- Capital expenditure is only used to refer to one-off purchases of new items or improvements to existing assets which are kept and used by the business. So the cost of buying a truck for your business is a capital expenditure, but the cost of hiring a truck is not.
- It is possible to claim tax relief on a percentage of most capital expenditure, using allowances such as "first year allowance" or "writing down allowance."
- One classic example of capital expenditure is the start-up expenses incurred when you buy or create a new business venture. These expenses are considered capital expenditure because the owner incurs them to acquire property that will be kept. These expenses may be fully deducted in year one, or may be amortized over several years.

MORE INFO
Website:
HMRC (UK) Business Income Manual section on capex: www.hmrc.gov.uk/manuals/bimmanual/BIM35000.htm

Capitalization Ratios

Capitalization ratios, also widely known as financial leverage ratios, provide a glimpse of a company's long-term stability and ability to withstand losses and business downturns.

WHAT THEY MEASURE

By comparing debt to total capitalization, these ratios reflect the extent to which a corporation is trading on its equity, and the degree to which it finances operations with debt.

Calculations

While not the focus here, capitalization ratio also refers to the percentage of a company's total capitalization contributed by debt, preferred stock, common stock, and other equity.

WHY THEY ARE IMPORTANT
By itself, any financial ratio is a rather useless piece of information. Collectively, and in context, though, financial leverage ratios present analysts and investors with an excellent picture of a company's situation, how much financial risk it has taken on, its dependence on debt, and developing trends. Knowing who controls a company's capital tells one who truly controls the enterprise!

HOW THEY WORK IN PRACTICE
A business finances its assets with either equity or debt. Financing with debt involves risk, since debt legally obligates a company to pay off the debt, plus the interest the debt incurs. Equity financing, on the other hand, does not obligate the company to pay anything. It pays investors dividends—but this is at the discretion of the board of directors. To be sure, business risk accompanies the operation of any enterprise. But how that enterprise opts to finance its operations—how it blends debt with equity—may heighten this risk.

Various experts include numerous formulas among capitalization financial leverage ratios. Three are discussed separately: debt-to-capital ratio, debt-to-equity ratio, and interest coverage ratios. What's known as the capitalization ratio *per se* can be expressed in two ways:

Long-term debt ÷ (Long-term debt + Owners' equity)

and

Total debt ÷ (Total debt + Preferred and common equity)

For example, a company whose long-term debt totals $5,000 and whose owners hold equity worth $3,000 would have a capitalization ratio of:

$5,000 ÷ (5,000 + 3,000) = 5,000 ÷ 8,000 = 0.625$

Both expressions of the capitalization ratio are also referred to as "component percentages," since they compare a company's debt with either its total capital (debt plus equity) or its equity capital. They readily indicate how reliant a company is on debt financing.

TRICKS OF THE TRADE
- Capitalization ratios need to be evaluated over time, and compared with other data and standards. A gross profit margin of 20%, for instance, is meaningless—until one knows that the average profit margin for an industry is 10%; at that point, 20% looks quite attractive. Moreover, if the historical trend of that margin has been climbing for the last three years, it strongly suggests that a company's management has sound and effective policies and strategies in place.
- Also, all capitalization ratios should be interpreted in the context of a company's earnings and cash flow, and those of its competitors.
- Take care in comparing companies in different industries or sectors. The same figures that appear to be low in one industry can be very high in another.
- Some less frequently used capitalization ratios are based on formulas that use the book value of equity (the stock). When compared with other ratios, they can be misleading, because there usually is little relation between a company's book value and its market value—which is apt to be many times higher, since market value reflects what the investment community thinks the company is worth.

MORE INFO
Book:
Walsh, Ciaran. *Key Management Ratios*. 4th ed. London: FT Prentice Hall, 2008.

See Also:
- Debt/Equity Ratio (pp. 384–385)
- Interest Coverage (pp. 395–396)

Calculations

Contribution Margin

Finding the contribution margin unearths an important comparison that otherwise would lie hidden in an income statement.

WHAT IT MEASURES
The amounts that individual products or services ultimately contribute to net profit.

WHY IT IS IMPORTANT
Contribution margin helps a business to decide how it should direct or redirect its resources.

When managers know the contribution margin—or margins, as is more often the case—they can make better decisions about adding or subtracting product lines, investing in existing products, pricing products or services (particularly in response to competitors' actions), structuring sales commissions and bonuses, where to direct marketing and advertising expenditures, and where to apply individual talents and expertise.

In short, contribution margin is a valuable decision-support tool.

HOW IT WORKS IN PRACTICE
Its calculation is straightforward:

Contribution margin = Sales price − Variable cost

Or, for providers of services:

Contribution margin = Total revenue − Total variable cost

For example, if the sales price of a good is $500 and the variable cost is $350, the contribution margin is $150, or 30% of the sales price.

This means that 30 cents of every sales dollar remains to contribute to fixed costs and to profit after the costs directly related to the sales are subtracted.

Contribution margin is especially useful to a company comparing different products or services (see the example below).

	Product A	Product B	Product C
Sales price	$260	$220	$140
Variable costs	$178	$148	$65
Contribution margin	$82	$72	$75
	31.5%	32.7%	53.6%

Obviously, Product C has the highest contribution percentage, even though Product A generates more total profit. The analysis suggests that the company might do well to aim to achieve a sales mix with a higher proportion of Product C. It further suggests that prices for Products A and B may be too low, or that their cost structures need attention. Notably, none of this information appears on a standard income statement.

Contribution margin can also be tracked over a long period of time using data from several years of income statements. It can also be invaluable in calculating volume discounts for preferred customers, and break-even sales or volume levels.

TRICKS OF THE TRADE
Contribution margin depends on accurately accounting for all variable costs, including shipping and delivery, or the indirect costs of services. Activity-based cost accounting systems aid this kind of analysis. Variable costs include all direct costs (usually labor and materials). Contribution margin analysis is only one tool to use. It will not show so-called loss leaders, for example. And it doesn't consider marketing factors like existing penetration levels, opportunities, or mature markets being eroded by emerging markets.

MORE INFO
See Also:
Marginal Cost (pp. 398–399)

Conversion Ratio

Calculations

Conversion ratio and conversion price work in tandem and should be considered together.

WHAT IT MEASURES
The number of shares of common stock an investor will receive on converting a convertible security—a bond, debenture, or preferred stock.

The conversion price may be set when the convertible security is issued, depending on its terms.

WHY IT IS IMPORTANT
Like conversion price, the conversion ratio is an investment strategy tool which is used to determine what the value of a convertible security would be if it were converted immediately. By knowing a convertible's value, an investor can compare it with the prevailing price of the issuing company's common stock and decide whether it is best to convert or to continue holding the convertible.

By the same token, holders of common stock in the company issuing the convertible can use the conversion ratio to help to monitor the value of their stock. For example, a relatively high ratio could mean that the value of their shares would be diluted if large numbers of convertible holders were to exercise their options.

HOW IT WORKS IN PRACTICE
In the same way as conversion price, the conversion ratio may be established when the convertible is issued. If that is the case, the ratio will appear in the indenture, the binding agreement that details the convertible's terms.

If the conversion ratio is not set, it can be calculated quickly: divide the par value of the convertible security (typically $1,000) by its conversion price:

$1,000 ÷ $40 per share = 25 shares

In this example, the conversion ratio is 25:1, which means that every bond held with a $1,000 par value can be exchanged for 25 shares of common stock.

Knowing the conversion ratio enables an investor to decide quickly whether his convertibles (or group of them) are more valuable than the shares of common stock they represent. If the stock is currently trading at $30, the conversion value is $750, or $250 less than the par value of the convertible. It would therefore be unwise to convert.

TRICKS OF THE TRADE
- Although it is rare, a convertible's indenture can sometimes contain a provision stating that the conversion ratio will change over the years.
- A conversion ratio that is set when a convertible is issued usually protects against any dilution from stock splits. However, it does not protect against a company issuing secondary offerings of common stock.

- "Forced conversion" means that the company can make holders convert into stock at virtually any time. Convertible holders should also pay close attention to the price at which the bonds are callable.

- Conversion ratio also describes the number of shares of one common stock to be issued for each outstanding share of another common stock when a merger takes place.

Creditor and Debtor Days

These financial measures are two sides of the same coin, since they respectively measure the flow of money out of and into a business. As such, they are reliable indicators of both efficiency and problems.

WHAT THEY MEASURE

Creditor days is a measure of the number of days on average that a company requires to pay its creditors, while debtor days is a measure of the number of days on average that it takes a company to receive payment for what it sells. It is also called accounts receivable days.

WHY THEY ARE IMPORTANT

Creditor days is an indication of a company's creditworthiness in the eyes of its suppliers and creditors, since it shows how long they are willing to wait for payment. Within reason, the higher the number the better because all companies want to conserve cash. At the same time, a company that is especially slow to pay its bills (100 or more days, for example) may be a company having trouble generating cash, or one trying to finance its operations with its suppliers' funds. Ultimately, companies whose creditor days soar have trouble obtaining supplies.

Debtor days is an indication of a company's efficiency in collecting monies owed. In this case, obviously, the lower the number the better. An especially high number is a telltale sign of inefficiency or worse. It may indicate bad debts, dubious sales figures, or a company being bullied by large customers out to improve their own cash position at another company's expense. Customers whose credit terms are abused also risk higher borrowing costs and related charges.

Changes in both measures are easy to spot, and easy to understand.

HOW THEY WORK IN PRACTICE

To determine creditor days, divide the cumulative amount of unpaid suppliers' bills (also called trade creditors) by sales, then multiply by 365. So the formula is:

$$\text{Creditor days} = \text{Trade creditors} \div \text{Sales} \times 365$$

For example, if suppliers' bills total $800,000 and sales are $9,000,000, the calculation is:

$$800{,}000 \div 9{,}000{,}000 \times 365 = 32.44 \text{ days}$$

The company takes 32.44 days on average to pay its bills.

To determine debtor days, divide the cumulative amount of accounts receivable by sales, then multiply by 365. For example, if accounts receivable total $600,000 and sales are $9,000,000, the calculation is:

$$600{,}000 \div 9{,}000{,}000 \times 365 = 24.33 \text{ days}$$

The company takes 24.33 days on average to collect its debts.

TRICKS OF THE TRADE

- Cash businesses, including most retailers, should have a much lower debtor days figure than noncash businesses, since they receive payment when they sell the goods. A typical target for noncash businesses is 40–50 days.
- An abnormally high creditor days figure may not only suggest a cash crisis, but also the management's difficulty in maintaining revolving credit agreements.
- An increasing number of debtor days also suggests overly generous credit terms (to bolster sales) or problems with product quality.

Calculations

Current Ratio

The current ratio is a key liquidity ratio and a staple for anyone who borrows or lends money.

WHAT IT MEASURES

A company's liquidity and its ability to meet its short-term debt obligations.

WHY IT IS IMPORTANT

By comparing a company's current assets with its current liabilities, the current ratio reflects its ability to pay its

upcoming bills in the unlikely event of all creditors demanding payment at once. It has long been the measurement of choice among financial institutions and lenders.

HOW IT WORKS IN PRACTICE

The current ratio formula is simply:

$$\text{Current ratio} = \text{Current assets} \div \text{Current liabilities}$$

Current assets are the ones that a company can turn into cash within 12 months during the ordinary course of business.

Current liabilities are bills due to be paid within the coming 12 months.

For example, if a company's current assets are $300,000 and its current liabilities are $200,000, its current ratio would be:

$$300,000 \div 200,000 = 1.5$$

As a rule of thumb, the 1.5 figure means that a company should be able to get hold of $1.50 for every $1.00 it owes.

TRICKS OF THE TRADE

- The higher the ratio, the more liquid the company. Prospective lenders expect a positive current ratio, often of at least 1.5. However, too high a ratio is cause for alarm, because it indicates declining receivables and/or inventory—signs that portend declining liquidity.
- A current ratio of less than 1 suggests pressing liquidity problems, specifically an inability to generate sufficient cash to meet upcoming demands.
- Managements use current ratio as well as lenders; a low ratio, for example, may indicate the need to refinance a portion of short-term debt with long-term debt to improve a company's liquidity.

- Ratios vary by industry, however, and should be used accordingly. Some sectors, such as supermarket chains and restaurants, perform nicely with low ratios that would keep others awake at night.
- One shortcoming of the current ratio is that it does not differentiate assets, some of which may not be easily converted to cash. As a result, lenders also refer to the quick ratio.
- Another shortcoming of the current ratio is that it reflects conditions at a single point in time, such as when the balance sheet is prepared. It is possible to make this figure look good just for this occasion: lenders should not, therefore, appraise these conditions by the ratio alone.
- A constant current ratio and falling quick ratio signal trouble ahead, because this suggests that a company is amassing assets at the expense of receivables and cash.

MORE INFO
See Also:
✔ Measuring Liquidity (pp. 299–300)
⇄ Liquidity Ratio Analysis (pp. 396–397)

Debt/Equity Ratio

Debt/equity is the most commonly used method of assessing corporate debt, but in fact there is more than one way of expressing essentially the same thing.

WHAT IT MEASURES
How much money a company owes compared with how much money it has invested in it by principal owners and stockholders.

WHY IT IS IMPORTANT
The debt/equity ratio reveals the proportion of debt and equity a company is using to finance its business. It also measures a company's borrowing capacity. The higher the ratio, the greater the proportion of debt—but also the greater the risk.

Some even describe the debt/equity ratio as "a great financial test" of long-term corporate health, because debt establishes a commitment to repay money throughout a period of time, even though there is no assurance that sufficient cash will be generated to meet that commitment.

Creditors and lenders, understandably, rely heavily on the ratio to evaluate borrowers.

HOW IT WORKS IN PRACTICE
The debt/equity ratio is calculated by dividing debt by owners' equity, where equity is, typically, the figure stated for the preceding calendar or fiscal year. Debt, however, can be defined either as long-term debt only, or as total liabilities, which include both long- and short-term debt.

The most common formula for the ratio is:

Debt/equity ratio = Total liabilities ÷ Owners' equity

In our example, a company's long-term debt is $8,000,000, its short-term debt is $4,000,000, and owners' equity totals $9,000,000. The debt/equity ratio would therefore be (calculating in thousands):

$$(8,000 + 4,000) \div 9,000 = 12,000 \div 9,000 = 1.33$$

An alternative debt/equity formula considers only long-term liabilities in the equation. Accordingly:

$$8,000 \div 9,000 = 0.889$$

There is also a third method, which is the reciprocal of the debt-to-capital ratio; its formula is:

Debt/equity ratio = Owners' equity ÷ Total funds

However, this would be more accurately defined as "equity/debt ratio."

TRICKS OF THE TRADE
- It is important to understand exactly how debt is defined in the ratio presented.
- When calculating the ratio, some prefer to use the market value of debt and equity rather than the book value, since book value often understates current value.

- For this ratio, a low number indicates better financial stability than a high one does; if the ratio is high, a company could be at risk, especially if interest rates are rising.
- A ratio greater than one means assets are mainly financed with debt; less than one means equity provides most of the financing. Since a higher ratio generally means that a company has been aggressive in financing its growth with debt, volatile earnings can result owing to the additional cost of interest.

- Debt/equity ratio is somewhat industry-specific, and often depends on the amount of capital investment required.

MORE INFO
See Also:
⇄ Capital Expenditure (p. 380)

Depreciation

GETTING STARTED

Depreciation is a basic expense of doing business, reducing a company's earnings while increasing its cash flow. It affects three key financial statements: balance sheet; cash flow; and income (or profit and loss). It is based on two key facts: the purchase price of the items or property in question, and their "useful life."

Depreciation values and practices are governed by the tax laws of both national governments, and state or provincial governments, which must be monitored continuously for any changes that are made. Accounting bodies, too, have developed standard practices and procedures for conducting depreciation.

Depreciating a single asset is not difficult: The challenge lies in depreciating the many assets possessed by even small companies, and it is intensified by the impact that depreciation has on income and cash flow statements, and on income statements. It is essential to depreciate with care and to rely on experts, ensuring that they fully understand the current government rules and regulations.

FAQS
What is depreciation?
It is an allocation of the cost of an asset over a period of time for accounting and tax purposes. Depreciation is charged against earnings, on the basis that the use of capital assets is a legitimate cost of doing business. Depreciation is also a noncash expense that is added into net income to determine cash flow in a given accounting period.

What is straight-line depreciation?
One of the two principal depreciation methods, it is based on the assumption that an asset loses an equal amount of its value each year of its useful life. Straight-line depreciation deducts an equal amount from a company's earnings each year throughout the life of the asset.

What is accelerated depreciation?
The other principal method of depreciation is based on the assumption that an asset loses a larger amount of its value in the early years of its useful life. Also known as the "declining-balance" method, it is used by accountants to reduce a company's tax bills as soon as possible, and is calculated on the basis of the same percentage rate each year of an asset's useful life. Accelerated depreciation better reflects the economic value of

the asset being depreciated, which tends to become increasingly less efficient and more costly to maintain as it grows older.

What can be depreciated?
To qualify for depreciation, assets must:
- be used in the business;
- be items that wear out, become obsolete, or lose value over time from natural causes or circumstances;
- have a useful life beyond a single tax year.
Examples include vehicles, machines and equipment, computers and office furnishings, and buildings, plus major additions or improvements to such assets. Some intangible assets can also be included under certain conditions.

What cannot be depreciated?
Land, personal assets, inventory, leased or rented property, and a company's employees.

MAKING IT HAPPEN
In order to determine the annual depreciation cost of assets, it is necessary first to know the initial cost of those assets, how many years they will retain some value for the business, and what value, if any, they will have at the end of their useful life.

For example, a company buys a truck to carry materials and finished goods. The vehicle loses value as soon as it is purchased, and then loses more with each year it is in service, until the cost of repairs exceeds its overall value. Measuring the loss in the value of the truck is depreciation.

Straight-line depreciation is the most straightforward method, and is still quite common. It assumes that the net cost of an asset should be written off in equal amounts over its life. The formula used is:

(Original cost − Scrap value) ÷ Useful life

For example, if the truck cost $30,000 and can be expected to serve the business for 7 years, its original cost less its scrap value would be divided by its useful life:

(30,000 − 2,000) ÷ 7 = $4,000 per year

The $4,000 becomes a depreciation expense that is reported on the company's year-end income statement under "operation expenses."

In theory, an asset should be depreciated over the actual number of years that it will be used, according to its actual drop

Calculations

in value each year. At the end of each year, all the depreciation claimed to date is subtracted from its cost in order to arrive at its "book value," which would equal its market value. At the end of its useful business life, any undepreciated portion would represent the salvage value for which it could be sold or scrapped.

For tax purposes, some accountants prefer to use accelerated depreciation to record larger amounts of depreciation in the asset's early years in order to reduce tax bills as soon as possible. In contrast to the straight-line method, the accelerated or declining balance method assumes that the asset depreciates more in its earlier years of use. The table compares the depreciation amounts that would be available, under these two methods, for a $1,000 asset that is expected to be used for five years and then sold for $100 in scrap.

| Year | Straight-line method | | Declining-balance method | |
	Annual depreciation	Year-end book value	Annual depreciation	Year-end book value
1	$900 × 20 per cent = $180	$1,000 − $180 = $820	$1,000 × 40 per cent = $400	$1,000 − $400 = $600
2	$900 × 20 per cent = $180	$820 − $180 = $640	$600 × 40 per cent = $240	$600 − $240 = $360
3	$900 × 20 per cent = $180	$640 − $180 = $460	$360 × 40 per cent = $144	$360 − $144 = $216
4	$900 × 20 per cent = $180	$460 − $180 = $280	$216 × 40 per cent = $86.40	$216 − $86.40 = $129.60
5	$900 × 20 per cent = $180	$280 − $180 = $100	$129.60 × 40 per cent = $51.84	$129.60 − $51.84 = $77.76

While the straight-line method results in the same deduction each year, the declining-balance method produces larger deductions in the first years and far smaller deductions in the later years. One result of this system is that, if the equipment is expected to be sold for a higher value at some point in the middle of its life, the declining-balance method can produce a greater taxable gain in that year because the book value of the asset will be relatively lower.

The depreciation method to be used for a particular asset is fixed at the time that the asset is first placed in service. Whatever rules or tables are in effect for that year must be followed as long as the asset is owned.

Depreciation laws and regulations change frequently over the years as a result of government policy changes, so a company owning property over a long period may have to use several different depreciation methods.

TRICKS OF THE TRADE

- With very specific exceptions, it is not possible to deduct in one year the entire cost of an asset if that asset has a useful life substantially beyond the tax year.
- To qualify for depreciation, an asset must be put into service. Simply purchasing it is not enough. There are rules that govern how much depreciation can be claimed on items put into service after a year has begun.
- It is common knowledge that if a company claims more depreciation than it is entitled to, it is liable for stiff penalties in a tax audit, just as failure to allow for depreciation causes an overestimation of income. What is not commonly known is that if a company does not claim all the depreciation deductions it is entitled to, it will be considered as having claimed them when taxable gains or losses are eventually calculated on the sale or disposal of the asset in question.
- While leased property cannot be depreciated, the cost of making permanent improvements to leased property can be (remodeling a leased office, for example). There are many rules governing leased assets; they should be depreciated with care.
- Another common mistake is to continue depreciating property beyond the end of its recovery period. Cars are common examples of this.
- Conservative companies depreciate many assets as quickly as possible, despite the fact that this practice reduces reported net income. Knowledgeable investors watch carefully for such practices.

MORE INFO

Book:

Wolf, Frank K., and W. Chester Finch. *Depreciation Systems*. Ames, IA: Iowa State University Press, 1994.

Websites:

Bankrate.com on Section 179 of the United States Internal Revenue Code: tinyurl.com/y4lc

Business Owner's Toolkit: www.toolkit.com

See Also:

⇄ Residual Value (p. 407)

Discounted Cash Flow

WHAT IT MEASURES

Discounted cash flow (DCF) is a way of measuring the net present value (NPV) of future cash flow. This allows companies to express the value of an investment today based on predicted future returns. The idea behind discounted cash flow is that $1 today is worth more than $1 you might receive in the future. The money you have now can be invested and might generate interest whereas money you haven't yet received can't be used in this way, and there is a risk it might not be received. Therefore, discounted cash flow is a way of adjusting the value of future money over time to reflect its "real" value today.

WHY IT IS IMPORTANT
Discounted cash flow is most useful when future operating conditions and cash flow are variable, or where trading conditions are expected to change significantly over time. It is a good way of assessing the likely value of money the business will receive in future, and therefore DCF is considered one of the best ways of valuing an investment.

HOW IT WORKS IN PRACTICE
To calculate discounted cash flow, you must first determine the forecasted cash flow of a company, and choose a discount rate based on the expected or desired rate of return. The discount rate chosen should reflect the risk that the return will not be achieved—a higher risk should result in a higher discount rate.

Next, use the discount rate for each year to discount cash flow to the "correct" adjusted present value, as shown in the example below. Remember, cash flow will lose value over time because it is discounted for a longer period.

For example:

$$NPV = CF1 \div (1 + r) + CF2 \div (1 + r)^2 + CF3 \div (1 + r)^3$$

where NPV is the net present value of cash flows, CF1, CF2, and CF3 are predicted cash flows in years 1, 2, and 3, respectively, and r is the discount rate. It's worth remembering that, unless the series of cash flows has a known finite endpoint, a terminal value will need to be assumed.

TRICKS OF THE TRADE
- Cash flows may represent interest payments or repayments, or in the case of stocks can relate to dividends.
- There are many variations to the calculation illustrated above, and different ways to measure cash flow and discount rates in a DCF calculation. All the different approaches are basically ways of estimating the return from an investment, adjusted for the time value of money.
- Like many calculations, a DCF figure is only as good as the figures used for cash flow and discount rates. Small changes in these figures can result in enormous variation in NPV figures, so it's often wiser to use DCF over a relatively short period of time and to adopt a terminal value approach, rather than discounting to infinity.
- DCF analysis of cash flow should be used when a business case deals with two potential uses of money, and wherever cash flow timing is different.

MORE INFO
Websites:
Investopedia tutorial on DCF analysis:
www.investopedia.com/university/dcf/
Solution Matrix on DCF:
www.solutionmatrix.com/discounted-cash-flow
See Also:
✔ Understanding the Relationship between the Discount Rate and Risk (pp. 308–309)

Distinguishing between a Capital and an Operating Lease

GETTING STARTED
Determining whether a lease obligation is an operating or capital lease, for financial reporting purposes, requires that it be evaluated on the basis of four criteria established by the FASB (Financial Accounting Standards Board). The criteria are objective rules for making a judgment about who, the lessor or the lessee, bears the risks and benefits of ownership of the leased property.

If a lease is determined to be a capital lease, an asset and corresponding liability are recorded at the present value of the minimum lease payments. The capital asset is depreciated over time, while the liability is amortized as lease payments are made. Rental payments under operating leases are simply expensed as incurred. Due to the complexity of lease agreements, management judgment still plays a large role in distinguishing between operating and capital leases.

FAQS
What are minimum lease payments?
The minimum lease payments are the rental payments to be made during the lease term, plus the amount of the bargain

price, guaranteed residual value, or penalty for failure to renew the lease at the end of its original term.

In determining whether a lease should be classified as an operating or capital lease, what interest rate should be used?
The interest rate used to discount the minimum lease payments to their present value is the incremental borrowing rate of the lessee, this being the interest rate that the lessee would have been charged if the assets had been acquired by borrowing the purchase price. If the lessor's implied interest rate for the lease is known and is lower than the lessee's estimated incremental borrowing rate, then the lessee uses the implied rate to discount.

MAKING IT HAPPEN
The Four FASB Criteria
Until the 1970s, many companies used leasing as a means to purchase tangible assets without recognizing their ownership or the lease obligation on the balance sheet. In substance,

Calculations

leases were off-balance-sheet financing. Although all leases were required to be disclosed in the footnotes to the financial statements, even long-term finance leases did not appear as a liability. Because the basic measures of leverage do not consider off-balance-sheet obligations, the accounting profession and the investment community believed that there needed to be more stringent guidelines for classifying leases as operating or financing, and in 1976 the FASB issued Statement no. 13, "Accounting for leases." The statement sets out four criteria to distinguish between an operating and a capital (finance) lease:

- The lease agreement transfers ownership of the assets to the lessee during the term of lease.
- The lessee can purchase the assets leased at a bargain price, such as $1, at the end of the lease term.
- The lease term is at least 75% of the economic life of the leased asset.
- The present value of the minimum lease payments is 90% or greater of the asset's value.

If a lease agreement does not meet any of these criteria, the lessee treats it as an operating lease for accounting purposes. If, however, the agreement meets one of the above criteria, it is treated as a capital lease.

Accounting for a Capital Lease

Capital leases are reported by the lessee as if the assets being leased were acquired and the monthly rental payments as if they were payments of principal and interest on a debt obligation. Specifically, the lessee capitalizes the lease by recognizing an asset and a liability at the lower of the present value of the minimum lease payments or the value of the assets under lease. As the monthly rental payments are made, the corresponding liability decreases. At the same time, the leased asset is depreciated in a manner that is consistent with other owned assets having the same use and economic life.

Accounting for an Operating Lease

If the lease is classified as an operating lease, the monthly lease payments are simply treated as rental expenses and recognized on the income tax return as they are incurred. There is no recognition of a leased asset or liability.

Clearing Up Remaining Confusion

The FASB's attempt to establish objective criteria for distinguishing between operating and capital leases was a good first step. This has enabled companies to make prudent financial decisions in lease versus buy situations, based on the accounting treatment afforded a specific lease structure. Furthermore, financial professionals now have a framework within which to determine what lease terms create a capital lease. However, the use of financial engineering still occurs. Consequently, many leases that are truly financing leases are recorded as operating leases, because their provisions have been altered to avoid qualification as capital leases.

When in doubt, a manager should always ask whether the risks and benefits of ownership have truly been passed from the lessor to the lessee. Facts indicating that the transfer has occurred are when maintenance, insurance, and property tax expenses are borne by the lessee, or when the lessee guarantees a specific residual value on the leased property.

MORE INFO

Websites:

Institute of Chartered Accountants in England and Wales (ICAEW): www.icaew.com

Securities and Exchange Commission (SEC; US): www.sec.gov

See Also:

★ Classification and Treatment of Leases (pp. 66–69)

Calculations

Dividend Yield

WHAT IT MEASURES

An investment's dividend yield is a measure of the dividend paid on stock, expressed as a percentage over one year. This measure is frequently used in stock quotes and financial reports, and is based upon the company's annual cash dividend per share and the current stock price.

WHY IT IS IMPORTANT

A stock's dividend yield is a crucial measure for potential investors in any company, since it illustrates how much cash flow is generated for each dollar invested in equity, on top of any capital gains made from a rising stock price. A relatively high-paying, stable stock will attract income investors, and the higher the dividend yield, the greater expected return for income investors. Historical data also show that stocks which pay a dividend have generally outperformed non-dividend-paying stocks in the long term.

HOW IT WORKS IN PRACTICE

To calculate a dividend yield, you will need to use the following formula:

Dividend yield = Annual dividend per share ÷ Stock price per share

For example, Company A has an annual dividend per share of $10, and the average quarterly value of its stock per share is $75. To assess the company's dividend yield, we would divide the dividend by the stock price, as follows:

10 ÷ 75 = 0.1333 = 13.33%

On this basis, the stock has a dividend yield of 13.33%.

Company B might also pay an annual dividend per share of $10, but if its stock is trading at $20 per share, then its dividend yield will be 50%—considerably higher than Company A's dividend yield. Assuming other factors are equal, income investors would find Company B a more attractive investment opportunity.

TRICKS OF THE TRADE
- Dividend yield is often simply referred to as a "yield" in financial markets.
- The dividend yield helps to explain a company's value to investors but can vary widely depending on a company's market position, industry, earnings, cash flow, and dividend policy. Therefore, this measure is not always important for long-term investors who are concerned with a company's long-term growth.
- It isn't a guarantee, but many studies show a strong correlation between yield and returns over five years—companies with higher yields tend to offer higher returns, while lower yields lead to lower returns.
- It is common for newspapers to include yield figures in tables showing stock performance and share prices. In general, a yield of around 2–4% is considered average, and most attractive to longer-term growth investors.
- High yields are generally offered by mature, well-established companies while younger companies tend to

pay lower yields because they are focused on growth. Many young companies will not pay any dividend at all.
- If a company has a low yield compared to others in the same industry, this could mean the company's stock is over-valued because investors are confident of future growth. Alternatively, it can suggest that the company can't afford to pay the expected dividends.
- If a company has a high yield in comparison to others in the same sector, it could suggest imminent dividend cuts.

MORE INFO
Websites:
Biz/ed on dividend yield:
www.bized.co.uk/compfact/ratios/investor8.htm
Investopedia dividend yield calculator:
www.investopedia.com/calculator/DivCYield.aspx

See Also:
Earnings per Share (pp. 389–390)
Yield (p. 416)

Earnings per Share

Earnings per share (EPS) is perhaps the most widely used ratio there is in the investing realm.

WHAT IT MEASURES
The portion of a company's profit allocated to each outstanding share of a company's common stock.

WHY IT IS IMPORTANT
Earnings per share is simply a fundamental measure of profitability that shows how much profit has been generated on a per-share-of-stock basis. Were the term worded as profit per share, the meaning certainly would be much clearer, if not self-evident.

By itself, EPS doesn't reveal a great deal. Its true value lies in comparing EPS figures across several quarters, or years, to judge the growth of a company's earnings on a per-share basis.

HOW IT WORKS IN PRACTICE
Essentially, the figure is calculated after paying taxes and dividends to preferred stockholders and bondholders. Barring extraordinary circumstances, EPS data are reported quarterly, semiannually, and annually.

To calculate EPS, start with net income (earnings) for the period in question, subtract the total value of any preferred stock dividends, then divide the resulting figure by the number of shares outstanding during that period:

Earnings per share =(Net income − Dividends on preferred stock)
÷ Average number of shares outstanding

By itself, this formula is simple enough. Alas, defining the factors used in the formula invariably introduces complexities and—as some allege on occasion—possible subterfuge.

For instance, while companies usually use a weighted average number of shares outstanding over the reporting period, shares outstanding can still be either "primary" or "fully diluted." Primary EPS is calculated using the number of shares that are currently held by investors in the market and able to be traded. Diluted EPS is the result of a complex calculation that determines how many shares would be outstanding if all exercisable warrants and options were converted into common shares at the end of a quarter. Suppose, for example, that a company has granted a large number of share options to employees. If these options are capable of being exercised in the near future, that could alter significantly the number of shares in issue and, thus, the EPS—even though the E part (the earnings) is the same. Often in such cases, the company might quote the EPS both on the existing shares and on the fully diluted version. Which one a person considers depends on their view of the company and how they wish to use the EPS figure. In addition, companies can report extraordinary EPS, a figure which excludes the financial impact of unusual occurrences, such as discontinued operations or the sale of a business unit.

Net income or earnings, meanwhile, can be defined in a number of ways, based on respective nations' generally accepted accounting principles.

For example, "pro-forma earnings" tend to exclude more expenses and income used to calculate "reported earnings."

Pro-forma advocates insist that these earnings eliminate all distortions and present "true" earnings that allow pure apples-with-apples comparisons with preceding periods. However, "nonrecurring expenses" seem to occur with such increasing regularity that one may wonder if a company is deliberately trying to manipulate its earnings figures and present them in the best possible light, rather than in the most accurate light.

"Cash" earnings are earnings from operating cash flow—notably, not EBITDA. In turn, cash EPS is usually these earnings divided by diluted shares outstanding. This figure is very reliable because operating cash flow is not subject to as much judgment as net earnings or pro-forma earnings.

TRICKS OF THE TRADE
- Given the varieties of earnings and shares reported today, investors need to determine first what the respective figures represent before making investment decisions. There are cases of a company announcing a pro-forma EPS that differs significantly from what is reported in its financial statements. Such discrepancies, in turn, can affect how the market values a given stock.
- Investors should check to see if a company has issued more shares during a given period, since that action, too, can affect EPS. A similar problem occurs where there have been a number of shares issued during the accounting period

being considered. Which number of issued shares do you use, the opening figure, the closing figure, or the mean? In practice the usual method is to use the weighted mean number of shares in issue during the year (weighted, that is, for the amount of time in the year that they were in issue).
- "Trailing" earnings per share is the sum of EPS from the last four quarters and is the figure used to compute most price-to-earnings ratios.
- Diluted and primary shares outstanding can be the same if a company has no warrants or convertible bonds outstanding, but investors should not assume anything, and need to be sure how "shares outstanding" is being defined.

MORE INFO
Article:
Wayman, Rick. "The 5 types of earnings per share." *Investopedia*. Online at: www.investopedia.com/articles/analyst/091901.asp

See Also:
⇄ Dividend Yield (pp. 388–389)
⇄ Price/Earnings Ratio (pp. 405–406)
⇄ Return on Stockholders' Equity (pp. 409–410)

EBITDA

EBITDA—an acronym that stands for "earnings before interest, taxes, depreciation, and amortization"—is slightly less inclusive than "EBIT"—earnings before interest and taxes. Both focus on profitability, and have gained popularity in the past decade as measures of operating success. But as this popularity has grown, so has the number of the measure's critics.

WHAT IT MEASURES
A company's earnings from ongoing operations, before net income is calculated.

WHY IT IS IMPORTANT
EBITDA's champions contend it gives investors a sense of how much money a young or fast-growing company is generating before it pays interest on debt, taxes, and accounts for noncash changes. If EBITDA grows over time, champions argue, investors gain at least a sense of long-term profitability and, in turn, the wisdom of their investment.

Business appraisers and investors also may study EBITDA to help to gauge a company's fair market value, often as a prelude to its acquisition by another company. It is also frequently applied to companies that have been subject to leveraged buyouts—the strategy being that EBITDA will help to cover loan payments needed to finance the transaction.

EBITDA, and EBIT, too, are claimed to be good indicators of cash flow from business operations, since they report earnings before debt payments, taxes, depreciation, and amortization

charges are considered. However, that claim is challenged by many—often rather vigorously.

HOW IT WORKS IN PRACTICE
EBITDA first appeared as leveraged buyouts soared in popularity during the 1980s. It has since become well established as a financial analysis measure of telecommunications, cable, and major media companies.

Its formula is quite simple. Revenues less the cost of goods sold, general and administrative expenses, and the deductions of items expressed by the acronym EBITDA:

EBITDA = Revenue − Expenses (excluding interest, taxes, depreciation, and amortization)

or

EBIT = Revenue − Expenses (excluding taxes and interest)

This formula does not measure true cash flow. A communications company, for example, once reported $698 million in EBIT but just $324 million in cash from operations.

TRICKS OF THE TRADE
- As yet no definition of EBITDA is enforced by standards-making bodies, so companies can all but create their own. As a result, EBITDA can easily be manipulated by aggressive accounting policies, which may erode its reliability.

- Ignoring capital expenditures could be unrealistic and horribly misleading, because companies in capital-intensive sectors such as manufacturing and transportation must continually make major capital investments to remain competitive. High-technology is another sector that may be capital-intensive, at least initially.
- Critics warn that using EBITDA as a cash flow indicator is a huge mistake, because EBITDA ignores too many factors that have an impact on true cash flow, such as working capital, debt payments, and other fixed expenses. Interest and taxes can, and do, cost a company cash, they point out,

while debt holders have higher claims on a company's liquid assets than investors do.
- Critics further assail EBITDA as the barometer of choice of unprofitable firms because it can present a more optimistic view of a company's future than it has a right to claim. *Forbes* magazine, for instance, once referred to EBIDTA as "the device of choice to pep up earnings announcements."
- Even so, EBITDA may be useful in terms of evaluating firms in the same industry with widely different capital structures, tax rates, and depreciation policies.

Economic Value Added

WHAT IT MEASURES
A company's financial performance—specifically, whether it is earning more or less than the total cost of the capital supporting it.

WHY IT IS IMPORTANT
Economic value added measures true economic profit, or the amount by which the earnings of a project, an operation, or a corporation exceed (or fall short of) the total amount of capital that was originally invested by the company's owners.

If a company is earning more, it is adding value, and that is good. If it is earning less, the company is in fact devouring value, and that is bad, because the company's owners (stockholders, for example) would be better off investing their capital elsewhere.

The concept's champions declare that EVA forces managers to focus on true wealth creation and maximizing stockholder investment. By definition, then, increasing EVA will increase a company's market value.

HOW IT WORKS IN PRACTICE
EVA is conceptually simple and easy to explain: From net operating profit, subtract an appropriate charge for the opportunity cost of all capital invested in an enterprise—the amount that could have been invested elsewhere. It is calculated using this formula:

EVA = Net operating profit less applicable taxes − Cost of capital

A company is considering building a new plant whose total weighted cost over 10 years is $80 million. If the expected annual incremental return on the new operation is $10 million, or $100 million over 10 years, then the plant's EVA would be positive, in this case $20 million:

100,000,000 − 80,000,000 = $20,000,000

An alternative but more complex formula for EVA is:

EVA =[Return on invested capital (%) − Cost of capital (%)]
   × Original capital invested

TRICKS OF THE TRADE
- EVA is a measure of dollar surplus value, not the percentage difference in returns.
- Purists describe EVA as "profit the way stockholders define it." They further contend that if stockholders expect a 10% return on their investment, they "make money" only when their share of after-tax operating profits exceeds 10% of equity capital.
- An objective of EVA is to determine which business units best utilize their assets to generate returns and maximize stockholder value; it can be used to assess a company, a business unit, a single plant, an office, or even an assembly line. This same technique is equally helpful in evaluating new business opportunities.

MORE INFO
Website:
EVA at Stern Stewart & Co: www.sternstewart.com/?
 content=proprietary&p=eva

See Also:
★ Creating Value with EVA (pp. 255–258)

Calculations

Enterprise Value

In the financial world, enterprise value has a precise meaning and calculation. It is important to remember this, as many conference planners and consultants routinely rely on "enterprise value" to promote whatever concept they happen to be selling.

WHAT IT MEASURES
It measures what financial markets believe a company's ongoing operations are worth.

Some people also define enterprise value as what it would actually cost to purchase an entire company at a given moment.

WHY IT IS IMPORTANT

Enterprise value is not a theoretical valuation but a firm and finite value, logically determined. It tells an individual investor the underlying value of his stake in an enterprise. For potential acquirers considering a takeover of a company, enterprise value helps them to determine a reasonable price for their desired acquisition.

HOW IT WORKS IN PRACTICE

Although it is a finite figure, enterprise value can be calculated in two ways. One method is quicker, but the other is more thorough and thus more reliable.

The quick way is simply to multiply the number of a company's shares outstanding by the current price per share. Using this approach, the enterprise value of a company with 2 million shares outstanding, and a share price of $25, would be:

Enterprise value $= 2,000,000 \times 25 = \$50,000,000$

However, this value is based on the market's perception of the value of its shares of stock; it also ignores some important factors about a company's fiscal health. The second, more complete, method is therefore preferred by many experts. This method calculates enterprise value as the sum of market capitalization, plus debt and preferred stock, minus cash and cash equivalents:

Enterprise value $=$ Market capitalization $+$ Long-term debt

$+$ Preferred stock $-$ Cash and equivalents

If market capitalization is $6.5 million, debt totals $1 million, the value of preferred stock is $1.5 million, and cash and equivalents total $2 million, enterprise value would be:

$6.5 + 1 + 1.5 - 2 = \$7$ million

This more thorough calculation recognizes the existence of both a company's debt and of the amount of cash and liquid assets on hand. No matter how a stock may fluctuate, these sums are relatively constant, and the amount of debt can be very significant. Debt—and cash too—can be just as important during a company's sale, since new owners assume existing debt and receive any cash on hand. Indeed, more than a few acquisitions are financed in part with funds of the acquired company.

TRICKS OF THE TRADE

- Financial markets often use the market capitalization figure for enterprise value, but they really are not the same thing.
- Experts will occasionally refer to "total enterprise value," but its definition and formula are virtually identical to this second formula for enterprise value. Total enterprise value is only meaningful to those who use the quick method to compute enterprise value.
- A company's value is sometimes expressed as "the total funds being used to finance it." This is increasingly used in place of the price/earnings ratio, and indicates the economic rather than the accounting return that the company is generating on the total value of the capital supporting it. Companies that have borrowed heavily to finance growth, or that have paid large premiums for acquisitions or assets, are more frequently evaluated by this method.

MORE INFO

See Also:

✔ Estimating Enterprise Value with the Weighted Average Cost of Capital (pp. 293–294)

Fair Value Calculations

WHAT IT MEASURES

Fair value is the value of an asset or liability in a transaction between two parties. It can be used to refer to the complete assets and liabilities of a company that is being acquired by another company, or to calculate the fair value of stock market securities. However, fair value can be applied to almost any assessment of something's value.

WHY IT IS IMPORTANT

In the securities market, fair value explains the relationship between the futures contract on a market and the actual value of the index. In other words, if futures are trading above fair value, investors believe the index will rise. The opposite is true if futures are trading below fair value. If your business invests in futures, this can be crucial in your ability to raise finance. There will always be some variation around fair value because of short-term issues of supply and demand, but futures should generally be close to fair value.

HOW IT WORKS IN PRACTICE

The calculation of fair value is relatively simple as long as you have access to the necessary underlying data. The formula most often used is:

Fair value $=$ Cash $\times (1 + r \times x) \div 360 -$ Dividends

where Cash is the closing index value, r is the current interest rate, and x is the time remaining until the contract expires, in days.

For example, the fair value calculation for the FTSE 100 where the closing price is 1157 points with a cash index of 1146, the interest rate is 0.57%, with 78 days before expiry of the contract, and a dividend value of 3.47 points, would be calculated as follows:

Fair value $= 1146 \times (1 + 0.0057 \times 78) \div 360 - 3.47$

This calculation gives a fair value of 1156.68 points. If the FTSE is trading at 1157 then the difference between the two figures is 0.32. At this time, the stock is trading below fair value.

TRICKS OF THE TRADE

- Remember that fair value will change on a daily basis depending on the money markets.
- The key purpose of a fair value figure is to give investors a feel for the initial move of the markets "on the open." Futures trading above the fair value number indicate a positive open for the grouping discussed, while numbers below fair value are indicative of negative openings.

- Fair value can also be used to refer more generally to a stock trading at a reasonable level considering price/earning ratios.
- Many financial news websites publish fair value data daily for key global markets, which means that you may not need to do all the calculations manually.

MORE INFO

Website:
Mark Hanes on fair value: tinyurl.com/3lglrxf

Future Value

Future value is simply the estimated value of a sum of money at a given point in the future, as in, "What will the $1,000 we have today be worth in two years' time?"

WHAT IT MEASURES

Any amount of any currency.

WHY IT IS IMPORTANT

Future value is a fundamental of investment. Understanding it helps any organization or individual to determine how a sum will be affected by changes in inflation, interest rates, or currency values. Inflation, for instance, will always reduce a sum's value. Interest rates will always increase it. Exchanging the sum for an identical amount in another currency will increase or decrease it, depending on how the respective currencies perform on the world market.

Armed with this knowledge, an organization can make more informed decisions about how to generate the maximum value from its funds in a given period of time: Would it be best to deposit them in simple interest-bearing accounts, exchange them for funds in another currency, use them to expand operations, or use them to acquire another company?

HOW IT WORKS IN PRACTICE

Start with three figures: the sum in question, the percentage by which it will increase or decrease, and the period of time. In this case: $1,000, 11%, and two years.

At an interest rate of 11%, our $1,000 will grow to $1,232 in two years:

$1,000 × 1.11 = $1,110 (first year) × 1.11 = $1,232 (second year)

Note that the interest earned in the first year generates additional interest in the second year, a practice known as compounding. When large sums are involved, the effect of compounding can be significant.

At an inflation rate of 11%, by contrast, our $1,000 will shrink to $812 in two years:

$1,000 ÷ 1.11 = $901 (first year) ÷ 1.11 = $812 (second year)

TRICKS OF THE TRADE

- Express the percentage as 1.11 and multiply and divide by that figure, instead of using 11%. Otherwise, errors will occur.
- Calculate each year, quarter, or month separately, as in our examples.
- It is important always to use the *annual* rates of interest and inflation.
- A more useful tool is "present value," which estimates what value future cash flows would have if they occurred today.

MORE INFO

Website:
Future value calculator: www.calculator.net/future-value-calculator.html

See Also:
 Time Value of Money (p. 411)

Calculations

Goodwill and Patents

One could define both goodwill and patents as figments of the imagination, the former a financier's and the latter an inventor's. The accounting realm assigns real value to both,

based on the theory that both will deliver real benefits in the future.

WHAT IT MEASURES
The value of two intangible assets.

WHY IT IS IMPORTANT
Since both goodwill and patents are intangible assets, their values will be whatever negotiators conclude. Still, their values need to be reflected in financial statements. Goodwill is created in the aftermath of an acquisition, and must appear on a balance sheet. The acquisition of a patent has a cost of its own, be it the price of internal development costs, or the purchase price paid to an inventor.

HOW IT WORKS IN PRACTICE
Ultimately, the assigned values of both assets are matters of opinion, however learned the opinions may be. Each must be considered separately.

Ordinarily, goodwill is completely ignored by accountants. Only when a company has been acquired by another does goodwill become an intangible asset. It then appears on a balance sheet in the amount by which the price paid by the acquiring company exceeds the net tangible assets of the acquired company. In other words:

Goodwill = Purchase price − Net assets

If, for example, an airline is bought for $12 billion and its net assets are valued at $9 billion, $3 billion of the purchase would be allocated to goodwill on the balance sheet.

The buyer will attribute the difference to any number of reasons that give a competitive advantage, such as a loyal and long-standing customer base, a strong brand, strategic location, or productive employees.

A patent's value, meanwhile, will probably be the sum of its development costs, or its purchase price if acquired from someone else. It is usually to a company's advantage to spread the patent's value over several years. If so, the critical time period to consider is not the full life of the patent (17 years in the United States), but its estimated useful life.

For example, let's say that in January 2000 a company acquired a patent issued in January 1995 at a cost of $100,000. It concludes that the patent's useful commercial life is 10 years, not the 12 remaining before the patent expires. In turn, patent value would be $100,000, and it would be spread (or amortized in accounting terms) over 10 years, or $10,000 each year.

TRICKS OF THE TRADE
- Accounting for goodwill can vary by country, an issue that needs to be considered when evaluating or negotiating acquisitions of foreign-based companies. Moreover, the rules may change from time to time. In the United States, for example, goodwill no longer has to be amortized over 40 years.
- The total value of a patent's development costs may stretch over several years.
- The cost of a patent ultimately may have little bearing on the future revenues and profits it brings.

MORE INFO
Websites:
UK Intellectual Property Office on patents:
  www.ipo.gov.uk/patent.htm
US Patent and Trademark Office on patents:
  www.uspto.gov/patents/

Gross Profit Margin Ratio

WHAT IT MEASURES
The gross profit margin ratio measures how efficiently a company uses its resources, materials, and labor in the production process by showing the percentage of net sales remaining after subtracting the cost of making and selling a product or service. It is usually expressed as a percentage, and indicates the profitability of a business before overhead costs.

WHY IT IS IMPORTANT
A high gross profit margin ratio indicates that a business can make a reasonable profit on sales, as long as overheads do not increase. Investors pay attention to the gross profit margin ratio because it tells them how efficient your business is compared to competitors. It is sensible to track gross profit margin ratios over a number of years to see if company earnings are consistent, growing, or declining.

For businesses, knowing your gross profit margin ratio is important because it tells you whether your business is pricing goods and services effectively. A low margin compared to your competitors would suggest you are under-pricing, while a high margin might indicate over-pricing. Low profit margin ratios can also suggest the business is unable to control production costs, or that a low amount of earnings is generated from revenues.

HOW IT WORKS IN PRACTICE
To calculate gross profit margin ratio, use the following formula:

Gross profit margin ratio = Gross profit margin ÷ Net sales

First, determine the gross profit for the business during a specific period of time, such as a financial quarter. This is total revenue minus the cost of sales. The cost of sales includes variable costs associated with manufacturing, packaging, and freight, and should not include fixed overheads such as rent or utilities.

For example, if Company A has net sales of $10 million, while costs for inventory or production total $7 million, then the gross profit margin is $3 million. Next, divide this by net sales. In our example:

3,000,000 ÷ 10,000,000 = 0.3 = 30%

(Simply multiply the result by 100 to see it expressed as a percentage, here a gross profit margin ratio of 30%.) Tracking several subsequent quarters will allow you to create a more accurate profit margin ratio. A more detailed version of the formula is:

Gross profit margin ratio = (Total revenue − Cost of sales) ÷ Total sales

TRICKS OF THE TRADE
- Gross profit margins tend to remain stable over time. Significant irregularities or sudden variations might be a potential sign of financial fraud, accounting irregularities, or problems in the business.
- Gross profit margin ratios can be calculated alongside net profit margin ratios (net profit after tax ÷ sales), pre-tax

profit margins (net profit before tax ÷ sales), and operating profit margins (net income before interest and taxes ÷ sales) to provide a more comprehensive insight into margins. Net profit margins and gross profit margins can be significantly different because of the impact of interest and tax expenses.
- Profit margin ratios are a popular way to benchmark against competitors. Industries will generally have standard gross profit margin ratios, which are easily discovered.
- If you use an accounting program such as QuickBooks, the software can calculate gross profit margin ratios for you, making it easier to track margin ratios over several years. If you discover fluctuations regularly occur at a particular time of year, you might try to adjust pricing to encourage greater sales at that period.

MORE INFO
Websites:
About.com on gross profit margin: tinyurl.com/e5b3b
BizWiz.com on profit margin ratios: tinyurl.com/6aykdyk

Interest Coverage

Interest coverage, or interest cover, describes several ratios used to assess a company's financial strength and capital structure.

WHAT IT MEASURES
The amount of earnings available to make interest payments after all operating and nonoperating income and expenses—except interest and income taxes—have been accounted for.

WHY IT IS IMPORTANT
Interest coverage is regarded as a measure of a company's creditworthiness because it shows how much income there is to cover interest payments on outstanding debt. Banks and financial analysts also rely on this ratio as a rule of thumb to gauge the fundamental strength of a business.

HOW IT WORKS IN PRACTICE
Interest coverage is expressed as a ratio, and reflects a company's ability to pay the interest obligations on its debt. It compares the funds available to pay interest—earnings before interest and taxes, or EBIT—with the interest expense. The basic formula is:

Interest coverage ratio = EBIT ÷ Interest expense

If interest expense for a year is $9 million, and the company's EBIT is $45 million, the interest coverage would be:

45,000,000 ÷ 9,000,000 = 5

The higher the number, the stronger a company is likely to be. Conversely, a low number suggests that a company's fortunes are looking ominous. Variations of this basic formula also exist. For example, there is:

Cash flow interest coverage ratio = (Operating cash flow + Interest + Taxes) ÷ Interest

This ratio indicates the company's ability to use its cash flow to satisfy its fixed financing obligations. Finally, there is the fixed-charge coverage ratio, which compares EBIT with fixed charges:

Fixed-charge coverage ratio = (EBIT + Lease expenses) ÷ (Interest + Lease expense)

"Fixed charges" can be interpreted in many ways, however. It could mean, for example, the funds that a company is obliged to set aside to retire debt, or dividends on preferred stock.

TRICKS OF THE TRADE
- A ratio of less than 1 indicates that a company is having problems generating enough cash flow to pay its interest expenses, and that either a modest decline in operating profits or a sudden rise in borrowing costs could eliminate profitability entirely.
- Ideally, interest coverage should at least exceed 1.5; in some sectors, 2.0 or higher is desirable.
- Interest coverage is widely considered to be more meaningful than looking at total debt, because what really

matters is what an enterprise must pay in a given period, not how much debt it has.

- As is often the case, it may be more meaningful to watch interest coverage over several periods in order to detect long-term trends.

- Cash flow will sometimes be substituted for EBIT in the ratio, because EBIT includes not only cash but also accrued sales and other unrealized income.
- Interest coverage also is called "times interest earned."

Internal Rate of Return

Internal rate of return (IRR) is another analytical tool based on the time value of money principle. Some regard it as the companion to net present value.

WHAT IT MEASURES
Technically, the interest rate that makes the present value of an investment's projected cash flows equal to the cost of the project; practically speaking, the rate that indicates whether or not an investment is worth pursuing.

WHY IT IS IMPORTANT
The calculation of internal rate of return (IRR) is used to appraise the prospective viability of investments and capital projects. It is also called dollar-weighted rate of return.

Essentially, IRR allows an investor to find the interest rate that is equivalent to the monetary returns expected from the project. Once that rate is determined, it can be compared to the rates that could be earned by investing the money elsewhere, or to the weighted cost of capital. IRR also accounts for the time value of money.

HOW IT WORKS IN PRACTICE
How is IRR applied? Assume, for example, that a project under consideration costs $7,500 and is expected to return $2,000 per year for five years, or $10,000. The IRR calculated for the project would be about 10%. If the cost of borrowing money for the project, or the return on investing the funds elsewhere, is less than 10%, the project is probably worthwhile. If the alternate use of the money will return 10% or more, the project should be rejected, since from a financial perspective it will break even at best.

Typically, management requires an IRR equal to or higher than the cost of capital, depending on relative risk and other factors.

The best way to compute an IRR is by using a spreadsheet (such as Excel) or a financial calculator, which do it automatically, although it is crucial to understand how the calculation should be structured. Calculating IRR by hand is tedious and time-consuming, and requires the process to be repeated to run sensitivities.

If using Excel, for example, select the IRR function. This requires the annual cash flows to be set out in columns, and

the first part of the IRR formula requires the cell reference range of these cash flows to be entered. Then a guess of the IRR is required. The default is 10%, written 0.1.

If a project has the following expected cash flows, then guessing IRR at 30% returns an accurate IRR of 27%, indicating that if the next best way of investing the money gives a return of − 20%, the project should go ahead.

Now	− 2,500
Year 1	1,200
Year 2	1,300
Year 3	1,500

TRICKS OF THE TRADE
- IRR analysis is generally used to evaluate a project's cash flows rather than income because, unlike income, cash flows do not reflect depreciation and therefore are usually more instructive to appraise.
- Most basic spreadsheet functions apply to cash flows only.
- As well as advocates, IRR has critics who dismiss it as misleading, especially as significant costs will occur late in the project. The rule of thumb that "the higher the IRR the better" does not always apply.
- For the most thorough analysis of a project's investment potential, some experts urge using both IRR and net present value calculations, and comparing their results.

MORE INFO
Book:
Walsh, Ciaran. *Key Management Ratios.* 4th ed. London: FT Prentice Hall, 2008.

Article:
Baker, Samuel L. "The internal rate of return." March 28, 2006. Online at: hadm.sph.sc.edu/COURSES/ECON/irr/irr.html

See Also:
★ Comparing Net Present Value and Internal Rate of Return (pp. 16–19)

Liquidity Ratio Analysis

WHAT IT MEASURES
Liquidity ratios are a set of ratios or figures that measure a company's ability to pay off its short-term debt obligations.

This is done by measuring a company's liquid assets (including those that might easily be converted into cash) against its short-term liabilities.

There are a number of different liquidity ratios, which each measure slightly different types of assets when calculating the ratio. More conservative measures will exclude assets that need to be converted into cash.

WHY IT IS IMPORTANT

In general, the greater the coverage of liquid assets to short-term liabilities, the more likely it is that a business will be able to pay debts as they become due while still funding ongoing operations. On the other hand, a company with a low liquidity ratio might have difficulty meeting obligations while funding vital ongoing business operations.

Liquidity ratios are sometimes requested by banks when they are evaluating a loan application. If you take out a loan, the lender may require you to maintain a certain minimum liquidity ratio, as part of the loan agreement. For that reason, steps to improve your liquidity ratios are sometimes necessary.

HOW IT WORKS IN PRACTICE

There are three fundamental liquidity ratios that can provide insight into short-term liquidity: current, quick, and cash ratios. These work as follows:

Current Ratio

This is a way of testing liquidity by deriving the proportion of assets available to cover current liabilities, as follows:

Current ratio = Current assets ÷ Current liabilities

Current ratio is widely discussed in the financial world, and it is easy to understand. However, it can be misleading because the chances of a company ever needing to liquidate all its assets to meet liabilities are very slim indeed. It is often more useful to consider a company as a going concern, in which case you need to understand the time it takes to convert assets into cash, as well as the current ratio.

The current ratio should be at least between 1.5 and 2, although some investors would argue that the figure should be above 2, particularly if a high proportion of assets are stock. A ratio of less than 1 (that is, where the current liabilities exceed the current assets) could mean that you are unable to meet debts as they fall due, in which case you are insolvent. A high current ratio could indicate that too much money is tied up in current assets—for example, giving customers too much credit.

Cash Ratio

This indicates liquidity by measuring the amount of cash, cash equivalents, and invested funds that are available to meet current short-term liabilities. It is calculated by using the following formula:

Cash ratio = (Cash + Cash equivalents + Invested funds) ÷ Current liabilities

The cash ratio is a more conservative measure of liquidity than the current ratio, because it only looks at assets that are already liquid, ignoring assets such as receivables or inventory.

Quick Ratio

The third liquidity ratio is a more sophisticated alternative to the current ratio, which measures the most liquid current assets—excluding inventory but including accounts receivable and certain investments.

Quick ratio = (Cash equivalents + Short-term investments
+ Accounts receivable) ÷ Current liabilities

The quick ratio should be around 0.7–1, with very few companies having a cash ratio of over 1. To be absolutely safe, the quick ratio should be at least 1, which indicates that quick assets exceed current liabilities. If the current ratio is rising and the quick ratio is static, this suggests a potential stockholding problem.

TRICKS OF THE TRADE

- All of these ratios have advantages and disadvantages. It is important to remember that any ratio that includes accounts receivable assumes a liquidation of accounts receivable—this may not be possible, practical, or desirable in many situations.
- Liquidity ratios should therefore be considered alongside ratios demonstrating the time it would take to convert assets to cash—a conversion time of several months compared to a few days would seriously affect liquidity.
- Some analysts use a fourth liquidity ratio to measure business performance, known as the "defensive interval." This measures how long a business can survive without cash coming in—and ideally should be between 30 and 90 days.

MORE INFO

Book:
Berman, Karen, and Joe Knight, with John Case. "Liquidity ratios: Can we pay our bills?" In *Financial Intelligence: A Manager's Guide to Knowing What the Numbers Really Mean*. Boston, MA: Harvard Business School Press, 2005. Also available separately.

Website:
Business Link on using accounting ratios to assess business performance: tinyurl.com/67y3xtp

See Also:
✔ Measuring Liquidity (pp. 299–300)
✥ Current Ratio (pp. 383–384)

Calculations

Management Accounts

WHAT THEY MEASURE

Company accounts fall into two categories: financial and management. While financial accounts are regulated and audited reports of financial transactions and processes, the management accounts are designed to help key business executives understand the overall performance of the business. Most companies produce these reports monthly or quarterly.

WHY THEY ARE IMPORTANT

Rather than focusing on financial metrics, management accounting focuses on operations and the value chain, as opposed to the historical activities of external financial reporting and auditing. They tend to be forward-looking and focused on identifying new revenue, cash flow, profit forecasts, and growth opportunities. Management accounts help executives carry out planning, control, and administration duties effectively. They mean you can see whether profitable parts of the business are subsidizing less successful activities, you can compare performance with forecasts, can identify trends, and manage resources better.

HOW THEY WORK IN PRACTICE

At their most basic, management accounts are reports that provide analysis of business performance and strategy broken down into different business activities or products. Each section of the report should provide an overview of cash flow, profit margins, liabilities, and forecasts for key business metrics.

In practice, management accounts are usually more complex than this. Management accountants may follow any of a number of management accounting methodologies, which will dictate what information is collected, and how it might be presented. Popular approaches to management accounting include:

Lifecycle costing: A form of management accounting that analyses the cost of manufacturing an individual product or service, and looks for how this might be improved.

Activity-based costing: Considers the costs involved in key manufacturing and business processes, such as running a single payroll, or a single product manufacturing cycle.

GPK: A German methodology for management accounting, sometimes known as marginal planned cost accounting. This system was created to provide a consistent, accurate view of how managerial costs are calculated and assigned to a company's products and services.

Lean accounting: A management accounting methodology that was designed in the 1990s for use in just-in-time manufacturing environments and service businesses.

Resource consumption accounting: Focuses on identifying areas with potential for business optimization. Governed by the RCA Institute, this approach to accounting

promotes consistency and professionalism in management accounts.

Throughput accounting: Recognizes the relationships between the various elements of the modern manufacturing process, and uses calculations to measure the contribution each part makes per unit of resource.

Management accounting can be applied to virtually any business, and each methodology can be tailored to meet the needs of different industries and sizes of company. However, any management accounting program should incorporate most of the following elements:
- variance analysis;
- rate and volume analysis;
- price modeling and profit margin analysis;
- cost analysis;
- cost/benefit analysis;
- lifecycle cost analysis;
- capital budgeting;
- strategic analysis;
- annual budgeting;
- sales and financial forecasting;
- cost allocation.

TRICKS OF THE TRADE
- Management accounting is easier if you build in regular systems to capture key information on a daily or weekly basis. Day to day, business managers should record information into a management accounts spreadsheet or application, including details of transactions made, results of financial changes, and projections of future trade.
- There are many off-the-shelf software packages that can be used for this purpose. The key is to select something easy to use—it's not an effective use of resources to spend weeks learning the intricacies of a financial reporting tool if your job is not financial.
- There is no pre-determined format for management accounts, nor any legal requirement to prepare them—but few businesses can survive without them.

MORE INFO
Website:
Business Link on management accounts:
  tinyurl.com/28zw3r6

Marginal Cost

Marginal cost is based on the economic theory that the more goods are produced, the lower will be the per-unit cost.

WHAT IT MEASURES
The additional cost of producing one more unit of product, or providing service to one more customer.

WHY IT IS IMPORTANT
Sometimes called incremental cost, marginal cost shows how much costs increase from making or serving one more unit, an essential factor when contemplating a production increase, or seeking to serve more customers.

If the price charged is greater than the marginal cost, then the revenue gain will be greater than the added cost. That, in

Calculations

turn, will increase profit, so the expansion in production or service makes economic sense and should proceed. Of course, the reverse is also true: If the price charged is less than the marginal cost, expansion should not go ahead.

HOW IT WORKS IN PRACTICE
The formula for marginal cost is:

Marginal cost = Change in cost ÷ Change in quantity

If it costs a company $260,000 to produce 3,000 items, and $325,000 to produce 3,800 items, the change in cost would be:

325,000 − 260,000 = $65,000

The change in quantity would be:

3,800 − 3,000 = 800

When the formula to calculate marginal cost is applied, the result is:

65,000 ÷ 800 = $81.25

If the price of the item in question were, say, $99.95, expansion should proceed.

TRICKS OF THE TRADE
- A marginal cost that is lower than the price shows that it is not always necessary to cut prices to sell more goods and boost profits.
- Using idle capacity to produce lower-margin items can still be beneficial, because these generate revenues that help cover fixed costs.
- Marginal cost studies can become quite complicated, because the basic formula does not always take into account variables that can affect cost and quantity. Software programs are available, many of which are industry-specific.
- At some point, marginal cost invariably begins to rise; typically, labor becomes less productive as a production run increases, while the time required also increases.
- Marginal cost alone may not justify expansion. It is best to determine also average costs, then chart the respective series of figures to find where marginal cost meets average cost, and thus determine optimum cost.
- Relying on marginal cost is not fail-safe; putting more product on a market can drive down prices and thus cut margins. Moreover, committing idle capacity to long-term production may tie up resources that could be directed to a new and more profitable opportunity.
- An important related principle is contribution: the cash gained (or lost) from selling an additional unit.

Market/Book Ratio

WHAT IT MEASURES
Market/book ratio, sometimes called price-to-book ratio, is a way of measuring the relative value of a company compared to its stock price or market value.

WHY IT IS IMPORTANT
Market/book ratio is a useful way of measuring your company's performance and making quick comparisons with competitors. It is an essential figure to potential investors and analysts because it provides a simple way of judging whether a company is under or overvalued. If your business has a low market/book ratio, it's considered a good investment opportunity.

HOW IT WORKS IN PRACTICE
At its simplest, market/book ratio measures the market capitalization (expressed as price per stock) of a business divided by its book value (the value of assets minus liabilities). The book value of a company refers to what would be left if the business paid its liabilities and shut its doors, although, of course, a growing business will always be worth more than its book value because it has the ability to generate new sales.

To calculate market/book ratio, take the current price per stock and divide by the book value per stock:

Market/book ratio = Market price per stock ÷ Book value per stock

For example, Company A might be trading at $2.20 per stock. However, the book value per stock is actually $3.00. This results in a market/book ratio of 0.73, suggesting the company's assets may in fact be undervalued by 27%.

Market-to-book value can alternatively be calculated as follows:

Market/book ratio = Market price per stock ÷ Net asset value per stock

TRICKS OF THE TRADE
- Like the price-to-earnings ratio, the lower the price-to-book ratio or market/book ratio, the better the value. Investors would use a low price-to-book ratio on stock screens, for instance, to identify potential candidates for new investment. As a rule of thumb, a market/book ratio above one suggests the company is undervalued, while a ratio over one suggests the company might be overvalued.
- A low market/book ratio could suggest a company's assets are undervalued, or that the company's prospects are good and earnings/value should grow.

Finance Essentials

- Market/book ratios are most useful when valuing knowledge-intensive companies, where physical assets may not accurately or fully reflect the value of the business. Technology companies and other businesses that don't have a lot of physical assets tend to have low book-to-market ratios.

MORE INFO
See Also:
⇄ Book Value (pp. 378–379)

Net Added Value (NAV) and Adjusted NAV

WHAT IT MEASURES
Net added value, or net asset value, is the value of a corporate asset or business based on its assets minus its liabilities. Adjusted NAV refers to the value once it has been adjusted for any known or suspected differences between market value and book value. In share dealing, NAV refers to the value of a portfolio minus its liabilities.

WHY IT IS IMPORTANT
For investors, the NAV gives an idea of appropriate share prices. For example, if a fund's NAV is $10, you should expect that you can buy the fund's shares for $10 each, although there are exceptions to this rule, such as a newly launched fund. NAV is particularly important when valuing shares in companies where much of the value comes from assets rather than the profit stream—such as investment trusts, but also property companies.

HOW IT WORKS IN PRACTICE
To calculate NAV for an investment portfolio, you should use the following formula:

Net added value = (Market value of all securities + Cash
+ Equivalent holdings − Liabilities)
÷ Total shares outstanding

For example, if a mutual fund holds $10.5 million in securities, $2 million in cash, and has liabilities totaling $0.5 million, with one million shares outstanding, then the NAV calculation would be as follows:

$(10.5 + 2 - 0.5) \div 1 = \$12$

TRICKS OF THE TRADE
- When calculating NAV for collective investments such as mutual funds, NAV is the total value of the portfolio less liabilities, calculated on a daily basis. Another alternative measurement for NAV is to add together unit capital and reserves held by a fund.

- In corporate valuations, NAV is the value of assets less liabilities. Assets include anything owned, whether in possession or not, while a liability is anything that is a potential cost to the business. Obviously this means calculating NAV for corporate entities is more difficult, and might be based on book value, carrying value, historical costs, amortized cost, or market value.
- NAV is a good way to keep track of price changes and asset valuations. However, you should keep in mind that the NAV calculation will change from day to day, and does not necessarily reflect the performance of the fund. In the early days of a fund, NAV will rise and fall as the fund's managers take their fees, and each time the fund makes a payout to shareholders. When a fund opens, it often trades at a premium to NAV, later falling to a discount.
- In general, a low NAV is considered a better investment opportunity than a high NAV. However, because NAV values on investment portfolios are calculated daily, critics argue that they are not a good performance indicator.
- In mutual funds, NAV per share is calculated at the close of trading each day based on closing share prices of securities held in the fund's portfolio. Any buy and sell orders are processed based on the day's NAV.
- The price that investors pay to purchase unit trust units is based on the approximate NAV per unit, plus fees that will be imposed by the unit's managers such as purchase fees.
- While you can calculate NAV for almost any business or fund, it is not of any real use when applied to service companies where there are few assets of value, such as plants, property, or equipment.

MORE INFO
Websites:
Money Terms on NAV: moneyterms.co.uk/nav/
US SEC on NAV: www.sec.gov/answers/nav.htm

Net Present Value

Net present value (NPV) expresses the sum total of an investment's future net cash flows (receipts less payments) minus the investment's initial costs. It is an investment appraisal tool.

WHAT IT MEASURES
The projected profitability of an investment, based on anticipated cash flows and discounted at a stated rate of interest.

WHY IT IS IMPORTANT

Net present value helps management or potential investors weigh the wisdom of an investment—in new equipment, a new facility, or other type of asset—by enabling them to quantify the expected benefits. Those evaluating more than one potential investment can compare the respective projected returns to find the most attractive project.

A positive NPV indicates that the project should be profitable, assuming that the estimated cash flows are reasonably accurate. A negative NPV, of course, indicates that the project will probably be unprofitable and therefore should be adjusted, if not abandoned altogether.

Equally significantly, NPV enables a management to consider the time value of money it will invest. This concept holds that the value of money increases with time because it can always earn interest in a savings account. Therefore, any other investment of that money must be weighed against how the funds would perform if simply deposited and saved.

When the time value of money concept is incorporated in the calculation of NPV, the value of a project's future net cash receipts in "today's money" can be determined. This enables proper comparisons between different projects.

HOW IT WORKS IN PRACTICE

Let's say that Global Manufacturing Inc. is considering the acquisition of a new machine. First, its management would consider all the factors: Initial purchase and installation costs; additional revenues generated by sales of the new machine's products; and the taxes on these new revenues. Having accounted for these factors in its calculations, the cash flows that Global Manufacturing projects will generate from the new machine are:

Year 1	− $100,000 (initial cost of investment)
Year 2	$30,000
Year 3	$40,000
Year 4	$40,000
Year 5	$35,000
Net total	$145,000

At first glance, it appears that cash flows total a whopping 45% more than the $100,000 initial cost, a strikingly sound investment indeed.

Alas, it's not that simple. Time value of money shrinks return on the project considerably, since future dollars are worth less than present dollars in hand. NPV accounts for these differences with the help of present value tables. These user-friendly tables, readily available on the internet and in references, list the ratios that express the present value of expected cash flow dollars, based on the applicable interest rate and the number of years in question.

In our example, Global Manufacturing's cost of capital is 9%. Using this figure to find the corresponding ratios in the present value table, the $100,000 investment cost, and expected annual revenues during the five years in question, the NPV calculation looks like this:

Year	Cash flow	Table factor (at 9%)	Present value
1	− $100,000	× 1.000000	= − $100,000.00
2	$30,000	× 0.917431	= $27,522.93
3	$40,000	× 0.841680	= $33,667.20
4	$40,000	× 0.772183	= $30,887.32
5	$35,000	× 0.708425	= $24,794.88
NPV			$16,873.33

Summing the present values of the cash flows and subtracting the investment cost from the total, the NPV is still positive. So, on this basis at least, the investment should proceed.

TRICKS OF THE TRADE

- Beware of assumptions. Interest rates change, of course, which can affect NPV dramatically. Moreover, fresh revenues (as well as new markets) may not grow as projected. If the cash flows in years 2–5 of our example fall by $5,000 a year, for instance, NPV shrinks to $5,260.89, which is still positive but less attractive.
- NPV calculations are performed only with cash receipts payments and discounting factors. In turn, NPV is a tool, not *the* tool. It ignores other accounting data, intangibles, sheer faith in a new idea, and other factors that may make an investment worth pursuing despite a negative NPV.
- It is important to determine a company's cost of capital accurately.

MORE INFO

Book:

Walsh, Ciaran. *Key Management Ratios*. 4th ed. London: FT Prentice Hall, 2008.

See Also:

★ Capital Budgeting: The Dominance of Net Present Value (pp. 12–16)

★ Comparing Net Present Value and Internal Rate of Return (pp. 16–19)

Nominal and Real Interest Rates

WHAT THEY MEASURE

When calculating interest rates, the nominal rate of interest refers to an interest rate calculated without any adjustment for inflation or for the full effect of compounding. The real interest rate includes compensation for value lost through inflation, whereas the nominal rate excludes this. Finally, the effective interest rate (sometimes known as the annual equivalent rate, or AER) is a rate that takes account of the impact of compounding.

If you purchase a bond for one year that pays 6% interest at the end of the 12 months, a $100 investment would return $106. The 6% interest is a nominal interest rate—it does not account for inflation during that year.

Imagine investing in the same bond and accounting for a 3% inflation rate for the year. If you buy an item for $100 at the start of the year, the same item would cost $103 at the end of the year. If we then invest the $100 into the 6% bond for one year, we lose $3 to inflation—meaning the real interest rate of the bond is actually 3%.

Alternatively, imagine investing the same $100 into the bond over 12 months. At 6%, your money would return $106 after one year. However, if interest is compounded every six months, you will actually earn slightly more. After six months, you would earn $3 interest. At the end of the year, the bond will pay 3% of your new investment total of $103, or $3.09. Your investment would then return $106.09 over a year, making the effective annual rate 6.09%, slightly higher than the nominal interest rate of 6%.

WHY THEY ARE IMPORTANT

When calculating interest rates, most calculations ignore the cost to the lender of not having funds available for a period of time—by the time a loan is repaid, the cost of items may have increased so that the money is now worth less. If you know what inflation is going to be, real interest rates are a powerful tool in analyzing the value of potential investments, because they take account of the erosion of spending power over the lifetime of an investment.

Calculating the effective rate is important because interest on different investments might be paid weekly, monthly, or annually. The effective annual interest rate can compare the returns or costs of different loans more accurately than a nominal interest rate.

HOW THEY WORK IN PRACTICE

The difference between real and nominal interest rates is simply expressed as: Real interest rate = Nominal rate − Inflation. More formally, it can also be described in the equation:

$$(1 + N) = (1 + r) - (1 + i)$$

where:
N is the nominal interest rate;
r is the real interest rate;
i is the rate of inflation.

This calculation is sometimes referred to as the Fisher equation. If you do not know the rate of inflation, it can be predicted using the following formula:

$$i = (\text{CPI this year } - \text{CPI last year}) \div \text{CPI last year}$$

If you know the nominal interest rate and the number of compounding periods, it is possible to calculate the effective annual rate using the following formula:

$$EAR = (1 + N \div P)^{P-1}$$

where:
N is the nominal rate;
P is the number of compounding periods.

TRICKS OF THE TRADE

- If inflation is positive then the real interest rate will be lower than the nominal interest rate. If the economy is experiencing deflation and the inflation rate is negative, then real interest is higher than nominal interest rates.
- When calculating effective interest rates, remember they will generally not include one-off charges such as set-up fees. In addition, while financial regulators closely control how the APR is expressed, there are fewer controls on the AER.
- The Fisher hypothesis states that, over time, inflation and nominal interest rates move together, so real interest rates are stable in the long term. This theory—sometimes called the Fisher effect, was devised by Irving Fisher.
- Some bonds and savings products link payments to an inflation index, so in effect pay a real interest rate. An example would be government-issued gilt.
- Sometimes it can be beneficial to value investments without taking inflation into account. This can be done by discounting using real interest rates.

MORE INFO

Article:
Moffatt, Mike. "What's the difference between nominal and real? Real variables and nominal variables explained." *About.com*. Online at: tinyurl.com/q25tt

See Also:
⚏ Annual Percentage Rate (pp. 374–375)

Option Pricing

WHAT IT MEASURES

There are two sorts of options in stock market trading: call and put. Option pricing uses mathematical models to calculate the value of a stock option and how it changes in response to changing conditions.

There are two key components to option pricing: the intrinsic value, which measures the amount by which an option is "in the money;" and the time value, which measures the amount paid for the time the option has before it expires.

WHY IT IS IMPORTANT

Stock traders use option pricing models to predict which options can be used to capture a potential move in a stock, and gain advantage in a trade. Option pricing is also important in risk management, because it can be used to quantify the risk associated with buying, selling, owning, and trading specific options with a high level of accuracy.

HOW IT WORKS IN PRACTICE

To understand option pricing, you must understand the four basic drivers of option prices: current stock price, intrinsic value, time to expiration, and volatility.

Stock price is important because if the price of a stock rises, the cost of a call option will also rise (though not necessarily at the same rate).

Intrinsic value is important because it measures how far an option is "in the money" (ITM), or what proportion of the option's value isn't lost over time. The intrinsic value of the call option is the stock price minus the call strike price.

Time value is the difference between the option's price and its intrinsic value. The more time an option has until it expires, the greater chance it will become "in the money"—and therefore the option becomes more valuable.

Option pricing is related to volatility expected in the market up to the time of expiration. If the market expects little movement in a stock's value, volatility is low, which results in a lower time value.

The most well-known method of modeling option pricing was developed by Fischer Black and Myron Scholes in 1973. The Black–Scholes model works as follows:

$$C = SN(d_1) - Ke^{(-rt)}N(d_2)$$

where:
C = call premium;
S = current stock price;
t = time to expiration;
K = option price;
r = risk-free interest rate;
N = normal distribution;
e = exponential term.
The first part of the calculation, $SN(d_1)$, shows the expected benefit of buying the stock outright. This is calculated by multiplying together the stock price and the change in call premium caused by a change in the underlying stock price.

The second part of the equation shows the present value of paying the exit price on the day the option expires. The fair value of the option price is then calculated by looking at the difference between the option's current value and value at expiration.

The Black–Scholes model of option pricing relies on several assumptions, which should be taken into account. These are:
- the stock pays no dividends during the option's life;
- the stock can only be exercised on the expiration date;
- markets are efficient;
- no commissions are charged;
- interest rates are consistent, predictable, and known;
- returns are normally distributed.

TRICKS OF THE TRADE
- A major potential limitation of the Black–Scholes model is the assumption that no dividends are paid on stock during the lifetime of the option—because most stocks do pay dividends. One way to resolve this is to subtract the discounted value of a future dividend from the stock price.
- In Europe, it is common that options can only be exercised on the expiration date, whereas in the United States they might be exercised at any time. This makes American options more flexible and therefore more valuable.
- The Black–Scholes model has been refined over time by a number of financial scholars, including Merton (who devised a model to take account of dividends) and Ingerson (who devised a model that did not require constant interest rates).

MORE INFO
Article:
Wagner, Hans. "Understanding option pricing." *Investopedia* (April 20, 2009). Online at: tinyurl.com/6l3n837

Website:
Risk Glossary on option pricing theory: tinyurl.com/6gq7u3f

See Also:
✔ Swaps, Options, and Futures: What They Are and Their Function (pp. 303–304)

Payback Period

At first glance, payback is a simple investment appraisal technique, but it can quickly become complex.

WHAT IT MEASURES

How long it will take to earn back the money invested in a project.

WHY IT IS IMPORTANT

The straight payback period method is the simplest way of determining the investment potential of a major project. Expressed in time, it tells a management how many months or years it will take to recover the original cash cost of the project—always a vital consideration, and especially so for managements evaluating several projects at once.

This evaluation becomes even more important if it includes an examination of what the present value of future revenues will be.

HOW IT WORKS IN PRACTICE

The straight payback period formula is:

Payback period = Cost of project ÷ Annual cash revenues

Thus, if a project costs $100,000 and is expected to generate $28,000 annually, the payback period would be:

$100,000 \div 28,000 = 3.57$ years

If the revenues generated by the project are expected to vary from year to year, add the revenues expected for each succeeding year until you arrive at the total cost of the project.

For example, say the revenues expected to be generated by the $100,000 project are:

Year	Revenue	Total
1	$19,000	$19,000
2	$25,000	$44,000
3	$30,000	$74,000
4	$30,000	$104,000
5	$30,000	$134,000

Thus, the project would be fully paid for in year 4, since it is in that year that the total revenue reaches the initial cost of $100,000.

The picture becomes complex when the time value of money principle is introduced into the calculations. Some experts insist this is essential to determine the most accurate payback period. Accordingly, present value tables or computers (now the norm) must be used, and the annual revenues have to be discounted by the applicable interest rate, 10% in this example. Doing so produces significantly different results:

Year	Revenue	Present value	Total
1	$19,000	$17,271	$17,271
2	$25,000	$20,650	$37,921
3	$30,000	$22,530	$60,451
4	$30,000	$20,490	$80,941
5	$30,000	$18,630	$99,571

This method shows that payback would not occur even after five years.

TRICKS OF THE TRADE

- Clearly, a main defect of the straight payback period method is that it ignores the time value of money principle, which, in turn, can produce unrealistic expectations.
- A second drawback is that it ignores any benefits generated after the payback period, and thus a project that would return $1 million after, say, six years might be ranked lower than a project with a three-year payback that returns only $100,000 thereafter.
- Another alternative to calculating by payback period is to develop an internal rate of return.
- Under most analyses, projects with shorter payback periods rank higher than those with longer paybacks, even if the latter promise higher returns. Longer paybacks can be affected by such factors as market changes, changes in interest rates, and economic shifts. Shorter cash paybacks also enable companies to recoup an investment sooner and put it to work elsewhere.
- Generally, a payback period of three years or less is desirable; if a project's payback period is less than a year, some contend it should be judged essential.

MORE INFO
See Also:
✔ Appraising Investment Opportunities (p. 358)
⇄ Return on Investment (pp. 408–409)

Payout Ratio

Dividend cover, and its US equivalent, payout ratio, is a quick reflection of profitability, which is used to evaluate and select investments.

WHAT IT MEASURES
Dividend cover expresses the number of times a company's dividends to common stockholders could be paid out of its net after-tax profits.

Payout ratio expresses the total dividends paid to stockholders as a percentage of a company's net profit in a given period of time.

WHY IT IS IMPORTANT
Whether defined as dividend cover or payout ratio, it measures the likelihood of dividend payments being sustained, and thus is a useful indication of sustained profitability. However, each ratio must be interpreted independently.

A low dividend cover suggests it might be difficult to pay the same level of dividends in a downturn, and that a company is not reinvesting enough in its future. High cover, therefore,

implies just the opposite. Negative dividend cover is unusual, and a clear sign of trouble.

The payout ratio, expressed as a percentage or fraction, is an inverse measure: A high ratio indicates a lack of reinvestment in the business, and that current earnings cannot sustain the current dividend payments. In other words, the lower the ratio, the more secure the dividend—and the company's future.

HOW IT WORKS IN PRACTICE
Dividend cover is so named because it shows how many times over the profits could have paid the dividend. If the figure is 3, for example, a firm's profits are three times the level of the dividend paid to shareholders. To calculate dividend cover, divide earnings per share by the dividend per share:

Dividend cover = Earnings per share $\div$ Dividend per share

If a company has earnings per share of $8, and it pays out a dividend of $2.10, dividend cover is:

$8 \div $2.10 = 3.80$

An alternative formula divides a company's net profit by the total amount allocated for dividends. So a company that earns $10 million in net profit and allocates $1 million for dividends has a dividend cover of 10, while a company that earns $25 million and pays out $10 million in dividends has a dividend cover of 2.5:

$10,000,000 ÷ $1,000,000 = 10

$25,000,000 ÷ $10,000,000 = 2.5

The payout ratio is calculated by dividing annual dividends paid on common stock by earnings per share:

Payout ratio = Annual dividend ÷ Earnings per share

Take the company whose earnings per share is $8 and dividend payout is $2.10. Its payout ratio would be:

2.10 ÷ 8 = 0.263 = 26.3%

TRICKS OF THE TRADE
- A dividend cover ratio of 2 or higher is usually adequate, and indicates that the dividend is affordable. By the same token, the payout ratio should not exceed two-thirds of earnings. Like most ratios, however, both vary by industry. US real estate investment trusts, for example, pay out almost all their earnings in dividends because US tax laws exempt them from taxes if they do so. American utilities also offer high payout rates.

- A dividend cover ratio below 1.5 is risky, and a ratio below 1 indicates that a company is paying the current year's dividend with retained earnings from a previous year—a practice that cannot continue indefinitely.
- The higher the dividend cover figure, the less likely the dividend will be reduced or eliminated in the future, should profits fall. Companies that suffer sharp declines or outright losses will often continue paying dividends to indicate that their substandard performance is an anomaly.
- On the other hand, a high dividend cover figure may disappoint an investor looking for income, since the figure suggests directors could have declared a larger dividend.
- A high payout ratio clearly appeals to conservative investors seeking income. However, when coupled with weak or falling earnings it could suggest an imminent dividend cut, or that the company is short-changing reinvestment to maintain its payout.
- A payout ratio above 75% is a warning. It suggests the company is failing to reinvest sufficient profits in its business, that the company's earnings are faltering, or that it is trying to attract investors who otherwise would not be interested.
- Newer and faster-growing companies often pay no dividends at all in order to reinvest earnings in the company's development.
- Historically, dividends have provided more than 40% of a stock investor's total portfolio return. However, the figure has been about half that over the last 20 years.

Price/Earnings Ratio

WHAT IT MEASURES
The price/earnings (P/E) ratio is simply the stock price divided by earnings per share (EPS). While EPS is an actual amount of money, usually expressed in cents per share, the P/E ratio has no units—it is just a number. Thus if a quoted company has a stock price of $100 and EPS of $12 for the last published year, then it has a historical P/E of 8.3. If analysts are forecasting for the next year an EPS of, say, $14 then the forecast P/E is 7.1.

WHY IT IS IMPORTANT
Since EPS is the annual earnings per share of a company, it follows that dividing the stock price by EPS tells us how many years of current EPS are represented by the stock price. In the above example, then, the P/E of 8.3 tells us that investors at the current price are prepared to pay 8.3 years of historical EPS for the stock, or 7.1 years of the forecast next year's EPS. Theoretically, the faster a company is expected to grow, the higher the P/E ratio that investors would award it. It is one measure of how cheap or expensive a stock appears to be.

HOW IT WORKS IN PRACTICE
Forecasts can go wrong, of course, resulting in the infamous profit warnings that are issued by some companies. In these they warn that expected profit targets, for various reasons, will

not be met. Understandably, a slump in the stock price is the normal reaction, and analysts would then downgrade their existing forecast EPS. If, in the above example, our forecast of $14 for next year was halved to $7 following a profit warning, the forecast P/E on the same price of $100 would immediately double to 14.3—but in practice the price would usually fall substantially, thus cutting back the forecast P/E.

The P/E ratio is mainly useful in comparisons with other stocks rather than in isolation. For example, if the average P/E in the market is 20, there will be many stocks with P/Es well above and well below this, for a variety of reasons. Similarly, in a particular sector, the P/Es will frequently vary quite widely from the sector average, even though the constituent companies may all be engaged in broadly similar businesses. The reason is that even two businesses doing the same thing will not always be doing it as profitably as each other. One may be far more efficient, as demonstrated by a history of rising EPS compared with the flat EPS picture of the other over a series of years, and the market might recognize this by awarding the more profitable stock a higher P/E.

TRICKS OF THE TRADE
- Take care. The market frequently gets it wrong and many high-P/E stocks have in the past been the most awful long-term investments, losing investors huge amounts of money

when the promise of future rapid growth proved to be a chimera. In contrast, many low-P/E companies, often in what are perceived as dull industries, have proved over time to be outstanding investments.

- The P/E is an investment tool that is both invaluable and yet requires extreme caution in its application when comparing and selecting investments. It remains, however, by far the most commonly utilized ratio in investment analysis.

MORE INFO
Book:

Walsh, Ciaran. *Key Management Ratios*. 4th ed. London: FT Prentice Hall, 2008.

See Also:

⇄ Earnings per Share (pp. 389–390)

Rate of Return

This may well be as basic and important a computation as there is in finance.

WHAT IT MEASURES
The annual return on an investment, expressed as a percentage of the total amount invested. It also measures the yield of a fixed-income security.

WHY IT IS IMPORTANT
Rate of return is a simple and straightforward way to determine how much investors are being paid for the use of their money, so that they can then compare various investments and select the best—based, of course, on individual goals and acceptable levels of risk.

Rate of return has a second and equally vital purpose: As a common denominator that measures a company's financial performance, for example, in terms of rate of return on assets, equity, or sales.

HOW IT WORKS IN PRACTICE
There is a basic formula that will serve most needs, at least initially:

Rate of return = (Current value of amount invested

− Original value of amount invested)

÷ Original value of amount invested

If \$1,000 in capital is invested in stock, and one year later the investment yields \$1,100, the rate of return of the investment is calculated like this:

$$(1100 − 1000) ÷ 1000 = 0.1 = 10\%$$

Now, assume \$1,000 is invested again. One year later, the investment grows to \$2,000 in value, but after another year the value of the investment falls to \$1,200. The rate of return after the first year is:

$$(2000 − 1000) ÷ 1000 = 1 = 100\%$$

The rate of return after the second year is:

$$(1200 − 2000) ÷ 2000 = −0.4 = −40\%$$

The average annual return for the two years (also known as average annual arithmetic return) can be calculated using this formula:

Average annual return = (Rate of return for year 1 + Rate of return for year 2) ÷ 2

Accordingly:

$$(100\% + −40\%) ÷ 2 = 30\%$$

Be careful, however! The average annual rate of return is a percentage, but one that is accurate over only a short period, so this method should be used accordingly.

The geometric or compound rate of return is a better yardstick for measuring investments over the long run, and takes into account the effects of compounding. As one might expect, this formula is more complex and technical, and beyond the scope of this article.

TRICKS OF THE TRADE
- The real rate of return is the annual return realized on an investment, adjusted for changes in the price due to inflation. If 10% is earned on an investment but inflation is 2%, then the real rate of return is actually 8%.
- Do not confuse rate of return with internal rate of return, which is a more complex calculation.
- Some mutual fund managers have been known to report the average annual rate of return on the investments they manage. In the second example, that figure is 30%, yet the value of the investment is only \$200 higher than it was two years ago, or 20%. So, read such reports carefully.

MORE INFO
Book:
Walsh, Ciaran. *Key Management Ratios*. 4th ed. London: FT Prentice Hall, 2008.

See Also:
⇄ Internal Rate of Return (p. 396)
⇄ Risk-Adjusted Rate of Return (p. 410)

Residual Value

WHAT IT MEASURES

Residual value is the value an asset will have after it has been depreciated, or amortized. Residual value is sometimes referred to as "salvage" value.

WHY IT IS IMPORTANT

According to international financial reporting standards, residual value is the value an asset should have if it is in the expected condition at the end of its useful life, after the cost of selling it.

HOW IT WORKS IN PRACTICE

When calculating the residual value of a business asset, the salvage value is used in conjunction with the purchase price and accounting methods to determine the amount by which the asset depreciates each period. For example, with a straight-line basis, an asset that cost $5,000 and has a salvage value of $1,000 and a useful life of five years would be depreciated at $800 ([5,000 − 1,000] ÷ 5) each year.

This straight-line method uses the following formula to calculate residual value:

$$\text{Depreciation expense} = (\text{Cost of fixed asset} - \text{Scrap value}) \div \text{Lifespan}$$

An alternative approach is to use the declining-balance method, which assumes that an asset loses value more rapidly in the early part of its useful lifetime. In the case of machinery, this is often a more realistic approach. To calculate residual value using this methodology, each period of depreciation is based on the previous year's net book value, estimated lifespan, and a factor of 2 (known as the double-declining balance). For example:

$$\text{Depreciation expense} = \text{Previous period NBV} \times \text{Factor} \div \text{N}$$

For the double-declining balance method, using the vehicle example from above, we compute the depreciation after the first year:

$$17000 \times 2 \div 5 = \$6800$$

In business accounting there are three common methods of calculating the residual value of a business:

Perpetuity business valuation: Using this methodology, the business assumes the company's future cash flow will continue indefinitely, and the residual value of the asset is calculated according to the following formula:

$$\text{Residual value} = \text{Free cash flow in year } n \div r$$

1 where r is the discount rate and n is the last year of the analysis period.

2 Liquidation business valuation: Using this methodology assumes the most conservative way to calculate residual value is to assume the asset will be liquidated at the end of the forecasting period. So, residual value is calculated as being the net liquidation value—the asset's value (including cash, inventory, plant) less liabilities. This value is discounted for the beginning of the period, before adding it to the discounted cash flow, to calculate the company's value.

3 Price earnings valuation: Assumes the best way to determine a venture's residual value is to calculate its market price using the relevant price earning factor as follows:

$$\text{Residual value} = \text{Net profit in year } n \times \text{Comparative PE} \div r$$

where r is the discount rate and n is the selected year. Comparative PE refers to the PE of any similar company, or the industry average. The result is then discounted to the beginning of the plan period and added to discounted cash flow.

TRICKS OF THE TRADE

- Residual values should be reviewed annually alongside the useful life of assets, and depreciation adjusted if the residual value of an asset has changed.
- Intangible assets have a zero residual value. Some tangible assets may also have a zero residual value if they cannot be resold, or if there are costs associated with their disposal that outstrip the residual value.
- Residual values used for calculating depreciation should be calculated per asset, but most companies would simplify the calculations by grouping together items into categories.
- Residual value can be built into leases. The residual value of leased assets is the cost of the asset minus less repayments of capital made over the lifetime of the lease.

MORE INFO

Article:

White, Diane. "Depreciation of fixed assets: Straight line, units-of-production, and double declining method." *Suite101.com* (September 15, 2008). Online at: tinyurl.com/5w6625f

Website:

Money Terms on residual value: moneyterms.co.uk/residual-value/

See Also:

≒ Depreciation (pp. 385–386)

Calculations

408 Return on Assets

Return on assets—or simply ROA—may also be termed return on total assets (ROTA) or return on net assets (RONA). Whatever its designation, it is often referred to as the No. 1 ratio in finance.

WHAT IT MEASURES
A company's profitability, expressed as a percentage of its total assets.

WHY IT IS IMPORTANT
Return on assets measures how effectively a company has used the total assets at its disposal to generate earnings. Because the ROA formula reflects total revenue, total cost, and assets deployed, the ratio itself reflects a management's ability to generate income during the course of a given period, usually a year.

Naturally, the higher the return, the better the profit performance. ROA is a convenient way of comparing a company's performance with that of its competitors, although the items on which the comparison is based may not always be identical.

HOW IT WORKS IN PRACTICE
To calculate ROA, divide a company's net income by its total assets, then multiply by 100 to express the figure as a percentage:

Return on assets = Net income ÷ Total assets

If net income is $30, and total assets are $420, the ROA is:

$30 \div 420 = 0.0714 = 7.14\%$

A variation of this formula can be used to calculate return on net assets (RONA):

Return on net assets = Net income ÷ (Fixed assets + Working capital)

And, on occasion, the formula will separate after-tax interest expense from net income:

Return on assets = (Net income + Interest expense) ÷ Total assets

It is therefore important to understand what each component of the formula actually represents.

TRICKS OF THE TRADE
- Some experts recommend using the net income value at the end of the given period, and the assets' value from the beginning of the period, or an average value taken over the complete period, rather than an end-of-the-period value; otherwise, the calculation will include assets that have accumulated during the year, which can be misleading.
- While a high ratio indicates a greater return, it must still be balanced against such factors as risk, sustainability, and reinvestment in the business through development costs. Some managements will sacrifice the long-term interests of investors in order to achieve an impressive ROA in the short term.
- A climbing return on assets usually indicates a climbing stock price, because it tells investors that a management is skilled at generating profits from the resources that a business owns.
- Acceptable ROAs vary by sector. In banking, for example, a ROA of 1% or better is a considered to be the standard benchmark of superior performance.
- ROA is an effective way of measuring the efficiency of manufacturers, but can be suspect when measuring service companies, or companies whose primary assets are people.
- Other variations of the ROA formula do exist.

MORE INFO
See Also:
 Asset Turnover (p. 375)
 Asset Utilization (pp. 375–376)

Calculations

Return on Investment

Return on investment (ROI) is a ratio that is used frequently—perhaps too frequently. Its definition can vary widely. Indeed, ROI today is not only a family of measurements of the performance of invested capital but also a concept, one used to justify expenditure on almost everything.

WHAT IT MEASURES
In the financial realm, the overall profit or loss on an investment expressed as a percentage of the total amount invested or total funds appearing on a company's balance sheet.

WHY IT IS IMPORTANT
Like return on assets or return on equity, return on investment measures a company's profitability and its management's ability to generate profits from the funds investors have placed at its disposal.

One opinion holds that if a company's operations cannot generate net earnings at a rate that exceeds the cost of borrowing funds from financial markets, the future of that company is grim.

HOW IT WORKS IN PRACTICE
The most basic expression of ROI can be found by dividing a company's net profit (also called net earnings) by the total investment (total debt plus total equity), then multiplying by 100 to arrive at a percentage:

Return on investment = Net profit ÷ Total investment

If, say, net profit is $30 and total investment is $250, the ROI is:

30 ÷ 250 = 0.12 = 12%

A more complex variation of ROI is an equation known as the Du Pont formula:

ROI = Net profit after taxes ÷ Total assets
= Net profit after taxes ÷ Sales × Sales ÷ Total assets

If, for example, net profit after taxes is $30, total assets are $250, and sales are $500, then:

30 ÷ 250 = 30 ÷ 500 × 500 ÷ 250 = 12% = 6% × 2 = 12%

Champions of this formula, which was developed by the Du Pont Company in the 1920s, say that it helps to reveal how a company has both deployed its assets and controlled its costs, and how it can achieve the same percentage return in different ways.

For stockholders, the variation of the basic ROI formula used by investors is:

ROI = (Net income + Current value − Original value) ÷ Original value

If, for example, somebody invests $5,000 in a company and a year later has earned $100 in dividends, while the value of the stock is $5,200, the return on investment would be:

(100 + 5,200 − 5,000) ÷ 5,000 = 300 ÷ 5,000 = 0.06 = 6%

TRICKS OF THE TRADE
- Securities investors can use yet another ROI formula: net income divided by common stock and preferred stock equity plus long-term debt.
- It is vital to understand exactly what a return on investment measures—for example, assets, equity, or sales. Without this understanding, comparisons may be misleading or suspect. A search for "return on investment" on the internet, for example, harvests everything from staff training to e-commerce to advertising and promotions!
- Be sure to establish whether the net profit figure used is before or after provision for taxes. This is important for making ROI comparisons accurate.

MORE INFO
See Also:
✔ Appraising Investment Opportunities (p. 358)
⇄ Payback Period (pp. 403–404)

Return on Stockholders' Equity

Return on equity (ROE) is probably the most widely used measure of how well a company is performing for its stockholders.

WHAT IT MEASURES
Profitability, specifically the percentage return that was delivered to a company's owners.

WHY IT IS IMPORTANT
ROE is a fundamental indication of a company's ability to increase its earnings per share and thus the quality of its stock, because it reveals how well a company is using its money to generate additional earnings.

It is a relatively straightforward benchmark, easy to calculate, and is applicable to a majority of industries. ROE allows investors to compare a company's use of their equity with other investments, and to compare the performance of companies in the same industry. ROE can also help to evaluate trends in a business.

Businesses that generate high returns on equity are businesses that pay off their stockholders handsomely and create substantial assets for each dollar invested.

HOW IT WORKS IN PRACTICE
To calculate ROE, divide the net income shown on the income statement (usually of the past year) by stockholders' equity, which appears on the balance sheet:

Return on equity = Net income ÷ Owners' equity

For example, if net income is $450 and equity is $2,500, then:
450 ÷ 2,500 = 0.18 = 18%

TRICKS OF THE TRADE
- Because new variations of the ROE ratio do appear, it is important to know how the figure is calculated.
- Return on equity for most companies certainly should be in the double digits; investors often look for 15% or higher, while a return of 20% or more is considered excellent.
- Seasoned investors also review five-year average ROE, to gauge consistency.
- A word of caution: Financial statements usually report assets at book value, which is the purchase price minus depreciation; they do not show replacement costs. A business with older assets should show higher rates of ROE than a business with newer assets.

Calculations

- Examining ROE with return on assets can indicate if a company is debt-heavy. If a company has very little debt, it is reasonable to assume that its management is earning high profits and/or using assets effectively.
- A high ROE also could be due to leverage (a method of corporate funding in which a higher proportion of funds is raised through borrowing than issuing stock). If liabilities are high the balance sheet will reveal it, hence the need to review it.

MORE INFO

Book:
Walsh, Ciaran. *Key Management Ratios*. 4th ed. London: FT Prentice Hall, 2008.

See Also:
⇄ Dividend Yield (pp. 388–389)
⇄ Earnings per Share (pp. 389–390)

Risk-Adjusted Rate of Return

Knowing an investment's risk-adjusted return goes a long way toward determining just how much "bang for the buck" is really being generated.

WHAT IT MEASURES
How much an investment returned in relation to the risk that was assumed to attain it.

WHY IT IS IMPORTANT
Being able to compare a high-risk, potentially high-return investment with a low-risk, lower-return investment helps to answer a key question that confronts every investor: Is it worth the risk?

By itself, the historical average return of an investment, asset, or portfolio can be quite misleading and a faulty indicator of future performance. Risk-adjusted return is a much better barometer.

The calculation also helps to reveal whether the returns of the portfolio reflect smart investment decisions, or the taking on of excess risk that may or may not have been worth what was gained. This is particularly helpful in appraising the performance of money managers.

HOW IT WORKS IN PRACTICE
There are several ways to calculate risk-adjusted return. Each has its strengths and shortcomings. All require particular data, such as an investment's rate of return, the risk-free return rate for a given period (usually the performance of a 90-day US Treasury bill over 36 months), and a market's performance and its standard deviation.

Which one to use? It often depends on an investor's focus, principally whether the focus is on upside gains or downside losses.

Perhaps the most widely used is the **Sharpe ratio**. This measures the potential impact of return volatility on expected return and the amount of return earned per unit of risk. The higher a fund's Sharpe ratio, the better its historical risk-adjusted performance, and the higher the number the greater the return per unit of risk. The formula is:

$$\text{Sharpe ratio} = \text{(Portfolio return} - \text{Risk-free return)} \div \text{Standard deviation of portfolio return}$$

Take, for example, two investments, one returning 54%, the other 26%. At first glance, the higher figure clearly looks the better choice, but because of its high volatility it has a Sharpe

ratio of 0.279, while the investment with a lower return has a ratio of 0.910. On a risk-adjusted basis the latter would be the wiser choice.

The **Treynor ratio** also measures the excess of return per unit of risk. Its formula is:

$$\text{Treynor ratio} = \text{(Portfolio return} - \text{Risk-free return)} \div \text{Portfolio's beta}$$

In this formula (and others that follow), beta is a separately calculated figure that describes the tendency of an investment to respond to marketplace swings. The higher the beta, the greater the volatility, and vice versa.

A third formula, **Jensen's measure**, is often used to rate a money manager's performance against a market index, and whether or not an investment's risk was worth its reward. The formula is:

$$\text{Jensen's measure} = \text{Portfolio return} - \text{Risk-free return} - \text{Portfolio beta} \times \text{(Benchmark return} - \text{Risk-free return)}$$

TRICKS OF THE TRADE
- A fourth formula, the **Sortino ratio**, also exists. Its focus is more on downside risk than potential opportunity, and its calculation is more complex.
- There are no benchmarks for these values. In order to be useful the numbers should be compared with the ratios of other investments.
- No single measure is perfect, so experts recommend using them broadly. For instance, if a particular investment class is on a roll and does not experience a great deal of volatility, a good return per unit of risk does not necessarily reflect management genius. When the overall momentum of technology stocks drove returns straight up in 1999, Sharpe ratios climbed with them, and did not reflect any of the sector's volatility that was to erupt in late 2000.
- Most of these measures can be used to rank the risk-adjusted performance of individual stocks, various portfolios over the same time, and mutual funds with similar objectives.

MORE INFO
Website:
Kalengo tutorial on risk-adjusted return: tinyurl.com/5s6z5er

See Also:
⇄ Treynor Ratio (pp. 412–413)

Time Value of Money

WHAT IT MEASURES

Time Value of Money (TVM) is one of the most important concepts in the financial world. If a business is paid $1 million for something today, that money is worth more than if the same $1 million was paid at some point in the future. The reason money given today is worth more is straightforward: If I have money today, I have the potential to earn interest on the capital.

TVM values how much more a given sum of money is worth now (or at a specific future date) compared to in the future (or, in the case of a future payment, a date that is even further in the future). TVM calculations take into account likely interest gains, discounted cash flow, and potential risk, to create a value figure for a specific amount of money or investment opportunity.

There are several calculations commonly used to express the time value of money, but the most important are present value and future value.

WHY IT IS IMPORTANT

If company A has the opportunity to realize $10,000 from an asset today, or two years in the future, TVM allows the company to calculate exactly how much more that $10,000 is worth if it's received today, as opposed to in the future. It is important to know how to calculate the time value of money because it means you can distinguish between the value of investment opportunities that offer returns at different times.

HOW IT WORKS IN PRACTICE

If a business has the option of receiving a $1 million investment today or a guaranteed payment of the same amount in two years' time, you can use TVM calculations to show the relative value of the two sums of money.

Option A, take the money now: The business might accept the $1,000,000 investment immediately and put the capital into an account paying a 4.5% annual return. In this account, the $1,000,000 would earn $92,025 interest over two years (annually compounded), making the future value of the investment $1,092,025. This can be expressed using the following formula:

$$\text{Future value} = 1,000,000 \times (1 + 0.045)^2$$

which might be expressed as:

$$\text{Future value} = \text{Original sum} \times (1 + \text{Interest rate per period})^{\text{No. of periods}}$$

Obviously, the present value of the $1 million if it is received today would be $1 million. But if the money isn't received for another two years, we can still calculate its present and future values.

The present value of a future $1 million investment is based on how much you would need to receive today to receive $1 million in two years' time. This is done by discounting the $1,000,000 by the interest rate for the period. Assuming an annual interest rate of 4.5%, we can calculate the present value using the following formula:

$$\text{Present value} = \text{Future value} \div (1 + \text{Interest rate per period})^{\text{No. of periods}}$$

Using this formula, we can see that the present value of a future payment of $1 million in two years' time is:

$$1,000,000 \div (1 + 0.045)^2 = \$915,730$$

In other words, the investment in two years time is the equivalent of receiving $915,730 today, and investing it at 4.5% for two years.

TRICKS OF THE TRADE

- There are five key components in TVM calculations. These are: present value, future value, the number of periods, the interest rate, and a payment principal sum. Providing you know four of these values, you can rearrange the TVM formulae to calculate the fifth.
- When calculating TVM, you may sometimes need to supplement the calculation to discount future payments to take account of risk as well as time value. Discount rates can be adjusted to take account of risks like the other party not paying you back (default risk) or the fact that the item you intended to purchase has become more expensive, reducing the buying power of the money. In this case, the company lending the principal sum might insist on a higher interest rate to compensate for the risk.
- If a future payment is not certain, you can use the capital asset pricing model to calculate the risk involved.

MORE INFO

Websites:
Money-zine TVM calculator: tinyurl.com/6cmtjql
TVMCalcs.com guide: www.tvmcalcs.com/tvm/tvm_intro

See Also:
⇄ Future Value (p. 393)

⇄ Future Value (p. 393)

Calculations

Total Return

Total return is one more way to evaluate investment decisions, and because it totals all factors it is perhaps a calculation that investors value most—or should.

WHAT IT MEASURES

The total percentage change in the value of an investment over a specified time period, including capital gains, dividends, and the investment's appreciation or depreciation.

WHY IT IS IMPORTANT

Total return furnishes fundamental information that every investor seeks sooner or later: All things considered, just how much did my investment return?

That in itself makes total return rather important. In addition, there are several sound reasons for paying close attention to each of its components. For those who invest to maximize income, dividends will be very important. For those who invest for long-term growth, capital appreciation will be equally important.

Knowing how much of an investment's total return is attributable to each of the components can help in assessing how volatile the fund is likely to be, how tax-efficient it is, and how much steady income it can be expected to produce.

HOW IT WORKS IN PRACTICE

The total return formula reflects all the ways in which an investment may earn or lose money: dividends as income, capital gains distributions, and capital appreciation—the increase or decrease in the investment's net asset value (NAV):

$$Total return = (Dividends + Capital \ gains \ distributions \pm Change \ in \ NAV) \div Initial \ NAV$$

If, for instance, you buy a stock with an initial NAV of $40, and after one year it pays an income dividend of $2 per share and a capital gains distribution of $1, and its NAV has increased to $42, then the stock's total return would be:

$$(2 + 1 + 2) \div 40 = 5 \div 40 = 0.125 = 12.5\%$$

TRICKS OF THE TRADE

- The total return time-frame is usually one year, and it assumes that dividends have been reinvested.
- If a fund's capital gains exceed its capital losses for the year, most of the net gain must be distributed to stockholders as a capital gains distribution.
- Total return measures past performance only; it cannot predict future results.
- Total return generally does not take into account any sales charges that an investor paid to invest in a fund, or taxes he or she might owe on the income dividends and capital gains distributions received.
- Rules of the US Securities & Exchange Commission require a company to show a comparison of the total return on its common stock for the last five fiscal years with the total returns of a broad market index and a more narrowly focused industry or group index.
- Total return can be a key yardstick in selecting funds once an investor has set objectives and a time horizon, and made decisions about risk and reward.

Treynor Ratio

WHAT IT MEASURES

The Treynor ratio, as devised by Jack Treynor, is a measurement of a portfolio's return earned in excess of what would be earned on a risk-free investment. The higher the Treynor ratio, the better the performance of the portfolio or stock being analyzed.

WHY IT IS IMPORTANT

The Treynor ratio is used to calculate returns over and above what would be generated by a risk-free investment. Whenever the Treynor ratio is high, it denotes that the investor received high yields for each unit of market risk. One of the key advantages of Treynor is that it shows how a fund will perform not in relation to its own volatility but the volatility it brings to an overall portfolio.

HOW IT WORKS IN PRACTICE

The Treynor Ratio divides a portfolio's excess return by its "beta." This is the widely used measure of market-related risk in a stock or collection of stocks. If a stock has a beta of 0.5, it tends to move up or down with the market, but only half as far as the overall market. If a stock has a beta of 1.25 and the market moves up by 10%, that stock would move up by 12.5%.

The formula for the Treynor Ratio is as follows:

$$Treynor \ ratio = (Average \ portfolio \ return \\ - Average \ risk \ return \ of \ risk\text{-}free \ investment) \\ \div Beta \ of \ portfolio$$

The formula can be applied to any fund or portfolio where you can find a beta value—the beta is a measurement of market-related risk.

An investor might use the Treynor ratio to calculate the return generated by a fund over the return of short-term Treasury bills. If the fund returns 12% over three years, while the Treasury bill rate is 1.5% and the fund's beta is 0.5, then we can see the Treynor ratio is 21 (= [12 − 1.5] ÷ 0.5).

TRICKS OF THE TRADE

- Like the Sharpe ratio, the Treynor ratio doesn't quantify the value added—it is simply a ranking mechanism. Where the two mechanisms differ is that the Sharpe ratio considers total risk (the standard deviation of the portfolio) while the Treynor ratio considers systematic risk (the beta of a portfolio versus the benchmark).
- In practice, it's possible to simply look up Treynor ratios for many listed equity funds. For example, many newspapers and financial websites will list Treynor figures under "performance" data, usually over three, five, and 10 years.

- It is worth considering how Treynor Ratios change over time and in relation to similar funds—a three-year ratio may be negative while five-year and 10-year figures are positive. This could be because the fund is mismanaged but also could reflect a market downturn or a short-term problem.

MORE INFO
See Also:
⇄ Risk-Adjusted Rate of Return (p. 410)

Value at Risk

WHAT IT MEASURES
Value at risk (VAR) is a useful tool for anyone looking to quantify the risk of a particular project or investment opportunity by measuring the potential loss that might be incurred over a certain period of time. VAR measures what is the most that an investor might lose, based on a specific level of confidence, over a specific period of time. For example, "What's the most I can—with a 95% level of confidence—expect to lose over the next 12 months?"

WHY IT IS IMPORTANT
Most risk measurements focus on volatility whereas VAR focuses specifically on losses. It is commonly used to evaluate risk across a portfolio, but can also be applied to single indexes or anything that trades like a stock. VAR is important because it provides financial executives with a method of quantifying risk that is rigorous but also easily understood by nonfinancial executives.

HOW IT WORKS IN PRACTICE
The most common method of calculating VAR is the variance-covariance approach, sometimes referred to as "parametric VAR." Parametric VAR is a percentile-based risk measure that measures the expected loss of a portfolio over a specific period of time, depending on the confidence. To calculate parametric VAR, use the following formula:

Value at risk = Mean × HPR + [Z-score × Std Dev × SQRT (HPR)]

where Mean is the average expected (or actual) rate of return, HPR is the holding period, Z-score is the probability, Std Dev is the standard deviation, and SQRT is the square root (of time).

To calculate the VAR of a portfolio worth $1 million with an expected average annual return of 13%, a standard annual deviation of 20% (equal to a daily deviation of 1.26%), and a 95% confidence score, therefore, you would perform the following calculation:

13 × 1 + (95 × 1.26 × SQRT) = 6.037%

This results in a 10-day VAR of $60,370. This means that your biggest potential loss over any 10-day period should not exceed $60,370 more than 5% of the time, or approximately once a year.

TRICKS OF THE TRADE
- VAR is now increasingly accepted as the *de facto* standard for risk measurement. In 1993, when the Bank of International Settlements members met in Basel, they amended the Basel Accord to require banks to hold in reserve enough capital to cover 10 days of losses based on a 95% 10-day VAR.
- A simpler alternative approach to calculating VAR is using the historical method—this simply takes all empirical profit and loss history and puts the returns in order of size. If we had 100 historical returns, the VAR for a 99% confidence score would simply be the second largest loss. Critics argue that very few portfolios have enough historical data to make this approach reliable, however.
- A third approach to calculating VAR is the simulation or Monte Carlo method, which uses computerized simulation to generate thousands of possible returns from a parametric assumption, then ordering them in the same way as with an historical calculation.
- Although VAR is often described as the "maximum possible" loss, this only applies at a single percentage confidence score. It is always possible to lose more by applying a higher confidence level—this is known as the conditional value at risk (CVAR), expected shortfall, or extreme tail loss.

MORE INFO
Books:
Butler, Cormac. *Mastering Value at Risk: A Step-by-Step Guide to Understanding and Applying VAR*. London: FT Prentice Hall, 1999.
Choudhry, Moorad. *An Introduction to Value-at-Risk*. 4th ed. Chichester, UK: Wiley, 2006.
Websites:
Investopedia on VAR: www.investopedia.com/articles/04/092904.asp
Risk Glossary on VAR: www.riskglossary.com/link/value_at_risk.htm

414   Weighted Average Cost of Capital

WHAT IT MEASURES

The weighted average cost of capital (WACC) is the rate of return that the providers of a company's capital require, weighted according to the proportion each element bears to the total pool of capital.

WHY IT IS IMPORTANT

WACC is one of the most important figures in assessing a company's financial health, both for internal use (in capital budgeting) and external use (valuing companies on investment markets). It gives companies an insight into the cost of their financing, can be used as a hurdle rate for investment decisions, and acts as a measure to be minimized to find the best possible capital structure for the company. WACC is a rough guide to the rate of interest per monetary unit of capital. As such, it can be used to provide a discount rate for cash flows with similar risk to that of the overall business.

HOW IT WORKS IN PRACTICE

To calculate the weighted average cost of capital, companies must multiply the cost of each element of capital for a project—which may include loans, bonds, equity, and preferred stock—by its percentage of the total capital, and then add them together.

For example, a business might consider investing $40 million in an expansion program. The financing is raised through a combination of equity (such as $10m of stock with an expected 10% return) and debt (for example, $30m bond issue, with 5% coupon).

In this simple scenario, WACC would be calculated as follows:

Equity ($10m) divided by total capital ($40m)
= 25%, multiplied by cost of equity (10%) = 2.5%

Debt ($30m) divided by total capital ($40m)
= 75%, multiplied by cost of debt (5%) = 3.75%

The two results added together give a weighted cost of capital of 6.25%.

In reality, interest payments are tax deductible, so a more accurate formula for WACC is:

$$WACC = DP \times DC - T + EP \times EC$$

where DP is the proportion of debt financing, DC is the cost of debt financing, T is the company's tax rate, EP is the proportion of equity finance, and EC is the cost of equity finance.

TRICKS OF THE TRADE

- To accurately calculate WACC, you need to know the specific rates of return required for each source of capital. For example, different sources of finance may attract different levels of taxation, or interest, which should be accounted for. A true WACC calculation could therefore be much more complex than the example provided here.
- Critics of WACC argue that financial analysts rely on it too heavily, and that the algorithm should not be used to assess risky projects, where the cost of capital will necessarily be higher to reflect the higher risk.
- Investors use WACC to help decide whether a company represents a good investment opportunity. To some extent, WACC represents the rate at which a company produces value for investors—if a company produces a return of 20% and has a WACC of 11%, then the company creates 9% additional value for investors. If the return is lower than the WACC, the business is unlikely to secure investment.
- Although the WACC formula seems simple, different analysts will often come up with different WACC calculations for the same company depending on how they interpret the company's debt, market value, and interest rates.

MORE INFO

Book:
Pratt, Shannon P., and Roger J. Grabowski. *Cost of Capital: Applications and Examples*. Hoboken, NJ: Wiley, 2008.

Websites:
Money Terms on WACC: moneyterms.co.uk/wacc/
12 Manage on WACC: www.12manage.com/methods_wacc.html

See Also:
✔ Estimating Enterprise Value with the Weighted Average Cost of Capital (pp. 293–294)
✔ Obtaining an Equity Value Using the Weighted Average Cost of Capital (WACC) (pp. 331–332)
✔ Understanding the Weighted Average Cost of Capital (WACC) (pp. 309–310)

Calculations

Working Capital Cycle

WHAT IT MEASURES

The working capital cycle measures the amount of time that elapses between the moment when your business begins investing money in a product or service, and the moment the business receives payment for that product or service. This doesn't necessarily begin when you manufacture a product—businesses often invest money in products when they hire people to produce goods, or when they buy raw materials.

WHY IT IS IMPORTANT

A good working capital cycle balances incoming and outgoing payments to maximize working capital. Simply put, you need to know you can afford to research, produce, and sell your product.

A short working capital cycle suggests a business has good cash flow. For example, a company that pays contractors in 7 days but takes 30 days to collect payments has 23 days of working capital to fund—also known as having a working capital cycle of 23 days. Amazon.com, in contrast, collects money before it pays for goods. This means the company has a negative working capital cycle and has more capital available to fund growth. For a business to grow, it needs access to cash—and being able to free up cash from the working capital cycle is cheaper than other sources of finance, such as loans.

HOW IT WORKS IN PRACTICE

The key to understanding a company's working capital cycle is to know where payments are collected and made, and to identify areas where the cycle is stretched—and can potentially be reduced.

The working capital cycle is a diagram rather than a mathematical calculation. The cycle shows all the cash coming in to the business, what it is used for, and how it leaves the business (i.e., what it is spent on).

A simple working capital cycle diagram is shown in Figure 1. The arrows in the diagram show the movement of assets through the business—including cash, but also other assets such as raw materials and finished goods. Each item represents a reservoir of assets—for example, cash into the business is converted into labor. The working capital cycle will break down if there is not a supply of assets moving continually through the cycle (known as a liquidity crisis).

The working capital diagram should be customized to show the way capital moves around your business. More complex diagrams might include incoming assets such as cash payments, interest payments, loans, and equity. Items that commonly absorb cash would be labor, inventory, and suppliers.

The key thing to model is the time lag between each item on the diagram. For some businesses, there may be a very long delay between making the product and receiving cash from sales. Others may need to purchase raw materials a long time before the product can be manufactured. Once you have this information, it is possible to calculate your total working capital cycle, and potentially identify where time lags within the cycle can be reduced or eliminated.

TRICKS OF THE TRADE

- For investors, the working capital cycle is most relevant when analyzing capital-intensive businesses where cash flow is used to buy inventory. Typically, the working capital cycle of retailers, consumer goods, and consumer goods manufacturers is critical to their success.
- The working capital cycle should be considered alongside the cash conversion cycle—a measure of working capital efficiency that gives clues about the average number of days that working capital is invested in the operating cycle.

MORE INFO

Articles:

Harper, David. "Financial statements: Working capital." *Investopedia*. Online at: tinyurl.com/5sgvfau

Johnson, Millard. "Revving up the working capital cycle." *Corporate Report Wisconsin* (July 1, 2004). Online at: www.allbusiness.com/accounting/959776-1.html

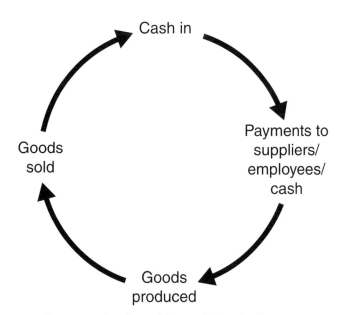

Figure 1. A simple working capital cycle diagram

416 Yield

WHAT IT MEASURES
Stocks that pay dividends (note that not all do) will produce an annual cash return to the investor. Simply dividing this cash return by the current stock price and expressing that as a percentage is known as the "yield"—that is, the annual percentage income at the current price. As far as newspapers are concerned, the yield figure they publish is usually the historical one.

Analysts will often provide forecasts for dividends in terms of earnings per share (EPS), and thus the forecast yield can then be calculated. Forecasts can, of course, go wrong, and consequently there is some risk in relying on them.

WHY IT IS IMPORTANT
Yield, after the price/earnings ratio, is one of the most common methods of comparing the relative value of stocks, and that is why it is so widely quoted in the press. The majority of investors like to see a cash income from their stocks, although to some extent this is a cultural thing. There are more companies in the United States, for example, that pay no dividends than in the United Kingdom.

HOW IT WORKS IN PRACTICE
You can compare yields against the market average or against a sector average, which in turn gives you some idea of the relative value of the stock against its peers, much like other ratios. Other things being equal, a higher-yield stock is preferable to that of an identical company with a lower yield. The higher-yield stock is cheaper. In practice, of course, there may well be good reasons why the market has decided that the higher yielder should be so—possibly it has worse prospects, is less profitable, and so on. This is not always the case; the market is far from being a perfectly rational place.

An additional feature of the yield (unlike many of the other stock analysis ratios) is that it enables comparison with cash. When you put cash into an interest-bearing source like a bank account or a government stock, you get a yield—the annual interest payable. This is usually a pretty safe investment. You can compare the yield from this cash investment with the yield on stocks, which are far riskier. This produces a valuable basis for stock evaluation. If, for example, you can get 4% in a bank without capital risk, you can then look at stocks and ask yourself how this yield compares—given that, as well as the opportunity for long-term growth of both the stock price and the dividends, there is plenty of capital risk.

TRICKS OF THE TRADE
- Care is necessary, however, because unlike banks paying interest, companies are under no obligation to pay dividends at all. Frequently, if they go through a bad patch, even the largest and best-known household name companies will cut dividends or even abandon paying them altogether. So, stock yield is much less reliable than bank interest or government stock interest yield.
- Despite this, yield is an immensely useful feature of stock appraisal. It is the only ratio that tells you about the cash return to the investor, and you cannot argue with cash. EPS, for example, is subject to accountants' opinions, but a dividend once paid is an unarguable fact.

MORE INFO
Websites:
Accounting Standards Board (ASB; UK): www.frc.org.uk/asb
Securities and Exchange Commission (SEC; US): www.sec.gov

See Also:

DICTIONARY

a-z

A

AAA[1] *abbr* ACCOUNTING American Accounting Association

AAA[2] STOCKHOLDING & INVESTMENTS **top investment rating** the maximum safety rating given to potential investments by Standard & Poor's or Moody's, the two best-known rating agencies. *Also called* ***triple A***

AAD *abbr* CURRENCY & EXCHANGE Arab Accounting Dinar

AASB *abbr* ACCOUNTING Australian Accounting Standards Board

AAT *abbr* ACCOUNTING Association of Accounting Technicians

ABA *abbr* BANKING American Bankers Association

abacus FINANCE **frame holding rods strung with beads for calculating** a counting device used for making basic arithmetic calculations, that consists of parallel rods strung with beads. Still widely used in education worldwide and for business and accounting in China and Japan, its origins can be traced back to early civilizations. Australia's oldest accounting journal bears the same name.

abandonment option STOCKHOLDING & INVESTMENTS **early investment-termination option** the option of terminating an investment before the time that it is scheduled to end

abandonment value STOCKHOLDING & INVESTMENTS **value of investment terminated early** the value that an investment has if it is terminated at a particular time before it is scheduled to end

ABA routing number BANKING **number allocated to US financial institution** in the United States, a nine-digit number allocated to a financial institution, such as a bank. It appears on US checks in the bottom-left corner. *Also called* ***routing number***. *See also* ***sort code***

abatement FINANCE **decrease in debt obligation** a reduction in an amount of a liability, for example, in the amount of a person's debts, or in a company's costs of paying employee benefits

ABB *abbr* TREASURY MANAGEMENT activity based budgeting

abbreviated accounts ACCOUNTING **abridged UK company accounts** in the United Kingdom, a shortened version of a company's ***annual accounts*** that a company classified as small- or medium-sized under the ***Companies Act*** (1989) can file with the ***Registrar of Companies***, instead of having to supply a full version

ABC *abbr* ACCOUNTING activity based costing

abnormal loss ACCOUNTING **loss exceeding normal allowance** any loss which exceeds the normal loss allowance. Abnormal losses are generally accounted for as though they were completed products.

abnormal shrinkage ACCOUNTING **shrinkage contributing to abnormal loss** the unexpectedly high level of reduction in inventory that has contributed to an abnormal loss

abnormal spoilage ACCOUNTING **shortfall contributing to abnormal loss** the unexpectedly high level of shortfall that has contributed to an abnormal loss

abnormal waste ACCOUNTING **waste contributing to abnormal loss** the unexpectedly high level of waste that has contributed to an abnormal loss

above par STOCKHOLDING & INVESTMENTS **trading above face value** used to describe a security that trades above its ***nominal value*** or ***redemption value***

above-the-line 1. ACCOUNTING **indicating exceptional items in accounts** used to describe entries in a company's profit and loss accounts that appear above the line separating those entries that show the origin of the funds that have contributed to the profit or loss from those that relate to its distribution. Exceptional and extraordinary items appear above the line. *See also* ***below-the-line*** *(sense 1)* **2.** ECONOMICS **indicating country's revenue transactions** in macroeconomics, used to describe a country's revenue transactions, as opposed to its below-the-line or capital transactions. *See also* ***below-the-line*** *(sense 2)* **3.** MARKETING **relating to marketing costs for advertising** used to describe marketing expenditure on advertising in media such as the press, radio, television, film, and the World Wide Web, on which a commission is usually paid to an agency. *See also* ***below-the-line*** *(sense 3)*

abridged accounts ACCOUNTING **provisional UK company financial statement** in the United Kingdom, financial statements produced by a company that fall outside the requirements stipulated in the ***Companies Act***. Abridged accounts are often made public through the media.

ABS *abbr* **1.** STOCKHOLDING & INVESTMENTS asset-backed security **2.** STATISTICS Australian Bureau of Statistics

absolute advantage ECONOMICS **favorable position of regions having low production costs** an advantage enjoyed by a country or area of the world that is able to produce a product or provide a service more cheaply than any other country or area

absorb ACCOUNTING **merge production overhead costs** to assign an overhead to a particular cost center in a company's production accounts so that its identity becomes lost. *See also* ***absorption costing***

absorbed account ACCOUNTING **account merged with related accounts** an account that has lost its separate identity by being combined with related accounts in the preparation of a financial statement

absorbed business MERGERS & ACQUISITIONS **firm combined with another** a company that has been merged into another company with which it is not on an equal footing

absorbed costs ACCOUNTING **indirect manufacturing costs** the indirect costs associated with manufacturing, for example, insurance or property taxes

absorbed overhead ACCOUNTING **locally adjusted overhead** an overhead attached to products or services by means of absorption rates

absorption costing ACCOUNTING **method allocating overhead costs to product** an accounting practice in which fixed and variable costs of production are absorbed by different cost centers. Providing all the products or services can be sold at a price that covers the allocated costs, this method ensures that both fixed and variable costs are recovered in full. However, if sales are lost because the resultant price is too high, the organization may lose revenue that would have contributed to its overhead. *See also* ***marginal costing***

absorption rate ACCOUNTING **rate of merging production overhead costs** the rate at which overhead costs are absorbed into each unit of production

ACA 1. ACCOUNTING **ICAEW Associate Chartered Accountant** an Associate (member) of the Institute of Chartered Accountants in England and Wales **2.** *abbr* REGULATION & COMPLIANCE Australian Communications Authority

Academy of Accounting Historians ACCOUNTING **US institution for accounting history** a US organization founded in 1973 that promotes "research, publication, teaching, and personal interchanges in all phases of Accounting History and its interrelation with business and economic history"

ACAUS *abbr* ACCOUNTING Association of Chartered Accountants in the United States

ACCA *abbr* ACCOUNTING Association of Chartered Certified Accountants

accelerated cost recovery system ACCOUNTING **use of asset depreciation to reduce US taxes** in the United States, a system used for computing the depreciation of some assets acquired before 1986 in a way that reduces taxes. *Abbr* **ACRS**

accelerated depreciation ACCOUNTING **assigning higher depreciation to new assets** a system used for computing the depreciation of some assets in a way that assumes that they depreciate faster in the early years of their acquisition. The cost of the asset less its residual value is multiplied by a fraction based on the number of years of its expected useful life. The fraction changes each year and charges the highest costs to the earliest years. *Also called* ***declining balance method, sum-of-the-year's digits depreciation***

acceptance FINANCE **signature guaranteeing payment for bill of exchange** the signature on a bill of exchange, indicating that the drawee (the person to whom it is addressed) will pay the face amount of the bill on the due date

acceptance bonus FINANCE **bonus paid to new employee** a bonus paid to a new employee on acceptance of a job. An acceptance bonus can be a feature of a golden hello and is designed both to attract and to retain staff.

acceptance credit BANKING **facility for seller to draw bill of exchange** a letter of credit granted by a bank to a buyer (the "applicant") against which a seller (the "beneficiary") can draw a bill of exchange

acceptance house UK BANKING **institution guaranteeing financial instruments** an institution that accepts financial instruments and agrees to honor them should the borrower default

accepting bank BANKING **bank accepting letter of credit** a bank in an exporter's own country to which an issuing bank sends a ***letter of credit*** for the exporter

accepting house BANKING **firm accepting bills of exchange** a company, usually an investment bank, that accepts bills of exchange at a discount, in return for immediate payment to the issuer

Accepting Houses Committee BANKING **banks linked to Bank of England for lending** the main London investment banks that organize the lending of money with the Bank of England and receive favorable discount rates

acceptor FINANCE **addressee of signed bill of exchange** a person who has accepted liability for a bill of exchange by signing its face

accommodation bill FINANCE **bill of exchange facilitating loan for another company** a bill of exchange where the drawee who signs it is helping another company (the drawer) to raise a loan. The bill is given on the basis of trade debts owed to the borrower.

account 1. FINANCE **arrangement for deferred payment** a business arrangement involving the exchange of money or credit in which payment is deferred **2.** FINANCE **record of financial dealings** a record maintained by a financial institution itemizing its dealings with a particular customer **3.** ACCOUNTING **record of monetary value of transactions** a structured record of transactions in monetary terms, kept as part of an accounting system. This may take the form of a simple list or that of entries on a credit and debit basis, maintained either manually or as a computer record. **4.** MARKETING **advertising firm's client** a client of an advertising or public relations agency **on account** FINANCE used to describe a transaction where something is received that is to be paid for later

accountability CORPORATE GOVERNANCE **responsibility for actions** the allocation or acceptance of responsibility for one's own actions or those of others lower in the hierarchy

accountancy ACCOUNTING **professional activities of accountants** the work and profession of accountants

accountancy bodies UK ACCOUNTING = ***accounting bodies***

accountancy profession UK ACCOUNTING = ***accounting profession***

accountant ACCOUNTING **somebody responsible for financial records** a professional person who maintains and checks the business records of a person or organization and prepares forms and reports for financial purposes

accountant's letter ACCOUNTING **independent statement about financial report** a written statement by an independent accountant that precedes a financial report, describing the scope of the report and giving an opinion on its validity

accountant's opinion ACCOUNTING audit report on firm's accounts a report of the audit of a company's books, carried out by a certified public accountant

account day ACCOUNTING day of settlement of executed order the day on which an executed order is settled by the delivery of securities, payment to the seller, and payment by the buyer. This is the final day of the *accounting period*.

account debtor ACCOUNTING body responsible for paying for something a person or organization responsible for paying for a product or service

accounting ACCOUNTING range of activities undertaken by accountants a generic term for the activities such as bookkeeping and financial accounting conducted by accountants. Accounting involves the classification and recording of monetary transactions; the presentation and interpretation of the results of those transactions in order to assess performance over a period and the financial position at a given date; and the monetary projection of future activities arising from alternative planned courses of action. Accounting in larger businesses is typically carried out by financial accountants, who focus on formal, corporate issues such as taxation, and management accountants, who provide management reports and guidance.

Accounting and Finance Association of Australia and New Zealand ACCOUNTING organization for accountancy and financial professionals an organization for accounting and finance academics, researchers, and professionals. The Association has a variety of objectives, including the promotion of information on accounting to the public, and the provision of programs in continual professional development to both members and nonmembers. The Association's name was changed in 2002 to incorporate the Accounting Association of Australia and New Zealand and the Australian Association of University Teachers in Accounting. *Abbr* **AFAANZ**

accounting bases ACCOUNTING fundamental accounting methods the methods used for applying fundamental accounting concepts to financial transactions and items; preparing financial accounts; determining the accounting periods in which revenue and costs should be recognized in the profit and loss account; and determining the amounts at which material items should be stated in the balance sheet

accounting bodies US ACCOUNTING professional organizations for accountants professional institutions and associations for accountants. These include such bodies as the Accounting Standards Board in the United Kingdom and the American Institute of Certified Public Accountants in the United States. *UK term* **accountancy bodies**

accounting concept ACCOUNTING accepted basis for preparing accounts any of the general assumptions on which accounts are prepared. The main concepts are: that the business is a going concern; that revenue and costs are noted when they are incurred and not when cash is received or paid; that the present accounts are drawn up following the same principles as the previous accounts; and that the revenue or

costs are only recorded if it is certain that they will be received or incurred.

accounting cost ACCOUNTING cost of proper financial records the cost of maintaining and checking the business records of a person or organization and of preparing forms and reports for financial purposes

accounting cycle ACCOUNTING process of regularly updating financial records the regular process of formally updating a firm's financial position by recording, analyzing, and reporting its transactions during the accounting period

accounting date ACCOUNTING end date of accounting period the date on which an accounting period ends. This can be any date, though it is usually 12 months after the preceding accounting date.

accounting department US ACCOUNTING company department dealing with finance the department in a company which deals with money paid, received, borrowed, or owed. *UK term* **accounts department**

accounting equation ACCOUNTING formula relating assets, liabilities, and equity a formula in which a firm's assets must be equal to the sum of its liabilities and the owners' equity. *Also called* **balance sheet equation**

accounting exposure ACCOUNTING risk from changing exchange rates the risk that foreign currency held by a company may lose value because of exchange rate changes when it conducts overseas business

accounting fees ACCOUNTING fees for preparing accounts fees paid to an accountant for preparing accounts. Such fees are tax-deductible.

accounting insolvency ACCOUNTING condition of liabilities exceeding assets the condition that a company is in when its liabilities to its creditors exceed its assets

accounting manager US ACCOUNTING manager of accounting department the manager of the accounting department in a business or institution. *UK term* **accounts manager**

accounting manual ACCOUNTING set of instructions for keeping accounts a collection of accounting instructions governing the responsibilities of persons, and the procedures, forms, and records relating to the preparation and use of accounting data. There can be separate manuals for the constituent parts of the accounting system, for example, budget manuals or cost accounting manuals.

accounting period ACCOUNTING time between financial reports a length of time for which businesses may prepare internal accounts so as to monitor progress on a weekly, monthly, or quarterly basis. Accounts are generally prepared for external purposes on an annual basis.

accounting policies ACCOUNTING options for financial reporting the specific accounting methods selected and consistently followed by an entity as being, in the opinion of the management, appropriate to its circumstances and best suited to present fairly its results and financial position. For example, from the various possible methods of *depreciation*, the accounting policy may be to use *straight line depreciation*.

accounting principles ACCOUNTING **rules of financial reporting** the rules that apply to accounting practices and provide guidelines for dealing appropriately with complex transactions

Accounting Principles Board ACCOUNTING **former US organization with oversight of accounting** in the United States, the professional organization which issued opinions that formed much of *Generally Accepted Accounting Principles* until 1973, when the Financial Accounting Standards Board (FASB) took over that role. *Abbr* **APB**

accounting procedure ACCOUNTING **method of keeping financial records** an accounting method developed by a person or organization to deal with routine accounting tasks

accounting profession *US* ACCOUNTING **set of organizations overseeing accountants** collectively, the professional bodies of accountants that establish and regulate training entry standards and professional examinations, as well as ethical and technical rules and guidelines. These bodies are organized on national and international levels. *UK term* **accountancy profession**

accounting profit ACCOUNTING **difference between revenue and costs** the difference between total revenue and explicit costs. Accounting profits exclude costs such as *opportunity costs*.

accounting rate of return ACCOUNTING **ratio of unadjusted profit to capital employed** the ratio of profit before interest and taxation to the percentage of capital employed at the end of a period. Variations include using profit after interest and taxation, equity capital employed, and average capital for the period. *Abbr* **ARR**

accounting ratio ACCOUNTING **ratio of one accounting result to another** an expression of accounting results as a ratio or percentage, for example, the ratio of *current assets* to *current liabilities*

accounting records ACCOUNTING **materials for preparing financial statements** all documentation and books used during the preparation of financial statements. *Also called* **books of account**

accounting reference date ACCOUNTING **last day included in financial record** the nominal last day of a company's *accounting reference period*, which ends on that date or on one no more than seven days on either side of it

accounting reference period ACCOUNTING **12 months that annual accounts cover** the period covered by a company's annual accounts, which is usually one full year

accounting software ACCOUNTING **programs for electronic accounts** computer programs used to help maintain accounting records electronically. Such software can be used for a variety of tasks, including preparing statements and recording transactions.

accounting standard ACCOUNTING **approved method of presenting financial information** an authoritative statement of how specific types of transaction and other events should be reflected in financial statements. Compliance with accounting standards will usually be necessary for financial statements to give a true and fair view.

Accounting Standards Board ACCOUNTING **UK standard-setting organization** in the United Kingdom, a standard-setting organization established on August 1, 1990, to develop, issue, and withdraw accounting standards. Its objectives are "to establish and improve standards of financial accounting and reporting, for the benefit of users, preparers, and auditors of financial information." *Abbr* **ASB**

accounting system ACCOUNTING **everything used in producing accounting information** the means, including staff and equipment, by which an organization produces its accounting information

accounting technician ACCOUNTING **qualified person working in finance industry** a qualified person who works in accounting and finance alongside certified public accountants. Accounting technicians have a variety of jobs, including accounts clerk, credit controller, and financial manager. Their professional body is the *Association of Accounting Technicians*.

accounting year *UK* ACCOUNTING, TAX = *fiscal year*

account reconciliation ACCOUNTING **1. comparing balances of transactions** a procedure for ensuring the reliability of accounting records by comparing balances of transactions **2. comparing checkbook records with bank statement** a procedure for comparing the register of a checkbook with an associated bank statement

accounts ACCOUNTING **record of monetary value of transactions** a structured record of transactions in monetary terms, kept as part of an accounting system. This may take the form of a simple list or that of entries on a credit and debit basis, maintained either manually or as a computer record.

accounts department *UK* ACCOUNTING = *accounting department*

accounts manager *UK* ACCOUNTING = *accounting manager*

accounts payable ACCOUNTING **amount owed through credit** the amount that a company owes for goods or services obtained on credit. *Abbr* **AP**

accounts receivable ACCOUNTING **amount owed by customers** the money that is owed to a company by those who have bought its goods or services and have not yet paid for them. *Abbr* **AR**

accounts receivable aging ACCOUNTING **money owed grouped by month and customer** a periodic report that classifies outstanding receivable balances according to customer and month of the original billing date

accounts receivable factoring ACCOUNTING **buying of discounted invoiced debts** the buying of *accounts receivable* at a discount with the goal of making a profit from collecting them

421

a–z

Dictionary

accounts receivable financing ACCOUNTING **using money owed as collateral for loan** a form of borrowing in which a company uses money that it is owed as collateral for a loan it needs for business operations

accounts receivable turnover ACCOUNTING **ratio indicating length of time before customers pay** a ratio that shows how long the customers of a business wait before paying what they owe. This can cause cashflow problems for small businesses.

The formula for accounts receivable turnover is straightforward. Simply divide the average amount of receivables into annual credit sales:

Sales/Receivables = Receivables turnover

If, for example, a company's sales are $4.5 million and its average receivables are $375,000, its receivables turnover is:

$4,500,000/375,000 = 12$

A high turnover figure is desirable, because it indicates that a company collects revenues effectively, and that its customers pay bills promptly. A high figure also suggests that a firm's credit and collection policies are sound. In addition, the measurement is a reasonably good indicator of cashflow, and of overall operating efficiency.

accredited investor STOCKHOLDING & INVESTMENTS **investor with income of specific size** an investor whose wealth or income is above a specific amount. It is illegal for an accredited investor to be a member of a private limited partnership.

accreted value STOCKHOLDING & INVESTMENTS **bond's value at present interest rate** the theoretical value of a bond if interest rates remained at the current level

accretion MERGERS & ACQUISITIONS **firm's asset growth** the growth of a company through additions or purchases of plant or value-adding services

accrual ACCOUNTING **unpaid charge in accounting results** a charge that has not been paid by the end of an accounting period but must be included in the accounting results for the period. If no invoice has been received for the charge, an estimate must be included in the accounting results.

accrual basis or **accrual concept** or **accrual method** ACCOUNTING **recording transactions for period they refer to** an accounting method that includes income and expense items as they are earned or incurred irrespective of when money is received or paid out. See also **cash accounting** (sense 1)

accrual bond STOCKHOLDING & INVESTMENTS = **zero coupon bond**

accrual of discount STOCKHOLDING & INVESTMENTS **annual gain for bond bought below face value** the annual gain in value of a bond owing to its having been bought originally for less than its **nominal value**

accrual of interest FINANCE **addition of interest to principal** the automatic addition of interest to the original amount loaned or invested. Accrual of interest costs match the cost of capital with the provision of capital.

accruals basis or **accruals concept** ACCOUNTING see **accrual basis**

accrue 1. FINANCE **increase with time** to increase and be due for payment at a later date, for example, interest **2.** ACCOUNTING **include item when earned or incurred** to include an income or expense item in transaction records at the time it is earned or incurred

accrued dividend STOCKHOLDING & INVESTMENTS **dividend earned since previous dividend payment** a dividend earned since the date when the last dividend was paid

accrued expense ACCOUNTING **expense incurred but not paid** an expense that has been incurred within a given accounting period but not yet paid

accrued income FINANCE **income due** income that has been earned or accumulated over a period of time but not yet received

accrued interest STOCKHOLDING & INVESTMENTS **interest accumulated since previous interest payment** the amount of interest earned by a bond or similar investment since the previous interest payment

accrued liabilities FINANCE **recorded but unpaid liabilities** liabilities which are recorded, although payment has not yet been made. This can include liabilities such as rent and utility payments.

accruing FINANCE **increasing with time** added as a periodic gain, for example, as interest on an amount of money

accumulated depreciation ACCOUNTING **cumulative depreciation claimed as expense** the cumulative annual depreciation of an **asset** that has been claimed as an expense since the asset was acquired. Also called **aggregate depreciation**

accumulated dividend STOCKHOLDING & INVESTMENTS **dividend earned since previous dividend payment** the amount of money in dividends earned by a stock or similar investment since the previous dividend payment

accumulated profit ACCOUNTING **profit carried over into next year** profit which is not paid as dividend but is taken over into the accounts of the following year

accumulated reserves FINANCE **annual reserves put aside** reserves which a company has put aside over a period of years

accumulating shares STOCKHOLDING & INVESTMENTS **common stock issued in place of dividend** common stock issued by a company equivalent to and in place of the net dividend payable to holders of common stock

accumulation unit STOCKHOLDING & INVESTMENTS **unit with dividends used for more units** a share in a mutual fund for which dividends accumulate and form more units, as opposed to an **income unit**, where the investor receives the dividends as **income**

ACH abbr E-COMMERCE, BANKING automated clearing house

acid test 1. ACCOUNTING **test of organization's liquidity** a test used to measure an organization's liquidity. See also **acid-test ratio 2.** GENERAL MANAGEMENT **decisive test** a stringent test of the worth or reliability of something

acid-test ratio ACCOUNTING **measure of organization's liquidity** an accounting ratio used to measure an organization's liquidity. The most common expression of the ratio is:

Acid-test ratio = (Current assets – Inventory) ÷ Current liabilities

If, for example, current assets total $7,700, inventory amounts to $1,200, and current liabilities total $4,500, then:

(7,700 – 1,200) ÷ 4,500 = 1.44

A variation of this formula ignores inventories altogether, distinguishes assets as cash, receivables, and short-term investments, then divides the sum of the three by the total current liabilities, or:

Acid-test ratio = (Cash + Accounts receivable + Short-term investments) ÷ Current liabilities

If, for example, cash totals $2,000, receivables total $3,000, short-term investments total $1,000, and liabilities total $4,800, then:

(2,000 + 3,000 + 1,000) ÷ 4,800 = 1.25

In general, the ratio should be 1:1 or better. It means a company has a unit's worth of easily convertible assets for each unit of its current liabilities.

acquirer 1. FINANCE **buyer** an organization or individual that buys a business or asset **2.** BANKING, E-COMMERCE **institution handling credit card transactions** a financial institution, commonly a bank, that processes a merchant's credit card authorizations and payments, forwarding the data to a credit card association, which in turn communicates with the issuer. *Also called* **acquiring bank, clearing house** (sense 3)

acquiring bank BANKING = *acquirer* (sense 2)

acquisition MERGERS & ACQUISITIONS **when one organization buys another** the process of one organization taking control of another, by the direct purchase of the net assets or liabilities of the other. *See also* **merger**

acquisition accounting MERGERS & ACQUISITIONS, ACCOUNTING = *purchase acquisition*

acquisition integration MERGERS & ACQUISITIONS **merging of new company into existing company** the process by which a company plans for and implements a successful integration of a newly acquired company

ACRS *abbr* ACCOUNTING accelerated cost recovery system

active account BANKING **account regularly used for transactions** an account such as a bank account or investment account that is used to deposit and withdraw money frequently

active asset FINANCE **asset in daily use** an asset that is used in the daily operations of a business

active fund management STOCKHOLDING & INVESTMENTS **proactive managing of mutual fund** the managing of a mutual fund by making judgments about stock valuations instead of relying on automatic adjustments such as indexation. *See also* **passive investment management**

active portfolio strategy STOCKHOLDING & INVESTMENTS **proactive managing of investment portfolio** the managing of an investment portfolio by making judgments about stock valuations instead of relying on automatic adjustments such as indexation

activist fiscal policy TREASURY MANAGEMENT **institutional intervention to affect exchange rate** the policy of a government or national bank that tries to affect the value of its country's money by such measures as changing interest rates for loans to banks and buying or selling foreign currencies

activity based budgeting TREASURY MANAGEMENT **allocation of resources to individual activities** the determination of which activities incur costs within an organization, establishing the relationships between them, and then deciding how much of the total budget should be allocated to each activity. *Abbr* **ABB**

activity based costing ACCOUNTING **calculating business's cost from cost of activities** a method of calculating the cost of a business by focusing on the actual cost of activities, thereby producing an estimate of the cost of individual products or services.

An ABC cost-accounting system requires three preliminary steps: converting to an accrual method of accounting; defining cost centers and cost allocation; and determining process and procedure costs.

Businesses have traditionally relied on the cash basis of accounting, which recognizes income when received and expenses when paid. ABC's foundation is the accrual-basis income statement. The numbers this statement presents are assigned to the various procedures performed during a given period. Cost centers are a company's identifiable products and services, but also include specific and detailed tasks within these broader activities. Defining cost centers will of course vary by business and method of operation. What is critical to ABC is the inclusion of all activities and all resources.

Once cost centers are identified, management teams can begin studying the activities each one engages in and allocating the expenses each one incurs, including the cost of employee services.

The most appropriate method is developed from time studies and direct expense allocation. Management teams who choose this method will need to devote several months to data collection in order to generate sufficient information to establish the personnel components of each activity's total cost.

Time studies establish the average amount of time required to complete each task, plus best- and worst-case performances. Only those resources actually used are factored into the cost computation; unused resources are reported separately. These studies can also advise management teams how best to monitor and allocate expenses that might otherwise be expressed as part of general overheads, or go undetected altogether. *Abbr* **ABC**

activity based management TREASURY MANAGEMENT **management based on cost of activities** a management control technique that focuses on the resource costs of organizational activities and processes, and the improvement of quality, profitability, and customer value. This technique uses *activity based costing* information to identify strategies for removing resource waste from operating activities. Main tools employed include: **strategic analysis**, **value analysis**, **cost analysis**, **life-cycle costing**, and **activity based budgeting**.

activity cost pool TREASURY MANAGEMENT **total cost of activity** a grouping of all of the cost elements associated with an activity

activity driver analysis TREASURY MANAGEMENT **assessing financial demands of activity** the identification and evaluation of the activity drivers used to trace the cost of activities to cost objects. It may also involve selecting activity drivers with potential to contribute to the cost management function, with particular reference to cost reduction.

activity indicator ECONOMICS **measure of economic productivity** a calculation used to measure labor productivity or manufacturing output in an economy

actuals 1. FINANCE **commodities immediately available** commodities that can be bought and used, as contrasted with commodities traded on a **futures contract 2.** ACCOUNTING **past earnings and expenses** earnings and expenses that have occurred rather than being only projected

actual to date ACCOUNTING **cumulative value already realized** the cumulative value realized by something between an earlier date and the present

actual turnover FINANCE **times person spends average available sum** the number of times during a specific period that somebody spends the average amount of money that he or she has available to spend during that period

ACU *abbr* CURRENCY & EXCHANGE Asian Currency Unit

ADB *abbr* BANKING **1.** African Development Bank **2.** Asian Development Bank

ADDACS *abbr* BANKING Automated Direct Debit Amendment and Cancellation Service

addend FINANCE **number added to complete sum** the initial number added to an **augend** in order to complete an **addition**

addition FINANCE **adding together numbers to make sum** an arithmetical operation consisting of adding together two or more numbers to make a sum

additional principal payment US ACCOUNTING **making larger than necessary loan payment** the payment of a lump sum to reduce the capital borrowed on a mortgage or other loan, thereby reducing the term of the loan and saving a large amount of interest expense, or the amount paid. *UK term* **overpayment**

adjustable rate preferred stock STOCKHOLDING & INVESTMENTS **preferred stocks linked to Treasury interest rate** preferred stocks on which dividends are paid in line with the interest rate on Treasury bills. *Abbr* **ARPS**

adjusted book value ACCOUNTING **current value of firm's assets and liabilities** the value of a company in terms of the current market values of its assets and liabilities. *Also called* **modified book value**

adjusted futures price STOCKHOLDING & INVESTMENTS **current value of futures contract** the current value of a futures contract to buy a commodity at a fixed future date

adjusted gross income ACCOUNTING **income after adjustments for tax purposes** the amount of annual income that a person or company has after various adjustments for income or corporation tax purposes. *Abbr* **AGI**

adjusted present value ACCOUNTING **separated discounted cashflows for operations and finance** where the capital structure of a company is complex, or expected to vary over time, discounted cashflows may be separated into (i) those that relate to operational items, and (ii) those associated with financing. This treatment enables assessment to be made of the separate features of each area. *Abbr* **APV**

adjustment FINANCE **change in financial condition** a change, often a significant downward turn, in the financial condition of a business, business sector, stock market, economy, etc.

adjustment credit BANKING **short-term loan from US Federal Reserve** a short-term loan from the US Federal Reserve to a commercial bank and the most common borrowing method to meet reserve requirements

adjustment trigger CURRENCY & EXCHANGE **factor triggering adjustment in exchange rates** a factor such as a specific level of inflation that triggers an adjustment in exchange rates

administration 1. FINANCE = **receivership 2.** GENERAL MANAGEMENT **management of firm's operations** the management of the affairs of a business, especially the planning and control of its operations

administration costs TREASURY MANAGEMENT **management costs** costs of management, not including production, marketing, or distribution costs

administrative receiver FINANCE **receiver representing long-term creditor** a receiver appointed by a **debenture** holder to liquidate the assets of a company on his or her behalf

ADR *abbr* STOCKHOLDING & INVESTMENTS American depository receipt

ADS *abbr* STOCKHOLDING & INVESTMENTS American depository share

advance FINANCE **1. money loaned or paid before due date** money paid as a loan or as a part of a payment scheduled to be made later **2. rise in price or rate** an increase in the price, rate, or value of something **3. pay money as loan or part payment** to pay an amount of money to somebody as a loan or as a part of a payment scheduled to be made later **4. become higher in price or rate** to increase in price, rate, or value

advance payment FINANCE **prepaid amount** an amount paid before it is earned or incurred, for example, a prepayment by an importer to an exporter before goods are shipped, or a cash advance for travel expenses

advance payment bond FINANCE made under a contract or order if the supplier fails to fulfill its contractual obligations.

advance payment guarantee *or* advance payment bond FINANCE **guarantee for recovery of advance payment** a guarantee that enables a buyer to recover an advance payment made under a contract or order if the supplier fails to fulfill its contractual obligations

adverse action FINANCE **refusal of credit** the action of refusing somebody credit or of canceling somebody's credit

adverse balance ACCOUNTING **deficit on account** a deficit on an account

adverse opinion ACCOUNTING **auditor's statement that accounts are misleading** a statement in the auditor's report of a company's annual accounts indicating a fundamental disagreement with the company to such an extent that the auditor considers the accounts misleading

advice of fate BANKING **notification as to whether check will be honored** immediate notification from a drawer's bank as to whether a check is to be honored or not

advising bank BANKING, INTERNATIONAL TRADE **bank facilitating firm's overseas credit** a bank in an exporter's own country to which an issuing bank sends a letter of credit. *Also called* **notifying bank**

advisory funds STOCKHOLDING & INVESTMENTS **funds invested at intermediary's discretion** funds placed with a financial institution to invest on behalf of a client as the institution sees fit

advisory management STOCKHOLDING & INVESTMENTS **stockbroker's provision of investment advice** an advisory service offered by some stockbrokers through which clients are able to discuss a variety of investment options with their broker and receive appropriate advice. No resulting action may be taken, however, without a client's express approval.

AER *abbr* FINANCE Annual Equivalent Rate

AEX *abbr* MARKETS, STOCKHOLDING & INVESTMENTS Amsterdam Exchange = ***Euronext Amsterdam***

AEX Index MARKETS, STOCKHOLDING & INVESTMENTS **main Dutch stock market index** an index of the 25 most-actively traded stocks on the Euronext Amsterdam exchange. It was established on January 3, 1983, with a base value of 45.38.

AFAANZ *abbr* ACCOUNTING Accounting and Finance Association of Australia and New Zealand

AfDB *abbr* BANKING African Development Bank

AFP *abbr* FINANCE Association for Financial Professionals

African Development Bank BANKING **bank supporting development in African countries** a bank set up by African countries to provide long-term loans to help agricultural development and improvement of infrastructure. *Abbr* **ADB**

after-acquired collateral FINANCE **collateral obtained after loan agreed** collateral for a loan that a borrower obtains after making the contract for the loan

after date FINANCE **after date stated on bill** after the date specified on a bill of exchange. Wording on a bill will state when payment has to be made, for example, "60 days after date, we promise to pay…" means 60 days after the date of the bill. *See also* **bill of exchange**

after sight FINANCE **after bill's acceptance** after acceptance of a bill of exchange. Wording on a bill will state when payment has to be made, for example, "60 days after sight, we promise to pay…" means 60 days after acceptance of the bill. *See also* **bill of exchange**

AG FINANCE **public limited company in German-speaking country** used after the name of a German, Austrian, or Swiss business to identify it as a public limited company. *Full form* **Aktiengesellschaft**

against actuals STOCKHOLDING & INVESTMENTS **relating to futures trade in cash** relating to a trade between owners of futures contracts that allows both to reduce their positions to cash instead of commodities

aged debt FINANCE **debt that is overdue** a debt that is overdue by one or more given periods, usually increments of 30 days

aged debtor FINANCE **somebody with overdue debt** a person or organization responsible for a debt that is overdue

agency bank BANKING **bank that is foreign bank's agent** a bank that does not accept deposits, but acts as an agent for another, usually foreign, bank

agency bill BANKING **bill of exchange drawn on local bank** a bill of exchange drawn on the local branch of a foreign bank

agency broker STOCKHOLDING & INVESTMENTS **dealer trading in shares for commission** a dealer who acts for a client, buying and selling stock for a commission

agent bank BANKING **1. bank participating in partner bank's credit card program** a bank that takes part in another bank's credit card program, acting as a depository for merchants **2. bank acting on foreign bank's behalf** a bank that acts on behalf of a foreign bank

agent's commission FINANCE **money paid for agent's services** money, often a percentage of sales, paid to an agent

agflation ECONOMICS **rapidly rising food prices** an economic situation occurring when the cost of food rises rapidly

aggregate demand ECONOMICS **total money spent or invested in economy** the sum of all expenditures in an economy that makes up its **GDP**, for example, consumers' expenditure on goods and services, investment in **capital stock**, and government spending

aggregate depreciation ACCOUNTING = ***accumulated depreciation***

aggregate income FINANCE **total of all incomes in economy** the total of all incomes in an economy without adjustments for inflation, taxation, or types of ***double counting***

aggregate output ECONOMICS **all goods and services produced in economy** the total value of all the goods and services produced in an economy. *Also called* **aggregate supply**

a–z

Dictionary

aggregate supply ECONOMICS = *aggregate output*

aggregator 1. FINANCE **firm selling product packages** a company that combines similar products or services into larger packages, making a profit by cost savings, by reaching a larger market, or by charging more for the combined package. In the secondary mortgage market, aggregators buy individual mortgages from financial institutions and turn them into *mortgage-backed securities*, pooling them and selling them on at a higher price. **2.** E-COMMERCE **middleman between producers and online customers** an organization that acts as an intermediary between producers and customers in an Internet business web. The aggregator selects products, sets prices, and ensures fulfillment of orders.

aggressive STOCKHOLDING & INVESTMENTS **describing high-risk investment strategy** used to describe an investment strategy marked by willingness to accept high risk while trying to realize higher than average gains. Such a strategy involves investing in rapidly growing companies that promise capital appreciation but produce little or no income from dividends and de-emphasizes income-producing instruments such as bonds.

aggressive accounting ACCOUNTING **deliberately inaccurate accounting to improve firm's position** inaccurate or unlawful accounting practices used by an organization in order to make its financial position seem healthier than it is in reality (slang)

aggressive growth fund STOCKHOLDING & INVESTMENTS **mutual fund pursuing large profits riskily** a mutual fund that takes considerable risks in the hope of making large profits

AGI *abbr* ACCOUNTING adjusted gross income

agio 1. FINANCE **difference between two related values** the difference between two values, for example, between the interest charged on loans made by a bank and the interest paid by the bank on deposits, or between the values of two currencies **2.** CURRENCY & EXCHANGE **charge for exchanging currency** a charge made for changing money of one currency into another, or for changing paper money into coins

AGM *UK* CORPORATE GOVERNANCE = *annual meeting*

agreement among underwriters STOCKHOLDING & INVESTMENTS **document forming syndicate of underwriters** a document which forms a syndicate of underwriters, linking them to the issuer of a new stock issue

agricultural produce ACCOUNTING **slaughtered animals and harvested plants** farm animals and plants once they have been slaughtered or harvested. Before this they are classified as *biological assets*

AIA *abbr* ACCOUNTING Association of International Accountants

AIB *abbr* BANKING American Institute of Banking

AIC *abbr* STOCKHOLDING & INVESTMENTS Association of Investment Companies

AICPA *abbr* ACCOUNTING American Institute of Certified Public Accountants

AIFA *abbr* FINANCE Association of Independent Financial Advisers

air bill *US* FINANCE **documents accompanying shipments by air** the documentation issued by an airline for the shipment of goods by air freight. *UK term* **air waybill**

air waybill *UK* FINANCE = *air bill*

AITC *abbr* FINANCE Association of Investment Trust Companies. *See* **Association of Investment Companies**

Aktiengesellschaft FINANCE *see* **AG**

all equity rate FINANCE **interest rate charged for high-risk project** the interest rate that a lender charges because of the apparent risks of a project that are independent of the normal market risks of financing it

allocate 1. FINANCE **assign item to single cost unit** to assign a whole item of *cost*, or of *revenue*, to a single cost unit, center, account, or time period **2.** STOCKHOLDING & INVESTMENTS **choose between different investments** to assign assets to different investment types such as equities, bonds, or cash

allonge FINANCE **attachment to bill of exchange allowing more signatures** a piece of paper attached to a bill of exchange, so that more endorsements can be written on it

allotment STOCKHOLDING & INVESTMENTS **UK issue of new company's stock to applicants** in the United Kingdom, the act of selling shares of stock in a new company to people who have applied for them

allowable losses ACCOUNTING **losses rightly offset against gains** losses such as those on the sale of assets that can be used to reduce the amount of income on which tax is paid

allowance for bad debt ACCOUNTING **accounting arrangement covering unpaid debt** a provision made in a company's accounts for potentially unrecoverable debts

alpha STOCKHOLDING & INVESTMENTS **number measuring price increase** a number representing an estimate of the anticipated price increase of a stock. A high alpha suggests a stock is likely to produce a good return. *See also* **beta**

alpha rating STOCKHOLDING & INVESTMENTS **expected return when market's rate is zero** the return a security or a portfolio would be expected to earn if the market's rate of return were zero. Alpha expresses the difference between the return expected from a stock or mutual fund, given its beta rating, and the return actually produced. A stock or trust that returns more than its beta would predict has a positive alpha, while one that returns less than the amount predicted by beta has a negative alpha. A large positive alpha indicates a strong performance, while a large negative alpha indicates a dismal performance.

To begin with, the market itself is assigned a beta of 1.0. If a stock or trust has a beta of 1.2, this means its price is likely to rise or fall by 12% when the overall market rises or falls by 10%; a beta of 7.0 means the stock or trust price is likely to move up or down at 70% of the level of the market change.

In practice, an alpha of 0.4 means the stock or trust in question outperformed the market-based return estimate by

0.4%. An alpha of −0.6 means the return was 0.6% less than would have been predicted from the change in the market alone.

Both alpha and beta should be readily available upon request from investment firms, because the figures appear in standard performance reports. It is always best to ask for them, because calculating a stock's alpha rating requires first knowing a stock's beta rating, and beta calculations can involve mathematical complexities. *See also* **beta rating**

alpha value STOCKHOLDING & INVESTMENTS **money given to departing employee for investment** in Australia and New Zealand, a sum paid to an employee when he or she leaves a company that can be transferred to a concessionally taxed investment account such as an ***Approved Deposit Fund***

alternate director CORPORATE GOVERNANCE **absent director's representative at board meeting** a person who is allowed to act for an absent named director of a company at a board meeting

alternative investment STOCKHOLDING & INVESTMENTS **investment not in bonds or stock** an investment other than in bonds or stock of a large company or one listed on a stock exchange

alternative order STOCKHOLDING & INVESTMENTS **instruction for either of two specified actions** an order given to a broker to do one of two things, for example, to sell a stock either when it goes up to a specified price or down to a specified price, thereby limiting gains and losses

AM *abbr* STOCKHOLDING & INVESTMENTS asset management

amalgamation MERGERS & ACQUISITIONS **joining of organizations for mutual benefit** the process of two or more organizations joining together for mutual benefit, either through a ***merger*** or ***consolidation***

amanah FINANCE **trust arrangement between parties** in Islamic financing, an arrangement in which one person holds funds or property in trust for another

ambit claim *ANZ* FINANCE **excessive arbitration claim anticipating compromise** a claim made to an arbitration authority for higher pay or improved conditions that is deliberately exaggerated because the claimants know that they will subsequently have to compromise

American Accounting Association ACCOUNTING **organization promoting accounting research** a voluntary organization for those with an interest in accounting research and best practice. Its mission is "to foster worldwide excellence in the creation, dissemination, and application of accounting knowledge and skills." The association was founded in 1916. *Abbr* **AAA**

American Bankers Association BANKING **US association representing banks** an association that represents banks in the United States and promotes good practice. *Abbr* **ABA**

American depository receipt STOCKHOLDING & INVESTMENTS **document indicating ownership of foreign stock** a document that indicates a US investor's ownership of stock in a foreign corporation. *Abbr* **ADR**

American depository share STOCKHOLDING & INVESTMENTS **foreign stock owned by US investor** a share of stock in a foreign corporation, whose ownership by a US investor is represented by an ***American depository receipt***. *Abbr* **ADS**

American Institute of Banking BANKING **US association training bankers** the part of the American Bankers Association that organizes training for people who work in the banking industry. *Abbr* **AIB**

American Institute of Certified Public Accountants ACCOUNTING **US association for certified public accountants** in the United States, the national association for certified public accountants, founded in New York in 1887. *Abbr* **AICPA**

American option *or* American style option STOCKHOLDING & INVESTMENTS **option contract running to expiration date** an option contract that can be exercised at any time up to and including the expiration date. Most exchange-traded options are of this style. *See also* ***European option***

amortization FINANCE **1. method of recovering costs of assets** a method of recovering (deducting or writing off) the capital costs of intangible assets over a fixed period of time.

For tax purposes, the distinction is not always made between amortization and depreciation, yet amortization remains a viable financial accounting concept in its own right.

It is computed using the straight-line method of depreciation: divide the initial cost of the intangible asset by the estimated useful life of that asset.

Initial cost/Useful life = Amortization per year

For example, if it costs $10,000 to acquire a patent and it has an estimated useful life of 10 years, the amortized amount per year is $1,000.

The amount of amortization accumulated since the asset was acquired appears on the organization's balance sheet as a deduction under the amortized asset.

While that formula is straightforward, amortization can also incorporate a variety of noncash charges to net earnings and/or asset values, such as depletion, write-offs, prepaid expenses, and deferred charges. Accordingly, there are many rules to regulate how these charges appear on financial statements. The rules are different in each country, and are occasionally changed, so it is necessary to stay abreast of them and rely on expert advice.

For financial reporting purposes, an intangible asset is amortized over a period of years. The amortizable life, or "useful life," of an intangible asset is the period over which it gives economic benefit.

Intangibles that can be amortized can include:

Copyrights, based on the amount paid either to purchase them or to develop them internally, plus the costs incurred in producing the work (wages or materials, for example). At present, a copyright is granted to a corporation for 75 years, and to an individual for the life of the author plus 50 years. However, the estimated useful life of a copyright is usually far less than its legal life, and it is generally amortized over a fairly short period.

Cost of a franchise, including any fees paid to the franchiser, as well legal costs or expenses incurred in the acquisition. A

a–z

Dictionary

franchise granted for a limited period should be amortized over its life. If the franchise has an indefinite life, it should be amortized over a reasonable period not to exceed 40 years.

Covenants not to compete: an agreement by the seller of a business not to engage in a competing business in a certain area for a specific period of time. The cost of the not-to-compete covenant should be amortized over the period covered by the covenant unless its estimated economic life is expected to be less.

Easement costs that grant a right of way may be amortized if there is a limited and specified life.

Organization costs incurred when forming a corporation or a partnership, including legal fees, accounting services, incorporation fees, and other related services. Organization costs are usually amortized over 60 months.

Patents, both those developed internally and those purchased. If developed internally, a patent's "amortizable basis" includes legal fees incurred during the application process. A patent should be amortized over its legal life or its economic life, whichever is the shorter.

Trademarks, brands, and trade names, which should be written off over a period not to exceed 40 years.

Other types of property that may be amortized include certain intangible drilling costs, circulation costs, mine development costs, pollution control facilities, and reforestation expenditures.

Certain intangibles cannot be amortized, but may be depreciated using a straight-line approach if they have "determinable" useful life. Because the rules are different in each country and are subject to change, it is essential to rely on specialist advice. **2. equal payment of principal and interest** the payment of the principal and interest on a loan in equal amounts over a period of time

amortize FINANCE **gradually repay debt or reduce value of assets** to reduce the value of an *asset* gradually by systematically writing off its cost over a period of time, or to repay a *debt* in a series of regular installments or transfers

amortized value FINANCE **value of amortized financial instrument** the value at a specific time of a financial instrument that is being amortized

amortizing swap STOCKHOLDING & INVESTMENTS **interest rate swap with decreasing notional principal amount** an *interest rate swap* in which the *notional principal amount* declines over the period of the contract

AMPS *abbr* STOCKHOLDING & INVESTMENTS auction market preferred stock

Amsterdam Stock Exchange MARKETS, STOCKHOLDING & INVESTMENTS = *Euronext Amsterdam*

analysis STOCKHOLDING & INVESTMENTS **evaluation of markets** a systematic examination and evaluation of the financial markets and the performance of securities

analyst STOCKHOLDING & INVESTMENTS **somebody who evaluates investments** a person whose job is to analyze the performance of securities and make recommendations about buying and selling

analytical review TREASURY MANAGEMENT **examination of trends between financial periods** the examination of ratios, trends, and changes in balances from one period to the next, to obtain a broad understanding of the financial position and results of operations and to identify any items requiring further investigation

Andersen effect ACCOUNTING **overcautious checking of data** the tendency to be more careful than usual in scrutinizing data, especially when carrying out financial audits, in order to avoid errors being found later. The term comes from the name of the firm Arthur Andersen which was involved in a major accounting scandal.

angel investing FINANCE **investing in unproven business venture** willingness of an individual or network of individuals to invest in an unproven but well-researched startup business, taking an advisory role without making demands

angel investor *or* angel FINANCE **investor in unproven business venture** an individual or group of individuals willing to invest in an unproven but well-researched startup business. Angel investors are typically the first port of call for Internet startups looking for financial backing, because they are more inclined to provide early funding than *venture capital* firms are. After investing in a company, angel investors take an advisory role without making demands.

angel network *or* angel investment group FINANCE **network of potential investors for entrepreneurs** a network of backers, organized through a central office which keeps a database of suitable investors and puts them in touch with entrepreneurs who need financial backing

announcement STOCKHOLDING & INVESTMENTS **statement of company's trading prospects** a statement that a company makes to provide information on its trading prospects, which will be of interest to its existing and potential investors

announcement date STOCKHOLDING & INVESTMENTS = *declaration date*

annual accounts CORPORATE GOVERNANCE, ACCOUNTING **document showing company's financial performance** a profit and loss account and balance sheet, and, where a company has subsidiaries, the company's group accounts, included in the *annual report and accounts* for stockholders. *See also annual report*

annual charge STOCKHOLDING & INVESTMENTS **management fee covering administrative costs** a management fee paid yearly to a stockbroker or collective fund manager by a client to cover a variety of administrative costs and *commission*

annual depreciation ACCOUNTING **reduction in book value of asset** a reduction in the book value of a fixed asset at a specific rate per year, based on the estimated useful life of that asset. *See also straight line depreciation*

annual depreciation provision ACCOUNTING **allocation of cost of asset to specific year** the allocation of the cost of an asset to a single year of the asset's expected lifetime

Annual Equivalent Rate FINANCE UK notional annual compound interest rate in the United Kingdom, a way of expressing different interest rates charged over different periods as an annual rate equivalent to a single payment of interest made on the anniversary of the loan and each subsequent year to repayment. *Abbr* **AER**. *See also compound annual return*

annual general meeting UK CORPORATE GOVERNANCE = *annual meeting*

annual income FINANCE money received in one year the money received from earnings or investments during a calendar year

annualized percentage rate FINANCE monthly rate times twelve the percentage rate over a year, calculated by multiplying the monthly rate by twelve. It is not as accurate as the annual percentage rate, which includes fees and other charges. *Abbr* **APR**

annual management charge STOCKHOLDING & INVESTMENTS charge made for managing investment account a charge made by the financial institution that is managing an investment account

annual meeting US CORPORATE GOVERNANCE stockholders' yearly business meeting a yearly meeting at which a company's management reports the year's results and stockholders have the opportunity to vote on company business, for example, the appointment of directors and auditors. Other business, for example, voting on dividend payments and board/stockholder-sponsored resolutions, may also be transacted. *Also called* **annual stockholders' meeting**. *UK term* **AGM**

annual percentage rate FINANCE hypothetical rate based on simple interest the interest rate that would exist if it were calculated as simple rather than compound interest.

Different investments typically offer different compounding periods, usually quarterly or monthly. The APR allows them to be compared over a common period of time: one year. This enables an investor or borrower to compare like with like, providing an excellent basis for comparing mortgage or other loan rates.

APR is calculated by applying the formula:

APR = [(1 + i)/m]m − 1

In the formula, *i* is the interest rate quoted, expressed as a decimal, and *m* is the number of compounding periods per year.

The APR is usually slightly higher than the quoted rate, and should be expressed as a decimal, that is, 6% becomes 0.06. When expressed as the cost of credit, other costs should be included in addition to interest, such as loan closing costs and financial fees. *Abbr* **APR**

annual percentage yield FINANCE effective annual return on investment the effective or true annual rate of return on an investment, taking into account the effect of *compounding*. For example, an annual percentage rate of 6% compounded monthly translates into an annual percentage yield of 6.17%. *Abbr* **APY**

annual report *or* annual report and accounts CORPORATE GOVERNANCE, ACCOUNTING document reporting company's business performance a document prepared each year to give a true and fair view of a company's state of affairs.

Annual reports are issued to shareholders and filed at the Securities and Exchange Commission in accordance with the provisions of company legislation. Contents include a profit and loss account and balance sheet, a cash flow statement, auditor's report, directors' report, and, where a company has subsidiaries, the company's group accounts. The financial statements are the main purpose of the annual report, and usually include notes to the accounts. These amplify numerous points contained in the figures and are critical for anyone wishing to study the accounts in detail.

annual return ACCOUNTING in UK, firm's report to Registrar of Companies in the United Kingdom, an official report that a registered company has to make each year to the Registrar of Companies

annual stockholders' meeting US CORPORATE GOVERNANCE = *annual meeting*

anticipation note STOCKHOLDING & INVESTMENTS bond repaid with future receipts or borrowings a bond that a borrower intends to pay off with money from taxes due or money to be borrowed in a later and larger transaction

anticipatory hedging STOCKHOLDING & INVESTMENTS hedging before relevant transaction occurs hedging conducted before the transaction to which the *hedge* applies has taken place. *See also* **hedge** (sense 2)

anti-inflationary ECONOMICS restricting inflation restricting or trying to restrict an increase in inflation

AP *abbr* ACCOUNTING accounts payable

APACS *abbr* BANKING Association for Payment Clearing Services

APB *abbr* ACCOUNTING Accounting Principles Board

applied economics ECONOMICS use of economic theories for practical policies the practical application of theoretical economic principles, especially in formulating national and international economic policies

apportionment ACCOUNTING distribution of costs the sharing of costs between different internal parties, cost centers, etc.

appreciation 1. ACCOUNTING value that asset accrues over time the value that some assets such as land and buildings accrue over time. Directors of companies are obliged to reflect this in their accounts. **2.** CURRENCY & EXCHANGE relative increase in currency value the increase in value of a currency with a *floating exchange rate* relative to another

appropriation ACCOUNTING sum set aside a sum of money that has been allocated for a specific purpose

appropriation account ACCOUNTING section of account showing treatment of profits the part of a *profit and loss account* that shows how a company's profit has been dealt with, for example, how much has been given to the stockholders as dividends and how much is being put into the reserves

approved accounts ACCOUNTING **accounts agreed on by company directors** accounts that have been formally accepted by a company's board of directors

approved securities STOCKHOLDING & INVESTMENTS **state bonds as bank reserves** state bonds that can be held by banks to form part of their reserves

APR *abbr* FINANCE **1.** hypothetical rate based on simple interest annual percentage rate **2.** annualized percentage rate

APS *abbr* BANKING, INSURANCE Asset Protection Scheme

APV *abbr* ACCOUNTING adjusted present value

APY *abbr* FINANCE annual percentage yield

AR *abbr* FINANCE accounts receivable

Arab Accounting Dinar CURRENCY & EXCHANGE **accounting unit of Arab Monetary Fund** a bookkeeping unit used between member states of the Arab Monetary Fund, equal to three IMF Special Drawing Rights. *Abbr* **AAD**

arbun FINANCE **nonrefundable deposit allowing buyer right to cancel** in Islamic financing, a nonrefundable down payment paid by a buyer to a seller upon the signing of a sale contract in which the buyer has the right to cancel the contract at any time

armchair economics ECONOMICS **casual economic opinion** economic forecasting or theorizing based on insufficient data or knowledge of a subject (informal)

ARPS *abbr* STOCKHOLDING & INVESTMENTS adjustable rate preferred stock

ARR *abbr* ACCOUNTING accounting rate of return

arrangement fee BANKING **bank charge for arranging credit** a charge made by a bank to a client for arranging credit facilities

arrears FINANCE **money owed but unpaid** money that is owed, but that has not been paid at the time when it was due **in arrears** FINANCE still owing money that should have been paid, especially in a series of payments

articles of association *UK* CORPORATE GOVERNANCE = *bylaws*

articles of incorporation CORPORATE GOVERNANCE **legal document creating US corporation** in the United States, a legal document that creates a corporation and sets forth its purpose and structure according to the laws of the state in which it is established. *Also called* **charter**

articles of partnership CORPORATE GOVERNANCE = *partnership agreement*

ASB *abbr* ACCOUNTING Accounting Standards Board

A share STOCKHOLDING & INVESTMENTS **share issued to raise additional capital** in the United States, a share of stock in a company issued to raise additional capital without diluting control of the company. *Also called* **nonvoting share**. *See also* **B share**

Asian Currency Unit ACCOUNTING **unit for recording transactions in Asian Dollar market** a bookkeeping unit used for recording transactions made by approved financial institutions operating in the Asian Dollar market. *Abbr* **ACU**

Asian Development Bank BANKING **bank supporting development in Asia** a bank set up by various Asian countries, with other outside members, to assist countries in the region with money and technical advice. *Abbr* **ADB**

Asian dollar BANKING, CURRENCY & EXCHANGE **US dollar deposited in Asian bank** a dollar deposited in a bank in Asia or the Pacific region

Asian option STOCKHOLDING & INVESTMENTS, RISK = *average option*

ask 1. *US* MARKETS **security's selling price** the price at which a security is offered for sale. *UK term* **asked price** **2.** STOCKHOLDING & INVESTMENTS **value of mutual fund** the net asset value of a mutual fund plus any sales charges

assessed value FINANCE **value calculated by professional adviser** a value for something that is calculated officially by somebody such as an investment adviser

assessor FINANCE **somebody who establishes something's worth** a person who determines the value of something such as real estate for tax or insurance purposes

asset ACCOUNTING **item to which value is assigned** any tangible or intangible item to which a value can be assigned. Assets can be physical, such as machinery and consumer durables, or financial, such as cash and accounts receivable, or intangible, such as brand value and goodwill.

Assets are typically broken down into five different categories. *Current assets* include cash, cash equivalents, marketable securities, inventories, and prepaid expenses that are expected to be used within one year or a normal operating cycle. All cash items and inventories are reported at historical value. Securities are reported at market value. *Noncurrent assets*, or long-term investments, are resources that are expected to be held for more than one year. They are reported at the lower of cost and current market value, which means that their values will vary. *Fixed assets* include property, plant and facilities, and equipment used to conduct business. These items are reported at their original value, even though current values might well be much higher. *Intangible assets* include legal claims, patents, franchise rights, and accounts receivable. These values can be more difficult to determine. Accounts receivable, for example, reflect the amount a business expects to collect, such as, say, $9,000 of the $10,000 owed by customers. Deferred charges include prepaid costs and other expenditures that will produce future revenue or benefits.

asset allocation STOCKHOLDING & INVESTMENTS **strategy maximizing return while minimizing risk** an investment strategy that distributes investments in a portfolio so as to achieve the highest investment return while minimizing risk. Such a strategy usually apportions investments among cash equivalents, stock in domestic and foreign companies, fixed-income investments, and real estate.

asset-backed security STOCKHOLDING & INVESTMENTS **security backed by loans** a security based on the collateral of outstanding loans for which the investor receives the payments

asset backing STOCKHOLDING & INVESTMENTS **assets supporting stock price** support for a stock price provided by the value of the company's assets

asset base STOCKHOLDING & INVESTMENTS **tangible assets of firm or person** the *tangible assets* held by a company or individual investor at any point in time

asset-based lending FINANCE **loans repaid with proceeds from acquired assets** the lending of money with the expectation that the proceeds from an asset or assets will allow the borrower to repay the loan

asset class STOCKHOLDING & INVESTMENTS **investment category** a category into which an investment falls, for example, stocks, bonds, commodities, or real estate

asset conversion loan FINANCE **loan repaid with proceeds from sale of asset** a loan that the borrower will repay with money raised by selling an asset

asset cover *or* asset coverage FINANCE **ratio showing company's solvency** a ratio, derived from the net assets of a company divided by its debt, that indicates the company's solvency

asset demand ECONOMICS **assets held in cash** the amount of assets held as cash, which will be low when interest rates are high and high when interest rates are low

asset financing FINANCE **borrowing that uses assets as collateral** the borrowing of money by a company using its assets as collateral

asset for asset swap FINANCE **exchange of bankrupts' debts** an exchange of one bankrupt debtor's debt for that of another

asset management STOCKHOLDING & INVESTMENTS **investment service combining banking and brokerage** an investment service offered by some financial institutions that combines banking and brokerage services. *Abbr* **AM**—*asset manager*

asset play STOCKHOLDING & INVESTMENTS **stock purchase assuming unknown assets** the purchase of a company's stock in the belief that it has assets that are not properly documented and therefore unknown to others

asset pricing model FINANCE **pricing model determining asset's future profit** a pricing model that is used to determine the profit that an asset is likely to yield

Asset Protection Scheme BANKING, INSURANCE **UK insurance plan supporting banks** in the United Kingdom, a government program established in 2009 that, for a fee, supports banks which have many bad loans and whose capital base is therefore compromised. It provides insurance against further losses, on the security of agreed assets, so that banks can continue to lend money. *Abbr* **APS**

asset protection trust FINANCE **trust protecting funds from creditors** a trust, often established in a foreign country, used to make the trust's principal inaccessible to creditors

asset restructuring FINANCE **purchase or sale of valuable assets** the purchase or sale of assets worth more than 50% of a listed company's total or net assets

asset side ACCOUNTING **side of balance sheet showing assets** the side of a balance sheet that shows the economic resources a firm owns, for example, cash in hand or in bank deposits, products, or buildings and fixtures

assets requirements FINANCE **assets needed to trade** the tangible and intangible assets needed for a business to continue trading

asset stripping MERGERS & ACQUISITIONS **practice of selling acquired firm's assets piecemeal** the purchase of a company whose market value is below its asset value, usually so that the buyer can sell the assets for immediate gain. The buyer usually has little or no concern for the purchased company's employees or other stakeholders, so the practice is generally frowned upon. —**asset stripper**

asset substitution FINANCE **purchase of risky assets undisclosed to lender** the purchase of assets that involve more risk than those a lender expected the borrower to buy

asset swap 1. FINANCE **exchange of assets allowing easy diversification** an exchange of assets between companies so that they may dispose of parts no longer required and enter another product area **2.** STOCKHOLDING & INVESTMENTS **exchange of fixed for varying payment** in capital markets, the exchange of a fixed coupon payment associated with a bond for a floating rate payment, usually based on LIBOR

asset turnover ACCOUNTING **measure of firm's business efficiency** the ratio of a company's sales revenue to its total assets, used as a measure of the firm's business efficiency

asset valuation ACCOUNTING **total value of firm's assets** the aggregated value of the assets of a firm, usually the capital assets, as entered on its balance sheet

asset value MERGERS & ACQUISITIONS **firm's value as combined value of assets** the value of a company calculated by adding together all its assets

assign FINANCE **transfer ownership of asset** to transfer ownership of an *asset* to another person or organization

associate director CORPORATE GOVERNANCE **unelected director attending board meetings** a director who attends board meetings, but has not been elected by the stockholders

Association for Financial Professionals FINANCE **US organization for professionals in finance industry** in the United States, an organization for corporate financial managers that provides training and certification to members and represents their interests to government. *Abbr* **AFP**

Association for Payment Clearing Services BANKING **UK organization for payments industry** the professional organization for providers of payment services to customers in the United Kingdom. *Abbr* **APACS**

Association of Accounting Technicians ACCOUNTING **UK accounting organization** a professional organization founded in the United Kingdom in 1980 and offering qualifications in subjects related to accounting. It now has members and students worldwide. *Abbr* **AAT**

Association of Chartered Accountants in the United States ACCOUNTING **association representing US chartered accountants** a nonprofit professional and educational organization that represents over 5,000 chartered accountants based in the United States. The Association was founded in 1985. *Abbr* **ACAUS**

Association of Chartered Certified Accountants ACCOUNTING **international organization representing accountants** an international accounting organization with over 300,000 members in more than 160 countries. It was formed in 1904 as the London Association of Accountants. *Abbr* **ACCA**

Association of Independent Financial Advisers FINANCE **UK trade association for financial advisers** a UK trade association that represents the interests of independent financial advisers to the UK government and in the European Union. *Abbr* **AIFA**

Association of International Accountants ACCOUNTING **organization for accountants** a professional accounting organization founded in the United Kingdom in 1928 and offering qualifications in international accounting. *Abbr* **AIA**

Association of Investment Companies STOCKHOLDING & INVESTMENTS **UK organization for investment industry** the professional organization for UK investment trust companies. It was founded in 1932 and until 2006 was called the Association of Investment Trust Companies. *Abbr* **AIC**

Association of Unit Trusts and Investment Funds STOCKHOLDING & INVESTMENTS *see* **Investment Management Association**

assumed bond STOCKHOLDING & INVESTMENTS **bond for which new firm takes responsibility** a bond for which a company other than the issuer takes over responsibility

asymmetric risk RISK **investment risk where gains and losses differ widely** the risk an investor faces when the gain realized from the move of an *underlying asset* in one direction is significantly different from the loss incurred from its move in the opposite direction

at call FINANCE **repayable on demand** used to describe a short-term loan that is repayable immediately upon demand

ATM BANKING **electronic machine for withdrawing money** an electronic machine at which bank customers can withdraw money or access an account using an encoded plastic card. *Full form* **automated teller machine**. *UK terms* **cash machine, cashpoint**

ATM card US BANKING **plastic card used in ATM** a plastic card used to withdraw money or access an account at an ATM. *UK term* **cash card**

at par MARKETS, STOCKHOLDING & INVESTMENTS **describing security sold at face value** used to describe a security that sells at a price equal to its face value

ATS *abbr* BANKING automatic transfer service

at sight FINANCE **immediately** as soon as presented. A negotiable instrument which is payable at sight is called a *sight draft*. *See also* **bill of exchange**

attention economy ECONOMICS **theory that website viewing is tradable commodity** a view of the economy in the late 20th century that suggests that people's attention to websites is a valuable and tradable commodity

attestation clause FINANCE **clause showing that signature has been witnessed** a clause showing that the signature of the person signing a legal document has been witnessed

at-the-money STOCKHOLDING & INVESTMENTS **describing option where trading price matches stock price** used to describe an option with a *strike price* roughly equivalent to the price of the underlying stock

attributable profit ACCOUNTING **profit generated by specific business activity** a profit that can be shown to come from a specific area of the company's operations

auction FINANCE **sale of goods by competitive bidding** a sale of goods or property by competitive bidding on the spot, by mail, by telecommunications, or over the Internet

auction market preferred stock STOCKHOLDING & INVESTMENTS **UK stock with dividends tracking money-market index** stock in a company owned in the United Kingdom that pays dividends which track a money-market index. *Abbr* **AMPS**

AUD *abbr* CURRENCY & EXCHANGE **Australian dollar** The currency of Australia, introduced on February 14, 1966, replacing the Australian pound.

audit ACCOUNTING **systematic examination of firm's activities and records** a systematic examination of the activities and status of an entity, based primarily on investigation and analysis of its systems, controls, and records

audit committee ACCOUNTING, GENERAL MANAGEMENT **committee monitoring firm's finances** a committee of a company's board of directors, from which the company's executives are excluded, that monitors the company's finances

audited accounts ACCOUNTING **accounts passed by auditor** a set of accounts that have been thoroughly scrutinized, checked, and approved by a team of auditors

auditing ACCOUNTING **official examination of firm's accounts** the work of officially examining the books and accounts of a company to see that they follow generally accepted accounting practices

auditor ACCOUNTING **person auditing accounts** a person who audits companies' accounts or procedures

Auditor-General FINANCE **official responsible for legality of Australian government expenditure** an officer of an Australian state or territory government who is responsible for ensuring that government expenditure is made in accordance with legislation

auditors' fees ACCOUNTING **approved payment to firm's auditors** fees paid to a company's auditors, which are approved by the stockholders at an annual meeting

auditors' qualification ACCOUNTING **auditors' statement that firm's financial position is misrepresented** a form of words in a report from the auditors of a company's accounts, stating that in their opinion the accounts are not a true reflection of the company's financial position. *Also called* **qualification of accounts**

auditor's report ACCOUNTING **auditor's confirmation of firm's financial records** a certification by an auditor that a firm's financial records give a true and fair view of its profit and loss for the period

audit report ACCOUNTING **official summary of audit** the summary submission made by auditors of the findings of an *audit*. An audit report is usually of the financial records and accounts of a company. An auditor's report normally takes one of the forms approved by the accountancy professional organizations to cover all requirements imposed by law on the auditor. If reports do not support the company's records, they may be termed "qualified." A report is qualified if it contains any indication that the auditor has failed to satisfy himself or herself on any of the points that the law requires. The qualification may, for example, add a rider stating that the appointed auditor has had to rely on secondary information supplied by other auditors under circumstances in which it has been inappropriate to do otherwise. Qualifications may also refer to the inadequacy of information or explanations supplied, or to the fact that the auditor is not satisfied that proper books or other records are being kept.

audit risk ACCOUNTING, RISK **danger of auditors' mistaken view** the risk that auditors may give an inappropriate audit opinion on financial statements

audit trail ACCOUNTING **record of steps in transaction** the records of all the sequential stages of a transaction. An audit trail may trace the process of a purchase, a sale, a customer complaint, or the supply of goods. Tracing what happened at each stage through the records can be a useful method of problemsolving. In financial markets, audit trails may be used to ensure fairness and accuracy on the part of the dealers.

augend FINANCE **number added to complete sum** the number added to an *addend* in order to complete an addition

austerity budget TREASURY MANAGEMENT **budget to discourage consumer spending** a budget imposed on a country by its government with the goal of reducing the national deficit by way of cutting consumer spending

Austrade FINANCE **Australian government organization promoting trade** Australian Trade Commission, a federal government body responsible for promoting Australian products abroad and attracting business to Australia. It currently has 108 offices in 63 countries.

Australian Accounting Standards Board ACCOUNTING **agency overseeing accounting standards** the body that is responsible for setting and monitoring accounting standards in Australia. It was established under Corporations Law in 1988, replacing the Accounting Standards Review Board. *Abbr* **AASB**

AUT *abbr* STOCKHOLDING & INVESTMENTS authorized unit trust

authority chart CORPORATE GOVERNANCE **diagram of organization's hierarchical relationships** a diagram showing the hierarchical lines of authority and reporting within an organization. *Organization charts* are similar.

authority to purchase FINANCE **bill bearing authorization for bank to buy it** a bill drawn up and presented with shipping documentation to the purchaser's bank, allowing the bank to purchase the bill

authorization FINANCE **giving approval for financial transaction** the process of assessing a financial transaction, confirming that it does not raise the account's debt above its limit, and allowing the transaction to proceed. This would be undertaken, for example, by a credit card issuer. A positive authorization results in an authorization code being generated and the relevant funds being set aside. The available credit limit is reduced by the amount authorized.

authorized capital FINANCE **firm's money raised from selling shares** the money made by a company from the sale of authorized shares of common and preferred stock. It is measured by multiplying the number of authorized shares by their par value.

authorized share STOCKHOLDING & INVESTMENTS **share issued legitimately** a share that a company issued with the authority to do so

authorized share capital UK STOCKHOLDING & INVESTMENTS **stock firm has approval to issue** the type, class, number, and amount of the stocks that a company may issue, as empowered by its memorandum of association. *See also* **nominal share capital**

authorized signatory STOCKHOLDING & INVESTMENTS **issuer of documents approving financial transactions** the most senior issuer of authorization certificates in an organization, recognized by a signatory authority and designated in a signatory certificate

authorized stock US STOCKHOLDING & INVESTMENTS **stock firm has approval to issue** the number of shares of stock that a corporation is allowed to issue, as stated in its articles of incorporation. *See also* **authorized share**

authorized unit trust STOCKHOLDING & INVESTMENTS **UK mutual fund** in the United Kingdom, a mutual fund that complies with the regulations of the Financial Services Authority. Different rules apply to different categories of mutual fund. *Abbr* **AUT**

AUTIF STOCKHOLDING & INVESTMENTS *see* **Investment Management Association**

automated clearing house BANKING, E-COMMERCE **computerized network for interbank transactions** *ATM* systems for interbank clearing and settlement of financial transactions. The network is also used for electronic fund transfers from a checking or savings account. *Abbr* **ACH**

Automated Direct Debit Amendment and Cancellation Service BANKING **UK computerized system for changing direct debits** in the United Kingdom, a *BACS* service that allows paying banks to inform direct debit payees of a change of instruction, for example, an amendment to the customer's account details or a request to cancel the instructions. *Abbr* **ADDACS**

automated teller machine BANKING *see* **ATM**

automatic debit US BANKING **bank customer's instruction for regular payments** an instruction given by an account holder to a bank to make regular payments on given dates to the same payee. *Also called* **banker's order**. *UK term* **standing order**

automatic transfer service BANKING **automatic funds transfer protection** an arrangement by which money from a depositor's savings account can be transferred automatically to his or her checking account to cover an overdraft or maintain a minimum balance. *Abbr* **ATS**

availability float ACCOUNTING **money representing checks written but not cashed** money that is available to a company because checks that it has written have not yet been charged against its accounts

aval FINANCE **guarantee of payment of bill or note** in Europe, an endorsement by a third party guaranteeing the payment of a bill or promissory note

average 1. STATISTICS **arithmetic mean** the arithmetic mean of a sample of observations **2.** STOCKHOLDING & INVESTMENTS **purchase stock regularly over period of changing prices** to purchase additional shares of a stock whose price is rising or falling at intervals during the period of changing prices, in order to affect the average price paid for the stock

average accounting return ACCOUNTING **percentage return of asset based on recorded value** the percentage return realized on an asset, as measured by its *book value*, after taxes and depreciation

average collection period ACCOUNTING **average time for cashing accounts receivable** the mean time required for a firm to liquidate its accounts receivable, measured from the date each receivable is posted until the last payment is received.
   Its formula is:

Accounts receivable/Average daily sales = Average collection period

   For example, if accounts receivable are $280,000, and average daily sales are 7,000, then:

280,000/7,000 = 40

average cost of capital FINANCE **average cost of getting money** the average of what a company is paying for the money it borrows or raises by selling stock

average down STOCKHOLDING & INVESTMENTS **purchase stock regularly over period of falling prices** to purchase additional shares of a security whose price is falling at intervals during the price drop period, in order to lower the average price paid for the stock

average due date FINANCE **date around which several payments are due** the average date when several different payments fall due

average nominal maturity FINANCE **average time for mutual fund to provide return** the average length of time until the *financial instruments* of a mutual fund mature

average option *or* average price option STOCKHOLDING & INVESTMENTS, RISK **option determined by commodity's average price** an option whose value depends on the average price of a commodity during a specific period of time. *Also called* **Asian option**

average up STOCKHOLDING & INVESTMENTS **purchase stock regularly over period of rising prices** to purchase additional shares of a security whose price is rising at intervals during the price rise period, in order to raise the average price paid for the stock

averaging STOCKHOLDING & INVESTMENTS **stock trading at intervals to get average price** the buying or selling of stocks at different times and at different prices to establish an average price

AWB *abbr* UK FINANCE air waybill = *air bill*

ax STOCKHOLDING & INVESTMENTS **expert in a particular investment** a financial adviser who is the current expert on a particular security or market sector

B

BAA *abbr* ACCOUNTING British Accounting Association

baby bonds US STOCKHOLDING & INVESTMENTS **bonds with low values** bonds in small denominations, usually less than $1,000, which small investors can afford to buy (informal)

backdoor selling FRAUD **1. illegal wholesaler selling directly to consumers** the practice by wholesalers of selling products directly to consumers in violation of contracts with retailers **2. selling tactic bypassing competitive bid requirement** the practice by salespeople of persuading buyers who are required to obtain competitive bids to purchase goods and services without them

back-end loading STOCKHOLDING & INVESTMENTS **sales fee paid by investor** a management charge or commission that is levied when an investor sells some types of investments such as funds and annuities. *See also* **front-end loading**

backer FINANCE **provider of financial or moral support** a person or company that gives somebody financial or moral support

back interest FINANCE **interest not yet paid** interest that is due but has not yet been paid

backlog depreciation ACCOUNTING **extra depreciation on revalued asset** the additional depreciation required when an asset is revalued to make up for the fact that previous depreciation had been calculated on a now out-of-date valuation

back pay FINANCE **overdue pay from earlier time period** pay that is owed to an employee for work carried out before the current payment period and is either overdue or results from a backdated pay increase

back payment FINANCE **payment due but not yet paid** a payment that is due to somebody but has not yet been paid

back-to-back loan FINANCE, CURRENCY & EXCHANGE **arrangement for two matching loans in different currencies** an arrangement in which two companies in different countries borrow offsetting amounts in each other's currency and each repays their loan at a specific future date in its domestic currency. Such a loan, often between a company and its foreign subsidiary, eliminates the risk of loss from fluctuations in exchange rates.

backup credit BANKING **secondary source of credit** a line of credit to be used as a standby should the primary credit source become unavailable. *Also called* **standby credit** (sense 1)

BACS BANKING **UK electronic clearing system for straightforward payments** in the United Kingdom, an electronic bulk clearing system generally used by banks and building societies for low-value and/or repetitive items such as standing orders, direct debits, and automated credits such as salary payments. It was formerly known as the Bankers Automated Clearing Service.

bad bank BANKING **government bank accepting other banks' risky loans** a government-owned bank created to buy and hold risky assets from other banks, in order to re-activate lending and stimulate economic activity

bad check *or* bad cheque BANKING **check returned unpaid** a check that is returned uncashed for any reason to the person who wrote it

bad debt FINANCE **debt that has to be written off** a debt that is or is considered to be uncollectable and is, therefore, written off either as a charge to the **profit and loss account** or against an existing doubtful debt provision

bad debt provision ACCOUNTING **estimate of uncollectable debts** an accounting estimate of the amount of debts thought likely to have to be written off

bad debt reserve FINANCE **firm's money set aside for uncollectable debts** an amount of money that a company sets aside to cover bad debts

bad debts recovered FINANCE **money written off then recovered** money formerly written off as uncollectable debt that has since been recovered either wholly or in part

badwill FINANCE **negative goodwill** a situation in which the value of the **separable net assets** of a company is greater than the total value of the business (slang)

bai al-bithaman ajil FINANCE **installment sale of goods arranged by bank** in Islamic financing, a sale of goods in which a bank purchases the goods on behalf of the buyer from the seller and sells them to the buyer at a profit, allowing the buyer to make installment payments. *Also called* **bai muajjal**

bailment FINANCE **delivery of something on loan** the delivery of goods from the owner to another person on the condition that they will eventually be returned

bail out FINANCE **give help to firm in financial difficulty** to provide sufficient financial support to a company that is having financial difficulties to ensure its survival

bailout FINANCE **financial backing for firm in crisis** the provision of sufficient financial support to a company that is having financial difficulties to ensure its survival

bai muajjal FINANCE = **bai al-bithaman ajil**

balance 1. BANKING **money in bank account** the state of a bank account at any one time, indicating whether money is owed (a debit) or owing (a credit balance) **2.** ACCOUNTING **discrepancy between debit and credit figures** in double-entry bookkeeping, the amount required to make the debit and credit figures in the books equal each other **3.** ACCOUNTING **difference between money paid and received** the difference between the totals of the debit and credit entries in an account

balance billing FINANCE **charging person for own insurance shortfall** the practice of requesting payment from a receiver of a service such as medical treatment for the part of the cost not covered by the person's insurance

balance brought down ACCOUNTING **figure in account to balance income and expenditure** an amount entered in an account at the end of a period to balance income and expenditure

balanced budget ACCOUNTING **spending plan in which income equals expenses** a budget in which planned expenditure on goods and services and debt interest can be met by current income

balanced fund STOCKHOLDING & INVESTMENTS **mutual fund with diversified investments** a mutual fund that invests in a variety of types of companies and financial instruments to reduce the risk of loss through poor performance of any one type

balanced investment strategy STOCKHOLDING & INVESTMENTS **spreading types of investment** the practice of investing in a variety of types of companies and financial instruments to reduce the risk of loss through poor performance of any one type

balance off ACCOUNTING **find balance by adding up totals** to add up and enter the totals for both sides of an account at the end of an accounting period in order to determine the balance

balance sheet ACCOUNTING **statement of total assets, liabilities, and owners' equity** a financial report stating the total assets, liabilities, and owners' equity of an organization at a given date, usually the last day of the accounting period. The credit side of the balance sheet states assets, while the debit side states liabilities and equity, and the two sides must be equal, or balance.

Assets include cash in hand and cash anticipated (receivables), inventories of supplies and materials, properties, facilities, equipment, and whatever else the company uses to conduct business. Assets also need to reflect depreciation in the value of equipment such as machinery that has a limited expected useful life.

Liabilities include pending payments to suppliers and creditors, outstanding current and long-term debts, taxes, interest payments, and other unpaid expenses that the company has incurred.

Subtracting the value of aggregate liabilities from the value of aggregate assets reveals the value of owners' equity. Ideally, it should be positive. Owners' equity consists of capital invested by owners over the years and profits (net income) or internally generated capital, which is referred to as "retained earnings"; these are funds to be used in future operations. *Abbr* **B/S**

balance sheet audit ACCOUNTING **partial audit to check compliance with rules** a limited audit of the items on a company's balance sheet in order to confirm that it complies with the relevant standards and requirements. Such an audit involves checking the value, ownership, and existence of assets and liabilities and ensuring that they are correctly recorded.

balance sheet date ACCOUNTING **annual date for balance sheet preparation** the date, usually the end of a financial or accounting year, when a company's balance sheet is drawn up

balance sheet equation ACCOUNTING = *accounting equation*

balance sheet total ACCOUNTING **total at bottom of UK firm's balance sheet** in the United Kingdom, the total of assets shown at the bottom of a balance sheet and used to classify a company according to size

balancing item *or* balancing figure ACCOUNTING **number making one total equal another** a number added to a series of numbers to make the total the same as another total. For example, if a debit total is higher than the credit total in the accounts, the balancing figure is the amount of extra credit required to make the two totals equal.

balloon FINANCE **1.** = *balloon loan* **2.** = *balloon payment*

balloon loan FINANCE **loan with large final payment** a loan repaid in regular installments with a single larger final payment including interest

balloon payment FINANCE **large final payment on loan** a large final payment including interest on a loan, after a number of periodic smaller payments have been made

ballpark *or* ballpark figure FINANCE **rough total** a rough, estimated figure. The term was derived from the approximate assessment of the number of spectators at a sporting event that might be made on the basis of a glance around. (slang)

BALO FINANCE **French financial publication** a French government publication that includes financial statements of public companies. *Full form* **Bulletin des Annonces Légales Obligatoires**

BAN *abbr* STOCKHOLDING & INVESTMENTS bond anticipation note

bang for the/your buck FINANCE **financial benefit** the leverage provided by an investment (slang)

bank BANKING **institution holding and lending money** a commercial institution that keeps money in accounts for individuals or organizations, makes loans, exchanges currencies, provides credit to businesses, and offers other financial services

bankable BANKING **acceptable as security for loan** acceptable by a bank as security for a loan

bankable paper BANKING **document accepted by bank as security** a document that a bank will accept as security for a loan

bank account BANKING **facility for depositing and withdrawing money at bank** an arrangement that a customer has with a bank, by which the customer can deposit and withdraw money

bank advance BANKING = *bank loan*

bank balance BANKING **money in bank account** the state of a bank account at any one time, indicating whether money is owed (a debit) or owing (a credit balance)

bank base rate BANKING **interest rate determining bank's rate to customers** the basic rate of interest on which the actual rate a bank charges on loans to its customers is calculated

bank bill BANKING **1.** US = *banknote* **2.** = *banker's bill*

bank book BANKING **booklet recording deposits and withdrawals** a small booklet formerly issued by banks and some other financial institutions to record deposits, withdrawals, interest paid, and the balance on savings and deposit accounts. In most cases, it has now been replaced by statements. *Also called* **passbook**

bank card BANKING **payment card issued by bank** a plastic card issued by a bank and accepted by merchants in payment for transactions. The most common types are *credit cards* and *debit cards*. Bank cards are governed by an internationally recognized set of rules for the authorization of their use and the clearing and settlement of transactions.

bank certificate BANKING **confirmation of firm's bank balance** a document, often requested during an audit, that is signed by a bank official and confirms the balances due to or from a company on a specific date

bank charge BANKING = *service charge*

bank confirmation BANKING **verification of firm's bank balances** verification of a company's balances requested by an auditor from a bank

bank credit BANKING **maximum credit** the maximum credit available to somebody from a specific bank

bank deposits BANKING **money deposited in banks** all money placed in banks by private or corporate customers

bank discount basis BANKING **income from US Treasury bills expressed over 360 days** the expression of yield that is used for US Treasury bills, based on a 360-day year

bank draft BANKING = *banker's draft*

bank-eligible issue BANKING US Treasury bonds available to commercial banks US Treasury obligations with a remaining maturity of ten years or less, eligible for purchase at any time by commercial banks

banker BANKING owner or senior executive of bank somebody who owns or is an executive of a bank or group of banks

banker's acceptance BANKING = *banker's credit*

Bankers Automated Clearing Service BANKING *see BACS*

banker's bill BANKING bank's order to another bank to pay money an order by one bank telling another bank, usually in another country, to pay money to somebody. *Also called bank bill*

banker's check BANKING = *banker's draft*

banker's credit BANKING financial instrument guaranteed by bank a financial instrument, typically issued by an exporter or importer for a short term, that a bank guarantees. *Also called banker's acceptance*

banker's draft BANKING check drawn by bank on itself a *bill of exchange* payable on demand and drawn by one bank on another. Regarded as being equivalent to cash, the draft cannot be returned unpaid. *Also called bank draft, banker's check. Abbr* B/D

bankers' hours BANKING short working day short hours of work. The term refers to the relatively short time that a bank is open to customers in some countries. (informal)

banker's lien BANKING bank's right to hold client's property as security the right of a bank to hold some property of a customer as security against payment of a debt

banker's order BANKING = *automatic debit*

banker's reference BANKING bank's report on customer's creditworthiness a report issued by a bank regarding a particular customer's creditworthiness

bank fee BANKING administrative charge for transaction a charge that is either paid in advance or is included in the gross capitalized cost, usually covering administrative costs such as the costs of obtaining a credit report, verifying insurance coverage, and checking documentation

Bank for International Settlements BANKING bank dealing with international finance a bank that promotes cooperation between central banks, provides facilities for international financial operations, and acts as agent or trustee in international financial settlements. The 17-member board of directors consists of the governors of the central banks of Belgium, Canada, France, Germany, Italy, Japan, the Netherlands, Sweden, Switzerland, the United Kingdom, and the United States. *Abbr* BIS

bank giro BANKING = *giro*

bank guarantee BANKING bank's undertaking to pay debt a commitment that a bank will pay a debt if the debtor defaults, for example, a bank may guarantee to pay an exporter for goods shipped if the buyer defaults

bank holding company BANKING firm owning bank or banks a company that owns one or more banks as part of its assets

bank holiday UK BANKING public holiday on weekday a weekday, especially a Monday, that is a public holiday when the banks are closed

bank identification number BANKING international number identifying individual bank n internationally agreed six-digit number that formerly identified a bank for credit card purposes. *Abbr* BIN. *See also issuer identification number*

banking account BANKING facility for depositing and withdrawing money at bank an arrangement that a customer has with a bank, by which the customer can deposit and withdraw money

Banking Code BANKING UK banks' voluntary code of practice a voluntary code of best practice for the banking and financial services industry, which is developed and revised by the *British Bankers' Association*

banking house BANKING financial institution providing banking services a financial organization such as a bank or *credit union* that is in the business of providing banking services to the public

Banking Ombudsman BANKING Australian or New Zealand official handling banking complaints an official of the Australian or New Zealand government responsible for dealing with complaints relating to banking practices

banking passport BANKING passport for holding assets abroad a second passport in another name used to hold assets confidentially and for banking transactions in another country

banking products BANKING items provided by banks for customers goods and services that banks provide for their customers, for example, statements, direct debits, and automatic debits

banking syndicate BANKING investment banks jointly offering new security a group of investment banks that jointly underwrite and distribute a new security offering

banking system BANKING network of banks providing financial services a network of commercial, savings, and specialized banks that provide financial services, including accepting deposits and providing loans and credit, money transmission, and investment facilities

bank investment contract BANKING contract between bank and investors a contract that specifies what a bank will pay its investors

bank line FINANCE = *line of credit*

bank loan BANKING loan made to bank's customer a loan made by a bank to a customer, usually against the security of a property or asset. *Also called bank advance*

bankmail BANKING agreement by bank not to finance customer's rival an agreement by a bank not to finance any rival's attempt to take over the same company that a particular customer is trying to buy (slang)

bank mandate BANKING **written order for opening bank account** a written order to a bank that asks the bank to open an account, names the person(s) allowed to sign checks on behalf of the account holder, and provides specimen signatures, etc.

banknote BANKING **1. item of paper money** a piece of paper money printed by a bank and approved as legal tender. *Also called **bank bill*** **2. note from Federal Reserve Bank usable as cash** in the United States, a non-interest bearing note, issued by a Federal Reserve Bank, that can be used as cash

Bank of England BANKING **UK central bank** the central bank of the United Kingdom, established in 1694. Originally a private bank, it became public in 1946 and increased its independence from government in 1997, when it was granted sole responsibility for setting the base rate of interest.

bank rate BANKING **1. central bank's discount rate** the discount rate offered by a country's central bank **2. formerly, Bank of England's lending rate** formerly, the rate at which the Bank of England lent to other banks, now replaced by the base rate. *Also called **minimum lending rate***

bank reconciliation BANKING **comparison of bank statement with firm's ledger** the process of comparing a bank statement with a company's ledger to verify that the balances are the same

bank reserve ratio BANKING = **required reserve ratio**

bank reserves BANKING **bank's ready money** the money that a bank has available to meet the demands of its depositors

bankroll FINANCE **1. finance for project** the money used for financing a project or business **2. give money to support something** to provide the financing for a project or business

bankruptcy-remote RISK **not likely to risk bankruptcy** used to describe a strategy or business structure designed to isolate a valuable asset or entity from financial risk

bank statement BANKING **statement of transactions on customer's bank account** a written statement from a bank showing the balance of an account and transactions over a period of time

bank term loan BANKING **bank loan lasting at least one year** a loan from a bank that has a term of at least one year

bank transfer BANKING **transference of money to another account** an act of moving money from one bank account to another

bar UK CURRENCY & EXCHANGE **£1,000,000** one million pounds sterling, used by traders (slang)

barbell STOCKHOLDING & INVESTMENTS **portfolio with no medium-term bonds** a portfolio that concentrates on very long-term and very short-term bonds only

barefoot pilgrim US STOCKHOLDING & INVESTMENTS **inexperienced and unsuccessful investor** an unsophisticated investor who has lost everything trading in securities (slang)

bargaining chip FINANCE **useful factor in negotiation** something that can be used as a concession or inducement in negotiation

barometer FINANCE **indicator of trend** an economic or financial indicator that forecasts a trend in the economy or in financial markets

barren money STOCKHOLDING & INVESTMENTS = **idle capital**

barrier option STOCKHOLDING & INVESTMENTS **option with trigger for trading in others** an option that includes automatic trading in other options when a commodity reaches a specific price

barter FINANCE **exchange of goods or services** the direct exchange of goods or services between two parties without the use of money as a medium

base currency CURRENCY & EXCHANGE **way of expressing income from investment** the currency used for measuring the return on an investment, usually the currency of the country in which the investment is made

base interest rate FINANCE **US minimum expected interest rate** in the United States, the minimum interest rate that investors will accept for investing in a non-Treasury security. *Also called **benchmark interest rate***

base pay US FINANCE **basic salary before additional benefits** a guaranteed sum of money given to an employee in payment for work, disregarding any fringe benefits, allowances, or extra rewards from an *incentive plan*. UK term **basic pay**

base period FINANCE **period against which current financial period is measured** a period of time against which financial or economic comparisons are made

base rate BANKING **1. US Federal Reserve's interest rate** the interest rate set by the US Federal Reserve that dictates the rate at which money is lent to other banks and which they in turn charge their customers **2. Bank of England's interest rate** the interest rate at which the Bank of England lends to other UK banks and which they in turn charge their customers

base-weighted index ECONOMICS **price index comparing prices against standard time period** a price index that is weighted according to prices from the base period

base year ECONOMICS **benchmark year for index calculations** the reference year from which an index is calculated

basic balance FINANCE **relationship of current and long-term capital accounts** the balance of current and long-term capital accounts in a country's balance of payments, which by implication must be financed with short-term *capital flows* such as short-term securities, money funds, and bank deposits

basic pay UK FINANCE = **base pay**

basic wage FINANCE **in Australia, minimum allowable pay for particular job** in Australia, the minimum rate of pay set by an industrial court or tribunal for a specific occupation

basic wage rate FINANCE **minimum pay in UK job** in the United Kingdom, the wages paid for a specific number of hours' work per week, excluding overtime payments and any other incentives

basis FINANCE **starting point for calculations** a point, price, or number from which calculations are made. For example, the purchase price of a security would be used as the basis for calculating gains or losses.

basis point STOCKHOLDING & INVESTMENTS **in bond interest rates, one hundredth of 1%** one hundredth of 1%, used in relation to changes in bond interest rates. Thus a change from 7.5% to 7.4% is 10 basis points.

basis price STOCKHOLDING & INVESTMENTS **1. price on which investment return is based** the price used for calculating the gain on any investment when selling it, based on purchase price and any other costs **2. price of bond given as yield to maturity** the price of a bond shown as its annual percentage yield to maturity rather than being quoted in a currency **3. over-the-counter securities price** the price agreed between a buyer and seller on the over-the-counter market

basket of currencies CURRENCY & EXCHANGE **group of currencies providing benchmark** a group of currencies, each of which is weighted, calculated together as a single unit in establishing a standard of value for another unit of currency. *Also called* **currency basket**

basket of prices FINANCE **group of prices used as benchmark** a group of prices used as a standard for measuring value over time

basket of securities STOCKHOLDING & INVESTMENTS **set of securities traded together** a group of securities that is treated as a single unit and traded together

basket of shares US STOCKHOLDING & INVESTMENTS **set of shares of stock sold together** a fixed number of shares of stock that is treated as a single unit and traded together. *UK term* **parcel of shares**

bath **take a bath** FINANCE to experience a serious financial loss

BBA *abbr* BANKING British Bankers' Association

BC *abbr* TREASURY MANAGEMENT budgetary control

BCCS *abbr* CURRENCY & EXCHANGE Board of Currency Commissioners

B/D *abbr* BANKING banker's draft

bean counter ACCOUNTING **accountant** an accountant, used to refer in a derogatory way especially to an accountant who works in a large organization (slang)

bear STOCKHOLDING & INVESTMENTS **exploiter of unfavorable business conditions** somebody who anticipates unfavorable business conditions, especially somebody who practices **short selling**, or selling stocks or commodities expecting their prices to fall, with the intention of buying them back cheaply later. *See also* **bull**

bear CD STOCKHOLDING & INVESTMENTS **CD paying more in falling market** a **certificate of deposit** that pays a higher interest rate when an underlying market index falls in value

bearer BANKING **person holding check or certificate** a person who holds a check or certificate that is redeemable for payment

bearer bond STOCKHOLDING & INVESTMENTS **bond owned by physical possessor of it** a negotiable bond or security whose ownership is not registered by the issuer, but is presumed to lie with whoever has physical possession of the bond

bearer check US BANKING **blank check** a check with no name written on it, so that the person who holds it can cash it. *Also called* **check to bearer**. *UK term* **cheque to bearer**

bearer instrument FINANCE **financial document entitling its presenter to payment** a financial instrument such as a check or bill of exchange that entitles the person who presents it to receive payment

bearer security STOCKHOLDING & INVESTMENTS **security owned by physical possessor of it** a stock or bond that is owned by the person who possesses it.

bear raid STOCKHOLDING & INVESTMENTS = **raid**

bed and breakfast deal STOCKHOLDING & INVESTMENTS **selling and buying back security overnight** a transaction in which somebody sells a security at the end of one trading day and repurchases it at the beginning of the next. This is usually done to formally establish the profit or loss accrued to this security for tax or reporting purposes.

bed and spouse STOCKHOLDING & INVESTMENTS **method for couples to reduce capital gains tax** in the United Kingdom, a method used by married taxpayers to reduce capital gains tax. A spouse who has a capital gain and has not used all their capital gains tax allowance may sell a security, and the other spouse may buy the same security back the next day, thereby allowing the spouse who sold to offset all or part of the gain with their tax allowance, while still holding onto the stock.

beginning inventory US ACCOUNTING **inventory carried over to next balance sheet** the closing inventory at the end of the balance sheet from one accounting period that is transferred forward and becomes the opening inventory in the one that follows. *UK term* **opening stock**

behavioral accounting US ACCOUNTING **accounting emphasizing psychological and social aspects** an approach to the study of accounting that emphasizes the psychological and social aspects of the profession in addition to the more technical areas

bells and whistles (slang) **1.** FINANCE **features appealing to investors or producers** special features attached to a derivatives instrument or securities issue that are intended to attract investors or reduce issue costs **2.** MARKETING **extra unnecessary features** peripheral features of a product that are unnecessary but desirable

bellwether STOCKHOLDING & INVESTMENTS **security with representative price** a security whose price is viewed by investors as an indicator of future developments or trends

belly **go belly up** FINANCE to fail financially or go bankrupt

below par STOCKHOLDING & INVESTMENTS **selling at less than face value** describes a stock with a market price that is lower than its par value

below-the-line 1. ACCOUNTING **showing profit distribution or sources of bottom line** used to describe entries in a company's *profit and loss account* that show how the profit is distributed, or where the funds to finance the loss originate. *See also* **above-the-line** *(sense 1)* **2.** ECONOMICS **showing country's capital transactions** in macroeconomics, used to describe a country's capital transactions, as opposed to its **above-the-line** or revenue transactions. *See also* **above-the-line** *(sense 2)* **3.** MARKETING **connected with marketing costs for everything but advertising** relating to the proportion of marketing expenditure allocated to activities that are not related to advertising, such as public relations, sales promotion, printing, presentations, sponsorship, and salesforce support. *See also* **above-the-line** *(sense 3)*

belt and braces man FINANCE **lender wanting extra safeguards** a very cautious lender who asks for extra collateral as well as guarantees for a loan (slang)

BEL 20 MARKETS, STOCKHOLDING & INVESTMENTS **main Belgian stock market index** an index of the 20 most-highly capitalized companies on the Euronext Brussels exchange. It was established on December 30, 1990, with a base value of 1,000.

benchmark accounting policy ACCOUNTING **one of two possible approved policies** one of a choice of two possible policies within an International Accounting Standard. The other policy is marked as an "allowed alternative," although there is no indication of preference.

benchmark interest rate FINANCE = *base interest rate*

beneficial interest FINANCE **benefiting from house as if its owner** an arrangement whereby somebody is allowed to occupy or receive rent from a house without owning it

beneficial owner STOCKHOLDING & INVESTMENTS **receiver of benefits of another's stock** a person who receives all the benefits of a stock such as dividends, rights, and proceeds of any sale but is not the registered owner of the stock

beneficiary FINANCE **somebody who will receive assets or proceeds** a person who is designated to receive assets or proceeds from, for example, an estate or insurance policy

beneficiary bank BANKING **bank dealing with gift** a bank that handles a gift such as a bequest

benefit 1. FINANCE **something extra offering improvement or reward** something that improves the profitability or efficiency of an organization or reduces its risk **2.** HR & PERSONNEL **nonmonetary reward for employee** any nonmonetary reward such as a paid vacation or employer contribution to a pension that is given to employees

benefit–cost ratio ACCOUNTING = *cost–benefit analysis*

bequest FINANCE **item left in will** a gift that has been left to somebody in a will

Berne Union FINANCE = *International Union of Credit and Investment Insurers*

beta *or* **beta coefficient** STOCKHOLDING & INVESTMENTS **number measuring changes in value** a number representing an estimate of the fluctuations in value of a stock in relation to the market as a whole. A high beta indicates that a stock is likely to

be more sensitive to market movements and therefore has a higher risk. *See also* **alpha, beta rating**

beta rating STOCKHOLDING & INVESTMENTS **means of measuring market risk** a means of measuring the volatility (or risk) of a stock or fund in comparison with the market as a whole.

The beta of a stock or fund can be of any value, positive or negative, but usually is between +0.25 and +1.75. Stocks of many utilities have a beta of less than 1. Conversely, most high-tech NASDAQ-based stocks have a beta greater than 1; they offer a higher rate of return but are also risky. Both alpha and beta ratings should be readily available upon request from investment firms, because the figures appear in standard performance reports. *See also* **alpha rating**

b/f *abbr* ACCOUNTING brought forward

bid 1. FINANCE **highest realistic price** the highest price a prospective buyer for a good or service is prepared to pay **2.** STOCKHOLDING & INVESTMENTS **offer for most of firm's capital shares** an offer to buy all or the majority of the capital shares of a company in an attempted takeover **3.** OPERATIONS & PRODUCTION **statement outlining acceptable price for job** a statement of what a person or company is willing to accept when selling a product or service. *Also called* **quote**. *See also* **tender**

bid bond FINANCE **guarantee of finance for international tender offer** a guarantee by a financial institution of the fulfillment of an international tender offer

bid costs MERGERS & ACQUISITIONS **professional fees paid during takeover** costs incurred during the takeover of a company as a result of professional advice to the purchasing company from, for example, lawyers, accountants, and bankers

bid rate FINANCE, CURRENCY & EXCHANGE **interest rate on Eurocurrency deposits** a rate of interest paid on Eurocurrency deposits

big bath ACCOUNTING **deliberately making bad income statement worse** the practice of making a particular year's poor income statement look even worse by increasing expenses and selling assets. Subsequent years will then appear much better in comparison. (slang)

Big Four 1. BANKING **largest UK banks** the United Kingdom's four largest commercial banks: Barclays, HSBC, Lloyds Banking Group, and NatWest (owned by Royal Bank of Scotland) **2.** ACCOUNTING **largest accounting firms** the four largest international auditors: PricewaterhouseCoopers, Deloitte Touche Tohmatsu, Ernst & Young, and KPMG **3.** BANKING **largest Australian banks** Australia's four largest banks: the Commonwealth Bank of Australia, Westpac Banking Corporation, National Australia Bank, and the Australia and New Zealand Banking Group Limited

Big GAAP ACCOUNTING **in US, accounting principles for large firms** in the United States, the *Generally Accepted Accounting Principles* that apply to large companies. It is sometimes felt that they are unnecessarily complex for smaller companies. (slang)

big-ticket FINANCE **expensive** used to describe something that costs a lot of money (slang)

Bilanzrichtliniengesetz ACCOUNTING **German law covering accounting** the 1985 German accounting directives law. *Abbr* **BiRiLiG**

bilateral clearing BANKING **central banks' settling of accounts between countries** the system of annual settlements of accounts between some countries, where accounts are settled by the central banks

bilateral credit BANKING **credit to banks during clearing of checks** credit allowed by banks to other banks in a clearing system to cover the period while checks are being cleared

bilateral facility BANKING **arrangement for lending to single borrower** a facility for making loans from one bank to one borrower, especially a corporate borrower

bilateral monopoly ECONOMICS **market with one seller and one buyer** a market in which there is a single seller and a single buyer

bilateral netting BANKING **significant settling of contracts between banks** the settling of contracts between two banks to give a new position

bill 1. FINANCE **document promising payment** a written paper promising to pay money **2.** *US* FINANCE **piece of paper money** a piece of paper currency printed by a bank and approved as legal tender. *UK term* **note 3.** LEGAL **draft of new law** a draft of a new law that will be discussed in a legislature **4.** OPERATIONS & PRODUCTION **list of charges payable to supplier** a written list of charges to be paid by a customer to a supplier **5.** OPERATIONS & PRODUCTION **give bill to customer for payment** to present a bill to a customer so that it can be paid

bill broker FINANCE **dealer in bills of exchange** an agent who buys and sells *promissory notes* and *bills of exchange*

bill discount BANKING **Federal Reserve's interest rate to banks** the interest rate that the Federal Reserve charges banks for short-term loans. This establishes a de facto floor for the interest rate that banks charge their customers, usually a little above the *discount rate*.

bill discounting rate FINANCE **reduction in cost of US Treasury bill** the amount by which the price of a Treasury bill is reduced to reflect expected changes in interest rates

billing cycle FINANCE **time between requests for payment** the period of time, often one month, between successive requests for payment

billion FINANCE **1. thousand millions** a sum equal to one thousand millions **2.** *UK* **million millions** a sum equal to one million millions (dated)

billionaire FINANCE **person with income over one billion** a person whose net worth or income is more than one billion dollars, pounds, or other unit of currency

bill of exchange FINANCE **negotiable instrument** a negotiable instrument, drawn by one party on another, for example, by a

supplier of goods on a customer, who, by accepting (signing) the bill, acknowledges the debt, which may be payable immediately (a *sight draft*) or at some future date (a *time draft*). The holder of the bill can thereafter use an accepted time draft to pay a bill to a third party, or can discount it to raise cash.

bill of goods FINANCE **1. in US, batch of goods** in the United States, a consignment of merchandise for transportation and delivery **2. in US, statement about batch of goods** in the United States, a statement of the nature and value of a consignment of goods to be transported and delivered

bill of lading FINANCE **document acknowledging shipment of goods** a document prepared by a consignor by which a carrier acknowledges the receipt of goods and which serves as a document of title to the goods consigned

bill of sale FINANCE **document confirming purchase** a document confirming the transfer of goods or services from a seller to a buyer

bills payable FINANCE **bills that firm must pay to creditors** bills, especially bills of exchange, that a company will have to pay to its creditors. *Abbr* **B/P**

bills receivable FINANCE **bills that firm's debtors will pay** bills, especially bills of exchange, that are due to be paid by a company's debtors. *Abbr* **B/R**

BIN *abbr* FINANCE bank identification number

biological assets ACCOUNTING **live animals and growing plants** farm animals and plants classified as assets. International Accounting Standards require that they are recorded on balance sheets at market value. Once they have been slaughtered or harvested, the assets become *agricultural produce*.

bionomics ECONOMICS **economics considered as ecosystem** a theory suggesting that economics can usefully be thought of as similar to an evolving ecosystem

BiRiLiG *abbr* ACCOUNTING Bilanzrichtliniengesetz

BIS *abbr* BANKING Bank for International Settlements

black in the black FINANCE **making a profit, or having more assets than debt**

black economic empowerment ECONOMICS **encouraging S. African black economic participation** the promotion of black ownership and control of South Africa's economic assets

black economy ECONOMICS **unofficial, untaxed economic activity** economic activity that is not declared for tax purposes and is usually carried out in exchange for cash

black knight MERGERS & ACQUISITIONS **former friendly firm involved in takeover** a former *white knight* that has disagreed with the board of the company to be acquired and has established its own hostile bid. *See also* **knight**

black market economy 1. ECONOMICS **illegal trading** a system of illegal trading in officially controlled goods **2.** CURRENCY & EXCHANGE **illicit parallel currency market** an illicit secondary currency market that has rates markedly different from those in the official market

black money ECONOMICS **untaxed money earned unofficially or illegally** money circulating in the *black economy* in payment for goods and services

Black-Scholes model STOCKHOLDING & INVESTMENTS **formula for determining option call price** a complex mathematical formula for calculating an option's *call price* using the current price of the security, the *strike price*, volatility, time until expiration, and the risk-free interest rate

Black Wednesday ECONOMICS **09.16.1992 when sterling crashed** Wednesday, September 16, 1992, when the pound sterling left the European Exchange Rate Mechanism and was devalued against other currencies

blank check *or* blank cheque BANKING **signed check with amount left blank** a check with the amount of money and the name of the payee left blank, but signed by the drawer

blended rate FINANCE **intermediate interest rate** an interest rate charged by a lender that is between an old rate and a new one

blind entry 1. ACCOUNTING **uninformative bookkeeping entry** a bookkeeping entry that records a debit or credit but fails to show other essential information **2.** *ANZ* FINANCE **statement of cost of goods and tax** a document issued by a supplier that stipulates the amount charged for goods or services as well as the amount of *Goods and Services Tax* payable

blind trust STOCKHOLDING & INVESTMENTS **trust without participation of beneficiary** a trust that manages somebody's business interests, with contents that are unknown to the beneficiary. People assuming public office use such trusts to avoid conflicts of interest.

block STOCKHOLDING & INVESTMENTS **10,000 or more shares of stock** a very large number of shares of stock, typically 10,000 or more

blocked account BANKING **frozen bank account** a bank account from which funds cannot be withdrawn for any of a number of reasons, for example, bankruptcy proceedings, liquidation of a company, or government order when freezing foreign assets

blocked currency CURRENCY & EXCHANGE **currency hard to exchange** a currency that people cannot easily trade for other currencies because of foreign *exchange controls*

blocked funds CURRENCY & EXCHANGE **money frozen in one place** money that cannot be transferred from one place to another, usually because of foreign *exchange controls* imposed by the government of the country in which the funds are held

block grant FINANCE **1. in US, federal money for local government** in the United States, money that the federal government gives to a local government to spend in ways that the recipient determines **2. in UK, government money for local authorities** in the United Kingdom, money that the government gives to local authorities to fund local services

blockholder STOCKHOLDING & INVESTMENTS **investor with large stake in firm** an individual or institutional investor who holds a large number of shares of stock or a large dollar amount of bonds in a given company

block investment *ANZ* STOCKHOLDING & INVESTMENTS **taking or having large stake in firm** the purchase or holding of a large number of shares of stock or a large dollar amount of bonds in a given company

block trade STOCKHOLDING & INVESTMENTS **sale of many stocks or bonds** the sale of a large round number of stocks or large amount of bonds

Blue Book FINANCE **UK national statistics of incomes and expenditure** national statistics of personal incomes and spending patterns in the United Kingdom, published annually

blue chip STOCKHOLDING & INVESTMENTS **profitable and low risk** used to describe an equity or company which is of the highest quality and in which an investment would be considered as low risk with regard to both dividend payments and capital values

blue-chip stocks STOCKHOLDING & INVESTMENTS **common stock in safe firm** common stock in a company that is considered to be well established, highly successful, and reliable, and is traded on a stock market

Blue Dogs FINANCE **fiscally conservative democrats in US Congress** members of a coalition of fiscally conservative Democrats in the House of Representatives of the US Congress

blue-sky laws FRAUD, REGULATION & COMPLIANCE **US state laws protecting investors from fraudulent deals** in the United States, state laws designed to protect investors against fraudulent traders in securities

blue-sky securities STOCKHOLDING & INVESTMENTS **worthless stocks and bonds** stocks and bonds that have no value, being worth the same as a piece of "blue sky" (slang)

BO *abbr* BANKING branch office

board CORPORATE GOVERNANCE = *board of directors*

board dismissal CORPORATE GOVERNANCE **removal of firm's whole board** the dismissal and removal from power of an entire board or *board of directors*

board meeting CORPORATE GOVERNANCE **directors' meeting** a meeting of the board of directors of a company

Board of Currency Commissioners CURRENCY & EXCHANGE **issuer of Singaporean currency** the sole currency issuing authority in Singapore, established in 1967. *Abbr* **BCCS**

board of directors CORPORATE GOVERNANCE **firm's highest management board** the people selected to sit on an authoritative standing committee or governing body, taking responsibility for the management of an organization. Members of the board of directors are officially chosen by stockholders, but in practice they are usually selected on the basis of the current board's recommendations. The board usually includes major stockholders as well as directors of the company. *Also called* **board**

board of trustees STOCKHOLDING & INVESTMENTS **group managing funds, assets, or property for others** a committee or governing body that takes responsibility for managing—and holds in trust—funds, assets, or property belonging to others, for example, charitable or pension funds or assets

boardroom CORPORATE GOVERNANCE **room for board meetings** a room in which board meetings are held. A boardroom may be a room used only for board meetings or can be a multiuse room that becomes a boardroom for the duration of a board meeting.

boardroom battle CORPORATE GOVERNANCE **struggle between board members** a conflict or power struggle between individual board members or between groups of board members

board seat CORPORATE GOVERNANCE **position on firm's board** a position of membership of a board, especially a *board of directors*

board secretary CORPORATE GOVERNANCE **organization's senior administrative officer** a senior employee in a public organization, with a role similar to that of a *company secretary*

body corporate CORPORATE GOVERNANCE **group acting as individual** an entity such as a company or institution that is legally authorized to act as if it were one person

body of shareholders STOCKHOLDING & INVESTMENTS **shareholders regarded as single unit** the shareholders of a company treated as a single shareholder in dealing with the company

boiler room fraud FRAUD **illegal selling of worthless stock** the illegal practice of calling people and pressing them to buy worthless stock in companies that do not exist or are virtually bankrupt

Bolivarism ECONOMICS **socialist vision of Venezuelan president** the new socialist and pan-South American vision of President Hugo Chávez of Venezuela, named for Simón Bolívar, the South American revolutionary leader who fought against Spanish colonial rule

Bolsa de Valores de Lisboa e Porto MARKETS, STOCKHOLDING & INVESTMENTS = *Euronext Lisbon*

bona fide FINANCE **undertaken in good faith** used to describe a sale or purchase that has been conducted in good faith, without collusion or fraud

bona vacantia FINANCE **goods of intestate person with no heirs** the goods of somebody who has died intestate and has no traceable living relatives. In the United Kingdom, these goods become the property of the state.

bond 1. FINANCE **money given as deposit** a sum of money paid as a deposit, especially on rented premises **2.** STOCKHOLDING & INVESTMENTS **contract promising loan repayment with interest** a certificate issued by a company or government that promises repayment of borrowed money at a set rate of interest on a particular date **3.** S. AFRICA MORTGAGES = *mortgage bond*

bond anticipation note STOCKHOLDING & INVESTMENTS **loan repaid through bonds issued later** a loan that a government agency receives to provide capital that will be repaid from the proceeds of bonds that the agency will issue later. *Abbr* **BAN**

bond covenant STOCKHOLDING & INVESTMENTS **promise by lender to limit activities** part of a bond contract whereby the lender promises not to do some things such as borrow beyond a specified limit

bond discount STOCKHOLDING & INVESTMENTS **gap between price and higher face value** the difference between the face value of a bond and the lower price at which it is issued

bond equivalent yield STOCKHOLDING & INVESTMENTS **compound interest conversion for bond comparison** the interest rate on a Treasury bill, commercial paper, or discount note, usually quoted as simple interest, converted to compound interest in order to compare it with the interest on a bond. *Also called equivalent bond yield. See also compound annual return*

bond fund STOCKHOLDING & INVESTMENTS **mutual fund with bonds** a mutual fund with an investment *portfolio* made up of bonds

bondholder STOCKHOLDING & INVESTMENTS **entity owning bonds** an individual or institution owning bonds issued by a government or company. Bondholders are entitled to payments of the interest as due and the return of the *principal* when the bond matures.

bond indenture STOCKHOLDING & INVESTMENTS **document describing bond** a document that specifies the terms and conditions of a bond

bond indexing STOCKHOLDING & INVESTMENTS **matching yield from bonds and specific index** the practice of investing in bonds in such a way as to match the yield of a designated index

bond issue STOCKHOLDING & INVESTMENTS **sale of bonds to investors** an occasion when a company or government offers *bonds* to investors in order to raise funding

bond premium STOCKHOLDING & INVESTMENTS **gap between price and lower face value** the difference between the face value of a bond and a higher price at which it is issued

bond quote STOCKHOLDING & INVESTMENTS **up-to-date statement of bond's price** a statement of the current price of a bond when traded on the open market

bond rating STOCKHOLDING & INVESTMENTS **assessment of bond-issuer's reliability** the rating of the reliability of a company, government, or local authority that has issued a bond. The highest rating is AAA (triple A).

bond swap STOCKHOLDING & INVESTMENTS **simultaneous sale and purchase of bonds** an exchange of some bonds for others, usually to gain a tax advantage or to diversify a portfolio

bond value ACCOUNTING **value stated in accounts** the value of an *asset* or *liability* as recorded in the accounts of a person or organization

a–z

Dictionary

bond-washing STOCKHOLDING & INVESTMENTS **avoidance of tax on dividend income** the practice of selling a bond before its dividend is due and buying it back later in order to avoid paying tax on the dividend

bond yield STOCKHOLDING & INVESTMENTS **yield of bond in relation to market price** the annual return on a bond (the rate of interest) expressed as a percentage of the current market price of the bond. Bonds can tie up investors' money for periods of up to 30 years, so knowing their yield is a critical investment consideration.

bonus FINANCE **extra money given as reward to employee** a financial incentive given to employees in addition to their base pay in the form of a one-time payment or as part of a bonus plan

bonus dividend STOCKHOLDING & INVESTMENTS **irregular additional dividend** a one-time extra dividend in addition to the usual payment

bonus issue STOCKHOLDING & INVESTMENTS **proportionate issue of new shares to stockholders** the capitalization of the reserves of a company by the issue of additional shares to existing stockholders, in proportion to their holdings. Such shares are usually fully paid up with no cash called for from the stockholders.

bonus plan US FINANCE **program for rewarding employees with extra money** a form of incentive plan under which a bonus is paid to employees in accordance with rules concerning eligibility, performance targets, time period, and size and form of payments. A bonus plan may apply to some or all employees and may be determined on organization, business unit, or individual performance, or on a combination of these. A bonus payment may be expressed as a percentage of salary or as a flat-rate sum. *UK term* ***bonus scheme***

bonus scheme UK FINANCE = ***bonus plan***

bonus shares STOCKHOLDING & INVESTMENTS **1. increased number of shares not affecting total value** shares issued to stockholders in a stock split, with at least one more share for every share owned, without affecting the total value of each holding. *See also* ***stock split*** **2. UK government reward to loyal founding stockholders** in the United Kingdom, extra shares paid by the government as a reward to founding stockholders who did not sell their initial holding within a specific number of years

book STOCKHOLDING & INVESTMENTS **record of trader's investments and amounts owed** a statement of all the holdings of a trader and the amount he or she is due to pay or has borrowed **cook the books** FRAUD to use accounting methods to hide aspects of a company's financial dealings such as losses or illegal activities **do the books** ACCOUNTING to keep records of expenditure and income

book-building STOCKHOLDING & INVESTMENTS **gathering information to determine offering price** the research done among potential institutional investors to determine the optimum offering price for a new issue of stock

book cost STOCKHOLDING & INVESTMENTS **total cost of stocks** the price paid for a stock, including any payments to intermediaries such as brokers

book entry ACCOUNTING **account entry unsupported by documentation** an accounting entry indicated in a record somewhere but not represented by any document

book-entry security STOCKHOLDING & INVESTMENTS **security without paper certificate** a security that is recorded as a ***book entry*** but is not represented by a paper certificate

book inventory ACCOUNTING **stock level recorded in accounts** the number of items in stock according to accounting records. This number can be validated only by a physical count of the items.

bookkeeper ACCOUNTING **maintainer of business's financial records** a person who is responsible for maintaining the financial records of a business

bookkeeping ACCOUNTING **recording income and expenditure** the activity or profession of recording the money received and spent by an individual, business, or organization

bookkeeping barter ACCOUNTING **exchange of goods treated as money transaction** the direct exchange of goods between two parties without the use of money as a medium, but using monetary measures to record the transaction

book of original entry *or* book of prime entry ACCOUNTING **chronological and classified record of transactions** a chronological record of a business's transactions arranged according to type, for example, cash or sales. The books are then used to generate entries in a double-entry bookkeeping system.

books ACCOUNTING **record of sales and receipts** the set of records that a business keeps, showing what has been spent and earned

books of account UK ACCOUNTING = ***accounting records***

book-to-bill ratio ACCOUNTING **relationship between orders received and bills issued** the ratio of the value of orders that a company has received to the amount for which it has billed its customers

book transfer STOCKHOLDING & INVESTMENTS **recorded change in security's ownership without transfer documents** a transfer of ownership of a security without physical transfer of any document that represents the instrument

book value 1. ACCOUNTING **recorded value of asset** the value of an asset as recorded in a company's balance sheet, usually the original cost with an allowance made for depreciation. Book value is not usually the same as ***market value*** (the amount it could be sold for). **2.** STOCKHOLDING & INVESTMENTS, ACCOUNTING **firm's own valuation of its stock** the value of a company's stock according to the company itself, which may differ considerably from the ***market value***. Book value is calculated by subtracting a company's liabilities and the value of its debt and preferred stock from its total assets. All of these figures appear on a company's balance sheet. For example:

$	
Total assets	1,300
Current liabilities	– 400
Long-term liabilities, preference shares	– 250
Book value	**= 650**

Book value represents a company's net worth to its stockholders. When compared with its market value, book value helps reveal how a company is regarded by the investment community. A market value that is notably higher than the book value indicates that investors have a high regard for the company. A market value that is, for example, a multiple of book value suggests that investors' regard may be unreasonably high. *Also called* **carrying amount, carrying value**

book value per share STOCKHOLDING & INVESTMENTS, ACCOUNTING firm's own valuation of each share the value of one share of a stock according to the company itself, which may differ considerably from the market value. It is calculated by dividing the *book value* by the number of shares in issue.

boom FINANCE significant increase in business a period of time during which business activity increases significantly, with the result that demand for products grows, as do prices, salaries, and employment

boom and bust *or* boom or bust FINANCE extreme economic or market upswings and downswings a regular pattern of alternation in an economy or market between extreme growth and collapse and recession

borrow 1. FINANCE arrange to use another's assets for a time to be given money by a person or financial institution for a fixed period of time, usually paying it back in installments and with interest **2.** STOCKHOLDING & INVESTMENTS buy at delivery price and sell forward simultaneously to buy a commodity or security at the present spot price and sell forward at the same time

borrower FINANCE somebody borrowing money from lender a person who receives money from a lender with the intention of paying it back, usually with interest

borrowing FINANCE receipt of money from lender the act of borrowing money from a lender

borrowing capacity *or* borrowing power FINANCE amount firm can borrow in loans the amount of money available as a loan to a company at a particular time, based on the company's financial situation

borrowing costs FINANCE expense of taking out loan expenses such as interest payments incurred from taking out a loan or any other form of borrowing. In the United States, such costs are included in the total cost of the asset whereas in the United Kingdom, and in International Accounting Standards, this is optional.

borrowings FINANCE money borrowed money borrowed, usually in the form of long-term loans

bottleneck 1. FINANCE process that holds up others an activity within an organization which has a lower capacity than preceding or subsequent activities, thereby limiting throughput. Bottlenecks are often the cause of a buildup of work in progress and of idle time. **2.** OPERATIONS & PRODUCTION somebody or something that slows down process a limiting factor on the rate of an operation. A workstation operating at its maximum capacity becomes a bottleneck if the rate of production elsewhere in the plant increases but throughput at that workstation cannot be increased to meet demand. An understanding of bottlenecks is important if the efficiency and capacity of an assembly line are to be increased. The techniques of fishbone charts, flow charts, and Pareto charts can be used to identify where and why bottlenecks occur.

bottom line ACCOUNTING firm's net profit or loss the net profit or loss that a company makes at the end of a specific period of time, used in the calculation of the earnings-per-share business ratio

bottom-up approach 1. STOCKHOLDING & INVESTMENTS describing investment on individual potential independent of trends used to describe an approach to investing that seeks to identify individual companies that are fundamentally sound and whose stock will perform well regardless of general economic or industry-group trends **2.** GENERAL MANAGEMENT involving employee participation at all levels used to describe a consultative leadership style that promotes employee participation at all levels in decisionmaking and problemsolving. A bottom-up approach to leadership is associated with *flat* organizations and the empowerment of employees. It can encourage creativity and flexibility. *See also* **top-down approach**

bottom-up budgeting TREASURY MANAGEMENT = *participative budgeting*

bought day book ACCOUNTING record of items bought on credit a book used to record purchases for which cash is not paid immediately

bought deal STOCKHOLDING & INVESTMENTS purchase of new issue for resale to investors a method of selling stock in a new company or selling an issue of new shares in an existing company, in which an underwriter purchases all the shares at a fixed price for resale to investors

bought-in goods FINANCE goods from outside supplier components and subassemblies that are purchased from an outside supplier instead of being made within the organization

bought ledger ACCOUNTING firm's book recording expenditure a book in which all of a company's expenditure is logged

bounce BANKING **1.** fail to honor check to refuse payment of a check because the account for which it is written holds insufficient money (slang) *Also called* **dishonor 2.** be refused by bank (of a check) to be returned by a bank because there are insufficient funds in the account to meet the demand (informal)

bounced check BANKING check that bank fails to honor a draft on an account that a bank will not honor, usually because there are insufficient funds in the account

boutique 1. STOCKHOLDING & INVESTMENTS **small specialist firm** a small firm that offers a limited number of investments or services. *See also **boutique investment house* 2.** BANKING **small investment bank** a small investment banking firm

boutique investment house STOCKHOLDING & INVESTMENTS **specialist broker** a brokerage that deals in securities of only one industry. *Also called **niche player** (sense 2)*

Bowie bond STOCKHOLDING & INVESTMENTS, RISK **bond backed by intellectual property** an ***asset-backed security*** for which the right to royalties from intellectual property is the collateral

B/P *abbr* FINANCE bills payable

B/R *abbr* FINANCE bills receivable

Brady bond STOCKHOLDING & INVESTMENTS **emerging country's bond backed by Treasury bonds** a bond issued by an emerging nation that has US Treasury bonds as collateral. It is named for Nicholas Brady, banking reformer and former Secretary of the Treasury.

branch accounts ACCOUNTING **financial records for firm's subsidiary operations** the ***accounting records*** or ***financial statements*** for the component parts of a business, especially those that are located in a different region or country from the main enterprise

branch office BANKING **organization in different location from headquarters** a bank or other financial institution that is part of a larger group and is located in a different geographic area from the parent organization. *Abbr* **BO**

break even ACCOUNTING **make neither profit nor loss** to balance income and expense, so as to show neither a net gain nor a loss

breakpoint 1. FINANCE **investment size that triggers reduced charges** the size of investment at which the ***front-end loading*** on larger investments in a mutual fund starts to be reduced **2.** BANKING **account balance that causes interest rate change** a balance reached in an account that triggers the payment of either a higher or lower interest rate

break-up value MERGERS & ACQUISITIONS **value of company's assets sold individually** the combined market value of a firm's assets if each were sold separately, as contrasted with selling the firm as an ongoing business. Analysts look for companies with a large break-up value relative to their market value to identify potential takeover targets.

Bretton Woods ECONOMICS **agreement establishing IMF and IBRD** an agreement signed at a conference at Bretton Woods, in the United States, in July 1944, that established the ***IMF*** and the ***IBRD***

bribery FRAUD **offer of gift or cash to gain advantage** the act of persuading somebody to exercise his or her business judgment in your favor by offering cash or a gift and thereby gaining an unfair advantage. Many organizations have codes of conduct that expressly forbid the soliciting or payment of bribes.

bridge financing FINANCE **borrowing in expectation of later loans** short-term borrowing that the borrower expects to repay with the proceeds of later, larger loans. *See also **takeout financing***

bridge loan *US* FINANCE **temporary loan while waiting for money** a short-term loan providing funds until further money is received, for example, for buying one property while trying to sell another. *UK term **bridging loan***

bridging FINANCE **borrowing short-term until finance is arranged** the obtaining of a short-term loan to provide a continuing source of financing in anticipation of receiving an intermediate or long-term loan. Bridging is routinely employed to finance the purchase or construction of a new building or property until an old one is sold.

bridging loan *UK* FINANCE = ***bridge loan***

bring forward ACCOUNTING **carry sum to next column or page** to carry a sum from one column or page to the next, or from one account to the next

British Accounting Association ACCOUNTING **UK association for accountancy education and research** an organization for the promotion of accounting education and research in the United Kingdom. The BAA has more than 800 members, a large proportion of which work in higher education institutions. Founded in 1947, the BAA also organizes conferences and publishes the *British Accounting Review*. *Abbr* **BAA**

British Bankers' Association BANKING **nonprofit financial organization** a not-for-profit trading association for the financial services and banking industries. The Association was established in 1919 and has 260 members, including 57 associate members. It addresses a variety of industry issues, including the development and revision of the voluntary *Banking Code*, which aims to set standards of best practice. *Abbr* **BBA**

British Private Equity and Venture Capital Association FINANCE **UK organization for equity and venture firms** the official organization representing UK-based private equity and venture capital firms and their advisers. *Abbr* **BVCA**

broker 1. FINANCE, GENERAL MANAGEMENT **intermediary in transaction** an agent who arranges a deal, sale, or contract **2.** STOCKHOLDING & INVESTMENTS = ***stockbroker* 3.** FINANCE, GENERAL MANAGEMENT **act as intermediary in transaction** to act as an agent in arranging a deal, sale, or contract

brokerage 1. FINANCE **fee for arranging deal** a fee paid to somebody who acts as an agent for somebody else. For example, brokers who arrange deals for the purchase and sale of real estate, those who execute orders for securities, and those who sell insurance receive commissions. *Also called **broker's commission* 2.** STOCKHOLDING & INVESTMENTS **broker's business** the business of being a broker, trading on a stock exchange on behalf of clients **3.** *US* STOCKHOLDING & INVESTMENTS **firm trading in securities for others** a company whose business is buying and selling stocks and other securities for its clients. *Also called **brokerage firm**, **brokerage house**. UK term **broking house***

broker-dealer STOCKHOLDING & INVESTMENTS **broker who also holds stocks for resale** a dealer who buys stocks and other securities and holds them for resale, and also deals on behalf of investor clients

broker loan rate BANKING **interest charged for buying derivatives** the interest rate that banks charge brokers on money that they lend for purchases *on margin*

broker recommendation STOCKHOLDING & INVESTMENTS **advice to trade or hold security** a recommendation to buy, hold, or sell a stock, made by an analyst who is employed by a brokerage firm to research specific companies' strengths and weaknesses

broker's commission STOCKHOLDING & INVESTMENTS = *brokerage (sense 1)*

broking UK STOCKHOLDING & INVESTMENTS = *brokering*

broking house UK STOCKHOLDING & INVESTMENTS **firm trading in stocks and bonds for others** a company whose business is buying and selling stocks and bonds for its clients. *US term* **brokerage**

brought forward ACCOUNTING **carried to next column or page** indicating a sum carried from one column or page to the next, or from one account to the next. *Abbr* **b/f**. *See also* **bring forward**

Brussels Stock Exchange MARKETS, STOCKHOLDING & INVESTMENTS = *Euronext Brussels*

B/S *abbr* ACCOUNTING balance sheet

B share STOCKHOLDING & INVESTMENTS **1. US share with limits on voting** in the United States, a share that has limited voting power. *See also* **A share 2. Australian mutual fund share with fee payable on redemption** in Australia, a share in a mutual fund that has no front-end sales charge but carries a redemption fee, or *back-end loading*, payable only if the share is redeemed. This load, called a *contingent deferred sales charge*, declines every year until it disappears, usually after six years.

bubble economy ECONOMICS **booming economic activity before crash** an unstable boom based on speculation in any market, often followed by a financial crash

buck US CURRENCY & EXCHANGE (slang) **1. US dollar** a United States dollar **2. one million** one million of any currency unit, used by traders

budget TREASURY MANAGEMENT **statement of predicted income and expenditure** a quantitative statement, for a defined period of time, that may include planned revenues, expenses, assets, liabilities, and cashflows. A budget provides a focus for an organization, as it aids the coordination of activities, allocation of resources, and direction of activity, and facilitates control. Planning is achieved by means of a fixed master budget, whereas control is generally exercised through the comparison of actual costs with a flexible budget.

Budget FINANCE **UK government's annual statement of financial plans** in the United Kingdom, the government's annual spending plan, which is announced to the House of Commons by the Chancellor of the Exchequer. The government is legally obliged to present economic forecasts twice a year, and since the 1997 general election the main Budget has been presented in the spring while a *pre-Budget report* is given in the autumn. This outlines government spending plans prior to the main Budget, and also reports on progress since the last Budget.

budget account UK BANKING **bank account for regular expenses** a bank account established to control a person's regular expenditure, such as the payment of insurance premiums, mortgage, utilities, or telephone bills. The annual expenditure for each item is paid into the account in equal monthly installments, bills being paid from the budget account as they become due.

budgetary TREASURY MANAGEMENT **of future financial plans** relating to a detailed plan of financial operations, with estimates of both revenue and expenditure for a specific future period

budgetary control TREASURY MANAGEMENT **regulation of spending** regulation of spending according to a planned budget

budget committee TREASURY MANAGEMENT **committee that prepares budgets** the group within an organization responsible for drawing up budgets that meet departmental requirements, ensuring they comply with policy, and then submitting them to the board of directors

budget deficit ACCOUNTING **amount expenditure exceeds income** the extent by which expenditure exceeds revenue, especially that of a government. *Also called* **deficit**

budget director TREASURY MANAGEMENT **person responsible for budget preparation** the person in an organization who is responsible for running the budget system

budgeted capacity TREASURY MANAGEMENT **output level in budget** an organization's available output level for a budget period according to the budget. It may be expressed in different ways, for example, in machine hours (the number of hours for which a machine is in production) or standard hours.

budgeted revenue TREASURY MANAGEMENT **expected income in budget** the income that an organization expects to receive in a budget period according to the budget

budgeting TREASURY MANAGEMENT **preparation of budget** the preparation of a budget in planning the management of income and expenditure

budget management TREASURY MANAGEMENT **adjusting activities to meet budgets** the comparison of actual financial results with the estimated expenditures and revenues for the given time period of a budget and the taking of corrective action as necessary

budget surplus ACCOUNTING **amount income exceeds expenditure** the extent by which revenue exceeds expenditure, especially that of a government. *Also called* **surplus**

budget variance ACCOUNTING **difference between budget estimate and reality** the difference between the financial value of something estimated in the budget, such as costs or revenues, and its actual financial value

building and loan association BANKING = *savings and loan association*

building society BANKING UKfinancial institution supporting real estate purchases in the United Kingdom,a financial institution that offers interest-bearing savings accounts, the deposits being reinvested by the society in long-term loans, primarily mortgage loans for the purchase of real estate

bulk handling FINANCE **financing of moneys due in bulk** the financing of a group of receivables together to reduce processing costs

bull STOCKHOLDING & INVESTMENTS **exploiter of favorable business conditions** somebody who anticipates favorable business conditions, especially somebody who buys specific stocks or commodities in anticipation that their prices will rise, often with the expectation of selling them at a large profit at a later time. *See also bear*

bull CD STOCKHOLDING & INVESTMENTS **CD paying more in rising market** a *certificate of deposit* that pays a higher interest rate when an underlying market index rises in value. *See also bear CD*

bulldog bond STOCKHOLDING & INVESTMENTS **foreign sterling bond in UK market** a bond issued in sterling in the UK market by a non-British corporation

bullet FINANCE **final large loan repayment** a single large repayment of the outstanding *principal* of a loan at maturity

bullet bond STOCKHOLDING & INVESTMENTS **bond repaid with single payment** a bond that can be redeemed only when it reaches its maturity date

Bulletin des Annonces Légales Obligatoires FINANCE *see BALO*

bullet loan FINANCE **loan with only interest payments until maturity** a loan that involves specific payments of interest until maturity, when the *principal* is repaid

bullion FINANCE **precious metal in bars** gold, silver, or platinum produced and traded in the form of bars

Bund STOCKHOLDING & INVESTMENTS, RISK **German government bond** a bond issued by the German government with a maturity of 8.5 to 10 years

bundle FINANCE **combination of products or services** a package of financial products or services offered to a customer

burn rate FINANCE **rate at which firm's capital is used** the rate at which a new business spends its initial capital before it becomes profitable or needs additional funding, used by investors as a measure of a company's ability to survive, or the rate at which a mature business spends its accumulated cash and liquid securities. *Also called cash burn*

business angel FINANCE **investor in new company** an individual who is prepared to invest money in a startup company. The amount offered by angels is typically much less than that offered by *venture capitalists*, but angels are often willing to take greater risks.

business combinations MERGERS & ACQUISITIONS **acquisitions or mergers** in the United States, acquisitions or mergers involving two or more business enterprises

business cycle ECONOMICS **regular repeating pattern of economic activity** a regular pattern of fluctuation in national income, moving from upturn to downturn in about five years

business expenses ACCOUNTING **money spent on firm's running costs** money spent on running a business, not on stock or assets

business risk RISK **possible risk to firm's standing** the uncertainty associated with the unique circumstances of a particular company which might affect the price of that company's securities, for example, the introduction of a superior technology by a competitor

business segment ACCOUNTING **distinct part of business or enterprise** a distinguishable part of a business or enterprise which is subject to a different set of risks and returns from any other part. Listed companies are required to declare in their annual reports information such as sales, profits, and assets, for each segment of an enterprise.

business unit ACCOUNTING **distinct part of business organization** a part of an organization that operates as a distinct function, department, division, or stand-alone business. Business units are usually treated as a separate *profit center* within the overall business.

bust go bust FINANCE to become bankrupt (informal)

bust up MERGERS & ACQUISITIONS **divide or subdivide firm** to split up a company or a division of a company into smaller units

bust-up proxy proposal MERGERS & ACQUISITIONS **approach to stockholders for leveraged buyout** an overture to a company's stockholders for a *leveraged buyout* in which the acquirer will sell some of the company's assets in order to repay the debt used to finance the takeover

butterfly spread STOCKHOLDING & INVESTMENTS **simultaneously buying and selling variety of options** a complex option strategy based on simultaneously purchasing and selling calls at different exercise prices and maturity dates, the profit being the premium collected when the options are sold. Such a strategy is most profitable when the price of the underlying security is relatively stable.

buy FINANCE **1. pay to get something** to get something in exchange for money **2. something you pay for** something that you pay for relative to its being worth or not worth the amount you pay

buy and hold STOCKHOLDING & INVESTMENTS **investment for long term** an investment strategy based on retaining securities for a long time

buy and write STOCKHOLDING & INVESTMENTS **buying stock and selling options as safeguard** an investment strategy involving buying stock and selling options to eliminate the possibility of loss if the value of the stock goes down

buyback 1. MARKETS **purchase by firm of its own stock** an arrangement whereby a company buys its own stock on the stock market. *Also called* **stock buyback 2.** STOCKHOLDING & INVESTMENTS **agreed repurchase of bonds or stock** the repurchase of bonds or stock, as agreed by contract. The seller is usually a *venture capitalist* who helped finance the forming of the company.

buydown 1. FINANCE **initial payment to secure favorable interest rate** an initial lump-sum payment made on a loan in order to get a more favorable ongoing rate, especially a loan secured by a mortgage **2.** MORTGAGES **partial repayment of principal on mortgage** the payment of principal amounts which reduces the monthly payments due on a mortgage

buy in STOCKHOLDING & INVESTMENTS **acquire controlling interest in firm** to buy stock in a company so as to have a controlling interest. This is often done by or for executives from outside the company.

buying economies of scale FINANCE **lower cost involved in large transactions** a reduction in the cost of purchasing raw materials and components or of borrowing money due to the increased size of the purchase

buying power FINANCE **assessment of ability to purchase products and services** the assessment of a person's or organization's disposable income, regarded as determining the quantity and quality of products and services that person or organization can afford to buy

buy on margin STOCKHOLDING & INVESTMENTS, RISK **borrow to pay for part of security purchase** to purchase securities by paying cash for part of the purchase and borrowing, using the security as collateral, for the remainder

buy out MERGERS & ACQUISITIONS **1. buy and take over business** to purchase the entire stock of, or controlling financial interest in, a company **2. buy all somebody's share** to pay somebody to relinquish his or her interest in a property or other enterprise

buyout 1. MERGERS & ACQUISITIONS **buying and taking over of business** the purchase and *takeover* of an ongoing business. It is more formally known as an *acquisition*. If a business is purchased by managers or staff, it is known as a *management buyout*. **2.** MERGERS & ACQUISITIONS **buying all of somebody's stock ownership** the purchase of somebody else's entire stock ownership in a firm. It is more formally known as an *acquisition*. **3.** PENSIONS **leaver's ability to move pension assets** an option to transfer benefits of a pension plan on leaving a company

buy-to-let *UK* FINANCE = *buy-to-rent*

buy-to-rent *US* FINANCE **purchase of property for rental purposes** an investment in property with the intention of renting it to produce income, often to pay the original mortgage used to purchase it. *UK term* **buy-to-let**

BVCA *abbr* FINANCE British Private Equity and Venture Capital Association

BVLP MARKETS, STOCKHOLDING & INVESTMENTS = *Euronext Lisbon*

by-bidder FINANCE **somebody bidding at auction to benefit seller** somebody who bids at an auction solely to raise the price for the seller

bylaws *US* CORPORATE GOVERNANCE **rules for corporation's internal procedures** rules governing the internal running of a corporation, such as the number of meetings, the appointment of officers, and so on. *UK term* **articles of association**

C

CA *abbr* ACCOUNTING **1.** chartered accountant **2.** certified accountant

C/A *abbr* FINANCE capital account

c/a *abbr* BANKING checking account

cable CURRENCY & EXCHANGE **exchange rate between US dollar and pound** a spot exchange rate between the US dollar and the pound sterling

CAC 40 MARKETS, STOCKHOLDING & INVESTMENTS **main French stock market index** an index of 40 stocks selected from those traded on the Euronext Paris exchange based on capitalization and turnover. It was established on December 31, 1987, with a base value of 1,000.

calendar spread STOCKHOLDING & INVESTMENTS, RISK = *horizontal spread*

calendar variance ACCOUNTING **accounting difference from calendar months versus working days** a variance that occurs if a company uses calendar months for the financial accounts but uses the number of actual working days to calculate overhead expenses in the cost accounts

call STOCKHOLDING & INVESTMENTS **1. option to buy stock** an *option* to buy stock at an agreed price or before a particular date. *Also called* **call option 2. demand for agreed partial payment of share capital** a request made to the holders of partly paid-up share capital for the payment of a predetermined sum due on the share capital, under the terms of the original subscription agreement. Failure on the part of the stockholder to pay a call may result in the forfeiture of the relevant holding of partly paid shares. *Also called* **call up**

callable STOCKHOLDING & INVESTMENTS **able to be repurchased before maturity** used to describe a security that the issuer has the right to buy back before its maturity date. *See also* **noncallable**

callable bond STOCKHOLDING & INVESTMENTS **bond able to be bought back** a bond that may be bought back by the issuer prior to its maturity date

callable capital FINANCE **capital from unpaid sale of stock** the part of a company's capital from the sale of stock for which the company has not yet received payment

a–z

Dictionary

callable preferred stock *US* STOCKHOLDING & INVESTMENTS = *redeemable preferred stock*

call date STOCKHOLDING & INVESTMENTS **pre-maturity deadline for repurchase of bond** the date before maturity on which the issuer of a **callable bond** has the right to buy it back

called-up share capital STOCKHOLDING & INVESTMENTS **stock not paid for by stockholders** the proportion of stock issued by a company that has not yet been paid for. *See also fully paid share capital*

call in BANKING **request payment of debt** to ask for a debt to be paid at once

call loan BANKING **bank loan repayable on demand** a bank loan that must be repaid as soon as repayment is requested

call option STOCKHOLDING & INVESTMENTS = **call** *(sense 1)*

call payment STOCKHOLDING & INVESTMENTS **sum in partial payment for stock** an amount that a company demands in partial payment for stock such as a rights issue that is not paid for at one time

call price STOCKHOLDING & INVESTMENTS **early redemption cost of US bond** a price to be paid by an issuer for the early redemption of a US bond

call provision STOCKHOLDING & INVESTMENTS **clause allowing bond to be redeemed early** a clause in an **indenture** that lets the issuer of a bond redeem it before the date of its maturity

call purchase FINANCE **purchase where either party can establish price** a transaction where either the seller or purchaser can fix the price for future delivery

call risk STOCKHOLDING & INVESTMENTS, RISK **risk of premature repurchase of bond** the possibility that the issuer of a **callable bond** will buy back the bond and the bondholder will be forced to reinvest at a lower interest rate

calls in arrears STOCKHOLDING & INVESTMENTS **outstanding money for shares** money called up for shares, but not paid at the correct time. The shares may be forfeited or a special calls in arrears account is established to debit the sums owing.

call up STOCKHOLDING & INVESTMENTS = **call** *(sense 2)*

Canadian Institute of Chartered Accountants ACCOUNTING **main professional body for accountants** in Canada, the principal professional accountancy body that is responsible for setting accounting standards. *Abbr* **CICA**

cancellation price STOCKHOLDING & INVESTMENTS **price at which mutual fund will redeem securities** the lowest value possible in any one day of a mutual fund. In the United Kingdom, it is regulated by the *Financial Services Authority*.

cap FINANCE **upper limit** an upper limit such as on a rate of interest for a loan

CAPA *abbr* ACCOUNTING Confederation of Asian and Pacific Accountants

capacity usage variance FINANCE **difference in result caused by working hours** the difference in gain or loss in a given

period compared to budgeted expectations, caused because the hours worked were longer or shorter than planned

capacity utilization 1. OPERATIONS & PRODUCTION **measure of equipment actually used for production** a measure of the plant and equipment of a company or an industry that is actually being used to produce goods or services. Capacity utilization is usually measured over a specific period of time, for example, the average for a month, or at a given point in time. It can be expressed as a ratio, where utilization = actual output divided by design capacity. This measure is used in both **capacity planning** and **capacity requirements planning** processes. **2.** ECONOMICS **degree of production capability being used** the output of an economy, firm, or plant divided by its output when working at full capacity

Caparo case ACCOUNTING **English ruling on auditors' responsibilities** in England, a court decision made by the House of Lords in 1990 that auditors owe a duty of care to present, not prospective, stockholders as a body but not as individuals

CAPEX *abbr* ACCOUNTING capital expenditure

capital FINANCE **investment money** money that is available to be invested by a person, business, or organization in order to make a profit

capital account FINANCE **firm's total capital** the sum of a company's **capital** at a specific time. *Abbr* **C/A**

capital adequacy ratio FINANCE **percentage of bank's assets represented by capital** an amount of money which a bank has to hold in the form of stockholders' equity, shown as a proportion of its risk-weighted assets, agreed internationally not to fall below 8%. *Abbr* **CAR**. *Also called* **capital to risk-weighted assets ratio**

capital appreciation FINANCE **increase in wealth** the increase in a company's or individual's wealth at market values

capital appreciation fund STOCKHOLDING & INVESTMENTS **mutual fund concentrating on capital not income** a mutual fund that aims to increase the value of its holdings without regard to the provision of income to its owners

capital asset ACCOUNTING **real estate owned but not traded** real estate that a company owns and uses but that the company does not buy or sell as part of its regular trade

capital asset pricing model STOCKHOLDING & INVESTMENTS **theory about relationship between cost and expected return** a model of the market used to assess the cost of capital for a company based on the rate of return on its assets.

The capital asset pricing model holds that the expected return on a security or portfolio equals the rate on a risk-free security plus a risk premium. If this expected return does not meet or beat a theoretical required return, the investment should not be undertaken. The formula used for the model is:

Risk-free rate + (Market return − Risk-free rate) × Beta value = Expected return

The risk-free rate is the quoted rate on an asset that has virtually no risk. In practice, it is the rate quoted for 90-day US

Treasury bills.The market return is the percentage return expected of the overall market, typically a published index such as Standard & Poor's. The beta value is a figure that measures the volatility of a security or portfolio of securities compared with the market as a whole. A beta of 1, for example, indicates that a security's price will move with the market. A beta greater than 1 indicates higher volatility, while a beta less than 1 indicates less volatility.

Say, for instance, that the current risk-free rate is 4%, and the S&P 500 index is expected to return 11% next year. An investment club is interested in determining next year's return for XYZ Software, a prospective investment. The club has determined that the company's beta value is 1.8. The overall stock market always has a beta of 1, so XYZ Software's beta of 1.8 signals that it is a more risky investment than the overall market represents. This added risk means that the club should expect a higher rate of return than the 11% for the S&P 500. The CAPM calculation, then, would be:

$$4\% + (11\% - 4\%) \times 1.8 = 16.6\% \text{ expected return}$$

What the results tell the club is that, given the risk, XYZ Software has a required rate of return of 16.6%, or the minimum return that an investment in XYZ should generate. If the investment club does not think that XYZ will produce that kind of return, it should probably consider investing in a different company. *Abbr* **CAPM**

capital base FINANCE funding structure as basis of firm's worth the funding structure of a company (stockholders' equity plus loans and retained profits) used as a way of assessing the company's worth

capital budget ACCOUNTING part of firm's budget concerned with capital expenditure a subsection of a company's master budget that deals with expected capital expenditure within a defined period. *Also called* **capital expenditure budget**, **capital investment budget**

capital budgeting TREASURY MANAGEMENT preparing budget for capital expenditure the process concerned with decision making with respect to the following issues: the choice of specific investment projects, the total amount of *capital expenditure* to commit, and the method of financing the investment portfolio

capital buffer FINANCE sufficient capital to counter risk the amount of capital a financial institution needs to hold above minimum requirements, calculated on an assessment of forecast risk

capital commitments ACCOUNTING authorized but unspent capital expenditure expenditure on assets which has been authorized by directors, but not yet spent at the end of a financial period

capital consumption FINANCE depreciation of fixed assets in a given period, the total depreciation of the fixed assets of a company or national economy, based on replacement costs

capital costs ACCOUNTING expenses on buying fixed assets expenses associated with the purchase of fixed assets such as land, buildings, and machinery

capital deepening ECONOMICS increase in country's capital-to-labor ratio the process whereby capital increases but the number of employed people falls or remains constant

capital employed FINANCE stockholders' funds plus long-term loans an amount of *capital* consisting of stockholders' equity plus the long-term loans taken out by a business. *See also* **return on assets**

capital equipment ACCOUNTING equipment used for everyday operations the equipment that a factory or office uses in operating its business

capital expenditure ACCOUNTING spending on fixed assets the cost of acquiring, producing, or enhancing fixed assets such as land, buildings, and machinery. *Abbr* **CAPEX**. *Also called* **capital investment**

capital expenditure budget ACCOUNTING = *capital budget*

capital expenditure proposal ACCOUNTING application for capital expenditure a formal request for authority to undertake *capital expenditure*. This is usually supported by the case for expenditure in accordance with capital investment appraisal criteria. Levels of authority must be clearly defined and the reporting structure of actual expenditure must be to the equivalent authority level.

capital flight STOCKHOLDING & INVESTMENTS withdrawal of investments from country the transfer of large sums of money between countries to seek higher rates of return or to escape a political or economic disturbance

capital flow STOCKHOLDING & INVESTMENTS international movement of money the movement of investments from one country to another. *Also called* **capital movement**

capital formation STOCKHOLDING & INVESTMENTS adding to capital by investment the creation of long-term assets, such as long-dated bonds or shares

capital funding planning TREASURY MANAGEMENT determining of means to finance capital expenditure the process of selecting suitable funds to finance long-term assets and *working capital*

capital gain ACCOUNTING money made from disposing of asset the financial gain made upon the disposal of an asset. The gain is the difference between the cost of its acquisition and the net proceeds upon its sale.

capital gains distribution STOCKHOLDING & INVESTMENTS allocation of capital gains to investors a sum of money that a body such as a mutual fund pays to its owners in proportion to the owners' share of the organization's capital gains for the year

capital gains expenses ACCOUNTING cost of buying or selling assets expenses incurred in buying or selling assets, which can be deducted when calculating a capital gain or loss

capital gearing STOCKHOLDING & INVESTMENTS firm's debt per share the amount of debt of all kinds that a company has for each share of its common stock

capital goods ECONOMICS assets used for producing other goods physical assets that are used in the production of other goods

capital growth FINANCE increase in value of assets an increase in the value of assets in a fund, or of the value of stock

capital inflow FINANCE money entering country from services overseas the amount of capital that flows into an economy from services rendered abroad

capital instrument FINANCE means of raising money a security such as stocks or *debentures* that a business uses to raise finance

capital-intensive FINANCE requiring money rather than labor used to describe economic activities that primarily require a high proportion of *capital* as opposed to needing labor. *See also labor-intensive*

capital investment ACCOUNTING = *capital expenditure*

capital investment budget ACCOUNTING = *capital budget*

capitalism ECONOMICS economic system where citizens own means of production an economic and social system in which individuals can maximize profits because they own the means of production

capitalist FINANCE investor in business a person who invests *capital* in trade and industry, for profit

capitalist economy ECONOMICS economy giving great commercial and financial freedom an economy in which each person has the right to invest money, to work in business, and to buy and sell products and services, without major government restrictions

capitalization 1. FINANCE raising funds through stock split the conversion of a company's reserves into *capital* through a stock split **2.** STOCKHOLDING & INVESTMENTS amount invested in firm the amount of money that is invested in a company **3.** STOCKHOLDING & INVESTMENTS firm's worth the worth of the bonds and stocks issued by a company

capitalization issue *UK* STOCKHOLDING & INVESTMENTS = *stock split*

capitalization rate FINANCE rate of raising capital through stock split the rate at which a company's *reserves* are converted into *capital* by way of a *stock split*

capitalization ratio FINANCE proportion of firm's value in capital the proportion of a company's value represented by debt, stock, assets, and other items.

By comparing debt to total capitalization, these ratios provide a glimpse of a company's long-term stability and ability to withstand losses and business downturns.

A company's capitalization ratio can be expressed in two ways:

$$= \frac{\text{Long-term debt}}{(\text{Long-term debt} + \text{Owners' equity})}$$

and

$$= \frac{\text{Total debt}}{(\text{Total debt} + \text{Preferred} + \text{Common equity})}$$

For example, a company whose long-term debt totals $5,000 and whose owners hold equity worth $3,000 would have a capitalization ratio of:

$$\frac{5,000}{(5,000 + 3,000)} = \frac{5,000}{8,000} = 0.625$$

Both expressions of the ratio are also referred to as *component percentages*, since they compare a firm's debt with either its total capital (debt plus equity) or its equity capital. They readily indicate how reliant a firm is on debt financing. Capitalization ratios need to be evaluated over time, and compared with other data and standards. Care should be taken when comparing companies in different industries or sectors. The same figures that appear to be low in one industry can be very high in another.

capitalize 1. FINANCE invest money in business to provide investment money for a business, in expectation of making a profit **2.** ACCOUNTING enter cost of asset in balance sheet to include money spent on the purchase of an *asset* as an element in a *balance sheet*

capital loss ACCOUNTING loss on sale of fixed asset a loss made through selling a *capital asset* for less than its market price

capital maintenance concept ACCOUNTING principle underpinning inflation accounting a concept used to determine the definition of profit, which provides the basis for different systems of *inflation accounting*

capital movement STOCKHOLDING & INVESTMENTS = *capital flow*

capital outlay ACCOUNTING = *capital expenditure*

capital profit ACCOUNTING profit from sale of asset a profit that a company makes by selling a *capital asset*

capital property ACCOUNTING, TAX type of asset under Canadian tax law under Canadian tax law, assets that can depreciate in value or be sold for a capital gain or loss

capital ratio ACCOUNTING firm's income as fraction of fixed assets a company's income expressed as a fraction of its *tangible assets*. These assets include leases and company stock, as well as physical assets such as land, buildings, and machinery.

capital rationing FINANCE **1.** firm's limiting of new investment the restriction of new investment by a company because of a shortfall in its capital budget **2.** imposition of limit on capital expenditure a restriction on an organization's ability to invest capital funds, caused by an internal budget ceiling being imposed by management (*soft capital rationing*), or by external limitations being applied to the company, as when additional borrowed funds cannot be obtained (*hard capital rationing*)

capital reconstruction MERGERS & ACQUISITIONS closing down then reconstituting firm the act of placing a company into voluntary liquidation and then selling its assets to another company with the same name and same stockholders, but with a larger capital base

capital redemption reserve ACCOUNTING **in UK, firm's account underpinning trade in own stock** in the United Kingdom, an account required by law to prevent a reduction in capital, where a company purchases or redeems its own stock out of *distributable profits*

capital reduction FINANCE **withdrawal of capital funds** the *retirement* or redemption of capital funds by a company

capital reorganization STOCKHOLDING & INVESTMENTS **restructuring firm's share holdings** the act of changing the capital structure of a company by amalgamating or dividing existing shares to form shares of a higher or lower nominal value

capital reserves FINANCE **1. UK funds unavailable for dividend payments** reserves not legally available for distribution to stockholders as dividends according to the Companies Act (1985) **2.** *US* **funds for future investment** money that a company holds in reserve for future investment or expense

capital resource planning TREASURY MANAGEMENT **assessing assets for strategic purposes** the process of evaluating and selecting long-term assets to meet established strategies

capital shares STOCKHOLDING & INVESTMENTS **shares with increasing value but no income** shares in a mutual fund that rise in value as the capital value of the individual stocks rises, but do not receive any income

capital stock STOCKHOLDING & INVESTMENTS **stock authorized by US firm's charter** in the United States, the stock authorized by a company's charter, including *common stock* and *preferred stock*. *See also* **share capital**

capital structure ACCOUNTING **relationship of equity capital and debt capital** the relative proportions of *equity capital* and *debt capital* in a company's *balance sheet*

capital surplus STOCKHOLDING & INVESTMENTS **difference between current and nominal value of stock** the value of all of the stock in a company that exceeds the nominal value of the stock

capital-to-asset ratio *or* **capital/asset ratio** FINANCE = *capital adequacy ratio*

capital to risk-weighted assets ratio FINANCE = *capital adequacy ratio*

capital transaction FINANCE **transaction bearing on non-current items** a transaction affecting non-current items such as fixed assets, long-term debt, or share capital, rather than revenue transactions

capital turnover FINANCE **annual sales in relation to stock value** the value of annual sales as a multiple of the value of a company's stock

capital widening ECONOMICS **increase in country's capital per person employed** the process whereby capital is increased as a result of an increase in the number of people being employed

CAPM *abbr* **1.** OPERATIONS & PRODUCTION computer-aided production management **2.** STOCKHOLDING & INVESTMENTS capital asset pricing model

capped floating rate note FINANCE **floating rate note with limited interest rate** a *floating-rate note* that has an agreed maximum rate of interest

capped rate FINANCE **variable interest rate with upper limit** an interest rate on a loan that may change, but cannot be greater than an amount fixed at the time when the loan is taken out by a borrower

captive finance company FINANCE **provider of credit for customers of parent company** an organization that provides credit and is owned or controlled by a commercial or manufacturing company, for example, a retailer that owns its store card operation or a car manufacturer that owns a company for financing the vehicles it produces

CAR *abbr* FINANCE capital adequacy ratio

cardholder BANKING **named user of credit card** an individual or company that has an active credit card account with an *issuer* with which transactions can be initiated

card-issuing bank BANKING = *issuer*

caring economy ECONOMICS **friendly relationships between firms and individuals** an economy based on amicable and helpful relationships between businesses and people

carried interest FINANCE **profit paid to private equity partners** the profit that partners in a private equity enterprise receive for the services they provide

carry FINANCE = *carrying charge*

carry forward ACCOUNTING **use as opening balance for next accounting period** to use an account balance at the end of the current period or page as the starting point for the next period or page

carrying amount STOCKHOLDING & INVESTMENTS = *book value* (sense 2)

carrying charge FINANCE **interest paid on money borrowed** the interest expense on money borrowed to finance a purchase. *Also called* **carry**

carrying value STOCKHOLDING & INVESTMENTS = *book value* (sense 2)

carryover STOCKHOLDING & INVESTMENTS **amount of commodity at beginning of fiscal year** the amount of a commodity that is being held at the beginning of a new fiscal year, to be added to the next year's supply. The amount of carryover may have an impact on price.

carry trade MARKETS, CURRENCY & EXCHANGE **borrowings in one currency purchasing assets in another** the practice of borrowing at low interest rates in one currency and using the loan to buy assets offering higher yields in another country

carve-out STOCKHOLDING & INVESTMENTS = *equity carve-out*

cash BANKING **1. exchange check for cash** to present a check and receive banknotes and coins in return **2. banknotes and coins** money in the form of banknotes and coins that are legal tender. This includes cash in hand, deposits repayable on demand with any bank or other financial institution, and deposits denominated in foreign currencies.

cash account 1. ACCOUNTING **record of money transactions** a record of receipts and payments of cash, checks, or other forms of money transfer **2.** STOCKHOLDING & INVESTMENTS **type of brokerage account** an account with a broker that does not allow *buying on margin*

cash accounting 1. ACCOUNTING **recording money transactions as they occur** an accounting method in which receipts and expenses are recorded in the period when they actually occur. *See also accrual basis* **2.** TAX **UK system giving automatic VAT relief on debts** in the United Kingdom, a system for *value-added tax* that enables the taxpayer to account for tax paid and received during a given period, thus allowing automatic relief for bad debts

cash advance BANKING **1. loan of cash against future payment** a loan given in cash as early part payment of a larger sum to be received in the future **2. loan on credit card** a sum of money taken as a loan on a credit card account

cash at bank BANKING **money in bank accounts** the total amount of money held at the bank by a person or company

cash available to invest STOCKHOLDING & INVESTMENTS **total amount available for investment with broker** the amount, including cash on account and balances due soon for outstanding transactions, that a client has available for investment with a broker

cashback FINANCE **1. giving purchaser cash refund** a sales promotion technique offering customers a cash refund after they buy a product **2. service allowing debit card payment to include cash** a facility that allows consumers who pay for items by debit card in a supermarket or some other stores to add a small amount of money to the amount of their purchase and receive that amount in cash

cash balance ACCOUNTING **account balance representing held cash only** an account balance that represents cash alone, as distinct from an account balance that includes money owed but as yet unpaid

cash basis ACCOUNTING **recording money in account only for actual transactions** the bookkeeping practice of accounting for money only when it is actually received or spent

cash bonus STOCKHOLDING & INVESTMENTS **extra dividend payment** an unscheduled dividend that a company declares because of unexpected income

cashbook ACCOUNTING **account book for cash transactions** a book in which all cash payments and receipts are recorded. In a double-entry bookkeeping system, the balance at the end of a given period is included in the trial balance and then transferred to the balance sheet itself.

cash budget TREASURY MANAGEMENT **estimate of cash transactions** a detailed budget of estimated cash inflows and outflows incorporating both revenue and capital items. *Also called cash flow projection*

cash burn FINANCE = *burn rate*

cash card *UK* BANKING = *ATM card*

cash conversion cycle ACCOUNTING **period between buying materials and selling product** the time between the acquisition of a raw material and the receipt of payment for the finished product. *Also called cash cycle*

cash cow 1. FINANCE **mature product generating cash** a product characterized by a high market share but low sales growth, whose function is seen as generating cash for use elsewhere within the organization **2.** MARKETING **very profitable product requiring little investment** a product that sells well and makes a substantial profit without requiring much advertising or investment (slang) **3.** GENERAL MANAGEMENT **slow-growing firm with high market share** in the *Boston Box* model, a business with a high market share with low growth rate, which could yield significant but short-term gain. *See also Boston Box*

cash crop ECONOMICS **plants grown in quantity and sold for cash** a crop such as tobacco, that is typically sold for cash rather than used by the producer

cash cycle ACCOUNTING = *cash conversion cycle*

cash deficiency agreement FINANCE **agreement to supply cash shortfall** a commitment to supply whatever additional cash is needed to complete the financing of a project

cash discount FINANCE **discount for paying promptly or in cash** a discount offered to a customer who pays for goods or services with cash, or who pays an invoice within a particular period

cash dispenser *UK* BANKING = *ATM*

cash dividend STOCKHOLDING & INVESTMENTS **dividend in cash not shares** a share of a company's current earnings or accumulated profits distributed to stockholders in cash, not in the form of *bonus shares*

cash economy ECONOMICS **sector of economy avoiding tax** an unofficial or illegal part of the economy, where goods and services are paid for in cash, and therefore not declared for tax

cash equivalents STOCKHOLDING & INVESTMENTS **investments convertible into cash immediately** short-term investments that can be converted into cash immediately and that are subject to only a limited risk. There is usually a limit on their duration, for example, three months.

cash float FINANCE **banknotes and coins for giving change** banknotes and coins held by a retailer for the purpose of supplying customers with change

cash flow ACCOUNTING **money from sales** the movement through an organization of money that is generated by its own operations, as opposed to borrowing. It is the money that a business actually receives from sales (the cash inflow) and the money that it pays out (the cash outflow).

cash flow accounting ACCOUNTING **accounting that considers only cash receipts and payments** the practice of measuring the financial activities of a company in terms of cash receipts and payments, without recording *accruals*, advance payments, debtors, creditors, and stocks

cash flow coverage ratio ACCOUNTING **ratio of cash received and required** the ratio of income to outstanding obligations which must be paid in cash

cash flow forecast TREASURY MANAGEMENT **estimate of money coming in and going out** a prediction of the amount of money that will move through an organization. This is an important tool for monitoring its solvency. *See also* **cash budget**

cash flow per common share STOCKHOLDING & INVESTMENTS **cash generated for each share of common stock** the amount of cash that a company derives from its activities, less any dividends paid, for each share of its common stock

cash flow projection TREASURY MANAGEMENT = *cash budget*

cash flow risk RISK **danger of receiving less cash than required** the risk that a company's available cash will not be sufficient to meet its financial obligations

cash flow statement ACCOUNTING **account of cash transactions** a record of a company's cash inflows and cash outflows over a specific period of time, typically a year.

It reports funds on hand at the beginning of the period, funds received, funds spent, and funds remaining at the end of the period. Cash flows are divided into three categories: cash from operations; cash investment activities; and cash-financing activities. Companies with holdings in foreign currencies use a fourth classification: effects of changes in currency rates on cash.

cash fraction STOCKHOLDING & INVESTMENTS **cash sum for allocation of part of share** a small amount of cash paid to a stockholder to make up the full amount of part of a share which has been allocated in a stock split

cash-generating unit FINANCE **smallest set of assets involved in cash transactions** the smallest identifiable group of assets generating cash inflows and outflows that can be measured

cash hoard FINANCE, MERGERS & ACQUISITIONS (informal) = *cash reserves*

cashier UK BANKING = *teller*

cashier's check BANKING **check drawn by bank on itself** a bank's own check, drawn on itself and signed by the cashier or other bank official

cash in STOCKHOLDING & INVESTMENTS **sell investments for cash** to sell stock or other property for cash

cash in hand FINANCE, ACCOUNTING **available money** money that is held in coins and banknotes, not in a bank account

cash ISA STOCKHOLDING & INVESTMENTS **UK tax-free account for savings** in the United Kingdom, a savings account for which tax is not paid on interest earned. The maximum that can be invested per tax year is capped, at £5,640 for 2012–13. Stocks

and shares ISAs are also available, instead of or alongside cash ISAs. *See also* **stocks and shares ISA**, **ISA**

cashless society ECONOMICS **community in which all payments are electronic** a society in which all bills and debits are paid by electronic money media such as bank and credit cards, direct debits, and online payments

cash limit 1. FINANCE **fixed sum available to spend** a fixed amount of money that can be spent during a specific period or on a specific project 2. BANKING **limit on single ATM withdrawal** a maximum amount somebody can withdraw at one time from an ATM using an ATM card

cash loan company FINANCE **S. African provider of unsecured short-term loans** in South Africa, a *microcredit* business that provides short-term loans without collateral, usually at high interest rates

cash machine UK BANKING = *ATM*

cash offer FINANCE 1. **offer to buy firm for cash** an offer to buy a company for cash rather than for stock 2. **offer of cash payment** an offer to pay for something in cash

cash payments journal BANKING **chronological record of payments from firm's bank account** a chronological record of all the money paid out from a company's bank account

cashpoint UK BANKING = *ATM*

cash position 1. ACCOUNTING **amount of cash currently available to firm** a statement of the amount of cash that a company currently has available to spend 2. STOCKHOLDING & INVESTMENTS **holdings in short-term debt** the extent to which a portfolio of assets includes short-term debt securities

cash price FINANCE 1. **better deal offered to customer paying cash** a lower price or better terms that apply to a sale if the customer pays cash rather than using credit 2. = *spot price*

cash ratio FINANCE **liquid assets divided by total liabilities** the ratio of a company's liquid assets such as cash and securities divided by total liabilities. *Also called* **liquidity ratio**

cash receipts journal BANKING **chronological record of deposits into firm's bank account** a chronological record of all the receipts that have been paid into a company's bank account

cash reserves FINANCE, MERGERS & ACQUISITIONS **available cash** a large amount of cash that a company holds in order to facilitate an expected project. Cash reserves are often attractive to a company looking to make an acquisition. *Also called* **cash hoard**

cash sale FINANCE **sale paid for in cash** a sale in which payment is made immediately in cash rather than put on credit

cash settlement STOCKHOLDING & INVESTMENTS 1. **early payment on options contract** an immediate payment on an options contract without waiting for expiration of the normal, usually five-day, settlement period 2. **paying for securities bought** the completion of a transaction by paying for securities, rather than physical delivery of them

cash transaction FINANCE **dealing involving cash payment** a transaction in which the method of payment is cash, as distinct from a transaction paid for by means of a transfer of a *financial instrument*

cash voucher FINANCE **document exchangeable for cash** a piece of paper that can be exchanged for cash

casino bank BANKING **bank taking large investment risks** a bank that is regarded as pursuing an unreasonably high-risk investment strategy

casino banking BANKING **high-risk investment practices by banks** the activity of pursuing a high-risk investment strategy for profit rather than providing a balanced range of banking services

casino capitalism FINANCE **high-risk financial dealings** a global phenomenon of increased financial risk-taking and instability, as an outcome of financial markets becoming very large and introducing many new investment products, and financial institutions being self-regulated, among other factors

catastrophe bond STOCKHOLDING & INVESTMENTS **bond with lower value in event of disaster** a bond with a very high interest rate which may be worth less or give a lower rate of interest if a disaster occurs, whether it be natural or otherwise

catastrophe future STOCKHOLDING & INVESTMENTS, RISK **futures contract covering insurance losses from catastrophes** a futures contract used by insurers to hedge their risk for low-probability catastrophic losses due to natural causes

catastrophe swap STOCKHOLDING & INVESTMENTS, RISK **option contract covering insurance losses from catastrophes** an option contract in which an investor exchanges a fixed periodic payment for part of the difference between an insurance company's premiums and its losses caused by claims due to a catastrophe

cats and dogs US STOCKHOLDING & INVESTMENTS **stocks with doubtful origins** speculative stocks with dubious sales histories (slang)

CBO *abbr* STOCKHOLDING & INVESTMENTS, RISK collateralized bond obligation

CCA *abbr* ACCOUNTING current cost accounting

ccc UK FINANCE **public limited company** the Welsh term for a public limited company *Full form* **cwmni cyfyngedig cyhoeddus**

CD *abbr* BANKING certificate of deposit

CDO *abbr* STOCKHOLDING & INVESTMENTS collateralized debt obligation

CDS *abbr* STOCKHOLDING & INVESTMENTS credit default swap

CDSC *abbr* STOCKHOLDING & INVESTMENTS contingent deferred sales charge

center US ACCOUNTING **chargeable unit of organization** a department, area, or function to which costs and/or revenues are charged

central bank ECONOMICS, BANKING **bank controlling country's monetary system** a bank that controls the credit system and money supply of a country

central bank discount rate BANKING **central bank's rate for discounting bills** the rate at which a central bank discounts bills such as Treasury bills

centralization FINANCE **concentration of shared functions at main office** the gathering together, at a corporate headquarters, of specialist functions such as finance, personnel, centralized purchasing, and information technology. Centralization is usually undertaken in order to effect economies of scale and to standardize operating procedures throughout the organization. Centralized management can become cumbersome and inefficient, and may produce communications problems. Some organizations have shifted toward *decentralization* to try to avoid this.

central planning ECONOMICS **economy planned by government** the use of an economic system in which the government plans all business activity, regulates supply, sets production targets, and itemizes work to be done

Central Registration Depository STOCKHOLDING & INVESTMENTS **US searchable database of investment advisers and brokers** a computerized database of brokers, investment advisers, and brokerage firms that is maintained by the US Securities and Exchange Commission and is accessible to the public. *Abbr* **CRD**

CEO *abbr* CORPORATE GOVERNANCE chief executive officer

certificate STOCKHOLDING & INVESTMENTS **document of share ownership** a document representing partial ownership of a company which states the number of shares that the document is worth and the names of the company and the owner of the shares

certificate of deposit BANKING **document giving guaranteed interest rate for deposit** a document from a bank showing that money has been deposited at a guaranteed interest rate for a specific period of time. *Abbr* **CD**

certified accountant ACCOUNTING **UK accountant qualified by practical training** in the United Kingdom, an accountant trained in industry, the public service, or in the offices of practicing accountants, who is a member of the *Association of Chartered Certified Accountants*. Such an accountant fulfills much the same role as a *chartered accountant* and is qualified to audit company records. *Abbr* **CA**

certified check BANKING **check bank guarantees to pay** a check that a bank guarantees is good and will be paid out of money put aside from the payer's bank account.

certified public accountant ACCOUNTING **US professional licensed accountant** in the United States, an accountant who has passed the exam administered by the American Institute of Certified Public Accountants and has met all other educational and experience requirements to be licensed by the state in which he or she practices. Certified public accountants fulfill much the same role as *chartered accountants* in the

United Kingdom and are qualified to audit company records. *Abbr* **CPA**

CFD *abbr* **1.** STOCKHOLDING & INVESTMENTS contract for difference (sense 1) **2.** CURRENCY & EXCHANGE contract for difference (sense 2)

CFO *abbr* TREASURY MANAGEMENT chief financial officer

chair CORPORATE GOVERNANCE *see* **chairman**

chairman CORPORATE GOVERNANCE **organization's highest executive** the most senior executive in an organization, responsible for running the annual meeting and meetings of the **board of directors**. He or she may be a figurehead, appointed for prestige or power, and may have no role in the day-to-day running of the organization. Sometimes the roles of chairman and **chief executive officer** are combined, and the chairman then has more control over daily operations; sometimes the chairman is a retired chief executive. In the United States, the person who performs this function is often called a **president**. Historically, the term **chairman** was more common. The terms **chairwoman** or **chairperson** are later developments, although **chair** is now the most generally acceptable. Chairman, however, remains in common use, especially in the corporate sector.

chairman's report *or* **chairman's statement** CORPORATE GOVERNANCE **chair's review of year's performance and prospects** a statement included in the annual report of most large companies in which the chair of the board of directors gives an often favorable overview of the company's performance and prospects

chairperson CORPORATE GOVERNANCE *see* **chairman**

chairwoman CORPORATE GOVERNANCE **woman who is organization's highest executive** a woman who is the most senior executive in an organization, responsible for running the annual meeting, and meetings of the **board of directors**. *See also* **chairman**

Chancellor of the Exchequer FINANCE **UK's chief finance minister** the United Kingdom's senior finance minister, based at HM Treasury in London. The office of Chancellor dates back to the 13th century. Some of the most famous names in British politics have served in this very senior government position, including William Gladstone and David Lloyd George.

channel stuffing FINANCE **making special offers at end of fiscal year** the artificial boosting of sales at the end of a fiscal year by offering distributors and dealers incentives to buy a greater quantity of goods than they actually need (slang)

CHAPS BANKING **means of rapid electronic transfer of substantial funds** Clearing House Automated Payment System: a method for the rapid electronic transfer of funds between participating banks on behalf of large commercial customers, where transfers tend to be of significant value. *Full form* **Clearing House Automated Payment System**

Chapter 11 bankruptcy FINANCE **bankruptcy protected from creditors** a bankruptcy declared under the US Bankruptcy

Reform Act (1978) which entitles enterprises experiencing financial difficulties to apply for protection from creditors

charge account FINANCE **arrangement for customer to buy on credit** a facility with a retailer that enables the customer to buy goods or services on credit rather than pay in cash. The customer may be required to settle the account within a month to avoid incurring interest on the credit. *Also called* **credit account**

charge and discharge accounting ACCOUNTING **former bookkeeping system** formerly, a bookkeeping system in which a person charges himself or herself with receipts and credits himself or herself with payments. This system was used extensively before the advent of double-entry bookkeeping.

charge card FINANCE **card used for buying store items on account** a card issued to customers by a store, bank, or other organization, used to charge purchases to an account for later payment. *See also* **credit card**

chargee FINANCE **1. creditor with legal interest in land** a person who holds a **charge** over a property, and who therefore has first claim on proceeds from the sale of the property **2. person with enforcement rights** a person who has the right to force a debtor to pay

charge off ACCOUNTING **unrepeated expense or bad debt** an uncollectable debt or a one-time expense that appears on a company's income statement

charitable contribution ACCOUNTING **firm's gift to charity** a donation by a company to a charity, deductible against tax

charity accounts ACCOUNTING **records of charity's financial activities** the accounting records of a charitable institution, which include a statement of financial activities rather than a profit and loss account. In the United Kingdom, the accounts should conform to the requirements stipulated in the Charities Act (1993).

chartered accountant ACCOUNTING **UK accountant qualified by professional examination** in the United Kingdom, a qualified professional accountant who is a member of an Institute of Chartered Accountants. Chartered accountants are qualified to audit company accounts and some hold management positions in companies. *Abbr* **CA**

Chartered Association of Certified Accountants ACCOUNTING **formerly, UK certified accountants' association** the former name of the *Association of Chartered Certified Accountants* in the United Kingdom

chartered bank BANKING **N. American bank established by government charter** in the United States and Canada, a bank that has been set up by government charter

Chartered Institute of Management Accountants ACCOUNTING *see* **CIMA**

Chartered Institute of Public Finance and Accountancy ACCOUNTING *see* **CIPFA**

charter value BANKING **worth of bank's capacity to continue operating** the value of a bank being able to continue to do business in the future, reflected as part of its share price

cheap money FINANCE money lent at low interest money that is lent at low interest rates, used as a government strategy to stimulate an economy either at the initial signs of, or during, a recession. *Also called* **easy money**. *See also* **dear money**, **expansionary monetary policy**

check US BANKING written instruction to bank to pay money an order in writing requiring the banker to pay on demand a specific sum of money to a specified person or bearer. Although a check can theoretically be written on anything (in a P. G. Woodhouse story, one was written on the side of a cow), banks issue preprinted, customized forms for completion by an account holder who inserts the date, the name of the person to be paid (the payee), the amount in both words and figures, and his or her signature. The customer is the drawer. *UK term* **cheque**

checkbook US BANKING book of blank cheques a booklet with new blank checks for a bank's customer to complete. *UK term* **cheque book**

check card US BANKING = **debit card**

check digit BANKING reference number for validating transactions the last digit of a string of computerized reference numbers, used to validate a transaction

checking account US BANKING flexible bank account with easy withdrawal a bank account in which deposits can be withdrawn at any time by writing checks but do not usually earn interest, except in the case of some online accounts. It is the most common type of bank account. *Abbr* **c/a**. *UK term* **current account**

check register US BANKING record of check transactions a control record of checks issued or received, maintained by a person or organization. *UK term* **cheque register**

check routing symbol BANKING number on US check identifying Federal Reserve district a number shown on a US check that identifies the Federal Reserve district through which the check will be cleared

check stub US BANKING part of check left in checkbook a piece of paper left in a checkbook after a check has been written and taken out. *UK term* **cheque stub**

check to bearer US BANKING = **bearer check**

cheque UK BANKING = **check**

cheque book UK BANKING = **checkbook**

cheque card BANKING UK card guaranteeing payment of check a plastic card from a UK bank that guarantees payment of a check up to some amount, even if the user has no money in his or her account

cheque register UK BANKING = **check register**

cheque stub UK BANKING = **check stub**

cheque to bearer UK BANKING = **bearer check**

Chicago School ECONOMICS school of conservative economic thought a school of conservative economic thought, promoting free markets and capitalism and relying heavily on mathematical analysis. It is associated with the University of Chicago and was for many years led by Professor Milton Friedman.

chief executive officer *or* chief executive CORPORATE GOVERNANCE executive ultimately responsible for firm's management the person with overall responsibility for ensuring that the daily operations of an organization run efficiently and for carrying out strategic plans. The chief executive of an organization normally sits on the *board of directors*. In a limited company, he or she is usually known as a managing director. *Abbr* **CEO**

chief financial officer TREASURY MANAGEMENT executive responsible for firm's financial management the officer in an organization responsible for handling funds, signing checks, the keeping of financial records, and financial planning for the company. *Abbr* **CFO**

Chief Secretary to the Treasury FINANCE UK government minister controlling public expenditure in the United Kingdom, a government minister responsible to the Chancellor of the Exchequer for the control of public expenditure

Chinese wall STOCKHOLDING & INVESTMENTS obstacle to exchange of inside information the procedures enforced within a securities firm to prevent the exchange of confidential information between the firm's departments so as to avoid the illegal use of inside information

CHIPS BANKING US international wire transfer system in the United States, the computerized domestic and international wire transfer system that also serves to convert all pending payments into a single transaction *Full form* **Clearing House Interbank Payments System**

CHIS *abbr* FRAUD covert human intelligence source

chose in action FINANCE personal right treated like property a personal right such as a patent, copyright, debt, or check that can be enforced or claimed as if it were property

chose in possession FINANCE object that can be owned a physical item such as a piece of furniture that can be owned

churn 1. STOCKHOLDING & INVESTMENTS encourage investor to change portfolio frequently to encourage an investor to change stock frequently because the broker is paid every time there is a change in the investor's portfolio (slang) **2.** INSURANCE encourage somebody to change insurance policy to encourage a client to change his or her insurance policy solely to earn the salesperson a commission **3.** GENERAL MANAGEMENT successive purchases of different brands of products to purchase a quick succession of products or services without displaying loyalty to any of them, often as a result of competitive marketing strategies that continually undercut rival prices, thus encouraging customers to switch brands constantly in order to take advantage of the cheapest or most attractive offers **4.** HR & PERSONNEL experience high employee turnover to suffer a high turnover rate of executives or other employees

churn rate 1. STOCKHOLDING & INVESTMENTS measure of change in investment portfolio a measure of the frequency and volume of trading of stocks and bonds in a brokerage account

2. GENERAL MANAGEMENT rate at which customers abandon new product the rate at which new customers try a product or service and then stop using it

CICA *abbr* ACCOUNTING Canadian Institute of Chartered Accountants

CIFAS *abbr* FRAUD Credit Industry Fraud Avoidance System

CIMA ACCOUNTING UK institution awarding financial degree to businesspeople a UK organization that is internationally recognized as offering a financial degree for business, focusing on strategic business management. Founded in 1919 as the Institute of Cost and Works Accountants, it has offices worldwide, supporting over 128,000 members and students in 156 countries. *Full form* ***Chartered Institute of Management Accountants***

CIPFA ACCOUNTING UK professional accountancy organization in the United Kingdom, one of the leading professional accountancy bodies and the only one that specializes in the public services, for example, local government, public service bodies, and national audit agencies, as well as major accounting firms. It is responsible for the education and training of professional accountants and for their regulation through the setting and monitoring of professional standards. CIPFA also provides a variety of advisory, information, and consulting services to public service organizations. It is the leading independent commentator on managing accounting for public money. *Full form* ***Chartered Institute of Public Finance and Accountancy***

circular flow of income ECONOMICS model of relationship between income and spending a model of a country's economy showing the flow of resources when consumers' wages and salaries are used to buy goods and so generate income for manufacturing firms

circularization of debtors ACCOUNTING auditors' approach to debtors to identify assets the sending of letters by a company's auditors to debtors in order to verify the existence and extent of the company's assets

circular letter of credit BANKING bank's authorization of payment to every branch a letter of credit sent to all branches of the bank which issues it

circular merger MERGERS & ACQUISITIONS joining of firms sharing distribution channels a merger involving firms that have different products but similar distribution channels. *See also* **merger**

circulating capital FINANCE = ***working capital***

circulation of capital FINANCE transfer of capital between investments the movement of ***capital*** from one investment to another, or between one country and another

City *or* **City of London** FINANCE area of London containing UK financial center the United Kingdom's financial center found in the historic center of London, where most banks and many large companies have their main offices. *Also called* ***Square Mile***. *See also* **Wall Street**

City bonus FINANCE annual financial reward for UK employee a very large sum of money, in addition to salary, paid to an employee in London's financial industry for effective performance in increasing his or her company's profits. *See also* **Wall Street bonus**

City Code on Takeovers and Mergers MERGERS & ACQUISITIONS UK code for fairness in takeovers in the United Kingdom, a code issued on behalf of the ***City Panel on Takeovers and Mergers*** that is designed principally to ensure fair and equal treatment of all stockholders in relation to ***takeovers***. The Code also provides an orderly framework within which takeovers are conducted. It is not concerned with the financial or commercial advantages or disadvantages of a takeover, nor with issues such as competition policy which are the responsibility of the government. The Code represents the collective opinion of those professionally involved in the field of takeovers on how fairness to stockholders can be achieved in practice.

City Panel on Takeovers and Mergers MERGERS & ACQUISITIONS independent UK group supervising takeovers in the United Kingdom, an independent nonstatutory group whose job is to supervise and regulate ***takeovers*** according to the ***City Code on Takeovers and Mergers***. *Also called* ***Takeover Panel***

claimant FINANCE somebody who makes benefit claim to government a person who claims a government benefit such as an unemployment or disability benefit

class STOCKHOLDING & INVESTMENTS classification for common stock a type of common stock issued by a company, usually with the designations A and B, and conferring different voting rights

classical economics ECONOMICS economic theory stressing importance of free enterprise a theory focusing on the functioning of a market economy and providing a rudimentary explanation of consumer and producer behavior in particular markets. The theory postulates that, over time, the economy would tend to operate at full employment because increases in supply would create corresponding increases in demand.

classified stock STOCKHOLDING & INVESTMENTS US firm's common stock divided into classes in the United States, a company's ***common stock*** divided into classes such as Class A and Class B

class of assets ACCOUNTING categorization of assets the grouping of similar assets into categories. This is done because, under International Accounting Standards Committee rules, ***tangible assets*** and ***intangible assets*** cannot be revalued on an individual basis, only within a class of assets.

claw back FINANCE take back money previously allocated to recover money that has already been assigned to a specific use, especially money given in grants or tax incentives

clawback 1. FINANCE money reclaimed money taken back, especially money taken back by the government from grants or tax incentives which had previously been made **2.** MARKETS

allocation of new stock to existing stockholders the allocation of new shares of stockto existing stockholders, so as to maintain the value of their holdings

clean float CURRENCY & EXCHANGE **exchange rate unrestricted by government** a *floating exchange rate* that is allowed to vary without any intervention from the country's monetary authorities

clean opinion *or* **clean report** ACCOUNTING **auditor's report without reservations** an auditor's report that is not qualified because of concern about the scope or treatment of some matter

clean surplus concept FINANCE **advocating statements showing all gains and losses** the idea that a company's income statement should show the totality of gains and losses, without any of them being taken directly to equity

clearing 1. BANKING **process of passing check through banking system** an act of passing of a check through the banking system, including the transfer of money from one account to another **2.** MARKETS **completion of transactions and payments** the process of verifying and settling orders between buyers and sellers in securities transactions

clearing bank BANKING **in UK, bank employing clearing house** in the United Kingdom, a bank that deals with other banks through a *clearing house*

clearing house *or* **clearing firm** *or* **clearing corporation 1.** BANKING **institution handling bank transactions** an institution that settles accounts between banks, using the *clearing system* **2.** MARKETS **institution handling securities transactions** an organization that coordinates the confirmation, delivery, and settlement of securities transactions on behalf of exchanges **3.** BANKING, E-COMMERCE = *acquirer (sense 2)*

Clearing House Automated Payment System BANKING *see* CHAPS

Clearing House Interbank Payments System BANKING *see* CHIPS

clearing system BANKING **system for handling bank transactions** the system of settling accounts among banks through *clearing houses*. It allows member banks to offset claims against each other.

clear profit FINANCE **profit after paying expenses** the profit remaining after all expenses have been paid

clientele effect STOCKHOLDING & INVESTMENTS **influence of investors on choice of securities** the preference of an investor or group of investors for buying a particular type of security

Clintonomics ECONOMICS **Clinton's policy of economic intervention** the policy of former US President Clinton's Council of Economic Advisers to intervene in the economy to correct market failures and redistribute income

CLO *abbr* STOCKHOLDING & INVESTMENTS collateralized loan obligation

clone fund STOCKHOLDING & INVESTMENTS **mutual fund matching established fund by using derivatives** a mutual fund that, by the use of derivatives, is able to duplicate the strategy and performance of a successful established mutual fund

close 1. MARKETS **end of stock trading for day** the end of a day's trading on a stock exchange **2.** MARKETS **have a particular price at end of trading** of a stock, to end the day's trading at a particular price **3.** *US* REAL ESTATE **pay balance on real estate** to pay off the balance owed on real estate in exchange for a deed showing ownership of the real estate. *UK term* **complete close a position** MARKETS to arrange affairs so that there is no longer any liability to pay, for example, by selling all securities held **close the accounts** FINANCE to come to the end of an accounting period and make up the profit and loss account

closed economy ECONOMICS **economic system isolated from international trade** an economic system in which little or no external trade takes place

closed-end credit FINANCE **credit with fixed date for full repayment** a loan, plus any interest and finance charges, that is to be repaid in full by a specific future date. Loans that have real estate or motor vehicles as collateral are usually closed-end. *See also* ***open-end credit***

closed-end fund *or* **closed-end investment company** STOCKHOLDING & INVESTMENTS **investment company with fixed number of shares** an investment company such as an investment trust that has a fixed number of shares that can be bought and sold in the marketplace. *See also* ***open-end fund***

closed fund STOCKHOLDING & INVESTMENTS **mutual fund in US closed to new investors** in the United States, a mutual fund that is no longer accepting new investors, because it has become too large

closely held shares STOCKHOLDING & INVESTMENTS **publicly traded US stock with few holders** in the United States, stock that is publicly traded but held by very few people

closing balance 1. ACCOUNTING **amount carried forward to next accounting period** the difference between credits and debits in a ledger at the end of one accounting period that is carried forward to the next **2.** BANKING **bank balance at end of business day** the amount in credit or debit in a bank account at the end of a business day

closing entries ACCOUNTING **entries at very end of accounting period** in a double-entry bookkeeping system, entries made at the very end of an ***accounting period*** to balance the expense and revenue ledgers

closing rate CURRENCY & EXCHANGE **exchange rate at end of accounting period** the exchange rate of two or more currencies at the close of business at the end of an accounting period, for example, at the end of the fiscal year

closing rate method CURRENCY & EXCHANGE **currency conversion method in accounts** a technique for translating the figures from a set of financial statements into a different currency using the ***closing rate***. This method is often used for the accounts of a foreign subsidiary of a parent company.

closing sale FINANCE **sale that reduces seller's risk** a sale that reduces the risk that the seller has through holding a greater number of shares or a longer term contract

closing stock ACCOUNTING **inventory at end of accounting period** a business's remaining stock at the end of an *accounting period*. It includes finished products, raw materials, or work in progress and is deducted from the period's costs in the balance sheets.

CMBS *abbr* STOCKHOLDING & INVESTMENTS, MORTGAGES commercial mortgage-backed securities

CN *or* **C/N** *abbr* FINANCE credit note

co-creditor FINANCE **one of several people to whom firm owes money** one of two or more people or organizations that are owed money by the same company

co-director CORPORATE GOVERNANCE **person involved in controlling firm** one of two or more people who direct the same company

co-financing FINANCE **joint provision of finance** the provision of money for a project jointly by two or more parties

cohesion fund FINANCE **EU fund to equalize members' economies** in the European Union, the main financial instrument for reducing economic and social disparities within by providing financial help for projects in the fields of the environment and transport infrastructure

coincident indicator ECONOMICS **indicator of current economic activity** a factor that provides information on economic activity taking place at the current time

COLA *abbr* FINANCE cost-of-living adjustment

collar STOCKHOLDING & INVESTMENTS, RISK **preset limit** a contractually imposed lower limit on a *financial instrument*

collateral FINANCE **resources providing security against loan** property or goods used as security against a loan and forfeited to the lender if the borrower defaults

collateralize FINANCE **provide loan with security** to secure a loan by pledging assets. If the borrower defaults on loan payments, the pledged assets can be taken by the lender. — collateralization

collateralized bond obligation STOCKHOLDING & INVESTMENTS, RISK **investment grade pool of bonds carrying risk** an *investment grade asset-backed security* that consists of a portfolio of bonds, some of which may carry high risk. Pooling bonds with different degrees of risk is thought to provide enough diversification to qualify the security for an investment grade rating. *Abbr* **CBO**

collateralized debt obligation STOCKHOLDING & INVESTMENTS **investment combining bonds and loans** a complex investment vehicle based on a portfolio of bonds and loans, which may include assets with an underlying risk. *Abbr* **CDO**. *Also called* **debt obligation**

collateralized loan obligation STOCKHOLDING & INVESTMENTS **asset-backed security formed when loan is** repackaged an asset-backed security that is created by repackaging loans, usually commercial loans made by a bank, at an attractive rate of interest. *Abbr* **CLO**

collateralized mortgage obligation STOCKHOLDING & INVESTMENTS, MORTGAGES **instrument with mortgages on property** a financial instrument that has mortgages on property given as security in case of default. CMOs are issued against the collective value of pooled mortgages, offering interest payments based on the overall cash flow. *Abbr* **CMO**

collateral trust certificate STOCKHOLDING & INVESTMENTS **bond with stock in another firm as security** a bond for which stock in another company, usually a subsidiary, is used as collateral

collecting bank BANKING **bank receiving check for processing** a bank into which a person has deposited a check, and which has the duty to collect the money from the account of the writer of the check

collection FINANCE **collecting payments on unpaid debts** the process of collecting payments on unpaid loans or bills

collection agency FINANCE **business collecting outstanding payments** a business that collects payments on unpaidloans or on bills

collection ratio ACCOUNTING **average time for invoice to be paid** the average number of days it takes a firm to convert its accounts receivable into cash.

Ideally, this period should be decreasing or constant. A low figure means the company collects its outstanding receivables quickly. Collection ratios are usually reviewed quarterly or yearly.

Calculating the collection ratio requires three figures: total accounts receivable, total credit sales for the period analyzed, and the number of days in the period (annual, 365; six months, 182; quarter, 91). The formula is:

$$\frac{\text{Accounts receivable}}{\text{Total credit sales for the period}} \times \text{Number of days in the period}$$

For example: if total receivables are \$4,500,000, total credit sales in a quarter are \$9,000,000, and number of days is 91, then:

$$\frac{4,500,000}{9,000,000} \times 91 = 45.5$$

Thus, it takes an average of 45.5 days to collect receivables.

Properly evaluating a collection ratio requires a standard for comparison. A traditional rule of thumb is that it should not exceed a third to a half of selling terms. For instance, if terms are 30 days, an acceptable collection ratio would be 40 to 45 days.

Companies use collection ratio information with an *accounts receivable aging* report. This lists aged categories of receivables, for example, 0–30 days, 30–60 days, 60–90 days, and over 90 days. The report also shows the percentage of total accounts receivable that each group represents, allowing for an analysis of delinquencies and potential bad debts. *Also called* **days' sales outstanding**

a–z

Dictionary

collusive tendering FINANCE **when job offerers share inside information** the illegal practice among companies making offers for a job of sharing privileged information between themselves, with the objective of fixing the end result

combination bond STOCKHOLDING & INVESTMENTS **bond secured by project's revenue and government credit** a government bond for which the collateral is both revenue from the financed project and the government's credit

combined financial statement FINANCE **summary of financial position of related firms** a written record covering the assets, liabilities, net worth, and operating statement of two or more related or affiliated companies

comfort letter 1. FINANCE **parent company's support for subsidiary's loan** a letter from the parent company of a subsidiary that is applying for a loan, stating the intention that the subsidiary should remain in business **2.** ACCOUNTING **in US, endorsement of financial statement** in the United States, a statement from an accounting firm provided to a company preparing for a public offering, which confirms that the unaudited financial information in the *prospectus* follows *Generally Accepted Accounting Principles*

command economy ECONOMICS **economic system controlled by government** an economy in which all economic activity is regulated by the government, as formerly in China or the Soviet Union

commerce FINANCE **trading on large scale** the large-scale buying and selling of goods and services, usually applied to trading between different states orcountries

commerce integration FINANCE **marrying of old and new ways of trading** the blending of Internet-based commerce capabilities with the *legacy systems* of a traditional business to create a seamless transparent process

commercial FINANCE **of trading** relating to the buying and selling of goods and services

commercial bank BANKING **privately owned bank offering range of facilities** a bank that provides financial services such as checking andsavings accounts and loans to individuals and businesses. *See also investment bank*

commercial bill FINANCE **bill of exchange not issued by government** a *bill of exchange* issued by a company (a *trade bill*) or accepted by a bank (a *banker's bill*), as opposed to a *Treasury bill*, which is issued by a government

commercial hedger STOCKHOLDING & INVESTMENTS **producer investing in commodities it needs** a company that holds *options* in the commodities it uses or produces, usually in order to ensure the price stability of the commodity

commercialization FINANCE **conversion of something into business** the application of business principles to something in order to run it as a business

commercial loan FINANCE **short-term renewable loan to firm** a short-term renewable loan or line of credit used to finance the seasonal or cyclical working capital needs of a company

commercial paper FINANCE **unsecured short-term loan note** an unsecured loan note issued by a company for a short period, generally maturing within nine months

commercial report FINANCE **background financial report on applicant** an investigative report made by an organization such as a *credit bureau* that specializes in obtaining information regarding a person or organization applying for something such as credit or employment

commercial substance FINANCE **economic reality behind piece of business** the economic reality that underlies a transaction or arrangement, regardless of its legal or technical denomination. For example, a company may sell an office block and then immediately lease it back: the commercial substance may be that it has not been sold.

commercial year FINANCE **12 months of 30 days** an artificial year treated as having 12 months of 30 days each, used for calculating such things as monthly sales data and inventory levels

commission 1. FINANCE **sum paid to intermediary** a payment made to an intermediary, often calculated as a percentage of the value of goods or services provided. Commission is most often paid to sales staff, brokers, or agents. **2.** *US* MARKETS **broker's fee for sale** a fee that a broker receives for a sale of securities. *Also called placement fee*

commission agent FINANCE **agent paid percentage of sales** an agent whose payment is based on a specific percentage of the sales made

commission house FINANCE **firm charging commission on futures contracts** a business that buys or sells *futures contracts* for clients and charges a commission for this service

commitment STOCKHOLDING & INVESTMENTS **agreement to underwrite credit** an agreement by an underwriting syndicate to underwrite a *note issuance facility* or other credit facility

commitment fee FINANCE **payment to fix interest rate on forthcoming loan** a fee that a lender charges to guarantee a rate of interest on a loan a borrower is soon to make. *Also called establishment fee*

commitment letter FINANCE **official confirmation of US loan** in the United States, an official notice from a lender to a borrower that the borrower's application has been approved and confirming the terms and conditions of the loan

commitments basis FINANCE **way of recording expenditure before outlay** the method of recording the expenditure of a public sector organization at the time when it commits itself to it rather than when it actually pays for it

commitments for capital expenditure FINANCE **amount committed to fixed assets in future** the amount a company has committed to spend on fixed assets in the future. In the United Kingdom, companies are legally obliged to disclose this amount, and any additional commitments, in their *annual report*.

Committee on Accounting Procedure ACCOUNTING **former US committee establishing accounting principles** in the United

States, a committee of the American Institute of Certified Public Accountants that was responsible between 1939 and 1959 for issuing accounting principles, some of which are still part of the *Generally Accepted Accounting Principles*

commodity-backed bond STOCKHOLDING & INVESTMENTS **bond linked to price of commodity** a bond tied to the price of an underlying commodity such as gold or silver, often used as a hedge against inflation

commodity paper FINANCE **loan secured by commodities** a loan or advance for which commodities or financial documents relating to them are collateral

commodity pool FINANCE **group trading in commodity options** a group of people who join together to trade in *options* on commodities

commodity-product spread FINANCE **trading in commodity and product** coordinated trades in both a commodity and a product made from it

common cost 1. ACCOUNTING **cost recorded in more than one center** a cost that is allocated to two or more cost centers within a company **2.** OPERATIONS & PRODUCTION **cost associated with multiple items** cost relating to more than one product or service and unable to be allocated to any individual one

common equity STOCKHOLDING & INVESTMENTS **common stock in a company** the ownership interest in a company that consists only of the common stock

common-size financial statements ACCOUNTING **statements with everything in percentages** statements in which all the separate parts are expressed as percentages of the total. Such statements are often used for making performance comparisons between companies.

common stock *US* STOCKHOLDING & INVESTMENTS **stock without first call on dividends** a stock that provides voting rights but only pays a dividend after dividends for preferred stock have been paid. *UK term* **ordinary share**

common stock ratio STOCKHOLDING & INVESTMENTS **in US, proportion of capital represented by share** in the United States, a measure of the interest each stockholder has in the company's capital

community property FINANCE **asset to be shared equally on divorce** any asset that is acquired during marriage by either spouse and that, in some states of the United States, must be divided equally between them if they should divorce. *Also called* **marital property**

companion bond STOCKHOLDING & INVESTMENTS **US bond secured by mortgages** in the United States, a class of a *collateralized mortgage obligation* that is paid off first when interest rates fall, leading to the underlying mortgages being prepaid. Conversely, the *principal* on these bonds will be repaid more slowly when interest rates rise and fewer mortgages are prepaid.

company director CORPORATE GOVERNANCE **somebody appointed to help run company** a person appointed by the stockholders to help run a company

company law CORPORATE GOVERNANCE **legislation governing firms** the body of legislation that relates to the formation, status, conduct, and *corporate governance* of companies as legal entities

company policy CORPORATE GOVERNANCE **firm's guidelines for behavior or procedure** a statement of desired standards of behavior or procedure applicable across an organization. Company policy defines ways of acting for staff in areas where there appears to be latitude in deciding how best to operate. This may concern areas such as time off for special circumstances, drug or alcohol abuse, workplace bullying, personal use of Internet facilities, or business travel. Company policy may also apply to customers, for example, policy on complaints, customer retention, or disclosure of information. Sometimes a company policy may develop into a *code of practice*.

company registrar CORPORATE GOVERNANCE **person maintaining firm's share register** the person who is responsible for maintaining the share register records of a company

company report CORPORATE GOVERNANCE **statement of firm's activities and performance** a document giving details of the activities and performance of a company. Companies are legally required to produce specific reports and submit them to the competent authorities in the country of their registration. These include *annual reports* and financial reports. Other reports may cover specific aspects of an organization's activities, for example, environmental or social impact.

company secretary CORPORATE GOVERNANCE **UK firm's senior administrative officer** a senior employee in an organization with director status and administrative and legal authority. The appointment of a company secretary is a legal requirement for most limited companies, except the smallest. A company secretary can also be a *board secretary* with appropriate qualifications. In the United Kingdom, many company secretaries are members of the Institute of Chartered Secretaries and Administrators.

comparative advantage ECONOMICS, BUSINESS **benefit of higher, more efficient production** an instance of higher, more efficient production in a particular area. A country that produces far more cars than another, for example, is said to have the comparative advantage in car production. It has been suggested that specialization in activities in which individuals or groups have a comparative advantage will result in gains in trade.

comparative balance sheet TREASURY MANAGEMENT **financial statement compared with one of different date** one of two or more financial statements prepared on different dates that lend themselves to a comparative analysis of the financial condition of an organization

comparative credit analysis RISK **assessment of financial risk** an analysis of the risk associated with lending to different companies

compensating balance BANKING **1. money required in bank account** the amount of money a bank requires a customer to maintain in a non-interest-bearing account, in exchange for which the bank provides free services **2. money required in bank account allowing credit** the amount of money a bank requires a customer to maintain in an account in return for holding credit available, thereby increasing the true rate of interest on the loan

compensating errors ACCOUNTING **mistakes after which accounts still balance** two or more errors that are set against each other so that the accounts still balance

compensation FINANCE **1. payment for work** pay given to somebody in recompense for work performed **2. money paid to unfairly dismissed employee** in the United Kingdom, money paid by an employer on the order of an employment tribunal to an employee who has been unfairly dismissed

compensation fund STOCKHOLDING & INVESTMENTS **fund compensating investors when stock exchange members default** a fund operated by a stock exchange to compensate investors for losses incurred when members of the stock exchange default (lose more on their trading positions than they hold in capital)

compensatory financing FINANCE **IMF financial assistance** financing from the *International Monetary Fund* to help a country in economic difficulty

competition ECONOMICS, BUSINESS **struggle between firms to win business** rivalry between companies to achieve greater *market share*. Competition between companies for customers will lead to product innovation and improvement and, ultimately, lower prices. The opposite of market competition is either a *monopoly* or a *controlled economy*, where production is governed by quotas. A company that is leading the market is said to have achieved *competitive advantage*.

competitive advantage ECONOMICS, BUSINESS **benefit of being more competitive** a factor giving an advantage to a nation, company, group, or individual in competitive terms

competitive bid STOCKHOLDING & INVESTMENTS **selling new securities at competing prices or terms** a method of auctioning new securities whereby various underwriters offer the stock at competing prices or terms

competitive devaluation CURRENCY & EXCHANGE **currency devaluation to increase competitiveness** the devaluation of a currency to make a country's goods more competitive on the international markets

competitive forces ECONOMICS, BUSINESS **external factors forcing organization to become more competitive** the external business and economic factors that compel an organization to improve its competitiveness

competitiveness index ECONOMICS, BUSINESS **ranking of countries in order of competitive advantage** an international ranking of states which uses economic and other information to list countries in order of their competitive performance. A competitiveness index can show which countries have overall or industrysector *competitive advantage*.

compliance department 1. STOCKHOLDING & INVESTMENTS, REGULATION & COMPLIANCE **department in stockbroking firm**

enforcing stock exchange rules a department in a stockbroking firm that makes sure that the stock exchange rules are followed and that confidentiality is maintained in cases when the same firm represents rival clients **2.** REGULATION & COMPLIANCE **department in firm enforcing business regulations** a department that ensures that the company it is part of is adhering to any relevant laws and regulations relating to its business

compliance documentation STOCKHOLDING & INVESTMENTS, REGULATION & COMPLIANCE **documents required for stock issues** documents that a stock-issuing company publishes in line with regulations on stock issues

component percentage FINANCE **proportion of firm's value in capital** the proportion of a company's value represented by debt, stock, assets, and other items. *See also capitalization ratio*

compound FINANCE **1. pay part of debt** in the United Kingdom, to agree with creditors to settle a debt by paying part of what is owed **2. calculate compound interest** to calculate compound interest, based on the initial sum plus any interest that has accrued

compound annual return *or*compounded annual return STOCKHOLDING & INVESTMENTS **return on investment including reinvestment returns** the annual return on an investment after allowing for the return on reinvested intermediate *cash flows*

compounding FINANCE **1. calculating compound interest** the calculation of *compound interest*, based on the initial sum plus any interest that has accrued **2. using compound interest** the making of a transaction involving the payment or receipt of *compound interest*

compound interest FINANCE **interest calculated after inclusion of accrued interest** interest calculated on the sum of the original borrowed amount and the accrued interest. *See also simple interest*

compound option STOCKHOLDING & INVESTMENTS, RISK **option with underlying asset another option** an option that has a second option as the underlying asset. If the first option is exercised, the second option acts like an ordinary option.

compound rate FINANCE **rate using compound interest** the interest rate of a loan based on its *principal*, the amount remaining to be paid, or any interest payments already received

comprehensive auditing ACCOUNTING = *value for money audit*

comprehensive income FINANCE **firm's income reflecting any changes in owner equity** a company's total income for a given accounting period, including all gains and losses, not only those included in a normal income statement but also any that reflect a change in the value of an owner's interest in the business. In the United States, comprehensive income must be declared, whereas in the United Kingdom it appears in the statement of total recognized gains and losses.

comptroller ACCOUNTING **organization's senior accountant** an accountant who is responsible for maintaining an organization's accounts

Comptroller of the Currency BANKING **US official responsible for federal banks** an official of the government responsible for the regulation of banks that are members of the Federal Reserve

compulsory acquisition STOCKHOLDING & INVESTMENTS **purchasing last 10% of stocks at original price** in the United Kingdom, the purchase by a bidder of the last 10% of stocks in an issue by right, at the offer price

computational error ACCOUNTING **calculation mistake** a mistake that was made in doing a calculation

computer model STOCKHOLDING & INVESTMENTS **training using Internet, intranet, or standalone computer** a system for calculating investment opportunities, used by fund managers to see the right moment to buy or sell

concealment of assets FRAUD **hiding of assets from creditors** the dishonest act of hiding assets so that creditors do not know they exist

concentration risk RISK **risk related to lack of variety in lending** the risk of loss to a financial institution as a result of having too many outstanding loans concentrated in a particular instrument, with a particular type of borrower, or in a particular country

concentration services BANKING **moving money into single account** the placing of money from various accounts into a single account

concepts ACCOUNTING **principles of accounting** principles and abstract ideas underpinning the preparation of accounting information. *See also* ***fundamental accounting concepts***

concert party MERGERS & ACQUISITIONS **secret plan to acquire company** an arrangement by which several people or companies work together in secret, usually to acquire another company through a takeover bid

concession 1. FINANCE **price reduction for selected group** a reduction in price for a specific group of people, not for everyone **2.** BUSINESS **right to operate in another's premises** the right of a retail outlet to operate within the premises of another establishment **3.** GENERAL MANAGEMENT **agreement to ignore product's nonconformity to specification** an agreement to ignore the failure of a product or service to conform to its specification, with a possible resultant deterioration in the quality of the product or service **4.** GENERAL MANAGEMENT **compromise** a compromise in opinion or action by a party to a dispute

Confederation of Asian and Pacific Accountants ACCOUNTING **Asia-Pacific organization for accountants** an umbrella organization for a number of accounting associations. *Abbr* **CAPA**

confidence indicator ECONOMICS, MARKETS **number that shows how economic market will perform** a number that gives an indication of how well a market or an economy will fare

confirmation STOCKHOLDING & INVESTMENTS, OPERATIONS & PRODUCTION **document confirming transaction or agreement** a written acknowledgment of a transaction or agreement, for example, from a broker confirming and detailing a securities transaction

conglomerate diversification MERGERS & ACQUISITIONS **starting different types of subsidiaries** the ***diversification*** of a ***conglomerate company*** through the setting-up of ***subsidiary companies*** with activities in various areas

conglomerate merger MERGERS & ACQUISITIONS **merger of companies in unrelated industries** a merger of organizations that belong to different types of industry

consideration FINANCE **payment for service** a sum of money paid in return for a service

consignment stock STOCKHOLDING & INVESTMENTS **stock held by dealer for somebody** stock held by one party (the "dealer") but legally owned by another (the "manufacturer") on terms that give the dealer the right to sell the stock in the normal course of its business, or, at its option, to return it unsold to the legal owner

consistency ACCOUNTING **using same accounting rules every year** the concept that a company should apply the same rules and standards to its accounting procedures for similar items and from one year to the next. In the United Kingdom, deviation from consistency must be noted in the company's ***annual report***.

consolidate ACCOUNTING **combine accounts of holding company and its subsidiaries** to combine the accounts of several subsidiary companies as well as their ***holding company*** in a single financial statement

consolidated accounts ACCOUNTING = ***consolidated financial statement***

consolidated balance sheet ACCOUNTING **outline of firm's finances** a balance sheet containing the most significant details of a company's finances, including those of subsidiaries

consolidated debt FINANCE **debt incorporating smaller debts** a single large debt into which smaller ones have been subsumed

consolidated financial statement ACCOUNTING **outline of finances of parent company and subsidiaries** a listing of the most significant details of the finances of a company and of all its subsidiaries. *Also called* ***consolidated accounts***

consolidated loan FINANCE **large loan for paying off smaller loans** a large loan, the proceeds of which are used to eliminate smaller ones

consolidated stock STOCKHOLDING & INVESTMENTS *see* ***consols***

consolidation 1. MERGERS & ACQUISITIONS **joining several firms together** the uniting of two or more businesses into one company **2.** STOCKHOLDING & INVESTMENTS **creating fewer but costlier shares** the combination of a specific number of lower-priced shares into one higher-priced one

a–z

Dictionary

consolidation accounting ACCOUNTING **combining financial statements for parent firm and subsidiaries** the process of adjusting and combining financial information from the individual financial statements of a parent undertaking and its subsidiary undertakings to prepare consolidated financial statements that present financial information for the group as a single economic entity

consols STOCKHOLDING & INVESTMENTS **UK government bonds with no maturity date** in the United Kingdom, government bonds that pay interest but do not have a maturity date *Full form* ***consolidated stock***

consumer ECONOMICS **somebody using product or service** somebody who uses a product or service. A consumer may not be the purchaser of a product or service and should be distinguished from a customer, who is the person or organization that purchased the product or service.

consumer confidence ECONOMICS **how people feel about economic future** a measure of how people feel about the future of the economy and their own financial situation, obtained through polling

consumer credit FINANCE **credit provided for purchase of goods** credit given by stores, banks, and other financial institutions to consumers so that they can buy goods

Consumer Credit Act, 1974 FINANCE **UK legislation regulating provision of loans** in the United Kingdom, an Act of Parliament that licenses lenders and requires them to state clearly the full terms of loans that they make, including the APR

consumer price index ECONOMICS **benchmark of basic retail prices** an index of the prices of goods and services purchased by consumers, used to measure the cost of living or the rate of inflation in an economy. *Abbr* **CPI**

consumption ECONOMICS **amount of products and services used** the quantity of resources used by consumers to satisfy their current needs and wants, measured by the sum of the current expenditure of the government and individual consumers

contagion ECONOMICS **spreading effect of downturn across economies** a situation in which a weakening economy in one country causes economies in other countries to weaken

contested takeover bid MERGERS & ACQUISITIONS **takeover bid resisted by board of target firm** a takeover bid where the board of the target company does not recommend it to the stockholders and tries to fight it. *Also called* ***hostile bid***

contingency fund ACCOUNTING **money held for unplanned expenditure** money set aside from normal expenditure in case it is needed for unplanned expenses

contingent deferred sales charge STOCKHOLDING & INVESTMENTS **fee payable on redemption** a redemption fee, or ***back-end loading***, payable on a share in a mutual fund only if the share is redeemed. It declines every year until it disappears, usually after six years. *Abbr* **CDSC**. *See also* ***B share***

contingent liability ACCOUNTING **potential liability provided for in company's accounts** a liability that may or may not occur, but for which provision is made in a company's accounts, as opposed to "provisions," for which money is set aside for an anticipated expenditure

continuous budget TREASURY MANAGEMENT = ***rolling budget***

continuous compounding ACCOUNTING **continuous calculation and addition of interest** a system in which interest is continuously calculated and added to the initial sum plus any interest that has already accrued on a debt

continuous disclosure STOCKHOLDING & INVESTMENTS **in Canada, providing full information about public firm** in Canada, the practice of ensuring that complete, timely, accurate, and balanced information about a public company is made available to shareholders

continuous inventory *or* continuous stocktaking ACCOUNTING **comparing actual inventory to accounting records throughout year** regular and consistent stocktaking throughout the fiscal year in order to ensure that the physical reality of the stock situation at any given time tallies with the accounting records. Any discrepancies will highlight errors or losses of stock and the accounts are adjusted to reflect this. Continuous inventory may preclude the need for an annual inventory.

contra account ACCOUNTING **account offsetting another account** an account that offsets another account, for example, when a company's supplier is not only a creditor in that company's books but also a debtor because it has purchased goods on credit

contract costing ACCOUNTING **attributing costs to individual contracts** a form of ***specific order costing*** in which costs are attributed to individual contracts

contract for difference 1. STOCKHOLDING & INVESTMENTS **swapping of fixed-price assets for floating-price assets** an exchange of a fixed-price asset for one that has a price that varies **2.** CURRENCY & EXCHANGE **currency exchange contract** a forward exchange rate contract for currency. *Abbr* **CFD**

contractual savings STOCKHOLDING & INVESTMENTS **money saved regularly in long-term investments** savings in the form of regular payments into long-term investments such as pension plans

contra entry ACCOUNTING **account entry offsetting earlier entry** an entry made in the opposite side of an account to offset an earlier entry, for example, a debit against a credit

contrarian STOCKHOLDING & INVESTMENTS **investing against market trends** used to describe an investor who purchases securities in opposition to the current market trend, buying when most others are selling and vice versa

contrarian research STOCKHOLDING & INVESTMENTS **investigation of purchases against market trends** research on market trends resulting in advice to potential buyers to purchase stocks against the current trend

contrarian stockpicking STOCKHOLDING & INVESTMENTS **choosing stocks against market trends** the practice of purchasing stocks against the current market trend

contributed surplus FINANCE **money from sources other than earnings** the part of company profits that comes from sources other than earnings, for example, from selling stock above its nominal value

contribution 1. FINANCE, PENSIONS **money paid into fund** an amount of money placed in a fund of any kind, for example, money paid regularly into a pension **2.** FINANCE **amount extra unit gains or loses** the amount of money gained or lost from selling an additional unit of a product

contribution center FINANCE **profitable section of business** a *profit center* in which marginal or direct costs are equal to or less than revenue

contribution margin FINANCE **profit from individual product** the amount of money that an individual product or service contributes to net profit

contribution of capital FINANCE **money paid as additional capital** money paid to a company as additional capital

control CORPORATE GOVERNANCE **power to run organization** the authority to direct an organization's operations and activities

control environment CORPORATE GOVERNANCE **organization's management style** the corporate culture of the directors and senior management of an organization

controlled disbursement FINANCE **payment once daily** the practice of presenting checks for payment only once each day

controlled economy ECONOMICS **economy with production quotas** an economy in which production is governed by quotas. Controlled economies and *monopolies* are the opposite of market competition. *See also* *competition*

controller ACCOUNTING **organization's senior accountant** an accountant who is responsible for maintaining an organization's accounts

control procedures CORPORATE GOVERNANCE **rules for running organization** the policies and procedures in addition to the *control environment* which are established to achieve an organization's specific objectives. They include procedures designed to prevent or to detect and correct errors.

control risk RISK **likelihood of firm's control system allowing errors** the part of an *audit risk* that relates to a client's internal control system

control security STOCKHOLDING & INVESTMENTS **security held by somebody with management power** a security held by a person who has an affiliation with the issuing company and the power to direct its management and policies, and whose resale must meet US Securities and Exchange Commission conditions

convergence 1. ECONOMICS **movement toward similarity in countries' economies** a situation in which the economic factors in two countries become more alike, for example, when basic interest rates or budget deficits become more similar

2. MARKETS **coming together of futures and spot prices** a situation in which the price of a commodity on the futures market moves toward the *spot price* as settlement date approaches

conversion costs FINANCE **expense of changing raw materials into products** the cost of changing raw materials into finished or semi-finished products. Conversion costs include wages, other direct production costs, and the production overhead.

conversion discount *or* conversion premium STOCKHOLDING & INVESTMENTS **price difference between convertible and common stock** the difference between the price of convertible stock and the common stock into which it is to be converted

conversion issue STOCKHOLDING & INVESTMENTS **offer of new bonds as older bonds expire** the issue of new bonds, timed to coincide with the date of maturity of older bonds, with the intention of persuading investors to reinvest

conversion of funds FRAUD **improper use of somebody else's money** the act of using money that does not belong to you for a purpose for which it is not supposed to be used

conversion period STOCKHOLDING & INVESTMENTS **period for converting loan stock into common stock** a time during which convertible loan stock may be changed into common stock

conversion price 1. CURRENCY & EXCHANGE **exchange rate for currency** the price at which a currency is changed into a foreign currency. *Also called* **conversion rate** (sense 2) **2.** STOCKHOLDING & INVESTMENTS **price offered for converting preferred stock** the price at which preferred stock is converted into common stock

conversion rate 1. STOCKHOLDING & INVESTMENTS = **conversion price** (sense 2) **2.** CURRENCY & EXCHANGE = **conversion price** (sense 1) **3.** MARKETING **how many people buy after consideration** the percentage of inquiries by potential customers or sales calls by sales staff that results in actual sales

conversion ratio 1. STOCKHOLDING & INVESTMENTS **relative value of two convertible investment products** an expression of the quantity of one security that can be obtained for another, for example, shares for a *convertible bond*.

The conversion ratio may be established when the convertible is issued. If that is the case, the ratio will appear in the indenture, the binding agreement that details the convertible's terms.

If the conversion ratio is not set, it can be calculated quickly by dividing the nominal value of the convertible security (typically $1,000) by its conversion price.

$$\frac{\$1,000}{\$40 \text{ per share}} = 25$$

In this example, the conversion ratio is 25:1, which means that every bond held with a $1,000 nominal value can be exchanged for 25 shares of common stock.

Knowing the conversion ratio enables an investor to decide whether convertibles (or a group of them) are more valuable than the shares of common stock they represent. If the stock is currently trading at 30, the conversion value is $750, or $250

a–z

Dictionary

less than the nominal value of the convertible. It would therefore be unwise to convert.

A convertible's indenture can sometimes contain a provision stating that the conversion ratio will change over the years. **2.** MERGERS & ACQUISITIONS **number of shares traded for others during merger** the number of shares of one common stock to be issued for each outstanding ordinary share of a different type when a merger takes place

conversion value STOCKHOLDING & INVESTMENTS **value of investment if changed for another type** the value that a security would have if converted into another type of security

convertibility CURRENCY & EXCHANGE **ease of currency exchange** the ability of one currency to be easily exchanged for another currency

convertible bond STOCKHOLDING & INVESTMENTS **bond that can be traded for another investment** a bond that the owner can convert into another asset, especially common stock

convertible currency CURRENCY & EXCHANGE **easily exchanged currency** a currency that can easily be exchanged for another

convertible debenture STOCKHOLDING & INVESTMENTS **debenture exchangeable for stock** a debenture or *loan stock* that can be exchanged for stock at a later date

convertible loan stock STOCKHOLDING & INVESTMENTS **in UK, money loaned and redeemable as stock** in the United Kingdom, money lent to a company which can be converted into shares at a later date

convertible preference shares UK STOCKHOLDING & INVESTMENTS = *convertible preferred stock*

convertible preferred stock US STOCKHOLDING & INVESTMENTS **stock that can be traded for another investment** stocks that give the holder the right to exchange them at a fixed price for another security, usually common stock.

Preferred stocks and other convertible securities offer investors a hedge: fixed-interest income without sacrificing the chance to participate in a company's capital appreciation.

When a company does well, investors can convert their holdings into common stock that is more valuable. When a company is less successful, they can still receive interest and principal payments, and also recover their investment and preserve their capital if a more favorable investment appears.

Conversion ratios and prices are important facts to know about preferred stocks. This information is found on the indenture statement that accompanies all issues. Occasionally the indenture will state that the conversion ratio will change over time. For example, the conversion price might be $50 for the first five years, $55 for the next five years, and so forth. Stock splits can affect conversion considerations.

In theory, convertible preferred stocks (and convertible exchangeable preferred stocks) are usually perpetual. However, issuers tend to force conversion or induce voluntary conversion for convertible preferred stocks within ten years. Steadily increasing common stock dividends is one inducement tactic used. As a result, the conversion feature for preferred stocks often resembles that of debt securities. Call

protection for the investor is usually about three years, and a 30 to 60-day call notice is typical.

About 50% of convertible equity issues also have a "soft call provision." If the common stock price reaches a specified ratio, the issuer is permitted to force conversion before the end of the normal protection period. *UK term* **convertible preference shares**

convertibles STOCKHOLDING & INVESTMENTS **securities convertible to common stock** corporate bonds or shares of preferred stock that can be converted into common stock at a set price on set dates

convertible security STOCKHOLDING & INVESTMENTS **investment product that can be converted to another** a bond, warrant, or share of preferred stock that can be converted into another type of security, especially common stock

convexity ECONOMICS, FINANCE **relationship of values** the convex shape of a curve. The theory is that if points in a set are connected and the line between any two points is included in the set, then the set is convex. In economics, this corresponds to diminishing *marginal utility*. In finance it can represent a convex curve in the price yield relationship of a bond or any non-linear price function, for example, that of an option.

corporate action STOCKHOLDING & INVESTMENTS **firm's action that affects its shares** a measure that a company takes that has an effect on the number of shares outstanding or the rights that apply to shares

corporate bond STOCKHOLDING & INVESTMENTS **bond issued by firm** a long-term bond with fixed interest issued by a corporation

corporate finance FINANCE **financial affairs of businesses** the financial affairs of companies and institutions

corporate fraud FRAUD **dishonest behavior at company level** a type of fraud committed by large organizations rather than individuals, for example, auditing irregularities. Since the collapse of Enron and WorldCom in 2001 and 2002, respectively, auditing practice around the world, but especially in the United States, has come under much scrutiny. Both companies had overstated their profits, but the auditors, Arthur Andersen, had approved accounts in each case.

corporate governance CORPORATE GOVERNANCE **system for running firm** the system by which companies are directed and controlled. Boards of directors are responsible for the governance of their companies. The stockholders' role in governance is to appoint the directors and the auditors and to satisfy themselves that an appropriate governance structure is in place. The responsibilities of the board include setting the company's strategic goals, providing the leadership to put them into effect, supervising the management of the business, and reporting to the stockholders on their stewardship. The board's actions are subject to laws, regulations, and the wishes of the stockholders in the general meeting.

corporate identity CORPORATE GOVERNANCE **firm's distinctive features as expressed to outsiders** the distinctive characteristics or personality of an organization, including corporate culture, values, and philosophy as perceived by those within the organization and presented to those outside. Corporate identity is expressed through the name, symbols, and logos used by the organization, and the design of communication materials, and is a factor influencing the *corporate image* of an organization. The creation of a strong corporate identity also involves consistency in the organization's actions, behavior, products, and brands, and often reflects the *mission statement* of an organization. A positive corporate identity can promote a sense of purpose and belonging within the organization and encourage employee commitment and involvement.

corporate image CORPORATE GOVERNANCE **public's ideas about what firm is like** the perceptions and impressions of an organization by the public as a result of interaction with the organization and the way the organization presents itself. Organizations have traditionally focused on the design of communication and advertising materials, using logos, symbols, text, and color to create a favorable impression on target groups, but a variety of additional activities contribute to a positive corporate image. These include public relations programs such as community involvement, sponsorship, and environmental projects, participation in quality improvement schemes, and good practice in industrial relations.

corporate planning CORPORATE GOVERNANCE **process of making plans to achieve firm's objectives** the process of drawing up detailed action plans to achieve an organization's goals and objectives, taking into account the resources of the organization and the environment within which it operates. Corporate planning represents a formal, structured approach to achieving objectives and to implementing the corporate strategy of an organization. It has traditionally been seen as the responsibility of senior management. The use of the term became predominant during the 1960s but has now been largely superseded by the concept of *strategic management*.

corporate raider MERGERS & ACQUISITIONS **somebody buying stake prior to hostile takeover** a person or company that buys a stake in another company with a view to making a *hostile takeover* bid

corporate resolution CORPORATE GOVERNANCE **document saying who can manage firm's money** a document signed by the officers of a corporation naming those persons who can sign checks, withdraw cash, and have access to the corporation's bank account

correction FINANCE **adjustment in valuation of something** a change in the valuation of something that is thought to be overvalued or undervalued which results in its being more realistically valued

correspondent bank BANKING **bank operating as foreign bank's agent** a bank that acts as an agent for a foreign bank

cost FINANCE **1. money paid for product** the amount of money that is paid to secure a good or service. Cost is the amount paid from the purchaser's standpoint, whereas the price is the amount paid from the vendor's standpoint. **2. calculate cost of**

something to ascertain what must be paid to acquire a specific thing or engage in a specific activity

cost account ACCOUNTING **accounting record of section of business** a record of revenue and/or expenditure of a cost center or cost unit

cost accountant ACCOUNTING **accountant advising on business costs** an accountant who gives managers information about their business costs

cost accounting ACCOUNTING **preparation of accounts detailing business costs** the process of preparing special accounts of manufacturing and sales costs

cost allocation ACCOUNTING **assignment of fixed expenses to cost centers** the way in which overhead expenses are assigned to different cost centers

cost audit ACCOUNTING **check on cost records and accounts** the verification of cost records and accounts, and a check on adherence to prescribed *cost accounting* procedures and their continuing relevance

cost basis ACCOUNTING **price paid including purchase costs** the price paid for an asset plus any expenses such as commissions associated with it at the time of purchase

cost–benefit analysis ACCOUNTING **comparison of activity's costs against results** a comparison between the cost of the resources used, plus any other costs imposed by an activity, for example, pollution or environmental damage, and the value of the financial and non-financial benefits derived, to establish whether there is a positive outcome. *Also called benefit–cost ratio*

cost center ACCOUNTING **section of business that costs firm money** a department, function, section, or individual whose cost, overall or in part, is an accepted overhead of a business in return for services provided to other parts of the organization. A cost center is usually an *indirect cost* of an organization's products or services.

cost driver ACCOUNTING **something that affects cost of activity** a factor that determines the cost of an activity. Cost drivers are analyzed as part of *activity based costing* and can be used in *continuous improvement* programs. They are usually assessed together as multiple drivers rather than singly. There are two main types of cost driver: the first is a *resource driver*, which refers to the contribution of the quantity of resources used to the cost of an activity; the second is an *activity driver*, which refers to the costs incurred by the activities required to complete a specific task or project.

cost-effectiveness analysis TREASURY MANAGEMENT **measurement of how much positive results cost** a method for measuring the benefits and effectiveness of a particular item of expenditure. Cost-effectiveness analysis requires an examination of expenditure to determine whether the money spent could have been used more effectively or whether the resulting benefits could have been attained through less financial outlay.

a–z

Dictionary

cost factor ACCOUNTING **activity or item incurring business cost** an activity or item of material, equipment, or personnel that incurs a cost

cost function ECONOMICS **ratio of total cost to quantity produced** a mathematical function relating a firm's or an industry's total cost to its output and factor costs

cost inflation ECONOMICS = *cost-push inflation*

cost of capital TREASURY MANAGEMENT **interest paid on operating capital** interest paid on the capital used in operating a business

cost of internal failure TREASURY MANAGEMENT **cost of correcting quality of products before sale** the costs arising from inadequate quality which are identified before the transfer of ownership from supplier to purchaser. *See also* ***cost of external failure***

cost of living FINANCE **money spent on housing, food, and basics** the average amount spent by somebody on accommodations, food, and other basic necessities. In the United States, a broad definition might sometimes include education and healthcare. Salaries are usually increased annually to cover rises in the cost of living.

cost-of-living adjustment *US* FINANCE, HR & PERSONNEL = *cost-of-living increase*

cost-of-living allowance *UK* FINANCE, HR & PERSONNEL = *cost-of-living increase*

cost-of-living increase FINANCE, HR & PERSONNEL **extra pay to cover price rises** a small increase in salaries made to account for rises in the ***cost of living***

cost-of-living index FINANCE, HR & PERSONNEL **information on changes in prices over time** an index that shows changes in the cost of living by comparing current prices for a variety of goods with the prices paid for them in previous years

cost-push inflation ECONOMICS **price increases caused by rise in production costs** inflation in which price rises result from increased production costs or similar factors rather than from customer demand

costs ACCOUNTING **amounts of money paid out for something** amounts of money that are paid out for something, especially on a regular basis

counterbid FINANCE **1. higher bid competing with another bid** a higher bid made in reply to a previous bid by another bidder **2. make counterbid** to make a higher bid in reply to a previous bid

countercyclical ECONOMICS **falling when other factor rises** tending to increase as another factor decreases and decreasing as it increases. *See also* ***procyclical***

countercyclical stock STOCKHOLDING & INVESTMENTS **stock price moving against economic trend** a stock that tends to rise as the economy weakens and fall as it strengthens

counterfeit FRAUD **illegally produce imitation goods or money** to produce forged or imitation goods or money intended to

deceive or defraud. Counterfeited goods of inferior quality are often sold at substantially lower prices than genuine products and may bear the brand or trade name of the company. Counterfeiting violates trademark and intellectual property rights and may damage the reputation of producers of authentic goods. National and international legislation provides some recourse to companies against counterfeiters, but strategies such as consumer warnings and labeling methods are also used to minimize the impact of counterfeiting. Efforts to eliminate counterfeiting are coordinated by the International Anti-Counterfeiting Coalition. **counterfeited relating to illegally produced imitations** used to describe goods or money illegally produced but appearing authentic

counterfoil BANKING **small paper record of transaction** a slip of paper kept after writing a check, an invoice, or a receipt, as a record of the deal that has taken place

counterparty risk RISK **risk associated with other party to contract** the possibility that the person or persons with whom a contract exists will fail to fulfill the terms of their side of the contract

countersign FINANCE **sign document after other signatory** to sign a document that has already been signed by somebody else

coupon STOCKHOLDING & INVESTMENTS **1. paper requesting bond payment** a piece of paper attached to a government bond certificate which a bondholder presents to request payment **2. interest rate of bond** the rate of interest paid on a bond issued at a fixed rate. *Also called* ***coupon rate*** **3. interest payment on bond** an interest payment made to a bondholder, originally on presentation of a dated coupon to the company or an agent of the issuer **clip coupons** FINANCE to collect periodic interest on a bond

coupon rate STOCKHOLDING & INVESTMENTS = *coupon* (sense 2)

coupon security STOCKHOLDING & INVESTMENTS **government security carrying coupon and paying interest** a government security that carries a coupon and pays interest, as opposed to a ***zero-coupon security***, that pays no interest but is sold at a discount from its face value. *See also* ***zero-coupon security***

covenant FINANCE **legal financial agreement** a financial agreement conditional on future events, for example, changes in the capital structure and rating of a firm, or fundamental changes in business strategy such as to divest of a major asset or to acquire another company. Covenants are frequently included in bond offerings or bank loan/syndication terms. In the United Kingdom, when payments are made by an individual under covenant to a charity, the charity can reclaim the tax paid by the donor.

covered bond STOCKHOLDING & INVESTMENTS **bond with loan as security** a bond that has mortgage or other loans given as security in case of default

covered option STOCKHOLDING & INVESTMENTS **option backed by actual stock** an ***option*** whose owner holds the stock for the option. A covered option can be either a **call option** or a **put option**.

covered warrant STOCKHOLDING & INVESTMENTS **futures contract** a type of **futures contract** issued by a financial institution allowing the holder to buy or sell a quantity of its **financial instruments**

covert human intelligence source FRAUD **somebody providing information about illegal activity** in the United Kingdom, a person who supplies information about somebody being investigated, for example, for fraud, without the knowledge of the person being investigated. *Abbr* **CHIS**

CP *abbr* FINANCE commercial paper

CPA *abbr* ACCOUNTING certified public accountant

CPI *abbr* ECONOMICS consumer price index

CPI inflation ECONOMICS **inflation rate of economy using consumer price index** the rate of **inflation** in an economy calculated using data from a **consumer price index**

CPIX *ANZ* ECONOMICS **consumer price index** the **consumer price index** excluding interest costs, on the basis that these are a direct outcome of monetary policy

crash 1. MARKETS **very large drop in stock price** a precipitous drop in value, especially of the stocks traded in a market **2.** ECONOMICS **large and sudden economic decline** a sudden and catastrophic downturn in an economy. While there were several in the 20th century, the crash in the United States in 1929 is one of the most famous. However, the events of 2008 have had even more severe global consequences.

crawling peg CURRENCY & EXCHANGE **incremental control on exchange rates** a method of controlling exchange rates, allowing them to move up or down slowly

CRD *abbr* STOCKHOLDING & INVESTMENTS Central Registration Depository

creative accounting FRAUD **accounting methods used to conceal firm's true state** the use of accounting methods to hide aspects of a company's financial dealings in order to make the company appear more or less successful than it is in reality (slang). *See also* **corporate fraud**

creative destruction MERGERS & ACQUISITIONS **process of new firms and products replacing old** a way of describing the endless cycle of innovation, which results in established goods, services, or organizations being replaced by new models. The term was first mentioned by Joseph Schumpeter in *Capitalism, Socialism and Democracy* (1942), but used heavily during the dot-com boom of the late 1990s and early 2000s.

credit FINANCE **1. positive amount of assets after liabilities are deducted** the amount of money left over when a person or organization has more **assets** than **liabilities**, and those liabilities are subtracted from the total of the assets **2. lender's belief that borrower will repay loan** the trust that a lender has in a borrower's ability to repay a loan, or a loan itself **3. arrangement to pay later for product bought now** a financial

arrangement between the vendor and the purchaser of a good or service by which the purchaser may buy what he or she requires, but pay for it at a later date **post a credit** ACCOUNTING in bookkeeping, to enter a credit item in a ledger

credit account FINANCE = **charge account**

credit availability FINANCE **ease of borrowing** the ease with which money can be borrowed at a given time

credit balance FINANCE **sum owed on credit account** the amount of money that a customer owes on a **charge account**

credit bureau FINANCE **US firm evaluating people's ability to repay loans** a company that assesses the creditworthiness of people for businesses or banks. *See also* **mercantile agency**

credit capacity FINANCE **total amount somebody can borrow and repay** the amount of money that a person or organization can borrow and be expected to repay

credit card BANKING **card from bank used to pay for things** a card issued by a bank or financial institution and accepted by a merchant in payment for a transaction for which the cardholder must subsequently reimburse the issuer. *See also* **charge card**

credit ceiling FINANCE = **credit limit**

credit column ACCOUNTING **accounting column recording money received** the right-hand column in accounts showing money received

credit committee RISK **group assessing creditworthiness** a committee that evaluates a potential borrower's credit status and ability to repay loans

credit company FINANCE **firm that lends money** a company that extends credit to people. It may be an independent company or a subsidiary of a parent company such as an automobile manufacturer whose products are being bought.

credit control RISK **monitoring of customers' credit management** a system of checks designed to ensure that customers pay on time and do not owe more than their credit limit

credit controller FINANCE **employee who manages payment of overdue invoices** a member of staff whose job is to expedite the payment of overdue invoices

credit cooperative FINANCE **group borrowing together** an organization of people who join together to gain advantage in borrowing

credit creation FINANCE **ability of banks to lend more money** the collective ability of finance companies, banks, and other lenders of money to make money available to borrowers. While a central bank can create money, it cannot create credit.

credit crunch FINANCE **inability or reluctance of banks to lend money** the collective inability or unwillingness of finance companies, banks, and other lenders to make money available to borrowers (informal). *Also called* **credit squeeze**, **liquidity squeeze**

credit default swap STOCKHOLDING & INVESTMENTS, RISK assumption of credit risk in return for payments a *derivative instrument* similar in structure to an insurance policy, in which the buyer of the instrument agrees to make payments to the seller in return for a guarantee that the seller will assume the credit risk of a third party. *Abbr* **CDS**

credit derivative STOCKHOLDING & INVESTMENTS, RISK **contract transferring lender's risk** a *financial instrument* or *derivative* by which the lender's risk is devolved to a third party and separately traded

credit entity FINANCE **person borrowing or lending** a borrower from a finance company, bank, or other lender of money, or the lender of the funds

credit entry ACCOUNTING **entry for income or value** an item in a financial statement recording money received or the value of an asset

credit exposure RISK **lender's risk that borrower will not repay** the risk to a lender that a borrower will default and not fulfill their contractual payment

credit facility BANKING **arrangement to supply credit** an arrangement with a bank or supplier that enables a person or organization to be given credit or borrow money when it is needed, for example, a *letter of credit*, *revolving credit* or a *term loan*. *Also called* **lending facility**

credit freeze FINANCE **period when government limits banks' lending** a period during which lending by banks is restricted by government

credit granter FINANCE **lender** a person or organization that lends money

credit history FINANCE **record of somebody's repayment of loans** a potential borrower's record of debt repayment. Individuals or organizations with a poor credit history may find it difficult to find lenders who are willing to give them a loan.

Credit Industry Fraud Avoidance System FRAUD **UK fraud prevention service** in the United Kingdom, a nonprofit membership organization established for the purpose of preventing financial crime. *Abbr* **CIFAS**

crediting rate STOCKHOLDING & INVESTMENTS **interest rate on insurance policy** the interest rate paid on an insurance policy which is an investment

credit limit FINANCE **total amount somebody is allowed to borrow** the highest amount that a lender will allow somebody to borrow, for example, on a credit card. *Also called* **credit ceiling**

credit line FINANCE = *line of credit*

credit-linked note RISK **fixed-income security with embedded credit default swap** a fixed-income security with an embedded *credit default swap* which is sold to investors willing to take the risk of default in return for a high yield on their investment

credit note CANADA UK FINANCE = *credit slip*

creditor FINANCE **somebody you owe money for goods or services** a person or an entity to whom money is owed as a consequence of the receipt of goods or services in advance of payment

creditor days FINANCE **number of days firm takes to pay creditors** the number of days on average that a company requires to pay its creditors.

To determine creditor days, divide the cumulative amount of unpaid suppliers' bills (also called trade creditors) by sales, then multiply by 365. If suppliers' bills total $800,000 and sales are $9,000,000, the calculation is:

$$\frac{800,000}{9,000,000} \times 365 = 32.44 \text{ days}$$

The company takes 32.44 days on average to pay its bills.

Creditor days is an indication of a company's creditworthiness in the eyes of its suppliers and creditors, since it shows how long they are willing to wait for payment. Within reason, the higher the number the better, because all companies want to conserve cash. At the same time, a company that is especially slow to pay its bills (100 or more days, for example) may be a company having trouble generating cash, or one trying to finance its operations with its suppliers' funds. *See also* **debtor days**

creditors' committee FINANCE **lenders' group seeking money from bankrupt borrower** a group that directs the efforts of creditors to receive partial repayment from a bankrupt person or organization. *Also called* **creditors' steering committee**

creditors' meeting FINANCE **meeting of bankrupt's creditors** a meeting of those to whom a bankrupt person or organization owes money

creditors' settlement FINANCE **agreement for partial repayment by bankrupt borrower** an agreement on partial repayment to those to whom a bankrupt person or organization owes money

creditors' steering committee FINANCE = *creditors' committee*

credit rating or **credit ranking** FINANCE **1. evaluation of creditworthiness** an assessment of a person's or an organization's ability to pay back money that they owe according to the terms on which it was borrowed, based on a broad assessment of financial health including previous loans and other outstanding financial obligations **2. process of evaluating creditworthiness** the process of assessing a person's or an organization's ability to pay back money that they owe according to the terms on which it was borrowed

credit rating agency US FINANCE **firm evaluating creditworthiness** a company that assesses a person's or an organization's ability to pay back money that they owe according to the terms on which it was borrowed, on behalf of businesses or banks. *UK term* **credit-reference agency**

credit rationing FINANCE, RISK **process of making it harder to borrow money** the process of making credit less easily available or subject to high interest rates

credit receipt *US* FINANCE = *credit slip*

credit-reference agency *UK* FINANCE = *credit rating agency*

credit references FINANCE **list of previous lenders when opening credit account** details of individuals, companies, or banks who have given credit to a person or company in the past, supplied as references when somebody is opening a credit account with a new supplier

credit report FINANCE **information concerning person's or organization's creditworthiness** information about the ability of a person or organization to pay back money that they owe, used by financial institutions in determining decisions relevant to granting credit

credit risk RISK **possibility that debtor will default** the possibility that a person or an organization will not be able to pay back money that they owe according to the terms on which it was borrowed

credit sale FINANCE **sale for which buyer can pay later** a sales transaction by which the buyer is allowed to take immediate possession of the purchased goods and pay for them at a later date

credit scoring FINANCE **calculation during credit rating** a calculation done in the process of assessing a person's or an organization's ability to pay back money that they owe according to the terms on which it was borrowed

credit side ACCOUNTING **part of financial statement with assets** the section of a financial statement that lists assets. In double-entry bookkeeping, the right-hand side of each account is designated as the credit side. *See also* **debit side**

credit slip *US* FINANCE **statement that store owes customer money** a receipt saying that a store owes a customer an amount of money for returned goods and entitling the person to goods of that value. *Also called* **credit receipt**. *UK term* **credit note**

credit spread RISK **difference between debt yield of firm and benchmark** the difference between the yield on the debt of a particular company and the yield on a risk-free asset such as a US *Treasury bond* having the same maturity

credit spread option STOCKHOLDING & INVESTMENTS, RISK **option contract based on firm's credit spread** an option contract on the **credit spread** of the debt of a particular company whose payoff is based on changes in the credit spread

credit spread swap STOCKHOLDING & INVESTMENTS, RISK **exchange of fixed for credit-spread payment** a *swap* in which one party makes a fixed payment to the other on the swap's settlement date and the second party pays the first an amount based on the actual credit spread

credit squeeze FINANCE = *credit crunch*

credit standing FINANCE **somebody's reputation for repaying debt** the reputation that somebody has with regard to meeting financial obligations

credit system FINANCE **means of making loans** a set of rules and organizations involved in making loans on a commercial basis

credit union BANKING **financial institution providing banking services to members** a cooperative financial organization that provides banking services, including loans, to its members at relatively low rates of interest

creditworthiness FINANCE **reliability in repaying debt** the extent to which a person or organization is financially reliable enough to borrow money or be given credit

creditworthy FINANCE **reliable in repaying debt** regarded as being reliable in terms of ability to pay back money owed according to the terms on which it was borrowed

creeping takeover MERGERS & ACQUISITIONS **takeover through gradual acquisition** a takeover of a company achieved by the gradual acquisition of small amounts of stock over an extended period of time (slang)

creeping tender offer MERGERS & ACQUISITIONS **gradual acquisition of firm's stock** an acquisition of many shares in a company by gradual purchase, especially to avoid US restrictions on tender offers

crony capitalism ECONOMICS **system in which well-connected people control wealth** a form of capitalism in which business contracts are awarded to the family and friends of the government in power rather than by open-market tender

crossborder services ACCOUNTING **accounting services for client in another country** accounting services provided by an accounting firm in one country on behalf of a client based in another country

cross currency swap CURRENCY & EXCHANGE = *currency swap* (sense 1)

crossed cheque *UK* BANKING **check that can only be deposited** a check with two lines across it showing that it can only be deposited at a bank and not exchanged for cash

cross holdings STOCKHOLDING & INVESTMENTS, MERGERS & ACQUISITIONS **reciprocal stockholdings designed to combat takeovers** a situation in which two companies own stock in each other in order to stop either from being taken over

cross rate CURRENCY & EXCHANGE **exchange rate of two currencies against third currency** the rate of exchange between two currencies expressed in terms of the rate of exchange between them and a third currency, for example, sterling and the peso in relation to the dollar. *Also called* **exchange cross rate**

crown jewels FINANCE **company's most valuable properties** an organization's most valuable *assets*, often the motivation behind *takeover bids*

cum FINANCE **with** the Latin word for "with." Its opposite is "ex-."

cum-all STOCKHOLDING & INVESTMENTS **including all normal benefits of stock ownership** including all of the entitlements that are attached to owning a share of stock. *See also* **ex-all**

cum coupon STOCKHOLDING & INVESTMENTS **with coupon attached or before payment of interest** with a coupon attached or before interest due on a security is paid

cum dividend *or* **cum div** STOCKHOLDING & INVESTMENTS **including unpaid dividend** including the next dividend still to be paid

cum rights STOCKHOLDING & INVESTMENTS **including rights** an indication that the buyer of the stock is entitled to participate in a forthcoming *rights issue*

cumulative interest FINANCE **total interest** the total interest added to capital originally invested

cumulative preference share *UK* STOCKHOLDING & INVESTMENTS = *cumulative preferred stock*

cumulative preferred stock *US* STOCKHOLDING & INVESTMENTS **preferred stock whose dividends accumulate if not paid** a type of *preferred stock* that will have the dividend paid at a later date even if the company is not able to pay a dividend in the current year. *UK term* **cumulative preference share**

cumulative voting CORPORATE GOVERNANCE **system of election of directors** a voting system that allows a stockholder one vote per share of stock owned multiplied by the number of directors to be elected. Stockholders may distribute these votes among the candidates in any way they choose.

currency CURRENCY & EXCHANGE **money of particular country** the system of money in general circulation in a particular country

currency backing CURRENCY & EXCHANGE **gold or securities supporting currency** gold, other valuable metal, or government securities, that support the strength of a country's currency

currency band CURRENCY & EXCHANGE **allowable range of variation in exchange rate** exchange rate levels between which a *currency* is allowed to move without full revaluation or devaluation

currency basket CURRENCY & EXCHANGE = *basket of currencies*

currency clause CURRENCY & EXCHANGE **clause fixing exchange rate for contract** a clause in a contract that avoids problems of payment caused by exchange rate changes by fixing in advance the exchange rate for the various transactions covered by the contract

currency future STOCKHOLDING & INVESTMENTS **option on currency** a contract for buying or selling currency at a particular exchange rate within a set period

currency hedging STOCKHOLDING & INVESTMENTS, RISK **reducing risk by diversifying currency holdings** a method of reducing *exchange rate risk* by diversifying currency holdings and adjusting them according to changes in exchange rates

currency mismatching CURRENCY & EXCHANGE **depositing low-interest loan in country with high-interest** the practice of borrowing money in the currency of a country where interest rates are low and depositing it in the currency of a country with higher interest rates. The potential profit from the interest rate margin may be offset by changes in the exchange rates, which increase the value of the loan in the company's balance sheet.

currency note CURRENCY & EXCHANGE **paper money** a piece of paper money, representing a promise to pay the bearer a specific sum on demand

currency reserves CURRENCY & EXCHANGE **government's reserves of foreign currency** foreign money held by a government to support its own currency and to pay its debts

currency risk CURRENCY & EXCHANGE, RISK **likelihood of adverse exchange rate** the possibility of a loss due to future changes in exchange rates

currency swap CURRENCY & EXCHANGE **1. agreement to use one currency for another** an arrangement between two parties to exchange an amount of one currency for another currency, later returning the original amounts. This is useful, for instance, where both parties hold a currency other than the one they need at a specific time. *Also called* **cross currency swap 2. selling and buying same amount of foreign currency** the selling or buying of a particular amount of a foreign currency for immediate delivery, accompanied by selling or buying the same amount of the same currency on the *futures market*

currency unit CURRENCY & EXCHANGE **coin or bill in specific monetary system** each of the notes and coins that are the medium of exchange in a country

current account BANKING **1. record of transactions between two parties** a record of transactions between two parties, for example, between a bank and its customer, or a branch and head office, or two trading nations. *Abbr* **c/a 2.** *UK* = *checking account*

current assets FINANCE **cash, or asset to be converted to cash** cash or other assets, such as stock and long-term investments, held for conversion into cash in the normal course of trading

current assets financing FINANCE **using current assets to back loan** the use of current assets such as cash, debtors, and stock as collateral for a loan

current cash balance STOCKHOLDING & INVESTMENTS **money that broker's client has available to invest** the amount, which excludes balances due soon for outstanding transactions, that a client has available for investment with a broker

current cost accounting ACCOUNTING **accounting based on current replacement cost of assets** a method of accounting that notes the cost of replacing assets at current prices, rather than valuing assets at their original cost. *Abbr* **CCA**. *See also* *historical cost accounting*

current earnings FINANCE **firm's most recent annual earnings** the annual earnings most recently reported by a company, which exclude interest and tax

current liabilities FINANCE **debt to be repaid within one year** liabilities which fall due for payment within one year. They include that part of any long-term loan due for repayment within one year.

current principal factor FINANCE part of original loan left to be paid the portion of the initial amount of a loan that remains to be paid

current ratio FINANCE ratio of current assets to current liabilities a ratio of *current assets* to *current liabilities*, used to measure a company's liquidity and its ability to meet its short-term debt obligations.

The current ratio formula is a simple one:

$$\frac{\text{Current assets}}{\text{Current liabilities}} = \text{Current ratio}$$

Current assets are the ones that a company can turn into cash within 12 months during the ordinary course of business. Current liabilities are bills due to be paid within the coming 12 months.

For example, if a company's current assets are $300,000 and its current liabilities are $200,000, its current ratio would be:

$$\frac{300,000}{200,000} = 1.5$$

As a rule of thumb, the 1.5 figure means that a company should be able to get hold of $1.50 for every $1.00 it owes.

The higher the ratio, the more liquid the company. Prospective lenders expect a positive current ratio, often of at least 1.5. However, too high a ratio is cause for alarm too, because it indicates declining receivables and/or inventory, which may mean declining liquidity. *Also called* **working capital ratio**

current stock value STOCKHOLDING & INVESTMENTS value of all stock held the value of all stock in an investor's set of holdings, including stock in transactions that have not yet been settled

current value FINANCE current assets minus current liabilities a ratio indicating the amount by which *current assets* exceed *current liabilities*

current yield STOCKHOLDING & INVESTMENTS interest on bond divided by market price the interest being paid on a bond divided by its current market price, expressed as a percentage. *Also called* **income yield**

cushion FINANCE firm's surplus money money left after a company has serviced its debts and therefore available to meet unexpected demands

cushion bond STOCKHOLDING & INVESTMENTS high-interest bond a bond that pays a high rate of interest and so depreciates less when interest rates rise but is at risk of being *called* if interest rates fall

custodial account BANKING bank account for child in the United States, a bank account opened, normally by a parent or guardian, in the name of a minor who is too young to control it

custodian BANKING manager of trust funds a legal guardian, whether a person or an institution, whose principal function is to maintain and grow the assets contained in a trust

customer capital FINANCE value of firm's customer relationships the value of an organization's relationships with its customers, which involves factors such as market share, customer retention rates, and profitability of customers

customer equity FINANCE value of firm's customer relationships the total asset value of the relationships that an organization has with its customers. The term was coined by Robert C. Blattberg and John Deighton in their article "Manage marketing by the customer equity test," *Harvard Business Review* 74:4 (Jul/Aug 1996), pp. 136–144. Customer equity is based on customer lifetime value, and an understanding of customer equity can be used to optimize the balance of investment in the acquisition and retention of customers. It is also known as customer capital and forms one component of the intellectual capital of an organization.

customer lifetime value FINANCE expected profit from customer over time the *net present value* of the profit an organization expects to realize from a customer for the duration of their relationship. Customer lifetime value focuses on customers as assets rather than sources of revenue; the volume of purchases made, customer retention rates, and profit margins are factors taken into account in calculations. Strategies for increasing customer lifetime value aim to improve customer retention and lengthen the life of the relationship with the customer. It is a key factor in the customer equity of an organization.

customer profitability FINANCE amount of firm's profits due to customers the degree to which a *customer* or segment of customers contributes toward an organization's profits. Customer profitability has been shown to be produced primarily by a small proportion of customers, perhaps 10% to 20%, who generate up to 80% of a company's profits. Up to 40% of customers may generate only moderate profits, and the other 40% may be lossmaking. Such data enables companies to focus efforts on the most profitable segments.

cyclical stock STOCKHOLDING & INVESTMENTS stock affected by business cycles a stock whose value rises and falls in line with economic cycles

cyclical unemployment ECONOMICS recurring temporary lack of employment unemployment, usually temporary, caused by a lack of *aggregate demand*, for example, during a downswing in the business cycle

D

D/A *abbr* BANKING deposit account

Daimyo bond CURRENCY & EXCHANGE Japanese bond for European investors a Japanese *bearer bond* that can be cleared through European clearing houses

daman FINANCE contract whereby one person underwrites obligation of another in Islamic financing, a contract of guarantee in which the guarantor agrees to be responsible for a debt or obligation of another. *Also called* **dhaman**

dated date STOCKHOLDING & INVESTMENTS **start date for calculation of interest** the date on which interest begins to accrue on a fixed-income security, which is also the date the security is issued

date of maturity STOCKHOLDING & INVESTMENTS = *maturity date*

dawn raid STOCKHOLDING & INVESTMENTS **large morning purchase of firm's stock** a sudden, planned purchase of a large amount of a company's stock at the beginning of a day's trading. Up to 15% of a company's stock can be bought in this way, and the purchaser must wait for seven days before buying more. A dawn raid may sometimes be the first step toward a *takeover*.

day book ACCOUNTING **book for recording daily sales and purchases** a book in which an account of sales and purchases made each day can be recorded

dayn FINANCE **debt obligation** in Islamic financing, a debt incurred as the result of any contract or financial transaction

Day of the Jackal Fraud FRAUD **UK identity fraud using dead child's birth certificate** in the United Kingdom, a form of identity fraud in which a person obtains the birth certificate of a dead child and uses it to acquire a false identity and passport

day order CURRENCY & EXCHANGE **in dollar trading, order with one day's validity** an order that is valid only during one trading day

days' sales outstanding ACCOUNTING = *collection ratio*

DC *abbr* BANKING documentary credit

D/C *abbr* BANKING documentary credit

DCF *abbr* FINANCE discounted cash flow

DD *abbr* 1. BANKING direct debit 2. ACCOUNTING due diligence

dead account BANKING **inactive account** an account that is no longer used

deadweight loss ECONOMICS **inefficiency caused by imbalance** economic inefficiency caused by a fall in quantities of a product produced, for example, when a monopoly producer keeps production low to maintain high prices, or by a tax

deal flow STOCKHOLDING & INVESTMENTS **presentation of new investments** the rate at which new offers of investments are being presented to underwriters

dear money FINANCE **money lent at high interest to restrict spending** money that is lent at a high interest rate and will therefore restrict a borrower's expenditure. *See also* *cheap money*

debenture bond FINANCE 1. **documentation of unsecured bond** a certificate showing that a *debenture* has been issued, and giving its terms and conditions 2. **US loan without security** in the United States, a long-term unsecured loan, a common type taken out by companies

debenture capital FINANCE **loan that company secures with assets** money borrowed by a company, using its fixed assets as security

debenture holder FINANCE **somebody holding a bond** a person who holds a bond or certificate of debt for money lent

debenture stock FINANCE **stock paying fixed interest on fixed schedule** a form of debt instrument in which a company guarantees payments on a fixed schedule or at a fixed rate of interest

debit ACCOUNTING **charge against account in bookkeeping** a bookkeeping entry that shows an increase in assets or expenses, or a decrease in liabilities, revenue, or capital. It is entered in the left-hand side of an account in double-entry bookkeeping.

debit balance ACCOUNTING **balance showing more money owed than received** the difference between debits and credits in an account where the value of *debits* is greater

debit card BANKING **bank card that functions like check** a card issued by a bank or financial institution and accepted by a merchant in payment for a transaction. Unlike the procedure with a *credit card*, purchases are deducted from the cardholder's account at the time when the transaction takes place. *Also called* *check card*

debit column ACCOUNTING **left side of double-entry bookkeeping system** the left-hand side of an account, showing increases in a company's assets or decreases in its liabilities

debit entry ACCOUNTING **entry for expenditure** an item in a financial statement recording money spent

debit note FINANCE **document showing that customer owes money** a document that shows how much money a person or company owes. *Abbr* **D/N**

debits and credits ACCOUNTING **record of firm's financial transactions** figures entered in a company's accounts to record increases and decreases in *assets*, expenses, liabilities, revenues, or capital

debit side ACCOUNTING **accounting column for money owed or paid out** the section of a financial statement that lists payments made or owed. In *double-entry bookkeeping*, the left hand side of each account is designated as the debit side. *See also* *credit side*

debt FINANCE 1. **money owed** an amount of money owed to a person or organization 2. **money borrowed** money borrowed by a person or organization to finance personal or business activities

debt bomb ECONOMICS **economic volatility caused by default of major institution** instability in an economy as a result of a major financial institution defaulting on its obligations

debt capital FINANCE **money raised as loan** capital that is raised that carries an obligation to pay back the principal together with interest

debt collection agency FINANCE **business specializing in getting debts repaid** a business that secures the repayment of debts for third parties on a commission or fee basis

debt-convertible bond STOCKHOLDING & INVESTMENTS **bond convertible from variable to fixed interest** a floating-rate bond that can be converted to a fixed rate of interest. *See also* *droplock bond*

debt counseling FINANCE **guidance for people in financial difficulty** a service offering advice and support to individuals who are financially stretched

debt factoring FINANCE **purchase of firm's accounts receivable at discount** the business of buying debts at a discount. A factor collects a company's debts when due, and pays the creditor in advance part of the sum to be collected, thus "buying" the debt.

debt finance *UK* FINANCE = *debt financing*

debt financing *US* FINANCE **raising of capital by long-term borrowing** the activity of raising capital from long-term borrowing such as the sale of bonds or notes. *UK term* *debt finance*

debt forgiveness FINANCE **lender's canceling of debt** the writing off of all or part of a nation's debt by a lender

debt instrument FINANCE **written agreement between borrower and lender** any document used or issued for raising money, for example, a bill of exchange, bond, or promissory note

debt market FINANCE **market trading in debts** a market in which corporate or municipal, government, or public debts are bought and sold

debtnocrat BANKING **person in position to make very large loans** a senior bank official who specializes in lending extremely large sums, for example, to emerging nations (slang)

debt obligation STOCKHOLDING & INVESTMENTS = *collateralized debt obligation*

debtor FINANCE **person owing money** a person or organization owing money to another. *Also called* *obligor*

debtor days FINANCE **average time it takes to collect payment** the number of days on average that it takes a company to receive payment for what it sells.

To determine debtor days, divide the cumulative amount of accounts receivable by sales, then multiply by 365. If accounts receivable total $600,000 and sales are $9,000,000, the calculation is:

$$\frac{600{,}000}{9{,}000{,}000} \times 365 = 24.33 \text{ days}$$

The company takes 24.33 days on average to collect its debts.

Debtor days is an indication of a company's efficiency in collecting monies owed. Obviously, the lower the number the better. An especially high number is a telltale sign of inefficiency or worse. *See also* *creditor days*

debtors' control FINANCE **systems for prompt repayment** strategies used to ensure that borrowers pay back loans on time

debt ratio FINANCE **relationship between firm's debts and assets** the debts of a company shown as a percentage of its *equity* plus loan capital

debt rescheduling FINANCE **negotiation of new terms for debt repayment** the renegotiation of debt payments. Debt rescheduling is necessary when a company can no longer meet its debt payments. It can involve deferring debt payments, deferring payment of interest, or negotiating a new loan. It is usually undertaken as part of *turnaround management* to avoid *business failure*. Debt rescheduling is also undertaken in less developed countries that encounter national debt difficulties. Such arrangements are usually overseen by the *International Monetary Fund*.

debt security STOCKHOLDING & INVESTMENTS **security issued as evidence of debt to purchaser** a security issued by a company or government which represents money borrowed from the security's purchaser and which must be repaid at a specified maturity date, usually at a specified interest rate

debt service FINANCE **combined interest and principal due on money borrowed** the payments due under a loan agreement, i.e. interest payable and payments of principal

debt/service ratio ECONOMICS **measurement of debt against gross income** the ratio of a country's or company's borrowing to its equity or *venture capital*

debt swap FINANCE **exchange of country's debt for local currency** a method of reducing exposure to long-term debt of nations with undeveloped economies by purchasing the debt at a discount and exchanging it with the central bank for local currency

declaration date STOCKHOLDING & INVESTMENTS **day when firm sets next dividend** in the United States, the date when the directors of a company meet to announce the proposed dividend per share that they recommend be paid

declaration of dividend STOCKHOLDING & INVESTMENTS **firm's official announcement of next dividend** a formal announcement by a company's directors of the proposed dividend per share that they recommend be paid. It is subsequently put to a stockholders' vote at the company's annual meeting.

declining balance method ACCOUNTING = *accelerated depreciation*

deduction FINANCE **deducting from total, or amount deducted** a subtraction of money from a total, or an amount of money subtracted from a total

deed of transfer STOCKHOLDING & INVESTMENTS **documentation of transfer of stock ownership** in the United Kingdom, a legal document that attests to the transfer of stock ownership

deep-discount bond STOCKHOLDING & INVESTMENTS **bond selling at far less than value** a bond offered at a large discount on the face value of the debt so that a significant proportion of the return to the investor comes by way of a capital gain on redemption, rather than through interest payments

deep-discounted rights issue STOCKHOLDING & INVESTMENTS **new shares priced below market value** a rights issue where the new shares are priced at a very low price compared to their

a–z

Dictionary

current market value to ensure that stockholders take up the rights

deep-in-the-money call option STOCKHOLDING & INVESTMENTS **profitable contract to buy securities** a *call option* that has an exercise price below the market price of the underlying asset and has therefore become very profitable. *See also **deep-out-of-the-money call option***

deep-in-the-money put option STOCKHOLDING & INVESTMENTS **profitable contract to sell securities** a *put option* that has an exercise price above the market price of an underlying asset and has therefore become very profitable. *See also **deep-out-of-the-money put option***

deep-out-of-the-money call option STOCKHOLDING & INVESTMENTS **unprofitable contract to buy securities** a *call option* that has an exercise price above the market price of the underlying asset and has little intrinsic value. *See also **deep-in-the-money call option***

deep-out-of-the-money put option STOCKHOLDING & INVESTMENTS **unprofitable contract to sell securities** a *put option* that has an exercise price below the market price of an underlying asset and has little intrinsic value. *See also **deep-in-the-money put option***

defalcation FINANCE **misuse of money entrusted to somebody's care** the improper and illegal use of funds by a person who does not own them, but who has been charged with their care

default 1. STOCKHOLDING & INVESTMENTS **be unable to cover loss on trades** as a member of an exchange, to lose more on a trading position than is held in capital **2.** LEGAL **not do what you have contracted to do** to fail to comply with the terms of a contract, especially to fail to pay back a debt

defaulter FINANCE **person failing to make scheduled payments** a person who defaults, for example, somebody who fails to make scheduled payments on a loan

default risk STOCKHOLDING & INVESTMENTS, RISK **risk of non-payment** the possibility that the issuer of a bond will be unable to make payments of principal and interest when they are due

defended takeover bid MERGERS & ACQUISITIONS **offer to buy firm that opposes being sold** a bid for a company takeover in which the directors of the target company oppose the action of the bidder

defensive security STOCKHOLDING & INVESTMENTS **security providing earnings despite falling market** a security that has very little risk and provides a return even when the stock market is weak

defensive stock STOCKHOLDING & INVESTMENTS **stock not affected by external factors** stock that prospers predictably regardless of external circumstances such as an economic slowdown, for example, the stock of a company that markets a product everyone must have

deferment FINANCE **putting off of something** a postponement of something, for example, taxes or interest on a loan, until a later date

deferred annuity STOCKHOLDING & INVESTMENTS **investment offering return 12 + months after last premium** an investment that does not pay out until at least one year after the final premium has been paid

deferred common stock *US* STOCKHOLDING & INVESTMENTS **stock paying dividends only after others are paid** a type of stock usually held by founding members of a company, often with a higher dividend that is only paid after other shareholders have received their dividends and, in some cases, only when a specific level of profit has been achieved. This type of stock is rarely issued in the United States. *Also called **deferred share**. UK term **deferred ordinary share***

deferred coupon STOCKHOLDING & INVESTMENTS **bond that delays interest payments** a *coupon* that pays no interest at first, but pays relatively high interest after a specific date

deferred credit *or* deferred income ACCOUNTING **money received but not yet recorded as income** revenue received but not yet reported as income in the profit and loss account, for example, payment for goods to be delivered or services provided at a later date, or government grants received for the purchase of assets. The deferred credit is treated as a credit balance on the balance sheet while waiting to be treated as income. *See also **accrual basis***

deferred creditor FINANCE **creditor paid after all others** a person who is owed money by a bankrupt person or organization but who is paid only after all other creditors

deferred interest bond STOCKHOLDING & INVESTMENTS **bond that delays interest payments** a bond that pays no interest at first, but pays relatively high interest after a specific date

deferred month STOCKHOLDING & INVESTMENTS **distant month for option** a month relatively late in the term of an *option*

deferred ordinary share *UK* STOCKHOLDING & INVESTMENTS **1. stock paying no dividend in early years** a type of stock that pays no dividend for a specific number of years after its issue date but then is treated the same as the company's common stock **2.** = *deferred common stock*

deferred payment 1. FINANCE **money to be repaid later** money owed that will be repaid at a later date **2.** OPERATIONS & PRODUCTION **payment in installments** payment for goods by installments over a period of time

deferred revenue ACCOUNTING **income carried into next accounting period** revenue carried forward to future accounting periods

deferred share STOCKHOLDING & INVESTMENTS = *deferred common stock*

deficiency FINANCE **amount of shortfall** the amount by which something such as a sum of money is less than it should be

deficit ACCOUNTING = *budget deficit*

deficit financing FINANCE **covering shortfall** the borrowing of money because expenditure will exceed receipts

deficit spending FINANCE spending financed by borrowing government spending financed through borrowing rather than through taxation or other current revenue

deflation ECONOMICS long-term decline in prices a reduction in the general level of prices sustained over several months, usually accompanied by declining employment and output

deflationary ECONOMICS causing drop in prices causing a decline in the prices of goods and services

deflationary fiscal policy ECONOMICS government policy of raising taxes and reducing spending a government policy that raises taxes and reduces public expenditure in order to reduce the level of *aggregate demand* in the economy

deflationary gap ECONOMICS failure in exploiting economic potential a gap between *GDP* and the potential output of the economy

deflator ECONOMICS inflation-related reduction in national income the amount by which a country's *GDP* is reduced to take into account *inflation*

del credere FINANCE extra charge to protect against nonpayment an amount added to a charge to cover the possibility of its not being paid

del credere agent FINANCE sales agent who guarantees purchaser's payment an agent who agrees to sell goods on commission and pay the principal even if the buyer defaults on payment. To cover the risk of default, the commission is marginally higher than that of a general agent.

deleverage FINANCE pay off debt to reduce the size of a company's debt, possibly by selling off some assets

delivery 1. FINANCE handing over of bill of exchange for payment the transfer of a bill of exchange or other negotiable instrument to the bank that is due to make payment **2.** OPERATIONS & PRODUCTION act of delivering commodity to buyer the transportation of a commodity by a seller to a purchaser as set out in a futures contract

delta STOCKHOLDING & INVESTMENTS option price change compared with associated asset the amount of change in the price of an option as compared to a corresponding change in the price of its underlying asset

demand 1. FINANCE request for payment an act of asking somebody for payment of money owed **2.** MARKETING measure of consumers' willingness to buy the need that consumers have for a product or their eagerness and ability to buy it

demand bill FINANCE bill of exchange payable on demand a *bill of exchange* that must be paid when payment is asked for

demand deposit BANKING account balance available for writing checks money in a deposit account that the holder can withdraw at any time by writing a check

demand forecasting FINANCE estimation of consumer demand for product or service the activity of estimating the quantity of a product or service that consumers will purchase. Demand forecasting involves techniques including both informal methods such as educated guesses and quantitative

methods such as the use of historical sales data or current data from test markets. Demand forecasting may be used in making pricing decisions, in assessing future capacity requirements, or in making decisions on whether to enter a new market.

demand note FINANCE promissory note that is payable on demand a promissory note that has no specific date for payment but instead must be paid when it is presented

demand price FINANCE price buyer is willing to pay the price that purchasers are willing to offer to pay for a given quantity of goods

demand-pull inflation ECONOMICS inflation caused by increased demand inflation caused by rising demand that cannot be met

demand risk RISK risk of customer demand not matching firm's forecast the risk for a company that demand for a product will either exceed their expectations and ability to meet the demand or fall short of their expectations and leave them with product they cannot sell

demerge MERGERS & ACQUISITIONS separate parts of firm to split up an organization into a number of separate parts

demerger MERGERS & ACQUISITIONS separation of company into independent parts the separation of a company into several distinct entities, especially used of companies that have grown by acquisition

demonetize CURRENCY & EXCHANGE discontinue coin or note to withdraw a coin or note from a country's currency

demutualization BANKING conversion of mutual society to public corporation the process by which a mutual society becomes a publicly owned corporation

denomination CURRENCY & EXCHANGE value on coin, banknote, or stamp a unit of money imprinted on a coin, banknote, or stamp

departmental budget ACCOUNTING budget for department a budget of income and/or expenditure applicable to a specific department. *See also functional budget*

dependency ratio ECONOMICS proportion of society economically dependent on work force a measure of the proportion of a population that is too young or too old to work and is therefore economically dependent on that part of the population that is productively working. *Also called support ratio*

deposit 1. BANKING money added to bank account money placed in a bank for safekeeping or to earn interest **2.** BUSINESS partial payment to reserve something part of the price of an item given by a customer in advance so that the item will not be sold to somebody else before the full price is paid **3.** OPERATIONS & PRODUCTION add money to bank account to pay money into a bank account

deposit account BANKING **1.** interest-paying account requiring prior notice for withdrawal a bank account that pays interest on deposited funds but on which prior notice must be given in order to withdraw money. *Abbr* **D/A**

a–z

Dictionary

2. interest-paying UK building society account in the United Kingdom, a building society account that is held by somebody who is not a member of the society. Deposit accounts are generally paid a lower rate of interest, but in the event of the society going into liquidation deposit account holders are given preference. *See also* ***share account***

depositor BANKING **somebody who deposits money in financial institution** a person or business that places money in a bank, savings and loan, or other type of financial institution

depository BANKING **institution responsible for keeping valuable items safe** a bank or organization with whom money or documents can be placed for safekeeping

deposit slip *or* deposit receipt *US* BANKING **receipt for deposits made in bank account** the slip of paper that accompanies money or checks being paid into a bank account. *UK term* ***paying-in slip***

deposit-taking institution BANKING **banking institution serving general public** an institution that is licensed to receive money on deposit from private individuals and to pay interest on it, for example, a bank or savings and loan

depreciable cost ACCOUNTING **expense spread over several accounting periods** an expense that may be set against the profits of more than one accounting period

depreciate 1. FINANCE **lose value over time** to lose value, or decrease the value of something, usually over a period of time **2.** ACCOUNTING **make allowance for asset's progressive loss of value** to make an allowance in business accounts for the loss of value of an asset over time

depreciation 1. ACCOUNTING **loss of value** an allocation of the *cost* of an ***asset*** over a period of time for accounting and tax purposes. Depreciation is charged against earnings, on the basis that the use of capital assets is a legitimate cost of doing business. Depreciation is also a non-cash expense that is added into net income to determine cash flow in a given accounting period.

To qualify for depreciation, assets must be items used in the business that wear out, become obsolete, or lose value over time from natural causes or circumstances, and they must have a useful life beyond a single tax year. Examples include vehicles, machines, equipment, furnishings, and buildings, plus major additions or improvements to such assets. Some intangible assets also can be included under certain conditions. Land, personal assets, stock, leased or rented property, and a company's employees cannot be depreciated.

Straight line depreciation is the most straightforward method. It assumes that the net cost of an asset should be written off in equal amounts over its life. The formula used is:

$$\frac{\text{(Original cost–Scrap value)}}{\text{Useful life in years}}$$

For example, if a vehicle cost $30,000 and can be expected to serve the business for seven years, its original cost would be divided by its useful life:

$$\frac{30,000 - 2,000}{7} = 4,000 \text{ per year}$$

The $4,000 becomes a depreciation expense that is reported on the company's year-end income statement under "operation expenses."

In theory, an asset should be depreciated over the actual number of years that it will be used, according to its actual drop in value each year. At the end of each year, all the depreciation claimed to date is subtracted from its cost in order to arrive at its ***book value***, which would equal its market value. At the end of its useful business life, any portion not depreciated would represent the salvage value for which it could be sold or scrapped.

For tax purposes, some accountants prefer to use the ***declining balance method*** to record larger amounts of depreciation in the asset's early years in order to reduce tax bills as soon as possible. In contrast to the straight-line method, this assumes that the asset depreciates more in its earlier years of use. The table below compares the depreciation amounts that would be available, under these two methods, for a $1,000 asset that is expected to be used for five years and then sold for $100 as scrap.

The depreciation method to be used for a particular asset is fixed at the time that the asset is first placed in service. Whatever rules or tables are in effect for that year must be followed as long as the asset is owned.

Depreciation laws and regulations change frequently over the years as a result of government policy changes, so a company owning property over a long period may have to use several different depreciation methods. **2.** CURRENCY & EXCHANGE **decrease in value of currency** a reduction of a currency's value in relation to the value of other currencies

depreciation rate ACCOUNTING **annual rate at which asset loses value** the rate at which the value of an asset decreases each year in business accounts

depression ECONOMICS **long-term decline in economic activity** a prolonged slump or downturn in the business cycle, marked by a high level of unemployment

deprival value FINANCE = ***value to the business***

derivative STOCKHOLDING & INVESTMENTS **security with price link to underlying asset** a ***security*** such as an ***option***, the price

Straight-line method of depreciation		
Year	Annual depreciation	Year-end book value
1	$900 × 20% = $180	$1,000 − $180 = $820
2	$900 × 20% = $180	$820 − $180 = $640
3	$900 × 20% = $180	$640 − $180 = $460
4	$900 × 20% = $180	$460 − $180 = $280
5	$900 × 20% = $180	$280 − $180 = $100

Declining-balance method of depreciation		
Year	Annual depreciation	Year-end book value
1	$1,000 × 40% = $400	$1,000 − $400 = $600
2	$600 × 40% = $240	$600 − $240 = $360
3	$360 × 40% = $144	$360 − $144 = $216
4	$216 × 40% = $86.40	$216 − $86.40 = $129.60
5	$129.60 × 40% = $51.84	$129.60 − $51.84 = $77.76

a–z

Dictionary

of which has a strong correlation with an underlying commodity, currency, or *financial instrument*

derivative instruments *or* derivatives STOCKHOLDING & INVESTMENTS **securities based on other securities or market conditions** forms of traded securities, such as option contracts, which are derived from ordinary bonds and shares, exchange rates, or stock market indices.

designated account BANKING **account requiring second person for extra identification** an account opened and held in one person's name, but that also includes another person's name for extra identification purposes

devaluation ECONOMICS **reduction of official currency exchange rate** a reduction in the official fixed rate at which one currency exchanges for another under a fixed-rate regime, usually to correct a balance of payments deficit

developing country ECONOMICS **poor nation with little industrial development** a country, often a producer of primary goods such as cotton or rubber, that cannot generate investment income to stimulate growth and that possesses a national income that is vulnerable to change in commodity prices

development capital FINANCE **money for expansion** financing acquired or provided for the expansion of an established business

dhaman FINANCE = *daman*

Diagonal Street *S. AFRICA* FINANCE **financial district of Johannesburg** the financial center of Johannesburg or, by extension, South Africa (informal)

DIAMONDs STOCKHOLDING & INVESTMENTS **shares in selected firms on American Stock Exchange** shares in a fund, traded on NYSE Amex Equities, that is made up of the 30 companies represented in the Dow Jones Industrial Average

differential costing FINANCE **way to determine costs based on production levels** a costing method that shows the difference in costs that results from different levels of activity such as making one thousand or ten thousand extra units of a product

digital economy ECONOMICS **economic system based on online business transactions** an economy in which the main productive functions are in electronic commerce, for example, trade on the Internet

dilution levy FINANCE **charge to compensate for effect of investors' transactions** an extra charge levied by fund managers on investors buying or selling units in a fund, designed to offset any potential effect on the value of the fund of such purchases or sales

dilution of equity *US* STOCKHOLDING & INVESTMENTS **sale of additional stock resulting in reduced value** a situation in which a company makes more shares of common stock available without an increase in its assets, with the end result that each share is worth less than before. *UK term dilution of shareholding*

dilution of shareholding *UK* STOCKHOLDING & INVESTMENTS = *dilution of equity*

direct debit BANKING **arrangement for charging customer's account automatically** a system by which a customer allows a company to make charges to his or her bank account automatically and where the amount charged can be increased or decreased with the agreement of the customer. *Abbr* **DD**. *See also* **automatic debit**

direct labor cost percentage rate FINANCE **product overhead attributed to labor costs** an *overhead absorption rate*, based on labor costs, which can readily be allocated to individual units of production

direct labor hour rate FINANCE **product overhead attributed to labor hours** an *overhead absorption rate*, based on labor hours, which can readily be allocated to individual units of production

directorate CORPORATE GOVERNANCE **group directing firm's course** the governing or controlling body of an organization responsible for the organization's corporate strategy and accountable to its stakeholders for business results. A directorate may also be known as a *board of directors* or council, or, at an inner level, the executive or management committee.

director's dealing STOCKHOLDING & INVESTMENTS **stock transactions by firm's director** the purchase or sale of a company's stock by one of its directors

director's fees FINANCE **money paid to company director** money paid to a director of a company for attendance at board meetings

directors' report CORPORATE GOVERNANCE **board of directors' annual report** the annual report prepared by the board of directors and distributed to the company's stockholders

direct share ownership *UK* STOCKHOLDING & INVESTMENTS = *direct stock ownership*

direct stock ownership *US* STOCKHOLDING & INVESTMENTS **ownership of stock by private individuals** the ownership of stock by private individuals, buying or selling through brokers, and not via holdings in mutual funds. *UK term direct share ownership*

dirty float CURRENCY & EXCHANGE **exchange rate influenced by central bank's actions abroad** a floating exchange rate that cannot float freely because a country's central bank intervenes on foreign exchange markets to alter its level

dirty price FINANCE **cost of debt plus unpaid interest** the price of a debt instrument that includes the amount of accrued interest that has not yet been paid

disaggregation MERGERS & ACQUISITIONS **breaking up group of allied firms** the breaking apart of an alliance of companies to review their strengths and contributions as a basis for rebuilding an effective business web

disbursement FINANCE **paying out of money** the payment of money, for example, as an expense or to get rid of a debt

disbursing agent FINANCE = *paying agent*

disclosure of shareholding STOCKHOLDING & INVESTMENTS **public disclosure of holdings in firm** a public announcement of a shareholding in a company, required by the regulatory authorities and stock exchanges if a shareholding exceeds a given percentage

discount 1. FINANCE **price reduction to encourage buying** a reduction in the price of goods or services in relation to the standard price. A discount is a selling technique that is used, for example, to encourage customers to buy in large quantities or to make payments in cash. It can also be used to improve sales of a slow-moving line. The greater the purchasing power of the buyer, the greater the discounts that can be negotiated. Some companies inflate original list prices to give the impression that discounts offer value for money; conversely too many genuine discounts may harm profitability.
2. STOCKHOLDING & INVESTMENTS **reduced share price offered by investment trust** the difference between the share price of an investment trust and its *net asset value*

discount broker STOCKHOLDING & INVESTMENTS **broker with lower fees offering fewer services** a broker who charges relatively low fees because he or she provides restricted services

discount brokerage US FINANCE **finance firm offering fewer, cheaper services** a brokerage that offers fewer services for a reduced commission than a standard brokerage

discounted bond STOCKHOLDING & INVESTMENTS **low-yield bond priced below face value** a bond that is sold for less than its face value because its yield is not as high as that of other bonds

discounted cash flow FINANCE **forecast return on investment subject to cost-of-funds adjustment** a calculation of the forecast return on capital investment by discounting future cash flows from an investment, usually at a rate equivalent to the company's minimum required rate of return. *Abbr* **DCF**

discounted dividend model STOCKHOLDING & INVESTMENTS **calculation of stock's value by discounting future dividends** a method of calculating a stock's value by reducing future dividends to the present value. *Also called* ***dividend discount model***

discounted value STOCKHOLDING & INVESTMENTS = *present value*

discount house FINANCE **firm trading in discounted bills of exchange** in the United Kingdom, a financial company that specializes in buying and selling ***bills of exchange*** at a reduced price

discount loan FINANCE **loan issued with interest payments deducted** a loan that amounts to less than its face value because payment of interest has been subtracted

discount rate 1. BANKING **interest rate banks pay for loans** the rate charged by a central bank on any loans it makes to other banks **2.** E-COMMERCE **fee seller pays for credit card transaction settlement** a percentage fee that an e-commerce merchant pays to an account provider or independent sales organization for settling an electronic transaction

discount security FINANCE **low-priced security not paying interest** a security that is sold for less than its face value in lieu of bearing interest

discount window BANKING **Federal Reserve loans to member banks** in the United States, the system by which the Federal Reserve grants loans to a member bank by giving advances on the security of Treasury bills that the bank is holding

discretionary account STOCKHOLDING & INVESTMENTS **account allowing broker to make trading decisions** a securities account in which the broker has the authority to make decisions about buying and selling without the customer's prior permission. *Also called* ***managed account***

discretionary client STOCKHOLDING & INVESTMENTS **client who lets broker manage funds without consultation** a client whose funds are managed at the discretion of a broker without the broker needing to refer to the client for prior permission

discretionary funds STOCKHOLDING & INVESTMENTS **funds broker can manage without consulting client** funds managed at the discretion of a broker without the broker needing to refer to the owner for prior permission

discretionary management STOCKHOLDING & INVESTMENTS **investment agreement allowing broker to make decisions** an arrangement between a stockbroker and his or her client whereby the stockbroker makes all investment decisions. It is the opposite of an ***advisory management*** arrangement.

discretionary order STOCKHOLDING & INVESTMENTS **transaction handled by broker alone** a security transaction in which a broker controls details such as the time of execution

discretionary spend UK FINANCE = ***discretionary spending***

discretionary spending US FINANCE **money for things you want but don't need** the amount of money available after direct taxation to an individual or family to spend on items other than necessities such as food, clothing, and homes. *UK term* ***discretionary spend***

discretionary trust FINANCE **trust arrangement giving trustee full decision-making power** a trust where the trustees decide how to invest the income and when and how much income should be paid to the beneficiaries

discriminating monopoly ECONOMICS **sole producer tailoring prices to markets** a company able to charge different prices for its output in different markets because as the only producer it has power to influence prices for its goods

disequilibrium FINANCE **imbalance in economy, as between supply and demand** an imbalance in the economy when supply does not equal demand, or when a country's balance of payments is in deficit

disequilibrium price ECONOMICS **product price causing supply and demand imbalance** the price of a good set at a level at which demand and supply are not in balance

dishonor BANKING **not pay check because funds are inadequate** to refuse payment of a check because the account for which it is written does not contain enough money. *Also called bounce (sense 1)*

disinflation ECONOMICS **removal of inflation through monetary policies** the elimination or reduction of inflation or inflationary pressures in an economy by fiscal or monetary policies

disintermediation 1. FINANCE **direct trading in money market** the process of savers and borrowers making transactions directly in the money market rather than by making deposits and taking loans from banks **2.** E-COMMERCE **removing middlemen to sell directly to customer** the elimination of intermediaries, for example, the wholesalers found in traditional retail channels, in favor of direct selling to the consumer. *See also reintermediation*

disinvest 1. FINANCE **reduce investment by non-replacement of capital assets** to reduce investment by not replacing capital assets when they wear out **2.** STOCKHOLDING & INVESTMENTS **reduce investment by selling stock** to reduce investment overall or in a specific area by selling stock

disinvestment FINANCE **1. reduction in investment through non-replacement of capital assets** a process of reducing investment by not replacing capital assets when they wear out **2. reduction in investment by selling stock** a process of reducing investment overall or in a specific area by selling stock

distressed property FINANCE **property subject to repossession** property originally purchased with the aid of a loan on which payments have stopped and the borrower has defaulted

distributable profit STOCKHOLDING & INVESTMENTS **profit usable as dividends** profit that can be distributed to stockholders as dividends if the directors decide to do so

distributed profit STOCKHOLDING & INVESTMENTS **profit passed on as dividends** profit passed to stockholders in the form of dividends

distribution of income 1. STOCKHOLDING & INVESTMENTS **payment of dividends to stockholders** the payment of accumulated dividends to stockholders on record, usually on an annual basis **2.** ECONOMICS **wealth range in society** the way income is spread across society as a whole, as a measure of the equality or inequality of wealth

distributions STOCKHOLDING & INVESTMENTS **income from investment** any income arising from a bond fund or an equity

District Bank BANKING **member bank of Federal Reserve** in the United States, one of the 12 banks that make up the *Federal Reserve*. Each District Bank is responsible for all banking activity in its assigned region.

diversification GENERAL MANAGEMENT, MERGERS & ACQUISITIONS **developing new areas for growth or risk reduction** a strategy to increase the variety of business, service, or product types within an organization. Diversification can be a growth strategy, taking advantage of market opportunities, or it may be aimed at reducing risk by spreading interests over different areas. It can be achieved through *acquisition* or through internal research and development, and it can involve managing two, a few, or many different areas of interest. Diversification can also be a corporate strategy of investment in acquisitions within a broad portfolio range by a large *holding company*. One distinct type is *horizontal diversification*, which involves expansion into a similar product area, for example, a domestic furniture manufacturer producing office furniture. Another is *vertical diversification*, in which a company moves into a different level of the *supply chain*, for example, a manufacturing company becoming a retailer.

diversified investment company FINANCE **varied mutual fund** a mutual fund with a range of types of investments

divestiture FINANCE **firm's sale of asset** the sale by a company of an asset, for example, to get money to pay off a debt

divestment 1. MERGERS & ACQUISITIONS **selling or closing part of firm** the sale or closure of one or several businesses, or parts of a business. Divestment often takes place as part of a rationalization effort to cut costs or to enable an organization to concentrate on core business or competences, and may take the form of a *management buyout*. **2.** STOCKHOLDING & INVESTMENTS **giving up ownership in firm** the proportional or complete reduction in an ownership stake in an organization

dividend STOCKHOLDING & INVESTMENTS **profits paid to stockholders** part of a company's net profits paid out to qualified stockholders at a fixed amount per share

dividend check *US* STOCKHOLDING & INVESTMENTS **check in payment of dividend** a check issued to qualified stockholders that makes payment of a dividend. *UK term dividend warrant*

dividend clawback STOCKHOLDING & INVESTMENTS **arrangement for reinvestment of dividends** an agreement that dividends will be reinvested as part of the financing of a project

dividend cover STOCKHOLDING & INVESTMENTS **ability of net profit to pay firm's dividend** the number of times a company's dividends to ordinary stockholders could be paid out of its net after-tax profits. This measures the likelihood of dividend payments being sustained, and is a useful indication of sustained profitability.

If the figure is 3, a firm's profits are three times the level of the dividend paid to stockholders.

Dividend cover is calculated by dividing earnings per share by the dividend per share:

$$\frac{\text{Earnings per share}}{\text{Dividend per share}} = \text{Dividend cover}$$

If a company has earnings per share of $8, and it pays out a dividend of 2.1, dividend cover is

$$\frac{8}{2.1} = 3.80$$

An alternative formula divides a company's net profit by the total amount allocated for dividends. So a company that earns

$10 million in net profit and allocates $1 million for dividends has a dividend cover of 10, while a company that earns $25 million and pays out $10 million in dividends has a dividend cover of 2.5:

$$\frac{10,000,000}{1,000,000} = 10$$

and

$$\frac{25,000,000}{10,000,000} = 2.5$$

A dividend cover ratio of 2 or higher is usually adequate, and indicates that the dividend is affordable. A dividend cover ratio below 1.5 is risky, and a ratio below 1 indicates a company is paying the current year's dividend with retained earnings from a previous year's, a practice that cannot continue indefinitely. On the other hand, a high dividend cover figure may disappoint an investor looking for income, since the figure suggests directors could have declared a larger dividend. *See also **payout ratio***

dividend discount model STOCKHOLDING & INVESTMENTS = *discounted dividend model*

dividend forecast STOCKHOLDING & INVESTMENTS **predicted amount of next dividend** a prediction of the amount that an expected dividend will pay per share

dividend limitation STOCKHOLDING & INVESTMENTS **restriction on dividend payments for bond** a provision in a bond limiting the dividends that may be paid

dividend mandate STOCKHOLDING & INVESTMENTS **permission to directly deposit dividends in bank account** an authorization by a stockholder to the company in which he or she has a holding to pay dividends directly into his or her bank account

dividend payout STOCKHOLDING & INVESTMENTS **money paid as dividends to stockholders** money distributed by a company in the form of dividends to qualified stockholders

dividend payout ratio STOCKHOLDING & INVESTMENTS = *payout ratio*

dividend per share STOCKHOLDING & INVESTMENTS **amount of dividend per share of stock held** an amount of money paid by a company as dividend for each share of stock held

dividend reinvestment plan STOCKHOLDING & INVESTMENTS **arrangement for reinvesting dividends in firm's stock** a plan that provides for the reinvestment of dividends in the stock of the company paying the dividends. *Abbr* **DRIP**

dividend rights STOCKHOLDING & INVESTMENTS **rights to receive dividends** the entitlement of a stockholder to receive a share of the company's profits

dividends-received deduction STOCKHOLDING & INVESTMENTS, TAX **tax break on dividends from subsidiary company** a tax advantage on dividends that a company receives from a company it owns

dividend warrant UK STOCKHOLDING & INVESTMENTS = *dividend check*

dividend yield STOCKHOLDING & INVESTMENTS **relative size of dividend** dividends paid out expressed as a percentage of a stock's price

D/N *abbr* FINANCE debit note

documentary credit *or* documentary letter of credit BANKING **provision for payment in international transactions** an arrangement, used in the finance of international transactions, whereby a bank undertakes to make a payment to a third party on behalf of a customer. *Abbr* **D/C**

dollar CURRENCY & EXCHANGE **currency unit in US and some other countries** a unit of currency used in the United States and other countries such as Australia, Bahamas, Barbados, Bermuda, Brunei, Canada, Fiji, Hong Kong, Jamaica, New Zealand, Singapore, and Zimbabwe

dollar area CURRENCY & EXCHANGE **region using US dollar for trading** an area of the world where the US dollar is the main trading currency

dollar cost averaging US FINANCE **regular repeating of investment** the regular periodic purchase of the same amount in dollars of the same security regardless of its price. *UK term **pound cost averaging***

dollar gap CURRENCY & EXCHANGE **shortage of US dollars** a situation in which the supply of US dollars is not enough to satisfy the demand for them from overseas buyers

dollars-and-cents US FINANCE **influenced by money** used to describe a situation in which cost and return are considered the determining factors

dollar stocks STOCKHOLDING & INVESTMENTS **stocks in US companies** stocks issued by companies incorporated in the United States

domestic consumer ECONOMICS **user of product for personal purposes** a *consumer* who uses a product for personal, domestic, or household purposes

domestic currency CURRENCY & EXCHANGE **money legally accepted in home country** the legal *currency* of the jurisdiction that issued it

domestic economy ECONOMICS **economy of home country** the production, consumption, and distribution of wealth within a specific country

domicilium citandi et executandi S. AFRICA FINANCE **address for delivering legal documents** the address where a summons or other official notice should be served if necessary, which must be supplied by somebody applying for credit or entering into a contract

dominant influence TREASURY MANAGEMENT **undisputed influence over financial policy** influence that can be exercised to achieve the operating and financial policies designed by the holder of the influence, notwithstanding the rights or influence of any other party

donor FINANCE **giver of gift** a person who gives a gift, especially money

dormant account BANKING **inactive bank account** a bank account that is no longer used by the account holder

dormant company ACCOUNTING **firm not doing business for a while** a company that has not made any transactions during a specific *accounting period*

double counting ACCOUNTING **using same cost or benefit twice in calculation** the counting of a cost or benefit element twice when carrying out analysis. This can happen when the total sales in a market is calculated as the sum of all sales made by companies, without deducting the purchases companies make from other firms in the market.

double-digit growth ECONOMICS **rapid growth of firm or economy** an increase of between 10% and 99% in the productivity or size of a company, business activity, or economy within a specific period of time

double-digit inflation ECONOMICS **rapid growth of inflation rate** a rate of inflation between 10% and 99%, usually calculated on an annual basis

double dipping FRAUD **fraudulently receiving two incomes from government** in the United States, the illegal practice of receiving income from a government pension as well as social security payments, or of holding a government job while receiving a government pension

double-dip recession ECONOMICS **brief recovery preceding further recession** a pattern in an economic cycle that shows two periods of recession separated by a brief period of growth. *Also called* ***W-shaped recession***

double-entry bookkeeping ACCOUNTING **type of bookkeeping system used by most businesses** the most commonly used system of bookkeeping, based on the principle that every financial transaction involves the simultaneous receiving and giving of value, and is therefore recorded twice

double-one-touch option STOCKHOLDING & INVESTMENTS **option paying at one of two preset levels** an option that gives an investor a payment if the price of the underlying asset reaches or exceeds one of two preset levels. *See also* ***no-touch option, one-touch option***

Dow Jones 1. BUSINESS, FINANCE **Dow Jones & Company** US publishing and financial information corporation, Dow Jones & Company. It was established in 1882 by reporters Charles Dow, Edward Jones, and Charles Bergstresser, and is now a subsidiary of News Corporation. It publishes the Wall Street Journal. **2.** MARKETS **Dow Jones Indexes** US index provider Dow Jones Indexes, established as a spin-off from Dow Jones & Company in 1997, it is now 90% owned by CME Group. Its best-known product is the Dow Jones Industrial Average, which was created in 1896. **3.** MARKETS **Dow Jones Industrial Average** abbreviated name sometimes used for the Dow Jones Industrial Average stock market index produced by Dow Jones Indexes the company

down payment FINANCE **partial payment at time of purchase** a part of the full price of something paid at the time it is bought, with the remaining part to be paid later

downside factor *or* downside potential STOCKHOLDING & INVESTMENTS **possibility of loss in value** the possibility of incurring a loss when an investment declines in value

downside risk STOCKHOLDING & INVESTMENTS **risk of loss in value** the risk that an investment will decline in value. *See also* ***upside potential***

downturn FINANCE, MARKETS **downward trend** a downward trend in sales, profits, a stock market, or an economy

draft BANKING **document ordering payment** a written order to pay a particular sum from one account to another, or to a person. *See also* ***sight draft, time draft***

drawdown FINANCE **decision to use money made available earlier** the act of obtaining money that has previously been made available under a credit agreement

drawee BANKING **payer of bill of exchange or check** the individual or institution to whom a bill of exchange or check is addressed, who will pay the sum indicated

drawer BANKING **person who writes check or bill** the person who writes a check or a bill asking an individual or institution to pay money to the payee indicated

drawing account BANKING **account for tracking money withdrawn** an account that permits the tracking of withdrawals, used, for example, by a ***sole proprietor*** or ***partner***

drawing rights FINANCE **member country's right to borrow from IMF fund** a right of a member country of the ***International Monetary Fund*** to borrow money from the fund in a foreign currency. *See also* ***Special Drawing Right***

DRIP *abbr* STOCKHOLDING & INVESTMENTS dividend reinvestment plan

drip feed 1. FINANCE **gradual provision of capital** a method of providing capital to a small startup company in which investors contribute capital as needed over a period of time **2.** STOCKHOLDING & INVESTMENTS **regular increase in investment** a method of investing in securities in which investors invest a specific amount of money on a regular basis

drop lock FINANCE **change from floating to fixed interest rate** the automatic conversion of a debt instrument with a floating rate to one with a fixed rate when interest rates fall to an agreed percentage

droplock bond STOCKHOLDING & INVESTMENTS **bond becoming fixed rate if interest rate falls** a floating-rate bond that will convert to a fixed rate of interest if interest rates fall to a specific level. *See also* ***debt-convertible bond***

dual currency bond CURRENCY & EXCHANGE **bond issued and paying interest in different currencies** a bond that pays interest in a currency other than the one used to buy it

dual economy ECONOMICS **different growth rates for manufacturing and services** an economy in which the manufacturing and service sectors are growing at different rates

dual trading FINANCE **working as agent for buyer and seller** the practice of acting as agent for both a broker's firm and its customers

dud check BANKING check not honored because of insufficient funds a check that cannot be cashed because the person writing it does not have enough money in the account to pay it

due bill STOCKHOLDING & INVESTMENTS notice of transfer from seller to buyer a notification that a security has been transferred from the seller to the buyer, giving details of the amounts such as cost, dividends, or interest owed either the seller or buyer

due date FINANCE deadline for payment of debt the date on which a debt is required to be paid

due diligence 1. ACCOUNTING detailed check of firm's accounts before sale the examination of a company's accounts prior to a potential takeover by another organization. This assessment is often undertaken by an independent third party. *Abbr* **DD** **2.** GENERAL MANAGEMENT investigation of firm before purchase or investment the collection, verification, analysis, and assessment of information about the operations and management of a company undertaken by a potential purchaser or investor. Due diligence aims to confirm that the purchaser or investor has an accurate picture of the target company and to identify risks and benefits associated with the prospective deal. Due diligence usually starts after the signing of a letter of intent by both parties and information disclosed during the process is normally protected by the signing of a confidentiality agreement. Due diligence often leads on to negotiations on the detailed terms of the agreement. The process may cover the financial, legal, commercial, technical, cultural, and environmental aspects of the organization's operations as well as its assets and liabilities, and may be conducted with the assistance of professional advisers.

duopoly ECONOMICS market with only two sellers of product a market in which only two sellers of a good exist. If one decides to alter the price, the other will respond and influence the market's response to the first decision.

duration STOCKHOLDING & INVESTMENTS time to receive current value of payments the time in years that it will take to receive the present value of all the payments from a fixed-income investment, calculated using the effect that a 1% change in the interest rate will have on the investment. This calculation is mainly used to measure the sensitivity of changes in bond prices to changes in interest rates.

Dutch auction FINANCE auction in which price bidding goes down an auction in which the lot for sale is offered at an initial price that, if there are no bidders, is then reduced until there is a bid

dynamic pricing FINANCE pricing from demand pricing that changes in line with patterns of demand

E

EAA *abbr* ACCOUNTING European Accounting Association

E&O *abbr* ACCOUNTING errors and omissions

early withdrawal BANKING taking money out of time deposit account early the removal of money from a deposit account before the due date. Early withdrawal often incurs a penalty that the account holder must pay.

earned income FINANCE money earned for work performed money generated by a person's or organization's labor, for example, wages, salaries, fees, royalties, and business profits. *See also* **unearned income**

earning potential 1. BUSINESS amount person can earn the amount of money somebody should be able to earn in his or her professional capacity **2.** STOCKHOLDING & INVESTMENTS potential dividend earnings the amount of dividend that a share potentially can produce

earnings 1. ACCOUNTING money available to business after expenses income or profit from a business, quoted gross or net of tax, which may be retained and distributed in part to the stockholders **2.** FINANCE money obtained through work a sum of money gained from paid employment, usually quoted before tax, including any extra rewards such as *fringe benefits*, allowances, or incentives

earnings before interest and taxes ACCOUNTING *see* **EBIT**

earnings before interest, tax, depreciation, and amortization ACCOUNTING *see* **EBITDA**

earnings credit BANKING in US, amount offsetting bank charges in the United States, an allowance that reduces bank charges on checking accounts

earnings drift FINANCE pay increases outstripping official rates a situation in which an increase in pay is greater than that of officially negotiated rates

earnings growth STOCKHOLDING & INVESTMENTS increase in profit per share of stock an increase in the profit a company earns as expressed on a per-share basis

earnings momentum STOCKHOLDING & INVESTMENTS change in profit per share of stock an increase or decrease in a company's earnings per share as compared to the same period of time in the previous year, used by investors as a measure of how its stock will perform

earnings performance STOCKHOLDING & INVESTMENTS dividend-yielding pattern of stock a measure of how well a specific stock does in providing dividends

earnings per share STOCKHOLDING & INVESTMENTS profit allotted to each share of common stock a financial ratio that measures the portion of a company's profit allocated to each outstanding share of common stock. It is the most basic measure of the value of a share, and also is the basis for calculating several other important investment ratios.

EPS is calculated by subtracting the total value of any preferred stock from net income (earnings) for the period in question, then dividing the resulting figure by the number of shares outstanding during that period.

$$\frac{(\text{Net income} - \text{Dividends on any preferred stock})}{\text{Average number of shares outstanding}}$$

a–z

Dictionary

Companies usually use a weighted average number of shares outstanding over the reporting period, but shares outstanding can either be "primary" or "fully diluted." Primary EPS is calculated using the number of shares that are currently held by investors in the market and able to be traded. Diluted EPS is the result of a complex calculation that determines how many shares would be outstanding if all exercisable warrants and options were converted into shares at the end of a quarter.

Suppose, for example, that a company has granted a large number of share options to employees. If these options are capable of being exercised in the near future, that could significantly alter the number of shares in issue and thus the EPS, even though the net income is the same. Often in such cases, the company might quote the EPS on the existing shares and the fully diluted version. *Abbr* **EPS**

earnings-related contributions FINANCE **payments into social security fund based on earnings** contributions to social security that rise as the person's earnings rise, especially *National Insurance* contributions in the United Kingdom

earnings report *US* STOCKHOLDING & INVESTMENTS **published financial report of US firm** a company's financial statements, which must be published according to US law. *UK term published accounts*

earnings retained ACCOUNTING = *retained profits*

earnings season STOCKHOLDING & INVESTMENTS **time when firms announce earnings** the time of year when major companies declare their results for the previous period

earnings surprise STOCKHOLDING & INVESTMENTS **gap between actual and expected earnings** a considerable difference in size between a company's actual and anticipated earnings

earnings yield FINANCE **earnings as percentage of stock price** money earned by a company during a year, expressed as a percentage of the price of one of its shares

easy money FINANCE = *cheap money*

easy money policy FINANCE **government policy to encourage borrowing** a government policy that aims to expand the economy by making money more easily accessible to the public. This is done by strategies such as lowering interest rates and offering easy access to credit.

easy terms *UK* FINANCE = *installment plan*

EBIT ACCOUNTING **income minus costs** revenue minus the cost of goods sold and normal operating expenses. *Full form earnings before interest and taxes*

EBITDA ACCOUNTING **use of earnings to measure firm's performance** the earnings generated by a business's fundamental operating performance, frequently used in accounting ratios for comparison with other companies. Interest on borrowings, tax payable on those profits, depreciation, and amortization are excluded on the basis that they can distort the underlying performance.

It is calculated as follows:

EBITDA = Revenue – Expenses (excluding tax and interest, depreciation, etc.)

It is important to note that EBITDA ignores many factors that impact on true cash flow, such as working capital, debt payments, and other fixed expenses. Even so, it may be useful for evaluating firms in the same industry with widely different capital structures, tax rates, and depreciation policies. *Full form earnings before interest, tax, depreciation, and amortization*

EBRD BANKING **European bank helping to develop market economies** a bank, established in 1991, to develop programs to tackle a variety of issues. These included the creation and strengthening of infrastructure; industry privatization; the reform of the financial sector, including the development of capital markets and the privatization of commercial banks; the development of productive competitive private sectors of small and medium-sized enterprises in industry, agriculture, and services; the restructuring of industrial sectors to put them on a competitive basis; and the encouragement of foreign investment and cleaning up the environment. The EBRD had 41 original members: the European Commission, the European Investment Bank, all the then EU countries, and all the countries of Eastern Europe except Albania, which finally became a member in October 1991, followed by all the republics of the former USSR in March 1992. *Full form European Bank for Reconstruction and Development*

ECB BANKING **bank responsible for EU monetary policy** the financial institution that replaced the European Monetary Institute in 1998 and that is responsible for carrying out EU monetary policy and administering the euro. *Full form European Central Bank*

ECBC *abbr* FINANCE European Covered Bond Council

ECOA *abbr* FINANCE **US law ensuring equal treatment for borrowers** Equal Credit Opportunity Act

econometric model ECONOMICS **set of mathematical equations representing economic relationships** a way of representing the relationship between economic variables as an equation or set of equations with statistically precise parameters linking the variables

econometrics ECONOMICS **study of mathematical equations for representing economic relationships** the branch of economics concerned with using mathematical models to describe relationships in an economy, for example, between wage rates and levels of employment

economic assumption ECONOMICS **belief on which economic model is based** an assumption built into an economic model, for example, that output will grow at 2.5% in the next tax year

economic benefit FINANCE **benefit measurable in money** a benefit to a person, business, or society that can be measured in financial terms

economic cycle ECONOMICS **recurrent expansion and slowdown of trade** a repeated sequence of business activity expanding, then slowing down, and then expanding again

economic development ECONOMICS **rise in country's living standards** improvements in the living standards and wealth of the citizens of a country

a–z

Dictionary

economic forecaster ECONOMICS **person predicting future economic performance** a person whose job is to predict how a country's economy will perform in the future

economic goods ECONOMICS **products or services sold in market** services or physical objects that can command a price in the market

economic growth ECONOMICS **increase in country's economic activity and income** an increase in the national income of a country created by the long-term productive potential of its economy

economic indicator ECONOMICS **statistical measurement of country's economy** a statistic that may be important for a country's long-term economic health, for example, rising prices or falling exports

economic life ECONOMICS **country's manufacturing and trade conditions** the conditions of trade and manufacture in a country that contribute to its prosperity or poverty

economic miracle ECONOMICS **dramatic rebuilding of economies after World War II** the rapid growth after 1945 in countries such as Germany and Japan, where in ten years economies shattered by World War II were regenerated

economic model ECONOMICS **computerized forecast of economic trends** a computerized plan of a country's economic system, used for forecasting economic trends

economic paradigm ECONOMICS **fundamental economic belief** a basic unchanging economic principle, one that governs the way economists view the world

economic planning ECONOMICS **government's plans for future of economy** plans made by a government for the financial state of a country over different future time periods

economic pressure ECONOMICS **country's negative economic conditions** a condition in a country's economy in which economic indicators are unfavorable

economic profit ACCOUNTING **total revenue less total cost** the difference between the total revenue and total cost associated with a specific business

economics ECONOMICS **study of society's wealth** the study of the consumption, distribution, and production of wealth in societies

economic surplus ECONOMICS **positive balance of costs against output** the positive difference between an economy's output and the costs incurred in factors such as wages, raw materials, and depreciation

economic theory of the firm ECONOMICS **idea that firm's responsibility is to serve stockholders** the theory that the only duty that a company has to those external to it is financial. The economic theory of the firm holds that stockholders should be the prime beneficiaries of an organization's activities. The theory is associated with *top-down leadership* and *cost cutting* through rationalization and *downsizing*. With immediate stock price dominating management activities, the economic theory of the firm has been criticized as being too

short-term, as opposed to the longer-term thinking behind *stakeholder theory*.

economic value added FINANCE **evaluating performance by comparing earnings to capital investment** a way of judging financial performance by measuring the amount by which the earnings of a project, an operation, or a corporation exceed or fall short of the total amount of capital that was originally invested by its owners.

EVA is conceptually simple: from net operating profit, subtract an appropriate charge for the opportunity cost of all capital invested in an enterprise (the amount that could have been invested elsewhere). It is calculated using this formula:

Net operating profit less applicable taxes − Cost of capital = EVA

If a company is considering building a new plant, and its total weighted cost over ten years is $80 million, while the expected annual incremental return on the new operation is $10 million, or $100 million over ten years, then the plant's EVA would be positive, in this case $20 million:

$100million − $80million = $20million

An alternative but more complex formula for EVA is:

(%Return on invested capital − %Cost of capital)
× Original capital invested = EVA

EVA is frequently linked with shareholder value analysis, and an objective of EVA is to determine which business units best utilize their assets to generate returns and maximize shareholder value; it can be used to assess a company, a business unit, a single plant, office, or even an assembly line. This same technique is equally helpful in evaluating new business opportunities. *Abbr* **EVA**

economic welfare ECONOMICS **society's well-being in economic terms** the level of prosperity in an economy, as measured by employment and wage levels

economies of scale ECONOMICS **savings achieved by mass production** the cost advantages of a company producing a product in larger quantities so that each unit costs less to make. *See also diseconomies of scale*

economies of scope ECONOMICS **savings achieved when multiple products share same technology** the cost advantages of a company producing a number of products or engaging in a number of profitable activities that use the same technology

economist ECONOMICS **somebody who studies society's wealth** a person who studies the consumption, distribution, and production of wealth in societies

economy ECONOMICS **production, consumption, and distribution of society's wealth** the distribution of wealth in a society and the means by which that wealth is produced and consumed

economy efficiency principle ECONOMICS **theory about relationships in efficient economy** the principle that if an economy is efficient, no one can be made better off without somebody else being made worse off

e-economy ECONOMICS **economy based largely on online business transactions** an economy that is characterized by extensive use of the Internet and information technology

effective annual interest rate FINANCE **average annual interest rate on deposit** the average interest rate paid on a deposit for a period of a year. It is the total interest received over 12 months expressed as a percentage of the principal at the beginning of the period.

effective date FINANCE, OPERATIONS & PRODUCTION **actual starting date** the date when an action such as the issuing of new stock is effective

effective demand FINANCE **demand for product by those able to buy** demand for a product made by people and organizations with sufficient wealth to pay for it

effective exchange rate CURRENCY & EXCHANGE **exchange rate of one currency against others** a rate of exchange for a currency calculated against a group of currencies whose values have been weighted

effective price STOCKHOLDING & INVESTMENTS **stock price adjusted for rights issue** the price of a stock adjusted to take into account the effects of existing stockholders being offered a rights issue. *See also* **rights issue**

effective rate FINANCE **true interest rate including all factors** the real interest rate to be paid on a loan or deposit, which includes compounding and other factors

effective spread STOCKHOLDING & INVESTMENTS **difference between new issue price and underwriter's price** the difference between the price of a newly issued stock and what the underwriter pays, adjusted for the effect of the announcement of the offering

effective strike price STOCKHOLDING & INVESTMENTS **actual price paid when option is exercised** the price of an option at a specific time, adjusted for fluctuation since the initial offering

effective yield *UK* STOCKHOLDING & INVESTMENTS = *yield to maturity*

efficiency ratio FINANCE **measure of relationship between income and overhead expenses** a way of measuring the proportion of operating revenues or fee income spent on overhead expenses.

Often identified with banking and financial sectors, the efficiency ratio indicates a management's ability to keep overhead costs low. In banking, an acceptable efficiency ratio was once in the low 60s. Now the goal is 50, while better-performing banks boast ratios in the mid-40s. Low ratings usually indicate a higher return on equity and earnings.

This measurement is also used by mature industries, such as steel manufacture, chemicals, or car production, that must focus on tight cost controls to boost profitability because growth prospects are modest.

The efficiency ratio is defined as operating overhead expenses divided by turnover. If operating expenses are $100,000, and turnover is $230,000, then

$$\frac{100{,}000}{230{,}000} = 0.43 \text{ efficiency ratio}$$

However, not everyone calculates the ratio in the same way. Some institutions include all non-interest expenses, while others exclude certain charges and intangible asset amortization.

A different method measures efficiency simply by tracking three other measures: accounts payable to sales, days' sales outstanding, and stock turnover. This indicates how fast a company is able to move its merchandise. A general guide is that if the first two of these measures are low and the third is high, efficiency is probably high; the reverse is likewise true.

To find the stock turnover ratio, divide total sales by total stock. If net sales are $300,000, and stock is $140,000, then

$$\frac{300{,}000}{140{,}000} = 2.14 \text{ stock turnover ratio}$$

To find the accounts payable to sales ratio, divide a company's accounts payable by its annual net sales. A high ratio suggests that a company is using its suppliers' funds as a source of cheap financing because it is not operating efficiently enough to generate its own funds. If accounts payable are $50,000, and total sales are $300,000, then

$$\frac{50{,}000}{300{,}000} = 0.14 = 14\% \text{ accounts payable to sales ratio}$$

efficiency variance FINANCE **disparity between actual and standard cost of production** the difference between the standard cost of making a product and actual costs of production. A separate variance can be calculated for materials, labor, and overhead.

efficient markets hypothesis ECONOMICS **theory on limitations of financial information** the hypothesis that exploiting stock market information cannot bring an investor unexpected returns because stock prices already reflect all the information available to the market about future economic trends and company profitability. *Abbr* **EMH**

EGM *abbr* CORPORATE GOVERNANCE extraordinary general meeting

EIB BANKING **organization that finances EU development** a financial institution whose main task is to further regional development within the EU by financing capital projects, modernizing or converting undertakings, and developing new activities. *Full form* **European Investment Bank**

either-way market CURRENCY & EXCHANGE **currency market buying and selling at same price** a currency market with identical prices for buying and selling, especially for the euro

elastic ECONOMICS **sensitive to price changes** responsive to changes in the price of a product

elasticity ECONOMICS **relationship between supply, demand, and price** a measurement of the relationship between supply, demand, and price.

In practical terms, elasticity indicates the degree to which consumers respond to changes in price. It is obviously important for companies to consider such relationships when contemplating changes in supply, demand, and price.

Demand elasticity measures how much the quantity demanded by a customer changes when the price of a product or service is increased or lowered. This measurement helps companies to find out whether the quantity demanded will remain constant despite price changes. Supply elasticity measures the impact on supply when a price is changed. The reverse can also be calculated, that is, how much the market clearing price for a good or service changes in response to changes in the supply or demand function. This is called the price elasticity, or demand or supply elasticity, respectively.

The general formula for elasticity is:

$$\text{Elasticity} = \frac{\%\ \text{change in x}}{\%\ \text{change in y}}$$

In theory, x and y can be any variable. However, the most common application measures price and demand. If the price of a product is increased from $20 to $25, or 25%, and demand in turn falls from 6,000 to 3,000, elasticity would be calculated as:

$$\frac{-50\%}{25\%} = -2$$

A value greater than 1 means that demand is strongly sensitive to price, while a value of less than 1 means that demand is not price-sensitive.

electronic banking BANKING **remote bank transactions by computer** the use of computers to carry out banking transactions such as withdrawals through ATMs or transfer of funds at point of sale

electronic trading STOCKHOLDING & INVESTMENTS **securities trading using computers** the buying and selling of investment instruments using computer systems

elephant FINANCE **financial institution whose high-volume trading increases prices** a very large financial institution such as a bank that makes trades in high volumes, thereby increasing prices (slang)

eligible liabilities BANKING **liabilities considered when calculating bank's reserves** liabilities that must be taken into account in the calculation of a bank's reserves

eligible paper FINANCE **1.** US **financial instruments accepted for rediscounting** in the United States, first class paper, such as a bill of exchange or a check, acceptable for rediscounting by the Federal Reserve System **2.** UK **financial instruments accepted as loan security** in the United Kingdom, bills of exchange or securities accepted by the Bank of England as security for loans to discount houses. *See also lender of last resort*

eligible reserves BANKING **total amount of money held by US bank** the sum of the cash held by a US bank plus the money it holds at its local Federal Reserve Bank

embezzlement FRAUD **illegal use of money for personal benefit** the illegal use of somebody else's money for personal benefit by the person to whom it has been entrusted

emergency credit FINANCE **special credit given by US Federal Reserve** in the United States, credit given by the *Federal Reserve* to an organization that has no other means of borrowing capital

emerging country *or* emerging nation ECONOMICS **country experiencing development and economic growth** a country in the early stages of becoming industrialized and undergoing economic growth and foreign investment

emerging economy ECONOMICS *see emerging market (sense 1)*

emerging market 1. ECONOMICS **country experiencing development and economic growth** a country that is becoming industrialized and undergoing economic growth. *Also called emerging economy* **2.** MARKETS **financial market in emerging nation** a financial market in a newly industrialized country, often with a high growth rate but with some risks

EMH *abbr* ECONOMICS efficient markets hypothesis

emoluments FINANCE **payments from employment** wages, salaries, fees, or any other monetary benefit derived from employment

employee ownership STOCKHOLDING & INVESTMENTS **when shares are in employees' hands** the possession of shares in a company, in whole or in part, by the workers. There are various forms of employee ownership that give employees a greater or lesser stake in the business. These include: employee stock ownership plans, employee buyouts, cooperatives, and employee trusts. Ownership does not necessarily lead to greater employee participation in decisionmaking, although the evidence suggests that where employees are involved in this, the company is more successful.

employee share ownership plan UK STOCKHOLDING & INVESTMENTS = *employee stock ownership plan*

employee share scheme STOCKHOLDING & INVESTMENTS **making stock available to employees** in the United Kingdom, a plan to give, or encourage employees to buy, a stake in the company that employs them by awarding free or discounted stock. Such plans may be available to some or all employees, and plans approved by HM Revenue & Customs enjoy tax advantages. Types of plan include *employee share ownership plans*, stock options, *Save as You Earn*, and employee share ownership trusts. Among the potential benefits are improved employee commitment and productivity, but the success of a plan may depend on linking it to employee performance and the performance of the price of stock.

employee stock fund STOCKHOLDING & INVESTMENTS US **firm's fund for buying stock for employees** in the United States, a fund from which money is taken to buy shares of a company's stock for its employees

employee stock ownership plan US STOCKHOLDING & INVESTMENTS **system of allocating stock to employees** a plan sponsored by a company by which a trust holds stock in the company on behalf of *employees* and distributes that stock to employees. In the United States, stock can only be sold when an employee leaves the organization, and is thus thought of as a form of pension provision. In the United Kingdom, stock can be disposed of at any time. There are two types of employee stock ownership plans in the United Kingdom: the case-law employee stock ownership plan, which can benefit all or some employees but may not qualify for tax benefits; and the employee stock ownership trust. *UK term* **employee share ownership plan**. *Abbr* **ESOP**

employee stock purchase plan STOCKHOLDING & INVESTMENTS **making stock available to employees** in the United States, a plan to encourage employees to buy a stake in the company that employs them by awarding free or discounted stock. Such plans may be available to some or all employees, and plans approved by the Internal Revenue Service enjoy tax advantages. Among the potential benefits are improved employee commitment and productivity, but the success of a plan may depend on linking it to employee performance and the performance of the price of stock. *Abbr* **ESPP**

EMS CURRENCY & EXCHANGE **first stage in European monetary union** the first stage of economic and monetary union of the EU, which came into force in March 1979, giving stable, but adjustable, exchange rates. *Full form* **European Monetary System**

EMU ECONOMICS **movement toward common European currency** a program for the integration of European economies and the introduction of a common currency. The timetable for European monetary union was outlined in the Maastricht Treaty in 1991. The criteria were that national debt must not exceed 60% of GDP; budget deficit should be 3% or less of GDP; inflation should be no more than 1.5% above the average rate of the three bestperforming economies of the EU in the previous 12 months; and applicants must have been members of the *ERM* for two years without having realigned or devalued their currency. The ERM was abandoned with the introduction of the *euro* in 12 countries in 2002. *Full form* **European Monetary Union**

encash *UK* CURRENCY & EXCHANGE = *cash* (*sense 1*)

endorse BANKING **sign reverse side of check** to sign a bill or check on the back to show that its ownership is being passed to another person or company

endowment FINANCE **donation of money for specified purpose** a gift of money, especially to a nonprofit organization, to be used for a specific purpose

endowment fund FINANCE **fund for nonprofit organization** a mutual fund established to provide income for a nonprofit institution

enterprise risk management RISK **procedure for reducing risk to organization** the process of planning and establishing control systems in order to minimize the risks that an organization faces, including financial, strategic, operational, and hazard risks. *Abbr* **ERM**

enterprise zone FINANCE, BUSINESS **district where government gives incentives for economic development** an area in which the government offers financial incentives such as tax relief to encourage new business activities. *Abbr* **EZ**

entitlement offer FINANCE **nontransferable offer** an offer that cannot be transferred to anyone else

entry ACCOUNTING **item written in accounts ledger** an item of written information put in an accounts ledger

environmental accounting ACCOUNTING **including costs to environment in decisionmaking** the practice of including the indirect costs and benefits of a product or activity, for example, its environmental effects on health and the economy, along with its direct costs when making business decisions. *Also called* **full cost accounting**, **green accounting**

EOQ *abbr* FINANCE, OPERATIONS & PRODUCTION economic order quantity

EPS *abbr* STOCKHOLDING & INVESTMENTS earnings per share

Equal Credit Opportunity Act FINANCE **US law ensuring equal treatment for borrowers** in the United States, a federal law that gives all consumers an equal opportunity to obtain credit by requiring creditors to follow specific rules regarding the information they can obtain from applicants. *Abbr* **ECOA**

equilibrium ECONOMICS **balance in economy** the state of balance in the economy where supply equals demand or a country's balance of payments is neither in deficit nor in excess

equilibrium price ECONOMICS **product price causing balanced supply and demand** the price at which the supply of and the demand for a good are equal. Suppliers increase prices when demand is high and reduce prices when demand is low.

equilibrium quantity ECONOMICS **amount regulating supply and demand** the quantity that needs to be bought for supply to match demand at a specific price. Suppliers increase quantity when demand, and therefore the price, is high and reduce quantity when demand or price is low.

equilibrium rate of interest ECONOMICS **when expected and actual interest rates match** the rate at which the expected interest rate in a market equals the actual rate prevailing

equipment trust certificate STOCKHOLDING & INVESTMENTS **US bond issued to pay for equipment** in the United States, a bond sold for a 20% down payment and collateralized by the equipment purchased with its proceeds

equities STOCKHOLDING & INVESTMENTS **stock in corporation** a stockholder's holdings in a corporation

equity 1. FINANCE **value of asset minus outstanding loans** the value of an asset minus any loans outstanding on it **2.** FINANCE **value of company owned by stockholders** the value of a company that is the property of its stockholders, calculated as the value of the company's assets minus the value of its liabilities, not including the ordinary share capital **3.** STOCKHOLDING & INVESTMENTS **ownership of company's stock** ownership in a company in the form of stock **4.** STOCKHOLDING & INVESTMENTS **stockholder's right to share in company's profit** the right of a stockholder to receive dividends from the profit of a company in which the shares of stock are owned

equity accounting ACCOUNTING listing subsidiary's profits on parent company's books a method of accounting that puts part of the profits of a subsidiary into the parent company's books

equity capital STOCKHOLDING & INVESTMENTS stock owned by stockholders the part of the nominal value of the stock owned by the stockholders of a company. *See also* ***share capital***

equity carve-out STOCKHOLDING & INVESTMENTS sale of shares of stockto fund spin-off a situation in which an established company sells off shares of stockto investors in order to create an independent company from a subsidiary part of the business. *Also called* ***carve-out***

equity claim FINANCE claim on residual earnings a claim on earnings that remain after debts are satisfied

equity contribution agreement FINANCE agreement to contribute equity an agreement to buy a proportion of the capital stock of a company in order to provide funds for a project

equity derivative STOCKHOLDING & INVESTMENTS derivative instrument based on stock a ***derivative instrument*** whose ***underlying asset*** is a stock. The most common equity derivative is an ***option***.

equity dilution STOCKHOLDING & INVESTMENTS decrease in percentage of ownership in firm the reduction in the percentage of a company represented by each share for an existing stockholder who has not increased his or her holding in the issue of new common stock

equity dividend cover UK ACCOUNTING calculation of firm's ability to pay dividend an accounting ratio, calculated by dividing the distributable profits during a given period by the actual dividend paid in that period, that indicates the likelihood of the dividend being maintained in future years.

equity finance UK FINANCE = ***equity financing***

equity financing US FINANCE money contributed for share in business the money introduced into a business by its owners. If it is a for-profit company, then the equity is introduced in exchange for shares and investors can expect a share of any profit. In the case of limited companies, it takes the form of dividends. *UK term* ***equity finance***

equity fund STOCKHOLDING & INVESTMENTS mutual fund that is invested in equities a mutual fund that is invested mainly in stocks, not in government securities or other funds

equity gearing FINANCE relationship of borrowings to equity the ratio between a company's borrowings and its ***equity***

equity multiplier FINANCE US firm's worth as multiple of stock price in the United States, a measure of a company's worth, expressed as a multiple of each dollar of its stock's price

equity risk premium STOCKHOLDING & INVESTMENTS extra return expected on equities compared to bonds an extra return on equities over the return on bonds, because of the risk involved in investing in equities

equity swap STOCKHOLDING & INVESTMENTS, RISK agreement between parties to exchange cash flows an agreement in which one party agrees to exchange its cash flow, which is linked to a benchmark such as the ***London Interbank Offered Rate*** or the rate of return on an ***index***, for another party's fixed or floating rate of interest

equity sweetener FINANCE incentive for people to lend firm money an incentive to encourage people to lend a company money. The sweetener takes the form of a warrant that gives the lender the right to buy stock at a later date and at a specific price.

equivalent annual cash flow FINANCE return on annuity compared to other investment the value of an annuity required to provide an investor with the same return as some other form of investment

equivalent bond yield STOCKHOLDING & INVESTMENTS = ***bond equivalent yield***

ERDF *abbr* FINANCE European Regional Development Fund

ERM 1. CURRENCY & EXCHANGE former system for stabilizing European Community exchange rates a system to maintain exchange rate stability used in the past by member states of the European Community. *Full form* ***Exchange Rate Mechanism 2.*** *abbr* RISK enterprise risk management

ERR *abbr* STOCKHOLDING & INVESTMENTS expected rate of return

error account BANKING account for recording transactions made in error an account for the temporary placement of funds involved in a financial transaction known to have been executed in error

error rate ACCOUNTING proportion of errors made the number of mistakes per thousand entries or per page

errors and omissions ACCOUNTING bookkeeping mistakes mistakes arising from incorrect record keeping or accounting. *Abbr* **E&O**

escrow account BANKING account holding money until contract conditions are met an account where money is held until specific conditions, such as a contract being signed, or a consignment of goods being safely delivered, are met

ESOP *abbr* STOCKHOLDING & INVESTMENTS employee stock ownership plan

ESPP *abbr* STOCKHOLDING & INVESTMENTS employee stock purchase plan

essential industry ECONOMICS industry necessary to nation's economy an industry regarded as crucial to a country's economy and often supported financially by a government by way of tariff protection and tax breaks

establishment fee FINANCE = ***commitment fee***

estate FINANCE deceased person's assets the net assets of somebody who has died

estimate FINANCE **1.** approximation of something's value an approximate calculation of an uncertain value. An estimate may be a reasonable guess based on knowledge and experience or it may be calculated using more sophisticated techniques designed to forecast projected costs, profits, losses, or value. **2. approximation of cost of work** a written statement of an approximate price for work to be undertaken by a business

estimator FINANCE **person who calculates expected job costs** a person whose job is to calculate the likely cost for carrying out work

ethical fund FINANCE **fund providing money to firms having moral practices** a fund that invests in companies that operate by moral standards approved of by their investors, such as not manufacturing or selling weapons, not trading with countries with poor human rights records, or using only environmentally acceptable sources of raw materials

ethical index STOCKHOLDING & INVESTMENTS **list of stock in conscientious firms** a published index of stock in companies that operate by moral standards approved of by their investors

ethical investment STOCKHOLDING & INVESTMENTS **investing only in socially responsible firms** investment only in companies whose policies meet the ethical criteria of the investor. *Also called **socially conscious investing***

Ethical Investment Research Service STOCKHOLDING & INVESTMENTS **organization determining which firms have moral practices** an organization that does research into companies and recommends those that follow specific ethical standards

EU *abbr* ECONOMICS European Union. *See also **single market***

euro *or* Euro CURRENCY & EXCHANGE **currency of nations belonging to EU** the currency of 12 member nations of the European Union. The euro was introduced in 1999, when the first 11 countries to adopt it joined together in an Economic and Monetary Union and tied their currencies' exchange rate to the euro. Notes and coins were brought into general circulation in January 2002, although banks and other financial institutions had before that time carried out transactions in euro. The official plural of euro is "euro," although "euros" is widely used.

euro account BANKING **account operated in euro** a checking account or savings account in euro

Eurobank BANKING, CURRENCY & EXCHANGE **US bank dealing in Eurocurrency** a bank that handles transactions in Eurocurrency

Eurobond STOCKHOLDING & INVESTMENTS **bond issued and traded in different currencies** a bond issued in the currency of one country and sold to investors from another country. *Also called **global bond***

Eurocheque BANKING **check good in any European bank** a check that can be cashed at any bank in the world displaying the European Union crest. The Eurocheque system is based in Brussels.

Eurocredit BANKING, CURRENCY & EXCHANGE **credit in currency of another country** a loan made in a currency other than that of the lending institution

Eurocurrency BANKING, CURRENCY & EXCHANGE **deposits in currency of another country** money deposited in one country

but denominated in the currency of another country, for example, dollars deposited in a British bank

Eurodeposit BANKING, CURRENCY & EXCHANGE **deposit in Eurocurrency** a short-term deposit of Eurocurrency. Eurodeposits have a variable interest rate based on the Euro Interbank Offered Rate.

Eurodollar BANKING, CURRENCY & EXCHANGE **US dollar deposited in foreign bank** a dollar deposited in a European bank or other bank outside the United States

euroland ECONOMICS = *eurozone*

Euronext MARKETS, STOCKHOLDING & INVESTMENTS **pan-European stock exchange** the stock exchange formed by the merger of the Amsterdam, Brussels, and Paris stock exchanges on September 22, 2000. It expanded in 2002 to include the Lisbon Stock Exchange and London International Financial Futures and Options Exchange, before merging with the New York Stock Exchange in 2007 to form the NYSE Euronext group.

Euronext Amsterdam MARKETS, STOCKHOLDING & INVESTMENTS **Dutch stock exchange** considered the world's first stock exchange, the Amsterdam Stock Exchange has its origins in 1602 with the first stocks issued by the Dutch East India Company. It merged with the Hague and Rotterdam stock exchanges in 1972. It then merged with the Brussels and Paris stock exchanges on September 22, 2000, to create *Euronext*, the first pan-European exchange, and is now part of the NYSE Euronext group. The main index of stocks on the exchange is the *AEX Index*. *Also called **AEX, Amsterdam Stock Exchange***

Euronext Brussels MARKETS, STOCKHOLDING & INVESTMENTS **Belgian stock exchange** stock exchange based in Brussels, Belgium, established in 1801. The Brussels Stock Exchange merged with the Antwerp Stock Exchange in 1993 and with the Belgian Futures and Options Exchange in 1999. It then merged with the Amsterdam and Paris stock exchanges on September 22, 2000, to create *Euronext*, the first pan-European exchange, and is now part of the NYSE Euronext group. The main index of stocks on the exchange is the *BEL 20*. *Also called **Brussels Stock Exchange***

Euronext Lisbon MARKETS, STOCKHOLDING & INVESTMENTS **Portuguese stock exchange** stock exchange based in Lisbon, Portugal, established as the Business Man's Assembly in 1769. The Lisbon Stock Exchange merged with the Porto Derivatives Exchange in 1999 to form BVLP, then with the Euronext stock exchange in 2002, and is now part of the NYSE *Euronext* group. The main index of stocks on the exchange is the *PSI 20*. *Also called **Bolsa de Valores de Lisboa e Porto, BVLP, Lisbon Stock Exchange***

Euronext Paris MARKETS, STOCKHOLDING & INVESTMENTS **French stock exchange** stock exchange based in Paris, France, established in 1724. The Paris Stock Exchange merged with the Amsterdam and Brussels stock exchanges on September 22, 2000, to create *Euronext*, the first pan-European exchange, and is now part of the NYSE Euronext group. The main index of stocks on the exchange is the *CAC 40*. *Also called **Paris Bourse, Paris Stock Exchange***

a–z

Dictionary

Euro-note CURRENCY & EXCHANGE **security in Eurocurrency market** a form of Eurocommercial paper in the Eurocurrency market

European Accounting Association ACCOUNTING **European organization for accounting academics** an organization for accounting academics. Founded in 1977 and based in Brussels, the EAA aims to be a forum for European research in accounting. It holds an annual congress and since 1992 has published a journal, *European Accounting Review*. *Abbr* **EAA**

European Bank for Reconstruction and Development BANKING *see* **EBRD**

European Central Bank BANKING *see* **ECB**

European Covered Bond Council FINANCE **representative organization for various financial institutions** the official organization bringing together bond issuers, analysts, investment bankers, rating agencies, and a wide range of interested market participants. *Abbr* **ECBC**

European Investment Bank BANKING *see* **EIB**

European Monetary System CURRENCY & EXCHANGE *see* **EMS**

European Monetary Union CURRENCY & EXCHANGE *see* **EMU**

European option STOCKHOLDING & INVESTMENTS **option exercisable only on expiration date** an option that the buyer can exercise only on the day that it expires. *See also* *American option*

European Private Equity and Venture Capital Association FINANCE **group providing information for investors** an organization that provides information and networking opportunities for investors, entrepreneurs and policymakers in the equity financing industry. *Abbr* **EVCA**

European Regional Development Fund FINANCE **fund supporting less developed European areas** a fund set up to provide grants to less industrially developed parts of Europe. *Abbr* **ERDF**

European Social Charter ECONOMICS **charter containing rights of EU members** a charter adopted by the European Council of the EU in 1989. The 12 rights it contains are: freedom of movement, employment, and remuneration; social protection; improvement of living and working conditions; freedom of association and collective bargaining; worker information; consultation and participation; vocational training; equal treatment of men and women; health and safety protection in the workplace; pension rights; integration of those with disabilities; and protection of young people. *Abbr* **ESC**

European Union ECONOMICS **organization of European nations** a social, economic, and political organization involving 27 European countries. It came into effect in 1993 as a result of the signing of the Maastricht Treaty by 15 countries; other countries joined later. Precursors were the European Community (EC) and the European Economic Community (EEC). *Abbr* **EU**. *See also* *single market*

Euroyen CURRENCY & EXCHANGE **yen deposited in bank abroad** a Japanese yen deposited in a bank outside Japan

Euroyen bond STOCKHOLDING & INVESTMENTS **Eurobond in yen** a Eurobond denominated in yen but issued outside of Japan by a non-Japanese company

eurozone ECONOMICS **countries using euro** the area of Europe comprising those countries that have adopted the euro as a common currency. *Also called* **euroland**

EVA *abbr* FINANCE economic value added

EVCA *abbr* FINANCE European Private Equity and Venture Capital Association

event risk STOCKHOLDING & INVESTMENTS **chance of loss on bond** the possibility that a bond rating will drop because of an unexpected event such as a takeover or restructuring

evergreen loan FINANCE **loan supplying flow of capital** a series of loans providing a continuing stream of capital for a project

exact interest ACCOUNTING **annual interest calculated over 365 days** annual interest calculated on the basis of a full 365 days, as opposed to ordinary interest that is calculated on 360 days

ex-all STOCKHOLDING & INVESTMENTS **without rights to anything pending** having no right with respect to stocks in any pending transaction such as a split or the issuance of dividends. *Abbr* **xa**. *See also* **cum-all**

exceptional items ACCOUNTING **1. ordinary business costs of unusual size or nature** costs that arise from normal business dealings, but that must be recorded because of their unusual size or nature **2. unusual items included in pre-tax balance sheet** items in a balance sheet that do not appear there each year and that are included in the accounts before the pre-tax profit is calculated, as opposed to **extraordinary items** that are calculated after the pre-tax profit

excess 1. FINANCE **assets less liabilities** in a financial institution, the amount by which assets exceed liabilities **2.** *UK* INSURANCE = **deductible**

excess liquidity BANKING **cash in bank exceeding required amount** cash held by a bank above what is required by the regulatory authorities

excess profit FINANCE **unusually high profit** a level of profit that is higher than a level regarded as usual

excess reserves BANKING **reserves in financial institution exceeding required amount** reserves held by a financial institution that are higher than those required by the regulatory authorities. As such reserves may indicate that demand for loans is low, banks often sell their excess reserves to other institutions.

excess return FINANCE **profit from investment** the amount received from an investment in excess of the basic interest rate or the cost of capital by which an activity is financed

exchange 1. MARKETS **place for buying and selling** a **market** where goods, services, or financial instruments are bought and sold **2.** STOCKHOLDING & INVESTMENTS **converting one form of security to another** the conversion of one type of security for another, for example, the exchange of a bond for stock **3.** E-COMMERCE **environment for conducting business** the main type of business-to-business marketplace. The **B2B exchange** enables suppliers, buyers, and intermediaries to come together and offer products to each other according to a set of criteria. **B2B Web exchanges** provide constant price adjustments in line with fluctuations of supply and demand. In E2E or "exchange-to-exchange" e-commerce, buyers and sellers conduct transactions not only within exchanges but also between them. **4.** FINANCE **barter** to trade goods and services for other goods and services **5.** CURRENCY & EXCHANGE **trade one country's currency for another** to trade the currency of one country or economic zone for that of another

exchange controls CURRENCY & EXCHANGE **regulations governing foreign exchange dealings** the regulations by which a country's banking system controls its residents' or resident companies' dealings in foreign currencies and gold

exchange cross rate CURRENCY & EXCHANGE = **cross rate**

exchange dealer CURRENCY & EXCHANGE **foreign currency trader** a person who buys and sells foreign currency

exchange equalization account CURRENCY & EXCHANGE **bank account for regulating value of British pound** the Bank of England account that sells and buys sterling for gold and foreign currencies to smooth out fluctuations in the exchange rate of the British pound

exchange offer STOCKHOLDING & INVESTMENTS **offer of one security for another** an offer to trade one security for another, usually to stockholders of a company in financial trouble and at less favorable terms

exchange option STOCKHOLDING & INVESTMENTS **option allowing holder to exchange assets** an option that allows the holder to trade one asset for another. The option may be either a **European option**, which can be exercised only on the expiration date, or an **American option**, which can be exercised at any time up to and including the expiration date. *Also called* **Margrabe option**

exchange premium CURRENCY & EXCHANGE **surcharge for buying foreign currency** an extra cost above the usual rate for buying a foreign currency

exchange rate CURRENCY & EXCHANGE **rate for converting one currency to another** the rate at which one country's currency can be exchanged for that of another country

Exchange Rate Mechanism CURRENCY & EXCHANGE *see* **ERM**

exchange rate movements CURRENCY & EXCHANGE **changes in value between currencies** the fluctuations in value between currencies that can result in losses to businesses that import and export goods and to investors

exchange rate parity CURRENCY & EXCHANGE **relative value of currencies** the relationship between the value of one currency and another

exchange rate risk CURRENCY & EXCHANGE, RISK **chance of incurring loss on converting currencies** the risk of suffering loss on converting another currency to the currency of a company's own country.

Exchange rate risks can be arranged into three primary categories. (i) Economic exposure: operating costs will rise due to changes in rates and make a product uncompetitive in the world market. Little can be done to reduce this routine business risk that every enterprise must endure. (ii) Translation exposure: the impact of currency exchange rates will reduce a company's earnings and weaken its balance sheet. To reduce translation exposure, experienced corporate fund managers use a variety of techniques known as **currency hedging**. (iii) Transaction exposure: there will be an unfavorable move in a specific currency between the time when a contract is agreed and the time it is completed, or between the time when a lending or borrowing is initiated and the time the funds are repaid. Transaction exposure can be eased by **factoring** (transferring title to foreign accounts receivable to a third-party factoring house).

Although there is no definitive way of forecasting exchange rates, largely because the world's economies and financial markets are evolving so rapidly, the relationships between exchange rates, interest rates, and inflation rates can serve as leading indicators of changes in risk. These relationships are as follows. Purchasing Power Parity theory (PPP): while it can be expressed differently, the most common expression links the changes in exchange rates to those in relative price indices in two countries:

Rate of change of exchange rate = Difference in inflation rates

International Fisher Effect (IFE): this holds that an interest-rate differential will exist only if the exchange rate is expected to change in such a way that the advantage of the higher interest rate is offset by the loss on the foreign exchange transactions. Practically speaking, the IFE implies that while an investor in a low-interest country can convert funds into the currency of a high-interest country and earn a higher rate, the gain (the interestrate differential) will be offset by the expected loss due to foreign exchange rate changes. The relationship is stated as:

Expected rate of change of the exchange rate = Interest-rate differential

Unbiased Forward Rate Theory: this holds that the forward exchange rate is the best unbiased estimate of the expected future spot exchange rate.

Expected exchange rate = Forward exchange rate

exchange rate spread CURRENCY & EXCHANGE **difference in buying and selling price of currencies** the difference between the price at which a broker or other intermediary buys and sells foreign currency

Exchequer BANKING **UK government's bank account** in the United Kingdom, the government's account at the Bank of England into which all revenues from taxes and other sources are paid

Exchequer stocks STOCKHOLDING & INVESTMENTS **UK government stocks** UK government stocks used to finance government expenditure. They are regarded as a very safe investment.

exclusive economic zone ECONOMICS **area in country with special economic conditions** a zone in a country in which specific economic conditions apply. The Special Economic Zone in China, where trade is conducted free of state control, is an example.

ex coupon STOCKHOLDING & INVESTMENTS **without interest coupons** without the interest coupons or after interest has been paid

ex dividend STOCKHOLDING & INVESTMENTS **giving buyer no dividend right** used to describe bonds or stocks that, when they are sold, do not provide the buyer with the right to a forthcoming dividend

execution 1. STOCKHOLDING & INVESTMENTS **completion of securities trade** the process of completing an order to buy or sell securities **2.** LEGAL **carrying out contract** the process of carrying out the terms of a legal order or contract

executive CORPORATE GOVERNANCE **1. person in senior management** an employee in a position of senior responsibility in an organization. An executive is involved in planning, strategy, policy making, and *line management*. **2. any person with responsible job** a person with a significant role in an organization or project, for example, a *manager*, *consultant*, *executive officer*, or *agent*

executive chairman CORPORATE GOVERNANCE **organization's highest executive** the most senior executive in an organization when the roles of chair and chief executive are combined, and the executive chairman has some control over daily operations. *See also chairman*

executive director CORPORATE GOVERNANCE **director in senior management position** a senior employee of an organization, usually with responsibility for a specific function and usually, but not always, a member of the *board of directors*

executive officer CORPORATE GOVERNANCE = *executive* (sense 2)

executive share option scheme UK STOCKHOLDING & INVESTMENTS = *executive stock option plan*

executive stock option plan US STOCKHOLDING & INVESTMENTS **stock purchase arrangement for top employees** an arrangement whereby some directors and employees are given the opportunity to purchase stock in the company at a fixed price at a future date. In some jurisdictions, such arrangements can be tax efficient if specific local tax authority conditions are met. *UK term executive share option scheme*

exempt purchaser STOCKHOLDING & INVESTMENTS **institutional investor exempt from securities commission filing requirements** an institutional investor who may buy newly issued securities without filing a prospectus with a securities commission

exempt security STOCKHOLDING & INVESTMENTS **security exempt from legal requirement** a security that is not subject to a provision of law such as margin or registration requirements

exercise STOCKHOLDING & INVESTMENTS **to use the right to act** to put into effect a right to carry out a transaction with previously agreed terms, especially in trading *options*

exercise date STOCKHOLDING & INVESTMENTS **date when option may be taken** the date on which the holder of an option can put its terms into effect

exercise notice STOCKHOLDING & INVESTMENTS **optionholder's notice of wish to exercise option** an optionholder's notification to the option writer of his or her desire to exercise the option

exercise of warrants STOCKHOLDING & INVESTMENTS **using warrant to buy stock** the process of activating the right given by a warrant to purchase stock at a specific date

exercise price STOCKHOLDING & INVESTMENTS **1. price at which option is taken** the price at which an option will be put into effect **2.** = *strike price*

exercise value STOCKHOLDING & INVESTMENTS **profit from cashing in option** the amount of profit that can be realized by cashing in an *option*

Eximbank BANKING **US bank lending money to foreign importers** a bank founded in 1934 that provides loans direct to foreign importers of US goods and services *Full form* ***Export-Import Bank***

exit STOCKHOLDING & INVESTMENTS **termination of investment** the way in which an investor can realize the gains or losses of an investment, for example, by selling the company they have invested in

exit charge *or* **exit fee** STOCKHOLDING & INVESTMENTS **fee charged to sell out of investment** a charge sometimes made by a trust when selling shares in a mutual fund

exit P/E ratio FINANCE **final price/earnings ratio** the *price/earnings ratio* when a company changes hands, as by a takeover or sale

ex-legal STOCKHOLDING & INVESTMENTS **US bond not displaying legal opinion** in the United States, a municipal bond that is issued without the legal opinion of a law firm printed on it

ex officio CORPORATE GOVERNANCE **by virtue of one's office** because of an office held. An officeholder such as a treasurer may attend a committee meeting "ex officio" because of the office held in the wider organization, even if they are not otherwise a member of that committee.

exotic option STOCKHOLDING & INVESTMENTS, RISK **complicated option traded in over-the-counter market** a complex option contract whose underlying asset or terms of payoff differ from those of either a standard *American option* or *European option*. Exotic options are usually traded in the *over-the-counter market*.

expansionary monetary policy FINANCE **lending at low interest to stimulate economy** a government strategy of lending money at low interest rates to stimulate an economy that is entering or experiencing a recession

expected rate of return *or* **expected return** STOCKHOLDING & INVESTMENTS **probable return on investment** the projected

percentage return on an investment, based on the weighted probability of all possible rates of return.

It is calculated by the following formula:

$$ERR = \sum_{i=1}^{n} = (P(i) \times r_i)$$

where P(i) is the probability of outcome i and ri is the return for outcome i.

The following example illustrates the principle that the formula expresses:

The current price of ABC, Inc. stock is trading at $10. At the end of the year, ABC shares are projected to be traded:

- 25% higher if economic growth exceeds expectations-a probability of 30%;
- 12% higher if economic growth equals expectations-a probability of 50%;
- 5% lower if economic growth falls short of expectations-a probability of 20%.

To find the expected rate of return, simply multiply the percentages by their respective probabilities and add the results:

$$(30\% \times 25\%) + (50\% \times 12\%) + (25\% \times -5\%) = 7.5 + 6 + -1.25 = 12.25\% \text{ ERR}$$

A second example:

- if economic growth remains robust (a 20% probability), investments will return 25%;
- if economic growth ebbs, but still performs adequately (a 40% probability), investments will return 15%;
- if economic growth slows significantly (a 30% probability), investments will return 5%;
- if the economy declines outright (a 10% probability), investments will return 0%.

Therefore:

$$(20\% \times 25\%) + (40\% \times 15\%) + (30\% \times 5\%) + (10\% \times 0\%)$$
$$= 5\% + 6\% + 1.5\% + 0\% = 12.5\% \text{ ERR}$$

Abbr **ERR**. *See also* ***capital asset pricing model***

expected return FINANCE **probable return on investment**

expected value FINANCE **future value based on probability of an occurrence** the future value of a course of action, weighted according to the probability that the course of action will actually occur. If the possible course of action produces income of $10,000 and has a 10% chance of occurring, its expected value is 10% of $10,000 or $1,000.

expenditure FINANCE **amount spent** an amount of money spent on a particular thing, or the total amount spent

expenditure switching ECONOMICS **switching government spending from one area to another** government action to divert domestic spending from one sector to another, for example, from imports to home-produced goods

expense ACCOUNTING **1. cost required** a cost incurred in buying goods or services **2. money spent** a charge against a company's profit

expense ratio STOCKHOLDING & INVESTMENTS **percentage of management costs passed on** the percentage of the assets held in a mutual fund that includes management fees and other

costs of operating the fund and that are passed on to stockholders

expiration date *US* STOCKHOLDING & INVESTMENTS **last day on which to exercise an option** the last day on which somebody who holds an option to buy or sell an asset can exercise that option. *UK term* ***expiry date***

expiry date *UK* STOCKHOLDING & INVESTMENTS = ***expiration date***

explicit cost FINANCE **cost of using resources not owned by producer** the cost of resources that are bought from outside the company producing the good or service. *See also* ***implicit cost***

exploding bonus FINANCE **potential recruits' bonus that diminishes with time** a bonus offered to recent graduates that encourages them to sign for a job as quickly as possible as it reduces in value with every day of delay (slang)

Export-Import Bank BANKING, INTERNATIONAL TRADE *see* ***Eximbank***

export-led growth ECONOMICS **increase in economy based on exports** growth in which a country's main source of income is from its export trade

ex-rights STOCKHOLDING & INVESTMENTS **sold without rights** for sale without rights such as voting or conversion rights. The term can be applied to transactions such as the purchase of new shares.

extendable bond STOCKHOLDING & INVESTMENTS **bond whose maturity can be postponed** a bond whose maturity can be delayed by either the issuer or the holder

extendable note STOCKHOLDING & INVESTMENTS **note whose maturity can be postponed** a note whose maturity can be delayed by either the issuer or the holder

extended credit FINANCE **1. credit with long repayment terms** credit that allows the borrower a long time before payment is required **2. long repayment term offered by US Federal Reserve** in the United States, an extra long period of credit offered to commercial banks by the Federal Reserve

extended fund facility ECONOMICS **time allowance for repaying IMF** a credit facility operated by the *International Monetary Fund* that allows a country up to eight years to repay money it has borrowed from the fund

Extensible Business Reporting Language FINANCE *see* ***XBRL***

external account BANKING **account of overseas resident in UK bank** an account held at a United Kingdom-based bank by a customer who is an overseas resident

external audit ACCOUNTING **periodic independent audit of firm's accounts** a periodic examination of the books of account and records of an entity conducted by an independent third party (an auditor) to ensure that they have been properly maintained; are accurate and comply with established concepts, principles, and accounting standards; and give a true and fair view of the financial state of the entity. *See also* ***internal audit***

external debt ECONOMICS country's debts to nonresidents the part of a country's debt that is owed to creditors who are not residents of the country

external finance FINANCE investors' money money that a company obtains from investors, for example, by loans or by issuing stock

external funds FINANCE third-party money money that a business obtains from a third party rather than from its own resources

extraordinary general meeting CORPORATE GOVERNANCE general meeting other than regular annual meeting any general meeting of an organization other than the *AGM*annual meeting. Directors can usually call an extraordinary general meeting at their discretion, as can company members who either hold not less than 10% of the paid-up voting shares, or who represent not less than 10% of the voting rights. Directors are obliged to call an EGM if there is a substantial loss of capital. Fourteen days' written notice must be given, or 21 days' written notice if a special resolution is to be proposed. Only special business can be transacted at the meeting, the general nature of which must be specified in the convening notice. *Abbr* **EGM**

extraordinary item ACCOUNTING exceptional inclusion in firm's accounts an item, such as an acquisition or a sale of assets, that is included in a company's accounts but is not likely to occur again. These items are not taken into account when a company's operating profit is calculated.

extraordinary resolution CORPORATE GOVERNANCE vote held on exceptional issue in the United Kingdom, an exceptional issue that is put to the vote at a company's general meeting, for example, a change to the company's articles of association, requiring 14 days' notice

EZ *abbr* FINANCE, BUSINESS enterprise zone

F

face value 1. FINANCE amount on banknote the amount printed on a banknote, showing its value **2.** STOCKHOLDING & INVESTMENTS value displayed the value shown on a *financial instrument* such as bonds or stocks, often different than the actual value

facility FINANCE total credit offered the total amount of credit that a lender will allow a borrower under a specific agreement

facility fee FINANCE charge for arranging credit a charge made by a lender to a borrower for arranging credit facilities

facility takeover UK FRAUD type of identity theft a type of fraud in which a person impersonates another person and falsely claims a change of address in order to gain access to and control that person's financial accounts

factor 1. FINANCE collector of corporate debt a business that purchases or lends money on *accounts receivable* based on an evaluation of the *creditworthiness* of prospective

customers of the business, for a small percentage of the debt amount **2.** STATISTICS statistical variable in a statistical study, a variable such as one affecting the price of an asset which can be isolated and modeled separately

factoring FINANCE **1.** transferring of foreign debts the practice of transferring title to foreign *accounts receivable* to a third-party *factor* that assumes responsibility for collections, administrative services, and any other services requested. Major exporters use factoring as a way of reducing exchange rate risk. The fee for this service is a percentage of the value of the receivables, anywhere from 5% to 10% or higher, depending on the currencies involved. Companies often include this percentage in selling prices to recoup the cost. **2.** selling firm's debts at discount the sale of *accounts receivable* to a third party (the *factor*) at a discount, in return for cash. A factoring service may be "with recourse," in which case the supplier takes the risk of the debt not being paid, or "without recourse," when the factor takes the risk. *See also invoice discounting* **3.** buying of debts the practice of buying up a business's *accounts receivable*, providing it with *working capital*

factoring charges FINANCE cost of selling debts to third party the cost of selling *accounts receivable* to an agent for a commission

factor market ECONOMICS place where capital or labor is traded a market in which *factors of production* are bought and sold, for example, the capital market or the labor market

Failure Mode and Effects Analysis RISK way of identifying and dealing with potential failures a method for identifying and ranking the seriousness of ways in which a product, process, or service could fail, and finding ways in which to minimize the risk of those potential failures. *Abbr* **FMEA**

fair market value *or* fair value FINANCE asset's or liability's worth in arm's length transaction the amount for which an asset or liability could be exchanged in an arm's length transaction between informed and willing parties, other than in a forced or liquidation sale.

fair value accounting UK ACCOUNTING = *historical cost accounting*

fallen angel STOCKHOLDING & INVESTMENTS highly rated security whose value has dropped a stock that was once very desirable but has now dropped in value (slang)

falling knife STOCKHOLDING & INVESTMENTS stock whose price has taken steep drop a stock whose price has fallen at a rapid rate over a short time period

false accounting ACCOUNTING, FRAUD criminal accounting practices the criminal offense of changing, destroying, or hiding accounting records for a dishonest purpose

false market MARKETS, FRAUD market influenced by illegal manipulation of stock prices a market in stocks caused by persons or companies conspiring to buy or sell and so influence the stock price to their advantage

falsification FRAUD making false accounting entries the activity of making false entries in financial accounts

family of funds STOCKHOLDING & INVESTMENTS **related group of mutual funds** a selection of mutual funds with different objectives that is offered by one investment company, allowing investors to easily transfer money from one fund to another with little cost. *Also called* *fund family*

FAS ACCOUNTING **US accounting standards** in the United States, the standards of financial reporting and accounting established by the FASB. *Full form* **Financial Accounting Standards**

FASB ACCOUNTING **US accounting organization** in the United States, an institution responsible for establishing the standards of financial reporting and accounting for companies in the private sector. The Securities and Exchange Commission performs a comparable role for public companies. *Full form* **Financial Accounting Standards Board**

FCA ACCOUNTING **ICAEW Fellow Chartered Accountant** a Fellow (long-term member) of the Institute of Chartered Accountants in England and Wales

FCCA ACCOUNTING **ACCA Fellow, Chartered Certified Accountant** a Fellow (long-term member) of the Association of Chartered Certified Accountants

FCM *abbr* STOCKHOLDING & INVESTMENTS futures commission merchant

FCMA ACCOUNTING **CIMA Fellow Chartered Management Accountant** a Fellow (long-term member) of the Chartered Institute of Management Accountants

FDI *abbr* STOCKHOLDING & INVESTMENTS foreign direct investment

Fed BANKING = *Federal Reserve*

Federal Funds FINANCE **US reserves** deposits held in reserve at the Federal Reserve by the US banks. The *Federal Funds rate*, the rate that the Federal Reserve charges banks for borrowing reserves, is the key US monetary policy rate.

Federal Home Loan Mortgage Corporation MORTGAGES, RISK *see* *Freddie Mac*

Federal National Mortgage Association MORTGAGES, RISK *see* *Fannie Mae*

Federal Open Market Committee ECONOMICS **committee that oversees US monetary policy** the 12-member committee of the *Federal Reserve Board* that meets eight times a year to determine US monetary policy by setting interest rates or by buying and selling government securities. *Abbr* **FOMC**

Federal Reserve BANKING **system of federal government control of US banks** the central banking system of the United States, founded in 1913 by an Act of Congress. The board of governors, made up of seven members, is based in Washington, DC, and 12 Reserve Banks are located in major cities across the United States. It regulates money supply, prints money, fixes the discount rate, and issues bonds for government debt. *Also called* **Federal Reserve System, Fed**

Federal Reserve bank BANKING **major US bank** any of the 12 banks that are members of the US *Federal Reserve*

Federal Reserve Board BANKING **supervisory board of the US Federal Reserve** the seven-member Board of Governors, appointed by the President of the United States and confirmed by the Senate, that supervises the *Federal Reserve* and formulates monetary policy. Appointees to the Board of Governors serve for 14 years. *Abbr* **FRB**

Federal Reserve note CURRENCY & EXCHANGE **US paper money** a piece of paper money issued by the Federal Reserve Bank and approved as the legal tender of the United States

Federal Reserve System BANKING = *Federal Reserve*

Fed funds rate BANKING **interest rate on interbank loans in Federal Reserve** the rate charged by US banks for lending money deposited with the *Federal Reserve* to other banks

Fed pass BANKING **US Federal Reserve's easing of credit** the addition of reserves to the *Federal Reserve* in order to increase availability of credit

Fedwire BANKING **US electronic transfer system** the US *Federal Reserve*'s electronic system for transferring funds

fee FINANCE **payment to professional for services** money paid for work carried out by a professional person such as an accountant

fee work FINANCE **work done for organization by non-employees** work on a project carried out by independent workers or contractors, rather than employees of an organization

fiat money FINANCE **government-recognized money** coins or banknotes that have little intrinsic value in the material of which they are made but that are recognized by a government or other issuing authority, such as the European Central Bank, as having value

FICO score FINANCE **US system for assessing credit rating** a score used by lenders in the United States to assess a person's ability to pay back a loan, based on the person's payment history, current debt, types of credit used, length of credit history, and new credit. Scores range from 300 to 850. The system was devised by the Fair Isaac Corporation (FICO).

fictitious assets ACCOUNTING **book assets with no resale value** assets such as pre-payments that do not have a resale value but are entered as assets on a company's *balance sheet*

fiduciary deposit BANKING **bank-managed deposit** a bank deposit that is managed for the depositor by the bank

figures ACCOUNTING **financial results** a company's financial results calculated for a particular period of time

fill STOCKHOLDING & INVESTMENTS **buy or sell an investment upon client's order** to carry out a client's instructions to buy or sell a security or commodity

final closing date MERGERS & ACQUISITIONS **final day for acceptance of takeover** the last date for the acceptance of a *takeover bid*, when the bidder has to announce how many stockholders have accepted the offer

final demand FINANCE **last reminder before legal action of debt** a last reminder from a supplier to a customer to pay an outstanding debt. Suppliers often begin legal proceedings if a final demand is ignored.

final discharge FINANCE **last debt payment** the final payment on the amount outstanding on a debt

final dividend STOCKHOLDING & INVESTMENTS **year-end dividend payment** the *dividend* paid at the end of a year's trading. The final dividend must be approved by a company's stockholders.

final sale *US* FINANCE **sale of nonreturnable items** a sale that does not allow the purchaser to return the goods. *UK term firm sale*

finance FINANCE **1. supply money for business or project** to provide an amount of money for a particular purpose. *See also fund* **2.** *UK* = *financing*

Finance and Leasing Association FINANCE **financing and leasing firms' UK organization** in the United Kingdom, an organization representing firms engaged in business financing and the leasing of equipment and cars

finance company FINANCE **business lending money for purchases** a business that lends money to people or companies against *collateral*, especially to make purchases of some kind. *UK term finance house*

finance house *UK* FINANCE = *finance company*

finance lease *UK* FINANCE = *capital lease*

finances FINANCE **money available for spending** the financial status of a person or organization

financial FINANCE **of finance** relating to the management of money

financial accountant TREASURY MANAGEMENT **UK accountant acting as adviser or financial director** a qualified accountant, a member of the Institute of Financial Accountants, who advises on accounting matters or who works as the financial director of a company

financial accounting 1. TREASURY MANAGEMENT **financial reports for investors and external parties** the form of accounting in which financial reports are produced to provide investors or others outside a company with information on a company's financial status. *See also management accounting* **2.** ACCOUNTING **process of producing financial statements** the process of classifying and recording a company's transactions and presenting them in the form of profit and loss accounts, balance sheets, and cash flow statements, for a given *accounting period*

Financial Accounting Standards ACCOUNTING *see FAS*

Financial Accounting Standards Board ACCOUNTING *see FASB*

financial adviser FINANCE **investment adviser** somebody whose job is to give advice about investments

financial aid FINANCE **money provided to help somebody or something** monetary assistance given to an individual, organization, or nation. International financial aid, from one country to another, is often used to fund educational, health-related, or other humanitarian activities.

financial analyst STOCKHOLDING & INVESTMENTS = *investment analyst*

financial capital FINANCE **funds for buying physical assets** funds that can be used for the purchase of assets such as buildings and equipment. *See also real capital*

financial control TREASURY MANAGEMENT **management of firm's finances** the policies and procedures established by an organization for managing, documenting, and reporting its financial transactions

financial correspondent FINANCE **reporter who covers money matters** a reporter who writes articles on money matters or reports on them on television or radio

financial distress FINANCE **situation close to bankruptcy** the condition of being in severe difficulties over money, especially being close to *bankruptcy*

financial economies of scale FINANCE **benefits gained by increasing scale of activity** financial advantages gained by being able to do things on a large scale

financial engineering STOCKHOLDING & INVESTMENTS **converting or creating financial instruments** the conversion of one form of financial instrument into another, such as the swap of a fixed-rate instrument for a floating-rate one, or the creation of a new type of financial instrument —financial engineer

financial incentive scheme FINANCE **in UK, money rewarding improved performance** in the United Kingdom, a program offering employees a cash bonus, share options or other monetary reward for improved commitment and performance and as a means of motivation. *See also non-financial incentive scheme*

financial institution FINANCE **organization investing large sums of money** an organization, such as a bank, savings and loan, pension fund, or insurance company, that invests large amounts of money in securities

financial instrument STOCKHOLDING & INVESTMENTS **contract that is evidence of financial transaction** any contract that gives rise to both a financial asset of one entity and a financial liability or equity instrument of another entity. Financial instruments include both primary financial instruments such as bonds, currency, and stocks, and derivative financial instruments, whose value derives from the underlying assets.

financial intermediary FINANCE **financial institution handling deposits and/or loans** an institution that accepts deposits or loans from individuals and lends money to clients. Banks, savings and loan associations, and finance companies are all financial intermediaries.

financial leverage FINANCE **relationship between firm's borrowings and stockholders' funds** the relationship between a company's borrowings (which includes both prior charge capital and long-term debt) and its stockholders' funds (common share capital plus reserves). Calculations can be made in a number of ways, and may be based on capital values or on earnings/interest relationships. Overdrafts and interest paid thereon may also be included:

$$\frac{\text{Profit before interest and tax}}{\text{Profit before tax}}$$

shows the effect of interest on the operating profit.

$$\frac{\text{Profit before interest and tax}}{\text{Interest expense}}$$

shows the number of times that profit will cover interest expense.

$$\frac{\text{Total long-term debt}}{\text{(Shareholders' funds + long-term debt)}}$$

shows the proportion of long-term financing which is being supplied by debt.

$$\frac{\text{Total long-term debt}}{\text{Total assets}}$$

a measure of the capacity to redeem debt obligations by the sale of assets.

$$\frac{\text{(Operating cashflows – Taxation paid – Returns on investment and servicing of finance)}}{\text{Repayments of debt due within one year}}$$

measures ability to redeem debt.

A company with a high proportion of prior charge capital to shareholders' funds is highly leveraged, and is lowly or lightly leveraged if the reverse situation applies. *Also called* **gearing**

financial obligation FINANCE **something you must pay** a sum of money that you are committed to pay, especially a debt. *See also* **collateralized debt obligation**

financial obligations FINANCE **things you must spend money on** things that you must use your money to pay for, such as rent, household expenses, dependent family members, etc.

financial performance FINANCE **firm's ability to generate revenue** a measure of a company's ability to generate income over a given period of time

financial planner FINANCE **somebody giving advice about money** a professional investment adviser who analyzes a person's financial situation and goals and prepares a plan to meet those goals. *See also* **independent financial adviser**

financial planning FINANCE **money management for future** the activity of producing strategies for the acquisition of funds to finance activities and meet established goals

Financial Planning Association of Australia FINANCE **Australian organization for financial planners** a national organization representing companies and individuals working in the Australian financial planning industry. Established in 1992, the Association is responsible for monitoring standards among its members. *Abbr* **FPA**

financial position FINANCE **value of firm's assets and liabilities** the amount of money that a person or organization has in terms of assets and liabilities

financial pyramid STOCKHOLDING & INVESTMENTS, RISK **investment pattern tapering from safe to risky** an investment strategy, typically having four levels of risk. The first and largest percentage of assets are in safe, liquid investments; the second, in investments that provide income and long-term growth; the third, in riskier investments with a chance of greater return; and the fourth and smallest percentage, in the riskiest investments with the chance of greatest return.

financial report ACCOUNTING **document detailing firm's financial position** a document that gives the financial position of a company or other organization

Financial Reporting Review Panel ACCOUNTING **UK group for examining questionable accounting practices** in the United Kingdom, a review panel established to examine contentious departures from accounting standards by large companies. It is a subsidiary body of the Financial Reporting Council.

Financial Reporting Standards Board ACCOUNTING **New Zealand accounting organization** in New Zealand, an organization that is responsible for setting and monitoring accounting standards. *Abbr* **FRSB**

financial resources FINANCE **money available for spending** the money that is available for a person or organization to spend

financial review FINANCE **examination of organization's finances** an examination of the state of an organization's finances

financial risk FINANCE, RISK **investors' chance of loss** the possibility of financial loss in an investment or speculation

Financial Services Compensation scheme FINANCE **fund compensating customers of insolvent UK financial firm** in the United Kingdom, an independent organization set up by law to pay compensation to customers who have made claims against an authorized financial services firm in the event that the firm is unable, or likely to be unable, to pay the claims

financial services industry FINANCE **financial institutions dealing in money management** the business activity of the financial institutions that offer money management services such as banking, investment, brokerage, and insurance

financial statements ACCOUNTING **documents reporting company's financial performance** summaries of accounts to provide information for interested parties. The most important financial statements are the balance sheet, income statement, statement of cash flows, and the shareholders' equity statement. *See also* **annual report**

financial supermarket FINANCE **firm providing many different financial services** a company that offers a variety of financial services. For example, a bank may offer loans, mortgages, retirement plans, and insurance alongside its existing range of normal banking services.

Financial Times BUSINESS, FINANCE **British financial newspaper** a respected British financial daily newspaper, first published on January 9, 1888. It is published in London but printed in 24 cities and available worldwide, as well as online.

a-z

Dictionary

It jointly owns the index company FTSE with the London Stock Exchange. *Abbr* **FT**

financial year *UK* **1.** ACCOUNTING, TAX = *fiscal year* **2.** TAX **for UK corporations, April 1–March 31** in the United Kingdom, for corporation tax purposes, the period from 1 April of a given year to 31 March of the following year

financier FINANCE **somebody who provides financing** a person who specializes in the provision of financing to other people or organizations

financing *US* FINANCE **money required to pay for something** the money needed by an individual or company to pay for something, for example, a project or inventory. *UK term* *finance*

financing gap 1. FINANCE **difference between money available and money needed** a shortfall between the funds available and the funds needed for a project. For example, a company planning expansion is able to finance some of this activity from internally generated cash and some from existing finance agreements but any shortfall requires the raising of new funds. **2.** ECONOMICS **funding shortfall from canceling poorer countries' debts** a gap in funding for institutions such as the *International Monetary Fund* caused by canceling the debts of poorer countries such as those in West Africa

financing vehicle FINANCE **product providing funds for activity** a method or product used to provide the funds for an activity

finder's fee FINANCE **fee for finding new client** a fee paid to somebody who finds a client for another person or company, for example, somebody who introduces a new client to a brokerage firm

fine-tuning ECONOMICS **making small changes to improve economic position** the process of making small adjustments in areas such as interest rates, tax bands, or the money supply, to improve a nation's economy

fire sale 1. FINANCE **sale of anything at a large discount** a sale of anything at a very low price, usually because the seller is facing *bankruptcy* **2.** OPERATIONS & PRODUCTION **sale of fire-damaged goods** a sale of goods that have been damaged during a fire

firm sale *UK* FINANCE = *final sale*

first quarter ACCOUNTING **first part of fiscal year** the period of three months from January to the end of March, or the period of three months at the start of any fiscal year. *Abbr* **Q1**

first-round financing FINANCE **initial funding** the first infusion of capital into a project

fiscal agent BANKING **agent in finance matters** a bank or trust that takes over the fiscal responsibilities of another party

fiscal balance ECONOMICS **balance of income and expenditure** the extent to which government receipts differ from government outlay. If outlays exceed receipts then the fiscal balance is negative or in deficit; if receipts exceed outlays then the balance is positive or in surplus.

fiscal consolidation ECONOMICS **policy for controlling government shortfall** a set of measures designed to reduce government deficits and the accumulation of debts

fiscal policy ECONOMICS, TAX **government's methods for managing economy** the central government's policy on lowering or raising taxation or increasing or decreasing public expenditure in order to stimulate or depress *aggregate demand*

fiscal year *US* ACCOUNTING, TAX **firm's 12-month accounting period** a twelve-month period used by a company for accounting and in some jurisdictions tax purposes. A fiscal year is not necessarily the same as a calendar year. *Abbr* **FY**. *UK terms* **accounting year**, *financial year*. *See also* *accounting period*

fixed asset ACCOUNTING **asset that firm keeps long-term** a long-term business asset such as a machine or building that will not usually be traded

fixed assets register ACCOUNTING **register of tangible assets** a record of individual tangible fixed assets belonging to a company or organization

fixed-asset turnover ratio ACCOUNTING **measure of how firm uses its assets** a measure of the use a business makes of its capital assets. It is calculated by dividing sales by net fixed assets.

fixed capital FINANCE **durable assets such as buildings and machinery** assets in the form of buildings and machinery, that are long-lasting and can be used repeatedly for production

fixed charge FINANCE **creditor's right to specific asset** the right of a creditor to a claim on a specific asset, as opposed to a *floating charge* that applies to all a company's assets. *Also called* **specific charge**

fixed cost ACCOUNTING **cost that remains fixed when sales fluctuate** a cost that does not change according to sales volumes, for example, overhead such as rent or production costs

fixed deposit BANKING **deposit paying fixed interest over set period** a deposit that pays a fixed rate of interest over a defined period

fixed exchange rate CURRENCY & EXCHANGE **set rate of exchange between currencies** a rate of exchange of one currency against another that cannot fluctuate, and can only be changed by devaluation or revaluation

fixed exchange rate system CURRENCY & EXCHANGE **currency exchange system with unchanging rates** a system of currency exchange in which there is no change of rate

fixed expenses FINANCE **unvarying overhead costs** costs that do not vary with different levels of production, for example, rent, staff salaries, and insurance

fixed income FINANCE **income that remains unchanged each year** income that does not change from year to year, for example, from an annuity

fixed interest FINANCE **1. with unvarying interest rate** used to describe a loan or financial product that has an interest rate that does not go up or down **2. interest rate that stays the same** interest that is paid at a rate that does not vary over a period of time

fixed-interest loan FINANCE **loan with unchanging interest rate** a loan whose rate of interest stays the same over the whole period of the loan

fixed-interest security STOCKHOLDING & INVESTMENTS **investment paying constant interest** an investment such as a government bond that produces an amount of interest that does not change with changes in short-term interest rates. *Also called **fixed-rate security***

fixed rate FINANCE **unchanging interest rate** an interest rate for loans that does not change with fluctuating conditions in the market and stays the same for the whole period of the loan

fixed-rate loan FINANCE **loan with unchanging interest rate** a loan with an interest rate that is set at the beginning of the term and remains the same throughout

fixed-rate security STOCKHOLDING & INVESTMENTS = *fixed-interest security*

fixed scale of charges FINANCE **range of standard charges** a set of charges that does not vary according to individual circumstances but is applied consistently in all cases of the same kind

fixed yield FINANCE **constant percentage return on investment** a percentage return on an investment which does not change over a period of time

flat rate FINANCE **unvarying standard rate** a price, payment or interest rate that remains the same regardless of other factors which may change

flat yield STOCKHOLDING & INVESTMENTS **interest rate as percentage of fixed-interest security price** an interest rate that is a percentage of the price paid for a *fixed-interest security*

flat yield curve FINANCE **graph using unified interest rate for bonds** a visual representation of relative interest rates that shows the same interest rates for long-term bonds as for short-term bonds. As investors are assumed to prefer shorter maturities to longer ones, other factors being equal, a flat yield curve is normally assumed to imply that investors can expect lower short-term rates in future.

flexed budget FINANCE **budget responsive to changes in trade** a budget that changes in response to changes in sales turnover and output

flexible exchange rate system CURRENCY & EXCHANGE **currency exchange system with fluctuating rates** a system of currency exchange in which rates change from time to time

flight of capital FINANCE **removal of investment money because of economic uncertainty** the rapid movement of investment money out of one country because of lack of confidence in that country's economic future

flight to quality STOCKHOLDING & INVESTMENTS **movement of investors to low-risk securities** a tendency of investors to buy safe well-established securities when the economic outlook is uncertain

float 1. FINANCE **delay between presentation of check and actual payment** the period between the presentation of a check as payment and the actual payment to the payee or the financial advantage provided by this period to the drawer of a check **2.** FINANCE **cash held for small transactions** a small cash balance maintained to facilitate low-value cash transactions. Records of these transactions should be maintained as evidence of expenditure, and periodically a float or petty cash balance will be replenished to a predetermined level. **3.** STOCKHOLDING & INVESTMENTS **sell stocks or bonds** to sell stocks or bonds. *See also **new issue***

floater FINANCE **variable-rate loan** a loan with an interest rate that varies over time

floating asset FINANCE **short-term asset replaced by another** an asset that it is assumed will be consumed during the company's normal trading cycle and then replaced by the same type of asset

floating capital FINANCE **amount of company's money invested in current assets** the portion of a company's money that is invested in current assets, as distinct from that invested in *fixed assets* or *capital assets*

floating charge FINANCE **charge linked to company's assets overall** a charge linked to any of the company's assets in a category, but not to a specific item

floating debenture FINANCE **debenture running for lifetime of firm** a *debenture* secured on all of a company's assets which runs until the company is closed down

floating debt FINANCE **loan frequently renewed** a borrowing for less than one year that is repeatedly renewed

floating exchange rate CURRENCY & EXCHANGE **currency exchange rate that is allowed to vary** an exchange rate for a specific currency that can vary according to market demand, and is not fixed by a government

floating rate FINANCE **interest rate fluctuating as market fluctuates** an interest rate that is not fixed and which changes according to fluctuations in the market

floating-rate note FINANCE, CURRENCY & EXCHANGE **Eurocurrency loan with variable interest rate** a Eurocurrency loan that is not given at a fixed rate of interest. *Abbr* **FRN**

floor 1. FINANCE **lower limit** a lower limit on an interest rate, price, or the value of an asset **2.** MARKETS = *trading floor*

floor limit BANKING **limit on credit card sale without bank authorization** the highest sale through a credit card that a retailer can accept without having to obtain authorization from the issuing bank

FMA *abbr* STOCKHOLDING & INVESTMENTS Fund Managers' Association

FMEA *abbr* RISK Failure Mode and Effects Analysis

folio ACCOUNTING **numbered page in account book** a page with a number, especially two facing pages in an account book which have the same number

FOMC *abbr* ECONOMICS Federal Open Market Committee

Forbes 500 FINANCE **list of largest US public companies** a list of the 500 largest public companies in the United States, ranked according to various criteria by *Forbes* magazine

forecast dividend STOCKHOLDING & INVESTMENTS **expected year-end dividend** a dividend that a company expects to pay at the end of the current trading year. *Also called* **prospective dividend**

foreclose *US* FINANCE **acquire mortgaged property when owner defaults** to acquire a property because the owner cannot or will not repay money that he or she has borrowed to buy the property.

foreclosure *US* FINANCE **act of recovering security on unpaid loan** the acquisition of property when an owner cannot or will not repay the loan that was taken out to buy the property. *UK term* **repossession**

foreign bill FINANCE **bill of exchange payable only overseas** a bill of exchange that is not payable in the country where it is issued

foreign currency CURRENCY & EXCHANGE **other country's money** the currency or interest-bearing bonds of a foreign country

foreign currency account BANKING, CURRENCY & EXCHANGE **bank account operated in foreign currency** a bank account in the currency of another country, for example, a dollar account in a bank in the United Kingdom

foreign currency reserves CURRENCY & EXCHANGE **foreign money held by government** foreign money held by a government to support its own currency and pay its debts. *Also called* **foreign exchange reserves, international reserves**

foreign debt CURRENCY & EXCHANGE **debt owed to other country** hard-currency debt owed to a foreign country in payment for goods and services

foreign direct investment STOCKHOLDING & INVESTMENTS **investment in firm by foreign company or government** investment in a company outside the country of the investor, who sets up subsidiaries or acquires usually about 10% of the stock with voting rights, thus gaining influence in the foreign company's management. *Abbr* **FDI**

foreign dividend STOCKHOLDING & INVESTMENTS **in UK, dividend paid from overseas** in the United Kingdom, a dividend paid from another country, possibly subject to special rules under UK tax codes

foreign draft CURRENCY & EXCHANGE **check drawn and payable in different countries** a check that is drawn in one country and payable in another

foreign exchange CURRENCY & EXCHANGE **1. foreign currencies** currencies and financial instruments used to buy goods abroad or as investments. *Also called* **forex 2. dealings in foreign currencies** dealings in the currencies of other countries, on foreign-exchange markets

foreign exchange broker *or* **foreign exchange dealer** CURRENCY & EXCHANGE **trader in foreign currencies** a person whose business is to buy and sell foreign currencies

foreign exchange dealing CURRENCY & EXCHANGE **trade in foreign currencies** the business of buying and selling currencies of other countries

foreign exchange market CURRENCY & EXCHANGE **1. market for trading foreign currencies** a market where people buy and sell foreign currencies **2. dealings in foreign currencies** dealings in the currencies of other countries

foreign exchange option CURRENCY & EXCHANGE **contract guaranteeing minimum rate in currency exchange** a contract that, for a fee, guarantees a worst-case exchange rate for the future purchase of one currency for another. Unlike a **forward transaction**, the option does not obligate the buyer to deliver a currency on the settlement date unless the buyer chooses to. These options protect against unfavorable currency movements while preserving the ability to participate in favorable movements.

foreign exchange reserves CURRENCY & EXCHANGE = **foreign currency reserves**

foreign exchange transfer CURRENCY & EXCHANGE **sending of money abroad** the process of sending money from one country to another

foreign income dividend STOCKHOLDING & INVESTMENTS **dividend from earnings abroad** a dividend paid from earnings in countries other than the one in which the investment was made

foreign investments STOCKHOLDING & INVESTMENTS **money invested abroad** money invested in countries other than your own

foreign money order CURRENCY & EXCHANGE **money order for somebody abroad** a money order in a foreign currency that is payable to somebody living in a foreign country

foreign reserve CURRENCY & EXCHANGE **centrally held foreign currency** the currency of other countries held by an organization, especially a country's central bank

forensic accounting 1. ACCOUNTING, FRAUD **accounting that assists in identifying financial fraud** an accounting practice that specializes in investigating and presenting expert court testimony concerning crimes involving financial matters **2.** ACCOUNTING **reference to accounts to check legality of activities** the use of accounting records and documents in order to determine the legality or otherwise of past activities

forex *or* **Forex** CURRENCY & EXCHANGE = **foreign exchange**

form 3 STOCKHOLDING & INVESTMENTS **US form for reporting first securities transactions** in the United States, a form that must be filed with the Securities and Exchange Commission within 10 days of the first securities transaction by officers, directors, or 10% shareholders in a company reporting their holdings in the company

form 4 STOCKHOLDING & INVESTMENTS **US form for reporting changes in securities holdings** in the United States, a form that must be filed with the Securities and Exchange Commission reporting any changes in the securities holdings of officers, directors, or 10% shareholders in a company

formal documents MERGERS & ACQUISITIONS **documents detailing takeover bid** documents that provide the full details of a takeover bid

form T STOCKHOLDING & INVESTMENTS **US form for reporting transactions after market close** in the United States, a required form used by brokers to report to the National Association of Securities Dealers all securities transactions that have taken place after the markets have closed

Fortune 500 FINANCE **list of largest US industrial companies** a list of the 500 largest industrial companies in the United States, compiled annually by *Fortune* magazine

forward cover FINANCE **cash purchase of commodity fulfilling futures contract** the purchase for cash of the quantity of a commodity needed to fulfill a futures contract

forward exchange rate CURRENCY & EXCHANGE **rate for future foreign currency purchase** a rate for purchase of foreign currency at a fixed price for delivery at a later date. *Also called* *forward rate* (sense 2)

forward interest rate FINANCE **interest rate set for future loan** an interest rate specified for a loan to be made at a future date

forward pricing STOCKHOLDING & INVESTMENTS **setting of investment price using future valuation** the establishment of the price of a share in a mutual fund based on the next asset valuation

forward rate 1. FINANCE **rate for loan** the rate at which there is no economic arbitrage between receiving an interest rate today and receiving an interest rate starting at some point in the future **2.** CURRENCY & EXCHANGE = *forward exchange rate*

forward rate agreement STOCKHOLDING & INVESTMENTS, RISK **contract trading fixed interest for variable interest** a contract traded in the *over-the-counter market* in which parties agree to exchange a fixed interest rate or currency exchange rate for a variable rate on an agreed amount of money for an obligation beginning at a future time

founders' shares UK STOCKHOLDING & INVESTMENTS **stock issued to firm's founders** stock held by founding members of a company, often with a higher dividend that is only paid after other stockholders have received their dividends and, in some cases, only when a specific level of profit has been achieved. *See also deferred common stock*

fourth quarter ACCOUNTING **last period of fiscal year** the period of three months from October to the end of the year, or the period of three months at the end of a fiscal year. *Abbr* **Q4**

FPA *abbr* FINANCE Financial Planning Association of Australia

fractional certificate STOCKHOLDING & INVESTMENTS **certificate relating to part of share** a certificate for less than a full share (*fractional share*)

fractional currency CURRENCY & EXCHANGE **paper money in very small denominations** the paper money that is in denominations smaller than one unit of a standard national currency

fractional share STOCKHOLDING & INVESTMENTS **less than full share of stock** one part of a full share of stock, usually created as the result of a dividend reinvestment plan or a *stock split*

franco FINANCE **free** available at no cost

franked payment STOCKHOLDING & INVESTMENTS **1. dividends with tax credits** dividends carrying tax credits paid by a company to stockholders **2. dividend free of UK corporation tax** in the United Kingdom, a dividend received by a company from another UK company, exempt from corporation tax

fraud FRAUD **dishonest methods used for personal benefit** the use of dishonesty, deception, or false representation in order to gain a material advantage or to injure the interests of others. Types of fraud include false accounting, theft, third party or investment fraud, employee collusion, and computer fraud. *See also corporate fraud*

fraud ring FRAUD **group organized to defraud others** an organized group of people or companies who defraud others, for example, by stealing identities to gain access to financial information, by forging mortgage documents, or by filing false insurance claims

FRB *abbr* BANKING Federal Reserve Board

Freddie Mac MORTGAGES, RISK **US institution financing housing** a stockholder-owned private company chartered in 1970 by the US Congress to fund home mortgages by issuing debt securities in US and international securities markets. On September 7, 2008, after Freddie Mac reported more than $2 billion in losses from subprime loans, its government regulatory agency, the Federal Housing Finance Agency, put Freddie Mac under its conservatorship. *Full form* *Federal Home Loan Mortgage Corporation*. *See also* *Fannie Mae*

free coinage CURRENCY & EXCHANGE **minting from donated metals** a government's minting of coins from precious metals provided by citizens

free currency CURRENCY & EXCHANGE **currency that can be traded without restriction** a currency that is allowed by the government to be bought and sold without restriction

free enterprise ECONOMICS **freedom to trade without government control** the trade carried on in a free-market economy, where resources are allocated on the basis of supply and demand

free gold FINANCE **government gold not part of national reserve** gold held by a government but not pledged as a reserve for the government's currency

free issue STOCKHOLDING & INVESTMENTS = *bonus issue*

a–z

Dictionary

free market ECONOMICS **system of trade without government controls** a market in which supply and demand are unregulated, except by the country's competition policy, and rights in physical and intellectual property are upheld

free market economy ECONOMICS **economic system operating without government controls** an economic system in which the government does not intervene or unduly regulate business activity

free period BANKING **permitted delay between credit card purchase and payment** the period allowed to credit card holders before payment for credit card purchases is requested

free reserves BANKING **bank reserves without restrictions** the part of a bank's reserves that are above the statutory level and so can be used for various purposes as the bank wishes

freeze-out STOCKHOLDING & INVESTMENTS **compulsory purchase of minor stockholdings in acquired company** the exclusion of minority stockholders in a company that has been taken over. A freeze-out provision may exist in a *takeover* agreement, which permits the acquiring organization to buy the noncontrolling shares held by small stockholders. A fair price is usually set, and the freeze-out may take place at a specific time, perhaps two to five years after the takeover. A freeze-out can still take place, even if provision for it is not made in a corporate charter, by applying pressure to minority stockholders to sell their shares to the acquiring company.

frictional unemployment ECONOMICS **temporarily between jobs** a situation in which people are temporarily out of the labor market. They could be seeking a new job, incurring search delays as they apply, attending interviews, and relocating.

friendly society BANKING **in UK, association whose dues help members in need** in the United Kingdom, a group of people forming an association to pay regular subscriptions to a fund that is used to help members of the group when they are in financial difficulties

FRN *abbr* FINANCE, CURRENCY & EXCHANGE floating-rate note

front company BUSINESS, FRAUD **firm hiding illegal activities of controlling firm** a company established as a legitimate business to conceal the illegal activities of the business controlling it

front-end loading FINANCE **early deduction of charges and commission** the practice of taking the commission and administrative expenses from the early payments made to an investment or insurance plan. *See also* **back-end loading**

frozen account BANKING **bank account made inoperable by court order** a bank account whose funds cannot be used or withdrawn because of a court order

frozen credits BANKING **credits that are not movable** credits in an account which cannot be moved, usually owing to a legal dispute

FRSB *abbr* ACCOUNTING Financial Reporting Standards Board

FT *abbr* BUSINESS, FINANCE Financial Times

full bank BANKING **bank offering full domestic and international services** a local or foreign bank permitted to engage in the full range of domestic and international services

full cost accounting ACCOUNTING = *environmental accounting*

full coupon bond STOCKHOLDING & INVESTMENTS **bond with competitive interest rate** a bond whose interest rate is competitive in the current market

full faith and credit FINANCE **US government debt repayment guarantee** an unconditional guarantee by the US government to repay the principal and interest on all its debt

full-service banking BANKING **provision of banking and financial services** a type of banking that offers a whole range of services including mortgages, loans, and pension plans

full-service broker FINANCE **broker managing portfolios and giving financial advice** a broker who manages portfolios for clients, and gives advice on stocks and financial questions in general

fully diluted earnings per (common) share STOCKHOLDING & INVESTMENTS **earnings including commitments to issue more stocks** the amount earned per share taking into account commitments to issue more shares, for example, as a result of convertibles, stock options, or warrants

fully diluted earnings per share STOCKHOLDING & INVESTMENTS **earnings per share taken over all ordinary shares** the amount earned per share calculated over the whole number of shares on the assumption that convertible shares and options have been converted to ordinary shares

fully diluted shares STOCKHOLDING & INVESTMENTS **total shares, including convertible shares and stock options** total number of shares that would be outstanding assuming that convertible shares have been converted to ordinary shares and that stock options have been exercised

fully distributed issue STOCKHOLDING & INVESTMENTS **issue fully sold out to investors** an issue of stocks sold entirely to investors rather than being held by dealers

full year ACCOUNTING **12 months** a 12-month period, especially with reference to financial information such as earnings, sales, profits, and outlook for the future

full-year forecast ACCOUNTING **prediction of future 12 months' earnings or losses** a prediction of the expected earnings or losses of a business for the future over a 12-month period

full-year results ACCOUNTING **past 12 months of financial data** the financial information of a business, especially its profits or losses, calculated for the preceding 12-month period

fully paid share capital *or* fully paid-up capital STOCKHOLDING & INVESTMENTS **total paid by investors for capital holdings** the amount of the share capital when all calls have been paid on all issued shares. *See also* **called-up share capital**, *paid-up capital*

functional budget TREASURY MANAGEMENT **budget for activity or department** a budget of income and/or expenditure applicable to a specific function. A function may refer to a process or a department. Functional budgets frequently include the following: production cost budget (based on a forecast of production and plant utilization); marketing cost budget; sales budget; personnel budget; purchasing budget; and research and development budget. *See also* **departmental budget**

fund FINANCE **1. money earmarked for something** an amount of money set aside for a particular purpose **2. money invested** money invested in an investment trust as part of a mutual fund, or given to a financial adviser to invest on behalf of a client. *See also* ***funds*** **3. supply money for purpose** to provide an amount of money for a particular purpose. *See also* ***finance***

fundamental accounting concepts ACCOUNTING **basic assumptions for accounts** broad basic assumptions that underlie the periodic financial accounts of business enterprises. *See also* ***concepts***

fundamental analysis STOCKHOLDING & INVESTMENTS **assessment of influences affecting firm's performance** an assessment of how the external and internal influences on a company's activities should affect investment decisions. *See also* ***technical analysis***

funded FINANCE **1. backed by long-term loans** supported by money in the form of long-term loans **2. based on a fund** a future financial commitment, such as the payment of a pension, that is supported by an existing fund of money

funded debt FINANCE **long- or medium-term debt** long-term debt or debt that has a maturity date in excess of one year. Funded debt is usually issued in the public markets or in the form of a private placement to qualified institutional investors.

fund family STOCKHOLDING & INVESTMENTS = ***family of funds***

funding FINANCE **1. finance for business or project** the financial support that is available for a business or project **2. changing short-term debt into long-term loan** the conversion of a short-term debt into a loan that has a maturity date in excess of one year

funding risk RISK **likelihood of difficulty in raising funds** the risk that it might be difficult to realize assets or otherwise raise funds to meet commitments associated with ***financial instruments***. *See also* ***liquidity risk***

fund management STOCKHOLDING & INVESTMENTS **business of investing clients' money** the business of dealing with the investment of sums of money on behalf of clients

fund manager STOCKHOLDING & INVESTMENTS **manager of investments** somebody who manages the investments of a mutual fund or other financial institution. *Also called* ***investment manager***

Fund Managers' Association STOCKHOLDING & INVESTMENTS **UK organization for fund managers** an association representing the interests of UK-based institutional fund managers. It now forms part of the ***Investment Management Association***. *Abbr* **FMA**

fund of funds STOCKHOLDING & INVESTMENTS **mutual fund investing in several underlying mutual funds** a registered mutual fund that invests in a variety of underlying mutual funds. Subscribers own units in the fund of funds, not in the underlying mutual funds.

funds FINANCE **money available to spend** money that is available to a person, business, or organization for spending. *See also* ***insufficient funds***

fungibility BUSINESS, FINANCE **interchangeability of product** the ability to be easily substituted for or combined with another similar product

fungible 1. FINANCE **substitutable** indistinguishable for business purposes from other items of the same type. Such products may be easily combined in making up shipments. **2.** STOCKHOLDING & INVESTMENTS **interchangeable** used to describe an asset, especially a security, that can be exchanged for a similar asset

funny money 1. CURRENCY & EXCHANGE **forged currency** money that is counterfeit or forged **2.** FRAUD **questionable money** money obtained from a legally or morally suspect source

future STOCKHOLDING & INVESTMENTS **contract for future delivery** a contract to deliver a commodity at a future date at a fixed price. *Also called* ***futures contract***

future option STOCKHOLDING & INVESTMENTS **contract for future trade at set price** a contract in which somebody agrees to buy or sell an option for purchasing or selling a commodity, currency, or security at a prearranged price for delivery in the future. *Also called* ***futures option***

futures STOCKHOLDING & INVESTMENTS **items traded now for later delivery** stock, currency, or commodities that are bought or sold now for delivery at a later date

futures commission merchant STOCKHOLDING & INVESTMENTS **broker for futures** somebody who acts as a broker for ***futures contracts***. *Abbr* **FCM**

futures contract STOCKHOLDING & INVESTMENTS *see* ***future***

futures exchange CURRENCY & EXCHANGE **exchange for futures** an exchange on which ***futures contracts*** are traded

futures option STOCKHOLDING & INVESTMENTS *see* ***future option***

future value FINANCE **projected value of sum of money** the value that a sum of money will have in the future, taking into account the effects of inflation, interest rates, or currency values.

Future value calculations require three figures: the sum in question, the percentage by which it will increase or decrease, and the period of time. In this example, these figures are $1,000, 11%, and two years.

At an interest rate of 11%, the sum of $1,000 will grow to $1,232 in two years:

$1,000 × 1.11 = $1,110 (first year) × 1.11
= $1,232 (second year, rounded to whole dollars)

a–z

Dictionary

Note that the interest earned in the first year generates additional interest in the second year, a practice known as compounding. When large sums are in question, the effect of compounding can be significant.

At an inflation rate of 11%, by comparison, the sum of $1,000 will shrink to $812 in two years:

$$\frac{\$1,000}{1.11} = \frac{\$901 \text{ (first year)}}{1.11} = \$812 \text{ (second year, rounded to whole dollars)}$$

In order to avoid errors, it is important to express the percentage as 1.11 and multiply and divide by that figure, instead of using 11%; and to calculate each year, quarter, or month separately. *See also* **present value**

fuzzy accounting ACCOUNTING, FRAUD **accounting practices that mislead investors** company accounting practices designed to inflate earnings or earnings estimates in order to attract investors

FY *abbr* ACCOUNTING fiscal year

G

G7 FINANCE **group of seven major industrial nations** the group of seven major industrial nations established in 1985 to discuss the world economy, consisting of Canada, France, Germany, Italy, Japan, the United Kingdom, and the United States. *Full form* **Group of Seven**

G8 FINANCE **G7 countries plus Russia** the group of eight major industrial nations consisting of the **G7** plus Russia. *Full form* **Group of Eight**

G10 FINANCE **nations contributing to General Arrangements to Borrow fund** the group of ten countries who contribute to the General Arrangements to Borrow fund: Belgium, Canada, France, Germany, Italy, Japan, the Netherlands, Sweden, the United States, and the United Kingdom. Switzerland joined in 1984. *Full form* **Group of Ten**. *Also called* **Paris Club**

G20 ECONOMICS **group of industrial and emerging countries** a forum for discussion between 20 industrialized and emerging-market countries on issues related to global economic stability. *Full form* **Group of Twenty**

GAAP *abbr* ACCOUNTING Generally Accepted Accounting Principles

GAB FINANCE **international fund providing large loans to countries** a fund financed by the **G10** that is used when the IMF's own resources are insufficient, for example, when there is a need for large loans to one or more industrialized countries. *Full form* **General Arrangements to Borrow**

gain FINANCE **increase in amount or value** an increase in the amount or level of something, for example, in a company's profit or in the value of stocks on a stock exchange

gain sharing FINANCE **sharing profits from efficiency improvements with employees** a group-based bonus plan to share profits from improvements in production efficiency between employees and the company

galloping inflation ECONOMICS **very rapid inflation** inflation that increases rapidly by large amounts

gamma STOCKHOLDING & INVESTMENTS **rate of change in option price** the rate of change in the **delta** of an option for a unit change in the price of the underlying asset. It is a measure of **convexity**.

gap analysis 1. FINANCE **analyzing shortfall between current results and ultimate goals** a method of improving a company's financial performance by analyzing the reasons for the gap between current results and long-term objectives **2.** MARKETING **investigation of gaps in market or availability** a marketing technique used to identify gaps in market or product coverage. In gap analysis, consumer information or requirements are tabulated and matched to product categories in order to identify product or service opportunities or gaps in product planning.

gap financing FINANCE **short-term loan arrangement** the process of arranging an extra loan such as a bridge loan in order to make a purchase not fully covered by an existing loan

garbatrage US STOCKHOLDING & INVESTMENTS **stocks benefiting from unrelated takeover** stocks that rise because of a **takeover** but that are not connected to the target company (slang)

garnishee FINANCE **person ordered to redirect debt payment to another** a person who owes money to a creditor and is ordered by a court to pay that money to a creditor of the original creditor, and not to the actual creditor

garnishment 1. FINANCE **withholding of income to repay debt** a procedure by which wages or salary are withheld from an employee in order to pay off the employee's debt **2.** LEGAL = **garnishee order**

GAS *abbr* ACCOUNTING Government Accountancy Service

GB pound CURRENCY & EXCHANGE = **pound sterling**

GDP ECONOMICS **all goods and services produced by economy** the total flow of goods and services produced by an economy over a quarter or a year, measured by the aggregate value of goods and services at market prices. *Full form* **gross domestic product**

GDP per capita ECONOMICS **total economic output divided by population** **GDP** divided by the country's population so as to achieve a figure per person in the population

GEAR ECONOMICS **redistributive economic program in S. Africa** the macroeconomic reform program of the South African government, intended to foster economic growth, create employment, and redistribute income and opportunities in favor of the poor. *Full form* **Growth, Employment, and Redistribution**

geared investment trust UK STOCKHOLDING & INVESTMENTS = **leveraged investment company**

gearing FINANCE, RISK = *financial leverage*

gearing ratios FINANCE = *leverage ratios*

geisha bond STOCKHOLDING & INVESTMENTS = *shogun bond*

General Arrangements to Borrow FINANCE *see* **GAB**

general audit ACCOUNTING comprehensive examination of firm's accounts an examination of all books and accounts belonging to a company

general expenses ACCOUNTING routine costs of running business minor expenses of various kinds incurred in the running of a business

general fund FINANCE mutual fund with wide-ranging investments a mutual fund that has investments in a variety of stocks

general ledger ACCOUNTING book listing firm's financial transactions a book that lists all of the financial transactions of a company

Generally Accepted Accounting Principles ACCOUNTING guidelines relating to fair accounting practices a summary of best practice in respect to the form and content of financial statements and auditors' reports, and of accounting policies and disclosures adopted for the preparation of financial information. GAAP has statutory or regulatory authority in the United States and Canada and some other countries, but not in the United Kingdom. *Abbr* **GAAP**

general meeting CORPORATE GOVERNANCE meeting of company's stockholders a meeting of all the stockholders of a company or of all the members of an organization

general obligation bond STOCKHOLDING & INVESTMENTS municipal bond financing public undertakings a municipal or state bond that is repaid out of general funds. *Abbr* **GO bond**

gensaki STOCKHOLDING & INVESTMENTS bond sale incorporating repurchase agreement the Japanese term for a bond sale incorporating a repurchase agreement at a later date

gharar FINANCE uncertainty prohibited in Islamic business dealings in Islamic financing, excessive uncertainty in a business transaction of any type. It is one of three prohibitions in Islamic law, the others being *maysir* and *riba*.

ghosting MARKETS, FRAUD illegal price fixing of stock an illegal practice in which two or more market makers, who are required by law to compete, join to influence the price of a stock

Giffen good ECONOMICS = *inferior good*

gift with reservation FINANCE gift that benefits donor in some way in the United Kingdom, a gift with some benefit retained for the donor, for example, the legal transfer of a dwelling when the donor continues in residence

gilt STOCKHOLDING & INVESTMENTS *see* *gilt-edged security*

gilt-edged STOCKHOLDING & INVESTMENTS issued by blue-chip company used to describe a security issued by a blue-chip company, which is therefore considered very secure (informal)

gilt-edged security STOCKHOLDING & INVESTMENTS UK government security paying regular fixed interest in the United Kingdom, a security issued by the government that pays a fixed rate of interest on a regular basis for a specific period of time until the redemption date, when the principal is returned. Their names, for example, Exchequer $10\frac{1}{2}$% 2005 (abbreviated to Ex $10\frac{1}{2}$% '05) or Treasury $11\frac{3}{4}$% 2003–07 (abbreviated to Tr $11\frac{3}{4}$% '03–'07) indicate the rate and redemption date. Thought to have originated in the 17th century to help fund the war with France, today they form a large part of the *national debt*. *Also called* **gilt**. *See also* **index-linked gilt**, **short-dated gilts**

gilt strip STOCKHOLDING & INVESTMENTS UK bond yielding single cash payment at maturity in the United Kingdom, a *zero coupon bond* created by splitting the interest payments from a gilt-edged security so that it produces a single cash payment at maturity

gilt unit trust STOCKHOLDING & INVESTMENTS UK mutual fund investing in gilts in the United Kingdom, a mutual fund where the underlying investments are *gilt-edged securities*

giro 1. BANKING UK bank transfer in the United Kingdom, a system of transferring money from one bank account to another. *Also called* **bank giro 2.** FINANCE UK state benefit in the United Kingdom, a benefit paid by the state (slang)

glamour stock STOCKHOLDING & INVESTMENTS fashionable investment a currently fashionable and popular security (slang)

global bank BANKING bank with worldwide business a bank that is active in the international markets and has a presence in several continents

global bond STOCKHOLDING & INVESTMENTS = *Eurobond*

global bond issue STOCKHOLDING & INVESTMENTS bond issue allowing transfer of titles between markets an issue of a bond that incorporates a settlement mechanism allowing for the transfer of titles between markets

global coordinator STOCKHOLDING & INVESTMENTS overall manager of global stock issue the lead manager of a global offering who is responsible for overseeing the entire issue and is usually supported by regional and national coordinators

global custody FINANCE bundle of financial services for institutional investors a financial service, usually available to institutional investors only, that includes the safekeeping of securities certificates issued in markets across the world, the collection of dividends, dealing with tax, valuation of investments, foreign exchange, and the settlement of transactions

global depositary receipt STOCKHOLDING & INVESTMENTS certificate for shares of stock traded abroad a certificate held by a bank in one country representing shares of stock that are traded on an exchange in a foreign country but can be purchased through various banks worldwide

global economy ECONOMICS, INTERNATIONAL TRADE **international trade relations** the economic relations between countries in a world where markets in individual countries have now spread beyond national boundaries and are more integrated with those of other countries. *Also called* **world economy**

global hedge STOCKHOLDING & INVESTMENTS = *macrohedge*

global marketplace ECONOMICS, INTERNATIONAL TRADE **market encompassing whole world** a worldwide trading system that has grown up since the 1970s, in which goods can be produced wherever the production costs are cheapest wherever they are ultimately sold

global offering STOCKHOLDING & INVESTMENTS **worldwide offering of securities** the offering of securities in several markets simultaneously, for example, in Europe, the Far East, and North America

GM *abbr* **1.** FINANCE gross margin (sense 1) **2.** ACCOUNTING gross margin (sense 2) **3.** OPERATIONS & PRODUCTION gross margin (sense 3)

gnomes of Zurich BANKING **Swiss bankers** bankers and currency dealers based in Switzerland, who have a reputation for secrecy. The term is often used to refer in a derogatory way to unknown currency speculators who cause upheavals in the currency markets (informal)

GNP ECONOMICS **country's total economic output plus foreign investment income** the *GDP* plus domestic residents' income from investment abroad less income earned in the domestic market accruing to noncitizens abroad. *Full form* **gross national product**

GNP per capita ECONOMICS **GNP divided by population** the *GNP* divided by the country's population so as to achieve a figure per person in the population

GO bond STOCKHOLDING & INVESTMENTS = *general obligation bond*

go-go fund STOCKHOLDING & INVESTMENTS, RISK **high-risk mutual fund** a mutual fund that trades heavily and predominantly in high-return, high-risk investments

going short FINANCE **selling asset for repurchase at lower price** borrowing and then selling an asset one does not own with the intention of acquiring it at a later date at a lower price for delivery to the purchaser. *See also* **bear**

gold bond STOCKHOLDING & INVESTMENTS **bond with gold as collateral** a bond for which gold is collateral, often issued by mining companies

gold bug STOCKHOLDING & INVESTMENTS **investor who believes gold prices will rise** a person who believes that gold is the best investment

gold bullion FINANCE **gold bars** gold in the form of bars

gold card BANKING **credit card for wealthy customer** a gold-colored credit card, generally issued to customers with above average incomes, that may include additional benefits such as

an overdraft at an advantageous interest rate. It may require an annual fee.

golden handcuffs FINANCE **financial incentive to remain in organization** a financial incentive paid to encourage employees to remain in an organization and dissuade them from leaving for a rival business or to start their own company (informal)

golden handshake *or* golden goodbye FINANCE **generous payment for departing senior executive** a sum of money given to a senior executive on his or her involuntary departure from an employing organization as a form of severance pay. A golden handshake can be offered when an executive is required to leave before the expiration of his or her contract, for example, because of a **merger** or corporate restructuring. It is intended as compensation for loss of office. It can be a very large sum of money, but often it is not related to the perceived performance of the executive concerned (informal)

golden hello FINANCE **1. generous financial arrangement for new employee** a welcome package for a new employee which may include a bonus and stock options. A golden hello is designed as an incentive to attract employees. Some of the contents of the welcome package may be contingent on the performance of the employee. **2. support for employer hiring new employee** a payment from a government to an employer who takes on new staff when jobs are hard to find in a recession

golden parachute *or* golden umbrella FINANCE **generous financial package on dismissal from employment** a clause inserted in the contract of employment of a senior employee that details a financial package payable if the employee is dismissed. A golden parachute provides an executive with a measure of financial security and may be payable if the employee leaves the organization following a **takeover** or **merger**, or is dismissed as a result of poor performance.

golden share STOCKHOLDING & INVESTMENTS **government's controlling interest in newly privatized company** a controlling interest retained by a government in a company that has been privatized after having been in public ownership

gold fix *or* gold fixing FINANCE **twice-daily setting of gold price** a system by which the world price for gold is set twice a day in US dollars on the London Gold Exchange and in Paris and Zurich

gold point CURRENCY & EXCHANGE **price variation in gold-backed currency** an amount by which a currency that is linked to gold can vary in price

gold reserve CURRENCY & EXCHANGE **central bank's gold holdings** gold coins or bullion held by a central bank to support a paper currency and provide security for borrowing

gold standard CURRENCY & EXCHANGE **system valuing currency against gold** a system in which a currency unit is defined in terms of its value in gold

good faith deposit FINANCE **sum given to confirm deal** a deposit made by a buyer to a seller to show a firm intention to complete the transaction

good for the day STOCKHOLDING & INVESTMENTS **describing instructions valid only on specific day** used to describe instructions to a broker that are valid only for the specific day indicated

good for this week or good for this month UK STOCKHOLDING & INVESTMENTS = *good this week, good this month*

goods and chattels FINANCE **movable personal property** movable personal possessions, as opposed to land and buildings

good this week or good this month US STOCKHOLDING & INVESTMENTS **valid only during specific week/month** used to describe instructions to a broker that are valid only for the duration of the week/month given. *Abbr* **GTW, GTM**. *UK terms* **good for this week, good for this month**

goodwill ACCOUNTING **business assets such as reputation and expertise** an *intangible asset* of a company which includes factors such as reputation, contacts, and expertise, for which a buyer of the company may have to pay a premium.

Goodwill becomes an intangible asset when a company has been acquired by another. It then appears on a balance sheet in the amount by which the price paid by the acquiring company exceeds the net tangible assets of the acquired company. In other words

Purchase price–Net assets = Goodwill

If an airline is bought for $12 billion and its net assets are valued at $9 billion, $3 billion of the purchase would be allocated to goodwill on the balance sheet.

go private STOCKHOLDING & INVESTMENTS **change to private status without stock market listing** to revert from being a public limited company quoted on a stock exchange to a private company without a stock market listing

go public STOCKHOLDING & INVESTMENTS **become public corporation** to place stock of a private company for sale on a stock exchange in order to raise funds

gourde CURRENCY & EXCHANGE **Haitian currency unit** a unit of currency used in Haiti

governance CORPORATE GOVERNANCE **management of firm** the process of managing a company, especially with respect to the soundness or otherwise of its management

Government Accountancy Service ACCOUNTING **body monitoring accounting practice in UK Civil Service** in the United Kingdom, a part of *HM Treasury* whose remit is to ensure that best accounting practice is observed and conducted across the whole of the Civil Service. *Abbr* **GAS**

government bond STOCKHOLDING & INVESTMENTS **investment product issued by government** a bond or other security issued by a government on a regular basis as a method of borrowing money for government expenditure

government borrowing FINANCE **money government borrows to fund public spending** the total amount of money that a country's central government has borrowed to fund its spending on public services and benefits. *See also national debt*

government securities/stock STOCKHOLDING & INVESTMENTS **securities or stock issued by government** securities or stock such as US Treasury bonds or UK gilt-edged securities that are issued by a government

grand total FINANCE **sum of all subtotals** the final total, which is a result of adding several subtotals

granny bond UK STOCKHOLDING & INVESTMENTS **savings type for older people** a long-term savings opportunity for older people, with a tax advantage or a return linked to the rate of inflation (informal). *See also index-linked savings certificate*

grant 1. FINANCE **money given to fund something** money given by a government or other organization to help pay for something such as education or research **2.** LEGAL **transfer something legally to somebody else** to transfer money, property, or rights to somebody in a legal transaction

grantor STOCKHOLDING & INVESTMENTS **seller of option** a person who sells an *option* to another person

gray knight US MERGERS & ACQUISITIONS **unreliable friendly firm involved in takeover** a *white knight* that does not have the confidence of the company to be acquired in a *takeover*. *UK term* **grey knight**. *See also knight*

Great Depression ECONOMICS **1930s global economic crisis** the world economic crisis that began after the US stock market collapsed in 1929 and continued through the 1930s, resulting in mass unemployment and poverty, especially in North America

greater fool theory STOCKHOLDING & INVESTMENTS **strategy assuming overpriced stock will attract buyer** the investing strategy that assumes it is wise to buy a stock that is not worth its current price. The assumption is that somebody will buy it from you later for an even greater price.

green accounting ACCOUNTING = *environmental accounting*

greenback CURRENCY & EXCHANGE **US paper money** a piece of US paper money of any denomination

green currency CURRENCY & EXCHANGE **former EU currency for agricultural prices** in the European Union, currency formerly used for calculating agricultural payments. Each country had an exchange rate fixed by the Commission, so before the introduction of the euro there were currencies such as "green francs" and "green marks."

green dollar US FINANCE **spending and investment based on environmental awareness** money spent on environmentally sound products and services and investing in companies with environmentally sound policies and practices. *UK term* **green pound**

green investing STOCKHOLDING & INVESTMENTS **investment in green technologies** investing in companies developing environmentally sound technologies and products to counter the economic effects of climate change

green pound 1. UK FINANCE = *green dollar* **2.** CURRENCY & EXCHANGE **monetary unit used for converting EU agricultural**

prices in the European Union, a currency unit formerly used for converting agricultural prices into pounds sterling

green shoe or **greenshoe** option STOCKHOLDING & INVESTMENTS **option in stock issue covering potential shortfall** an option offered by a company raising the capital for the issue of further shares of stock to cover a shortfall in the event of overallocation. It gets its name from the Green Shoe Manufacturing Company, which was the first to include the feature in a public offering. (slang)

Gresham's Law ECONOMICS **theory that cheaper money replaces more valuable money** the principle that "bad money will drive out good." If two forms of money with the same denomination exist in the same market, the form with the higher metal value will be driven out of circulation because people hoard it and use the lower-rated form to spend.

grey knight UK MERGERS & ACQUISITIONS = **gray knight**

gross ACCOUNTING **without deductions** before taxes and other deductions have been taken into account

gross borrowings ACCOUNTING **total of firm's loans and overdrafts** the total of all money borrowed by a company including items such as overdrafts and long-term loans but without deducting cash in bank accounts and on deposit

gross domestic product ECONOMICS see **GDP**

gross earnings FINANCE **total pay before deductions** a person's salary or wage before subtracting payroll deductions such as taxes and retirement savings

gross income FINANCE **total income before deductions** a person's salary or wage plus any other money received from other sources, before subtracting payroll deductions, such as taxes and retirement savings, and any other taxes

gross income yield ACCOUNTING **yield before tax** the yield of an investment before tax is deducted

gross interest ACCOUNTING **interest earned before tax is deducted** the interest earned on a deposit or security before the deduction of tax. See also **net interest**

gross lease FINANCE **lease that exempts lessee from some payments** a lease that does not require the lessee to pay for things the owner usually pays for. See also **net lease**

gross margin 1. FINANCE **difference between borrower's interest payments and lender's costs** the difference between the interest rate paid by a borrower and the cost of the funds to the lender **2.** ACCOUNTING **percentage difference between income and costs** the difference between revenue and cost of revenue expressed as a percentage **3.** OPERATIONS & PRODUCTION **difference between unit's manufacturing cost and sale price** the difference between the manufacturing cost of a unit of output and the price at which it is sold. Abbr **GM**

gross national product ECONOMICS see **GNP**

gross profit ACCOUNTING **difference between total sales revenue and production costs** the difference between an organization's sales revenue and the cost of goods sold. Unlike **net profit**, gross profit does not include distribution, administration, or finance costs. Also called **trading profit**

gross profit margin ACCOUNTING see **profit margin**

gross receipts ACCOUNTING **total revenue** the total revenue received by a business, before tax and other deductions have been taken into account. See also **net receipts**

gross redemption yield UK STOCKHOLDING & INVESTMENTS = **yield to maturity**

gross sales ACCOUNTING **sales before discounts** the total of all sales before discounts

gross turnover ACCOUNTING **total turnover** all of a business's income less statutory allowances, and other taxes on this income

gross yield STOCKHOLDING & INVESTMENTS **income derived from securities before tax** the income return derived from securities before the deduction of tax

gross yield to redemption UK STOCKHOLDING & INVESTMENTS = **gross redemption yield**

group balance sheet ACCOUNTING = **consolidated balance sheet**

group investment STOCKHOLDING & INVESTMENTS **shared investment** an investment made by more than one person

Group of Eight FINANCE see **G8**

Group of Seven FINANCE see **G7**

Group of Ten FINANCE see **G10**

Group of Twenty FINANCE see **G20**

growth 1. FINANCE **firm's economic increase** an increase in productivity, sales, or earnings that an organization experiences **2.** OPERATIONS & PRODUCTION **increase in demand for product** the second stage in a product life cycle, following the launch, when demand for the product increases rapidly

growth and income fund STOCKHOLDING & INVESTMENTS **mutual fund seeking capital increase with large dividends** a mutual fund that tries to maximize growth of capital while paying significant dividends

growth capital FINANCE **funding that firm uses to expand** funding that allows a company to accelerate its growth. For new startup companies, growth capital is the second stage of funding after **seed capital**.

growth equity STOCKHOLDING & INVESTMENTS **promising investment product** an equity that is thought to have good prospects of growth, usually with a high price/earnings ratio. Also called **growth stock**

growth fund STOCKHOLDING & INVESTMENTS **mutual fund focusing on capital increase** a mutual fund that tries to maximize growth of capital without regard to dividends

growth industry FINANCE **area of business expanding quickly** an industry that is developing and expanding at a faster rate than other industries

growth prospects FINANCE **potential for economic increase** the likelihood that something such as a specific stock or a country's economy will considerably improve its performance

growth rate ECONOMICS **how much and how fast economy is growing** the rate of an economy's growth as measured by its technical progress, the growth of its labor force, and the increase in its *capital stock*

growth stock STOCKHOLDING & INVESTMENTS = *growth equity*

GTC *abbr* STOCKHOLDING & INVESTMENTS good 'til cancel

GTM *abbr* STOCKHOLDING & INVESTMENTS **good this month**

GTW *abbr* STOCKHOLDING & INVESTMENTS good this week

guarantee FINANCE **promise to cover another person's contractual duties** a promise made by a third party, or guarantor, that he or she will be liable if one of the parties to a contract fails to fulfill their contractual obligations. A guarantee may be acceptable to a bank as security for borrowing, provided the guarantor has sufficient financial means to cover his or her potential liability.

guaranteed bond STOCKHOLDING & INVESTMENTS **bond with guaranteed principal and interest** a bond on which the principal and interest are guaranteed by an institution other than the one that issues it, or a stock in which the dividends are similarly guaranteed. *Also called* *guaranteed stock*

guaranteed fund STOCKHOLDING & INVESTMENTS **investment whose losses third party promises to cover** a fixed term investment where a third party promises to repay the investor's principal in full should the investment fall below the initial sum invested

guaranteed stock STOCKHOLDING & INVESTMENTS = *guaranteed bond*

guarantor of last resort FINANCE **person or entity guaranteeing bad debt repayment** a person, organization, or government that guarantees repayment of a debt that cannot otherwise be repaid

gun jumping FINANCE **profitable trading based on inside information** trading that takes place on the basis of privileged information (slang)

gunslinger STOCKHOLDING & INVESTMENTS **investment manager investing in high-risk stocks** a portfolio manager who invests in high-risk stocks hoping that they will yield high returns (slang)

H

haggle FINANCE **discuss to agree on price of item** to reach a price with a buyer or seller by the gradual raising of offers and lowering of the price asked until a mutually accepted figure is obtained

haircut 1. FINANCE **difference between loan amount and value of collateral** the difference between the market value of a

security and the amount lent to the owner using the security as collateral **2.** STOCKHOLDING & INVESTMENTS **estimate of investment loss** an estimate of possible loss in investments

half-stock STOCKHOLDING & INVESTMENTS **$50 stock** a stock that has a nominal value of fifty US dollars

half-year ACCOUNTING **half of accounting period** six months for which accounts are presented

handle 1. BUSINESS **to deal in particular product, service, or market** to buy, sell, or trade in a particular product, service, or market **2.** STOCKHOLDING & INVESTMENTS **whole-number price of share of stock or currency** the price of a stock or foreign currency, quoted as a whole number

hang out loan FINANCE **outstanding amount on loan** the amount of a loan that is still outstanding after the termination of the loan

hara-kiri swap FINANCE **exchange of interest rates with no profit margin** an interest rate swap made without a profit margin

hard capital rationing FINANCE *see* *capital rationing* (*sense 2*)

hard cash CURRENCY & EXCHANGE **money in bills** money in the form of bills and coins, as opposed to checks or credit cards

hard currency CURRENCY & EXCHANGE **money traded in foreign exchange market** a currency that is traded in a foreign exchange market and for which demand is persistently high relative to its supply. *See also* *soft currency*

hardening FINANCE **1. stabilizing after changes** becoming stable after a period of fluctuation **2. describing prices that are slowly rising** used to describe prices that are slowly moving upward

hard landing ECONOMICS **sudden economic recession after growth period** the rapid decline of an economy into recession and business stagnation after a sustained period of growth

harmonization 1. FINANCE **equality of financial and social regulation** the convergence of financial and social regulation in the countries of the European Union **2.** GENERAL MANAGEMENT **equalizing pay and conditions** the resolution of inequalities in the pay and conditions of employment between different categories of employees **3.** GENERAL MANAGEMENT **equalizing benefits of related companies** the alignment of the systems of pay and benefits of two companies that become one by merger, acquisition, or takeover **4.** GENERAL MANAGEMENT **equalizing treatment of full- and part-time employees** the process of removing differences between groups of employees, such as full- and part-time staff, with regard to terms and conditions of employment such as rates of pay, pension rights, and vacation entitlement

headline rate of inflation ECONOMICS **inflation measure including wide range of costs** a measure of inflation that attempts to take account of most costs and services. In the United States, the headline rate is based on the Consumer Price Index. In the United Kingdom, it is based on the Retail

a–z

Dictionary

Price Index, which takes account of homeowners' mortgage costs.

health saving account FINANCE US savings plan for medical expenses in the United States, a savings plan with tax benefits that is designed to help individuals accumulate money for qualified medical expenses. *Abbr* **HSA**

health warning STOCKHOLDING & INVESTMENTS message on UK advertisements about risks of investing in the United Kingdom, a legally required warning message printed on advertisements for investments, stating that the value of investments can fall as well as rise (slang)

heavy 1. MARKETS experiencing more activity than usual used to describe a market in which trading is more active than usual **2.** STOCKHOLDING & INVESTMENTS investing too much in one type of stock having too many investments in related industries or stock **3.** STOCKHOLDING & INVESTMENTS high-priced used to describe a stock that has such a high price that small investors are reluctant to buy it. In this case the company may decide to split the stock so as to make it more attractive.

hedge STOCKHOLDING & INVESTMENTS **1.** method of protecting against possible loss a protection against a possible loss on an investment which involves taking an action that is the opposite of an action taken earlier **2.** take action to reduce risk of investment loss to take measures to offset risk of loss on an investment, especially by investing in counterbalancing securities as a guard against price fluctuations

hedge fund STOCKHOLDING & INVESTMENTS, RISK risky type of investment fund an investment fund that takes considerable risks, including investment in unconventional instruments, in the hope of generating great profits. There are many types of hedge funds, using very different strategies. Some are highly geared and some use arbitrage, futures, and options to achieve their objectives.

hedging STOCKHOLDING & INVESTMENTS, RISK strategy for protecting against possible financial losses financial transactions intended to protect against possible losses from existing financial activities or investments, for example, buying investments at a fixed price for delivery later or investing in counterbalancing securities **hedging against inflation** STOCKHOLDING & INVESTMENTS investing in order to avoid the impact of inflation, thus protecting the purchasing power of capital. Historically, equities have generally outperformed returns from savings accounts in the long term and beaten the retail price index. They are thus considered as one of the best hedges against inflation, although no stock market investment is without risk.

held order STOCKHOLDING & INVESTMENTS large order that seller waits to process an order that a dealer does not process immediately, often because of its large size

Herstatt Risk CURRENCY & EXCHANGE, RISK risk of delivery failure in foreign currency transaction the risk in foreign currency exchange transactions that one party to the exchange will fail to make payment after having received payment from the other party

hidden asset ACCOUNTING firm's property recorded at lower than actual value an asset that is shown in a company's accounts as being worth much less than its true market value

hidden economy ECONOMICS = *black economy*

hidden reserves ACCOUNTING firm's unrecorded reserves funds that are set aside but not declared in the company's balance sheet

high finance FINANCE dealing with very large amounts of money the lending, investing, and borrowing of very large sums of money organized by financiers

high-flier *or* high-flyer STOCKHOLDING & INVESTMENTS stock that increases quickly in price a heavily traded stock that increases in value considerably over a short period

high gearing FINANCE when firm borrows a lot of money a situation in which a company has a high level of borrowing compared to its stock price

high-income STOCKHOLDING & INVESTMENTS describing fund yielding high returns used to describe a fund that yields a high rate of return

high net worth individual FINANCE somebody with at least $4 million a person whose net assets, excluding the value of a home, are worth more than $4 million, by some classifications. It is estimated that some 10 million worldwide fall into this category. *Abbr* **HNWI**

high-premium convertible debenture STOCKHOLDING & INVESTMENTS bond unlikely to be converted a convertible bond with an exercise price that makes it unlikely to be converted in the foreseeable future. It therefore has a low option premium.

high-risk company BUSINESS, RISK firm running high business risks a company that is exposed to high levels of business risk

High Street bank BANKING major UK bank with local offices a UK bank that provides *retail banking* services and has many local offices for customers to visit, as distinguished from an *investment bank* or a bank that provides services only on the Internet

high-tech crime FRAUD crime committed using computer technologies illegal activities using the Internet or other computer technologies. *Also called* **hi-tech crime**

high yield STOCKHOLDING & INVESTMENTS, RISK higher than usual yield a higher rate of return than is usual for a particular type of investment or company

high-yield bond STOCKHOLDING & INVESTMENTS RISK = *junk bond*

high yielder STOCKHOLDING & INVESTMENTS, RISK high-performing but risky investment product a security that has a higher than average rate of return and is consequently often a higher risk investment

hire 1. HR & PERSONNEL give job to somebody to employ somebody new to work for you or your organization **2.** *UK* FINANCE = *rent*

hire purchase *UK* FINANCE = *installment plan*

historical cost *or* historic cost ACCOUNTING original cost of item bought in past the record of the value of a firm's asset reflecting its original price when it was purchased

historical cost accounting ACCOUNTING record keeping based on original cost of items the preparation of accounts on the basis of historical cost, with assets valued at their original cost of purchase. *UK term* **fair value accounting**. *See also* **current cost accounting**

historical cost depreciation ACCOUNTING discounting asset's value based on original cost the accounting practice of depreciating a firm's asset based on its original cost

historical figures ACCOUNTING figures or values correct at the time figures or values that were correct at the time of purchase or payment, as distinct from a current value

historical summary ACCOUNTING UK report of firm's results in past in the United Kingdom, an optional synopsis of a company's results over a period of time, often five or ten years, featured in the annual accounts

historic pricing STOCKHOLDING & INVESTMENTS basing mutual fund prices on most recent holdings the establishment of the price of a share in a mutual fund on the basis of the most recent values of its holdings

hi-tech crime FRAUD = *high-tech crime*

HM Treasury FINANCE UK government department that manages public funds the UK government department responsible for managing the country's public revenues. While the incumbent prime minister holds the title of First Lord of the Treasury, the department is run on a day-to-day basis by the Chancellor of the Exchequer.

HNWI *abbr* FINANCE high net worth individual

hold STOCKHOLDING & INVESTMENTS own security for long time to own a security over a long period of time

holder FINANCE owner of financial obligation the person who is in possession of a **bill of exchange** or **promissory note**

holder of record STOCKHOLDING & INVESTMENTS official owner of stock the person who is registered as the owner of stock in a company

holding *or* holdings STOCKHOLDING & INVESTMENTS investment owned by somebody an investment, or set of investments, that a person owns at a specific time

holding period STOCKHOLDING & INVESTMENTS period between purchase and sale of asset the length of time an asset was held from the time of purchase to the time of sale, used for determining whether a capital gain or loss is taxed as short-term (less than one year) or long-term (one year or more)

home banking BANKING using computer at home for banking services a system of banking using a personal computer at home to carry out various financial transactions such as paying invoices or checking transactions in a bank account

home run FINANCE investment with rapid returns an investment that produces a high rate of return in a short time

honorarium FINANCE modest payment for simple duties a payment made to somebody for performing a specific service, often a token amount

horizontal equity ECONOMICS belief in similar taxation for similar incomes the theory that individuals in similar financial situations should be taxed at the same rate

horizontal merger MERGERS & ACQUISITIONS combining of firms in same industry the amalgamation of two or more organizations from the same industry under single ownership, through the direct **acquisition** by one organization of the net assets or liabilities of the other. *See also* **merger**

horizontal spread STOCKHOLDING & INVESTMENTS, RISK simultaneous buying and selling of two options a purchase of one **option** accompanied by the sale of another with the same **exercise price** but a different date of maturity. *Also called* **calendar spread**

hostile bid MERGERS & ACQUISITIONS = *contested takeover bid*

hostile takeover MERGERS & ACQUISITIONS unwelcome acquisition of firm the acquisition by a company of a controlling interest in the voting share capital of another company whose directors or stockholders are opposed to the action. *See also* **takeover**

hot card BANKING stolen credit card a credit card that has been stolen and might be used fraudulently

hot issue STOCKHOLDING & INVESTMENTS new investment product expected to perform well a new security that is expected to trade at a significant premium to its issue price. *See also* **hot stock**

hot money 1. FRAUD stolen money money that has been obtained by dishonest means. *See also* **money laundering 2.** STOCKHOLDING & INVESTMENTS funds transferred for short-term gain money that is moved on short notice from one financial center to another to secure the best possible return

house FINANCE finance firm a business organization, especially a financial institution that handles the purchase and sale of securities to investors

house call STOCKHOLDING & INVESTMENTS warning by brokerage firm of low margin account notice from a brokerage firm that the amount of money in a client's margin account is less than the required amount

house poor FINANCE with all money invested in house a situation in which the cost of owning a home is too high in proportion to the homeowner's income

HSA *abbr* FINANCE health saving account

hurdle rate 1. BANKING rate above which loan is profitable for bank a minimum rate of return needed by a bank to fund a loan, representing the rate below which a loan is not profitable for the bank **2.** STOCKHOLDING & INVESTMENTS minimum return before fees due the minimum rate of return required on a fund before the fund manager can begin taking fees **3.** *UK* STOCKHOLDING & INVESTMENTS **growth rate needed to repay stock's redemption price** the rate of growth in a portfolio required to repay the final fixed redemption price of zero dividend preference shares

hurricane bond STOCKHOLDING & INVESTMENTS, RISK **catastrophe bond for hurricane insurance risk** a type of *catastrophe bond* that transfers some of the insurance risk from insurers to investors in the event of a hurricane

hybrid STOCKHOLDING & INVESTMENTS **combination of investment types** a combination of financial instruments, for example, a bond with warrants attached, or a variety of cash and derivative instruments designed to mirror the performance of a financial market

hybrid financial instrument STOCKHOLDING & INVESTMENTS **investment type with features of other types** a *financial instrument* such as a convertible bond that has characteristics of multiple types of instruments, often convertible from one to another

hyperinflation ECONOMICS **extremely high rate of inflation** a very rapid growth in the rate of inflation so that money loses value and physical goods replace currency as a medium of exchange. This happened, for example, in Latin America in the early 1990s and in Zimbabwe in the 2000s.

hypothecate FINANCE **1. use real estate to back loan** to use the mortgage on real estate as collateral for a loan **2. use money for defined purpose** to designate money, especially public funds, to be used for a specific purpose only

hypothecation FINANCE **1. using assets as loan collateral without transferring ownership** an arrangement in which assets such as securities are used as collateral for a loan but without transferring legal ownership to the lender **2. designating money for specific purpose** the process of earmarking money derived from specific sources for related expenditure, for example, using taxes collected on gasoline sales solely on public transportation

hysteresis ECONOMICS **dependency of equilibrium on change** the way in which equilibrium is dependent on the changes that take place as an economy experiences change

I

IAS *abbr* TAX, STOCKHOLDING & INVESTMENTS installment activity statement

IASB *abbr* ACCOUNTING International Accounting Standards Board

IASC *abbr* ACCOUNTING International Accounting Standards Committee

IB *abbr* BANKING investment bank

IBRD BANKING **UN bank that helps poorest nations** a United Nations organization that provides funds, policy guidance, and technical assistance to facilitate economic development in its poorer member countries. *Full form* **International Bank for Reconstruction and Development**

ICAEW *abbr* ACCOUNTING Institute of Chartered Accountants in England and Wales

ICAI *abbr* ACCOUNTING Institute of Chartered Accountants in Ireland

ICANZ *abbr* ACCOUNTING Institute of Chartered Accountants of New Zealand

ICAS *abbr* ACCOUNTING Institute of Chartered Accountants of Scotland

ICSA *abbr* *UK* FINANCE Institute of Chartered Secretaries and Administrators

ICSID *abbr* BANKING International Centre for Settlement of Investment Disputes

IDA *abbr* FINANCE International Development Association

identity theft FRAUD **use of another's identity for criminal purpose** the use of another person's personal and financial information, such as credit card numbers, Social Security numbers, or passport information, without their knowledge, to commit a crime

idle capital *or* **idle cash** FINANCE **firm's unused money and property** the money and assets of a business that are not being invested productively. *Also called* **barren money, sideline cash**

IDR *abbr* STOCKHOLDING & INVESTMENTS International Depository Receipt

IFA *abbr* **1.** FINANCE independent financial adviser **2.** ACCOUNTING Institute of Financial Accountants

IFAD *abbr* FINANCE International Fund for Agricultural Development

IFC *abbr* FINANCE International Finance Corporation

IFRS *abbr* ACCOUNTING International Financial Reporting Standards

IIN *abbr* BANKING issuer identification number

ijara *or* **ijarah** FINANCE **agreement by bank to purchase then lease item** in Islamic financing, a leasing arrangement in which a bank or financier purchases an item for a customer, then leases it to the customer at a profit

ijara wa-iqtina FINANCE **agreement by customer to buy item after leasing it** in Islamic financing, a leasing arrangement with a bank similar to ijara in which the customer agrees to purchase the item at a prearranged price at the end of the lease term

ILG *abbr* STOCKHOLDING & INVESTMENTS index-linked gilt

illegal parking STOCKHOLDING & INVESTMENTS, FRAUD **concealing true ownership** an illegal stock market practice of using another company's name when purchasing securities (slang)

illiquid FINANCE **1. lacking easy access to cash** used to describe a person or business that lacks cash or assets such as securities that can readily be converted into cash **2. not easily convertible to cash** used to describe an asset that cannot be easily converted into cash

illiquid market STOCKHOLDING & INVESTMENTS **securities market with low trading volume** a securities market in which very little trading is taking place

IMA *abbr* STOCKHOLDING & INVESTMENTS **1.** investment management agreement **2.** Investment Management Association

IMF FINANCE **international lending organization** an international organization based in Washington, DC, that was established by industrialized nations to monitor economic and financial developments, lend to countries with balance of payments difficulties, and provide expert policy advice and technical assistance. *Full form* **International Monetary Fund**

impaired capital FINANCE **firm's total capital lower than stock value** a company's capital that is worth less than the nominal value of its stock

impaired credit FINANCE **when somebody's credit rating is reduced** a situation in which a person becomes less creditworthy than before

impairment of capital FINANCE **how much firm's stock value exceeds total capital** the extent to which the value of a company is less than the nominal value of its stock

impersonation of the deceased fraud FRAUD **fraud using deceased person's identity** in the United Kingdom, a situation in which a person uses the identity of somebody who has recently died to commit a crime such as accessing financial information or obtaining a passport. *Abbr* **IOD fraud**

implicit cost FINANCE **cost of using resources owned by producer** the cost of using resources that are owned by a company that is producing a good or service. *See also* **explicit cost**

imprest account ACCOUNTING **type of petty cash record** in the United Kingdom, a record of the transactions of a type of petty cash system. An employee is given an advance of money, an imprest, for incidental expenses and, when most of it has been spent, he or she presents receipts for the expenses to the accounts department and is then reimbursed with cash to the total value of the receipts.

imprest system ACCOUNTING **petty cash system involving written receipts** in the United Kingdom, a system of controlling a petty cash fund, in which cash is paid out against a written receipt, and the receipt is used to get more cash to bring the fund up to the original level

imputed interest FINANCE, TAX **taxable interest considered paid but not paid** interest that is considered to be paid and may be taxed, even though it has not yet been paid

inactive account BANKING **bank account that is not in use** a bank account that is not used over a particular period of time

incentive plan *US* FINANCE **program rewarding improved performance** a program set up to give benefits to employees to reward them for improved commitment and performance and as a means of motivation. An incentive plan is designed to supplement base pay and fringe benefits. A financial incentive plan may offer stock options or a cash bonus, whereas a nonfinancial incentive plan offers benefits such as additional paid vacations. Awards from incentive plans may be made on an individual or team basis. *UK term* ***incentive scheme***

incentive scheme *UK* FINANCE = ***incentive plan***

incentive stock option STOCKHOLDING & INVESTMENTS **US plan allowing employees to buy stock** in the United States, an employee stock option plan that gives each qualifying employee the right to purchase a specific number of the corporation's shares at a set price during a specific time period. Tax is only payable when the stocks are sold.

incestuous share dealing STOCKHOLDING & INVESTMENTS **stock trading among firms in same group** stock trading by companies within a group in the stock of the other companies within that group. The legality of such transactions depends on the objective of the deals.

inchoate instrument FINANCE **incomplete monetary contract** a ***negotiable instrument*** that is incomplete because, for example, the date or amount is missing. The person to whom it is delivered has the authority to complete it in any way he or she considers fit.

incidental expenses FINANCE **small amounts spent on unplanned items** small amounts of money spent at various times in addition to the usual larger budgeted amounts

income 1. FINANCE **money received** money received by a company or individual **2.** FINANCE **money created** money generated by a business **3.** STOCKHOLDING & INVESTMENTS **interest or dividends received from investments** money received from savings or investments, for example, interest on a bank account or dividends from stock

income bond STOCKHOLDING & INVESTMENTS **bond repaid from profits** a bond that a company repays only from its profits

income distribution 1. FINANCE, HR & PERSONNEL **levels of earnings across group or area** the distribution of income across a specific group such as a company or specific area such as a region or country, showing the various wage levels and the percentage of individuals earning at each level **2.** *UK* STOCKHOLDING & INVESTMENTS = ***income dividend***

income dividend *US* STOCKHOLDING & INVESTMENTS **money paid to investors from group investment earnings** payment to investors of the income generated by a collective investment, less management charges, tax, and expenses. It is distributed in proportion to the number of shares held by each investor. *UK term* **income distribution** *(sense 2)*

income elasticity of demand FINANCE **demand changing with income** a proportional change in demand in response to a change in income

income fund STOCKHOLDING & INVESTMENTS **fund focused on high income** a fund that attempts to provide high income rather than capital growth

income gearing FINANCE **ratio of firm's loan interest payments to profits** the ratio of the interest a company pays on its borrowing shown as a percentage of its pre-tax profits

income redistribution ECONOMICS **government policy to balance income levels through taxation** a government policy to redirect income to a targeted sector of a country's population, for example, by lowering the rate of tax paid by low-income earners

income shares *UK* STOCKHOLDING & INVESTMENTS = *income stock*

income smoothing ACCOUNTING **accounting method to make income appear steady** a form of *creative accounting* that involves the manipulation of a company's financial statements to show steady annual profits rather than large fluctuations

incomes policy ECONOMICS **UK government policy to limit wage and price increases** in the United Kingdom, any government policy that seeks to restrain increases in wages or prices by regulating the permitted level of increase

income statement ACCOUNTING = *profit and loss account*

income stock *US* **1.** STOCKHOLDING & INVESTMENTS **stock expected to pay high dividends** common stock sought because of its relatively high yield as opposed to its potential to produce capital growth **2.** MARKETS **split fund shares receiving income, not capital appreciation** certain funds, for example, investment trusts, that issue split level funds where holders of the income element receive all the income (less expenses, charges, and tax), while holders of the capital element receive only the capital gains (less expenses, charges, and tax). *UK term income shares*

income stream FINANCE **money received from product or activity** the income received by a company from a particular product or activity

income support FINANCE **UK government subsidy for people with low incomes** in the United Kingdom, a government benefit paid to low-income earners who are working less than 16 hours per week, and may be disabled or have family care responsibilities. *Abbr* **IS**

income unit STOCKHOLDING & INVESTMENTS **in UK, share in mutual fund** in the United Kingdom, a share in a mutual fund that makes regular dividendpayments to its stockholders

income yield STOCKHOLDING & INVESTMENTS = *current yield*

inconvertible CURRENCY & EXCHANGE **describing currency not easily converted** used to describe a currency that cannot be easily converted into other currencies

indebted FINANCE **owing money to somebody else** used to describe a person, company, or country that owes money to another person, a financial institution, or another country

indebtedness FINANCE **amount of debt** the degree to which a person, organization, or country owes money. High levels of

domestic and public indebtedness have an effect on economic growth. Mortgage indebtedness was major factor in the global financial crisis of 2007–8.

indemnity FINANCE **agreement to pay compensation** an agreement by one party to make good the losses suffered by another. *See also indemnity insurance, letter of indemnity*

indenture STOCKHOLDING & INVESTMENTS **agreement about bond** a formal document showing the terms of agreement on a *bond issue*

independent financial adviser FINANCE **somebody giving unbiased advice about money** a person who gives impartial advice to clients on financial matters and who is not employed by any financial institution, although commission for the sale of products may be received. *Abbr* **IFA**. *See also financial planner*

index 1. FINANCE **amount representing value of group** an amount calculated to represent the relative value of a group of things **2.** MARKETS **number indicating value of stocks in market** a standard that represents the value of stocks in a market, for example, the Dow Jones Industrial Average, FTSE 100, or Hang Seng Index. *Also called stock market index. UK term share index*

indexation FINANCE **connecting rate to standard price index** the linking of a rate to a standard index of prices, interest rates, stock prices, or similar items

indexed portfolio STOCKHOLDING & INVESTMENTS **stock in all firms in stock exchange index** a portfolio of stock in all the companies that form the basis of a specific stock exchange index

index fund STOCKHOLDING & INVESTMENTS **mutual fund linked to stock exchange index** a mutual fund composed of companies listed in an important stock market index in order to match the market's overall performance. *Also called index tracker, tracker fund. See also managed fund*

index futures STOCKHOLDING & INVESTMENTS **futures contract on stock exchange index** a futures contract trading in one of the major stock market indices such as the S&P 500

index-linked FINANCE **changing in relation to numerical scale** varying in value in relation to an index, especially the *consumer price index*, or the *retail price index* for index-linked securities in the United Kingdom

index-linked bond STOCKHOLDING & INVESTMENTS **investment product with index tied to index** a security where the income is linked to an index such as a financial index. *See also index-linked gilt, index-linked savings certificate*

index-linked gilt STOCKHOLDING & INVESTMENTS **UK bond with payments linked to retail prices** in the United Kingdom, an inflation-proof government bond, first introduced for institutional investors in 1981 and then made available to the general public in 1982. It is inflation-proof in two ways: the dividend is raised every six months in line with the *retail price index* and the original capital is repaid in real terms at redemption, when the indexing of the repayment is

a–z

Dictionary

undertaken. The nominal value of the stock, however, does not increase with inflation. Like other gilts, ILGs are traded on the market. Price changes are principally dependent on investors' changing perceptions of inflation and real yields. *Abbr* **ILG**

index-linked savings certificate STOCKHOLDING & INVESTMENTS **UK savings type with payments linked to inflation rate** a certificate issued by the UK National Savings & Investments organization, with a return linked to the retail price index. *See also* **granny bond**

index-linked security *UK* STOCKHOLDING & INVESTMENTS = **sinflation-proof security**

index number ECONOMICS **number indicating relative economic change** a weighted average of a number of observations of an economic attribute, for example, retail prices expressed as a percentage of a similar weighted average calculated at an earlier period

index of leading economic indicators ECONOMICS **predictor of future economic performance** a statistical measure that uses a set of economic variables to predict the future performance of an economy

index option STOCKHOLDING & INVESTMENTS **option to purchase shares in market index** an option to purchase shares in a stock market index. This allows an investor to trade within a particular sector and eliminates some of the risk of investing in individual stocks.

index tracker STOCKHOLDING & INVESTMENTS = **index fund**

indicated dividend STOCKHOLDING & INVESTMENTS **predicted annual dividends if current rate stays same** the forecast total of all dividends in a year if the amount of each dividend remains as it is

indicated yield STOCKHOLDING & INVESTMENTS **predicted annual income** the forecast yield at the current dividend rate

indifference curve ECONOMICS **curve on graph representing customers' product satisfaction** a line on a graph showing how consumers view different combinations of products. The line joins various points, each point representing a combination of two products, and each combination giving the customer equal satisfaction.

indirect cost ACCOUNTING **unchanging expense not directly related to production** a fixed or overhead cost that cannot be attributed directly to the production of a particular item and is incurred even when there is no output. Indirect costs may include the **cost center** functions of finance and accounting, information technology, administration, and personnel. *See also* **direct cost**

Individual Savings Account STOCKHOLDING & INVESTMENTS *see* **ISA**

industrial production ECONOMICS **total output of factories and mines** the output of a country's productive industries. Until the 1960s, this commonly related to iron and steel or coal, but since then lighter engineering in automobile or robotics manufacture has taken over.

industrial revenue bond STOCKHOLDING & INVESTMENTS **bond to pay for building** a bond that a private company uses to finance construction

ineligible bills FINANCE **bills unacceptable for discounting** those **bills of exchange** that cannot be **discounted** by a central bank

inferior good ECONOMICS **item demanded less as income rises** a good that a consumer buys in decreasing quantities as his or her income rises. *Also called* **Giffen good**

inflation ECONOMICS **increase in prices over time** a sustained increase in a country's general level of prices which devalues its currency, often caused by excess demand in the economy

inflation accounting ACCOUNTING **record-keeping method including effects of inflation** the adjustment of a company's accounts to reflect the effect of inflation and provide a more realistic view of the company's position

inflationary ECONOMICS **tending to cause increase in prices** characterized by excess demand or high costs creating an excessive increase in the country's money supply

inflationary gap ECONOMICS **situation where demand is greater than production capacity** a gap that exists when an economy's resources are utilized and **aggregate demand** is more than the full-employment level of output. Prices will rise to remove the excess demand.

inflationary spiral ECONOMICS **cycle of rising prices and wages** a situation in which, repeatedly, in inflationary conditions, excess demand causes producers to raise prices and employees to demand wage rises to sustain their living standards. *Also called* **wage-price spiral**

Inflationlinked bond STOCKHOLDING & INVESTMENTS, RISK **government bond with inflation protection** a bond issued by a government that is indexed to protect against inflation

inflation-proof ECONOMICS **indexed to inflation so as to preserve value** used to describe a pension, wage, or investment that is indexed to inflation so that its value is preserved in times of inflation

inflation-proof security *US* STOCKHOLDING & INVESTMENTS **security growing with inflation** a security that is indexed to inflation or a cost-of-living index. *UK term* **index-linked security**

inflation rate ECONOMICS **rate at which prices increase over time** the rate at which general price levels increase over a period of time

inflation target ECONOMICS **central bank's goal for increase in prices** a range or figure for the rate of increase in prices that the central bank of a country aims to reach at a specific date in the future

informal economy ECONOMICS **untaxed, unofficial economic activity** the economy that runs in parallel to the formal economy but outside the reach of the tax system, most transactions being paid for in cash or goods

ingot CURRENCY & EXCHANGE **gold or silver bar** a bar of gold or silver

inheritance FINANCE **property received from somebody who has died** property that is received from somebody through a will or by legal succession

initial capital FINANCE **money used for starting firm** the money that is used to start a business. Sources of initial capital might include personal funds, bank loans, grants, or credit from suppliers.

initial margin STOCKHOLDING & INVESTMENTS **required deposit on open positions** the deposit required of members of the *London Clearing House* on all open positions, long or short, to cover short-term price movements. It is returned to members when the position is closed. *See also* *variation margin*

initial offer STOCKHOLDING & INVESTMENTS **in UK, first offer on another firm's stock** in the United Kingdom, the first offer that a company makes to buy the stock of another company

initial public offering STOCKHOLDING & INVESTMENTS **first time firm's stock are sold** the first instance of making particular stock available for sale to the public. *Abbr* **IPO**. *See also* *flotation*

initial yield STOCKHOLDING & INVESTMENTS **expected yield of new investment fund** the yield that an investment fund is estimated to provide at its launch

inland bill CURRENCY & EXCHANGE **in UK, bill belonging to one country** in the United Kingdom, a bill of exchange that is payable and drawn in the same country

inside director CORPORATE GOVERNANCE **full-time director of firm** a director who works full-time in a corporation. *See also* *outside director*

inside information *or* **insider information** STOCKHOLDING & INVESTMENTS **secret knowledge about firm** information that is of advantage to investors but is only available to people who have personal contact with a company.

insider dealing *or* **insider trading** MARKETS, FRAUD **trading stock using secret information** profitable, usually illegal, trading in securities carried out using information not available to the public

insolvency FINANCE **lacking money to pay debt** the inability to pay debts when they become due. Insolvency will apply even if total assets exceed total liabilities, if those assets cannot be readily converted into cash to meet debts as they mature. Even then, insolvency may not necessarily mean *business failure*. *Bankruptcy* may be avoided through *debt rescheduling* or *turnaround management*.

insolvency practitioner FINANCE **UK insolvency specialist** in the United Kingdom, a licensed professional who advises on or acts in all formal insolvency procedures

insolvent FINANCE **unable to pay debts** used to describe a person or business that is unable to pay debts, because the debts are more than the amount of assets that can be readily turned into cash

installment FINANCE **one of several payments for initial public offering** one of two or more payments made for the purchase of an initial public offering

installment activity statement TAX, STOCKHOLDING & INVESTMENTS **Australian form for reporting payments on investment income** a standard form used in Australia to report *pay-as-you-go* installment payments on investment income. *Abbr* **IAS**

installment loan US FINANCE **fixed-interest loan with regular payments** a loan that is repaid with fixed regular installments, and with a rate of interest fixed for the duration of the loan. *UK term* **instalment credit**

installment plan US FINANCE **method of paying for purchase with regular payments** a method of buying something by paying for it in regular equal amounts over a period of time. *UK terms* **hire purchase**, **easy terms**

instalment credit UK FINANCE = *installment loan*

instant access account BANKING **UK savings account with easily accessible funds** in the United Kingdom, a savings account that pays interest, but from which the account holder can withdraw money immediately whenever he or she needs it

Institute of Chartered Accountants in England and Wales ACCOUNTING **UK accounting organization** the largest professional accounting body in Europe, providing certification by examinations, ensuring high standards of education and training, and supervising professional conduct. *Abbr* **ICAEW**

Institute of Chartered Accountants in Ireland ACCOUNTING **Ireland-wide accounting organization** the oldest and largest professional body for accountants in Ireland, the ICAI was founded in 1888. Its many objectives include promoting best practice in chartered accountancy and maintaining high standards of professionalism among its members. It publishes a journal, *Accountancy Ireland*, and has offices in Dublin and Belfast. *Abbr* **ICAI**

Institute of Chartered Accountants of New Zealand ACCOUNTING **New Zealand accounting organization** the only professional accounting body in New Zealand, representing over 26,000 members in that country and abroad. ICANZ has overseas branch offices in Fiji, London, Melbourne, and Sydney. *Abbr* **ICANZ**

Institute of Chartered Accountants of Scotland ACCOUNTING **Scottish accounting organization** the world's oldest professional body for accountants, based in Edinburgh. *Abbr* **ICAS**

Institute of Chartered Secretaries and Administrators UK FINANCE **association of administrators and administrative assistants** an organization that works to promote the efficient administration of commerce, industry, and public affairs. Founded in 1891 and granted a royal charter in 1902, it represents the interests of its members to government, publishes journals and other materials, promotes the standing of its members, and provides educational support and qualifying programs. *Abbr* **ICSA**

Institute of Directors CORPORATE GOVERNANCE **UK organization for directors of firms** in the United Kingdom, an individual membership association whose stated objective is to "serve, support, represent, and set standards for directors." Founded in 1903 by Royal Charter, the IoD it is an independent, nonpolitical body. It is based in London, but also has offices in Belfast, Birmingham, Bristol, Edinburgh, Manchester, and Nottingham. *Abbr* **IoD**

Institute of Financial Accountants ACCOUNTING **UK organization for accountants** a UK professional organization, established in 1916, that works to set technical and ethical standards in financial accounting. *Abbr* **IFA**

Institute of Financial Services BANKING **UK organization for financial education** in the United Kingdom, the trading name of the Chartered Institute of Bankers, especially when involved with education

institutional buyout MERGERS & ACQUISITIONS **purchase of firm by financial institution** the *takeover* of a company by a financial institution that backs a group of managers who will run it

institutional investor STOCKHOLDING & INVESTMENTS **organization that invests** an institution such as an insurance company, bank, or labor union that makes investments

instrument 1. FINANCE **way of achieving something** a means to an end, for example, a government's expenditure and taxation in its quest for reducing unemployment **2.** STOCKHOLDING & INVESTMENTS **investment product** a generic term for either securities or derivatives. Instruments can be negotiable or nonnegotiable. *See also financial instrument, negotiable instrument* **3.** LEGAL **legal document** an official or legal document

insufficient funds FINANCE **too little money in bank account for check** a lack of enough money in a bank account to pay a check drawn on that account

insured bond STOCKHOLDING & INVESTMENTS **bond protected by insurance** a bond whose principle and interest payments are insured against default

intangible asset FINANCE **non-material resource** an asset such as intellectual property or *goodwill*. *Also called invisible asset*. *See also tangible asset*

intangibles FINANCE **non-material costs and benefits to business** the benefits to a business such as customer goodwill and employee loyalty, and costs such as training time and lost production, that cannot easily be quantified

intellectual assets FINANCE **knowledge, experience, and skills of workers** the knowledge, experience, and skills of its staff that an organization can make use of

intellectual capital FINANCE **firm's combined intangible assets** the combined intangible assets owned or controlled by a company or organization that provide *competitive advantage*. Intellectual capital assets can include the knowledge and expertise of employees, brands, customer information and relationships, contracts, *intellectual*

property such as patents and copyright, and organizational technologies, processes, and methods. Intellectual capital can be implicit and intangible, stored in people's heads, or explicit and documented in written or electronic format.

intellectual property FINANCE **ownership of items such as copyrights and patents** the ownership of rights to ideas, designs, and inventions, including *copyrights*, *patents*, and *trademarks*. Intellectual property is protected by law in most countries, and the World Intellectual Property Organization is responsible for harmonizing the law across different countries and promoting the protection of intellectual property rights.

intellectual property crime FRAUD **crime involving counterfeiting and copyright piracy** illegal activities involving the manufacture and distribution of counterfeit and copyrighted products

interbank loan BANKING **loan made to another bank** a loan that one bank makes to another bank

interbank market MARKETS, BANKING **lending of money amongst banks** a market in which banks lend money to or borrow money from each other for short periods

interchange E-COMMERCE, BANKING **transaction between issuing and acquiring banks** a transaction between an *acquirer* and an *issuer*

interchangeable bond STOCKHOLDING & INVESTMENTS **bond whose form can be changed** a bond whose owner can change it at will between registered and coupon form, sometimes for a fee

interchange fee E-COMMERCE, BANKING **charge on interchange, paid by acquiring bank** the charge on a transaction between the acquiring bank and the issuing bank, paid by the acquirer to the issuer

intercommodity spread STOCKHOLDING & INVESTMENTS **options for purchase and sale of related goods** a combination of purchase and sale of options for related commodities with the same delivery date

inter-dealer broker STOCKHOLDING & INVESTMENTS **intermediary between dealers** a broker who arranges transactions between dealers in government securities

interest FINANCE **borrowing charge or payment** the rate that a lender charges for a loan or *credit facility*, or a payment made by a financial institution for the use of money deposited in an account

interest arbitrage UK FINANCE **switching funds between countries for higher interest rates** transactions in two or more financial centers in order to make an immediate profit by exploiting differences in interest rates. *See also arbitrage*

interest assumption FINANCE **predicted amount of interest** the expected rate of return on a portfolio of investments

interest-bearing FINANCE **paying or requiring interest** used to describe a deposit, account, shares, etc., that pay interest, or a loan that requires interest

interest-bearing account *or* **interest-bearing deposit** BANKING **money in bank account that earns interest** a deposit of money, or a bank account, that receives interest

interest charge BANKING **fee paid for borrowing money** an amount of money paid by a borrower as interest on a loan

interest cover FINANCE **amount of money available for payment of interest** the amount of earnings available to make interest payments after all operating and nonoperating income and expenses, except interest and income taxes, have been accounted for.

Interest cover is regarded as a measure of a company's creditworthiness because it shows how much income there is to cover interest payments on outstanding debt.

It is expressed as a ratio, comparing the funds available to pay interest (earnings before interest and taxes, or EBIT) with the interest expense. The basic formula is

$$\frac{\text{EBIT}}{\text{Interest expense}} = \text{Interest coverage ratio}$$

If interest expense for a year is $9 million, and the company's EBIT is $45 million, the interest coverage would be

$$\frac{45 \text{ million}}{9 \text{ million}} = 5:1$$

The higher the number, the stronger a company is likely to be. A ratio of less than 1 indicates that a company is having problems generating enough cashflow to pay its interest expenses, and that either a modest decline in operating profits or a sudden rise in borrowing costs could eliminate profitability entirely. Ideally, interest coverage should at least exceed 1.5; in some sectors, 2.0 or higher is desirable.

Variations of this basic formula also exist. For example, there is:

$$\frac{(\text{Operating cash flow} + \text{Interest} + \text{Taxes})}{\text{Interest}} = \text{Cashflow interest coverage ratio}$$

This ratio indicates the firm's ability to use its cashflow to satisfy its fixed financing obligations. Finally, there is the fixed-charge coverage ratio, that compares EBIT with fixed charges:

$$\frac{(\text{EBIT} + \text{Lease expenses})}{(\text{Interest} + \text{Lease expenses})} = \text{Fixed-charge coverage ratio}$$

"Fixed charges" can be interpreted in many ways, however. It could mean, for example, the funds that a company is obliged to set aside to retire debt, or dividends on preferred stock.

interest-elastic investment STOCKHOLDING & INVESTMENTS **investment with variable rate of return** an investment with a rate of return that varies with the rise and fall of interest rates

interest expense FINANCE **cost of borrowing money** the cost of the interest payments on borrowed money

interest-free credit FINANCE **loan for which no fee is charged** credit or a loan on which no interest is paid by the borrower

interest-inelastic investment STOCKHOLDING & INVESTMENTS **investment with fixed rate of return** an investment with a rate of return that does not vary with the rise and fall of interest rates

interest in possession trust FINANCE **UK trust whose income can be distributed immediately** in the United Kingdom, a trust that gives one or more beneficiaries an immediate right to receive any income generated by the trust's assets. It can be used for real estate, enabling the beneficiary either to enjoy the rent generated by the property or to reside there, or as a life policy, a common arrangement for inheritance tax planning.

interest payment FINANCE **borrowing or lending charge** an amount of money paid by a financial institution for the use of money deposited in an account, or money paid by a borrower as interest on a loan

interest rate FINANCE **percentage of money charged for borrowing** the amount of interest charged for borrowing a sum of money over a specific period of time

interest rate effect ECONOMICS **interest rate change leading to increased investment** the increase in investment that takes place when companies take advantage of lower interest rates to invest more

interest rate exposure *UK* FINANCE **possible loss related to changes in interest rates** the risk of a loss associated with movements in the level of interest rates. *See also* **bond**

interest rate guarantee FINANCE **1. limit on fluctuation** a limit that is set to prevent interest rates moving outside a specific range **2. legal protection from interest-rate changes** a tailored indemnity protecting the purchaser against future changes in interest rates

interest rate option STOCKHOLDING & INVESTMENTS **contract for interest** a contract conferring the right but not an obligation to pay or receive a specific interest rate under stated terms. *See also* **option**

interest rate risk FINANCE **risk of investment loss due to rising interest** the risk that the value of a fixed-income investment will decrease if interest rates rise

interest rate swap FINANCE **trade of loans with different interest rates** an exchange of two debt instruments with different rates of interest, made to tailor cash flows to the participants' different requirements. Most commonly a longer-term fixed rate is swapped for a shorter-term floating one.

interest-sensitive FINANCE **affected by changes in interest rates** used to describe assets, generally purchased with credit, that are in demand when interest rates fall but considered less attractive when interest rates rise

interest yield FINANCE **set rate of return paid on investment** a rate of gain generated by an investment that pays a fixed rate of return, usually a percentage of the amount invested

interim dividend STOCKHOLDING & INVESTMENTS **dividend for part of tax year** a dividend whose value is determined on the basis of a period of time of less than a full fiscal year

interim financial statement FINANCE **financial statement for part of tax year only** a financial statement that covers a period other than a full fiscal year. Although UK companies are not legally obliged to publish interim financial statements, those listed on the London Stock Exchange are obliged to publish a half-yearly report of their activities and a profit and loss account that may either be sent to stockholders or published in a national newspaper. In the United States, the practice is to issue quarterly financial statements. *Also called* **interim statement**

interim financing FINANCE **providing of temporary finance** financing by means of bridge loans, between the purchase of one asset and the sale of another

interim payment STOCKHOLDING & INVESTMENTS **partial payment of dividend early in year** a distribution to stockholders of part of a dividend in the first part of a financial year

interim statement FINANCE = *interim financial statement*

intermediary FINANCE **agent for financial transactions** a person or organization that arranges financing, insurance, or investments for others

intermediation FINANCE **acting as agent in financial transaction** the process of arranging financing through an intermediary. Financial institutions act as intermediaries when they lend depositors' money to borrowers.

internal audit RISK **audit by firm's own employees** an audit of a company undertaken by its employees, usually to check on its internal controls. *See also* **external audit**

internal cost analysis ACCOUNTING **investigation into organization's activities to establish profitable areas** an examination of an organization's value-creating activities to determine sources of profitability and to identify the relative costs of different processes. Internal cost analysis is a tool for analyzing the *value chain*. Principal steps include identifying those processes that create value for the organization, calculating the cost of each value-creating process against the overall cost of the product or service, identifying the cost components for each process, establishing the links between the processes, and working out the opportunities for achieving relative cost advantage.

internal rate of return FINANCE **interest rate indicating worthwhile profit** in a discounted cash flow calculation, the rate of interest that reduces future income streams to the cost of the investment; practically speaking, the rate that indicates whether or not an investment is worth pursuing.

Let's assume that a project under consideration costs $7,500 and is expected to return $2,000 per year for five years, or $10,000. The IRR calculated for the project would be about 10%. If the cost of borrowing money for the project, or the return on investing the funds elsewhere, is less than 10%, the project is probably worthwhile. If the alternative use of the money will return 10% or more, the project should be rejected, since from a financial perspective it will break even at best.

Typically, managements require an IRR equal to or higher than the cost of capital, depending on relative risk and other factors.

The best way to compute an IRR is by using a spreadsheet (such as Excel) or financial calculator.

If using Excel, for example, select the IRR function. This requires the annual cashflows to be set out in columns and the first part of the IRR formula requires the cell reference range of these cashflows to be entered. Then a guess of the IRR is required. The default is 10%, written 0.1.

If a project has the following expected cashflows, then guessing IRR at 30% returns an accurate IRR of 27%, indicating that if the next best way of investing the money gives a return of -20%, the project should go ahead.

Now	− 2,500
Year 1	1,200
Year 2	1,300
Year 3	1,500

IRR can be misleading, especially as significant costs will occur late in the project. The rule of thumb "the higher the IRR the better" does not always apply. For the most thorough analysis of a project's investment potential, some experts urge using both IRR and net present value calculations, and comparing their results. *Abbr* **IRR**

International Accounting Standards Board ACCOUNTING **organization that sets accounting standards** an independent and privately funded standard-setting organization for the accounting profession, based in London. The Board, whose members come from nine countries and a variety of backgrounds, is committed to developing a single set of high quality, understandable, and enforceable global standards that require transparent and comparable information in general purpose financial statements. It also works with national accounting standard setters to achieve convergence in accounting standards around the world. *Abbr* **IASB**

International Accounting Standards Committee ACCOUNTING **former organization promoting international agreement on accounting standards** formerly, an organization based in London that worked toward achieving global agreement on accounting standards, replaced by the *International Accounting Standards Board*. *Abbr* **IASC**

International Bank for Reconstruction and Development BANKING *see* **IBRD**

International Centre for Settlement of Investment Disputes BANKING **part of World Bank Group** one of the five institutions that comprise the World Bank Group, based in Washington, DC. It was established in 1966 to undertake the role previously undertaken in a personal capacity by the president of the World Bank in assisting in mediation or conciliation of investment disputes between governments and private foreign investors. The overriding consideration in its establishment was that a specialist institution could help to promote increased flows of international investment. Although ICSID has close links to the World Bank, it is an autonomous organization. *Abbr* **ICSID**

International Depository Receipt STOCKHOLDING & INVESTMENTS **outside US, document indicating ownership of stock** the equivalent of an *American depository receipt* in the rest of the world, an IDR is a negotiable certificate issued by a bank that indicates ownership of stock. *Abbr* **IDR**

International Development Association FINANCE **agency helping poorest nations** an agency administered by the International Bank for Reconstruction and Development to provide assistance on concessionary terms to the poorest countries. Its resources consist of subscriptions and general replenishments from its more industrialized and developed members, special contributions, and transfers from the net earnings of the International Bank for Reconstruction and Development. *Abbr* **IDA**

International Finance Corporation FINANCE **UN agency encouraging private investment in developing nations** a United Nations organization promoting private sector investment in developing countries to reduce poverty and improve the quality of people's lives. It finances private sector projects that are profit-oriented and environmentally and socially sound, and helps to foster development. The International Finance Corporation has a staff of 2,000 professionals around the world who seek profitable and creative solutions to complex business issues. *Abbr* **IFC**

International Financial Reporting Standards ACCOUNTING **standards for preparing financial statements** a set of rules and guidelines established by the *International Accounting Standards Board* for standardizing the preparation of financial statements so that investors, organizations, and governments have a basis for comparison. *Abbr* **IFRS**

international fund FINANCE **mutual fund with domestic and foreign investments** a mutual fund that invests in securities both inside and outside a country

International Fund for Agricultural Development FINANCE **UN agency in poor countries** a specialized United Nations agency with a mandate to combat hunger and rural poverty in countries with developing economies. Established as an international financial institution in 1977 following the 1974 World Food Conference, it has financed projects in over 100 countries and independent territories, to which it has committed US$7.7 billion in grants and loans. It has three sources of finance: contributions from members, loan payments, and investment income. *Abbr* **IFAD**

International Monetary Fund FINANCE *see* ***IMF***

international money market MARKETS, CURRENCY & EXCHANGE **exchange of foreign currencies** a market in which currencies can be borrowed and lent and converted into other currencies

international reserves CURRENCY & EXCHANGE = *foreign currency reserves*

International Swaps and Derivatives Association STOCKHOLDING & INVESTMENTS **organization for derivative traders** a professional association for international traders in derivatives, founded in 1985. *Abbr* **ISDA**

intervention ECONOMICS **government action to influence market forces** government action to manipulate market forces for political or economic purposes

intervention mechanism CURRENCY & EXCHANGE **central banks' means of maintaining fixed exchange rates** a method such as buying or selling of foreign currency used by central banks in maintaining equivalence between exchange rates

inter vivos trust FINANCE **trust set up between living people** a legal arrangement for managing somebody's money or property, set up by one living person for another living person

in the money STOCKHOLDING & INVESTMENTS **having intrinsic value** used to describe an option that, if it expired at the current market price, would have significant *intrinsic value*. *See also* ***out of the money***

intrinsic value STOCKHOLDING & INVESTMENTS **gap between share price and option price** with reference to an option or convertible, the value at which a security would trade if there were no *option premium*, i.e. the share price less the option price

introducing broker STOCKHOLDING & INVESTMENTS **broker not paid directly by customers** a person or organization acting as a broker but not able to accept payment from customers

inventory depreciation ACCOUNTING **reduction in value of stored stock** a reduction in value of inventory that is held in a warehouse for some time

inventory financing FINANCE **obtaining loans against product inventory** a method by which manufacturers of consumer products obtain a loan by using their inventory as collateral

inventory turnover 1. ACCOUNTING **replacement rate of commercial assets** an accounting ratio of the number of times *inventory* is replaced during a given period. The ratio is calculated by dividing net sales by average inventory over a given period. Values are expressed as times per period, most often a year, and a higher figure indicates a more efficient manufacturing operation.

It is calculated as follows:

$$\frac{\text{Cost of goods sold}}{\text{Inventory}}$$

If COGS is $2 million, and inventory at the end of the period is $500,000, then

$$\frac{2,000,000}{500,000} = 4$$

Also called **stock turns 2.** *US* STOCKHOLDING & INVESTMENTS **measure of how quickly inventory needs replacing** the total value of inventory sold in a year divided by the average value of goods held in stock. This checks that cash is not tied up in inventory for too long, losing its value over time. *UK term* ***stock turnover***

inventory valuation *US* ACCOUNTING **estimation of stock value** an estimation of the value of inventory at the end of an accounting period. *UK term* ***stock valuation***

inverse floating rate note STOCKHOLDING & INVESTMENTS **security with interest varying inversely with base rate** a security whose interest rate varies inversely with a *base interest rate*, rising as it falls and vice versa

inverted yield curve STOCKHOLDING & INVESTMENTS **showing lower interest rates for long-term bonds** a visual representation of relative interest rates that shows lower interest rates for long-term bonds than for short-term bonds. *See also* ***yield curve***

invested capital FINANCE firm's stock, retained earnings plus debt the total amount of a company's stock, retained earnings, and long-term debt

investment 1. FINANCE expenditure on assets and securities the spending of money on stocks and other securities, or on assets such as plant and machinery **2.** FINANCE something invested in something such as stocks, real estate, or a project in which money is invested in the expectation of making a profit **3.** STOCKHOLDING & INVESTMENTS money invested an amount of money invested in something in the expectation of making a profit

investment analyst STOCKHOLDING & INVESTMENTS researcher into investment possibilities an employee of a stock exchange company who researches other companies and identifies investment opportunities for clients. *Also called* **financial analyst**

investment appraisal STOCKHOLDING & INVESTMENTS assessment of future value of new assets analysis of the future profitability of capital purchases as an aid to good management

investment bank BANKING **1.** bank for corporate borrowers a bank that specializes in providing funds to corporate borrowers for startup or expansion **2.** *US* bank for investors and their backers a bank that does not accept deposits but provides services to those who offer securities to investors, and to those investors. *See also* **commercial bank**. *UK term* **merchant bank**. *Abbr* **IB**

investment borrowing ECONOMICS borrowing money to promote economic growth the borrowing of funds intended to encourage a country's economic growth or to support the development of particular industries or regions by adding to physical or human capital

investment center STOCKHOLDING & INVESTMENTS section responsible for profitable investment a profit center with additional responsibilities for capital investment, and possibly for financing, whose performance is measured by its return on investment

investment club STOCKHOLDING & INVESTMENTS group combining to invest in securities a group of people who join together to make investments in securities

investment committee BANKING bank employees assessing proposals for investment in the United States, a group of employees of an investment bank who evaluate investment proposals

investment company STOCKHOLDING & INVESTMENTS firm investing money of several investors a company that pools for investment the money of several investors. *See also* **investment fund**

investment dealer *CANADA* STOCKHOLDING & INVESTMENTS securities broker a broker dealing in stock, bonds, debentures, and other securities. *Also called* **broker**

investment fund STOCKHOLDING & INVESTMENTS savings plan that makes investments a savings plan that invests its clients' funds in, for example, corporate start-up or expansion projects. *See also* **investment company**

investment grade STOCKHOLDING & INVESTMENTS refers to highly rated bond relating to a bond issued by a company, government, or local authority with a rating of BBB or higher, carrying relatively little risk. Trusts or pension funds may be restricted to investing in investment grade securities.

investment grade rating STOCKHOLDING & INVESTMENTS opinion of quality of bond as safe investment an assessment by a *rating agency* that a bond carries little risk for the investor. Bonds with ratings between AAA and BBB are considered investment grade.

investment grant STOCKHOLDING & INVESTMENTS government money given to firms for capital assets a government grant to a company to help it invest in capital assets such as buildings, equipment, or new machinery

investment horizon STOCKHOLDING & INVESTMENTS period of time for holding investment the length of time an investor expects to hold an investment, or the holding period over which an investment is analyzed

investment income STOCKHOLDING & INVESTMENTS money earned on investments revenue paid to investors that is derived from their investments, for example, dividends and interest on securities. *See also* **earned income**

investment management agreement STOCKHOLDING & INVESTMENTS contract between investor and fund manager a contract between an investor and an investment manager. *Abbr* **IMA**

Investment Management Association STOCKHOLDING & INVESTMENTS association for UK investment professionals the trade body for the UK investment industry, formed in February 2002 following the merger of the Association of Unit Trusts and Investment Funds and the Fund Managers' Association. *Abbr* **IMA**. *See also* **Fund Managers' Association**

investment manager STOCKHOLDING & INVESTMENTS = **fund manager**

investment objective STOCKHOLDING & INVESTMENTS long-term financial goal of investments the financial goal that determines how an individual or institution invests its assets, for example, for long-term growth or income

investment portfolio STOCKHOLDING & INVESTMENTS = **portfolio**

investment professional STOCKHOLDING & INVESTMENTS somebody legally qualified to give investment advice a person who is licensed to offer advice on, and sell, investment products

investment properties FINANCE buildings bought to rent out either commercial buildings such as stores, factories, or offices, or residential dwellings such as houses or apartments, that are purchased by businesses or individuals for renting to third parties

a–z

Dictionary

investment revaluation reserve *UK* FINANCE **reserve created by firm investing in property** the capital reserve where changes in the value of a business's investment properties are disclosed when they are revalued

Investment Services Directive STOCKHOLDING & INVESTMENTS **former EU regulations governing investment and market conduct** formerly, an EU directive regulating the conduct and operation of investment companies and markets, replaced by the Markets in Financial Instruments Directive. *Abbr* **ISD**

investment trust STOCKHOLDING & INVESTMENTS **investment firm with limited shares** an investment company with a fixed number of shares available. Investment trusts are *closed-end investment companies*.

investment vehicle STOCKHOLDING & INVESTMENTS **product or firm to invest in** a financial product such as stocks, bonds, funds, or futures, or a company, in which somebody can invest money

investor STOCKHOLDING & INVESTMENTS **person or organization spending money for financial return** a person or organization that invests money in something, especially in the stock of publicly owned corporations

investor relations research STOCKHOLDING & INVESTMENTS **research into how financial markets view firm** research carried out on behalf of an organization in order to gain an understanding of how financial markets regard the organization, its stock, and its sector

invisible asset FINANCE = *intangible asset*

invisible hand ECONOMICS **power of market forces** according to the 18th century British economist Adam Smith, the force of the market which drives the economy

invoice FINANCE **document requesting payment** a document that a supplier sends to a customer detailing the cost of products or services supplied and asking for payment

invoice date FINANCE **official date of sending of invoice** the date on which an invoice is issued. The invoice date may be different from the delivery date.

invoice discounting FINANCE **sale of invoices for less than stated value** the selling of invoices at a discount for collection by the buyer, or the payment of invoices at a discount by an intermediary with the customer's eventual payment routed through the intermediary, who takes a fee

invoice register ACCOUNTING **record of invoices for things bought** a list of purchase invoices recording the date of receipt of the invoice, the supplier, the invoice value, and the person to whom the invoice has been passed to ensure that all invoices are processed by the accounting system

invoicing FINANCE **requesting payment** the process of sending out invoices to customers

involuntary liquidation preference STOCKHOLDING & INVESTMENTS **payment to particular stockholders before liquidation** a payment that a company must make to holders of its preferred stock if it is forced to sell its assets when facing bankruptcy

inward investment STOCKHOLDING & INVESTMENTS **investment in local area** investment by a government or company in its own country or region, often to stimulate employment or develop a business infrastructure

IoD *abbr* CORPORATE GOVERNANCE Institute of Directors

IOD fraud *abbr* FRAUD impersonation of the deceased fraud

IOU FINANCE **note of money borrowed personally** a representation of "I owe you" that can be used as legal evidence of a debt, although it is most commonly used as an informal reminder of a minor transaction

IP-backed STOCKHOLDING & INVESTMENTS, RISK **describes securities backed by intellectual property** used to describe securities whose underlying assets are intellectual property such as patents, copyrights, and trademarks

IPO *abbr* STOCKHOLDING & INVESTMENTS initial public offering

IRR *abbr* FINANCE internal rate of return

irrecoverable debt FINANCE **loan that will never be repaid** a debt that will never be paid to the person to whom it is owed and must be written off, either as a charge to the profit and loss account or against an existing doubtful debt provision

irredeemable bond STOCKHOLDING & INVESTMENTS **indefinite government bond** a government bond that has no date of maturity but provides interest

irrevocable letter of credit BANKING **permanent credit authorization** a *letter of credit* that cannot be canceled

irrevocable trust FINANCE **unalterable trust** a trust that cannot be canceled or revised without the agreement of its beneficiary

IS *abbr* FINANCE income support

ISA STOCKHOLDING & INVESTMENTS **UK tax-free account for savings and investment** in the United Kingdom, a tax-free savings or investment account. Both cash ISAs and stocks and shares ISAs are available. The maximum that can be invested per tax year is capped, at £11,280 for 2012–13, up to £5,640 of which can be saved in cash. Formerly, Mini ISAs allowed investment in either cash or stocks, and Maxi ISAs investment in both together. *Full form* **Individual Savings Account**

ISD *abbr* STOCKHOLDING & INVESTMENTS Investment Services Directive

ISDA *abbr* STOCKHOLDING & INVESTMENTS International Swaps and Derivatives Association

issuance costs FINANCE **money spent issuing debt** the underwriting, legal, and administrative fees required to issue a debt. These fees are significant when issuing debt in the public markets, such as the bond market. However, other types of debt, such as private placements or bank loans, are cheaper to issue because they require less underwriting, legal, and administrative support.

issue STOCKHOLDING & INVESTMENTS **stocks or bonds for sale at one time** a set of stocks or bonds that a company offers for sale at one time

issue by tender STOCKHOLDING & INVESTMENTS = *sale by tender*

issued capital STOCKHOLDING & INVESTMENTS = *share capital*

Issue Department BANKING **part of Bank of England issuing currency** the department of the Bank of England that is responsible for issuing currency

issued price STOCKHOLDING & INVESTMENTS **price of firm's first stock issue** the price of shares of stock in a company when they are offered for sale for the first time

issued share capital STOCKHOLDING & INVESTMENTS **amount representing shares** the type, class, number, and amount of the shares held by stockholders. *See also* **stockholders' equity**

issued shares STOCKHOLDING & INVESTMENTS **shares held by investors** those shares that comprise a company's authorized capital that has been distributed to investors. They may be either fully paid or partly paid shares.

issue price STOCKHOLDING & INVESTMENTS **original price of securities** the price at which securities are first offered for sale

issuer bid STOCKHOLDING & INVESTMENTS **offer to buy own securities** an offer made by an issuer for its own securities when it is disappointed by the offers of others

issuer identification number BANKING **international number identifying individual bank** an internationally agreed six-digit number that uniquely identifies a bank in electronic transactions. *Abbr* **IIN**

issuing house FINANCE **UK financial institution that launches private companies** in the United Kingdom, a financial institution that specializes in the flotation of private companies. *See also* **investment bank, merchant bank**

item ACCOUNTING **unit of accounting information** a single piece of information included in a company's accounts

J

J curve CURRENCY & EXCHANGE **line representing falling exchange rate's effect on trade** a line on a graph shaped like a letter "J," with an initial short fall, followed by a longer rise, used to describe the effect of a falling exchange rate on a country's balance of trade

Jensen's measure FINANCE = *risk-adjusted return on capital*

jobbing backward *UK* STOCKHOLDING & INVESTMENTS **review of actions** the analysis of an investment transaction with the benefit of hindsight

job cost ACCOUNTING **describes accounting allowing determination of profit per job** used to describe a method of accounting whereby a project-oriented business allocates costs to a specific project, thereby having the ability to determine the profitability of individual projects

job lot FINANCE **varied items bought or sold together** a miscellaneous assortment of items, including securities, that are offered as a single deal

joint account BANKING **account shared by two or more people** an account, such as one held at a bank or by a broker, that two or more people own in common and can access

joint bond STOCKHOLDING & INVESTMENTS **bond guaranteed by third party** a bond that is guaranteed by a party other than the company or government that issued it

joint float CURRENCY & EXCHANGE **shared exchange relationship within set of currencies** a group of currencies that maintains a fixed internal relationship and moves jointly in relation to another currency

joint stock bank BANKING **formerly, commercial bank** a term that was formerly used for a commercial bank that is a partnership, as opposed to one that is a publicly held corporation

journal ACCOUNTING **consolidated record of transactions** a record of original entry, into which transactions are usually transferred from source documents. The journal may be subdivided into: sales journal/day book for credit sales; purchases journal/day book for credit purchases; cash book for cash receipts and payments; and the journal proper for transactions which could not appropriately be recorded in any of the other journals.

ju'alal FINANCE **contract for payment for services performed** in Islamic financing, a contract for performing a specified act for a specified fee

junior capital STOCKHOLDING & INVESTMENTS **capital representing stockholders' equity** capital in the form of stockholders' equity which is repaid only after the secured loans forming the senior capital have been paid if the firm goes into liquidation

junior debt FINANCE **debt with low priority for repayment** a debt that has no claim on a debtor's assets, or less claim than another debt. *See also* **senior debt**. *Also called* *subordinated debt*

junior security STOCKHOLDING & INVESTMENTS **security that is subordinate to another** a security whose interest or dividend payment has a lower priority than that of another security issued by the same company

junk bond STOCKHOLDING & INVESTMENTS, RISK **high-interest but high-risk bond** a high-yielding bond issued on a low-grade security. The issue of junk bonds has most commonly been linked with takeover activity.

junk-rated STOCKHOLDING & INVESTMENTS, RISK **describes bond that is risky investment** used to describe a bond that is considered by a *rating agency* to not be *investment grade* and therefore has a higher than average risk. Junk-rated bonds have a rating of BB or less.

527

a–z

Dictionary

K

K FINANCE **1,000** one thousand: used especially after numbers expressing a sum of money. It derives from kilo-.

kafalah FINANCE **agreement to pay debt of another who defaults** in Islamic financing, an agreement in which one party assumes responsibility for the debt of another if the debtor should fail to pay

kappa STOCKHOLDING & INVESTMENTS **relationship between option price change and asset's volatility** a ratio between the expected change in the price of an option and a one percent change in the expected volatility of the underlying asset. *Also called **lambda**, **vega***

ker-ching FINANCE **expression suggesting financial success** an expression suggesting that something will be very successful financially (slang)

Keynesian economics ECONOMICS **economic philosophy of John Maynard Keynes** the economic teachings and doctrines associated with *John Maynard Keynes*

Keynes, John Maynard ECONOMICS **British economist with influential theories on macroeconomics** a British economist who lived from 1883–1946. He is best known for his theories regarding *macroeconomics*. He believed that in a *recession*, the only way to reduce unemployment and improve the economy was for the government to increase spending, even if it meant running a deficit, and to reduce interest rates to encourage borrowing.

key rate FINANCE **interest rate on which other rates are based** an interest rate that gives the basic rate on which other rates are calculated, for example, the Bank of England's bank rate or the Federal Reserve's discount rate in the United States

kickback FRAUD **illicit payment to facilitator in transaction** a sum of money paid illegally to somebody in order to gain concessions or favors (slang)

kicker STOCKHOLDING & INVESTMENTS **attractive extra to standard security** an addition to a standard security that makes it more attractive, for example, options and warrants (slang). *See also **bells and whistles**, **sweetener***

kill FINANCE **stop instruction** to stop an instruction or order from being carried out (slang)

killing make a killing FINANCE to make a lot of money very quickly

kitchen sink bond STOCKHOLDING & INVESTMENTS, RISK **bond created from collection of collateralized mortgage obligations** a high-risk bond created by combining *tranches* of existing collateralized mortgage obligations

kite 1. FRAUD **fraudulent check, bill, or receipt** a fraudulent financial transaction, for example, a bad check that is dated to take advantage of the time interval required for clearing **2.** FINANCE **sign fraudulent checks** to write bad checks in order to take advantage of the time interval required for clearing

fly a kite1. FRAUD to use a fraudulent financial document such as a bad check**2.** GENERAL MANAGEMENT to make a suggestion in order to test people's opinion of it

kiwibond CURRENCY & EXCHANGE **Eurobond in NZ dollars** a *Eurobond* denominated in New Zealand dollars

knight MERGERS & ACQUISITIONS **firm involved in takeover** a term borrowed from chess strategy to describe a company involved in the politics of a *takeover* bid. There are three main types of knights. A *white knight* is a company that is friendly to the board of the company to be acquired. If the white knight gains control, it may retain the existing *board of directors*. A *black knight* is a former white knight that has disagreed with the board of the company to be acquired and has established its own hostile bid. A *gray knight* is a white knight that does not have the confidence of the company to be acquired.

knockout option STOCKHOLDING & INVESTMENTS **option with condition attached** an option to which a condition relating to the underlying security's or commodity's present price is attached so that it effectively expires when it goes *out of the money*

knowledge capital FINANCE **knowledge applicable for profit** knowledge that a company possesses and can put to profitable use

krona CURRENCY & EXCHANGE **Swedish and Icelandic currency unit** a unit of currency used in Sweden and Iceland

Krugerrand CURRENCY & EXCHANGE **South African gold coin** a South African coin consisting of one ounce of gold, first minted in 1967, bearing the portrait of 19th-century South African president Paul Kruger on the obverse

L

L ECONOMICS **measurement of money supply** a measure of the money supply, calculated as the broad money supply plus short-term Treasury securities, savings bonds, and commercial paper

laddering 1. STOCKHOLDING & INVESTMENTS **selling after raising stock price by continued buying** the investment strategy of repeatedly buying shares in a newly launched corporation so as to force up the price, then selling the whole investment at a profit **2.** STOCKHOLDING & INVESTMENTS, RISK **timed purchase, sale, and reinvestment strategy reducing risk** the action of making a series of investments that mature at different times, cashing each one at maturity, then reinvesting the proceeds, thereby reducing the risk of losing large amounts all at once

ladder option STOCKHOLDING & INVESTMENTS, RISK **option whose profit is locked in set level** an option whose *strike price* is reset when the underlying asset breaks through a specified level, locking in the profit between the old and new strike price

Laffer curve ECONOMICS, TAX **graph showing effects of tax rate changes** a graph showing that cuts in tax rates increase output in the economy and thus increase overall tax revenues

lagging indicator ECONOMICS economic factor confirming change in economic trend a measurable economic factor, for example, corporate profits or unemployment, that changes after the economy has already moved to a new trend, which it can confirm but not predict

laissez-faire economy ECONOMICS economic system in which government does not intervene an economy in which the government does not interfere because it believes that market forces should determine the course of the economy

lambda STOCKHOLDING & INVESTMENTS relationship of option price to underlying asset's volatility a ratio between the expected change in the price of an option and a one percent change in the expected volatility of the underlying asset. *Also called* **kappa, vega**

land bank FINANCE undeveloped land owned by builder or developer the land that a builder or developer has that is available for development

land banking FINANCE acquiring land for future development the practice of buying land that is not needed immediately, but with the expectation of using it in the future

lapping US ACCOUNTING way of concealing missing funds an attempt to hide missing funds by delaying the recording of cash receipts in a business's books. *UK term* **teeming and lading**

lapse STOCKHOLDING & INVESTMENTS expiry of option without trading the termination of an option without trade in the underlying security or commodity

lapsed option STOCKHOLDING & INVESTMENTS expired right to buy or sell investment an option to buy or sell a security or commodity that is no longer valid because it has expired

lapse rights STOCKHOLDING & INVESTMENTS rights of somebody allowing offer to lapse rights, such as those to a prearranged premium, owned by the person who allows an offer to lapse

last quarter ACCOUNTING final period of fiscal year a period of three months from October to the end of the year, or the period of three months at the end of the fiscal year

laundering FRAUD concealing illegal origins of money the process of passing the profits of illegal activities such as tax evasion into the normal banking system via apparently legitimate businesses

law of diminishing marginal utility ECONOMICS increased consumption of product decreases consumer's satisfaction a general theory in economics stating that each unit of a product consumed adds less satisfaction to the consumer than the previous one, i.e., the **marginal utility** of any good or service diminishes as each new unit of it is consumed

law of diminishing returns ECONOMICS increase in one area has limited effect a rule stating that as one factor of production is increased, while others remain constant, the extra output generated by the additional input will eventually fall. The law of diminishing returns therefore means that extra workers, extra capital, extra machinery, or extra land may not necessarily raise output as much as expected. For example,

increasing the supply of raw materials to a production line may allow additional output to be produced by using any spare capacity workers have. Once this capacity is fully used, however, continually increasing the amount of raw material without a corresponding increase in the number of workers will not result in an increase of output.

law of supply and demand ECONOMICS *see* **supply and demand**

lay-away US FINANCE paying for product in installments before taking ownership the reservation of an article for purchase by the payment of an initial deposit followed by regular interest-free installments, on completion of which the article is claimed by the buyer

LBO *abbr* MERGERS & ACQUISITIONS leveraged buyout

LC *or* L/C *abbr* BANKING letter of credit

LCM *abbr* ACCOUNTING lower of cost or market

LDC *abbr* ECONOMICS **1.** less developed country **2.** least developed country

LDT *abbr* FINANCE licensed deposit-taker

lead bank BANKING main bank in loan syndicate the primary bank in a loan syndicate, which organizes the transaction in question

leading economic indicator *or* leading indicator ECONOMICS early indication of change in economic trends an economic variable, such as private-sector wages, that tends to show the direction of future economic activity earlier than other indicators. *See also* **lagging indicator**

lead manager UK STOCKHOLDING & INVESTMENTS = **lead underwriter**

leads and lags CURRENCY & EXCHANGE adjusting speed of transactions with exchange rates in businesses that deal in foreign currencies, the practice of speeding up the receipt of payments (leads) if a currency is going to weaken, and slowing down the payment of costs (lags) if a currency is thought to be about to strengthen, in order to maximize gains and reduce losses

lead time 1. FINANCE, OPERATIONS & PRODUCTION time between starting and finishing the time interval between the start of an activity or process and its completion, for example, the time between ordering goods and their receipt, or between starting manufacturing of a product and its completion **2.** OPERATIONS & PRODUCTION period between order placement and delivery in inventory control, the time between placing an order and its arrival on site. Lead time differs from delivery time in that it also includes the time required to place an order and the time it takes to inspect the goods and receive them into the appropriate store. Inventory levels can afford to be lower and orders smaller when purchasing lead times are short. **3.** OPERATIONS & PRODUCTION, MARKETING period from new product idea to sales readiness in **new product development** and manufacturing, the time required to develop a product from concept to market delivery. Lead time increases as a result of the poor sequencing of dependent activities, the lack

a–z

Dictionary

of availability of resources, poor quality in the component parts, and poor plant layout. The technique of **concurrent engineering** focuses on the entire concept-to-customer process with the goal of reducing lead time. Companies can gain a **competitive advantage** by achieving a leadtime reduction and so getting products to market faster. *Also called* **cycle time** (sense 2)

lead underwriter US STOCKHOLDING & INVESTMENTS **institution in charge of new issue** the financial institution with overall responsibility for a new issue of shares of stockincluding its coordination, distribution, and related administration. *UK term* **lead manager**

LEAPS STOCKHOLDING & INVESTMENTS **options with one to three-year expiry dates** options that expire between one and three years in the future *Full form* **long-term equity anticipation securities**

leaseback LEGAL, FINANCE *see* **sale and leaseback**

least developed country ECONOMICS **very poor country with little economic development** a country that is not economically advanced, especially a country that borrowed heavily from commercial banks in the 1970s and 1980s to finance its industrial development, and so helped to create an international debt crisis. *Abbr* **LDC**

ledger ACCOUNTING **1. book for accounts** a book in which account transactions are recorded **2. book with record of account transactions** a collection of accounts, or book of accounts. Credit sales information is recorded, for example, by debtor, in the sales ledger. **3. book of consolidated accounts** a collection of accounts, maintained by transfers from the books of original entry. The ledger may be subdivided as follows: the sales ledger/debtors' ledger contains all the personal accounts of customers; the purchases ledger/creditors' ledger contains all the personal accounts of suppliers; the private ledger contains accounts relating to the proprietor's interest in the business such as capital and drawings; the general ledger/nominal ledger contains all other accounts relating to assets, expenses, revenue, and liabilities.

leg STOCKHOLDING & INVESTMENTS **price for security** either the highest price offered for a security or the lowest price a seller will accept for a security

legal currency LEGAL, CURRENCY & EXCHANGE **legally accepted money** money that is recognized by a government to be legally acceptable for payment of a debt

legal list LEGAL, STOCKHOLDING & INVESTMENTS **securities that financial institutions can legally invest in** a list of blue-chip securities in which banks and financial institutions are allowed to invest by the state in which they are based

legal tender LEGAL, CURRENCY & EXCHANGE **legally accepted paper money and coins** paper money and coins that have to be accepted within a given jurisdiction when offered as payment of a debt. *See also* **limited legal tender**

lender FINANCE **somebody who lends money** a person or financial institution that lends money

lender of last resort BANKING **bank lending to troubled commercial banks** a central bank that lends money to banks that cannot borrow elsewhere

lending facility BANKING = **credit facility**

lending limit BANKING **maximum amount of money bank can lend** a restriction placed on the amount of money a bank can legally lend

lending margin BANKING **spread above base rate borrowers agree to pay** an agreed spread for lending paid by borrowers, based on a reference rate such as the London Interbank Offered Rate

less developed country ECONOMICS **poorer country with limited economic development** a country whose economic development is held back because it lacks the technology and capital to make use of its natural resources to produce goods demanded on world markets. *Abbr* **LDC**

letter of comfort UK BANKING = **letter of moral intent**

letter of credit BANKING **letter of authorization from one bank to another** a letter issued by a bank that can be presented to another bank to authorize the issue of credit or money. *Abbr* **LC**

letter of license LEGAL, FINANCE **letter giving debtor more time for repayment** a letter from a creditor to a debtor who is having problems repaying money owed, giving the debtor a specific period of time to raise the money and an undertaking not to bring legal proceedings to recover the debt during that period

letter of moral intent US BANKING **parent company's support for subsidiary's loan** a letter from a holding company addressed to a bank where one of its subsidiaries wishes to borrow money. The purpose of the letter is to support the subsidiary's application to borrow funds and offer reassurance—although not a guarantee—to the bank that the subsidiary will remain in business for the foreseeable future, often with an undertaking to advise the bank if the subsidiary is likely to be sold. *UK term* **letter of comfort**

letter of renunciation STOCKHOLDING & INVESTMENTS **document transferring new stock** a form used to transfer an allotment of shares in a **rights issue** to another person

letter security STOCKHOLDING & INVESTMENTS **unregistered security salable under certain conditions** in the United States, a security that has not been registered with the **SEC** but can be sold privately if the buyer signs a letter of intent stating that the security is for investment, not resale, or can be traded publicly if the owner files a Form 144 with the SEC showing that the sale meets conditions that exempts it from registration with the SEC

level load STOCKHOLDING & INVESTMENTS **decreasing annual fee** an annual fee that is deducted from the assets in a mutual fund to cover management costs and that decreases gradually over time

leverage FINANCE **corporate funding mainly through borrowing** a method of corporate funding in which a higher proportion of funds is raised through borrowing than through stock issue. *Also called* **gearing**. *See also* **financial leverage**

leveraged bid MERGERS & ACQUISITIONS **takeover bid with borrowed finance** a takeover bid financed by borrowed money, rather than by a stock issue

leveraged buyout MERGERS & ACQUISITIONS **takeover with borrowed finance** a takeover using borrowed money, with the purchased company's assets as collateral. *Abbr* **LBO**

leveraged investment company *US* STOCKHOLDING & INVESTMENTS **investment company using borrowed money to expand** an investment company that borrows money in order to increase its portfolio. When the market is rising, stocks in a leveraged investment trust rise faster than those in an unleveraged trust, but they fall faster when the market is falling. *UK term* ***geared investment trust***

leveraged required return STOCKHOLDING & INVESTMENTS **income from investment exceeding cost of loan** the rate of return from an investment of borrowed money needed to make the investment worthwhile

leverage ratios FINANCE, RISK **means of quantifying risk from capital** ratios that indicate the level of risk taken by a company as a result of its capital structure. A number of different ratios may be calculated, for example, debt ratio (total debt divided by total assets), debt-to-equity or leverage ratio (total debt divided by total equity), or interest cover (earnings before interest and tax divided by interest paid). *Also called* ***gearing ratios***

liabilities FINANCE **firm's debts** the debts of a business, including dividends owed to stockholders

liability FINANCE **money lent without guarantee of repayment** a debt that has no claim on a debtor's assets, or less claim than another debt

liability management FINANCE **investigation of impact of liabilities on profitability** any exercise carried out by a business with the objective of controlling the effect of liabilities on its profitability. This will typically involve controlling the amount of risk undertaken, and ensuring that there is sufficient liquidity and that the best terms are obtained for any funding needs.

licensed deposit-taker FINANCE **UK institution that took deposits and paid interest** formerly in the United Kingdom, a type of ***deposit-taking institution*** that was licensed to receive money on deposit from private individuals and to pay interest on it, for example, a bank or savings and loan. *Abbr* **LDT**

licensed institution FINANCE = ***licensed deposit-taker***

lifeboat 1. FINANCE = ***lifeboat scheme* 2.** *S. AFRICA* BANKING **loan to rescue commercial bank** a low-interest emergency loan made by a central bank to rescue a commercial bank in danger of becoming insolvent

lifeboat scheme FINANCE **rescue measure for business or fund** a measure designed to protect or rescue a failing business or fund. *Also called* ***lifeboat** (sense 1)*

life-cycle costing ACCOUNTING **way of assessing asset's cost over time** a method of calculating the total cost of a physical asset throughout its life. Life-cycle costing is concerned with all costs of ownership and takes account of the costs incurred by an asset from its acquisition to its disposal, including design, installation, operating, and maintenance costs.

life-cycle fund STOCKHOLDING & INVESTMENTS **mutual fund linked to investor's age** a mutual fund whose investments vary according to the age of the investor

life-cycle savings motive ECONOMICS **reason for saving money over lifetime** a reason that a household or individual has for saving at specific times in life so as to have sufficient funds available to spend on anticipated expenses, for example, when starting a family or nearing retirement

limit STOCKHOLDING & INVESTMENTS **specified minimum or maximum price for transaction** an amount above or below which a broker is not to conclude the purchase or sale of a security for the client who specifies it

limited legal tender LEGAL, CURRENCY & EXCHANGE **bills and coins only usable in small transactions** in some jurisdictions, low denomination bills and all coins that may only be submitted up to a specific sum as legal tender in any one transaction

limit order STOCKHOLDING & INVESTMENTS **order to buy or sell security** an order to a broker to sell a security at or above an agreed price, or to buy a security at or below an agreed price

line of credit FINANCE **means of borrowing money** an agreed finance facility that allows a company or individual to borrow money. *Also called* ***bank line, credit line***

liquid FINANCE **easy to convert to cash** describes an asset that is easily converted to cash

liquid asset ratio FINANCE **ratio of liquid to total assets** the ratio of liquid assets to total assets. This is an indicator of a company's solvency.

liquid assets FINANCE **possible sources of cash** cash, and other assets readily convertible into cash without significant loss of capital

liquidate 1. BUSINESS **end existence of firm** to close a company by selling its assets, paying off any outstanding debts, distributing any remaining profits to the stockholders, and then ceasing trading **2.** STOCKHOLDING & INVESTMENTS **convert into cash** to sell assets in order to be able to have cash

liquidity FINANCE **ability to obtain cash from assets** an assessment of the ease with which assets can be converted to cash

liquidity agreement FINANCE **agreement to cash in asset** an agreement to allow a company to convert an asset into cash

liquidity event FINANCE **exit strategy of startup business** the means by which founders and initial investors in a new company are able to obtain the money the business has earned by changing their *equity* into cash. The company may be sold or there may be a public offering of stock.

liquidity preference FINANCE **desire for cash over other investments** a choice made by people to hold their wealth in the form of cash rather than bonds or stocks. A general increase in liquidity preference is symptomatic of a financial crisis whereas a general decrease is associated with increased appetite for risk.

liquidity ratio FINANCE = *cash ratio*

liquidity risk RISK **danger of inability to cash in assets** the risk that an entity will encounter difficulty in realizing assets or otherwise raising funds to meet commitments associated with financial instruments. *See also funding risk*

liquidity squeeze FINANCE **time when money is hard to borrow** a situation or period in which money for borrowing is unavailable from finance companies, banks, and other lenders of money. *Also called credit squeeze*

liquidity trap BANKING **inability to push interest rates lower** a central bank's inability to lower interest rates once investors believe rates can go no lower

liquid savings FINANCE **money saved** money held in deposit and savings accounts that is easily available if needed and not usually subject to large fluctuations in value

Lisbon Stock Exchange MARKETS, STOCKHOLDING & INVESTMENTS = *Euronext Lisbon*

listed security STOCKHOLDING & INVESTMENTS, MARKETS **security traded on exchange** a security that is quoted on a recognized stock exchange

living wage FINANCE **amount of pay needed for normal life** a level of pay that provides enough income for normal day-to-day basic requirements

load STOCKHOLDING & INVESTMENTS **administration charge for investment** a charge in some investment funds to cover administration, profit, and incidentals. When the primary cost is paid at the beginning this is *front-end loading*; at the end it is *back-end loading*. *See also load fund*

load fund STOCKHOLDING & INVESTMENTS **mutual fund requiring payment for transactions** a mutual fund that charges a fee for the purchase or sale of shares. *See also no-load fund*

loading 1. *ANZ* FINANCE **extra pay for exceptional skills or work environment** a payment made to employees over and above the basic wage in recognition of special skills or unfavorable conditions, for example, for overtime or shiftwork **2.** OPERATIONS & PRODUCTION **giving particular jobs to workstation** the assignment of tasks or jobs to a workstation. The loading of jobs is worked out through the use of *master production scheduling*.

loan FINANCE **borrowing arrangement with fixed schedule** a borrowing either by a business or a consumer where the amount borrowed is repaid according to an agreed schedule at an agreed interest rate, typically by regular installments over a set period of years. However, the principal may be repayable in one installment. *See also balloon loan, fixed-rate loan, interest-only mortgage, variable interest rate*

loanable funds theory ECONOMICS **interest rates are determined by supply and demand** the theory that interest rates are determined solely by supply and demand. It assumes

that consumers must be offered interest on their savings to induce them not just to spend their income and to make funds available for investment.

loanback 1. FINANCE **in US, return of money to lender** in the United States, the return to somebody of money that has been given as a loan, often as a way of illegally masking the money's true owner **2.** PENSIONS **in UK, arrangement to borrow from pension fund** in the United Kingdom, the ability of a holder of a pension fund to borrow money from it

loan capital FINANCE **money firm borrows for operations** a part of a company's capital that is a loan to be repaid at a later date

loan committee FINANCE **group considering nonstandard loan applications** a committee that examines applications for special loans, such as higher loans than usually allowed by a bank

loan constant ratio FINANCE **ratio of annual payments to original balance** the total of annual payments due on a loan as a fraction of the amount of the principal

Loan Council FINANCE **Australian federal committee overseeing borrowing by states** an Australian federal body, made up of treasurers from the states and the Commonwealth of Australia, that monitors borrowing by state governments

loan loss reserves BANKING **sum held by bank to cover bad debts** the money a bank holds to cover losses through defaults on loans that it makes

loan note FINANCE **written details of loan** a written agreement between parties describing the terms of repayment, interest if applicable, and due date of a loan

loan participation BANKING **collaboration by banks to make single large loan** the grouping together by several banks to share a very large loan to one single customer

loan production cycle FINANCE **time between loan application and lending of money** the period that begins with an application for a loan and ends with the lending of money

loan schedule FINANCE **details of loan payments** a list of the payments due on a loan and the balance outstanding after each has been made

loan shark FINANCE **lender charging excessively high interest rates** somebody who lends money at excessively, often illegally, high rates of interest (informal)

loan stock STOCKHOLDING & INVESTMENTS **bonds and debentures** a fixed-income security given in exchange for a loan

loan to value ratio FINANCE **ratio of worth of loan to collateral** the ratio of the amount of a loan to the value of the collateral for it. *Abbr* **LTV ratio**

loan value FINANCE **sum available to borrower** the amount that a lender is willing to lend a borrower

local authority bond STOCKHOLDING & INVESTMENTS **UK local government's fixed-interest bond** in the United Kingdom, a loan raised by a local authority in the form of a fixed-interest bond, repayable at a specific date. Local authority bonds are similar to US *Treasury bonds*.

local authority deposits FINANCE **money lent to UK local government** in the United Kingdom, money deposited with a local authority to earn interest for the depositor

lockbox BANKING **banking service for checks sent by mail** a banking system in which checks sent to a Post Office box rather than to a company are picked up by a bank and deposited in a bank account

Lombard loan RISK **loan with securities pledged as collateral** a loan granted by a financial institution against pledged collateral in the form of securities

long STOCKHOLDING & INVESTMENTS **having more shares than wanted** having a positive holding as a trader in a security

long bond *or* **long coupon bond** STOCKHOLDING & INVESTMENTS **bond that matures after 10 years or more** a bond which will mature in more than ten years' time, usually a 30-year bond issued by the US Department of the Treasury

long credit FINANCE **loan that borrower can repay over long time** credit terms which allow the borrower a long time to pay back the money he or she has borrowed

long-dated STOCKHOLDING & INVESTMENTS **maturing after 15 years or more** used to describe securities such as bonds that mature after fifteen years or more. *See also* **short-dated**

long-dated bill STOCKHOLDING & INVESTMENTS **bill payable after three or more months** a bill that is payable at a date that is not less than three months away

long-dated gilt STOCKHOLDING & INVESTMENTS **UK government security maturing in 15 years or more** a security issued by the UK government that pays a fixed rate of interest on a regular basis until the redemption date, in 15 years or more, when the principal is returned. *See also* **gilt-edged security**

long-dated stocks STOCKHOLDING & INVESTMENTS = *longs*

long firm fraud FRAUD **crime of business buying on credit, then disappearing** in the United Kingdom, a criminal activity in which somebody sets up an apparently legitimate wholesaling business, obtains fake credit references, trades on credit with wholesale suppliers with no intention of paying for the goods, and then disappears

longs STOCKHOLDING & INVESTMENTS **long-term government stocks** government stocks that will mature more than 15 years after the date of purchase

long-term bond STOCKHOLDING & INVESTMENTS **bond maturing in 7 years or more** a bond that has at least seven years before its redemption date, or, in some markets, a bond with more than seven years until its redemption date

long-term borrowings FINANCE **borrowings repayable in several years' time** money that is borrowed that does not have to be repaid for a number of years

long-term debt FINANCE **loans for more than one year** loans and debentures that are not due until after at least one year

long-term equity anticipation securities STOCKHOLDING & INVESTMENTS *see* **LEAPS**

long-term financing FINANCE **provision of funding with extended credit** forms of funding, such as loans or stock issue, that do not have to be repaid immediately

long-term liabilities FINANCE **debts with extended credit** forms of debt such as loans that do not have to be repaid immediately

loose change CURRENCY & EXCHANGE **coins of little value** money in the form of coins, especially when the value is small

loose credit ECONOMICS **easily available credit to encourage growth** a central banking policy to make borrowing easier by lowering interest rates in order to stimulate economic activity

loss ACCOUNTING **when costs of activity exceed income from it** a financial position in which the *costs* of an activity exceed the *income* derived from it

loss carryback ACCOUNTING **application of current-year loss to prior year** the process of applying a net operating loss to a previous accounting year in order to reduce tax liability in that year

loss carryforward ACCOUNTING **application of current-year loss to future year** the process of applying a net operating loss to a following accounting year in order to reduce tax liability in that year

loss control FINANCE, RISK **methods of limiting impact of loss of asset** the implementation of safety procedures to prevent or limit the impact of a complete or partial loss of an organization's physical assets. Loss control is based on safety audit and prevention techniques. It is concerned with reduction or elimination of losses caused by accidents and occupational ill health. The extent to which it is implemented is usually decided by calculating the total organizational asset cost and weighing this against the likelihood of failure and its worst possible effects on the organization. Loss control was developed in the 1960s as an approach to *risk management*.

lower of cost or market ACCOUNTING **accounting method treating stocks at lower value** a method used by manufacturing and supply firms when accounting for their homogenous stocks which involves valuing them either at their original cost or the current market price, whichever is lower. *Abbr* **LCM**

low gearing UK FINANCE **low ratio of firm's debt to assets** a situation in which a company has only a small amount of debt in proportion to its assets

loyalty bonus STOCKHOLDING & INVESTMENTS **extra shares given after UK privatizations** in the United Kingdom in the 1980s, a number of extra shares, calculated as a proportion of the shares originally subscribed, given to original subscribers of privatization issues providing the shares were held continuously for a given period of time

LTV ratio *abbr* FINANCE loan to value ratio

lump sum FINANCE **1. repaid in one installment** used to describe a loan that is repayable with one installment at the end of its term. *See also **balloon loan, interest-only mortgage*** **2. money received in single payment** an amount of money received in one payment, for example, the sum payable to the beneficiary of a life insurance policy on the death of the policyholder

M

M0 ECONOMICS **money available to public for spending** an estimate of the amount of money in public circulation, available for use as a means of exchange. *Also called **narrow money** (sense 2)*

M1 ECONOMICS **cash plus bank accounts** an estimate of the amount of money held by the public in coins, banknotes, and checking accounts. *Also called **narrow money** (sense 1)*

M2 ECONOMICS **cash plus easily available deposits** an estimate of the amount of money held by the public in coins, currency, checking and savings accounts, and deposits

M3 ECONOMICS **M1, M2 plus international money** an estimate of the amount of money in M1, M2 and large denomination repurchase agreements, institutional money market accounts, and some Eurodollar time deposits

Macaulay duration MARKETS, RISK **measure of interest-rate risk in owning bonds** a measure of a bond's sensitivity to changes in interest rates. It is calculated by dividing the present value of the cash flows received by the current market value of the bond. *See also **modified duration***

machine hour rate FINANCE **proportion of overhead costs** an *overhead absorption rate* based on the number of hours a machine is used in production

macroeconomics ECONOMICS **study of national economic systems** the study of national income and the economic systems of nations. *See also **microeconomics***

macroeconomy ECONOMICS **national economy as whole** the broad sectors of a country's economic activity, for example, the financial or industrial sectors, that are aggregated to form its economic system as a whole. *See also **microeconomy***

macrohedge RISK **reduction of risk on whole portfolio** a *hedge* that aims to cover the overall risk to an entire investment *portfolio*. *Also called **global hedge**. See also **microhedge***

macroprudential risk RISK **risk of collective action causing instability** the risk that individual companies acting prudently will nevertheless cause instability in a financial system by their collective action in a particular area, for example, all lenders restricting lending or all companies selling assets at the same time

mail ballot *US* FINANCE **election accepting votes returned by mail** an election of officers of a company in which the voters send in their ballot papers by mail. *UK term **postal vote***

maintenance bond STOCKHOLDING & INVESTMENTS **guarantee for period after complete transaction** a bond that provides a

guarantee against defects for some time after a contract has been fulfilled

majority shareholder STOCKHOLDING & INVESTMENTS **stockholder with controlling interest** a shareholder with a controlling interest in a company. *See also **minority interest***

majority shareholding STOCKHOLDING & INVESTMENTS **stockholding in excess of 50%** a group of shares of stockthat are more than half the total and enough to give control to the person or entity holding them

managed account STOCKHOLDING & INVESTMENTS = *discretionary account*

managed currency fund CURRENCY & EXCHANGE **managed fund investing in currencies** a managed mutual fund that makes considered investments in foreign exchange

managed derivatives fund STOCKHOLDING & INVESTMENTS **fund investing in derivatives** a fund that uses mainly *futures* and *options* instead of investing in the underlying securities

managed economy ECONOMICS **economy controlled by government** an economy directed by a government rather than the free market

managed float ECONOMICS **exchange rate affected by government action** the position when the exchange rate of a country's currency is influenced by government action in the foreign exchange market

managed fund STOCKHOLDING & INVESTMENTS **mutual fund investing after research** a mutual fund with professional managers who make considered investments, as opposed to an *index fund*. *Also called **managed mutual fund***

managed mutual fund *US* STOCKHOLDING & INVESTMENTS = *managed fund*

managed rate BANKING **financial institution's independently established interest rate** a rate of interest charged by a financial institution for borrowing that it sets itself from time to time, rather than following a prescribed margin over base rate

managed unit trust STOCKHOLDING & INVESTMENTS = *managed fund*

management accountant TREASURY MANAGEMENT **financial adviser on management decisions** a person who contributes to management's decision-making processes by, for example, collecting and processing data relating to a business's costs, sales, and the profitability of individual activities

management accounting TREASURY MANAGEMENT **use of accounting principles to benefit organization** the application of the principles of accounting and financial management to create, protect, preserve, and increase value so as to deliver that value to the stakeholders of profit and nonprofit enterprises, both public and private. Management accounting is an integral part of management, requiring the identification, generation, presentation, interpretation, and use of information relevant to formulating business strategy;

planning and controlling activities; decisionmaking; efficient resource usage; performance improvement and value enhancement; safeguarding tangible and intangible assets; and corporate governance and internal control.

management accounts TREASURY MANAGEMENT **financial report prepared for manager** financial information prepared for a manager so that decisions can be made, including monthly or quarterly financial statements, often in great detail, with analysis of actual performance against the budget

management buyin MERGERS & ACQUISITIONS **purchase of business by external managers** the purchase of an existing business by an individual manager or management group outside that business. *Abbr* **MBI**

management buyout MERGERS & ACQUISITIONS **takeover of business by its management** the purchase of an existing business by an individual manager or management group from within that business. *Abbr* **MBO**

management charge *UK* STOCKHOLDING & INVESTMENTS = *annual management charge*

management fee STOCKHOLDING & INVESTMENTS **fee for managing mutual fund** a fee paid to a mutual fund manager by a client to cover their services and a variety of administrative costs

managing director CORPORATE GOVERNANCE **limited company's director in charge of daily business** the *chief executive officer* of a *limited company* in the United Kingdom and other countries, who has overall responsibility for its day-to-day operations. *Abbr* **MD**

M&A *abbr* MERGERS & ACQUISITIONS mergers and acquisitions

mandatory bid STOCKHOLDING & INVESTMENTS **compulsory bid for remaining stock** an offer to purchase the remaining shares of a company that a stockholder has to make if he or she acquires at least 30% of that company's stock

manufacturing account ACCOUNTING **accounts showing only production costs** a financial statement that shows production costs only, as opposed to a *profit and loss account*, which shows sales and costs of sales. A manufacturing account will include direct materials and labor costs and the production overhead.

margin FINANCE **1. gap between cost and selling price** the difference between the cost and the selling price of a product or service **2.** *ANZ* **extra pay for employees' special skills** a payment made to workers over and above the basic wage in recognition of special skills

margin account FINANCE **account with investment broker who lends money** an account with a broker who lends money for investments, held in the name of an investor who pays only a percentage of the price of purchases

marginal 1. FINANCE **not worth money spent** producing very little benefit in relation to the amount of money spent (informal) **2.** OPERATIONS & PRODUCTION **barely covering production cost** nearly unable to cover the cost of production when selling goods or when goods are being sold

marginal analysis ECONOMICS **investigation into economic effects of small changes** the study of how small changes in an economic variable will affect an economy

marginal costing ACCOUNTING **accounting system treating variable and fixed costs differently** the accounting system in which variable costs are charged to cost units and fixed costs of the period are written off in full against the aggregate contribution. Its special value is in recognizing cost behavior, and hence assisting in decisionmaking. *Also called* ***variable costing***

marginal costs and benefits ECONOMICS **losses and gains resulting from incremental changes** the losses or gains to a person or household arising from a small change in a variable, such as food consumption or income received

marginalization ECONOMICS **process of becoming less important in world economy** the process by which countries lose importance and status because they are unable to participate in mainstream activities such as industrialization or the Internet economy

marginal lender FINANCE **lender with lower limit on interest rate** a lender who will make a loan only at or above a particular rate of interest

marginal utility ECONOMICS **satisfaction in using one additional unit** satisfaction gained from using one more unit of a product or service

margin call STOCKHOLDING & INVESTMENTS **request for additional deposit to margin account** a request for a purchaser of a futures contract or an option to deposit more money in his or her *margin account*, since the fall in the price of the securities or commodity has brought the value of the original deposit below the minimum required

margining STOCKHOLDING & INVESTMENTS, RISK **way London Clearing House controls risk** the system by which the London Clearing House controls the risk associated with the position of a member of the London International Financial Futures and Options Exchange on a daily basis. To achieve this, members deposit cash or collateral with the London Clearing House in the form of initial and variation margins. The initial margin is the deposit required on all open positions, long or short, to cover short-term price movements and is returned to members by the London Clearing House when the position is closed. The variation margin is the members' profits or losses, calculated daily from the marked-to-market-close value of their position, whereby contracts are revalued daily for the calculation of variation margin and credited to or debited from their accounts.

margin of safety TREASURY MANAGEMENT **level of firm's performance above break-even point** the difference between the level of activity at which an organization breaks even and the level of activity greater than this point. For example, a margin of safety of $300,000 is achieved when the break-even point is $900,000 and sales reach $1,200,000. This measure can be expressed as a proportion of sales value, as a number of units sold, or as a percentage of *capacity*.

Margrabe option STOCKHOLDING & INVESTMENTS, RISK = *exchange option*

marital property FINANCE = *community property*

marked cheque *UK* BANKING (slang) = *certified check*

market 1. FINANCE **rate of financial sales** the rate at which financial commodities or securities are being sold **2.** ECONOMICS, MARKETING **group of consumers with shared need** a group of people or organizations unified by common requirements **3.** ECONOMICS **group of buyers and sellers trading goods** a gathering of sellers and purchasers to exchange commodities **make a market** MARKETS to be prepared as a dealer to buy or sell a particular security at the quoted bid or ask price

marketable security STOCKHOLDING & INVESTMENTS **security easily sold or exchanged** a security that can easily be sold and converted into cash, or exchanged for a different type of security

market economy ECONOMICS **economic system not controlled by government** an economy in which a free market in goods and services operates

market if touched STOCKHOLDING & INVESTMENTS **instruction to trade at specific price** an order to trade a security if it reaches a specific price. *Abbr* **MIT**

market-neutral funds STOCKHOLDING & INVESTMENTS **hedge funds exploiting temporary fluctuations** hedge funds that are not related to general market movements but that are used to find opportunities to take advantage of temporary slight changes in the relative values of particular financial assets

market price 1. MARKETS **price consumers are paying** the price that buyers are currently paying for a good, service, commodity, etc. **2.** ECONOMICS **price at which supply equals demand** the theoretical price at which supply equals demand

market risk MARKETS, RISK **risk inherent in securities market or economy** investment risk that is attributable to the performance of the stock market or of the economy and cannot be removed by diversification

market risk premium RISK, STOCKHOLDING & INVESTMENTS **return needed to compensate for risk** the extra return required from a high-risk investment to compensate for its higher-than-average risk

market valuation 1. MARKETS = *market capitalization* **2.** STOCKHOLDING & INVESTMENTS **worth of portfolio on selling** the value of a portfolio if all its investments were to be sold at current market prices **3.** REAL ESTATE **professional assessment of current value of real estate** the opinion of an expert professional as to the current worth of a piece of real estate

market value FINANCE **worth of asset if sold** the value of an asset based on what price would be received for it if it were sold

massaging ACCOUNTING **presentation to suggest better performance** the adjustment of financial figures to create the impression of better performance (slang)

matador bond STOCKHOLDING & INVESTMENTS **foreign bond in Spain** a foreign bond issued into the Spanish domestic market by a non-Spanish company (slang)

matched bargain *UK* STOCKHOLDING & INVESTMENTS **connected sale and rebuying** the linked sale and repurchase of the same quantity of the same security. *See also* **bed and breakfast deal**

matching convention ACCOUNTING **accounts basis with matching of sales with costs** the basis for preparing accounts that says that profits can only be recognized if sales are fully matched with costs accrued during the same period

matrix trading STOCKHOLDING & INVESTMENTS **trading taking advantage of differences in yields** a *bond swap* strategy that takes advantages of discrepancies in yields of bonds of different classes

mature FINANCE **due for payment** having reached maturity

mature economy ECONOMICS **economy that has slowed down** an economy that is no longer developing or growing rapidly. Such economies tend to have increased consumer spending rather than industrial and manufacturing investment.

maturity STOCKHOLDING & INVESTMENTS **period before repayment date of financial instrument** the period that will elapse before a financial instrument such as a bond becomes due for repayment or an option expires

maturity date STOCKHOLDING & INVESTMENTS **expiration date of option** the date on which a financial instrument such as a bond becomes due for repayment or an option expires

maturity value STOCKHOLDING & INVESTMENTS **amount payable on mature financial instrument** the amount payable when a bond or other financial instrument matures

maturity yield STOCKHOLDING & INVESTMENTS = *yield*

Maxi ISA STOCKHOLDING & INVESTMENTS **former UK tax-free account for savings and investment** formerly, in the United Kingdom, an ISA in which savers invested tax-free mainly in stocks with a limited cash component. Savers could own only one Maxi ISA. *See also* **Mini ISA**, **ISA**

maximize FINANCE **increase financial gain as much as possible** to take measures to increase something such as your gain on an investment or profit in a business as much as possible

maysir FINANCE **gambling or speculation prohibited by Islamic law** in Islamic financing, gambling with the intention of making an easy profit. It is one of three prohibitions in Islamic law, which is extended to such financial practices as speculation, insurance, futures, and options; the others are *gharar* and *riba*.

MBI *abbr* MERGERS & ACQUISITIONS management buyin

MBO *abbr* **1.** MERGERS & ACQUISITIONS management buyout **2.** GENERAL MANAGEMENT management by objectives

MBS *abbr* MORTGAGES, STOCKHOLDING & INVESTMENTS mortgage-backed security

MD *abbr* CORPORATE GOVERNANCE managing director

means test FINANCE **1. examination of somebody's eligibility for government aid** an inquiry into how much money somebody earns or has in savings to see if they are eligible for government benefits **2. bankruptcy test in US courts** a test used by US courts to see whether somebody wishing to file for bankruptcy has enough income to repay some of the debt, determining which type of bankruptcy that person is eligible for

means-test FINANCE **determine if somebody is eligible for government aid** to find out how much money somebody earns or has in savings and assets to see if they are eligible for government benefits

medium-dated STOCKHOLDING & INVESTMENTS **maturing in 5–10 years** used to describe securities such as bonds that mature in five to ten years. *See also* ***long-dated, short-dated***

medium-dated gilt STOCKHOLDING & INVESTMENTS **UK government security with 5–10 years' maturity** a security issued by the UK government that pays a fixed rate of interest on a regular basis for at least five but no more than ten years until the redemption date, when the principal is returned. *See also* ***gilt-edged security***

medium of exchange FINANCE **means of paying for goods** anything that is used to pay for goods. Nowadays, this usually takes the form of money (banknotes and coins), but in ancient societies it included anything from cattle to shells.

medium-term bond STOCKHOLDING & INVESTMENTS **bond redeemed in 5–10 years** a bond that has at least five but no more than ten years before its redemption date. *See also* ***long-term bond***

medium-term note FINANCE **borrowing repaid within 5 years** borrowing arranged over a period of up to five years. *Abbr* **MTN**

medium-term noteholder FINANCE **investor repaying borrowings within 5 years** an investor who borrows money over a period of up to five years

member 1. STOCKHOLDING & INVESTMENTS **shareholder in firm** somebody who owns stock in a limited liability company **2.** BUSINESS **organization belonging to larger group** a business organization that is part of a larger group

member bank BANKING **bank in US Federal Reserve System** a bank that is a member of the US Federal Reserve System

member of a company STOCKHOLDING & INVESTMENTS **in UK, registered stockholder** in the United Kingdom, a stockholder whose name is recorded in the register of members

mercantile ECONOMICS **relating to trading** relating to trade or commercial activity

mercantile paper STOCKHOLDING & INVESTMENTS = ***commercial paper***

mercantilism ECONOMICS **economic theory based on importance of international trade** the body of economic thought developed between the 1650s and 1750s, based on the belief that a country's wealth depended on the strength of its foreign trade

merchant bank 1. E-COMMERCE **bank accepting proceeds from seller's credit card transactions** a financial institution at which a trader has opened a ***merchant account*** into which the proceeds of credit card transactions are credited after the institution has subtracted its fee **2.** *UK* BANKING = ***investment bank***

merger MERGERS & ACQUISITIONS **when one organization buys and combines with another** the amalgamation of two or more organizations under single ownership, through the direct acquisition by one organization of the net assets or liabilities of the other. A merger can be the result of a friendly ***takeover***, which results in the combining of companies on an equal footing. After a merger, the legal existence of the acquired organization is terminated. There is no standard definition of a merger, as each is different, depending on what is expected from the merger, and on the negotiations, strategy, stock and assets, human resources, and stockholders of the players. Four broad types of mergers are recognized. A ***horizontal merger*** involves firms from the same industry, while a ***vertical merger*** involves firms from the same supply chain. A ***circular merger*** involves firms with different products but similar distribution channels. A ***conglomerate company*** is produced by the union of firms with few or no similarities in production or marketing but that come together to create a larger economic base and greater profit potential. *See also* ***acquisition, consolidation, joint venture, partnership***

merger accounting ACCOUNTING **accounting treating combined firm as result of merger** a method of accounting that regards a business combination as the acquisition of one company by another. The identifiable assets and liabilities of the company acquired are included in the consolidated balance sheet at their fair value at the date of acquisition, and its results included in the profit and loss account from the date of acquisition. The difference between the fair value of the consideration given and the fair values of the net assets of the entity acquired is accounted for as ***goodwill***.

merger arbitrage MERGERS & ACQUISITIONS **trading securities of merging companies simultaneously** in a merger, a hedge fund trader sells short the high-priced securities of the target company and buys the underpriced ones of the acquiring company, and then at a time when prices have reverted to true value, the trade can be liquidated at a profit

merger arbitrageur MERGERS & ACQUISITIONS **trader in securities of merging firms** a trader or fund dealing in merger arbitrage

mergers and acquisitions MERGERS & ACQUISITIONS **ways in which organizations change ownership** a blanket term covering the main ways in which organizations change hands. *Abbr* **M&A**

mezzanine capital FINANCE = ***mezzanine financing***

mezzanine debt FINANCE **additional borrowing** debt that derives from a mezzanine financing arrangement

mezzanine finance *UK* FINANCE = ***mezzanine financing***

mezzanine financing FINANCE **firm's additional borrowing** capital provided to a company that cannot borrow more from banks. Mezzanine financing usually gives the lender the right to either ownership of the company or an equity interest in the company if the loan is not repaid. *UK term* ***mezzanine finance***

microcredit BANKING **financing those not eligible for standard bank loans** the extension of credit to entrepreneurs and ***microbusinesses*** that are too poor to qualify for conventional bank loans. *Also called* ***microlending***

microeconomic incentive ECONOMICS **financial encouragement to improve market performance** a tax benefit or subsidy given to a business to achieve a specific objective such as increased sales overseas

microeconomics ECONOMICS **study of consumers' and firms' roles in economy** the branch of economics that studies the contribution of groups of consumers or firms, or of individual consumers, to a country's economy. *See also* ***macroeconomics***

microeconomy ECONOMICS **individual areas of economy that influence whole economy** the narrow sectors of a country's economic activity that influence the behavior of the economy as a whole, for example, consumer choices. *See also* ***macroeconomy***

microfinance UK FINANCE = ***microfinancing***

microfinancing US FINANCE **providing variety of financial services to poor** the provision of a range of financial resources such as small loans, insurance, and savings to low-income families in order to help them build businesses and increase their income. *UK term* ***microfinance***. *See also* ***microcredit***

microhedge STOCKHOLDING & INVESTMENTS **hedge for one asset or liability** a ***hedge*** that relates to a single asset or liability in an investment ***portfolio***. *See also* ***macrohedge***

microlending BANKING = ***microcredit***

microloan FINANCE **small loan to low-income borrower** a very small loan made to somebody who has a low or no income and nothing to offer as collateral, or to the owner of a small unprofitable business

micromort RISK **measure of risk of death** a one-in-a-million risk of dying

micro-profits FINANCE **profits after microfinancing** the profits made by businesses that have been financed by microfinancing

middle price *or* mid-price UK STOCKHOLDING & INVESTMENTS **price between bid price and offer price** a price, halfway between the bid price and the offer price, that is generally quoted in the press and on information screens

MIGA *abbr* BANKING Multilateral Investment Guarantee Agency

million FINANCE **thousand thousands** a sum equal to one thousand thousands

millionaire FINANCE **person with income over one million** a person whose net worth or income is more than one million dollars, pounds, or other unit of currency

Mini ISA STOCKHOLDING & INVESTMENTS **former UK tax-free account for savings or investment** formerly, in the United Kingdom, an ISA in which savers held either cash or stocks tax-free. Savers could have up to two Mini ISAs, one for cash and one for stocks. *See also* ***Maxi ISA***, ***ISA***

minimum balance BANKING **least amount of money required in account** the smallest amount of money which must be kept in an account to qualify for the services provided

minimum lending rate BANKING **lowest UK central bank interest rate** formerly, the rate at which the Bank of England lent to other banks, now replaced by the base rate. *Abbr* **MLR**. *Also called* ***bank rate*** *(sense 2)*

minimum reserves BANKING **least amount that bank must have in reserve** the smallest amount of reserves which a commercial bank must hold with a central bank

minimum subscription STOCKHOLDING & INVESTMENTS **minimum bid for new issue** the smallest number of shares or securities that may be applied for in a new issue

minimum wage FINANCE **least hourly pay rate legally allowed** the lowest hourly rate of pay, usually set by government, to which all ***employees*** are legally entitled

minority interest *or* minority ownership CORPORATE GOVERNANCE **holding less than half of firm's common stock** ownership of less than 50% of a company's common stock, which is not enough to control the company

minority shareholder STOCKHOLDING & INVESTMENTS **stockholder with less than 50% of firm's stock** a person who owns a group of shares of stockbut less than half of the stock in a company. *Also called* ***minority stockholder***

minority shareholding STOCKHOLDING & INVESTMENTS **less than 50% of firm's stock** a group of shares of stockthat somebody has which account for less than half the total shares in a firm

minority stockholder STOCKHOLDING & INVESTMENTS = ***minority shareholder***

minutes CORPORATE GOVERNANCE **official notes from meeting** an official written record of the proceedings of a meeting. Minutes usually record points for action, and indicate who is responsible for implementing decisions. Good practice requires that the minutes of a meeting be circulated well in advance of the next meeting, and that those attending that meeting read the minutes in advance. Registered companies are required to keep minutes of meetings and make them available at their registered offices for inspection by company members and shareholders.

mirror fund STOCKHOLDING & INVESTMENTS **investment trust and mutual fund under same control** an investment trust where the manager also runs a mutual fund with the same objectives

misappropriation FRAUD **fraudulent use of somebody else's money** the illegal use of money by somebody who is not the owner but who has been trusted to look after it

MIT *abbr* STOCKHOLDING & INVESTMENTS market if touched

mixed economy ECONOMICS **combination of government and private business ownership** an economy in which both public and private enterprises participate in the production and supply of goods and services

MLR *abbr* BANKING minimum lending rate

MMDA *abbr* BANKING money market deposit account

mobile money FINANCE **use of cell phones for financial transactions** a facility that allows people to use their cell phones and other hand-held devices to handle financial transactions

modern portfolio theory STOCKHOLDING & INVESTMENTS = *portfolio theory*

modified accounts ACCOUNTING = *abbreviated accounts*

modified book value ACCOUNTING = *adjusted book value*

modified cash basis ACCOUNTING **different accounting for short- and long-term assets** the bookkeeping practice of accounting for short-term assets on a cash basis and for long-term assets on an accrual basis

modified duration MARKETS, RISK **measure of interest-rate risk in owning bonds** a measure of a bond's sensitivity to changes in interest rates, based on the assumption that interest rates and bond prices move in opposite directions

mom and pop investors US STOCKHOLDING & INVESTMENTS **inexperienced investors** people who hold or wish to purchase stock but have little experience withor knowledge of the stock market (slang)

momentum investor STOCKHOLDING & INVESTMENTS **buyer of stock rising in price** an investor who buys stock that seems to be moving upward in price

monetarism ECONOMICS **belief that increased money causes inflation** an economic theory that states that inflation is caused by increases in a country's money supply

monetarist ECONOMICS **1. believer in monetarism** a person who believes that inflation is caused by increases in a country's money supply and that the money supply should remain fairly steady **2. according to monetarism** according to the economic theory of *monetarism*

monetary FINANCE **of money, cash, or liquid assets** relating to or involving cash, currency, or assets that are readily convertible into cash

monetary assets ACCOUNTING **assets corresponding to amounts in accounts** assets such as accounts receivable, cash, and bank balances that are realizable at the amounts stated in the accounts. Other assets such as facilities and machinery, inventories, and marketable securities will not necessarily realize the sum stated in a business's balance sheet.

monetary base ECONOMICS **nation's total cash supply** the stock of a country's coins, notes, and bank deposits held by the central bank

monetary base control ECONOMICS **government restrictions on cash availability** the restricting of the amount of *liquid assets* in an economy through government controls

monetary items ACCOUNTING **items worth the same regardless of inflation** monetary assets, such as cash and debtors, and monetary liabilities, such as overdrafts and creditors, whose values stay the same in spite of inflation

monetary policy ECONOMICS **government policy regarding money and currency** government economic policy concerning a country's rate of interest, its exchange rate, and the amount of money in the economy

Monetary Policy Committee ECONOMICS **Bank of England committee that sets interest rates** a committee of the Bank of England, chaired by the Governor of the Bank, that has responsibility for setting UK interest rates independently of the British government. Its goal is to set rates with a view to keeping inflation at a defined level and avoiding deflation. *Abbr* **MPC**

monetary reserve BANKING **currency and bullion in central bank** the foreign currency and precious metals that a country holds, that provide a cushion for central banking functions

monetary standard CURRENCY & EXCHANGE **value on which currency system is based** the value underlying the currency in a specific country's monetary system, for example, the *gold standard*, which in the past many countries used to set the value of their currencies

monetary system ECONOMICS **set of government rules controlling nation's money** the set of government regulations concerning a country's monetary reserves and its holdings of notes and coins

monetary targets FINANCE **government financial targets** figures that are given as targets by the government when setting out its budget for the forthcoming year

monetary unit CURRENCY & EXCHANGE **standard unit of nation's currency** the standard unit of a country's currency, such as the dollar in the United States, the pound sterling in the United Kingdom, or the euro in many other countries of the European Union

monetary working capital adjustment ACCOUNTING **adjustment in accounts for inflation** an adjustment in *current cost accounting* to the historical cost balance sheet to take account of the effect of inflation on the value of debtors, creditors, and stocks of finished goods. *Abbr* **MWCA**

monetize 1. FINANCE **change securities into money** If a government monetizes its debt, it converts interest-bearing securities into money, therefore expanding the money supply and reducing the value of money in circulation. **2.** CURRENCY & EXCHANGE **designate as official currency** to establish a currency as a country's legal tender

money CURRENCY & EXCHANGE **current medium of exchange** a medium of exchange that is accepted throughout a country as payment for services and goods and as a means of settling debts **at the money** MARKETS, RISK a situation in which the price an option holder must pay to exercise an option is the same as the current market price of the underlying security or commodity **at the money forward** MARKETS, RISK a situation in which the price an option holder must pay to exercise an option is the same as the forward price of the underlying security or commodity

money at call and short notice BANKING **1. in UK, advances repayable on demand or soon** in the United Kingdom, advances made by banks to other financial institutions, or corporate and personal customers, that are repayable either upon demand (call) or within 14 days (short notice) **2. in UK, balances available on demand or soon** in the United Kingdom, balances in an account that are either available upon demand (call) or within 14 days (short notice)

moneyer CURRENCY & EXCHANGE **coiner of money** an archaic term for somebody who is authorized to mint money

moneylender FINANCE **lender of money at interest** a person whose business is lending money to others for interest

money lying idle FINANCE **uninvested money producing no interest** money that is not being used to produce interest and that is not invested in business

money management FINANCE, STOCKHOLDING & INVESTMENTS **business of investing clients' money** the activity of making decisions about income and expenditure, including budgeting, banking arrangements, making investments, and tax payments, either for yourself or on behalf of clients

money manager STOCKHOLDING & INVESTMENTS **specialist in investment management** a person or company that manages an investment *portfolio*, usually of *money market instruments*, on behalf of investors. *See also* ***portfolio manager***

money market account BANKING **account with high interest rate** an account with a financial institution that requires a minimum deposit, and pays a rate of interest, related to the wholesale money market rates, generally higher than retail rates. Most institutions offer a variety of term accounts, with either a fixed rate or variable rate, and notice accounts, with a variety of notice periods at variable rates.

money market deposit account BANKING **US savings account** in the United States, a type of savings account with deposits invested in the money market and having a high yield. There is often a high minimum deposit and withdrawals require notice. *Abbr* **MMDA**

money market fund STOCKHOLDING & INVESTMENTS **mutual fund investing in short-term securities** a mutual fund that invests in short-term debt securities. In the United States these are strictly regulated by the ***Securities and Exchange Commission***.

money market instruments STOCKHOLDING & INVESTMENTS **financial products traded on money markets** short-term assets and securities, usually maturing within 12 months, that are traded on money markets, for example, certificates of deposit, commercial papers, and Treasury bills

money men FINANCE **people working in finance industry** the people who provide finance for a venture, campaign, etc.

money national income ECONOMICS **unadjusted value of nation's annual output** *GDP* measured using money value, not adjusted for the effect of inflation

money of account ACCOUNTING **unit for accounting purposes** a monetary unit that is used in keeping accounts but is not necessarily an actual currency unit

money order BANKING **instruction to make payment to someone** a written order to pay somebody a sum of money, issued by a bank or post office

money substitute CURRENCY & EXCHANGE **trading goods used to replace currency** any goods used as a medium of exchange because of the degree of devaluation of a country's currency

money supply ECONOMICS **nation's cash available for purchases** the stock of *liquid assets* in a country's economy that can be given in exchange for services or goods

monies *or* **moneys** CURRENCY & EXCHANGE **sums of money** amounts of money, especially those that come from a specific place or have a specific purpose

monopoly ECONOMICS **economic situation in which one firm controls market** a *market* in which there is only one producer or one seller. A company establishes a monopoly by entering a new market or eliminating all competitors from an existing market. A company that holds a monopoly has control of a market and is able to fix prices. For this reason, governments usually try to avoid monopoly situations. However, some monopolies such as government-owned utilities are seen as beneficial to *consumers*.

month-end ACCOUNTING **of end of month** relating to the end of each month when financial transactions for the current month are finalized

Moody's STOCKHOLDING & INVESTMENTS **US firm that rates credit risk of investments** a US organization that rates the reliability of a debtor organization on a scale from AAA to C. It also issues ratings on municipal bonds, running from MIG1, the highest rating, to MIG4. *See also* ***Standard & Poor's***

moral hazard RISK **danger through protection from consequences of actions** a risk that somebody will behave immorally because insurance, the law, or some other agency protects them against loss that the immoral behavior might otherwise cause

moratorium FINANCE **postponement** a period of delay, for example, additional time agreed onby a creditor and a debtor for recovery of a debt

more bang for your buck US FINANCE **greater financial benefit** greater leverage provided by an investment (slang)

mortgage-backed security STOCKHOLDING & INVESTMENTS, MORTGAGES **security backed by mortgages** a security for which the collateral is the principal and interest on a set of mortgages

mortgage bank BANKING **bank dealing in mortgages** a financial institution that trades in mortgages

mortgage bond STOCKHOLDING & INVESTMENTS, MORTGAGES **debt backed by real estate** especially in the United States, a debt secured by real estate

mortgage indebtedness FINANCE **money borrowed against property** money owed on loans using a property, especially a residence, as collateral

mortgage securitizer STOCKHOLDING & INVESTMENTS firm creating and selling groups of mortgage loans as securities a company that collects residential mortgage loans into a package for sale to investors

MPC *abbr* ECONOMICS Monetary Policy Committee

MSB *abbr* BANKING mutual savings bank

MTN *abbr* FINANCE medium-term note

multicurrency FINANCE offering number of currencies used to describe a loan that gives the borrower a choice of currencies

multifunctional card BANKING plastic card with more than one use a plastic card that may be used for two or more purposes, for example, as an ATM card, a check card, and a debit card

Multilateral Investment Guarantee Agency BANKING part of World Bank Group one of the five institutions that constitute the World Bank Group. MIGA was created in 1988 to promote foreign direct investment into emerging economies by insuring against political risk, with the objective of improving people's lives and reducing poverty. Apart from offering political risk insurance to investors and lenders, MIGA assists emerging countries to attract and retain private investment. *Abbr* **MIGA**

multilateral netting CURRENCY & EXCHANGE consolidating sums from various sources into one currency a method of putting together sums from various international sources to reduce currency transaction costs, used by groups of companies or banks trading in several currencies at the same time

multiple application STOCKHOLDING & INVESTMENTS more than one application for new share issue the submission of more than one share application for a new issue that is expected to be oversubscribed. In most jurisdictions, this practice is illegal.

multiple exchange rate CURRENCY & EXCHANGE exchange rate varying with transaction's purpose a two-tier rate of exchange used in some countries where the more advantageous rate may be for tourists or for businesses proposing to build a factory

multiplier FINANCE factor that multiplies another number or value a number that multiplies another, or a factor that tends to multiply something, for example, the effect of new expenditure on total income and reserves

multiplier effect ECONOMICS effect of increased investment or spending on income a situation in which a small initial change in investment or spending produces a proportionately larger change in national income

mum and dad investors ANZ STOCKHOLDING & INVESTMENTS = *mom and pop investors*

municipal bond *or* muni *or* muni-bond STOCKHOLDING & INVESTMENTS US government security in the United States, a security issued by states, local governments, and municipalities

municipal bond fund STOCKHOLDING & INVESTMENTS fund investing in municipal bonds a fund that is invested in municipal bonds

murabaha *or* murabahah FINANCE when Islamic bank purchases item for customer in Islamic financing, an arrangement in which a bank purchases an item for a customer provided the customer agrees to purchase it from the bank at a prearranged higher price. *See also* **tawarruq**

mutual fund US STOCKHOLDING & INVESTMENTS firm trading in investments for clients an investment company that holds a range of stocks in which investors can buy units. *UK term* **unit trust**

mutual savings bank BANKING US savings bank run by trustees in the United States, a state-chartered savings bank run in the interests of its members. It is governed by a local board of trustees, not necessarily the legal owners. Most of these banks offer accounts and services that are typical of full-service banks. *Abbr* **MSB**

muzara'a *or* muzara'ah FINANCE payment for land rent by crop share in Islamic financing, an agreement in which a landowner lets somebody farm an area of land in return for part of the crop

MWCA *abbr* ACCOUNTING monetary working capital adjustment

N

NAIC *abbr* **1.** INSURANCE, REGULATION & COMPLIANCE National Association of Insurance Commissioners **2.** STOCKHOLDING & INVESTMENTS National Association of Investors Corporation

naked option STOCKHOLDING & INVESTMENTS = *uncovered option*

naked position STOCKHOLDING & INVESTMENTS holding with unhedged securities a situation in which an investor holds securities some of which are not *hedged*

naked writer STOCKHOLDING & INVESTMENTS offerer of option on another's shares a person selling an option who does not own the underlying shares

narrow bank BANKING bank with safely invested deposits a proposed type of bank that has all its deposits invested in safe assets, and which does not involve itself in investment banking

narrow money ECONOMICS **1.** *US* = *M1* **2.** *UK* = *Mo*

National Association of Investors Corporation STOCKHOLDING & INVESTMENTS US organization promoting investment clubs in the United States, an organization that fosters the creation and development of *investment clubs*. *Abbr* **NAIC**

national bank BANKING **1.** central bank of state a bank owned or controlled by the state that acts as a bank for a government and implements its monetary policies **2.** US bank in Federal Reserve in the United States, a bank that operates under federal charter and is legally required to be a member of the *Federal Reserve*

national debt ECONOMICS amount of government borrowing the total amount of money that a country's central government has borrowed and is still unpaid

a–z

Dictionary

national demand ECONOMICS **overall need for products in country's economy** the total demand for goods and services made by consumers in an economy

national income ECONOMICS **country's total earnings from goods and services** the total earnings from a country's production of goods and services in a specific year

national income accounts FINANCE **statistical information on country's economy** economic statistics that show the state of a nation's economy over a given period of time, usually a year. *See also* **GDP, GNP**

National Savings & Investments STOCKHOLDING & INVESTMENTS **UK government agency for savings and investment** in the United Kingdom, a government agency accountable to the Treasury that offers a variety of savings and investment products directly to the public or through post offices. The funds raised finance government borrowing (the national debt).

National Savings Bank BANKING **UK savings plan** in the United Kingdom, a savings plan established in 1861 as the Post Office Savings Bank and now operated by National Savings & Investments. *Abbr* **NSB**

National Savings Certificate STOCKHOLDING & INVESTMENTS **UK investment providing tax-free income** in the United Kingdom, either a fixed-interest or an index-linked certificate issued for two- or five-year terms by National Savings & Investments with returns that are free of income tax. *Abbr* **NSC**

National Society of Accountants ACCOUNTING **US association of financial professionals** in the United States, a non-profit organization of some 17,000 professionals who provide accounting, tax preparation, financial and estate planning, and management advisory services to an estimated 19 million individuals and business clients. Most of the NSA's members are individual practitioners or partners in small to mid-size accounting and tax firms. *Abbr* **NSA**

natural capitalism ECONOMICS **capitalism incorporating environmentalism** an approach to capitalism in which protection of the Earth's resources is a strategic priority

NAV *abbr* STOCKHOLDING & INVESTMENTS net asset value

NBV *abbr* ACCOUNTING net book value

NDP *abbr* ECONOMICS net domestic product

nearby futures contract STOCKHOLDING & INVESTMENTS **option with closest delivery date** a futures option with the earliest delivery date of those being considered. *See also* **most distant futures contract**

nearby month STOCKHOLDING & INVESTMENTS **next month with futures contract available** the earliest month for which there is a *futures contract* for a specific commodity. *Also called* **spot month**. *See also* **far month**

near-cash STOCKHOLDING & INVESTMENTS **easy to convert to cash** used to describe an investment that can be quickly converted to cash

near money STOCKHOLDING & INVESTMENTS **assets easily cashed in** assets such as some types of bank deposit, short-dated bonds, and certificates of deposit that can quickly be turned into cash. *See also* **quick asset**

negative amortization FINANCE **addition to principal following incomplete interest payments** an increase in the *principal* of a loan due to the inadequacy of payments to cover the interest

negative carry FINANCE **when interest payments exceed income on loan** interest that is so high that the borrowed money does not return enough profit to cover the cost of borrowing

negative cash flow FINANCE **higher expenditures than income** a cash flow in which expenditures are higher than income

negative equity FINANCE **when property is worth less than it cost** a situation in which a fall in prices leads to a property being worth less than was paid for it

negative gearing FINANCE, TAX **borrowing money that earns less than interest payments** the practice of borrowing money to invest in property or stocks and claiming a tax deduction on the difference between the income and the interest payments

negative goodwill MERGERS & ACQUISITIONS **value of company's assets above price paid** the gain that a company has when a company it acquires has assets with a market value greater than the price the acquiring company paid for them

negative pledge clause STOCKHOLDING & INVESTMENTS **condition preventing bond issuer from disadvantaging holders** a provision in a bond agreement that prohibits the issuer from doing something that would give an advantage to holders of other bonds

negative yield curve STOCKHOLDING & INVESTMENTS **graph plotting interest rates against different maturities** a visual representation of relative interest rates showing that they are higher for short-term bonds than they are for long-term bonds

negotiable FINANCE **transferable or cashable** able to be transfered from one person to another or exchanged for cash

negotiable certificate of deposit FINANCE **certificate of deposit that can change hands freely** a certificate of deposit with a very high value that can be freely traded

negotiable instrument *or* negotiable paper FINANCE **document promising to pay cash to holder** a document that can be exchanged for cash, for example, a bill of exchange or a check

negotiable order of withdrawal BANKING **in US, check drawn on savings account** in the United States, a check drawn on a type of savings account that bears interest but allows withdrawals

negotiable order of withdrawal account BANKING = *NOW account*

negotiable security STOCKHOLDING & INVESTMENTS **security that can change ownership** a security that can be freely traded to bring its owner some benefit

negotiate FINANCE **1. sell financial instruments** to transfer ownership of financial instruments such as bearer securities, bills of exchange, checks, and promissory notes to somebody else in exchange for money **2. discuss to agree price of item** to reach an agreed price with a buyer or seller by the gradual raising of offers and lowering of the price asked until a mutually agreeable price is reached

negotiated commission FINANCE **brokers' commission discussed and agreed with customers** a commission that results from bargaining between brokers and their customers, typically large institutions

negotiated issue STOCKHOLDING & INVESTMENTS = *negotiated offering*

negotiated offering STOCKHOLDING & INVESTMENTS **offer at price negotiated with underwriting syndicate** a *public offering* of stock, the price of which is determined by negotiations between the issuer and an *underwriting syndicate*. *Also called* *negotiated issue*

negotiated sale FINANCE **offer at price negotiated with one underwriter** a *public offering* of stock, the price of which is determined by negotiations between the issuer and a single underwriter

neoclassical economics ECONOMICS **economic theory emphasizing free markets** an economic theory that emphasizes the need for the free operation of market forces through supply and demand

nest egg FINANCE **savings for retirement** savings, usually other than a pension plan or retirement account, that have been set aside for use in somebody's retirement (*informal*)

net 1. FINANCE **remaining after deductions have been made** used to describe the amount of something such as a price or salary remaining after all deductions have been made **2.** ACCOUNTING **earn amount as profit** to make a profit after all expenses have been taken into account

net advantage of refunding ACCOUNTING **money raised by replacing debt** the amount gained by renewing the funding of debt after interest rates have fallen

net advantage to leasing ACCOUNTING **cost difference between leasing and borrowing to buy** the amount by which leasing something is financially better than borrowing money and purchasing it

net advantage to merging MERGERS & ACQUISITIONS **value gained after merging firms** the amount by which the value of a merged enterprise exceeds the value of the preexisting companies, minus the cost of the merger

net assets ACCOUNTING **value of assets minus liabilities** the amount by which the value of a company's assets exceeds its liabilities, representing its capital

net asset value STOCKHOLDING & INVESTMENTS **firm's net market value** the value of a company's stock assessed by subtracting any liabilities from the market value. *Abbr* **NAV**

net asset value per share ACCOUNTING, STOCKHOLDING & INVESTMENTS **firm's net market value divided by share number** the value of a company's stock assessed by subtracting any liabilities from the market value and dividing the remainder by the number of shares of stock issued

net book value ACCOUNTING **original cost of asset minus depreciation** the historical cost of an asset less any accumulated depreciation or other provision for diminution in value, for example, reduction to net realizable value, or asset value which has been revalued downward to reflect market conditions. *Abbr* **NBV**. *Also called* *written-down value*

net borrowings ACCOUNTING **borrowings minus cash available** the total of all borrowings less the cash in bank accounts and on deposit

net capital ACCOUNTING **net assets minus noncash assets** the amount by which net assets exceed the value of assets not easily converted to cash

net cash balance ACCOUNTING **value of ready cash** on a balance sheet, the amount of cash recorded as on hand

net cash flow ACCOUNTING **difference between cash inflows and outflows** the difference between the amount of money coming in and going out of an organization

net current assets ACCOUNTING **assets minus liabilities** the amount by which the value of a company's current assets exceeds its current liabilities. *Also called* *net working capital*

net dividend STOCKHOLDING & INVESTMENTS **worth of dividend after tax** the value of a dividend after the recipient has paid tax on it

net domestic product ECONOMICS **total national economic output with factors deducted** the figure produced after factors such as depreciation have been deducted from *GDP*. *Abbr* **NDP**

net errors and omissions ACCOUNTING **size of discrepancies in accounting** the net amount of the discrepancies that arise in the calculation of a balance of payments

net exports FINANCE **total exports minus total imports** a figure showing the total value of exports less the total value of imports

net fixed assets ACCOUNTING **worth of fixed assets after depreciation** the value of fixed assets after depreciation as shown on a balance sheet

net foreign factor income FINANCE **gross national minus gross domestic product** income from outside a country, constituting the amount by which a country's gross national product exceeds its gross domestic product

net income ACCOUNTING **1. income minus expenditures** an organization's income less the costs incurred to generate it **2. income after tax** gross income less tax that has been deducted **3. earnings after tax and other deductions** a salary or wage less tax and other statutory deductions such as Social Security contributions. *See also* *disposable income*

net interest FINANCE **interest after tax** gross interest less tax that has been deducted

net investment STOCKHOLDING & INVESTMENTS **capital invested minus estimated capital consumption** an increase in the total capital invested. It is calculated as gross capital invested less an estimated figure for capital consumption or depreciation.

net liquid funds ACCOUNTING **money plus salable investments minus short-term borrowings** an organization's cash plus its marketable investments less its short-term borrowings such as overdrafts and loans

net loss ACCOUNTING **loss taking all expenses into consideration** a loss calculated after the deduction of overhead and other expenses

net margin ACCOUNTING **percentage of income that is profit** the percentage of revenues that is profit, often used an an indicator of cost control

net national product FINANCE **national income** a country's *GNP* adjusted to deduct capital depreciation during the period in question. *Abbr* **NNP**

net operating income ACCOUNTING **income minus expenses** the amount by which income exceeds expenditure, before considering taxes, interest, and other expenses

net operating margin ACCOUNTING **income minus expenses as percentage of revenues** *net operating income* as a percentage of revenues. It is an indicator of profitability.

net pay FINANCE **total pay minus deductions** the amount of pay an employee receives after all deductions such as income tax, social security, or pension contributions. *Also called* ***take-home pay***. *See also* ***disposable income***

net position STOCKHOLDING & INVESTMENTS **balance of long and short positions** the difference between an investor's long and short *positions* in the same security

net present value ACCOUNTING **cash inflows minus cash outflows** the value of an investment calculated as the sum of its initial cost and the ***present value*** of expected future cashflows

A positive NPV indicates that the project should be profitable, assuming that the estimated cashflows are reasonably accurate. A negative NPV indicates that the project will probably be unprofitable and therefore should be adjusted, if not abandoned altogether.

NPV enables management to consider the time-value of money it will invest. This concept holds that the value of money increases with time because it can always earn interest in a savings account. When the time-value-of-money concept is incorporated in the calculation of NPV, the value of a project's future net cash receipts in "today's money" can be determined. This enables proper comparisons between different projects.

For example, if Global Manufacturing Inc. is considering the acquisition of a new machine, its management will consider all the factors: initial purchase and installation costs; additional revenues generated by sales of the new machine's products, plus the taxes on these new revenues. Having accounted for these factors in its calculations, the cashflows that Global Manufacturing projects will generate from the new machine are:

Year 1	− 100,000 (initial cost of investment)
Year 2	30,000
Year 3	40,000
Year 4	40,000
Year 5	35,000
Net Total	145,000

At first glance, it appears that cashflows total 45% more than the $100,000 initial cost, a sound investment indeed. But the time-value of money shrinks the return on the project considerably, since future dollars are worth less than present dollars in hand. NPV accounts for these differences with the help of present-value tables, which list the ratios that express the present value of expected cashflow dollars, based on the applicable interest rate and the number of years in question.

In the example, Global Manufacturing's cost of capital is 9%. Using this figure to find the corresponding ratios on the present value table, the $100,000 investment cost and expected annual revenues during the five years in question, the NPV calculation looks like this:

Year	Cashflow	Table factor (at 9%)	Present value
1	($100,000) ×	1.000000 =	($100,000)
2	$30,000 ×	0.917431 =	$27,522.93
3	$40,000 ×	0.841680 =	$33,667.20
4	$40,000 ×	0.772183 =	$30,887.32
5	$35,000 ×	0.708425 =	$24,794.88
NPV =	$16,873.33		

NPV is still positive. So, on this basis at least, the investment should proceed. *Abbr* **NPV**

net proceeds ACCOUNTING **gains from transaction minus its cost** the amount received from a transaction minus the cost of making it

net profit ACCOUNTING **income after expenses** an organization's income as shown in a ***profit and loss account*** after all relevant expenses have been deducted. *Also called* ***profit after tax***

net profit margin ACCOUNTING, OPERATIONS & PRODUCTION *see **profit margin***

net profit ratio ACCOUNTING **ratio of net profit to net sales** the ratio of an organization's net profit to its total net sales. Comparing the net profit ratios of companies in the same sector shows which are the most efficient.

net realizable value ACCOUNTING **selling price minus costs** the value of an asset if sold, allowing for costs

net receipts ACCOUNTING **income after all deductions have been made** receipts calculated after the deduction of commission, tax, discounts, and other associated expenses. *See also* ***gross receipts***

net residual value ACCOUNTING **value of asset being disposed of** the anticipated proceeds of an asset at the end of its useful life, less the costs such as transportation and the commission associated with selling it. It is used when calculating the annual charge for *straight line depreciation*. *Abbr* **NRV**

net return ACCOUNTING **profit from investment after expenditures** the amount received from an investment, taking taxes and transaction costs into account

net salary FINANCE **earnings after all deductions have been made** the salary remaining after deductions for taxes, social security, medicare, and any employee share of insurance premiums. *See also* *disposable income*

net sales ACCOUNTING **actual value of sales** a company's total sales less any relevant discounts such as those given to retailers

net salvage value ACCOUNTING **value of project being abandoned, after tax** the amount of money remaining after a project has been terminated, taking tax consequences into consideration

net tangible assets ACCOUNTING **firm's total assets minus intangible assets** the total assets of a company less its intangible assets such as goodwill or intellectual property. *Abbr* **NTA**

net working capital ACCOUNTING = *net current assets*

net worth ACCOUNTING **assets minus liabilities** the difference between the assets and liabilities of a person or company

net yield ACCOUNTING **rate of return after costs and tax** the amount produced by an investment after deducting all costs and taxes

new economy ECONOMICS **economic system based on e-commerce** a term used in the late 1990s and 2000s to describe the e-commerce sector and the *digital economy*, in which firms mostly trade online rather than in the bricks and mortar of physical premises

new issue STOCKHOLDING & INVESTMENTS **1. new security on sale for first time** a new security, such as a bond or stock, being offered to the public for the first time. *See also* *float*, *initial public offering* **2. issue of new security** an additional issue of an existing security, for example, a *rights issue*

newly industrialized economy ECONOMICS **nation benefiting from industrialization** a country whose industrialization has recently started to develop. Mexico and Malaysia are examples of newly industrialized economies.

new money FINANCE **financing from a new source** financing provided by an issue of new shares of stock or by the transfer of money from one account to another

New Zealand Trade Development Board FINANCE **New Zealand agency promoting exports and inward investment** a government body responsible for promoting New Zealand exports and facilitating foreign investment in New Zealand. *Also called* **TRADENZ**

next futures contract STOCKHOLDING & INVESTMENTS **option for following month** an *option* to buy or sell for the month after the current month

niche bank *or* niche banker BANKING **specialist banker** a bank or banker specializing in a specific field such as management buyouts

niche player (informal) 1. BANKING = *niche bank* **2.** STOCKHOLDING & INVESTMENTS = *boutique investment house*

nickel *US* FINANCE **small margin** five hundredths of one percent, expressing a fine margin (slang)

NIF *abbr* FINANCE note issuance facility

nil paid STOCKHOLDING & INVESTMENTS **nothing paid yet** with no money yet paid. In the United Kingdom, the term is used in reference to the purchase of newly issued stocks, or to the stocks themselves, when the stockholder entitled to buy new stocks has not yet made a commitment to do so and may sell the rights instead.

ninja loan FINANCE **loan made to somebody with poor credit rating** a loan made to somebody who has No INcome, No Job, and no Assets (slang). *See also* *subprime loan*

NNP *abbr* FINANCE net national product

no-load fund STOCKHOLDING & INVESTMENTS **mutual fund with no fee for trading** a mutual fund that does not charge a fee for the purchase or sale of shares. *See also* *load fund*

nominal 1. FINANCE **very much lower than usual level** very small when compared with what would be considered usual, especially with reference to a sum of money **2.** ACCOUNTING **relating to current prices** considered in terms of the stated or original value only, without adjustment for inflation and other changes **3.** GENERAL MANAGEMENT **assigned by name** assigned to a specific name or category

nominal account ACCOUNTING **account recording items according to category** a record of revenues and expenditures, liabilities and assets classified by their nature, for example, sales, rent, rates, electricity, wages, or share capital

nominal annual rate FINANCE = *annual percentage rate*

nominal capital STOCKHOLDING & INVESTMENTS = *nominal share capital*

nominal cash flow ACCOUNTING **cash flow disregarding inflation** cash flow in terms of currency, without adjustment for inflation

nominal exchange rate CURRENCY & EXCHANGE **stated exchange rate** the exchange rate as specified, without adjustment for transaction costs or differences in purchasing power

nominal interest rate FINANCE **stated interest rate** the interest rate as specified, without adjustment for compounding or inflation

nominal ledger *UK* ACCOUNTING **ledger recording money values** a record of revenue, operating expenses, assets, and capital

nominal share capital STOCKHOLDING & INVESTMENTS **maximum amount of firm's share capital** the total value of all of a corporation's stock at *nominal value*. *Also called* *nominal capital*. *See also* *authorized share capital*

a–z

Dictionary

nominal value STOCKHOLDING & INVESTMENTS **original value of new stock** the original value officially given to a newly issued stock. *Also called* ***par value***. *See also* ***capitalization, reserves***

nominal yield STOCKHOLDING & INVESTMENTS **dividend as percentage of face value** the dividend paid on a share of stock expressed as a percentage of its face value

nominee 1. FINANCE **in US, somebody acting for another** in the United States, a person who is appointed to deal with financial matters on your behalf **2.** *US* STOCKHOLDING & INVESTMENTS **holder of security on another's behalf** a financial institution, or an individual employed by such an institution, that holds a security on behalf of the actual owner. While this may be to hide the owner's identity, for example, in the case of a celebrity, it is also to allow an institution managing any individual's portfolio to conduct transactions without the need for the owner to sign the required paperwork. *UK term* ***nominee name***

nominee account BANKING **account not in owner's name** an account held not in the name of the real owner of the account, but instead in the name of another person, organization, or financial institution. Stocks can be bought and held in nominee accounts so that the owner's identity is not disclosed.

nominee name *UK* STOCKHOLDING & INVESTMENTS = ***nominee***

nonacceptance BANKING **rejection of bill of exchange on presentation** a refusal to accept a bill of exchange when it is presented, by the person on whom it is drawn

nonbusiness days BANKING **days when banks are closed** those days when banks are not open for business, for example, public holidays, or Saturdays and Sundays in Western countries

noncallable STOCKHOLDING & INVESTMENTS **not able to be repurchased before maturity** used to describe a security that the issuer cannot buy back before its maturity date. *See also* ***callable***

noncash item 1. ACCOUNTING **entry in income statement not representing cash** an item, such as a gain or loss from an investment or depreciation expenses, that occurs on an income statement and is not a receipt of actual money **2.** BANKING **financial instruments representing money** checks, drafts, and similar items that have money value but are not money themselves

noncurrent assets FINANCE **long-term investments** resources that are expected to be held for more than one year. They are reported at the lower of cost and current market value, which means that their values will vary.

nondeductible ACCOUNTING **not admissible as deduction** not allowed to be deducted from a payment, especially not acceptable as an allowance against income tax

nonexecutive director CORPORATE GOVERNANCE **board member without day-to-day involvement** a part-time, nonsalaried member of the ***board of directors***, involved in the planning, strategy, and policymaking of an organization but not in its day-to-day operations. The appointment of a

nonexecutive director to a board is usually made in order to provide independence and balance to that board, and to ensure that good ***corporate governance*** is practiced. A nonexecutive director may be selected for the prestige they bring or for their experience, contacts, or specialist knowledge. *Also called* ***part-time director***. *See also* ***outside director***

nonfinancial asset ACCOUNTING **not money or financial contract** an asset such as real estate or personal property that is neither money nor a financial instrument

non-financial incentive scheme FINANCE **UK program rewarding performance other than with money** in the United Kingdom, a program offering benefits such as additional paid vacations, set up to reward employees for improved commitment and performance and as a means of motivation. *See also* ***financial incentive scheme***

noninterest-bearing bond STOCKHOLDING & INVESTMENTS **bond with discount rather than interest** a bond that is sold at a discount instead of with a promise to pay interest

nonnegotiable instrument FINANCE **financial contract that cannot change hands** a financial instrument that cannot be signed over to anyone else. These include ***bills of exchange*** and ***crossed cheques***.

nonoperational balances BANKING **Bank of England deposits that cannot be withdrawn** accounts that banks maintain at the Bank of England without the power of withdrawal

nonparticipating preferred stock STOCKHOLDING & INVESTMENTS **preferred stock paying fixed dividend** the most common type of preferred stock that pays a fixed dividend regardless of the profitability of the company. *See also* ***participating preferred stock***

nonperforming asset STOCKHOLDING & INVESTMENTS **asset providing no income** an asset that is not producing income, for example, one that is no longer accruing interest

nonperforming loan FINANCE **loan made to borrower likely to default** a loan made to a borrower who is not likely to pay any interest nor to repay the principal

nonrecourse debt FINANCE **debt with no liability** a debt for which the borrower has no personal responsibility, typically a debt of a limited partnership

nonrecoverable FINANCE **that will never be paid back** used to describe a debt that will never be paid, for example, because of the borrower's bankruptcy

nonrecurring charge ACCOUNTING **unique charge** a charge that is made only once

nonrecurring item ACCOUNTING **unique item in account** in a set of accounts an item that is included on only one occasion

non-sufficient funds *UK* BANKING = ***insufficient funds***

nonsystematic risk RISK **risk related to particular firm** investment risk that is attributable to the performance of a specific company, not to the performance of the stock market or economy, and can be reduced by diversification

nonvoting share STOCKHOLDING & INVESTMENTS **common stock receiving dividend but not voting rights** common stock that is paid a dividend from the company's profits, but that does not entitle the stockholder to vote at any meeting of stockholders. Such stock is unpopular with institutional investors. *Also called **A share***

normal profit ECONOMICS **minimum profit required for business** the minimum level of profit that will attract an entrepreneur to begin a business or remain trading

normal yield curve STOCKHOLDING & INVESTMENTS **showing lower yields for short-term bonds** a visual representation of interest rates showing higher yields for long-term bonds than for short-term bonds. *See also **yield curve***

nostro account BANKING **account with bank abroad** an account that a bank has with a ***correspondent bank*** in another country

note 1. CURRENCY & EXCHANGE **item of paper money** a piece of paper money printed by a bank and approved as legal tender. *Also called **banknote** (sense 1), **bill** (sense 2)* **2.** FINANCE **document promising to repay borrowed money** a written promise to repay money that has been borrowed

note issuance facility FINANCE **facility for buying and reselling Eurocurrency notes** a credit facility where a company obtains a loan underwritten by banks and can issue a series of short-term ***Eurocurrency*** notes to replace others that have expired. *Abbr* **NIF**

note of hand FINANCE = ***promissory note***

notes to the accounts *or* notes to the financial statements ACCOUNTING **information supporting account entries** an explanation of specific items in a set of accounts

not-for-profit FINANCE **not operated to generate income** organized typically for a charitable, humanitarian, or educational purpose and not generating profits for shareholders. In the United States, not-for-profit corporations can apply for tax-exempt status at both the federal and state levels of government. *See also **nonprofit organization***

notifying bank BANKING, INTERNATIONAL TRADE = ***advising bank***

notional income ACCOUNTING **income not physically received** invisible benefit that is not actual money, goods, or services

notional principal amount FINANCE **value of loan** the value used to represent a loan in calculating ***interest rate swaps***

notional rent ACCOUNTING **theoretical rent for firm's own premises** an amount of money noted in accounts as rent where the company owns the building it is occupying and so does not pay an actual rent

not negotiable FINANCE **not able to change hands absolutely** used to describe a check or bill of exchange that cannot be transferred to somebody else. If such a document is given by one person to another, the recipient obtains no better title to it than the signatory. *See also **negotiable instrument***

no-touch option STOCKHOLDING & INVESTMENTS **option paying if preset level not reached** an option that gives an investor a payment only if the price of the underlying asset has not reached or exceeded a preset level. *See also **double-one-touch option, one-touch option***

not sufficient funds *UK* BANKING = ***insufficient funds***

NOW account BANKING **interest-paying US account with checks** in the United States, an interest-bearing account with a bank or savings and loan association, on which checks (called ***negotiable orders of withdrawal***) can be drawn. *Full form* ***negotiable order of withdrawal account***

NPV *abbr* ACCOUNTING net present value

NRV *abbr* ACCOUNTING net residual value

NSA *abbr* ACCOUNTING National Society of Accountants

NS&I *abbr* STOCKHOLDING & INVESTMENTS National Savings & Investments

NSB *abbr* BANKING National Savings Bank

NSC *abbr* STOCKHOLDING & INVESTMENTS National Savings Certificate

NSF *abbr* BANKING non-sufficient funds *or* not sufficient funds

NTA *abbr* ACCOUNTING net tangible assets

numbered account BANKING **bank account without holder's name** a bank account identified by a number to allow the holder to remain anonymous

numbers FINANCE **financial data** financial results or forecasts calculated for a particular period of time or project

O

obligor FINANCE = ***debtor***

OBSF *abbr* FINANCE off-balance-sheet financing

obsolescence 1. FINANCE **loss through becoming out of date** the loss of value of a fixed asset due to advances in technology or changes in market conditions **2.** MARKETING **becoming out of date** the decline of products in a market due to the introduction of better competitor products or rapid technology developments. Obsolescence of products can be a planned process, controlled by introducing deliberate minor cosmetic changes to a product every few years to encourage new purchases. It can also be unplanned, however, and in some sectors the pace of technological change is so rapid that the rate of obsolescence is high Obsolescence is part of the product life cycle, and if a product cannot be turned around, it may lead to product abandonment.

OCF *abbr* ACCOUNTING operating cash flow

OCR *abbr* BANKING official cash rate

O/D *abbr* BANKING overdraft

a–z

Dictionary

OEIC *abbr* STOCKHOLDING & INVESTMENTS open-ended investment company

off-balance-sheet financing FINANCE **raising money through items not on balance sheet** financing obtained by means other than debt and equity instruments, for example, by partnerships, joint ventures, and leases. *Abbr* **OBSF**

offer STOCKHOLDING & INVESTMENTS **1.** *see offering price* **2. net value of mutual fund** the *net asset value* of a mutual fund plus any sales charges. It is the price investors pay when they buy a security.

offer by prospectus STOCKHOLDING & INVESTMENTS **UK means of selling securities to public** in the United Kingdom, one of the ways available to a *lead underwriter* of offering securities to the public. *See also float, initial public offering, new issue, offer for sale*

offer document STOCKHOLDING & INVESTMENTS = *prospectus*

offer for sale STOCKHOLDING & INVESTMENTS **invitation to buy stock** an invitation to apply for stock in a company, based on information contained in a prospectus

offering circular STOCKHOLDING & INVESTMENTS = *prospectus*

offering price *US* STOCKHOLDING & INVESTMENTS **selling price of share of stock** the price at which somebody offers a share of a stock, especially a new issue, for sale. *UK term offer price*

offeror STOCKHOLDING & INVESTMENTS **maker of bid** somebody who makes a bid to buy a *financial obligation* such as a debt

offer period MERGERS & ACQUISITIONS **time span when takeover bid is open** the time after a *takeover bid* for a company is first announced until the deal is closed or the offer lapses

offer price *UK* STOCKHOLDING & INVESTMENTS = *offering price*

official books of account ACCOUNTING **institution's financial records** the official financial records of an organization set up for educational, professional, religious, or social purposes

official cash rate BANKING **government interest rate** the current interest rate as set by a central bank. *Abbr* **OCR**

official development assistance FINANCE **money made available to emerging country** money that the *OECD*'s Development Assistance Committee gives or lends to an emerging country

official intervention CURRENCY & EXCHANGE **government action to affect exchange rate** an attempt by a government to influence the exchange rate by buying or selling foreign currency

official return ACCOUNTING **legally required financial report** a financial report or statement required by law and made by a person or company, for example, a tax return

offset STOCKHOLDING & INVESTMENTS **counterbalancing transaction in security** a transaction that balances all or part of an earlier transaction in the same security

offshore banking BANKING **banking in foreign banks** banking in a foreign country, especially one that has favorable taxation regulations and is considered as a *tax haven*

offshore financial center FINANCE **finance hub in foreign country** a country or other political unit that has banking laws intended to attract business from industrialized nations

offshore fund STOCKHOLDING & INVESTMENTS **fund based abroad** a fund that is based in a foreign country, usually a country that has favorable taxation regulations

OI ACCOUNTING *see EBIT*

oil economy ECONOMICS **1. economy based on oil revenues** an economy that is funded by the revenues from oil resources **2. economy based on oil** an economy that depends on oil supplies for its transportation, agricultural, and energy needs

Old Lady of Threadneedle Street *UK* BANKING **Bank of England** the Bank of England, which is located in Threadneedle Street in the City of London (informal)

oligarch FINANCE **rich powerful businessman** one of a small group having financial and political power, especially nowadays somebody with extreme personal wealth (slang)

omitted dividend STOCKHOLDING & INVESTMENTS **unpaid regular dividend** a regularly scheduled dividend that a company does not pay

omnibus account STOCKHOLDING & INVESTMENTS **combined account for broker's convenience** an account of one broker with another that combines the transactions of multiple investors for the convenience of the brokers

on account FINANCE **by advance payment** used to describe an amount of money paid that represents part of a sum of money due to be paid in the future

oncost ACCOUNTING **general cost of running business** a business cost that cannot be charged directly to a particular good or service and must be apportioned across the business

on demand 1. BANKING **allowing immediate withdrawals** used to describe an account from which withdrawals may be made without giving a period of notice **2.** FINANCE **allowing demand for immediate repayment** used to describe a loan, usually an overdraft, that the lender can request the borrower to repay immediately **3.** FINANCE **payable immediately to holder** used to describe a bill of exchange that is paid upon presentation

one-stop shopping FINANCE **provision of complete variety of financial services** the ability of a single financial institution to offer a full variety of financial services

one-touch option STOCKHOLDING & INVESTMENTS **option paying at preset level** an option that gives an investor a payment if the price of the underlying asset reaches or exceeds a preset level. *See also double-one-touch option, no-touch option*

one-year money STOCKHOLDING & INVESTMENTS **investment for fixed period of one year** money placed on a money market for a fixed period of one year, with either a fixed or variable rate of

a–z

Dictionary

interest. It can be removed during the fixed term only upon payment of a penalty.

online banking E-COMMERCE, BANKING banking service accessible by computer over Internet a system by which customers have bank accounts that they can access directly from their home computers, using the Internet, and can carry out operations such as checking on their account balances, paying invoices, and receiving their salaries electronically

onshore FINANCE located in home country based in the home country, especially referring to a company that is registered in the country in which it conducts most of its business, or to funds or activities that are held or located in the home country. *See also* **offshore**

on-target earnings FINANCE commission equaling amount aimed at the amount earned by somebody working on *commission* who has achieved the targets set. *Abbr* **OTE**

open account FINANCE **1.** credit offered to buyer without requiring security a credit account offered by a supplier to a purchaser for which the supplier does not require security **2.** unpaid credit an account offered by a business to a customer that is as yet unpaid

open check US BANKING blank signed check a signed check where the amount payable has not been indicated

open cheque UK BANKING uncrossed check a check that is not crossed and so may be cashed by the payee at the branch of the bank where it is drawn. *See also* **crossed cheque**

open credit FINANCE credit offered without requiring security credit given by a supplier to a good customer without requiring security

open-end credit US FINANCE arrangement allowing borrowing and repaying at will a credit facility that allows the borrower, within an overall credit limit and for a set period, to borrow or repay debt as required. *Also called* **revolving credit**. *UK term* **open-ended credit**

open-ended credit UK FINANCE = **open-end credit**

open-ended fund UK STOCKHOLDING & INVESTMENTS = **open-end fund**

open-ended investment company UK STOCKHOLDING & INVESTMENTS **1.** = **open-end fund 2.** = **open-end investment company**

open-ended management company UK STOCKHOLDING & INVESTMENTS = **open-end management company**

open-end fund US STOCKHOLDING & INVESTMENTS mutual fund with varying share numbers a mutual fund that has a variable number of shares. *UK term* **open-ended fund**. *See also* **closed-end fund**

open-end investment company US STOCKHOLDING & INVESTMENTS firm pooling funds for mutual funds a company with a variable number of shares that it sells to investors and pools for investment in mutual funds. *UK term* **open-ended investment company**. *See also* **open-end fund**

open-end management company US STOCKHOLDING & INVESTMENTS firm selling mutual funds a company that sells mutual funds. *UK term* **open-ended management company**

opening balance ACCOUNTING amount at beginning of record the value of a financial quantity at the beginning of an accounting period

opening balance sheet ACCOUNTING record of opening balances a record giving details of an organization's financial balances at the beginning of an accounting period

opening entry ACCOUNTING first record in account the first entry recorded in an account, for example, the first entry when starting a new business

opening purchase STOCKHOLDING & INVESTMENTS first in series of option purchases the first of a series of purchases to be made in options of a specific type for a specific commodity or security

opening stock UK ACCOUNTING = **beginning inventory**

open interest STOCKHOLDING & INVESTMENTS total of options not yet closed the number of *options* contracts that have not yet been exercised, offset, or allowed to expire

operating budget ACCOUNTING plan for firm's income and expenses a forecast of income and expenses that result from the day-to-day activities of a company over a period of time

operating cash flow ACCOUNTING money used and generated in firm's operations the amount used to represent the money moving through a company as a result of its operations, as distinct from its purely financial transactions. *Abbr* **OCF**

operating costs *or* operating expenses ACCOUNTING expenses for firm's ordinary business activities the costs arising from the day-to-day activities of running a company. *Also called* **running costs**

operating income ACCOUNTING = **EBIT**

operating leverage ACCOUNTING ratio of fixed to total costs the ratio of a business's fixed costs to its total costs. Fixed costs have to be paid regardless of output, the higher the ratio, the higher the risk of losses in an economic downturn.

operating loss ACCOUNTING firm's loss during ordinary business activities a loss incurred by a company during the course of its usual business

operating margin ACCOUNTING = **profit margin**

operating profit ACCOUNTING standard income minus standard costs the difference between a company's revenues and any related costs and expenses, not including income or expenses from any sources other than its normal methods of providing a good or service

operating risk ACCOUNTING poor ratio of fixed to total costs the risk of a high *operating leverage*, when each sale makes a significant contribution to fixed costs

operational costs ACCOUNTING costs of running business the costs incurred by a company during the course of its usual business

549

a–z

Dictionary

operational gearing ACCOUNTING ratio of fixed to total costs the relationship between a company's fixed costs and its total costs. Fixed costs have to be paid before profit can be made, so high operational gearing increases a company's risk.

operational risk OPERATIONS & PRODUCTION, RISK risk of loss from internal or external failures the risk of economic loss that an organization faces, resulting from failed or inadequate controls, processes, or systems, or from human or external events

opportunity cost STOCKHOLDING & INVESTMENTS loss through choice of investment an amount of money lost as a result of choosing one investment rather than another

optimal portfolio STOCKHOLDING & INVESTMENTS best possible investments a theoretical set of investments that would be the most profitable for an investor

option 1. STOCKHOLDING & INVESTMENTS contract for trading rights a contract for the right to buy or sell an asset, typically a commodity, under agreed terms. *Also called* ***option contract***, ***stock option*** **2.** BUSINESS opportunity to buy or sell on agreed terms an agreement that somebody may buy or sell a specific asset on predetermined terms on or before a future date

option account STOCKHOLDING & INVESTMENTS account for buying and selling options an account that an investor holds with a broker and uses for trading in ***options***

optionaire STOCKHOLDING & INVESTMENTS millionaire in terms of stock options a millionaire whose wealth consists of or is derived from stock ***options*** (slang)

optional redemption provision STOCKHOLDING & INVESTMENTS bond early redemption clause the terms in a bond agreement that allow the issuer (usually) or the lender (less frequently) to redeem it before the final redemption date

option buyer STOCKHOLDING & INVESTMENTS buyer of option an investor who acquires an ***option*** to buy or sell a security, currency, or commodity

option class STOCKHOLDING & INVESTMENTS group of options of same type a set of ***options*** that are identical with respect to type and underlying asset

option contract STOCKHOLDING & INVESTMENTS = ***option***

option elasticity STOCKHOLDING & INVESTMENTS relative changing values of option and underlying asset the relative change in the value of an ***option*** as a function of a change in the value of the underlying asset

option income fund STOCKHOLDING & INVESTMENTS mutual fund with options a mutual fund that derives income from investing in ***options***

option premium STOCKHOLDING & INVESTMENTS cost of each share in option the amount per share that a buyer pays for an ***option*** to buy or sell a security, currency, or commodity above the exercise price

option price STOCKHOLDING & INVESTMENTS price of option the price of an ***option*** to buy or sell a security, currency, or commodity

option pricing model STOCKHOLDING & INVESTMENTS means of establishing value of options a model that is used to determine the fair value of ***options***. *See also* ***Black-Scholes model***

option seller STOCKHOLDING & INVESTMENTS = ***option writer***

option series STOCKHOLDING & INVESTMENTS group of options representing same thing a collection of options that are identical in terms of class, ***exercise price***, and date of maturity

options on physicals STOCKHOLDING & INVESTMENTS options on physical assets a type of ***option*** that is on real assets rather than financial assets

option writer STOCKHOLDING & INVESTMENTS seller of option a person, institution, or other organization that sells an ***option*** to buy or sell a security, currency, or commodity. *Also called* ***option seller***

order 1. STOCKHOLDING & INVESTMENTS instruction to trade for investor's own account an occasion when a broker is told to buy or sell a financial product for an investor's own account **2.** OPERATIONS & PRODUCTION arrangement between customer and supplier a ***contract*** made between a customer and a supplier for the supply of a variety of goods or services in a determined quantity and quality, at an agreed price, and for delivery at or by a specific time

orders pending STOCKHOLDING & INVESTMENTS, OPERATIONS & PRODUCTION unfulfilled orders orders that have not yet resulted in transactions

ordinary interest FINANCE interest based on 360-day year interest calculated on the basis of a year having only 360 days

ordinary resolution CORPORATE GOVERNANCE general issue put to vote at annual meeting a resolution put before an annual meeting, usually referring to some general procedural matter, that requires a simple majority of votes to be accepted

ordinary share *UK* STOCKHOLDING & INVESTMENTS = ***common stock***

original cost ACCOUNTING total cost of asset the total cost of acquiring an asset

original issue discount STOCKHOLDING & INVESTMENTS discount at bond's first sale the discount offered on the day of sale of a debt instrument

original maturity STOCKHOLDING & INVESTMENTS date for payment of bond a date on which a ***debt instrument*** is due to mature

OTC *abbr* FINANCE over-the-counter

OTE *abbr* FINANCE on-target earnings

other capital ACCOUNTING uncategorized capital capital that is not listed in specific categories

other current assets ACCOUNTING non-cash assets maturing within year assets that are not cash and are due to mature within a year

a–z

Dictionary

other long-term capital ACCOUNTING **uncategorized long-term assets** long-term capital that is not listed in specific categories in accounts

other long-term liabilities FINANCE **obligations with no interest charge in next year** obligations such as deferred taxes and employee benefits with terms greater than one year and on which there is no charge for interest in the next year

other prices FINANCE **unlisted prices** prices that are not listed in a catalog

other short-term capital ACCOUNTING **uncategorized short-term assets** a residual category in the balance of payments that includes financial assets of less than one year such as currency, deposits, and bills

outgoings *UK* ACCOUNTING = *costs*

outlay ACCOUNTING **money spent for specific purpose** money spent on something such as capital assets or operating costs

out-of-pocket expenses ACCOUNTING **amount of employee's own money spent on business** an amount of an employee's personal money that he or she has spent on company business, especially when considered for reimbursement

out of the money STOCKHOLDING & INVESTMENTS **having no intrinsic value** used to describe an *option* that, if it expired at the current market price, would have no intrinsic value. *See also* **in the money**

output gap ECONOMICS **difference between economy's production capacity and actual production** the difference between the amount of activity that is sustainable in an economy and the amount of activity actually taking place

output method ACCOUNTING **accounting technique categorizing costs by output purpose** an accounting system that classifies costs according to the outputs for which they are incurred, not the inputs they have bought

outside director CORPORATE GOVERNANCE **director not employed by firm** a member of a company's *board of directors* neither currently nor formerly in the company's employment. An outside director is sometimes described as being synonymous with a *nonexecutive director*, and as usually being employed by a holding or associated company. In the United States, an outside director is somebody who has no relationships at all to a company. In US public companies, compensation and audit committees are generally made up of outside directors, and use of outside directors to select board directors is becoming more common.

outstanding check ACCOUNTING **check issued but not cashed** a check which has been written and therefore has been entered in the company's ledgers, but which has not been presented for payment and so has not been debited from the company's bank account

outstanding share STOCKHOLDING & INVESTMENTS **share allotted to applicant** a share that a company has issued and somebody has bought

outstanding share capital STOCKHOLDING & INVESTMENTS **value of stock available to trade** the value of all of the stock of a company minus the value of retained shares

overall capitalization rate FINANCE **income minus most costs divided by value** *net operating income* other than debt service divided by value

overall market capacity ECONOMICS **amount of product that market can absorb** the amount of a service or good that can be absorbed in a market without affecting the price

overall rate of return *or* **overall return** STOCKHOLDING & INVESTMENTS **return relative to investment** the aggregate of all the dividends received over an investment's life together with its capital gain or loss at the date of its realization, calculated either before or after tax. It is one of the ways an investor can look at the performance of an investment.

overbid FINANCE **1. bid too much** to bid more than necessary to make a successful purchase **2. too high a bid** an amount that is offered that is unnecessarily high for a successful purchase to be made

overborrowed FINANCE **having too much debt in comparison to assets** used to describe a company that has very high borrowings compared to its assets, and has difficulty in meeting its interest payments

overcapitalized FINANCE **having surplus capital** used to describe a business that has more capital than can profitably be employed. An overcapitalized company could buy back some of its own stock in the market; if it has significant debt capital it could repurchase its bonds in the market; or it could make a large one-time dividend to stockholders.

overdraft BANKING **1. deficit in bank account** the amount by which the money withdrawn from a bank account exceeds the balance in the account. *Abbr* **O/D 2.** = *overdraft facility*

overdraft facility BANKING **agreement for deficit in bank account** a credit arrangement with a bank, allowing a person or company with an account to use borrowed money up to an agreed limit when nothing is left in the account

overdraft line BANKING **agreed amount of overdraft** an amount in excess of the balance in an account that a bank agrees to pay in honoring checks on the account

overdraft protection BANKING **guarantee of payment from overdrawn account** a bank service, amounting to a *line of credit*, that assures that the bank will honor overdrafts, up to a limit and for a fee

overdraw BANKING **create deficit in bank account** to withdraw more money from a bank account than it contains or than was agreed could be withdrawn

overdrawn BANKING **having deficit in bank account** in debt to a bank because the amount withdrawn from an account exceeds its balance

overdue FINANCE **still owing** still to be paid after the date due

overfunding ECONOMICS **when UK government sells more stock than necessary** in the United Kingdom, a situation in which the government borrows more money than it needs for expenditure, as a result of selling too much government stock

overgeared FINANCE **with greater financial commitments than common stock capital** describing a company with debt capital and preferred stock that outweigh its **common stock capital**

overhead US ACCOUNTING = *overhead costs*

overhead absorption rate ACCOUNTING **proportion of overhead attributed to product or service** a means of attributing overhead to a product or service, based for example on direct labor hours, direct labor cost, or machine hours (the number of hours for which a machine is in production). The choice of overhead absorption base may be made with the objective of obtaining "accurate" product costs, or of influencing managerial behavior; for example, overhead applied to labor hours or part numbers appears to make the use of these resources more costly, thus discouraging their use.

overhead capacity variance ACCOUNTING **gap between budgeted and required overhead** the difference between the overhead absorbed, based on budgeted hours, and actual hours worked

overhead costs ACCOUNTING **costs incurred in upkeep or running** the indirect costs of the day-to-day running of a business, i.e. not money spent on producing goods, but money spent on such things as renting or maintaining buildings and machinery. *Also called* **overhead, overheads**

overhead expenditure variance ACCOUNTING **misjudgment of indirect costs** the difference between the budgeted *overhead costs* and the actual expenditure

overheads UK ACCOUNTING = *overhead costs*

overindebtedness FINANCE **unsustainable debt** the situation in which borrowers, including individuals, companies and countries, have borrowed more money than they are able to pay back

overinvested 1. STOCKHOLDING & INVESTMENTS **with too much invested** having a higher than desired amount invested in a security, or having a higher amount committed to tracking an index or matching a model portfolio than the index or model suggests **2.** BUSINESS **with investment predicated on higher demand** used to describe a business that invests heavily during an economic boom only to find that when it starts to produce an income, the demand for the product or service has fallen

overlap profit ACCOUNTING **profit assignable to two accounting periods** profit that arises in two overlapping accounting periods and on which tax relief can be claimed

overnight rate MARKETS, RISK **interest rate on interbank overnight loans** the interest rate charged by financial institutions on overnight loans to each other

overnight repo BANKING **arrangement for temporary sale for cash** a repurchase agreement where banks sell securities for cash and repurchase them the next day at a higher price. This type of agreement is used by central banks as a means of regulating the *money markets*.

overpayment 1. FINANCE **paying too much** an act of paying more than is required or reasonable, or the sum paid in such a situation **2.** UK ACCOUNTING = *additional principal payment*

overrated FINANCE **with value set too high** used to describe something that is valued more highly than it should be

overriding commission *or* override *or* overrider FINANCE **further additional commission** a special extra commission which is above all other commissions

overseas funds FINANCE **investment products in foreign countries** investment funds that are based in other countries and are not subject to regulation in the home country

overspend ACCOUNTING **1. spend more than planned** to spend more money than was budgeted or planned or than can be afforded **2. excess amount spent** an amount that is more than was budgeted for spending

over-the-counter FINANCE **of trading between dealers** used to describe the trade of securities directly between licensed dealers, rather than through an auction system. *Abbr* **OTC**

over-the-counter security STOCKHOLDING & INVESTMENTS **security traded directly between dealers** a security that is traded directly between licensed dealers on the *over-the-counter market*

overvalue FINANCE, GENERAL MANAGEMENT **give something too high a value** to give a higher value to something or somebody than is justified

owner's equity ACCOUNTING **total assets minus total liabilities** a business's total assets less its total liabilities, being the funds provided by the owners. *See also* **capital, common stock**

P

package and sell STOCKHOLDING & INVESTMENTS **sell combined loans** to combine a number of loans and sell them to investors as *mortgage-backed securities*

Pac Man defense MERGERS & ACQUISITIONS **offer to purchase buyer to avoid firm's takeover** a strategy by a company seeking to avoid a hostile takeover, in which the target company makes an offer to purchase the prospective buyer

paid-in capital STOCKHOLDING & INVESTMENTS **firm's capital received from investors for stock** capital in a business that has been provided by its stockholders

paid up FINANCE **fully paid** having paid all the money owed

paid-up capital *or* paid-up share capital STOCKHOLDING & INVESTMENTS **stock issued and paid for** an amount of money paid for the issued capital shares of stock, which does not include *called-up share capital*. *See also* **fully paid share capital, partly paid capital**

paid-up share STOCKHOLDING & INVESTMENTS **stock paid for in full** a stock for which stockholders have paid the full contractual amount. *See also* **call, called-up share capital, paid-up capital, share capital**

panda CURRENCY & EXCHANGE **Chinese gold or silver collector coin** one of a series of Chinese gold and silver bullion collector coins, each featuring a panda, that were first issued in 1982. Struck with a highly polished surface, the smallest gold coin weighs 0.05 ounces, the largest 12 ounces.

P&L *abbr* ACCOUNTING profit and loss

Panel on Takeovers and Mergers MERGERS & ACQUISITIONS **UK group overseeing fairness in takeovers** in the United Kingdom, the group that issues the *City Code on Takeovers and Mergers*, a code designed principally to ensure fair and equal treatment of all stockholders in relation to takeovers. *See also* **City Code on Takeovers and Mergers**

panic buying FINANCE **exceptional buying because of fear of shortages** an unusual level of buying caused by fear or rumors of product shortages or by severe price rises

panic dumping CURRENCY & EXCHANGE **selling currency because of devaluation fears** a rush to sell a currency at any price because of fears of a possible devaluation

paper 1. FINANCE **record of holdings** a certificate of deposits and other securities **2.** STOCKHOLDING & INVESTMENTS **issue of stock or bonds to raise capital** a rights issue or an issue of bonds launched by a company to raise additional capital **3.** FINANCE **all debt issued by firm** all funding instruments issued by a company, other than *equity*

paper gain STOCKHOLDING & INVESTMENTS = *paper profit*

paper loss STOCKHOLDING & INVESTMENTS **drop in value of unsold investment** a loss made when an asset has fallen in value but has not been sold. *Also called* **unrealized loss**

paper millionaire STOCKHOLDING & INVESTMENTS **person owning stock valued currently at one million** an individual who owns stock that is worth in excess of a million in currency at a specific date, but which may fall in value. In 2001 many of the founders of dot-com companies were paper millionaires. *See also* **paper profit**

paper money 1. CURRENCY & EXCHANGE **bills** currency that is not coins **2.** BANKING **checks** payments in paper form such as checks

paper offer MERGERS & ACQUISITIONS **takeover bid with stock rather than cash** a takeover bid in which the purchasing company offers its stock in exchange for stock in the company being taken over, as opposed to a cash offer

paper profit ACCOUNTING **increase in value on investment not yet sold** an increase in the value of an investment that the investor has no immediate intention of realizing

PAR *abbr* BANKING prime assets ratio

paradox of saving *or* **paradox of thrift** ECONOMICS **cutbacks in expenditure lead to increased expenditure elsewhere** the observation that savings made by individuals in their consumption lead to a drop in overall demand which in turn leads to increased spending by a business or government

parallel economy ECONOMICS = *black economy*

parallel loan FINANCE = *back-to-back loan*

parcel STOCKHOLDING & INVESTMENTS **set of securities sold together** a group of related securities that are sold at one time

parcel of shares *UK* STOCKHOLDING & INVESTMENTS = *basket of shares*

Pareto's Law ECONOMICS **idea that income will be distributed similarly everywhere** a theory of income distribution that states that regardless of political or taxation conditions, income will be distributed in the same way across all countries

Paris Bourse MARKETS, STOCKHOLDING & INVESTMENTS = *Euronext Paris*

Paris Club FINANCE = *G10*

Paris Interbank Offered Rate BANKING **bank releasing money against check** the French equivalent of the London Interbank Offered Rate. *Abbr* **PIBOR**

Paris Stock Exchange MARKETS, STOCKHOLDING & INVESTMENTS = *Euronext Paris*

parity value STOCKHOLDING & INVESTMENTS = *conversion value*

park STOCKHOLDING & INVESTMENTS (slang) **1. illegally disguise ownership of stock** to place owned stock with third parties to disguise their ownership, usually illegally **2. invest money safely for short time** to put money into safe investments while deciding where to invest it in the longer term

parking STOCKHOLDING & INVESTMENTS (slang) **1. illegal transfer of stock to nominee** the transfer of stock in a company to a third party such as a nominee or the name of an associate, often illegally **2. temporarily keeping money in safe investments** the practice of putting money into safe investments while deciding where to invest it in the longer term

part exchange *UK* FINANCE = *trade-in*

participating bond STOCKHOLDING & INVESTMENTS **bond yielding dividends and interest** a bond that pays the holder dividends as well as interest

participating preference share *UK* STOCKHOLDING & INVESTMENTS = *participating preferred stock*

participating preferred stock *US* STOCKHOLDING & INVESTMENTS **stock yielding dividend and share of surplus profit** a type of *preferred stock* that entitles the holder to a fixed dividend and, in addition, to the right to participate in any surplus profits after payment of agreed levels of dividends to holders of *common stock* has been made. *See also* *nonparticipating preferred stock*. *UK term* **participating preference share**

participative budgeting TREASURY MANAGEMENT **system allowing budget holders to draft own budgets** a budgeting system in which all budget holders are given the opportunity to participate in setting their own budgets. *Also called* **bottom-up budgeting**

partly paid capital *or* partly paid share capital STOCKHOLDING & INVESTMENTS **capital not paid in full** capital composed of shares for which the stockholders have not paid the full value at once, but have paid in installments. *See also fully paid share capital, paid-up capital*

partly paid share STOCKHOLDING & INVESTMENTS **stock not paid in full** a stock for which stockholders have not paid the full value at once, but have paid in installments. *See also call, partly paid capital*

partnership accounts 1. BANKING **accounts of business partners** the capital and checking accounts of each partner in a partnership **2.** ACCOUNTING **record of financial activities** accounts that record the business activities of each partner in a partnership

part payment FINANCE **amount paid to cover part of debt** a partial payment that leaves a balance to pay at some future time

part-time director CORPORATE GOVERNANCE = nonexecutive director

par value STOCKHOLDING & INVESTMENTS = *nominal value*

passbook BANKING = *bank book*

passing off FRAUD **intentionally making one product appear to be another** a form of fraud in which a company tries to sell its own product by deceiving buyers into thinking it is another product

passive investment management STOCKHOLDING & INVESTMENTS **managing investment portfolio by automatic adjustments** the managing of a mutual fund or other investment portfolio by relying on automatic adjustments such as tracking an index instead of making personal judgments. *See also active fund management*

passive portfolio strategy STOCKHOLDING & INVESTMENTS **relying on automatic adjustments to manage investments** a plan for managing an investment portfolio that relies on automatic adjustments such as tracking an index

pass-through security STOCKHOLDING & INVESTMENTS **security made up of pool of securities** a security that represents an interest in a pool of securities, most commonly *mortgage-backed securities*, in which the earnings are passed through to investors

pathfinder prospectus UK STOCKHOLDING & INVESTMENTS **preliminary prospectus to test market** a preliminary prospectus used in initial public offerings to gauge the reaction of investors. *US term red eye*

pawnbroker FINANCE **person lending money against personal items** a person who lends money against the security of a wide variety of chattels, from jewelry to cars. The borrower may recover the goods by repaying the loan and interest by a specific date. Otherwise, the items pawned are sold and any surplus after the deduction of expenses, the loan, and interest is returned to the borrower.

pay FINANCE **money paid for work done** a sum of money given in return for work done or services provided. Pay, in the form of salary or wages, is generally provided in weekly or monthly fixed amounts, and is usually expressed in terms of the total sum earned per year. It may also be allocated using a **piece rate** system, where employees are paid for each unit of work they perform.

payables ledger US ACCOUNTING **record of accounts to be paid** a ledger in which a company records its **accounts payable**. *UK term purchase ledger*

payable to order FINANCE **indicating that payee may be changed** the statement on a bill of exchange or check, used to indicate that the payee is able to endorse it to a third party

payback FINANCE **1. repayment of borrowed money** the act of paying back money that has been borrowed **2. time taken for investment project to break even** the time required for the cash revenues from a capital investment project to equal the cost

payback period ACCOUNTING **time needed to recover project investment costs** the length of time it will take to earn back the money invested in a project.

The straight payback period method is the simplest way of determining the investment potential of a major project. Expressed in time, it tells a management how many months or years it will take to recover the original cash cost of the project. It is calculated using the formula:

$$\frac{\text{Cost of project}}{\text{Annual cash revenues}} = \text{Payback period}$$

Thus, if a project cost $100,000 and was expected to generate $28,000 annually, the payback period would be:

$$\frac{100,000}{28,000} = 3.57 \text{ years}$$

If the revenues generated by the project are expected to vary from year to year, add the revenues expected for each succeeding year until you arrive at the total cost of the project.

For example, say the revenues expected to be generated by the $100,000 project are:

Revenue	Total	Cum. total
Year 1	$19,000	$19,000
Year 2	$25,000	$44,000
Year 3	$30,000	$74,000
Year 4	$30,000	$104,000
Year 5	$30,000	$134,000

Thus, the project would be fully paid for in Year 4, since it is in that year the total revenue reaches the initial cost of $100,000. The precise payback period would be calculated as:

$$\frac{100,000 - 74,000}{1000,000 - 74,000} \times 365 = 316 \text{ days} + 3 \text{ years}$$

The picture becomes complex when the time-value-of-money principle is introduced into the calculations. Some experts insist this is essential to determine the most accurate payback period. Accordingly, the annual revenues have to be discounted by the applicable interest rate, 10% in this example. Doing so produces significantly different results:

Revenue	Present value	Total	Cum. total
Year 1	$19,000	$17,271	$17,271
Year 2	$25,000	$20,650	$37,921
Year 3	$30,000	$22,530	$60,451
Year 4	$30,000	$20,490	$80,941
Year 5	$30,000	$18,630	$99,571

This method shows that payback would not occur even after five years.

Generally, a payback period of three years or less is desirable; if a project's payback period is less than a year, some contend it should be judged essential.

pay down FINANCE **reduce loan amount through payments** to reduce the amount of the *principal* on a loan by making payments

paydown FINANCE **partial repayment of loan** a repayment of part of a sum which has been borrowed

payee 1. FINANCE **person being paid** the person or organization to whom a payment has to be made **2.** BANKING **person to whom check is payable** the person or organization to whom a check is specified as payable. *Also called* ***drawee***

payer BANKING **person paying** the person or organization making a payment

paying agent FINANCE **institution paying interest or repaying capital** the institution responsible for making interest payments on a security and repaying capital at redemption. *Also called* ***disbursing agent***

paying banker UK BANKING **bank releasing money against check** the bank on which a bill of exchange or check is drawn

paying-in book UK BANKING **book of slips for listing bank deposits** a book of detachable slips that accompany money or checks being paid into a bank account

paying-in slip UK BANKING = ***deposit slip***

paymaster FINANCE **person issuing pay** the person responsible for paying an organization's employees or the members of a country's armed services

payment FINANCE **1. giving of money for goods or services** the act of giving an amount of money in exchange for goods or services **2. money paid for goods or services** an amount of money paid in exchange for goods or services

payment by results FINANCE **making pay dependent on work output** a system of pay that directly links an employee's salary to his or her work output

payment in advance FINANCE **payment made before goods are delivered** a payment made for goods when they are ordered and before they are delivered. *See also* ***prepayment***

payment in due course FINANCE **payment on fixed future date** the payment of a bill of exchange on a fixed date in the future

payment in kind FINANCE **something of equivalent value instead of money** an alternative form of pay given to employees in place of monetary reward but considered to be of equivalent value. A payment in kind may take the form of use of a car, purchase of goods at cost price, or other nonfinancial exchange that benefits the employee. It forms part of the total pay package rather than being an extra benefit. *See also* ***PIK note***

payment-in-kind note FINANCE *see* ***PIK note***

payment-in-lieu FINANCE **money as substitute** payment that is given in place of an entitlement

payoff FINANCE **1. final repayment** a final payment for something that is owed, for example, the outstanding balance of principal and interest on a mortgage or loan **2. profit or reward of some sort** a profit or reward, for example, from a plan or project that is financially successful

payout FINANCE **1. money given to somebody in difficulties** money that is given to help a company or person experiencing difficulties **2. amount paid** a particular sum of money offered, for example, in compensation, or from an insurance policy

payout ratio STOCKHOLDING & INVESTMENTS **amount of firm's earnings paid as dividends** an expression of the total dividends paid to stockholders as a percentage of a company's net profit in a specific period of time. This measures the likelihood of dividend payments being sustained, and is a useful indication of sustained profitability. The lower the ratio, the more secure the dividend, and the company's future.

The payout ratio is calculated by dividing annual dividends paid on common stock by earnings per share:

$$\frac{\text{Annual dividend}}{\text{Earnings per share}} = \text{Payout ratio}$$

Take the company whose earnings per share are $8 and its dividend payout is 2.1. Its payout ratio would be:

$$\frac{2.1}{8} = 0.263 \text{ or } 26.3\%$$

A high payout ratio clearly appeals to conservative investors seeking income. When coupled with weak or falling earnings, however, it could suggest an imminent dividend cut, or that the company is short-changing reinvestment to maintain its payout. A payout ratio above 75% is a warning. It suggests the company is failing to reinvest sufficient profits in its business, that the company's earnings are faltering, or that it is trying to attract investors who otherwise would not be interested. *Also called* ***dividend payout ratio***. *See also* ***dividend cover***

payroll ACCOUNTING **record of pay and deductions for each employee** a record showing for each employee his or her gross pay, deductions, and net pay. The payroll may also include details of the employer's associated employment costs.

PBR *abbr* FINANCE pre-Budget report

PBT *abbr* ACCOUNTING profit before tax

P/C *abbr* ACCOUNTING petty cash

PDR *abbr* STOCKHOLDING & INVESTMENTS price/dividend ratio

a–z

Dictionary

P/E STOCKHOLDING & INVESTMENTS *see price/earnings multiple, price/earnings ratio*

pecuniary FINANCE **of money** relating to or involving money

peg 1. CURRENCY & EXCHANGE **fix exchange rate of currency against others** to fix the exchange rate of one currency against that of another or of a basket of other currencies **2.** FINANCE **fix wages and salaries to control inflation** to fix wages and salaries during a period of inflation to help prevent an inflationary spiral

P/E multiple *abbr* STOCKHOLDING & INVESTMENTS price/earnings multiple

penalty FINANCE **money paid for breaking contract** an arbitrary prearranged sum that becomes payable if one party breaks a term of a contract or an undertaking. A common penalty is a high rate of interest on an unauthorized **overdraft**. *See also* **overdraft**

penalty rate *ANZ* FINANCE **high rate of overtime pay** a higher than normal rate of pay awarded for work performed outside normal working hours

penny share *UK* STOCKHOLDING & INVESTMENTS = **penny stock**

penny stock *US* STOCKHOLDING & INVESTMENTS **very low-priced stock** very low-priced stock, typically under one dollar, that is a speculative investment. *UK term* **penny share**

PEP *abbr* STOCKHOLDING & INVESTMENTS **former UK stock-based investment** in the United Kingdom, a stock-based tax-effective investment replaced by ISAs in 1999. *Full form* **Personal Equity Plan**

PER *abbr* STOCKHOLDING & INVESTMENTS price/earnings ratio

per annum FINANCE **in a year** in one year

P/E ratio *abbr* STOCKHOLDING & INVESTMENTS price/earnings ratio

per capita FINANCE **per person** average for each person

per capita income ECONOMICS **average income of group of people** the average income of each of a specific group of people, for example, the citizens of a country

perception of risk RISK = **risk perception**

per diem FINANCE, HR & PERSONNEL **rate allowed for each day** an amount of money paid per day, for example, for expenses when an employee is working away from the office

perfect capital market ECONOMICS **when buying and selling do not affect prices** a situation in which the decisions of buyers and sellers have no effect on market price in a **capital market**

perfect competition ECONOMICS **when no single buyer or seller affects price** a situation in which no individual buyer or seller can influence prices. In practice, perfect markets are characterized by few or no barriers to entry and by many buyers and sellers.

perfect hedge STOCKHOLDING & INVESTMENTS **investment with balanced risks** an investment that exactly balances the risk of another investment

performance bond BANKING **guarantee against third party failure to perform** a guarantee given by a bank or insurance company to a third party stating that it will pay a sum of money if its customer, the account holder, fails to complete a specific contract

performance fund STOCKHOLDING & INVESTMENTS **higher-risk investment fund expecting high returns** an investment fund designed to produce a high return, reflected in the higher risk involved

performance-related pay FINANCE **payment related to the quality of work** a payment system in which the level of pay is dependent on the employee's performance. Performance-related pay can be entirely dependent or only partly dependent on performance. There are usually three stages to a performance-related pay system: determining the criteria by which the employee is assessed, establishing whether the employee has met the criteria, and linking the employee's achievements to the pay structure. Performance measures can incorporate skills, knowledge, and behavioral indicators. The system can be compared to **payment by results**, which is based solely on quantitative productivity measures.

performance share *UK* STOCKHOLDING & INVESTMENTS = **performance stock**

performance stock *US* STOCKHOLDING & INVESTMENTS **higher-risk stock showing capital growth** a stock which is likely to show capital growth rather than income, which is a characteristic of stocks with a higher risk. *UK term* **performance share**

period bill *UK* FINANCE **bill of exchange with specific payment date** a bill of exchange payable on a specific date rather than on demand. *Also called* **term bill**

period-end ACCOUNTING **of end of accounting period** relating to the end of an accounting period when financial transactions for that period are finalized

period of account ACCOUNTING **time span covered by UK firm's accounts** the period covered by a UK firm's accounts, sometimes coinciding with the firm's **accounting period**

permanent interest-bearing shares STOCKHOLDING & INVESTMENTS **UK stock issued by credit union** in the United Kingdom, stock issued by the UK equivalent of a credit union to raise capital because the law prohibits it from raising capital in more conventional ways. *Abbr* **PIBS**

perpetual bond STOCKHOLDING & INVESTMENTS **bond without maturity date** a **bond** that has no date of maturity and pays interest in perpetuity

perpetual debenture FINANCE **debenture without maturity date** a **debenture** that has no date of maturity and pays interest in perpetuity

personal account 1. ACCOUNTING **record of amounts for or from individual** a record of amounts receivable from or payable to a person or an entity. In the United Kingdom, a collection of these accounts is known either as a sales/debtor ledger or a purchases/creditors ledger, or, more simply, as a **revenue**

ledger or a *purchase ledger*. In the United States, the terms *receivables ledger* and *payables ledger* are used. **2.** BANKING **bank account for individual** a bank account designed for a private individual rather than a business entity

Personal Equity Plan STOCKHOLDING & INVESTMENTS *see PEP*

personal financial planning FINANCE **person's short- and long-term financial arrangements** short- and long-term financial planning by somebody, either independently or with the assistance of a professional adviser. It will include the use of tax-efficient plans such as Individual Retirement Accounts, ensuring adequate provisions are being made for retirement, and examining short- and long-term borrowing requirements such as overdrafts and mortgages.

Personal Identification Number BANKING *see PIN*

personal income FINANCE **money person receives from earnings and other payments** the income received by somebody from various sources such as earnings, retirement funds, disability benefits, and dividends from investments

personal loan FINANCE **loan used for personal purpose** a loan from a financial institution to somebody for a personal use such as making home improvements or purchasing an automobile

personal property FINANCE **things belonging to somebody** property other than real estate that a person owns

person-to-person lending FINANCE = *social lending*

petty cash ACCOUNTING **amount kept for small payments** a small accessible store of cash used for minor business expenses. *Abbr* **P/C**

petty cash account ACCOUNTING **record of small cash receipts and payments** a record of relatively small cash receipts and payments, the balance representing the cash in the control of an individual, usually dealt with under an *imprest system*

petty cash voucher ACCOUNTING **document recording petty cash payments** a document supporting payments of small amounts of cash to employees under a petty cash system

petty expenses ACCOUNTING **small amounts spent on small items** small sums of money spent on such items as postage, taxi fares, or copying charges

phantom bid MERGERS & ACQUISITIONS **rumored company purchase** a reported but nonexistent attempt to buy a company

pharming E-COMMERCE, FRAUD **fraudulent poaching of online bank customers** the hijacking of online bank customers by infecting web browsers and redirecting them to fake websites, where they are asked to disclose their account details

phishing E-COMMERCE, FRAUD **fraud to obtain financial information** the fraudulent use of e-mail and fake websites to obtain financial information such as credit card numbers, passwords, and bank account information

physical asset ACCOUNTING **asset that is not cash or securities** an asset such as a building or equipment that has a physical presence, as opposed to cash or securities

PIBOR *abbr* BANKING Paris Interbank Offered Rate

PIBS *abbr* STOCKHOLDING & INVESTMENTS permanent interest-bearing shares

piece rate FINANCE **payment according to units completed** payment of a predetermined amount for each unit of output by an employee. The rate of pay is usually fixed subjectively, rather than by more objective techniques. Rates are said to be tight when it is difficult for an employee to earn a bonus and loose when bonuses are easily earned. Piece-rate systems are a form of *payment by results* or *performance-related pay*.

piecework FINANCE **work paid according to items produced** work for which employees are paid in accordance with the number of products produced or pieces of work done and not at an hourly rate

piggyback loan FINANCE **loan against same security as existing loan** a loan that is raised against the same security as an existing loan

piggyback rights STOCKHOLDING & INVESTMENTS **permission to sell existing shares with new shares** permission to sell existing shares in conjunction with the sale of similar shares in a new offering

PIK note FINANCE **debt finance paying interest on note redemption** a form of debt financing that pays interest only when the note is redeemed, although the interest rate is usually much higher than on ordinary debt. The issue of PIK notes constitutes the payment of interest for tax purposes, so if the notes are issued in the accounting period in which the interest accrues, the interest is tax deductible on an accrual basis and does not affect cash flow. *Full form* **payment-in-kind note**

PIN BANKING **number verifying card transaction** a set of numbers that is used to access an account at an ATM, a computer, or a telephone system, or to verify a credit or debit card at an electronic point of sale. *Full form* **Personal Identification Number**

pink dollar *US* FINANCE **money spent by gays and lesbians** money spent by gays and lesbians on goods and services that appeal to them. *UK term* **pink pound**

pink form STOCKHOLDING & INVESTMENTS **in the UK, stock application form for employees** in the United Kingdom, a preferential application form for an initial public offering that is reserved for the employees of the company being floated. *Also called* **preferential form**

pink paper *UK* FINANCE (informal) = *Financial Times*

pink pound *UK* FINANCE = *pink dollar*

Pink 'Un *UK* FINANCE **Financial Times** an informal name for the London-based newspaper the *Financial Times*. It is printed on pink paper. (informal)

pip CURRENCY & EXCHANGE **smallest unit in currency price** the smallest unit of change in the bid or ask price of a currency

piracy FRAUD **illegal copying** illegal copying of a product such as software or music

a–z

Dictionary

placement *US* STOCKHOLDING & INVESTMENTS = *private placement*

placement fee *UK* STOCKHOLDING & INVESTMENTS = *commission*

plain vanilla FINANCE **standard form of financial product** a basic or standard form of a *financial instrument* such as an *option*, *bond*, or *swap* (slang)

planned economy ECONOMICS **economic system completely controlled by government** an economic system in which the government plans all business activity, regulates supply, sets production targets, and itemizes work to be done. *Also called* **command economy**. *See also* **central planning**

plant ACCOUNTING **fixed assets producing goods** the capital assets used to produce goods, typically factories, production lines, and large equipment

plastic *or* plastic money BANKING **debit or credit card** a payment system using a debit or credit card, not cash or checks (informal). *See also* **credit card, debit card, multifunctional card**

plenitude ECONOMICS **hypothetical situation with abundant supply of products** a hypothetical condition of an economy in which manufacturing technology has been perfected and scarcity is replaced by an abundance of products

plough back *UK* FINANCE = *plow back*

ploughed back profits *UK* FINANCE = *plowed back profits*

plow back *US* FINANCE **reinvest earnings instead of paying dividends** to reinvest a company's earnings in the business instead of paying them out as dividends. *UK term* **plough back**

plowed back profits *US* FINANCE **retained profits** the amount of profit kept within the company for reinvestment, not distributed. *UK term* **ploughed back profits**

plum *UK* STOCKHOLDING & INVESTMENTS **successful investment** an investment that yields a good return (slang)

PN *abbr* FINANCE promissory note

point FINANCE **1. unit used in calculating a value** a unit used for calculation of a value, such as a hundredth of a percentage point for interest rates **2. unit on scale** a single unit on any scale of measurement, such as a salary scale or range of prices

poison pill MERGERS & ACQUISITIONS **deterrent measure taken to avoid hostile takeover** a measure taken by a company to avoid a hostile takeover, for example, the purchase of a business interest that will make the company unattractive to the potential buyer (slang). *Also called* **show stopper**

political economy ECONOMICS **study of government and economics** the study of the ways in which the politics and economic organization of a country interact

political price ECONOMICS **bad effect on government of decision** the negative impact on a government of a policy decision such as raising interest rates

political risk ECONOMICS **possible bad effect on government of decision** the potential negative impact on a government of a policy decision such as raising interest rates

Ponzi scheme FRAUD **banking fraud** a fraudulent pyramid selling activity that offers investors high returns which are paid directly from the money deposited by new investors. When new deposits cannot match payments, the organization fails. The fraud is named after Charles Ponzi, who first set up such a scheme in the United States in 1920.

pool FINANCE **collateral underpinning loan** a group of mortgages and other collateral that is used to back a loan

poop *US* FINANCE **somebody with privileged information** a person who has *inside information* on a financial deal (slang)

pork bellies FINANCE **meat of pigs traded as commodity** meat from the underside of pig carcasses used to make bacon, traded as *futures* on some US commodities exchanges

portfolio STOCKHOLDING & INVESTMENTS **investments held by one owner** a set of investments, such as stocks and bonds, owned by one person or organization. *Also called* **investment portfolio**

portfolio immunization STOCKHOLDING & INVESTMENTS **measures to maintain investment value** measures taken by traders to protect their holdings against loss or undue risk

portfolio insurance STOCKHOLDING & INVESTMENTS **options protecting portfolio** the use of *options* that provide *hedges* against the set of investments held

portfolio investment STOCKHOLDING & INVESTMENTS **investment seeking spread of assets** a form of investment that attempts to achieve a mixture of securities in order to minimize risk and maximize return

portfolio management STOCKHOLDING & INVESTMENTS **trading to maximize investor's profit** the professional management of investment portfolios with the goal of minimizing risk and maximizing return

portfolio manager STOCKHOLDING & INVESTMENTS **specialist in investment management** a person or company that specializes in managing an investment portfolio on behalf of investors. *See also* **money manager**

portfolio theory STOCKHOLDING & INVESTMENTS **idea that variety of investments bring best results** a strategy for managing a portfolio of investments in order to minimize risk and maximize return by having a variety of types of investments. *Also called* **modern portfolio theory**. *See also* **CAPM**

position STOCKHOLDING & INVESTMENTS **size of holding of one owner** the number of shares of a security that are owned by a person or organization

position limit STOCKHOLDING & INVESTMENTS **maximum holding for individual or group** the largest amount of a security that any group or individual may own

positive carry STOCKHOLDING & INVESTMENTS **when investment return is greater than cost** a situation in which the cost of financing an investment is less than the return obtained from it

positive cash flow FINANCE **when firm's income is greater than outflow** a situation in which more money is coming into a company than is going out

positive economics ECONOMICS **study of verifiable economic theories** the study of economic propositions that can be verified by observing the real economy

positive yield curve STOCKHOLDING & INVESTMENTS **when long-term investment return exceeds short-term** a visual representation of a situation in which the yield on a short-term investment is less than that on a long-term investment. In a long-term investment, an investor expects a higher return because his or her money is tied up and at risk for a longer period of time.

postal account BANKING **account operated only by mail** an account for which all dealings are done by post, thereby reducing *overhead costs* and allowing a higher level of *interest* to be paid

postal vote UK FINANCE = *mail ballot*

post-balance sheet event ACCOUNTING **incident affecting accounts after balance sheet completed** something that happens after the date when a balance sheet is completed but before it is officially approved by the directors, that affects a company's financial position

postindustrial society ECONOMICS **economy not reliant on heavy industry** a society in which the resources of labor and capital are replaced by those of knowledge and information as the main sources of wealth creation. The postindustrial society involves a shift in focus from manufacturing industries to service industries and is enabled by technological advances.

pot 1. STOCKHOLDING & INVESTMENTS **unreleased portion of stock issue** the part of a new stock issue that is not released to the public and is only available for purchase by institutional investors **2.** US FINANCE **amount collected for specific use** an amount of money collected from the members of a group for a specific purpose **pot of gold** FINANCE a large amount of money, especially one that is achieved by accident or good luck **pot of money** FINANCE an amount of money assigned to a specific purpose **pots of money** FINANCE an extremely large amount of money

potential GDP ECONOMICS **full value of country's production capacity** a measure of the real value of the services and goods that can be produced when a country's factors of production are fully employed. *See also GDP*

pot trust FINANCE **trust for group of people** a trust, typically created in a will, for a group of beneficiaries

pound CURRENCY & EXCHANGE **main currency unit in UK and other countries** a unit of currency used in the United Kingdom and many other countries including Cyprus, Egypt, Lebanon, Malta, Sudan, and Syria

pound cost averaging UK STOCKHOLDING & INVESTMENTS = *dollar cost averaging*

pound sterling CURRENCY & EXCHANGE **official UK currency** the official term for the currency used in the United Kingdom

PPP *abbr* **1.** CURRENCY & EXCHANGE purchasing power parity **2.** BUSINESS public private partnership

preauthorized electronic debit US BANKING **agreed transfer between bank accounts** a system in which a payer agrees to let a bank make payments from an account to somebody else's account. *UK term direct debit*

pre-Budget report FINANCE **fall forecast of UK government's economic plans** in the United Kingdom, an economic forecast the government has to present in the fall of each year, reporting on progress since the Budget in the spring and outlining government spending plans prior to the next Budget. *Abbr* **PBR**

preceding year ACCOUNTING **previous fiscal year** the year before the fiscal year in question

preceding year basis ACCOUNTING **using previous year's accounts** the principle of assessing income or profits based on the figures for the year before the fiscal year in question. *Abbr* **PYB**

precious metals FINANCE **high value metals** rare metals with a high economic value, especially gold, silver, and platinum

predatory lending FINANCE **unfair lending practices** the practice of encouraging people to borrow in an unfair or unprincipled way, especially if the loan is greater than a borrower can reasonably be expected to repay, or is based on personal property such as a house or car which will be lost if the borrower defaults

pre-emption right UK STOCKHOLDING & INVESTMENTS = *pre-emptive right*

pre-emptive right US STOCKHOLDING & INVESTMENTS **right of stockholder to first purchase of new stock** the right of a stockholder who already owns stock in a company to maintain proportional ownership by being first to purchase stock in a new issue. *UK term pre-emption right*

preference share UK STOCKHOLDING & INVESTMENTS = *preferred stock*

preferential creditor FINANCE **creditor who must be paid before others** a creditor who is entitled to payment, especially from a bankrupt, before other creditors

preferential form STOCKHOLDING & INVESTMENTS = *pink form*

preferential issue STOCKHOLDING & INVESTMENTS **stock for specific buyers** an issue of stock available only to designated buyers

preferential payment FINANCE **payment to priority creditor** a payment to a *preferential creditor*, whose debt has first claim on a bankrupt or company that is winding up

preferred stock US STOCKHOLDING & INVESTMENTS **stock receiving dividend or repayment before others** stock that entitles the owner to preference in the distribution of dividends and the proceeds of liquidation in the event of bankruptcy. *UK term* **preference share**

pre-financing FINANCE **securing funding before project begins** the practice of arranging funding in advance of the start date of a project

preliminary announcement ACCOUNTING **initial announcement of firm's financial results** an announcement of a company's full-year financial results, which are given out to the press before the detailed annual report is released

preliminary prospectus STOCKHOLDING & INVESTMENTS **details about firm given before initial public offering** a document issued prior to an ***initial public offering*** that provides details about the company and its financial situation. *Also called* **red herring**

Premiers' Conference FINANCE **annual meeting of Australian federal and state heads** an annual meeting at which the premiers of the states and territories of Australia meet with the federal government to discuss their funding allocations

premium 1. FINANCE **extra cost for scarcity** a higher price paid for a scarce product or service **2.** FINANCE **extra charge for high quality** a pricing method that uses high price to indicate high quality **3.** STOCKHOLDING & INVESTMENTS **price paid for option** the price a purchaser of a traded ***option*** pays to its seller **4.** STOCKHOLDING & INVESTMENTS **difference between futures price and cash price** the difference between the futures price and the cash price of an underlying asset **5.** INSURANCE **price of insurance contract** the amount paid for an insurance contract, which is needed before the contract is valid **at a premium 1.** FINANCE of a fixed interest security, at an issue price above its nominal value **2.** FINANCE at a price that is considered expensive in relation to others **3.** STOCKHOLDING & INVESTMENTS of a new issue, at a trading price above the one offered to investors

Premium Bond STOCKHOLDING & INVESTMENTS **non-interest-bearing UK security eligible for prize draw** in the United Kingdom, a nonmarketable security issued by National Savings & Investments at £1 each that pays no interest but is entered into a draw every month to win prizes from £25 to £1 million. There are many lower value prizes, but only one £1 million prize. The bonds are repayable upon demand.

premium pay plan FINANCE **higher pay scale for top employees** an enhanced pay scale for high performing employees. A premium pay plan can be offered as an incentive to motivate employees, rewarding such achievements as high productivity, long service, or completion of training with an increased pay package.

premoney valuation *or* **premoney value** FINANCE **firm's value before capital investors contribute** the assessed value of a business before ***venture capital*** or other capital investors make their investment

prepaid interest FINANCE **interest paid early** interest paid in advance of the date on which it is due

prepayment FINANCE **payment of debt before due date** the payment of a debt before it is due to be paid

prepayment penalty FINANCE **charge made for early payment** a charge that may be levied if a payment, such as one on a mortgage or loan, is made before it is due to be paid. The penalty compensates the lender or seller for potential lost interest.

prepayment privilege FINANCE **payment before due date without penalty** the right to make a payment, such as one on a loan or mortgage, before it is due to be paid, without penalty

prepayment risk FINANCE, RISK **risk that prepayment will reduce interest income** the risk that a debtor will avoid interest charges by making partial or total payment in advance on a mortgage or loan, especially when interest rates fall

prequalification 1. FINANCE, MORTGAGES **evaluation of likely borrower** the process of establishing the financial circumstances of a borrower or mortgage customer before a loan is formally applied for **2.** MARKETING **evaluation of likely customer** a sales technique in which the potential value of a prospect is carefully evaluated through research

prerefunding STOCKHOLDING & INVESTMENTS **using funds from new bond to repay another** the process of issuing a longer-term bond in order to take advantage of a drop in interest rates and use the funds to pay off another bond issued earlier

present value FINANCE **1. future value of asset, discounted for inflation** the amount that a future interest in a financial asset is currently worth, discounted for inflation. *Also called* **discounted value 2. current value of future income, minus accruing interest** the value now of an amount of money that somebody expects to receive at a future date, calculated by subtracting any interest that will accrue in the interim

preservation of capital STOCKHOLDING & INVESTMENTS **cautious investment strategy** an approach to financial management that protects a person's or company's capital by arranging additional forms of finance

pre-syndicate bid STOCKHOLDING & INVESTMENTS **advance bid on NASDAQ exchange** in the *NASDAQ* system, a bid made before a public offering in order to stabilize the price of the stock on offer

previous balance ACCOUNTING **closing balance of previous accounting period** a balance in an account at the end of the *accounting period* before the current one

price-book ratio STOCKHOLDING & INVESTMENTS = ***price-to-book ratio***

price controls ECONOMICS **government limits on prices to control inflation** measures used by a government to set prices in order to protect consumers from rapidly rising prices. Many economists believe that price controls actually hurt the economy by creating shortages and should only be used in an emergency.

price discovery ECONOMICS **establishment of price in free market** the process by which price is determined by negotiation in a free market

price/dividend ratio STOCKHOLDING & INVESTMENTS **price of stock divided by annual dividend paid** a ratio derived from the price of a stock divided by the annual dividend paid on a share, which gives an indication of how much has to be paid to receive $1 of dividends. *Abbr* **PDR**

price/earnings multiple STOCKHOLDING & INVESTMENTS **stock price divided by its earnings** the number of times by which the price of stock is greater than the earnings per share. *Abbr* **P/E multiple**. *See also* **price/earnings ratio**

price/earnings ratio STOCKHOLDING & INVESTMENTS **price of stock divided by earnings per share** a company's stock price divided by earnings per share.

While earnings per share (EPS) is an actual amount of money, usually expressed in cents per share, the P/E ratio has no units, it is just a number. Thus if a quoted company has a stock price of $100 and EPS of $12 for the last published year, then it has a historical P/E ratio of 8.3. If analysts are forecasting for the next year EPS of, say, $14, then the forecast P/E ratio is 7.1.

The P/E ratio is predominantly useful in comparisons with other stocks rather than in isolation. For example, if the average P/E ratio in the market is 20, there will be many stocks with P/E ratios well above and well below this, for a variety of reasons. Similarly, in a particular sector, the P/E ratios will frequently vary from the sector average, even though the constituent companies may all be engaged in similar businesses. The reason is that even two businesses doing the same thing will not always be doing it as profitably as each other. One may be far more efficient, as demonstrated by a history of rising EPS compared with the flat EPS picture of the other over a series of years, and the market might recognize this by awarding the more profitable stock a higher P/E ratio. *Abbr* **PER**

price effect ECONOMICS **how price changes affect economy** the impact of price changes on a market or economy

price elasticity of demand ECONOMICS **how demand responds to price changes** the percentage change in demand divided by the percentage change in price of a good

price elasticity of supply ECONOMICS **how supply responds to price changes** the percentage change in supply divided by the percentage change in price of a good

price index ECONOMICS **index measuring inflation** an index such as the consumer price index that measures inflation

price indicator ECONOMICS **measure of general price trends** a measurable variable that can be used as an indicator of the price of something, for example the number of home loans arranged can be an indicator for rising or falling house prices

price-insensitive ECONOMICS **describing essential goods or services with unvarying sales** used to describe a good or service for which sales remain constant no matter what its price because it is essential to buyers

price instability ECONOMICS **situation in which prices change frequently** a situation in which the prices of goods alter daily or even hourly

prices and incomes policy ECONOMICS **government regulations on prices and wages** a policy that limits price or wage increases through government regulations

price-sensitive ECONOMICS **describing goods or services with price-dependent sales** used to describe a good or service for which sales fluctuate depending on its price, often because it is a nonessential item

price stability ECONOMICS **insignificant changes in prices** a situation in which there is little fluctuation in the price of goods or services overall

price support ECONOMICS **government spending to keep prices from falling** government assistance designed to keep market prices from falling below a minimum level

price-to-book ratio STOCKHOLDING & INVESTMENTS **ratio of firm's market value to theoretical value** the ratio of the value of all of a company's stock to its *book value*. *Also called* **price-book ratio**

price-to-cash-flow ratio STOCKHOLDING & INVESTMENTS **ratio of firm's market value to cash flow** the ratio of the value of all of a company's stock to its cash flow for the most recent complete fiscal year

price-to-sales ratio STOCKHOLDING & INVESTMENTS **ratio of firm's market value to sales** the ratio of the value of all of a company's stock to its sales for the previous twelve months, a way of measuring the relative value of a stock when compared with others.

The P/S ratio is obtained by dividing the *market capitalization* by the latest published annual sales figure. So a company with a capitalization of $1 billion and sales of $3 billion would have a P/S ratio of 0.33.

P/S will vary with the type of industry. You would expect, for example, that many retailers and other large-scale distributors of goods would have very high sales in relation to their market capitalizations—in other words, a very low P/S. Equally, manufacturers of high-value items would generally have much lower sales figures and thus higher P/S ratios.

A company with a lower P/S is cheaper than one with a higher ratio, particularly if they are in the same sector so that a direct comparison is more appropriate. It means that each share of the lower P/S company is buying more of its sales than those of the higher P/S company.

It is important to note that a stock which is cheaper only on P/S grounds is not necessarily the more attractive stock. There will frequently be reasons why it has a lower ratio than another similar company, most commonly because it is less profitable.

price-weighted index ECONOMICS **index adjusted for price changes** an index of production or market value that is adjusted for changes that occur in prices

primary account number BANKING **credit card identifier** an identifier for a credit card used in secure electronic transactions

primary earnings per (common) share STOCKHOLDING & INVESTMENTS **profit from each current share of common stock** a measure of earnings per share calculated on the basis of the number of shares of **common stock** actually held by investors, not including exercisable warrants and options. *See also fully diluted earnings per (common) share, earnings per share*

primary liability FINANCE, INSURANCE **responsibility as first payer of financial claims** a responsibility to pay before anyone else who also has financial responsibility for financial claims such as damages covered by insurance

primary sector ECONOMICS **part of economy involved in production** businesses operating in the sector of a country's economy that is involved in producing goods

prime BANKING = *prime rate*

prime assets ratio BANKING **Australian banks' obligatory holding in secure assets** in Australia, the proportion of total liabilities that banks are obliged by the Reserve Bank to hold in highly secure assets such as cash and government securities. *Abbr* **PAR**

prime bill FINANCE **risk-free bill of exchange** an agreement that involves no risk of default, setting out an instruction to pay a particular person a fixed sum of money on a particular date or when the person requests payment

prime broker STOCKHOLDING & INVESTMENTS **investment bank servicing hedge fund** an investment bank that provides borrowing, lending, and settlement services to a *hedge fund*. Such financial services are often considered the most profitable activity for a major bank but great losses can be incurred if the hedge fund fails.

prime lending BANKING **safe lending to creditworthy borrower** lending to borrowers who have no delinquencies or defaults and no historical or current financial problems. *Also called vanilla lending*

prime loan BANKING **safe loan to creditworthy borrower** a loan to a borrower who is regarded as being highly creditworthy, has no obvious financial difficulties and a good payment record, and is therefore very likely to repay the loan. *Also called vanilla loan*

prime rate *or* **prime interest rate** BANKING **in US, best interest rate on offer** in the United States, the lowest interest rate that commercial banks offer on loans to well-regarded customers. It is analogous to the *base rate* in the United Kingdom. *Also called prime*

priming FINANCE = *pump priming*

principal FINANCE **original amount lent** the original amount of a loan or investment, not including any *interest*. *See also mortgage*

principal shareholders UK STOCKHOLDING & INVESTMENTS = *principal stockholders*

principal stockholders US STOCKHOLDING & INVESTMENTS **owners of majority of stock** the people who own the largest percentage of stock in a business or organization. *UK term principal shareholders*

prior charge percentage STOCKHOLDING & INVESTMENTS = *priority percentage*

priority percentage STOCKHOLDING & INVESTMENTS **share of profit paid to priority stockholders** the proportion of a business's net profit that is paid in interest to holders of *debt capital* and *preferred stock*. *Also called prior charge percentage*

prior lien bond STOCKHOLDING & INVESTMENTS **bond giving priority claim on debtor's assets** a bond whose holder has more claim on a debtor's assets than holders of other types of bonds

prior year adjustment ACCOUNTING **alteration to accounts of previous years** an adjustment made to accounts for previous years, because of changes in accounting policies or because of errors

private bank BANKING **1. bank owned by individual or small group** a bank that is owned by a single person or a limited number of private stockholders **2. bank for wealthy clients** a bank that provides banking facilities to high net worth individuals. *See also private banking* **3. independent bank in country with state-owned institutions** a bank that is not state-owned in a country where most banks are owned by the government

private banking BANKING **banking services offered to wealthy clients** a service offered by some financial institutions to high net worth individuals. In addition to standard banking services, it will typically include portfolio management and advisory services on taxation, including estate planning.

private cost ECONOMICS **cost to individual consumer or firm of consumption** the cost incurred by individuals or companies when they consume resources

private debt FINANCE **nongovernmental borrowings** money owed by individuals and organizations other than governments

private enterprise ECONOMICS **businesses not controlled by government** business or industry that is controlled by companies or individuals rather than the government

private equity financing FINANCE = *venture capital*

private income FINANCE **income separate from salary** income from dividends, interest, or rent which is not part of a salary

private investor STOCKHOLDING & INVESTMENTS **ordinary person investing money** an ordinary person who makes investments and who is not in the business of investing other people's money

private placement US STOCKHOLDING & INVESTMENTS **sale of securities directly to investors** the sale of securities directly to institutions for investment rather than resale. *UK term private placing*

private placing UK STOCKHOLDING & INVESTMENTS = *private placement*

private property FINANCE **property not for general public use** property or assets that are owned by a person or group and not for use by the general public

private sector ECONOMICS **part of economy not controlled by government** the section of the economy that is financed and controlled by individuals or private institutions such as companies, stockholders, or investment groups. *See also* ***public sector***

private sector investment ECONOMICS **non-government investment** investment by the private enterprise sector of an economy

private treaty FINANCE **land sale without auction** the sale of land arranged by seller and buyer without a public auction

probability measure RISK, STATISTICS **evaluation of chance of event occurring** in a statistical study, a calculation of the likelihood that a given event will occur

proceeds FINANCE **income from sale** the money derived from a sale or other commercial transaction

procyclical ECONOMICS **1. increasing in line with other factor** tending to increase and decrease in tandem with another factor. *See also* ***countercyclical* 2. promoting instability** likely to increase instability or fluctuation

procyclicality ECONOMICS **positive feedback in linked factors** a pattern of positive reinforcement in the behavior of linked factors that can intensify fluctuations in a system. For example, credit expands as the financial climate improves, but in a subsequent period of economic contraction credit shrinks and financial constraint increases

producer price index ECONOMICS **statistical measure of wholesale prices** the *weighted average* of the prices of commodities that firms buy from other firms

productive capital FINANCE **assets producing income** the part of a company's assets that generate an income

profit FINANCE **1. difference between higher selling price and lower purchase price** the difference between the selling price and the purchase price of a product when the selling price is higher. In the case of a security or financial instrument the profit will include any accrued interest. **2. income exceeding expenditure** in business transactions, the amount by which income is greater than expenditure **3. money made by activity** the amount of money that is made from a business undertaking or transaction **turn a profit** to make a profit from a business activity

profitability FINANCE **1. extent of profit** the degree to which an individual, company, or single transaction achieves financial gain **2. generation of profit** the ability to achieve financial gain from a sale or other commercial transaction

profitability index FINANCE **current value of investment divided by original investment** the present value of the amount of money an investment will earn divided by the amount of the original investment

profitability threshold FINANCE **start point of making profit** the point at which a business begins to make profits from its activities or from a specific product

profitable FINANCE **producing a profit** used to refer to a product, service, or business that achieves financial gain

profit after tax ACCOUNTING = *net profit*

profit and loss ACCOUNTING **difference between income and costs** the difference between a company's income and its costs as shown in its accounts. *Abbr* **P&L**

profit and loss account *or* profit and loss statement ACCOUNTING **record of firm's external financial transactions** the summary record of a company's sales revenues and expenses over a period, providing a calculation of profits or losses during that time. *Also called* ***trading account***

profit before tax ACCOUNTING **amount of profit before tax** the amount that a company or investor has made, before tax is deducted. *Abbr* **PBT**

profit center ACCOUNTING **business unit responsible for own costs and profits** a person, unit, or department within an organization that is considered separately when calculating profit. Profit centers are used as part of management control systems. They operate with a degree of autonomy with regard to marketing and pricing, and have responsibility for their own costs, revenues, and profits.

profit distribution STOCKHOLDING & INVESTMENTS, FINANCE **allocation of profits** the allocation of profits to different categories of recipients such as stockholders and owners, or for different purposes such as research or investment

profit from ordinary activities ACCOUNTING **profits gained from usual business** profits earned in the normal course of business, as opposed to profits from extraordinary sources such as windfall payments

profit margin ACCOUNTING, OPERATIONS & PRODUCTION **amount by which revenues exceed expenses** the amount by which income is greater than expenditure. The profit margin of an individual product is the sale price minus the cost of production and associated costs such as distribution and advertising. The *net profit margin* or *return on sales* is net income after taxes divided by total sales. On a larger scale, the profit margin is an accounting ratio of company income compared with sales. The profit margin ratio can be used to compare the efficiency and profitability of a company over a number of years, or to compare different companies. The *gross profit margin* or *operating margin* of a company is its operating, or gross, profit divided by total sales. The level of profit reported is also influenced by the extent of the application of accounting conventions, and by the method of product costing used, for example, *marginal costing* or *absorption costing*.

profit sharing FINANCE **allocation of some profit to employees** the allocation of a proportion of a company's profit to employees by an issue of stock or other means

profit-sharing debenture STOCKHOLDING & INVESTMENTS **employee debenture linking payouts to company performance** a *debenture* held by an employee, the payments from which depend on the employing company's financial success

profits warning STOCKHOLDING & INVESTMENTS **firm's prediction of low profits** an announcement by a company of lower than expected profits for a specific period. *Also called* ***profit warning***

profit-taking STOCKHOLDING & INVESTMENTS sale of investments the act of selling investments in order to receive money for the profit they have made

profit warning STOCKHOLDING & INVESTMENTS = *profits warning*

pro forma balance sheet ACCOUNTING statement of projected financial position after planned transaction in the United States, a projection showing a business's financial statements after the completion of a planned transaction

pro-forma financial statement UK ACCOUNTING statement of projected financial position after planned transaction a projection showing a business's likely financial statements after the completion of a planned transaction

pro-forma invoice ACCOUNTING initial basic invoice an invoice that does not include all the details of a transaction, often sent before goods are supplied and followed by a final detailed invoice

program trading STOCKHOLDING & INVESTMENTS electronic trading of securities the trading of securities electronically, by sending messages from the investor's computer to a market

progress payment FINANCE payment of project work in stages a payment of a portion of the total contracted price of a project that is made at a agreed stage of completion

project finance FINANCE funds raised for specific venture money raised for a specific self-contained venture such as a construction or development project

projection FINANCE financial forecast a forecast of conditions that will occur in the future, especially the ways in which they are likely to affect business operations

project risk analysis *or* project risk assessment GENERAL MANAGEMENT, RISK assessment of risks to activities the identification of *risks* to which a project is exposed, and the assessment of the potential impact of those risks on the project. Project risk analysis forms part of the process of *project management* and is a specialized type of *risk analysis*.

promissory note FINANCE agreement to pay for something received a written contract to pay money to a person or organization for a good or service received. *Abbr* **PN**

property FINANCE asset owned by somebody *assets*, such as real estate or goods, that a person or organization owns

property bond STOCKHOLDING & INVESTMENTS bond with property as collateral a bond for which real estate is collateral

proprietors' interest FINANCE owners' investment in business an amount of money which the owners of a business have invested in the business

pro rata FINANCE at a proportional rate at a rate that is in proportion to something. For example, several investors in a company may share the profits of that company in proportion to their ownership interest.

prospective dividend STOCKHOLDING & INVESTMENTS = *forecast dividend*

prospective P/E ratio STOCKHOLDING & INVESTMENTS P/E ratio forecast on expected dividends an assessment of the *price/earnings ratio* that can be expected for the future on the basis of forecast dividends

prospectus STOCKHOLDING & INVESTMENTS document accompanying sale of securities a description of a company's operations, financial background, prospects, and the detailed terms and conditions relating to an offer for sale or placing of its stock by notice, circular, advertisement, or any form of invitation which offers securities to the public

protective put buying STOCKHOLDING & INVESTMENTS purchase of options to sell something already owned the purchase of *options* to sell *financial instruments* that are the same as some the purchaser already owns

protest FINANCE proof that bill of exchange is unpaid an official document that proves that a bill of exchange has not been paid

provision ACCOUNTING money earmarked for potential future expense a sum set aside in the accounts of an organization in anticipation of a future expense, often for doubtful debts. *See also* **bad debt**

proxy CORPORATE GOVERNANCE surrogate voter at company meeting somebody who votes on behalf of another person at a company meeting

proxy fight CORPORATE GOVERNANCE consideration of proxy votes in settling disagreement the use of *proxy votes* to settle a contentious issue at a company meeting

proxy form *or* proxy card CORPORATE GOVERNANCE form that stockholders use to appoint proxy a form that stockholders receive with their invitations to attend an annual meeting, and that they fill in if they want to appoint somebody to vote for them on a resolution

proxy statement CORPORATE GOVERNANCE firm's notification to stockholders of voting rights a notice that a company sends to stockholders, allowing them to vote and giving them all the information they need to vote in an informed way

proxy vote CORPORATE GOVERNANCE vote made by somebody authorized by absent person a vote given by somebody who is present at a company meeting and has been authorized by a person who is not present to vote on his or her behalf

prudence TREASURY MANAGEMENT *see* **prudence concept**

prudence concept TREASURY MANAGEMENT principle of not anticipating profits in accounts the principle that revenue and profits are not anticipated but are included in the *profit and loss account* only when realized in the form either of cash or of other assets, the ultimate cash realization of which can be assessed with reasonable certainty. Provision is made for all known liabilities (expenses and losses) whether the amount of these is known with certainty or is a best estimate in the light of the information available.

prudent FINANCE careful and sensible about money careful and exercising good judgment, especially in financial matters

prudential ratio BANKING, REGULATION & COMPLIANCE in EU, ratio of capital to assets in the European Union, the regulations covering the ratio of capital to assets that a bank should have

prudent man rule FINANCE rule requiring trustees to act carefully the assumption that trustees who make financial decisions on behalf of other people will act carefully, as any prudent person usually would

PSBR *abbr* FINANCE public sector borrowing requirement (see *public sector cash requirement*)

PSI 20 MARKETS, STOCKHOLDING & INVESTMENTS main Portuguese stock market index an index of the 20 most-actively traded stocks on the *Euronext Lisbon* exchange. It was established on December 31, 1992, with a base value of 3,000.

Public Accounts Committee FINANCE UK House of Commons committee monitoring government spending in the United Kingdom, a committee of the House of Commons that examines the spending of each department and ministry

public debt FINANCE money owed by government the money that a government or a group of governments owes

public deposits FINANCE money of UK government departments in the United Kingdom, the balances to the credit of the government held at the Bank of England

public expenditure FINANCE government spending on citizens' needs spending by the government of a country on items such as pension provision and infrastructure enhancement

public financing FINANCE money that governments raise and spend the money raised by means of taxation and borrowing, and spent by governments, or the process of raising and spending this money

public funds FINANCE money that government spends money that a government has available for expenditure

public issue STOCKHOLDING & INVESTMENTS offer of stock to public offering a new issue of stock for sale to the public. An issue of this type is often advertised in the press. *See also offer for sale, offer by prospectus*

public offering STOCKHOLDING & INVESTMENTS raising of funds via offer of stock a method of raising money used by a company in which it invites the public to apply for shares

public placement US STOCKHOLDING & INVESTMENTS restricted selling of stock in public company the selling of stock in a publicly held corporation to a limited number of designated buyers. *UK term public placing. See also private placement*

public placing UK STOCKHOLDING & INVESTMENTS = *public placement*

public sector borrowing requirement FINANCE see *public sector cash requirement*

public sector cash requirement FINANCE difference between revenue and expenses of public sector the difference between the income and the expenditure of the public sector.

It was formerly called the *public sector borrowing requirement*.

public spending ECONOMICS government expenditure spending by the government of a country on publiclyprovided goods and services

published accounts UK ACCOUNTING = *earnings report*

pump-and-dump STOCKHOLDING & INVESTMENTS illegal exaggeration of value of stock for profit an illegal practice in which the owner of a stock makes false claims about the stock, exaggerating its value, then sells it at a profit (slang)

pump priming FINANCE injection of funds to boost business the injection of further investment in order to revitalize a company or economy in stagnation, or to help a *startup* business over a critical period. Pump priming has a similar effect to the provision of *seed capital*.

punter STOCKHOLDING & INVESTMENTS speculator in stock market a person who hopes to make a quick profit in a stock market (slang)

purchase FINANCE **1.** something bought a product or service that somebody is going to buy or has bought **2.** to buy something to buy a product or service

purchase acquisition MERGERS & ACQUISITIONS, ACCOUNTING accounting procedures for mergers the standard accounting procedures that must be followed when one company merges with another. *Also called acquisition accounting*

purchase ledger UK ACCOUNTING = *payables ledger*

purchasing power FINANCE measure of ability to buy goods and services a measure of the ability of a person, organization, or sector to buy goods and services

purchasing power parity CURRENCY & EXCHANGE theory linking exchange rate to purchasing power a theory that the exchange rate between two currencies is in equilibrium when the purchasing power of currency is the same in each country. If a basket of goods costs £100 in the United Kingdom and $150 for an equivalent in the United States, for equilibrium to exist, the exchange rate would be expected to be £1 = $1.50. If this were not the case, *arbitrage* would be expected to take place until equilibrium was restored. *Abbr* **PPP**

pure endowment FINANCE gift with conditions attached a gift that can only be used in the way laid down by its donor

purpose credit STOCKHOLDING & INVESTMENTS credit for purchasing securities credit obtained with the intention of buying and selling securities

put *or* put option STOCKHOLDING & INVESTMENTS option to sell stock an option to sell stock within an agreed time at a specific price

put bond STOCKHOLDING & INVESTMENTS bond redeemable at specific date before maturity a bond that can be redeemed at face value at a specified time before its maturity date

PV *abbr* FINANCE present value

PYB *abbr* ACCOUNTING preceding year basis

a–z

Dictionary

pyramiding 1. FINANCE **illegal payment of interest from new deposits** the illegal practice of using new investors' deposits to pay the interest on the deposits made by existing investors **2.** MERGERS & ACQUISITIONS **process of acquiring increasingly large companies** the process of building up a major group by acquiring controlling interests in many different companies, each larger than the original company

Q

Q1 *abbr* ACCOUNTING first quarter

Q2 *abbr* ACCOUNTING second quarter

Q3 *abbr* ACCOUNTING third quarter

Q4 *abbr* ACCOUNTING fourth quarter

qard *or* **qard hassan** FINANCE **interest-free loan** in Islamic financing, a loan, which under Islamic law is always free of profit. A qard may also be a bank deposit, which is considered a loan to a bank for its use but which must be returned to the depositor upon request.

qualification of accounts ACCOUNTING = *auditors' qualification*

qualification payment FINANCE **financial reward for academic qualification** an additional payment sometimes made to employees of New Zealand companies who have gained an academic qualification relevant to their job

qualified auditor's report ACCOUNTING = *adverse opinion*

qualified domestic trust FINANCE **trust giving benefits to non-US spouse** in the United States, a trust established by a US citizen for a noncitizen spouse that affords tax advantages to the spouse at the time of the citizen's death

qualified listed security STOCKHOLDING & INVESTMENTS **security that can be purchased by regulated entity** a security that is eligible for purchase by a regulated entity such as a trust

qualified valuer FINANCE **professional person conducting valuation** a person conducting a valuation who holds a recognized and relevant professional qualification. The person must also have recent post-qualification experience and sufficient knowledge of the state of the market with reference to the location and category of the tangible fixed asset being valued.

qualifying distribution STOCKHOLDING & INVESTMENTS **former UK dividend payment** formerly in the United Kingdom, the payment to a stockholder of a dividend on which *advance corporation tax* was paid

qualifying period FINANCE **period needed for eligibility** a period of time that has to pass before somebody is eligible for something, for example, a grant or subsidy

qualifying shares STOCKHOLDING & INVESTMENTS **stockholding required before rights are granted** the number of shares of

stocksomebody needs to hold to be eligible for something such as a bonus issue

quality bond STOCKHOLDING & INVESTMENTS **bond issued by safe firm** a bond issued by an organization that has an excellent credit rating

quality equity STOCKHOLDING & INVESTMENTS **equity with good performance history** an equity with a good track record of earnings and dividends. *See also* **blue chip**

quant FINANCE **1.** = *quantitative analyst* **2.** = *quantitative analysis*

quantitative analysis FINANCE **numerical assessment of financial variables** the use of mathematical and statistical models in the evaluation of financial data of all kinds. *Also called* **quant** (sense 2). *See also* **chartist, qualitative analysis, technical analysis**

quantitative analyst FINANCE **somebody assessing financial variables numerically** a person who uses econometric, mathematical, or statistical models to evaluate a project or investment. *Also called* **quant** (sense 1)

quantitative easing FINANCE **central bank's issue of money to other banks** the release by a central bank of sufficient funds to stimulate activity in a banking system that has become sluggish and generate an improvement in the economy. This sometimes means printing money in order to give banks more capital.

quantum meruit FINANCE **as much as has been earned** a Latin phrase meaning "as much as has been earned." A claim for quantum meruit can be for reasonable payment for work that has been done without a full estimate.

quarter 1. ACCOUNTING **three-month period** a three-month calendar period, often used as a period for reporting earnings, paying taxes, or calculating dividends **2.** CURRENCY & EXCHANGE **US coin worth 25 cents** a US coin worth one-fourth of a dollar or 25 cents

quarter-end ACCOUNTING **of end of three-month period** relating to the end of a three-month *accounting period* when financial transactions for that period are finalized

quarterly 1. GENERAL MANAGEMENT **happening every three months** taking place once in every period of three months **2.** ACCOUNTING **company's financial results** the results of a corporation, produced each quarter

quarterly report ACCOUNTING **financial statement for quarter of tax year** a financial statement that covers a quarter of a full fiscal year. In the United States the general practice is to issue quarterly reports. *See also* **interim financial statement**

quasi-loan FINANCE **arrangement to pay somebody else's debt** an arrangement whereby one party pays the debts of another, on the condition that the sum of the debts will be reimbursed by the indebted party at some later date

quasi-money *UK* STOCKHOLDING & INVESTMENTS = *near money*

quasi-rent FINANCE **difference between production cost and selling cost** excess earnings made by a company representing the difference between production cost (the cost of labor and materials) and selling cost

qubes STOCKHOLDING & INVESTMENTS **fund tracking NASDAQ-100** an exchange-traded fund that tracks the stocks in the NASDAQ-100 index, which consists mainly of the largest nonfinancial companies traded on the NASDAQ

question mark company STOCKHOLDING & INVESTMENTS **uncertain investment prospect** a company that offers a doubtful return on investment

quick asset FINANCE **asset easily cashed in** cash or any asset that can quickly be turned into cash, for example, a bank deposit of some types, a short-dated bond, or a certificate of deposit. *See also* **near money**

quick ratio FINANCE **1. measure of somebody's short-term borrowing potential** a measure of the amount of cash a potential borrower can acquire in a short time, used in evaluating creditworthiness **2. ratio of liquid assets to current debts** the ratio of a company's liquid assets to its current liabilities, used as an indicator of **liquidity**

quid pro quo FINANCE **something in exchange** a Latin phrase meaning "something for something," something given or done in exchange for something else. To be valid, a contract must involve a quid pro quo.

quorum CORPORATE GOVERNANCE **minimum number of attendees required for decision-making** the minimum number of people required in a meeting for it to be able to make decisions that are binding on the organization. For a company, this number is stated in its bylaws; for a partnership, in its partnership agreement.

quota 1. FINANCE **limit of investment by party in joint venture** the maximum sum to be contributed by each party in a joint venture or joint business undertaking **2.** STOCKHOLDING & INVESTMENTS **ceiling on investment in given situation or market** the maximum number of investments that may be purchased and sold in a specific situation or market, as in a US Treasury auction, where bidders may not apply for more than a specific percentage of the securities being offered **3.** INTERNATIONAL TRADE **limit of imports or exports** the maximum amount of a specific commodity, product, or service that can be imported into or exported out of a country

quote *or* **quotation** FINANCE **estimate of price** a statement of what a person or company is willing to accept when selling a product or service. *Also called* **bid**

R

racket FRAUD **illegal money-making deal** an illegal business deal that makes a lot of money, involving such activities as bribery or intimidation

raider MERGERS & ACQUISITIONS **maker of hostile takeover bids** a person or company that makes hostile takeover bids, wanted neither by directors nor stockholders

rand CURRENCY & EXCHANGE **S. African currency unit** the standard unit of currency of the Republic of South Africa, equal to 100 cents

ratchet effect ECONOMICS **adjusting more easily to income increases than decreases** the result when households adjust more easily to rising incomes than to falling incomes, as, for example, when their consumption drops by less than their income in a recession

rate FINANCE **assess value** to calculate or assess the value of something, for example, real estate for tax purposes

rateable value FINANCE **value calculated according to rule** the value of something calculated with reference to a rule. An example is the value of a commercial property taken as a basis for calculating local taxes.

rate cap FINANCE = **cap**

rate of exchange CURRENCY & EXCHANGE = **exchange rate**

rate of inflation ECONOMICS **percentage increase in prices over year** the percentage increase in the price of goods and services calculated over a twelve-month period

rate of interest FINANCE **percentage charged on loan or paid on investment** a percentage charged on a loan or paid on an investment for the use of the money

rate of return ACCOUNTING, STOCKHOLDING & INVESTMENTS **ratio of investment profit to investment cost** an accounting ratio of the income from an investment to the amount of the investment, used to measure financial performance.

There is a basic formula that will serve most needs, at least initially:

$$\frac{(\text{Current value of amount invested} - \text{Original value of amount invested})}{\text{Original value of amount invested}} \times 100\% = \text{Rate of return}$$

If \$1,000 in capital is invested in stock, and one year later the investment yields \$1,100, the rate of return of the investment is calculated like this:

$$\frac{1,100 - 1,000}{1,000} \times 100\% = \frac{100}{1,000} \times 100\% = 10\%$$

Now, assume \$1,000 is invested again. One year later, the investment grows to \$2,000 in value, but after another year the value of the investment falls to \$1,200. The rate of return after the first year is:

$$\left[\frac{(2,000 - 1,000)}{1,000}\right] \times 100\% = 100\%$$

The rate of return after the second year is:

$$\left[\frac{(1,200 - 2,000)}{2,000}\right] \times 100\% = -40\%$$

The average annual return for the two years (also known as average annual arithmetic return) can be calculated using this formula:

$$\frac{(\text{Rate of return for year 1} + \text{Rate of return for year 2})}{2} = \text{Average annual return}$$

Accordingly:

$$\frac{(100\% + -40\%)}{2} = 30\%$$

The average annual rate of return is a percentage, but one that is accurate over only a short period, so this method should be used accordingly.

The geometric or compound rate of return is a better yardstick for measuring investments over the long term, and takes into account the effects of compounding. This formula is more complex and technical.

The real rate of return is the annual return realized on an investment, adjusted for changes in the price due to inflation. If 10% is earned on an investment but inflation is 2%, then the real rate of return is actually 8%. *Also called* **return**

rate tart FINANCE somebody often changing to accounts with better rates somebody who changes loan providers or savings accounts regularly to benefit from better interest rates (slang)

rating FINANCE relative assigned value the value or quality that something is assessed as having, for example, the status of a person or company in terms of creditworthiness, or a company or product in terms of suitability for investment. *See also* **credit rating**

rating agency STOCKHOLDING & INVESTMENTS organization rating firms issuing bonds an organization that gives a *rating* to companies or other organizations issuing bonds

ratio analysis FINANCE using ratios in financial analysis the use of ratios to measure a company's financial performance, for example, the **current ratio** or the leverage ratios

RBA *abbr* BANKING Reserve Bank of Australia

RBNZ *abbr* BANKING Reserve Bank of New Zealand

RD *or* **R/D** *abbr* UK BANKING refer to drawer

RDG *abbr* ECONOMICS regional development grant

RDP FINANCE government policies addressing economic aftermath of apartheid a policy framework by means of which the South African government intends to correct the socioeconomic imbalances caused by apartheid. *Full form* ***Reconstruction and Development Program***

RDPR *abbr* BANKING refer to drawer please re-present

ready money FINANCE money immediately available cash or money that is immediately available for use

Reaganomics ECONOMICS 1980s economic policies of Ronald Reagan the economic policy of former US President Reagan in the 1980s, who reduced taxes and social security support and increased the national budget deficit to an unprecedented level

real FINANCE after considering inflation after the effects of inflation are taken into consideration

real asset FINANCE physical asset an asset with a physical presence such as land or a building. *See also* **tangible asset**

real balance effect ECONOMICS results of falling prices and increased consumption the effect on income and employment when prices fall and consumption increases

real capital FINANCE assets with monetary value assets such as buildings or equipment that are used in creating products and can be assigned a monetary value. *See also* ***financial capital***

real earnings FINANCE available income after deductions income that is available for spending after tax and other contributions have been deducted, adjusted for inflation. *Also called* **real income, real wages**

real economy ECONOMICS goods, services, and jobs the production of goods and services on which jobs, incomes, and consumer spending depend

real estate investment trust REAL ESTATE, STOCKHOLDING & INVESTMENTS trust investing in properties and mortgages a publicly traded ***investment trust*** that uses investors' money to invest in properties and mortgages. *Abbr* **REIT**

real exchange rate CURRENCY & EXCHANGE exchange rate adjusted for inflation a current exchange rate that has been adjusted for inflation

real GDP ECONOMICS GDP adjusted for prices a measure of ***GDP*** adjusted for changes in prices

real growth ECONOMICS economic growth adjusted for prices the increase in productivity, sales, or earnings of a country or a household adjusted for changes in prices

real income FINANCE = ***real earnings***

real interest rate FINANCE interest rate adjusted for inflation an interest rate after a deduction for inflation has been made

real investment FINANCE purchase of real estate or plant, not securities the purchase of assets such as land, real estate, and plant and machinery, as opposed to the acquisition of securities

realize FINANCE sell asset for cash to change an ***asset*** into an amount of money by selling it

realized profit FINANCE profit from sale of something profit made when something has been sold, as opposed to ***paper profit***

real money FINANCE **1.** capital from investors who have not borrowed investment capital provided by investors such as pension funds, some insurance companies, retail mutual funds, and high net worth individuals who are not borrowing it from other sources **2.** bills and coins money available as bills and coins to spend, rather than existing only as items on financial accounts **3.** lots of money a very large amount of money (informal)

real option STOCKHOLDING & INVESTMENTS, RISK **choice available to investor in tangible investment** the opportunity to choose a course of action that an investor has when investing in something tangible such as a business project

real purchasing power ECONOMICS **how much consumer is able to buy** the purchasing power of a country or a household adjusted for changes in prices

real rate of return FINANCE **rate of return allowing for inflation** the rate of return received after a deduction for inflation

real return after tax FINANCE, TAX **net income or profit** the income or profit made after deductions for taxes and inflation

real value FINANCE **value of investment in real terms** a value of an investment that is maintained at the same level, for example, by making it *index-linked*

real wages FINANCE = *real earnings*

rebate 1. FINANCE **money returned when payment is excessive** money returned because a payment exceeded the amount required, for example, a tax rebate **2.** FINANCE **discount** a reduction in the price of goods or services in relation to the standard price **3.** STOCKHOLDING & INVESTMENTS **reduce client's commission charge** of a broker, to reduce part of the commission charged to the client as a promotional offer

recapitalization FINANCE **reorganization of firm's capital** the process of changing the way a company's capital is structured, in terms of the balance between debt and equity, usually in response to a major financial problem such as *bankruptcy*

recapture 1. FINANCE **sale with right to buy back** a situation in which a seller of an asset retains the right to buy back part or all of the asset **2.** TAX, ACCOUNTING **treatment of past deduction as income** a situation in which a deduction taken in a previous tax year must be reported as income, for example, when a depreciated asset is sold at a gain

recd *or* **rec'd** *abbr* FINANCE received

receipts FINANCE **money from sales** the total amount a retailer takes from sales. *Also called* **takings**. *See also* **gross receipts, net receipts**

receivables ACCOUNTING **money owing but not paid** money that has been billed to customers or clients but has not yet been received

receivables ledger *US* ACCOUNTING **record of accounts receivable** a ledger in which a company records its *accounts receivable*. *See also* **payables ledger**. *UK term* **purchase ledger**

received FINANCE **referring to money taken in** used in recording payments or sums of money. *Abbr* **recd**

receivership FINANCE, LEGAL **management of insolvent company by court-appointed official** a state of insolvency prior to liquidation. During receivership, receivers may attempt to undertake turnaround management or decide that the company must go into liquidation. *Also called* **administration** (sense 1)

recession ECONOMICS **slowdown of economic activity** a stage of the *business cycle* in which economic activity is in slow decline. Recession usually follows a boom, and precedes a *depression*. It is characterized by rising unemployment and falling levels of output and investment.

recessionary gap ECONOMICS **shortfall of demand needed to ensure full employment** a shortfall in the amount of *aggregate demand* in an economy needed to create full employment

reciprocal holdings STOCKHOLDING & INVESTMENTS **mutual stockholdings that prevent takeover bids** a situation in which two companies own stock in each other to prevent takeover bids

reconciliation ACCOUNTING **accounting adjustment in line with authoritative information** adjustment of a record, such as somebody's own record of bank account transactions, to match more authoritative information

reconciliation statement ACCOUNTING **document verifying date of independently recorded transaction** a document used to verify that two independent records of the same financial transactions agree as of a particular date

Reconstruction and Development Program FINANCE *see* **RDP**

recourse FINANCE **right of lender to demand repayment of loan** a right of a lender to compel a borrower to repay money borrowed, or, in some cases, to take assets belonging to the borrower if the money is not repaid

recourse agreement FINANCE **installment plan agreement allowing retailer to repossess** an agreement in an installment plan whereby the retailer repossesses the goods being purchased in the event that the purchaser fails to make regular payments

recoverable amount ACCOUNTING **value of asset if sold or when used** the value of an asset, either the price it would bring if sold, or its value to the company when used, whichever is the larger figure

recovery ECONOMICS **return to normal economic activity after downturn** the return of a country to economic health after a crash or a depression

recovery fund STOCKHOLDING & INVESTMENTS **fund investing in recovery stock** a fund that invests in *recovery stock* that it considers likely to return to a previous higher price

recovery stock STOCKHOLDING & INVESTMENTS **underperforming stock now recovering** a stock that has fallen in price because of poor business performance, but is now expected to climb as a result of an improvement in the company's prospects

red BANKING **color for debits** the color of debit or overdrawn balances in some bank statements **in the red** FINANCE, BANKING, ACCOUNTING in debt, or losing money

Red Book FINANCE **copy of UK finance minister's Budget speech** a copy of the Chancellor of the Exchequer's speech published on the day of the Budget. It can be regarded as the United Kingdom's financial statement and report.

Red chips STOCKHOLDING & INVESTMENTS **good Chinese companies** Chinese companies that are considered risk-free and worth investing in

red day *US* FINANCE **unprofitable day** a day on which no profit has been made (slang)

redeem 1. FINANCE **pay off loan or debt** to carry out the repayment of a loan or a debt **2.** BUSINESS **exchange voucher for something** to exchange a voucher, coupon, or stamp for a gift or a reduction in price **3.** STOCKHOLDING & INVESTMENTS **exchange security for cash** to exchange a security for cash

redeemable bond STOCKHOLDING & INVESTMENTS **bond that will be repaid** a bond that is redeemable

redeemable gilt STOCKHOLDING & INVESTMENTS **gilt that will be repaid** a gilt that is redeemable

redeemable government stock STOCKHOLDING & INVESTMENTS **stock redeemable for cash** government stock that can be redeemed for cash at some time in the future

redeemable preference share *UK* STOCKHOLDING & INVESTMENTS = *redeemable preferred stock*

redeemable preferred stock *US* STOCKHOLDING & INVESTMENTS **preference share that firm may buy back** a type of preferred stock that a company has the right to buy back at a specific date and for a specific price. *Also called* **callable preferred stock**. *UK term* **redeemable preference share**

redeemable security STOCKHOLDING & INVESTMENTS **security redeemable at face value** a security that can be redeemed at its face value at a specific date in the future

redeemable shares STOCKHOLDING & INVESTMENTS **shares of stock that may be repurchased** stock that is issued on terms that may require it to be bought back by the issuer at some future date, at the discretion either of the issuer or of the holder

redemption STOCKHOLDING & INVESTMENTS **ending of financial obligation** repayment of a financial obligation, frequently used in connection with preferred stock, debentures, and bonds

redemption date STOCKHOLDING & INVESTMENTS **date for repayment of redeemable security** the date on which a redeemable security is due to be repaid

redemption value STOCKHOLDING & INVESTMENTS **value of security at redemption** the value of a security at the time it is redeemed

redemption yield STOCKHOLDING & INVESTMENTS **yield on security up to redemption** a yield on a security including interest and its value up to the time it is redeemed. *See also* *yield to maturity*

red eye *US* STOCKHOLDING & INVESTMENTS **preliminary prospectus to test market** information in the form of a *preliminary prospectus* used in *initial public offerings* to gauge the reaction of investors (slang). *UK term* **pathfinder prospectus**

red herring STOCKHOLDING & INVESTMENTS = *preliminary prospectus*

rediscount FINANCE **discount bill of exchange for second time** to discount a bill of exchange that has already been discounted by a commercial bank

redistribution of wealth ECONOMICS **sharing of wealth across population** the process of sharing wealth among the entire population, often through taxation

redistributive effect ECONOMICS, TAX **wealth equalization resulting from taxes and benefits** the tendency toward equalization of people's wealth that results from a *progressive tax* or selective benefit

redlining FINANCE, LEGAL **discrimination against borrowers because of neighborhood of residence** the illegal practice by financial institutions of discriminating against prospective borrowers because of the area of the town or city in which they live

reducing balance depreciation CURRENCY & EXCHANGE *see depreciation*

reducing balance method ACCOUNTING = *accelerated depreciation*

redundancy payment *UK* FINANCE, HR & PERSONNEL = *severance pay*

reference BANKING = *banker's reference*

reference rate FINANCE **rate used as benchmark** a benchmark interest rate, for example, a bank's own set rate or the *London Interbank Offered Rate*. Lending rates are often expressed as a margin over a reference rate.

referred share STOCKHOLDING & INVESTMENTS **ex dividend stock** a stock that is *ex dividend*, the right to dividends remaining with the vendor

refer to drawer *UK* BANKING **refuse to pay check from underfunded account** to refuse to pay a check because the account from which it is drawn has too little money in it. *Abbr* **RD**, **R/D**

refer to drawer please re-present BANKING **shown on refused UK check** in the United Kingdom, marked on a check by the paying banker to indicate that there are currently insufficient funds to meet the payment, but that the bank believes sufficient funds will be available shortly. *See also* *refer to drawer*. *Abbr* **RDPR**

refinance FINANCE **replace loan** to replace one loan with another, especially at a lower rate of interest or at a longer maturity

refinancing FINANCE **1. replacing one loan with another** the process of taking out a loan to pay off other loans **2. new loan that repays old loan** a loan taken out for the purpose of repaying another loan or loans

reflation ECONOMICS **increasing employment by increasing demand** a method of reducing unemployment by increasing an economy's *aggregate demand*. *See also* *recession*

refugee capital FINANCE resources entering country through necessity people and other financial resources that come into a country because they have been forced to leave their own country for economic or political reasons

refunding FINANCE issuance of new bonds to replace old the process of a government's renewing of the funding of a debt by issuing new bonds to replace those that are about to mature

regeneration ECONOMICS revitalization of rundown industrial or business areas the redevelopment of industrial or business areas that have suffered decline, in order to increase employment and business activity

regional development grant ECONOMICS grant encouraging business in UK regions in the United Kingdom, a grant given to encourage a business to establish itself in a specific part of the country. *Abbr* **RDG**

regional fund STOCKHOLDING & INVESTMENTS mutual fund investing in geographic region a mutual fund that invests in the markets of a particular geographic region

registered bond STOCKHOLDING & INVESTMENTS bond with ownership recorded by issuer a bond the ownership of which is recorded on the books of the issuer

registered capital FINANCE = authorized capital

registered check BANKING check written on temporary bank account a check written on a bank's account on behalf of a customer who does not have a bank account but who gives the bank funds to hold to cover the check

registered investment adviser STOCKHOLDING & INVESTMENTS professionally recognized US financial manager a person or company that is registered with the US Securities and Exchange Commission and usually manages the portfolios of others

registered representative STOCKHOLDING & INVESTMENTS qualified US seller of securities a person who is licensed by the US Securities and Exchange Commission to sell securities, after having passed the required examinations

registered security *or* **registered share** STOCKHOLDING & INVESTMENTS security with holder's name recorded by issuer a security for which the holder's name is recorded in the books of the issuer. *See also* **nominee**

registered share capital STOCKHOLDING & INVESTMENTS = authorized share capital

register of directors' interests REGULATION & COMPLIANCE, STOCKHOLDING & INVESTMENTS firm's record of directors' holdings a record that every *registered company* in the United Kingdom must maintain of the stocks and other *securities* that have been issued by the company and are held by its directors. It has to be made available for inspection during the company's annual meeting.

registrar CORPORATE GOVERNANCE keeper of official records a person or organization responsible for keeping official records, for example, the person who keeps a record of stockholders in a company

Registrar of Companies LEGAL, CORPORATE GOVERNANCE official holding record of registered UK companies the person charged with the duty of holding and registering the official startup and constitutional documents of all *registered companies* in the United Kingdom

regulatory pricing risk INSURANCE, RISK risk that government will regulate insurance company's prices the risk an insurance company faces that a government will regulate the prices it can charge

rehypothecation FINANCE pledge of client's securities as loan collateral an arrangement in which a broker pledges securities in a client's margin account as collateral for a loan from a bank

reimbursement FINANCE repayment of expense incurred repayment of money spent for an agreed or official purpose or taken as a loan, or money paid as compensation for a loss

reinvestment STOCKHOLDING & INVESTMENTS **1.** investing of money again the act of investing money again in the same securities **2.** firm's investing of earnings in own business the act of investing a company's earnings in its own business by using them to create new products for sale

reinvestment rate FINANCE interest rate available for reinvested income the interest rate at which an investor is able to reinvest income received from an investment

reinvestment risk FINANCE, RISK risk that reinvestment will be at lower rate the risk that an investor will be unable to earn the same rate of return on the proceeds of an investment as he or she earns on the investment as a result of declining interest rates

reinvestment unit trust STOCKHOLDING & INVESTMENTS mutual fund using dividends to buy more stock in the United Kingdom, a mutual fund that uses dividends to buy more shares in the company issuing them. *See also* **accumulation unit**

REIT *abbr* REAL ESTATE, STOCKHOLDING & INVESTMENTS real estate investment trust

relative income hypothesis ECONOMICS belief that people care about others' incomes the theory that consumers are concerned less with their absolute living standards than with consumption relative to other consumers

relevant interest *ANZ* STOCKHOLDING & INVESTMENTS legal position enabling investor to buy and sell the legal status held by stock investors who can legally dispose of, or influence the disposal of, stocks

reminder BUSINESS, FINANCE letter reminding of obligation to pay invoice a letter to remind a customer that he or she has not paid an invoice

remittance BUSINESS, FINANCE money sent as payment money that is sent to pay a debt or to pay an invoice

remittance advice *or* **remittance slip** BUSINESS, FINANCE detailed document accompanying payment a document sent with payment, giving details of what invoices are being paid and credits, if any, being taken

remitting bank BANKING = *collecting bank*

remuneration FINANCE, HR & PERSONNEL = *earnings*

rent 1. FINANCE **arrangement to use equipment for money** an arrangement whereby customers pay money to be able to use a car, boat, or piece of equipment owned by another person or firm for a period of time **2.** REAL ESTATE **arrangement to use buildings or land for money** money paid to use an office, building, or piece of farmland, for example, owned by another person for a period of time **3.** FINANCE **allow somebody use of something for money** to use or allow somebody to use, an office, building, or piece of farmland, for example, in return for a regular payment. *Also called* **let**

renting back FINANCE = *sale and leaseback*

renunciation STOCKHOLDING & INVESTMENTS = *letter of renunciation*

reorganization bond STOCKHOLDING & INVESTMENTS **US bond for creditors of firm being reorganized** in the United States, a bond issued to creditors of a business that is undergoing a form of **Chapter 11** reorganization. Interest is normally only paid when the company can make the payments from its earnings.

repatriation FINANCE **return of foreign investment earnings to home country** the act of sending money earned on foreign investments to the home country of their firm or owner

repayable FINANCE **to be repaid** used to describe money that is to be paid back, usually in a particular way, for example, in monthly installments

repayment FINANCE **1. repaying of money** the act of paying money back, usually in a particular way, for example, in monthly installments **2. money repaid** money that is paid back, usually in a particular way, for example, in monthly installments

replacement cost *or* replacement price ACCOUNTING **today's cost of replacing something** the cost of replacing an asset or service with its current equivalent

replacement cost accounting ACCOUNTING **means of evaluating firm's assets** a method of valuing company assets based on their replacement cost

replacement cost depreciation ACCOUNTING **depreciation based on current replacement cost** depreciation based on the actual cost of replacing the asset in the current year

replacement ratio ECONOMICS **difference between wages and unemployment benefits** the ratio of the total resources received when unemployed to those received when in employment

repo 1. FINANCE, MARKETS = *repurchase agreement* **2.** BANKING, MARKETS **open-market buying and selling by US Federal Reserve** in the United States, an open market operation undertaken by the Federal Reserve to purchase securities and agree to sell them back at a stated price on a future date **3.** BANKING, MARKETS **Bank of England's repurchase agreement** in the United Kingdom, a Bank of England

repurchase agreement with market makers in gilt-edged securities. It is used to provide securities for short positions.

reporting entity CORPORATE GOVERNANCE **organization providing financial information to stockholders** any organization such as a limited company that reports its accounts to its stockholders

repossession FINANCE **return of merchandise after default on time payments** the return of goods purchased through an installment plan when the purchaser fails to make the required regular payments. *See also* **recourse agreement**

repudiation FINANCE **refusing to honor debt** a refusal to pay or acknowledge a debt or similar contract

repurchase FINANCE **buy back shares in mutual fund** to buy back shares, for example, when a fund manager buys back the shares in a mutual fund after an investor sells, or when companies repurchase shares instead of or in addition to paying a dividend to shareholders

required rate of return FINANCE **lowest acceptable return** the minimum return for a proposed project investment to be acceptable. *See also* **discounted cash flow**

required reserve ratio *or* required reserves BANKING **ratio of bank's reserves to deposits** the proportion of a bank's deposits that must be kept in reserve.

In the United Kingdom and in certain European countries, there is no compulsory ratio, although banks will have their own internal measures and targets to be able to repay customer deposits as they forecast they will be required. In the United States, specified percentages of deposits—established by the Federal Reserve Board—must be kept by banks in a non-interest-bearing account at one of the twelve Federal Reserve Banks located throughout the country.

In Europe, the reserve requirement of an institution is calculated by multiplying the reserve ratio for each category of items in the reserve base, set by the European Central Bank, with the amount of those items in the institution's balance sheets. These figures vary according to the institution.

The required reserve ratio in the United States is set by federal law, and depends on the amount of checkable deposits a bank holds. Up to $9.3M the required reserve ratio is 0%, from $9.3M to $43.9M it is 3% and above $43.9M it is 10%. These breakpoints are reviewed annually in accordance with money supply growth. No reserves are required against certificates of deposit or savings accounts.

The reserve ratio requirement limits a bank's lending to a certain fraction of its demand deposits. The current rule allows a bank to issue loans in an amount equal to 90% of such deposits, holding 10% in reserve. The reserves can be held in any combination of till money and deposit at a Federal Reserve Bank. *Also called* **bank reserve ratio, reserve ratio, reserve requirement**

reschedule FINANCE **arrange new payment schedule for debt** to arrange a new payment schedule and new conditions for the repayment of a debt

research STOCKHOLDING & INVESTMENTS **evaluation of information to aid investing** the examination of statistics and other information regarding past, present, and future trends or performance that enables analysts to recommend to investors which stocks to buy or sell in order to maximize their return and minimize their risk. It may be used either in the top-down approach (where the investor evaluates a market, then an industry, and finally a specific company) or the bottom-up approach (where the investor selects a company and confirms his or her findings by evaluating the company's sector and then its market). Careful research is likely to help investors find the best deals, in particular **value shares** or *growth equities*. *See also* **technical analysis**

reserve FINANCE business profits withheld to cover unexpected costs profits in a business that have not been paid out as dividends but have been set aside in the business to cover any unexpected costs. *Also called* **reserve fund**

reserve bank BANKING bank that holds money for other banks in the United States, a bank such as a Federal Reserve bank that holds the reserves of other banks

Reserve Bank of Australia BANKING central bank of Australia Australia's central bank, which is responsible for managing the Commonwealth's monetary policy, ensuring financial stability, and printing and distributing currency. *Abbr* **RBA**

Reserve Bank of New Zealand BANKING central bank of New Zealand New Zealand's central bank, which is responsible for managing the government's monetary policy, ensuring financial stability, and printing and distributing currency. *Abbr* **RBNZ**

reserve currency CURRENCY & EXCHANGE foreign currency kept for international trading foreign currency that a central bank holds for use in international trade

reserve for fluctuations CURRENCY & EXCHANGE money to absorb exchange rate differences money set aside to allow for changes in the values of currencies

reserve fund FINANCE = **reserve**

reserve price FINANCE minimum price in auction a price for a particular lot, set by the vendor, below which an auctioneer may not sell

reserve ratio BANKING = **required reserve ratio**

reserve requirement BANKING = **required reserve ratio**

reserves 1. FINANCE money held for contingencies and opportunities a sum of money held by a person or organization to finance unexpected business opportunities. *See also* **war chest 2.** BANKING money that bank holds for withdrawals the money that a bank holds to ensure that it can satisfy its depositors' demands for withdrawals **3.** ACCOUNTING, STOCKHOLDING & INVESTMENTS profit not distributed plus stock subscriptions in a company balance sheet, the total of profits not yet distributed to shareholders and the amount subscribed for stock in excess of the **nominal value**

residual value ACCOUNTING value of asset after depreciation a value of an asset after it has been depreciated in the company's accounts

residue FINANCE money left over money that has not been spent or paid out

resolution CORPORATE GOVERNANCE proposal to be voted on at meeting a proposal put to a meeting, for example, an annual meeting of shareholders, on which those present and eligible can vote. *See also* **extraordinary resolution**, **special resolution**

resource driver ACCOUNTING **1.** *see* **cost driver 2.** unit for measuring usage and assignment of resources a measurement unit that is used to assign resource costs to **activity cost pools** based on some measures of usage. For example, it may be used to assign office occupancy costs to purchasing or accounting services within a company.

responsibility accounting ACCOUNTING record-keeping that shows individual responsibilities the keeping of financial records with an emphasis on who is responsible for each item

restated balance sheet ACCOUNTING accounts reorganized to emphasize selected feature a balance sheet reframed to serve a specific purpose such as highlighting depreciation on assets

restatement ACCOUNTING revised financial statement a revision of a company's earlier financial statement

restricted security STOCKHOLDING & INVESTMENTS security bought in unregistered sale a security acquired in an unregistered private resale from the issuer or an affiliate of the issuer, and whose sale must meet certain conditions laid down by the **Securities and Exchange Commission**

restricted surplus US FINANCE funds unavailable for dividend payments reserves that are not legally available for distribution to stockholders as dividends. *UK term* **undistributable reserves**

restricted tender STOCKHOLDING & INVESTMENTS conditional offer for stock an offer to buy stock only under specific conditions

restrictive covenant FINANCE agreement to retain loan collateral an agreement by a borrower not to sell an asset that he or she has used as collateral for a loan

result ACCOUNTING account produced at end of trading period a profit or loss account for a company at the end of a trading period

retail banking BANKING financial services for individuals services provided by commercial banks to individuals as opposed to business customers that include current accounts, deposit and savings accounts, as well as credit cards, mortgages, and investments. In the United Kingdom, although this service was traditionally provided by high street banks, separate organizations, albeit offshoots of established financial institutions, more recently began to provide Internet and telephone banking services, though the credit crunch of 2008 has set back their operations. *See also* **wholesale banking**

retail deposit BANKING money held in bank on somebody's behalf a sum of money held in a bank on behalf of an individual

a–z

Dictionary

retail depositor BANKING **individual bank customer** an individual who deposits money in a bank, as opposed to a business customer

retailer number BANKING **retailer's identification number for depositing credit card payments** the identification number of the retailer, printed at the top of the report slip when depositing credit card payments

retail investor STOCKHOLDING & INVESTMENTS **small investor** a private investor who buys and sells stock

retail price index ECONOMICS **list of average prices charged to consumers** a listing of the average levels of prices charged by retailers for goods or services. The retail price index is calculated on a set variety of items, and usually excludes luxury goods. It is updated monthly, and provides a running indicator of changing costs. *Abbr* **RPI**

retained earnings *US* ACCOUNTING = *retained profits*

retained profits ACCOUNTING **firm's profits kept as reserves, expansion, or investment** the amount of profit remaining after tax and distribution to stockholders that is retained in a business and used as a reserve or as a means of financing expansion or investment. *Also called* **retained earnings, retentions**

retainer FINANCE **money advanced to retain somebody's services** money paid in advance to somebody so that they will work for you and not for someone else

retention 1. FINANCE **withholding of payment** the holding back of money due until a condition has been fulfilled **2.** HR & PERSONNEL **keeping existing employees** the process of keeping the loyalty of existing employees and persuading them not to work for another company

retentions ACCOUNTING = *retained profits*

retire 1. FINANCE **pay off loan** to pay the balance owed on a loan **2.** HR & PERSONNEL **stop working at end of career** to leave a job or career voluntarily at the usual age or time for doing so

retirement 1. FINANCE **payment of loan balance** the act of paying the balance owed on a loan **2.** HR & PERSONNEL **act of retiring** the act of leaving a job or career voluntarily at the usual age or time for doing so **3.** HR & PERSONNEL **time after retiring** the time that follows the end of a person's working life

retrenchment FINANCE **cost reductions to improve profitability** the reduction of costs or spending in order to maintain or improve profitability, especially in response to changed economic circumstances

return 1. ACCOUNTING, STOCKHOLDING & INVESTMENTS = *rate of return* **2.** TAX = *tax return*

return date ACCOUNTING **in UK, date for required annual return** in the United Kingdom, a date by which a company's annual return has to be made to the *Registrar of Companies*

return on assets ACCOUNTING **net income as percentage of total assets** a measure of profitability calculated by expressing a company's net income as a percentage of total assets. *Abbr* **ROA**

return on capital *or* return on capital employed ACCOUNTING **ratio used for measuring profitability by UK firms** in the United Kingdom, a ratio of the net profit made in a fiscal year in relation to the *capital employed*. It is used as a measure of business profitability. *Abbr* **ROC, ROCE**

return on equity FINANCE **relationship between net income and stockholders' funds** the ratio of a company's net income as a percentage of shareholders' funds.

Return on equity is easy to calculate and is applicable to the majority of industries. It is probably the most widely used measure of how well a company is performing for its shareholders.

It is calculated by dividing the net income shown on the income statement (usually of the past year) by shareholders' equity, which appears on the balance sheet:

$$\frac{\text{Net income}}{\text{Owners' equity}} = \text{Return on equity}$$

For example, if net income is \$450 and equity is \$2,500, then:

$$\frac{450}{2,500} = 0.18 \times 100\% = 18\% \text{ return on equity}$$

Return on equity for most companies should be in double figures; investors often look for 15% or higher, while a return of 20% or more is considered excellent. Seasoned investors also review five-year average ROE, to gauge consistency. *Abbr* **ROE**

return on invested capital *or* return on investment FINANCE **profit as percentage of investment** a ratio of the profit made in a financial year as a percentage of an investment.

The most basic expression of ROI can be found by dividing a company's net profit (also called net earnings) by the total investment (total debt plus total equity), then multiplying by 100 to arrive at a percentage:

$$\frac{\text{Net profit}}{\text{Total investment}} = \text{ROI}$$

If, say, net profit is \$30 and total investment is \$250, the ROI is:

$$\frac{30}{250} = 0.12 \times 100\% = 12\%$$

A more complex variation of ROI is an equation known as the Du Pont formula:

$$\frac{\text{Net profit after taxes}}{\text{Total assets}} = \frac{\text{Net profit after taxes}}{\text{Sales}} \times \frac{\text{Sales}}{\text{Total assets}}$$

If, for example, net profit after taxes is \$30, total assets are \$250, and sales are \$500, then:

$$\frac{30}{250} = \frac{30}{500} \times \frac{500}{250} = 12\% = 6\% \times 2 = 12\%$$

Champions of this formula, which was developed by the Du Pont Company in the 1920s, say that it helps reveal how a company has both deployed its assets and controlled its costs, and how it can achieve the same percentage return in different ways.

For shareholders, the varition of the basic ROI formula used by investor is:

$$\frac{(\text{Net income} + \text{Current value} - \text{Original value})}{\text{Original value}} = \text{ROI}$$

If, for example, somebody invests $5,000 in a company and a year later has earned $100 in dividends, while the value of the shares is $5,200, the return on investment would be:

$$\frac{(100 + 5,200 - 5,000)}{5,000} = \frac{300}{5,000} = 0.06 \times 100\% = 6\% \text{ ROI}$$

It is vital to understand exactly what a return on investment measures, for example, assets, equity, or sales. Without this understanding, comparisons may be misleading. It is also important to establish whether the net profit figure used is before or after provision for taxes. *Abbr* **ROI**, **ROIC**

return on net assets FINANCE **profit as percentage of firm's assets** a ratio of the profit made in a fiscal year as a percentage of the assets of a company. *Abbr* **RONA**

return on sales ACCOUNTING **profit or loss as percentage of sales** a company's operating profit or loss as a percentage of total sales for a given period, typically a year. *Abbr* **ROS**. *See also* ***profit margin***

returns to scale ECONOMICS **increase in output related to increases in inputs** the proportionate increase in a country's or company's output as a result of increases in all its inputs

revaluation CURRENCY & EXCHANGE **increase in value of nation's currency** a rise in the value of a country's currency in relation to other currencies

revaluation method ACCOUNTING **asset depreciation using change in value over year** a method of calculating the depreciation of assets by which the asset is depreciated by the difference in its value at the end of the year over its value at the beginning of the year

revaluation of assets ACCOUNTING **asset depreciation using change in value since acquisition** the revaluation of a company's ***assets*** to take account of inflation or changes in value since the assets were acquired. The change in value is credited to the ***revaluation reserve account***.

revaluation of currency CURRENCY & EXCHANGE **altering currency value to affect balance of payments** an increase in the value of a currency in relation to others. In situations where there is a ***floating exchange rate***, a currency will usually find its own level automatically but this will not happen if there is a ***fixed exchange rate***. Should a government have persistent ***balance of payment*** surpluses, it may exceptionally decide to revalue its currency, making imports cheaper but its exports more expensive.

revaluation reserve CURRENCY & EXCHANGE **money held to cover fluctuations in foreign currencies** money set aside to account for the fact that the value of assets may vary as a result of accounting in different currencies

revaluation reserve account ACCOUNTING **account for asset depreciation** an account to which the change in value of a company's assets is credited during a ***revaluation of assets***

revalue ACCOUNTING **reassess value of something** to value something again, usually setting a higher value on it than before

revenue FINANCE **income from product or service** the income generated by a product or service over a period of time

revenue account ACCOUNTING **business account for recording income** an account in a business used for recording receipts from sales, services, commissions, and other income associated with the business's activities

revenue anticipation note STOCKHOLDING & INVESTMENTS, TAX **government means of raising money** a government-issued ***debt instrument*** for which expected income from taxation is collateral

revenue bond STOCKHOLDING & INVESTMENTS **US government bond** a bond that a US state or a local government issues, to be repaid from the money made from the project financed with it

revenue center FINANCE **center for generating income without costs** a part of a business that raises revenue but has no responsibility for costs, for example, a sales center

revenue expenditure ACCOUNTING **money spent on inventory purchases for current-year sale** expenditure on purchasing stock, but not on capital items, which is then sold during the current accounting period

revenue ledger ACCOUNTING **record of total income** a record of all the income received by an organization. *Also called* ***sales ledger***

revenue recognition ACCOUNTING **determination of when income becomes revenue** an accounting principle that determines when income is recognized as revenue. In ***cash accounting***, revenue is recognized not when services were performed or products delivered but when payment is actually received. Following the ***accrual concept***, revenue is recognized when payment is earned no matter when it is actually received.

revenue reserves FINANCE, ACCOUNTING **undistributed earnings held as stockholders' funds** retained profits that are shown in the company's balance sheet as part of the stockholders' funds

reversal FINANCE **change in status** a change to the opposite, for example, from being profitable to unprofitable, or, in the case of a stock price from rising to falling

reverse leverage FINANCE **1. higher expenditures than income** a cash flow in which expenditures are higher than income **2. borrowing at higher interest rate than investments pay** the borrowing of money at a rate of interest higher than the expected rate of return on investing the money borrowed

reverse split STOCKHOLDING & INVESTMENTS **exchange of fewer new shares for old shares** the issuing to stockholders of a fraction of one share for every share that they own. *See also* ***stock split***

reverse takeover MERGERS & ACQUISITIONS **takeover by lesser company** the ***takeover*** of a large company by a smaller one, or the takeover of a public company by a private one

a–z

Dictionary

reverse yield gap FINANCE, STOCKHOLDING & INVESTMENTS **amount by which expenditure exceeds yield or income** the amount by which bond yield exceeds equity yield, or interest rates on loans exceed rental values as a percentage of the costs of properties

reversing entry ACCOUNTING **final debit or credit entry reversing earlier entry** a debit or credit entry in a chart of accounts that is made at the end of an accounting period to reverse an entry

revocable trust FINANCE **trust that can be revoked** a trust whose provisions can be amended or canceled

revolving charge account FINANCE **account with renewable credit for buying goods** a charge account with a company for use in buying that company's goods with *revolving credit*

revolving credit FINANCE = *open-end credit*

revolving fund FINANCE **fund receiving revenue from projects it finances** a fund the resources of which are replenished from the revenue of the projects that it finances

revolving loan BANKING **loan allowing money repaid to be borrowed again** a loan facility whereby the borrower can choose the number and timing of withdrawals against their bank loan and any money repaid may be reborrowed at a future date. Such loans can be made available to both businesses and personal customers.

riba FINANCE **interest charge or unfair profit** in Islamic financing, interest or any unjust profit made by a lender in a financial transaction. It is one of three prohibitions in Islamic law, the others being *gharar* and *maysir*.

rights issue STOCKHOLDING & INVESTMENTS **raising capital by offering existing stockholders additional stock** the raising of new capital by giving existing stockholders the right to subscribe to new shares or *debentures* in proportion to their current holdings. These shares of stock are usually issued at a discount to market price. A stockholder not wishing to take up a rights issue may sell the rights. *Also called rights offer*

rights offer STOCKHOLDING & INVESTMENTS = *rights issue*

rights offering STOCKHOLDING & INVESTMENTS **offering additional stock to existing stockholders** an offering for sale of a *rights issue*, in proportion to the holdings of existing stockholders

ring-fence 1. FINANCE **separate profitable elements to safeguard business** to separate valuable assets or profitable businesses from others in a group that are unprofitable and may make the whole group collapse **2.** FINANCE **use money for specific projects** to identify money from specific sources and only use it in agreed areas or for specific projects. *See also hypothecation* **3.** BUSINESS **not let firm's liquidation affect others in group** to allow one company within a group to go into liquidation without affecting the viability of the group as a whole or any other company within it

risk RISK **1. possibility of suffering harm or loss** the possibility of suffering damage or loss in the face of uncertainty about the outcome of actions, future events, or circumstances.

Organizations are exposed to various types of risk, including damage to property, injury to personnel, financial loss, and legal liability. These may affect profitability, hinder the achievement of objectives, or lead to business interruption or failure. Risk may be deemed high or low, depending on the probability of an adverse outcome. Risks that can be quantified on the basis of past experience are insurable and those that cannot be calculated are uninsurable. **2. potential for negative outcome** a condition in which there exists a quantifiable dispersion in the possible outcomes from any activity

risk-adjusted return on capital STOCKHOLDING & INVESTMENTS, RISK **return on capital evaluated in terms of risks** return on capital calculated in a way that takes into account the risks associated with income. *Also called Jensen's measure, Treynor ratio*

risk analysis RISK **determination of how risks might affect organization** the identification of risks to which an organization is exposed and the assessment of the potential impact of those risks on the organization. The goal of risk analysis is to identify and measure the risks associated with different courses of action in order to inform *decision making*. In the context of business decisionmaking, risk analysis is especially used in investment decisions and capital investment appraisal. Risk analysis may be used to develop an organizational *risk profile*, and also may be the first stage in a *risk management* program.

risk arbitrage MARKETS, RISK **trading without guaranteed profit** simultaneous buying and selling without certainty of profit, though at relatively low risk. It is particularly employed by *hedge fund* managers.

risk arbitrageur RISK **somebody engaged in risk arbitrage** a person whose business is *risk arbitrage*

risk assessment RISK **determination of how risky something is** the determination of the level of risk in a specific course of action. Risk assessments are an important tool in areas such as health and safety management and environmental management. Results of a risk assessment can be used, for example, to identify areas in which safety can be improved. Risk assessment can also be used to determine more intangible forms of risk, including economic and social risk, and can inform the scenario planning process. The amount of risk involved in a specific course of action is compared to its expected benefits to provide evidence for decisionmaking.

risk asset ratio BANKING, RISK **proportion of assets that carry risk** the proportion of a bank's total capital assets that carry risk. *See also risk-weighted asset*

risk-averse STOCKHOLDING & INVESTMENTS, RISK **having desire to avoid risk in investment** wanting to achieve the best return that can be had on an investment while taking the least possible risk

risk aversion STOCKHOLDING & INVESTMENTS, RISK **desire to avoid risk in investment** a desire to achieve the best return that can be had on an investment while taking the least possible risk

risk-based capital assessment BANKING, RISK **bank's value based on risk attached to assets** an internationally approved system of calculating a bank's capital value by assessing the risk attached to its assets. Cash deposits and gold, for example, have no risk, while loans to less-developed countries have a high risk.

risk-bearing economy of scale BUSINESS, RISK **employing diversification to reduce risk** conducting business on such a large scale that the risk of loss is reduced because it is spread over so many independent events, as in the issuance of insurance policies

risk capital FINANCE, RISK = *venture capital*

risk factor RISK **degree of risk in enterprise** the degree of risk in a project or other business activity

risk-free return STOCKHOLDING & INVESTMENTS, RISK **money from safe investment** the profit made from an investment that involves no risk

risk management RISK **1. actions intended to reduce or eliminate risks** the variety of activities undertaken by an organization to control and minimize threats to the continuing efficiency, profitability, and success of its operations. The process of risk management includes the identification and analysis of risks to which the organization is exposed, the assessment of potential impacts on the business, and deciding what action can be taken to eliminate or reduce risk and deal with the impact of unpredictable events causing loss or damage. Risk management strategies include taking out insurance against financial loss or legal liability and introducing safety or security measures. **2. understanding and dealing with inevitable risks** the process of understanding and managing the risks that an organization is inevitably subject to in attempting to achieve its corporate objectives. For management purposes, risks are usually divided into categories such as operational, financial, legal compliance, information, and personnel.

risk manager GENERAL MANAGEMENT, HR & PERSONNEL, RISK **employee managing business risk** the person in an organization who is in charge of assessing and managing business risks

risk perception RISK **nonobjective view of risk** the way in which people and organizations view risk, based on their concerns and experiences, but not necessarily on objective data. Risk perceptions can influence such things as business policies and investment decisions. *Also called* **perception of risk**

risk premium FINANCE, RISK **extra payment received by somebody taking risks** an extra payment, for example, increased dividend or higher than usual profits, for taking risks

Risk Priority Number RISK **number used to quantify risk** a measure used in *Failure Mode and Effects Analysis* to quantify risk. It is a product of the severity, probability of occurrence, and ability to detect failure. *Abbr* **RPN**

risk profile RISK **1. description of risks facing organization** an outline of the risks to which an organization is exposed. An organizational risk profile may be developed in the course of *risk analysis* and used for *risk management*. It examines the nature of the threats faced by an organization, the likelihood of adverse effects occurring, and the level of disruption and costs associated with each type of risk. **2. analysis of willingness to take risks** an analysis of the willingness of individuals or organizations to take risks. A risk profile describes the level of risk considered acceptable by an individual or by the leaders of an organization, and considers how this will affect decisionmaking and corporate strategy.

risk tolerance STOCKHOLDING & INVESTMENTS, RISK **ability to withstand stress of investing** the ability of an investor to handle the uncertainty and money losses inherent to investing

risk-weighted asset FINANCE, RISK **asset weighted by its riskiness** an asset weighted by factors relating to its riskiness, used by financial institutions in managing their capital requirements. *See also* **risk asset ratio**

ROA *abbr* ACCOUNTING return on assets

road show STOCKHOLDING & INVESTMENTS **events to interest potential investors** a series of presentations to potential investors and brokers given by the management of a company prior to issuing securities, especially in an *initial public offering*, intended to create interest in the offering

ROC *abbr* ACCOUNTING return on capital

ROCE *abbr* ACCOUNTING return on capital employed

rocket scientist FINANCE **innovative finance worker** an employee of a financial institution who creates innovative securities that usually include derivatives (slang)

rodo kinko FINANCE **Japanese provider of loans to small businesses** in Japan, a financial institution that specializes in providing credit for small businesses

ROE *abbr* FINANCE return on equity

ROI *abbr* FINANCE return on investment

ROIC *abbr* FINANCE return on invested capital

rolled-up coupon UK STOCKHOLDING & INVESTMENTS **interest coupon added to capital value of security** an interest coupon on a security that is not paid out, but added to the capital value of the security

rolling budget ACCOUNTING **budget that moves with time** a budget that moves forward on a regular basis, for example, a budget covering a twelve-month period that moves forward each month or quarter

rollover FINANCE **extension of credit or period of loan** an extension of credit or of the period of a loan, though not necessarily on the same terms as previously

roll up FINANCE **loan payments including interest** the addition of interest amounts to principal in loan payments

RONA *abbr* FINANCE return on net assets

a–z

Dictionary

ROS *abbr* ACCOUNTING return on sales

round figures FINANCE **numbers adjusted to nearest 10, 100, 1,000, etc.** figures that have been adjusted up or down to the nearest 10, 100, 1,000, and so on

routing number BANKING = *ABA routing number*

royalties FINANCE **share of income paid to creator of product** a proportion of the income from the sale of a product paid to its creator, for example, an inventor, author, or composer

RPI *abbr* ECONOMICS retail price index

RPIX ECONOMICS **indicator of inflation excluding mortgages** in the United Kingdom, an index based on the *retail price index* that excludes mortgage interest payments and is regarded as an indication of the *underlying rate of inflation*

RPIY ECONOMICS **indicator of inflation excluding indirect tax and mortgages** in the United Kingdom, an index based on the *retail price index* that excludes mortgage interest payments and indirect taxation

RPN *abbr* RISK Risk Priority Number

R-squared STOCKHOLDING & INVESTMENTS **benchmarked measure of investment performance** a measure of how much of the performance of an investment can be explained by the performance of a *benchmark index*

rubber check BANKING **check returned because of insufficient funds** a check that cannot be cashed because the person writing it does not have enough money in the account to pay it (slang)

rule of 72 STOCKHOLDING & INVESTMENTS **method of calculating growth of investment** a calculation that an investment will double in value at compound interest after a period shown as 72 divided by the interest percentage, so interest at 10% compounded will double the capital invested in 7.2 years

rule of 78 STOCKHOLDING & INVESTMENTS **calculation of interest rebate on loan repaid early** a method used to calculate the rebate on a loan with front-loaded interest that has been repaid early. It takes into account the fact that as the loan is repaid, the share of each monthly payment related to interest decreases, while the share related to principal increases.

run 1. BANKING, CURRENCY & EXCHANGE **simultaneous withdrawal of money by bank customers** an incidence of bank customers, or owners of holdings in a specific currency, simultaneously withdrawing their entire funds because of a lack of confidence in the institution **2.** STATISTICS **unbroken sequence in statistical series** an uninterrupted sequence of the same value in a statistical series

running account credit BANKING **UK arrangement for borrowing and reborrowing limited sum** in the United Kingdom, an overdraft facility, credit card, or similar system that allows customers to borrow up to a specific limit and reborrow sums previously repaid by either writing a check or using their card

running costs ACCOUNTING = *operating costs*

running total ACCOUNTING **total carried over to next column** a total carried from one column or set of figures to the next

running yield STOCKHOLDING & INVESTMENTS = *current yield*

run-off STOCKHOLDING & INVESTMENTS **reduction in value of mortgage-backed securities** a decline in the value of *mortgage-backed securities*, caused by borrowers refinancing at lower interest rates or defaulting on their loans, resulting in losses by investors in the securities

S

safe custody STOCKHOLDING & INVESTMENTS = *safe keeping*

safe hands STOCKHOLDING & INVESTMENTS **1. investors buying securities to hold for longer term** investors who buy securities and are unlikely to sell in the short- to medium-term **2. securities held by friendly investors** securities held by investors who are not likely to sell them

safe investment STOCKHOLDING & INVESTMENTS **investment unlikely to lose value** an investment such as a bond that is not likely to fall in value

safe keeping STOCKHOLDING & INVESTMENTS **holding by financial institutions of customers' valuable documents** a service provided by a financial institution in which stock certificates, deeds, wills, or a locked deed box are held by it on behalf of customers. Securities are often held under the customer's name in a locked cabinet in the vault so that if the customer wishes to sell, the bank can forward the relevant certificate to the broker. A will is also usually held in this way so that it may be handed to the executor on the customer's death. Deed boxes are always described as "contents unknown to the bank." Most institutions charge a fee for this service. *Also called* **safe custody**

salam FINANCE **agreement to pay now for goods delivered later** in Islamic financing, a contract for the purchase of goods to be delivered at a specified time in the future. Payment for the goods is made in advance.

salary FINANCE **payment for work** a form of pay given to employees at regular intervals in exchange for the work they have done. Traditionally, a salary is a form of remuneration given to professional employees on a monthly basis. In modern usage, the word refers to any form of pay that employees receive on a regular basis. A salary is usually paid straight into an employee's account.

sale and leaseback FINANCE **seller's leasing of previously sold asset** the leasing back by the former owner of an asset, usually buildings, that has been sold to a third party. *Also called* **leaseback**, **renting back**

sale by tender FINANCE **sale to party invited to make offer** the sale of an asset to interested parties who have been invited to make an offer. The asset is sold to the party that makes the highest offer. *See also* **tender**

sales charge STOCKHOLDING & INVESTMENTS **purchase fee on some mutual funds** a fee charged to the purchaser of some types of mutual funds

sales ledger ACCOUNTING = *revenue ledger*

sales mix profit variance FINANCE **varying profitability of products in range** the differing profitability of different products within a product range

sales revenue FINANCE **income from sales** the income generated by sales of goods or services

sales turnover FINANCE **amount of sales in specific period** the total amount sold within a specific time period, usually a year. Sales turnover is often expressed in monetary terms but can also be expressed in terms of the total amount of stock or products sold.

sales volume FINANCE **number of items sold** the number of units of a product sold

sales volume profit variance FINANCE **difference between actual and forecast profits** the difference between the profit on the number of units actually sold and the forecast figure

Sallie Mae FINANCE **US company investing in student loans** the largest source of student loans and administrator of college savings plans in the United States. Created in 1972 as a government-sponsored entity, it became completely privatized in 2004 and is a stockholder-owned company traded on the New York Stock Exchange. Sallie Mae purchases loans from lenders, pools them, and sells them to investors. *Full form* **Student Loan Marketing Association**

salvage value ACCOUNTING = *scrap value*

samurai bond STOCKHOLDING & INVESTMENTS **bond sold by foreign institution in Japan** a bond issue denominated in yen and issued in Japan by a foreign institution. *See also* **shibosai bond**, **shogun bond**

sandbag MERGERS & ACQUISITIONS **prolong negotiations in hostile takeover** in a hostile *takeover* situation, to enter into talks with the bidder and attempt to prolong them as long as possible, in the hope that a *white knight* will appear and rescue the target company (slang)

S&L *abbr* BANKING savings and loan association

S&P *abbr* STOCKHOLDING & INVESTMENTS Standard & Poor's

sarf CURRENCY & EXCHANGE **currency trading** in Islamic financing, the buying and selling of currencies

Save as You Earn STOCKHOLDING & INVESTMENTS **method of saving attracting tax relief** in the United Kingdom, a system for employees to save on a regular basis toward buying shares in their company that is encouraged by the government through tax concessions. *Abbr* **SAYE**

savings FINANCE **money reserved for future use** money set aside by consumers for various purposes such as meeting contingencies or providing an income during retirement. Savings (money in deposit and savings accounts) differ from

investments such as stocks in that they are not usually subject to price fluctuations and are thus considered safer. *Also called* *liquid savings*

savings account BANKING **account paying interest** an account with a bank or savings and loan association that pays interest. *See also* **fixed rate, gross interest, net interest**

savings and loan association BANKING **chartered bank offering services for consumers** in the United States, a *chartered bank* that offers savings accounts, pays dividends, and invests in new mortgages. *Abbr* **S&L**. *Also called* **building and loan association**. *See also* **thrift institution**

savings bank BANKING **bank managing small investments** a bank that specializes in managing small deposits from customers with personal savings. *See also* **thrift institution**

savings bond STOCKHOLDING & INVESTMENTS = *US savings bond*

savings certificate STOCKHOLDING & INVESTMENTS = *National Savings Certificate*

savings function ECONOMICS **measurement of how much people will save** an expression of the extent to which people save money instead of spending it

savings ratio ECONOMICS **measurement of proportion of income saved** the proportion of the income of a country or household that is saved in a particular period

savings-related share option scheme STOCKHOLDING & INVESTMENTS **arrangement allowing UK employees to buy stock** in the United Kingdom, an arrangement that allows employees of a company to buy company shares of stock with money which they have contributed to a savings scheme

SAYE *abbr* STOCKHOLDING & INVESTMENTS Save as You Earn

scarce currency CURRENCY & EXCHANGE **money traded in foreign exchange market** a currency that is traded in a foreign exchange market and for which demand is persistently high relative to its supply

scarcity ECONOMICS **situation in which demand exceeds supply** a situation in which the demand for something exceeds the supply. This can apply to anything from consumer goods to raw materials.

scarcity value FINANCE **value of rare item in great demand** the value something has because it is rare and a large demand exists for it

schedule 1. FINANCE **long-term plan** a plan of how an activity will be carried out over a period of time, drawn up in advance. For example, a repayment schedule sets out how debts will be paid. **2.** FINANCE **list of interest rates** a list of rates of interest that apply to a range of investments **3.** LEGAL **list attached to contract** a list, especially a list forming an additional document attached to a contract **4.** TAX **form relating to UK income tax** in the United Kingdom, a form relating to a particular kind of income liable for income tax **5.** INSURANCE **details of insurance cover** details of the items covered by insurance, sent with the policy

scheme of arrangement FINANCE UK plan for avoiding bankruptcy proceedings in the United Kingdom, a plan offering ways of paying debts, drawn up by a person or company to avoid bankruptcy proceedings

scrap value ACCOUNTING value of asset if scrapped the value of an asset if it is sold for scrap. *Also called* **salvage value**

scrip dividend STOCKHOLDING & INVESTMENTS dividend paid with stock a dividend paid by the issue of additional company shares, rather than by cash

scrip issue *UK* STOCKHOLDING & INVESTMENTS = **stock split**

scripophily STOCKHOLDING & INVESTMENTS collecting of old stocks and bonds the collecting of stock or bond certificates that have been canceled, for their historical, aesthetic, or rarity value

SDR *abbr* CURRENCY & EXCHANGE Special Drawing Right

seasonal adjustment ACCOUNTING accounts adjustment for seasonal distortion of figures an adjustment made to accounts to allow for any short-term seasonal factors such as Christmas sales that may distort the figures

seasoned equity STOCKHOLDING & INVESTMENTS stocks traded for 90 days stocks that have traded for more than 90 days on a regulated market, long enough to be purchased by **retail investors**

seasoned issue STOCKHOLDING & INVESTMENTS offering from established company a stock issue that has traded for more than 90 days on a regulated market, long enough to be purchased by **retail investors**. *See also* **unseasoned issue**

SEC fee STOCKHOLDING & INVESTMENTS US SEC trading fee in the United States, a small fee that the Securities and Exchange Commission charges for the sale of securities listed on a stock exchange

secondary bank BANKING finance company funding installment-plan deals a finance company that provides money for installment-plan deals

secondary issue STOCKHOLDING & INVESTMENTS offer of already traded stock an offer of listed stocks that have previously been publicly traded

second half ACCOUNTING second 6-month period in fiscal year the period of six months that is the second part of any fiscal year

second quarter ACCOUNTING second of four divisions of fiscal year the period of three months from April to the end of June, or the period of three months following the first quarter of the fiscal year. *Abbr* **Q2**

secretary of the board CORPORATE GOVERNANCE *see* **company secretary**

Secretary of the Treasury FINANCE US government official overseeing finance a senior member of the US government in charge of financial affairs

secret reserves FINANCE = **hidden reserves**

sector 1. ECONOMICS businesses in economy providing similar products or services a part of the economy in which businesses produce the same type of product or provide the same type of service **2.** STOCKHOLDING & INVESTMENTS securities in particular industry or market a group of securities in one type of industry or market, for example, the banking sector or the industrial sector

sector fund STOCKHOLDING & INVESTMENTS fund invested in a particular sector a fund that is invested in only one sector of the stock market

secular STOCKHOLDING & INVESTMENTS developing over many years underlying movement over a long period, usually a number of years

secured FINANCE *see* **collateral, security**

secured bond STOCKHOLDING & INVESTMENTS bond with asset as collateral a bond for which real estate or goods have been pledged as collateral

secured creditor FINANCE creditor with legal claim on defaulting debtor's assets a person or organization that is owed money and has a legal claim to some or all of the borrower's assets if the borrower fails to repay the money owed

secured debt FINANCE debt backed by assets a debt that is guaranteed by assets that have been pledged. *See also* **unsecured debt**

secured loan FINANCE loan guaranteed by borrower's assets as security a loan that is guaranteed by the borrower giving assets as security

securities account TREASURY MANAGEMENT account record of financial assets an account that shows the value of financial assets held by a person or organization

securities analyst FINANCE professional studying effectiveness of firms and their securities a professional person who studies the performance of securities and the companies that issue them

securities deposit account BANKING electronic deposit account for securities a brokerage account in which deposits of securities are registered electronically, without receipt of an actual certificate

Securities Institute of Australia FINANCE organization of Australian financial industry professionals a national professional body that represents people involved in the Australian securities and financial services industry. *Abbr* **SIA**

securities lending FINANCE lending of securities between brokers the loan of securities from one broker to another in the process of **selling short**

securitization MORTGAGES, STOCKHOLDING & INVESTMENTS changing debt into securities the process of changing financial assets such as mortgages and loans into securities. The practice of selling mortgages to investors by repackaging the loans as loan notes paying a rate of interest that international banks and fund managers found attractive became widespread and eventually contributed to the financial difficulties experienced by banks and other financial institutions worldwide in 2008.

securitized mortgage STOCKHOLDING & INVESTMENTS **mortgage exchanged for securities** a mortgage that has been converted into securities. *See also* ***securitization***

securitized paper STOCKHOLDING & INVESTMENTS **documents representing securitization** the ***bond*** or ***promissory note*** resulting from changing financial ***assets*** such as mortgages and loans into ***securities***

security 1. STOCKHOLDING & INVESTMENTS **financial asset that can be bought and sold** a tradable financial asset, for example, a bond, stock, or a warrant **2.** FINANCE **guarantee of payment of debt** an asset pledged as collateral for a loan or other borrowing

security deposit FINANCE **deposit forfeited in transaction if buyer backs out** an amount of money paid before a transaction occurs to compensate the seller in the event that the transaction is not concluded because the buyer defaults

security printer FINANCE **printer of valuable documents** a printer who prints paper money, stock prospectuses, and confidential government documents

seed capital *or* seed money FINANCE **money needed to start new business** a usually modest amount of money used to convert an idea into a viable business. Seed capital is a form of ***venture capital***.

seigniorage CURRENCY & EXCHANGE **difference between money's production cost and its value** the difference between the cost of producing a currency and the face value of the currency. If the money is worth more than it cost to produce, the government makes a profit.

selective pricing FINANCE **pricing according to market** setting different prices for the same product or service in different markets. This practice can be broken down as follows: category pricing, which involves cosmetically modifying a product such that the variations allow it to sell in a number of price categories; customer group pricing, which involves modifying the price of a product or service so that different groups of consumers pay different prices; peak pricing, setting a price which varies according to the level of demand; and service level pricing, setting a price based on the specific level of service chosen from a range.

self-certification FINANCE **borrower's unconfirmed statement of income** a statement by a borrower of their income, without confirmation by an employer or accountant, made in order to obtain a loan

self-financing FINANCE **financing of project from own resources** the process by which a company finances a project or business activity from its own resources, rather than by applying for external financing

self-liquidating FINANCE **paying for itself** providing enough income to pay off the amount borrowed for financing

self-tender STOCKHOLDING & INVESTMENTS **US firm's offer to buy back stock** in the United States, the repurchase by a corporation of its stock by way of a tender

semiannual FINANCE **paying or payable twice a year** paying, or requiring payment, every six months

senior capital FINANCE **loan capital with priority for payment** capital in the form of ***secured loans*** to a company that, in the event of liquidation, is repaid before ***junior capital*** such as stockholders' equity

senior debt FINANCE **debt with higher claim on assets than others** a debt whose holder has more claim on the debtor's assets than the holder of another debt. *See also* ***junior debt***

sensitivity analysis ACCOUNTING **analysis of effect of small adjustments to calculation** the analysis of the effect of a small change in a calculation on the final result

separable net assets ACCOUNTING **assets that can be sold separately** assets that can be separated from the rest of the assets of a business and sold off

series STOCKHOLDING & INVESTMENTS **bonds or savings certificates issued over time** a group of bonds or savings certificates, issued over a period of time but all bearing the same interest

Serious Fraud Office FRAUD, REGULATION & COMPLIANCE **UK government department investigating major commercial fraud** in the United Kingdom, a government department in charge of investigating major fraud in companies. *Abbr* **SFO**

service charge 1. FINANCE, BANKING **sum or additional sum paid for service** a fee for any service provided, or an additional fee for any improvements to an existing service. For example, residents in apartment buildings may pay an annual maintenance fee, or banks may charge a fee for operating an account or obtaining foreign currency for customers (also called a ***bank charge***). **2.** MARKETING **payment to serving staff** a gratuity usually paid in restaurants and hotels. A service charge may be voluntary or may be added as a percentage to the bill.

service cost center FINANCE **cost center serving other cost centers in organization** a cost center providing services to other cost centers. When the output of an organization is a service rather than goods, an alternative name is usually used, for example, support cost center or utility cost center.

service/function costing ACCOUNTING **cost accounting for services within organization** ***cost accounting*** for services or functions, for example, canteens, maintenance, or personnel

servicing borrowing FINANCE **paying interest** the process of paying the interest that is due on a loan

set-aside ACCOUNTING = ***reserves***

set-off FINANCE **offset of debts or loss against gain** an agreement between two parties to balance one debt against another or a loss against a gain

settle STOCKHOLDING & INVESTMENTS **finalize security sale** to transfer property such as securities from a seller to a buyer in return for payment

settlement 1. FINANCE **payment** the payment of an outstanding debt, invoice, account, or charge **2.** STOCKHOLDING & INVESTMENTS **finalizing security sale** the transfer of property such as securities from a seller to a buyer in return for payment **3.** E-COMMERCE **transfer of payment to account of e-business** the portion of an electronic transaction during which the customer's credit card is charged for the transaction and the proceeds are deposited into the *merchant account*

settlement date FINANCE **due date for paying debt or charge** the date on which an outstanding debt or charge is due to be paid, or when cash offered for securities or derivatives of them must be delivered

setup costs ACCOUNTING **amount spent to make equipment usable** the costs associated with making a workstation or equipment available for use. Setup costs include the personnel needed to set up the equipment, the cost of downtime during a new setup, and the resources and time needed to test the new setup to achieve the specification of the parts or materials produced.

severance pay *US* FINANCE **payment to dismissed or discharged employee** a payment made by an employer to an employee when the employee who has been dismissed or discharged leaves the organization. *Also called* **unemployment compensation**. *UK term* **redundancy payment**

SFO *abbr* FRAUD, REGULATION & COMPLIANCE Serious Fraud Office

shadow economy ECONOMICS = *black economy*

shadow price ECONOMICS **estimated cost of new economic activity** the amount that engaging in a new economic activity is likely to cost a person or an economy. *See also* **opportunity cost**

share STOCKHOLDING & INVESTMENTS = *stock*

share account 1. BANKING **member's account in UK building society** in the United Kingdom, an account at a building society where the account holder is a member of the society. Account holders who are not members are offered a deposit account. *See also* **deposit account 2.** STOCKHOLDING & INVESTMENTS **account with credit union paying dividends** in the United States, an account with a credit union that pays dividends rather than interest

share at par STOCKHOLDING & INVESTMENTS **stock valued at face value** a share whose value on the stock market is the same as its face value

share buyback STOCKHOLDING & INVESTMENTS = *buyback*

share capital STOCKHOLDING & INVESTMENTS **capital from sale of stock** the amount of *nominal share capital* that a company raises by issuing shares of stock. Share capital does not reflect any subsequent increase or decrease in the value of stock sold; it is capital raised, irrespective of changes in stock value in the secondary markets. *Also called* **issued capital**. *See also* **stockholders' equity**, *reserves*

share certificate *UK* STOCKHOLDING & INVESTMENTS = *stock certificate*

share exchange STOCKHOLDING & INVESTMENTS **exchange of individual stockholdings for shares in fund** a service provided by some collective investment plans whereby they exchange investors' existing individual stockholdings for shares in their funds. This saves the investor the expense of selling holdings, which can be uneconomical when dealing with small stockholdings.

share-for-share offer STOCKHOLDING & INVESTMENTS **bidder's offer of shares as payment for company** a type of *takeover bid* where the bidder offers its own shares, or a combination of cash and shares, for the target company

shareholder STOCKHOLDING & INVESTMENTS **1. somebody owning stock in corporation** a person or organization that owns shares in a limited company or partnership. A shareholder has a stake in the company and becomes a member of it, with rights to attend the annual meeting. Since shareholders have invested money in a company, they have a vested interest in its performance and can be a powerful influence on company policy; they should consequently be considered *stakeholders* as well as shareholders. Some pressure groups have sought to exploit this by becoming shareholders in order to get a particular viewpoint or message across. At the same time, in order to maintain or increase the company's market value, managers must consider their responsibility to shareholders when formulating strategy. It has been argued that on some occasions the desire to make profits to raise returns for shareholders has damaged companies, because it has limited the amount of money spent in other areas (such as the development of facilities, or health and safety). *Also called* **stockholder 2. participant in pooled investment** a person who owns shares of a fund or *investment trust*

shareholders' equity *or* shareholders' funds STOCKHOLDING & INVESTMENTS = *stockholders' equity*

shareholders' perks STOCKHOLDING & INVESTMENTS **benefits for stockholders besides dividends** benefits offered to stockholders in addition to dividends, often in the form of discounts on the company's products and services. *Also called* **stockholder perks**

shareholder value STOCKHOLDING & INVESTMENTS **total return to stockholders including dividends and appreciation** the total return to the stockholders in terms of both dividends and share price growth, calculated as the present value of future free cash flows of the business discounted at the weighted average cost of the capital of the business less the market value of its debt. *Also called* **stockholder value**

shareholder value analysis STOCKHOLDING & INVESTMENTS **firm's value based on return to stockholders** a calculation of the value of a company made by looking at the returns it gives to its stockholders. *Abbr* **SVA**. *Also called* **stockholder value analysis**

shareholding UK STOCKHOLDING & INVESTMENTS = *stockholding*

share issue STOCKHOLDING & INVESTMENTS **offer to sell shares in business** the offering for sale of shares in a business. The capital derived from share issues can be used for investment in the core business or for expansion into new commercial ventures.

share option UK STOCKHOLDING & INVESTMENTS = *stock option*

share option scheme UK STOCKHOLDING & INVESTMENTS = *stock option plan*

shareowner STOCKHOLDING & INVESTMENTS = *shareholder*

share premium STOCKHOLDING & INVESTMENTS **amount paid for share above declared value** the amount payable for a share above its *nominal value*. Most shares are issued at a *premium* to their nominal value. Share premiums are credited to the company's *share premium account*.

share premium account ACCOUNTING **account where firms credit share premiums** the special reserve in a company's balance sheet to which *share premiums* are credited. Expenses associated with the issue of shares may be written off to this account.

share register STOCKHOLDING & INVESTMENTS **list of stockholders** a list of the stockholders in a particular company

share shop STOCKHOLDING & INVESTMENTS **office where stock is traded** the name given by some financial institutions to an office open to the public where stock may be bought and sold

shares of negligible value STOCKHOLDING & INVESTMENTS **worthless shares in defunct firm** shares that are considered as having no value in income tax terms because the company has ceased to exist. The shares of companies in receivership are not deemed to be of negligible value, although they may eventually end up as such.

share split STOCKHOLDING & INVESTMENTS = *scrip issue* stock split

share tip UK STOCKHOLDING & INVESTMENTS = *stock tip*

share warrant STOCKHOLDING & INVESTMENTS **document stating right to hold stock** a document stating that somebody has the right to a number of shares of stockin a company

shariah-compliant FINANCE **in accordance with Islamic law** used to describe financial activities and investments that comply with Islamic law, which prohibits the charging of interest and involvement in any enterprise associated with activities or products forbidden by Islamic law

Sharpe ratio STOCKHOLDING & INVESTMENTS **formula for calculating relationship between risk and return** a method of determining the relationship between investment risk and return, calculated by subtracting the return on a risk-free investment from the rate of return on a portfolio of investments and dividing the result by the standard deviation of the return

sharp practice FRAUD **underhand business methods** business methods that are not illegal but are not entirely open and honest

shelf registration STOCKHOLDING & INVESTMENTS **in US, statement registering future securities sale** in the United States, a *registration statement* filed with the *Securities and Exchange Commission* two years before a corporation issues securities to the public. The statement, which has to be updated periodically, allows the corporation to act quickly when it considers that the market conditions are right without having to start the registration procedure from scratch.

shibosai STOCKHOLDING & INVESTMENTS **sale of securities direct to investors** the Japanese term for a private placement, which is the sale of securities direct to institutions for investment rather than resale

shibosai bond STOCKHOLDING & INVESTMENTS **yen-denominated bond sold direct by issuing company** a bond denominated in yen sold direct to investors by the foreign issuing company. *See also samurai bond, shogun bond*

shift differential FINANCE **extra pay for working unpopular shift** payment made to employees over and above their basic rate to compensate them for the inconvenience of working in shifts. A shift differential usually takes account of the time of day when the shift is worked, the duration of the shift, the extent to which weekend working is involved, and the speed of rotation within the shift.

shinyo kinku BANKING **Japanese bank financing small businesses** in Japan, a financial institution that provides financing for small businesses

shinyo kumiai BANKING **Japanese credit union financing small businesses** in Japan, a credit union that provides financing for small businesses

shirkah FINANCE **contract between people going into business for profit** in Islamic financing, a contract between two or more people who launch a business or financial enterprise in order to make a profit. *Also called musharaka*

shogun bond STOCKHOLDING & INVESTMENTS **non-yen bond sold in Japan by non-Japanese institution** a bond denominated in a currency other than the yen that is sold on the Japanese market by a non-Japanese financial institution. *Also called geisha bond. See also samurai bond, shibosai bond*

short 1. FINANCE **asset behind security benefiting from asset's fall** an asset underlying a security in which a dealer has a short position and so gains by a fall in the asset's value **2.** MARKETS **investor selling short** an investor who is holding a short position **3.** MARKETS = *sell short*

short bill FINANCE **bill payable at short notice** a bill of exchange that becomes payable at short notice

short-change FRAUD **give customer too little change** to give a customer less change than is right, either by mistake or in the hope that it will not be noticed, or to treat somebody less than fairly

short credit FINANCE **credit terms demanding repayment soon** terms of borrowing that allow the customer only a little time to pay

short-dated STOCKHOLDING & INVESTMENTS **maturing in 5 years or less** used to describe securities such as bonds that mature in five years or less. *See also **long-dated, medium-dated***

short-dated bill FINANCE **bill payable almost immediately** a bill that is payable within a few days

short-dated gilts STOCKHOLDING & INVESTMENTS **UK government security maturing within 5 years** fixed-interest securities issued by the UK government that mature in less than five years from the date of purchase. *Also called **shorts**. See also **gilt-edged security***

shortfall FINANCE **amount missing from expected total** an amount that is missing that would make the total expected sum

short interest STOCKHOLDING & INVESTMENTS **quantity of security sold and not repurchased** the total number of shares of a specific security that investors have sold short and have not repurchased in anticipation of a price decline

short position STOCKHOLDING & INVESTMENTS **selling unbought security hoping price will decline** a situation in which somebody sells commodities, currencies, or securities they have borrowed for a fee in the expectation that they will be able to buy them back and return the loan at a lower price, so making a profit. *See also **long position***

shorts STOCKHOLDING & INVESTMENTS = ***short-dated gilts***

short sale STOCKHOLDING & INVESTMENTS **sale of borrowed security anticipating cheap repurchase** a sale of borrowed commodities, currencies, or securities in the expectation that prices will fall before they have to be bought back and then returned to the original owner

short-term bond STOCKHOLDING & INVESTMENTS **bond maturing within 2 years** a bond on the corporate bond market that has an initial maturity of less than two years

short-term capital FINANCE **money on short-term loan** funds raised for a period of less than 12 months, for example, by a bank loan, to cover a short-term shortage. *See also **working capital***

short-term debt FINANCE **debt due within year** debt that has a term of one year or less

short-term economic policy ECONOMICS **economic planning for near future** an economic policy with objectives that can be met within a period of months or a few years

short-term loan FINANCE **loan repayable in weeks** a loan that has to be repaid within a year, usually within a few weeks

short-term security STOCKHOLDING & INVESTMENTS **security maturing within 5 years** a security that matures in less than five years

show stopper MERGERS & ACQUISITIONS (slang) = ***poison pill***

SIA *abbr* FINANCE Securities Institute of Australia

sideline cash FINANCE = ***idle capital***

sight bill FINANCE **bill of exchange payable immediately** a bill of exchange payable when it is presented, rather than at a given length of time after presentation or after a date indicated on the bill

sight deposit BANKING **bank deposit withdrawable immediately** a bank deposit against which the depositor can immediately make a withdrawal

sight draft FINANCE **bill of exchange payable immediately** a bill of exchange that is payable on delivery. *See also **time draft***

sight letter of credit FINANCE **letter of credit presented along with required documents** a ***letter of credit*** that is paid when the necessary documents have been presented

signature guarantee BANKING **stamp or seal validating signature** a stamp or seal, usually from a bank or a broker, that vouches for the authenticity of a signature

signature loan FINANCE = ***unsecured loan***

silly money FINANCE **excessively high or low sum** an amount of money that is regarded as excessively large or, occasionally, small (informal)

simple interest FINANCE **interest paid on principal only** interest charged simply as a constant percentage of the principal and not compounded. *See also **compound interest***

Singapore dollar CURRENCY & EXCHANGE **Singapore's unit of currency** Singapore's unit of currency, whose exchange rate is quoted as S$ per US$

single-currency CURRENCY & EXCHANGE **denominated in same currency** used to describe an international transaction denominated entirely in one currency

single entry ACCOUNTING **book-keeping system using only one entry per transaction** a type of bookkeeping where only one entry, reflecting both a credit to one account and a debit to another, is made for each transaction

single-figure inflation ECONOMICS **inflation below 10%** inflation that is rising at less than 10% per annum

single market ECONOMICS **organization of European nations** the European Union in its role as an economic organization. *See also **European Union***

single-payment bond STOCKHOLDING & INVESTMENTS **bond redeemed with single payment at maturity** a bond redeemed with a single payment combining principal and interest at maturity

sinker STOCKHOLDING & INVESTMENTS **bond paid from debt repayment reserve** a bond whose principal and interest payments are paid out of the issuer's ***sinking fund***

sinking fund FINANCE **money set aside for debt payments** money put aside periodically to settle a liability or replace an asset. The money is invested to produce a required sum at an appropriate time.

SIV *abbr* STOCKHOLDING & INVESTMENTS structured investment vehicle

skimming FRAUD stealing small amounts from customer accounts the unethical and usually illegal practice of taking small amounts of money from accounts that belong to other individuals or organizations

skin in the game FINANCE amount of entrepreneur's money invested in business the amount of an entrepreneur's own money that they have invested in their business, considered by *venture capitalists* as an indication of the entrepreneur's commitment to making the business successful

sleeper 1. STOCKHOLDING & INVESTMENTS stock with potential to rise in value a stock that has not risen in value for some time, but may suddenly do so in the future **2.** BUSINESS product that sells after period of sluggish sales a product that does not sell well for some time, then suddenly becomes very popular

slippage STOCKHOLDING & INVESTMENTS discrepancy between estimated and actual costs the difference between the estimated costs of buying or selling a security and the actual costs of the transaction

slowdown ECONOMICS minor decrease in economic activity a fall in demand that causes a lowering of economic activity, less severe than a *recession* or *slump*

slow payer FINANCE somebody slow to pay debts a person or company that does not pay debts on time

slump ECONOMICS major decrease in economic activity a severe downturn phase in the business cycle

slumpflation ECONOMICS decrease in economic activity with increased inflation a collapse in all economic activity accompanied by wage and price inflation. This happened, for example, in the United States and Europe in 1929. (slang)

slush fund FINANCE fund used for bribery or corruption a fund used by a company for illegal purposes such as bribing officials to obtain preferential treatment for planned work or expansion

small change FINANCE money in coins a small quantity of coins of mixed value that somebody might carry, often used to suggest a sum of no significance

smurf FRAUD somebody involved in money-laundering someone who passes money obtained illegally through banks or businesses in order to make it appear legitimate

snake CURRENCY & EXCHANGE currencies formerly in European Exchange Rate Mechanism formerly, the group of currencies within the European Exchange Rate Mechanism whose exchange rates were allowed to fluctuate against each other within specific bands or limits

social lending FINANCE direct lending between people the practice of one person offering to lend money to another, without the involvement of a bank or other institution, especially through the Internet. *Also called* ***person-to-person lending***. *See also* **ZOPA**

socially conscious investing STOCKHOLDING & INVESTMENTS = *ethical investment*

social marginal cost ECONOMICS cost to society of change in economic variable the additional cost to a society of a change in an economic variable, for example, the price of gas or bread

Society for Worldwide Interbank Financial Telecommunication BANKING *see* **SWIFT**

socioeconomic ECONOMICS relating to social and economic factors involving both social and economic factors. Structural unemployment, for example, has socioeconomic causes.

soft capital rationing ACCOUNTING management's imposition of limit on capital investment a restriction on an organization's ability to invest capital funds caused by an internal budget ceiling being imposed by management. *See also* ***capital rationing***

soft commissions FINANCE brokerage commissions rebated to institutional customer brokerage commissions that are rebated to an institutional customer in the form of, or to pay for, research or other services

soft currency CURRENCY & EXCHANGE currency that is weak or expected to fall a currency that is weak, usually because there is an excess of supply and a belief that its value will fall in relation to others. *See also* ***hard currency***

soft landing ECONOMICS slowdown of economic activity without recession the situation when a country's economic activity has slowed down but demand has not fallen far enough or rapidly enough to cause a recession

soft loan FINANCE loan on highly favorable terms a loan on exceptionally favorable terms, for example, for a project that a government considers worthy

sold short STOCKHOLDING & INVESTMENTS borrowed and sold anticipating price drop used to refer to commodities, currencies, or securities that somebody borrows and sells, then buys back and repays in the expectation that prices will have fallen. *See also* ***sell short***

solicit FINANCE request money to ask another person or company for money

solvency FINANCE situation of being able to pay all debts situation in which a person or organization is able to pay all debts on their due date. *See also* ***insolvency***

solvency margin FINANCE business's assets minus liabilities a business's *liquid assets* that exceed the amount required to meet its liabilities

solvency ratio 1. FINANCE ratio of assets to liabilities a ratio of assets to liabilities, used to measure a company's ability to meet its debts **2.** INSURANCE in UK, measure of insurance company's financial condition in the United Kingdom, the ratio of an insurance company's net assets to its non-life premium income

solvent FINANCE able to pay all one's debts used to refer to a situation in which the assets of an individual or organization are worth more than their liabilities

sort code UK BANKING **number identifying UK bank branch** a combination of numbers that identifies a bank branch on official documentation such as bank statements and checks. *See also* **ABA routing number**

source and application of funds statement ACCOUNTING = *cash flow statement*

sources and uses of funds statement ACCOUNTING = *cash flow statement*

sovereign bond STOCKHOLDING & INVESTMENTS **government bond in foreign currency** a bond issued by a national government denominated in a foreign currency

sovereign debt FINANCE **borrowing by government** borrowing that has been undertaken by a government

sovereign default FINANCE **government not repaying debt** the inability or refusal of a government to pay back money it has borrowed

sovereign loan FINANCE **bank loan to foreign government** a loan by a financial institution to an overseas government, usually of an emerging country. *See also* **sovereign risk**

sovereign money STOCKHOLDING & INVESTMENTS **money in sovereign wealth funds** the money that is invested in *sovereign wealth funds*

sovereign risk FINANCE **risk that government defaults on loan** the risk that a government may refuse to repay or be unable to repay money it has borrowed

sovereign wealth fund STOCKHOLDING & INVESTMENTS **very wealthy state investment fund** an investment fund owned by a government with very large amounts of money at its disposal. There is concern that such a fund would be able to buy stakes in another country's strategic industries. *Abbr* **SWF**

special clearing BANKING = *special presentation*

special damages FINANCE **damages awarded for calculable loss** damages awarded by a court to compensate for a loss that can be calculated, for example, the expense of repairing something

special deposit 1. MORTGAGES **in US, mortgage money for home improvements** in the United States, an amount of money set aside for the renovation or improvement of a property as part of a mortgage **2.** BANKING **commercial bank's required deposit in Bank of England** a large sum of money that a commercial bank has to deposit with the Bank of England

Special Drawing Right CURRENCY & EXCHANGE **country's entitlement to receive IMF loans** an accounting unit used by the *International Monetary Fund*, allocated to each member country for use in loans and other international operations. The value is calculated daily on the weighted values of a group of currencies shown in dollars. *Abbr* **SDR**

special notice STOCKHOLDING & INVESTMENTS **late announcement of proposal for stockholder meeting** notice of a proposal to be put before a meeting of the stockholders of a company that is issued less than 28 days before the meeting

special presentation BANKING **direct delivery of check to paying banker** the sending of a check directly to the paying banker rather than through the clearing system. *Also called* **special clearing**. *See also* **advice of fate**

special purpose bond STOCKHOLDING & INVESTMENTS **bond for one particular project** a bond for one particular project, financed by levies on the people who benefit from the project

special resolution CORPORATE GOVERNANCE **vote held on exceptional issue** in the United Kingdom, an exceptional issue that is put to the vote at a company's general meeting, for example, a change to the company's articles of association, requiring 21 days' notice

special situation STOCKHOLDING & INVESTMENTS **expectation of stock price rise** the expectation that a stock will increase in value as a result of a change in the company such as a merger

specie CURRENCY & EXCHANGE **coins that are legal tender** coins, as opposed to pieces of paper money, that are legal tender

specific charge FINANCE = *fixed charge*

specific order costing ACCOUNTING **way to track costs billed by separate contractors** the basic cost accounting method used where work consists of separately identifiable contracts, jobs, or batches

speculation FINANCE **purchase made on basis of large anticipated gain** a purchase made solely to make a profit when the price or value of something increases

spending money CURRENCY & EXCHANGE **personal money** money that is available for small ordinary personal expenses

split STOCKHOLDING & INVESTMENTS = *stock split*

split-capital investment trust *or* split-capital trust STOCKHOLDING & INVESTMENTS = *split-level investment trust*

split commission FINANCE **transaction fee divided among multiple parties** commission that is divided between two or more parties in a transaction

split coupon bond STOCKHOLDING & INVESTMENTS = *zero coupon bond*

split-level investment trust *or* split-level trust STOCKHOLDING & INVESTMENTS **investment trust combining income shares and capital shares** an investment trust with two categories of shares: *income shares*, which receive income from the investments, but do not benefit from the rise in their capital value, and *capital shares*, which increase in value as the value of the investments rises. Income shareholders receive all or most of the income generated by the trust and a predetermined sum at liquidation, while capital shareholders receive no interest but the remainder of the capital at liquidation. *Also called* **split trust, split-capital investment trust, split-capital trust**

split payment FINANCE **payment greatly subdivided** a payment that is divided into small units

split trust STOCKHOLDING & INVESTMENTS = *split-level investment trust*

sponsor 1. FINANCE **person or company giving money for venture** a person or company that pays money to help with an activity or to pay for a business venture **2.** FINANCE **firm giving money to sport for advertising rights** a company that pays to help a sport, in return for advertising rights **3.** STOCKHOLDING & INVESTMENTS **backer of an initial public offering** an organization such as an investment bank that backs an initial public offering **4.** BUSINESS **somebody giving job recommendation** somebody who recommends another person for a job **5.** MARKETING **company purchasing advertising on TV program** a company that pays part of the cost of making a television program by taking advertising time on the program

sponsorship 1. FINANCE **financial support** financial backing for an activity or business venture **2.** MARKETING **financial support as means of advertising** a form of advertising in which an organization provides funds for something such as a television program or sports event in return for exposure to a target audience

spot cash CURRENCY & EXCHANGE **cash paid on the spot** cash paid immediately for something bought

spot currency market CURRENCY & EXCHANGE, MARKETS **market for currency deliverable at time of sale** a market that deals in foreign exchange for immediate rather than future delivery. *See also* ***spot market***

spot exchange rate CURRENCY & EXCHANGE, MARKETS **current exchange rate** the exchange rate used for immediate currency transactions

spread 1. MARKETS **difference between buying and selling price for security** the difference between the buying and selling price of a security achieved by a ***market maker*** on a stock exchange **2.** STOCKHOLDING & INVESTMENTS **mix of investments** the range of the investments in a particular portfolio

spread betting STOCKHOLDING & INVESTMENTS **betting on stock movements within specified range** betting on the movement of a stock price in relation to a range of high and low values. If the price moves outside the range on a specific day, the bettor wins a multiple of the original stake times the number of points outside the range.

sprinkling trust STOCKHOLDING & INVESTMENTS **trust in which trustees have discretion over distributions** a trust with multiple beneficiaries where the trustees have discretion over how the trust's income is distributed

Square Mile FINANCE = ***the City***

squeeze ECONOMICS **government restriction of available credit** a government policy of restriction, commonly affecting the availability of credit in an economy

SSAPs *abbr* REGULATION & COMPLIANCE, ACCOUNTING Statements of Standard Accounting Practice

stabilization fund ECONOMICS **government reserve for international financial support** a fund created by a government for use in maintaining its official exchange rate when necessary

stag STOCKHOLDING & INVESTMENTS **somebody buying new stock for immediate resale** somebody who buys initial public offerings at the offering price and sells them immediately to make a profit

staged payments FINANCE **payments made in stages** payments that are made in stages over a period of time

stagflation ECONOMICS **situation with high unemployment and inflation** a situation in which both inflation and unemployment exist at the same time in an economy. There was stagflation in the United Kingdom and the United States in the 1970s, for example.

stagnation ECONOMICS **situation with no economic progress** a situation in which no progress is being made, especially in economic matters

stakeholder theory STOCKHOLDING & INVESTMENTS **theory that stockholders' interests needn't harm stakeholders** the theory that an organization can enhance the interests of its stockholders without damaging the interests of its wider ***stakeholders***. Stakeholder theory grew in response to the ***economic theory of the firm***. One of the difficulties of stakeholder theory is allocating importance to the values of different groups of stakeholders, and a solution to this is proposed by ***stakeholder value analysis***.

stakeholder value analysis STOCKHOLDING & INVESTMENTS **assessment of stakeholders' views for corporate planning purposes** a method of determining the values of the ***stakeholders*** in an organization for the purposes of making strategic and operational decisions. Stakeholder value analysis is one method of justifying an approach based on ***stakeholder theory*** rather than the ***economic theory of the firm***. It involves identifying groups of stakeholders and eliciting their views on particular issues in order that these views may be taken into account when making decisions.

stale bull STOCKHOLDING & INVESTMENTS **investor seeking to sell nonperforming security** an investor who bought stocks hoping that they would rise, and now finds that they have not risen and wants to sell them

Standard & Poor's STOCKHOLDING & INVESTMENTS **major US bond-rating corporation** in the United States, a corporation that rates bonds according to the creditworthiness of the organizations issuing them. Standard & Poor's also issues stock market indices, for example, the S&P 500. *Abbr* **S&P**. *See also* ***Moody's***

Standard & Poor's rating STOCKHOLDING & INVESTMENTS **US stock rating service** a stock rating service provided by the US agency Standard & Poor's

standard cost FINANCE **calculated future cost as basis of estimates** a future cost that is calculated in advance and against which estimates are measured

standard costing ACCOUNTING **comparison of standard and actual costs** a control procedure that compares standard costs and revenues with actual results to obtain variances, which are used to stimulate improved performance

a–z

Dictionary

standard of living ECONOMICS **people's ability to buy desired goods and services** a measure of economic well-being based on the ability of people to buy the goods and services they desire

standby credit 1. BANKING = *backup credit* **2.** ECONOMICS **credit that can be used by emerging countries** credit drawing rights given to an emerging country by an international financial institution, to fund industrialization or other growth policies

standby fee FINANCE **fee for additional loan** a fee paid to obtain *standby credit*

standby loan ECONOMICS **loan to emerging country for specific purposes** a loan given to an emerging country by an international financial institution, to fund technology hardware purchase or other growth policies

standing order UK BANKING = *automatic debit*

staple commodity FINANCE **basic item of trade** any basic food or a raw material that is important in a country's economy

star 1. STOCKHOLDING & INVESTMENTS **outstanding investment** an investment that is performing extremely well **2.** BUSINESS **fast-growing business with high market share** in the *Boston Box* model, a business with a high market share and high growth rate. *See also* **Boston Box**

startup costs FINANCE **money required to launch new business** the initial sum required to establish a business or to get a project under way. The costs will include the capital expenditure and related expenses before the business or project generates revenue.

startup financing *or* **start-up financing** FINANCE **first stage in financing new project** the first stage in financing a new project, which is followed by several rounds of investment capital as the project gets under way

state bank BANKING **bank chartered by US state** in the United States, a commercial bank chartered by one of the states rather than having a federal charter

state capitalism ECONOMICS **capitalistic system where government controls most production** a way of organizing society in which the state controls most of a country's means of production and capital

statement BANKING **list of bank account transactions** a summary of all transactions, for example, deposits or withdrawals, that have occurred in an account at a bank or savings and loan association over a given period of time

statement of account ACCOUNTING **1. list of recent transactions** a summary of transactions that have occurred between two parties over a given period of time **2. list of commercial transactions** a list of sums due, usually comprising unpaid invoices, items paid on account but not offset against particular invoices, credit notes, debit notes, and discounts

statement of affairs ACCOUNTING **list of assets and liabilities showing financial condition** a statement in a prescribed form, usually prepared by a receiver, showing the estimated financial position of a debtor or a company that may be unable to meet its debts. It contains a summary of the debtor's assets and liabilities, with the assets shown at their estimated realizable values. The various classes of creditors, such as preferential, secured, partly secured, and unsecured, are shown separately.

statement of cash flows ACCOUNTING **list of cash transactions** a statement that documents actual receipts and expenditures of cash

statement-of-cash-flows method ACCOUNTING **accounting system based on business's cash flow** a method of accounting that is based on flows of cash rather than balances on accounts

statement of changes in financial position ACCOUNTING **list of business's income and expenditures** a financial report of a company's incomes and outflows during a period, usually a year or a quarter

statement of source and application of funds ACCOUNTING = *cash flow statement*

statement of total recognized gains and losses ACCOUNTING **list of changes in stockholders' equity** a financial statement showing changes in stockholders' equity during an accounting period

Statements of Standard Accounting Practice REGULATION & COMPLIANCE, ACCOUNTING **UK rules for preparation of financial statements** rules laid down by the UK Accounting Standards Board for the preparation of financial statements. *Abbr* **SSAPs**

state of indebtedness FINANCE **situation of owing money** the situation that exists when somebody owes money

status inquiry FINANCE **credit check** the act of checking on a customer's credit rating

statute-barred debt FINANCE **debt that is uncollectable after time limit** a debt that cannot be pursued as the time limit laid down by law has expired

statutory auditor ACCOUNTING, REGULATION & COMPLIANCE **in UK, officially qualified auditor** in the United Kingdom, a professional person qualified to conduct an audit required by the Companies Act

statutory voting CORPORATE GOVERNANCE **system granting one vote per share** a system of voting in which stockholders in a company have one vote per share of stock owned

sterling CURRENCY & EXCHANGE **UK currency** the standard currency (pounds and pence) used in the United Kingdom

sterling area CURRENCY & EXCHANGE **formerly, countries using sterling as trading currency** formerly, the area of the world where the pound sterling was the main trading currency

sterling balances CURRENCY & EXCHANGE **trade balances expressed in sterling** a country's trade balances expressed in pounds sterling

sterling index CURRENCY & EXCHANGE **index measuring sterling against other currencies** an index that shows the current value of sterling against a group of other currencies

stipend FINANCE **regular payment to office-holder** a regular remuneration or allowance paid as a salary to an office-holder such as a member of the clergy

stock 1. STOCKHOLDING & INVESTMENTS **fixed interest investment** a form of security issued in fixed units at a fixed rate of interest. The technical difference between stocks and shares is that a company that fixes its capital in terms of a monetary amount and then sells different proportions of it to investors creates stock, while a company that creates a number of shares of equal nominal value and sells different numbers of them to investors creates shares. For all practical purposes they are the same. In the United States, all equity instruments are called stocks, whereas in the United Kingdom, they are called shares. **2.** UK OPERATIONS & PRODUCTION = **inventory**

stockalypse STOCKHOLDING & INVESTMENTS **collapse in stock prices** a sudden and dramatic drop in the price of stock (slang)

stockbroker STOCKHOLDING & INVESTMENTS **professional agent for securities** a person or company that arranges the sale and purchase of stocks and other securities, usually for a commission. *Also called* **broker**

stockbroking STOCKHOLDING & INVESTMENTS **dealing in stock** the business of dealing in stocks and other securities for clients

stock buyback STOCKHOLDING & INVESTMENTS = **buyback**

stock certificate US STOCKHOLDING & INVESTMENTS **document representing ownership in firm** a document that certifies ownership of stock in a company. *UK term* **share certificate**

stock depreciation UK ACCOUNTING = **inventory depreciation**

stock dividend STOCKHOLDING & INVESTMENTS **dividend paid as additional shares of stock** a dividend paid to a stockholder in the form of additional stock rather than cash

stockholder US STOCKHOLDING & INVESTMENTS **somebody with shares in company** a person or organization that owns one or more shares of stock in a company. *UK term* **shareholder** (sense 1)

stockholder perks US STOCKHOLDING & INVESTMENTS = **shareholders' perks**

stockholders' equity US FINANCE **firm's share capital and reserves** the part of a company's financial assets consisting of share capital and retained profits. *Also called* **shareholders' equity, shareholders' funds**

stockholder value US STOCKHOLDING & INVESTMENTS = **shareholder value**

stockholder value analysis US STOCKHOLDING & INVESTMENTS = **shareholder value analysis**

stockholding US STOCKHOLDING & INVESTMENTS **ownership of shares in firm** the stock in a corporation owned by a stockholder. *UK term* **shareholding**

stock option STOCKHOLDING & INVESTMENTS **right to buy or sell on agreed terms** the right of an option holder to buy or sell a specific stock on predetermined terms on, or before, a future date. *Also called* **option**. *UK term* **share option**

stock option plan US STOCKHOLDING & INVESTMENTS **employees' right to buy company stock** a program in which an employee is given the option to buy a specific number of shares of stock at a future date, at an agreed price. Stock options provide a financial benefit to the recipient only if the stock price rises over the period the option is available. If the stock price falls over the period, the employee is under no obligation to buy. There may be a tax advantage to the employees who participate in such a program. Share options may be available to all employees or operated on a discretionary basis. *UK term* **share option scheme**

stockpicker STOCKHOLDING & INVESTMENTS **buyer choosing stock** somebody who is choosing which stock to buy. *See also* **bottom-up approach**

stocks and shares STOCKHOLDING & INVESTMENTS **firms' capital owned by public** the units of ownership in public companies. The technical difference between stocks and shares is that a company that fixes its capital in terms of a monetary amount and then sells different proportions of it to investors creates stock, while a company that creates a number of shares of equal nominal value and sells different numbers of them to investors creates shares. For all practical purposes they are the same. In the United States, all equity instruments are called stocks, whereas in the United Kingdom, they are called shares.

stocks and shares ISA STOCKHOLDING & INVESTMENTS **UK tax-free account for investment** in the United Kingdom, an investment account for which interest is not paid on dividends, and capital gains tax is not paid on any profits. The maximum that can be invested per tax year is capped, at £11,280 for 2012–13, although this is reduced by the amount invested in any cash ISA also held. *See also* **cash ISA, ISA**

stock split US STOCKHOLDING & INVESTMENTS **numerical increase of shares without affecting total value** an act of issuing stockholders with at least one more share for every share owned, without affecting the total value of each holding. A stock split usually occurs because the stock price has become too high for easy trading. *Also called* **share split, split**. *See also* **bonus shares, reverse split**. *UK term* **scrip issue**

stock tip US STOCKHOLDING & INVESTMENTS **expert's recommendation on stock** a recommendation about a stock published in the financial press, usually based on research published by a financial institution. *UK term* **share tip**

stock turnover UK STOCKHOLDING & INVESTMENTS = **inventory turnover**

stock turns ACCOUNTING = **inventory turnover**

stock valuation UK ACCOUNTING = **inventory valuation**

stokvel BANKING **S. African savings association** in South Africa, an informal, widely used cooperative savings program that provides small-scale loans

stop-go ECONOMICS **alternately tightening and loosening economic policies** the alternate tightening and loosening of fiscal and monetary policies, characteristic of the UK economy in the 1960s and 1970s

store card FINANCE **credit card used exclusively in department store** a credit card issued by a large department store, which can only be used for purchases in that store

story stock STOCKHOLDING & INVESTMENTS **stock reported on in press** a stock that is the subject of a press or financial community story that may affect its price

straddle STOCKHOLDING & INVESTMENTS **simultaneous security purchase of put and call options** the act of buying a *put option* and a *call option* for the same number of shares of the same security at the same time with the same *strike price* and expiration date. This allows the buyer to make a profit if the price rises or falls. *See also strangle*

straight line depreciation ACCOUNTING **reducing value of asset evenly over its lifetime** a form of *depreciation* in which the cost of a fixed asset is spread equally over each year of its anticipated lifetime

strategic financial management FINANCE **handling firm's money to achieve firm's goals** the identification of the strategies capable of maximizing an organization's net present value, the allocation of scarce capital resources, and the implementation and monitoring of a particular strategy

stress test BANKING **review of system's stability** a stringent set of checks on the stability and security of a system or of an organization such as a bank

strike price STOCKHOLDING & INVESTMENTS **price fixed by seller** the price for a security or commodity that underlies an *option*. *Also called exercise price (sense 2)*

strip STOCKHOLDING & INVESTMENTS **separation of coupons from bond for sale individually** the separation of the coupons from the principal of a bond in order to sell them separately as a package of interest coupons and a bond that repays principal without interest. *See also strips*

strippable bond STOCKHOLDING & INVESTMENTS **bond separable into principal and interest payments** a bond that can be divided into separate zero-coupon bonds, representing its principal and interest payments, which can be traded independently

stripped bond STOCKHOLDING & INVESTMENTS **bond separated into principal and interest payments** a bond that has been divided into separate zero-coupon bonds, representing its principal and interest payments, which can be traded independently

stripped stock STOCKHOLDING & INVESTMENTS **stock without dividend rights** stock for which the rights to dividends have been split off and sold separately

stripping STOCKHOLDING & INVESTMENTS **splitting bond into two parts for separate trading** the process of separating the coupons from the principal of a bond in order to sell them separately as a package of interest coupons and a bond that repays principal without interest. *See also strips*

strips STOCKHOLDING & INVESTMENTS **bond parts allowing interest or principal payments only** the parts of a *stripped bond* that entitle the owner to interest payments only, or to the payment of principal only

strong currency CURRENCY & EXCHANGE **currency with relatively high value** a currency that has a high value against other currencies

structural adjustment ECONOMICS **change in basic framework of economy** the reallocation of resources in response to alterations in the composition of the output of an economy as it experiences changes between the contribution of different business sectors. *Also called structural change*

structural change ECONOMICS = *structural adjustment*

structural fund STOCKHOLDING & INVESTMENTS **mutual fund invested in EU economic development** a type of mutual fund that invests in projects that contribute to the economic development of poorer nations in the European Union

structural inflation ECONOMICS **inflation with no specific cause** inflation that naturally occurs in an economy, without any particular triggering event

structural reform FINANCE **improve and strengthen system** reorganization of a system by which something such as the financial services industry is managed in order to strengthen it

structural unemployment ECONOMICS **unemployment caused by change in basic economic framework** unemployment resulting from a change in demand or technological advances, which cause a surplus of labor in a particular location or skills area

structured finance FINANCE **nonstandard form of borrowing** complex financial arrangements individually designed to support a client's needs for which the normal sources of financing are not suitable

structured investment vehicle STOCKHOLDING & INVESTMENTS **product with short-term borrowing funding high-yielding securities** a product that borrows money in the short-term credit market to invest in high-yielding, longer-dated securities. *Abbr SIV*

structured note FINANCE **debt with derivative component** typically, a senior unsecured debt obligation with a derivative component, reflecting the terms of the transaction and specifying payments, normally including the return of the principal amount at maturity (for principal protected notes), or possibly some principal loss (in the case of nonprincipal protected notes), depending on the performance of the underlying investment

structured product STOCKHOLDING & INVESTMENTS **customized financial contract** a legally binding financial contract between a client and an investment bank, designed to meet a client's specific needs and stating the specific terms that have been agreed. The legal form of the transaction is called a wrapper.

stub equity STOCKHOLDING & INVESTMENTS **1. money from high risk bond sales** the money raised through the sale of large quantities of high risk bonds, as in a *leveraged buyout* **2. stock with greatly reduced price** a stock whose price has seriously fallen due to major financial problems. Stub stock is a risky investment with great potential if the company regains its strength.

Student Loan Marketing Association FINANCE *see Sallie Mae*

subject to collection FINANCE **depending on repayment** dependent upon the ability to collect the amount owed

subordinated debt FINANCE = *junior debt*

subordinated loan FINANCE **debt whose repayment ranks after all others** a loan that ranks below all other borrowings with regard to both the payment of interest and principal. *See also pari passu*

subprime loan FINANCE **loan made to borrower unlikely to repay** a loan made to somebody who does not meet the usual or standard qualifications for borrowing the amount in question. In 2007–8, a world financial crisis was precipitated by defaults on subprime mortgage loans.

subscribed capital *or* subscribed share capital STOCKHOLDING & INVESTMENTS = *issued share capital*

subscriber 1. STOCKHOLDING & INVESTMENTS **somebody who buys stocks in new firm** a buyer, especially one who buys stocks in a new company or new issues **2.** BUSINESS **original stockholder** a person who signs a company's *memorandum of association*

subscription price STOCKHOLDING & INVESTMENTS **price of new stock offered for sale** the price at which new shares of stock in an existing company are offered for sale

subscription share STOCKHOLDING & INVESTMENTS **share of stock in new firm** a stock purchased by a subscriber when a new company is formed

subsidiary account BANKING **individual account for one owner of joint account** an account for one of the individual people or organizations that jointly hold another account

subsidized FINANCE **having financial assistance** for which a *subsidy* has been paid

subsidy FINANCE **financial assistance for activity or firm** financial assistance to a company or group of people, usually given by a government, to encourage new developments of benefit to the public or to support an industry for a period of time. Subsidies are regarded as restrictive in international trade if by supporting a domestic industry they make imports more expensive.

subsistence allowance FINANCE **money for living expenses away from home** *expenses* paid by an employer, usually within preset limits, to cover the cost of accommodations, meals, and incidental expenses incurred by employees when away on business

subtreasury FINANCE **subordinate treasury** a place where some of a nation's money is held

subvention FINANCE **financial support given officially** money given by a government or official body to support an activity

sukuk FINANCE **asset-backed interest-free bond** in Islamic financing, the equivalent of a bond, which represents undivided shares in ownership of tangible assets. Under Islamic law it cannot earn interest.

sum FINANCE **1. money** a particular amount of money **2. total amount of something** the total amount of any given item, such as stocks or securities **3. total of added numbers** the total arising from the addition of two or more numbers

sum at risk FINANCE, RISK **how much of something investors might lose** an amount of any given item, such as money, stocks, or securities, that an investor might lose

sum of digits method *or* **sum-of-the-year's-digits depreciation** ACCOUNTING = *accelerated depreciation*

sums chargeable to the reserve ACCOUNTING **sums debited to company's reserves** sums that can be debited to a company's reserves

sunk cost ACCOUNTING **completed cost unrelated to future decisions** a cost that has been irreversibly incurred or committed prior to a decision point, and cannot therefore be considered relevant to subsequent decisions

supplementary capital BANKING = *Tier 2 capital*

supply and demand ECONOMICS **quantity of available goods and desire for them** the quantity of goods available for sale at a given price, and the level of consumer need for those goods. The balance of supply and demand fluctuates as external economic factors—for example, the cost of materials and the level of competition in the marketplace—influence the level of demand from consumers and the desire and ability of producers to supply the goods. Supply and demand is recognized as an economic force, and is often referred to as the law of supply and demand.

supply shock ECONOMICS **event causing reduced supply of necessity** an event that causes a sudden reduction, or perceived reduction, in the production or availability of a product or resource necessary to an economy

supply-side economics ECONOMICS **economic theory stressing incentives for suppliers** a branch of economics that emphasizes the production of goods through incentives as a means of stimulating economic growth

support price ECONOMICS **product price subsidized by government** the price of a product that is fixed or stabilized by a government so that it cannot fall below a specific level

support ratio ECONOMICS = *dependency ratio*

surety FINANCE **1. guarantor** somebody who promises to cover another person's obligations **2. guarantee for loan** the *collateral* given as security when a person, business, or organization takes out a loan

a–z

Dictionary

surplus ACCOUNTING = *budget surplus*

surrender charge FINANCE **penalty for early withdrawal of invested money** a charge levied when somebody withdraws money invested before the date allowed

sushi bond STOCKHOLDING & INVESTMENTS **Japanese bond** a bond that is not denominated in yen and is issued in any market by a Japanese financial institution. This type of bond is often bought by Japanese institutional investors. (slang)

suspense account BANKING **temporary holding account** an account in which debits or credits are held temporarily until sufficient information is available for them to be posted to the correct accounts

SVA *abbr* STOCKHOLDING & INVESTMENTS shareholder value analysis

swap 1. FINANCE, STOCKHOLDING & INVESTMENTS **trade of payment terms between two firms** an arrangement whereby two organizations contractually agree to exchange payments on different terms, for example, in different currencies, or one at a fixed rate and the other at a floating rate. *See also **asset swap, bond swap, interest rate swap*** **2.** FINANCE **exchange** an exchange of credits or liabilities

swap book STOCKHOLDING & INVESTMENTS **list of exchanges wanted** a broker's list of stocks or securities that clients wish to swap

swaption STOCKHOLDING & INVESTMENTS **right to exchange** an *option* giving the right but not the obligation to enter into a *swap* contract (slang)

sweat equity FINANCE **unpaid work by firm's founder** work done for little or no pay by the owner or partners of a new company in the early stages of the company's activities

sweep facility BANKING **automatic service moving money to different account** the automatic transfer of sums from a checking account to a deposit account, or from any low interest account to a higher one. For example, a personal customer may have the balance transferred just before receipt of their monthly salary, or a business may stipulate that when a balance exceeds a specific sum, the excess is to be transferred.

sweetener 1. STOCKHOLDING & INVESTMENTS **high-yield investment added to lower yield collection** a security with a high yield that has been added to a portfolio to improve its overall return. *See also **kicker*** **2.** GENERAL MANAGEMENT **incentive** an incentive offered to somebody to take a particular course of action **3.** STOCKHOLDING & INVESTMENTS **attractive extra feature on investment product** a feature added to a security to make it more attractive to investors

SWF *abbr* STOCKHOLDING & INVESTMENTS sovereign wealth fund

SWIFT BANKING **society supporting common global financial transactions network** a nonprofit cooperative organization with the mission of creating a shared worldwide data processing and communications link and a common language for international financial transactions. Established in Brussels in 1973 with the support of 239 banks in 15 countries, it now has over 7,000 live users in 192 countries, exchanging millions of messages valued in trillions of dollars every business day. *Full form* ***Society for Worldwide Interbank Financial Telecommunication***

switch 1. STOCKHOLDING & INVESTMENTS **replace one investment product in set with another** to exchange a specific security with another within a portfolio, usually because the investor's objectives have changed **2.** STOCKHOLDING & INVESTMENTS **swap involving exchange rates** a type of *swap* that involves different currencies and interest rates. *See also **swap*** **3.** OPERATIONS & PRODUCTION **move goods elsewhere** to move a commodity from one location to another

Switch BANKING **UK debit card** a debit card formerly used in the United Kingdom

switching STOCKHOLDING & INVESTMENTS **buying and selling different futures contracts simultaneously** the simultaneous sale and purchase of contracts in futures with different expiration dates, as, for example, when a business decides that it would like to take delivery of a commodity earlier or later than originally contracted

switching discount STOCKHOLDING & INVESTMENTS **lower charge to existing customers for exchanging funds** the discount available to holders of collective investments who move from one fund to another offered by the same fund manager. The discount is usually a lower initial charge compared to the one made to new investors, or to existing investors who make a further investment.

SYD *abbr* ACCOUNTING sum-of-the-year's-digits depreciation = *accelerated depreciation*

syndicate 1. BUSINESS **group joining together for business activity** a group of people or companies that come together for a specific business activity, especially when they jointly contribute capital to a project **2.** GENERAL MANAGEMENT **distribute item to several outlets** to agree to distribute an article, a cartoon, a television show, or other work to several different outlets, publications, or broadcasting companies **3.** BANKING **get large loan underwritten by international banks** to arrange for a large loan to be underwritten by several international banks

synthetic CDO FINANCE **investment backed by derivatives** a collateralized debt obligation that is based on credit derivatives rather than bonds or loans

systematic risk RISK **risk related to securities market or economy** investment risk that is attributable to the performance of the stock market or the economy

systematic withdrawal STOCKHOLDING & INVESTMENTS **regular payment from mutual fund to shareholder** an arrangement in which a mutual fund pays out a specific amount to the shareholder at regular intervals. *See also **withdrawal plan***

T

T + FINANCE **number of days for completing business deal** an expression of the number of days allowed for settlement of a transaction

tail 1. MARKETS **difference between acceptable yields in US Treasury auction** the spread between the average yield accepted in an auction of US government securities and the highest yield accepted **2.** STOCKHOLDING & INVESTMENTS **numbers after decimal point in bond price** the figures that come after the decimal point in the quoted price of a bond

take a flier FINANCE **guess** to speculate about what might happen (slang)

take a hit FINANCE **lose money** to make a loss on an investment (slang)

take-home pay FINANCE (informal) = *net pay*

takeout STOCKHOLDING & INVESTMENTS **selling stock in firm** the act of removing capital that was originally invested in a new company by selling stock

takeout financing FINANCE **long-term borrowing** long-term loans taken out to replace short-term financing

takeover MERGERS & ACQUISITIONS **1. when one firm takes control of another** the acquisition by a company of a controlling interest in the voting share capital of another company, usually achieved by the purchase of a majority of the voting stocks **2.** = *takeover bid*

takeover approach UK MERGERS & ACQUISITIONS **price offered for takeover** the price at which a prospective buyer offers to purchase a controlling interest in a business or corporation. *US term* **tender offer**

takeover battle MERGERS & ACQUISITIONS **result of firm's resistance to acquisition** the activities surrounding a *contested takeover bid*. The bidder may raise the offer price and write to the stockholders extolling the benefits of the takeover. The board may contact other companies in the same line of business, hoping that a *white knight* may appear. It could also take action to make the company less desirable to the bidder. *See also* **poison pill**

takeover bid MERGERS & ACQUISITIONS **firm's attempt to buy another** an attempt by one company to acquire another. A takeover bid can be made either by a person or an organization, and usually takes the form of an approach to shareholders with an offer to purchase. The bidding stage is often difficult and fraught with politics, and various forms of *knight* may be involved.

Takeover Panel MERGERS & ACQUISITIONS, REGULATION & COMPLIANCE = *City Panel on Takeovers and Mergers*

takeover ratio UK MERGERS & ACQUISITIONS **indicator of likelihood that firm is acquisition target** the *book value* of a company divided by its market capitalization. If the resulting figure is greater than one, then the company is a candidate for a takeover. *See also* **appreciation, asset stripping**

takeover target MERGERS & ACQUISITIONS **firm another company wants to purchase** a company that another company has chosen to acquire by buying enough of its stock to control it

taker 1. STOCKHOLDING & INVESTMENTS **buyer of option** the buyer of an *option* to buy or sell at a particular price and time **2.** FINANCE **borrower** somebody who takes out a loan

take-up rate STOCKHOLDING & INVESTMENTS **percentage of stockholders agreeing to buy more stock** the percentage of acceptances of an offer to existing stockholders to buy more stock in a specific company

takings FINANCE = *receipts*

talon STOCKHOLDING & INVESTMENTS **form for ordering bond coupons** a form attached to a *bearer bond* that the holder of the bond uses to order new coupons when those attached to the bond have been depleted

tangible asset ACCOUNTING **firm's material resource** an asset that has a physical presence, for example, buildings, cash, and stock. Leases and securities, although not physical in themselves, are classed as tangible assets because the underlying assets are physical. *See also* **intangible asset**

tangible asset value *or* **tangible net worth** ACCOUNTING **asset value expressed per share** the value of all the assets of a company less its intangible assets such as goodwill, shown as a value per share

tangible book value ACCOUNTING **value of all firm's material resources** the book value of a company after intangible assets, patents, trademarks, and the value of research and development have been subtracted

tank STOCKHOLDING & INVESTMENTS **drop steeply in price** to fall suddenly and steeply, especially with reference to stock prices (slang)

tap CD FINANCE **certificate of deposit issued on demand** an issue of a *certificate of deposit*, normally in a large denomination, at the request of a specific investor

tape don't fight the tape STOCKHOLDING & INVESTMENTS **don't go against the direction of the market**

tap stock STOCKHOLDING & INVESTMENTS **UK government stock issued over time** in the United Kingdom, a government stock that is made available over a period of time in varying amounts

target 1. GENERAL MANAGEMENT **goal of effort** an end toward which effort is directed and on which resources are focused, usually to achieve an organization's strategy. **2.** MERGERS & ACQUISITIONS = *target company*

target cash balance FINANCE **amount of money firm wants available** the amount of cash that a company would like to have readily available

target company MERGERS & ACQUISITIONS **firm subject to acquisition** a company that is the object of a *takeover bid*

targeted repurchase MERGERS & ACQUISITIONS **buying back stock from firm's potential buyer** a company's purchase of its own stock from somebody attempting to buy the company

target savings motive ECONOMICS **desire to save money for particular goal** the wish to have a specific item or to achieve a specific goal that gives people a reason to save

TARP *abbr* FINANCE Troubled Asset Relief Program

tawarruq FINANCE **sale for cash of item purchased by installments** in Islamic financing, an arrangement in which somebody purchases an item from a bank on a deferred payment plan, then sells it immediately to obtain money. *See also* **murabaha**

tax and price index ECONOMICS, TAX **UK measure of household buying power** in the United Kingdom, an index number showing the percentage change in gross income that taxpayers need if they are to maintain their real *disposable income*

Tax-Exempt Special Savings Account STOCKHOLDING & INVESTMENTS *see* **TESSA**

tax revenue FINANCE, TAX **money from taxes** the money that a government receives in taxes from any source

T-bill *abbr* STOCKHOLDING & INVESTMENTS Treasury bill

T-bond *abbr* STOCKHOLDING & INVESTMENTS Treasury bond

TDB *abbr* FINANCE Trade Development Board

technical analysis STOCKHOLDING & INVESTMENTS **examination of changes in investment prices** the analysis of past movements in the prices of financial instruments, currencies, commodities, etc., with a view to predicting future price movements by applying analytical techniques. *See also* **fundamental analysis, qualitative analysis, quantitative analysis**

Technology and Human Resources for Industry Programme FINANCE *see* **THRIP**

technology stock STOCKHOLDING & INVESTMENTS **shares in technology firms** stock issued by a company that is involved in new technology

teeming and lading *UK* ACCOUNTING = *lapping*

telebanking BANKING = *telephone banking*

telegraphic transfer BANKING **means of moving money abroad** a method of transferring funds from a bank to a financial institution overseas, using telephone or cable. *Abbr* **TT**

telephone banking BANKING **accessing bank account by telephone** a system in which customers can access their accounts and a variety of banking services 24 hours a day by telephone. *Also called* **telebanking**

telephone number salary FINANCE **very high salary** a six- or seven-figure salary, especially one aspired to or considered undeserved (informal)

teller *US* BANKING **bank employee dealing with customers face to face** an employee in a bank or savings and loan association

who deals in person with customers' deposits and withdrawals. *UK term* **cashier**

tenbagger STOCKHOLDING & INVESTMENTS **investment with big increase in value** an investment that increases in value ten times over its purchase price (slang)

tender 1. STOCKHOLDING & INVESTMENTS **make offer for investment product at auction** to bid for securities at auction. The securities are allocated according to the method adopted by the issuer. In the standard auction style, the investor receives the security at the price they tendered. In a Dutch style auction, the issuer announces a strike price after all the tenders have been examined. This is set at a level where all the issue is sold. Investors who submitted a tender above the strike price just pay the strike price. The Dutch style of auction is increasingly being adopted in the United Kingdom. US Treasury bills are also sold using the Dutch system. *See also* **offer for sale, sale by tender 2.** GENERAL MANAGEMENT **submit price to do work** to offer to undertake work or supply goods at a specific price, usually in response to an invitation to bid for a work contract in competition with other suppliers **3.** OPERATIONS & PRODUCTION **statement outlining acceptable price for job** a statement of what a person or company is willing to accept when offering to undertake a major piece of work or supply goods, given in response to request to bid competitively for the work. *See also* **quote**

tender offer *US* MERGERS & ACQUISITIONS **price offered for takeover** the price at which a prospective buyer offers to purchase a controlling interest in a business or corporation. *UK term* **takeover approach**

10-K ACCOUNTING **US firm's official yearly financial statement** the filing of a US company's annual accounts with the New York Stock Exchange

tenor FINANCE **period before bill of exchange can be paid** the period of time that has to elapse before a bill of exchange becomes payable

10-Q ACCOUNTING **US firm's official quarterly financial statement** the filing of a US company's quarterly accounts with the New York Stock Exchange

term STOCKHOLDING & INVESTMENTS **period before investment product is fully payable** the period of time that has to elapse from the date of the initial investment before a security or other investment such as a term deposit or endowment insurance becomes redeemable or reaches its maturity date

term bill FINANCE = *period bill*

term deposit BANKING **savings held for a specified period** in the United Kingdom, a deposit account held for a fixed period. Withdrawals are either not allowed during this period, or they involve a fee payable by the depositor.

terminal date *UK* STOCKHOLDING & INVESTMENTS **end date for futures contract** the day on which a *futures contract* expires and the buyer must take delivery. *Also called* **delivery date**

term loan FINANCE **debt arrangement for specified period** a loan for a fixed period, usually called a *personal loan* when it is for non-business purposes. While a personal loan is usually at a fixed rate of interest, a term loan to a business may be at either a fixed or variable rate. Term loans may be either secured or unsecured. An early payment fee is usually payable when such a loan is repaid before the end of the term. *See also* **balloon loan, bullet loan**

terms STOCKHOLDING & INVESTMENTS **conditions attached to new issue** the conditions that apply to an issue of shares of stock

term share BANKING **building society account for specified period** in the United Kingdom, a share account in a building society that is for a fixed period of time. Withdrawals are usually not allowed during this period. However, if they are, then a fee is usually payable by the account holder.

term structure of interest rates STOCKHOLDING & INVESTMENTS **discount pattern for each year to maturity** a set of interest rates for each year to maturity of fixed-rate securities such as bonds of differing *term*. *See also* **yield to maturity**

tertiary sector ECONOMICS **part of economy involving nonprofit organizations** the part of the economy made up of nonprofit organizations such as consumer associations

TESSA STOCKHOLDING & INVESTMENTS **former untaxed UK bank account** a former UK savings account in which investors could save up to £9,000 over a period of five years and not pay any tax, provided they made no withdrawals over that time. TESSAs were replaced by ISAs in 1999. *Full form* **Tax-Exempt Special Savings Account**

test STOCKHOLDING & INVESTMENTS **assessment of likely stock price movements** in technical analysis, a way of determining whether to buy or sell a stock by observing if it is likely to rise above or drop below specific price levels that it has had difficulty breaking through in the past

test level STOCKHOLDING & INVESTMENTS **barrier price level** a specific price level that a stock has had difficulty breaking through in the past. In technical analysis, it is used in determining whether to buy or sell a stock.

theta STOCKHOLDING & INVESTMENTS **ratio of option's decreasing value to decreasing time** a ratio between the rate of decrease in the value of an option and the decrease in time as it approaches expiration. *Also called* **time decay**

third quarter ACCOUNTING **third of four divisions of fiscal year** the period of three months from July to the end of September, or the period of three months following the second quarter of the fiscal year. *Abbr* **Q3**

third sector ECONOMICS **part of economy involving nonprofit organizations** the part of the economy made up of nonprofit organizations such as charities, professional associations, labor unions, and religious, arts, community, research, and campaigning bodies

360 degree branding LEGAL, STOCKHOLDING & INVESTMENTS **supporting brand identity by all marketing activity** taking an inclusive approach in branding a product by bringing the brand to all points of consumer contact

3i BANKING **bank-owned group providing company finance** a finance group owned by the big British commercial banks which provides finance to other companies, especially small ones

threshold agreement FINANCE **UK contract promising pay raise in specific situation** in the United Kingdom, a contract that says that if the cost of living goes up by more than an agreed amount, pay will go up to match it

thrift 1. FINANCE **care in managing money** a cautious attitude toward the management of money, shown by saving, or spending it carefully and looking for good value **2.** BANKING **private local US bank for small investors** in the United States, a private local bank, savings and loan association, or credit union, that accepts and pays interest on deposits from small investors

thrift institution BANKING **US institution acting like savings bank** in the United States, an institution that is not a bank but accepts savings deposits and makes loans to savers. *See also* **savings and loan association, savings bank**

THRIP FINANCE **S. African program supporting industry research and development** in South Africa, a collaborative program involving industry, government, and educational and research institutions, which supports research and development in technology, science, and engineering. *Full form* **Technology and Human Resources for Industry Programme**

tick STOCKHOLDING & INVESTMENTS **smallest amount price or rate can change** the least amount by which a value such as the price of a stock or a rate of interest can rise or fall, for example, a hundredth of a percentage point or an eighth of a dollar **have ticks in all the right boxes** GENERAL MANAGEMENT to be on course to meet a series of objectives

tied loan FINANCE **loan to foreign country to buy lender's products** a loan made by one national government to another on the condition that the funds are used to purchase goods from the lending nation

Tier 1 capital BANKING **bank's core capital funds** the core capital of a bank, mainly consisting of stockholders' funds, which is used by regulators as a measure of a bank's stability

Tier 1 capital ratio BANKING **ratio of bank's core to supplementary funds** the relationship between the amount of Tier 1 capital and other capital held by a bank. *See also* **capital adequacy ratio**

Tier 2 capital BANKING **bank's supplementary funds** funds such as undisclosed reserves, held by a bank in addition to its core capital of stockholders' funds. *Also called* **supplementary capital**

tight money ECONOMICS **situation where borrowing money is difficult** a situation where it is expensive to borrow because of restrictive government policy or high demand

tight money policy ECONOMICS **government policy restricting money supply** a government policy to restrict money supply, usually by raising interest rates, making it more difficult to borrow and spend money

time and material pricing FINANCE **determining price based on work and materials** a form of *cost-plus pricing* in which price is determined by reference to the cost of the labor and material inputs to the product or service

time decay STOCKHOLDING & INVESTMENTS = *theta*

time deposit BANKING **US savings arrangement for specified period** a US savings account or a certificate of deposit, issued by a financial institution. While the savings account is for a fixed term, deposits are accepted with the understanding that withdrawals may be made subject to a period of notice. Banks are authorized to require at least 30 days' notice. While a certificate of deposit is equivalent to a term account, passbook accounts are generally regarded as funds readily available to the account holder.

time draft BANKING **type of US bill of exchange** a bill of exchange drawn on and accepted by a US bank. It is either an *after date* bill or *after sight* bill.

times covered STOCKHOLDING & INVESTMENTS **ability of net profit to pay firm's dividend** the number of times a company's dividends to ordinary stockholders could be paid out of its net after-tax profits. This measures the likelihood of dividend payments being sustained, and is a useful indication of sustained profitability. *Also called* *dividend cover*

time value of money FINANCE **potential growth in value over time** the principle that a specific amount of money is worth more now than it will be at a date in the future, because the sum available now can be invested and will have grown in value by the date in the future

tip STOCKHOLDING & INVESTMENTS **recommendation given by expert** a piece of useful expert information, for example, a recommendation about a product or a stock tip

tip-off STOCKHOLDING & INVESTMENTS **confidential information** a piece of confidential information about something that is going to happen, or a warning based on confidential financial or commercial information. *See also* **insider dealing, money laundering**

toasted FINANCE **having suffered financial losses** used to refer to someone or something that has lost money (slang)

toehold purchase *or* **toehold** MERGERS & ACQUISITIONS **small stake in corporation** in the United States, the acquisition of less than 5% of the outstanding stock in a company that is targeted for a takeover. At the 5% level, the acquiring company must notify the Securities and Exchange Commission and the targeted company of its plans.

token payment FINANCE **small payment made as token gesture** a small payment made only so that a payment of some sort is seen to be made

tombstone FINANCE **newspaper notice detailing large loan for business** a notice in the financial press giving details of a large lending facility, or large equity or debt securities offerings, to a business. It may relate to a management buyout or to a package that may include an *interest rate cap* and *collars* to finance a specific package. More than one bank may be involved. Although it may appear to be an advertisement, technically in most jurisdictions it is regarded as a statement of fact and therefore falls outside the advertisement regulations. The borrower generally pays for the advertisement, though it is the financial institutions that derive the most benefit.

top slicing 1. STOCKHOLDING & INVESTMENTS **sale of holding yielding original cost of investment** selling part of a stockholding that will realize a sum that is equal to the original cost of the investment. What remains therefore represents potential pure profit. **2.** TAX in **UK, assessment of tax on mature investments** in the United Kingdom, a complex method used by HM Revenue & Customs for assessing what tax, if any, is paid when some investment bonds or endowment policies mature or are cashed in early

total absorption costing ACCOUNTING **accountant's method of pricing goods and services** a method used by a cost accountant to price goods and services, allocating both direct and indirect costs. Although this method is designed so that all of an organization's costs are covered, it may result in opportunities being missed because of high prices. Consequently sales may be lost that could contribute to overheads. *See also* **marginal costing**

total assets FINANCE **sum of assets owned by person or organization** the total value of all current and long-term assets owned by a person or organization

total overhead cost variance ACCOUNTING **difference between actual and absorbed overhead costs** the difference between the overhead costs absorbed and the actual overhead costs incurred, both fixed and variable

total return STOCKHOLDING & INVESTMENTS **percentage change in overall value of investment** the total percentage change in the value of an investment over a specified time period, including capital gains, dividends, and the investment's appreciation or depreciation.

The total return formula reflects all the ways in which an investment can earn or lose money, resulting in an increase or decrease in the investment's *net asset value* (NAV):

$$\frac{\text{(Dividends} + \text{Capital gains distributions} \pm \text{Change in NAV)}}{\text{Beginning NAV}} = \text{Total return}$$

If, for instance, you buy a stock with an initial NAV of $40, and after one year it pays an income dividend of $2 per share and a capital gains distribution of $1, and its NAV has increased to $42, then the stock's total return would be:

$$\frac{2 + 1 + 2}{40} = \frac{5}{40} = 0.125 \times 100\% = 12.5\%$$

The total return time frame is usually one year, and it assumes that dividends have been reinvested. It does not take into account any sales charges that an investor paid to invest in a fund, or taxes they might owe on the income dividends and capital gains distributions received.

total revenue FINANCE **total income from all sources** all income from all sources

total utility ECONOMICS **consumer's total satisfaction from good or service** the overall satisfaction that a consumer receives from consuming a particular quantity of a specific good or service

touch barrier *or* **touch level** STOCKHOLDING & INVESTMENTS **preset price point triggering option payment** the preset point that the price of an underlying asset must reach, exceed, or fail to reach before a touch option will pay an investor

touch option STOCKHOLDING & INVESTMENTS **option paying at different preset levels** a type of option that gives an investor a payment dependent on the price of the underlying security reaching, exceeding, or not reaching a preset level. *See also double-one-touch option, no-touch option, one-touch option*

toxic FINANCE, STOCKHOLDING & INVESTMENTS **adversely affecting financial status** damaging to financial health. The term as applied to loans, debt, assets, and financial instruments such as mortgages, bonds and other securities refers to finance that is risky and potentially seriously damaging not only to the owner but to the financial system as a whole (informal)

toxic waste STOCKHOLDING & INVESTMENTS **high-risk securities** new securities with unusually high risk, often notes that have as collateral the riskiest portions of numerous issues of otherwise relatively low-risk debt (slang)

tracker fund STOCKHOLDING & INVESTMENTS = *index fund*

tracking 1. STOCKHOLDING & INVESTMENTS **investing to match a market index** the practice of buying investments in order to achieve the same or a similar return to a market index **2.** MARKETING **research into changing perception of product or organization** research designed to monitor changes in the public perception of a product or organization over a period of time

tracking error STOCKHOLDING & INVESTMENTS **degree to which fund fails to track index** the deviation by which an *index fund* fails to replicate the index it is aiming to mirror

tracking stock STOCKHOLDING & INVESTMENTS **stock with dividends linked to performance of subsidiary** a stock whose dividends are tied to the performance of a subsidiary of the corporation that owns it

trade bill FINANCE **bill of exchange between trading partners** a bill of exchange between two businesses that trade with each other. *See also acceptance credit*

trade credit FINANCE **credit offered to trading partner** credit offered by one business when trading with another. Typically this is for one month from the date of the invoice, but it could be for a shorter or longer period.

trade date STOCKHOLDING & INVESTMENTS **date of a purchase or sale** the date on which a buyer and seller reach an agreement for the purchase and sale of an asset

trade debt FINANCE **debt from normal trading** a debt that originates during the normal course of trade

trade debtor FINANCE **debtor with debt incurred through normal trading** a person or company that owes money to a company as a result of the normal activities of trading

traded option STOCKHOLDING & INVESTMENTS **option bought and sold on exchange** an option that can be continuously traded on an exchange

trade-in *US* FINANCE **using old product as partial payment for new** the act of giving an old product as part of the payment for a new one. *UK term* **part exchange**

trade investment STOCKHOLDING & INVESTMENTS **investment of one business in another** the action or process of one business making a loan to another, or buying stock in another. The latter may be the first stages of a friendly **takeover bid**.

trade-weighted index CURRENCY & EXCHANGE **measure of country's currency against trading partners' currencies** an index that measures the value of a country's currency in relation to the currencies of its trading partners

trading account ACCOUNTING = *profit and loss account*

trading loss FINANCE **sales income lower than expenditure** a situation in which the amount of money an organization receives in sales is less than its expenditure

trading profit ACCOUNTING = *gross profit*

tranche STOCKHOLDING & INVESTMENTS **one installment in series** one of a series of installments, used, for example, when referring to loans to companies, government securities that are issued over a period of time, or money withdrawn by a country from the IMF

tranche CD BANKING **certificate of deposit sold in series over time** a *certificate of deposit* that is part of a set that is sold by the issuing bank over a period of time. Each of the CDs in a tranche has the same maturity date.

transaction costs STOCKHOLDING & INVESTMENTS **direct costs of buying or selling asset** incremental costs that are directly attributable to the buying or selling of an asset. Transaction costs include commissions, fees, and direct taxes.

transaction exposure CURRENCY & EXCHANGE, RISK **risk in international trade from changing exchange rates** the risk that an organization may incur major losses from the effects of foreign exchange rate changes during the time it takes to arrange the export or import of goods or services. Transaction exposure is present from the time a price is set.

transaction history STOCKHOLDING & INVESTMENTS **record of trades with broker** a record of all of an investor's transactions with a broker

transactions motive ECONOMICS **desire to keep cash for upcoming purchases** the motive that consumers have to hold money for their likely purchases in the immediate future

transfer 1. BANKING **movement of money between banks** the movement of money through the domestic or international banking system, between banks in a *clearing system*, or between particular bank accounts. *See also BACS, Fedwire,*

SWIFT 2. STOCKHOLDING & INVESTMENTS **change of ownership** the change of ownership of an asset or security

transfer agent STOCKHOLDING & INVESTMENTS **agent handling transfers of ownership** an agent employed by a corporation to keep a record of the owners of securities and handle transfers of ownership

transfer out fee STOCKHOLDING & INVESTMENTS **fee for closing broker's account** a fee payable when an investor closes an account with a broker

translation exposure CURRENCY & EXCHANGE, RISK **risk on business from changing exchange rates** the risk that the balance sheet and income statement may be adversely affected by foreign exchange rate changes

traveler's checks BANKING **checks for cashing in foreign country** checks bought by a traveler that are valid for use at home or abroad, but are generally cashed in a foreign country. Only a countersignature is required from the holder for verification. *UK term* **traveller's cheques**

traveller's cheques BANKING = *traveler's checks*

treasurer TREASURY MANAGEMENT **officer responsible for money** a person who is responsible for the funds and other assets of an organization

Treasurer FINANCE **Australian government minister responsible for financial and economic matters** in Australia, the minister responsible for financial and economic matters in a national, state, or territory government

treasuries STOCKHOLDING & INVESTMENTS **US government securities** negotiable debt instruments issued by the US government. *See also* **Treasury bill, Treasury bond, Treasury note**

treasury TREASURY MANAGEMENT **section of firm responsible for financial matters** the department of a company or corporation that deals with all financial matters

Treasury FINANCE **government department responsible for finance and economy** in some countries, the government department responsible for the nation's financial policies as well as the management of the economy

Treasury bill STOCKHOLDING & INVESTMENTS **discounted short-term security** a short-term security issued by the US or UK government that is sold at a discount from face value and pays no interest but can be redeemed for full face value at maturity. *Abbr* **T-bill**

Treasury bill rate STOCKHOLDING & INVESTMENTS **effective interest earned from holding Treasury bill** the rate of interest obtainable by holding a **Treasury bill**. Although Treasury bills are non-interest bearing, by purchasing them at a discount and holding them to redemption, the discount is effectively the interest earned by holding these instruments. The Treasury bill rate is the discount expressed as a percentage of the issue price. It is annualized to give a rate per annum.

Treasury bond STOCKHOLDING & INVESTMENTS **US government bond** a bond issued by the US government that bears fixed interest. *Abbr* **T-bond**

treasury direct STOCKHOLDING & INVESTMENTS **trading system for US Treasury bills** in the United States, a system offered through Federal Reserve banks that allows investors to buy and sell **Treasury bills** directly from the Federal Reserve

treasury inflation protected security STOCKHOLDING & INVESTMENTS **US government security protected from inflation** a security issued by the US government with principal and coupon payments that are increased automatically to protect against inflation

treasury management TREASURY MANAGEMENT **firm's handling of all financial matters** the corporate handling of all financial matters, the generation of external and internal funds for business, the management of currencies and cash flows, and the complex strategies, policies, and procedures of corporate finance

Treasury note STOCKHOLDING & INVESTMENTS **1. US 2–10-year government security** a fixed-interest security issued by the US government that can mature within two to ten years **2. short-term debt instrument issued by Australian government** a short-term debt instrument issued by the Australian federal government. Treasury notes are issued on a tender basis for periods of 13 and 26 weeks.

treasury stock STOCKHOLDING & INVESTMENTS **shares of firm's stock bought back by firm** shares of a company's stock that have been bought back by the company and not canceled. In the United States, these shares are shown as deductions from equity; in the United Kingdom, they are shown as assets in the balance sheet.

Treynor ratio ECONOMICS = *risk-adjusted return on capital*

trial balance ACCOUNTING **draft balance in bookkeeping** in a double-entry bookkeeping system, a draft calculation of debits and credits to see if they balance

trickle-down theory ECONOMICS **belief that benefits spread downward in economy** the theory that financial and other benefits received by big businesses and wealthy people eventually spread down through an economy to the rest of society

triple A STOCKHOLDING & INVESTMENTS = *AAA*

Troubled Asset Relief Program FINANCE **federal government support for lenders** in the United States, a federal government program established in response to the credit crunch of 2007–8 by which the Treasury was authorized to buy mortgage-backed securities from financial institutions in an attempt to provide them with funds that would enable them to return to lending. *Abbr* **TARP**

troubleshooter FINANCE **consultant employed by firm in difficulty** an independent person, often a consultant, who is called in by a company in difficulties to help formulate a strategy for recovery

trough ECONOMICS **low point in economic cycle** the lowest point or period in an economic cycle before the situation begins to improve

troy ounce FINANCE **unit of weight for precious metals** the traditional unit used when weighing precious metals such as gold or silver. It is equal to approximately 1.097 ounces avoirdupois or 31.22 grams.

true and fair view UK ACCOUNTING **auditor-confirmed statement of firm's financial position** a correct statement of a company's financial position as shown in its accounts and confirmed by the auditors

true interest cost FINANCE **real interest rate paid on debt security** the effective rate of interest paid by the issuer on a debt security that is sold at a discount

trust 1. US BUSINESS **cartel** a group of companies that act together with the effect of reducing competition and controlling prices **2.** FINANCE **assets held for somebody else** money or property held by one person or a group of people (the trustees) with a legal obligation to administer them for another person's benefit. *See also* **blind trust**

trust account BANKING **account held for somebody else** money held by one person (the trustee), often a professional, on behalf of the owner of the funds in it, for example, a minor

trust bank BANKING **Japanese bank offering banking and trustee services** a Japanese bank that acts commercially in the sense of accepting deposits and making loans and also in the capacity of a trustee

trust corporation BANKING **US institution sometimes performing banking activities** a US state-chartered institution that may undertake banking activities

trustee FINANCE **somebody holding assets in trust** a person who, either individually or as a member of a board, has a legal obligation to administer assets for another person's benefit

trustee in bankruptcy FINANCE **somebody managing bankrupt's finances** somebody appointed by a court to manage the finances of a bankrupt person or company

trustee investment STOCKHOLDING & INVESTMENTS **investment made by trustee** an investment that is made by a trustee and is subject to legal restrictions

trusteeship FINANCE **1. status of trustee** the position of a *trustee* with a legal obligation to administer assets for another person's benefit **2. time as trustee** the term during which somebody acts as a *trustee*

trust fund FINANCE **set of assets held in trust** assets held in trust by a *trustee* or board of trustees for the trust's beneficiaries

trust officer FINANCE **manager of assets of trust** somebody who manages the assets of a trust, especially for a bank that is acting as a *trustee*

TT *abbr* BANKING telegraphic transfer

turkey FINANCE **poor performer** an investment or business that is performing badly (informal)

turnaround US **1.** FINANCE **return of profitability** a term for the act of making a company profitable again **2.** OPERATIONS &

PRODUCTION **value of sales divided by value of inventory** a term for the value of goods sold during a year divided by the average value of goods held in stock **3.** OPERATIONS & PRODUCTION **preparation of vehicle for another commercial trip** a term for the process of emptying a ship, plane, etc., and getting it ready for another commercial trip **4.** OPERATIONS & PRODUCTION **processing and dispatching of orders** a term for the time it takes to process orders and send out the goods. *UK term* ***turnround***

turnover 1. ACCOUNTING **firm's total sales revenue** the total sales revenue of an organization for an accounting period. This is shown net of VAT, trade discounts, and any other taxes based on the revenue in a profit and loss account. **2.** MARKETS **total value of stocks traded during year** the total value of stocks bought and sold on an exchange during the year. This covers both sales and purchases, so each transaction is counted twice. **3.** HR & PERSONNEL **rate of change of staff** the rate at which staff leave and are replaced in an organization

turnround UK = ***turnaround***

two-tier tender offer MERGERS & ACQUISITIONS **offering premium for initial stock in acquisition attempt** in the United States, a ***takeover bid*** in which the acquirer offers to pay more for shares bought early than for those acquired at a later date, in order to encourage stockholders to accept the offer, thus gaining control quickly. This form of bidding is outlawed in some jurisdictions, including the United Kingdom.

U

UCITS STOCKHOLDING & INVESTMENTS **EU rules for mutual funds** a set of directives that regulate mutual funds throughout all the countries of the European Union. *Full form* ***Undertakings for Collective Investment in Transferable Securities***

UHNWI *abbr* FINANCE ultra high net worth individual

UIT *abbr* STOCKHOLDING & INVESTMENTS unit investment trust

UKFI *abbr* FINANCE UK Financial Investments Ltd

UK Financial Investments Ltd FINANCE **firm managing UK government's banking investments** a company that manages the UK government's investments in the Royal Bank of Scotland plc, Lloyds Banking Group, Bradford & Bingley, Northern Rock plc and Northern Rock Asset Management plc. It was set up in 2008 after the government had to step in to overcome serious difficulties in independent banks. *Abbr* **UKFI**

ultra high net worth individual FINANCE **person with $30 million plus** a person whose net assets, excluding the value of a home, are worth more than $30 million. About 100,000 people worldwide fall into this category. *Abbr* **UHNWI**

ultra vires activity FINANCE **something disallowed by rules** an act that is not permitted by applicable rules such as those of a corporate charter. Such acts may lead to contracts being void.

umbrella fund STOCKHOLDING & INVESTMENTS **offshore investment in other offshore concerns** a collective investment based offshore that invests in other offshore collective investments

unbalanced growth ECONOMICS different parts of economy growing at different rates the situation that occurs when some sectors of an economy grow at different rates from others

unbundling 1. MERGERS & ACQUISITIONS dividing of firm before selling it off the dividing of a company into separate constituent companies, often to sell all or some of them after a takeover **2.** STOCKHOLDING & INVESTMENTS splitting returns on security for separate sale the separation of the components of a security in order to sell them separately

uncalled share capital STOCKHOLDING & INVESTMENTS unpaid proportion of stock value the amount of the *nominal value* of shares for which the company has not requested payment. It may not be intended that this payment should be requested unless the company goes into *liquidation*.

uncollectable FINANCE describing debt that is written off used to describe a debt that must be written off, either as a charge to the profit and loss account or against an existing doubtful debt provision

uncollected funds BANKING value residing in deposit that bank cannot negotiate money deriving from the deposit of an instrument that a bank has not been able to negotiate

unconditional bid MERGERS & ACQUISITIONS takeover bid offering payment irrespective of stock volume in a takeover battle, a situation in which a bidder will pay the offered price irrespective of how many shares are acquired, typically after the acquisition of a majority of the shares

unconsolidated STOCKHOLDING & INVESTMENTS not grouped together used to describe shares, holdings, loans, or subsidiaries that are not combined into a single unit

uncovered bear STOCKHOLDING & INVESTMENTS person selling stock not yet acquired a person who sells stock which he or she does not hold, hoping to be able to buy stock back at a lower price when it is time to settle

uncovered option STOCKHOLDING & INVESTMENTS option whose seller does not own associated asset a type of option in which the underlying asset is not owned by the seller, who risks considerable loss if the price of the asset falls. *Also called naked option*

undated bond STOCKHOLDING & INVESTMENTS bond without maturity date a bond to which no maturity date has been assigned

underbanked STOCKHOLDING & INVESTMENTS describing new issue with few sellers used to describe a new issue without enough brokers to sell it

undercapitalized FINANCE with insufficient capital used to describe a business that has insufficient capital for its requirements

underemployed capital FINANCE capital not producing enough income capital that is not being used effectively to produce income

underlying asset STOCKHOLDING & INVESTMENTS asset with option an asset that is associated with an *option* or other derivative or structured note

underlying security STOCKHOLDING & INVESTMENTS security with option a security that is associated with an *option*

undermargined account BANKING account with funds insufficient for margin requirements an account that does not have enough funds to cover its margin requirements, resulting in a *margin call*

underspend FINANCE **1.** spend less than intended or allowed to spend less than the amount that was budgeted for spending **2.** smaller amount spent than expected an amount that is less than the amount that was budgeted for spending

undersubscribed STOCKHOLDING & INVESTMENTS describing stock issue with some stock unsold used to describe a new issue in which not all shares are sold, and part of the issue remains with the underwriters

Undertakings for Collective Investment in Transferable Securities STOCKHOLDING & INVESTMENTS *see UCITS*

underused liquidity FINANCE cash not being optimally used available capital that is not being put to effective use in developing a business

undervaluation FINANCE valuation at less than true worth the assessment of an asset as having a value that is less than its expected value or worth

undervalued FINANCE describing asset available for less than value used to describe an asset that is offered for sale at a price lower than its expected value or worth

undervalued currency CURRENCY & EXCHANGE currency available cheaply a currency that costs less to buy with another currency than it is worth in goods

underwrite STOCKHOLDING & INVESTMENTS, INSURANCE, RISK be liable for potential losses to assume risk, especially for a new issue or an insurance policy. *Also called write*

underwriter 1. STOCKHOLDING & INVESTMENTS guarantor of public offering an institution or group of institutions who, for a fee, guarantee a public offering from a corporation and, if it fails to find enough buyers, will purchase the remaining shares **2.** INSURANCE insurance risk assessor a person who establishes insurance risk and issues insurance policies for an *insurance company* or syndicate, paying the insured party if a specified loss occurs. *Also called writer (sense 1). See also Lloyd's underwriting syndicate*

underwriters' syndicate STOCKHOLDING & INVESTMENTS group guaranteeing public offering a group of institutions who, for a fee, guarantee a public offering from a corporation and, if it fails to find enough buyers, will purchase the remaining shares

underwriting STOCKHOLDING & INVESTMENTS guaranteeing of public offering the activity of guaranteeing a public offering from a corporation for a fee, agreeing to buy any shares that remain unsold

underwriting commission *or* underwriting fee STOCKHOLDING & INVESTMENTS **fee guaranteeing purchase of new stock** a fee paid by a company to the **underwriters** for guaranteeing the purchase of new shares in that company.

underwriting spread STOCKHOLDING & INVESTMENTS **difference between stock costs and income from sale** an amount that is the difference between what an organization pays for an issue and what it receives when it sells the issue to investors

underwriting syndicate STOCKHOLDING & INVESTMENTS **group of institutions selling new securities to investors** a group of financial institutions who join to sell new securities to investors, and agree to buy any that are unsold themselves

undistributable reserves *UK* FINANCE = **restricted surplus**

undistributed profit STOCKHOLDING & INVESTMENTS **profit not paid out as dividend** profit that has not been distributed as dividends to stockholders

UNDP ECONOMICS **UN agency providing human development grants** a part of the United Nations system with goals that include the elimination of poverty, environmental regeneration, job creation, and advancement of women. It is the world's largest source of grants for sustainable human development. *Full form* **United Nations Development Programme**

unearned income FINANCE **money not received from employment** income received from sources such as investments or interest on savings rather than from employment. *See also* **earned income**

uneconomic FINANCE **not producing profits** not profitable for a country, firm, or investor in the short or long term

unemployment ECONOMICS **people wanting to work but not finding jobs** the situation in which some members of a country's labor force are willing to work but cannot find employment

unfunded debt FINANCE **debt to be repaid within a year** short-term debt requiring repayment within a year of being issued

ungeared *UK* FINANCE = **unleveraged**

ungluing MERGERS & ACQUISITIONS **splitting up established networks** the process of breaking up traditional supply chains or groups of cooperating organizations after taking control of the element of mutual interest that holds them together

unissued share capital *or* unissued capital *UK* STOCKHOLDING & INVESTMENTS = **unissued stock**

unissued stock *US* STOCKHOLDING & INVESTMENTS **capital stock not yet issued** the proportion of a company's capital stock that is authorized but has not been issued. *UK term* **unissued share capital**

unit STOCKHOLDING & INVESTMENTS **1. securities traded together** a collection of securities traded together as a single item **2. single mutual fund share of stock** a share in a mutual fund

United Nations Development Programme ECONOMICS *see* **UNDP**

unit investment trust STOCKHOLDING & INVESTMENTS **investment company offering units in unmanaged portfolio** an investment company that offers an unmanaged portfolio of securities to investors through brokers, typically in units of $1,000 each. *Abbr* **UIT**

unit of account CURRENCY & EXCHANGE **currency unit used for payments** a unit of a country's currency that can be used in payment for goods or in a firm's accounting

unit of trade STOCKHOLDING & INVESTMENTS **smallest amount that can be traded** the smallest quantity that can be bought or sold of a share of stock, or a contract included in an **option**

unit trust *UK* STOCKHOLDING & INVESTMENTS = **mutual fund**

unleveraged *US* FINANCE **describing firm with no borrowings** used to describe a company that has no borrowed money. *UK term* **ungeared**

unlimited liability FINANCE **full responsibility for debts** full responsibility for the obligations of a **general partnership**. This may include the use of personal assets to pay debts.

unlimited risk RISK **risk with unlimited potential loss** a risk whose potential loss is unlimited, for example, in futures trading

unlisted securities STOCKHOLDING & INVESTMENTS **stocks not listed on exchange** stocks that are not listed on an exchange. *Also called* **unquoted investments, unquoted shares**

unprofitable FINANCE **not profitable** not producing a profit

unquoted investments STOCKHOLDING & INVESTMENTS = **unlisted securities**

unquoted shares STOCKHOLDING & INVESTMENTS = **unlisted securities**

unrealized capital gain ACCOUNTING **profitable investment not yet sold** a profit from the holding of an asset worth more than its purchase price, but not yet sold

unrealized loss ACCOUNTING = **paper loss**

unrealized profit ACCOUNTING = **paper profit**

unremittable gain ACCOUNTING **in UK, capital gain that cannot be imported** in the United Kingdom, a capital gain that cannot be imported into the taxpayer's country, especially because of currency restrictions

unseasoned issue STOCKHOLDING & INVESTMENTS **issue of stocks to SEC-approved investors** an issue of stocks that a dealer may only sell to specific qualifying investors as agreed by the US Securities and Investment Commission. *See also* **seasoned issue**

unsecured creditor FINANCE **creditor making unsecured loans** a creditor who is owed money, but has no security from the debtor for the debt. Unsecured creditors are at risk of losing everything, as official procedures may absorb most of the money remaining after a business failure and small creditors may not be paid.

unsecured debt FINANCE **money borrowed without collateral** an amount of money borrowed without the borrower providing **collateral** to the lender

unsecured loan FINANCE **loan provided without collateral** a loan made without **collateral** provided to the lender by the borrower. *Also called* **signature loan**

unstable equilibrium ECONOMICS **easily disrupted balance of supply and demand** a market situation in which, if there is a movement of price or quantity away from the equilibrium, existing forces will push the price even further away

unsubsidized FINANCE **without financial assistance** for which no **subsidy** has been paid. *See also* **subsidized**

upside potential STOCKHOLDING & INVESTMENTS **potential for value of security to go up** the possibility that a security will increase in value. *See also* **downside risk**

upturn ECONOMICS **upward trend** an upward trend in sales, profits, a stock market, or an economy

urbun FINANCE **forfeitable deposit paid by buyer to seller** in Islamic financing, money paid by a buyer to a seller at the time of execution of a contract that will be forfeited if the contract is canceled by the buyer

used credit FINANCE **used part of offered credit** the portion of a **line of credit** that is no longer available for use

use of proceeds FINANCE **details of intended investment use** detailed information for investors on how money invested in an undertaking will be put to use

U-shaped recovery ECONOMICS **slow exit from recession** a pattern of recovery after a recession shaped like the letter U, showing a gradual improvement of conditions. *See also* **V-shaped recovery**

US savings bond STOCKHOLDING & INVESTMENTS **US Federal government savings product** in the United States, a bond that can be bought from the Federal government. *Also called* **savings bond**

usury FINANCE **lending money at high rates** the practice of lending money at a rate of interest that is either unlawful or considered to be excessively high

utility 1. BUSINESS **company that provides a service to community** a public service company, for example, one that supplies water, gas, or electricity or that runs public transportation **2.** ECONOMICS **customer satisfaction** the usefulness or satisfaction that a consumer gets from a product

V

valuation FINANCE **estimate of worth** an estimate of how much something is worth

value FINANCE **1. worth measured in money** the amount of money that something is worth **2. estimate worth of something in money** to estimate how much money something is worth

value-at-risk STOCKHOLDING & INVESTMENTS, RISK *see* **Var**

value date FINANCE **transfer date** a date on which a transaction takes place

value driver FINANCE **something adding value to product or service** an activity or organizational focus that enhances the value of a product or service in the perception of the consumer and which therefore creates value for the producer. Advanced technology, reliability, or reputation for customer relations can all be value drivers.

value for money audit ACCOUNTING **examination of firm's effectiveness in using resources** an investigation into whether proper arrangements have been made for securing economy, efficiency, and effectiveness in the use of resources. *Abbr* **VFM**. *Also called* **comprehensive auditing**

value investing STOCKHOLDING & INVESTMENTS **investing based on company's value** an investment strategy based on the value of a company rather than simply on its stock price

value proposition FINANCE **proposed profit-making plan** a proposed plan for making a profit, presented, for example, to a potential investor

value share *or* **value stock** STOCKHOLDING & INVESTMENTS **currently underpriced stock** a stock that is considered to be currently underpriced by the market, and therefore an attractive investment prospect

value to the business *or* **value to the owner** FINANCE **asset's minimum assessable value** the lower of the figures for the **recoverable amount** and the **replacement cost** of an asset. *Also called* **deprival value**

vanilla lending FINANCE = **prime lending**

vanilla loan FINANCE = **prime loan**

Var *or* **VAR** STOCKHOLDING & INVESTMENTS, RISK **assessment of likely depreciation of asset or investment** a risk assessment measure that is used to establish how much the market value of an asset or a portfolio is likely to decrease over a specific period of time. *Full form* **value-at-risk**

variable costing ACCOUNTING = **marginal costing**

variable interest rate FINANCE **interest rate that fluctuates during loan period** an interest rate that changes, usually in relation to a standard index, during the period of a loan

variable rate FINANCE **interest rate that fluctuates** a rate of interest on a loan that is not fixed, but can change with the current bank interest rates. *Also called* **floating rate**

variable rate note FINANCE **note with interest rate linked to index** a note whose interest rate is tied to an index, such as the prime rate in the United States or the London Interbank Offering Rate in the United Kingdom. *Abbr* **VRN**

variance 1. GENERAL MANAGEMENT **difference between actual and predicted performance** a measure of the difference between actual performance and forecast, or standard, performance **2.** ACCOUNTING **difference between planned and actual cost** the difference between a planned, budgeted, or standard cost and the actual cost incurred. The same comparisons may be made for revenues.

variation margin STOCKHOLDING & INVESTMENTS, RISK **daily profits or losses** the profits or losses of members of the *London Clearing House*, calculated daily from the marked-to-market-close value of their position. *See also initial margin*

vault cash BANKING **cash used for bank's everyday needs** cash held by a bank in its vaults, used for day-to-day needs

VC *abbr* FINANCE venture capitalist

vega STOCKHOLDING & INVESTMENTS **relationship of option price to underlying asset's volatility** a ratio between the expected change in the price of an option and a 1% change in the expected volatility of the underlying asset. *Also called kappa, lambda*

velocity of circulation of money ECONOMICS **how quickly money moves around economy** the rate at which money circulates in an economy

vendor FINANCE **seller** a person or organization that sells goods, services, shares, or property

vendor placing STOCKHOLDING & INVESTMENTS **business vendor's exchanging of acquired stock for cash** the practice of issuing stock to acquire a business, where an agreement has been made to allow the vendor of the business to place the stock with investors for cash

venture capital FINANCE **finance for new businesses or projects** money used to finance new companies or projects, especially those with high earning potential and high risk. *Also called risk capital*

venture capital fund FINANCE **fund providing venture capital** a fund that invests in finance houses providing *venture capital*

venture capitalist FINANCE **firm or individual providing venture capital** a finance company or private individual specializing in providing venture capital. *Abbr* **VC**

venture funding FINANCE **second round of funding for new firm** the round of funding for a new company that follows the provision of seed capital by venture capitalists

venturer FINANCE **partner in joint venture** one of two or more parties involved in a *joint venture*

verification ACCOUNTING **in-depth examination of firm's assets and liabilities** in an audit, a substantive test of the existence, ownership, and valuation of a company's assets and liabilities

vertical diversification GENERAL MANAGEMENT, MERGERS & ACQUISITIONS **developing new areas in supply chain diversification** in which a company moves into a different level of the *supply chain*, for example, a manufacturing company becoming a retailer. *See also diversification*

vertical form ACCOUNTING **presentation of debits and credits in single column** the presentation of a financial statement in

which the debits and credits are shown in one column of figures

vertical merger MERGERS & ACQUISITIONS **combining of firms in same supply chain** the amalgamation of two or more organizations from the same supply chain under single ownership, through the direct acquisition by one organization of the net assets or liabilities of the other. *See also merger*

vested interest FINANCE **personal interest in maintaining status quo** a special interest in keeping an existing state of affairs for personal gain

VFM *abbr* ACCOUNTING value for money audit

v-form FINANCE **graph line showing value falling then rising** a graphic representation of something that had been falling in value and is now rising

virement *UK* ACCOUNTING **transfer of money between accounts or budgets** a transfer of money from one account to another or from one section of a budget to another

virtual bank BANKING, E-COMMERCE **bank only accessible electronically** a financial institution that offers banking services via the Internet, ATMs, and telephone but does not have a physical location for customers to visit

voetstoots FINANCE **in S. Africa, at buyer's risk** in South Africa, used to describe a sale or purchase for which there is no warranty or guarantee

Volcker rule BANKING **US restriction on banks' investment activities** in the United States, a federal government proposal, in response to the global banking crisis of 2007–8, that no bank or financial institution that contains a bank can own, invest in, or sponsor, for its own profit, hedge funds, private equity funds, or proprietary trading operations that are unrelated to serving customers. The effect of this is to separate banking operations from trading activities.

volume variances ACCOUNTING **monetary differences when actual and budgeted activity diverges** differences in costs or revenues compared with budgeted amounts, caused by differences between the actual and budgeted levels of activity

voluntary arrangement FINANCE **agreement with terms not legally binding** an agreement the terms of which are not legally binding on the parties

vostro account BANKING **local bank account held for foreign bank** an account held by a local bank on behalf of a foreign bank

votes on account FINANCE **extra money for UK government department** in the United Kingdom, money granted by Parliament to allow government departments to continue spending in a fiscal year before final authorization of the totals for the year

voting shares *UK* STOCKHOLDING & INVESTMENTS = *voting stock*

voting stock *US* STOCKHOLDING & INVESTMENTS **stock giving voting rights** stock whose owners have the right to vote at the company's annual meeting and any extraordinary meetings. *UK term* ***voting shares***

voting trust STOCKHOLDING & INVESTMENTS **group with voting rights from stockholders** a group of individuals who have collectively received voting rights from stockholders

voucher ACCOUNTING **evidence for accounting entry** a document supporting an entry in a company's accounts

vouching ACCOUNTING **auditor's matching of vouchers with accounting entries** an auditing process in which documentary evidence is matched with the details recorded in an accounting record in order to check for validity and accuracy

VRN *abbr* FINANCE variable rate note

V-shaped recovery ECONOMICS **rapid exit from recession** a pattern of recovery after a recession shaped like the letter V, showing rapid smooth improvement in conditions. *See also* ***U-shaped recovery***

vulture capitalist FINANCE **venture capitalist benefiting investors, not entrepreneur client** a ***venture capitalist*** who exploits entrepreneurs by structuring deals on their behalf in such a way that the investors benefit rather than the entrepreneurs (slang)

vulture fund STOCKHOLDING & INVESTMENTS **investment fund specializing in discounted items** a mutual fund that specializes in acquiring investments such as bonds that have been downgraded or ***distressed property***

W

wage FINANCE **money regularly paid for work done** the money paid to an employee in return for work done, especially when it is based on an hourly rate and is paid weekly

wage drift FINANCE = ***earnings drift***

wage freeze ECONOMICS **government restraints on wage increases** a government policy of preventing pay raises in order to combat inflation

wage incentive FINANCE **monetary reward for employee's performance** a monetary benefit offered as a reward to those employees who perform well in an agreed way

wage indexation ECONOMICS **linking of pay raises to cost of living** the linking of increases in wages to the percentage rise in the cost of living

wage policy *US* ECONOMICS **government policy on wage levels** a government policy setting wages and wage increases for workers, for example, setting minimum wage requirements. *UK term* ***wages policy***

wage-price spiral ECONOMICS = ***inflationary spiral***

wage restraint FINANCE **curbs on pay raises** the act of keeping increases in wages under control and in proportion to increases in workers' productivity

wages FINANCE **money in return for work** a form of pay given to employees in exchange for the work they have done. Traditionally, the term wages applied to the weekly pay of manual, or nonprofessional workers. In modern usage, the term is often used interchangeably with salary.

wages costs ACCOUNTING **costs of paying employees** the costs of paying employees for their work. Along with other costs such as pension contributions, these costs typically form the largest single cost item for a business.

wages payable account ACCOUNTING **in UK, account showing expenditure on employees** in the United Kingdom, an account showing the gross wages and employer's ***National Insurance*** contributions paid during a specific period

wages policy *UK* ECONOMICS = ***wage policy***

wakalah FINANCE **contract appointing agent** in Islamic financing, a contract in which one person appoints another person to act as an agent on their behalf in a transaction

wallflower STOCKHOLDING & INVESTMENTS **unappealing investment** an investment that does not attract a lot of interest from potential investors (slang)

wallpaper STOCKHOLDING & INVESTMENTS **major stock issue financing takeovers** a disparaging term used to describe a situation where a company issues and sells many new shares in order to finance a series of takeovers (slang)

Wall Street bonus FINANCE **large financial reward for US employee** a very large sum of money, in addition to annual salary, paid to an employee in New York's financial industry for effective performance in increasing his or her company's profits. *See also* ***City bonus***

Wall Street Journal FINANCE **US financial newspaper** a respected US daily newspaper, first published on July 8, 1889. It is published in New York by Dow Jones & Company, now a subsidiary of News Corporation, with Asian and European editions.

war babies STOCKHOLDING & INVESTMENTS **defense industry securities** securities in companies that work as contractors in the defense industry (slang)

war chest MERGERS & ACQUISITIONS **reserves for financing takeovers** a large amount of money held by a person or a company in ***reserves*** that can be used to finance the ***takeover*** of other companies (slang)

war loan STOCKHOLDING & INVESTMENTS **UK government bond paying fixed interest** a UK government bond that pays a fixed rate of ***interest*** and has no final ***redemption date***. War loans were originally issued to finance military expenditure.

warrant STOCKHOLDING & INVESTMENTS **contract to buy stocks in future** a contract that gives the right to buy a predetermined number of shares of stock in the future

warrant premium STOCKHOLDING & INVESTMENTS **extra paid for buying and exercising warrant** a premium paid to buy and exercise a warrant, above the price of buying the shares of stock directly without the warrant

warrants risk warning notice STOCKHOLDING & INVESTMENTS **broker's statement of risks of options trading** a statement that a broker in the United Kingdom gives to clients to alert them to the risks inherent in trading in options

wash sale STOCKHOLDING & INVESTMENTS **sale and repurchase of same stock** the sale and then immediate repurchase of a block of stock. In the United States it may be used as a means of creating fictitious trading volume. *See also bed and breakfast deal*

wasting asset ACCOUNTING **asset that is consumed to earn income** a *fixed asset* that is consumed or exhausted in the process of earning income, for example, a mine or a quarry

waterbed effect FINANCE **linked fall and rise** the effect of a reduction in one area creating an increase in another area. For example, if the price for one service provided by a company is fixed at a particular level, the price for another of its services rises.

watered stock STOCKHOLDING & INVESTMENTS **stock with value lower than capital invested** stock in a company that is worth less than the total *capital* invested

WC *abbr* FINANCE working capital

WDA *abbr* ACCOUNTING, TAX writing-down allowance

WDV *abbr* ACCOUNTING written-down value = *net book value*

wealth ECONOMICS **real estate or investments** physical assets such as a house or financial assets such as stocks and bonds that can yield an income for their holder

wear and tear ACCOUNTING **degeneration of asset owing to normal use** the deterioration of a tangible *fixed asset* as a result of normal use. This is recognized for accounting purposes by *depreciation*.

WEF *abbr* ECONOMICS World Economic Forum

weighted average cost of capital FINANCE **average cost of firm's capital** the average cost of a company's financing (equity, debentures, bank loans) weighted according to the proportion each element bears to the total pool of capital. Weighting is usually based on market valuations, current yields, and costs after tax. The weighted average cost of capital is often used as the *hurdle rate* for investment decisions, and as the measure to be minimized in order to find the optimal capital structure for the company.

weighted average cost price FINANCE **cost of each item in inventory** a value for the cost of each item of a specific type in an inventory, taking into account what quantities were bought at what prices

weighted average number of ordinary shares UK STOCKHOLDING & INVESTMENTS = *weighted average number of shares outstanding*

weighted average number of shares outstanding US STOCKHOLDING & INVESTMENTS **figure used for calculating earnings per share** the number of shares of common stock at the beginning of a period, adjusted for shares canceled, bought back, or issued during the period, multiplied by

a time-weighting factor. This number is used in the calculation of *earnings per share*. UK term **weighted average number of ordinary shares**

weighted index ECONOMICS **index with importance affecting value** an index in which some important items are given more value than less important ones

Wheat Report ACCOUNTING **report examining principles and methods of US accounting** a report produced by a committee in 1972 that set out to examine the principles and methods of accounting in the United States. Its publication led to the establishment of the *FASB*.

whisper number *or* whisper estimate FINANCE **rumored earnings** an estimate of a company's earnings that is based on rumors.

whisper stock STOCKHOLDING & INVESTMENTS **stock predicted to rise in value** a stock about which there is talk of a likely change in value, usually upward and often related to a takeover

white-collar crime FRAUD **crime by white-collar worker** a crime committed by somebody in the course of doing a white-collar job, for example, embezzlement

white knight MERGERS & ACQUISITIONS **preferred buyer whose action thwarts takeover** a person or company liked by a company's management, who buys the company when a hostile company is trying to buy it. *See also knight*

whitemail MERGERS & ACQUISITIONS **issue of cheap shares of stock to prevent takeover** a method used by a company that is the target of a takeover bid to prevent the takeover, in which the target company issues a large number of shares of stock below the market price to friendly investors. The company wanting to acquire the target must buy the shares in order to be successful.

white squire MERGERS & ACQUISITIONS **shareholder whose stock purchases prevent takeover bid** somebody who purchases a significant, but not controlling, number of shares of stock in order to prevent a *takeover bid* from succeeding. A white squire is often invited to purchase the shares by the company to be acquired, and may be required to sign an agreement to prevent him or her from later becoming a *black knight*.

wholesale banking BANKING **banking services provided by merchant banks** banking services between investment banks and other financial institutions. *See also retail banking, commercial bank*

wholesalefunded BANKING **funded by short-term borrowing** used to describe a bank whose funds come from other banks and financial institutions in the form of short-term loans rather than from long-term deposits

wholesale funding BANKING **funding of banks through short-term borrowing** a method of funding banks by short-term borrowing from other banks and financial institutions

wholesale market MARKETS, BANKING = *interbank market*

wholesale price index ECONOMICS **government indicator of inflation level** a government-calculated index of wholesale prices, indicative of inflation in an economy

whoops US FINANCE **disparaging name for Washington state power company** a disparaging way of referring to the Washington Public Power Supply System, a municipal corporation in the US state of Washington that built and operated power plants. Delays, cost overruns, and mismanagement in the construction of nuclear power plants caused the company to default on the $2.25 billion in bonds, the largest bond default in US history before the events of 2008.

widow-and-orphan stock US STOCKHOLDING & INVESTMENTS **dependable stock** a stock considered extremely safe as an investment

windfall gains and losses FINANCE **unforeseen gains and losses** large financial gains and losses that occur unexpectedly

windfall profit FINANCE **large unexpected profit** a large profit that is made unexpectedly and may be subject to extra tax

wire room 1. BANKING **bank department dealing with payment orders** the department in a financial institution that originates, receives, and transmits payment orders **2.** MARKETS **brokerage department dealing with securities orders** the department in a brokerage firm that receives and transmits securities orders to the floor of the exchange or the trading department

withdraw 1. BANKING **take money from account** to remove money from an account **2.** FINANCE **rescind offer** to retract an offer that has been made

withdrawal STOCKHOLDING & INVESTMENTS **income disbursement from open-end mutual fund** the regular disbursement of dividend or capital gain income from an open-end mutual fund

withdrawal plan STOCKHOLDING & INVESTMENTS **regular payment to shareholder from mutual fund** an arrangement in which a mutual fund pays out a specific amount to a shareholder at regular intervals. *See also* ***systematic withdrawal***

working capital FINANCE **firm's money available for trading** the funds that are readily available to operate a business.

Working capital comprises the total net ***current assets*** of a business minus its ***current liabilities***.

$$\text{Current assets} - \text{Current liabilities}$$

Current assets are cash and assets that can be converted to cash within one year or a normal operating cycle; current liabilities are monies owed that are due within one year.

If a company's current assets total $300,000 and its current liabilities total $160,000, its working capital is:

$$\$300,000 - \$160,000 = \$140,000$$

Abbr WC

working capital productivity FINANCE **measure of firm's productivity** a way of measuring a company's efficiency by comparing working capital with sales or turnover.

It is calculated by first subtracting ***current liabilities*** from ***current assets***, which is the formula for working capital, then dividing this figure into sales for the period.

$$\frac{\text{Sales}}{\text{Current assets} - \text{Current liabilities}} = \text{Working capital productivity}$$

If sales are $3,250, current assets are $900, and current liabilities are $650, then:

$$\frac{3250}{900 - 650} = \frac{3250}{250} = 13 \text{ working capital productivity}$$

In this case, the higher the number the better. Sales growing faster than the resources required to generate them is a clear sign of efficiency and, by definition, productivity.

The working capital to sales ratio uses the same figures, but in reverse:

$$\frac{\text{Working capital}}{\text{Sales}} = \text{Working capital to sales ratio}$$

Using the same figures in the example above, this ratio would be calculated:

$$\frac{250}{3250} = 0.077 \times 100\% = 7.7\%$$

For this ratio, obviously, the lower the number the better.

Some experts recommend doing quarterly calculations and averaging them for a given year to arrive at the most reliable number.

working capital ratio ACCOUNTING = ***current ratio***

working capital turnover FINANCE **sales divided by average working capital** a figure equal to sales divided by average working capital

World Bank BANKING **group of institutions funding less developed countries** one of the largest sources of funding for the less industrially developed countries in the world. It is made up of five organizations: the International Bank for Reconstruction and Development, the International Development Association, the International Finance Corporation, the Multilateral Investment Guarantee Agency, and the International Centre for Settlement of Investment Disputes. The World Bank was founded at the 1944 Bretton Woods Conference and has over 180 member countries. Its head office is located in Washington, DC, but the Bank has field offices in over 100 countries. Its focus has shifted dramatically since the 1980s, when over one-fifth of its lending was made up of investment in the energy industry. Its current priorities are education, health, and nutrition in the most economically challenged countries of the world.

World Economic Forum ECONOMICS **organization seeking to effect global economic improvement** an independent economic organization whose goal is to "improve the state of the world." Based in Switzerland, the WEF was formed in the 1970s by Professor Klaus Schwab, who set out to bring together the CEOs of leading European companies in order to discuss strategies that would enable Europe to compete in the global marketplace. Since then, over 1,000 companies around the world have become members of the WEF and its interests have diversified to cover health, corporate citizenship, and peace-building activities. However, it has attracted criticism from some quarters, and antiglobalization protesters gather regularly at its meetings. *Abbr* **WEF**

world economy ECONOMICS = *global economy*

wrap account STOCKHOLDING & INVESTMENTS **brokerage account charging periodic fee** a client account with a broker in which the broker charges a set quarterly or annual fee covering transaction and management costs instead of charging per transaction

wrap fund STOCKHOLDING & INVESTMENTS **fund investing in various underlying mutual funds** a registered fund that, while not itself a mutual fund, has similar status to that of a stockbroker's portfolio and invests in a variety of underlying mutual funds, each of which is treated as a discrete holding, often in the form of an insurance bond. *Also called* **wrapper**

wrapper 1. FINANCE **financial contract** a legally binding financial contract between a client and an investment bank, stating the specific terms that have been agreed. Common wrappers are structured notes, swaps, and over-the-counter transactions. **2.** STOCKHOLDING & INVESTMENTS = **wrap fund**

write STOCKHOLDING & INVESTMENTS, RISK = **underwrite**

write-down ACCOUNTING **assignment of lower value to asset** the recording of an asset at a lower value than previously

write-off 1. ACCOUNTING **reduction in recorded value of asset** a reduction in the recorded value of an asset, usually to zero **2.** INSURANCE **cancellation of debt** the total loss or cancellation of a bad debt **3.** INSURANCE **something damaged beyond repair** for insurance claims, something that is so badly damaged that it cannot be repaired and will have to be replaced

writer 1. INSURANCE = **underwriter 2.** STOCKHOLDING & INVESTMENTS **seller of traded option** somebody who is selling a traded option

write-up ACCOUNTING **increase in book value of asset** an increase made to the book value of an asset to adjust for an increase in market value

writing-down allowance ACCOUNTING, TAX **tax relief on acquired assets that lose value** in the United Kingdom, a form of capital allowance giving tax relief to companies acquiring *fixed assets* that are then depreciated. This allowance forms part of the system of *capital allowances*. *Abbr* **WDA**

written-down value ACCOUNTING = *net book value*

W-shaped recession ECONOMICS = *double-dip recession*

X

X STOCKHOLDING & INVESTMENTS **with no dividend right** a symbol used in newspapers to designate a stock or bond that is trading *ex dividend*

xa *abbr* STOCKHOLDING & INVESTMENTS ex-all

XBRL FINANCE **computer language for financial reporting** a computer language used for financial reporting. It allows companies to publish, extract, and exchange financial information through the Internet and other electronic means. *Full form* **Extensible Business Reporting Language**

xd *abbr* STOCKHOLDING & INVESTMENTS ex dividend

xr *abbr* STOCKHOLDING & INVESTMENTS ex-rights

xw STOCKHOLDING & INVESTMENTS **trading without a warrant to buy shares** a symbol used in newspapers to designate a stock that is trading without a *warrant* to buy shares of stock

Y

Yankee bond STOCKHOLDING & INVESTMENTS **foreign bond in US market** a bond issued in the US domestic market by a non-US company

yard CURRENCY & EXCHANGE **one billion currency units** used by traders for one billion units of any currency (slang)

year end ACCOUNTING **end of fiscal year** the end of the financial year, when a company's accounts are prepared

year-end ACCOUNTING **of end of fiscal year** relating to the end of a fiscal year

year-end closing ACCOUNTING **statements at end of firm's fiscal year** the financial statements issued at the end of a company's fiscal year

year to date ACCOUNTING **period from start of fiscal year to now** the period from the start of a fiscal year to the current time. A variety of financial information, such as a company's profits, losses, or sales, may be displayed on this basis. *Abbr* **YTD**

yen CURRENCY & EXCHANGE **Japanese currency** the basic unit of currency used in Japan

yield STOCKHOLDING & INVESTMENTS **percentage that is annual income from investment** a percentage of the amount invested that is the annual income from an investment.

Yield is calculated by dividing the annual cash return by the current share price and expressing that as a percentage.

Yields can be compared against the market average or against a sector average, which in turn gives an idea of the relative value of the share against its peers. Other things being equal, a higher yield share is preferable to that of an identical company with a lower yield.

An additional feature of the yield (unlike many of the other share analysis ratios) is that it enables comparison with cash. Cash placed in an interest-bearing source like a bank account or a government stock produces a yield—the annual interest payable. This is usually a safe investment. The yield from this cash investment can be compared with the yield on shares,

Dictionary

which are far riskier. This produces a valuable basis for share evaluation.

Share yield is less reliable than bank interest or government stock interest yield, because, unlike banks paying interest, companies are under no obligation at all to pay dividends. Frequently, if they go through a bad patch, even the largest companies will cut dividends or abandon paying them altogether.

yield curve STOCKHOLDING & INVESTMENTS **graph showing comparable interest on bonds** a visual representation of relative interest rates of short- and long-term bonds. It can be normal, flat, or inverted.

yield gap STOCKHOLDING & INVESTMENTS **difference in return between equities and bonds** an amount representing the difference between the yield on a safe equity investment and the yield on a riskier bond investment. *See also* **reverse yield gap**

yield management FINANCE **price adjustment that secures maximum profits** securing maximum profits from available capacity by manipulating pricing to gain business at different times, and from differing market segments. Yield management is used particularly in service industries such as the airline, hotel, and equipment rental industries, where there are heavy fixed overheads and additional revenue has a big impact on bottom line profitability. Increasing computing power has enabled organizations to integrate complex information from different sources (for example, customer travel histories and current information on bookings) and use mathematical models to analyze the possibility of increasing profitability. Hotel businesses, for example, can use price offers to increase "revenue per available room," or "RevPAR," on the basis of yield management analysis.

yield to call STOCKHOLDING & INVESTMENTS **yield on bond at potential call date** the yield on a bond at a date when the bond can be called

yield to maturity *US* STOCKHOLDING & INVESTMENTS **investor's total return if security held to maturity** the total return to an investor if a fixed interest security is held to maturity, in other words, the aggregate of gross interest received and the capital gain or loss at redemption, annualized. *Abbr* **YTM**. *UK term* **gross redemption yield**

YTD *abbr* ACCOUNTING year to date

YTM *abbr* STOCKHOLDING & INVESTMENTS yield to maturity

Z

ZBB *abbr* ACCOUNTING zero-based budgeting

Z bond STOCKHOLDING & INVESTMENTS **bond paying interest after paying all other holders** a bond whose holder receives no interest until all of the holders of other bonds in the same series have received theirs

zero-balance account BANKING **bank account for outgoings, holding no residual funds** a bank account that does not hold funds continuously, but has money automatically transferred into it from another account when claims arise against it

zero-based budgeting ACCOUNTING **budgeting method requiring costs to be justified** a method of budgeting that requires each cost element to be specifically justified, as though the activities to which the budget relates were being undertaken for the first time. Without approval, the budget allowance is zero. *Abbr* **ZBB**

zero coupon bond STOCKHOLDING & INVESTMENTS **discounted bond paying no interest** a bond that pays no interest and is sold at a large discount. *Also called* **accrual bond, split coupon bond**

zero-coupon security STOCKHOLDING & INVESTMENTS **government security without interest** a government security that pays no interest but is sold at a discount from its face value

zero-fund FINANCE **provide no money for project** to assign no money to a business project without actually canceling it (slang)

zero growth ECONOMICS **no increase in output** a lack of increase in the output of a business or economy between one period, such as one quarter, and the next. *See also* **recession**

zero-sum game FINANCE **gain by one results in loss by another** a situation in which a gain by one participant results in another participant's equivalent loss

ZOPA BANKING, E-COMMERCE **website facilitating loans between users** a personal loan exchange website that allows web users to lend to and borrow from each other directly. *Full form* **Zone of Possible Agreement**

Z score STATISTICS, FINANCE **measure of bankruptcy risk** a statistical measure used to determine the likelihood of bankruptcy from a company's credit strength

Index